OXFORD MEDIEVAL TEXTS

General Editors
J. W. BINNS   D. D'AVRAY
M. S. KEMPSHALL   R. C. LOVE

NIGEL OF LONGCHAMP
SPECVLVM STVLTORVM

Burnellus imagines becoming a bishop. BL, Additional MS 38665, fo. 114^v.
© The British Library Board. Reproduced by permission

Nigel of Longchamp

SPECVLVM STVLTORVM

EDITED AND TRANSLATED BY
JILL MANN

CLARENDON PRESS · OXFORD

Great Clarendon Street, Oxford, OX2 6DP,
United Kingdom

Oxford University Press is a department of the University of Oxford.
It furthers the University's objective of excellence in research, scholarship,
and education by publishing worldwide. Oxford is a registered trade mark of
Oxford University Press in the UK and in certain other countries

© Jill Mann 2023

The moral rights of the author have been asserted

All rights reserved. No part of this publication may be reproduced, stored in
a retrieval system, or transmitted, in any form or by any means, without the
prior permission in writing of Oxford University Press, or as expressly permitted
by law, by licence or under terms agreed with the appropriate reprographics
rights organization. Enquiries concerning reproduction outside the scope of the
above should be sent to the Rights Department, Oxford University Press, at the
address above

You must not circulate this work in any other form
and you must impose this same condition on any acquirer

Published in the United States of America by Oxford University Press
198 Madison Avenue, New York, NY 10016, United States of America

British Library Cataloguing in Publication Data
Data available

Library of Congress Control Number: 2022944280

ISBN 978–0–19–285771–2

Printed and bound by
CPI Group (UK) Ltd, Croydon, CR0 4YY

Links to third party websites are provided by Oxford in good faith and
for information only. Oxford disclaims any responsibility for the materials
contained in any third party website referenced in this work.

To Michael

PREFACE

The *Speculum Stultorum* has occupied my attention for most of my scholarly life. I first read it in connection with my doctoral research on estates satire, and a comparison with Chaucer's *Nun's Priest's Tale* was the subject of one of my earliest articles. The interest in medieval beast literature which was kindled at that point persisted through the long years of research on the earlier Latin beast epic *Ysengrimus*, and culminated in my book on medieval British beast literature, *From Aesop to Reynard*, which was published in 2009, and in which a chapter was devoted to the *Speculum*. During this whole period I had been using the little spare time that was available to work on a translation of the *Speculum*; a draft was completed in 2002 and typed up by my Notre Dame graduate research assistant Ben Fischer. Meanwhile, at some point in the early 1990s (as far as I can remember), the late (and much lamented) Giovanni Orlandi asked if I could suggest a medieval Latin text whose textual transmission would make a suitable subject for investigation in a *laurea* dissertation by one of his pupils. I proposed the *Speculum*, and in due course I received in 1996 a copy of the dissertation ('La tradizione manoscritta della *Speculum Stultorum* di Nigello Wireker', Università degli Studi di Milano, 1994–1995), which was kindly sent to me by its author, Benedetta Marietti (Andreani). Administrative commitments, and other research projects, prevented me from giving attention to this work for a good many years, and it was only after 2009 that I was free to familarize myself with its contents. Dr Marietti's dissertation does not undertake a new edition, but it consists of a collation of seventeen of the manuscripts listed in Mozley and Raymo's edition of 1960, and provides an analysis of their textual relations and a provisional version of a stemma which differs significantly from that in the 1960 edition by J. H. Mozley and R. Raymo.

My original plan for a translation did not envisage the need to undertake a new edition, but Dr Marietti's dissertation, and the review by Karl Langosch to which it drew my attention, made clear that the Mozley–Raymo edition needed fundamental reassessment and reworking, as Langosch put it, from the beginning. I therefore set about acquiring photographs of the manuscripts, discovering in the process eight manuscripts, and five fragments, that were unknown to Mozley and Raymo. I am most grateful to Professor Anna Maria Fagnoni of the Facoltà di Lettere e Filosofia in Milan for sending me

viii PREFACE

most of the materials used by Dr Marietti, and to Benedetta Marietti herself for generously giving me *carte blanche* to use them and her dissertation in beginning the work afresh. Although my findings sometimes differ from hers, anyone who has confronted a case of complex textual transmission will know how helpful it is to have a second pair of eyes going over the same material and providing independent reactions to serve as stepping-stones to revised judgements.

In approaching this task, I had at first taken comfort from the thought that at least it would not need the extensive historical research that had been necessary for the *Ysengrimus*. To my surprise (and consternation), however, I found that this was not the case: the closer one looked at the text of the *Speculum*, the more important its Canterbury context became, and the more precisely focused was the implicit meaning on which Nigel insists at the beginning and the end of the poem. My historical investigations into the poem's context in time and place took the initial form of a paper delivered at the Fifth International Medieval Latin Congress at Toronto in 2006, which set out the details of this context and concluded by redating the poem. This paper was subsequently published in the *Journal of Medieval Latin*, xvii (2007), 1–37; portions of this article, in suitably adapted form, appear in the Introduction to this edition, and I am grateful to the Editorial Board of the journal, and to Brepols, its publishers, for permission to reuse this material.

In assembling the manuscript materials for this edition, I have been most grateful for the assistance of the staff of the relevant libraries, which are listed in the Manuscript Descriptions. I am also particularly grateful to the following librarians, who answered specific enquries about the manuscripts, their contents and/or provenance, and provided catalogue details which were not otherwise available: Julie Dietman and Matt Heintzelman at the Hill Museum and Manuscript Library in Collegeville, Minnesota; Marek Suchy and Tomáš Zubec in the Prague Castle Archives; Petr Slouka and Soňa Černocká in the Lobkowicz Library at Nelahozeves Castle; Petr Brůha in the Prague National Library; Michal Broda and Adam Poznański in the University Library, Wrocław; Silvano Groff in the Biblioteca comunale di Trento; Almuth Märker and Matthias Eifler at the Universitätsbibliothek, Leipzig; don Giacomo Cardinali in the Vatican Library; Bruce Barker-Benfield in the Bodleian Library, Oxford; Cressida Williams in the Canterbury Cathedral Archives; Susan Kleine at the Universitäts- und Landesbibliothek in Darmstadt, and Ulrike Spyra at the Stuttgart Handschriftenzentrum. Carolin Schreiber, head of the

PREFACE ix

Handschriftenzentrum in the Bayerische Staatsbibliothek in Munich, deserves special thanks, not only for the information which she has willingly provided on numerous occasions, but also for the warm and friendly welcome that she extended on my personal visits.

In the early stages Julia Walworth and Danuta Shanzer helped me to navigate the online catalogue of the Österreichische Nationalbibliothek. In the later stages, Tessa Webber devoted a session of her palaeographical seminar to examples of the *Speculum Stultorum* manuscripts. Rod Thomson generously scrutinized sample photos of all of them and gave his judgement on their dates.

In Cambridge, Mark Statham presided over my visit to the library of Gonville and Caius College, and Johanna Ward at the University Library provided images of Caius MS 427/427. The staff of the University Library have been consistently helpful. Ann Toseland and Simon Gates gave hands-on assistance with transforming microfilms into CDs and CDs into A3 print-outs. Especially in the last two years, I have often felt I should acknowledge a debt to Sir Tim Berners-Lee, since this project would have ground to a halt during the enforced isolation of the pandemic without the resources of the worldwide web. In these challenging circumstances, the Cambridge University Library provided indispensable support via its scan-and-deliver system for articles and book excerpts, backed up by the click-and-collect system for borrowing books, and the Virtual Reading Room facility which provided answers to specific enquiries and requests to check references.

Thanks are also due to those individuals who have responded to my enquiries on a whole variety of questions: Mike Watt (on the process of tanning); the late David Luscombe and Julia Barrow (on John of Salisbury's early career); Helen Clark, Simon Trew, and Matthew Bennet (on amblers); Andy Orchard (on Norns); Birgit Ebersperger (on the Fraterhaus at Weidenbach); Joan Greatrex and Michael Stansfield (on the archives of Christ Church Canterbury); and Piero Boitani (for checking Boccaccio references). Laura Amalasunta Gazzoli kindly checked some doubtful readings in Vienna manuscripts for me.

Tony Edwards introduced me to the Schoenberg manuscript database, and thus uncovered the existence of the Huntington manuscript. Tim Bolton gave me his invaluable help in tracing it from a Sotheby's sale to California, and put me in touch with Jonathan Reilly of Maggs Bros, the antiquarian booksellers who effected the sale to the Huntington Library.

At OUP, Cathryn Steele and Emma Slaughter handled the production process with exemplary efficiency. Bonnie Blackburn was an

X PREFACE

impressively thorough and amicable copy-editor. Thanks also to Nicola Sangster for her patient, cheerful, and eagle-eyed correction of the proofs. The general editors of the Oxford Medieval Texts series made welcome interventions in the final stages: David d'Avray and Rosalind Love made helpful suggestions on the Introduction, translation, and apparatus criticus, while Jim Binns went through the proofs with meticulous attention to detail.

Finally, a huge debt of thanks is due to Michael Reeve for allowing me to draw on his unrivalled knowledge of Latin textual transmission. He read and commented on the entire text and the first draft of the section on the textual transmission, drew attention to a number of metrical problems, and answered a long list of questions on specific problems. His interest and detailed assistance have been an invaluable support.

As ever, however, my greatest debt is to Michael Lapidge, who has been involved in this project every step of the way, and has brought to it the benefits of his learning, experience, and judgement. As a former general editor of Oxford Medieval Texts, and author of the style sheet of the series, he has also advised on the minutiae of OMT copy-editing and presentation. In addition, he contributed the entire section on Nigel's metre and style in the Introduction. He has patiently listened to my daily progress reports, and responded to a stream of detailed requests for his opinion. He has also given much practical help in recent years, when I have unfortunately suffered from reduced mobility due to chronic bursitis: at various times, as circumstances dictated, he has taken a taxi across town to pick up a click-and-collect order for me, or else has cheerfully tramped the long corridors of the University Library to bring me the books I needed. I owe him more than I can say, and this edition is dedicated to him.

J.M.

Cambridge, 2022

CONTENTS

LIST OF ILLUSTRATIONS	xiii
ABBREVIATED REFERENCES	xv
STEMMATA	xix
SIGLA	xxi
INTRODUCTION	xxvii
Text and Context	xxvii
The Poem	xxvii
The Author	xxx
The Dedicatee	xxxiv
The Context: Canterbury	xlii
The Date	l
The Motive	lv
The Manuscripts	lxiii
The Various Forms of the Poem in the Manuscripts	lxviii
Textual Transmission	lxxix
The Manuscript Groups	lxxix
Descent from a Common Archetype	lxxix
The α Group of Manuscripts	lxxxiii
The β Group of Manuscripts	lxxxvii
The γ Group of Manuscripts	lxxxviii
The δ Group of Manuscripts	xcii
'Mixed' Manuscripts	xcix
Manuscripts *Tr Ha La*	xcix
Manuscripts *G* and *I*	ci
Manuscripts *GI* and their relationship to *BH*	ciii
Manuscript *X*	cv
Manuscript *U*	cviii
Manuscripts *Q*, *Y*, and *Z*	cx
Conclusion	cxv
The Question of Revision	cxvi
The Stemma and the Construction of the Text	cxvii
The Evolution of the Poem: Conclusions	cxxv
Nigel's Place in the Tradition of Beast Epic	cxxvii
The Later Influence of the *Speculum Stultorum*	cxxxi
Manuscript Circulation	cxliii

xii CONTENTS

Nigel's Metre and Style cxliv
    Hexameter cxlvii
    Pentameter cli
    Prosody cliii
    Rhyme cliv
    Poetic Diction clvi
    Style clix
Earlier Editions and Translations of the *Speculum Stultorum* clxii
Editorial Conventions clxv
Headings clxix
Translation and Notes clxx

SPECVLVM STVLTORVM 1

APPENDICES
A. Manuscript Descriptions and Early Printed Editions 359
B. Interpolation on the Mendicant Friars 398
C. *Epistola ad Willelmum* in Österreichische
    Nationalbibliothek 3467, fols. 1ʳ–3ʳ 422
D. Borrowings from the *Speculum Stultorum* in Gower's
    Vox Clamantis 425
E. England and Sicily 427

BIBLIOGRAPHY 431

INDEX OF QUOTATIONS AND ALLUSIONS 457

INDEX OF MANUSCRIPTS 466

GENERAL INDEX 467

LIST OF ILLUSTRATIONS

Burnellus imagines becoming a bishop. BL, Additional
MS 38665, fo. 114ᵛ. © The British Library Board.
Reproduced by permission   *frontispiece*

Figures
Stemma 1   xix
Stemma 2   xx

ABBREVIATED REFERENCES

Albini	*Nigelli di Longchamps Speculum Stultorum*, ed. and trans. [Italian] Francesca Albini (Genoa, 2003)
Armstrong, *Francis*	*Francis of Assisi: Early Documents* [English translation], ed. Regis J. Armstrong, J. A Wayne Hellmann, and William J. Short (3 vols., New York, 1999–2002)
AV	Authorized Version of the Bible
Bächtold–Stäubli	*Handwörterbuch des deutschen Aberglaubens*, ed. Hanns Bächtold-Stäubli and Eduard Hoffman-Krayer (10 vols.; Berlin, 1927–42)
Becket Correspondence	*The Correspondence of Thomas Becket, Archbishop of Canterbury 1162–1170*, ed. and trans. Anne Duggan (2 vols.; OMT, 2000) [with consecutive pagination]
BL	British Library
BnF	Paris, Bibliothèque nationale de France
Blaise	Albert Blaise, *Dictionnaire latin-français des auteurs chrétiens* (Turnhout, 1954)
CCCM	Corpus Christianorum, Continuatio Mediaevalis
CCM	Corpus Consuetudinum Monasticarum
CCSL	Corpus Christianorum, Series Latina
1 Cel.	Thomas of Celano, *Vita prima Sancti Francisci*, in *Fontes Franciscani*, pp. 273–424; trans. Armstrong, *Francis*, i. 180–309
2 Cel.	Thomas of Celano, *Vita secunda Sancti Francisci*, in *Fontes Franciscani*, pp. 441–639; trans. Armstrong, *Francis*, ii. 239–393
CFMA	Classiques Français du Moyen Âge
Commedie	*Commedie latine del XII e XIII secolo*, general ed. Ferruccio Bertini (6 vols., Genoa, 1976–98)
CSEL	Corpus Scriptorum Ecclesiasticorum Latinorum
Disticha Catonis	*Dicta Catonis*, in *Minor Latin Poets*, ed. and trans. J. Wight Duff and Arnold Duff (2 vols., Cambridge, MA, 1934), ii. 585–639 [cited by Book, distich, and line of distich]
DMLBS	*Dictionary of Medieval Latin from British Sources*, ed. R. E. Latham, D. R. Howlett, and R. K. Ashdowne

	(Oxford, 1975–2013). Available online at http://www.dmlbs.ox.ac.uk/web/online.html
DOML	Dumbarton Oaks Medieval Library
Du Cange	Charles du Fresne du Cange, sieur, *Glossarium mediae et infimae latinitatis* [1681], rev. by Léopold Favre *et al.* (10 vols. in 5, Graz, 1954)
elegiac *Romulus*	*L'Esopus attribuito a Gualtero Anglico*, ed. and trans [Italian] Paola Busdraghi (Favolisti latini medievali e umanistici, x; Genoa, 2005)
Epigrams	*Epigrams*, in Nigel of Canterbury, *The Passion of St. Lawrence, Epigrams and Marginal Poems*, ed. and trans. Jan M. Ziolkowski (Leiden, 1994), pp. 248–81 [cited by Epigram number and line number]
Fontes Franciscani	*Fontes Franciscani*, ed. Enrico Menestò, Stefano Brufani, *et al.* (Assisi, 1995)
Forcellini	*Totius latinitatis lexicon*, ed. Egidio Forcellini, Jacopo Facciolati, Giuseppe Furlanetto *et al.* [1864–1926] (Padua, 1940)
Gerald of Wales, *Opera*	*Giraldi Cambrensis Opera*, ed. J. S. Brewer, J. F. Dimock, and G. F. Warner (RS xxi; 8 vols., London, 1861–91)
Gervase, *Chronicle*	*The Chronicle of the Reigns of Stephen, Henry II., and Richard I.*, in *The Historical Works of Gervase of Canterbury*, ed. William Stubbs (RS lxxiii; 2 vols., London, 1879–80), i
Gratian, *Decretum*	*Corpus Iuris Canonici*, ed. E. Friedberg (2nd edn.; 2 vols., Leipzig, 1879–81; repr. 1959) [cited as specified in Brundage, *Medieval Canon Law*, pp. 193–4]
Langosch	*Nigellus von Longchamps, Narrenspiegel oder Burnellus, der Esel, der einen längeren Schwanz haben wollt*, trans. Karl Langosch (Leipzig, 1982)
Langosch review	Karl Langosch, review of *Speculum Stultorum*, ed. Mozley and Raymo, *Mittellateinisches Jahrbuch*, iii (1966), 280–6
Latham	R. E. Latham, *Revised Medieval Latin Word-List from British and Irish Sources* (London, 1965)
Lawrence	*The Passion of St. Lawrence*, in Nigel of Canterbury, *The Passion of St. Lawrence, Epigrams and Marginal Poems*, ed. and trans. Jan M. Ziolkowski (Leiden, 1994), pp. 52–247 [cited by line number]

ABBREVIATED REFERENCES   xvii

Lewis and Short	*A Latin Dictionary Founded on Andrews' Edition of Freund's Latin Dictionary*, ed. Charlton T. Lewis and Charles Short (Oxford, 1897)
Mansi	*Sacrorum conciliorum nova et amplissima collectio*, ed. G. D. Mansi, cont. J. B. Martin, L. Petit (53 vols., Florence and Venice, 1759–98; Paris, 1899–1927)
Map Poems	*The Latin Poems Commonly Attributed to Walter Mapes*, ed. Thomas Wright (Camden Society; London, 1841) [cited by page number and line number of poem]
Matthew Paris, *Chronica*	*Matthaei Parisiensis monachi Sancti Albani Chronica majora*, ed. Henry Richards Luard (RS lvii; 7 vols., 1872–83)
MGH	Monumenta Germaniae Historica
Auct. Ant.	Auctores Antiquissimi
Epp.	Epistolae (in quarto)
Poetae	Poetae Latini Aevi Carolini
SS	Scriptores (in folio)
SS rer. Germ.	Scriptores rerum Germanicarum in usum scholarum separatim editi
Miracles	Nigel of Canterbury, *Miracles of the Virgin Mary, in Verse*, ed. Jan Ziolkowski (Toronto, 1986) [cited by line number]
Niermeyer	*Mediae Latinitatis Lexicon Minus*, ed. J. F. Niermeyer (2 vols., Leiden, 1976)
ODNB	*Oxford Dictionary of National Biography*. Online version at https://www.oxforddnb.com
OLD	*Oxford Latin Dictionary*, ed. P. G. W. Glare (Oxford, 1968–82; 2nd edn., 2012)
OMT	Oxford Medieval Texts
PL	Patrologiae cursus completus, series latina, ed. J.-P. Migne (221 vols., Paris, 1841–64)
Paul	Leo M. Kaiser, 'A critical edition of Nigel Wireker's *Vita Sancti Pauli Primi Eremitae*', *Classical Folia*, xiv (1960), 63–81
Publilius Syrus	in *Minor Latin Poets*, ed. and trans. J. Wight Duff and Arnold Duff (2 vols., Cambridge, MA, 1934), i. 3–111
RS	Britain and Ireland during the Middle Ages, published . . . under the direction of the Master of the Rolls (99 vols.; London, 1858–96)

xviii   ABBREVIATED REFERENCES

Rule of St Benedict	*Benedicti Regula*, ed. and trans. P. Schmitz (4th edn.; Maredsous, 1975) [cited by chapter number]
Sancti Bernardi Opera	*Sancti Bernardi Opera*, ed. Jean Leclercq, C. H. Talbot, and H. M. Rochais (8 vols. in 9; Rome, 1957–77) [cited by letter number if relevant, volume and page number]
SC	Sources chrétiennes
Singer, *Thesaurus*	*Thesaurus proverbiorum medii aevi. Lexikon der Sprichwörter des romanisch-germanischen Mittelalters*, ed. Samuel Singer and others (13 vols. in 14, Berlin, 1995–2002) [cited by Singer's numbering system for proverbs, plus volume and page numbers]
SS	*Speculum Stultorum*
Statuta Petri Venerabilis	*Statuta Petri Venerabilis Abbatis Cluniacensis IX (1146/7)*, ed. Giles Constable, in *Consuetudines Benedictinae Variae (Saec. XI–Saec. XIV* (CCM vi, Siegburg, 1975), pp. 19–106
Stubbs, *Introductions*	William Stubbs, *Historical Introductions to the Rolls Series*, ed. Arthur Hassall (London, 1902) [page references to this volume are followed by an equal sign and a reference to the page number of the introduction in the original edition (e.g., Stubbs, *Introductions*, p. 000 = Roger of Howden, *Chronica*, iii. 000)]
TLL	*Thesaurus linguae Latinae*, ed. Internationale Thesaurus-Kommission (Munich, 1896–)
Tractatus, ed. Boutemy	Nigellus de Longchamp dit Wireker, *Tractatus contra curiales et officiales clericos*, ed. André Boutemy (Paris, 1959)
Walther, *Initia*	Hans Walther, *Initia carminum ac versuum Medii Aevi posterioris latinorum* (Göttingen, 1969)
Walther, *Proverbia*	Hans Walther, *Proverbia Sententiaeque Latinitatis Medii Aevi* (6 vols.; Göttingen, 1963–9); *Nachträge*, supplementary vols., vii–ix, ed. Paul Gerhardt Schmidt (Göttingen, 1982–6) [cited by proverb number]
Werner, *Sprichwörter*	Jakob Werner, *Lateinische Sprichworter und Sinnsprüche des Mittelalters* (Heidelberg, 1912)

STEMMATA

For the reader's convenience, stemmata (1) and (2) represent in diagrammatical form the relations between the main manuscript groups as indicated by the surviving manuscripts. Since so many intervening stages in the development of the poem have disappeared in the centuries between the date of the poem's composition and the date of these manuscripts, the stemmata should not be taken as a complete factual representation of the textual transmission of the poem. The Greek letter ω represents the author's original version of the poem, while β represents the first extended version (see Introduction, pp. cxxv–cxxvii). The letters αβγδ represent the hypothetical originals of each branch of the transmission, with the addition of a tentatively hypothesized original for an intermediate stage between γ and δ which could have been a source for the 'mixed' manuscripts ZQY. Some 'mixed' manuscripts (GI, UX) appear at more than one point in the stemma, reflecting their complex affiliations; dotted lines indicate connections created by contamination.

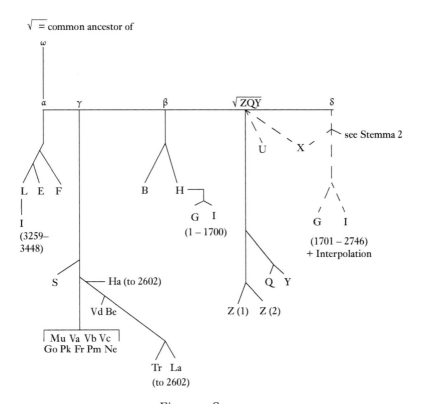

Figure 1. Stemma 1

STEMMATA

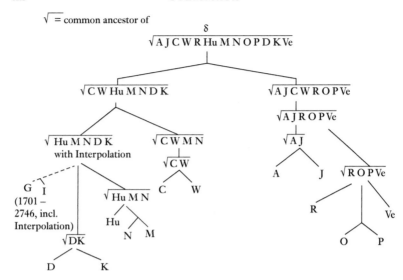

Figure 2. Stemma 2

SIGLA

INDIVIDUAL MANUSCRIPTS

Mozley's sigla are given only in cases where they differ from the ones used in this volume; * = a manuscript not known to Mozley

A   London, British Library, Harley 2422, fos. 2^r–81^v

B   London, British Library, Arundel 23, fos. 1^r–66^v

Be*   Berlin, Staatsbibliothek zu Berlin, Preussischer Kulturbesitz, theol. qu. 214, fos. 181^r–234^r

C   London, British Library, Cotton Titus A. XX, fos. 4^r–50^v

D   Dublin, Trinity College Library, 440, pp. 1–130 (paginated)

E   Oxford, Bodleian Library, Bodley 761 (S.C. 2535), fos. 160^r–180^r

F   Oxford, Bodleian Library, Bodley 851 (S.C. 3041), fos. 97^v–115^v

Fr*   Frankfurt am Main, Universitätsbibliothek, Barth. 62, fos. 150^r–162^v

G   Oxford, Bodleian Library, Digby 27 (S. C. 1628), fos. 1^r–61^v

Go   Erfurt, Forschungsbibliothek Gotha, Chart. B 517, fos. 136^r–195^v (Mozley's k)

H   Oxford, Bodleian Library, Bodley 496 (S.C. 2159), fos. 146^r–192^r

Ha*   Halle, Universitäts- und Landesbibliothek, Stolb.-Wern. Za 89, fos. 1^r–47^v

Hu*   Huntington Library, San Marino, California, MS HM80250, fos. 168^v–184^r

I   Oxford, Bodleian Library, Bodley 780 (S.C. 2583), fos. 1^r–33^v

J   Oxford, All Souls College, 37, fos. 171^r–196^r

K   London, British Library, Additional 38665, fos. 85^r–156^r

L   London, Lambeth Palace Library, 357, fos. 78^r–111^r

La*   Sankt Paul im Lavanttal (Kärnten), Stiftsbibliothek, Codex 239/4, fos. 101^r–151^v, 161^r–184^v

M   Lincoln, Cathedral Chapter Library, 105, fos. 91^r–116^v

Mu   Munich, Bayerische Staatsbibliothek, clm 23820, fos. 243^r–282^v (Mozley's m)

N   Lincoln, Cathedral Chapter Library, 191, fos. 228^v–255^r

Ne*   Lobkowicz Library, Nelahozeves Castle, Czech Republic, Sig. VI Fb 29, pp. 87–125

O   Brussels, KBR, 2695–719, fos. 34^r –93^v

P   Brussels, KBR, 1701–4, fos. 122^v–138^v

xxii SIGLA

Pk* Prague, Archiv Prazského Hradu, Knihovna Metropolitni Kapituly, M. CXXI (catalogue 1482), fos. 43^r–86^v

Pm* Prague, Knihovna Národního muzea, XIV. D. 4, fos. 144^r–180^v

Q Copenhagen, Det Kongelige Bibliotek, GKS 1634 quarto, fos. 85^r–133^r

R Città del Vaticano, Biblioteca Apostolica Vaticana, reg. lat 1379, fos. 1^r–70^r

S Paris, Bibliothèque nationale de France, lat. 16519, fos. 51^r–106^v

T Wrocław, Biblioteka Uniwersytecka we Wrocławiu, IV.Q.126, fos. 154^r–183^r

Tr Trento, Biblioteca comunale, W 3154, fos. 211^r–235^v (Mozley's s)

U London, British Library, Sloane 1831 B, fos. 1^r–47^v

Va Vienna, Österreichische Nationalbibliothek, 3487, fos. 1^r–43^r (Mozley's V)

Vb Vienna, Österreichische Nationalbibliothek, 12531, fos. 85^r–133^r (Mozley's z)

Vc Vienna, Österreichische Nationalbibliothek, 3283, fos. 1^r–87^r (Mozley's t)

Vd Vienna, Österreichische Nationalbibliothek, 3467, fos. 1^r–56^r (Mozley's u)

Ve Vienna, Österreichische Nationalbibliothek, 3529, fos. 1^r–74^v (Mozley's x)

W* Oxford, Bodleian Library, Lat. misc. c. 75 (*olim* Phillips 3119), fos. 1^r–23^v

X London, British Library, Cotton Vespasian E. XII, fos. 10^v–77^r

Y Wolfenbüttel, Herzog-August Bibliothek, Helmst. 616, fos. 93^r–137^v

Z Leipzig, Universitäts-Bibliothek, 1591, fos. 1^r–62^v

FRAGMENTS

fb* Bonn, Universitäts- und Landesbibliothek, S 220, fos. 252^v–258^v, 356^v–358^v

fc* Canterbury Cathedral Archives CCA-DCc/AddMS/127/4

fg Paris, Bibliothèque de Sainte Geneviève, 3196, fos. 115^r–116^r (Mozley's e)

fh* Giessen, Universitätsbibliothek 1251, fos. 51^v–52^v

fm Munich, Bayerische Staatsbibliothek, clm 237, fos. 218^r–220^v (Mozley's n)

fn Munich, Bayerische Staatsbibliothek, clm 14529, fos. 154v, 160^r–166^r (Mozley's o)

SIGLA xxiii

fp   Prague, Národní Knihovna, III. D. 17, unnumbered guard-leaf, r–v (= 469) (Mozley's p)

fq   Prague, Národní Knihovna, X. D. 9, fos. 94^v–96^v (=1888) (Mozley's q)

ft*   Trier, Stadtbibliothek 1898, fo. 90$^{r–v}$

fu*   Uppsala, Universitets-Bibliotek, Lat. 931, fo. 86$^{r–v}$

MANUSCRIPT GROUPS

L E F = α
B H = β
S Mu Va Vb Vc Vd T Go Be Pk Fr Pm Ne = γ *(minus Fr from 2052–464)*; *when with Tr Ha La (up to line 2602)* = γ+; *when minus S* = γ-
A C J W R Hu M N O P D K Ve = δ

When a reading is shared by some but not all members of the group (so that the Greek letter cannot be used), the sigla of the relevant MSS are listed in the *apparatus criticus* without spaces in between, but a space separates them from the succeeding group, e.g. *SMuVaVb ACJWR*.

The following 'mixed manuscripts' are grouped according to their general character but not assigned a Greek letter since they derive from more than one ancestor:
G I
Tr Ha La (after line 2602, when γ ends, they are always listed separately)
U Z X Q Y
These are listed without spaces between the individual sigla, but with a space separating them from other groups.

The sigla for the manuscript groups in the *Epistle to William* have slightly different referents, since it is lacking in *LECOPUZQY*. Manuscripts containing the *Epistle* are *F BH* (= β); *SMuVaVbVcVdTGoBePkFrPmNe* (= γ); *AJWRHuMNDKVe* (= δ); *GI TrHaLa X*. The *Epistle* follows the poem in *D*, *F*, and *R*. *Vd* has an abridged version,which is printed separately in Appendix C; its readings are not included in the *apparatus criticus*.

EDITORIAL PRACTICE IN THE *APPARATUS CRITICUS*

Scribal corrections are not usually recorded if they seem to be in the main hand and to have been made at the time of original copying

xxiv   SIGLA

(or very close to it), *unless* the corrections shed light on the manuscript groupings and thus on the textual transmission. Superscript [ac] and [pc] are used for corrections or alternative readings which can with reasonable confidence be identified as made by the original scribe at or near the time of original copying (even if these variants derive from a different exemplar).

Superscript [2] is used to designate corrections or additions which seem to have been made at a later time than the original copying, as suggested by a different script, different pen, or erasures and additions which indicate large-scale revision resulting from consultation of a different exemplar.

If a variant is identified as [ac] (before correction), but no [pc] (after correction) version is given, this means that after correction the reading is identical with the lemma. If a variant is identified as [pc], but no [ac] version is given, this means that *either* the previous version of the word is illegible, *or* that the reading still differs from the lemma after correction.

Where a scribe has copied the same material twice (whether single lines or larger portions of text), deliberately or inadvertently, variants in the first and second versions are indicated by the addition of (1) or (2) (not superscript) to the sigil, respectively. For details of repeated material, see the *apparatus criticus*.

Ha and *La* frequently record alternative readings, most often in the margin, prefaced by 'uel' (written out in full, as 'ul', or simply as 'l'). Since these alternative readings have significance for the textual transmission, they are recorded in the *apparatus criticus*; a forward slash (/) indicates the placing in the margin. However, it should be noted that it is not always easy to distinguish between the letter l with a diagonal stroke through it as representing an abbreviation for 'uel' and the *signe de renvoi*, a forward slash with one or two marks to the right of it. When it appears that this sign indicates an alternative, it is represented in the apparatus criticus by '[*uel*]'; when it indicates a correction (the original reading being deleted), this is indicated by superscript [ac] or [pc] in the usual way. When the original word is struck through, the intention to correct is clear, but sometimes it is underlined, and it is not clear whether this is a way of indicating expunction or a way of drawing attention to the lemma of the variant reading. On a few occasions, the alternative word is incorporated within the line, with or without preceding 'uel' (see, for example, *La* 3703, *Ha* 1250, 1252). The above format(s) are very occasionally used for alternatives and corrections in other manuscripts.

SIGLA

OTHER ABBREVIATIONS USED IN THE
APPARATUS CRITICUS

add.   added
corr.   corrected
om.   omitted
transp. transposed

INTRODUCTION

TEXT AND CONTEXT

The Poem

A DONKEY NAMED Burnellus conceives an overwhelming desire for a longer tail which will match his splendid ears. He asks a doctor (Galen) for help; having tried in vain to persuade Burnellus to be content with what nature has given him, Galen invents a list of absurd medicines which he says will do the trick, and sends the ass off to Salerno to buy them. On arrival, he encounters a London merchant who fraudulently claims to have the medicines all assembled in ten glass jars, and Burnellus joyfully pays up without opening the jars to test his claim. On the way home, a Cistercian monk called Fromundus sets his dogs on Burnellus; in the fray, the glass jars are broken, the ass loses all his imaginary medicines, and in addition the dogs bite off half his tail. Claiming to be a papal legate, Burnellus angrily threatens Fromundus that the pope will punish him severely. Fromundus tries to appease him by offering to take him to a garden of delights where his every desire will be catered for; secretly, he plans to murder him. Burnellus guesses his plan and hurls Fromundus into the sea from a high cliff. Burnellus then decides that if he cannot have a longer tail, he will have learning instead, and sets out for the university of Paris. He studies for seven years but learns nothing; leaving Paris, he cannot even remember its name. He next resolves to enter a religious order, and assesses the suitability for a donkey of each of the existing orders, but he does not actually put this plan into action. After another brief encounter with the doctor Galen, his old master suddenly appears and reclaims him for his old life of drudgery. He cuts off the ass's ears (so that instead of acquiring a longer tail to match his ears, he ends up with shorter ears to match his truncated tail). The concluding moral is that no one can escape nature.

This is the simple narrative outline of the *Speculum Stultorum*, a twelfth-century beast epic in 3,900 lines of Latin elegiac verse. The best-known examples of beast epic at this period centre on the persistent antagonism between Reynard the fox and his supposed 'uncle', the

xxviii INTRODUCTION

wolf Ysengrimus.[1] The *Speculum Stultorum* is a surprising exception: its central figure is not the cunning fox but a very stupid ass. As the opening of the poem makes clear (57–80), the seminal idea for his story is Avianus's fable of the ass who clothes himself in a lion's skin; he may terrify the other animals, says the farmer who owns him, but 'to me you'll always be a donkey'.[2] Burnellus does not, however, yearn to be a lion, but to be even more 'asinine' than nature made him. And his subsequent adventures—his journey to Salerno, his encounter with the evil monk Fromundus, and his seven-year sojourn at the university of Paris—are all without parallel in other beast literature.

The same could be said of the lengthy interpolations of various kinds with which the basic narrative is filled out. First, there are a number of inset narratives:

(1) Galen tells the story of two cows whose tails get stuck in some freezing mud; one cow rashly amputates her tail, so that when summer comes she dies of insect stings, while the other patiently waits until the sun thaws the mud and she can return home unharmed (205–594).

(2) On the way to Paris, a fellow-traveller tells Burnellus the story of a cock whose leg was accidentally broken by Gundulf, a priest's son, when it was a young chick, and many years later took revenge by failing to crow on the day when the young man was himself to be ordained a priest, so that he slept in and missed the ceremony (1251–502).

(3) Burnellus tells how he once rescued three thieves from execution by opening their prison and carrying them to safety. One of them is now mayor of his home town, and *because* Burnellus did him this favour, Burnellus is sure that he will be his enemy, since the man whose life you have saved always hates you for having put him under an obligation (1805–912).

(4) Burnellus tells the story of the Three Fates who travel through the world with the aim of lavishing the gifts of Fortune on those suffering from the defects of Nature. The two junior Fates wish to aid two girls who are distinguished by their beauty and virtue, but who suffer from emotional or physical distress. The senior Fate refuses, on the grounds that Nature has already given them so much; instead, she

---

[1] The earliest example is the Latin poem *Ysengrimus* (ed. Mann), which was the model and source for the earliest branches of the French *Roman de Renart*, the Dutch *Van den Vos Reinaerde*, and many others. See Knapp, *Das lateinische Tierepos*; Foulet, *Le Roman de Renard*; Flinn, *Le Roman de Renart*. For a succinct survey of the development of Latin and vernacular beast epic, see Mann, *From Aesop to Reynard*, pp. 17–20. For discussion of Nigel's predecessors and later influence, see below, pp. cxxvii–cxliv.

[2] Avianus, *Fabulae*, v. 18: 'semper asellus eris'. Cf. *SS* 58, 'semper asellus erit'.

TEXT AND CONTEXT   xxix

insists that they should shower riches and honours on a coarse and ignorant peasant girl whom they encounter defecating by the side of the road (3281–458).

(5) The poem concludes with the story of the Grateful Animals and the Ungrateful Man, in which the central figure is Burnellus's master Bernard, and the ass himself is given only a passing mention. A rich man called Dryanus falls into a pit which has been dug to trap wild animals; already in the pit are a lion, a monkey, and a snake. Attracted by Dryanus's cries, Bernard throws down a rope to him, but is horrified when, one after another, the three animals use it to escape. Persuaded by Dryanus's promises of rich reward, he tries one last time and pulls him out of the pit, but when he tries to collect the promised reward, he is driven from the rich man's door. Meanwhile, the lion brings him fresh meat daily; the monkey cuts and stacks firewood for him, and the snake gives him a magic jewel which returns to his purse every time he tries to sell it. Hearing of this magical stone, the king enquires about its origin, and when Bernard tells him the story, he decrees that Dryanus should either fulfil his promise or else be put back in the same pit with the same three animal companions. Naturally, Dryanus chooses the first option (3561–870).

In addition, there are a number of rhetorical set-pieces:

(6) Burnellus discourses on the duties of a bishop (1669–778).

(7) Burnellus surveys all the religious orders in turn as he tries to decide which is best for a donkey to join, and then proposes a new order combining the features he finds most attractive (2051–464).

(8) Burnellus laments the moral decay of the court of Rome, and the failings of kings, bishops, abbots, and priors (2559–872).

(9) Burnellus then relates a debate between birds that he once overheard, about whether the disasters of the world are to be blamed on avian sins (2873–3236).

The story of the two cows dimly recalls the episode in which Reynard persuades the wolf to go fishing in a wintry river, using his tail as 'fishing-rod'; the freezing ice holds him fast, and he escapes only when a peasant woman cuts off his tail with an axe (*Ysengrimus*, i. 665–ii. 135). The focus in the story of the two cows has, however, shifted to the comically elaborate speeches in which each cow justifies its own course of action. The story of Gundulf and the cock has no known parallel, and neither has the story of the three thieves. The story of the Three Fates reflects a motif of Scandinavian folklore, but is not part of medieval beast literature. And although animals play a major role in the story of the Grateful Animals and the Ungrateful Man, its background

xxx INTRODUCTION

is not in western European beast literature, but in the oriental tale-collection known as *Kalila and Dimna* or the *Pañchatantra*.[3] It was first introduced to England by Richard I on his return from the Third Crusade (on which, more later).

These narrative insertions and rhetorical set-pieces are tied to the main story by only the slenderest of threads. The tale of the two cows has some potential relevance to Burnellus's rash ambition, but the same cannot be said for any of the other mini-narratives. The tale of the chick with the broken leg, for example, has no relevance to Burnellus, and the traveller who tells it disappears from the narrative soon after it is ended. Even when an inset story involves Burnellus himself, such as the account of how he rescued the three thieves from prison, it is of no further consequence to the main narrative and is not an obvious illustration of the ass's folly. The reader might therefore conclude that the poem's rambling structure is due to the primary desire to entertain—that it is no more than a fairly casual assemblage of amusing anecdotes and rhetorical elaborations of conventional satiric topics. Closer examination of the themes and motifs of the poem, and a more detailed knowledge of its historical context, its author and its dedicatee, will, however, reveal the underlying motives and concerns that tie all these disparate elements together and make coherent sense of the whole.

The Author

In contrast to the anonymity that cloaks so many medieval texts, the author of the *Speculum Stultorum* makes plain his identity at the very beginning of his poem:

> Suscipe pauca tibi ueteris, Willelme, Nigelli
> scripta, minus sapido nuper arata stylo.
> Hoc modicum nouitatis opus tibi mitto legendum,
> maxima pars animae dimidiumque meae. (1–4)

Accept, William, these scanty writings, lately scribbled in unembellished style by your old friend Nigel. To you, who are half my soul, and the more important part, I send this little novelty to read.

The identities of 'Nigel' and 'William' are specified in more detail at the beginning of another work by Nigel, the *Tractatus contra Curiales et Officiales Clericos*:[4] he identifies himself as a monk of Christ Church,

---

[3] See below, pp. cxxxiv–cxli, and n. to lines 3561–866.
[4] The *Tractatus* was edited by André Boutemy in 1959. On the manuscripts of the *Tractatus* and the verse epistle which was probably intended as a poetic envoy to this work, see pp. 92–6, 131–43 of Boutemy's edition.

TEXT AND CONTEXT   xxxi

Canterbury ('Cantuariensis ecclesie fratrum minimus frater Nigellus veste monachus, vita peccator, gradu presbyter sed indignus').[5] He addresses the *Tractatus* to 'Reverendo patri et domino Willelmo, Dei gratia Eliensi episcopo, apostolicae sedis legato, regis Angliae cancellario'—that is, William of Longchamp, chancellor of King Richard I of England, and bishop of Ely from 1189 until his death in 1197.[6] Also addressed to William is a prose epistle which accompanies the *Speculum* in many of its manuscripts and offers an interpretation of its meaning (see below, pp. lv–lxiii, for a discussion of the *Epistle*). On the principle of Ockham's razor, it has generally been assumed that the 'William' to whom the *Speculum Stultorum* is addressed is also William of Longchamp.[7]

Various other poetic works are attributed to Nigel, as follows: *Miracles of the Virgin Mary*; *Passion of St Lawrence*; *Epigrams* and other poems; and a *Life of St Paul of Thebes*.[8] The attribution rests on the

---

[5] Two Canterbury rentals of around 1200 mention an Agatha, sister of 'Nigel our monk' ('Nigelli monachi nostri'). See Urry, *Canterbury under the Angevin Kings*, pp. 296–7 (Rental D266 and Rental E42), and for the dates of the rentals, see pp. 9, 13. Two references to monks named Nigel occur in an early 13th-c. Canterbury obituary (BL, Cotton Nero C. IX, fos. 3^r–18^v, dated 1225 × 1240 by Boutemy, 'Two obituaries', pp. 292–3). See the edition of this obituary by Fleming, 'Christchurch's sisters and brothers', pp. 130–48, which supersedes the 18th-c. edition by Dart, *History and Antiquities of the Cathedral Church of Canterbury*, pp. xxxii–xli: fo. 9^v (Fleming, p. 138), 'Obierunt [other names] et Nigellus sacerdotes et monachi nostre congregationis'; fo. 12^v (Fleming, p. 141), 'Obierunt Godefridus et Nigellus sacerdotes et monachi nostre congregationis'. (The entry on fo. 11^r (Fleming, p. 140) for 'Nigellus frater noster' must refer to a lay member of the fraternity rather than a monk.) Since the obits are of different dates (18 Kal. Mai. and 6 Kal. Oct.), they must refer to two different monks of this name, although there is no indication of the year of death; Jan Ziolkowski's assertion that 'there is no reason to believe that more than one Nigel belonged to Christ Church in the late twelfth century' (*Lawrence*, p. 9) is thus questionable.

Joan Greatrex's *Biographical Register* (p. 244) notes the two obits on p. 244. On p. 320, she also notes two references in a Canterbury cathedral accounts book (CCA-DCc/MA/1, fos. 56^v and 58^v), under the years 1215 and 1216, to 'Nigel' as almoner of the monastery ('Nigello elemosinar[io] xiiii lib[ras]'); given the two entries in the obit list, this may or may not be the author of *SS*, but it is very possible.

[6] For a brief summary of William's life, see Turner, 'Longchamp, William de (*d.* 1197)', *ODNB*. The fullest study is the PhD dissertation by David Balfour, ' William Longchamp: Upward Mobility and Character Assassination'. I cited this study as forthcoming with the Davenant Press in my article 'Does an author?' in 2007, but unfortunately the Press's website still lists it as 'coming soon'. Balfour's study supersedes the older monograph by Champeaux (*Notice*).

[7] Though this is (implicitly) not accepted by Rigg, 'Nigel of Canterbury', who speaks of Nigel sending the *Speculum Stultorum*, 'with an introductory explication', to 'a William', while the *Tractatus* is addressed to 'the Chancellor William de Longchamps' (p. 306).

[8] For editions of these works, see *Miracles*, ed. Ziolkowski; *Lawrence*, ed. Ziolkowski (which includes the *Epigrams*); Boutemy, 'Une vie inédite de Paul de Thèbes'; Kaiser, 'Nigel Wireker's *Vita Sancti Pauli Primi Eremitae*'.

xxxii INTRODUCTION

sole manuscript witness of these works, BL, Cotton Vespasian D. XIX,[9] which identifies them as the work of 'Nigel of Longchamp' ('Nigelli de Longo Campo').[10] The alternative name 'Wireker', by which Nigel was

[9] There is, however, another copy of one of the *Miracles* ('De puero cum alio ludente') in BL, Arundel 23, fo. 67[r] (my MS *B*), which also contains the *Speculum Stultorum*. The contents list of Vespasian D. XIX (see following note) also attributes to Nigel a versified list of the archbishops of Canterbury which does not, however, appear in this manuscript; the full list of 75 leonine-rhymed hexameters is to be found in BL, Vitellius A. XI, fo. 37[v], and was printed by Boutemy, 'À propos d'un manuscrit', pp. 1001–3, and *Tractatus*, pp. 46–8. Another version, signalled by Boutemy on p. 74 of his edition of the *Tractatus*, is contained in Oxford, Bodleian Library, Douce 95, fos. 20[v]–22[v]; it consists of 74 lines, of which the first 68 agree with the version in Vitellius A. XI, ending with Archbishop Richard, who died in 1184. The last six are replaced by new lines which take the list up to the death of Hubert Walter in 1205, as follows: 'Isti successit Baldewinus cum requiescit/ Mundus ei cessit dum se pro praesule gessit/ Hic betel (?) accessit ad Arcon [=Acre] post fata quiescit/ Hinc dat Hubertus largus per dona repertus/ Iudicio iustus vir strenuus atque venustus/ Moribus et fultus propria nunc sede sepultus.' An eleven-line excerpt from this list, representing lines 65–75 of the version in Vitellius, is contained in Arundel 23, fo. 66[v]; Cambridge, Gonville and Caius College 427/427 (s. xii/xiii), p. 230; Cambridge, Gonville and Caius College 191/224, p. 345 (s. xvi); and Cambridge, Corpus Christi College 287, fo. 131[v]. The above details, which do not entirely agree with the descriptions in the catalogues of M. R. James for Corpus and Caius colleges, have been verified in person, except for the Corpus manuscript, which has been verified by consultation of the digitized version of Corpus manuscripts entitled Parker on the Web (https://parker.stanford.edu). James suggested that Caius 427/427 might have come from Christ Church, but Graham and Watson (*Recovery of the Past*, p. 48, n. 156) indicate that it more probably came from St Augustine's. (This casts doubt on Boutemy's suggestion that Caius 427/427 is Nigel's rough draft, in his own hand; see *Tractatus*, pp. 138–9.) See also Catherine Hall ('One-way trail', p. 282), who suggests that the eleven-line excerpt in Caius 427 may be in the hand of Matthew Parker, who later owned this manuscript.

Ziolkowski's erroneous statement (*Miracles*, p. 4, n. 16) that these eleven lines are also found in MS Corpus 441 (which, like Corpus 287, contains Nigel's *Tractatus*, at pp. 253–310) apparently derives from a similar statement by Boutemy in 'À propos d'un manuscrit', p. 997, where Boutemy seems to have allowed his memory to trick him into substituting one Corpus manuscript number for another.

Also attributed to Nigel are some marginal glosses and poems in a copy of Peter Comestor's *Historia scholastica* in Cambridge, Trinity College B.15.5, which are edited by Ziolkowski in *Lawrence*, pp. 282–302; see also O'Daly, 'Reading the *Historia Scholastica*'. Finally, Arundel 23 also contains a 'Life of St Eustace' in elegiac distichs (ed. Varnhagen in 'Zwei lateinische metrische versionen'), which Boutemy (*Tractatus*, pp. 69–70) very tentatively ascribed to Nigel, while admitting that there was nothing in the text to support this attribution, and it rested solely on the presence in Arundel 23 of other works by Nigel or associated with Canterbury. However, even a cursory inspection of the St Eustace poem reveals not only its unsophisticated narrative style but also a level of metrical incompetence sufficient to rule out Nigel's authorship.

[10] See Mozley, 'Unprinted poems of Nigel Wireker', p. 398. A fuller account of the manuscript is given in Ward, *Catalogue of Romances*, ii. 691–5. At the top of fo. 1[v], in small letters, is the Canterbury *ex libris*: 'hic liber est ecclesie Xti Cant.: qui illum inde abstulerit auferat eum dominus de libro uite'. Nigel's name, in large black and red letters, is under the *ex libris*. Beneath his name, in a much later hand, are details about Nigel, and under that again, a list of contents, written in blue ink, appears on a small pasted-in slip. The manuscript is listed in the catalogue of Christ Church library; see James, *Ancient Libraries*, p. 48, no. 278, and Ker, *Medieval Libraries*, p. 36.

TEXT AND CONTEXT

xxxiii

long known, seems to be a misreading of 'Witeker',[11] which is attested in a fine rental of Canterbury holdings at London.[12] J. H. Mozley explains this name as a mistake by the sixteenth-century antiquarian John Bale, misled by a contents list on fo. 2ʳ of BL, Cotton Julius A. VII (fifteenth-century) which refers to 'the verses of Nigel Wetekre' ('versus Nigelli Wetekre monachi Cantuariensis').[13] The competing claims of these differing ascriptions have been assessed by A. G. Rigg,[14] whose concluding suggestion was that Nigel should be called 'of Canterbury', though this name is nowhere associated with him in medieval sources. If I prefer the designation 'of Longchamp', it is because this name is linked to his literary works in an early manuscript,[15] and one which belonged to his own monastery.

[11] Mozley ('Nigel Wireker or Wetekre?', p. 314) ascribes the misreading to the 16th-c. antiquary John Bale, whose *Index Britanniae Scriptorum* has an entry referring to 'Nigellus de Werekere, monachus Cantuariensis' (ed. Poole and Bateson, p. 311).

[12] The rental is dated c.1230 by Urry, *Canterbury under the Angevin Kings*, p. 2. Nigel is there called 'de Wetehekere', possibly referring to Whiteacre ('wheat-acre'), the name of a hamlet in Waltham, a few miles from Canterbury. Nigel's sister Agatha (see above, n. 5) is called 'filia Gileberti de Sarneis', which may refer to Sarness Farm in Waltham, half a mile from Whiteacre (though 'Sarneia' is also the Latin name for Guernsey). See Urry, *Canterbury under the Angevin Kings*, p. 154, especially n. 4.

[13] See Mozley, 'Nigel Wireker or Wetekre?'. Urry (*Canterbury under the Angevin Kings*, p. 154, n. 4) suggested a family connection between Nigel and one Emma of Whiteacre (Wettekera), whose husband Geoffrey was 'of Lisors', a village in Normandy not far from Longchamps (Urry, p. 59, p. 154, n. 4). Urry also suggested (p. 154, n. 4) that this might be the Emma whose death is lamented in Nigel's *Epigram* no. ix. However, she most likely earned this poetic commemoration, not by any family relationship to Nigel, but because she and her husband agreed with Wibert, prior of Christ Church Canterbury, to exchange a piece of land north of the cathedral precincts for property in central Canterbury (Urry, pp. 148, 221). This would explain why 'Emma soror nostra' appears in the 13th-c. obituary list of Christ Church Canterbury (Fleming, 'Christchurch's sisters and brothers', p. 140) at 15 Kal. Oct. (= 17 Sept.). The obit given in Nigel's poem (12 Kal. Oct. = 20 Sept.) is not identical, but is close enough to make the identification probable. Two other references to an 'Emma soror nostra', at Kal. Sept (= 1 Sept.) on fo. 11ʳ (Fleming, p. 139), and at 5 Kal. Ian. (= 28 Dec.) on fo. 18ᵛ (Fleming, p. 148) are too far distant in date to be relevant.

[14] Rigg ('Nigel of Canterbury', p. 305) thinks that in Nigel's case, 'de Longo Campo' is a Latinization of 'Whiteacre', not because all wheat-fields are long, but because 'if (as is perfectly possible) the wheat-field at Sarness Farm happened to be long, someone from that farm could well have been described as being 'de longo campo'. This explanation is unconvincing: toponyms need to be distinctive to serve their purpose and long fields must have occurred more or less everywhere.

[15] Cotton Vespasian D. XIX is ascribed to the late 12th or early 13th c. (see the references to James, Ker, and Ward in n. 10 above). It is included in the online collection of digitized manuscripts in the British Library.

xxxiv INTRODUCTION

The Dedicatee

One of the most intriguing things about Nigel's surname 'de Longo Campo' is that he shared it with his dedicatee, William of Longchamp.[16] It does not seem likely that they were related by birth. William's family is well documented, and since William came from Normandy, while Nigel's origins seem to have been in Kent, it has not proved possible to demonstrate even a likely connection between them.[17] In the *Speculum Stultorum*, Nigel addresses William in terms of personal affection, echoing Horace in calling him 'half my soul'.[18] In his *Tractatus*, while praising William's learning, he implies that he has frequently been in company with him.[19] It is possible that they had known each other when young, perhaps at the university of Paris (though there is no evidence for this).[20] But there are other, more important reasons why an author might choose William as the dedicatee of a literary work.

---

[16] Stubbs suggested that the inscription in Cotton Vespasian D. XIX might be a mistake, influenced by Nigel's association with William (*Introductions*, p. 414, n. 2 = *Epistolae Cantuarienses*, Introduction, p. lxxxv, n. 2), but as Ward pointed out, 'this appears hardly likely, considering that the MS. belonged to Nigel's own monastery', and he preferred Stubbs's alternative hypothesis, that 'they were either relations or fellow-townsmen' (*Catalogue of Romances*, ii. 692).

[17] William's family 'took its name from the vill known today as Longchamps, located in eastern Normandy immediately upon what in the twelfth century was the southeastern edge of the forest of Lions' (Balfour, 'Origins of the Longchamp family', p. 78). Tantalizingly, Nigel mentions having heard some gossip 'in Normannia' (*Tractatus*, ed. Boutemy, p. 190), but it is impossible to say when or for how long he was there. He may, for example, have been one of the Canterbury monks who went to Normandy in 1187 in order to plead the monastery's case to Henry II (Gervase, *Chronicle*, i. 377, 380–1).

[18] *SS* 4: 'Maxima pars animae dimidiumque meae'. Cf. Horace, *Odes*, i. 3. 8: 'et serves animae dimidium meae', and ii. 17. 5: 'a, te meae si partem animae rapit'. On this phrase, see below, p. xliii, n. 79. At the opening of his *Tractatus*, Nigel insists that he is addressing William 'non quem animi impetus aut spiritus exacerbatus excitet, sed quem intimae dilectionis devotio propinet' (ed. Boutemy, p. 151), and twice addresses him as 'dilectissime' (ibid. pp. 155, 177).

[19] Nigel says he fears that he will be charged with insolence or temerity in presuming to write something for William's benefit, 'qui tot scripturarum scientiam penes te non tantum in codicibus sed <etiam> in corde tuo habes reconditam, ita tamen quod omni loco et tempore quantumvis et quomodovis proferas de thesauro tuo nova et vetera non praemunitus aut praemeditatus, et talia quidem quae et aedificent audientes, et ex operis venustate commendent artificem.... Rem igitur tam mirandam, immo tam miraculosam, tibi insitam primo in tantum mirabar, quod nec credidi sed neque adhuc credidissem, nisi *ex commoratione familiari crebra experientia* vulnus incredulitatis amputasset' (ed. Boutemy, p. 152; my italics). He also comments on William's eating habits in such a way as to imply he has often been at table with him (ibid.). Cf. p. 205: 'ipse aliquando *dicere consueveras*' (my italics). It is possible that these observations might be based on William's visits to Canterbury (see below, pp. xliii, xlvi) but they suggest rather more.

[20] Boutemy (*Tractatus*, p. 87) conjectures that they may have met in Paris. In the *Tractatus*, Nigel refers to William's education: 'Liberalium artium studiis satis olim indulsisti' (ed. Boutemy, p. 155), but does not say where these studies were conducted. Balfour thinks it more likely that William studied at Bologna (*William Longchamp*, ch. 2).

TEXT AND CONTEXT   XXXV

William first reached prominence as chancellor of Richard, son of Henry II, count of Poitou and duke of Aquitaine.[21] When Richard became king of England in 1189, William continued to be his chancellor, and at the Council of Pipewell (15 September 1189) held two days after Richard's coronation, he was made bishop of Ely.[22] In December 1189, when Richard left on crusade to the Holy Land, he made William a colleague of the justiciar, Hugh of Puiset (bishop of Durham), giving him control of the royal seal and custody of the Tower of London.[23] Shortly afterwards, in March 1190, Richard increased his power even further by making him sole justiciar south of the Humber, leaving Hugh of Puiset as justiciar of the northern part of the realm.[24] In June 1190, at the king's request, William was made a papal legate,[25] and since Archbishop Baldwin of Canterbury was accompanying Richard on crusade, William thus became the highest-ranking cleric in England.

William did not enjoy this high position for long. He seems to have been resented by members of the old baronial families in England because he was a foreigner who despised the English and also because (they claimed) he was of low and indeed servile origin.[26] He was typical of a number of men at this period whose careers were based on administrative ability and personal service rather than aristocratic lineage and ancient wealth.[27] Regarding him as an upstart, his enemies accused him of arrogant high-handedness and a failure to consult.[28] In September–October 1191 they united against William under the leadership of John, count of Mortain, Richard's younger brother, whose ultimate aim was to secure the crown for himself,[29] acting in concert

[21] For William's early career, see below, n. 121.

[22] Stubbs, *Introductions*, p. 206 = Roger of Howden, *Chronica*, iii. xxvi. William was one of a series of bishops of Ely who had 'distinguished themselves in the service of the King', rather than as churchmen; see Karn, 'The twelfth century', pp. 5–9 (quotation on p. 9).

[23] Roger of Howden, *Gesta* ii. 101; Roger of Howden, *Chronica*, iii. 28; West, *Justiciarship*, p. 67.

[24] Roger of Howden, *Gesta* ii. 106; Roger of Howden, *Chronica*, iii. 32; West, *Justiciarship*, p. 68.

[25] Roger of Howden, *Gesta* ii. 106, 108; Roger of Howden, *Chronica*, iii. 33–4.

[26] On William's contempt for the English, see, for example, Gerald of Wales, *De vita Galfridi*, ii. 19, *Opera*, iv. 424. William's origins were not, however, as humble as his opponents claimed; see Balfour, 'Origins of the Longchamp family'.

[27] For the hostility of conservative critics from old-established families towards the new type of administrators who made their way by ability, see Turner, 'Changing perceptions'. See also Turner, *Men Raised from the Dust*, a study of the careers of six men whose careers are of the same general type as William of Longchamp's.

[28] For these accusations, see Roger of Howden, *Gesta* ii. 143; repeated in Roger of Howden, *Chronica*, iii. 72. West (*Justiciarship*, pp. 71–2) thinks that the latter accusation is unlikely to be true.

[29] For suggestions as to John's reasons for hating William, see Stubbs, *Introductions*, pp. 226–7 = Roger of Howden, *Chronica*, iii. lv–lvi).

xxxvi INTRODUCTION

with Geoffrey, bastard son of Henry II (and thus Richard's half-brother), and Hugh of Nonant, bishop of Coventry. After much complicated manoeuvring on both sides they deprived William of the justiciarship and eventually forced him to leave the country in a hurried and undignified manner and take refuge across the Channel.[30]

Nigel of Longchamp was not the only writer to dedicate works to William. Richard Barre, archdeacon of Ely, dedicated to him a *Compendium* of the Old and New Testaments.[31] In 1191, Gerald of Wales, who had served under William as a royal clerk, dedicated to him his *Itinerarium Cambriae*.[32] Around the same time, it would seem, Ralph de Diceto wrote him a congratulatory letter, celebrating his elevation to the offices of legate and justiciar, which was later (1194–5?) prefaced, 'as a sort of dedication', to the manuscript containing Ralph's *Opuscula*.[33] Gerald's motivation was undoubtedly to win his own ecclesiastical promotion; he is notorious for his sycophantic approaches to anyone who he thought might favour his case, and in fact William did offer him the bishopric of Bangor (which Gerald turned down as not

---

[30] The immediate cause of this sequence of events was William's attempt to prevent Geoffrey from landing in England during Richard's absence. Both Geoffrey and John had sworn to Richard that they would stay on the Continent for three years, to avoid any suspicion that they would try to seize power, but John had later been given permission to be in England; Geoffrey now wished to come to England in order to be consecrated as archbishop of York. Unfortunately, those sent to arrest Geoffrey for this violation of his promise dragged him by force from the chapel of Dover Priory, in a scene that was compared by contemporaries to the murder of Becket in his cathedral. William claimed he had not given orders for this violence (*Epistolae Cantuarienses*, no. ccclxxi), but it gave William's enemies the perfect pretext for expressing their outrage and acting against him.

The contemporary historical accounts of this series of events are as follows: Roger of Howden, *Gesta*, ii. 207–21; Roger of Howden, *Chronica*, iii. 134–55; Gervase, *Chronicle*, i. 497, 504–8; Richard of Devizes, *Chronicle*, pp. 29–35, 39–43, 45–6, 48–54; William of Newburgh, *Historia*, iv. 14–17; Gerald, *De vita Galfridi*, ii. 1–13, *Opera*, iv. 386–413. For a detailed synthesis of these sources, see Stubbs, *Introductions*, pp. 218–45 (= Roger of Howden, *Chronica*, iii. xliii–lxxxii), and for a more recent account, see Turner and Heiser, *The Reign of Richard Lionheart*, pp. 110–29.

[31] Sharpe, 'Richard Barre's *Compendium Veteris et Noui Testamenti*'.

[32] For Gerald as a royal clerk, see Bartlett, *Gerald of Wales*, p. 15 (pp. 20–1). For the dedication to William, see ibid. pp. 60–2 (pp. 55–7), and Gerald of Wales, *Itinerarium Kambriae*, *Opera*, vi. xxxiv–xxxvi, and ibid. p. 3, n. 1. See also below, n. 51.

[33] Stubbs, *Introductions*, p. 80 = Ralph de Diceto, *Historical Works*, i. p. lxxiv. For the letter, see Ralph de Diceto, *Opuscula*, ii. 177–80. Interestingly, in this letter Ralph excuses William for devoting himself to the chancery rather than his bishopric, citing the example of Pope Gregory VI. William was still in touch with Ralph in 1196, when he sent him the letter allegedly written by the 'Old Man of the Mountain', leader of the tribe of assassins, exculpating Richard I from having plotted the assassination of Conrad of Montferrat, king of Jerusalem, so that Ralph might include it in his chronicles ('ut de illo agatis in cronicis vestris'; Ralph de Diceto, *Historical Works*, ii. p. viii; *Ymagines*, ii. 128).

TEXT AND CONTEXT

xxxvii

up to his expectations).[34] Jan Ziolkowski has denied, however, that Nigel's dedications to William of Longchamp were inspired by similar motives. Although Mozley and Raymo referred to William as Nigel's patron, Ziolkowski says, 'it would be forcing the facts to present Nigel in any way as a client poet in the patronage of William'.[35] 'Client poet' suggests a stronger relationship of financial dependency than is necessarily implied in the word 'patron'; it might be thought that the dedication of a literary work to someone is enough in itself to justify calling that person an actual or potential patron.[36] But Ziolkowski vigorously denies that 'Nigel viewed William as a potential personal benefactor', apparently supposing that Nigel is writing simply as one old friend to another, motivated purely by a moralist's desire to excoriate the failings of the contemporary world.[37]

Rather than quibbling over the meaning of the word 'patron', however, I think it would be more profitable to investigate further the possible significance of William of Longchamp for a monk of Canterbury, especially at the time that Nigel's two major works were written. Ziolkowski claims that the two works that Nigel dedicated to William were produced at 'exceptionally inopportune moments' for any expectation of patronage.[38] I propose to examine this claim by considering the two works and their date of production in turn, beginning with the *Tractatus*. Internal evidence shows that it was written after William's expulsion in 1191 (to which Nigel makes sorrowing reference),[39] and also after King Richard's capture in Austria on the way home from the crusade in December 1192, but apparently before his release and return to England in March 1194.[40] At this point, says Ziolkowski,

---

[34] Bartlett, *Gerald of Wales*, pp. 48 and n. 97, 60–2 (pp. 45–6 and n. 97, 55–7).

[35] *Lawrence*, ed. Ziolkowski, p. 40.

[36] Cf. Haskins, 'Henry II. as a patron of literature', p. 71: 'In the earlier Middle Ages, evidence of literary patronage is found chiefly in dedications and sporadic references.'

[37] *Lawrence*, p. 40.

[38] Ibid.

[39] *Tractatus*, ed. Boutemy, pp. 198–201. The tone of these passages is one of sorrow over the sudden reversals of fickle Fortune: e.g. 'Defluentibus igitur amicis quasi sub prima hieme arborum foliis, et in locum suum recedentibus aquis apparuit arida et frons prius capillata repente decalvata'...(p. 200). The account of William's discomfiture uses similarly general and conventional phrasing throughout, and in no way justifies George Rigg's claim that the *Tractatus* is 'a satire, in which the downfall of William, with all its indignities, is fully recounted' ('Nigel of Canterbury', p. 306). On the contrary, Nigel compares William's abandonment by his friends to Peter's denial of Christ, and the intended violence that his enemies would have visited on him had he not retreated to France, to the murder of Becket (*Tractatus*, ed. Boutemy, p. 200).

[40] *Tractatus*, ed. Boutemy, p. 98. Nigel also speaks (ibid. pp. 196–7) of the expulsion of the monks of Coventry, which took place at the end of 1190 (see below, pp. xlvi–xlvii).

xxxviii INTRODUCTION

'William's brief heyday as England's most powerful figure had ended conclusively in a humiliating exile', and in these circumstances, we could only suppose that Nigel dedicated the *Tractatus* to William 'either because he had no other plausible dedicatee or because he clung to the hope that William would recover politically'.[41] 'Conclusively' is, however, too strong a word; in 1193 it might have seemed entirely likely that William would 'recover politically', and so long as the king was overseas and William was at his side, 'exile' does not seem the appropriate word either. William was still Richard I's chancellor and remained so until his death in 1197.[42] The débâcle of 1191 did not cost him the king's favour, and he continued to act as Richard's right-hand man.[43] He was one of the first to reach him in his captivity and was warmly received; he first negotiated Richard's transfer from the castle of Trifels to the more comfortable surroundings of the imperial court at Hagenau, and was then charged with collecting the ransom to free his master.[44] William returned to England for this purpose in 1193,[45] and was not well received in London (where he ordered the seizure of some houses belonging to his enemy the bishop of Coventry) and St Albans, so he soon returned to Richard's side.[46] But when Richard returned to England in 1194, William came with him, and at the solemn crown-wearing that took place in

---

[41] *Lawrence*, p. 40.

[42] William died at Poitiers, on his way to Rome to conduct the king's business at the papal court, at the end of January 1197 (Turner, 'Longchamp, William de (*d.* 1197)', *ODNB*).

[43] In 1193 (at Mantes) and 1194 (at Tillières), William was commissioned by Richard to negotiate truce terms with the king of France (see Landon, *Itinerary of King Richard I*, pp. 78–9, 96–7); in 1195, Richard sent him to the German emperor to discuss with him his offer of support against the French king (ibid. pp. 103–4). The only discordant note is Roger of Howden's report that Richard withdrew his seal from William because he was dissatisfied with the terms of the French truce, but the new seal was not brought into use until after William's death, several years later, and it seems that the motive for introducing it and demanding that all existing documents be re-authenticated 'must have been to bring money into the exchequer', which would mean that Richard's 'dissatisfaction' with William's handling of the truce, if Roger's report has any foundation, was only a front to cover the real motive. See Landon, *Itinerary of King Richard I*, Appendix A, especially pp. 176–80 (the quotation is on p. 180).

[44] Stubbs, *Introductions*, p. 252 = Roger of Howden, *Chronica*, iii. xciii, referring to Roger of Howden, *Chronica*, iii. 209 (a letter from Richard to his mother: 'venit ad nos carissimus cancellarius noster Willelmus Eliensis episcopus'); Gerald, *De vita Galfridi*, ii. 17, *Opera*, iv. 415; William of Newburgh, *Historia*, iv. 33; Gillingham, *Richard I*, p. 239; id. 'The kidnapped king', pp. 22–3.

[45] He had already returned briefly in early 1192, in an attempt to resume his old position, but was unsuccessful since John, having accepted a bribe from William in return for his support, accepted an even larger bribe to withdraw it (Gervase, *Chronicle*, i. 512; Stubbs, *Introductions*, pp. 249–50 = Roger of Howden, *Chronica*, iii. lxxxviii–xc).

[46] Stubbs, *Introductions*, pp. 253–4 = Roger of Howden, *Chronica*, iii. xcv–xcvi; Appleby, *England without Richard*, pp. 114–15.

TEXT AND CONTEXT
xxxix

Winchester on 17 April, in a splendid procession made up of archbishops, bishops, abbots, and other clergy, along with earls, barons, knights, and the king of Scotland, 'William, bishop of Ely, his chancellor' walked at the king's right hand.[47] Richard also took care to punish those who had plotted against William: Hugh of Nonant, bishop of Coventry, Godfrey de Lucy, bishop of Winchester, and Gerard Camville, sheriff of Lincolnshire and constable of Lincoln Castle.[48] It was now Hugh of Nonant's turn to beat a prudent retreat to the Continent.[49]

So if William's fortunes underwent a reversal in 1191, there was no reason to suppose that it would be permanent.[50] It is true that Gerald of Wales, switching sides with his usual alacrity, seems to have changed the dedication of his *Itinerarium Cambriae*,[51] and that around 1193 he wrote a slavishly sycophantic life of Geoffrey, archbishop of York, the king's half-brother, in which he included a vicious and indeed scurrilous attack on William (borrowed from a malicious epistle written by his enemy Hugh of Nonant).[52] In the absence of Richard, Gerald was

---

[47] 'a dextris ejus ibat Willelmus Eliensis episcopus, cancellarius suus'; Roger of Howden, *Chronica*, iii. 247; cf. Gillingham, *Richard I*, p. 272.

[48] For the actions of these people against William, see Stubbs, *Introductions*, pp. 227–32, 237–8, and 244 (= Roger of Howden, *Chronica*, iii. lvi–lxiv, lxxi–lxxii, lxxxi). For Richard's punishments, see Stubbs, *Introductions*, pp. 256–7 (= Roger of Howden, *Chronica*, iii. xcix–c).

[49] Franklin, 'Nonant, Hugh de (*d.* 1198)', *ODNB*: 'On hearing of the captivity of Richard I in 1193 Bishop Hugh is said to have started immediately for Germany with funds, but to have been robbed en route. And although he reached Richard in Germany, he found it prudent to return almost immediately to France, since his relations with the king appear to have become strained, a situation almost certainly exacerbated by the treasonable behaviour of the bishop's brother Robert...After Richard had returned to England he issued instructions, on 31 March 1194, that Hugh de Nonant should answer for his crimes both as bishop and as sheriff. Bishop Hugh was able to obtain pardon by paying the immense sum of 5000 marks...'. Although Hugh seems to have visited England at some point between 1193 and 1196, he apparently spent most of his time in France and died at the abbey of Bec in March 1198.

[50] Peter of Blois wrote to William *c.*1191, commiserating with him on his ill-treatment at the hands of his envious enemies, and predicting his eventual return to power (*Epistolae*, no. lxxxvii, PL ccvii. 272–6; he also wrote a strongly worded letter to Hugh of Nonant, threatening him with divine judgement for having engineered the downfall of this 'vir sapiens, amabilis, generosus, benignus et mitis, et in omnes liberaliter effusus' (*Epistolae*, no. lxxxix, PL ccvii. 278–81, quotation at 279A).

[51] On the changed dedication, see Gerald of Wales, *Itinerarium Kambriae, Opera*, vi. xxxvii–xxxix, and ibid., p. 3, n. 1. The *Itinerarium* is an account of Gerald's travels through Wales with Archbishop Baldwin in 1190, preaching the Third Crusade; the changed dedication and Gerald's flattering remarks about Baldwin (ii. c. 14) were doubtless part of his attempts to win friends and influence people.

[52] For Gerald's attack, see *De vita Galfridi*, ii. 18–19, *Opera*, iv. 417–31. Hugh's epistle is quoted in full in Roger of Howden, *Gesta*, ii. 215–20, and Roger of Howden, *Chronica*, iii. 141–7; Roger also includes the reply written in defence of William by Peter of Blois (*Chronica*, iii. 148–50). Hugh's epistle has been freshly edited in *English Episcopal Acta xvii. Coventry and Lichfield 1183–1208*, ed. Franklin, Appendix II, 'Bishop Hugh's Open Letter'.

xl INTRODUCTION

obviously changing his allegiance to the party of Count (later King) John and Geoffrey. 'At this time', Robert Bartlett says, '[Gerald] was a *familiaris* of Count John'.[53] But he seems to have been backing the wrong horse; as Bartlett says, it is significant that 'John's unsuccessful rebellion and Richard's return from captivity in 1194' were shortly followed by 'Gerald's retirement from court'.[54]

Gerald's habitual switches of loyalty seem to have left him, in this instance, on the wrong side of the fence. But a monk of Canterbury such as Nigel would have had powerful reasons for continuing to be loyal to William of Longchamp. For it was precisely in 1193 that there seemed to many people to be a strong possibility that William might become archbishop of Canterbury. Archbishop Baldwin (who had, as mentioned earlier, gone on crusade with Richard) died in the Holy Land at the siege of Acre in November 1190;[55] the news reached Canterbury in March 1191.[56] The right of electing a new archbishop technically belonged to the monks (or so at least they vigorously claimed),[57] but the kings of England exerted a strong influence in the matter and generally it was well for the monks if their choice coincided with the king's.[58] In March 1191, the monks petitioned the king for a free election,[59] but in May William of Longchamp presented them with a letter from Richard ordering them to elect the archbishop of Monreale (in Sicily, where King Richard currently was).[60] The monks made no moves towards obeying this order, however, and instead resorted to delaying tactics.[61] Eventually in early December, when the convent was forced to move to an election, they obliged Reginald, the

---

[53] Bartlett, *Gerald of Wales*, p. 65 (p. 59).

[54] Ibid.

[55] Fryde *et al.*, ed., *Handbook of British Chronology*, p. 232.

[56] Gervase, *Chronicle*, i. 490; Stubbs, *Introductions*, p. 413 = *Epistolae Cantuarienses*, Introduction, p. lxxxiv.

[57] See, for example, Gervase, *Chronicle*, i. 490–1, and cf. Roger of Howden, *Chronica*, ii. 287.

[58] Despite his almost continual absence from England, Richard exerted a strong influence over English episcopal elections, and managed to ensure that a large number of the elections during his reign went to his *curiales* (Turner, 'Richard Lionheart and English episcopal elections'; on regal influence over episcopal elections in general, see p. 3).

[59] *Epistolae Cantuarienses*, no. ccccli.

[60] *Epistolae Cantuarienses*, no. cccxlviii (the letter had been written in January); Gervase, *Chronicle*, i. 493–4. See Stubbs, *Introductions*, p. 231 = Roger of Howden, *Chronica*, iii. lxi–lxii. For Stubbs's suggestions as to why Richard nominated the archbishop of Monreale, see *Introductions*, p. 415 = *Epistolae Cantuarienses*, Introduction, p. lxxxvi.

[61] Stubbs, *Introductions*, p. 417; Gervase, *Chronicle*, i. 494. They claimed that the news of Baldwin's death was unreliable and needed to be confirmed before they proceeded with the election (*Epistolae Cantuarienses*, no. cccliv, pp. 333–4).

TEXT AND CONTEXT
xli

elderly bishop of Bath, who had shown himself sympathetic to them in the past,[62] to accept the archiepiscopal office, but he died before the month was out.[63] During the whole of 1192 the see remained vacant (since permission to fill it had again to be sought), and it was not until May 1193 that Hubert Walter was elected, on the king's orders, and not until November of that year that he was consecrated. For almost the whole of the period from March 1191 to May 1193, therefore, the archiepiscopal see was vacant. What is more, not only did William of Longchamp desire the post ('he was sniffing after the archbishopric', said Jocelin of Brakelond),[64] but there is little doubt, as the great historian William Stubbs said, that 'had the election been free the monks would have elected him'.[65] Count John was so alarmed at the possibility that he wrote them a letter forbidding them to elect William, as he had heard they intended to do.[66] Having elected Reginald of Bath (probably as a stopgap) only when Count John and his other enemies had driven William out of the country,[67] they wrote William an apologetic letter explaining that they had acted under duress, when they were deprived of William's 'protection'.[68] After Reginald's death, the hope of electing William revived, and the monks immediately wrote to him again, sympathizing with him in his recent troubles, which they can well understand as they have troubles of their own. Since they have been deprived of his patronage ('vestro destituti sumus patrocinio'), they

---

[62] See Gervase, *Chronicle*, i. 410–11, 477.

[63] Ibid. i. 511–12.

[64] 'Dicebatur olfacere archiepiscopatum' (Jocelin of Brakelond, *Chronicle*, ed. Butler, p. 52). William of Newburgh (*Historia*, iv. 15) also reports that after Baldwin's death, William forbade Walter, archbishop of Rouen, to go to Canterbury to arrange the election of a new archbishop, because William was 'already aspiring to the honour of that see' ('ad ejusdem jam sedis praerogativam aspirans'). William's letter to Walter is reproduced in Gerald, *De vita Galfridi*, ii. 6, *Opera*, iv. 399–400, and Ralph de Diceto, *Ymagines*, ii. 92–3; it is also reprinted in Stubbs's Appendix to the *Epistolae Cantuarienses* as no. dlxvi (p. 548). William of Newburgh (*Historia*, iv. 18) also records the continuation of William of Longchamp's aspirations after his expulsion in 1191: the archbishop of Rouen and others arranged for the filling of the vacant primacy 'ad quam tyrannus [= William] aspiraverat et forte adhuc aspirabat'. On Reginald's death, William of Newburgh comments: 'spemque cancellarii, sua forte electione mortuam, moriendo resuscitavit'.

[65] Stubbs, *Introductions*, p. 414 = *Epistolae Cantuarienses*, Introduction, p. lxxxv.

[66] *Epistolae Cantuarienses*, no. ccclxxiv.

[67] The Canterbury monks were still stalling the election of anyone else even after William's expulsion: when summoned to London in October and pressed to elect the Archbishop of Monreale, the prior declined on the grounds that it was an insult to all the clerics of England to pass them over in favour of a 'personam ignotam' (Gervase, *Chronicle*, i. 508). The justiciars thanked the monks for their sensible response and sent them home.

[68] 'parvitas nostra...vestrae...protectionis quoque gratiam abesse persensit' (*Epistolae Cantuarienses*, no. ccclxxxvi).

xlii INTRODUCTION

say, William's enemies have risen against them. To make matters worse, they hear that William is angry with them (obviously because they elected Reginald), and they beg him to understand that their actions were coerced.[69] It seems that in 1192 or 1193 Richard I actually sent the monks a letter supporting William's election, though he later changed his mind and ordered the election of Hubert Walter (another royal servant).[70] (Two months after Hubert's election a letter arrived forbidding them to elect *him*,[71] testifying to a fair amount of dithering on Richard's part; he seems to have been under pressure from various interest groups.[72]) Possibly Richard thought his chancellor's services too valuable to lose.[73]

The Context: Canterbury

Why were the monks of Canterbury so keen to have William as their archbishop? One important reason is that he had shown himself sympathetic to their interests. In October 1190, while Archbishop Baldwin was on crusade, the Canterbury monks complained at a council of bishops held in Westminster, under the aegis of William in his role as papal legate, that a new bishop had been elected at Worcester without Canterbury's consent or knowledge. They insisted that the consecration should be performed only by the bishop of Rochester, nominated

---

[69] *Epistolae Cantuarienses*, no. cccxcii, written in January 1192. Note that in this letter they proclaim themselves 'memores beneficiorum quae nobis contulistis, pro quibus omnibus condigne vobis respondere speramus, et expectamus in tempore opportuno' (p. 357).

[70] This is implied by a letter written by Richard to his mother Eleanor of Aquitaine, charging her to go to Canterbury and secure the election of Hubert Walter, and to ignore any previous letters of his recommending the election of William of Longchamp or the bishop of Bath ('Et si forte aliquid mandatum a nobis accepistis in contrarium, pro cancellario vel pro Bathoniensi episcopo, vel pro aliquo alio, proculdubio vos scire volumus quod illud cassamus, et omne mandatum quod de caetero de cancellaria nostra emanabit, in contrarium': *Epistolae Cantuarienses*, no. cccciii (p. 365); cf. Gervase, *Chronicle*, i. 517–18).

[71] *Epistolae Cantuarienses*, no. ccccv.

[72] Stubbs, *Introductions*, p. 418 = *Epistolae Cantuarienses*, Introduction, pp. xc–xci. In the letter already quoted, Richard writes to his mother: 'Satis enim vestra novit dilectio, quod dum in custodia tenemur, oportet nos precibus magnorum virorum cedere, et pro quibusdam supplicare, quos nullatenus promovere vellemus': *Epistolae Cantuarienses*, no. cccciii (p. 365). This probably refers to Savaric, bishop of Bath, a relative of the German/Roman emperor; for Savaric's career, see Stubbs, *Introductions*, p. 415, n. 4 = *Epistolae Cantuarienses*, Introduction, p. lxxxvii, n. 1. However, Richard sent contradictory letters on other occasions, suggesting a degree of chronic indecisiveness. See Richard of Devizes, *Chronicle*, p. 14 (on the quarrel between the bishop of Salisbury and the monastery of Malmesbury) and pp. 13–14 (Richard's change of heart on the question of whether his brother John was to be allowed to come to England for three years after he had left on crusade).

[73] For Richard's later employment of William on important business, see above, nn. 42 and 43.

TEXT AND CONTEXT
xliii

by Baldwin as deputy in his absence, and should take place at Canterbury, not in London. William responded tactfully and declared his willingness to uphold the rights of Canterbury; the following month he visited Canterbury and was received by the convent 'with honour' ('honorifice').[74] The dispute rumbled on, however,[75] and was finally settled at a meeting of bishops held at Canterbury in May 1191, when William agreed to perform the consecration himself, in his capacity as papal legate,[76] the new bishop having promised obedience to the archbishop and church of Canterbury.[77] Similarly, at about the same time, when news came that the king's half-brother Geoffrey was preparing to be consecrated archbishop of York in France, William wrote a circular letter forbidding any Continental archbishops or bishops to perform the consecration, since this was to be done only in Canterbury by the archbishop.[78]

Even more important, it seems that William was prepared to take the monks' part in their bitter and protracted dispute with Archbishop Baldwin, which was probably the most dramatic ecclesiastical quarrel of the twelfth century after the row between Henry II and Thomas Becket (and lasted much longer). The quarrel is documented in the *Epistolae Cantuarienses*, a collection of letters and documents compiled by the monastery shortly after the event (Nigel is mentioned in two of them and may have been the author of another),[79] and in Gervase of

---

[74] Gervase, *Chronicle*, i. 485–8.

[75] Ibid. 490.

[76] Technically speaking William's legateship terminated with the death of Pope Clement III in March 1191, but Gervase's account of this episode consistently refers to William as legate (*Chronicle*, i. 491–3), and it was only on this basis that he can have been accepted as qualified to perform the consecration. Pope Celestine III renewed the legateship without question. A full list of the contemporary references to William as legate, and an analysis of their significance, is given in Landon, *Itinerary of King Richard I*, Appendix G (pp. 215–18). William's commission finally lapsed in 1194, when the title was transferred to Hubert Walter, the newly appointed archbishop of Canterbury (the primate was the usual holder of the office, and it was because of Baldwin's absence in the Holy Land that it had been given to William).

[77] Gervase, *Chronicle*, i. 492–3. See also Richard of Devizes, *Chronicle*, p. 27. It was on this occasion that William presented the monks with the king's letter instructing them to elect the archbishop of Monreale (see above, p. xl); neither he nor they would have been willing that the king's instructions should be carried out.

[78] Gervase, *Chronicle*, i. 497; *Epistolae Cantuarienses*, no. cccxliv; but cf. no. cccxlii. In 1191, William also supported the monks' claim to a whale that had been washed up on their land in Kent, in gratitude for which they sent him the tongue and part of the head (Gervase, *Chronicle*, i. 489).

[79] Nigel is mentioned in *Epistolae Cantuarienses*, no. cccxxvi, where he is said to have been threatened by Archbishop Baldwin ('Nigellus valde minatus est ab archiepiscopo': p. 312) and no. cccxxix (p. 317). The case for his authorship of *Epistolae Cantuarienses*, no. cccxxii rests on the second of the four lines of verse with which the letter ends: 'Maxima pars nostri

xliv INTRODUCTION

Canterbury's *Chronicle*.[80] It arose from Baldwin's proposal to found a college of canons at Hackington, a suburb to the north of Canterbury, less than half a mile from the cathedral.[81] It was a peculiarly English system that the religious communities serving the major cathedrals were convents of monks, rather than chapters of canons.[82] This meant that the bishop or archbishop was the titular abbot as an automatic consequence of his episcopal appointment, whether he himself was a monk or not. The day-to-day running of the monastery was under the charge of the prior. Archbishop Baldwin was a monk, but he was a Cistercian, whereas the Canterbury monks were Benedictines. The hostility between black and white monks which was ubiquitous in the twelfth century probably fuelled the quarrel. Baldwin's aims in seeking to establish a college of canons are easily understandable: it was not very convenient for archbishops to have a body of monks at their disposal, since so much of their time was taken up with the divine office, and their mobility was restricted because they were in theory supposed to remain cloistered. It was far more useful to have a body of secular clerics, who could perform the administrative tasks that the primate's role in national affairs necessarily entailed.[83] Also, it was useful to be able to reward or recruit public servants by giving them a prebend— which the archbishop clearly could not do with a monastic community.

The Canterbury monks were, predictably, violently opposed to Baldwin's proposal. In the first place, they objected that this new community was to be funded out of their endowments. This was a knotty

---

dimidiumque mei', which echoes *SS* line 4 (quoted in n. 18 above). See Stubbs, *Introductions*, p. 414, n. 2 = *Epistolae Cantuarienses*, Introduction, p. lxxxv, n. 2. However, the phrase 'dimidium animae meae' seems to have been a cliché in current use at Canterbury and elsewhere. Already in the 11th c. Guibert of Nogent remarked 'amicos animarum nostrarum dimidium . . . appellare solemus', 'we customarily call our friends "half our souls"' (*De sanctis et eorum pigneribus*, ii. line 117 (ed. Huygens, CCCM cxxvii, p. 113), and Thomas Becket uses it in several of his letters (*Becket Correspondence*, i. 606, 610 (no. cxxvi), i. 646 (no. cxl), i. 788 (no. clxxii), ii. 840 (no. clxxxix)), so it does not conclusively prove Nigel's authorship.

[80] Gervase, *Chronicle*, i. 332–502. Gervase lays out the grounds of the dispute in the first of the two *Imaginationes* included in his *Chronicle* (i. 29–68, and see Stubbs's Introduction, pp. xvii–xix). For a detailed account of the sequence of events in the quarrel, with special emphasis on its local dimensions in Canterbury, see Sweetinburgh, 'Caught in the cross-fire'.

[81] 'dominus Baldewinus . . . congregationem secularium clericorum sub festinatione proposuit statuere in ecclesia Sancti Stephani, quae tribus fere stadiis a Cantuaria distat ad aquilonem' (Gervase, *Chronicle*, i. 337).

[82] See Knowles, *Monastic Order*, ch. 36: 'The cathedral monasteries and the bishops' abbeys', and Stubbs, *Introductions*, pp. 371–8 = *Epistolae Cantuarienses*, Introduction, pp. xxi–xxxi.

[83] As was explained by Peter of Blois in arguing Baldwin's case to Pope Urban III (Gervase, *Chronicle*, i. 368).

TEXT AND CONTEXT

xlv

point. It was customary for the income from certain estates to be earmarked for individual monastery offices (prior, cellarer, etc.) or for particular uses (the monks' table, alms-giving). On this system, the archbishop had controlled his own individual income, which was certainly large enough for him to finance his proposed foundation.[84] The problem was that Baldwin's predecessors had over time surrendered their rights to this income, not out of liberal impulses, but to prevent it falling into the king's hands during periods when the see was vacant.[85] So while Baldwin felt he had moral rights over this income, the monks could point to the titular rights they had acquired over it. Secondly, this college of canons was going to be dedicated to Saints Stephen and Thomas Becket, and the monks were afraid that the archbishop was going to transfer Becket's body (the source of considerable wealth to them) to the new foundation.[86] Thirdly, they feared that they would lose the right to elect the archbishop of Canterbury.[87]

The battle over these matters was violent and lengthy (the quarrel revived under Hubert Walter, Baldwin's successor, and was finally settled only in 1201).[88] The monks appealed to the pope, sending representatives from the convent to plead their case in person;[89] the prior Honorius and several other monks spent a considerable amount of time in Italy between 1186 and 1188, dragging themselves from Verona to Pisa to Rome in pursuit of various popes (two of whom died in 1187).[90] Five of these monks died of plague in July 1188, and Honorius himself died of the same cause in October 1188.[91] (One of Nigel's *Epigrams* is in praise of Honorius, and another laments his death.)[92]

---

[84] See the detailed discussion of the complex relations between archiepiscopal and conventual revenues at Canterbury in Crosby, *Bishop and Chapter*, pp. 66–105, especially pp. 95–102 on Archbishop Baldwin. Similar tussles between monks and their bishop over their relative endowments occurred in 12th-c. Ely, and William of Longchamp played a part in achieving an acceptable solution (Karn, 'The twelfth century', pp. 13–14).

[85] Stubbs, *Introductions*, p. 377 = *Epistolae Cantuarienses*, Introduction, p. xxx.

[86] Pope Urban III mentions having heard a rumour to this effect (Gervase, *Chronicle*, i. 368–9; cf. i. 431). Later, Hubert Walter tried to assuage the monks' fears by promising not to do this (Gervase, *Chronicle*, i. 546).

[87] Gervase (*Chronicle*, i. 337) claims that Henry II perceived Baldwin's proposal as a means of subverting the convent's right to a free election of their archbishop ('cernens itaque subtilissimus rex hoc commento jura Cantuariensis ecclesiae et libertatem quam maxime in electione sui pontificis usque ad haec habuerat tempora posse subnervari'). Again, Hubert Walter later assured the monks that he would not try to destroy this right (Gervase, *Chronicle*, i. 546).

[88] Stubbs, *Introductions*, p. 430 = *Epistolae Cantuarienses*, Introduction, p. cix.

[89] Gervase, *Chronicle*, i. 345, 356, 366.

[90] Stubbs, *Introductions*, pp. 386, 396, 399–402 = *Epistolae Cantuarienses*, Introduction, pp. xliii, lviii, lxiii–lxvii.

[91] *Epistolae Cantuarienses*, no. cclxxxix; Gervase, *Chronicle*, i. 429.

[92] *Epigrams*, nos. ii and xi, ed. Ziolkowski, *Lawrence*, pp. 250, 260–3.

xlvi INTRODUCTION

The archbishop looked for help from the king, and also sent his own representatives to the papal curia.[93] Half England seems to have been dragged into the dispute one way or another, and prelates on the Continent also became involved (for example, the case was brought to the general chapter of the Cistercian order at Cîteaux in 1188, where, predictably, the abbot of Cîteaux found it hard to believe that Baldwin had behaved so badly).[94] At home, matters reached such a pitch that at one point the monks were physically imprisoned in the monastery by the setting of guards on the gates to the close and the cemetery; they were thus immured for 84 weeks, during which time they were dependent on the gifts of pilgrims for food. During most of this time, divine service was suspended.[95]

In late 1189, Richard I interested himself in the Canterbury quarrel and tried to persuade the monks to submit their case to arbitrators (one of whom was William of Longchamp, in his capacity as bishop-elect of Ely).[96] At the end of November, Richard 'and his whole court', including William, came to Canterbury and effected a temporary settlement.[97] Baldwin agreed to remove the prior, Roger Norreys, whom he had forced on the convent, and to demolish the chapel at Hackington. However, shortly afterwards he re-established it at Lambeth and the quarrel started up again.[98] William himself seems not to have started out as a strong partisan of the monks' cause, since he presided over a council held at Westminster in October 1190 which licensed Hugh of Nonant, the bishop of Coventry, to expel the monks of his cathedral

---

[93] Among these representatives was Peter of Blois, who was then in the archbishop's service; Peter argued Baldwin's case before Pope Urban III in 1187 and incurred the hatred of the Canterbury monks on this account (see Gervase, *Chronicle*, i. 356, 368–9). In a letter to the bishop of Soissons and the abbots of Igny and Pontigny (dated to the 1190s by Revell), Peter mounted a vigorous defence of Baldwin's proposed college of canons (at this date intended for Lambeth); see Peter of Blois, *Later Letters*, ed. Revell, Letter 10 = *Epistolae*, no. ccxi, PL ccvii. 492–5, also printed in the Appendix to *Epistolae Cantuarienses*, no. dlxxi (pp. 554–7). Peter later humbly apologized to the monks for having acted against their interests, and promised to make amends (*Epistolae*, no. ccxxxiii, PL ccvii. 534–5, also included in *Epistolae Cantuarienses*, no. ccclv). See also Cotts, *Clerical Dilemma*, pp. 36–7, 90, 149–50, 158–60.

[94] *Epistolae Cantuarienses*, no. cclxxiv.

[95] Gervase, *Chronicle*, i. 398–405. Nigel's *Epigram* 11 refers to this crisis in the monastery's life: 'Ouibus sua pascua tollit/ pastor et impastas carcere claudit eas . . . a cantu Cantica mesta silet' (25–6, 40).

[96] Gervase, *Chronicle*, i. 461–81. On William as arbitrator, see p. 469.

[97] Stubbs, *Introductions*, p. 408 = *Epistolae Cantuarienses*, Introduction, p. lxxvi. Cf. Gervase, *Chronicle*, i. 474–83. Charters sealed by William in his official capacity as chancellor show that he was in Canterbury from 29 November until 5 December (Landon, *Itinerary of King Richard I*, pp. 18–21).

[98] Gervase, *Chronicle*, i. 484.

TEXT AND CONTEXT   xlvii

chapter and replace them by canons.[99] The final expulsion at Coventry
took place around Christmas 1190,[100] and in his *Tractatus* Nigel refers
to it with horror and asks William to examine his conscience and decide
what responsibility he bears in the matter.[101] William, however, seems
to have changed his position—perhaps shocked by the expulsion, perhaps influenced by Hugh of Nonant's enmity to him in late 1191.[102]
The very last document in the *Epistolae Cantuarienses* (a statement of
the monastery's case in response to some proposals from Hubert
Walter for settlement of the conflict in 1198) ends with a story about
William, relating his response when he was urged by some important
men to establish in his own memory a college of canons on some of the
cleared land on the estates of his church at Ely.[103] He replied that he
had often thought of doing this, but had rejected the idea because it
would have been a cause of scandal between him and the monks of Ely,
who had accepted him, a secular cleric, although they themselves were
monks, while none of the vacant sees appropriate for secular clerics

---

[99] Richard of Devizes, *Chronicle*, p. 13. See Knowles, *Monastic Order*, pp. 322–4. There
had been an earlier 'trial run' of the expulsion in October 1189; Gervase of Canterbury
(*Chronicle*, i. 461) vividly describes the physical violence inflicted on the monks. However, at
a council held at Westminster in the same month, Hugh of Nonant had complained to his
fellow-bishops that his monks had laid violent hands on *him* (Richard of Devizes, *Chronicle*,
p. 8). Possibly William had been at first convinced by this that Hugh was the victim rather
than the aggressor.

[100] Gervase, *Chronicle*, i. 488–9.

[101] *Tractatus*, ed. Boutemy, p. 197. Since he was present at the Westminster meeting in
November 1189 which was held to discuss the Canterbury quarrel (*Epistolae Cantuarienses*,
no. cccxxix, pp. 315, 317), Nigel must have heard Hugh of Nonant's sardonic comment to
King Richard, as reported by Gervase of Canterbury (*Chronicle*, i. 470): 'Cestrensis [= Hugh]
autem exclamans et subsannans dixit ad regem: "Heohe! Nonne dixi vobis de monachis? Si
michi velletis adquiescere, infra breve spatium temporis nec unus remaneret in Anglia.
Monachos ad diabolos".' Cf. *Epistolae Cantuarienses*, no. cccxxix (p. 318).

[102] William of Newburgh (*Historia*, iv. 36) comments on William's initial support for
Hugh on the expulsion, but says that Hugh soon changed sides and went over to Count
John's party. Stubbs (*Introductions*, p. 226 = Roger of Howden, *Chronica*, Introduction, iii.
liv–lv) thought that William may have 'hesitated to sanction the oppressive means by which
the change was carried out', or perhaps, when the see of Canterbury became vacant, he pru-
dently decided to take the side of cathedral monasteries; for whatever cause, the friendship
between Hugh and William was abruptly converted into violent enmity. The *Annales
Wintonienses*, in recording William's death, mention his connivance at the Coventry expulsion as a blot on his otherwise impeccable record as 'a father of monks': 'homo quidem pru-
dentia saeculi et gratia labiorum mira aestimatione insignis, et quo nemo unquam in
integritate semel conceptae dilectionis fidelior extitit; qui et merito pater monachorum
poterat appellari, nisi cum olim utrumque teneret gladium apostolica auctoritate et regia,
consiliis consensisset religioni adversantium, ut in magno concilio suo apud Londonias ejec-
tionem monachorum de Coventre quantum in ipso fuerat confirmasset' (*Annales Monastici*,
ed. Luard, ii. 64).

[103] *Epistolae Cantuarienses*, no. dlvii (p. 538).

xlviii INTRODUCTION

had appointed him at that time; he therefore felt bound by gratitude to them to introduce no cause of dissension. He also remembered Archbishop Baldwin, and the disturbances that his attempts to found a college of canons had caused. When it was suggested that Baldwin's mistake was to found a canonry so near to the monastery, he said the distance was immaterial, so long as the new foundation diminished the wealth of the monastery. This story gives us a good indication of why the Canterbury monks would have thought of William as a friend and supporter, and why, in 1192–3, they were anxious to have him as their archbishop, despite the fact that he was not a monk.[104]

So, it is not really the case that the *Tractatus* was written at an 'exceptionally inopportune' moment to address William. On the contrary, it was written at a time when he seemed to be poised to play a major role in the Canterbury community and also in the nation at large. The *Tractatus* reflects at various points the concerns of the Canterbury monks between 1191 and 1193: most notably, it insists on the right to the free election of bishops or abbots and complains at the interference of kings in the electoral process.[105] Its appeal to William to give up affairs of state and devote himself to his duties as a bishop, and the final exhortation to him to imitate Thomas Becket, who gave up his chancellorship when he became archbishop of Canterbury, look like very strong hints as to the desirable course of action if William in his turn were to become archbishop.[106]

---

[104] The 13th-c. Christ Church obituary in London, British Library, MS Cotton Nero C. IX, fo. 4ᵛ, records William's death as follows: 'II Kal. Feb. Willelmus eliensis episcopus frater et b[enefactor]' (*Tractatus*, ed. Boutemy, p. 112).

[105] See *Tractatus*, ed. Boutemy, pp. 178–81. The complaint that bishops who are completely unknown to the electors are forced on them by the king (p. 178) seems likely to refer to the king's proposal of the Archbishop of Monreale.

[106] 'Sed et ille [Thomas Becket] aliquando regis fuerat cancellarius tantaeque potestatis ut post regem ipsum videretur totius regni dominus. Verumtamen, ex quo ordinatus est in episcopum, ulterius non est reversus ad cancellariae officium, sed nec etiam voluit ecclesiam quae eum vocaverat ingredi, aut consentire electioni, nisi omnino liber et absolutus ab omni potestate et exactione fisci, sciens quod utraque officia pariter non posset sine ordinis sui periculo expedire. Unde altero non transitorie neque ad tempus relicto, sed in perpetuum relegato, altero fideliter adhaesit et in eo usque in finem perseveravit; nec tamen id fecit coactus, sed spontaneus, cum adhuc eo tempore a regis gratia non excidisset, sed in ulteriorem ipsius amicitiam receptus, posset, si vellet, non solum cancellariam retinere, sed etiam quidquid a rege peteret impetrare. Hunc utinam non quasi per speculum et in aenigmate intuearis, sed ita facie ad faciem ut opera eius imiteris…' (*Tractatus*, ed. Boutemy, pp. 206–7). This passage best fits a situation when it seemed possible that William might become archbishop of Canterbury, but as a general admonition it would also be applicable to Hubert Walter, the king's eventual choice for the archbishopric, who was just as important a royal servant as William. In the earlier part of the *Tractatus*, where Nigel talks about the inappropriateness of

TEXT AND CONTEXT   xlix

What about the *Speculum Stultorum?* The quarrel with Baldwin seems to have left its mark on the poem at several points. In the first place, Nigel takes the opportunity of being rude about the Cistercians (the order to which Baldwin belonged). Fromundus, the monk who sets the dogs on Burnellus, is a Cistercian, and Nigel describes him as having the cruelty of his kind (877–80). In his survey of the monastic orders, Burnellus admits that the Cistercians are hard-working, but accuses them of being greedy for land and wealth, and secretly breaking the rule against meat-eating. Having made fun of them for wearing no breeches under their monastic habits, Burnellus moves into a long diatribe against 'false brethren' (2161–80) who are the source of every evil, and who are as little entitled to be in the cloister as Satan was to be in Paradise.

Anti-Cistercianism is of course pervasive in twelfth-century satirical literature, so that not too much can be read into these attacks. Much more unusual is the vitriolic attack on secular canons, which accuses them of subverting the order of the Church, and, significantly, of corrupting bishops and the king:[107]

There are also those called secular canons, who have earned their name from their function [i.e. secular = worldly]. For them, whatever pleases them is lawful and legitimate; this is the canon under which the whole pack of them has determined to live. They do not rule out or hold in contempt anything which ministers to the flesh. And this thing in particular they have set up as something to be observed by all for all time: that, as the old law commanded, no male should be without a female, and that each male can have two females. They hold to the world, and lest its drooping flower should quickly wither, they take care to water it frequently. These are they who do whatever the wantonness of the flesh commands, so that the path to their vices may be smooth. They lead the whole world into error; they go first and take a headlong tumble. The world does not possess them but rather they the world, and because they drive it downwards, it topples from its foundations. Ready to undermine the foundations of the faith, what they recommend in their teaching they demolish in their practice. It is through them that the force, rule, and power of

---

a secular head of a monastic community, he may even be suggesting to William that he should become a monk if he wishes to be an archbishop who can act as a true head of the Canterbury community. Most of the preceding archbishops had been monks, and as he was dying, Reginald of Bath expressed a wish to become a monk; Richard of Devizes reports that he actually did so (*Chronicle*, p. 56), but the *Epistolae Cantuarienses* (nos. ccclxxxviii–ccclxxxix) make clear that he died before the prior bringing him the monastic cowl reached him.

[107] Richard of Devizes (*Chronicle*, pp. 70–1) has some equally acerbic, though much briefer, comments on secular canons, but they too are prompted by particular historical circumstances— viz., the replacement of monks by secular canons at Coventry (see above, pp. xlvi–xlvii).

INTRODUCTION

bishops falters and the order of the church becomes disordered. Through them, respect for the clergy grows faint and dies, and the glory of religious life dwindles to nothing. By their counsel kings plan wicked deeds, and give free rein to what they should hold back. They are the evil associates of bishops and kings—a wandering foot, a lying tongue, a grasping hand, a double heart, counterfeit love, a godless name, a concealed wrath, a real turbulence and a false calm, a bottomless purse, a robber without the name of robbery, a lying scale of truth and a truthful measure of fraud, law without the law of God, and canon without the rule of Christ, the preceding cause of evil, a page on which guile is written. They are the ones who have prostituted virgin justice, and have taught their tongues to utter falsehoods. While they endeavour to prop up the tottering world, they stagger when it staggers and fall when it falls. Their life is toil, their path slippery, their glory is shit and their end doubtful, grief their sure reward. (2315–54)

This tirade is clearly inspired by Baldwin's proposal to set up a college of canons that would undermine the rights of the Canterbury community.[108] But this supposition runs into an obvious difficulty, namely that it cannot be squared with Boutemy's suggested date for the *Speculum Stultorum*, 1179–80.[109] Baldwin did not become archbishop until 1184, and it was not until 1186 that he first put forward his proposal for the new college of canons at Hackington. The passage on the secular canons as well as several other pieces of evidence speak in favour of placing it considerably later than Boutemy thought.[110]

The Date

Burnellus's survey of the monastic orders contains an even clearer indication of a date in the late 1180s or even later: the section on the Grandmontines makes clear reference to a legal dispute within the order which first broke out in 1185:

They trouble the public law courts with quarrels and various lawsuits, and a simple case is dragged out at length. Having no property, they yet run up expenses, and a long-buried case turns into a marathon [lit. 15 years long]. Divided into two, they work hard and long, and continually put themselves to

---

[108] John Cotts discusses Nigel's outburst against the secular clergy, comparing it with Peter of Blois's vacillating attitudes to the same body (see Cotts, 'Critique'). However, Cotts assumes that Nigel's description of secular canons is a reflection of his previous experience, based on encounters with those of them who were in archiepiscopal service; in my view, even if his experience played a part in his attitude, his deliberately and obviously exaggerated description is far more proactive—that is, it is a violent attempt to ward off the threat of Baldwin's proposed college of canons.

[109] Boutemy, 'Prologue en prose', pp. 72–85; this date is accepted in *Lawrence*, ed. Ziolkowski, p. 40.

[110] I argued this in 'Does an author?'.

TEXT AND CONTEXT

li

unnecessary expenses. For in a reversal of order the lay-brother rules, while the cleric performs the sacred duties of his office. Disturbed on this account, Grandmont went to Rome, but there too the lawsuit had no end. Their outlay was large, but the Mount is fat and rich, providing them with all things from its milk, and although no one ploughs it, sows it, or reaps it, it miraculously brings forth at will whatever they want. So why is it that the man who lives like an angel inwardly is so often battered about in the public court? (2211–26)

As Raymo's note (to 2211–22) points out, Nigel's reference to the expenditure of time and money suggests that the quarrel has been running for some time, pointing to 1187 or 1188 at the earliest. It would be possible to suggest that this passage, and the section on the secular canons, were later additions to the poem, but the textual transmission of the poem yields no sign of an earlier version from which these passages were absent.[111] The α group of manuscripts lacks lines 2483–3258 and 3449–900, and the γ group breaks off at line 2602, but both groups contain the monastic survey in lines 2051–464.[112]

The section on the Carthusians points the same way, though more unobtrusively. In the late twelfth century, there was only one Carthusian foundation in England: the monastery at Witham, Somerset, in the diocese of Wells, established by Henry II (supposedly as part of his penances for the murder of Thomas Becket). References to this monastery date from 1179/80, but the foundations for its permanent buildings seem to have been begun only in 1181/82.[113] It is therefore rather surprising, to say the least, that Nigel includes the Carthusians in the survey of monastic orders, and also that he seems to be so well informed about the everyday practices of this comparatively recent order. Although Burnellus is supposed to be Italian, the monastic orders listed in the survey display a particularly English bias (especially as regards the Gilbertines), and there is no reason to think that Nigel would have had any acquaintance with Carthusian houses on the Continent. And whereas he comments on the Gilbertine order as a 'noua res' (2452), although it was founded around 1130, he does not comment on the recent arrival of the Carthusians in England. His description of Carthusian life is therefore more easily accounted for if it was composed at some time in the 1190s when the Carthusian community had become a more familiar part of the English monastic scene.

---

[111] The monastic survey is present in all manuscript versions of the poem except *Fr*; for a possible explanation of its lack in this manuscript, see below, p. lxxi.

[112] See below, pp. lxiii–lxvii for details of all the manuscripts.

[113] Thompson, *Carthusian Order*, pp. 59–60.

lii   INTRODUCTION

What, then, was Boutemy's evidence for the earlier dating? It hinges on a passing reference to 'Louis, king of the French' near the beginning of the poem. When Galen is trying to dissuade Burnellus from his desire for a longer tail, he tells him that 'Louis, king of the French' has no longer a tail than he has (201–2). Louis VII died on 18 September 1180, and was succeeded by Philip Augustus. There are several possible explanations for this discrepancy in dating indications. One might argue (though I am not sure that I would) that the action of the poem takes up a number of years (Burnellus spends seven years in Paris, and at least two or three more years are implied) so that a strict timescale would place its opening action ten years in the past. Or one might see it as some kind of private joke, specially aimed at or involving Louis, who visited Canterbury to pray for his health in August 1179 and who was granted fraternity with the community; after his death, he was to be remembered in the prayers of the monks, and there was to be a memorial service celebrated on its anniversary.[114] More plausibly, we might suppose that the composition of the *Speculum Stultorum* occupied a number of years, and this reference belongs to an early stage in its composition.[115] The late addition of the story of the Grateful Animals and the Ungrateful Man supports the view that the poem evolved in stages, the first of which might have comprised only the ass's desire for a longer tail and the story of the two cows, which includes Galen's remark about Louis VII. However we choose to account *either* for this reference *or* for the passages in the monastic survey, one or the other has to be 'explained away' in fixing a date.[116]

[114] Gervase, *Chronicle*, i. 293; *English Episcopal Acta ii. Canterbury 1162–1190*, ed. Cheney and Jones, no. 164. The *Epistolae Cantuarienses* often invoke Louis's name in appealing to Philip Augustus for assistance in the dispute with Baldwin. Recalling the reference, in the account of Burnellus's time in Paris, to the popular myth that the English have tails (1533–8), one might wonder if Louis had made this joke during his visit.

[115] The episodic structure of the poem means that it could well have evolved over a number of years, and in successive stages; the point that is important to my argument is that the dedication to William, and a large amount of material in the poem, fit a date in the 1190s.

[116] The other dating indication mentioned by Boutemy ('Prologue en prose', pp. 73–5), the reference to Saladin at *SS* line 2065, in the section on the Templars in the survey of monastic orders, is not decisive. Saladin had, as Boutemy pointed out, already acquired fame in the West through his destruction of the Templar castle at Jacob's Ford in 1179. On this event, see Barber, 'Frontier warfare in the Latin kingdom of Jerusalem'. However, Saladin's greatest triumph was his capture of Jerusalem in 1187, which led to the Third Crusade, in which Richard I played a leading role and had personal contacts with Saladin. See also n. to line 2065. It is interesting that Burnellus's survey of the monastic orders does not begin, as one would expect, with the Benedictines, Cistercians, etc., but with the crusading orders, the Templars and Hospitallers. This would make sense if the *SS* was written during or immediately after the crusade. Saladin died in 1193.

TEXT AND CONTEXT

liii

A particularly clear piece of evidence in favour of the later date was overlooked by Boutemy (and also by me, in my article of 2007). Burnellus's travelling companion Arnoldus prefaces his story of Gundulf and the cock by mentioning that it took place in Puglia (Apulia) 'in the time of William, the grandfather/ancestor of the present king' ('tempore Willelmi principis huius aui'; 1255–6). Boutemy does not mention this very specific indication of date; Raymo's note on these lines glosses 'Willelmus' as 'William the Bad (1154–1166)'. William was the second king of Sicily, whose territory at that date embraced the whole of Apulia.[117] This would mean that the 'present ruler' of Sicily was Tancred (1190–4), which would be at odds with Mozley and Raymo's date of 1179–80 for the composition of the *Speculum*, though Raymo does not seem to notice this. The dukes of Apulia/kings of Sicily in the second half of the twelfth century were as follows: William I (the Bad), 1154–66; his son, William II (the Good), 1166–89; William II's (illegitimate) cousin Tancred, 1190–4; Tancred's son William III, 1194.[118] Strictly speaking, none of these kings was the grandfather or grandson of any other; 'auus' may simply mean 'ancestor', or it may be supposed that Nigel assumed a direct line of descent and was not accurately informed on their exact relation to each other. But what is clear is that to allow for two changes in succession to the throne after a king called William, 'the present prince' must be either Tancred or William III, and in either case this would fix the date of *SS* well after 1179–80. It seems unlikely that 'the present prince' is William III, who was a child of four and whose reign lasted only from February 1194 to November of the same year, when he was deposed by the Hohenstaufen emperor Henry VI.[119] This would mean dating *SS* to a very brief period in 1194, and it seems more probable that the 'William' in question is William I, and 'the present prince' is Tancred. The reign of 'the present prince' then stretches from 1189 to 1194, and would comfortably fit a date in the early 1190s for the *Speculum*.

Another small pointer in favour of the early 1190s is Burnellus's description of the city of Paris, as he looks back on it, as a 'turreted

---

[117] This William was son of Count Roger II of Sicily, the first to hold the title of king. Roger was crowned king in 1130 and died in 1154.

[118] See the genealogical tables in *Roger II*, ed. Loud, p. xii, and Norwich, *The Kingdom in the Sun*, p. 394, and n. to *SS* line 1256.

[119] Henry's claim to Sicily was based on his marriage to Constance, daughter of Roger II, first king of Sicily (1130–54). Duke Leopold VI of Austria, who had captured Richard I in late 1192 on his way home from the crusade, transferred his captive to Henry in March 1193; Henry used the enormous ransom raised for Richard's release in February 1194 to finance his capture of the kingdom of Sicily.

liv   INTRODUCTION

city', 'surrounded with mighty walls' (1921–2). The construction of the great walls of Paris was ordered by Philip Augustus in 1190, before he left on crusade to the Holy Land (see n. to these lines). The walls on the Right Bank were built with great rapidity, and would presumably be noticeable and a matter for comment by travellers in the early 1190s.

The final reason for thinking that the *Speculum Stultorum* is more plausibly dated after 1190, rather than to 1179–80, is the dedication to William of Longchamp itself. Jan Ziolkowski has said that it is implausible to think of William as Nigel's patron (in whatever sense of the word) in 1179–80, because at that point 'William was still an unimportant bureaucrat in France'.[120] True, and for that very reason it is hard to imagine why at that date Nigel should dedicate his poem to him, even if (and this is mere speculation) they had met while studying in Paris and become friends. As noted earlier, Nigel certainly uses the language of affection in addressing William. But twelfth-century writers do not usually dedicate their works to old school chums; rather, they aim to give them prestige and influence by addressing them to the great and the good. In 1180, Richard was duke of Aquitaine, and his activities were entirely Continent-based.[121] Richard did not become

---

[120] *Lawrence*, ed. Ziolkowski, p. 40.

[121] Richard visited England (and Canterbury) briefly in 1179, after his victory at Taillebourg (Gillingham, *Richard I*, p. 62) but it is not at all clear that William was in his service at this time. According to Gerald of Wales (*De vita Galfridi*, ii. 1, *Opera*, iv. 388), William started his career as a clerk in the service of Geoffrey Plantagenet, natural son of Henry II and his chancellor, while Geoffrey was archdeacon of Rouen: 'Praefecerat enim eum officialem per archidiaconatum suum Rothomagensem.' Gerald had earlier explained (*De vita Galfridi*, i. 4, *Opera*, iv. 368) that Henry made Geoffrey his chancellor when the latter resigned the see of Lincoln in 1182, and conferred on him the archdeaconry of Rouen, along with several other offices, to provide him with an income. Gerald (*De vita Galfridi*, ii. 19, *Opera*, iv. 420–1) attributes the departure from Geoffrey's service to William's unpopularity with Henry II, placing it at the time of a rupture between Henry and Richard, caused by the latter's sins. The major breaches between Henry II and his sons occurred in 1173–4 and in 1187–9, but these dates are difficult to reconcile with the rest of Gerald's account. According to David Spear, the only documentary attestation of Geoffrey as archdeacon of Rouen occurs in 1183, though Spear speculates that he may have held the archdeaconry until his election as archbishop of York in 1189 ('Les Archidiacres de Rouen', p. 29; *The Personnel of the Norman Cathedrals*, p. 216). Professor Nicholas Vincent, who is preparing an edition of Richard's charters for the period before he became king, informs me (pers. comm., 17 December 2006, 15 January 2007, 24 September 2022) that William appears as witness to two charters issued by Richard while he was count of Poitou, one dated 1188, the other (in favour of St Peter's, La Réole) undated. On the other hand, a charter issued by Richard on the VI Kal. Januarii (= 27 December), 1181, is said to have been written 'per manum Iohannis cancellarii' (the date of 1181 is confirmed by the inclusion of Pope Lucius III—who was enthroned only on 1 September 1181—in the dating clause); see *Chartes et documents pour servir à l'histoire de l'abbaye de Saint-Maxent*, ed. Richard, 375–6, no. 362. Taken together with Gerald's testimony, this would suggest a date of 1182 or later for William's transfer from

TEXT AND CONTEXT

lv

king until 1189, at which point William accompanied him to England. What is more, in 1180 no one could reasonably have *expected* Richard to become king, since his older brother Henry was clearly marked out as the heir, and was actually crowned, well in advance of Henry II's death, on 14 June 1170; until the Young King (Henry) died in 1183, the natural assumption was that he would succeed his father. For these reasons it is hard to see why Nigel—or anyone else—should have dedicated a work to William in 1179–80. If, however, we follow the dating indications in the survey of monastic orders and the allusion to 'William, ruler of Sicily', and place the poem some time in the early 1190s, not only these passages but also the dedication make sense.[122]

The Motive

A clue to Nigel's motives in dedicating the *Speculum* to William is provided by the prose epistle that accompanies the poem in 32 of the 41 surviving medieval manuscripts. This epistle gives a rather surprising explanation of the poem's narrative:

This ass is a monk, or any man of religion situated in a cloister, who is charged with the service of God as an ass is with bearing burdens, and who, not content with his condition, as the ass is not with his tail, yearns passionately for what he does not naturally have or is totally incapable of having because nature forbids it, who pursues his desire in every way possible, and takes advice from a doctor, that is, from anyone who he thinks is able to give it to him, which in his deluded mind he thinks is possible. He wants his old tail to be torn out and a new one to be implanted, because he totally despises the monastic life in which he ought to persevere to the end in order to be saved, exploring every possible way in which he may be uprooted from it and transplanted to where a

---

Geoffrey to Richard. Balfour ('William de Longchamp', ch. 2) proposes that William moved to Richard's service in 1184, when relations between Henry and Richard were openly hostile as a result of Richard's refusal to obey Henry's order to surrender Aquitaine to his brother John. (NB: in its entry for 'Longchamp, William de (*d*. 1197)', *ODNB* misleadingly supplies the obit 1186 for Geoffrey, confusing him with Henry's legitimate son Geoffrey, count of Brittany.) I am grateful to David Balfour, the late Richard Sharpe, Ralph V. Turner, and Nicholas Vincent for helping me to trace William's early career.

[122] There seem to be two possibilities. The poem might have been written around 1190–1, when William was at the height of his power; it might also have been written after 1194, after Richard's release from captivity and William's restoration to a position of power and influence (in which case it would post-date the *Tractatus*). A strong piece of evidence in favour of the latter possibility is the concluding story of the Grateful Animals and the Ungrateful Man, which was brought to England by Richard I in 1194 (see below for details).

This dating shift is also consistent with O'Daly's 'revised chronology' of Nigel's life, which suggests the possibility that his annotations of Peter Comestor's *Historia Scholastica* 'took place in several stages from the early 1170s to [their] completion by 1194' ('Reading the *Historia Scholastica*', p. 291).

lvi INTRODUCTION

new and luxuriant tail may grow on him, that is, that he may be able to get
himself a prioracy or abbacy, where he can first introduce a numerous retinue
of his relatives, and then drag them after him like a tail wherever he goes.
(*Epistle to William*, 10–13)

Nothing in the poem suggests that Burnellus represents a monk
(unlike the *Ysengrimus*, where the other animals consistently address
the wolf as 'abbot'). And the idea that his desire for a longer tail represents a desire for a prioracy or abbacy so that he can drag after himself
a long retinue of his relatives seems to be on a par with the wilder
excesses of medieval biblical exegesis. Equally unexpected allegorical
explanations are proposed for other episodes of the poem. Galen's
story of the two cows is said to represent two types of men in religious
life. The first represents those who are

excessively indiscreet and very rash, who when any adversity comes along, as
if constricted by a frost, are enslaved and blinded by a tenderness for their
relatives, as the cow is by love for her calf, and immediately cut off their tails,
that is, they cast far from them the remembrance of death, with which they
ought to protect themselves from the flies that fly about and sting. Not looking
to the future nor calculating the outcome of events in their frenzy, they cut off
without hope of recovery their old friends, who could come to them in their
need, and completely uproot them (*Epistle to William*, 21–3).

The second cow represents those 'ruled by a riper counsel', who look
to the future, and 'patiently bear the onslaughts of the impatient', calling to their mind 'those who are forgetful and ungrateful for benefits'
(*Epistle to William*, 24, 26). Protected by their tails (that is, the thought
of their last end), they will survive the torments of heat—that is, the
Last Judgment (*Epistle to William*, 29). Next, Nigel explains that
Burnellus buying the ten glass jars represents a monk who desperately
seeks, by a mixture of flattery and bribery, to acquire men's favour,
which is as fragile as glass, but having been 'whirled above his station
to a position where he may fulfil his foolish and empty desires, he loses
even the little he possessed before' (*Epistle to William*, 37).

These surprising explanations are, as Fritz Peter Knapp says, 'over-
interpretations' ('Überinterpretationen').[123] That is, they are not so
much allegory as allegoresis or 'imposed allegory'.[124] True allegory
brings together two areas of discourse in a metaphorical relationship

---

[123] 'Das mittelalterliche Tierepos', p. 59.
[124] See Tuve, *Allegorical Imagery*, ch. 4, 'Imposed Allegory', and, for the distinction
between allegory and allegoresis, Quilligan, *The Language of Allegory*, pp. 25–6, 29–32.

TEXT AND CONTEXT   lvii

that seems to be grounded in an existential similarity (such as the progress through life and going on pilgrimage, or making love to a woman and plucking a rose). As William Empson astutely said: 'Part of the function of an allegory is to make you feel that two levels of being correspond to one another in detail, and indeed that there is some underlying reality, something in the nature of things, which makes this happen. Either level may illuminate the other.'[125] Allegoresis, on the other hand, proceeds by interpreting individual episodes, characters, features of landscape, and so on, in piecemeal fashion, finding ingenious and unsuspected equivalents for the details of the narrative. The ad hoc impression made by these particular allegorical explanations is strengthened by the fact that at this point in the epistle Nigel switches to explanations of a straightforwardly literal type (that is, they do not involve metaphor). Fromundus (who, of course, is not a metaphorical monk but a real one) is said to signify those who try to outwit and trick their simpler brethren by cunning and who often fall into the nets that they themselves have spread. The ass's 'foolish' and 'imprudent' boasts (about his cleverness in outwitting Fromundus) are said to signify (because they *are*) 'imprudent and futile meditations' (*Epistle to William*, 40). The story of the vengeful cock, Nigel says, does not need any explanation because it is 'self-explanatory' (*Epistle to William*, 42)—that is, it is about those who do not forget injuries. The ass's inability to learn anything at the university signifies—again, in a quite unmetaphorical way—those who have not the wit to learn anything and who hypocritically lay claim to a knowledge they do not possess (*Epistle*, 44–8). Burnellus's survey of the monastic orders is said to be a way of criticizing them by means of a comic pretence (that the ass wishes to become a monk) (*Epistle to William*, 50).

At this point, the explanatory epistle breaks off, leaving the last 1,400 lines of the poem without authorial comment. Various explanations for its abrupt ending have been proposed: that the exemplar of the epistle lost a final folio,[126] or that the poem itself was originally

---

[125] Empson, *The Structure of Complex Words*, p. 346.

[126] André Boutemy, 'Prologue en prose', p. 69. Boutemy draws attention to the word 'interserit' ('inserts'), used in the penultimate sentence of the epistle ('Vnde Burnellus quaedam de diuersis ordinibus interserit, uolens iocosa quaedam insimulatione reprehendere quae nouerat aspera increpatione nequaquam se posse extirpare. Multa enim genera morborum sunt quae utilius unguentum quam cauterium ad medelam admittunt'; *Epistle to William*, 49–50). Boutemy thinks that if the survey of the religious orders is 'inserted' into the narrative, this implies that something followed it, and therefore the poem must have continued past this point.

lviii   INTRODUCTION

much shorter.[127] But it is hard not to feel that the rest of the poem
might come under the 'self-explanatory' heading. So far from feeling
that we have been deprived of the key to the end of the poem, we may
well feel that we have been provided with a key to its beginning that we
did not really need and do not quite know what to do with. Although,
in his verse prologue at the opening of the poem, Nigel urges the reader
to pay attention not to the words of his poem but to their inner meaning
(9–10), this seems to be no more than the conventional fable-writer's
claim that his absurd animal anecdotes embody moral wisdom. The
allegorical explanations do not strike us as opening up the true meaning
of the narrative, and they cannot be sustained beyond an individual
episode. If, for example, Burnellus *signifies* a monk in the opening
episode, how are we to interpret his later decision to *become* a monk?[128]
And how are we to know when an episode is to be interpreted allegorically,
and when it is supposed to be 'self-explanatory'? The *Epistle* seems to
need as much interpreting as the poem.

Yet if we look at the prose epistle, not as a decipherment of the
Speculum Stultorum, but as putting a number of threads into our hands,
we shall see that they form part of a complex web of meaning which
encompasses both the poem and its context. First, the epistle's various
interpretations stress the centrality of monastic life: those episodes of
the poem in which monks or monasticism appear are interpreted literally, while in those episodes where monks and monasticism do not
appear they are 'read in' allegorically. Since Nigel of Longchamp was
a monk this is not surprising, but it does suggest that he is writing not
as a disembodied moral observer but from a particular social (and perhaps individual) stance. Secondly, if we piece together the various
interpretations in the epistle, a set of overlapping concerns begins to
emerge: desire for promotion to the position of abbot or prior;
favouritism or fondness for relatives; neglect of old friends in favour of
relatives; ingratitude; vengeance for old injuries; monastic ambition;
monastic deviousness; monastic hypocrisy and false pretensions to

---

[127] Nigel of Longchamp, '*Epistola ad Willelmum*', ed. Mozley, p. 14. Mozley cited in support of this hypothesis the 'remarkable lack of firmness in the manuscript tradition in the
latter part of the poem'; some manuscripts (*LEF*) have a long lacuna from 2483 to 3258, while
the original of the manuscript group c (my γ) 'must have stopped at 2602', and in MS *Y* lines
3233–458 are missing. However, he later abandoned the hypothesis that the shorter manuscripts represented earlier versions of the poem, and suggested instead that they derived
from defective exemplars. See below, p. cxvi.

[128] Cf. C. S. Lewis's comment: 'allegory is *idem in alio*. Only a bungler, like Deguileville,
would introduce a monastery into his [allegorical] poem if he were really writing about
monasticism' (*The Allegory of Love*, p. 323).

TEXT AND CONTEXT

learning. This composite picture suggests that the prose epistle carries a lightly coded message, which can be expressed roughly as follows: asses are winning promotion in monastic life; they do so by using flattery and bribery, and by parading a false and superficial learning; favours are handed out to family relatives, while old friends are forgotten and the benefits they have rendered are not met with gratitude; such injuries rankle and may one day be avenged.

I suggested long ago that this coded message refers to Nigel's own situation:[129] he is appealing to an old friend, drawing attention to his own suitability for promotion, and providing, in the poem itself, a demonstration of the true learning which his more successful rivals can only counterfeit. It is not of course possible to provide cast-iron proof of this claim (though I shall shortly try to support it with some historical and literary evidence), but I should like to draw attention to the way that it provides a coherent motivation for some important thematic motifs in the poem, which appear also in the parts that the epistle does not discuss. The story of how Burnellus saved the three thieves, and consequently earned the mayor's enmity, seems on the face of it rather pointless (since the mayor's enmity is only a fantasy on Burnellus's part), but it of course illustrates the theme of ingratitude, and this is also the central theme of the concluding tale of the Grateful Animals and the Ungrateful Man. The story of the Three Fates tells how they seek to distribute the gifts of Fortune in such a way that they will counterbalance the gifts of Nature. Ignoring one girl who has many virtues but is desperately unhappy, and another who is very beautiful but unable to walk, they shower Fortune's gifts on the stupid brutish peasant girl whom they find emptying her bowels by the side of the road. Considered as an autonomous anecdote, this story seems to be nothing more than an expression of cynicism, but when it is related to the epistle, it is easy to see it as an ironic demonstration of the universal principle that rewards go only to those who are totally unworthy of them. And in fact Burnellus's concluding comments on the story insist on its applicability to religious life in particular, and the manifold wrongs that spring from a sense of injured merit:

On models such as this, many things often come about in religious life which are not in accord with reason. This is often the way in religious life, O teacher, and you too will often have to put up with it. That is the general rule; these characteristics are shared by many, and this is generally the evil practice of bishops. This is what produces many improprieties, and sets the pastor and his

[129] Mann, 'The *Speculum Stultorum* and the *Nun's Priest's Tale*'.

lx INTRODUCTION

flock at odds with each other. These are the things that produce disasters in religious life, scandals, contempt, schisms, injuries, guile. Although virtue can disregard other things which are harmful to many, it cannot disregard its own contemptuous treatment. Nothing wounds the mind more grievously, nothing burns more deeply, than when virtue's gifts are scorned.[130] Although other things wear off over time, this never leaves the mind. This is a type of wound that gets worse with treatment, and becomes a bigger sore with the passage of time. This causes snake poison to drip into the mind, and no antidote has power against it. Anyone who can patiently bear his own contempt can easily endure other things. Although patience conquers by bearing everything, beneath this burden she falls conquered. (3435–58)

Similar comments emerge at odd moments in the various satiric outpourings of the poem: for example, Burnellus's speech on the faults of bishops declares:

Not despising a care for flesh and blood, they attentively look after both themselves and their family. The one whom they especially ought to have promoted, barely manages to skulk in some remote corner. He who gave what might alleviate another's hunger now burns, freezes, and is needy, thirsts, hungers, and is full of sores. (2711–16)

Talking about the defects of abbots and priors, the ass claims that they are beset by three things in particular: 'the first is the effort to rise in life, after which come the indiscriminate love of their relatives, and an anxiety that knows no peace' (2837–8). In contrast, the ideal confessor will not be swayed by favour for his relatives ('causa parentum': 2997). And when he is praising the Benedictines (Nigel's own order), he says: 'They give outside postings only to those who have been long and thoroughly tried by the discipline of the cloister. Neither the abbot's favour, nor any blood-relationship can prevail against the monks' interest' (2097–100). Insofar as the prose epistle functions to draw attention to them, these passages serve as indications that the poem's moral strictures and satiric criticisms are not the results of a detached observation of the human scene but emanate from, and lead back to, a particular standpoint.

In dedicating his poem to William, Nigel might just have been trying to win the goodwill of an influential and powerful supporter for the monks of Canterbury in their quarrel with Baldwin. But the prose epistle, with its insistent emphasis on monastic promotion and the neglect of people distinguished by solid learning and true merit, suggests that

---

[130] This is the point at which manuscripts *LEF* end; for the claim that this was the original end of the poem, see below.

TEXT AND CONTEXT

lxi

Nigel might also have been thinking of his own advancement. And the passionate outburst at the end of the story of the Three Fates, which I quoted earlier, also points in the same direction. William's enemies said of him when he was justiciar that there was 'no monk who longed for an abbey who was not obliged to become subservient to his power and influence'.[131] Even when deprived of the justiciarship, William would have retained considerable influence on English religious affairs, both as papal legate and as bishop of Ely, which was one of the wealthiest and most important English dioceses.[132] In 1193, we find Robert, abbot-elect of the Benedictine abbey of Thorney, travelling all the way to Worms to receive the episcopal benediction from William, who was in Germany to negotiate Richard's release from captivity.[133] Still more interesting, William was notorious for securing promotion, secular or religious, for his family,[134] and two of his brothers were made heads of religious houses. His brother Henry was made abbot of Crowland (in Lincolnshire) in 1190, and his brother Robert became prior of Ely, at an uncertain date (but not before 2 December 1189, when his predecessor is attested as having been in post).[135] In 1191 William tried to get Robert made abbot of Westminster (the king had written a letter giving him carte blanche in the affair),[136] but this plan was foiled by his expulsion from England, and it may have been at this point that Robert was made prior of Ely, as a kind of compensation prize.[137]

---

[131] Roger of Howden, *Chronica*, iii. 142: 'nec erat rusticus qui agrum, nec civis qui fundum, nec miles qui praedium, nec clericus qui ecclesiam, nec monachus qui abbatiam affectaret, quem in jus et potestatem ejus transire non oporteret'. The comment is not made by Roger of Howden himself but is contained in Hugh of Nonant's malicious letter attacking William, which Roger quotes in full. Cf. Gerald, *De vita Galfridi*, ii. 19, *Opera*, iv. 425: 'Proinde et super matrimoniis, super honoribus et dignitatibus, tam ecclesiasticis quam saecularibus, pro animi sui motu, ad libitum et nutum cuncta disponebat.'

[132] Ely's income in the late 12th c. has been estimated as approximately £800 (eight times larger than Hugh of Nonant's diocese of Coventry); see Crosby, *Bishop and Chapter*, p. 370.

[133] *Victoria County History of the County of Cambridge and the Isle of Ely*, ii. 213.

[134] 'Laicis vero et clericis ecclesias, terras et possessiones suas abstulit, quas aut nepotibus suis aut clericis et servientibus erogabat, aut damnabiliter sibi retinebat, aut in usus extraordinarios dilapidabat' (Roger of Howden, *Gesta* ii. 143; repeated in Roger of Howden, *Chronica*, iii. 72).

[135] See Conway, 'The family of William Longchamp', pp. 39–40; Knowles et al., *Heads of Religious Houses*, pp. 42 (Crowland) and 46 (Ely). Confusingly, William seems to have had *two* brothers named Henry; the other one held secular offices (Conway, pp. 31–3).

[136] See Richard of Devizes, *Chronicle*, p. 29 ('De abbatia uero Westmonasterii iam uacante solo cancellario permittitur ordinare pro libito') and pp. 39, 54.

[137] Since Richard of Devizes (*Chronicle*, p. 39) calls Robert a monk of Caen at the time of the Westminster attempt, it may have been after this attempt failed that he went to Ely.

lxii INTRODUCTION

David Knowles has noted that the monastery of Christ Church, Canterbury, because of its position at the centre of things, 'naturally became a nursery whence, often at the suggestion of the primate, superiors were drawn for other houses, and even occasionally bishops for sees over which Canterbury desired to secure influence'.[138] He lists eleven monks who in the course of the twelfth century became abbots elsewhere: at the latter end of the century we find Odo sent to Battle in 1175, Ralph sent to Shrewsbury in 1175, Roger sent to St Augustine's Canterbury in 1175/6, Benedict sent to Peterborough in 1177, Alan sent to Tewkesbury (although this was the result of his being 'kicked upstairs' by Baldwin to get him out of the way) in 1186/7,[139] and Roger Norreys sent to Evesham in 1190.[140] It might well have seemed to Nigel therefore that a stream of his fellow-monks were winning promotion while he was being neglected. Was he perhaps put out that he had not been promoted prior of Ely himself? (or was he writing before Robert had been appointed?) A poem that accompanies the *Tractatus* in one manuscript suggests he knew the monastery and its monks rather well: imitating Ovid's *Tristia* (i. 1–128), he imagines his poem travelling through the fens to Ely; after being hospitably received by the bishop, it will proceed to the monastery where one of the monks, 'my Nicholas', will greet it with embraces and kisses (lines 153–6, 223–6).[141] An entry

---

[138] Knowles, *Monastic Order*, pp. 176–7.

[139] Stubbs, *Introductions*, p. 384 = *Epistolae Cantuarienses*, Introduction, p. xl. Cf. Gervase, *Chronicle*, i. 335. Baldwin wanted to replace him with a prior who would he thought be more amenable to his wishes, but in choosing Honorius for this purpose he was very much mistaken (see above, pp. xlv, lxxiv–lxxv).

[140] Knowles, *Monastic Order*, p. 177, n. 1. Ziolkowski thinks that this stream of promotions drained the strength of the mother house (*Lawrence*, p. 35); Knowles obviously sees it in quite the opposite terms, as increasing Canterbury's network of influence.

[141] 'Postquam transieris [addressing the *Tractatus*] pontes, vada, stagna, paludes,/ Est quibus Elysii gloria septa loci,/ Virginis Eldredae venies devotus ad aram,/ Dignaque pro meritis dona precesque dabis/ ... Si licet atque vacat monachorum claustra subibis,/ Portans multiplicis verba salutis eis./ Protinus occurret meus ille tibi Nicholaus,/ Dicere nec Petro vix patietur "ave"./ Totus in amplexus et in oscula tantus abibit,/ Cedat ut anguillae filia febris ei' (lines 153–6, 223–8). The poem precedes the *Tractatus* in London, BL, MS Cotton Cleopatra B. III, and is found independently in BL, MS Cotton Julius A. VII, fos. 60^v–65^r (see the digitized version of this manuscript); *Tractatus*, ed. Boutemy, pp. 94–5. As Boutemy points out, in the 14th-c. catalogue of Dover Priory, the poem is listed as an independent item (James, *Ancient Libraries*, p. 463, no. 202, fo. 1*a*, 'Nigellus ad cancellarium a[nglie]', inc. 'Postquam tristis hyemps'), while on the other hand incipits show that it did not preface any of the five examples of the *Tractatus* included in the same catalogue (ibid. p. 441, no. 59; p. 443, no. 79; p. 449, nos. 105 and 106; p. 455, no. 135). Boutemy argues that the poem was not conceived as a preface to the *Tractatus* and was probably written for a different work, now lost (*Tractatus*, p. 96).

THE MANUSCRIPTS   lxiii

in Bale's *Index* tantalizingly calls him 'Nigellus Eliensis monachus'.[142] At any rate, if William was indeed an old friend, his rise to power, whether as a trusted servant of the king, as justiciar, or as papal legate, must have seemed like a golden opportunity for Nigel.

The *Epistle to William* thus helps us to see some of the threads that run through the *Speculum Stultorum*, and it also gives us some hints as to the nature of their importance for Nigel, even if it does not answer all the questions that it raises.[143] It is now time to return to the poem, and to try to identify the reasons behind the different shapes it assumes in the manuscripts.

THE MANUSCRIPTS

The following is a list of the 41 manuscripts of the *Speculum Stultorum* which have been collated for the present edition.[144]

A London, British Library, Harley 2422, fos. 2^r–81^v
  s. xiii^2. Ends at 3542 (missing leaves).

B London, British Library, Arundel 23, fos. 1^r–66^v
  s. xv med. Omits 849–1386 (missing leaves); ends at 3864.

*Be Berlin, Staatsbibliothek zu Berlin, Preussischer Kulturbesitz, theol. qu. 214, fos. 181^r–234^r
  s. xv. Ends at 2602.

C London, British Library, Cotton Titus A. XX, fos. 4^r–50^v
  AD 1367 × 1400. Complete.

D Dublin, Trinity College Library, 440, pp. 1–130 (paginated)
  s. xiv med. Complete. Contains the Interpolation on the Mendicant Orders.

E Oxford, Bodleian Library, Bodley 761 (S.C. 2535), fos. 160^r–180^r
  c.1360–70. Like *LF*, lacks 2483–3258; ends at 3448.

---

[142] Bale, *Index Britanniae Scriptorum*, ed. Poole and Bateson, p. 310; cf. Mozley, 'Nigel Wireker or Wetekre?', p. 314. Bale's entry may be a mistake, influenced by the reference in the following line to 'Guillelmum Eliensem episcopum', but since the entry relates to the poem cited in n. 141 above, Bale may have picked up the internal indications that Nigel had some association with Ely.

[143] See below, pp. lxxv–lxxviii on the possible relevance of the debate between birds.

[144] An asterisk before the manuscript entry signifies that it was not known to Mozley when he was producing his edition of *SS* (in the case of *Ha*, he learned of it before the edition was published but too late to make use of it). Fragments and prose paraphrases are not included in this list, nor is the 17th-c. transcription by Richard James, Cotton Librarian (Mozley's h); for a fuller list, and details of dates, indications of origin, ownership, general character of contents, and bibliographical references, see the Manuscript Descriptions in Appendix A.

lxiv INTRODUCTION

F   Oxford, Bodleian Library, Bodley 851 (S.C. 3041), fos. 97^v–115^v

s. xiv^{ex}. Like *LE*, lacks 2483–3258, and ends at 3448, but also transposes 3259–78 to follow 3432, after which 3323–8 are repeated.

*Fr   Frankfurt am Main, Universitätsbibliothek, Barth. 62, fos. 150^r–162^v

s. xv$^{3/4}$. Lacks 2053–464; ends at 2602.

G   Oxford, Bodleian Library, Digby 27 (S.C. 1628), fos. 1^r–61^v

s. xv. Ends at 2746 (missing leaves). Contains the Interpolation on the Mendicant Orders.

Go   Erfurt, Forschungsbibliothek Gotha, Chart. B 517, fos. 136^r–195^v (Mozley's k)

s. xv. Ends at 2602.

H   Oxford, Bodleian Library, Bodley 496 (S.C. 2159), fos. 146^r–192^r

s. xv med. Ends at 3864.

*Ha   Halle, Universitäts- und Landesbibliothek, Stolb.-Wern. Za 89, fos. 1^r–47^v

s. xv. Complete.

*Hu   Huntington Library, San Marino, California, MS HM80250, fos. 168^v–184^r

s. xiv^1. Complete. Contains the Interpolation on the Mendicant Orders.

I   Oxford, Bodleian Library, Bodley 780 (S.C. 2583), fos. 1^r–33^v

s. xv. Lacks 1116–744 (missing leaves); lacks 2747–3258 (like *G*); copies 3259–448 from an exemplar closely related to *L*; ends at 3448 (like *LEF*). Contains the Interpolation on the Mendicant Orders.

J   Oxford, All Souls College, 37, fos. 171^r–196^r

s. xv^{in}. Complete.

K   London, British Library, Additional 38665, fos. 85^r–156^r

s. xv^{in}. Complete. Contains the Interpolation on the Mendicant Orders.

L   London, Lambeth Palace Library, 357, fos. 78^r–111^r

s. xv^1. Like *EF*, lacks 2483–3258; ends at 3448.

THE MANUSCRIPTS

lxv

*La Sankt Paul im Lavanttal (Kärnten), Stiftsbibliothek, Codex 239/4, fos. 101^r–151^v, 161^r–184^v

s. xv med. Complete.

M Lincoln, Cathedral Chapter Library, 105, fos. 91^r–116^v

s. xiv. Transposes 3602–896 after 3320.

Mu Munich, Bayerische Staatsbibliothek, clm 23820, fos. 243^r–282^v (Mozley's m)

AD 1462. Ends at 2602. Contains the Interpolation on the Mendicant Orders.

N Lincoln, Cathedral Chapter Library, 191, fos. 228^v–255^r

s. xiv. Like M, transposes 3602–896 after 3320. Contains the Interpolation on the Mendicant Orders.

*Ne Lobkowicz Library, Nelahozeves Castle, Czech Republic, Sig. VI Fb 29, pp. 87–125

s. xv. Ends at 2602.

O Brussels, KBR, 2695–719, fos. 34^r –93^v

s. xv. Transposes 3761–825 after 3853. Complete.

P Brussels, KBR, 1701–4, fos. 122^v–138^v

s. xv. Omits 55–666 in situ, but adds 205–594 after line 3900 at the end of the poem (so only 56–204 and 595–666 are completely lacking); 2859–3097 are repeated.

*Pk Prague, Archiv Prazského Hradu, Knihovna Metropolitni Kapituly, M. CXXI (catalogue 1482), fos. 43^r–86^v

s. xv. Ends at 2602.

*Pm Prague, Knihovna Národního muzea, XIV. D. 4, fos. 144^r–180^v

s. xv$^{1/4}$. Transposes 1599–2476 after 721. Ends at 2602.

Q Copenhagen, Det Kongelige Bibliotek, GKS 1634 quarto, fos. 85^r–133^r

s. xv. Like Y, lacks 1249–502, 2401–12, 3233–458.

R Città del Vaticano, Biblioteca Apostolica Vaticana, reg. lat 1379, fos. 1^r–70^r

s. xv^{in}. Complete.

S Paris, Bibliothèque nationale de France, lat. 16519, fos. 51^r–106^v

AD 1391. Ends at 2522.

lxvi INTRODUCTION

T Wrocław, Biblioteka Uniwersytecka we Wrocławiu, IV.Q.126, fos. 154^r–183^r

s. xv². Ends at 2602; a torn leaf means that lines 934–1022 are largely missing.

Tr Trento, Biblioteca comunale, W 3154, fos. 211^r–235^v (Mozley's s)

s. xv¹. Complete.

U London, British Library, Sloane 1831 B, fos. 1^r–47^v

s. xv. Very defective (missing leaves); lacks 1–1042, 2351–677, 3359–412. Ends at 3864.

Va Vienna, Österreichische Nationalbibliothek, 3487, fos. 1^r–43^r (Mozley's V)

s. xv. Lacks 618–81, 1177–234. Lines 33–96 follow line 617, lines 229–92 follow line 1176. Ends at 2602.

Vb Vienna, Österreichische Nationalbibliothek, 12531, fos. 85^r–133^r (Mozley's z)

s. xv^{in}. Ends at 2602. The *Epistle to William* ends at section 15.

Vc Vienna, Österreichische Nationalbibliothek, 3283, fos. 1^r–87^r (Mozley's t)

AD 1478. Ends at 2602.

Vd Vienna, Österreichische Nationalbibliothek, 3467, fos. 1^r–56^r (Mozley's u)

s. xv. Ends at 2602.

Ve Vienna, Österreichische Nationalbibliothek, 3529, fos. 1^r–74^v (Mozley's x)

s. xv. Complete.

*W Oxford, Bodleian Library, Lat. misc. c. 75 (olim Phillips 3119), fos. 1^r–23^v

s. xiv. Complete.

X London, British Library, Cotton Vespasian E. XII, fos. 10^v–77^r

s. xv². Complete.

Y Wolfenbüttel, Herzog-August Bibliothek, Helmst. 616, fos. 93^r–137^v

AD 1419. Like Q, lacks 1249–502, 2401–12, 3233–458.

Z Leipzig, Universitäts-Bibliothek, 1591, fos. 1^r–62^v

THE MANUSCRIPTS lxvii

s. xv. Ends at 3882 (missing leaf). Between 822 and 1154 lines are disordered: 822, 936–92, 883–935, 823–82, 1103–53, 1049–102, 993–1048, 1154.

In the above list, I have adhered as far as possible to the sigla established in the 1960 edition of the *Speculum Stultorum* by Mozley and Raymo, but I have been obliged to alter them in certain cases where they are confusing or misleading. In the first place, Mozley's sigla jumble together complete (or originally complete) copies of the poem with fragments, excerpts, or prose paraphrases; secondly, his manuscript sigla vary between capital and lower-case letters in an apparently random way.[145] I have followed conventional practice by separating main manuscripts from fragments and excerpts (listed in Manuscript Descriptions in Appendix A) and designating the latter by lower-case letters preceded by 'f'. This means that it has been necessary to devise new sigla for the five Vienna manuscripts, now labelled *Va–Ve*, and also for Munich 23820, now *Mu*. The nine manuscripts signalled by asterisks in the list above were not collated by Mozley. The Halle manuscript became known to him only after the Mozley–Raymo edition of *SS* went to press, via two articles published by Anton Blaschka.[146] Blaschka suggested giving this manuscript the sigil U, which Mozley had already assigned to BL, Sloane 1831; I therefore use *Ha* for the Halle manuscript. The remaining eight manuscripts were not known to Mozley, although five of them (*BePkFrPmNe*) were listed in Walther's *Initia carminum ac uersuum* under the incipit of the *Speculum* (Walther 18944).[147]

---

[145] I attribute responsibility for the sigla to Mozley, though Raymo's account of the division of labour between the two editors (see their Preface) states that the description of the manuscripts was a joint endeavour, with Mozley taking responsibility for the Continental manuscripts and Raymo for the British ones. The errors that pervade the description of the manuscripts are so characteristic of Mozley that I assume he was responsible for its final form. Karl Langosch's review of this edition in *Mittellateinisches Jahrbuch* iii (1966), 280–6 complained about the strangely random distribution of capital and lower-case letters in Mozley's sigla. Conventional practice would be to use capital letters for the main manuscripts and lower-case letters for the fragments and excerpts. Examination suggests that the lower-case letters are used for most of the group Mozley calls c̲ (my group γ) which end at line 2602 (that is, Mozley's STkmtuVz). But even so there is no complete consistency and no explanation is given.

[146] See *SS*, p. 128.

[147] Walther's *Initia* was published in 1959, but Mozley and Raymo's edition of 1960 was probably in press by then. Mozley's list also includes a 17th-c. transcription by Richard James (now Bodleian Library, James 15), who was Sir Robert Cotton's librarian. Mozley gave this manuscript the sigil h, but he does not seem to have collated it and it is not included in his stemma (*SS*, p. 23). I have not collated it for this edition.

lxviii INTRODUCTION

It should be noted that Mozley's list of manuscripts is riddled with errors: shelfmarks, folio numbers, accounts of the final line of the poem in particular manuscripts, even information as to whether a manuscript is written in double or single columns, are all liable to be erroneous. Discrepancies between Mozley's list and my own may be attributed to these errors.

THE VARIOUS FORMS OF THE POEM IN THE MANUSCRIPTS

The manuscripts listed above contain an initially bewildering variety of versions of the poem, differing in length and order. To begin with, I am focusing on these large-scale differences in the general outlines of the poem, and their possible connections with its evolution; for that reason I have given details of where each manuscript ends, and of any major lacunae. (Omissions of smaller units, from one to ten lines, say, have been ignored for these purposes.) Analysis of their variant readings and textual affiliations will follow, concluding with a summary sketching the probable stages in the evolution of the poem.

Many of the idiosyncratic forms of the poem can be accounted for in a quite straightforward manner. The main cause is loss of leaves, which occurred in the case of manuscripts *A*, *B*, *G*, *I* (first lacuna), *T*, and *U*. *I* derives from an exemplar shared with *G*, which explains the absence of 2747–3258; it then draws on a manuscript related to *L* (if not *L* itself) and therefore cannot fill most of *G*'s major gap, and ends where *L* does at 3448 (see below, pp. ci–cii). Loss of leaves is also the most probable explanation for the large group of manuscripts which end at 2602, and which derive from a common exemplar (see below on group γ). Line 2602 is in the middle of the long tirade against the corrupting influence of 'munera'; ending at this point leaves the narrative without a conclusion, and makes no sense. The end of the poem thus seems most likely to have been lost as a result of physical mutilation. *S*, which belongs to this group, has suffered a further loss, apparently of only two folios,[148] but it would seem more likely that it lost lines 2523–602 than that the other manuscripts in the group added these lines. The exemplar of *Be*, which ends at 2595, also seems to have lost a final folio, since the scribe confidently adds not one explicit but two: 'Explicit speculum stultorum', and underneath 'Speculi stultorum est hic finis'. *U* is a complicated case, but physical loss is the likeliest cause, as Boutemy attempted

---

[148] See Boutemy, 'The manuscript tradition', p. 519 n. 1.

VARIOUS FORMS OF THE POEM   lxix

to explain.[149] The truncation of the *Epistle to William* at the bottom of fo. 85^v in *Vb* is more puzzling: the quires are regular gatherings of twelve folios, as is indicated by the catchwords at the foot of fos. 28^v, 40^v, 52^v, 64^v, 76^v, 88^v, 100^v, 112^v, etc.[150] This would suggest that if anything was lost, the loss must have occurred in the exemplar, though the scribe of *Vb* gives no sign of being conscious of it.

Transposition of lines may be simply a result of scribal error in copying, as is the case with *O*,[151] but can also be the result of misbinding. This is evidently the case with *Z*, whose severe disordering is, as Mozley explained (*SS*, p. 15), the result of the first and the third bifolia (each with 25–30 lines to a page) in a quire having changed places (see MS *Z* in Manuscript Descriptions in Appendix A). Misbinding is evidently the cause of the jumbled order of the text in *Pm*: fos. 144^r–55^v have lines 1–721; fos. 156^r–167^v have lines 1599–2476; fos. 168^r–179^v have lines 722–1598. This is easily accounted for by assuming three quires of twelve folios each, of which the second and third have changed places. Lines 2477–602 (the end of the poem in this version) are squeezed into double columns to make them fit into a single folio, ending nine lines down on the verso; the blank is then filled up with the beginning of the *Liber Occultus*, in a different, very untidy hand. The transposition shared by *M* and *N* must likewise be the result of misplaced leaves in their common exemplar since it results in nonsense; the text jumps from 3320, in the story of the Three Fates, to 3602, in the story of the Grateful Animals and the Ungrateful Man, and then back again to fill in the gaps in both stories and tack the four last lines of the poem on to line 3601 (see the entry for MS *M* in the Manuscript Descriptions in Appendix A). Loss can also occur as a result of misbinding. A severe dislocation of the text in *Va*, resulting in the loss of lines 618–81 and 1177–234, is most likely a result of the loss of two folios during the process of binding (in each case, involving a single folio).[152]

The practice of leaving manuscripts as a group of unbound quires, to allow members of religious houses to borrow segments of a work for private reading, or to facilitate copying, doubtless precipitated this sort of loss and misbinding. This may well account for the textual confusion in *P*, which omits 55–666 in place, but after concluding *SS* at line

---

[149] Ibid., pp. 511–12. See the entry for MS *U* in the Manuscript Descriptions in Appendix A.

[150] Laura Amalasunta Gazzoli has kindly checked the manuscript for me and confirmed that there is no sign of any missing folios.

[151] See the entry for MS *O* in the Manuscript Descriptions in Appendix A.

[152] See the entry for MS *Va* in Manuscript Descriptions in Appendix A.

lxx   INTRODUCTION

3900 at the bottom of column a on fo. 136^r, the scribe adds 205–594, beginning at column b of the same folio, so only lines 56–204 and 595–666 are completely lacking. Lines 205–594 exactly encompass the story of the two cows, Brunetta and Bicornis, and it seems very likely that the quires containing this narrative had been borrowed for private amusement and so were unavailable for copying;[153] when they were later returned, the scribe would have been able to supply the missing text, while discarding lines 56–204 and 595–666, which contain material that is not strictly part of this story. The repetition of lines 2859–3097, which appear on both fo. 132$^{r–v}$ and fo. 138$^{r–v}$, is rather harder to explain, but there are clues in the manuscript that a scribal error is the probable source. P is quired in 8s, and the last quire begins on fo. 131. Stitching appears, as would be expected, between fos. 134^v and 135^r, and the final folio of the quire, again as expected, is fo. 138, which is the counterpart to fo. 131 in the initial bifolium. What one would not expect, however, is that the text on fos. 131 and 138 is continuous: fo. 131^v contains lines 2744–858 and fo. 138^r continues with lines 2859–980, and fo. 138^v has lines 2981–3097. The obvious explanation is that the scribe was copying the text by bifolium (as was a frequent practice), using his exemplar as a guide to the distribution of text, rather than proceeding from recto to verso of each folio. Possibly he just made a mechanical error and simply carried on copying across the centrefold, or perhaps he mistakenly thought the bifolium was the centre of a quire rather than the outer leaves of a new quire. In any case, when he realized his mistake, he corrected it by replacing it with a new bifolium, the present fos. 132 and 137, in which fo. 132$^{r–v}$ reproduces fo. 138$^{r–v}$ by recopying lines 2859–3097, and fo. 137 was originally left blank, as we shall see. Folio 132 reveals itself as a replacement through the fact that at the second time around the lines did not take up so much space, so the scribe left four empty lines at the bottom of column b, and wrote 'hic nichil deficit' (that is, the space does not imply missing text). This shows that he had already written lines 3098–347 on the succeeding folio, the present fo. 133$^{r–v}$. He followed up with lines 3348–900 (the end of the poem) on fos. 134$^{r–v}$, 135$^{r–v}$, and 136^r, finishing at the bottom of column a. The explicit with his name that appears at the bottom of this column shows that he thought he had completed copying the text, leaving fo. 136rb and fo. 137$^{r–v}$ blank. When the story of the two cows became available, he entered it on these blank leaves, ending, significantly, in the middle

---

[153] The scribe most probably knew that the story was missing, as later in the poem he omits lines 1239–40 which refer back to it.

VARIOUS FORMS OF THE POEM

lxxi

of column b on fo. 137ᵛ. Folio 138 remained as the last leaf of the quire because of its attachment to fo. 131; instead of cutting it away he indicated that it should be ignored by writing a note in the upper margin, beginning 'Istud folium omnis vacat et est post...' [the text then is cut away]; 'this text is all void...'.

The absence of lines 2053–464 in *Fr* may also be a result of the separate circulation of certain parts of the poem, since these lines exactly match the extent of the survey of monastic orders. *Fr* is the only manuscript in which this section of the poem is missing, so it does not seem likely to have been a late addition, and its excision is rather surprising, since it seems to have been one of the features of the poem that ensured its later popularity, having been excerpted at least three times for independent circulation (see *fh*, *fm*, and *fn* in the list of fragments below, pp. 391–2, all of which derive from the same manuscript group as *Fr*). There are no missing leaves at this point in *Fr* but a line is left empty between 2052 and 2465, signalling that the scribe was conscious that part of the text was absent. It may have been censored because of its anti-religious import, but a more likely explanation is that this section of the poem had been removed to serve as exemplar for an independent copy of the monastic survey.

The omissions in *Q* and *Y* are a rather different matter, and appear to be the result of an overriding desire to abbreviate the poem. These two manuscripts (and especially *Y*) constantly omit two or more lines where the omission can be made without loss of sense. This suggests that the omission of the Gundulf story (1249–502), and of the section stretching from the bird debate to the story of the Three Fates (3233–458) was a deliberate attempt at abridgement (see below, pp. cx–cxi).

It remains to account for the distinctive shape of *LEF*, whose major gaps can plausibly be attributed to other causes. In the first place, they do not make nonsense of what remains. The first major lacuna (2483–3258) covers Burnellus's long diatribe against the misdeeds of the Roman curia, kings, and bishops, followed by his account of the bird debate that he once overheard. The second lacuna runs from line 3449 to the end of the poem (3900) and comprises the story of the Grateful Animals and the Ungrateful Man.

It is easy to show that this latter section must have been a late addition to the poem, rather than having disappeared through physical loss or deliberate abridgement. As was mentioned above, this story has an eastern origin (it first appears in the eighth-century Arabic version of the eastern tale-collection *Kalila and Dimna*), and Michael Chesnutt, who has studied its diffusion, suggested that Sicily is the most likely

lxxii INTRODUCTION

source of its transmission to the west.[154] By an extraordinary stroke of fortune, we know exactly when and how this happened. Matthew Paris introduced it into his chronicles,[155] where he describes it as a favourite story of Richard I: 'Haec saepe referebat rex Ricardus munificus, ingratos redarguendo' (p. 416). A marginal note reads 'Apologus Ricardi regis quem abbati Sancti Albani Guarino et ipse nobis enarravit'—that is, Richard told it to Warin, abbot of St Albans (1183–95), who repeated it to the monks of St Albans. Matthew places the story in his account of 1195: having reported a letter from the pope on behalf of the Holy Land, he goes on to comment on Richard's exhortations to all and sundry to take up the crusading cause, which he reinforces, 'praedicatoris formam induens', by telling this 'parabolam' (pp. 412–13). Since Richard I wintered in Sicily in 1190–1 on his way to the Holy Land,[156] he could easily have picked up the story there, and put it into circulation on his return to England in 1194 (where the first place he visited was Canterbury).[157] Nigel could not, therefore, have encountered this story before 1194.[158] As has been demonstrated above, ingratitude is a major theme of the *Speculum Stultorum*, and is heavily emphasized in the *Epistle to William* that Nigel added to the poem. Significantly, the *Epistle* is not included in manuscripts *LE*—a further indication that they represent a first version of the poem, and that Nigel tells the truth when he says that the *Epistle* was written after it had been sent to William of Longchamp.[159] When the story of the Grateful Animals reached Nigel, he would immediately have realized that it was perfectly adapted to one of the major themes of his poem, and would make a fitting conclusion to it, even though the ass Burnellus had to be relegated to a walk-on part. The story of the Three Fates will therefore have been the original conclusion of the *Speculum*; appropriately, this tale makes Nigel's self-interested point that it is specially in monastic life that the unjust distribution of rewards takes place

---

[154] Chesnutt, 'The Grateful Animals', pp. 40, 51–3.

[155] Matthew Paris, *Chronica majora*, ii. 413–16.

[156] Landon, *Itinerary of King Richard I*, pp. 41–8.

[157] Matthew Paris, *Chronica majora*, ii. 403.

[158] Mozley briefly rehearsed these facts in his *Speculum* article of 1930 ('On the text and manuscripts', p. 261), when he was prepared to see *LEF* as an early version of the poem, but he did not recognize the relevance of the story to the themes of the *Speculum* and by the time his edition appeared in 1960 he had changed his mind on the development of the poem (see below).

[159] The *Epistle* refers to the poem having been sent to William of Longchamp in the recent past ('Librum tibi nuper misi'). *F* can thus be taken to represent a slightly later stage in the development of the poem.

VARIOUS FORMS OF THE POEM   lxxiii

(3435–48).[160] When the new ending was added, Nigel appended to it a new conclusion, again stressing the need to give merit its just reward, and in addition threatening dire consequences for those who fail to do so:

See, this is how ingrates often pay for not bestowing worthy rewards on services rendered. So it's better on occasion to have given a gift with a willing heart than to have stayed one's hand. To pay due recompense for services is a deed of the greatest piety, commanded by God. Let not a man's toil or assistance hang on you until the morrow, that there be no complaint of it in the ear of God. The New Testament says that a man is worthy of the hire to which his labour entitles him. So whoever does not give, when time and cause require it, creates injurious harms for himself... So, happy is the man who is made prudent by another's perils, and is taught to be ruled by moderation. (3867–94)

Internal indications suggest that lines 2483–3258 are likewise a later addition to the *LEF* version. Having declared his intention to enter a monastic order at lines 2023–4 ('Hinc ego disposui me tradere religioni,/ ut ualeat saluus spiritus esse meus'), Burnellus embarks on his survey of the monastic orders in order to determine which is most suitable for a donkey. The survey ends at line 2464; Burnellus then by chance meets Galen and briefly laments his hard life. At this point he launches into a long and impassioned tirade against the failings of the Roman curia, the wickedness of kings, the power of bribes ('munera'), and the shortcomings of bishops (2483–872). He declines to complete this tirade by relating the sins of the laity, and instead recounts the bird debate that he once overheard (2875–3232). He is still supposedly addressing Galen, and at the end of this long interpolation he returns to his complaint about his broken health, his sinful life, and his decision to become a monk, in words which closely echo line 2023: 'Hinc est quod statui me tradere religioni, /cuius ero primus doctor et auctor ego' (3259–60); he advises Galen to join his new order and not to mind if he is subject to his inferior (Burnellus), since this is quite common in religious life (3259–78). Lines 3259 and following therefore follow on quite smoothly and naturally from the survey of monastic orders, and the *LE* version of the poem, in which they do just that, presents an entirely coherent sequence. *F* is a slightly different case, since the concluding advice to Galen in lines 3259–78 has been shifted to follow the story of the Three Fates rather than preceding it, perhaps in an early attempt to strengthen this as the concluding moral of the entire poem. It is also significant that the *Epistle to William* in *F* deals with all the

---

[160] The passage is quoted above, pp. lix–lx.

lxxiv INTRODUCTION

episodes of the poem up to the end of the monastic survey; the only episode of the *LE* version that it does not cover is the story of the Three Fates. This looks like further confirmation of the supposition that the two major passages that are lacking in *LEF* were not part of the original version of the poem.

The rationale behind the addition of the long diatribe against the papal curia, kings, bishops, abbots, and priors, becomes clear if we set it against the background of Canterbury's long struggle with its archbishop over his proposal to establish a college of secular canons. The *Epistolae Cantuarienses* show clearly that Henry II was a staunch supporter of Baldwin in the dispute. Baldwin himself was of course both abbot and archbishop. Much of this long passage of complaint is conventional, but the repeated accusations that bribes corrupt bishops as well as kings, perverting the course of justice (2595, 2623), resonate with the local situation at Canterbury. Significantly, bishops and kings are the two groups of people that Nigel had earlier claimed are corrupted by secular canons.[161] The accusations against the papal curia are harder to account for in these terms (although much of the content of this passage echoes the conventional topoi of contemporary satire),[162] since a succession of popes were in fact supporters of the monks rather than of Archbishop Baldwin. They issued a stream of mandates ordering the archbishop to demolish the new church at Hackington (later at Lambeth) and to restore the sequestered income to the monks.[163] However, a clue to the criticisms of the curia in this passage may be discerned in the comment in *Epistolae Cantuarienses*, no. ccxxxiv, written by the prior Honorius to the convent at home when he was trying to get Pope Clement to appoint a sympathetic legate who would travel to England and implement the papal mandates. Honorius tells his fellow-monks that there are good prospects of getting one of the two candidates for the post who would be favourable to them, 'since we

---

[161] 'It is through them [secular canons] that the force, rule and power of bishops falters and the order of the church becomes disordered. Through them, respect for the clergy grows faint and dies, and the glory of religious life dwindles to nothing. By their counsel kings plan wicked deeds, and give free rein to what they should hold back. They are the evil associates of bishops and kings' (2335–41).

[162] See n. to line 2496.

[163] The actions of the relevant popes (Urban III, 1185–7; Gregory VIII, 1187; Clement III, 1187–91; Celestine III, 1191–8) can be most easily traced through the chronological list of items in the *Epistolae Cantuarienses* provided by Stubbs at the beginning of the volume (pp. cxxi–clxvii). The letter-collection itself does not follow exact chronological order. In contrast to his predecessor and successors, Gregory VIII took Baldwin's side; see Cotts, *Clerical Dilemma*, p. 37.

VARIOUS FORMS OF THE POEM

lxxv

have offered the lord pope, from the prior and the brethren, venerable relics of the martyrs Albinus and Rufinus'.[164] Readers of medieval Goliardic literature will be well aware that the 'relics' of these mythical saints are a euphemism for '(red) gold' and '(white) silver'; that is, Honorius and the monks have offered the pope a large bribe to appoint the right man. It seems entirely likely, therefore, that papal support for the convent was purchased by the expenditure of large sums, which would explain Nigel's complaints about the insatiable greed of the curia. The rapid succession of four popes within the space of fifteen years would have compounded the problem; no sooner had the good will of one pope been assured by these means, than he died and the monks had to start all over again with the next one.

The targets of this long satiric tirade—kings, bishops, abbots, and priors—are thus chosen by virtue of their role as persecutors of the monastic community. The laity are left to one side because they played no part in this particular quarrel. Why the bird debate takes the place of the laity is rather more puzzling,[165] but a veiled meaning makes itself felt. The raven, who speaks first, laments the disasters currently afflicting the world, and blames them on avian wrongdoing. The debate gradually shifts to the dangers of revealing one's misdemeanours, rather than keeping silent. The raven is a classic example of the dangers of speaking out: because of his garrulity, his white feathers were turned black and his beautiful voice became a squawk (3002–22). Nowadays, he says, no one can confess their sins without having them broadcast to the world at large (2957–82). An ideal confessor remembers how weak the flesh is (2989), and he supports the sinner rather than inflicting punishment. The debate then returns to the peccadilloes of birds; the list culminates with the parrot, whose garrulity again gives trouble, when it repeats to the mistress of the household what her maids said when she was out of the room. This is why birds are often poisoned, to keep them quiet. Significantly, the raven then mentions birds who live in monasteries, and are for the same reason exposed to dangers of this kind.

---

[164] 'Cum itaque venerandas martyrum reliquias Albini et Rufini domino papae, per priorem et fratres porrexerimus, indubitanter scimus quod alter eorum veniet, aut litterae emanabunt cum poena suspensionis inflicta domino Cantuariensi, nisi fecerit quod in mandatis accipiet' (*Epistolae Cantuarienses*, no. ccxxxiv, p. 215). Bishop Stubbs's learning does not seem to have extended to Goliardic literature, since he takes this euphemism literally (ibid., Introduction, p. xcix). Cf. Nigel's allusion to the 'merits of the blessed Rufinus' at *SS*, lines 1317–18, and n.

[165] There have been attempts to solve the problem by claiming that the bird debate is a disguised attack on the sins of the laity, but they are not convincing.

lxxvi INTRODUCTION

There are other birds too, who all their lives inhabit the blessed cloisters of the monks, and I am incapable of enumerating now the dangers they inflict on them on many occasions through the year. (3063–6)

The cock then indignantly repudiates the raven's accusations: he himself is a model of virtue. He lists the benefits he provides to humankind: he gives them eggs, feather-beds, and a reliable alarm clock. But then he reverts to the topic of keeping quiet about the misdoings of other people:

But I don't want to be ungrateful or undutiful to those whom fate has made my masters. For if I wanted to speak slander, and if—which heaven forbid!— I didn't know how to put a rein on my tongue, many people would come to a sticky end and would suffer the penalties of prison or the gallows which befitted their deserts. Many crimes which are committed in the darkness of night, and which are far blacker than black night—what the master does, what the wicked servant says—if the whole town knew as well as I do, the morrow might well see many men, and many women too, hanged on the gallows. What the peasant speaks quietly in his wife's ear, he can't conceal from me, whether he likes it or not. The gods forbid that it should be my fate to harm anyone, or to betray another's crime with my voice. Let me not be like the raven, who betrayed the one who was the major source of his well-being. May Jupiter hurl his thunderbolts against me first, and the earth swallow up me and my kin, may the wave of the sea engulf me and may I tumble headlong into the depth of hell's abyss, before I reveal any secrets committed to me, or any wicked speech comes out of my mouth. Anyone who does not praise, speak well of, honour, and love those people with whom he is obliged to live, is a fool, and lacks a human being's understanding, statue-like, although possessing a sentient body. This is what I think, this is my true opinion, and this I will say for my part, speaking for myself alone. (3137–66)

The cock then suggests that the sparrow-hawk and the falcon should be asked for their opinion, since he knows nothing of court life:

Since the sparrow-hawk and the falcon live in the hall, they are party to the discussions of kings and dukes. To them it is granted to inhabit secret places, free from the noise of common people and far from the throng. They are placed high up in the prince's chamber, so that they can see many things from their perch. The remotest corner of the chamber, a place suitable for business that has to be conducted in private, is assigned to them. There wicked plots are often hatched, and vile deeds set in train. Sometimes, the corner is more agreeable than the hall to young lads, and girls too, and dark night more agreeable than day. Here is often hidden the secret love, which, when the womb opens up and it emerges, suffers an untimely end. Here too are confessions made which have been uttered to no priest, nor ought to be, as I think. Here lurk poisons, sought with long effort, here flourish the baleful spells of

VARIOUS FORMS OF THE POEM   lxxvii

stepmothers. This place requires a boy to come at dead of night to visit a sick hawk. This place cures asthmatics and heals epileptics, and often makes dawn at night. These are the places where a lamp is unwelcome, and which earn the rewards of praise by their claim to wickedness. The sparrow-hawk and the falcon, who frequent these unholy places, know well what the case is and what I speak of. (3173–98)

The sparrow-hawk replies with aristocratic hauteur: whatever the 'pueri' do, the hawks would never betray their secrets, mindful of all the benefits they receive from them. Since the eyes, not the tongue, see the misbehaviour, let the tongue keep quiet until the eyes speak. On this note, the bird debate ends. I have quoted the above passages at length because their length is surprising (and I have not quoted them in their entirety). Tale-telling is traditionally associated with the story of the raven, but not with the cock or the hawks.

Tentative speculation is all that is possible here, but it may be that a little polite blackmail is going on. Is Nigel hinting at some sexual misbehaviour that William of Longchamp committed in his youth, and promising to keep his mouth shut about it (for which he would of course expect the reward that he has been hinting that he deserves)? Admittedly, although William's enemies accused him of sexual aberrations, they were of a homosexual rather than heterosexual nature. Gerald of Wales claims that this 'nefandum ... et enorme crimen' was characteristic of William's Norman background, and was practised by him with such vigour that in his court anyone who did not despise 'naturalis copula' was held in contempt. With relish, Gerald relates an anecdote about a beautiful young girl who disguised herself as a man and was introduced into William's bedchamber; when he found out her true sex, he threw her out. At dinner, Gerald says, he would prick with a pointed stick whichever of the noble boys who served him at table was later to be 'pricked by him with another kind of stick' ('alio a se ... pungendum aculeo').[166] When Gerald, borrowing from Hugh of Nonant's letter, relates the story of William's flight from England in 1191, he echoes Hugh in mocking the fact that William dressed as a woman, 'a sex he always loathed'.[167] They both take prurient pleasure in telling how William's true sex was revealed by a sailor who made advances to

---

[166] *De vita Galfridi* ii. 19, *Opera*, iv. 423.

[167] 'Sese feminam simulavit, cuius sexum semper odit' ('Bishop Hugh's Open Letter', *English Episcopal Acta xvii. Coventry and Lichfield 1183–1208*, ed. Franklin, p. 128). The phrase is echoed by Giraldus when he remarks on the irony that his true sex was discovered by two women who tried to buy the bolt of cloth that he was carrying, to make it appear he was a cloth-seller (*De vita Galfridi*, ii. 12, *Opera*, iv. 412).

lxxviii INTRODUCTION

him as he waited for a boat on the seashore; with his left arm round William's neck, with the other hand the sailor explored his lower regions, and was shocked by what he found.[168]

These allegations may simply be malicious fabrications; Gerald's description of William's appearance, for example, is clearly a grotesque exaggeration.[169] And as already noted, the sexual misdemeanours that Nigel hints at involve girls, rather than (or as well as?) other boys. But the insistence on hushing up nocturnal misdemeanours, when nothing in the immediate context seems to warrant the topic, arouses suspicion.[170]

Since evidence supports the theory that the story of the Grateful Animals was added to the poem at a relatively late stage, it is reasonable to suppose that Nigel took the opportunity to bolster his attack on the secular canons with the long diatribe against the powerful authorities who supported their cause. It is hard to see why Nigel should have deleted these two long passages in a late revision, and it is equally hard to imagine that their absence is due to loss of leaves in the exemplar of *LEF*, since there is no consequent incoherence in the narrative. The natural conclusion is that *LEF* represents the earliest version of the poem, and the longer versions are later expansions. The minor disorder and repetition in *F* may be attributed to its representing a preliminary stage of revision on the way to the expanded versions; the fact that it contains the *Epistle to William*, whereas *LE* do not, and that in *F* the *Epistle* follows the poem, and refers to 'the poem I sent you the other day', supports the hypothesis that *F* is a later version than *LE*, although closely related to them.

---

[168] 'Bishop Hugh's Open Letter', *English Episcopal Acta xvii. Coventry and Lichfield 1183–1208*, ed. Franklin, p. 128; *De vita Galfridi*, ii. 12, *Opera*, iv. 411.

[169] *De vita Galfridi*, ii. 19, *Opera*, iv. 420, 'Descriptio beluae multiformis'.

[170] It is also interesting that *c*.1171/2, a group of clerks who had been in the service of Thomas Becket (now dead) wrote to William, archbishop of Sens, making a complaint against Roger, archbishop of York (another Norman cleric, and formerly archdeacon of Canterbury), who was acting against them in the papal curia, and in order to blacken Roger's name, reminded William that he (Roger) had formerly enjoyed a homosexual relationship with a beautiful young boy named Walter. When the young man later repented of it and made it public, Roger engineered a lawsuit against him which resulted in his eyes being put out and eventually his execution by hanging. When this came to light, Roger was obliged to clear himself by oath, which was taken in the Canterbury cathedral chapter. As Frank Barlow says, 'it is just possible that Walter could have been a Canterbury monk' (Barlow, *Thomas Becket*, p. 34; for bibliography, see Barlow, *English Church 1066–1154*, p. 94 n. 175, and for the letter written to William, see John of Salisbury, *Letters*, no. cccvii (ed. Millor and Brooke, ii. 742–9; the editors' comments are on p. xliv) Cf. Elliott, *The Corrupter of Boys*, pp. 138–9. While there is no hard evidence of homosexual activity at Canterbury, and of course William of Longchamp was never a Canterbury monk, the suggestion that Nigel is hinting at something in William's past, or his own, which should remain under the seal of silence, is tantalizing.

TEXTUAL TRANSMISSION

lxxix

This hypothesis needs, however, to be further supported by a full analysis of the surviving manuscripts, identification of their stemmatic groups, and determination of their probable relations to each other.

TEXTUAL TRANSMISSION

The Manuscript Groups

The manuscripts fall into four main groups; I use the Greek letters α (*LEF*), β (*BH*), γ (*SMuVaVbVcVdTGoBePkFrPmNe*), and δ (*AJCWRHuMNOPDKVe*) to designate the hypothetical common ancestors of each group. The remaining manuscripts (*GITrHaLaUXZQY*) are classified as 'mixed', since they either switch allegiance from one main group to another at a definite point in the text, or show mixed affiliations throughout.

Descent from a Common Archetype

A number of errors which are found in all manuscripts indicate that they all derive from a common archetype (ω).[171] They are as follows:

---

[171] Mozley gives a list (Introduction, pp. 16–17) of errors common to his two main groups (a = ACJMNDKOP and b = EFLSBH), which he says are found 'either without exception or with sufficient unanimity to warrant descent from a common archetype'. He does not specify which manuscripts lack which errors in this list, or what he takes to be the reason for their absence (such as correction by an intelligent scribe). My list includes some examples which can be added to Mozley's; conversely, the following further examples need to be removed from Mozley's list:

1 193–4 coget senior. This should be 'senior coget', as 'senior' is construed with 'discam' rather than 'coget':

> Nec pudor annorum, quamuis puerilia discam
> iam senior, coget deseruisse scholas.

However the error is by no means universal; no fewer than twenty-one manuscripts read 'senior coget'.

1598 uenerunt. The correct reading is 'neuerunt' but this is the reading of *VcOpc* (glossed 'filauerunt') *Q*.

2502 inopis. The correct reading 'inopi' is found in all the γ manuscripts (except *Mu*, which has 'inopum'), and also in *TrHaLaZ*. Mozley's *apparatus criticus* records only *S*; clearly he did not collate the other γ manuscripts.

2801–2 Litibus impensa breuis est quaeuis mora longa
moxque quod est Domini taedia magna parit.

Sedgwick proposed emending 'Moxque quod est' to 'Hora breuis' ('Textual criticism', p. 293), but this is unlikely to have become corrupted to 'Moxque quod est', which in any case is not necessarily erroneous. Translate as 'What pertains to God quickly produces great boredom'. Compare the similar construction at *Lawrence*, 953: '*quod est carnis* caro perficit absque labore'.

3057–8 Quod fuerant secum tacite timideque locutae
auribus et tutis, et sine teste *loco*.

INTRODUCTION

(1) 491–2   Cauda *nocet* capiti proprio, prohibetque timeri
cornua, dum metuunt posteriora sequi.

All manuscripts read 'nocet' except for *Fr* which has 'nos' (meaning-less), and *QY* which omit these lines. Their meaning is not clear (see Raymo's Notes, *SS* p. 147), and they seem to have defeated Langosch, who simply omits 491–2 from his translation. Mozley thinks that they may be spurious and/or may have been displaced from the *Commendatio caudae* (pp. 16, 130). He suggests that 'proprio' 'should perhaps be 'pro-pior'. Shackleton Bailey proposed emending 'nŏcet' to 'căuet' ('Textual notes', p. 282); that is, the tail protects the cow from the horns of the cow following behind it. In whatever way the difficulty is resolved, it seems clear that line 491 is erroneous as it stands in the manuscripts.

(2) 525   Terra parit *pulices* pariuntque cadauera uermes

All the manuscripts read 'pūlices', 'fleas', but its long first syllable is unmetrical. Skutsch (according to Mozley, *SS*, p. 130; in a private com-munication?) proposed to emend to 'cŭlices', 'gnats, midges', which is metrically acceptable; air-borne insects also suit the context better.

(3) 543–4   These lines are transposed after 546 in all the manu-scripts; this makes it seem that 545–6 ('Haec abit, illa uolat...'), which describe the cow fleeing from the flies, apply to Brunetta rather than (as they should) to Bicornis.

(4) 769–70   Vror amore tamen patriae, tantoque reuerti
anxius exopto quo magis ire uetor.

In 770, a comparative is needed to complement 'quo magis ire uetor'. Accordingly, Mozley emends 'anxius' to 'acrius'. Cf. 236, where the manuscripts divide between 'anxius' and 'acrius', and 864, where they divide between 'anxius', 'acrius', and 'arcius'; see my Notes.

(5) 787   *Gula* mihi soror est, multis notissima regnis.

Gŭla has a short first syllable, so its position here is unacceptable met-rically. This is unlikely to be an authorial mistake, as the word is scanned correctly at line 3101: 'Tē gŭlă tē uēntēr, tē uīcĭt ĭnēptă uŏlūptās'. One

Except for *RO*, which have 'locis', all witnesses have 'loco'. Mozley's Textual notes (*SS*, p. 138) assume that 'loco' was induced by 'locutae' in line 3057, and suggest emending to 'malo', but this seems unnecessary.

3673–4 Cum prope iam putei foret egressurus ab ore,
inque pedem laetus depositurus humo

All the manuscripts read 'inque'. Mozley emended to 'iamque', but Michael Reeve has pointed out to me that if 'inque' is taken with 'humo', this is unnecessary.

TEXTUAL TRANSMISSION

lxxxi

might propose emendation to Gīla, but that has already been given as the name of the London merchant's mother in the preceding line.[172] The manuscripts have a number of variants (goula, bula, boula, bolla, toudla, oula), suggesting scribal uncertainty.

(6) 863   Angit utrumque malum, misero satis esset *in* unum

The reading of the manuscripts, 'in', does not make sense; Mozley emends to 'et'. The error could, however, be polygenetic.

(7) 1709–10   qui ne pontifices fiant sunt apocopati,
ne sint abbates syncopa mitra facit.

Most manuscripts read 'ne', which makes no sense; the alternative readings 'nec/ni/et/me' are no better. Mozley emended to 'ut'.

(8) 2034   *ens* in flore suo prodiga facta sui

According to Mozley's *apparatus criticus*, 'spes' is a conjecture by Skutsch, but it is not to be found in Skutsch's 'Three rare words' and must therefore result from personal communication (unless it is simply a mistake on Mozley's part). The majority reading in the manuscripts is 'ens', with 'mens', 'eius', 'eius et' and 'quos' as alternatives. None of them makes obvious sense.

(9) 2072   et uenter uacuus et *cophinellus* erit.

'Cophinellus' is a conjecture by Skutsch ('Three rare words', pp. 29–30). The variants at this point show considerable confusion on the part of the scribes: 'prophinellus/prosinellus' are unattested; 'fămēlĭcŭs' ('hungry, famished') fits the context but is unmetrical. Skutsch's 'cophinellus', 'little basket' (as a receptacle for food) is an economical attempt at repair.

(10) 2117   *Lac et lana* greges ouium pecorumque ministrant.

Almost all the manuscripts read 'lăc ēt lānă', which is unmetrical. (*Ne*'s 'lac lanam' and *K*'s 'his lac lana' look like scribal attempts at repair.) Mozley emended to 'Lac lanamque'.

(11) 2359–60   In medio fornacis agunt, flammaeque uorantis
in girum stadium constituere suum.

The manuscripts read 'in girum' ($\alpha\gamma HaLaZ$), 'ignitum' ($\beta\delta GITrXQY$), or 'ignium' (*J*), the last two evidently provoked by the references to fire

---

[172] NB 'gila' is not included in *OLD* or medieval Latin dictionaries, except for *DMLBS*, which has one example, dated 1235. Mozley does not list it in his article on Nigel's Latinity.

lxxxii INTRODUCTION

in line 2359. In line 2360, 'stadium' also has a variant 'studium', complicating matters further. Mozley conjecturally emends 'girum' to 'giro', which is the best that can be suggested.

> (12) 2475–6 Rusticus atque schola duo sunt tormenta *doloris*
> intus et exterius quae mihi ferre solent.

Most of the manuscripts read 'doloris', which Skutsch emended to 'dolores' in order to provide an object for 'ferre' ('Three rare words', p. 31), with a comma added after 'tormenta'. 'Dolores' is, however, the reading of *Vc*; it may be a scribal correction made *ope ingenii*, or simply the result of scribal variation (see also the note on this line).

> (13) 2583–4 In quorum manibus crebro tractantur iniqua,
> dextera muneribus esse referta solet.

In the manuscripts these lines are placed after line 2644, where they interrupt the succession of clauses beginning 'Munera si cessent'. Conversely, at 2583–4, 'quorum' matches the beginning of lines 2579 and 2581, so Mozley transferred them to this point. If this is accepted, the kings' hands must be envisaged as stuffed with bribes they have accepted, rather than offered.

> (14) 2687–8 Et quoniam pascunt mercedis amore, secundi
> officio *similes* sors facit esse pares.

All manuscripts read 'similes' but Shackleton Bailey saw that 'similis', modifying 'sors', makes better sense ('Textual notes', p. 284).

> (15) 2744 Plus et amat lucrum quam *facit ipse* Lucam

Mozley's Textual notes state that 'sapuisse' is Sedgwick's conjectural emendation of 'facit ipse' which is the reading of all the manuscripts, but it is not to be found in Sedgwick's 'Textual criticism'. (Possibly, however, lines 2743–4 are spurious, and 'facit ipse' is very bad Latin for 'he does'; 'he loves lucre more than he does Luke').

> (16) 2956 et tamen absorptum constitit esse *canem*

A reference to some kind of food or drink is involved here, so 'canem', the reading of most of the manuscripts, makes no sense. (*K*'s 'ciphum' is an obvious attempt at repair.) Skutsch ('Three rare words', p. 29) conjectured 'camum', 'a kind of beer' (see *OLD*, Du Cange, *DMLBS*).

> (17) 3197 Nisus et ancipiter, loca *qui male sancta frequentant*

TEXTUAL TRANSMISSION   lxxxiii

The various manuscript readings show the scribes to be at a loss: qui male sancta frequentant] que mala fata (facta X multa U) frequentant β $UXQY$ que mala (male R Ha) facta sequantur δ $TrHaLa$ mala sacraque frequentant Z. Skutsch conjectured 'qui malefata frequentant' ('Three rare words', p. 30); however, 'malefata' (which he explains as meaning 'ill spoken of, ill reputed') is an otherwise unattested word. Mozley's suggestion, 'male sancta' is more plausible, since 'male' placed before an adjective functions as a negative (*OLD*, s.v. male 6). So 'male sanus' = 'insane', 'male sancta' = 'unholy, profane'.

> (18) 3467   *Omni* mane suo currens lepus et capra clauda

All the manuscripts read 'omni'; Sedgwick conjectured 'omine' ('Textual criticism', p. 293).

> (19) 3705–6   Sicque uicem meritis referens gratesque rependens,
>   et quacumque potest parte iuuare *iuuat*

Mozley emended 'iuuat' to 'iuuans' (Textual notes, *SS* p. 139), so that it is parallel with the other present participles. (The main verb does not arrive until line 3707.) As usual, the scribe's horizon is bounded by the end of the line and he completes the syntactic unit prematurely.

Almost all of these examples are undoubted errors, and it is significant that they occur throughout the full extent of the poem; errors in the shorter versions α and γ must have been carried over to the archetypes of the longer versions β and δ.

The α Group of Manuscripts

The α group comprises MSS *LEF.* The existence of the group is attested in the first instance by the distinctive shape of the poem in these three manuscripts: all three lack lines 2483–3258 and end at 3448. That is, they lack the sustained attack on the Roman curia, kings, bishops, and abbots, and Burnellus's account of the debate between birds (lines 2483–3258), as well as the concluding narrative of the Grateful Animals and the Ungrateful Man (3449–900); for my argument that this shorter version represents the earliest form of the poem, see pp. lxxi–lxxviii above. *LEF* also preface the poem with the same rubric: 'Burnelli speculum (*F*: Speculum Burnelli) merito liber iste vocatur/ Cuius sub specie stultorum vita notatur'.

LEF share the following omissions: 528–31 (*eyeskip* 'oester'); 929–30; 1076–7 (*eyeskip* 'aselli'); 3445–6. In addition, 2377–82 are transposed after 2386 (lines 2377–8 follow on best from 2375–6, since both concern singing the divine office), and 2433–4 are transposed after 2435–6

lxxxiv INTRODUCTION

(Burnellus is describing his new order in the same sequence that he had described the old ones, which means the Regular Canons should follow the Carthusians).

The following examples of shared errors constitute further evidence of the existence of the group; the lemma that the α variants replace is given in parentheses after each variant. In the examples from lines 3259–448, the group is joined by MS *I* (see nn.176–7, 201, and p. ci below).[173]

1. Variants unacceptable because of sense or syntax: 385 discrimine (discrimina); 398 arta (atra); 427 sibi (mihi);[174] 451 deuexit (deuexus) (*the finite verb does not fit the syntax of the sentence*); 485 mors (mora); 488 sed (res) (*without 'res', 'uoluptas' becomes the subject of 'docet'*); 547 nescia lugubris (se lugubris et); 650 adulta (adepta); 715 manifeste (manifestum); 763 hic emerem (emimus hic) (*the merchant is not proposing to buy the medicines but is claiming that he already possesses them*); 764 lucra darent (cura foret) (*the merchant says he has the medicines but to get them home would be very difficult*); 1043 dictat/dicat (dicet) (*surrounding verbs are all in the future tense*); 1054 quod (ut); 1131 ob hoc (adhuc); 1157 sed quod (si quod); 1175 dedecus est redeam si sic (est melius quod non redeam) (*the conjunction 'donec' in line 1176 requires a negative; 'it is best that I do not return until...'*); 1186 domi (domum); 1194 cogitet (coget); 1311 et (in²); 1391 dominus (domine) (*vocative required for sense and metre*); 1493 fassus (fatus); 1609 sub (ceu); 1610 dolent (dolet); 1660 aliquo (alio); 1756 quoque (quia); 1902 esse (ipse); 1905 primum (proprium); 2025 iuuencula (iuuenalia); 2214 fit quoque claustralis (fitque trilustralis); 2267 non (ne); 3273 uiuit (uiuunt); 3349 obumbrarem (obumbrarer); 3378 quam sic ditauit gratia totque dedit (cui natura potens tot pretiosa dedit) (*'natura potens' is a theme of the poem and the allusion to Boethius (Cons. III.2) is characteristic of Nigel*); 3392 *different version of whole line.*

2. Variants unacceptable for metrical reasons[175] 772 et *om.*; 1328 īndūlgēnt nĭmīs (īndūlgēntquĕ nĭmīs); 1678 quāmuīs ĕt ōffĭcĭī (quāmuīs ōffĭcĭī); 1742 stŭdĕăt ŏnĕrī (ŏnĕrī stŭdĕăt//) 1799 mātēr (părēns); 2363 uĕlŭt (sīcŭt).

---

[173] *I*'s readings in lines 3405–6 are illegible.

[174] Here as elsewhere I ignore the occasional agreement of one of the 'mixed manuscripts' (*GITrHaLaUZXQY*), which are subject to contamination.

[175] For the reader's convenience, I give quantities as they would be reckoned within the relevant line, where some naturally short syllables are lengthened by following consonants, and also at the caesura, which I indicate by a double forward slash.

TEXTUAL TRANSMISSION   lxxxv

3. Easier substitutions (*lectiones faciliores*)
522 amena (amoma); 2460 mihi (libens).

4. Variants which are not otherwise identifiable as error but are rejected because agreement between two or more other branches of the stemma provides support for the alternatives:[176]

1 tui (tibi); 54 reor (puto); 171 dictis sed (sed dictis); 184 quod (quem); 191 aper (caper); 204 poteris (posses); 262 tenererer (retinerer); 393 ueris ueniunt (ueniunt ueris); 418 mundata bene (bene mundata); 443 cauda tenear (tenear cauda); 662 istud (illud); 666 humo (humi); 672 pariter (tota); 757 dimidio (aequo); 771 de patris (patris de); 772 dicit (fingit); 779 quod (quia); 833 ingentes (immensos); 860 uie (suus); 950 pariter (grauiter); 952 et (quod); 971 nec cocta (nisi cruda); 1033 celer (semel); 1068 rui (uehi); 1084 arte sua texuit ante sibi (ipse sibi texuit arte sua); 1269 pulli matrem (matrem pulli); 1273 magis (plus); 1304 iuuat (leuat); 1306 et (uel); 1461 talibus auditis (talia dicenti); 1529 notata (referta); 1534 quo (cur); 1771 uentres (uentrem); 1829 simul (quos²); 1841 nociuior (nocentior); 2092 id (uel); 2212 trahitur (teritur); 2379–80 pectore...corpore (corpore...pectore); 2388 ferunt (gerunt); 2390 cetera (candida); 2392 *whole line*; 2395 quaedam sunt (sunt quedam); 2476 cruciare (mihi ferre); 3259 reddere (tradere); 3264 meus (nouus); 3325 aliena uenari (quaerere...aliena); 3352 sociam (dominam); 3362 refellantur (repellantur); 3406 festinato (festinando); 3440 consuetudo frequens (mos malus esse solet).

A Subgroup of α: *Manuscripts L and E*

Manuscripts *L* and *E* form a subgroup of α, as is shown by the following shared errors:[177]

1. Variants unacceptable because of sense or syntax
88 putabit (putabat); 109 restat (praestat); 138 magnum (magnis; *F* magno); 149–50 *transp. after 154*; 296 tempora (tempore); 317 a (et²); 345 sociali (socialia); 391 sum/sim tamen (sim uel; *F* sum quodcum sum); 394 ad hec (adhuc); 407 facies (faciet); 409 Bicornes (Bicornem); 455 cibus (siluis); 462 qua (quam; *F* quo); 480 ita (cita); 701 multas (multos); 804 cunctus (cinctus); 845 seuus (serius; *F* segnius); 852 ita (onus); 891 manus (nouus); 900 pretereunte (praeeunte; *F* preente); 961 possim (passim); 1031 apes medicas (opes medicos); 1036 causitus

---

[176] In lines 3259–448, *I* shares these α readings (see below, n. 201), but its readings in lines 3405–6 are doubtful.

[177] In lines 3293–447, *I* shares the *LE* readings, but as already noted, its readings in lines 3405–6 are doubtful.

(consitus); 1139 quod nisi (et si); 1305 nunc...nunc (non...non; *F* nec...nec); 1353 bibendum (bibentum; *om. F*); 1426 in (en²); 1651 ad (ob); 1745 sit *om.*; 1747 sed (si); 1862 sui (mihi; *F* sua); 2059 pede seruas (pedem seruans); 2071 sicut (scutica); 2132 sed (sit); 2237 minister (frequenter); 2350 docuisse (docuere); 2364 aura (aurum); 2447 bona *om.*; 3293 ipso (ipse); 3311 quoque (quia); 3366 pondus...inerte (pondere...mersa; *F* pondere iuncta) (*failure to recognize that the grammatical subject is 'uirgo' in line 3363, as implied in 'mersa', so 'pondus' is turned into a nominative to replace it*); 3369 uisus (uocis); 3405 non *om.*; 3447 militem (mentem).

2. Variants unacceptable for metrical reasons

663 et *om.*; 1782 et *om.*; 1854 uīcōs (uĭās; *F* uĭcēs); 3361 nōn sūnt sēd iūstă (sēd iūstā// nōn sūnt; *FBI* sēd nōn sūnt iūsta).

Some of the *F* variants specified above may be attempts to correct the *LE* readings, in which case the erroneous *LE* readings will have been inherited from α.

There are some agreements between *L* and *F*, and also between *E* and *F*, which on the face of it contradict the suggested existence of *LE* as a separate subgroup of α, but on closer examination these agreements can be plausibly accounted for in other ways. Convergent variation seems the most likely explanation in the following instances (correct reading given in parentheses).

LF agreement: 296 sanantur (sanatur); 1597 per te (Parcae).

EF agreement: 32 necdum (nondum); 969 fuerat (fuerit); 1732 ut (cur; *L* quid); 2015 morte (mortem).

In many cases this explanation is confirmed by the fact that the variant in question also appears in other manuscripts not belonging to the α group, as in the following examples:

LF agreement: 383 et *om.*; 1429 cella (sella); 2373 coactis (coactus) (*influenced by neighbouring 'uiduisque'*).

EF agreement: 354 sceleres (celeres); 427 qui (quae); 881 nec (ut) (*prompted by preceding 'non'?*); 1553 discere (dicere); 1714 menstrua (monstrua).

In other examples, the *LF/EF* agreement seems to be instigated by corruption in or misreading of α (the hypothetical common ancestor of *LEF*):

LF agreement: At 1043, it seems that α read 'dictat' (instead of 'dicet'), preserved in *LF* but misread as 'dicat' by *E*. At 1583, Mozley prints 'Gallosque' but *LF* 'gallosue', which is supported by αβγ and other manuscripts, can be taken as original, misread by *E* as 'gallos ut'. At 1755, *E*'s 'suadeat' may reflect an α variant of original 'suaserit'

TEXTUAL TRANSMISSION   lxxxvii

(perhaps changed to present subjunctive to match preceding 'faciat'?), which was then simplified to 'suadet' by L and F independently. At 3355, $LFIU$ have 'posset propriisque' instead of archetypal 'propriis possetque'; the homoeoarchon that provoked the reversed word order seems also to have led E to return it to its original state.

EF agreement: At 262, original 'tunc' seems to have been varied to 'tum' in α, copied by L but misread as 'cum' by E and F.

Neither L nor E is copied from the other, as is shown by the following unique variants:

L: 299 cadunt *om.*; 780 precibus *om.*; 1199 ueniam *om.*; 1289 dedicere (dedidicere); 1307 aues (auet) 1420 luat *om.*; 1705 meis *om.*; 1747 habet *om.*; 1893 et^2 *om.*; 2449 in eis *om.*

E: 148 magna (iuncta); 335 scito (cito); 595 tibi (igitur); 595 iam que nos (tibi quae); 1167 uerbo (uerbi); 1312 fugens (fungens); 1358 si (sed); 1457 laqueus (laqueo); 2446 et ouam...meam (zonam... meam).

F is not the exemplar of L or E, as is shown, most importantly, by its containing the *Epistle to William*, which L and E lack, and also by its following unique variants:

310–11 *om.* (*eyeskip 'Casibus in laetis'*); 415–16 *om.* (*eyeskip 'Illa dies'*); 421 enim (est); 425–6 *om.* (*eyeskip 'Haec est illa dies*); 809 dixit (dicit); 1045 quas (cras); 1072 *four extra lines added*; 1419–20 *om.*; 1430 subito (solito); 1484 *two extra lines added;* 1506 mensaque (mensa calixque); 1628 fudere (fuere); 1771 sociare petentum (satiare potentum); 2335 uigor *om.*; 2389 sacro (nigro).

In addition, L and E have no trace of F's major textual dislocation, which transposes lines 3259–78 after lines 3279–432, and then repeats lines 3323–8. As suggested above, one possible explanation of F's idiosyncratic arrangement is that it represents an early attempt at rearrangement, as a basis for the expanded version of the poem.

The β Group of Manuscripts

The core of this group consists of two manuscripts, B and H. Once again, the most distinctive feature of these manuscripts is their overall shape and length. Loss of leaves means that B lacks lines 849–1386, but like H, it contains the major sections of the poem that α lacks: the attack on the Roman curia, kings, bishops, and abbots, followed by the bird debate (2483–3258), and the concluding narrative of the Grateful Animals and the Ungrateful Man (3449–864). For an account of the probable motives behind these major additions to the poem, see above pp. lxxi–lxxviii. At line 3864 both B and H end, without the last 36 lines

lxxxviii INTRODUCTION

of the poem in which Nigel re-emphasizes the importance of gratitude and the need to give merit its just reward.

B's major loss of leaves means that shared errors are less numerous than they might have been, but the following provide evidence of the textual affiliations of *B* and *H*.

Errors common to *BH* (*B* out in lines 849–1386): Variants unacceptable because of sense or syntax.

222 prius (patet); 254 ne sic (hic ego); 1576 ruina (Cremona); 1926 qualis (talis); 2018 potest (solet; *GI* potest uel solet); 2178 eis (eum); 2369 etiam cito (et cerea); 2446 zona...mea (zonam...meam); 2911 fixo pede (et fixo); 2990 grauis (graui).

BH variants which are not so evidently identifiable as error but which show the agreement between these two manuscripts in clear contrast to the δ readings (α and γ being out in this section of the poem): 2640 intus (iunctus); 2749 proprium (primum); 2959 cuncta (facta); 3515 diceret (dixerit).

Although *BH* undoubtedly belong to the same branch of the stemma, it is worth noting that there are frequent disagreements between them; sometimes one has the correct reading, sometimes the other. Nor do their variants regularly align with one branch of the stemma (α, γ, or δ) rather than another.

The γ Group of Manuscripts

The core of this group comprises thirteen manuscripts:

S Mu Va Vb Vc Vd T Go Be Pk Fr Pm Ne.

The most obvious feature linking these manuscripts is the fact that they terminate at line 2602 of the poem (except for *S*, which terminates even earlier, at line 2522), in the middle of the long tirade against the corrupting influence of *munera*. The likely reasons for this feature have already been discussed. As will be shown later, textually the group is often linked to α and β, as opposed to δ, but it also has a set of exclusive shared variants which mark it out as a separate branch of the stemma.[178]

---

[178] Although it clearly belongs to the γ group, *S* is sometimes absent; its readings are somewhat closer to the archetype than the other γ manuscripts. Note that *Fr* lacks 2053–464, *Va* lacks 618–81 and 1177–234, lines 934–1022 are largely missing in *T*, and *S* ends at 2522, so these manuscripts will inevitably be absent from the entries for these stretches of text. It should also be noted that on occasion the γ readings vary slightly among themselves (the variation is indicated in the examples if not too complicated, as it is at 1085, 1536, etc.), but their common origin, and separation from the other groups, is still unmistakable. Further details are to be found in the *apparatus criticus*.

TEXTUAL TRANSMISSION   lxxxix

Up to line 2602, the readings of these thirteen core manuscripts are frequently shared by a further three manuscripts, *Tr Ha La*, which, however, do not terminate at line 2602 but continue to line 3900. After line 2602, their main affiliation switches to the δ group, which has, however, already supplied some of their readings. See the section on Mixed Manuscripts below for more details.

A number of omissions are shared by this group (provocations to eyeskip are indicated in parentheses): 221–2, 435–6 (?Sed), 479–80 (solet), 1324–5 (parentes), 2011–12 (scient), 2347–8 (not *T*) (doli),[179] 2408–9 (Canonici, sorores).

The following examples of γ variants are identifiable as shared errors:

1. Variants unacceptable because of sense or syntax[180]

219 alcius (artius); 546 sternit* (*om. S*) (urget); 865 labori/e (dolori) (*repeats 'labor' from earlier in the line and makes poor sense*); 944 uulneris (criminis); 1205 nullo (alio); 1372 ipse/ille (inde); 1381 silet (ruit); 1404 tempora (singula) (*repetitive*); 1407–9 *lines disordered, 1407 om., new 1409a added*; 1419 lux* (lex); 1570 fessa/fossa (falsa); 1584 heu calidos (hos calices); 1709 sunt protinus* (fiant sunt); 1978 liqui/loqui (destruo); 2024 sanus/sanius (saluus); 2063 defert (desint) (*subject of the verb is lacking*); 2070 scindere ligna domus (ligna referre domum) (*a donkey is more suited to carry logs than to split them*); 2088 quinta[181] (sexta) (*eating meat on Friday is worse than eating meat on Thursday, so 'sexta' makes better sense*); 2103 premia* (praedia); 2145 de facili (qua facie); 2196 alias (hamis); 2219 mox (mons); 2266 infirmum (aut), mane *om.*; 2284 mente (ueste); 2312 curam (causam); 2516 *whole line*; 2524 *whole line* (*S is out*); 2565 forte (terre); 2567 saluacione/saluatore (*prompted by 'in cruce suspendi'*) (sumpta carne); 2580 deficit (desipit).

2. Variants unacceptable for metrical reasons

709 sī fŏrtĕ uīna* (uīnŭm sī fŏrtĕ) (*'forsan' in Fr is perhaps an attempt at repair*); 785 gŭlă* (gīlă); 1501 sic *om.*; 2495 quārūmquĕ māxĭmă (quārūm prāēmāxĭmă).

3. Easier substitutions (*lectiones faciliores*)

831 aspexit (aspiciens) (*scribal preference for early completion of the syntactical unit*); 1322 est (*om. S*) (urbs); 1455 mater* (genetrix); 1938 talia dixit (obuius inquit); 2160 debet nam (frater habet); 2517 fuit* (sui) (*scribal preference for early completion of the syntactical unit*).

---

[179] See my Notes on this line.
[180] In this and following sets of examples, asterisks indicate variants not shared by *S*.
[181] *VdT* read 'sexta' but this could be a scribal correction.

xc INTRODUCTION

4. Misreadings of the exemplar

700 lata (not *Vc*) (lauta); 922 iudicet (not *Vc*) (uindicet); 1854 tresque (not *MuT*) (transque); 2380 dogmate (smigmate).

Many of the variants exclusive to γ are acceptable in themselves and are rejected only because agreement between other branches of the stemma provides more support for the alternatives. See, for example, the following:

15 ministrat* (propinat); 91 prolixior* (productior); 190 petis* (rogas); 193 es tu (unus); 283 respondet Bruneta sibi[182] (postea respondens dixit); 335 soluisse si possem (priuasse possem sed); 355 euertit* (subuertit); 357 leui (breui); 379 omnia sola* (omnibus una); 419–20 *transp. after 422* (not *Go*); 422 pessimus (maximus); 444 effrangar adhuc* (tamen effrangar); 472 rutilis/rutibus/uitibus (missis); 552 ala (penna); 595 modo (tibi); 608 uel...nequit (nec...potest); 610 si tamen in (dummodo cum); 642 subito (obiter); 695 sunt hec/hic (constant); 772 clamat (fingit); 782 plena...uasa (uasa...plena); 810 rusticus...furcifer (furcifer...rusticus); 908 culpa tamen (fuit culpa); 957 non pereat solus (soluendo fuerit); 966 ultus ero (ulciscar); 984 dematurque/demanturque (damneturque); 1023 rogabo* (precabor); 1039 et (ut); 1040 arbitrii uotis/uocis/rotis/uoci (sederit arbitrio); 1085 stolidum morti dare fraude (stultum delere scienter); 1150 non emendata (nondum mutata); 1155 dicetur de me/ad me (diceturque mihi); 1162 toti/toto (magno); 1201 post hec/hoc* (postea); 1226 rogo (precor); 1228 precor (peto); 1231 iunctis...dextris* (dextris...iunctis); 1245 casumque/casuque (saltumque); 1262 ualet/uellet (licet); 1275–6 *transp after 1278**; 1286 sepe (posse); 1287 labente (crescente); 1307 cupit (auet); 1311 iam lustrum fecerat ille/ipse (sextum iam pullus in annum); 1335 cunctis...prefigitur (tempus...praescribitur); 1347 includit* (excludit); 1363 subiecit (not *Vc*) (suggessit); 1395 absorptus (absumptus); 1414 preteriisse (dissiluisse); 1418 in hoc (ego); 1457 et si (quamuis); 1535 pro/pre (de); 1536 accrescat siquidem (cur nihil accrescet); 1538 non (cur); 1606 sunt (nam); 1607 pectus (latus est); 1693 portat/portant* (gestat); 1707 et plus (quoniam); 1732 illius/illos esto memor* (esto memor uerbi); 1782 inflexo/inflexio (obstipo); 1822 fugam/fudam (not *Vc*) (uiam); 2014 estque docere (est docuisse); 2089 multa (plura); 2190 faceret (facit ad); 2200 boni (sibi); 2253 iure/iura (lite); 2326 usque* (saepe); 2346 mali* (doli); 2352 cadunt* (labant); 2457 bona que si non (quae si non nunc); 2514 larga (longa);

---

[182] Despite variations in the readings here, the γ pattern remains distinctive. The same holds good at lines 335, 444, 810, and 1085.

TEXTUAL TRANSMISSION xci

2555 *whole line**; 2556 nam sicut populi uox* (quae sit uox populi quae); 2562 breuis* (not *T*) (leuis) (*S is out*).

There are, however, five cases where a γ variant probably preserves the original reading:

152 cōmmodius (făcilius). There is no evidence of 'facilius' being scanned with a long 'a', which would be needed at the beginning of the line, where the word is placed. 'Commodius' may well be the archetypal reading.

434 cōnsŏcĭīsquĕ/ cūm sŏcĭīsquĕ (pāstōrĭbūsquĕ). A short 'o' is required at this position in the foot.

1055 dūcens/dīcens (mĭnans). 'Mĭnans' is metrically unacceptable; either 'dūcens' or 'dīcens' is preferable.

1700 Mozley prints the δ reading 'ut non sit', but γ's 'et sic non' is supported by αβ's 'et non sic'.

2545 Mozley prints the δ reading, 'Sīc ŏuĭs ūnă grĕgēm tōtūm măcŭlāndŏ rĕspērgīt'. At first it seems that this version could be rejected on metrical grounds, but shortening of the final -o in a gerund is common, and Nigel regularly shortens the ĕ in the prefix 're'. See the comment in Lewis and Short, p. 1528: 'The orthography and quantity of words compounded with *re* are in general somewhat arbitrary, especially in the ante- and post-class. poets'. However, the γ version of the line, which ends 'măcŭlāt măcŭlōsā', seems more characteristic of Nigel's fondness for polyptoton (see Introduction, pp. clix–clx).

A Subgroup of γ: Manuscripts Vd and Be

The γ group is in general remarkably cohesive, and subgroups are hard to distinguish. However, *Vd* and *Be* certainly form a pair, and are also frequently joined by *Tr* or *La* or both.

Examples of *VdBe* agreement: 716 plangendo (plangendus); 801 uilium (multum); 911 in indignissima (etiam dignissima); 917 pacificis (pontificis); 1499 factum *om.*; 1555 cedit (quatit); 1777 ergo (sibi); 2016 redocuisse (dedocuisse); 2025 ut qui (utque); 2222 modo (suo); 2567 saluatore (sumpta carne); 2595 *repeated after 2602*.

Examples where *VdBe* readings are shared by *Tr* and *La*: 679 puluis te nunc (*La alt.*)[183] (pluuiae tecum); 1007 quam (nam); 1235–6 *transp.*; 1330 exultans (*La alt.*) (exhilarans); 1419 potuit (poterit); 1517 multumque (*La*ac) (uultuque); 1561 preciosa (*La*ac) (uitiosa); 1620 satum (*La alt.*) (citum); 2067 scindet (*La alt.*) (fundet); 2106 mala (multa);

---

[183] '(*La alt.*)' means that the *La* reading is one of two proffered alternatives. See below, pp. xcix–c.

xcii INTRODUCTION

2164 indicat (inserit); 2220 finem (*La alt.*) (modum); 2243 ter *om.*; 2428 liqueat (liceat); 2592 uitulus (titulus).

Examples where *VdBe* readings are shared by *La*: 1257 discedens (digressus); 1756 *om.* (*La*ᵃᶜ); 2047 declino (*La alt.*) (deseruio); 2354 mente (incerto); 2385 ante tenus (aure tenus); 2394 percussint (percutiunt); 2505 uotum/uocum (*La alt.*) (morum); 2563 huius/eius (eris); 2571 sic² *om.*

Examples where *VdBe* readings are shared by *Tr*: 153 ut (nunc); 258 hic (hoc); 444 effrangor (effrangar); 1147 futurum (futuri); 1202 regales (legales); 1203 mecum (necnon); 1459 culpamque tibi (tibi culpam); 1580 iordanum/iordanem (Rodanum); 1809 modo (meo); 1922 turrida (turrita).

It seems that the γ manuscript(s) used by *Tr* and *La* were closely related to an ancestor of *VdBe*.

The δ Group of Manuscripts

The δ group comprises thirteen manuscripts, *AJCWRHuMNOPDKVe*. These manuscripts contain the fullest extent of the poem, taking it up to line 3900, and they agree with each other with remarkable consistency. The first evidence of their group agreement is the omissions they share but which are not found in the αβγ manuscripts;[184] most are self-evidently the result of eyeskip (that is, they are not likely to have been authorial additions in the other branches of the stemma). The list, with indications of the words responsible for eyeskip if relevant, is as follows: 247–8 (mihi); 941–4 (erit); 1070–1; 1169–72; 1185–6; 1275–6 (ira/modum); 1409–10 (noctis); 1885–6; 2105–6; 2109–10; 2145–6; 2310–11; 2407–8 (sorores); 2419–20 (mihi); 2555–8; 2619–20 (Munera); 2918b–2920a; 3122b–24a (Per me...datur); 3127–9 (*followed by reordering of lines 3130–4 and addition of a new 3134a*); 3518–19; 3643–4. Strictly speaking, eyeskip introduces the possibility of polygenesis (convergent variation), but the group attestation is both conjunctive (an indication of a link between these manuscripts) and disjunctive (an indication of their separation from the other main groups).

As before, I give a list of variants which are characteristic of the manuscripts of the δ group, with the corresponding readings in the edited text supplied in parentheses. The variants selected are supported by all or almost all of the δ manuscripts, but not by other groups; in

---

[184] Mozley gives an incomplete list on p. 24 of his Introduction. The only instance in this list of agreement with δ by a manuscript from the αβγ group is *Fr* at 247–8, which is probably a polygenetic instance of eyeskip.

TEXTUAL TRANSMISSION

most cases, therefore, they are unlikely to be original readings, and in many cases this is confirmed by unacceptable sense, metre, or probable *lectiones faciliores* (of course these categories may overlap). For further examples and discussion of inferior readings in δ, see pp. cxvii–cxxv below.

1. Variants unacceptable because of sense or syntax

222 placet (patet); 371 prestant (praestat); 723 porteque (sportaeque); 848 eripiens (arripiens); 972 culpa (culpae); 1025 accipiam (decipiam); 1285 hincque (inde); 1295 sanum (sura); 1637 pareat/pariat/pateat (calleat); 1926 qualis ego (talis erat); 2019 paribus/peribet (partitur); 2244 carnes (pisces); 2353 stat quasi (gloria); 2481 uerum mea (neuerunt); 2507 ordine (omnia); 2593 reseruant/ reformant (serenant); 2756 dedit (suas); 2824 Augustino (Augustini); 2901 sub ramis/ramos (ramos super); 2925 sanctior unus (stemmate maior); 3046 atque (immo); 3197 facta sequantur (sancta frequentant); 3501 sportellas eneas (sportellasque meas); 3516 factis uerba (uerbis facta)[185]; 3603 ait (ego); 3708 attulit (abstulit); 3726 tenore/tenere (timore).

2. Variant unacceptable for metrical reasons

2928 fŏrĕ (scīrĕ).

3. Easier substitutions (*lectiones faciliores*)

763 hic teneo (emimus hic); 773 et cuncta (tenus ore); 864 anxius (acrius); 940 criminis ultor erit (plus tamen istud eo); 955 illius/in huius (illata); 1504 ueniunt (subeunt); 1711 nomen habent sine re (re sine nomen habent); 1759 et ueniant (introeant); 1831 insistendo (infitiando); 1893 necnon (miser et); 2013 labor[2] *om.* (labor labor); 2047 nisi quod (quorsum); 2737 splendida (regia); 3848 rege iubente suo (infitiatur opus).

4. Misreadings of the exemplar

840 num/nam/non (sum); 1307 aue/auem (auet); 1327 mensis (mensas); 1737 uel (nil); 1750 nil ergo/igitur uitii (quidnam uirtutis);[186] 1979 peperit (periit); 2000 graues (magis);[187] 2038 bono (suo); 2071 trimordi (trinodi); 2253 scire (lite); 2259 semper (spernunt); 2277 albo (albedo); 2509 pudoris (prioris); 2612 ciues...gemunt (uices...gerunt); 2803 arcius (acrius); 2893 uidebar/uidebat (iuuabat).

The following δ variants are acceptable in themselves and are rejected only because there is more support from different manuscript groups for the alternatives:

---

[185] The reversal produces nonsense, as the scribes of *PK* probably saw.

[186] The change is likely to have been caused by β's substitution of 'adesse' for 'abesse', which seems to make virtue undesirable in a bishop.

[187] See Notes on this line.

xciv   INTRODUCTION

791 nomen burnellus mihi stat (nomine brunellus dicor); 924 laeditur et/in (laesa sed est); 989 sic (mihi); 1599 sed fata/facta (mea fata); 1700 ut non sit (et non sic);[188] 1714 cornua uana (menstrua membra); 1749 et uia duxque (omnia factus); 1797 pontificis tanti nunc tempora (praesule defuncto modo plurima; 1968 *whole line*; 2087–8 uorare... saepe licebit eis (uorarem... nam licet illud ibi); 2735 laceras/lateras (uacuas); 3360 uideo bene nunc (bene conspicio).

Subgroups of δ: Manuscripts Hu, M, and N

Manuscripts *Hu*, *M*, and *N* are particularly closely related, as is shown by the very numerous exclusive variants that they share throughout the length of the poem. All three contain the Interpolation on the Mendicant Orders (244 lines added between lines 2412 and 2413, and 14 lines added between lines 2456 and 2457). All three also transpose 708–11 to follow 728, and 1338 to follow 1344; they all omit 1434–5, 1920, 2631–2 and 3863–72.[189]

The following are some further examples of their agreement in error (with the received reading, as usual, in parentheses): Epistle 46 a patre (apprime); 27, 29 diuo (duro); 37 di <*space left empty*> (disertior); 39 semina (omnia); 52 utrumque (intumet); 259 crine (crure); 293 saperis (sapiens); 340 rure (iure); 659 apibus (Alpibus); 824 mare (mane); 875 amisso (a misero); 913 germinis (criminis); 993 eum *om.*; 1092 abiens (alueus); 1397 dicere (cantor); 1530 sallia (Gallia); 1555 querit iste (quatit ille); 1599 sed facta (mea fata); 1619 armis (annis); 1629 leonum (luporum); 3459 nare *om.*; 3574 cumque (quinque); 3627 finem (funem); 3715 facit (fuit); 3718 iuuenis (in nemus); 3746 spondere (pondere); 3825 sumpta (rupta); 3878 mihi (sibi).

The descent of all three manuscripts from a common ancestor is clear. Within this trio, *M* and *N* form a pair, most strikingly in that both transpose 3602–896 to follow 3320 (see p. lxix above, and the entry for MS *M* in the Manuscript Descriptions in Appendix A).[190] They also share a number of agreements in error which are absent from *Hu*, mainly of a trivial nature. Examples are: 3 nouiter (nouitatis); 221 ut *om.*; 680 nocui canina (noctu cana); 1085 de se (delere); 1092 unda *om.*; 1138, 1526 ecce (esse); 2609 uirtus (uirus); 2664 adest (abest); 2923 delicti (dilecti); 3117 non (nonnulla); 3167 nisi (nisus); 3280 soluta (solita); 3362 expellantur (repellantur); 3410 aget (eget).

---

[138] See above, p. xci.

[189] The absence of 3863–72 may go back to a stage in the poem's evolution (that is, these lines may have been added in order to stress the theme of ingratitude).

[190] Mozley's figures are inaccurate (*SS*, pp. 18–19): 3602–3892 should be 3602–3896, and 3859–3868 should be 3863–72.

TEXTUAL TRANSMISSION

Mozley did not know *Hu*, but he recognised that *M* and *N* are so close as to make a common origin certain,[191] although he thought that neither could be a direct copy of the other.[192] Although *M* and *N* share the major transposition of text at 3602–896, other idiosyncrasies of *M* are not reflected in *N*. For example, *M* omits part of *Epistle* 12–13 through eyeskip from 'possit sibi accrescere' to 'possit sibi apprehendere', and its headings from 448 onwards are out of step with the text, consistently lagging one section behind. For example, at 448, where other manuscripts (including *N*) have something along the lines of 'qualiter Brunetta liberata est', *M* has 'commendatio caude sue', and at 460 *M* has 'qualiter brunetta liberata est', while other manuscripts are signalling 'lamentatio Bicornis'. The discrepancies persist up to line 1048, where *M*'s heading 'dissimulacio Burnelli' at last catches up with *N*.

M also has dozens of trivial errors which are not reproduced in *N* (or any other manuscript).[193] *N* is closer to *Hu*, and shares its general level of correctness. *N* and *Hu* occasionally agree in error, as at line 123 where they read 'ab' for 'absque', 153 where they have 'disceris' for 'diceris', 980 'oculo' for 'oculos', 1017 'nam' for 'namque', 1355 'nectem' for 'noctem', 2767 'uente' for 'uentre', and 3007 'beatis' for 'beatus'. Particularly clear examples of dependency are the repetition of the entire phrase 'ualde sit difficile' at Epistle 31 and the spelling of 'Nigelli' as 'scigelli' at line 1. In contrast, the few examples of *HuM* agreement could well be instances of convergent variation through omission of abbreviation marks ('pauus' for 'proauus' at 795, 'cesura' for 'censura' at 1165, or the omission of 309–10 through eyeskip). On some occasions, *N* seems to have independently corrected a mistake in the joint exemplar of all three manuscripts: at Epistle 43, all three originally read 'naturam' instead of 'in naturam', but *N* has added 'in' later; at 291, *N* has changed 'grauius' to the correct 'grauibus' leaving *Hu* and *M* in agreement on the error; at 1279 *HuM* read 'sactu' (for 'iactu'), which *N* has corrected to 'saltu'. In such instances, *HuM* agreement is accidental rather than genetic.

---

[191] *SS*, p. 18; cf. p. 27.

[192] Despite the fact that Mozley's stemma on p. 23 of the *SS* edition shows *N* as deriving directly from *M*.

[193] For example, 513 aurora (aurore); 523 perstiuo (estiuo); 615 crederit (creuerit); 727 mutuque (mutique); 739 sergens (surgens); 903 feteor (fateor), and so on. *M* also frequently omits words: 97 mihi; 540 saepe; 576 perit; 691 ab; 749 tuus; 800 et; 2859 ex; 3131 uigili; 3157 unda. (However, it is not true that *M* omits lines 68–71, as Mozley claims (*SS*, p. 19); these lines are present in *Hu*, *M*, and *N*.) *N* has only a handful of errors which are not in *M* (e.g. 153 disceris for diceris).

xcvi INTRODUCTION

N's avoidance of *M*'s many characteristic errors show that it cannot be a direct copy of *M*. The absence of the *HuN* errors in *M* suggest that *N* is unlikely to have been *M*'s exemplar;[194] more likely, the two manuscripts derive from a common ancestor, to which *N* is much closer than *M*. The major dislocation of text at 3320 seems to have originated in this common ancestor; in *N* the scribe seemed originally unaware of the gap in continuity, but a marginal note by a later hand draws the reader's attention to it.[195] Accordingly, *M* leaves a line empty at this point, but gives no other indication of the problem, and possibly does not understand its nature.

Subgroups of δ: Manuscripts D and K, and the Subgroup HuMNDK

Manuscripts *D* and *K* form a rather idiosyncratic pair. The evidence is by no means as abundant as for *MN*, but it is of such a kind as to leave no doubt of their relationship. At 1678, for example, they add two spurious lines of comment on abbots who wear the pontificals. At 2315, they show their disapproval of the scansion of 'canonicus' with a long first syllable and 'secularis' with a short first syllable (Sūnt ēt cānŏnĭcī sĕcŭlārēs quīquĕ uŏcātī; but see n. 344 below) by rewriting 2315 and adding two lines that make the problem clear:

> Sūnt ēt cānŏnĭcī quōrūm nōmēn mĕtră spērnūnt
> nē lōngēnt brĕuĭā lōngăquĕ cŏrrĭpĭant
> sēd ērrāntĕ mĕtrō sūnt cānŏnĭcī sĕcŭlārēs.

There are also canons whose name metre repudiates, unless it lengthens short syllables and shortens long ones, but with defective metre, they are secular canons.

This sensitivity to prosody is also evident when, at line 1951, they replace the unmetrical δ variant 'uīcīnā' (for 'Vīennā') with 'prŏpīnquā'.[196] At 3296, *D* and *K* differ from each other, but are both clearly reflecting an incomprehension of 'si Styga iurasset' in their common source, which they render as 'si de saturno' (*D*) or 'quam si saturno' (*K*). As these examples show, the scribes of these two manuscripts are distinguished by their independent variations and willingness to 'improve' the text with their own interventions.

Such interventions aside, however, *DK* clearly belong to the subgroup *HuMNDK*, the most obvious evidence for which is the two

---

[194] Mozley will have excluded this possibility because he dated *M* to the 13th/14th c. and *N* to the 15th. Thomson, however, assigns both to the 14th c. (*Manuscripts of Lincoln Cathedral Chapter Library*, pp. 78–9, 153–4).

[195] See MS *M* in the Manuscript Descriptions in Appendix A.

[196] See below, p. cxxiii and n. 259.

TEXTUAL TRANSMISSION

Interpolations that these manuscripts contain. The first comprises the 244 lines on the Mendicant Orders which are added to Burnellus's survey of the monastic orders, after line 2412. The second comprises 14 lines, also concerning the friars, which are added to Burnellus's summary of his opinions on the advantages or disadvantages of each order, following line 2456. The first Interpolation also appears in manuscripts *G* and *I*, probably by contamination.[197] For analysis of the variant readings in these Interpolations, see p. 398 below.

Other examples of *HuMNDK* agreement are the following: 933 tam grande (damnumque); 1994–5 *om.*; 2001–4 *om.*; 2417 meum sumat de nomine nomen (meo nomen de nomine sumat); 2544 et uirus (et unus *M*) (toxicat et); 3682 seruando fidem (firmata fide); 3724 supposuitque (imposuitque); 3825 penultima cuncta (cuncta repente). Sometimes the group is perceptible only in unanimously rejecting the accepted reading, as at 2103–4:

> Non uendunt uel emunt sua praedia uel prioratus;
> omnia sed gratis distribuuntur ibi.

MNK change this to

> Non uendunt uel emunt cum symone predia gratis
> *atque prioratus* distribuuntur ibi.

D rewrites more thoroughly:

> *predia multa satis ibi gratis distribuuntur*
> *atque prioratus non comodant uel emunt.*

There is a similar situation at 2148, where the accepted reading is 'nunquam de reliquo monachus albus ero', which *MNK* replace with 'non albus monachus postea dictus (ductus *N*) ero', and *D* with 'nunquam post illud albus ero monachus'. A smaller example of a similar split occurs at 302, where *HuMND* read 'aspera' instead of 'prospera', and *K*, realizing that this does not supply the necessary contrast with 'duris', remedies the situation by changing 'aspera' to 'mitia'.

Subgroups of δ: Manuscripts C and W and the Subgroups CWHuMNDK and CWHuMN

There is abundant evidence for *CW* as a manuscript pair, and for its association with *HuMNDK*. For examples of the former, see 306 circumferri (certum fieri); 308 sui (frui); 999 discrescerit (discesserit);

---

[197] See below, p. civ.

xcviii INTRODUCTION

1191 carebit (cauebit); 1226 uita (uia); 1227 sunt *om.*; 1358 surripuit (supprimit); 1718 pacificetur (paciscetur); 2288 tenent (placent); 2810 socios (sanctos); 2867 aues (aries); 2886 proprius (propius); 3334 color (calor).

For examples of the group *CWHuMNDK*, see the following: 352 sibi (pari); 1828 opus (onus); 2304 raro (numquam); 2395 harum *om.*; 2476 nocuere mihi (mihi ferre solent); 2670 ipsemet istud (et quibus illud); 2890 sternere (stertere); 3020 mihi (mei); 3147 necnon (etiam); 3709 remanente (remeante); 3750 suppositum (impositum); 3861 itaque (igitur; *D is out*). Sometimes, however, *CWHuMN* appear as a group without *DK*: for example, 703 decipiunt (desipiunt); 1097 in aquis (et undis; *DK and others* in undis); 2683 sed alter (secundus; *sic D*); 2793 rupe (ripae); 3272 fuerit (seruit); 3388 renuens (reuerens); 3475 eiusdem (eisdem). Occasionally *DK* diverge but are still recognizably related to *CWHuMN*: 2914 simplice, simplici *D* (supplice); 3756 receptus, repertus *DK* (reuersus).

Subgroups of δ: the subgroup AJCWROPVe

This situation is further complicated by the fact that *CW* also appear as members of the main subgroup on the other side of the δ branch, namely *AJCWROPVe*. For examples of this group, see 933 *whole line*; 937 quanti sit dedecus at (hoc *R*) (dedecus at quanti sit); 1488 exteriorque (exteriora); 1994 reticere (retinere); 2412 mero (melo); 2609 sanabile (insanabile); 3472 talo (colo). The appearance of *CW* in both subgroups must be traced back to the first stages of development from the δ archetype, with one copy producing errors that characterize the ancestor of *AJCWROPVe* and another producing errors that characterize the ancestor of *CWHuMNDK*.

The later development of this branch of the tradition is difficult to determine, as the groupings of variant readings show no settled patterns, despite the fact that their δ parentage remains unmistakable. Presence or absence of individual manuscripts may be attributed to convergent variation, or else to scribal correction of errors *ope ingenii*. Stemma 2 (p. xx) tentatively suggests a relationship between *A* and *J* (see 2097, 2759, 3136). *ROPVe* occasionally appear as a group. They share some omissions:[198] 812–17 (perura(n)t); 963–4 (dabunt; also shared by *H Fr X*); 3172–3 (aula/m); 3662–5 (cupido). They also share some variant readings: 1016 cupit (cupis); 1538 ue retro (retroue); 2395 quaedam *om.*; 2887 pene (pone; *CW* pede). *O* and *P* regularly appear

---

[198] Provocations to eyeskip are given in parentheses.

TEXTUAL TRANSMISSION

together, but usually as part of a larger group, and in the few examples where they appear on their own, the variants are trivial and could perhaps be the result of polygenesis (e.g. 451 'claras' for 'clarus'; 2369 'terea' for 'cerea'; 2622 'precis' for 'procis'. The only substantive example is 'peraddit' for 'parabat' at 1103. Moreover, *O* shows no sign of *P*'s major omissions and dislocations of text. They cannot therefore be connected by direct descent, nor can they share an immediate common ancestor. *R* is difficult to place, since it is an idiosyncratic manuscript, with a great many unique variants, some of which, however, seem to be the only evidence of the original reading; see 2519 faciens (sitiens); 2779 impubes (shared only with *O*) (impuberes); 3161 cuiuis (cuius); 3242 fractus (factus). Some of these may be scribal corrections, but some seem to be genetically produced.

'Mixed' Manuscripts

Manuscripts Tr Ha La

As indicated above, up to line 2602, *TrHaLa* are regular members of group γ, and *La* is particularly close to *VdBe*. In the case of *Ha* and *La*, their 'mixed' quality is immediately apparent in the fact that at numerous points they each record alternative versions of words or phrases which sometimes reproduce the manuscript readings of group δ. These alternatives are usually added in the margin and indicated by 'uel' (see p. xxiv, above, for the different ways in which variations in this format are recorded). As far as one can judge from photographs, these alternatives are in the main hand and were entered at the time the main text was copied or shortly after. Interestingly, *Ha* and *La* almost never agree on these alternatives, so they must have been independently noted.

In line with *La*'s general affiliation with the γ group up to line 2602, at least one of *La*'s alternatives is usually drawn from that group. It is harder to locate the precise source of the other element in these pairings, since they most usually correspond to a majority reading found in two or more groups. And, surprisingly, on a number of occasions there is no other attestation for one element of the pair at all. For example: 41 discretum; 47 gemino; 63 fulsa; 112 impetit; 118 uita; 254 titius; 454 gelu (but cf. 452); 727 famuli; 880 caudam; 926 multus; 929 antiquis; 931 intuenda, and so on. This might suggest that the alternatives reflect the scribe's uncertainty as to the reading of his exemplar, rather than being the result of consulting more than one manuscript. However, on some occasions, it is clear that an *La* reading or one of the proffered alternatives derives from a δ manuscript. For example: 222

c INTRODUCTION

placet; 430 munda; 497 mihi dum coniuncta; 527 pariter conturbat (*alt.*[199]); 580 mundana; 600 tutius ire domum (*alt.*); 621 noli tardare pedester; 634 referes; 936 absque; 1295 sanum (*alt.*); 1567 periitque labor sed; 1619 cur; 1749 sicut et uia duxque (*alt.*); 1750 nil ergo uicii debet adesse sibi (*alt.*); 1926 qualis ego (*alt.*); 2047 nisi quod (*alt.*); 2087 uorare; 2277 albo. Other readings confirm the affiliation with δ, both before and after line 2602.

Ha has an even larger number of alternatives that are completely unattested elsewhere in the manuscript tradition. For example, 61 decepit; 885 ba ba; 932 quocumque; 951 decet; 997 non; 1042 idem; 1051 fraudes; 1052 suadet; 1081 periit; and so on and so on. However, unlike *La*, *Ha* has almost no clear connections with δ up to line 2602, the only possibilities being 114 opis; 159 est; 231 magnoque (shared with *DK*); 1252 dinumerare (shared with *RD*); these examples may be the result of polygenesis.

Tr does not record alternatives in the manner of *Ha* and *La*, but its mixed affiliations are clear from the large number of δ readings that are incorporated in its text, even before line 2602. For example: 159 est; 371 prestant; 468 ludibrio; 546 stimulant mordent; 580 mundana; 1295 sanum; 1325 generalia; 1432 qui; 1831 insistendo; 1926 qualis ego; 1951 uicina; 2013 labor et; 2047 nisi quod; 2087 uorare; 2168 spemque fidemque; 2206 nec licet; 2244 carnes; 2301 salubrius; 2352 cumque... labent...ruent; 2353 stat quasi; 2395 parturientes; 2407–8 *om.*; 2476 nocuere mihi; 2478 dat; 2481 uerum mea; 2507 ordine; 2551 in *om.* This makes it clear that when *Tr*'s readings diverge from γ (and also from *HaLa*) and agree with an archetypal αβδ reading, they must have been taken, not from α or β, but from a δ manuscript. This is the case, for example, with the following: 908 fuit culpa; 922 uindicet; 1286 posse; 1501 sic *not om.*; 1535 de; 1535 mores formantur; 1570 falsa; 2014 est docuisse; 2103 praedia; 2190 facit ad; 2284 ueste; 2326 saepe; 2567 sumpta carne. In addition, though *Tr* agrees with γ in omitting 221–2 and 435–6, it does not omit 479–80 or 1324–5, or transpose 419–20 after line 422.

After line 2602, it is obvious that *Tr Ha La* must have had access to a manuscript outside the γ group, since their text continues to the end of the poem at line 3900.[200] Their alternative source cannot be α, since

---

[199] This means that this reading is one of *La*'s two proffered alternatives.

[200] *La* marks the switch from one exemplar to another by a break in copying at almost exactly this point; fo. 151ᵛ ends with line 2592, and a note directs the reader to the continuation of *SS* eleven folios later, where the text picks up (in the same hand) with line 2593 and continues to line 3900. Originally, the intervening folios were apparently left blank, though

TEXTUAL TRANSMISSION

ci

LEF lack lines 2483–3258, and the only possible candidates are β or δ. Analysis of the *apparatus criticus* for lines 2603–3900 shows that when there is a clear split between β (*BH*) and δ, *Tr Ha La* regularly go with δ against *BH*. For example, they share all the characteristic δ omissions after line 2602: 2619–20; 2918b–20a; 3122b–24a; 3127–9 (and the accompanying re-ordering of lines 3130–4); 3518–19; 3643–4.

Manuscripts G and I

G and *I* are very closely related, and Mozley indeed believed that *I* was a copy of *G*. Significantly, *G* ends imperfectly at 2746 and *I* correspondingly lacks 2747–3258 and is obliged to derive 3259–448 from an α manuscript (most probably *L*).[201] Since *LEF* lack 2483–3258, *I* could not have derived this portion of the poem from α, nor could it derive from α the last 452 lines of the poem (3449–900), the story of the Grateful Animals and the Ungrateful Man. *I*'s lack of lines 1116–744, on the other hand, is due to loss of leaves, as is shown by its catchwords, which indicate quires of 8. The catchword at fo. 16ᵛ is 'Dixerat', the first word of line 1116, but fo. 17ʳ begins with 'Nam', the first word of line 1745.

GI both contain the Interpolation on the Mendicant Orders (also found in *MNDK*), which was obviously added to the survey of the monastic orders in the thirteenth century at the earliest, a good while after the original composition of the poem in the 1190s. *GI* also share some characteristic omissions, viz. (with possible causes of eyeskip indicated in parenthesis): 988 (added in *I²*) (haec); 1074–5 (1075 added in *I²*) (uocibus); 1876; 1989–90 (mihi); 2431; 2728. They also share a spurious couplet added after line 406.

Other substantial examples of *GI* agreement in error are as follows:

1. Variants unacceptable because of sense or syntax

119 abunde (abinde); 149 in nato (innatum); 229 conante (conatae); 332 prato (prata); 468 delubrium (ludibrium); 515 uite (uoce); 546 uergit (urget); 685 forti (portae); 784 poscentis (uendentis); 868 retinuisse

---

fos. 152ʳ–153ᵛ were later filled by various disconnected items (see the entry for MS *La* in Manuscript Descriptions in Appendix A). The only item that has a connection with *SS* is the fable 'De Catulo et Asello' (no. xvii of the popular collection now known as the elegiac *Romulus, L'Esopus attribuito a Gualtiero Anglico*, ed. Busdraghi, p. 80, Inc. 'Murmuris et caude studio testatus amorem'), which is copied on fo. 152ʳ; its link with *SS* is provided not only by the figure of the ass, but also by the moral, which begins 'Quod natura negat, nemo feliciter audet' (echoing *SS* 186).

[201] In 3259–448, *I* shares the following variants with α: 3291 eam *om.* (*L*); 3355 posset propriisque (*LF*); 3366 pondus inerte (*LE*); 3444 scanda (*L*); 3445–6 *om.* (*LEF*); 3447 militem (*LE*). *L* is the only manuscript that can have supplied all these variants. At line 184, *I²* also provides an alternative reading 'quod', which is the *LEF* reading, in place of 'quem'.

cii   INTRODUCTION

(restituisse); 1102 titulit (titulum); 1939 potenti (petendi); 2006 excutit (exerit); 2136 heu heu (her her); 2537 est nil tam facile (nil tam difficile); 2548 exinde (ex igne).

2. Variants unacceptable for metrical reasons
36 cōnstăt (cōnstĭtĭt); 214 rĕcŭbŭĕrĕ (prōcŭbŭĕrĕ).

However, when I's readings differ from G, I is often correct, which tells against Mozley's belief that I is a copy of G and suggests that it must be a cognate of it. The situation is complicated by the fact that some of these correct readings in I are due to revisions made by a later hand (I^2)[202] and some have been written over erasures, suggesting that original agreement with G may have been eradicated as a result of consultation with another manuscript. In the following examples, the I reading agrees with the lemma in my text but is written over an erasure (or a superfluous word has been erased, leaving a blank space): 8 et] in G; 196 si] si tibi G; 687 propinqui] parenti G; 728 sitque] sintque G; 963 sortem] mortem G; 979 conspexerit] confecerit G. Other examples where I has been visibly corrected are the following: 290 facit] *om. GI, added I^2*; 466 ue²] *om. GI, added I^2*; 481 soluat] *om. GI, added I^2*; 689 sequetur] sequatur G, *corrected I^2*; 836 strata] stra GI, *corrected I^2*; 887 numquam] num G, *corrected I^2*; 970 perpetuo] perpetua G, *corrected I^2*; 987 ego] sic G, *corrected I^2*; 1052 ora] hora GI^{ac}, *h erased I^2*; 1061 mora] mea GI, *corrected I^2*; 1066 mortibus] moribus G I^{ac}, *corrected in margin I^2*; 2259 spernunt] s<*erasure*> G *om. I, added I^2*. Lines 988 and 1074–5 were originally omitted in G and I, but 988 and 1075 (though not 1074) were added in the margin by I^2 (line 1075 is at the end of 1077, preceded by 'uel sic'). Lines 995–6 are transposed in G and I, but the order is corrected by I^2.

I's corrections could (almost) all have been made by consultation with lines 1–2482 of the α manuscript from which I derived lines 3259–448;[203] significantly, there are no corrections in lines 2483–746, which are absent from the α manuscripts LEF. And in 2527, where the correct reading would be 'aes' and G reads 'os', there is an erasure in I, left blank. There are, however, many other instances where G has a variant while I has the correct reading but there is no physical trace of correction in I. See, for example, 152 poterit] poteris G; 423 quae muscas] quo muscas G; 644 suo] suis G; 734 tempus] templus G; 885

---

[202] I^2's corrections also introduce some errors without parallel in other manuscripts; see 881 cumque I^2 (cum); 1048 omnia dat I^2 *over erasure* (uimque facit); 2710 neque I^2 *over erasure* (seque).

[203] The exception is line 1075, which could have been derived from L, but I^2 reads 'celebrantes' where L reads 'celebremus'. Is this an independent scribal error in I^2?

TEXTUAL TRANSMISSION

dicto] dico *G*; 1035 conterminus] cum terminis *G*; 1059 falluntur] fallantur *G*; 1062 extinctis] ex cunctis *G*; 2343 numine] munere *G*. *G* also shows signs of contamination, in several cases where δ readings are added as alternatives, but these are not carried over into *I*. See 317 sero/ uel raro; 473 fata/ uel facta; 742 *whole line* nec tamen inuenit que cupiebat ibi *add. as an alternative in upper margin*; 2632 cadet/ uel ruet. These additions are all in the original hand. Such instances cumulatively tell against the supposition that *I* was a copy of *G*.

It also seems improbable that the cases where *I* has the correct reading without any physical sign of correction can all be the result of *I*'s ingenious emendation of *G* at the time of original copying. One might assume that *G* and *I* share a common exemplar, but here too there are problems. *I*'s exemplar lacked 2747–3258 (*I* goes straight from 2748 to 3259, without any hesitation or break in copying), but *G*'s apparently did not: at the bottom of fo. 61ᵛ, where *G* breaks off at line 2746, is the catchword 'aliter', which clearly if imperfectly represents the first word of line 2747, 'qualiter'. However, fo. 61ᵛ is in the exact middle of a quire of six (*G* habitually adds catchwords at the bottom of each verso, rather than at the end of a quire),[204] and the remaining leaves of this quire were originally left blank,[205] so that if the truncation of the text is due to a simple loss of quires, this loss must have occurred in *G*'s exemplar, not in *G*. *G* clearly knew there was more text to come and expected to be able to fill the blank leaves. Whether he was thwarted by personal circumstance or by defects in his copy, it is impossible to say. One explanation that would solve this problem is to assume that the common ancestor of *G* and *I* was originally complete (perhaps even to line 3900) but later lost its final quires, and the surviving portion of text, lines 1–2746, was then copied not only by the exemplar of *G*, but also by a now lost manuscript which corrected some but not all of *G*'s errors, added lines 3259–448, and was then copied by *I*.

Manuscripts GI and their relationship to BH

In the first 1700 lines or so of the poem, *BH* errors are often shared by manuscripts *G* and *I*, though *I* lacks 1116–744 because of missing leaves. Errors common to *BHGI* are as follows (*B* out in lines 849–1386; *I* out in lines 1116–744):

---

[204] Some of these catchwords are absent, presumably cut off in rebinding.

[205] The blank leaves were filled by a later hand with prose excerpts from Isidore and others (Macray, *Bodleian Quarto Catalogues* IX: *Digby Manuscripts*). The collation of Digby 27 is as follows: 1¹⁰2¹⁰3¹⁰4¹²5¹⁶6⁶7³. The last three folios, a bifolium and a singleton, are clearly later additions. See the Manuscript Descriptions in Appendix A.

civ INTRODUCTION

1. Variants unacceptable because of sense or syntax

53 quisquam (cum quis); 139 cuncta (multa); 216 quod fuit ante lutum (mollia cuncta prius) (*near-repetition of line 217*); 440 ad (uel); 774 cura (charta); 1409 surgentes (surgendi); 1444 rediens (rediit).

2. Easier substitutions (*lectiones faciliores*)

438 in nullo (parue pari)

3. Variants which are not identifiable as error but are rejected because agreement between other branches of the stemma provides more support for the alternatives:

124 tibi (sibi); 218 habent (erant); 440 seua (nulla); 484 multos (stultos).

However, it is clear that *GI* could have derived all their β readings from *H* (or to be more precise, its exemplar) alone. In addition to the *BHGI* variants given above, the following readings demonstrate the *HGI* relationship (archetypal readings in parentheses as usual):[206]

91 iam (nam); 114 quem (quam); 139 soluere (uoluere); 232 solent (student); 302 sepe (mixta); 323 regum (regis); 362 putes (putas); 431 furor nimiumque (nimium feruorque); 541 hec (hinc); 663 collata (collecta); 828 facile (facilis). *GI* also contain the spurious lines added by *H* after the first half of line 405 (and then deleted). *HG* also agree in omitting 1710–11, without any cause for eyeskip (*I* is out at this point). The only counter-examples occur at line 739, where *BGI* have 'fori' for *H*'s 'forum', and in lines 1553–4, where *BG* render the donkey's 'heehaw' as 'iha', while *H* has 'yha', but the first could be an example of convergent variation, and the second is a mere spelling variant. Elsewhere, when *B* agrees with *GI* against *H*, it is because *BGI* preserve the correct reading of ω, the common archetype (see 2709, 'specula qua' *BGIX*; 2718 'tot uini cyati' *BGIY*).

In the second half of the poem, *GI* switch their allegiance to δ, as is shown in the first instance by the fact that they include after line 2412 the Interpolation on the Mendicant Orders, which is also found in *MNDK* (all of which are δ manuscripts). *GI* and δ also share the following examples of agreement in error:

1. Variants unacceptable because of sense or syntax

1843 sumptis (spretis); 1979 peperit (periit); 1994 talem...mihi (tamen...nihil); 2000 graues (magis); 2071 trimordi (trinodi); 2109–10 *om.*; 2253 scire (lite); 2267 pereat (pariat); 2277 albo (albedo); 2291 dura (duris); 2310–11 *om.* (*eyeskip*: si foret); 2317 lex noua lutumque (lex est licitumque); 2407–8 *om.* (*eyeskip*: Canoni–...sorores); 2419–20

---

[206] I restrict examples to the portions of the text where *BHGI* are all present, to show that the absence of *B* or *I* is not a result of their physical lacunae.

TEXTUAL TRANSMISSION

om. (*eyeskip*: mihi); 2478 sed pascit (depascit); 2481 fata...uerum mea facta (fila...neuerunt fata); 2509 pudoris (prioris); 2593 reseruant (serenant); 2609 sanabile (insanabile).

2. Variants unacceptable for metrical reasons
2013 lăbōr// ĕt ēst (lăbōr// lăbŏr ēst).

3. Easier substitutions (*lectiones faciliores*)
1877 seruus certissimus (tuus immo tuissimus); 1893 necnon (miser et); 2193 assumpto uellere (sicco cum subere).[207]

The following *GIδ* variants are acceptable in themselves but are rejected because there is more support from different manuscript groups for the alternatives:
1759 et ueniant (introeant); 1778 non sapienter (insipienter); 1797 pontificis tanti nunc tempora (praesule defuncto modo plurima); 1968 nomen surripuit urbis ubi studui (surripuit uerbum quod fuit ante meum); 2476 nocuere mihi (mihi ferre solent); 2735 laceras (uacuas).

The agreement with δ is not, however, complete: for example, 2619–20 are omitted in δ but not in *GI*. There are also other substantial agreements of *GI* with β in the second half of the poem: 2725 tendit sua brachia mundus *BHGIUXZQY* (quidam sua brachia tendit); 2743–4 *om. BHGIQY*. The common ancestor of *GI* must therefore have been closer to the common archetype of all the manuscripts (ω) than to the common ancestor of δ, and the agreements with δ may well result from contamination, since it is obvious that the scribe of the *GI* ancestor had access to both β and δ readings.

Manuscript X

As Mozley notes (p. 19), *X* is generally aligned with δ up to line 1500 or thereabouts—that is, at roughly the same point of the poem when *GI* shift allegiance from β to δ; from this point until the end of the poem, *X* shows frequent (though not constant) agreements with β. One explanation that has been proposed is that *GI* and *X* were each using one half of a split β manuscript, and for the missing halves were obliged to resort to a manuscript of the δ family. However this is untenable for a number of reasons, the most obvious being that *BH* end at 3864 but *X* continues after this point and ends at 3900, like the δ group. A number of δ readings also appear in this final section of the poem. Another reason is that *X* is consistently in agreement with β in the *Epistle to William* (examples given below), showing that it had access to β readings from the outset.

---

[207] See Notes on this line.

cvi   INTRODUCTION

Examples of characteristic δ variants appearing in X in the first half of the poem are the following: 17 reuoluo (recordor); 87 nequibat (negabat); 153 modo (nunc); 214 concubuere (procubuere); 317 raro (sero); 394 castigat (sepeliuit); 497 mihi dum coniuncta (dum me comitata); 527 pariter conturbat (pecudum turbator); 546 stimulant mordent (stimulos acuunt); 600 tutius ire domum (stulte redito domum); 621 noli tardare pedester (nocuit differre paratis); 763 hic teneo (emimus hic); 773 et cuncta (tenus ore); 791 nomen Burnellus mihi stat (nomine Burnellus dicor); 924 leditur et (laesa sed est); 940 criminis ultor erit (plus tamen istud eo); 955 illius (illata); 1295 sanum (sura); 1376 profert (promit); 1411 maxima (plurima); 1420 hic iaceat (ille bibat); 1462 dare (reddo); 1504 ueniunt (subeunt). X also shares the distinctive δ forms of lines 742 and 1062, and the distinctive δ omissions at 941–4, 1169–72, 1185–6, 1275–6, 1302–3,[208] 1409–10, 1885–6, 3518–19.

Manuscript D naturally contains all these δ variants, and it also appears in exclusive agreement with X in numerous variants up to line 1600 or so.[209] For example: 13 historia breuiter (historiae breuitas); 20 sepe (omne); 118 nocuisse (nocuere); 159 et paruo congruit ergo (breuis es, nihil utilitatis); 160 *whole line*; 240 et gemuit (ingemuit); 332 suum (statum); 444 sed non (non tamen); 527 urit (agit); 565 socios (comites); 720 ait (orat); 750 res manifesta docet (nec latuisse potes); 774 docet (notat); 864 alcius (acrius); 978 uera (certa); 979 perrexerit (conspexerit); 986 que quasi sint (uel potius); 1114 cibum (suum); 1124 mihi natura; 1194 *whole line*; 1223 dans oscula querit (dedit oscula quarens); 1292 cor retinet (corda tenent); 1293 patrias (proprias); 1307 sed nec (nec auet); 1477 uicto (uictor); 1510 roba (tunica); 1549 diu laborando (diuque laborans).[210]

This simple picture of δX agreement is, however, complicated not only by the fact that X lacks the Interpolation on the Mendicant Orders which appears in D (and the δ manuscripts MNK), but also by the numerous instances where X diverges both from D and from δ and

---

[208] On this particular omission, see n. 210 below.

[209] And even afterwards: at line 2072, X adds in the margin the D reading 'prope nullus' as an alternative to 'profinellus'.

[210] X's omission at lines 1302–4 is a good demonstration of the DX relationship: instead of simply omitting 1302–3, like most δ manuscripts, after writing the first word of 1302 ('Dum'), X continues with a wholly new line which replaces 1304. Evidently X's exemplar resembled D in that it lacked 1304 as well as 1302–3, so that when X noticed the lack of a pentameter to follow 1301 he could not (like the other δ manuscripts) go straight to 1304 and had to fill the gap with his own invention.

TEXTUAL TRANSMISSION cvii

aligns with other branches of the stemma.[211] Examples are: 24 et stabiles non habet (instabiles nunc habet); 114 opem (opis); 137 modico
(medico); 222 patet (placet); 397 nocentior (nociuior); 723 sportaeque
(porteque); 1025 decipiam (accipiam). In addition, X has lines 1070–1,
which are omitted from δ.

Nevertheless it is clear that X's main affiliation changes after 1600
or so. After 1409–10, it has none of the many δ omissions except the
final one at 3518–19. Instead, it almost always agrees with the αβγ tradition against δ. Examples are the following:[212] 1608 puto (meo); 1750
quidnam uirtutis (nil ergo uitii); 1831 infitiando (insistendo); 1877
tuus immo tuissimus (seruus certisssimus); 1994 tamen...nihil
(talem...mihi); 2175 falsi...ficti (ficti...furti); 2317 lex est licitumque (lex noua lutumque); 2412 melo (mero/metro); 2477–8 flagel-
lat/ sed (flagella /dat). Sometimes, as Mozley noted (*SS*, p. 19), the
variant is exclusive to β and X: 1693–4 genitalia mulus/ gestat *BHX*;
1990 sic maneat *BHX*; 2114 me *BHX*; 2408 quas simul in unum *BHX*;
2481–2 sed...nequeo *BHX*; 2652 morsibus *BHX*. However, at 2218 X
agrees with αγ ('iura') rather than β ('uita') against δ's 'uota', while at
1951 X reads 'uicina', with most of δ (but not D) against the correct
reading 'uienna'.[213] And from about line 2500 to the end of the poem,
X's allegiances fluctuate continually. It often reverts to δ, as in the following examples (δX reading given first, followed by the β reading): 2593
reseruant (serenant); 2893 uidebar (iuuabat); 2907 timendo (timere);
2925 sanctior unus (stemmate maior); 3385 composuere (compositurae); 3481 omni (esse) 3562 nocior urbe (nota Cremona). However, this
stretch of the poem in X also includes β readings[214] (βX readings given
first, followed by the δ reading), such as 2599 repellunt (refellunt);
2636 longe (iure); 2696 proiciuntque macrum[215] *BX* (quod uile despiciunt); 2723 ut (et); 2792 quod (hinc); 2911 fixo pede (et fixo); 3677
rapiens (capiens); 3690 sua (sui).

As mentioned above, X also shows steady agreement with groups
other than δ in the *Epistle*. It aligns with β, or with αβγ, in archetypal
readings against a δ variant in the following examples (X reading given

---

[211] In the following examples, the lemma is the reading of X, and the reading in parentheses is that of δ (including D). To save space, I have not specified the manuscript groups
that agree with X; they may be found in my *apparatus criticus*.
[212] The αβγ reading is given first, and the variant in parentheses is the δ reading.
[213] See above, p. xcvi, and below, p. cxxiii and n. 259.
[214] It will be recalled that α is out from 2483 to 3258, and γ ends at 2602.
[215] This β reading is that accepted in my text, not a rejected reading.

cviii   INTRODUCTION

first):[216] *Epistle* 1 et in christo (sibi in christo et semper); *Epistle* 9
inferri (inseri); *Epistle* 10 deputatus (mancipatus); *Epistle* 10 potest
(poterit); *Epistle* 12 omnimodis (omnibus modis); *Epistle* 14 audito
(audiat); *Epistle* 17 demoratae (commorate); *Epistle* 17 quo (ubi); *Epistle*
19 aduersis (angustiis); *Epistle* 24 nec aliquid infirmum—in minimo
(qui in aliquo leuiter seu grauiter); *Epistle* 33 inani (manuum); *Epistle*
37 ex toto (omnino confusus); *Epistle* 38 faceret (tolleret). *X* shares a
variant reading with β in the following examples: *Epistle* 3 meis *om.*
HGIX; *Epistle* 6 neque *HGIX* (nequaquam); *Epistle* 15 suadet omnino
HGIX (suadet; δ suadeat); *Epistle* 15 posse *om.* *HRKGIX*; *Epistle* 19
adquiescens (adquiescere); *Epistle* 30 caudam suam *HGIX* (caudam);
Epistle 44 discendo *om.* *HGIX*.

These fluctuating patterns cannot be explained by the theory of a
split manuscript. It might be supposed that *X* is a thoroughly contaminated manuscript, and this supposition might seem to be confirmed by the fact that it contains a large number of corrected readings.
However examination of the corrections shows that they do not arise
from the scribe's comparison of a manuscript from one branch of the
stemma with another. The only example that fits this description is line
3254, where 'flagitiosus', the reading of *BHUX*, has the marginal addition 'uel religiosus', the reading of δ. Elsewhere, by far the most usual
pattern is that a distinctive error in *X* (i.e., a reading with no parallel
elsewhere) is corrected to the majority reading, which could have been
derived from any of the branches of the stemma, or indeed simply
from renewed attention to X's exemplar.[217] Some of the *X* readings
before correction have parallels with *D* or *H* (or *HGI*),[218] but there is
no consistent pattern to these links. As with the alternative readings in
TrHaLa, it proves impossible to identify two competing stemmatic
affiliations in these corrections.

The only other explanation of the fluctuations between β and δ in *X*
that suggests itself is that this manuscript perhaps represents a stage in
the scribal evolution of the text from β to δ.

Manuscript U

Manuscript *U* presents a number of challenges. In the first place, as
noted earlier, it has a number of major lacunae as a result of missing
leaves: it lacks lines 1–1042, 2351–677, 3359–412. However, it concludes

---

[216] I omit simple changes in word order.
[217] See the examples in the *apparatus criticus* for lines 13, 33, 173, 241, 539, 542, 770, 836,
2010, 2093, 3092.
[218] See the *apparatus criticus* for lines 288, 362, 533, 952, 1360.

TEXTUAL TRANSMISSION

at line 3864, as do the β manuscripts *B* and *H*, which provides the first clue to its affiliation.

Closer examination produces a more complicated picture. *U* frequently omits one or two lines, most of which are added in the lower margin by a different hand (U^2). On the face of it, one would suppose it possible to identify the affiliation both of *U*'s exemplar and of the manuscript used to supply the missing lines, by comparing the omissions (or lack of them) in other branches of the stemma. However, most of *U*'s omissions are unique to this manuscript (see the *apparatus criticus* for lines 1579, 1588, 1947–8, 1966–7, 1978–9, 2049, 2154–5, 2895–6, 2960–1, 3722). All of these lines were later added by U^2, but it is not immediately clear from which of the other main branches of the stemma the corrector took them. Of the many omissions characteristic of the δ manuscripts (see p. xcii above), *U* shares only six (1070–1, 2109–10, 2310–11, 2918b–20a, 3122b–4a, 3643–4) but significantly in these six cases the missing lines are *not* supplied by U^2. This means that *U* cannot have been using a δ manuscript as its main exemplar, but could have been using one for the corrections. This impression is confirmed when one considers the lines omitted by *U* and also by other manuscript groups, viz.: 1076–7* (*aHTFrPmDUX*); 1302–3* (*FγδTrHaLaUZX*); 2743–4 (*βAGIUQY*); 3314–19* (*βδTrHaLaUZX*); 3785–6 (*BδTrHaLaUZQY*); 3810–11* (*BδTrHaLaUZQY*).[219] Of these omissions, only 1076–7 and 2743–4—that is, the omissions *not* shared by δ—are corrected by U^2.[220] So far, the picture agrees with Mozley's impression that *U* is a <u>b</u> (αβγ) manuscript which has been corrected by an <u>a</u> (δ) manuscript.

In addition to supplying missing lines, the correcting hand (U^2) has erased and rewritten numerous words and phrases throughout. In almost every instance, the corrections are recognizable as δ readings; for example, 1295 sanum; 1749 et uia duxque; 1831 insistendo; 1877 seruus certissimus; 1926 qualis ego; 2244 carnes; 2277 albo; 2718 uestibus ornati; 2737 splendida...aula; 2893 uidebar; 2901 sub; 3129 (=3134a) *whole line*. The αβγ substratum of *U*'s text is also very often in evidence, and becomes increasingly prominent towards the end of the poem, as if the corrector was becoming tired. See, for example, 1198 audentes; 1285 inde...stimulabat; 1376 promit; 1411 plurima;

---

[219] Asterisked numbers could have been caused by eyeskip.

[220] *U*'s unique omission of 1168b–69a is remedied by the insertion of two lines into the main text at 1185, but they agree with the αβγ version of these lines, not δ. It seems therefore that the main scribe omitted these in copying but soon noticed the error and inserted the missing lines at the point in copying that he had reached.

CX INTRODUCTION

1462 reddo; 1486 uices; 1504 subeunt; 1608 puto; 1714 monstrua membra; 1778 insipienter; 1951 uienna; 3197 frequentant; 3254 flagitiosus; 3472 colo; 3481 esse; 3501 -que meas; 3640 quas; 3708 abstulit; 3848 inficietur opus.

Since, however, the α manuscripts lack 2483–3258 and end at 3448, while the γ manuscripts end at 2602, neither of these branches of the stemma can have furnished U's exemplar, which must have been related to β (as is indicated by the ending at 3864). Variants shared with β include the following: 2684 decipiatque; 2686 primis; 2687 sed; 2725 tendit sua brachia mundus; 2907 timere; 3496 effectus. The initial readings of U do not, however, entirely coincide with those of β (BH); there are numerous δ readings which are not the result of correction but are part of the original text. Examples are: 1062 *whole line*; 1307 aue; 1434 largus; 1567 periitque labor sed; 1619 cur; 1759 et ueniant; 1797 pontificis tanti nunc tempora; 1893 necnon; 2047 nisi quod; 2088 sepe licebit eis; 2175 ficti...furti; 2193 assumpto uellere; 2253 scire; 2259 semper; 2735 laceras; 2756 dedit; 2803 arcius; 2848 nefas; 2925 sanctior unus; 3046 atque; 3053 beamur; 3563–4 *transp. after 3566*; 3701 adiret. It seems improbable to suppose, as Mozley seems to (SS, p. 22), that the scribe was working from both a β manuscript and a δ manuscript simultaneously, selecting readings from one or the other as the mood took him; the many corrections from δ, which are clearly in a different hand and entered some time after the copying of the main text, suggest that the δ manuscript was acquired only later and that U's exemplar emanated from the β tradition, but had already developed some variants characteristic of δ,[221] and had indeed moved rather further in that direction than X. Indicative of this is that whereas there is a sizable number of agreements between BHX, BX or HX, similar agreements between U and BH are lacking.

Manuscripts Q, Y, and Z

Manuscripts Q and Y are closely related, as is overwhelmingly clear from their shared omissions.[222] Both lack the story of Gundulf and the cock (1249–1502), and a large section stretching from the end of the

---

[221] I can find no evidence to support Mozley's assertion (SS, p. 22) that U is specially close to G, and such evidence would in any case necessarily be sparse, given that G ends at 2746 and U lacks 1–1042 and 2351–677, so they do not have much text in common. Their only similarity is their general relation to the β tradition.

[222] Mozley (SS, p. 20) notes the major omissions in Y, but fails to record that they are shared by Q, and also fails to comment on the very many minor omissions shared by this pair. He acknowledges that his collation of Y is 'only partial'.

TEXTUAL TRANSMISSION

bird debate to the end of the story of the Three Fates (3233–458). The latter omission would seem too large a jump to be caused by eyeskip, but it is significant that line 3459 in QY begins 'talia dicenti niso' (the first half of line 3233) instead of 'talia dicenti subito' (the correct beginning of line 3459); this suggests that the story of the Three Fates was deliberately omitted, the cut neatly effected by skipping between these near-identical phrases.[223]

QY also share many smaller omissions. First, the section on the Grandmontine order lacks lines 2211–12 and 2215–24, and the section on the order of Sempringham is cut entirely, both in Burnellus's initial survey and in the account of his own 'ideal' order (2401–12, 2451–8). This also looks like a deliberate excision, very probably because Sempringham was little known outside of England. And a deliberate intention to abbreviate can also be suspected in a number of the many two-line omissions, where Nigel's rhetorical repetitions signal his expansions on a limited theme, offering opportunities to cut. For example, the repetition of 'semper' at the beginning of lines 2233 and 2235 could have prompted the excision of lines 2233–6, similarly with 'sic' in lines 2279–82, or 'si foret' at the end of 2305–12. Whatever their cause, there are nearly 50 of these small omissions which are found only in QY, viz.: 403–4, 411–14, 421–2, 437–8, 475–8, 491–2, 585–6, 731–4, 770–2, 807–10, 816–18, 839–40, 863–4, 895–6, 917–18, 927–8, 937–40, 949–54, 963, 981–2, 1011–12, 1015–18, 1031–2, 1061–2, 1071, 1089–92, 1103–4, 1137–8, 1167–76, 1189–90, 1195–6, 1209–10, 2233–6, 2239–40, 2247–50, 2252–5, 2279–82, 2297–8, 2305–12, 2601–2, 2607–10, 2613–14, 2621–2, 2627–32, 2641–2, 2915–16, 3161–4. A few omissions are shared with other manuscripts, e.g. 407–8, 929–30, 2743–4, 3565–6, 3785–6, 3810–11, but they reveal no regular alignments. For example, QY share only three of the characteristic δ omissions, viz. 1185–6, 2918b–20a, 3122b–4a. There are three omissions shared with Z, which are significant in the light of the connections between Z and QY to be discussed below, but these pale in significance when compared to the number of QY omissions.

The close relationship between Q and Y is also demonstrated by their frequent exclusive agreements in error. Examples, with the correct readings given in parentheses, are as follows: 116 omnia dura (gratia diua); 272 recitat (resistit); 401 praua (inane; prata ZX); 587 dicite (discite); 790 ut quidem (duxeris ut); 1136 lassa (lapsa); 1887 uite (ante); 1923 roma (Iouis); 2126 nigra (uirga); 2189 loca (lata); 2259

---

[223] Cf. p. lxxi above. There is no sign of lost leaves at this point in either manuscript.

cxii INTRODUCTION

semperque (non spernunt); 2336 micat (nutat); 2369 poterit cito terrea (leuis est et cerea); 2527 inopis poculum (in os patulum); 2793 nisi (uisa); 2985 nemo (non); 3596 iniuncus (inuitus); 3890 recte (illud); 3891 qui fuit (quaesiuit).

Q and *Y*, however, each have a number of unique omissions which indicate that neither manuscript is a copy of the other: *Q* lacks 385, 624–5, 656, 1525–6, 1991b–2a, 2291b–2a, 2379b–80a, while *Y* lacks 1163–6 (*add. Y*[pc]), 2460, 2633–4, and 2838. In addition, the readings of *Q* and *Y* often diverge from each other, and each of them also has unique variants, of which *Q* has a far larger number (almost 300)[224] than *Y*, mostly of a trivial nature.

In terms of their relation with one or other of the larger manuscript groups (αβγ as against δ), *QY* fluctuate constantly throughout the poem. Examples of agreement with αβγ readings are the following (the δ variant is given in parenthesis):

17 recordor (reuoluo); 153 nunc (modo); 397 nocentior (nociuior); 430 praeterita (tunc munda); 527 pecudum turbator/ur (pariter conturbat); 660 fac (tu); 763 emimus hic (hic teneo); 791 nomine Burnellus dicor (nomen burnellus mihi stat); 902 ratus ipse (meditando);[225] 955 illata (illius); 1504 subeunt (ueniunt); 1608 puto (meo); 1877 tuus (debet *Q*) immo tuissimus (seruus certissimus); 1951 uienna (uicina/propinqua); 2038 suo (bono); 2244 pisces (carnes).

However, since *QY* go all the way to line 3900 (despite their large omissions), while α lacks 2483–3258 and 3449–900, and γ ends at 2602, the only possible sources for lines 2603–3259 and 3449–900 are β and δ. Agreements between *Q* and β are the following (δ reading in parentheses): 2725 tendit sua brachia mundus (quidam sua brachia tendit); 2737 regia...alta (splendida...aula); 2781 sicut ait (sic dixit); 2893 iuuabat (uidebar); 2928 scire (fore); 3197 frequentant (sequantur); 3481 esse (omni); 3501 sportellasque meas (sportellas eneas); 3603 ego (ait); 3710 tulit (ferens).

On the other hand, *QY* include a roughly equal number of typical δ readings, which appear all the way through the poem; for example (the αβγ reading is given in parentheses):

214 concubuere (procubuere); 394 castigat (sepeliuit); 497 mihi dum coniuncta (dum me comitata); 546 stimulant mordent (stimulos

---

[224] There are obviously too many to list them all, but for examples, see the *apparatus criticus* for lines 27, 36, 41, 48, 70, 81, 94, 135, 136, 139, 146, 148, etc.

[225] *B* is out from 849–1386 because of lost leaves, so that in these lines β is represented by *H* alone.

TEXTUAL TRANSMISSION

acuunt); 580 mundana (Q mundata) (discreta); 600 tutius ire domum (stultus adesto domi H, stultus es esto domi B); 621 noli tardare pedester (nocuit differre paratis); 723 porteque (sportaeque); 742 *whole line*; 773 et cuncta (tenus ore); 936 absque (atque);[226] 1025 accipiam (decipiam); 1968 *whole line*; 2000 graues (magis); 2019 paribus (partitur); 2088 sepe licebit eis (non licet illud ibi); 2175 ficti... furti (falsi... ficti); 2277 albo (albedo). In the following examples, where first α and then γ are absent (see above), Q agrees with δ against β: 2593 reseruant (serenant); 2612 ciues... gemunt (uices... gerunt); 2911 et fixo (fixo pede); 2925 sanctior unus (stemmate maior); 2959 facta (cuncta); 3046 atque (immo); 3516 factis uerba (uerbis facta); 3848 rege iubente suo (infitiatur (insisitatur H) opus).

While QY do not manifest their 'mixed' character by including alternative readings or corrections made as a result of consulting another manuscript after copying, it is clear that their allegiances are fairly evenly split between β and δ throughout the poem. This would suggest that like X they belong to a stage intermediate between β and δ, at a point when the poem had already been extended to 3,900 lines, but when the introduction of δ readings was not fully complete. That is, the δ readings are not the product of contamination, but represent an interstitial stage in the scribal development of the text.

Manuscript Z, on the other hand, is clearly contaminated, as is shown by the 35 instances where it provides two versions of the same line (see the *apparatus criticus* for lines 33, 229, 231, 325, 345, 385, 467, 472, 600, 601, 621, 634, 647, 742, 761, 923, 924, 933, 957, 1070, 1085, 1127, 1128, 1535, 1579, 1968, 2047, 2266, 2338, 2343, 2524, 2548, 2833, 3830, 3831). These alternative versions provide the first clue to the dual affiliations of Z. As with the alternative readings offered by Ha and La, the Z variants sometimes have no parallels at all elsewhere in the transmission,[227] but where they do reflect the readings of other manuscripts, they reveal that the affiliations are with QY on the one hand and γ on the other. The evidence in these 35 instances is too complicated to set out in detail but can be viewed in the *apparatus criticus* for the lines cited above with the exception of 33, 467, 647, 781, 1128, 1579, 2833, 3830–1. It is significant that there are no examples from lines 1249–1502, which are lacking in QY, and only two examples after line 2602, where the γ manuscripts end. Line 2833 has only minimal variations, which lack any parallels elsewhere and read like attempts on

---

[226] See preceding note.
[227] For example, line 33 'pro parcis' ($Z(2)$).

cxiv INTRODUCTION

the scribe's part to make sense of his exemplar; as for line 3830, $Z_{(2)}$ is very close to the variant version in *R Tr*, while $Z_{(1)}$ similarly reproduces a nearly exact copy of line 3831 in *R Tr*. What is striking is that no major δ variant plays a part in these two versions.

Z's twin affiliation to γ and to QY is amply confirmed in the rest of the poem. As a demonstration of Z's close relation to QY, one can cite examples of exclusive agreement between these three manuscripts, as follows (the text as printed in this edition is given in parenthesis): 86 flet dum per medicos (ante tamen quam); 415–18 *transp. after 420*; 419–20 *transp. after 410*; 451 clarus *om.*; 451 auras frigidasque calescat (frigidas calefecit QY) (deuexus in auras); 473 heu mihi quid faciam (quaeque nimis praeceps); 538 queque nimis tuta (queque tuta minus[228]); 636 male (bene); 649 liberam (libram); 750 res patet ipsa palam (nec latuisse potes); 905 necnon satis ampla platea (quam rebar et esse plateam); 911–12 *om.*; 919 si fateor (fatear XY) uerum (quod tamen auxerunt); 922 incommodum tantum (nostram papa suam); 1069 *new line added*: Et dare que uoluit premia dantur ei; 1105–6 *transp. after 1108*; [QY are out from 1249–1502] 1797 presule burnello (burnelle Y) (praesule defuncto); 2109a/2110 *whole line*; 2293–4 *om.*; 2315 seculares sunt uocitati (seculares quique uocati); 2344 fallit est quia (uera motio); 2735–6 *om.*; 2817 postposito (posthabito); 2917 nemorose (morosae); 3061 dixerunt queque (miscent aconita); 3125 erat cibus (et eunuchus); 3470 atque (atra); 3539 nostri *om.*; 3870 *whole line*; 3882 *whole line*. The list could be vastly extended if examples where ZQY are joined by one or two other manuscripts were to be added, but only D and X appear with any frequency and it seems best to avoid blurring the picture and to confine the examples to ZQY alone.

Up to line 2602, Z also shares numerous distinctive γ readings. See, for example, the following (alternative readings in parentheses):[229] 152 commodius* (facilius); 357 leui (breui); 434 consociisque* (pastoribusque); 772 clamat (fingit); 1262 ualet (licet); 1275–6 *transp. after 1278*; 1287 labente (crescente); 1311 iam lustrum fecerat ille (sextum iam pullus in annum); 1324–5 *om.*; 1335 cunctis (tempus); 1335 prefigitur (praescribitur); 1347 includit (excludit); 1363 subiecit (suggessit); 1395 absorptus (absumptus); 1407 *om.*; 1408–9 *transp.*; 1409a *new line added*; 1414 preteriisse (dissiluisse); 1418 in hoc (ego); 1455 mater (genetrix); 1457 et si (quamuis); 1591 multum si (uel multum); 1707 et

---

[228] This is the closest of the many variants at this point.

[229] Asterisked readings are those γ readings which probably derive from the ultimate archetype (see above, p. xci) and have been accepted into my text.

TEXTUAL TRANSMISSION CXV

plus (quoniam); 1822 fugam (uiam); 2070 scindere ligna domus (ligna referre domum); 2103 premia (praedia); 2219 mox (Mons); 2312 curam (causam); 2380 dogmate (smigmate); 2408–9 *om.*; 2516 *whole line*; 2524 *whole line*; 2567 saluacione (sumpta carne).

As already noted, it is striking that δ plays no significant role in Z's readings. Where Z does agree with a δ variant, this is for the most part because the variant in question is also in QY or β or γ. The few exceptions can plausibly be attributed to convergent variation; e.g., 2686 primo (primis); 2824 augustino[230] (Augustini); 3011 amisi (admisi); 3481 omni[231] (esse); 3603 ait (ego). It should be borne in mind, however, that Z cannot derive from Q or Y directly (as shown by its lack of QY's omissions, both major and minor), so that it must have taken its QY readings from their common ancestor, which did not necessarily contain either the minor or the major omissions of QY themselves. Examples where δZ agreement may reflect the reading of a common ancestor of QY are the following: 2609 sanabile[232] (insanabile); 2709 speculo...quo[233] (specula...qua). Significantly, the most substantial set of examples occurs in lines 3233–458 (the story of the Three Fates), which are lacking in QY, but which, as already suggested, may well have been in QY's ancestor (see above, pp. cx–cxi). This would account for the δZ agreements which suddenly appear in line 3250, and just as suddenly end at line 3439: 3250 reor (rear); 3254 religiosus (flagitiosus); 3259 statuo (statui); 3339 parasset (pararet); 3385 composuere (compositurae); 3399 uidetis (timetis); 3438 illud (istud); 3439 illud (istud).

In other words, Z, like X, represents a stage in the transmission between βγ and δ, before δ had assumed its final form.[234]

Conclusion

Close study of the 'mixed' manuscripts shows that they are not all of the same kind. Some switch allegiances in mid-stream; some originally belong to one manuscript group but were later corrected by reference to another; in other cases, the scribe had access to two (or more) manuscripts from the start; still others represent an intermediate stage in

---

[230] Which will have been influenced by 'Bernardo...Benedicto' in the preceding line.

[231] Following the comparative 'nocentior', 'omni' is an easier reading.

[232] The fact that this is the reading of H and X strengthens the presumption that it might have been in the QY ancestor.

[233] Again, H agrees with δZ, while Q has 'speculo...qui' and Y has 'speculo...qua'; they may be misreporting 'speculo...quo' in their exemplar.

[234] Z's isolated position is also indicated by its exceedingly large number of unique variants (even more than Q's), which were not taken over by any other manuscript.

cxvi INTRODUCTION

the development of the text, which could possibly be determined with greater accuracy if we were in possession of all the early manuscripts. The 'mixed' manuscripts do not play the most significant role in determining what Nigel originally wrote, but they help to explain how the major manuscript groups came into being, and thus to determine the relative weight to be attached to each of these groups.

The Question of Revision

In Mozley's first article (1929) on the manuscripts of the *Speculum Stultorum*, he suggested two explanations for the differences between the shape of the poem in *LEF* and other manuscripts: (1) physical damage—that is, the common exemplar of *LEF* had lost some leaves,[235] and (2) *LEF* represent the earliest form of the work and the portions of the poem that they lack are later additions.[236] In a later article (1930),[237] he reviews evidence in favour of (2), *but* although he concludes that some *LEF* variants are an improvement on their counterparts in MS *A* (treated as representative of the δ group), others are, in his opinion, the reverse.[238] Furthermore, the tradition of *A* variants continues through other manuscripts, such as *B*, which have all or nearly all the poem, suggesting (to Mozley) that the original of *LEF* had it too. He concludes that 'on the whole this evidence is against the hypothesis [that *LEF* represents an earlier and shorter edition of the poem]' and that this hypothesis 'must therefore be left unproved'.[239]

The logic behind this conclusion is hard to see. The fact that *A* resembles *B* in containing a full-length version of the poem, and that these two manuscripts (plus a number of others which are left unspecified by Mozley) share numerous variants in the portion of the poem not contained by *LEF*, in no way indicates the existence of a common ancestor of *A* and *B* which pre-dates the common ancestor of *LEF*. A full collation of all the manuscripts suggests rather that *B* is a first expansion of *LEF*, and that *A* is representative of a group that is later still (see, for example, its many omissions, which are not shared by *LEF* or *BH*).

---

[235] 'On the text of the *Speculum Stultorum*' (1929), p. 434.

[236] Ibid. p. 435.

[237] 'On the text and manuscripts of the *Speculum Stultorum*' (1930).

[238] For discussion of the *LEF* variants at 621 and 742, the two examples cited by Mozley, see below, p. cxxii.

[239] 'On the text and manuscripts of the *Speculum Stultorum*' (1930), p. 261.

TEXTUAL TRANSMISSION cxvii

It seems that Mozley has allowed himself to be unduly influenced by the fact that *A* is the oldest manuscript of the poem (thirteenth century). This influence is also perceptible in the stemma that he provides on p. 23 of the 1960 edition of the *Speculum Stultorum*, which gives a list of (putative) manuscript dates at the left-hand side. *A* thus takes pride of place, being placed highest against the date-list, and nearest to Nigel's autograph, with other manuscripts belonging to the same group (my δ) ranged below. Over to the right, Mozley places 'Nigel's revision', from which he derives *LEF*, *GIU*, *BHX*, and the manuscripts ending at 2602 (my group γ), with *YQZ* between the two groups, since they share features of both. This putative 'revision' does not account for the large-scale differences in the overall length and shape of the poem; it concerns only individual words and phrases. Recognizing that the readings of αβγ manuscripts are generally preferable to those of δ, Mozley does not draw the obvious conclusion that δ contains a larger number of scribal corruptions, and is therefore later than αβγ; instead, he explains it by assuming that αβγ represent Nigel's second thoughts. This hypothesis does not explain how the α archetype of this 'revised version' lost large portions of the poem which are nevertheless contained in manuscripts that both precede and follow *LEF*. Nor does it explain, for example, the presence of the Interpolation on the Mendicant Orders in *MNDKGI*, since Mozley's stemma shows *MN* and *DK* as deriving from the same ancestor as *RYPO* (which do not have the Interpolation), and *GI* as belonging to a different branch of the stemma altogether. Contamination might be invoked to explain this scattered pattern, but why should it operate in such a random manner?

The Stemma and the Construction of the Text

Bearing in mind my earlier discussion of the probable evolution of the poem from a shorter to a longer version, as well as the detailed analysis of the shared readings that establish the different manuscript groups and their interrelations, it is possible to sketch a different stemma (see Stemma 1, p. xix), and to use it in establishing the text.

The classic way of constructing a stemma is to identify an increasing number of errors in its various branches. If a hypothetical branch p has five errors, and branch q has the same five plus another five in addition, then evidently q derives from p. However if p and q are separately derived from the ultimate archetype, this neat pattern does not necessarily hold: q will probably not repeat all of p's five mistakes and instead will in some instances preserve the correct reading of the archetype.

cxviii INTRODUCTION

Conversely, *q* will have some mistakes of its own, where *p* preserves the readings of the archetype. Contamination, and the possibility that scribes may be able to correct simple errors on their own initiative, complicate the pattern still further. In a situation involving over 40 manuscripts, most of which are separated by two or three centuries from the author's original, the possible complications are dauntingly numerous. It is, however, possible to discern a general preponderance of error which suggests that αβγ are closer to the author's original than δ. The split between the two can be seen in Mozley's division of the manuscripts into two major groups, which he labelled <u>a</u> (comprising ACJMNDKOP) and <u>b</u> (comprising EFLSBH).[240] His list of the variant readings distinguishing these two groups is (characteristically) marred by inaccuracies; a corrected version is provided below.[241] My sigla reverse Mozley's <u>ab</u> order, using α for *LEF*, because I believe (as argued above) that *LEF* represents the earliest and shortest version of the poem, and that *BH* is a separate group containing the earliest version of the long redaction. In my view, the main function of Mozley's list is to illustrate the divergence between δ and αβγ; in every case the <u>a</u> reading is that of δ (or a substantial proportion of the δ group), joined, after 2602, by *TrHaLa*,[242] while Mozley's <u>b</u> list gives the readings of αβγ.[243]

Mozley's list, corrected:

<u>a</u> readings (= my δ)		<u>b</u> readings (= my αβγ)	
17	reuoluo	recordor	
33	prodigiosus	prodigiosos	
87	nequibat	negabat	
114	opis	opem	
153	modo	nunc	
222	*placet	patet	
262	quoque...nunc	quaque...tunc	
314	subtraxit	subtraheret	

[240] Mozley also identified a group he labelled <u>c</u>, which is identical with my group γ, but he gives it much less importance, and the 'mixed' manuscripts even less.

[241] In Mozley's Introduction, <u>a</u> and <u>b</u> are underlined, but in the *apparatus criticus* they are not, which can lead to confusion at various points between the Latin preposition 'a, ab' and the group sigils.

[242] In a few instances, δ is joined by manuscripts from α, β, or γ: 33 prodigiosus (*FSVdGo*); 545 comitantur (α and eight γ manuscripts); 1061 correptis (*HT*); 1411 maxima (*F*); 1504 ueniunt (*Go*); 1994 mihi (*Vd*). These examples could well be the result of accidental convergence. In contrast, the only example of a δ reading in Mozley's <u>b</u> list is at 262, where *DK* read 'tunc' for 'nunc', a likely example of convergent variation.

[243] Where these groups are represented; α is absent from lines 2483–3258 and lines 3449–900, while γ is absent after 2602.

394	†castigat[244]	sepeliuit
430	tunc munda	praeterita[245]
497	michi dum coniuncta	dum me comitata
527	pariter conturbat	pecudum turbator
545	comitantur	comitatur[246]
	et illi	et illa
580	†mundana	discreta
621	†noli tardare pedester	nocuit differre paratis
742	†nec tamen inuenit que	orbe quod in toto non fuit
	cupiebat ibi	usque petens
791	nomen Burnellus michi stat	nomine Burnellus dicor
808	decent	decens
846	soli	solo
924	leditur et	lesa sed est
936	absque	atque
1025	*accipiam	decipiam
1040	cederit, cesserit	sederit[247]
1061	†correptis fuste molossis	correpto fuste molossis
1062	disponit socium fallere	omnibus extinctis
	fraude suum	accelerauit iter
1149	in	ad
1285	*hincque...stimulauit	inde...stimulabat
1295	*†sanum	sura
1376	profert	promit
1411	maxima	plurima
1434	largus	lapsus
1462	dare	reddo
1504	*ueniunt	subeunt
1567	periitque labor sed	periit labor omnis
1608	meo	puto

[244] Mozley's list jumps from 'castigat' to 'tunc munda' (he places the latter in the b column, omitting the b readings 'sepeliuit' and 'praeterita', and the reference to line 430).

[245] For a defence of this reading, see my note to line 430.

[246] I have split this entry into two lemmata, since Mozley fails to make clear that so far from showing a clear plural/singular split, the manuscripts mix the two (α and seven γ manuscripts plus *La* have a plural verb and a singular subject). What seems to have happened is that the singular verb (which is correct) was erroneously written as a plural in α, the error was taken over into δ and half of γ, whereupon some scribes, but not all, corrected by changing the pronoun to match the verb. The result does not illustrate a division within group δ but rather its interconnections.

[247] This entry misrepresents the complicated range of variants at this point in the text, and should be disregarded.

1750	*nil ergo uitii . . . adesse	quidnam uirtutis . . . abesse
1831	*insistendo	infitiando
1951	*†uicina	uienna[248]
1994	*talem . . . michi	tamen . . . nichil
2088	sepe licebit eis	nam licet illud ibi
2175	ficti . . . furti	falsi . . . ficti
2218	uota	iura, uita
2317	*lex noua lutumque	lex est licitumque
2412	mero, metro	melo
2477–8	flagella/ dat	flagellat/ sed
2545	maculando	maculosa[249]
2593	*reseruant, reformant	serenant
2618	dubitet	dubitat
2718	†uestibus ornati	tot uini cyati
2893	*uidebar	iuuabat[250]
2925	*sanctior unus	stemmate maior
3197	facta sequantur	fata frequentant
3254	religiosus	flagitiosus
3385	composuere	compos!iture
3481	omni[251]	esse
3501	*eneas	-que meas
3640	que	quas
3708	*attulit	abstulit

As Mozley pointed out (*SS*, p. 24), a large number of the a/b variants 'are not the result of error and offer little or nothing to choose between them',[252] but in the case of others, reflection 'forces the admission that many b readings [that is, the readings of αβ] are older than those of the rival group [δ]'. Mozley reasonably concluded: 'This evidence as to the priority of b [αβ] readings and the greater correctness of the b text gives a presumption of superiority when other variants are considered' (p. 24).

[248] In Mozley's list, these readings are erroneously reversed.

[249] 'maculosa respergit/respersit' is the reading of β; α is out. γ has 'maculat maculosa', which I adopt as characteristic of Nigel's style (see below, p. clix).

[250] γ ends at 2602, α is out in 2483–3258 and 3449–900.

[251] Mozley's *omnis* is a typographical error.

[252] He instances 17 recordor/reuoluo; 317 raro/sero; 550 celeri/crebro; 670 fata/cuncta; 1376 promit/profert; 1608 meo/puto. He does not, however, indicate which readings he considers to be clearly errors, or give reasons for thinking so. In the lists above, I indicate with an asterisk items which are identified as errors in my analysis of δ readings above on pp. xciii, civ–cv, cvii, cxii, while items prefaced with an obelus (†) are identified as errors in my discussion below on pp. cxxi–cxxiii. For lines 87, 430, 2175, 2477–8, see the notes on these lines.

TEXTUAL TRANSMISSION   cxxi

Mozley acknowledged that the superiority of the b̲ [αβ] text partly derives from the fact that it more accurately reproduces the archetype: 'there are passages that occur in b̲ but not in a̲; in many it seems certain that they were in the common archetype of the two families, but were omitted by the archetype of a̲ through homoeoteleuton (or -archon)' (p. 24). However, as noted above, he went on to suggest that some of the preferable b̲ [αβ] readings are the result of an authorial revision of the text. This revision, he claimed, can be detected in isolated words and phrases, which somehow made their way into 'a revised text issued perhaps in [Nigel's] lifetime, a text that also avoided the many mistakes of which the a̲ [δ] text is guilty'. The conclusion to his Introduction repeats the hypothesis that 'some a̲ [δ] readings are apparently first drafts rather than alterations or corruptions, and that the corresponding changes in b̲ [αβ] manuscripts seem to be improvements, and were perhaps incorporated in the text at some time subsequent to the earliest edition as Nigel's own work' (p. 28). This account is both vague and implausible, in that it locates authorial intervention at both the beginning and the end of the process of scribal transmission, but has no explanation as to why the poem should have grown shorter rather than longer over time.[253] In my opinion, however, the major cause of the divergence between a̲ [δ] and b̲ [αβ] readings in Mozley's list is not authorial improvement but scribal corruption in a̲ [δ].

To demonstrate scribal corruption in δ, I begin with some examples where Mozley sees authorial improvement.[254] In line 394, Brunetta foresees the arrival of summer and the dangers it threatens, since the flies that have been killed by the winter cold will revive with the summer heat:

> Ecce dies ueniunt ueris, muscaeque resurgent,
> quas *castigat/sepeliuit* adhuc cana pruina gelu. (394–5)

Mozley prints the δ reading 'castigat' in favour of αβγ 'sepeliuit' (although, if he thought 'sepeliuit' a revised reading, he ought to have preferred it). Like the scribe of the δ archetype, he misses the metaphor

---

[253] The stemma on p. 23 shows *LEF* and the Vienna group of manuscripts (my γ) as all subsequent to the full-length versions of the poem in Mozley's group a̲. Mozley's only reference to this problem is his glancing acknowledgement that 'the b̲ texts are curiously incomplete' (p. 22).

[254] There are two versions of this list, one on p. 24, and an expanded version on p. 28. It has to be said that it is not entirely clear whether Mozley is opting for the a̲ or b̲ readings in this list, since he sometimes chooses one and sometimes the other in his text. At 430 he prints an emendation, eschewing both readings; at 394 and 621 he prints the a̲ (δ) reading, at 742, 791 and 1567 the b̲ (αβγ) reading.

cxxii   INTRODUCTION

that yields the contrast between 'burial' and 'resurrection'; 'castigat' loses this pointed contrast and produces a flabbier result. A similar flabbiness characterizes the δ version of line 742, summarizing Burnellus's fruitless quest for the non-existent medicines that will lengthen his tail; δ simply states the obvious, 'nec tamen inuenit que cupiebat ibi', 'he didn't find there what he was looking for', while the αβγ reading emphasizes the extreme nature of the donkey's folly: 'orbe quod in toto non fuit usque petens', 'constantly seeking what did not exist in the whole world'. In line 621, when Galienus is urging Burnellus to get to Salerno as quickly as possible, the αβγ reading is a half-line of Lucan (*De bello ciuili*, i. 281): 'nocuit differe paratis' ('to those who are ready [to start], delay is harmful'). Mozley objects to this 'crude insertion of the tag from Lucan', which 'does not seem quite in Nigel's manner' (p. 25). On the contrary, it is quite in keeping with other 'Goliardic' features of Nigel's style, such as wordplay, parody, and the comic use of learned allusion; the whole of this same line from Lucan ('Tolle moras; semper nocuit differre paratis') is found as a comic *auctoritas* in Walter of Châtillon's 'Missus sum in uineam'.[255] The δ reading (perhaps arising from a failure to recognize or understand the quotation) again reduces this to a banal repetition of the advice to waste no time: 'noli tardare pedester', 'don't dally in your walk'. At 1061–2, when Burnellus has insisted that the malicious monk Fromundus should kill the dogs he has let loose on him, the αγ reading reports the execution of this command: 'correpto fuste, molossis/ omnibus extinctis acceleer-auit iter' ('having seized a stick and killed all the dogs, [Fromundus] set off in haste'). The δ reading leaves the dogs alive (in contradiction to what Burnellus later says at lines 1079–80): 'correptis fuste molossis/ disponit socium fallere fraude suum' ('having restrained the dogs with a stick, [Fromundus] plans to deceive his companion').[256] Mozley suggests that Nigel may have forgotten (in the space of ten lines!) that the dogs were all to be killed, and when he remembered, he realized that 'he must change his first phrase "correptis fuste molossis"' (p. 26). Obviously the disjunction between noun and past participle is the work

---

[255] See Walter of Châtillon, *Poems*, no. xlii, stanza 14. 4 (p. 108). This stanza is also incorporated into the composite poem, made up of various stanzas from Walter's poetry, ibid., Appendix 1, stanza 17.4 (p. 300). Nigel's acquaintance with Lucan's line is also demonstrated by his use of its opening ('Tolle moras'; 'Away with delay!') as the beginning of *Lawrence*, 1701: 'Tolle moram'.

[256] The error seems to have originated with β: *H* agrees with δ, *B* is out. Although disliking the ablative absolute in both versions, Langosch attempted an unconvincing defence of the δ reading (review, p. 285). Boutemy, on the other hand, recognized that the αγ reading makes more sense ('The manuscript tradition', pp. 517–18).

TEXTUAL TRANSMISSION

of an inattentive scribe (anticipating/influenced by the ending of 'molossis') rather than an amnesiac author. At 2718, when describing the splendour of the bishops' daily life, Nigel envisages their luxurious dining habits: 'tot uini cyati' ('so many measures of wine') is the β reading,[257] which δ replaces by 'uestibus ornati' ('elaborately dressed'). The latter looks very like a *lectio facilior*, prompted perhaps by unfamiliarity with the word 'cyati'.

Moving on to other examples, the same could be said of δ's rendering of line 580, which in the αβγ version reads: 'gloria discreta quae ratione caret' ('glory which is devoid of prudent wisdom'). The δ scribe probably did not recognize 'discretus' in the sense of 'prudent',[258] and so did not realize that it modifies 'ratione' (as the long -a makes clear) rather than 'gloria', and changed it to the obvious cliché, 'gloria mundana' ('worldly glory'). In line 1295, in the description of a healing wound, δ's 'sanum' in place of αβγ's 'sura' ('calf of the leg') is another example of a *facilior*. In line 1951, in place of the αβγ reading 'ab urbe Vienna' ('from the town of Vienne'), δ has the vague 'ab urbe uīcīnā' (from the/a neighbouring town'), ignoring the fact that 'uīcīnā' does not scan at the end of a hexameter. The scribe of the ancestor of *DK* seems to have recognized this, and attempted to mend matters by substituting 'prŏpīnquā', which scans but unfortunately does not restore the original sense.[259] In line 1289, the young cock's broken leg is said to have recovered entirely from the injury: 'Ossa diu fracta iam dedidicere dolorem', but his sense of injury is unchanged. The δ manuscripts replace the last half-line with 'multum/nimium doluere dolore/dolere', completely inverting the sense of the phrase, apparently through failure to grasp that the mental sense of injury can survive the physical healing. The prize example of scribal dullness is, however, line 1877, where Burnellus is describing the heartfelt gratitude expressed by the three thieves whom he has saved from execution. 'We shall always be at your command', they assure him,

> Iure tuus debet, tuus, immo tuissimus esse,
> quem tu saluasti carcere, fune, cruce. (1877–8)

Rightly should the one whom you saved from prison, from the rope, from the gallows, be yours—yours to the nth degree.

---

[257] α and γ are both out at this point.

[258] See Niermeyer sense 3.

[259] The change was probably caused by the mistaken assumption that 'Vienna' is meant to refer to the city of Vienna, which is geographically inappropriate. Burnellus has at this point travelled twelve days on his journey home from Paris to Cremona, and as he is crossing the Alps meets the pilgrim who is travelling to Rome from Vienne (see lines 1951–2 and n.).

cxxiv INTRODUCTION

This is the reading of αβγ, but the δ manuscripts replace 'tuus, immo tuissimus' with the bland 'seruus certissimus', apparently failing to understand or appreciate the witty transformation of 'tuus' into a superlative. Astonishingly, Mozley fails to include this striking example in his list of significant divergences between δ and αβγ.

For large stretches of the text, however, α and γ are absent, since γ ends at 2602 (or 2522 in the case of *S*), while *LEF* lack 2483–3258, and end at 3448. For these portions of the text, β and δ, with whatever support can be gleaned from the 'mixed manuscripts', form the basis for the text, and on occasions when β is in error, the sole witness of δ has to be accepted. Sometimes the δ readings must be correct in the early part of the text as well. The following are instances where a δ reading is adopted in my text (with the rejected variant given in parentheses): 570 haec (hac); 863 unum (uno); 902 meditando (ratus ipse); 1175 est melius quod non redeam (dedecus est redeam si sic *and variants*[260]); 1442 restabat nulla (unica restabat); 1569 caudae superinstituendae (cauda superinficienda); 1804 nec (ne); 2457 si non nunc (si modo non *etc.*); 2568 *whole line*; 2686 primo (primis); 2687 secundi (secundis); 2725 quidam sua brachia tendit (tendit sua brachia mundus); 2791 auibus capiat (capiat auibus); 2792 hinc (quod); 2907 timendo (timere); 2911 et fixo (fixo pede); 2959 facta (cuncta); 3677 capiens (rapiens). The assumption here is that δ preserves the reading of the archetype ω.

Mozley describes his editorial method as follows: 'The text is based on the agreement of the four a̲ [δ] manuscripts AMDK and the 6 b̲ [αβγ] manuscripts EFLSBH. As a subordinate group of b̲ manuscripts, I have occasionally included readings in which the Central European manuscripts or a majority of them agree; these I call c̲ [γ]…Where the two families disagree, I have shown a general preference for b̲ [αβγ], a much sounder text on the whole; sometimes, but rarely, I have even preferred readings confined to BH or EFL, against all the others. I have tried to form the text in the light of what I consider to have been Nigel's attainments in grammar and prosody, to guard against later improvements in the former and corruptions in the latter' (*SS*, pp. 27–8). He concludes by repeating his hypothesis concerning evidence of authorial revision in selected phrases. Leaving aside the latter point, whose implausibility has, I hope, been sufficiently demonstrated above, this editorial method is generally satisfactory; the readings of *LEF* and *BH* are indeed usually preferable to those of the

---

[260] See the section on α above, p. lxxxiv.

TEXTUAL TRANSMISSION
CXXV

δ group, especially when αβ is supported by γ. In practice, however, Mozley's editorial method was quite eclectic: for example, from the list of <u>ab</u> readings given above, despite his expressed preference for <u>b</u> [αβγ], he prints the <u>a</u> [δ] reading at lines 17 (reuoluo); 87 (nequibat); 153 (modo); 394 (castigat); 497 (mihi dum coniuncta); 621 (noli tardare pedester); 924 (laeditur et); 1149 (in); 2218 (uota); 2545 (maculando); 2618 dubitet (dubitat).[261] There seems to be no compelling reason to choose the <u>a</u> [δ] readings in these instances, while sometimes there is good reason to choose the <u>b</u> [αβγ] alternative. He does provide a stemma, which gives a partially correct picture of the manuscript relations in some subordinate situations, but unfortunately (because of his 'revision' theory) gets the development of the transmission back-to-front, placing δ at its head, and αβγ at its latter end. As suggested above, he seems to have been unduly influenced by the fact that A is the earliest manuscript in date.[262] In any case, however, he does not make any detailed use of the stemma as an editorial tool.[263]

Like Mozley, I prefer the readings of αβγ to those of δ, and I also pay attention to sense, grammar, and metre in the choice of variants. But other things being equal, I also rely on a newly constructed stemma (see p. xix) to the extent that I treat agreement between two or more of its separate branches (αβγδ) as *a priori* testimony to an original reading (while recognizing of course that it may also be testimony to an error in the common archetype of all the manuscripts). When I speak of a reading as 'better supported', it is the number of separate branches, rather than the number of individual manuscripts, that is at issue.

The Evolution of the Poem: Conclusions

At this point it is possible to summarize the conclusions reached in the preceding account of the different forms of the poem and the relation of their hyparchetypes. Leaving aside the idiosyncratic arrangements

---

[261] Other δ readings retained in Mozley's text but rejected in this edition include the following: 1166 digito (digitis); 1187 non (nec); 1195 non (nec); 1200 non (nec); 1434 largus (lapsus); 1443 multumque (multoque); 1461 iniquam (iniquum); 1486 uicem (uices); 1700 ut non sit (et non sic); 1714 cornua uana (menstrua membra); 2095 et (sed); 2175 ficti...fures (falsi...ficti); 2193 assumpto uellere (sicco cum subere); 2789 festinus praesul (praesul festinus); 2848 nefas (scelus); 2883 esse (ipse); 3325 ediderit (ediderint); 3399 uidetis (timetis).

[262] Similar criticisms of Mozley's 'curious and even illogical' editorial procedure were made by Boutemy as early as 1933 ('The manuscript tradition', pp. 516–17).

[263] In his 1930 article ('On the text and manuscripts of the *Speculum Stultorum*', p. 260), Mozley speaks slightingly of the values of stemmata: 'I have not attempted to construct anything in the way of a stemma of M.SS; while undoubtedly a pleasing exercise of ingenuity, their practical value appears to be little.' One may agree that a stemma is a highly simplified representation of a complex situation, but it can still be of some practical value.

cxxvi INTRODUCTION

that are the result of physical loss or disordering, as described on pp. lxviii–lxxi above, its development may be traced through the four main manuscript groups, as follows.

(1) The earliest form of the poem is represented by manuscripts *LEF* (α), which lack 2483–3258 (containing the ass's diatribe against the Roman curia, kings, bishops, and abbots, and the following account of the bird debate overheard by Burnellus) and lines 3449–900 (containing the story of the Grateful Animals and the Ungrateful Man). As already noted, evidence that lines 2483–3258 did not form part of the original form of the poem, but were added later (rather than having been lost from the original for some reason), is provided by the visible nature of the join where the new material has been inserted: line 3259 ('Hinc est quod statuo me tradere religioni/ cuius ero primus doctor et auctor ego') clearly jumps all the way back to the monastic survey and Burnellus's decision to found his own order, and hence would follow on smoothly from line 2482. The α version then continues with (what are now) lines 3259–448—that is, the story of the Three Fates, and its moral conclusion warning of the evils that arise in religious life when rewards are distributed to the undeserving, which makes an entirely suitable end to the whole poem. Evidence that the story of the Grateful Animals was added later, as a kind of afterthought, is provided by the fact that Burnellus more or less disappears from the poem at this point, and the story itself only became known in England at a late date. Without this final story, the shape of the narrative in the α version generally corresponds to the account of it given in the *Epistle to William*, which appears in *F* but not *LE*, confirming what is said in the *Epistle* itself—namely, that it was written and sent to William after he had received the poem dedicated to him.

(2) The version of the poem in *BH* (β) represents the most important expansion of the poem, through the addition of lines 2483–3258 (the attacks on the curia, kings, bishops, and abbots, followed by the bird debate, which ends with a section on confessing secrets), and lines 3449–864 (the story of the Grateful Animals). It was probably Nigel's encounter with the latter, when Richard I brought it back from the Crusade, that prompted him to expand his poem, driving home the moral of gratitude which is one of its running themes, as is emphasized in the *Epistle*. Nigel then took the opportunity to add the satiric denunciation of the social elements that were responsible for the troubles of Christ Church Canterbury in the eyes of the monastic community. If Archbishop Baldwin was safely dead in the Holy Land, and Henry II had been replaced by a new king whose chancellor was the dedicatee

PLACE IN THE TRADITION OF BEAST EPIC   cxxvii

of *SS*, criticism of kings, bishops, and abbots could be indulged in more safely.

(3) The manuscripts belonging to group γ are more difficult to place with certainty: they continue past the point where the α manuscripts end, so their hyparchetype could well have resembled β in its overall shape, but they end in midstream, not far from the beginning of the criticism of kings, and while the tirade against the evil influence of 'munera' is in full flow. Unlike the endings of α and β, this does not read like a concluding moral to the poem, and it strongly suggests that the hyparchetype of this group had suffered loss of its final leaves, and could well have ended originally where β does—or even δ, but this is made less likely by γ's general textual alignment with αβ rather than δ.

(4) The manuscripts belonging to group δ follow the shape of β, but add a brief concluding section in lines 3865–900, which drive home the moral about the need to reward true merit, and the impossibility of seeking what nature denies. It is possible that these lines were already present in the β hyparchetype and were lost through missing leaves, or they may have been added in a final stage of revision, to provide a resounding finale to the poem by repeating yet again its moral and the 'hidden meaning' behind its surface (cf. 9–10 and 3881–2). The δ version will have appealed to scribal preference for the most complete version of a work, and this will have helped to boost its popularity.

The 'mixed manuscripts' (*TrHaLa, GI, X, QY, U, Z*) are the result of contamination and/or affiliation to two separate branches of the stemma. In the latter instance, the double affiliation might also reflect one or more intermediate stages in the development from the hyparchetype of β to the hyparchetype of δ. Given the length of time between the composition of the poem and the date of the surviving manuscripts, it is not surprising that most of the representatives of these intermediate stages should have disappeared, leaving only the isolated copies from the lost hyparchetypes.

NIGEL'S PLACE IN THE TRADITION OF BEAST EPIC

Beast fable is a genre that goes back to antiquity; beast epic is essentially a product of the twelfth century.[264] Its first full-scale example is

---

[264] The first work with some claim to be called a forerunner of beast epic is the *Ecbasis Captivi*, whose date is disputed: it may be 10th or 11th c. (probably the latter). However, although it contains a central episode (the flaying of the wolf to cure the sick lion) which later became the core of the *Ysengrimus*, its general structure and mood differ from the later Reynardian narratives, and it seems to have had little influence on the mainstream beast epic.

cxxviii INTRODUCTION

the *Ysengrimus*, a seven-book narrative in Latin elegiacs, written in Flanders (probably in the town of Ghent) around 1150. This brilliantly satirical work relates the evolving feud between the fox Reinardus and his supposed 'uncle', the wolf Ysengrimus, which culminates in the wolf's ignominious death (he is eaten alive by 66 pigs). The fox's cunning, exercised against the wolf and other animals, became the subject matter of a spate of later beast narratives in both Latin and the vernaculars, the best known of them being the many branches of the *Roman de Renart*.[265] As mentioned at the beginning of this Introduction, *SS* i highly unusual in stepping aside from this Reynardian tradition and inventing a wholly original set of episodes, with the ass Burnellus as the central figure.

Nevertheless, *SS* shows its affinity with the *Ysengrimus* in its rhetorical set-pieces and lengthy monologues. Such extreme verbal elaboration is the hallmark of *Ysengrimus* and its contribution to the tradition of beast epic. Beast fables, in contrast, are characteristically brief and sparing of narrative detail.[266] They aim to present a narrative which instructs by virtue of its structure, which is given a quasi-inevitability by the animal nature of the participants. Although the animals have the power of human speech, their words are revealed to be mere camouflage, a distraction from the real motive of self-interest. Any animal who is foolish enough to ignore physical realities is eventually brought up against the predominance of *facta* over *dicta*. In contrast, beast epic revels in *dicta*. As I expressed it on an earlier occasion, if beast fable is sparing of words, beast epic is prodigal of them.[267] This difference alters the whole thrust of the narrative and its relation to the copious moralizing that accompanies it, as becomes immediately clear in the opening of *SS*. Burnellus's desire for a longer tail at first seems to fit a familiar type of beast fable which presents an animal trying to transcend the limits of its nature (a crow wishing to be as beautiful as a peacock, a toad trying to blow itself up so it is as large as an ox, and so on), and discovering that its ambition is doomed to failure. The doctor Galen does indeed try to impress this lesson on Burnellus: 'Quod natura negat, reddere nemo potest' (186). If this were a beast fable, instead of Galen's attempt at dissuasion, the narrative would move immediately to the account of the thwarting of his desire and the loss of half of

---

[265] See above, n. 1.
[266] For more detailed analysis of the structural and stylistic differences between beast fable and beast epic, see Mann, *From Aesop to Reynard*, ch. 1, and *passim*.
[267] Ibid. p. 44.

PLACE IN THE TRADITION OF BEAST EPIC cxxix

his tail, with Galen's maxim quoted as the moral of the story. Instead, the narrative events are prolonged to inordinate lengths, not only by Galen's moral exhortations but also by his story of the two cows whose tails become stuck in some frozen mud, by Burnellus's journey to Salerno to buy the (imaginary) tail-lengthening medicines, by his misadventure with the monk Fromundus and revenge on him, by his decision to study at the university of Paris, and so on ad infinitum. The story of the two cows in itself breaks the bounds of beast fable by representing an animal confronted by a moral *choice* in advance of an action rather than being confronted in retrospect by a moral *lesson*. The inevitability in the chain of events, leading from foolish desire to consequent disaster, is broken, and the instructive force of the narrative itself is undermined.

The story of the two cows itself repeats this pattern. For a moral conclusion of the beast-fable type, it would be enough to show Brunetta patiently waiting for the sun to thaw the mud, while Bicornis cuts off her tail and is then driven to madness and death by the stinging clouds of summer insects. Here again, what breaks the bounds of fable is that both cows argue at length for the wisdom of their individual choice, drawing on apparently inexhaustible stores of proverbial wisdom and rhetorical argument which can, however, justify quite opposite conclusions. In fact, although the narrative outcome justifies Brunetta, it is easy to imagine different narrative conclusions—for example, Brunetta freezing to death overnight, or being attacked by a predator while she is immobilized. Bicornis's argument that 'half a loaf is better than no bread' is one that is offered seriously elsewhere in *SS* (3857–60) and in Nigel's *Tractatus*.[268] The fact that this is a story *about tails* confuses the issue even further by diverting attention to the surface of the narrative instead of its moral structure: why should not Burnellus conclude that it shows that the more tail an animal has, the better protected it is?

There is of course no point in preaching *to an animal* that one should be content with nature; in life, the animal has no choice. The towering rhetorical edifices that are erected on the flimsy basis of the narrative are entirely irrelevant to animal action in beast epic as in beast fable. The difference is that in beast epic, the gap between the two allows room for the entry of comedy and satire. Burnellus constantly aspires to inhabit the moral and intellectual world of human beings—to acquire a university education, to become a bishop, to forsake the world and

[268] Ed. Boutemy, p. 167.

CXXX INTRODUCTION

enter a monastic order—but he cannot get beyond the 'hee haw' that nature gave him. The moral conclusion in these instances attaches itself not to the ass but to the humans who take on these roles with as little success as Burnellus.[269]

In beast epic, the animal is constantly played off against the human, with comic results that are alien to the sober restraint of beast fable. The bird debate reported by Burnellus towards the end of the poem is a case in point: the raven claims that the disasters evident everywhere in the world are all brought about by avian sinfulness (2951–2). Chattering birds reveal confessional secrets (2973–6), just as he, the raven, once revealed the adultery of his mistress to Apollo. Birds pull up seedlings and destroy crops; they tear blossoms from the trees before fruit is formed. Chickens eat up the grain stored in barns; hawks fly away from their keepers, who incur danger as they pursue them; parrots tell tales on maidservants. This is why humans set traps for birds and attack them with slings and arrows. The cock meets this long recital of avian wickedness with a contrasting list of his own virtues: he provides feathers for beds, meat and eggs for the table, and a reliable alarm clock. There is no need to pursue further this application of human morality to natural animal behaviour; its comic absurdity is self-evident. The comedy does not apply criticism of the animal; rather it ridicules the human tendency to position human behaviour as the central explanation for all events.

Nigel could very well have learned from the *Ysengrimus* the comic potential created by the huge disparity between animal behaviour and the weight of rhetoric that it brings into play. There are occasional verbal echoes of *Ysengrimus* in *SS*,[270] and although the number of surviving manuscripts is relatively small, the relations between Canterbury and Flanders were close enough to make it quite possible that Nigel had some acquaintance with his distinguished forerunner.[271] Indeed, what other model could he have had? Original as the story of the two cows is, it seems clear that it is a 'rifacimento' of the story of the wolf 'fishing' with his tail in a river that freezes over and holds him fast,

---

[269] This is not to deny that fable can have a satiric *application*, but it occurs outside of the fable narrative and can be changed from one situation to another, whereas beast epic is designed for specific situations which are, as it were, built into it and clearly identifiable.

[270] See the notes to lines 825, 883.

[271] There are five manuscripts of the whole poem, but it also survives in numerous florilegia, suggesting that it had a wider circulation and other copies must have been lost (*Ysengrimus*, ed. Mann, pp. 188–9). On the close relations between Canterbury and Flanders at this period, see Mann, *From Aesop to Reynard*, p. 101.

INFLUENCE OF THE *SPECVLVM STVLTORVM*   cxxxi

until a peasant woman cuts off his tail with an axe. And the rhetorical elaborations of the bird debate could well have been inspired by similar disputations in *Ysengrimus*, such as the elaborate arguments at the lion's court in Book III.

THE LATER INFLUENCE OF THE *SPECVLVM STVLTORVM*

The bird debate in *SS* also exerted its own influence: although this has previously been overlooked, it is the only possible model for one of the liveliest productions of Middle English literature, *The Owl and the Nightingale*.[272] As in *SS*, the birds engage in animated debate in which they evaluate themselves and each other according to moral yardsticks which are quite inappropriate for animals. When pushed onto the back foot, however, they will switch their standards of judgement and defend as 'natural' avian behaviour which is unacceptable by human standards. In addition, this poem takes over one of Nigel's most original manoeuvres: whereas Galen tells the story of the two cows to try and persuade Burnellus of his folly—as if beast literature were the most suitable literary genre for transmitting moral wisdom to an animal— the *Owl and the Nightingale* takes the joke one stage further by making the *animals themselves* appeal to beast literature to bolster their arguments.[273] The nightingale cites Marie de France's fable of the owl in the hawk's nest as 'evidence' of the owl's filthy behaviour.[274] The owl accuses the nightingale of encouraging adultery, quoting the narrative of Marie's *Laüstic* as support.[275] Beast literature is no longer a genre *about* animals with a meaning for humans; instead it has become their own internal reference point. This confusion of human and animal is a rich source of comedy, which at the same time points up the arbitrariness and opportunism of human methods of argument.

Fourteenth-century England provides further proof of the popularity of Nigel's beast epic. In Chaucer's *Nun's Priest's Tale*, as the fox is flattering the cock Chauntecleer by saying he is even cleverer than his father, he cites the story of Gundulf in *SS* as a standard of comparison:

> 'I have wel rad, in Daun Burnel the Asse,
> Among his vers, how that ther was a cok,
> That, for a preestes sone yaf him a knok
> Upon his leg, whil he was yong and nice,

---

[272] Ed. Cartlidge. For discussion of this poem, see Mann, *From Aesop to Reynard*, ch. 4.
[273] See Mann, *From Aesop to Reynard*, pp. 123–4, 176.
[274] Ibid. pp. 177–8.
[275] Ibid. pp. 180–2.

cxxxii INTRODUCTION

> He made him for to lese his benefice.
> But certein, ther nis no comparisoun
> Bitwix the wisdom and discrecioun
> Of youre fader, and of his subtiltee!' (3312–19)

Chaucer evidently appreciated Nigel's joke about beast fables being addressed to animals: here we find that animals are now *reading beast literature*.[276] Indeed, the reference to 'his vers' even implies that they are writing it. The *Nun's Priest's Tale* also shows that Chaucer had thoroughly absorbed the comic use of rhetoric in *SS*: the simple narrative skeleton of the tale, which Chaucer borrowed from the *Roman de Renart*, is swollen to enormous proportions by the debate between the cock and his wife on the significance of dreams.[277] As in beast fable and beast epic, however, the action is not determined by rhetoric or reason, but by natural instinct: having fought off his wife's proposal to cure the fear his dream had caused him by dosing him with laxatives, the cock succumbs to her physical charms and totally forgets the impending disaster on which he had insisted. No matter, because when he catches sight of the fox, he instinctively flies up in fright—

> For naturelly a beest desireth flee
> Fro his contrarye, if he may it see,
> Though he nevere erst hadde seyn it with his eye. (3279–81)

Chauntecleer finally escapes disaster by persuading the fox to be momentarily as blinded by *verba* as he has been himself: forgetful of *facta*—that speaking involves opening one's mouth—the fox is persuaded to boast of his capture, and so allows his prey to escape.

The story of Gundulf and the cock also appears in medieval Scottish literature, in the poem known as *The Talis of the Fyve Bestis*, which is preserved in the early sixteenth-century Asloan manuscript.[278] The five beasts—horse, hart, unicorn, boar, and wolf—offer counsel to the lion-king in turn. The first four pieces of advice take the form of tales, each followed by a *moralitas*; in the fifth, the wolf duplicitously tries to persuade the lion that he needs to eat the flesh of the other animals, so that his own kin might take over the role of counsellors. Fortunately, the lion sees through this plan, and exiles the wolf and his fellow-predators.

---

[276] Ibid. p. 254.

[277] Ibid. pp. 255–61, especially p. 260.

[278] Now Edinburgh, National Library of Scotland, MS 16500 (*olim* Accession 4243). *The Talis of the Fyve Bestis* is edited by Wingfield and Purdie in *Six Scottish Courtly and Chivalric Poems*; the manuscript is defective and consequently the poem is fragmentary at two points, one of which is its opening.

INFLUENCE OF THE *SPECVLVM STVLTORVM* cxxxiii

The narrative framework of this poem is generally indebted to beast epic. The lion-king and his court form the major setting for Book III of *Ysengrimus*, in which the wolf makes a similarly duplicitous attempt to incite the lion against his enemy the fox, and to persuade him that he needs to eat the flesh of a sheep and a goat, the animals who are the fox's supporters. The tales that are set within this framework are of very varied nature: three of them exclusively concern human beings, but the unicorn's tale is obviously borrowed from the story of Gundulf and the cock in *SS*, although it is considerably simplified and shorn of some of its satiric aspects. The protagonist Gundulfus shares the same name as the boy in *SS*, but he is the son of a peasant, not a priest, so that the satiric allusion to the transmission of church livings to the illegitimate offspring of the clergy is discarded. As in *SS*, when young, Gundulfus accidentally breaks the leg of a chick, who later becomes a handsome cock, chief of the poultry yard. Gundulfus meanwhile has become a student at Oxford, and has learned to read and write, and studied canon law, logic, necromancy, and medicine. Returning home, he tells his parents that he has to travel to Rochester without delay, in order to be ordained priest the very next day. His mother persuades him to spend the night at home and leave at 3 a.m. Trusting in the cock to wake them, the family eat and drink their fill and fall into a heavy sleep. The cock of course refuses to crow, despite his wife's remonstrations; he sourly replies that although his leg has healed, his heart still bleeds at the injury. Gundulfus wakes up only in broad daylight, jumps on his horse in a panic, and sets off at breakneck speed, The horse stumbles and throws him in the mire; he lies there until noon, when the ordination ceremony is over, then returns home covered with shame. The cock rejoices at having revenged the old injury. The moral of the tale warns any 'lord and ruler of this land' not to oppress the poor, because the time may come when their victims have power over them and exact vengeance.

Nigel's story has been simplified by the omission of Gundulf's dream, in which he imagines that he has been ordained and is celebrating Mass, with the cock, robed in white, leading the choir. But what is not omitted is the lively exchange between the cock and his wife, Coppok.[279] Chaucer's influence joins with Nigel's in the relation between the two

---

[279] The name probably reflects the name of the hen in *SS*, which is Coppa, with the addition of the Scottish diminutive -ock (Henryson, *Poems*, ed. Fox, pp. 215–16). One of the hens in Henryson's retelling of Chaucer's *Nun's Priest's Tale*, *The Cock and the Fox*, is also called Coppok in the Bannatyne manuscript (ibid.).

cxxxiv INTRODUCTION

birds: as with Chaunticleer and Pertelote, it is first described in romantic terms (163–6), but then quickly devolves into comic marital bickering: 'Syng wald he nocht bot schrewily said, "Madame, / Wysest ye ar quhen that ye hald you still, / And yit ye wyfis evir speike ye will. / Dame, intromet you in your wyfis deid..."' (232–5).

The tales told by the horse, hart, unicorn, and boar conform to the conventional structure of beast fable: a short narrative followed by a *moralitas*. But the roles of animals and humans are interestingly reversed: instead of a narrative about animals which is told by a human being for the edification of other human beings, these narratives are told by animals to another animal (the lion), but are about human beings and are applied to other human beings in the *moralitas*.[280] It might seem that this is another joke in the line of descent that connects Galen's story of the two cows, told to Burnellus, to the use of animal stories by the owl and the nightingale in their debate, and the fox's claim to have read *SS* in the *Nun's Priest's Tale*, but neither comic intention nor comic effect is evident in this instance. The use of animals seems to depend on a vague sense that the beast fable makes them appropriate for moral teaching, but this is not derived from the narrative action: the four animals are no more than mouthpieces for pieces of 'advice to princes'. Their splendid appearance (silver tines, golden bristles) suits their role as courtiers, but their characterization goes no further. The Chaucerian exchange between the cock and his wife is the only glimmer of the humour that is abundant in *Ysengrimus*, the *Roman de Renart*, and *SS*. In this respect, the *Fables* of the Scots poet Robert Henryson, some of which were included in the Asloan manuscript, make a striking contrast in their fusion of epic humour and fable seriousness: the fable narrative is recounted with epic verve and wit, but a streak of savagery brings the 'game' back to 'earnest' in the *moralitas*.[281]

The tale of the Grateful Animals and the Ungrateful Man also had a successful afterlife. As noted earlier, its original home was in the

---

[280] The cock is the only animal to appear in these stories. The horse's (fragmentary) tale concerns two travellers, one wise and one foolish, who come to a forking of the ways, one fair and one perilous; the wise man is persuaded to take the more attractive path, which leads to a nest of thieves. This is allegorized as the soul mistakenly obeying the dictates of the body. The hart's tale (also fragmentary) is a paean of praise to William Wallace and the cause of Scottish independence. The boar's tale tells how Alexander the Great was tricked by a clerk into abandoning his intention to conquer the town of Lapsat.

[281] For detailed discussion of Henryson's *Fabillis*, see Mann, *From Aesop to Reynard*, ch. 7. A contents list in the Asloan manuscript shows that although it now contains only one of Henryson's *Fabillis* (The Two Mice), it formerly contained several more, including The Cock and the Fox (Henryson, *Poems*, ed. Fox, p. xxxix).

INFLUENCE OF THE *SPECVLVM STVLTORVM*   CXXXV

Eastern tale collection known as the *Pañchatantra* or *Kalila and Dimna*, and it first appears in the Arabic version of this collection by Abdullah Ibn al-Muquaffa', an eighth-century writer of Persian origin.[282] In this version, a goldsmith falls into a pit designed to trap animals, in which there are already a tiger, a snake, and a monkey. A passing hermit notices them and decides to win heaven's favour by saving the man. He gets a rope and lets it down into the pit, but first the monkey, then the tiger, and finally the snake seize it and climb out. They warn the hermit not to rescue the man, who is the most ungrateful creature alive. The animals (who, like all the animals in *Kalila and Dimna*, have the power of speech) tell the goldsmith they live near a town called Barajoun, and say that if he comes to find them he will be rewarded. Ignoring their warning, the hermit saves the goldsmith, who tells him that he lives in the same town mentioned by the animals and if the hermit visits him there he can claim his reward. After a while the hermit has business in this town, and on his way there he meets the monkey, who fetches him some delicious fruits as a sign of his gratitude. Next the hermit meets the tiger, who tells the hermit to wait until he comes back, then goes off and kills the king's daughter, steals her jewels and brings them back to the hermit, without revealing where he got them. The hermit then decides to call on the goldsmith, thinking that he is bound to match the generosity of the animals, and even if he is poor, he can sell the jewels on his behalf. The goldsmith, however, recognizes the jewels, and, pretending that he is going to fetch food, goes to the king and tells him that he has in his house the murderer of his daughter. The hermit is seized and brought before the king, who orders him to be beaten, paraded through the town, and then crucified. As he is being led round the town, the snake hears his loud laments and thinks of a plan to save him. He goes to the king's son and bites him. Magicians are summoned but cannot revive him, until (inspired by the snake's fairy sister who appears in a dream to the boy and tells him what to say) he recovers the power of speech and reveals that only the poor hermit can cure him by laying on his hands. The hermit is brought before the king, who asks what he was doing in the town and is told the whole history of his rescue of the man and the animals. With the aid of an antidote that the snake has given him, the hermit cures the boy and is rewarded with

---

[282] *Kalila et Dimna*, trans. Miquel, pp. 262–5. *Kalila and Dimna* also became known in the West via Rabbi Joel's Hebrew version and its translation into Latin by John of Capua as the *Directorium humanae vitae*, but since the latter work was not composed until the 13th c., this line of transmission cannot have influenced Nigel. For the process by which the Arabic version of this particular tale is likely to have reached the West, see n. to lines 3561–866.

cxxxvi INTRODUCTION

presents by the king, while the goldsmith is beaten and crucified. The story teaches us to do good only to grateful people, whether or not they are our relatives.[283]

This story is rather confusing, especially in the way it changes direction in mid-stream. The tiger does more harm than good by killing the king's daughter, and it is not clear at the end why the king overlooks the death of his daughter while rejoicing at the cure of his son. The goldsmith hardly qualifies as ungrateful, since he does not reject or beat the hermit, and genuinely believes he is guilty of murder, so it hardly seems that he deserves to be put to death. The business with the snake's fairy sister is a pointless digression. Other versions of the story in the *Kalila* tradition vary its details, but they all retain this oddly bifurcated plot, with the rescuer accused of murder and theft as a result of accepting jewellery from one of the animals.[284]

In *SS* the tale takes a different form from the Arabic original; most of its differences can be traced back to the version told by Richard I to the abbot of St Albans, as reported in the *Chronica majora* of Matthew Paris,[285] which can be summarized as follows. A rich and avaricious citizen of Venice named Vitalis went out hunting one day, hoping to get some game for his daughter's wedding feast. By chance he fell into a pit which had been dug to trap wild animals, and in which a lion and a snake had already been captured. Protecting himself from the beasts with the sign of the Cross, Vitalis remained there all night and the following day, uttering cries for help, which were eventually heard by a poor charcoal burner (unnamed) who was in the forest gathering oddments of wood, and asked who was there. Vitalis joyfully identified himself and explained that he had fallen into the pit, which already held two animals, but they had not harmed him. He promised the charcoal burner a reward of half his wealth if he got him out of the pit. Meanwhile the lion and the snake also begged by gestures to be released. The poor man went home and fetched a rope ladder ('scalam quandam cum funiculis'), which he let down into the pit. The lion and the snake came up first, and circling round him, made signs of gratitude to their rescuer. Finally Vitalis came up and the poor man enthusiastically kissed his hand, anticipating his reward. Vitalis told him to come to his

---

[283] The moral is therefore rather different from the Western versions, which highlight the animal/human contrast; this version heightens the predicament of the hermit as a result of saving the goldsmith because it aims to show the folly of ignoring the advice that one should not do good to the ungrateful.

[284] See Chesnutt, 'The Grateful Animals', pp. 44–6.

[285] See above, pp. lxxi–lxxiii and n. to lines 3561–866.

INFLUENCE OF THE *SPECVLVM STVLTORVM* cxxxvii

palace within four days and he would receive it. The poor charcoal burner went home, and as he sat at dinner the lion appeared with a (dead) young mule which he offered as reward. The poor man followed him back to his lair, the lion playing with him and licking his feet as they went. He then returned home and ate; after the meal the snake appeared, bearing in its mouth a precious stone which it placed on a dish, while showing its gratitude by playfully rolling itself in coils. As with the lion, the poor man tracked the snake back to its home. After two or three days, taking the stone, he went to Vitalis's house to ask for his reward, and found him celebrating his release at a feast for his neighbours. When asked for the promised reward, Vitalis mocked his rescuer and ordered him to be imprisoned. The poor man quickly left and went to the city judges, to whom he told the story, showing the precious stone as proof. One of those present, recognizing its worth, paid a great price for it. As further proof, the poor man led some of the citizens to the homes of the lion and the serpent, who again showed their gratitude to their liberator. Satisfied of the truth of the poor man's story, the judges compelled Vitalis to pay what he had promised. King Richard often told this story in reproach of ingratitude.

This version simplifies the structure and ties it more closely to the stated moral by excising the confusing sequence concerning the stolen jewels and keeping the focus on the contrast between the grateful animals and the ungrateful man. The role of the serpent's stone in leading to the denouement is more plausible in Matthew, and even more so in Nigel, who seems to have been responsible for inventing its magic power to return to the seller. The rich man's treatment of his rescuer is made even more brutal in *SS*, so as to demonstrate his ingratitude clearly. Nigel creates a connection with the larger narrative of *SS* by turning the charcoal burner into a woodcutter who is identified with Burnellus's master Bernard, and having the ass accompany him to the forest to collect wood. The daughter's wedding feast is discarded as irrelevant to the point of the story. Dryanus does not inform his potential rescuer of the presence of the other animals in the pit, presumably so as not to scare him off; this creates comedy as the animals emerge one by one, causing abject terror in Bernard, and increases the narrative tension as it seems he will decide the whole thing is a demonic illusion and give up the attempt. The account of the poor man tracking the animals to their lairs, which is obviously inherited from the Arabic, has no obvious function in Matthew's version, since the lion and the snake bring their rewards to the poor man's home; it is thus omitted in Nigel's account. Finally, the inclusion of a lion in both Matthew and

cxxxviii INTRODUCTION

Nigel deserves comment. Although the lion appears in John of Capua, it is not included in the older *Kalila* texts. Its presence is most probably due to the popular story of the grateful lion, which was part of the Western fable tradition and also, in somewhat different form, entered romance.[286] The descriptions of the lion fawning on his rescuer suggest a derivation from this latter tradition.

This comparison of the different versions of the story in the *Kalila* tradition, by Matthew Paris and Nigel, makes it possible to determine the affiliations of the story as it appears in the other texts identified by Chesnutt as belonging to an 'Anglo-French tradition': the *Compilatio singularis exemplorum*,[287] the Anglo-Latin *Gesta Romanorum*,[288] and Gower's *Confessio Amantis*. The *Compilatio* is a miscellany, containing a collection of exempla arranged according to the 'estates of the world'; the story of the grateful animals appears among the 'exempla de ruralibus' (ed. Hilka, pp. 21–3). The links with *SS* are as follows: the rich man is called Adrianus (with obvious similarity to Dryanus); the poor man is a woodcutter who goes to the forest to gather wood to sell; he has with him an ass; the same three animals as in *SS* (monkey, lion, and snake) have fallen into the pit, but the rich man does not reveal their presence and his would-be rescuer is terrified when they appear; the animals bring the same rewards (wood, fresh meat, a precious stone) as in *SS*; the poor man has a wife and four sons; the jewel brought by the snake miraculously returns to the seller, and this leads to the story of the rich man's rescue becoming public. The picture is complicated slightly by the inclusion of two details which appear in Matthew but

---

[286] The grateful lion story appears in the *Romulus vulgaris*, iii. 1; it tells how a shepherd removed a thorn from a lion's foot, and later, when thrown to the lions in the Roman circus, was recognized by the same lion and spared. The story of the lion who is saved from the clutches of a serpent, which is the pivotal episode of Chretien's *Yvain*, first appears in a letter of Peter Damian (s. xi). See Baist, 'Der dankbare Löwe'.

[287] Selected exempla from the *Compilatio* were edited by Hilka ('Beiträge', pp. 1–24) from two manuscripts, MS 468 in the Bibliothèque municipale de Tours (s. xv), and MS 679 in the Burgerbibliothek of Bern (s. xiii/xiv); a third manuscript is MS C 523 in the Universitetsbibliotek of Uppsala (s. xiv). Thirty-two of these exempla were re-edited by Carsten Wollin ('Geschichten'). The *Compilatio* was judged by Léopold Delisle to have been written in the late 13th c. by a Dominican preacher who was familiar with Touraine, Maine, and Anjou ('Notes sur quelques manuscrits', p. 604). See also Wolff, 'Unterwegs', especially pp. 62–3, 69, for the manuscript references and discussion of the current state of scholarship on this important collection, and its relations with others of similar nature. Delisle gave the Tours manuscript the number 205, but this was updated in Hilka, following the appearance of the *Catalogue descriptif et raisonné des manuscrits de la bibliothèque de Tours* by A. Dorange (Tours, 1875), pp. 251–2.

[288] The date of the *Gesta* is uncertain, but it is probably s. xiv[2/4]; see Bright's Introduction (*Gesta*, pp. xxii–xxviii), with arguments against Brigitte Weiske's claim for a 13th-c. date.

INFLUENCE OF THE *SPECVLVM STVLTORVM* cxxxix

not in *SS*: the rich man is out hunting for meat to serve at his daughter's wedding feast, and when the poor man goes to his house, he finds him among his friends and relatives holding a feast to celebrate his escape from the pit. Contamination seems the only way to account for these details. Other details which diverge from both Matthew and *SS* could well be due to the author's own invention: the rich man's horse runs off when he falls into the pit, so that he is known to be missing; the poor man is called Mados; Adrianus tells Mados to collect bark and tie it together to make a net or mesh ('laqueariam')[289] which he throws down into the pit; it is attached to Mados and his ass by two horse collars, one for himself and one for his ass, so that they can drag the net out of the pit; when asked for the reward, Adrianus mocks Mados, gives him the equivalent of one and a half days' pay, and says he will match whatever he gets from the animals (but does not beat him); the serpent's jewel is sold to the emperor, but returns, since it will do so unless the seller is paid at its true level of worth. The ending is entirely novel: Adrianus denies the whole story, so Mados challenges him to a duel; they meet on the edge of a wood and the three animals emerge and kill Adrianus. Mados inherits Adrianus's wealth. These unique variations have the stamp of original invention, ingeniously put to use to find an extra narrative role for the ass,[290] to increase the contrast between Adrianus and the grateful animals, to make the returning jewel seem less of a cheat, and to give the animals a decisive role in the ungrateful man's punishment. Despite the two details that come from Matthew, the story is clearly closer to *SS* in fundamentals, and has no special connection to the *Kalila* version.

The *Gesta Romanorum* is another exempla collection designed as a preacher's source book.[291] Its heavily didactic nature accounts not only for the long religious allegorization which is appended to the end of the story, but also for the introductory addition to its opening. This tells how the rich man Lenticulus had been raised to wealth and high position by the Roman emperor, on condition that he promise to be trustworthy; his failure to keep this promise in respect of his rescuer thus makes him doubly guilty of ingratitude. It is Lenticulus himself who has ordered the pits to be dug to trap animals, a detail obviously

---

[289] The word is not to be found in the major dictionaries, but it must derive from 'laqueus' = 'snare, noose'; *DMLBS* 4 glosses 'laquear' as 'tie, lace', and the dictionary of Firminus Verris includes 'laqueatus', meaning 'laqueis captus vel ligatus'.

[290] The ass is also given a role when the monkey and the lion bring their gifts: each of them loads them on to the ass.

[291] The Grateful Animals story is no. 83, ed. Bright, pp. 544–63.

cxl   INTRODUCTION

inspired by the biblical maxim that he who digs a pit shall fall into it himself.[292] The animals are the same three as in *SS*, but their gifts have been changed in nature, again in order to provide a basis for the final moralization. The lion brings ten asses laden with riches, which are later explained as the Ten Commandments; the serpent's stone is tri-coloured (symbolic of the Trinity), and it endows its owner with 'joy without sorrow, abundance without want, light without darkness' because it represents Christ, who does the same. These features are identifiable as the *Gesta* author's invention because they disrupt the narrative logic: since the poor man has already been made rich twice over, by the lion and the snake, the rich man's refusal of a reward for his rescue hardly seems to matter. Nevertheless, the underlying shape of the tale shows its derivation from *SS*: the absence of the snake-poisoning episode, the identification of the poor man as a woodcutter with an ass; the violence that the rich man inflicts on him when he claims his reward; the gift of wood from the ape, and the snake's miraculously returning stone as the means by which the story of the rescue becomes known.

The *Gesta* may have picked up the story from the *Compilatio*, or both may have relied on some intermediary exempla collection, but there is no doubt that John Gower knew *SS* directly and intimately. In addition to the *Confessio Amantis*, he is the author of a long Latin satir-ical poem in seven books titled the *Vox Clamantis*. This poem draws heavily on existing Latin poetry, both classical and medieval, including *SS*. Gower's editor Macaulay identified some of its borrowings, and Robert Raymo found many more, all of which are listed below in Appendix C. Gower also explicitly refers to *SS* on two occasions: in his opening account of a dream in which people are grotesquely trans-formed into animals (an allegory of the Uprising of 1381), he sees them aspiring to be horses but actually becoming asses:

> Ut vetus ipse suam curtam Burnellus inepte
>   Caudam longari de novitate cupit,
> Sic isti miseri nova tergaque longa requirunt,
>   Ut leo de cauda sint et asellus idem. (i. 201–4)

Just as old Burnellus, from a desire for novelty, stupidly wishes to lengthen his short tail, so these wretches seek new and long backs, so that the lion and the ass may be the same in respect of tails.

Later in the poem, he criticizes the friars for abandoning their own Rule and following the 'new order' created by Burnellus:

---

[292] See n. to lines 1087–8 for the biblical references.

INFLUENCE OF THE *SPECVLVM STVLTORVM* cxli

Set sacer ordo tamen remanet, quem sanxerat olim
   Frater Burnellus, crescit et ille magis.
Hec decreta modo, Burnellus que statuebat,
   Omnia non resero nec reserare volo.

...

Mollibus ornatus sic dignior ordo novellus
   Restat Burnelli, vult quia velle viri.
Nil michi Bernardus, nichil ammodo seu Benedictus
   Sint, set Burnellus sit Prior ipse meus. (iv. 1189–92, 1207–10)

But the holy order that Brother Burnellus sanctioned of old remains in being, and grows in size. I will not disclose all those decrees that Burnellus instituted, nor do I wish to do so.

...

So the more venerable new order, adorned with soft clothing, is still that of Burnellus, since man's desire wants it to be so. Bernard is nothing to me, nor is Benedict anything to me now, but Burnellus shall be my Prior.

Gower's retelling of the tale of the Grateful Animals and the Ungrateful Man appears in his major tale-collection, the *Confessio Amantis* (v. 4937–5162); although more briefly related, it clearly derives from *SS*. The names of the two principal actors are themselves clues to its origins: the rich man is named Adrianus (representing Nigel's Dryanus) and the poor man Bardus (representing Burnellus's master Bernardus). As in *SS*, the poor man is gathering wood with his ass when he hears the trapped man's cries for help, accompanied by a promise of half his wealth to his rescuer. Also as in *SS*, Adrianus does not tell his rescuer that there are animals in the pit with him, so that Bardus is amazed and terrified when first an ape and then a serpent come up the rope he has let down into the pit. Once rescued, Adrianus sets off for home without even saying 'thank you', and when Bardus asks for the reward, he receives only threats. Still following the *SS*, the next day the ape brings wood to Bardus and the serpent brings a precious stone which magically returns to him every time it is sold. The news of this reaches the emperor, the truth emerges, and Bardus is rewarded with half of Adrianus's possessions. The story shows 'What schame it is to be unkinde [ungrateful]' (v. 5160). The only major divergence from *SS* is the omission of the lion, which may have been due to the desire for brevity, but it is also possible that Gower was (like me) puzzled by the idea of a lion climbing a rope.[293]

---

[293] This would also account for Matthew's specification of a rope-*ladder*, and the *Compilatio*'s unique account of the making of the 'laquearia' which is attached to horse-collars and pulled up by the poor man and his ass.

cxlii   INTRODUCTION

Finally, Burnellus's survey of the monastic orders was, to judge by its survival in multiple florilegia, one of the most popular parts of the poem.[294] Its influence also seems to be apparent in the vernacular, namely in the early thirteenth-century *Bible* of Guiot de Provins. Written in 2,686 rhyming octosyllables, this is a satire on the 'estates of the world' model, beginning in the conventional manner at the top of

[294] Raymo claims several other examples of Nigel's influence on later writers (*SS*, p. 127, n. 50) but on examination almost all these claims turn out to be spurious; see the notes on lines 2481–2, 2508–10, 3893–4. The exception is Gerald of Wales (see n. to line 317). Raymo also claims (*SS*, p. 127, n. 50) that Boccaccio 'explicitly refers to the *SS* in a letter', citing *Le lettere autografe di Giovanni Boccaccio*, ed. Traversari, letter iv, p. 71. The reference is inaccurate, as becomes clear when Traversari's text is checked on archive.org: letter iv ends on p. 65, and there is nothing on p. 71 that relates to *SS*. The first Index (p. 78) shows that the word 'brunellitos' appears in letter iv on p. 61, as part of a description of the unpleasantness of peasant life, which includes their 'latratus brunellitos' (Traversari confesses that he does not understand this adjective). Massèra's standard edition of the letters (*Epistolarum quae supersunt*) renumbers this as letter ii, and emends the word to 'brunellicos'; he comments 'la spiegazione (da *Brunellus*, l'asino, del poema di Nigello Wireker) è del Cian' (p. 316), referring to Cian's note in *Bulletino della società dantesca italiana*, NS xvii, p. 139, which explains the word as an allusion to *SS*. Ginetta Auzzas's edition of the *Epistole* in vol. v.1 of the multivolume Mondadori edition of Boccaccio (ed. Branca) takes over Massèra's text, and translates the phrase as 'asinini latrati', but offers no further comment. Raymo has accepted Cian's explanation (without citing it), despite the fact that he was well aware (see his note to *SS*, line 595, on p. 149) that 'brunellus' was used as 'a popular synonym for *asellus* or *asinus*' (see the examples given in my note to *SS*, line 595). The word 'brunellicos' is therefore not an allusion, explicit or implicit, to *SS*, and there is thus no evidence at all that Boccaccio knew *SS*.

Raymo's claim (p. 127, n. 49) that Odo of Cheriton was one of those who drew on *SS* is also dubious at best. Raymo links *SS* 137–8 with 'Hervieux, II, p. 608', and his List of Abbreviations expands this as a reference to Hervieux, *Les Fabulistes latins* (5 vols., 1893–99). However this is the second edition, in which Odo of Cheriton's fables occupy a volume to themselves, namely vol. iv, which does not run to 600 pages. The fable of the town mouse and the country mouse appears on pp. 190–1, and the only verse line quoted there is 'Rodere malo fabam quam cura perpete rodi', which is taken from the same fable in the elegiac *Romulus* (ed. Busdraghi, 12. 23). In fact Raymo is referring to the first edition of Hervieux's *magnum opus*, in which Odo does indeed appear in vol. ii (1883), and on p. 608: in the fable of the town mouse and the country mouse, lines 137–8 of *SS* follow the line from the elegiac *Romulus* just quoted. Confusingly, in vol. iv these lines are still included in Hervieux's list of 'vers cités par Eudes' on p. 345, without any cross-reference to Odo's *Fables* or explanation of their removal in this new volume. The explanation of the discrepancy between the two editions of the *Fabulistes latins* is that the text of Odo's *Fables* in the first edition is taken from BL, Harley 219 (s. xv), while the text in the second edition is taken from Cambridge, Corpus Christi College, 441 (pp. 488–9). Checking with the digitized version of the latter manuscript in Parker on the Web confirms that the two lines from *SS* are indeed absent from the Corpus manuscript. Corpus 441 is a 13th-c. manuscript with Canterbury provenance: it belonged to Richard de Weynchepe, a monk, who became prior of the Benedictine priory of Dover in 1268, but it seems to have reverted to the library of Dover's mother house, Christ Church, Canterbury, since it is listed as no. 1420 in the early 14th-c. catalogue of Christ Church library by Henry of Eastry (James, *Ancient Libraries*, pp. 120–1, 511).

Further investigation of Odo manuscripts would be needed to determine whether Odo himself quoted Nigel's lines, or whether they were simply added by some alert scribe who picked up their appropriateness to the fable of the two mice.

MANUSCRIPT CIRCULATION   cxliii

the social scale with the Pope and the Roman curia and working downwards to the secular professions of medicine and law. The monastic
orders are dealt with in the following order: Benedictines, Cistercians,
Carthusians, Grandmontines, Premonstratensians, regular canons;
the Templars and Hospitallers are (understandably) demoted to the
end of the line, and followed by a new section on the canons regular of
St Anthony and the late twelfth-century order of the Capuchonnés du
Puy;[295] a final section deals with nuns and *conversi*. The content of the
satire is mostly confined to generalities, and only occasionally echoes
SS: for example, the narrator complains that the Cluniacs will wake
him up during the night when he wishes to sleep (1665–7; cf. *SS* 2079–
80); in the Grandmontine order, the *conversi* lord it over the choir
monks (cf. *SS* 2217–18). The erroneous statement that the Carthusians
'ne tiennent pas silence' (1514) is an echo of *SS* 'nulla silentia seruant'
(2187). These details may be mere coincidences, but the influence of
SS seems to be detectable in Guiot's separate treatment of each order;
in other medieval examples of estates satire, monks are all lumped
together.[296]

MANUSCRIPT CIRCULATION

Apart from Guiot, the writers who produced later imitations of portions
of *SS* were English or Scots, and the earliest surviving manuscripts
(thirteenth or fourteenth century) are also English. However, the
poem's later circulation and influence were by no means restricted to
the British Isles. The surviving fifteenth-century manuscripts testify
to an impressively wide geographical diffusion in Europe, ranging
from Paris in the east, through Germany, Austria, Poland, Bohemia
and Moravia, to Prague in the west. In the seventeenth century, Queen
Christina of Sweden acquired a copy (MS *R*), which with the rest of
her collection eventually passed to the Vatican; a century later, a copy
produced in Germany (MS *Q*), entered the Royal Library in Copenhagen.
Interest in the poem was fuelled by the Reformation, whose supporters
saw in its satire of the Roman curia, its critique of ecclesiastical failings
such as clerical marriage and the ordination of child priests and
bishops, and the survey of the monastic orders, ammunition for their
own criticism of the papacy and Catholic doctrine. Communications
between Wycliffites and the followers of the Bohemian Protestant

---

[295] As in *QY*, the section in *SS* on the order of Simplingham/Sempringham is understandably omitted by Guiot, since it was an exclusively English order.
[296] See the lists of estates in Mann, *Chaucer and Medieval Estates Satire*, pp. 203–6.

cxliv INTRODUCTION

Jan Hus, executed for heresy in 1415, were one strand in a web of relations between England and Bohemia which went back to the marriage of Anne of Bohemia to King Richard II, and continued through the first half of the fifteenth century.[297] The Croatian humanist and Lutheran reformer Matthias Flacius Illyricus owned a copy of the poem (MS Y), and included an account of it in his *Catalogus testium veritatis*, a conspectus of anti-clerical writings and documents dating from the beginnings of Christianity up to Matthias's own day.[298] Matthias quotes from the passage on the secular canons in the survey of monastic orders (2327–30, 2349–50), and from the passage on the greed of the Roman curia (2511–14, 2517, 2519–20, 2535–40, 2557–8).[299] Doubtless Nigel's poem was also enjoyed for its own literary merits, but its popularity some two hundred and fifty or three hundred years after its date of composition also had unexpected causes and effects far beyond what its author could have imagined.

NIGEL'S METRE AND STYLE

During the twelfth century, the study of Latin grammar—in monastic as well as cathedral schools—attained a level of excellence unparalleled since late antiquity, to the point that the Latin composed by many twelfth-century authors achieves a standard which makes their writings, from the point of view of grammatical correctness, virtually indistinguishable from those of their classical and Late Latin predecessors. The excellence of this Latin training was founded on the meticulous study of classical Latin authors, both prose and verse. Although it is not possible to determine where Nigel had received his schooling (some features of his poem might suggest Paris), the Latin of the *Speculum Stultorum* reveals that Nigel was the beneficiary of that excellent training in Latin which characterizes the writings of many of his contemporaries, notably the author of the *Ysengrimus*, John of Salisbury, and Walter of Châtillon (to name only three prominent twelfth-century

---

[297] See Hudson, *Transmission of Wyclif's Writings*, I–III; Van Dussen, *From England to Bohemia*; Hornbeck and Van Dussen, eds., *Europe after Wyclif*.

[298] *Catalogus testium veritatis* (1562 edition), pp. 539–40. See Haye, 'Der *Catalogus testium veritatis*', p. 39. Matthias's source for information on English writers seems to have been the English antiquary John Bale (who owned MS W). Both were in Basel in the mid-16th c., and shared the same publisher; see Huber-Rebenich, 'Die Rezeption der mittellateinischen Satire', pp. 182–3.

[299] Matthias also thinks Nigel is serious in praising clerical marriage, failing to take account of the fact that this approval is voiced by an ass and is therefore ironical.

NIGEL'S METRE AND STYLE   cxlv

Latin poets). An analysis of Nigel's Latin verse may begin by considering the classical and Late Latin poets whom he had evidently studied
with care.

Of classical Latin poets, Nigel was thoroughly familiar with all the
verse of Vergil (*Aeneid, Georgics, Eclogues*),[300] with most of the verse of
Horace (*Odes, Saturae, Epistulae*),[301] and the *De bello ciuili* of Lucan.[302]
He also had certainly studied the *Saturae* of Juvenal, and (probably) of
Persius.[303] But the poet whose verse he knew best, and was most deeply
influenced by, was Ovid: the *Speculum Stultorum* is permeated with
reminiscences, especially of the *Heroides* and *Metamorphoses*,[304] but
also (to a lesser extent) the *Amores, Ars amatoria, Fasti*, and *Tristia*.[305] It
is not simply that Nigel repeats phrases from Ovid's verse: it is that his
sense of metrical structure and rhythm is profoundly influenced by Ovid.

In addition to the principal classical Latin poets,[306] Nigel was also
widely read in Late Latin and (to a lesser extent) in Christian-Latin verse.
Thus his verse reveals debts to the following: the *Disticha Catonis*;[307]
Avianus, *Fabulae*;[308] Claudian, *De raptu Proserpinae* and *Panegyricus
de Quarto Consulatu Honorii Augusti*;[309] Maximian, *Elegies*,[310] and the
metra of Boethius, *De consolatione Philosophiae*.[311] The first four authors

---

[300] Vergil, *Aeneid*: see notes to lines 1493, 2924, and 3155–60 (and cf. also notes to lines
533, 1074, 1198, 1867, and 1975–6); for the *Georgics*, cf. the notes to lines 533, 1074, and
1197; and for the *Eclogues*, note to line 2617 (and cf. the note to line 3273).

[301] Horace, *Odes*: see note to line 4; *Saturae*: see notes to lines 137–8 and 1782 (and cf. note
to line 2253); and *Epistulae*: see notes to lines 668 and 2569–70 (and cf. note to line 3009).
There is a possible reminiscence of the *Ars poetica* at line 2369.

[302] Lucan, *De bello ciuili*: see note to line 621 (and cf. notes to lines 1147, 2637, and 2652).

[303] Juvenal, *Saturae*: see notes to lines 651 and 923; for Persius, cf. note to lines 1421–2.

[304] *Heroides*: see notes to lines 145, 300, 341, 391, 461, 544, 545, 571, 626, 1026, 1456,
1479, 2894, 3155–60, and 3542; and cf. also notes to lines 471–2, 1082, 1376, 2198, 2899,
3336, and 3520. *Metamorphoses*: see notes to lines 517, 547–8, 564, 2737, 3004, 3061, 3256,
and 3664; and cf. also notes to lines 401, 1029, 1867, 2475, and 2614.

[305] *Amores*: see notes to lines 153, 167, and 1700 (and cf. notes to lines 589–90, 1372, and
2609); *Ars amatoria*: see notes to lines 23 and 446; *Fasti*: see note to line 299; *Tristia*: see notes
to lines 459, 968, 1177, and 3649.

[306] Interestingly, Nigel's verse shows no knowledge of Lucretius or Silius Italicus, and
quotes Statius only once (289).

[307] *Disticha Catonis*: see notes to lines 1107, 1973–4, and 3877 (and cf. note to lines 1277–8).

[308] Avianus, *Fabulae*: see notes to lines 57–66, 740, 1300, 1617–21 (and cf. note to lines
3507–8). It is hardly surprising that Nigel should have been familiar with one of the principal
sources of Latin beast fables.

[309] Claudian, *De raptu Proserpinae*: see note to line 39; *Panegyricus de Quarto Consulatu
Honorii Augusti*: see note to line 2659.

[310] Maximian, *Elegies*: see notes to lines 76, 496, 571 (and cf. note to line 1030).

[311] Boethius: see notes to lines 3329 and 3378 (and cf. notes to lines 49–50, 3041–2, and
3357).

cxlvi INTRODUCTION

in this list form a regular part of the so-called Liber Catonianus, the group of texts which were usually studied by young students learning Latin.[312] The Christian-Latin poets whose verse formed the staple of the curriculum in the early Middle Ages (e.g. Juvencus, Caelius Sedulius, Cyprianus Gallus, Arator) appear not to have been studied by Nigel, given that the curriculum of Latin authors had changed substantially by the twelfth century; but he does show knowledge of Prudentius and Dracontius.[313]

Finally, Nigel seems to have been well acquainted with the Latin poetry of his contemporaries. Thus his verse contains frequent reminiscences of several Latin *comoediae* (the *Babio*, the *Geta* by Vitalis of Blois, and possibly the *Lidia* and the *Pamphilus*).[314] He was evidently familiar with the *Ysengrimus*, the twelfth-century master-piece which defined the genre of the Latin beast epic,[315] as well as with the so-called elegiac *Romulus*.[316] He knew the Latin verse of Hildebert of Tours,[317] John of Salisbury,[318] Hugh Primas,[319] Sextus Amarcius,[320] and numerous short satirical poems such as those by Walter of Châtillon.[321]

The *Speculum Stultorum* is composed in elegiac couplets, and so it is unsurprising that the earlier poets whose influence is most palpable throughout the poem also composed in elegiacs: Ovid (esp. the *Heroides*, but also the *Amores*, *Ars amatoria*, and *Tristia*), Avianus, Maximian, and (of twelfth-century verse) the *Ysengrimus*, the elegiac *Romulus*, and the elegiac *comoediae*. Since an elegiac couplet consists of a hexameter

---

[312] See Mann, 'He knew nat Catoun'.

[313] Prudentius, *Liber cathemerinon*: see notes to lines 401 and 517; *Contra Symmachum*: see note to line 1469 (and cf. note to line 945); *Psychomachia*: see note to line 1375. Line 46 possibly contains a reminiscence of the *Praefatio*, and line 1566 of the *Hamartigenia*. Dracontius, *De laudibus Dei*: see note to line 3412.

[314] *Babio*: see notes to lines 1876 and 2028 (and cf. notes to lines 56 and 703); Vitalis of Blois, *Geta*: see note to line 442; *Lidia*: cf. the note to lines 1051–2; and *Pamphilus*: cf. the note to line 1197.

[315] *Ysengrimus*: see note to line 825 (and cf. notes to lines 819–20 and 1055).

[316] Elegiac *Romulus*: see notes to lines 14, 137–8, and 359–60.

[317] Hildebert, *Carmina*: see note to line 3007.

[318] John of Salisbury, *Entheticus maior*: see note to line 1012 (and cf. note to line 1560); *Entheticus minor*: see note to line 1030.

[319] Hugh Primas, *Gedichte*: see note to line 1021 (and cf. note to lines 1837–8).

[320] Sextus Amarcius, *Satires*: see note to line 2187.

[321] Walter of Châtillon, *Poems*: cf. notes to lines 1999–2000, 2498, 2511–16, 2535, and 2663. Nigel also seems to have known the *Apocalipsis Goliae* and some of the poems included in the *Carmina Burana*.

NIGEL'S METRE AND STYLE

followed by a pentameter, it is convenient to consider Nigel's handling of each of these elements separately.

Hexameter

A hexameter consists of six metrical feet, of which the final two—at least during the Middle Ages—were invariably a dactyl (– ˘ ˘) in the fifth foot, followed by a spondee (– –) or trochee (–˘) in the final foot. The rhythm of the final cadence was therefore fixed. In the first four feet of a hexameter, however, there was considerable flexibility of choice: each of the first four feet could be either a dactyl (D) or a spondee (S). With two possibilities in each foot, there were a total of sixteen possible combinations of dactyl and spondee in the first four feet, ranging from DDDD, a combination which produces a rapid, often mellifluous, flow of syllables, to SSSS, which produces a sharp, staccato-like effect, with the other fourteen possible combinations lying in between these two extremes. In practice, of course, individual poets favoured individual combinations, particularly in the eight combinations which they used most frequently. As George Duckworth, who pioneered the analysis and recording of these metrical structures, observed, 'the percentages of the favorite pattern ... and especially the first eight, are extremely significant in that they help to establish the metrical "fingerprints" of the various poets'.[322] Analysis of the preferences in the first eight feet, therefore, helps to characterize each poet's individual poetic voice: Vergil, for example, always placed a spondee in the fourth foot of his hexameters, whereas Ovid invariably began his hexameters with a dactyl. In fact Ovid has been characterized by Duckworth as 'the master of dactylic rhythm'.[323] It is hardly surprising then that Nigel, who (as we have seen) was thoroughly familiar with Ovid, should have been deeply influenced by Ovid's preference for dactylic rhythms, as may be seen from the following table (where the statistics for Nigel are based on scansion of the first 500 hexameters of his poem; those for Ovid's *Metamorphoses* are taken from Duckworth;[324]

---

[322] Duckworth, *Vergil and Classical Hexameter Poetry*, p. 5.

[323] Ibid. pp. 71–80.

[324] Ibid. p. 73. It will be seen from the table that Duckworth did not provide percentages for nos. 3–8 among Ovid's preferences in the *Metamorphoses*. Since the percentages for the first two choices are so similar to those of Nigel, as are the overall percentages of the first eight, it did not seem worthwhile to scan all 11,995 hexameters of the *Metamorphoses* in order to supply the statistics which Duckworth omitted.

cxlviii INTRODUCTION

and those for the *Heroides* are based on scansion of the 766 hexameters of *Heroides* i–x):

Nigel, *SS* 1–999	totals (%)	Ovid, *Met.*	Ovid, *Heroides* i–x
1. DDSS	68 (13.6%)	1. DDSS (13.1%)	1. DDSD (14.4%)
2. DSSS	64 (12.8%)	2. DSSS (12.6%)	2. DSSD (13.8%)
3. DDSD	62 (12.4%)	3. DSSD	3. DSDS (10.3%)
4. DSSD	56 (11.2%)	4. DSDS	4. DSSS (10.0%)
5. DDDS	46 (9.2%)	5. DDSD	5. DDSS (9.5%)
6. DSDS	44 (8.8%)	6. DDDS	6. DSDD (9.1%)
7. DSDD	39 (7.8%)	7. DSDD	7. DDDD (8.0%)
8. DDDD	37 (7.4%)	8. DDDD	8. DDDS (6.9%)

The first eight patterns of *SS* make up 83.2 per cent of the total, a figure which closely resembles the totals for Ovid's *Metamorphoses* (81.6%) and *Heroides* (82.1%). The figures for the first two patterns of *SS* are virtually identical to those for the *Metamorphoses*. Like Ovid, Nigel almost never places a spondee in the first foot of his hexameters, and his first eight preferred rhythms are all dactylic.

The rhythm of the first four feet of Nigel's hexameters, then, was deeply influenced by Ovid. The rhythm of the final two feet—the five syllables which make up the cadence—of his hexameters, however, is not indebted to classical precedent. Classical Latin poets typically terminated their hexameters with either a trisyllable followed by a disyllable (*Metamorphoses*, i. 1: *dicere formas*) or a disyllable followed by a trisyllable (*Metamorphoses*, i. 17: *forma manebat*); only on exceptionally rare occasions was a hexameter terminated (say) by a single pentasyllable, and in such a case the word would characteristically be a Greek name. Medieval Latin poets began to experiment with different types of rhythm in their hexameter cadences, with the result that medieval hexameters often terminated in two monosyllables, or a monosyllable followed by a tetrasyllable, or a monosyllable followed by two disyllables, or a single pentasyllable. Terminations such as these, which are infrequent in classical Latin verse, characterize what is called 'the medieval hexameter'.[325] Nigel was well aware of this medieval development, and these cadences constitute a significant proportion of his hexameters: thus the *Speculum Stultorum* has 18 cadences consisting either of

---

[325] This aspect of the 'medieval hexameter' was first defined by Klopsch, *Einführung in die mittellateinische Verslehre*, pp. 68–74, and was further explored by Orlandi, 'Caratteri della versificazione dattilica', pp. 347–52 with the table on pp. 358–9, and Lapidge, 'Two notes on the "medieval" hexameter', pp. 123–34.

NIGEL'S METRE AND STYLE

two monosyllables or ending in a single monosyllable;[326] 42 cadences consisting of a monosyllable followed by a tetrasyllable;[327] 18 cadences consisting of a monosyllable followed by two disyllables;[328] and 83 cadences consisting of a single pentasyllable.[329] In sum, there are 161 'medieval' cadences in Nigel's hexameters, corresponding to 82 per 1,000 lines: a fairly substantial amount.

Classical Latin poets attempted to moderate the flow of syllables in their hexameters by the use of elision and by the placement of caesuras. Elision occurs when a word ending in a vowel (or a vowel + *m*) is followed by a word beginning with a vowel; in such cases the two vowels elide to become one. (Elision between two vowels is called *synaloepha*; that between a vowel + *m* and a following vowel is called *ecthlipsis*; hiatus is said to occur when vowels in these circumstances do not elide.[330]) Vergil, for example, employed elision in more than half his hexameters (52%), with as many as three elisions occurring in a single hexameter. Ovid used fewer elisions than Vergil; nevertheless, elision occurs in more than 20 per cent of Ovid's hexameters. The medieval Latin poets who modelled their verse closely on that of their classical predecessors tended to employ elision on a similar scale: Walter of Châtillon in his *Alexandreis*, 15.8 per cent; Joseph of Exeter in his *Ylias*, 21.0 per cent; and the author of the *Ysengrimus*, 18.4 per cent;[331] but there were other medieval Latin poets who avoided elision altogether: thus there is no example of elision in the *Geta* of Vitalis of Blois, and only one elision in 511 verses of Alan of Lille's *Anticlaudianus*, as scanned by Klopsch.[332]

---

[326] *SS* 107 (*non sunt*), 141 (*quis sis*), 173 (*per quem*), 809 (*uae uae*), 855 (*ha ha*), 1157 (*non est*), 1237 (*ad quid*), 1546 (*hy ha*), 1554 (*hy ha*), 1729 (*a me*), 2037 (*a spe*), 2393 (*aut res*), 3603 (*hic sum*), 3877 (*aut res*). More abrupt are the cadences which end in a single monosyllable: 2323 (*sua sit*), 2663 (*faciat nos*), 3521 (*super me*), and 3873 (*apud te*).

[327] For example, *SS* 51 (*ex alieno*), 67 (*ex alieno*), 71 (*ex alieno*), 79 (*non rapuisse*), 125 (*et speciebus*), 201 (*rex Ludouicus*), 315 (*non potuerunt*), 465 (*non miserandae*), 715 (*uult manifestum*), 777 (*de peregrino*), 887 (*tu benedictus*), 889 (*in peregrinos*), 927 (*tam manifesto*), 1005 (*est faciendum*), and so on.

[328] For example, *SS* 175 (*hoc minus illo*), 675 (*et tua cauda*), 753 (*est tua tota*), 1305 (*non lupus agnum*), 1609 (*quae tamen ictus*), 1627 (*me prece fusa*), 1881 (*nec suus esse*), 1923 (*Mons Iouis iste*), and so on.

[329] For example, *SS* 33 (*prodigiosos*), 35 (*prodigiosum*), 85 (*utilitatem*), 105 (*experimenta*), 123 (*praeueniente*), 153 (*auriculatus*), 159 (*utilitatis*), 183 (*sustinuisse*), 189 (*nobiliores*), 203 (*conditionem*), 253 (*materiatum*), 271 (*surripuere*), 295 (*praecipitandum*), 335 (*paenituisse*), 381 (*utilitatis*), 589 (*deficiente*), 611 (*enumerandis*), 625 (*experiemur*), 671 (*progredienti*), 693 (*ebrietati*), 743 (*Londoniensis*), 779 (*religiosum*), 861 (*dimidiatam*), 997 (*accelerato*), 1049 (*conditione*), and so on.

[330] There is no example of hiatus in the *Speculum Stultorum*, so the phenomenon requires no further discussion.

[331] See discussion by Klopsch, *Einführung in die mittellateinische Verslehre*, pp. 79–87.

[332] Ibid. p. 82.

cl INTRODUCTION

Nigel's practice is very similar to that of Alan of Lille: there are only three instances of elision, all involving the verb *est*, in the 1,950 hexameters of the *Speculum Stultorum*.[333] Concerning the caesura (that is, a break when the ending of a word occurs within a metrical foot): in classical Latin verse, a caesura was normally placed at approximately the midpoint of the hexameter, that is, after two and a half metrical feet, as in the opening three hexameters of Ovid's *Metamorphoses*:

> In nova fert animus | mutatas dicere formas
> corpora; di coeptis | (nam vos mutastis et illas)
> adspirate meis | (*Metamorphoses*, i. 1–3)

A caesura placed like this in the third metrical foot is referred to by metrists as a 'strong' or 'masculine' caesura, and is denoted as 3m. (Since the strong 3m caesura occurs after five metrical half-feet or measures—a measure consists of either one long (–) or two short ($\smile$ $\smile$) syllables—it is technically described as a 'penthemimeral' caesura.) In order to introduce some variety into the structure of their hexameters, and to avoid the monotony of repeated 3m caesuras, classical Latin poets also from time to time employed what is called a 'weak' or 'feminine' caesura (denoted 3f), that is, a caesura placed after the first long *plus* the following short syllable of a third-foot dactyl, as in these two examples from near the beginning of Ovid's *Metamorphoses*:

> nec quicquam nisi pondŭs | iners congestaque eodem (*Metamorphoses*, i. 8)

> ponderĭbus librată | suis, nec bracchia longo (*Metamorphoses*, i. 13)

Classical Latin poets used feminine 3f caesuras but sparingly, and principally to avoid the monotony of repeated 3m caesuras, as I have said: 11 per cent of caesuras in Vergil's *Aeneid* are feminine, and 9 per cent of those in Ovid's *Metamorphoses*.[334] Nigel was clearly aware of the classical practice of using occasional feminine caesuras for variety, but in fact he very rarely used them: there are only thirteen examples in the 1,950 hexameters of the *Speculum Stultorum*.[335]

---

[333] *SS* 169 (*multor(um) est*), 2495 (*caus(a) est*), and 2951 (*caus(a) est*).

[334] Statistics for the occurrence both of masculine (3m) and feminine (3f) caesuras in Latin poets from Lucretius to Abbo of Saint-Germain (end of 9th c.) are given in Lapidge, 'Two notes on the "medieval" hexameter', pp. 146–7.

[335] The following hexameters in *SS* have feminine (3f) caesuras: 3, 505, 747, 749, 1817, 1961, 1965, 2359, 2407, 2591, 3041, 3533, and 3835.

NIGEL'S METRE AND STYLE   cli

Associated with the almost invariable use of the strong (3m) caesura was the practice of treating as long a naturally short syllable when positioned as the caesural syllable (that is, the long syllable which occurs immediately before the caesura itself). This 'lengthening' of a naturally short syllable at the caesura is described as *productio ob caesuram*. Lengthening of this sort was avoided by classical Latin poets such as Vergil and Ovid; only with the Latin poets of the early Middle Ages, such as Eugenius of Toledo, does the practice become more common.[336] A good example of the practice can be seen in the following hexameter from *SS*:

> Prospera sint cunctā, sint cunctă salubria nobis (735)

In this example, the final short syllable of the first *cuncta* is lengthened at the strong (3m) caesura, but in the second occurrence of the word, *cuncta* is scanned correctly, with a short final syllable. Nigel's practice in this respect is comparable to that of his twelfth-century contemporaries: there are 90 occurrences of *productio ob caesuram* in his hexameters,[337] and a further 84 examples of lengthening of the caesural syllable in his pentameters;[338] overall, therefore, *productio* occurs in 4.4 per cent of his verses (cf. figures for the *Elegia* of Henry of Settimello (3.8%), Walter of Châtillon, *Alexandreis* (6.6%), Joseph of Exeter, *Ylias* (4.0%), etc.).[339]

Pentameter

The second element of the elegiac distich was the pentameter, which consisted of two more or less equal halves: the first half consisted of two feet, either of which could be a dactyl (– ⌣ ⌣) or spondee (– –), followed by a long caesural syllable; the second half of the pentameter consisted of two dactyls followed by a final caesural syllable. It will be seen that the only variation permissible was the choice of dactyl or spondee in the first two feet. Nigel in his pentameters followed the example of Ovid, particularly in the *Heroides*, in preferring dactyls over spondees, as may be seen from the following table:

---

[336] The most thorough study of this practice in classical and early medieval Latin poetry is by Friedrich Vollmer, *Zur Geschichte des lateinischen Hexameters*, esp. pp. 38–52.

[337] See, for example, *SS* 69, 163, 167, 175, 207, 227, 335, 391, 477, 547, 561, 565, 605, 637, 663, 675, 677, 695, 729, 735, 753, 835, 841, 945, 955, 981, 989, 1021, etc.

[338] See, for example, *SS* 12, 102, 122, 208, 268, 318, 418, 440, 470, 480, 528, 582, 606, 608, 650, 654, 656, 672, 678, 694, 806, 874, 878, 986, 1004, etc.

[339] For the practice of *productio* in 12th-c. Latin poets, see Klopsch, *Einführung in die mittellateinische Verslehre*, pp. 74–6, with Table VIII.

SS, 2–1000	totals (%)	Ovid, *Heroides* i–x	totals (%)
1. DS	209 (41.8%)	1. DS	394 (51.3%)
2. DD	184 (36.8%)	2. DD	231 (30.2%)
3. SD	82 (16.4%)	3. SD	83 (10.9%)
4. SS	25 (5.0%)	4. SS	59 (7.6%)

Ovid's pentameters have a slightly higher percentage of DS than Nigel's, but the proportions are very similar: as in their hexameters, pentameters begin in the majority of cases—some 80 per cent—with a dactyl (79% in Nigel, 81% in Ovid), as against a mere 20 per cent which begin with a spondee. In the second half of the pentameter, no variation of the two dactyls was allowed, but the arrangement of words which make up the dactyls was a matter of poetic choice. In Ovid, the final word of the pentameter was usually disyllabic, although occasionally he would place a monosyllabic word in the final caesural syllable (e.g. *Heroides*, ii. 74: 'hic est cuius amans | hospita capta dolo est', and iii. 22: 'nec repetor; cessas, | iraque lenta tua est', with elision of the preceding syllable in both cases). This practice is not followed by Nigel. But one arrangement, which Ovid apparently learned from Tibullus, was that of filling the entire second half of the pentameter with a pentasyllabic word followed by a disyllable: 'crimine te potui | demeruisse meo' (*Heroides*, ii. 28) or 'paenitet et lateri | conseruisse latus' (*Heroides*, ii. 58). This arrangement allows the end of the pentameter to flow smoothly as a unit. Sometimes the rapidity of the flow of syllables in the pentasyllable reproduces the speed of the action being described:

> cum grege pastores, praecipitando gradum (534)
> spargitur armentum, diffugiuntque greges (536)
> certauit celeri praecipitique pede (550)
> ut nostrum citius expediatur iter (736)
> certantes subita dissiluisse fuga (1820)

Of the 1,950 pentameters in SS, 314 end in this way, with a pentasyllable followed by a disyllable; this is the equivalent of one every six pentameters: a far greater frequency than is observable in earlier elegiac poets. Nigel can be observed exploring the possibilities of the pentameter cadence, as in the examples quoted above. On two striking but similar occasions, Nigel replaced the pentasyllabic word with five monosyllables: 'contigit, et dubito | ne sit et an sit ita' (2916), and 'uera rei series | quae sit et an sit ita' (3844). There is no antecedent in

NIGEL'S METRE AND STYLE   cliii

Ovid for this daring practice, and one can only conclude that Nigel was experimenting playfully with a fixed form.[340]

Prosody

On the whole, Nigel's prosody is correct by classical standards, and reveals remarkable attention to classical precedents.[341] On occasions when he departs from classical practice, there is usually abundant precedent in Late Latin and early medieval Latin verse. For example, he frequently scans the final long -*o* of first person verbs (present and future indicative, as well as future imperative) as short; but this practice is already well established in Ovid. It is evident that Nigel chose the form with -*ŏ* as a matter of metrical convenience, for forms with the short vowel often exist alongside forms with the (classical) long vowel: e.g. 'ergo gestabō sed non gustabŏ Lyaeum' (707). (There are 65 examples of final -*o* scanned as short, as against 44 examples of the correct classical long -*ō*.[342]) Similarly, the long -*ō* with which the ablative of the gerund terminated in classical Latin was frequently shortened by medieval poets as a metrical convenience. In the *Speculum Stultorum* there are 29 examples of the gerund with short final -*ŏ* against a mere three examples with the correct classical Latin long -*ō*.[343] By the same token, Nigel scans the final syllables of adverbs ending in -*ē* as short (*cautĕ* (3882), *maximĕ* (3871), *mysticĕ* (3881) *studiosĕ* (2705), *stultĕ* (130), and *ualdĕ* (2934)). He lengthens the naturally short first syllable of *statim* (1941, 3461) and the naturally short third syllable of *mulieres, -um* (2371, 2446, 3147). He shortens the naturally long first syllable of *feria* (2088, 2425; cf. 2175 *fĕrales*). With Greek loanwords that had long been naturalized in Latin he follows the practice of earlier Latin poets and ignores the original length of Greek vowels: thus the second syllable of *ecclesia* is scanned short (2336, 2755, 2775,

---

[340] On two occasions (*SS* 2844, 3064), Nigel filled the entire first half of a pentameter with a single hexasyllabic word: *religiosorum*. The only possible precedent for this practice in Ovid's *Heroides* is the hexasyllable *Hellespontiaci* (*Her.* xviii. 108, xix. 32).

[341] It is striking, for example, that he has mastered the rule (known as *brevis brevians*) by which the diphthong in the prefix *prae-* is scanned short when it is followed in a compound word by another vowel: 900 (*praeeunte*), 1205 (*praeeunte*), 1209 (*praeeunte*), 1321 (*praeeuntia*), 1345 (*praeoptabat*), 1475 (*praeeunte*), 1715 (*praeambula*), 2329 (*praeeuntibus*), and 2330 (*praeeunt*).

[342] For example, *SS* 3 (*mittŏ*), 119 (*estŏ*), 247 (*estŏ*), 259 (*malŏ*), 430 (*erŏ*), 445 (*malŏ*), 600 (*reditŏ*), 667 (*ibŏ*), 669 (*erŏ*), 707 (*gustabŏ*), 779 (*putŏ*), 794 (*seruiŏ*), 807 (*approbŏ*), 809 (*transeŏ*), 898 (*nesciŏ*), 899 (*nesciŏ*), 937 (*nesciŏ*), 1128 (*nesciŏ*), etc.

[343] For example, *SS* 537 (*fugiendŏ*), 682 (*dandŏ*), 778 (*dandŏ*), 830 (*meditandŏ*), 845 (*currendŏ*), 902 (*meditandŏ*), 1114 (*mendicandŏ*), 1115 (*memorandŏ*), 1167 (*redimendŏ*), 1199 (*uacandŏ*), etc.

cliv INTRODUCTION

2779), as is the penultimate syllable of *charactere* (2825); the short first syllable of *climata* is scanned long (601), as is the final syllable of *horizon* (3401). His treatment of *canon*, a Greek loanword with a naturally short first syllable, is variable: sometimes it is scanned correctly with a short first syllable (2250, 2347), but more frequently the first syllable is scanned as long (893, 2315, 2375, 2407, 2409, 2796, 2817).[344] The only unprecedented error of scansion in the *Speculum Stultorum* involves the word *oestrus* or *oester* (a 'horse fly'). The first syllable *oe-* reproduces the original Greek diphthong, and is correctly scanned as a single long syllable (as could have been observed in Vergil, *Georgics*, iii. 148 or Juvenal, *Saturae*, iv. 123); inexplicably, Nigel scans the first syllable as an iamb ($\smile$ –), thus *ŏēster*, etc. in 373, 421, 527, 531, 541, 556. But this is a rare exception.

Rhyme

Rhyme was an unostentatious feature of Latin verse from the time of Vergil onwards. The favoured site for monosyllabic rhyme in hexameter verse (disyllabic rhyme is virtually non-existent in classical Latin verse) was the caesural penthemimeral syllable and the final syllable (this type of internal, or horizontal, rhyme came in the twelfth century to be known as 'leonine' rhyme), as in the following line from near the beginning of Ovid's *Metamorphoses*: 'nam caelo terras et terris abscidit undas' (i. 22). Ovid uses rhyme of this sort in roughly 11 per cent of his hexameters, and this modest proportion is fairly typical of all hexameter verse from Vergil to the end of the ninth century.[345] From the tenth century onwards, particularly in poets such as Hrotswitha and Purchard of Reichenau, and the poet of the *Ecbasis captivi*, the amount of monosyllabic rhyme rises dramatically, to over 90 per cent of hexameters.[346] In the following century, a further development was initiated by a number of poets from the Loire valley—Hildebert of

[344] The scribes of *D* and *K* add a couple of spurious lines after 2315 (see above, p. xcvi), expressing their disapproval of the long ā in 'cānŏnĭcī', but there are parallels elsewhere. See the satirical couplet by Serlo of Wilton, *Poèmes*, ed. Öberg, p. 120, no. lxxiv: 'Nōstrī cānŏnĭcī dēbēnt ā cānŏnĕ dīcī –/ Nāmquĕ quŏd ēst cānōn bĕnĕ sērvānt, āppŏsĭtā "nōn" ', and the popular verses attributed to Hugh Primas (supposedly on the loss of his prebend): 'Cānŏnĭcūm quī cānŏnĭcē mē cānŏnĭcāstīs,/ Cānŏnĭcūm nōn cānŏnĭcē dēcānŏnĭcāstīs' (*Beiträge*, ed. Werner, no. clxiii, p. 78). On the appearance of these lines in other manuscripts, see Delisle, 'Notes', p. 605; Meyer, 'Les Manuscrits français', p. 349; Hugh Primas, *Gedichte*, ed. Meyer, p. 78. For another example of Nigel's use of variable vowel length, see the comments on 'pater' in the n. to line 1184.

[345] See discussion by Lapidge, 'Two notes on the "medieval" hexameter', pp. 134–42, with table at pp. 143–7, as well as the earlier study by Karl Strecker, 'Studien zu karolingischen Dichtern', pp 213–51 ('Leoninische Hexameter und Pentameter im 9. Jh.').

[346] Orlandi, 'The hexameter in the "aetas Horatiana" ', pp. 382–3, with table at pp. 385–9.

NIGEL'S METRE AND STYLE   clv

Tours, Marbod of Rennes, Baudri of Bourgueil—in which monosyllabic rhyme was replaced by disyllabic rhyme, and this striking practice subsequently spread throughout Europe, and was extended from disyllabic leonine rhyme to include rhyme of many kinds.[347] At Canterbury, for example, disyllabic rhyme characterizes the verse of the poet Reginald, particularly his metrical *Vita S. Malchi*. Reginald was resident at St Augustine's in the early twelfth century, but had received his training at the hands of the poets of the Loire, such as Hildebert.[348]

Nigel was well aware of the practice of using disyllabic rhyme. His own *Passio S. Laurentii* is composed of 2,348 hexameters, set out as couplets, each of which has disyllabic end-rhyme (called *versus caudati*).[349] In the *Speculum Stultorum*, however, rhyme of any kind is used only sporadically, and such rhyme as occurs is usually monosyllabic, and rarely disyllabic. Thus, at the very beginning of the poem, Nigel addresses William of Longchamp with the following lines, which have monosyllabic rhyme in both hexameter and pentameter:

> Suscipe pauca tibi ueteris, Willelme, Nigelli
> scripta, minus sapido nuper arata stylo. (*SS* 1–2)

Rhyme like this, where both hexameter and pentameter have monosyllabic leonine rhyme, but with a different rhyme in each line, is found in the following verses describing the iniquities of secular canons:

> bursa carens fundo, praedae sine nomine praedo,
> lanx mendax ueri, uera statera doli,
> lex sine lege Dei, canon sine canone Christi,
> praeuia causa mali, pagina plena doli.
> Hi sunt iustitiam qui prostituere pudicam,
> falsa loqui linguas qui docuere suas. (*SS* 2345–50)

A similar rhyme scheme, but with the same monosyllabic rhyme in both hexameter and pentameter, is used at various points in the poem, including these lines describing the abuses of bishops:

> totque domus domini, tot circumquaque ministri,
> tot stantes pueri, totque meando uagi;

---

[347] Klopsch, *Einführung in die mittellateinische Verslehre*, pp. 38–49. There is an admirably clear and succinct description of the various kinds of rhyme to be found in quantitative Latin verse composed in England from the 11th c. to the 15th, in Rigg, *Anglo-Latin Literature*, pp. 319–22.

[348] The most thorough study of Reginald's verse is Liebermann, 'Raginald von Canterbury'; see also the brief note by Lind, 'Reginald of Canterbury and the rhymed hexameter'.

[349] Ziolkowski discusses Nigel's *versus caudati* at *Lawrence*, pp. 65–8.

clvi   INTRODUCTION

> tot iuuenes compti uariisque modis redimiti,
> totque senes docti gesta priora loqui. (*SS* 2719–22)

It would appear from these examples that rhyme was randomly introduced, and was not employed in order to underline the message of the
lines in question.[350] The same randomness is seen on the very rare
occasions when Nigel employs disyllabic leonine rhyme, as in the
following distich:

> Saepius exosus ueniat post terga molossus!
> Oscula dando tamen, dixit asellus, Amen.[351] (681–2)

Usually disyllabic rhyme like this is found in single lines only;[352] but
there is one point of the *Speculum Stultorum* where disyllabic leonine
rhyme is used over a stretch of six lines (for no apparent purpose):

> Non sum Burnellus sapiens, sed iners et asellus
> semper, et in primis stultus hebesque nimis;
> stultus ego natus, sum stultus et ante creatus,
> quamque diu fuero non nisi stultus ero.
> Stultus et ipse pater meus et stultissima mater,
> dat mihi natura disipuisse mea. (*SS* 1119–24)

Even here, however, Nigel abandoned the disyllabic rhyme scheme
in the final verse. Nigel was clearly very responsive to the sounds of
Latin,[353] but this response did not encourage him to introduce rhyme
on any extensive scale.

Poetic Diction

The language of classical Latin poetry was strikingly different from
that of prose,[354] and many features of classical Latin poetic diction

---

[350] The same pattern of monosyllabic rhyme in hexameter and pentameter is found in
lines 23–4, 191–2, 475–6, 501–2, 573–4, 837–8, 861–2, 1101–2, 1135–6, 1161–2, 1517–18,
1971–2, 2041–2, 2173–4, 2231–2, 2235–6, 2247–8, 2783–4, and 3425–6.

[351] The same disyllabic rhyme (*tamen—Amen*) occurs in the final line of Nigel's *Passio S.
Laurentii*: 'cum genitore tamen prece martiris annuat, amen' (2348).

[352] *SS* 189 (*maiores—nobiliores*), 697 (*salmentis—mentis*), 791 (*Burnellus—asellus*), 1419–
20 (*fiat—dictat, bibat—luat*), 2171 (*carnalis—spiritualis*), 2259 (*induti—uti*), and 2323–4
(*suasit—sua sit, suas—duas*). The only occasion in the entire poem in which disyllabic vertical
rhyme between hexameter and pentameter occurs is the metrical epitaph of the cow Bicornis:
'Quae dum stulta fuit doctos docuisse probatur / haec postquam sapuit uermibus esca
datur' (*SS* 593–4). There are examples of monosyllabic vertical rhyme in lines 709–10, and
2061–2.

[353] Note, for example, the insistent repetition of sounds in lines 1151–2: 'error posterior
peior quandoque priore / esse solet uereor posteriora mea'. But this is an isolated occurrence.

[354] See the valuable studies by Janssen, 'Le caratteristiche della lingua poetica romana',
and Leumann, 'La lingua poetica latina'.

NIGEL'S METRE AND STYLE   clvii

were imitated by medieval Latin poets. Some, but not all, of the characteristic features of classical Latin poetic diction are to be found in the
Speculum Stultorum: the use of so-called 'poetic' compounds;[355] the use
of diminutives; the use in the fifth foot of hexameters of accusative and
ablative terminations in *-amina/-amine* from nouns in *-men*; Grecisms;
the use of the third person preterite plural termination in *-ere* (in lieu
of *-erunt*); and the use of the perfect infinitive with present meaning.
(Various other features of classical Latin poetic diction, such as passive
infinitives with the archaic termination *-ier*, the use of the *accusativus
graecus*, the genitive plural of second declension nouns in *-um*, are
almost totally absent from the Latin verse of Nigel.)[356] Nigel's use of
these various aspects of poetic diction is as follows. In the entirety of
the *Speculum Stultorum*, there are only six examples of 'poetic' compounds: *altisonis* (2377), *mortifero* (2615), *quadrifidi* (2408), *Romipeta*
(1951), and *ruricola* (729, 3169). Nigel uses diminutives only on rare
occasions (with the obvious exception of *asellus*, which occurs fourteen
times: 57–9, 61, 75, 81, 665, 791, 1063, 1075, 1077, 1099, 3187, 3570):
carbunculus (2499), *catulus* (728), *paruula* (265, 364), *paucula* (320,
2011, 3500), *pusillus* (2151, 2152), *sarcinula* (664, 1222), and *sportella*
(3501). Nouns in *-men* with acc./abl. terminations in *-amina/amine* (a
feature which is distinctively Ovidian) are used very rarely by Nigel:
medicamine (599, 613, 3451), *moderamine* (285, 1011), *modulamine*
(2377), and *stamine* (651). The poem contains a scattering of grecisms:
antiphrasim (1641, 1646, 2406) *apocopata* (86, 1709), *astmaticos* (3195),
charactere (2825), *climata* (601), *grammate* (592), *horizon* (3400),
hypocrisi (2434), *paradigmate* (11), *pedagogus* (2773), *phantasmate*
(3625, 3635), *psalmatis absque melo* (2412), *spermate* (653), and *syncopa*
(1710). While these features of classical Latin poetic diction are used
very sparingly by Nigel, there are two features which have a more
tangible presence in his poem, namely the use of the third-person
preterite plural in *-ēre* (rather than *-ērunt*),[357] and the use of the perfect

---

[355] On 'poetic' compounds (by which is meant tetrasyllabic, bipartite nouns or adjectives,
the first part of which is usually denominative, the second part deverbative, the entire word
having the metrical structure of a choriamb (–˘ ˘ –)), see Janssen, 'Le caratteristiche della
lingua poetica romana', pp. 121–6; Leumann, 'La lingua poetica latina', pp. 169–71, as well
as—for early medieval Latin verse—Lapidge, 'Poetic compounds'.

[356] There is one possible instance of an *accusativus graecus* in *SS*: *foemina nuda pedes*
(3472).

[357] See Janssen, 'Le caratteristiche della lingua poetica romana', p. 98, and Leumann, 'La
lingua poetica latina', pp. 156–7. Nigel could have observed this practice in the verse of Ovid;
e.g. *Heroides* v. 121–2: 'Dixerat, in cursu famulae *rapuere* furentem / at mihi flaventes
diriguere comae'; etc.

clviii INTRODUCTION

infinitive in lieu of the present.[358] Nigel uses the third-person preterite plural in *-ēre* some sixty-five times,[359] the regular preterite plural in *-ērunt* far less often.[360] As far as usage of the perfect infinitive is concerned, in some cases it is unambiguously clear that the sense is present rather than past, as in the following line, where the infinitive is placed in the context of present imperatives:

Ne perdas quod habes, quod habes *tenuisse* labora. (*SS* 131)

or in the following lines, where the perfect infinitive is used in parallel with a present infinitive, both of which are dependent on a verb in the present tense:

cantorisque uidet niueo sub tegmine gallum
obtinuisse uices atque *tenere* chorum. (*SS* 1387–8)

By my count there are some 89 examples where the perfect infinitive is quite likely being used with present meaning,[361] and a further 46 occasions where the perfect infinitive is (probably) being used correctly with past meaning.[362] But it is often difficult to be certain that the intended sense is present rather than past. Similarly, Nigel used various metrical 'helpmeets' which are characteristic of classical Latin

---

[358] Note the comment of Janssen ('Le caratteristiche della lingua poetica romana', p. 85), that the use of the perfect infinitive 'è così caro ai poeti dattilici proprio perché molti di questi infiniti perfetti, soprattutto quelli formati da perfetti in *-ui*, si adattano facilmente all'esametro, e viceversa parecchi infiniti presenti non vi trovano posto: *continere* non è possibile, *continuisse* invece sì.' Nigel could have observed this practice in the verse of Ovid; e.g. *Heroides* iii. 117–18: 'tutius est *iacuisse* toro, *tenuisse* puellam / Threiciam digitis *increpuisse* lyram'; etc.

[359] For examples, see *SS* 118 (*nocuere*), 214 (*procubuere*), 227 (*uoluere*), 230 (*continuere*), 270 (*consueuere*), 271 (*surripuere*), 626 (*ualuere*), 706 (*consueuere*), 853 (*periere*), 855 (*cecidere*), 860 (*deperiere*), 867 (*periere*), 875 (*continuere*), 895 (*conuenere*), 896 (*constituere*), 1071 (*periere*; but cf. 1079: *perierunt*), 1354 (*praeteriere*), 1359 (*siluere*), etc.

[360] But note *SS* 857: 'Illa remans**erunt** tantum quae nulla fu**erunt**', with disyllabic leonine rhyme.

[361] For examples, see *SS* 52 (*tumuisse*), 79 (*rapuisse*), 113 (*nocuisse*), 131 (*tenuisse*), 142 (*statuisse*), 145 (*habuisse*), 167 (*dixisse*), 168 (*fecisse*), 183 (*sustinuisse*), 305 (*praetimuisse*), 335 (*priuasse*, *paenituisse*), 354 (*detinuisse*), 360 (*nocuisse*), 407 (*meminisse*), 409 (*meminisse*), 410 (*habuisse*), 425 (*praetimuisse*), 428 (*euasisse*), 432 (*latuisse*), 436 (*nocuisse*), 554 (*succubuisse*), 750 (*latuisse*), 838 (*docuisse*), 868 (*restituisse*), 958 (*deperiisse*), 1014 (*latuisse*), and so on.

[362] On some occasions the past sense of the perfect infinitive is utterly unambiguous: e.g. 1928 (*studuisse*), 1929 (*didicisse*), and 1930 (*deperisse*). Elsewhere the past sense is probably, if not certainly, intended: for example, at 68 (*dedidicisse*), 72 (*perisse*), 210 (*rediisse*), 593 (*docuisse*), 862 (*deperiisse*), 1093 (*docuisse*), 1106 (*desipuisse*), 1131 (*desipuisse*), 1142 (*sapuisse*), 1391 (*fecisse*), 1392 (*fuisse*), 1588 (*dedidicisse*), 1744 (*diripuisse*), 1842 (*surripuisse*), 1858 (*tulisse*), 1865 (*seruasse*), 1866 (*exposuisse*), 1987 (*tenuisse*), etc.

NIGEL'S METRE AND STYLE

clix

poetry, such as syncope,[363] synizesis,[364] and tmesis.[365] It seems clear, however, that he employed these various devices as a matter of metrical convenience, and not in order to impart poetic resonance to his poem. Overall the diction of the *Speculum Stultorum* is prosaic rather than poetic, even though it is cast in metrical form. His overriding concern was with verbal witticism rather than with poetic nuance.

Style

Nigel's poem is animated by wordplay of many kinds; the ludicrous adventures and opinions of the donkey are pointed throughout by witty use of rhetorical schemata of various kinds. Some of these schemata, such as anaphora (the repetition of the same word at the beginning of verses) and epanaphora (the repetition of a word within a verse), occur so frequently that there is little point in recording them here. However, four kinds of rhetorical schemata were particularly favoured by Nigel, and these deserve individual discussion: polyptoton, asyndeton, alliteration, and paronomasia.

Polyptoton is a form of wordplay based on distinct but etymologically related forms of a word,[366] and is found throughout the *Speculum Stultorum*. The following list (which is not exhaustive) will give some idea of Nigel's penchant for this form of wordplay: 33–4 (*parit— partus—partu*), 78 (*pondera pondus*), 130 (*ulterius ulteriora*), 159 (*magnum magna*), 160 (*amplius ampla*), 177 (*qui facit et reficit, creat atque creata gubernat*), 224 (*lutosa lutum*), 321 (*dura—duranda*), 391 (*passa— passura*), 487 (*modicum modico*), 506 (*texerat intextis*), 814 (*crimine crimen*), 873 (*miser—miserabilis*), 878 (*non ferus immo fera*), 945–6 (*dignis digna*), 947 (*Causa grauis, grauior persona, grauissima damna*), 1107 (*fraus fraude, ars—arte*), 1376 (*sonare sonat*), 1468 (*derisus rideo*), 1539 (*studio studiosus*), 1602 (*conditio conditione*), 1644 (*sequente sequi*), 1749 (*omnibus omnia*), 1837–8 (*miseratio—miseris—misererer*), 1844 (*uicit et euicit*), 1857 (*pondera pondus*), 2011 (*de multis multi*), 2037 (*spes fuit in*

---

[363] Syncope involves the 'cutting out' of a syllable, for example the shortening *metri gratia* of *uincula* to *uincla* (280, 324, 326, 1892), or of *pericula* to *pericla* (107, 363, 3665, 3680, 3884).

[364] Synizesis involves the 'sinking together' of two vowels, as in *SS* 2771, where the verb *deest* is scanned as a monosyllable.

[365] Tmesis, or the 'separation' of one word into two, as in *SS* 1872, where the word *quocumque* is separated into its two elements for metrical reasons: *quo- tibi -cumque placet.*

[366] Leumann, Hofmann, and Szantyr, *Lateinische Grammatik*, ii. 707–8. Isidore defines polyptoton as the employment of one word in different cases: 'polyptoton est, cum diversis casibus sententia variatur' (*Etymologiae*, i. 36. 17).

clx   INTRODUCTION

flore, sed flos defloruit a spe), 2134 (*facti—facta*), 2155–6 (*suo sua, texisse—detexisse*), 2169–70 (*fidelis—infidum—fide*), 2172 (*fallitur—fallit*), 2229 (*solam solus*), 2272 (*mundis munda*), 2309 (*caro carnis*), 2331 (*mundum non mundus*), 2336 (*status absque statu*), 2352 (*labent labant, ruente ruunt*), 2545 (*maculat maculosa*), 2554 (*memorem—memoranda*), 2570–1 (*regna regunt, regnant, regum*), 2609 (*insanabile sanis*), 2654 (*armat inarmatas*), 2675 (*a pascendo—non depascendo*), 2807 (*paterentur quod patiuntur*), 3067 (*odio nos odit*), 3093 (*turbato cerebro turbantur*), 3131 (*uigili uigilantior*), 3144 (*nigra—nigriora*), 3291 (*superi superis*), 3292 (*magno—magna*), 3504 (*duxit et abduxit*), 3603 (*miser et miserabilis*), 3605 (*miserumque misertus*), 3797 (*de postfacto res est patefacta*), and 3822–3 (*grauis—grauem—grauiorem*).

Asyndeton is the stringing together of words of the same class (in Nigel's case, usually nouns) without the use of connectives.[367] On rare occasions Nigel will compose an entire hexameter by stringing together five nouns without any connective: e.g. *SS* 376 ('lancea funda lapis claua sagitta faces') or 3444 ('scandala contemptum schismata damna dolum'). But his favourite use of asyndeton was the so-called *asyndeton trimembre*, in which three words, usually nouns, are combined without a connective so as to constitute either the first or the second half of the pentameter. Examples of three-member asyndeton in the first half of the pentameter are the following: 218 (*stagna lacus fontes*), 808 (*risus uerba iocus*), 1228 (*uotum causa solum*), 1360 (*pocula nox somnus*), 1507 (*ossa cutem neruos*), and 3374 (*pectore uoce manu*); but more numerous are examples of three-member asyndeton in the second half of the pentameter: 1078 (*tympana sistra chori*), 1112 (*corpore mente pede*), 1232 (*pectore uoce pede*), 1446 (*pectore uoce manu*), 1508 (*balnea cura quies*), 1852 (*uerbera uerba cruces*), 1878 (*carcere fune cruce*), 2236 (*ligna legumen aqua*), 2478 (*uiscera corda latus*), 2830 (*brachia colla manus*), 2846 (*pascua prata greges*), 3094 (*lumina lingua manus*), 3162 (*laudet honoret amet*), 3430 (*pascua prata greges*), and 3680 (*damna pericla necem*). By the same token, three-member asyndeton is also used as the cadence of a hexameter: 2261 (*faba pisa legumen*), 2335 (*uigor ordo potestas*), and 3793 (*leo simia serpens*).

Alliteration, the repetition of the same sound (vocalic or consonantal) at the beginning of consecutive words, is a common feature of Latin verse of all periods.[368] Alliteration involving three or four consecutive words is frequent in the *Speculum Stultorum*: 438 (*parua pari*

---

[367] Leumann, Hofmann, and Szantyr, *Lateinische Grammatik*, ii. 828–31.
[368] Ibid., 700–4.

NIGEL'S METRE AND STYLE   clxi

poterit), 491 (*cauda cauet capiti*), 733 (*sint merces multae, sit multum cara moneta*), 752 (*in propria patria non peregrinus eris*), 1600 (*mala multa mihi*), 1613 (*cur mea me mater maledicta fudit ab aluo*), 2484 (*dolore meo mens mea mente caret*), 2574 (*trepidet terra timore*), 2746 (*dispensante Domino dissimulante diu*), 2880 (*cum canibus multis multa minando mihi*), 3033 (*ne faciant fructum flores*), 3181 (*consilia crebro capiuntur*), 3235 (*uolucres uerna uelocius*) 3365 (*pondere pressa pedum prohibetur*), 3409 (*munera magna manu*; repeated in 3428); 3510 (*uertice cum cauda conueniente mea*), 3585 (*uocis uox uerbi*) 3628 (*praemia ne pereant percipienda sibi*), 3654 (*deficiunt domino deficiente suo*), and 3665 (*uota uiamque uia*). In addition to striking examples such as these, involving three or four consecutive words, there are countless examples of pairs of alliterating words in the *Speculum Stultorum*.

Paronomasia is wordplay involving similar sounding, but etymologically unrelated words, what in English is called a pun.[369] Paronomasia is used throughout the *Speculum Stultorum*, sometimes with brilliant effect. I list some examples to indicate the nature of Nigel's use of this device. In speaking of peasants (820), whom Burnellus vigorously hates, he says that they are said to be born (*satus*) from Satan's excrement, which they prove sufficiently (*satis*); in speaking of his own qualifications for being a bishop, Burnellus states (1717) that he will tolerate no treaty (*foedus*) with the 'foul' (*foedo*) Simon (i.e. he will not be guilty of simony); he considers that the monastic order of Simplingham is named for their 'simplicity' (2405: 'Simplingham dictus de simplicitate uocatus'); at another point (2543–4) he observes that a headache (*dolor*) makes all limbs ache (*dolere*), just as a small amount of poison infects large receptacles (*dolia*); and finally that Bernardus has cut off Burnellus's ears so that he will in future be more 'cautious' (*cautior*) having been 'cauterized' (*cauteriatus*) in this way (3508). There are many more examples of paronomasia in the poem, but perhaps the most striking example concerns Burnellus's forgetting the name of Paris, at which he has just spent seven years studying; when asked by a wayfarer why he is now going to Paris, the mention of the name *Parisius* determines Burnellus to remember it; but, unfortunately, when the wayfarer later says his 'Pater noster', the word 'Pater' drives out from his mind the syllable *Par-*, and the name of Paris is lost with it. Nigel brilliantly illustrates Burnellus's predicament with a series of puns involving the syllables *par-* / *per-*:

---

[369] Ibid. 709–14.

clxii INTRODUCTION

Verbum quod periit nostrum uerbo peregrini
    par fuit in parte principioque sui.
Finis erat dispar

Partem pro toto poni docuere diserti,
    dummodo pars maneat sufficit una mihi.
Nec totum superest, ubi pars est una recisa,
    nec totum periit, parte manente sui. (1979–81; 1989–92).

At any moment it seems that the lost word will re-emerge, but it always remains unrealized. Passages such as this show plainly that one of Nigel's principal concerns in the *Speculum Stultorum* was the display of his verbal wit.

EARLIER EDITIONS AND TRANSLATIONS
OF THE *SPECVLVM STVLTORVM*

There have been only two editions of the *Speculum Stultorum* in modern times. In 1872 Thomas Wright published an edition in the first volume of his *Anglo-Latin Satirical Poets*. This was based on only three manuscripts, which Wright labelled A, B, and C (without divulging further details), and one printed edition, labelled P. Mozley ('On the text', 1929) identified the manuscripts as BL, Harley 2422 (A), BL, Arundel 23 (B), and BL, Cotton Titus A. XX (C), while P is the edition printed at Paris by A. Gaillant in 1485 or 1490 (at *SS*, p. 16, Mozley qualifies this and says it is either the Paris or the Utrecht edition). A and C belong to the same branch of the stemma (my δ), and P is, according to Mozley, closely related to R, also a δ manuscript, although an idiosyncratic one. Although B belongs to a different branch of the stemma (β), it has a substantial lacuna as a result of missing leaves (covering lines 849–1386), so that Wright did not have sufficient data to construct a critical edition. His text has several of the omissions characteristic of δ (941–4, 1070–1, 1169–72, 1185–6, 1275–6), although elsewhere he could rely on B to supply the missing lines; he also omits lines 1302–3, 3785–6, 3810–11. His text is also marred by misprints and the choice of inferior readings.

In 1960, J. H. Mozley (a British classicist) and Robert R. Raymo (an American medievalist whose PhD dissertation (University of Cambridge, 1953) was a translation and commentary on *SS*) published their edition of *SS*, which was based on a far larger number of manuscripts and included brief descriptions of them, a selective *apparatus criticus*, a discussion of the relation of the manuscripts and the development of the text, and 40 pages of explanatory notes. This edition was

EARLIER EDITIONS AND TRANSLATIONS   clxiii

generally greeted with an enthusiastic response from reviewers; only Karl Langosch published an extremely critical review, which concluded with the severe judgement that the work needed to be done all over again from the beginning. Close examination of this edition shows that Langosch was right.

To begin with Mozley and Raymo's list of manuscripts: this comprises 40 items, only 32 of which are medieval copies of the whole (or nearly the whole) poem. Five are fragments, containing only short excerpts; one is a transcript made in the seventeenth century by Richard James, the Cotton librarian; one is a prose paraphrase of the poem, and one is a copy of the so-called *Liber de moribus egregiisque dictis omnium philosophorum et poetarum*. This is a voluminous prose compendium of various moralizing texts, including *SS*; a résumé of the poem's narrative is followed by excerpts of its moralizing passages (e.g. 'de medicis', 'de miserabili statu curie romane'). The sigla assigned to these 40 items make no discrimination between their differing natures; they are all jumbled together in the list, and capital and lower-case letters are randomly assigned (instead of reserving lower-case letters for fragments, as is usual). Also, the information provided for each item is rife with error of various kinds: manuscript shelfmarks are inaccurate (for example, Munich 2380 should be 23820, and Konelige Bibliotek, Copenhagen S 1364 should be Det Kongelige Bibliotek Copenhagen, GKS 1634 quarto); Bodleian Library shelfmarks are given only as *Summary Catalogue* numbers, and the *SC* number for Bodley 761 should be 2535, not 2353. Folio references are inaccurate (for example, in Digby 27, SS ends at fo. 61^r, not fo. 67; in Bodley 780, the last folio is 33^v, not 36^v). Details of the poem contained in the manuscripts are sometimes ignored or misreported: for example, in Bodley 496, the poem ends at 3864, not 2746 as Mozley states, while Bodley 780 not only ends imperfectly but also lacks lines 1116–744 and 2747–3258 through loss of leaves.

This level of carelessness persists throughout: the reported readings in the *apparatus criticus* and the section of the Introduction dealing with manuscript relations contain too many errors to document.[370] Even the list of major differences in readings between the two branches of the textual transmission identified by Mozley (*SS*, pp. 17–18) jumps

---

[370] Working on Mozley's edition brings to mind David Knowles's comment on Cardinal Gasquet, that his 'capacity for carelessness amounted almost to genius' (*The Historian and Character and Other Essays*, p. 254).

clxiv INTRODUCTION

from line 430a to 497b, and reverses the entries for line 1951 (see above, pp. cxviii–cxx). Although it is obvious from his passing remarks that Mozley did not collate all the manuscripts fully, he never states clearly which ones were collated in full and which in part only. His treatment of the manuscript relations does not recognize that they are in the first instance to be established by agreement in error, and he never explains why some readings are to be regarded as error and others as correct (as Langosch points out). Mozley's text of the poem is also marred by frequent typographical errors. The following readings in Mozley's edition are assumed to be typographical errors, since either they are not Latin, or they make no sense in context, and/or are not found in any manuscript, and are not signalled as an editorial emendation. The correct reading is given in parentheses:

> 326 regis (reges); 383 capite (capiti); 784 noman (nomen); 1038 mins (mens); 1129 sum (cum); 1165 prohibit (prohibet); 1185 tenere (terrere); 1338 muntius (nuntius); 1359 silit (silet); 1363 accendens (accedens); 1482 victoria (victoris); 1704 praemutiliata (praemutilata); 1715 mulus (munus); 1749 quicque (quique); 1819 agressique (egressique); 1868 talis (talia); 1877 debit (debet); 1915 erge (ergo); 2336 absquo (absque); 2680 student (studet); 2829 voc (vox); 2852 omnis (omnia); 2930 nihi (mihi); 3054 malam (mala), 3111 maculum (maculam); 3228 moto (mota); 3305 uulta (uultu); 3331 abscendens (abscedens); 3348 haero (haereo); 3397 duae (duas); 3410 his (hic); 3421 sedem (eadem); 3440 his (hic); 3731 Barnardus (Bernardus); 3759 totiensque (quotiensque); 3835 hinc (haec); 3841 me (mi); 3885 nonnuli (nonnulli); 3887 ardua (ad ardua); Epistle: 1 seribentis (scribentis); 7 festucan (festucam); 12 ceberet (deberet); 18 erat (esset); 19 hieme (in hieme); 20 duo (duae); 21 uetuli (uituli); 22 eos...adire (eis...adesse); 39 hos (eos); 41 inutiles (instabiles); 44 excitatos (exercitatos); 44 uideantur et credantur (uideantur); 45 hominibus (ab hominibus); 45 aliquod (aliquid).

The following readings are found in a very small number of manuscripts but context nevertheless reveals them to be mistakes:

> 1038 parat (parit); 1190 accrescit (accrescet); 2049 agitur (igitur); 3353 minis (nimis); 3375 possit (posset); Epistle 43 enim (enim hodie).

Errors in the Interpolation on the Mendicant Friars (Appendix A in the Mozley–Raymo edition): the following readings in Mozley's edition are assumed to be simple errors, since they are neither to be found in any of the seven manuscripts nor are they signalled as editorial emendations. The correct reading is given in parentheses.

> 5 quod (quia); 17 quod (quia); 80 quod (quia); 87 sequentes (sequaces); 107 idem (etiam); 113 quidam (quondam); 125 uictu (uicti); 157 hic (hi); 161

EDITORIAL CONVENTIONS

clxv

sanctis (sanctus); 169 religionem (religionum); 180 quod (quos); 212 queant (queunt); 218 famam (finem); 235 quam (plus quam); 240 imprime (impune).

All the above errors (except Epistle 44) have been silently corrected without comment in my Notes.

Raymo's notes are not as defective as Mozley's text and *apparatus criticus*, but they also contain their fair share of erroneous references, which can send the unsuspecting researcher on many fruitless searches. Many of these slips are signalled in my Notes; others have been silently corrected.

As for translations, there is no existing English translation which satisfies the demands of completeness, accuracy, and scholarly presentation. Again, there are only two contenders: in 1959, Graydon W. Regenos published a translation which unfortunately was based on Wright's quite inadequate edition of the poem, and accordingly accepted numerous corrupt or doubtful readings, and also omitted clusters of lines, some of these omissions originating with Wright, others not. The fact that the translation is in iambic pentameters necessarily involved a fairly free treatment with frequent departures from the Latin original, and in addition there are numerous points where Regenos does not properly understand the Latin.

In 1963 Mozley published a translation in rhymed verse of various types (sometimes in couplets, sometimes stanzaic) which also treats the original with some freedom in order to reproduce its witty and comic aspects. Neither of these translations could be of much use to a reader who wished for help in understanding the Latin, for a reliable reflection of its contents, or for a commentary on its historical aspects.

Mention may also be made of the German translation by Karl Langosch, and the Italian translation by Francesca Albini (accompanying the Mozley–Raymo text, but correcting only a few of its typographical errors). Neither of these is of much help in solving difficulties, and the notes in both are of a perfunctory sort.

EDITORIAL CONVENTIONS

This edition is based on a full collation of the 41 manuscripts listed above (pp. lxiii–lxvii), and in Manuscript Descriptions in Appendix A; they comprise the 32 medieval copies of the poem listed by Mozley (leaving aside the seventeenth-century transcript by Richard James), plus the Halle manuscript and a further eight manuscripts that I traced myself. I have personally examined all the manuscripts in London (*A, B, C, K, U, X*), Oxford (*E, F, G, H, I, W*), Munich (*Mu, fm, fn*), and clxvi INTRODUCTION

Brussels (*O*, *P*), and I have photographic prints of all 41, with CDs or microfilms in most cases. I have also collated all the fragments except *fq*, and entered their readings in the *apparatus criticus*. Their textual affinities are indicated below in the Manuscript Descriptions in Appendix A, but I have not discussed them in detail or tried to place them in the stemma. Full collation of 41 manuscripts has inevitably resulted in an *apparatus criticus* of over 70,000 words, too extensive to be published in its entirety in an OMT edition. The methods I have used to reduce it to manageable size are outlined below. It has not been possible to reduce it by selecting a base manuscript and recording only important variations from it. This is because, in the first place, the manuscripts which (I argue above, pp. lxxi–lxxviii) stand closest to Nigel's original draft of the poem (*LEF*) for that very reason do not represent the fullest and final form of the poem. In the second place, other, later manuscripts have suffered large-scale mutilation or deliberate excisions which make them equally unsuitable as a base manuscript. And finally, the three centuries which separate most of these later manuscripts from the author have introduced a degree of scribal corruption which similarly disqualifies them from this role.

In order to demonstrate the evolution of the poem, it has therefore been necessary to analyse its textual transmission in its entirety and to construct a stemma which, although tentative and provisional, can serve as a working hypothesis for evaluating different readings. Fortunately, the relatively stable agreement within each of the various manuscript groups means that the branches of this stemma can be established with a degree of confidence that is sufficient to carry out this evaluation. The *apparatus criticus* is designed to provide the evidence for it, and the evidence is analysed in full above (pp. lxxix–cxxvii).

Nevertheless, in order to reduce the *apparatus criticus* to a manageable length, I have borrowed from other editors of medieval Latin texts (especially those in the OMT series) some principles by which many insignificant variants may be omitted. These are the following:

1. Unique variants (that is, readings found in only one manuscript) are omitted, unless they are in some way interesting from the point of view of the stemmatic grouping or textual transmission, especially those in manuscripts belonging to group α (*LEF*) or group β (*BH*), since these play an important part in the early development of the poem. However, all variants, even unique ones, which are, for various reasons, cited in the Introduction, are included in the *apparatus criticus*. Variants in the fragments are generally recorded, since they are needed to establish stemmatic affiliation of the fragment, as are

EDITORIAL CONVENTIONS clxvii

instances where manuscripts such as *Ha* and *La* give alternative readings, and instances where correction of individual manuscripts, such as
I or *U*, indicates scribal consultation of a manuscript other than the
original exemplar. Also, if a unique variant is accompanied by others
which are supported by two or more manuscripts, the unique variant is
cited as part of the larger group.

2. Common variations in spelling: e.g. c/t confusion; m/n variation
(numquam/nunquam); mihi/michi; nihil/nichil. Idiosyncratic spellings of less familiar words (e.g., thymiamata, amoma, psittacus, antidotum) are also ignored. Diphthongs are used in my printed text, but
not in the variants in the apparatus criticus, even though MS *Z* uses
them.

3. Simple variations in word order (with metrical analysis to support
deduction of the correct order) are omitted.

4. Common scribal variations, such as ipse/ille/iste; quod/quid/
quia/quam/que/qua/quo, etc.; nimis/minus, ergo/igitur, are omitted, unless there are other reasons for recording them.

5. Variants arising from obvious scribal error, caused by omission of
abbreviation marks, or inability to recognize unfamiliar words (unless,
in this latter case, the scribal confusion is shared by more than one
manuscript and thus shows interrelation between them); dittography
(repetition of a word or words).

6. Variant forms of proper nouns (of persons, places, or animals), are
dealt with as follows:
If the name appears only once or twice, the variants are allowed to stand
in the *apparatus criticus* (as, for example, with Saladinus, Lodowicus,
Carabella, Bolonia, Libanum), with manuscript sigla attached. If it
appears more frequently, variants are not recorded in the *apparatus
criticus* but are summarized below, with only occasional identification
of the line(s) in which the variant appears or the manuscript source(s).

Burnellus: The manuscripts are divided on whether the donkey's
name should be spelled Burnellus or Brunellus. The αβ manuscripts
prefer Burnellus, γ prefers Brunellus, while the δ manuscripts are split
between the two, some of them containing both forms. The very few
isolated variants are obvious errors (Brune, Brimellus, Brunullus), the
only one of interest being that Bernellus occurs at exactly the same
point (line 3880) in two manuscripts (*NVe*).

Other names which occur quite frequently but have only trivial and
infrequent variants are as follows: Brunetta (spelled Bruneta or
Brunecta/Brunicta in some manuscripts); Bicornis (spelled Bycornis
or Bicorna); Fromundus (Formundus); Galienus (Gallienus).

clxviii INTRODUCTION

Greater variation is found in other names, such as Gundulfus. It is frequently spelled Gundulphus in αβ and preponderantly in δ; the scribes do not seem to make a distinction between the two spellings. The other manuscripts contain a remarkable proliferation of variants, in which the alternation of f (sometimes ff) and ph can be assumed: Gondulfus, Gandolfus, Gandulphus, Gondolphus, Gendolphus, Gundolphus, Gendulphus, Gundelphus, Grundelphus, Grundulphus. Gundophus, Gundulpus, Gundulplus, Gundolplus, Guldulphus, Gudolfus, and Gundultus.

Other names which occur in limited sections of the poem but yield a surprising number of variants are as follows: Grimbaldus (thus in *L* and *Mu*, and almost universally in δ) elsewhere appears as Grummaldus, Grimwaldus, Grinwaldus, Gibaldus, Gilbaldus (the most popular form in γ), Gimbaldus, Grumbaldus, Crumbaldus, Cumbaldus, Galbaldus, Crimwaldus, Crimbaldus, Gilbardus, Gibbaldus, Giwaldus, Ginwaltus, Grimwaldus, Grumbaldus.

Arnoldus (thus in α and *B*, *H* being out in this section) in γ appears as Alnoldus or Alnodus (*Ne* has both forms). δ is divided: *CWD* have Arnaldus, *J* has Arnuldus, and the rest (including *J* on one occasion) have Arnoldus. Of the mixed manuscripts, *UQY* go with δ, while *Z* has Arnholdus and *X* has Alnardus.

Robekinus and Wileminus. These names exhibit a surprising number of examples within a few lines (2753–65). Substitution of y for i is frequent; other variations are Robikinus, Robokinus, Robkinus, Rolekinus, Robelinus, Rodelinus, Rebekinus, Rubekinus, Robibonus, and Willeminus, Wiliminus, Williminus, Willerminus, Wilekinus, Wilkinus, Velekinus, Vilekinus, Wilekinus, Willekinus, Willelmus, Wilhelminus, Gwylhelmus.

Place names seem to be particularly difficult for scribes to recognize; even when they get them right on some occasions, they falter on others. This is the case with Cremona, which is usually correctly spelled but can also appear as cremena, cremoma, crenona, tremona, tremore, or rinona. *BH* both have ruina; at 3562 *MN* have cremota, evidently induced by preceding 'nota'. At 2469, *Tr* inventively renders 'ab urbe cremona' as 'ab urbe romana', and at 3562, *CW^{ac}KX* replace 'in tota nota cremona fuit' with 'in tota nocior urbe fuit'. Rodanus (the river Rhône) is usually so spelled, but also appears as rodannus, rodanis, rodarius, radanus, rodonus, radonus, redanus. Its genitive form 'rodani' at 1035 is often misread as 'rodam' by scribes. At 1095, *Z* renders it as 'iordanus', and at 1580, 'Trans rodanum', which is written as one word in the manuscripts, appears in *VdBe^{ac}Tr* as 'transiordanem/um' (that

HEADINGS   clxix

is, the crusader kingdom of Transjordan). Lugdunum (Lyon) also appears as lugdumum, lugdinium, lugdinum, lugdunium, ludunum, ludunium, ludinium, lodunum, laudinium, londinium, londonum, dilunium, and ludibrium. Londoniis, ablative of Londoniae ('London'), also appears (at 785 and 1242) as londonia, londomia, ludonia, landonia, londonis, lodoniis, lundoniis, lundonis, landonis. Londonis, ablative of Londoni, adj. ('ciues Londoni', 'citizens of London') appears (at 755) mostly in this form, but frequently as londanis, and also as londinis, lodonis, lundanis, londanus, lundonis, landonis, and londonie. Parisius (Paris) usually indecl. (but see *apparatus criticus* at 1918), also adverbial ('at Paris, to Paris'; see *DMLBS* 3a–b), is also spelled 'parusius' by MS *T* and 'pariseus' or 'pariseos' by MS *Fr*. Simplingham (ignoring simple variation between y and i) appears as simplingham, simplingeham, symphlyngheham, simplegeham, simplegeam, simplegam, simplegepham, simpleiham, simpingham, simpringham, sempringham, semplingham, sempingham, semphinpham, sampingham, symphinigram, symphinigra, simpleinghamia, simphegeham, simpligama, simpligam, simplinga, simplingam, simplegia, simplegena, simpligea, semper lege ham.

HEADINGS

In most of the manuscripts, the text of the narrative is broken up by headings which indicate what follows. These headings vary considerably from manuscript to manuscript, to such an extent that there seems to be no possibility of reconstructing an original version (although it seems likely that Nigel's original had headings of some sort). Sometimes they occur on a separate line between the blocks of text, sometimes they are placed in the margin; sometimes they appear to have been written by the original scribe, sometimes some at least have been added later. In addition, later scribes and readers have added their own comments, narrative summaries, nota signs, and so on, making it difficult to know where to draw the line between a heading and a reader response.

Thomas Wright's edition included headings taken from the sources he used for his text (the three manuscripts *A*, *B*, and *C*, and the printed edition *P*); the sources are indicated in his footnotes. Mozley used the headings in *A* for a large part of the poem, but towards the end of the poem, he expanded some of *A*'s headings (apparently from *D*), and added others (apparently from some δ manuscript) where *A* lacked them. I have collated all the headings, but to include them in the *apparatus* clxx INTRODUCTION

criticus would take up a considerable amount of space (the variant readings take up some 6,000 words). I have therefore decided to follow Mozley in using *A*'s headings, supplemented by headings from *D* at the end of the poem, but italicizing all of them, in order to make it clear that they have not been reconstructed on the same basis as the surrounding text.

TRANSLATION AND NOTES

The translation is designed to be, as far as possible, an accurate reflection of the Latin, while free enough to be readable in its own right. The Notes explain difficulties in the text and provide information on its literary and historical aspects. It is hoped that the edition will be found useful by both historians and literary scholars; each group will doubtless find some of the information given superfluous, but they are asked to remember the needs of the other, as well as of neophytes in the field.

SPECVLVM STVLTORVM

EPISTOLA AD WILLELMVM

1 Dilecto et in Christo[1] diligendo fratri Willelmo suus Nigellus salutem et inniti sapientiae salutari. 2 Librum tibi nuper misi, cuius titulus et textus legentibus et non intelligentibus uidetur esse ridiculosus; sed si singula subtiliter inspexeris animumque scribentis et intentionem attenderis, licet stilus non minus sit rudis quam materia, in aliquo forsitan poteris erudiri. 3 Vnde ut tibi in lucem prodeant quae uerborum uelata sunt dissimulatione, pauca tibi breuiter de absconditis meis dignum duxi denudare.

4 Titulus igitur libelli talis est, Speculum Stultorum.[2] 5 Qui ideo sic appellatus est ut insipientes aliena inspecta stultitia tamquam speculum eam habeant, quo inspecto propriam corrigant discantque in seipsis id esse reprehendendum quod in aliis reprehensibile uiderint quasi per speculum. 6 Verumtamen, sicut speculum intuentibus faciem representat et formam, sed nequaquam in animo praeteritae representationis conseruat memoriam, sic et stultis familiare solet esse raro uel difficile reuocari a propria stultitia, quantumcumque fuerint eruditi ex aliena.

7 Dicitur ergo Speculum Stultorum, uel quia stulti inspecta sapientia statim obliuiscuntur eam[3] uel quia sapientes ex eo etiam proficiunt quod stultorum stoliditatem dum aspiciunt seipsos componunt, et ex

---

1 et in Christo] sibi in christo et semper δ *Tr* sibi in christo *GI* in christo *VbFr Ha* et in christo semper *Mozley*; diligendo fratri] fratri diligendo *I*; Willelmo] .W. *H VaVbPmNe GI HaLa* X Vo *Go* Wi *Be* Wo. S*Pk* Wilhelmo *MuVcT RVe Tr* om. *Fr*; suus Nigellus] om. *Fr*; Nigellus] .N. *H SVaVbBePkPmNe HaLa* X Ni *Go* Nigelli *Mu*; et inniti sapientiae salutari] et sapientie inniti salutari (salutaris *GI*) *F B GI* et intuti sapientie salutari *Go* in summo et uero salutari *AJWHuRMNDK* in summo et uero salute *Ve* in nomine saluatoris *H* 2–3 om. γ *HaLa* 2 cuius] cuius et *F AJRHuMNDVe*; sed] sed et *RVe Tr* 3 meis] om. *H GI X*; duxi] dixi *GI* 4 titulus igitur libelli talis est] titulum huius libelli sic pono (ponitur *Fr*) liber iste γ *HaLa*; igitur] ergo *J Tr* om. *WMNDK*; libelli] huius libelli δ *Tr* 5 ideo sic] igitur sic *H RVe* sic ideo *X*; est] om. *B M GI X*; insipientes] inspicientes *RVe*; eam] eum *VbVcT D*; seipsis] seipsa *W* semetipsis *VaVbVcGoBePkFrPmNe TrHaLa*; id] illud *GI*; reprehensibile uiderint] uiderent reprehensibile *F* reprehensibile uiderunt *FrNe D* 6 intuentibus] inspicientibus *MuVaVbVcTGoPkPm TrHa* insipientibus *BeFr La*ᵃᶜ inspicientium *Ne*; nequaquam] nequam *Pm* neque *H GI X*; stultis familiare] stultis famuliare *J* stultus simili a re *MuVc Ha* stultus similare *Fr* stultis simili re *T* stultis simili are *VaVb* stultis simili a re *PmNe* stulti similiare *Go*; reuocari a propria] a propria reuocari δ 7 statim] om. γ *MN Tr Ha*; obliuiscuntur] obliuiscantur *T R* obuiscuntur *Go* obliuiscens *Vc*; etiam] om. *GI*; quod stultorum stoliditatem dum] qui dum stultorum stoliditatem *VcTFr R* quod (quia *Tr*) dum stultorum stoliditatem (soliditatem *Pm* stultitiam *Mu*) *MuVaVbGoBePkPmNe TrHaLa*; et] ut *GI X*; conspecta] inspecta *RK*; festucam eiciunt] festucam eiciant *GI X* festucam inspiciunt *J* tollunt uestucam *Mu*

THE LETTER TO WILLIAM

1 To dear brother William, beloved in Christ,[1] his Nigel [wishes] health and zeal for healthful wisdom. **2** I recently sent you a book, the title and text of which have a ridiculous air to those who read and do not understand them; but if you carefully examine the details, and pay attention to the aim and intention of the author (even though the style is no less crude than the subject matter), you may perhaps be instructed in some respect. **3** Wherefore, so that the things which are cloaked by verbal dissembling should stand forth in the light for you, I have thought it worthwhile to unveil briefly a few of my secrets.

4 So, the title of the book is this, 'The Mirror for Fools'.[2] **5** It is so called for the reason that the foolish, having scrutinized the folly of others, may have it as a mirror, and having looked in it may correct their own folly, and may learn, as if through a mirror, that what they see to be deplorable in others is to be deplored in themselves. **6** Indeed, as a mirror reflects the face and figure of those who look into it, but keeps no memory at all in the soul of the reflection once it has passed away, so it is usual for fools rarely or with difficulty to be recalled from their own folly, however often they are instructed by that of other people.

7 So it is called 'The Mirror for Fools', either because fools, having once beheld wisdom, immediately forget it,[3] or because the wise also profit from it, because while they gaze at the idiocy of fools they make comparison with themselves, and by means of the beam beheld in

---

[1] This is the reading of *F* (the sole representative of α in the Epistle)βγ*LaX*. Mozley adds 'semper', though no manuscript has the phrase in this exact form. He has silently imported it from the δ reading, 'sibi in christo et semper'.

[2] On the vogue for mirror-titles in the Middle Ages and English Renaissance, see Grabes, *The Mutable Glass*. He speculates that *SS* was 'the first "literary" work' (as opposed to religious/didactic works) to bear a mirror-title (p. 25).

[3] Jas. 1: 24.

4 SPECVLVM STVLTORVM

trabe conspecta in oculo alieno festucam eiciunt de proprio.[4] 8 Haec de titulo sufficiant.

9 Introducitur autem asinus, animal scilicet stolidum, uolens caudam aliam et ampliorem quam natura contulerat contra naturam sibi inferri,[5] non respiciens quid necessitas exposcat sed quid inepta cupiditas suadeat, eo magis uota sua in uetitum exacuens quo ad impossibilia se conuertit desiderium[6] dilationis impatiens.

10 Asinus iste monachus est, aut uir quilibet religiosus in claustro positus, qui tamquam asinus ad onera portanda Domini seruitio est deputatus, qui non contentus conditione sua, sicut nec asinus cauda, quod naturaliter non accepit uel repugnante natura nequaquam potest accipere, amplius affectat, 11 ad illud modis omnibus anhelat, et consulit medicum, id est quemcumque putat id sibi posse conferre, quod mente captus aestimat esse possibile. 12 Caudam ueterem uult sibi auelli et nouam inseri, quia uitam claustralem in qua deberet usque in finem perseuerare ut saluus fieret[7] omnino fastidit, quaerens omnimodis qualiter ab ea euellatur et transplantetur ubi cauda noua et prolixa

---

8 *om.* MuVaVbVcTGoFrPm; haec] et hec *Tr* hoc *Be La* hic *Pk* hoc igitur *Ve*; sufficiant] *om.* F SBePkNe δ TrHaLa   9 *Fr here begins copying part of (9), beginning* 'inepta cupiditas', *and ending* 'innocitum' (*Fr*(1)); *this passage is repeated at the correct place* (*Fr*(2)); scilicet] *om.* MuVcTGo R GI uidelicet *F*; caudam aliam] caudam *GI* aliam caudam *X* caudam suam *H*; inferri] inseri *Vc* δ *TrLa* inferi *Pm* ui ferri *I* ui inferri *G* inferri uel inseri *S* miser *Fr*; respiciens] aspiciens *VcT* inspiciens *Go*; quid[1]] quod *Vc R*; necessitas] necessitatis *F Be om.* Mu; quid[2]] quod *Vc R* magis quod *Ve* quicquid *Mu*; eo] eo quod *La* et quod SMuVaVbVcTBePkFrPmNe *TrHa* et quid *Go*; in uetitum] innocitum *Fr*(1)*Fr*(2); exacuens] exacuit γ *TrHaLa*; quo] quod SMuVaGoPkFrPmNe *M La* quam *Be Ha* que *Ve* cum *VcT* eo *Be*[1]; dilationis impatiens] impatiens dilationis *A*(*hardly legible*)*JWRMNDVe* dilationis non patiens *X*   10 uir] etiam SMuVaVbVcTGoPkFrPmNe *TrHaLa* ut *D* quicumque *Be RVe*; quilibet religiosus] religiosus quilibet *HuMNK* religiosus *Ve* alius religiosus *R* quilibet alius religiosus MuVaVbTGoBePkFrPmNe *TrHaLa* quilibet positus *X*; in claustro positus] in claustro religiosus *X* in claustro *H*; deputatus] mancipatus δ; nec] *om.* Mu *RVe*; cauda] cauda sua *AJWHuMNDKVe Tr X*[ac] sua cauda *R om.* Mu; quod] quam *Be Tr* id quod *R*; naturaliter non] non naturaliter *GI* naturaliter *Be Tr*; nequaquam] nunquam MuVaVbVcTGoFrPm *Ha* nec nunquam *Ne* nec quam *BePk La*; potest] potuit *H* poterit δ   11 ad] et ad *VcT*; et] *om.* F β γ *GI TrHaLa*; putat id] putat *D* putat illud *Ne GI* id *HuMN*; posse] *om.* Pm *AJWRHuMNKVe La*; aestimat] existimat SMuVaVbVcGoBePkFrPmNe *TrLa*; esse possibile] possibile *T Ve* impossibile *D*   12 auelli] euelli *TBe TrLa X* uelli *D*; inseri] inferri MuVaVbGo *GI*; quia] qui *S* qua *Fr* et *F Ha*; deberet] debet γ *TrHaLa*; usque in finem] usque ad finem *SFr Tr* usque ad finem uite sue *T* in finem *Ne om. K*; saluus] sanus β *G!* salus *M*; omnino] omnia *HuMN*; quaerens] queris *Be* merens uiis *GI*; omnimodis] omnibus modis δ modis omnibus *F* omnimode VaVbVcTGoBePmNe *TrHaLa* omnino *MuFr*; ab ea] ab eo *R GI Tr*; euellatur] auellatur *B Go Ve GI* euelletur *BePkNe HaLa*; et transplantetur ubi] transplantetur ibi (ubi *F S Ha*) *F β S GI HaLa X* et transplantetur ut MuVbGoPkFrPm *RVe* et transportetur ubi *T*; cauda noua] noua cauda δ cauda *H*; possit sibi] posset sibi *F* sibi posset MuVbTGo[pc]PkFr *HaLa* sibi possit *SVaVcBeP Ne Tr*; accrescere— (13) abbatiam possit sibi] *om.* M Go[ac] *add. in lower margin* Go[pc]

SPECVLVM STVLTORVM

another's eye they pluck out the mote in their own.[4] 8 This is enough about the title.

9 So an ass is introduced—that is, a stupid animal, who in contradiction of nature wants to have given[5] to him another, and longer, tail than nature had conferred on him, not considering what necessity demands but rather what foolish greed counsels, with his wishes for the forbidden all the keener because his desire,[6] impatient of delay, is directed towards impossibilities.

10 This ass is a monk, or any man of religion situated in a cloister, who is charged with the service of God as an ass is with bearing burdens, and who, not content with his condition, as the ass is not with his tail, yearns passionately for what he does not naturally have or is totally incapable of having because nature forbids it, 11 who pursues his desire in every way possible, and takes advice from a doctor, that is, from anyone who he thinks is able to give it to him, which in his deluded mind he thinks is possible. 12 He wants his old tail to be torn out and a new one to be implanted, because he totally despises the monastic life in which he ought to persevere to the end in order to be saved,[7] exploring every possible way in which he may be uprooted from it and transplanted

---

[4] Matt. 7: 3.

[5] Mozley prints 'inseri', which may be thought preferable from the point of view of meaning ('implant, graft'), and is used at Epistle 12, 13, 37, but 'inferri' is supported by three manuscript groups.

[6] Mozley has 'desideria', presumably because he assumes it goes with the adjective 'impossibilia' (which I take to be a quasi-substantive). All manuscripts have the singular except *Ve*, which is corrected to 'desideriis'.

[7] Matt. 24: 13.

6 SPECVLVM STVLTORVM

possit sibi accrescere, **13** scilicet ut prioratum uel abbatiam possit sibi apprehendere, ubi parentum suorum sequelam copiosam possit prius inserere et postea quasi caudam post se quocumque ierit trahere.[8] **14** Medicus uero, id est ille qui desiderat infirmum curare dummodo sit curabilis, audito quid asinus petat, quid desideret, quo denique tendat, petitionem habet pro friuolo, desiderium pro stulto, id quo tendit omnino pro nihilo. **15** Vnde et ab inceptis[9] suadet desistere et naturalibus contentum bonis aliena non appetere, dicens de facili quemlibet posse bona quae possidet perdere, sed perdita nequaquam leuiter sed uix aut numquam recuperare.

16 Et ut hoc efficacius persuadeat, assumpta parabola[10] de duabus uaccis quid contigerit narrat. **17** Duae uaccae fuerunt cuidam patrifamilias, quae tempore hiemali in quodam prato lutoso de nocte demoratae, superueniente gelu acriori, per caudas lutosas terrae quae limosa erat adhaeserunt, itaque congelatae sunt quod mane, cum ad stabula reuerti conarentur, nullatenus potuerunt a terra caudas euellere, sed

---

13 scilicet] uidelicet *Tr om.* γ *AJWHuNDKVe GI HaLa*; possit sibi apprehendere] posset sibi apprehendere *AJ* possit apprehendere *F Vc* sibi possit apprehendere *SVaVbBePkPmNe HaLa* sibi posset apprehendere *TGo Tr* sibi apprehendere *Mu*; suorum sequelam copiosam] sequelam suorum copiosam *HuMN* suorum copiam sequelamque *S* suorum copiam sequelam *VaVbBePkFrNe Ha* suorum sequelam copiam *Pm* suorum copiam et sequelam *VcT* suorum copiosamque sequelam *Tr* suorum copiosam sequelam *Mu La* suorum capiam sequelam *Go* suorum sequelam pomposam *H GI*; trahere] trahere glorianter *AJWRHuNDK Tr* trahere gloriantur *Ve* trahere similanter *M*   **14** id est] *om. F VcBeFr La*; ille] iste *RVe Tr om. Fr*; sit] sic *Go Ve*; audito] audiat *AJWRHuMNDK* audeat *Ve*; quid[1]] quod *Vc X*; desideret] desiderat *H SMuVaVbVcTBePkFrPm*ᵃᶜ *WRK TrHaLa* desiderium? *Go*; tendat] tendat et *AWRHuMNDKVe* intendat *Vc* tendit *Go*; habet] habeat δ; friuolo] friuola *SMuVaVbVcGoBePkPm La* friuole *Hu*   **15** et[1]] *om. F R*; suadet] suadet omnino *H GI X* suadeat δ; quemlibet] quelibet *Fr I* eum *R*; posse] *om. H RK GI X* post se *B*; nequaquam] non δ; sed[2]] si *Vb* seu *Be Tr X om. Fr*; aut nunquam *Vb ends here (missing leaves?)*   **16** *om. RHuMNDKVe*; et ut] et ei ut *Fr om. I*; hoc] ei hac *Pm* ei hec *La* hec ei *Ha* hoc ei *S AJW* ei hoc *MuVaVcTPk* ei hic *BeNe* ei *Go Tr* hec *F H GI om. Fr*; narrat] narrando taliter declarat *AJW* narrat taliter declarans *La* narratis *I*   **17** Duae] fuerant *F B GoBePmNe TrLa*; cuidam] cuiusdam *VaVcTGoPkFrPmNe* quondam cuidam δ circumspecte cuiusdam *Be Tr* cuiusdam circumspecti *La*; patrifamilias] patrisfamilias *VaTGoFrPmNe La*; quodam prato] prato quodam *F* β *GI X*; demoratae] commorate *AJWRHuMNKVe* comorante *D* remorate *F SMuVaVcTPmNe Ha*ᵃᶜ*La* remorate sunt *BePk Tr* remorati *Go* remorare *Fr*; superueniente] superuenienti *X* ueniente *BePk Tr*; erat] erant *GI*; itaque] et ita δ ita *T* tamquam *F*; quod] adeo quod *SMuVaVcTGoPkPmNe TrHaLa* a deo quod *Be* cum *Fr*; ad stabula reuerti conarentur] ad stabula conarentur redire *S* conarentur ad stabula redire *MuVcTGoFrPm* conarentur ad stabula *Va* ad stabula conarentur *PkNe Ha* ad stabulum reuerti conarentur *La* ad stabulum conarentur *Be* ad stabulum ire conarentur *Tr*; potuerunt a terra caudas euellere] possent a terra caudas euellere *S* possent caudas euellere a terra *F* possent caudas a (e *Mu* in *Fr*) terra euellere (auellere *Go*) β *MuVaTGoBePkFrPmNe GI TrHaLa X* possent caudas euellere *Vc*; sed quo—inuitae residere] *om. Ve*; quo] ubi *AJWHuMNDK Tr om. Mu R*; uolentes et ultronee uenerant] uenerant uolentes et ultronee *AJWHuMNDK* uolentes ultronee uenerant *Mu om. R*

SPECVLVM STVLTORVM

to where a new and luxuriant tail may grow on him, **13** that is, that he may be able to get himself a priorate or abbacy, where he can first introduce a numerous retinue of his relatives, and then drag them after him like a tail wherever he goes.[8] **14** But the doctor, that is the man who wants to cure the sick man while he is still curable, having heard what the ass seeks, what he desires, whither he is aiming, considers his request frivolous, his desire foolish, and his goal completely futile. **15** So he tries to persuade him to desist from what he has embarked on,[9] and, being content with his natural endowments, not to seek others, saying that anyone can easily lose the goods he has, but once lost, he cannot recover them easily, but on the contrary with difficulty or not at all.

16 And so that he may more effectively persuade him of this, having chosen an instructive story,[10] he relates what happened to two cows. **17** There were two cows belonging to a certain householder, who in wintertime spent the night in a certain muddy field, and with the arrival of a sharp frost, they were stuck to the muddy ground by their muddy tails, and frozen so fast that in the morning, when they tried to go back to their byre, they were completely unable to pull their tails out of the earth; in the place to which they had come voluntarily, of

---

[8] For Nigel's criticisms of clerical nepotism, see n. to *SS*, lines 2711–12.

[9] Mozley has 'incepto', which is not found in any manuscript. There seems to be no good reason for emendation.

[10] Num. 23: 7.

8 SPECVLVM STVLTORVM

quo uolentes et ultroneae uenerant compulsae sunt inuitae residere.

18 Vnde cum altera earum fortunae suae nimis esset impatiens, illecta nihilominus amore uituli, quem nuper editum domi reliquerat inclusum, caudam suam nimis festina praescidit, domumque cucurrit, suadens sociae ut abscisa cauda ab impedimento se solueret et secum expedita rediret. 19 Sed illa magis circumspecta et secum pensans et ponderans quid cauda, quae oneri est in hieme, utilitatis conferat in aestate, consilio adquiescere supersedit, expectans donec sol circa meridiem incalescens glaciem solueret et gelu temperaret, eamque sineret immutilatam abscedere,[11] quae per discretionem se nouit in aduersis temperare.

20 Hae duae uaccae duo hominum genera in religione uiuentium significant. 21 Sunt enim quidam nimis indiscreti et ualde praecipites, qui cum aduersitate aliqua superueniente, quasi quodam gelu constricti uel parentum suorum teneritudine quadam, uelut uacca uituli amore, capti et excaecati, caudam suam statim abscidunt, id est, memoriam mortis, qua se a muscis praeteruolantibus et pungentibus deberent protegere, longe proiciunt; 22 sed et in futurum non prospicientes nec rerum exitus in ira sua metientes ueteres amicos suos, qui eis in

---

18 unde cum] unde et cum *SMuVaBePkPm La* unde cum et *VcT Ha* unde et tamen *Go* unde et *Ne*; nihilominus amore] amore nihilominus *MuTPm* nihilominus *Fr*; nihilominus] uero in *R* tamen *Ve*; editum] *om. RVe*; reliquerat] relinquerat *X* dereliquerat *SMuVaVcTGoBePkNe HaLa* derelinquerat *FrPm*; festina] festine *R X* festinanter *D*; domumque cucurrit] domique currens *MuVaGoFrPmNe* domumque currens *VcTPk Ha* et domi currens *Be TrLa*; suadens sociae ut] suadens prius socie ut *SMuVaGoBePkFrPmNe TrHaLa* suasit prius socie ut *VcT* suadens socie sue *R* suadens socient *M*; secum expedita] expedita secum *Go* secum expedite *Ve* statim secum expedita *Fr* statim expedita *Va*   19 illa magis] magis *D* magis illa *GI*; et ponderans] et se ponderans *T* ac ponderans *AJWHuMNDK om. RVe*; quid] quod *BeFr TrLa*; in hieme] hieme *RVe*; utilitatis] utilitatem *Be TrLa*; consilio] consilium *M* consilio socie *SMuVaVcTGoBePkFrPmNe TrHaLa*; adquiescere] adquiescens *H GI X* minime acquiescens *Mu*; donec sol circa meridiem incalescens] temporis beneficium quod sui temperamento *SMuVaVcTGoBePkFrPmNe TrHaLa*; immutilatam] immaculatam *MuVcTGo R*; abscedere] abscidere *La* gaudenter abscedere *AJHuMNDKVe* gaudenter abcedere *R Tr* gaudenter abscidere *W* redire *F*; quae] qui *W* et sic *SMuVaVcTGoBePkPmNe HaLa* sic *Fr*; discretionem] discripcionem *GI*; aduersis] angustiis *F SMuVaVcTGoBePkFrPmNe* δ *TrHaLa*   20 hae] hec autem *SNe La* hee autem *MuVaVcTGoBePkFrPm TrHa* nota hee *M*; hominum genera in religione uiuentium significant] genera hominum in religione uiuentium significant *F* genera hominum significant in religione uiuentium *SMuVaGoBePkFr HaLa* genera hominum sunt in religione uiuentium δ genera designant hominum in religione uiuentium *Tr*   21 enim] *om. WHuMND*; quadam] quidem *F* qui *K*; uelut] sicut *F SMuVaVcTGoBePkFrPmNe* δ *TrHaLa*; capti] capta *T La*; statim] *om. H GI X*; id est] hoc est *F* et *T om. GoBeFr La*; deberent] deberet *VcT M*; proiciunt] proiecit *VcT*   22 sed et] sed β *Va RVe GI Tr X*; prospicientes] prospiciens *VcT* conspicientes *La*; metientes] manentes *H GI* mentientes *D X* metiento *Fr* metiens *VcT*; eis…adesse] eius…aduenient *Fr* eos…adire *Mozley*; poterant] poterunt *D GI*; et penitus] penitus et δ et *MuVcTGoFr Tr* et omnino *Ha*

SPECVLVM STVLTORVM

their own free will, they were unwillingly compelled to stay put. **18** Whereupon one of them, too impatient of her lot, and driven by love of her newborn calf, whom she had left shut up at home, with excessive haste cut off her tail and ran home, persuading her companion that she should cut her tail off, free herself from any impediment, and so liberated, should return with her. **19** But the other, who was more cautious, and who reflected and considered in her mind what usefulness a tail, which is a burden in winter, provides in summer, refused to accede to this plan, and waited until the sun, around midday, should warm up the ice and melt it, counteracting the frost, and should allow her to depart unharmed,[11] knowing how to restrain herself by reason in adversities.

20 These two cows signify two types of men living the religious life. **21** For there are some who are excessively indiscreet and very rash, who when any adversity comes along, as if constricted by a frost, are enslaved and blinded by a tenderness for their relatives, as the cow is by love for her calf, and immediately cut off their tails, that is, they cast far from them the remembrance of death, with which they ought to protect themselves from the flies that fly about and sting. **22** Not looking to the future nor calculating the outcome of events in their frenzy, they

---

[11] Mozley has 'gaudenter abscedere', adopting 'gaudenter' from δ.

10 SPECVLVM STVLTORVM

necessitate adesse poterant, sine spe recuperationis praecidunt et penitus euellunt. 23 Vnde in tempore angustiae non immerito cadunt ante faciem subsequentis,[12] amicorum destituti adiutorio, qui noluerunt moderari quid facerent in furore suo. 24 Alii autem sunt qui maturiori reguntur consilio, spiritu sapientiae et intellectus,[13] in anteriora extensi,[14] et, quod maxime prudentiae est, fortuitos casus inopinatorum metuunt euentuum, nec aliquid infirmum putant uel sine robore quod aliquo tempore uel in minimo[15] possit nocere; 25 illud sapientis prae oculis interioribus habentes: 'a casu describe diem non solis ab ortu, non attendentes faciem scorpionis sed caudam'.[16] 26 Hi sunt qui in aduersis patienter impatientium impulsiones tolerant, qui beneficii ingratos humili expectatione ad memoriam immemores reuocant, qui rerum exitus plus quam principia ponderant. 27 Hi sunt qui, aestiui feruoris non immemores, caudam suam seruant, ut muscas abigant et elidant.

28 Cauda extrema pars est corporis, quae omnibus membris necessaria est in die incalescentis feruoris. 29 Cauda corporis est finis uitae praesentis; hunc qui bonum facit et bene custodit muscas, id est daemonum insidias, in die feruoris, immo furoris, scilicet in die Iudicii, non timebit. 30 Ille uero qui tempore hiemis, id est huius uitae frigescentis, caudam absciderit, id est, extrema sua corrigere neglexerit, ibi tormentis cum daemonibus subiacebit.

23 noluerunt] noluerint *Vc* non uoluerunt *Mu* uoluerunt *FrPm* nolunt *S*; moderari] moderare *H Fr TrHa* cognoscere *Mu*; furore] furore /uel futuro *La*; suo] *om.* *HuMN* 24 autem] *om.* δ; reguntur consilio] consilio reguntur *WHuMNDK* regentur consilio *Go* regunt consilio *Fr*; spiritu] spiritus *F* β *GI* spiritu enim *SMuVcTGoBePkFrPmNe HaLa*; est] *om.* *VcGo*; metuunt] metiuntur *SMuVaVcGoBePkFrPmNe* δ *TrHaLa* mentiuntur *F om.* *T*; euentuum] euentum *Go R La* euentu *MuFr*; nec aliquid infirmum—in minimo] qui in aliquo leuiter seu (uel *K*) grauiter δ; in minimo] minimo *H Tr* minime *MuVaVcTGoFrPm* nimio *La* in ieiunio *S*; possit nocere] posset nocere *F S* possent nocere *AJWHuMNKVe* possunt nocere *D* eis possent nocere *R* nocere poterint aut iuuare *Fr* nocere ualeat aut iuuare *SMuVaVcTGoBePkPmNe TrHaLa* 25 interioribus habentes] habentes interioribus unde uersus *R* habentes interioribus *T* anterioribus habentes *X*; describe] describere *Vc G* describis *Fr* 26–7 *transp.* *MuVcTFr*, *27 repeated in its correct position* *Fr*(2) 26 sunt qui] quidem *H* qui *GI X*; beneficii ingratos] beneficii ingratos benefieri *SBePk HaLa* beneficii ingratos beneficii *MuGoPm* beneficii ingratos beneficiis *Ne* beneficii ingratus beneficii *Fr*; ad memoriam] a memoriam *M* in memoriam *R om. H GI* 27 feruoris] furoris *HuMN*; suam seruant] seruant suam *HuMN*; abigant] ambigant *BePk* abiant *Fr* 28 pars est] est pars *WHuMN* pars *Fr*; necessaria est] necessaria *X* necesse est *Go La*; incalescentis] calescentis *Ve Tr X* 28–9 incalescentis—demonum insidias *om.* *D* 29 est[1]] *om. H GI X*; hunc] huic *GI* hic *Pm* hunc habet *Tr* habenti *Fr* significans hunc *R*; hunc qui—custodit] sed ille qui bene facit et perseuerarit usque in finem ex fine decedet et *F*; bonum facit] facit bonum *MuVcTGo* bene facit *Va* bonum fecerit *Fr*; feruoris immo furoris] feruoris *RHuMN* furoris uel feruoris *F*; scilicet] id est *N*[pc] *om. HuMK X* 30 hiemis id est] hiemis et *R GI* hiemis *Fr*; caudam] caudam suam *H GI X*; absciderit] abscidit *BeFr GI HaLa* exciderit *S*; id est[2]] et *GI*; corrigere] corrigere /uel porrigere *La*; ibi] in *R om. TrHa*; tormentis cum daemonibus] cum demonibus tormentis *F GI* eternis tormentis cum demonibus *Ha*

SPECVLVM STVLTORVM

cut off without hope of recovery their old friends, who could come to them in their need, and completely uproot them. 23 Whence, in the time of trial that follows, they not undeservedly fall in the sight of their persecutor,[12] deprived of the help of friends, since they would not restrain what they did in their fury. 24 There are, however, others who are ruled by a riper counsel, by the spirit of wisdom and understanding,[13] reaching forth unto those things which are before,[14] and who, as is the special characteristic of prudence, fear the chance incidents of unexpected events, and do not think that anything is so feeble or lacking strength that it cannot at some time, even in a small way,[15] do harm. 25 They keep before their eyes the wise man's saying: 'describe a day according to its ending, not according to its dawn', 'not looking to the scorpion's face but to its tail'.[16] 26 They are the ones who in adversity patiently bear the onslaughts of the impatient, who by their humble expectation recall to mindfulness those who are forgetful and ungrateful for benefits, considering the outcome of events rather than their beginnings. 27 They are the ones who, not forgetful of the summer heat, preserve their tail, so that they may whisk away and swat the flies.

28 The tail is the endmost part of the body, which is necessary to all the bodily members on the day of burning heat. 29 The tail is the end of this present life; whoever does well, and watches out for the flies, that is, for the traps of the devils, will have no fear on the day of heat, or rather of fury—that is, on the day of Judgement. 30 But he who in the wintertime (that is, this chilly life) cuts off his tail (that is, neglects to correct his end) will then be subject to tortures by demons.

---

[12] Lam. 1: 6.

[13] Isa. 11: 2.

[14] Cf. Phil. 3: 13.

[15] Mozley's text imports the δ reading, 'leuiter seu grauiter', which is clearly a rewriting of αβγ's 'in minimo', into the αβγ text, and so creates a tautologous hybrid.

[16] Both these sayings are proverbial (see Singer, *Thesaurus*, s.vv. 'Tag', 6. 2. 1 (xi. 257–8) and 'Skorpion' 1. 1–2 (x. 439)); they are found in combination in *Ysengrimus*, iii. 594–5: 'Vespere laudari debet amoena dies;/ Scorpio blanditur vultu, pars postera pungit.' The first of the two (which is a pentameter) is reproduced verbatim in Geoffrey of Vinsauf, *Poetria nova*, 383, who may be the 'sapiens' that Nigel refers to, but their relative dates would make it seem more likely that Geoffrey was the borrower.

SPECVLVM STVLTORVM

31 Galienus igitur uolens ut asinus saperet et intelligeret ac nouissima prouideret dissuasione usus est, sed considerans quod stulto aliquid contra uoluntatem suadere uel dissuadere ualde sit difficile, **32** cum eum uideret in proposito suo ita pertinaciter persistere, iuxta Saolomonem qui ait 'responde stulto iuxta stultitiam suam',[17] praecepit ei ut quaedam perquireret quae impossibilia erant reperiri. **33** Quasi manifeste ei diceret, consilio non acquiescis, exemplo non instrueris, necesse est ut labore inani erudiaris. **34** Multis enim uexatio dedit intellectum, quos prosperitas numquam potuit erudire. **35** Asinus igitur qui uadit emere uana et in uasis uitreis ea recondit monachus est qui, ut uanitatem quam desiderat assequatur, circumquaque discurrit, gratiam hominum quae quasi uitrum fragilis[18] est nunc adulationibus allicit nunc muneribus astringit, **36** totque laboribus et aerumnis afficitur pro nihilo quod longe minori pretio posset regnum sibi comparasse caelorum.

37 Vnde plerumque fit ut dum supra se quis rapitur quo stulta et inania desideria adquirat illud etiam modicum perdat quod antea possederat; sicut asinus qui dum nouam caudam sibi inseri laborauit ueterem ex toto amisit.

---

31 igitur] uero *H SMuVaVcTGoBePkFrPmNe TrHaLa*; usus] prius usus *SMuVaVcTGoBePkFrPmNe TrHaLa*; sed] et *VaAJWHuMNDKVe*; suadere uel dissuadere] suam suadere *D* persuadere *K* dissuadere uel suadere *SMuVaVcTGoBePkFrPmNe TrLa* dissuadere *Ha*; ualde sit difficile] ualde sic difficile *G* ualde difficile est *Fr* nimis sit difficile *R* difficile est *X* ualde sit difficile ualde sit difficile *HuN*   **32** iuxta] unde *HuMND* secundum illud quod *K*; Salomonem] salamonem *F I X* salomonis consilium *Go*; qui ait] ait *K om. MND*; praecepit] precipit *K* unde precepit *HuMN* unde recepit *D om. X*; impossibilia erant] impossibile erant *Vc AJWHuMNDVe* impossibile erat *F SMuVaTGoBePkPmNe HaLa* erant impossibile *RK*   **33** inani] manuum *AJWRHuMNDVe TrLa* me *F om. SVaVcTGoBePkFrPmNe K Ha*   **34** nunquam] nusquam *AJVe* unquam *Va* **35** igitur] ergo *K MuVaVcTGoFrPm* autem *GI om. F*; ea] *om. F β SMuVaVcTGoBePkFrPmNe GI TrHaLa X*; monachus] ille *SMuVaVcTGoBePkFrPmNe La* ille enim *Ha* et monachus *I*; ut] et *VaVcTPkPm Ha* ad *Fr om. Mu La*; assequatur] assequitur *MuVaVcTGoPkFrPmNe HaLa*; circumquaque] circumque *Pk* circum quam *VaPm*; hominum] hominum querens δ *La*; quae] qui *PkNe*; fragilis] fragile *R GI*; nunc¹] nuncque *AJRHuMNDKVe* nunc quia *W*; astringit] constringit *VcFr*   **36** afficitur] efficitur *VcBe La*; longe] longo *Be D Tr*   37 dum] de *VaGoBePkPmNe GI Ha* plus *H om. Fr*; supra] sensu *Be La*ᵃᶜ sua *Pk*; quis] *om. F β SMuVaVcTGoBePkFrPmNe GI HaLa X*; quo] quod *MuVaVcTGoBePkPmNe AJWRHuMNDVe TrHaLa* ut *Fr K*; desideria adquirat] desideria perficiat (perficit *T*) uel quod (*om. Go*) insipienter desiderat acquirat (acquirit *Fr*) *SMuVaVcTGoBePkFrPmNe TrHaLa*; etiam] in β *Be om. GI*; antea possederat] antea possiderat *Be La* ante possiderat *Go I Tr* ante possederat *X* ante ea possederat *VaT* ante possideat *Fr* prius habebat (habeat *M*) δ; qui dum] qui cum *R* quidam β *GI* quidam dum *X*; inseri] inferri β *SVaBePmNe GI HaLa X* inferre *Mu*; laborauit] laborabat *Fr* laborat *H T La*; ex toto] omnino confusus *AJWRHuNDKVe* animo confusus *M*

SPECVLVM STVLTORVM

31 So Galen, wanting the ass to be wise and understand and to provide for the end, resorted to dissuasion, but considering that it is very difficult to persuade or dissuade a fool of anything against his will, 32 when he saw him obstinately persist in his plan, in accordance with Solomon who says 'answer a fool according to his folly',[17] ordered him to look for certain things which were impossible to find. 33 As if he were saying to him plainly: you do not listen to advice, you are not taught by example, so it is necessary for you to be instructed by pointless labour. 34 For trouble gave understanding to many people whom prosperity could never make any wiser. 35 The ass who goes to buy vain things and stores them in glass jars is the monk who, so that he may acquire the foolishness he desires, runs about everywhere, and now by flattery, now by bribery, wins men's favour, which is as fragile[18] as glass, 36 and is worn down by so many toils and hardships, for nothing at all, that he could have won himself the kingdom of heaven for a far lesser price.

37 Whence it often happens that while anyone is whirled above his station to a position where he may fulfil his foolish and empty desires, he loses even the little he possessed before, just like the ass who, while he strove after the implantation of a new tail, lost the old one altogether.

---

[17] Prov. 26: 5. Also quoted in *Lawrence*, 914–16.

[18] The feminine ending of 'fragilis' is appropriate for 'gratia', the subject of the relative clause. The neuter form 'fragile', found in a few manuscripts and printed by Mozley, obviously arose by attraction to 'uitrum'.

14   *SPECVLVM STVLTORVM*

38 Item frater Fromundus, qui canes immisit in asinum et postea minis perterritus simulauit se in omnibus satisfacturum, cogitans quomodo clanculo eum de medio faceret, et dum hoc callide machinaretur ab asino in Rodanum praecipitatus est et submersus, **39** eos significat qui fratres simpliciores sua dum astutia circumuenire et decipere attentant saepius ipsi in laqueos incidunt quos aliis abscondunt;[19] iuxta illud

> neque enim lex aequior ulla est
> quam necis artifices arte perire sua.[20]

40 Verba quae asinus secum loquitur secundum animi sui motum[21] nunc fatua nunc indiscreta meditationes cordis eorum significant indiscretas et inutiles qui ponunt impossibilia in animo suo, et ea quae non sunt tamquam ea quae sunt sperant et expectant; **41** dies suos in uanitate consumentes,[22] circa seria desides et negligentes, circa[23] friuola solliciti et praecipites; quorum cogitationes stultas et instabiles opera quae sequuntur ostendunt, dicente scriptura 'a fructibus eorum cognoscetis eos'.[24]

42 Quod autem sequitur de filio presbiteri et pullo gallinae qui postea pro tibia fracta reddidit talionem, quia per se satis elucet, expositione

---

38 immisit] misit *SVa*; minis] minis eius *SMuVaVcTGoBeFrPm TrHaLa* minis est *Pk* nimis *MKVe G* nimis eius *Ne om. D*; cogitans] *om. HuMN*; quomodo clanculo eum] quomodo eum *R* clanculo quomodo eum *K* qualiter clanculo eum *X* quomodo eum clanculo *SMuVaVcTGoBePkPmNe TrHaLa* quomodo eum clam *Fr*; faceret] tolleret *F SMuVaVcTGoBePkFrPmNe δ TrHaLa*; et dum] et de *H GI* dumque *SVaGoBePkPmNe TrHaLa* cumque *MuVcT* demum *Fr*; hoc] hec *Mu AJWRHuMNK Tr* hic *VaVcGoBePkFrNe La om. T*; ab] *om. GᵃᶜI*   **39** simpliciores] simplices *WHuMNDK* aut homines simpliciores (simplices *VaBePk TrHa* simplicior *Pm* simces *Fr*) *SMuVaVcTGoBePkFrPmNe TrHaLa*; sua dum astutia] sua astutia dum *F B AJWHuMNKVe X* sua astutia *H RD GI* dum sua astutia *SMu* de sua astutia *VaVcTGoBePkBeFrPmNe TrHaLa*; ipsi in laqueos] ipsos in laqueos *GI* ipsius in laqueum *HuMN* in laqueos ipsi *X* ipsi in laqueum *D*; abscondunt] absconderunt *Va WDK* abscondent *GoBe La*; neque enim] non *MuVaVcTGoBePkFrPmNe TrHaLa* non etenim poterit fieri *X*; lex aequior ulla est] lex ulla equior est β lex equior ulla *SVc X* lex est equior illa *AJWHuMVe* lex est equior ulla *NK* est lex equior illa *GoBePkNe D TrLa* est lex equior ulla *MuVaTFrPm* est lex iustior ulla *Ha* lex equior est ulla *R*; necis artifices arte perire] necis arte artifices necis perire *F GI*; artifices] artificem *F N* auctorem *Ha*   **40** asinus secum loquitur] secum asinus loquitur δ asinus loquitur secum *VcTBe* asinus loquitur *VaFrPm TrLa*; indiscreta] discreta *F* β *SMuVaVcTGoBePkFrPmNe GI HaLa X*; eorum] *om. SMuVaVcTGoBePkFrPmNe TrHaLa*; qui] eorum qui *S* que *H Ha*; sperant] et sperant *SMuVaVcTGoBePkNe HaLa*   **41** dies] diesque *SMuVaVcT GoBePkFrPmNe TrHaLa*; consumentes] consumante β *AJWRHuMND X* inconsummantes *F* consumunt *SMuVaVcTGoBePkFrPmNe TrHaLa*; circa¹] certa *Go D*; seria] certa δ *GI X*; circa²] et circa δ; cognoscetis] cognosces *Ne K*; eos] *om. T M*   **42** pullo] de pullo *Vc Ha*; gallinae] *om. GI*; reddidit] reddit *H GI* redditur *Pk*; quia] qui *VaFr* est quia *Tr*

SPECVLVM STVLTORVM

38 Also brother Fromundus, who set the dogs on the ass and afterwards, terrified by threats, pretended he would make full satisfaction, plotting how he might secretly do away with him, and while he was cunningly plotting this was thrown by the ass into the Rhône and drowned, **39** signifies those who, while trying to outwit and trick their simpler brethren by cunning, often fall into the nets which they hide to catch others[19]—according to the saying

there is no juster law
Than that those who plot death should perish by their own trickery.[20]

40 The words, now foolish and now imprudent, that the ass speaks to himself, according to the promptings of his heart,[21] signify the imprudent and futile meditations of those who conceive impossibilities in their soul, and who hope for and expect things that are not as if they were, **41** wasting their days in idle pursuits,[22] lazy and careless about serious things and anxious and busy about[23] frivolities, whose meditations are shown to be foolish and giddy by the works which follow, as Scripture says, 'by their fruits ye shall know them'.[24]

42 What follows, about the priest's son and the hen's chick who afterwards took vengeance for its broken leg, does not need any

---

[19] Ps. 7: 16. Cf. lines 1083, 1087–8, and nn.

[20] Ovid, *Ars amatoria*, i. 655–6. Cf. lines 1072, 1082, and nn.

[21] A computer search of PL shows that '(secundum) motum animi (mei, sui, etc.)' is a favourite phrase in patristic authors.

[22] Ps. 77 (78): 33.

[23] Mozley adopts δ's 'et circa', which probably reflects scribal preference for grammatical explicitness.

[24] Matt. 7: 16.

16   SPECVLVM STVLTORVM

non indiget. **43** Hoc enim hodie ex consuetudine uersum est in naturam,[25] ut qui laeduntur uel etiam in minimo offenduntur in pueritia tempus retributionis usque ad annos ultimae senectutis reseruent in memoria nec acceptam aliquando obliuiscuntur iniuriam, quousque manifeste fuerit expiata per poenam.

44 Similiter asinus qui Parisius scholas frequentando et literas discendo operam perdit et expensas, quia discedens nomen urbis non potuit retinere in qua moram fecerat septennem, illos significat qui cum sensus non habeant exercitatos uel aptos ad literarum apices intelligendos tamen ut uideantur[26] in utroque testamento eruditi libros legunt quos non intelligunt, **45** quorum etiam nomina eis perlectis non meminerunt, cupientes potius ut ab hominibus multa et magna scire credantur ex assidua librorum inspectione quam ut aliquid sciant in rei ueritate.[27]

46 Hi in omnibus apprime eruditi sunt quousque articulus[28] emerserit ut res uerbis[29] fidem faciat et scientia diutius abscondita per operis effectum in publicum prodeat; cum turpe admodum et ridiculosum sit id aliquem profiteri non erubescere quod cum ad rei exhibitionem peruentum fuerit liquido appareat eum omnino nescire. **47** Sunt autem

---

43 enim hodie] enim homine *Fr* enim *F X*; uersum] uersus *M* hodie uersum *X*; in naturam] in natura *D* naturam *HuMN*[ac]; ut] non *H GI*; uel] sed *H om. GI*; etiam] etiam qui *Go* et in *Be om. X*; offenduntur] offendantur *B AJ GI X*; ultimae senectutis] senectutis ultime *X* senectutis *Ve* ultra senectutem *F*; reseruent] reseruant *MuVaVcTGoPkFrPm HaLa* seruent *S*; memoria] memoriam *AJWMND GI*; obliuiscuntur] obliuiscantur *AJRHuMNDK*; manifeste] manifesta *H Ne GI Ha* manifestam *B SMuVaTBePkFrPm La X* manifestum *Go*; fuerit expiata] fuerint expiata *Fr* expiata fuerit *F D Tr* fuerit et expiata *H* expietur *K* **44** similiter] similiter et *X* item *F* pariter *AJWRMNKVe* preterea *SMuVaVcTGoBePkFrPmNe TrHa* propter *La om. D*; Parisius] parum *SVaVcTGoBePkFrPmNe HaLa*; frequentando] frequentat *F B SMuVaVcGoBePkFrPmNe AJWRHuMNKVe TrHaLa* frequentauit *T* frequentabat *D*; discendo] discendo penam portat *Tr* pena discendo *WR* penam discendo *AJHuMNVe* adiscendo *D* cum pena discendo *K om. H GI X*; operam] et operam δ opera *X*; perdit] perdidit *H Fr om. X*; et expensas] impensam *AJWHuMNVe* et impensam *F SMuVaVcTGoBePkFrPmNe RK TrHaLa* et impensamque *D*; nomen urbis non] non nomen urbis β *SMuVaGoBePkFrPm GI HaLa* nisi nomen urbis *Ne* nec nomen urbis *F X*; non potuit retinere] potuit retinere *Ne X* retinuit uel retinere potuit *F*; habeant] habent *F H TFr* **45** eis perlectis] eis perlecta *Fr* eis prolectis *GI* propriis perlectis *Tr om. H*; meminerunt] meminerint *I* meminunt *VaPkFr*; credantur] uideantur et credantur β *GI X*; librorum inspectione] inspectione librorum *WHuMNDK* librorum aspectione *JR GI* laborum inspectione *Ne* **46** in] *om. Vc Ha*; apprime] a primo *H* a parte *AW Tr* aperte *RDVe* a patre *HuMN* apparenter *K* optime *VaVcGoPkFrPmNe Ha* opime *T om. SMuBe J La*; sunt] sunt optime *S*; articulus] articulos *Fr* articulis *HuMN* articuculus *K*; fidem faciat] faciat fidem *WHuMNDK* faciat *GI*; et scientia—effectum] *om. J*; in publicum prodeat] in publicum procedat *AWRMNDVe* in publicum prodat *Fr* aperte procedat *J* procedat in publicum *K*; admodum] *om. R Tr*; et[2]] *om. Be Ha*; id aliquem] id aliquid *Be La om. VaFr*; exhibitionem] executionem *Ve Tr* assecucionem *R*; liquido] liquide *A*[pc]*JRHuMNDKVe Tr*; appareat] apparet *F* β *SMuVaVcTGoBePkFrPmNe Ve TrLa X* **47** multi simulatores] simulatores multi *Tr* multe simulationes / uel multi simulatores *La*; <simu>latores—non sit aliqua] *om. Ne*; aut] at *M* nec *VcT Ve* quod *Pk illegible F*; aliqua non sit] non sit aliqua *SMuVaGo AJVe* non est aliqua *Vc R Ha* non sit *WHuMNDK*

SPECVLVM STVLTORVM   17

explanation, since it is quite self-explanatory. **43** For nowadays this has from custom become [a law of] nature,[25] that those who are injured or even offended in a small matter in youth will keep the time of retribution in their memory into the years of extreme old age and will not forget an injury received on any occasion, until it is clearly expiated by being punished.

44 Similarly the ass who in frequenting the Parisian schools and learning the arts loses his effort and expense, in that on his departure he cannot retain the name of the city in which he had stayed for seven years, signifies those who, not having wits sufficiently trained or suited for learning letters, nevertheless, in order that they might seem[26] to be learned in both Testaments, read books that they do not understand, **45** whose very names they do not remember once they have read them, preferring that men should believe that they know many important things from the diligent perusal of books than that they should know anything in very earnest.[27] **46** They are terribly learned in everything, until the moment[28] comes when reality should provide credence for their words[29] and the knowledge long hidden should come into the open through the medium of the deed, since it is totally base and ridiculous that anyone professing such a thing should not blush that when it comes to the demonstration of the thing it is crystal-clear that he knows nothing. **47** For there are many

---

[25] *ex consuetudine uersum est in naturam*: the phrase echoes Jerome, *Epistulae*, cxlvii, ed. Hilberg, iii. 321. The idea that custom becomes nature is proverbial; see Singer, *Thesaurus*, s. v. 'Gewohnheit' 3. 3. 4, v. 8–9.

[26] Mozley's text reads 'uideantur et credantur', which is not found in any manuscript at this point, though his *apparatus criticus* records it as omitted in a (= my δ), implying it is present in other branches of the stemma. In Epistle 45, however, *BHGIX* have 'uideantur et credantur', where Mozley reads simply 'credantur', without comment in his *apparatus criticus*. It is possible that he intended to change 'uideantur' to 'uideantur et credantur' in 45, but made the correction in the wrong place. In any case, in 45 'uideantur' is syntactically unacceptable in 45 since it does not fit the preposition 'ab' (which is found in all manuscripts but not in Mozley's text) in 'ab hominibus'; 'uideor' meaning 'to seem' normally takes the dative. Finally, the cross-branch evidence is actually in favour of the 24 manuscripts that read 'credantur' in 45, that is, *F*, all relevant γ manuscripts (*Vb* and *Vd* are out at this point), δ, and *TrHala*.

[27] Cf. the similar criticism in Nigel's *Tractatus*, ed. Boutemy, pp. 157, 204, of those who go to the university of Paris, but return with only a smattering of learning.

[28] *articulus* = '(critical) moment, (crucial) time' (*DMLBS* 5).

[29] *res uerbis*: see n. to line 153.

18   *SPECVLVM STVLTORVM*

hodie multi simulatores, nec est ars aut ordo in orbe uniuerso fere in quibus aliqua non sit simulatio; **48** qui enim artibus uacant simulant se scire quod nesciunt; qui in ordine religionis uiuunt id uolunt uideri quod non sunt. **49** Vnde Burnellus quaedam de diuersis ordinibus interserit, uolens iocosa quaedam insimulatione reprehendere quae nouerat aspera increpatione nequaquam se posse extirpare. **50** Multa enim genera morborum sunt quae utilius unguentum quam cauterium ad medelam admittunt.[30]

Prologus auctoris

Suscipe pauca tibi ueteris, Willelme, Nigelli
   scripta, minus sapido nuper arata stylo.
Hoc modicum nouitatis opus tibi mitto legendum,
   maxima pars animae dimidiumque meae.
5   Ipsa superficies quamuis uideatur inepta
   materiesque rudis, uerba diserta minus,

---

49 quaedam de] quedam *H* quidam de *VaVcTPkFrPmNe GI HaLa* quidem de *GoBe*; quaedam insimulatione] quadam insimulatione *B PkNe K* quadam simulatione *H MuVaVcTGoFrPmDGIHa X*; se]*om. SMuVaVcTGoBePkFrPmNe TrHaLa*   **50** morborum] morbi *F* β *SMuVaVcTGoBePkFrPmNe HaLa X* membrorum *AJWRHuMNDVe* membrorum uel morbi *GI*; cauterium] cauterium id est ferrum quo uruntur infirmi uel dampnati *R* cauteres *Ne*; ad medelam admittunt] admittunt β *SMuVaVcTGoPkFrPm Ha* ad medicinam admittunt *X* admittunt ad cautelam *Tr* admittunt et cetera *F Be* admittunt etc etc etc *La om. Ne*

1–1042 *om. U* (*missing leaves*)   **1** tibi] tui α; Willelme] Wilhelme *VaGo RO erased, hardly legible Y*; Nigelli] sigilli *M* scigelli *HuN* digellus *Go* nigelle *Q* nigrelle *Fr*   **2** minus] nimis *Pm^{ac} GI*; arata] arato *AHuM^{pc}N* aratro *M^{ac2}D* atrita *Vd* parata *Pm* arate *Q*   **3** nouitatis] nouiter *MN* leuitatis *X*   **4** maxima] maxime *GoBeNe* maximo *Vd*   **6** materiesque] materieque β *SMuVaVbTGoBePkFrPmNe* δ *GI HaLa ZXQY* materiaque *Vc* materie *Vd*; diserta] deserta *F BeFr I* deserta / uel diserta *La* discreta *Vd*; minus] nimis *L VaVbPkPm^{ac} P GI La X*

Heading   For the manuscript sources from which the headings are taken, see Introduction, pp. clxix–lxx.

  1 *ueteris*: Relying on his dating of *SS* to 1179–80, and his consequent conjecture that Nigel was born *c.*1140, Boutemy (*Tractatus*, p. 13) concluded that this means literally 'old'. My redating of *SS* to the 1190s, taken together with the indication that Nigel had been in company with Thomas Becket (at some point before his murder in 1170), would make the adjective even more appropriate, but it is also possible that 'ueteris' just means 'old friend'. *Willelme*: William of Longchamp, chancellor of Richard I, bishop of Ely 1189–97, and from 1190 to 1191, justiciar of England. See further Introduction, pp. xxxiv–xlviii, lxi–lxiii, lxxvii–lxxviii.

SPECVLVM STVLTORVM

19

hypocrites these days, as there is almost no branch of study or religious order in the whole world, almost, in which there is no hypocrisy, **48** since those who devote themselves to study pretend that they know what they do not, and those who live in a religious order want to seem to be what they are not. **49** Wherefore Burnellus inserts some things about the different orders, wishing to criticize by a comic pretence what he knew he could not root out by harsh reproof. **50** For there are many kinds of illnesses which respond better to unguents than to cauterization.[30]

Author's Prologue

Accept, William, these scanty writings, lately scribbled in unembellished style by your old friend Nigel. To you, who are half my soul, and the more important part, I send this little novelty to read. Although it may on the surface seem foolish, [5] its subject may seem crude, and its language uncouth, yet the attentive reader will be able to glean much

---

2 *arata*: 'arare' = 'to write' (*DMLBS* 2c); cf. *exarare. minus sapido*: 'plain, not savoury'. For 'minus' used to negate an accompanying adjective, see *DMLBS* 3b and cf. *SS*, 6 ('minus diserta'), 71 ('minus prudens'), 538 ('tuta minus'), 3079 ('minus diserta').

3 *nouitatis opus*: also in *SS*, 2908; *Miracles*, 423, 645; *Epigrams*, no. xi. 25.

4 Horace, *Odes*, i. 3. 8: 'et serves animae dimidium meae'. The phrase seems to have passed into general usage: see Introduction, pp. xliii–xliv, n. 79.

---

[30] An echo of the *Rule of Benedict*, c. xxviii, which describes an escalating series of means by which the abbot, like a wise doctor, can correct the faults of monks: 'fomenta...unguenta' = exhortation; 'medicamina' = the Scriptures; 'ustio' (cauterization) = excommunication or flogging; and only in the last resort 'ferro abscisio' (amputation) = expulsion from the monastic community.

20 SPECVLVM STVLTORVM

multa tamen poterit lector studiosus in illis
sensibus et studiis carpere digna suis.
Non quod uerba sonant, sed quae contraria uerbis
10 insita sensus habet sunt retinenda magis.
Quis uetet, ex nugis uario paradigmate sumpto,
seria quandoque plurima posse legi?
Saepius historiae breuitas mysteria magna
claudit, et in uili res pretiosa latet.
15 Quicquid ad exemplum morum scriptura propinat
doctrinae causa, debet habere locum.
Saepius admiror, dum tempora lapsa recordor,
quam fuerint nobis quamque notanda tibi.
Nil cum praeterito praesens mihi tempus habere
20 cernitur, in caudam uertitur omne caput.
Fit de nocte dies, tenebrae de luce serena,
de stulto sapiens, de sapiente nihil.
Fit Cato mentis hebes, linguam facundus Vlixes
perdidit, instabiles non habet aura uices.
25 Plusque Catone sapit, magis est facundus Vlixe,
qui modo mutus erat, mente manuque carens.
Quique fuit sapiens duro sub tempore belli,
hunc quasi delirum tempora pacis habent;
et qui nil sapuit nisi stultum tempore duro,
30 postquam pax rediit, incipit esse Cato.

---

8 et] *sic P over erasure* in *H G*   9 quae] quod *ZQY* quo *I*   10 habet] habent α
I Tr Z que *Mu*   11 uetet] uetat *R T ZQ* notet *L GI* uiget *Ha*; paradigmate]
paranigmate *GI* paradigate *T* paradimate *Ne*; sumpto] sumptis *Mu*ᵃᶜ*Go Ha*   13 historiae breuitas] historia breuiter *D X*; misteria] historia *X*ᵃᶜ miseria quoque *T*   15 exem-
plum] exempla *PD XY*; morum] mori *HuMN*; propinat] ministrat γ- *TrLa* propinat /uel
ministrat *Ha*   17 recordor] reuoluo δ *X*   18 quamque] quamquam *Tr* queque
D QY;   19 praesens mihi] mihi presens β *GI*   20 omne] sepe *D X*   21 fit]
fitque *MuV̄aVdGoBeFrPm* atque *Pk*; de¹] *om. VaBePkPm*   23 Vlixes] uluxes *Fr*
AHuMN Y eloquens *T*   24–5 *om. Go*   24 perdidit] perdit *VcVd*; instabiles non
habet] instabilis non habet *MuVaVb*ᵖᶜ*VcVdTBePkFrPmNe TrLa* instabiles nunc habet
AJCWROPDKVe instabiles habet et *MN* et stabiles non habet β *GI Ha ZXQY*; uices] uires
VdTr uoces *Fr*   25 magis est] magisque *AJCWPVe* magisque est *Hu*; facundus Vlixe]
uluxes facundus *Hu*; ulixe] uluxes *MN* uluxe *A Y*   26 mutus] mucus /uel mutus
La stultus *L*; erat] erit *AJCWRHuMNPKVe*; manuque] uera *Mu* namque *VaGo*
27 quique] qui *Ha Y* qui modo *Q*; fuit] fuerit *C* est *Q*; duro] duo *I* diuo *MN* domino *T*
29 duro] diuo *MN*

SPECVLVM STVLTORVM

that is worthy of his meditation and study. It is not what the words say, but the meaning smuggled in under their cover that is more to be retained. [10] Who would deny that on occasion many serious things can be learned from trifles, by the selection of various examples? Often a short tale holds great secrets, and a precious thing lurks in something despised. Whatever literature offers for our instruction as an illustration of morals [15] ought to be given its place. I often marvel, when I recall bygone times, at how much they should be taken notice of, both by me and by you. The present time appears to me to have nothing in common with the past; everything is turned head to tail. [20] Night is turned into day, daylight into darkness, a fool into a wise man, a wise man into nothing. Cato turns into a simpleton, eloquent Ulysses has lost his tongue, and the wind no longer shifts. The man who just now was dumb, lacking brains and courage, knows more than Cato and is more eloquent than Ulysses. [25] And the one who was wise in wartime is treated like a madman in time of peace; he who knew nothing but foolishness in times of hardship becomes Cato when peace returns.

5–12 Beast fables traditionally stress at their opening that despite their frivolous surface, they offer wise advice. See, for example, Phaedrus, *Fabulae*, i. Prol.; Avianus, *Fabulae*, Dedicatory Letter; elegiac *Romulus* (ed. Busdraghi), Prologue 1–6. However, Nigel's protestation that his words have an underlying meaning is probably also a pointer to the implicit message to William which is indicated in the *Epistle*; see Introduction pp. lv–lxiii. The insistence on what the poem signifies 'mystice' is repeated at its end, lines 3881–2.

14 *in uili res pretiosa iacet*: this is a near-verbatim echo of the fable of the cock and the jewel in the elegiac *Romulus* (ed. Busdraghi), Fable i. 3: the cock addresses the jewel as 'res uili pretiosa loco'. Cf. Walther, *Proverbia*, 27317.

17–48 These lines should be read in the light of Nigel's complaint in the *Epistola* that those who (like Burnellus) attend university and read books which they completely fail to understand, nevertheless make a false parade of their learning.

17 *recordor*: Mozley prints 'reuoluo', the δ reading, but 'reuoluo' is not found elsewhere in *SS* whereas 'recordor' appears at 391, 1464, 1846, 2935, and 3237.

20 *in caudam uertitur...caput*: for other examples of this popular phrase, see *SS*, 2508–10; Peter of Blois, *Epistolae*, no. ci (PL ccvii. 314C); John of Salisbury, *Letters*, no. ccxliv (ii. 484). The image of 'the world upside down' was a popular theme in medieval literature; see Curtius, *European Literature*, pp. 94–8.

23 *facundus Vlixes*: Ovid, *Ars amatoria*, ii. 123.

24 The line obviously gave difficulty to the δ scribes, but 'nunc' is clearly an easier substitution for 'non', reflecting a conventional attitude to the weather. Nigel inverts this conventional belief in the characteristic changeability of the weather: in the topsy-turvy world he is describing, the weather no longer changes. Cf. line 1796: 'uicis est non habuisse uicem', 'The absence of change constitutes a change'.

22 SPECVLVM STVLTORVM

Quodque magis miror, furantur Nestoris annos
    quos nondum partus edidit ipse suus.
Sic fortuna, parit dum partus prodigiosos,
    redditur ex partu prodigiosa suo.
35   Prodiga facta magis quam prouida, prodigiosam
    constitit ante suam se peperisse diem.
Nam puer impubes Cicerone disertior ipso
    fingitur, et magno scire Catone magis.
Omnia lunari subiecta globo reserare
40   nouit, et interdum mystica multa uidet.
Qualemcumque uirum cupias, quantumque disertum
    fingere mente, manu pingere, talis erit.
Talis apud tales, talis sub tempore tali,
    subque suo tali iudice talis erit.

31–2 *om. Ha QY*   31 furantur Nestoris annos] furantur uestoris annos *L* furatur nestoris annos *J La X* furantur nestoris annus *Go* furantur nectoris annos *Pk* sumpserunt nestoris annos *Z om. D*   32 nondum] necdum *EF* non *Go* modum *Vd* unde *Pk*; suus] suos *Be La* suas *Tr* sues *Vd*   33 *line repeated in alternative form* $Z_{(1)}Z_{(2)}$ sic] dum *D* Ha^{pc} $Z_{(1)}Z_{(2)}QY$ dic *X corr.* X^2; parit] patrit *Vb* perit RPW^{ac}(*corr. in margin*)*Ve*; dum partus] dum partu *Vc* partus sic *D* partus dum *X* de partis *MuVaTBe*(alias partu *add. interlinear* Be^2)*FrPmNe* departus *Vb* de partu *VdPk La* depcis *Go* de parcis *TrHa*^{ac} dum parcis Ha^{pc} pro parcis $Z_{(2)}$; prodigiosos] prodigiosus *F SVdGo AJCWRHuMNOPKVe GI* $Z_{(1)}Z_{(2)}$ prodigiosis *MuVaPk*   35–40 *end of lines illegible (rubbed) I*   35 prodiga] prodigia *Va C I* prouida *H*; prouida] prodiga *Vc M*; prodigiosam] prodigiosa *VdGo* prodigiosum F^{pc} *Vc X* prodigiosis (?) *J*   36 constitit] constit *Fr* constat *GI* cum sciat *R* conspicit *ed. Lips.*; se peperisse] sepe perisse *Vc R* sit peperisse *Q* deperiisse *B* deperuisse *H*   37 Cicerone] ordine *F* ticione *S* cicutone *M* citherone *WD* thitherone *Hu*; disertior] di <*space left empty*> *HuMN* discretior *SVaVcVdBePk Ve Ha*? discricior *Fr* discretior /[*uel*] disertior *La*; ipso] ipse *VdGo R* ipsa *Tr*   38 fingitur] fungitur *Go* fungitur /uel fingitur *La*; Catone] citerone *I* canone *M* et catone *Vd*   39 omnia] semina *HuMN*; reserare] reserari *SVaVdGoBePkFrPmNe TrHaLa X* reseratur *Z*   41 uirum] uix *Q*; cupias] capias *Vd* cupiat *D* cupia *R* cupies *Ha ZQY* cupiasque *Fr*; quantumque] quantumcumque CW^{pc} *Z* quamcumque *R Y* cautumque *SVbPk La* cantumque *Va* tantumque *MuVdTGoBePmNe* quantumque /uel cautum *Ha om. Fr*; disertum] desertum *F* discretum /uel disertum *La*; (*whole line*) qualem quandoque iure cupiat quantumque deserunt *F*   43–4 *om. Ne* *RO*(*add. in margin* O^{pc})   43 talis¹] tales *Vd I QY* esse talis *Fr*; talis²] tales *QY* tali *Va om. Fr*; tempore] specie *OPVe* parte *Z*; tali] talis *GI*   44 *om. Mu*

31–42 Nestor, one of the Greeks who fought against Troy, was famed for his great age and the wisdom it had brought. Nigel's complaint is that nowadays, even babes in arms pretend to similar wisdom. Similar complaints are to be found in *Carmina Burana*, no. vi (Inc. 'Florebat olim studium'): 'sed retro actis seculis/ vix licuit discipulis/ tandem nonagenarium/ quiescere post studium./ at nunc decennes pueri/ decusso iugo liberi/ se nunc magistros iactitant' (9–15); in John of Salisbury, who represents the young as rejecting the wisdom of the ancients and boasting that their youth teaches them all they need to know (*Entheticus maior*, ed. van Laarhoven, 40–64), and ridicules the speed with which new arrivals at the

SPECVLVM STVLTORVM
23

[30] Even more wonderful, those who were not yet born now assume Nestor's years. So fortune, while it gives birth to monstrous offspring, is made monstrous in its birth; prodigal rather than provident, [35] it has become clear that she has monstrously given birth before her time. For a beardless youth masquerades as more learned than Cicero himself, and as knowing more than great Cato. He knows how to explain everything under the moon, and along with this, sees many secrets. [40] Whatever kind of man, however learned, you want to imagine in your mind or paint with your hand, such he will be—of a piece with his fellows, with his age, and with those who judge him. So a whitewashed wall is painted on the outside,

schools of Paris turn into 'consummate philosophers, the pupil who had arrived illiterate generally not dallying longer in the class than the short space of time it takes little chicks to grow feathers' (*Metalogicon*, i. 3, ed. Hall, pp. 16–17; trans. Hall, p. 130); and in Peter of Blois, who criticizes those who skip the hard slog of elementary grammar and plunge into advanced topics of philosophy (*Epistolae*, no. ci, PL ccvii. 311–14). John of Hauville similarly criticizes the beardless youths who climb into the teacher's chair and 'lay claim to rewards held in store for age' (*Architrenius*, ed. Wetherbee, v. 72–9, trans. Wetherbee). However, when opening his poem, John sardonically inverts the topos, protesting that although he does not remember the days of Deucalion's flood, and does not have wrinkles or white hair, his book should nevertheless not be sneered at (*Architrenius*, ed. Wetherbee, i. 65–99). Joseph of Exeter similarly defends (his own) beardless youth against white-haired old age (*Ylias*, i. 15–23). (Raymo misreads these latter two passages, assigning them to the pro-age group.) Cf. Curtius, *European Literature*, p. 98.

35 *prodigiosam*: Shackleton Bailey's emendation to 'prodigiosa' ('Textual notes', p. 282) is tempting ('she has given birth prematurely to monsters'), but 'prodigiosam' is well attested in all manuscript groups and makes good sense in context. The shift from the nominatives 'prodiga... prouida' to the accusative 'prodigiosam' can be explained as anacoluthon.

36 *constitit*: this is the reading of all manuscripts except *Fr* ('constit'), *GI* ('constat'), and *R* ('cum sciat'). Mozley adopted 'conspicit' from Conrad Kachelofen's Leipzig edition of 1487/1495, but the emendation is unnecessary. In classical and medieval Latin, 'constat' is frequently used in an impersonal construction, usually with accusative and infinitive (here, 'prodigiosam... se peperisse'), to mean 'it is established (as fact), certain' (see *OLD* 9a–b, and *DMLBS* 2c); often the sense is weakened to mean little more than 'it is (was) the case that', or even simply '(*x*) is (was)' (*OLD* 5a), and Nigel often uses it in this way. For examples, see *SS*, lines 266, 695, 978, 999, 1561, 1832, 2178, 2578, 2956, 3092, 3108, 3849, etc. On the use of 'se' for 'eam' (less frequent than 'suus' for 'eius'), see Stotz, *Handbuch*, ix. 385.

37–8 Medieval writers referred to Cicero as a typical representative of eloquence, and Cato as a typical representative of wisdom. See *Ysengrimus*, v. 512 ('Fit uicibus certis Tullius atque Cato'); Matthew of Vendôme, *Commendatio militis*, PL ccv. 983 ('Tullius eloquio... rigore Cato'); Geoffrey of Vinsauf, *Poetria nova*, 1775–6 ('Es Cato mente,/ Tullius ore').

39 *lunari subiecta globo*: Claudian, *De raptu Proserpinae*, ii. 298.

41 *quantumque*: for 'quantumcumque'.

24   *SPECVLVM STVLTORVM*

45   Sicque dealbatus paries depingitur extra,
        interius plenus sordibus atque luto.
      Sic pictura lutum uestit, sic gemma uenustat
        stercora, sic aurum putrida ligna tegit.
      Qui nihil est per se, nec habet quo tendat in altum,
50   expedit alterius ut releuetur ope.
      Est tamen absurdum, cum quilibet ex alieno
        intumet ulterius quam tumuisse decet.
      Quamuis, de propria cum quis uirtute superbit,
        sit uitium, leuius hoc tamen esse puto.
55   Consuetudo tamen solet attenuare pudorem,
        reddit et audacem quem mora longa iuuat.
      Regna licet teneat sceptrumque leonis asellus,
        iuraque det populis, semper asellus erit.
      Asperior tamen est in sede leonis asellus
60   si positus fuerit, quam foret ipse leo.
      Pelle leonina tectum detexit asellum
        fastus, et excedens gloria uana modum.

---

46 *after 45, 63–4 transp. J*   47 gemma] gemino / uel gemma *La*   48 stercora] stercore *fb* stercore / uel stercora *La*; ligna] lingua *Vb CWHuMND Q*; tegit] tegunt *Z* terit *Q*   49 tendat] tendit *LE H Go GI Tr* tendet *P*   50 releuetur] reueletur *VdFr HuMN GI La*ac *Z corr Z*[2]   51 cum] quod γ *C TrLa* quod / uel cum *Ha* qui *HuMN*   52 intumet] utrumque *HuMN*; ulterius] alterius *SVcGoBe RHuMN TrHa*ac *QY*; quam] quem *TrHa* quasi *Go* quod *Fr*; tumuisse] timuisse *TGo HuMND GI X*   53 cum quis] quisquam β *GI*   54 sit] sic *SVa GI XY*; puto] reor α   55–56 *om. at this point* P, *205–594 are added at end of poem*   57 sceptrumque] sceptraque *VcFr A*pc*CWHuNDVe* sceptra *O fb* septrique *G*   58–9 *om. Fr HuMN*   61 detexit] deduxit *J* detexit / uel decepit *Ha* detexerit *Ne*   62 et] *om. VaVc*

    45–8 *dealbatus paries*: a biblical phrase; see Acts 23: 3, and cf. Matt. 23: 27. *pictura lutum...gemma...stercora*: cf. Walter of Châtillon, *Poems*, no. lvi. 18. 3–4 (= *Carmina Burana*, no. xlii. 18. 3–4), referring to someone who has bought a bishopric at the papal curia: 'Et accedit dignitas animali bruto,/ tamquam *gemma stercori uel pictura luto.*' Cf. also Geoffrey of Vinsauf, when insisting on the need for style to match subject matter: 'Se nisi conformet color intimus exteriori,/ Sordet ibi ratio: faciem depingere verbi/ Est *pictura luti*, res est falsaria, ficta/ Forma *dealbatus paries* et hypocrita verbum/ Se simulans aliquid, cum sit nihil' (*Poetria nova*, 741–5). Traill's note to Walter's poem (see p. lxxxix) suggests that Walter was Nigel's source, and Nigel was Geoffrey's. However, Traill's further suggestion that the motif of the jewel in the dunghill is taken from Christian writers, who used it 'to justify their study of pagan authors', overlooks the fable of the cock and the jewel, which is clearly alluded to by Nigel at line 14 (see n.).

    46 *sordibus atque luto*: cf. Prudentius, *Praefatio*, 11–12: 'luxus petulans...foedavit iuuenem nequitiae sordibus et luto'.

    49–50 Cf. Boethius, *De consolatione*, iii pr. 9: 'si quid est, quod in ulla re imbecillioris valentiae sit, in hac praesidio necesse est egeat alieno'. Nigel is here justifying himself for attacking those who falsely pretend to have qualities that they lack (viz., the pretentious

SPECVLVM STVLTORVM   25

[45] but is inwardly full of dirt and filth. So a painted exterior hides
dirt, a jewel adorns a dungheap, and gold covers rotten wood. Anyone
who is himself nothing and is incapable of rising in the world has to be
raised by someone else's help. [50] But it is ridiculous for someone to
puff himself up more than he should on account of another person's
merit. Although it is a vice for someone to be proud of his own abilities,
I think this is a less serious one. Yet habit customarily wears away mod-
esty, [55] and makes a man bold when long delay strengthens him.

Although the ass holds the lion's sceptre and his kingdom, and gives
laws to his people, he will always be an ass. But the ass is more cruel, if
he is placed on the lion's throne, than the lion himself would be. [60]
The ass who is cloaked in the lion's skin is unmasked by his pride and
the vainglory that passes all bounds. Were it only kept within limits, the

---

ignoramuses who win the rewards that are denied to him), and defending his own shameless-
ness in drawing attention to his own greater claims. The 'long delay' which he has been
forced to endure while waiting for recognition of his merits has made him bold enough to
draw attention to them. See Introduction, pp. lxi–lxiii.

56 Cf. *Babio*, 303–4 (*Commedie*, ii. 278): 'Est rea res venia: multis dedit ausa malorum;/
Ausa dedit Niobe tardior ira dee.'

57–66 A reference to and partial quotation of Avianus, *Fabulae*, v, which tells of an ass who
clothed himself in a lion's skin and in this disguise scared the other animals; however, the
farmer who owned him stripped the lion's pelt from him and said that although he might
terrify strangers, 'To me you will always be a donkey' ('semper asellus eris', 18). This phrase
is used by Serlo of Wilton to clinch his insulting exchange with Hugh Primas (*Serlon de
Wilton: Poèmes latins*, ed. Öberg, no. lxxv, p. 120). Avianus was read as a school text by begin-
ners in medieval Latin, and there were numerous modernizations in the period;
see Hervieux, *Les Fabulistes latins*, vol. iii, partially updated in *Favolisti latini medievali*;
see under Avianus in the Bibliography. The ass in the lion's skin in particular enjoyed quasi-
proverbial status in the Middle Ages; see the Archpoet, ed. Watenphul and Krefeld, iv. 24.
1–3 ('Vellem.../ non leonum spoliis asinos ornarent'); John of Salisbury, *Entheticus minor*,
196–7, ed. van Laarhoven ('pelle leonina dic quid asellus agat; / quid leo dum servit. quid
agit dum regnat asellus'); Alan of Lille, *Liber Parabolarum*, ed. Limone, lines 433–6 ('Nos
asinus ridere facit dum more leonis/ pingitur et vulpes subdola cogit idem;/ exuat is pellem
qua se putat esse leonem/ et patiens oneris, iussa sequatur heri'); Walter of Châtillon, *Poems*,
no. lvi. 1. 4 = *Carmina Burana*, no. xlii. 1. 4 ('et leonis spolium induunt aselli'). For other
examples in medieval literature, and references to Latin proverbs, see Dicke and Grubmüller,
Die Fabeln, no. 117, pp. 122–4.

60 After 60, *MuVcTGoPmNeft* have two extra lines: 'Ordine retrogrado si forsan dat rota
saltum/ asperius nichil est humili dum surgit in altum' ('If the wheel chances to make a
backward leap, nothing is harsher for the humble man who is rising upwards'). *Vc* has the
same lines in the top margin, marked for insertion after line 60. *Pm* has the lines in the margin next to line 62. *Go* has the lines in the margin at the side of line 65; *Ne* has the lines in the
margin beside lines 66–8. Variant readings are as follows: dat] det *T* dant *Vc*; si] *om. Go*; rota]
uota *MuVc*; nihil est humili] humili nihil est *ft*; est] *om. Go*; humili] misero *Ne*. *T* adds a third
line: Qui premit indigno libera colla pede. The second line is a widely cited proverb (Walther,
Proverbia, 1565), found *inter alia* in Alan of Lille's *Liber Parabolarum* (ed. Limone, line 299,
p. 70; PL ccx 587C). Its probable source is Claudian, *In Eutropium*, i. 181 (*Pm* adds an attribution to 'Claudianus').

26 SPECVLVM STVLTORVM

Si moderata foret saltem, sub imagine falsa
res simulata diu posset habere locum.

65   Sed nimis impatiens grauis in nouitate uetustas
praecipites saltus in sua damna dedit.

Dum miser ipse sibi factus suus ex alieno
fortunam didicit dedidicisse suam,
perdidit inuitus, male se simulante leonem,

70   quod bene siue male credidit esse bonum.

Si qua minus prudens male perdidit, ex alieno
perdidit, ex proprio nil periisse liquet.

Quae fuit ante sibi nullo mediante figura
permanet, ex nihilo perdidit ergo nihil.

75   Qui leo non potuit fieri, si fiat asellus
Sufficit; alterius sarcina pondus habet,

quoque magis fertur magis est onerosa ferenti.

Respectu uario pondera pondus habent;
sanius ergo foret alienum non rapuisse,

80   quam cum dedecore non retinere suum.

De asino qui uoluit caudam suam longiorem fieri

Auribus immensis quondam donatus asellus
institit ut caudam posset habere parem.

Cauda suo capiti quia se conferre nequibat,
altius ingemuit de breuitate sua,

85   non quia longa satis non esset ad utilitatem,
ante tamen quam sic apocopata foret.

63–4 *transp. after 45 J*   **63** falsa] fulsa / uel falsa *La*   **64** *om. Ne*   **64** posset] possit *GoFr O*   **65** sed] sic *GI* si *Fr J Ha*; uetustas] uenustas *F H Be R* tenenda *T*   **67** factus suos] factus suus *Mu* factus fuit α *AJCWRHuMNOKVe GI Ha ZQY* felix fuit *D Tr X* uel felix *add. interlinear* K^{pc} **68** *om. Fr*   dedidicisse] sic didicisse *MN* se didicisse *W ZQY*^{ac} didicisse *Vc* dedicisse *Mu CDVe X* uel dedecuisse *add.* X^2 **69–70** *transp. after 72,* 71 *om. Fr* (67, 72, 69, 70, 73)   **70** *transp. after 72 GoPmNe; om. Vd*; quod] quia *T* qui *Be Tr* quam *Ha*; credidit] credit *Q*   **71–2** *transp. Mu; transp. after* 69 *Va*; *transp. after 76 VdBePk Tr*; *transp. after 75 La*   **71** si qua] sicque *GI* si que β   **73** *om. Vd*   **73** quae] quod *H MuTPm* qui *VaBePkNe TrLa* quid *Go*; nullo] nulla *MuTGoFrPm AJCWHuMNODK Ha ZQY*   **74** nihilo] proprio *ZXQY* nihilo / uel proprio *Ha*   **75** fiat] fiet *Vc R* foret *T*   **77–8** *repeated, then line* 77 *deleted Mu; om. Go O* (77 *add. in margin* O^{pc})   **77** quoque] quodque α *Ha Y* queque *GI Z*; est] hec α   **78** habent] habet *GI*   **80** dedecore] decore *F VdGoFr Tr QZ*^{ac} **81** auribus] iuribus *G*; quondam] quemdam *Q*; donatus] dotatus *H MuVaVcTGoBe DK GI Tr ZXQ* donatus /uel dotatus *La* deuotus *VdFr* denominatus *Ve*   **82** posset] possit *H TGo O XY*   **83** cauda] caudam *QY*   **85** quia] quod α *GI*; non²] hec *ZQY om. Fr*   **86** ante tamen quam] flet dum per medicos *ZQY* aure tamen breuius *Vb* ante tamen breuius *Vc* perit dum / uel ante tamen quam sit *Ha*; sic] sit *SVdFrPm X om. Vb ZQY*

SPECVLVM STVLTORVM

fake could keep its position a long time under its disguised appearance. But solemn old age, impatient with a new situation, [65] leaps headlong to its own destruction. While a wretch takes another's characteristics as his own, and learns to forget his own lot, he unwillingly loses, by unsuccessfully pretending to be the lion, what—for good or ill—he thought to be good. [70] If the fool had the misfortune to lose anything, he lost what was another's, so it is clear that he lost nothing of his own. The condition that he had before, without anyone else's intervention, still remains, so he has lost nothing out of nothing. Anyone who cannot be a lion should be satisfied with being an ass; [75] another's burden weighs one down, and the longer it is carried the heavier it is to the bearer. The weight of burdens varies according to circumstance; so it would be wiser not to grab another's than to incur shame by failing to carry one's own. [80]

About the ass who wanted his tail to be made longer

Once upon a time, an ass endowed with enormous ears was determined that he should have a tail of equal size. Because his tail could not be compared with his head, he loudly bewailed its brevity—not because it was not long enough to do its job, [85] at least before it was cut short.

---

71 *qua*: see *OLD* s. v. qui¹, indef. pron. (neuter pl.) C. 24, after 'si' = anything'. *minus prudens*: see n. to line 2.

76 *sarcina pondus habet*: Maximian, *Elegies*, v. 70.

77 For a parallel construction to the first half-line, cf. line 1625.

79–80 Proverbial; see Singer, *Thesaurus*, s.v. 'Eigen' 5. 2. 5 (ii. 399). The warning against attempting to acquire more than one has, in case it leaves one with nothing, is a frequent moral in beast fables, such as the fable of the Dog and the Meat Reflected in the Water: see elegiac *Romulus* (ed. Busdraghi), v. 5–6: 'Non igitur debent pro vanis certa relinqui./ Non sua si quis avet, mox caret ipse suis.' See also Avianus, *Fabulae*, viii. 1–2: 'Contentum propriis sapientem vivere rebus/ Nec cupere alterius, nostra fabella monet.'

86 *apocopata*: a proleptic reference to the later incident in the narrative, in which the ass's tail is bitten in half by dogs.

28   SPECVLVM STVLTORVM

consuluit medicos, quia quod natura negabat,
artis ab officio posse putabat eos.

Responsio Galieni

Cui Galienus ait: 'Satis est bipedalis asello
90   cauda, quid ulterius poscis, inepte, tibi?
Sufficit ista tibi, nam quo productior esset,
sordidior fieret proximiorque luto.
Hac nisi contentus fueris, dum forte requiris
prolongare nimis, abbreuiabis eam.
95   Quod natura dedit non sit tibi uile, sed illud
inter diuitias amplius esse puta.
Crede mihi, uetus est tibi cauda salubrior ista
natibus innata quam foret illa noua.
Nec placet ista tamen, sed habere cupis meliorem;
100   artibus et curis insita peior erit.
Sed neque de facili posset noua cauda creari,
quamuis deposita cauda uetusta foret.
Vita breuis, morbus grauis est et tempus acutum,
ars est longa nimis, abdita causa latet.
105   Difficiles curae nimium, sed et experimenta
ipsa suos medicos fallere saepe solent.
Certa pericla manent, medicorum dogmata non sunt
qualia tu credis, qualia quisque putat.
Sed neque sic passim praestat medicina salutem,
110   quamuis distribuat arte peritus eam.
Pendet in ambiguo morbi medicina, dolorem
impedit atque parit conditione pari.
Quae prosunt aliis, aliis nocuisse probantur;
non est in medico quam cupit aeger opem.

---

87 consuluit] consiliit *JM I* consulit *N*; medicos] medicus *F GoFr*; negabat] nequibat
AJCWRHuMNODKVe X negabit *LE*   88 putabat] putabit *LE*   89 asello]
aselle *MuVaTBeFrPm RDM TrHa ZQY*   90 poscis] petis *MuFr* possis *Tr* posset *Z*
91 nam] iam *H GI*; productior] prolixior γ- *TrLa* productior / uel prolixior *Ha*   93 hac]
ac *GoBe* at *MuVaVbPkPmNe* ac / [uel] hac *La* hec *Z* hoc *fb*; dum] et *MuVaVdTGoFrPm* ac
BeNe Tr de *Pk*   94 nimis] modo *Q*   97 mihi] mihi mihi *Ne om. M*
99 tamen] tibi a *D La*   102 *om. Ne*   104 abdita] addita *VaTBePkFrPmNe* adita
Go   105 et] *om. F*ᵃᶜ *H VdT MK*   109 *om. Fr*   109 passim] possim *Pk*
possum *Z* passum *Ne Ve*; praestat] restat *LE* prestet *O*   110–11 *om. T*   110 dis-
tribuat] distribuit *MuFr? DVe X* destribuat *O*   112 impedit] imperat *T* impedit / uel
impetit *La*   113 quae] quod *Va* qui *Pm Q*   114 quam] quem *H GI* quod *O ZQY*
fb; opem] opis *AJCWRHuMNODKVe Ha Y fb* opes *Q* ipse *L*

SPECVLVM STVLTORVM

He sought advice from doctors, because he thought they could achieve, by the exercise of their art, what nature denied.

Galen's reply

Galen answered: 'A two-foot tail is enough for an ass. Why do you seek more, you fool? [90] This is enough for you, since, if it were longer, it would be dirtier from being nearer the mud. If you are not content with this one, you may well make it shorter while you are trying to lengthen it unduly. You should not hold cheap what nature gave, [95] but should rather look on it as riches. Believe me, this old tail that your backside was born with is more healthful to you than any new one would be. But you don't like this one, and you want to have a better one—when art and skill have set it in place, you will like it less. [100] Nor is it easy to create a new tail, even if the old tail were to be discarded. Life is short, sickness is serious, and its crisis is acute; medical art is very slow, and the hidden cause eludes it. Cures are hard to come by, [105] and doctors are cheated by their own experiments. Risk is a certainty, and medical teachings are not what you believe or what anyone thinks. Medicine can't always bring healing, even if it's administered by one learned in the art. [110] Medicine for an illness can go either way; it both removes pain and, by the same process, creates it. What is helpful to some proves to be harmful to others; the relief that the patient craves is not to be found in the doctor. The doctor can wish

---

87 Mozley prints the δ reading 'nequibat', which apparently arose from the influence of line 83; 'negabat' is widely attested in the manuscripts and 'quod natura negat reddere nemo potest' is a proverbial saying, quoted by Nigel at line 186 (see n. below).

89 *Galienus*: The archetypal name for a doctor. The historical Galen was a Greek physician who lived in the 2nd c. AD, and whose theories were influential throughout the Middle Ages. Raymo's assumption that Nigel is satirizing Galienus for his 'pompous loquacity' and his willingness to deceive Burnellus for the sake of a large fee, seems unjustified; in fact Galienus does his best to talk some sense into the ass, and only gives up when he sees that this is futile.

103–4 *Vita breuis...ars...longa*: an aphorism originating with the Greek doctor Hippocrates.

104 After 104, *R* adds two extra lines: 'Cotidie fallunt ars et praxis medicine/ si tres euadunt septem dant colla ruine' ('Daily, the art and practice of medicine fail; if three escape, seven succumb to disaster').

113 Proverbial; see Singer, *Thesaurus*, s.v. 'Schaden' 6. 5 (ix. 468).

114 Cf. Ovid, *Ex Ponto*, i. 3. 17: 'Non est in medico semper releuetur ut aeger'; quoted in a letter of John of Salisbury to Thomas Becket, *Becket Correspondence* i. 74–5 (no. xxiv).

SPECVLVM STVLTORVM

30

115
Velle potest medicus, sed non conferre, salutem;
gratia diua facit, ipse minister adest.

Saepe quidem medici fallunt, falluntur et ipsi,
et uice conuersa quae nocuere iuuant.

Esto, quod ars mandat, faciat, nec abinde recedat;
120
non tamen euenient quae cupis ipse tibi.

Solus enim Deus est morbis medicina salutis;
nos tantum uelle possumus, ille potest.

Nos nihil absque suo uel eo nos praeueniente
possumus; ipse sibi sufficit absque meo.

125
Nos herbis uariis, pigmentis et speciebus
utimur; hic uerbo singula sana facit.

Dicimur a populo medici, sed nomine solo;
sed Deus est medicus nomine reque simul.

Quam dedit ille tibi caudam retinere memento,
130
stulte, nec ulterius ulteriora petas.

Ne perdas quod habes, quod habes tenuisse labora,
ne ueniant subito deteriora tibi.

Quam tibi plantauit caudam qui contulit aures,
si mihi credideris, hanc retinere stude.

135
Inque statu quo te medicus tuus ille reliquit
sta, donec ueniat, mutet et ipse statum.

Tutius est certe modico gaudere salubri,
quam magnis tristi conditione frui.

Voluere multa solet animi meditatio stulta
140
quae magis impediunt quam sua uota iuuant.

---

116 gratia] omnia *QY*; diva] divina *F*ᵃᶜ *VcVdTPm DVe Tr* dei *Go ft* dura *QY*; ipse] ille β *GI Z*   117 quidem] quidam *H STNe CWR Ha*; medici fallunt] fallunt medici *VdBe La*   118 *om. Va*   uice] uita /uel uice *La*; conuersa] uersa *Fr Tr Q*; quae] qui *MuGoPm*; nocuere] necuere *Fr* nocuisse *D X*   119 mandat] mandauit *Vd La*ᵃᶜ mandant *C*; abinde] abunde *GI*; recedat] recedit *F O*   120 euenient] eueniet *C Fr* eueniunt *La* eueneant *Go* inueniet *Vc*; cupis ipse tibi] cupit ipse sibi *EF SMuVaVbVcVdTGoBePkPmNe AJCWRHuMNODKVe HaLa ZXQY* cupit sibi *L* capit ipse sibi *Fr* cupit ipse tibi *Tr*   121 morbis] morbus uis *Vb* morbi *TFr Tr X*; salutis] salutem *H Mu G Tr*   122 *om. Va*   tantum] tamen *Vd I*; ille] ipse *F H TFr JROD GI TrHa X*   123–4 *om. Vd*   123 absque] ab *HuN*   124 sibi] tibi β *GI om. Ne*   129 ille] ipse *Vb Ve GI* iste *X*   131 habes²] habeo *Go om. VcNe*   132 ueniant] uenient *T Ha Y* ueniat *Fr*   135 tuus ille] tuus ipse *H X* iste *Vc* ille *T*; reliquit] relinquit *Q*   136 ueniat] ueniet *Go TrHa Y* remeat *Q*; mutet] mutat *Q*   137 modico] de modico *E* medico *H VcTBeFr AJCWHuMDVe GI Ha QY*   138 magnis] magnum *LE* magno *F* magis *H VaFrPm Ha*   139 uoluere] soluere *H GI*; multa] cuncta β *GI*; solet] studet solet *Va om. Q*   140 que] qui *Ne* quo *GI*; impediunt] impediant *D* impendunt *F*; iuuant] iuuent *EF SMuVaVbVcVdTGoBePkPm La* iuuet *Ne*

SPECVLVM STVLTORVM   31

for health, but not bestow it; [115] divine grace does the work, he is its servant. Doctors often deceive, and they are themselves deceived, and conversely, things that were harmful turn out to be beneficial. Suppose the doctor does what medicine prescribes, and does not depart from it, even so the results you want will not follow. [120] God is the only healthful remedy for sicknesses; we can only wish, whereas He can act. We can do nothing without His will or His prior action, but He is self-sufficient, in no need of mine. We use various herbs, unguents, and spices; [125] He makes things whole by word alone. We are called healers by the people, but in name alone, while God is a healer in word and deed alike. Take care to preserve the tail He gave you, fool, and no longer seek for more. [130] Lest you lose what you have, strive to hold on to it, in case worse things suddenly come upon you. If you trust me, try to hang on to the tail that was fixed on you by the One who bestowed your ears. Remain in the state that that Healer left you [135], until He comes and changes your state Himself. It is certainly safer to be content with a healthful moderation than to enjoy great possessions in a state of misery. The mind's foolish imagining turns over many things which are more of an impediment than a help to its wishes. [140] From

116   The image of Christ the Physician, which derives from Augustine, is a favourite motif in medieval literature. See Arbesmann, 'The concept of "Christus medicus"'; Fichtner, 'Christus als Arzt'. For the role of the doctor as 'minister' of God's grace, see John of Salisbury, *Policraticus*, ii. 29 (ed. Webb, i. 168, line 16; trans. Pike, p. 150).

120   *cupis ipse tibi* is attested only in *BHGI*, but in the majority reading 'cupit ipse sibi' there is no obvious subject for the verb ('ars' would require 'ipsa', not 'ipse').

121   *medicina salutis*: also in *Miracles*, 1139.

125   *speciebus*: 'species' = 'spices' (*DMLBS* 13b), as used in medieval medicine (cf. *Ysengrimus*, iii. 312, 395).

127–8   On the 'nomen/res' contrast, see n. to line 153 below.

137–8   This resembles the moral of the well-known fable of the town mouse and the country mouse. See Horace, *Saturae*, ii. 6. 77–117; elegiac *Romulus* (ed. Busdraghi), xii. 31–2: 'Pauperies si leta venit, ditissima res est:/ tristior immensas pauperat usus opes.'

SPECVLVM STVLTORVM

32

Auribus ex propriis poteris cognoscere quis sis,
quamque sit absurdum quod statuisse cupis.
Auribus ex geminis tria corpora talia posses
inuestire satis et remaneret adhuc.

145 Non honor est sed onus tales aures habuisse,
quae pariant domino nil nisi damna suo.
Auribus ecce tuis si par tibi cauda fuisset,
quid nisi iuncta simul haec duo monstra forent?
Innatum solum satis est in corpore monstrum;

150 ingeminata magis deteriora forent.
Cum pateant oculis quae sunt manifesta, duabus
commodius poterit una latere lues.
Ex re nomen habens nunc diceris auriculatus,
risus et es populi ludibriumque fori.

155 Quid si cauda tibi fieret quasi pertica longa?
Per caput et caudam tunc trahereris item.
Si duo monstra simul corpus iungantur in unum,
a populo digito nonne notandus eris?
Magnum magna decent; breuis es, nihil utilitatis

160 quam tibi cauda breuis amplius ampla daret.
Tutius ergo puto caudam retinere uetustam

---

141 poteris] potes *VdBe La*; quis] quid *SMuVaVcVdTGoBePkFrPmNe CW La* quod *Vb*;
sis] sit *MuVbVcVdBePkFrPmNe*   **142** quamque sit] quam sit *T JCWND Y* quam
sit et *RMOVe TrHa ZQ* quemque sicut *S*   **143** corpora talia] talia corpora
SMuVaTGoFrPm   **145** est] *om. Fr CD*   **146** quae] qui *Pk I*; pariant] pariunt β
Be GI Tr pareant *Go JK X* parant *Y*; damna] damno *Q*   **148** iuncta simul] *om. Q*;
iuncta] magna *E*   **149–50** *transp. after 154 LE*; *transp. after 151 Pk*   **149** inna-
tum] in nato *GI*; solum] solo α β *SMuVaVdTGoBePkFrPmNe AJCWHuMNOVe GI
TrHa^{pc}La ZXQY* suo *Ha^{ac}*   **150** magis…forent] forent…magis *GI*   **151** dua-
bus] duobus *F* γ+ *ROD I ZQ*   **152** commodius] facilius α β *AJCWRHuMNODKVe
GI XQY* facilius /uel commodius *Ha*; poterit] poteris *G* poteret *Fr*   **153** re] te *QY*;
habens] habes *SVdBe D GI Tr*; nunc] modo *AJCWRHuMNODKVe X* ut *VdBe Tr*; diceris]
disceris *HuN*; auriculatus] auricularis *D* auriculatus /uel is *Ha*   **154** es] est *CWO La^{ac}*
om. Vc   **155** quid] quod *D X*; si cauda tibi fieret] si cauda tibi fiet *GoPm* si cauda fieret
tibi *VaVd* si cauda foret tibi *T* si tibi cauda fieret *Z* tibi si cauda fieret *F AJCWRHuMNODKVe
X*; pertica] partica *B Mu GI* pertita *BeNe La* (*marginal gloss:* 'uirga longa qua mensuratur
ager' *Pm*)   **156** trahereris] traheris *FrPm HuD I* traheretis *Vd*; item] iter *T M* idem *F
H VcGo QY* idem /uel item *Ha*   **157** corpus] *om. C X*   **158** eris] erit *VaVdBePm
La   after 158, Tr has 2 extra lines:* Magnum magna decent ac paruo congruit ergo/
cauda breuis oneri nam foret ampla magis. *These two lines replace 159–60 in D X, and Tr may
have imported them from D, whose scribe habitually tinkers with the text*   **159** magnum]
magnis *GI*; breuis es nihil utilitatis] et paruo congruit ergo *D X*; es] est *S AJCWROVe GI
TrHa ZY*   **160** *(whole line)* cauda breuis oneri nam foret ampla magis *D X*
161 ergo] esse *GI*; puto] puta *GoFr*

SPECVLVM STVLTORVM

33

your own ears you can recognize who you are, and how absurd is what you want to achieve. With those two ears you could completely cover three such bodies, and there would still be some left over. It's not an honour but a disadvantage to have such ears, [145] which bring nothing but trouble to their owner. See now, if your tail was equal to your ears, what would these add up to except two monstrosities? It's enough to have one monstrosity in a body; two would be even worse. [150] Since what is obvious strikes the eye, one defect can go unnoticed more comfortably than two. You are now called "Big-Ears", a name that fits the fact, and you are a joke to the public and a laughing-stock to the town. What if your tail were to become as long as a pole? [155] Then you would be dragged about by your head and tail as well. If two monstrosities are united in one body, will you not be pointed at by everyone? Big things befit a big creature, but you are small. A long tail would be of no greater usefulness to you than a short one. [160] So I think it safer to keep your old tail than to graft on a new one that would be less

145 *Non honor est sed onus*: Ovid, *Heroides*, ix. 31. The same wordplay also appears in *SS*, 246, 1741–2, 2010; *Miracles*, 663, 1621, 2431, and in Nigel's *Epigrams*, no. ii. 2, no. iii. 6–7; see also Walter of Châtillon, *Poems*, xliv. 18. 4; *Map Poems*, 'Nuper ductu serio', p. 250, line 228.

152 *commodius*: the majority reading 'facilius' has a short first syllable and is metrically impossible. 'Commodius' solves the problem, although it may be a scribal improvement by the ancestor of $\gamma TrLaHa$(alt.)Z. See Introduction, p. xci.

153 *Ex re nomen habens*: Ovid, *Amores*, i. 8. 3; *Metamorphoses*, xiii. 569–70. The idea that names ('nomina') should fit their referents ('res') is ubiquitous in *SS* (see lines 127–8, 792, 1695–1700, 1711–12, 2160, 2572, 2577–8, 2656, 2849–54) and also appears in his other poems (*Lawrence*, 337–8, 2238; *Miracles*, 732–8, 1018, 1769, 1875, 1891; *Epigrams*, no. ii. 12, 18; no. ivA. 7, no. ivB; *Paul*, 149, 613) and the *Tractatus* (ed. Boutemy, p. 204). It is a commonplace in medieval literature in general: for numerous examples in medieval Latin satiric poetry, see Walter of Châtillon, *Poems*, no. lvi. 13 = *Carmina Burana*, no. xlii. 13; further examples are cited in the notes to this stanza in the commentary volume of Hilka and Schumann's edition, ii/i), and in Mann, 'Satiric subject and satiric object', pp. 66–8 and nn. *auriculatus*: this line of *SS* is the only entry in *DMLBS* (s.v. 'auriculare' 2) with the meaning 'long-eared' for the past participle 'auriculatus', but Latham records it among the esoteric words in the (7th- or 8th-c.) poem *Rubisca*, which is preserved in Cambridge University Library, MS Gg.5.35, a mid-11th-c. manuscript compiled at St Augustine's Abbey, Canterbury (see n. to lines 2201–4 below).

34
SPECVLVM STVLTORVM

quam plantare nouam quae minus apta foret.
Sed neque cauda noua, quod et auditu nouitatem
   narrat inauditam, crescere posset ita.
165 Res facilis dictu, sed difficilis nimis actu;
   uerba ruunt subito, rem mora longa trahit.
Est leue dixisse quia uentus et aura ministrant,
   sed fecisse quidem non leue pondus habet.
Dicere multorum est, sed uox nisi crescat in actum,
170 est uento similis, uentus et ipsa leuis.
Dicere quisque potest, sed dictis iungere facta,
   si bene perpendas, non ita quisque potest.
Haec duo sunt eius cuius sunt omnia, per quem
   omnia, sub quo sunt omnia iure pari;
175 cuius idem posse quod uelle, nec hoc minus illo,
   qui solus cunctis contulit esse suum;
qui facit et reficit, creat, atque creata gubernat,
   non minor aut maior tempore siue loco.
Huius in arbitrio pendent mortalia quaeque;
180 hic et non alius praestitit esse tibi.
Quod dedit ipse tibi, qualem te contulit esse,
   etsi nolueris, improbe, talis eris.
Cur non sustineas quod oportet sustinuisse
   eius ad arbitrium, quem cohibere nequis?
185 Crede mihi, nihil est fieri quod posse putasti;
   quod natura negat reddere nemo potest.'

Increpatio Galieni

'Numquid enim ceruus, saliens in montibus altis,
   supplicat atque petit qualia, stulte, petis?

163–4 *transp. after 165 Vd*; *om.* T   **163** neque] nec *MuVaGoFrPm*; quod et auditu] quid et auditu *MuFr ZQ* quod et audita *Vd* auditu que *X*; nouitatem] nouitate *Fr Z* **164** narrat] narret *Va O*; posset] possit α *MNO*   **167** quia] que *ROVe fb*; uentus] uestus *CW* uetus *Go*; et] in *Vd M*; ministrant] ministrat *SVaVbVcVdTGoBePkPmNe AJCWRHuMNODKVe HaLa XQY fb* **169** est] *om.* α γ *TrLa Z*; **171** dicere] discere *F K Tr* diceris *Go*; sed dictis] dictis sed α   **172** si] sed *I Z*; perpendas] perpendis α γ *TrLa* **173** eius] ergo *X corr. X²* **174** omnia¹] omnia sunt *VaFr*; iure] in re *Be La* **175** hoc] hic *VaBe?PkPmNe Q om. Vc Z* **179** mortalia] moralia *TGo RO Tr* **181** quod dedit] que dedit *MuPm* qui dedit *VaGoBe Tr* nam quod *K²over erasure*; ipse] esse *VaTr* **182** nolueris] uolueris *MuVdGo Z* **184** eius] quis *GI*; quem] quod α *I² La^{ac}* que *VcBe* qua *Fr* cum *S* **185** nihil] non *LE* nec *F*; fieri quod posse] quod fieri *fb* **187** enim] ei α *B AJCWMODKVe G²over erasure XQY* **188** stulte] stulta *Go HuMN Q*

SPECVLVM STVLTORVM
35

suitable. Nor can a new tail—an unheard-of novelty—grow in such a manner. It is a thing easier said than done; [165] words trip off the tongue, but the deed is slow in coming. Saying is easy, for wind and air are at your service, but doing is a weightier matter. Saying is open to everyone, but unless speech grows into action it is like the wind, and is itself a puff of wind. [170] Anyone can say something, but not anyone can marry deeds with their words, if you consider the matter carefully. These two things belong to the One who is Lord of all, by Whom and likewise under Whom all things exist, Whose will is identical with His power, and not inferior to it, [175] Who alone gave all things their being; Who makes and remakes, creates and governs His creation, no lesser or greater in time or place. All mortal things are subject to His will; He and none other gave you existence. [180] What He Himself gave you, such as He made you to be, such you will be, you wretch, even if you do not like it. Why do you not endure what you should endure, by the will of Him Whom you cannot withstand? Believe me, what you thought could be done is nought. [185] What Nature denies, no one can supply.'

Galen's Scolding

'Does a stag, leaping over the high mountains, ask or petition for what you, fool, request? If those greater than you, and those more noble than

---

167 *uentus et aura*: Ovid, *Amores*, i. 8. 106. For the idea that words are only 'wind and air', cf. *SS*, 1767, 2562; *Lawrence*, 1437.

170 Nigel is alluding to the medieval commonplace that the spoken word ('uox') is defined in physical terms as 'broken air' ('aer ictus') or 'wind'. See *Grammatici Latini*, ed. Keil, ii. 5 (Priscian, *Institutiones grammaticae*, i. 1), and iv. 367 (Donatus, *Ars grammatica*, i. 1).

173–4 Cf. Heb. 2: 10.

186 Proverbial; cf. lines 3889–90 and see Walther, *Proverbia*, 25903, and Singer, *Thesaurus*, s.v. 'Natur' 1. 2. 2. 3 (viii. 428). Its source is Maximian, *Elegies*, no. v. 54; it is quoted in a letter to Thomas Becket, *Becket Correspondence*, ii. 1344 (no. cccxxv). See also *Miracles*, 1137–8. *reddere nemo potest*: an infinitive followed by 'nemo potest' is a convenient ending for a pentameter; see *SS*, 1012, 1908; *Miracles*, 1606.

SPECVLVM STVLTORVM

Si te maiores, si te quoque nobiliores
190   talia nulla rogant, tu quid, inepte, rogas?
Nil lepus aut ursus, caper aut capra, damula, ceruus,
   causantur caudae de breuitate suae.
Numquid es his melior, maior, uel sanctior unus?
   Et tamen his breuior quam tibi cauda manet.'

Consolatio Galieni

195   'Nobile corpus habes, non sit tibi cauda pudori;
   nam si cauda breuis, est tibi grande caput.
Nec breuis est adeo quod non aliis breuiorem
   esse liquet; satis est ergo remissa tibi.
Quod minus est caudae capitis supplebis honore;
200   non decet ut fiant illud et illa pares.
In titulo caudae Francorum rex Lodouicus
   non tibi praecellit pontificesue sui.
Firmiter ergo tene quod habes, quia conditionem
   de facili posses damnificare tuam.'

Narratio Galieni ut reuocet asinum a stultitia sua

205   'An nescis uaccis quid contigit ecce duabus,
   quas puer aspexi patris in aede mei?
Altera Brunetta fuit, altera dicta Bicornis,
   sed nigra Brunetta, flaua Bicornis erat.
Contigit has igitur hiemali tempore quodam
210   nocte retardatas non rediisse domum.
Per uada transibant limosa lutoque repleta,

---

189 *om. Fr*   **190** rogas] petis γ- *TrLa*   **191** lepus] lupus *LE Va*; caper] aper α *om. La*   **192** *om. Fr*   **193** es his] es *T* eis *SMuVaVbVcVdGoBeFrPmNe TrLa* eris *Pk* ex his *Q*; uel] aut *Vb La Z*; unus] es tu γ *TrLa* ullus *Z*^{pc} **194** manet] foret *H*^{ac} *GI*   **195** pudori] pudoris *TFr Z*   **196–7** *order reversed, and transp. after 195 (195, 197, 196, 198) Vd*   **196** *om. FrX*   si] *sic P over erasure* si tibi *G*   **197** nec] non *AJCWRHuMNODKVe X*; aliis] alius *H I*   **198** *om. F*   **199** supplebis] supplebit *F C*   **200** *om. Fr*; decet] decent *F Tr*; fiant] fiat *GI* faciat *O*   **201** Lodouicus] lodowicus *F MuVaGoBePm AJCMOD GI Q* ludowicus *Vb Ve TrHa* lodowigus *T* lodowycus *H WHuNK X* londouicus *E* ludouicus *B SVcVdPk R* ludobicus *La* ludwicus *Fr* lodewicus *Y* ladewicus *Z*   **202** tibi] te α *VdTGoBeFr TrLa*; pontificesue] pontificesque γ+(*Ha*^{ac}) *CWHuMNDK ZXQ*   **203–4** *om. Z*   **203** conditionem] conditioni *CWMD*   **204** posses] posse *Y* possis *Fr Q fb* poteris α posset *T*   **205** quid] quod *PD;* ecce] esse *F SVaVbVdGoBePkFrPm MNOD TrLa*   **209** igitur] ergo *VdTBe TrLa*; hiemali] hiemale *KVe*; quodam] quonam *Ve* quadam *SMuVaVbBePmNe La XQ*   **211** limosa] in linosa *M* linosa *HuN*

SPECVLVM STVLTORVM

you, do not ask anything of the sort, why do you do so, you nincompoop? [190] Neither the hare nor the bear, the male or female goat, the fallow-deer or the stag complains about the shortness of its tail. Are you better than they, greater or more virtuous? Yet their tails are shorter than yours.'

Galen's Consolation

'You have a noble body; don't be ashamed of your tail, [195] for if your tail is short, your head is large. Nor, clearly, is it so short that others don't have a shorter one, so what is granted you is enough. What is lacking in your tail, you will make up for with your head; it is not right that they should both be the same. [200] In the matter of a tail, Louis, king of France, does not surpass you, nor his bishops either. So hold fast to what you have, since you could easily worsen your condition.'

Galen's Story to Recall the Ass from his Foolishness

'Do you not know what once happened to two cows, [205] whom I observed as a boy in my father's house? One was called Brunetta, the other Bicornis; Brunetta was black and Bicornis was tawny. Well, one wintertime it happened that they did not get back home, having been prevented by nightfall. [210] They were wandering through the swampy shallows, filled with mud,

---

192 *causantur*: 'causari' = 'to complain about' (Niermeyer).

201 *Francorum rex Lodouicus*: King Louis VII of France (1137–80). For a discussion of the problem that this line poses for dating *SS*, see Introduction, pp. l–lv.

205 The story of the two cows seems to be Nigel's own invention. See Introduction, pp. xxix, cxxx–cxxxi.

207 *Brunetta*: 'Brownie', apparently a traditional name for a cow (cf. the fabliau *Brunain la vache au prestre*, in *Nouveau Recueil complet des fabliaux*, v. 39–48 (no. xl)). *Bicornis*: 'two-horned'.

38   *SPECVLVM STVLTORVM*

pascua cum peterent cotidiana sibi.
Vtque solent uaccae, caudis de more lutosis,
   in pratis luteis procubuere toris.

215 Nocte gelu subitum ueniens terramque perurgens
   contulit in solidum mollia cuncta prius.
Duruit in lapidem quicquid fuit ante lutosum;
   stagna, lacus, fontes, marmoris instar erant.
Quas fouet innatas ligat artius alueus undas,

220   nec sinit elabi flumina more suo.
Tot pontes quot aquae, liber nec ut ante negatus
   transitus est per aquas qua uia plana patet.
Haeserunt terrae cauda mediante iuuencae,
   artius astringit terra lutosa lutum.

225 Vndique terra riget caudas retinente rigore,
   surgere non poterant nec remeare domum.
Mane reuertente pariter uoluere reuerti,
   sed prohibet glacies conglutinata solo.
Plurima conatae, spem defrustrante labore,

230   tandem lassatas continuere manus.
Multa tamen querulae tacitoque dolore gementes
   attentare student et uariare uices.
Sed nihil est quod agunt, propria uirtute resolui
   non sinit obiecta uis uiolenta sibi.'

---

213 utque] ut quae *E Fr*; uaccae] nocte α; more] morte *MN*ᵃᶜ   **214** procubuere] proculonere *Fr* concubuere δ *ZXQY* recubuere *GI*   **215** *largely illegible in Ha as a result of water staining*; subitum ueniens] ueniens subitum β *GI* ueniens subito *H T*   **216** mollia cuncta prius] quod fuit ante lutum β *GI*   **217** duruit] diruit *J TrHa ZX*   **218** erant] habent β *GI* erat *Pm X* erit *Go*   **219** artius] alcius γ(*Vc*ᵖᶜ) *TrLa*; alueus] aut lucus *La*   **220** *transp. after* **223** *T*; *om. Ne*; nec] ne *Be Tr*; sinit] sinat *F Tr*   **221–2** *om.* γ *Tr*   **221** ut] *om. MN*; liber] libet *QY*; negatus] negatur *LE ROPVe* meatus *Ha ZQY*   **222** qua] quam *D* quia *CW*; plana] plena *H M*; patet] prius β placet δ *La* tenet *Ha ZQY*   **223** cauda] caude *P Tr* caudam *Go*; iuuencae] iuuente *MuVbVaBeNe WRM TrLa QY* iuuente /uel <*illegible*>ente *Ha* iuuante *Go* sua *T* iuuinta *Z* iumenta *Fr*   **224** astringit] astrinxit α *B* constringat *Fr*   **226** non] nec *VcVdBe TrLa*   **227** reuertente] reuertenti *H Q*; uoluere] noluere *VbFr*   **229** *line repeated in alternative form* (*marked* 'uel sic') *Z*(1)*Z*(2)   plurima conatae spem] plurimum conate spem *D* plurima conante spem *GI* plurimo conate sed spem *S* plurima conatae sed spem *Vc* plurima conate spe *Be* plurima conantur sed spe *Tr* tractu (tracta *Z*(1)) lassantur sed *Z*(1)*XQY* tracte lassantur sed /uel plurima conate spem *Ha*   **230** *om. Z*   **231** *line repeated in alternative form Z*(1)*Z*(2), *K*(1),*K*(2); multa tamen] multe tamen *Go CWHuMN* et (sed *QY*) rursus (rursum *QY*) *DK*(2) *XQY* sed sursum *Z*(1) multa tamen /uel sed sursum *Ha*; querulae] querulo *K*(1); tacitoque] tacioque *Be* tacito que *C* tactoque *G* tractoque *I* tantoque *M Z*(2) magnoque *DK*(2) *Z*(1)*XQY* magnoque uel <tacito?> *Ha*; dolore] labore *Fr Z*(2); gementes] reuerti *Tr*   **232** student] solent *H GI*   **234** sinit] sunt *VaNe Tr* fuit *Ha*; obiecta] abiecta *TGoFr Ha*

SPECVLVM STVLTORVM

while seeking their daily grazing. As cows are wont to do, they bedded down on muddy couches in the fields, with their tails (as usual) muddy. In the night a sudden frost came on, seizing the earth in its grip, [215] and turned solid everything that had previously been soft. Whatever was muddy before became as hard as stone; puddles, pools, springs, were like marble. The river-channel grips more tightly the brimming water that it held in its bosom, and does not allow the stream to flow in its normal way. [220] Every watercourse is a bridge, nor is free passage over the waters denied as it was before, where a level way offers itself. The ground had solidified with each heifer's tail in its midst, the muddy earth constricting mud the more tightly. The earth is stiff on all sides, the stiffness holding the tails fast; [225] they were unable to rise or return home. When morning returned, they too wanted to return, but the ice clamped on the earth prevented it. After many attempts, their efforts thwarting them of hope, they at length stayed their weary hands. [230] Greatly lamenting, and groaning in silent grief, they set themselves to struggle and change their condition. But what they do amounts to nothing; the strength of the opposing force does not allow them to be released by their own power.'

215 *perurgens*: 'perurgere' = 'to press greatly, press hard' (Lewis and Short).

219 *innatas*: 'innare' = 'to flow over' (*OLD*).

224 *lutum*: i.e. the mud–covered tails, which amalgamate with the mud that the cows are lying on; both freeze solid.

229 *defrustrante*: 'defrustrare' = 'to deprive of hope' (Niermeyer).

231 *Multa*: n. pl. adj., used adverbially: 'to a great extent, much, greatly' (*OLD*, s.v. 'multus' 3c). Cf. Vergil, *Georgics*, iii. 226; *Aeneid*, iii. 610.

234 *sibi*: refers to the logical subject (the cows) rather than to the grammatical subject ('uis').

SPECVLVM STVLTORVM

De Bicorne

235 'Anxia facta nimis uitulo clamante Bicornis,
  acrius instabat posse referre pedem.
Nam noua nata domi stabulis inclusa relicta
  hesterno fuerat, ne sequeretur eam.
Sed nil proficiens cum desperata laboris
240 iam foret, ingemuit altius, haec et ait:'

Consilium Bicornis

' "Vna salus superest, caudas resecare lutosas,
  quae retinent miseras nec remeare sinunt.
Quid mea cauda mihi uel quid sibi contulit umquam?
  Quis fructus uel quae gloria cauda mihi?
245 En per eam teneor tamquam captiua, quid ergo?
  Non honor est, sed onus, haec mea cauda mihi.
Esto quod hinc possem cauda remanente redire,
  semper erunt oneri cauda lutumque mihi.
Attrahit ipsa lutum pendens oneratque ferentem;
250 quod tribuat uideo nil nisi triste mihi.
Libera nunc essem nulloque tenente redirem,
  ni foret in causa sordida cauda mihi.
Tollere materiam, ne propter materiatum
  hic ego deficiam, tutius esse puto.
255 Causidici dicunt, quia legibus est ita cautum,
  causatum perimit causa perempta suum.
Sanius est partem quam totum perdere, caudam

---

236 acrius] *Mozley* anxius α β γ *AJCWRHuMNOPKVe GI TrLa* arcius *D Ha ZXQY*   **237** nam] non *M Q*; nata] nota *Q*; stabulis] stabilis *Ne Ve*   **239** cum] dum *ZY* tamen *Go*   **240** iam] nam *Vd La*; ingemuit] et gemuit *D X* ingemit *MuVc*; haec et] hɔc et *Ne M GI Ha* et hec *F*   **241** superest] nobis est *X corr. X²*; resecare] reserare *H GoFr*   **242** retinent] retinet *H Vd*; sinunt] sinat *G* sinant *I*   **243** sibi] mihi *SMᴜVaVbVcTGoBePkPmNe RD TrLa ZX* tibi *Ha QY om. VdFr*   **244** uel quae] uel etiam *S* etiam *MuVaVbVcVdGoBePkFrPmNe La* aut que *T*   **245–6** *om. B Pm J add. in margin Bᵖᶜ Pmᵖᶜ*   **245** en per eam] si pereo *Ha Z*; en] heu *SMuVaVbVcVdTBePkFrPmNe TrLa* hereo *Go*; per eam] peream *MuVaGoPmNe AHuNK* perio *D QY*   **246** est] *om. F Z*   **247–8** *om. Fr δ*   **247** possem] possim *Mu Q*   **249** pendens] pendet *MuPm*   **250** quod] quid β γ- *RDMNO GI HaLa ZXQY*   **251** nulloque tenente] nullo retinente *OD XQ*   **252** ni] ne *Va Tr* si *Pk* nil /[uel] ni *La <letter erased> >*i *J*; causa] cauda *Go R Zᵃᶜ* tanta *Tr*; cauda] causa *VdᵃᶜGo RMN Gᵃᶜ* causa /uel cauda *Ha*   **254** hic ego] hec ego *Z* hic ergo *GI* ne sic β; tutius] titius /uel tutius *La*; esse] ipse *F* ergo *fb*   **255** quia] quod α *X*   **257** totum] totam *F AJCWRHuMNPDKVe VaGoBePkFrPm TrHaLa ZXQY fb*

SPECVLVM STVLTORVM 41

About Bicornis

'Bicornis, made anxious by the cries of her calf, [235] was more eagerly intent on being able to return. For the day before, her newborn daughter had been left at home shut up in the byre, so she wouldn't follow her. But not succeeding, and now despairing of her efforts, she groaned deeply and said this:' [240]

Bicornis's Plan

' "One remedy remains, to cut off our muddy tails, which hold back us wretches and prevent us from returning. What did my tail ever do for me or for itself? What profit or glory does my tail represent to me? Look, I'm held by it like a captive—and so? [245] It's not an honour but a nuisance to me, my tail is. Suppose I could leave here with my tail in place, the tail and the mud will always be a burden to me. As it dangles, it attracts mud and encumbers its owner. I don't see that it brings me anything but vexation. [250] I would at this moment be free and would be returning with nothing to hold me, if it weren't for my dirty tail. I think it safer to take away the substance [of the trouble], lest I die here on account of what it has produced. The lawyers say—for it is so decreed by the laws [255]—that when the cause is removed the effect disappears. It is better to lose a part than a whole, my tail rather than

236 *acrius*: Mozley's conjecture. Most manuscripts read 'anxius'; six read 'arcius'. Since the subject is Bicornis, the correct form of the adjective would be 'anxia', but this has already been applied to the cow at the beginning of line 235, and has clearly influenced the erroneous reading at 236. See also Introduction, p. lxxx.

246 *honor... onus*: see n. to line 145.

250 As Shackleton Bailey points out ('Textual notes', p. 282), this is a statement, not a question, so Mozley's 'quid' should be 'quod'.

252 For 'esse in causa' meaning 'to be responsible (for something)', see *OLD* s.v. 'causa' 11b.

253 *materiam...materiatum*: Boethius, *De topicis differentiis*, ii. 7. 24, ed. Nikitas, p. 35: 'ubi materia deest, et quod ex materia efficitur desit' ('where the matter is lacking, what is made from the matter is also lacking'; trans. Stump, p. 53).

255–6 This is a reference to a well-known legal maxim 'cessante causa, cessat effectus'. It is not found in Justinian, and its exact origins are obscure, although phrases with a similar meaning occur in Gratian. André Gouron ('*Cessante causa cessat effectus*: À la naissance de l'adage', ascribes it to the same passage from Boethius's *De topicis differentiis* that is quoted in the note to 253 above. Cf. also Boethius, *In Ciceronis Topica*, ii (PL lxiv. 1080A–B): 'ab effectis vero non oportet aliud nisi causam probare...causas ab effectis suis non separari', 'an argument from effects proves nothing but a cause...causes are not separated from their effects'; trans. Stump, p. 70). According to Gouron, the familiar form of the phrase was developed in the work of 12th-c. legal glossators (which would explain Nigel's 'causidici'); cf. Brundage, *Medieval Canon Law*, p. 173. The maxim quickly gained general currency in the 12th c.: see Alan of Lille, *De fide catholica*, i. 31 (PL ccx. 333C): 'quamdiu enim causa est secundum quod est causa, nunquam cessat effectus?' and Andreas Capellanus, *De amore*, ed. Walsh, i. 6. 50: 'Cessante igitur causa eius de necessitate cessat effectus' (where, ironically, this learned maxim is supposedly addressed by a plebeian man to a plebeian woman).

SPECVLVM STVLTORVM

quam caput, hoc modicum quam meliora magis.
Malo mihi caudam pariter cum crure reuelli,
260   quam subito uitam claudere morte meam.
Forsitan hic alias simili ratione morarer,
quoque modo teneor tunc retinerer item.
Si mea cauda modo fuerit succisa, regressus
tutior hic aderit quam fuit ante mihi.
265   Paruula, si peream, mecum mea nata peribit,
quam nondum quintum constat habere diem.
Et si non pro me faciam mihi talia, saltem
propter eam facere cogor, oportet ita.
Corporis haec nostri pars est, quam dente procaci
270   consueuere canes dilacerare prius,
dimidiumque fere iam pridem surripuere;
heu mihi, quod reliquum restitit usque modo!
Quod superest canibus placet hoc impendere natae,
hocque pium satis est, hocque salubre mihi.
275   Ergo quid ulterius quae sum factura morabor?
Casibus in duris accelerare iuuat."
Dixit, et arreptam caudam pugione recidit,
festinansque domum carpere coepit iter.
Ante tamen studuit ferrum praestare sorori,
280   posset ut a simili soluere uincla sibi.
Sed minus haec praeceps prudensque magis patienter
uerba tulit, cohibens a pugione manum.'

---

258 hoc] et α *I* hec *MuFr* hic *VdBe Tr*; magis] nimis *CWHuMNODKVe Tr X* minus *AJRP La*   **259** crure reuelli] cruce reuelli *Vd* crine reuelli *HuMN* crere euelli *La* sanguine tolli *B* carne reuelli *Fr R* rure reuelli *Be Tr* aure reuelli *Vc*   **262** quoque] quaque α β *SMuVaVeVcTGoFrPmNe GI ZXQY* qua *Be Tr* quam *VdPk La*; tunc] nunc *H AJCWRHuMNOPVe* cum *EF* tum *L* iter *S* ?uenit *Fr*; retinerer] retinere *SGo Z* retiner *Ha* retineret *VaVbVcVdPkPmNe La* retinereret *Be* retinerem *T* tenererer α   **263** modo fuerit] mihi fuerit γ *K TrLa X²* meo fuerit *X*ᵃᶜ foret modo *C*; modo] mihi /uel modo *Ha*   **264** tutior] tutius *I Z*; hic] huc *T R* huc /uel hic *Ha* hec *H* hinc *Vc Z*   **265** paruula] per hanc *H*; si] sic β *Vb GI*; mecum] simul et *Vc*; nata] nacta *Go* natura *Ha*; (*whole line*) admouet et nata domi stabulisque relicta *Mu [cf. 237]*   **268** facere cogor oportet] fieri ratio cogit *XQY*; facere cogor] facere cogar *Pm* fieri cogit α β δ *GI*   **269** haec] hoc *VdPk MN* hoc / uel hec *La* hic *D GI QY* hac *Z*; dente] denti *MN QY*   **270** canes…prius] prius…canes *D ZXQY* carnes…prius *Vb*   **271** fere] uere *VcFr*   **272** quod] quid *T ZQY*; reliquum] reliqua α; restitit] destitit *SVbVdBePk TrLa* restat *P* recitat *QY*   **273** quod] quid *T M GI Tr Y*; hoc] hec *Ne JHu* hic *Be La Q*   **274** hocque¹] hecque *HuMN* hoc quia *F*; hocque²] hecque *HuMN* hicque *VdPk La* atque *DK ZXQY*   **275** quae] quod *H P* qua *Va* quem *Vd* ?qui *Z* quid *Fr Ha* sicut *Be Tr*; sum] sim *FrPm Tr* sit *E* sine *Pk*   **276** duris] dictis *GoFr*   **280** ut] et *Vd G*ᵃᶜ; a] hec α *I*; a simili] assimili *VaPkNe*   **281** haec] hoc *M I* hic *Pm*; patienter] sapienter *F H* γ+ *R GI* sapienter patienter *Y*

SPECVLVM STVLTORVM   43

my head, this little thing than far better ones. I'd rather my tail *and* leg were torn away together than that I should suddenly end my life in death. [260] Perchance I might be delayed here another day for the same sort of reason, and I would then be again held down in the manner I am held now. If my tail were cut off now, my return to this place will be safer than it was before. If I die, my little daughter—who is no more than five days old—will die with me. [265] If I don't do this much to myself for my own sake, I am at least obliged to do it for hers—and so it must be. This is the part of my body which the dogs used to tear first with their eager teeth. [270] They've already long ago torn off almost half—what a pity that the remainder has survived until now! What has survived the dogs is willingly sacrificed to my daughter; this is true mother-love, and also for my own good. So why shall I delay longer what I am to do? [275] In tough situations it's a good thing to act quickly." Having spoken, she seized her tail and cut it off with a knife, and in haste set off on her journey home. First, however, she was mindful to offer the knife to her sister, so that she could loosen her fetters in the same way. [280] But she, less rash and more prudent, restraining her hand from the dagger, patiently spoke her mind.'

257 Proverbial; see Singer, *Thesaurus*, s.vv. 'Verlieren' 5. 10 (xii. 184); 'Teil' 1. 3 (xi. 282). Cf. *Ysengrimus*, vi. 319: 'Sumere prestabat modicum quam perdere totum.' See also Nigel's *Tractatus*, ed. Boutemy, p. 167: 'Sicque ambitiosus partem amisit pro toto, immo partem et totum, et alter accepit partem pro toto, malens possidere partem quam totum.'

262 Mozley prefers 'quaque', which is well supported, but his assumption that 'ratione' is understood seems strained; it also involves taking 'mŏdŏ' to mean 'now', but since its second syllable is usually short, this is metrically unacceptable. 'Quōquĕ mŏdō' (abl. of 'mŏdus'), 'in the manner in which', is a better reading.

264 *quam fuit ante mihi*: also in *Miracles*, 2476 (with 'sibi'); cf. *SS*, 616 (with 'tibi'), and 1008 (with 'malum').

272 Mozley punctuates with an exclamation mark after 'mihi' and a question mark after 'modo', but the whole line is clearly an exclamation, not a question.

44 SPECVLVM STVLTORVM

Responsio Brunettae

'Postea respondens dixit, "Quid, inepta, laboras?
Quod mihi persuades absit ut illud agam!
285 Rebus in aduersis opus est moderamine multo,
non decet in grauibus praecipitare gradum.
Rebus in ambiguis quotiens fortuna laborat,
consilium praeceps non decet esse nimis.
Impetus, ut memini, grauis est, male cuncta ministrat;
290 si male cuncta facit, ergo nec ulla bene.
Non opus est grauibus, ubi res grauis est et acerba,
sed magis auxilio consilioque bono.
Mitius in duris sapiens Cato mandat agendum,
mollia ne pereant asperitate graui.
295 Res ubi difficilis, non est ita praecipitandum;
tempore sanatur quod ratione nequit.
Si fortuna modo grauis est, conuersa repente
quod graue portamus alleuiabit onus.
Tempora labuntur, dominique cadunt, renouantur
300 serui, uulgus abit, area lata patet.
Quae ueniunt subito subito quandoque recedunt;
prospera cum duris mixta uenire solent.
Fortuitos casus non est uitare uolentum,
nemo futurorum praescius esse potest.
305 Plus ualet interdum non praetimuisse futura

---

283 postea respondens dixit] postea respondens dicit *R* ostea respondens dixit *G* respondet bruneta sibi *SVaVbVdGoPm* respondens bruneta sibi *PkNe* respondet bruneta *Be* respondit bruneta sibi *VcT HaLa* responditque bruneta sibi *Fr* respondet modo bruneta *Tr* respondit bruneta *Mu*; inepta] inepte *VcVdFr CWRMNP Ha*; laboras] laborans *P* **284** quod] quid *F DM Y*; illud] istud *HuMNDK X* **286** gradum] ?grauis *Q* manum *fb* **288** consilium] concilium *H K Z*; decet] debet *D X corr. X²*; nimis] minus *TGo C* **289** male] mala *ZY fu*; cuncta] certa *LE* β *AJHuMNP* **290** male] mala *Go La QY*; facit] *om. GI added P²* **291** grauibus] grauius *HuMN*ac **292** consilioque] concilioque *Z fb* consuloque *Vd*; bono] pio α *SMuVbVcVdTGoBePkFrPmNe TrHaLa fu* pia *Vc* **293** sapiens] saperis *HuMN*; sapiens Cato] cato sapiens *VdBe La* sapiens cito *S* **296** tempore] tempora *LE*; sanatur] sanantur *LF* **297–300** *om. fu* **299** tempora] tempore *LE MN*; dominique] diu que *D* denique *Fr C* domini *Go P*; cadunt] *om. L*; renouantur] remouentur *MuVaVbVcVdTBePkFrNe HaLa* remenouentur *Go* remouerant *Pm* releuantur *Q* **300** area] aera *ZX corr. X²* **301** *first half of line illegible (water stain) Ha* quandoque] quocumque *fu* **302** prospera] aspera *HuMND* mitia *K*; mixta] sepe *H GI* iuxta *Ne*; uenire] quandoque uenire *fb* **303** uitare] mutare *Vc D X*; uolentum] uolantum *Mu* ualetum *Go* uolentem *Vd La* **304** futurorum] futuri *fu* **305** praetimuisse] pretimiisse *D* pretinuisse *Pm HuO* precinuisse *Va* presciuisse *TGoFr ZQY fu* pretimuisse /uel pretinuisse uel pres<ciuisse?> *La*

SPECVLVM STVLTORVM

Brunetta's Reply

'She then replied: "Why, silly girl, do you struggle? Heaven forbid that I should do what you urge me! In adverse circumstances, great moderation is called for; [285] in serious matters it's no good forcing the pace. Whenever one's fortune is struggling in difficult times, it's not a good idea to make up one's mind too quickly. Haste, as I've said, is troublesome; it handles everything badly—and if it does everything badly, then it doesn't do anything well. [290] When the situation is troublesome and nasty, troublesome things are not what's wanted—rather, assistance and good advice. The wise Cato prescribes that in tough situations one should go easier, lest comforts are wiped out by forbidding harshness. When the situation is difficult one should not rush at things in this way; [295] time cures what planning can't. If fortune is cruel now, she will suddenly turn about and lighten the heavy burden we now bear. The times pass, lords fall, and slaves are recreated [free men]; people vanish, and the waste land stretches wide. [300] What comes quickly sometimes departs quickly too; blessings usually come mixed with drawbacks. Chance events can't be avoided by those who wish it; no one can have foreknowledge of future things. Sometimes it's better not to have feared the future [305] than to be certain of it and

---

  284 *absit ut illud agam*: cf. Gen. 44: 17 ('absit a me ut sic agam)'.

  285–8 For the numerous proverbs in many languages warning against the dangers of haste and expressing the idea 'more haste, less speed', see Singer, *Thesaurus*, s.v. 'Eile' 3–4 (ii. 406–12).

  289 *Impetus...male cuncta ministrat*: Statius, *Thebaid*, x. 704–5.

  291–2 Cf. Publilius Syrus, *Sententiae*, 141: 'Consilium in dubiis remedium prudentis est.'

  293–4 It is not clear which Cato is meant here, or what text Nigel had in mind. Sanford ('Quotations from Lucan', p. 3) sees this as a deliberate 'howler'—that is, a comic inversion of Cato's speech to the soldiers in Lucan, *De bello civili*, ix. 379 ff., urging them to endure the hardships ahead of them; however, this seems too complicated to be convincing. Rather, Nigel may have been thinking of one of the frequent exhortations in the *Disticha* of (pseudo-) Cato which urge patience as a response to difficulties (*Disticha Catonis*, i. 21. 2; i. 38. 1–2; ii. 10. 1–2; iii. 17. 1).

  299 *Tempora labuntur*: Ovid, *Fasti*, vi. 771.

  300 *area lata patet*: Ovid, *Heroides*, i. 72.

  305 *praetimuisse futura*: also at *SS*, 425, 2021; cf. *Miracles*, 43, 'et timuisse futura'.

SPECVLVM STVLTORVM

quam certum fieri sollicitumque nimis.

Nam sua multotiens docuit uexatio multos,
obfuit et multis prosperitate frui.

Casibus in laetis minor est sollertia multis,
310   erudit incautos sollicitudo grauis.

Casibus in laetis magis est metuenda uoluptas,
segnius in uitium tristia corda ruunt.

Integra Troia fuit dum se suspectus utrimque
subtraheret durus hostis ab hoste suo.

315   Pax data subuertit quae praelia non potuerunt
moenia, plus nocuit rege remissa manus.

Sola uenire solent et uix et sero secunda;
turbine uallata sors inimica uenit.

Si fortuna dedit dudum mihi dulcia, quare
320   dedigner sub ea paucula dura pati?

Dura quidem patior, sed non duranda per annum;
nondum praeteriit tota uel una dies.

Principis aut regis si carcere tenta ligarer,
asperiora luto ferrea uincla forent.

325   Mollius esse lutum ferro quis nesciat? Ipsos
reges et satrapas ferrea uincla tenent.

Si leuiora luti quam regia uincula ferri,
est leuior certe sors mea sorte sua.

Illos sorte sua quinquennia uincula seruant,

---

306 certum fieri] iterum fieri S circumferri CW 307 *(whole line)* multotiens
docuit uexacio nam multus sua Go 308 et] in β Mu K GI; frui] sui CW
309–10 *transp. after 312* β GI Tr; *transp. after 311* C; *line order in* Vd *is 308, 311, 310, 309,
312; om.* $HuMK$ *fu. After 310,* Go *repeats 309 and first half of 310, then deletes this half-line and
continues on next line with 312, omitting 311*   310–11 *om.* F 311 metuenda]
metuendo E metuanda CW Z 313 dum] de H $VdBePk$ Tr; utrimque] utrumque E
$SMu^{ac}VaVdGoFr$ $RMPK$ $TrHa$ ZQY utremque Mu^{pc} utramque Be utrique X uterque $VcPk$
D *fu*   314 subtraheret] subtraxit δ   316 *om. fu*   rege] regi S Q ergo Z
317 et²] a LE aut P GI in Tr; sero] raro δ X uel raro *add. interlinear* G^{pc} raro uel sero I fero Z
318 uallata] fallata $VcGo$ Z uocato Tr uacato Vd uacata Be La 319 dudum mihi] mihi
dudum $HuMNDK$ X 320 dedigner] dedignar Go GI dedignor LE quare dedigner Y
dedignet Z 322 uel] nec γ+   323 regis] regum H GI regit M; ligarer] legarer
B ligaret $VdGoBe$ 324 asperiora] asperior GI 325 *line repeated in alternative
form* $Z_{(1)}Z_{(2)}$ esse] est L M GI Y; lutum] luto L S; quis nesciat ipsos] quis nesciat ipsi S
quod nesciat ipsos D scito reputari $Z_{(1)}XQY$ 326 satrapas] satrape S satraphas D
satrapes E 327 *om. Mu*   luti] luto TGo $TrHa$; ferri] ferrer $SVaBeNe$ $TrHaLa$ fer-
rem $VbVc$ fere? Pk ferrent $GoPm$ feretur Fr seruant Vd 328 certe] sorte G forte Vc I;
sors] mors $SVaVbVcVdGoPkFrPmNe$ $HaLa$ QY; sorte] forte $GoPm$; sua] tua $HuMN$ mea Tr
X uel sua *add. interlinear* X^2 329 sorte] forte α B $SMuVaVbVcVdGoBePkFrPmNe$
$A\mathcal{J}WRHuMNOPDKVe$ GI $TrLa$ XQY

SPECVLVM STVLTORVM

worry too much. For many have been taught a lesson by their troubles, while many have been harmed by the enjoyment of good fortune. In happy circumstances, many are less cautious, while serious anxiety is a lesson to the heedless. [310] In happy circumstances, pleasure is more to be feared; sad hearts rush less swiftly towards vice. Troy was unharmed while each side mistrusted its unflinching enemy and held back from the other; the agreeing of peace overthrew the walls that battle was unable to. [315] The slackened hand did more than the king. Blessings usually come singly, and little, and late; a hostile fate comes with an army around it. If Fortune has given me some nice things in the past, why do I scorn to suffer a few little inconveniences at her hands? [320] Certainly, I suffer inconveniences, but not ones that are to last the whole year; as yet, not even a whole day has gone by. If I were held imprisoned by a prince's or king's dungeon, then iron chains would be more cruel than mud. Who does not know that mud is softer than iron? [325] Iron chains hold kings and princes themselves. If mud chains are lighter than the king's iron chains, then my lot is certainly lighter than his. Chains restrain *them*, as their fate decrees, five years long, while

---

313–14 The fall of Troy was a major theme in medieval literature and art. See Scherer, *The Legends of Troy*. For a list of the most important works of literature dealing with the Trojan War, from Homeric times to the present day, see Scherer's Appendix A, pp. 219–31.

316 *rege*: probably referring to Agamemnon, leader of the Greek forces. *remissa manus*: cf. Heb. 12: 12: 'remissas manus'.

317 This line is the fifth in a set of eight verses (Inc. 'Semper adest homini quo pectoris ima gemiscant') quoted by Gerald of Wales in the *Symbolum electorum*, dist. ii. 5 (*Opera*, i. 354–5), in a *Letter to Stephen Langton* (*Opera*, i. 403), and in the *Speculum ecclesiae*, dist. iv. 19 (*Opera*, iv. 304), where Gerald claims that they are 'metricos sapientis cuiusdam versus' (see the improved edition of this chapter of the *Speculum*, edited by Pauli, MGH SS xxvii, 419–21; reproduced as an Appendix to Richard Kay, 'Gerald of Wales and the Fourth Lateran Council', pp. 92–3). The first six lines are also quoted in the *De vita Galfridi*, ii. Prol. (*Opera*, iv. 386), the *Topographia hibernica*, dist. iii. 49 (*Opera*, v. 193), and in *A Preface or Preparation to a Sermon on St Stephen* printed in the *Speculum duorum*, ed. Lefèvre et al., Letter 4, p. 180; lines 5–6 appear in some manuscripts of the *Itinerarium Kambriae*, i. 4 (*Opera*, vi. 51, n. 3). No other source for these lines has been found, and they seem most likely, as Pauli says, to be by Gerald himself, in which case, the reference to 'a certain wise man' to which they are attributed in all the instances except the *Letter to Langton*, the *Symbolum electorum*, and the *De vita Galfridi*, is a tongue-in-cheek compliment to himself. For other occasions where Gerald attributes proverbial lines to a 'sapiens' who is probably himself, see *Speculum duorum*, ed. Lefèvre et al., Part i, 669; Part ii, 449, 784, and Huygens's notes. All the above works by Gerald, except the *De vita Galfridi* and the *Speculum duorum*, are hard to date with any precision, though none seems to pre-date 1188 (see Bartlett, *Gerald of Wales*, Appendix I); it is therefore not possible to say if the fifth line originated with Gerald or with Nigel, or if it circulated independently as a proverb. Walther, *Proverbia*, 27890a, is citing Gerald.

318 *turbine uallata*: Literally, 'surrounded by a storm'.

48   *SPECVLVM STVLTORVM*

330   forsitan in triduo carcere soluar ego.
Flante leui Zephyro, Notus in sua regna redibit,
     percipientque statum prata lutosa suum.
Tunc dissoluentur per se mea uincula gratis,
     et remanebit adhuc haec mea cauda mihi.
335   Me cito priuasse possem, sed paenituisse
     forsitan aeternum perpetuumque foret.
Sorte pari poterit nox una resoluere uinctam,
     sicut et anterius una ligauit eam.
Non decet ut quotiens quaedam minus apta putantur,
340   quod quis perpetuo iure releget ea;
sed quibus obstat hiems aestatis gratia prosit,
     ut sua quem deicit sors aliena leuet.
Sicque uices uarias per se sua tempora mittunt,
     possit ut alterius alter honore frui.
345   Dulce relatiuum socialia foedera iungit,
     fortius incedunt foedera iuncta sibi.
Quod minus alter habet, sua quem fortuna grauauit,
     suppleat alterius copia grata magis.
Nil ita praecipuum uel tam sublime creatum
350   ut non alterius possit egere manu.
Tempora siue uices uario discrimine certant,
     nec coeunt nexu foedera quaeque pari.

---

332 *om. Ha*; percipientque] precipientque *GI* percipient *S*; statum] suum *D X* statim *Mu*; prata] prato *GI* praua *Q̣*; suum] statum *D X* lutum *F*   333 per se mea] mea per se *AJCWRHuMNODKVe X*   334 remanebit] remaneret *H G* remanet *I*; haec] hic *Vd* sic *Mu om. Go La Z*   335 cito] scito *E*; priuasse possem sed] soluisse possem sed *Tr* soluisse si possem *SMuVaVbVcTPkFrPm Ha* soluisse uel si possem *VdBe La* soluisse etsi possem *Ne* soluisse se possem *Go*   337 nox una] nox unam *SVb* uox una *VdNe* uox mea *M*; resoluere] soluere γ *AJCWHuMNO^{ac}PDVe TrHaLa ZX corr. X²*; uinctam] uincula *E Ha Z* iunctam *B*   339 quaedam] que dum *VbVcVd* quod *JP* quod que *Ve* quo *Tr* queque *O* que *Q*   340 quod quis] quod uis *CW* quisquis *Tr*; perpetuo] perpetua *Fr AJCWHuMNP*; iure] rure *HuMN*; releget] relegit *E AJCWRHuMND* religet *Vd GI* relegat *Go* religat *Fr*; ea] eam *Go GI* ea conditione *Fr*   341 sed quibus] si quibus *R* si quis *G* si quid *I*   342 ut] et *DVe X*; quem] quam α *H Go* que *SVaVbVdBePkNe HaLa*; leuet] michi *H* leuat *Go Tr* leuetur *Vd* louet *W*   343 mittunt] mutunt *S* mutant *F H VcGo DVe GI ZXQ* mutat *Y*   345 *line repeated in alternative form Z(1)Z(2)*; socialia] sociali *LE* solacia *Be CWHuMND Z(1)Z(2)QY* solaucia *K*; foedera] federe *Pk* dulcia *D Z(2)QY*; iungit] iungunt *VcFr Tr*   346 sibi] mihi *AJCWRHuMNPVe fb* simul *K* sibique *Go*   347 quod] quid *W* que *MuVaVbVcPm* qui *VdBe La* quidam *Go*; minus] unus *H G X*; quem] quam *VaGoPm*; fortuna grauauit] fortunia grauant *C* fortuna grauabit *Tr* fortuna grauat *VdFr illegible (water stain) Ha*   348 *om. Fr*   349 uel] nil β *TOK*   350 possit] posset *CRD Y*   352 pari] sibi *CWHuMNDK*

SPECVLVM STVLTORVM

I shall perhaps be set free from my prison in three days. [330] With the blowing of a gentle breeze, the South Wind will return to its kingdom, and the muddy fields will recover their normal state. Then my chains will be effortlessly unloosed all by themselves and I shall still keep my tail. I could rid myself of it quickly, but the regrets of having done so [335] would perhaps be eternal and never-ending. By an equal stroke of fate one night may release the captive, just as one night earlier bound her. It's not right that every time things seem inconvenient, someone should reject them on a lasting basis. [340] But let those to whom winter is a hardship be relieved by the blessing of summer, so that another's fortune may lift up the man whom his own fortune cast down. Thus the times bring their different changes of their own accord, so that one may profit from the advantage of another. Social alliances create a welcome interrelation, [345] and alliances joined to each other advance more boldly. What one had less of, being oppressed by his fortune, the ampler abundance of another should make up for. So there is nothing so exalted or created so lofty that it can manage without another's help. [350] Times and events contend with different dangers, and not all alliances are joined in equal yoke. Often we have seen little shrubs

---

341 *gratia prosit*: Ovid, *Heroides*, vii. 41.
344 *honore frui*: also at *SS*, 1670; *Miracles*, 606.

SPECVLVM STVLTORVM

50

Saepe breues frutices currentia sternere plaustra
uidimus, et celeres detinuisse boues.

355 Saepe breuis magnas subuertit machina turres,
impulsuque leui moenia summa ruunt.

Se premit imbre breui uiolentia maxima uenti,
atque procellosas mitigat Eurus aquas.

Nil contemnendum reputes quod tempore quouis
360 ferre uel auxilium uel nocuisse potest.

Vilius interdum quod carius esse putamus
constat, et est maius quod minus esse putas.

Obstitit interdum magnis res parua periclis,
terruit et rabidos paruula uirga canes.

365 Vrbibus in mediis incendia magna repente
extingui modica saepe uidemus aqua." '

Commendatio caudae

' "Corporis ergo mei quamuis pars ultima cauda,
utilius tamen hac nil reor esse mihi.

Quae quamuis oneri modo sit nulloque decori,
370 aestiuo redimit tempore damna sui.

Vnica cauda mihi plus quam duo cornua praestat
tempore muscarum, plusque salutis habet.

Ventilat haec uespes, saeuos dispergit oestros,
uerberat et muscas improbitate graues.

---

353 currentia] ad terram *R* curtericia *VdBe*   354 celeres] sceleres *EF VdBe JHuMN Q* steriles *Go Ha*ᵃᶜ fortes *D*   355 breuis] breues *Vd G Ha*; subuertit] euertit γ- *TrHaLa*ᵖᶜ; turres] *sic Pover erasure* turris *S* teres *G*   356 impulsuque] impulsu *H Ha*; summa] magna *K Tr om. T*   357–8 *transp. Vd*   357 se premit] depremit *F VcFr* se perimit *Ha*ᵃᶜ; breui] leui γ+ *Z*ᵖᶜ   358 mitigat] mitit *MND* micit *W* inicit *Hu* mittat *K* s:c mitigat *Go*   359 tempore] tempora *Pk La*   362 maius] magis *H I X corr. X*²; putas] putes *H GI*   363 magnis res] res magnis *D Tr X* magnis res res *Y* 364 rabidos] rabides *Y* rapidos β *SVaVbVdBePkPm AJCWRHuMNOPDVe GI La X* rapidus *Go* rapidas *Q* tepidos *Vc* rapuit *fb*; paruula uirga] parua uirgula *Go* uirgula parua *D Tr X* paruula terga *Q*   366 extingui] extinguit *VdPk Ha* extiguet *Fr* extigui *Q* 368 hac] hoc *Vd La* hanc *Be*; nil] non *VdGoBe Tr*; mihi] mei *RVe Tr* mea *Z* 369 nulloque] nullique *SMuVaVbVcVdTGoBePkFrPm DK TrLa ZX* nulliusque *Ne Ha Q* ulliusque *Y*; decori] decoris *MuGoNe D Ha QY*   370 aestiuo] estimo *VdFrPm ZQY*; redimit] redimet *MuVaVbVcVdGoBePkFrPmNe TrHaLa* redimi *Ve* redimat *Z* quod redimat *QY* redemit *O*; tempore] tempora *VdFr D Tr ZQ*   371 praestat] prestant *AJCWRHuMNOPK Tr ZQ*   372 muscarum plusque] niscarum plus *M* muscarum plusquam *VaFr Ve*   373 haec] hoc *M* hac *F* hic *Z*; seuos] seues *R I*; *(whole line)* uentilat oestros et seuas uerbere uespas *K*

SPECVLVM STVLTORVM

overturn a moving cart and bring swift oxen to a halt. Often a little war-engine topples great towers, [355] and high walls tumble under a light assault. The utmost violence of the wind subsides with a brief shower, and the East Wind subdues the stormy waters. You should not think that anything is to be despised if it can at any time be of assistance or do harm. [360] Sometimes what we think to be more precious is worth less, and what you think to be less is in fact the greater. Sometimes a little thing has averted great dangers, and a little stick has terrified raging dogs. In town centres we have often seen mighty fires suddenly [365] extinguished by a little water." '

Praise of the Tail

' "So although my tail is the least part of my body, I nevertheless think nothing is more useful to me than it is. Although it is now a nuisance and no advantage, in the summertime it makes up for its drawbacks. [370] In the time of flies, one tail is worth more to me than two horns, and is of more benefit. It whisks away the wasps, it scatters the savage gadflies, and swats the flies, whose boldness makes them troublesome.

---

357 Proverbial; cf. lines 2917–18, and see Singer, *Thesaurus*, s.v. 'Regen' 4. 2 (ix. 231–3). 12th-c. examples include *Pamphilus*, 480 ('Ingens ex parvis imbribus aura cadit': *Commedie*, iii. 106); Chretien de Troyes, *Perceval*, 5414 ('grans vens chiet a poi de pluie'); John of Salisbury, *Entheticus minor*, ed. van Laarhoven, 202 ('curque levi ventus grandis ab imbre cadat'); *Becket Correspondence*, i. 569 (no. cxviii) ('Fulmina eorum in tonitrus conuertentur, et turbo uentositatis huius facile soluetur imbre').

359–60 This corresponds to the moral of the fable of the lion and the mouse: 'Tu qui summa potes, ne despice parva potentem,/ nam prodesse potest, si quis obesse nequit' (elegiac *Romulus*, ed. Busdraghi, xviii. 23–4).

367–448 Brunetta's lengthy praise of her tail is in the style of a rhetorical topos, in which trivial or unattractive things were accorded exaggerated praise. See Pease, 'Things without honor'.

SPECVLVM STVLTORVM

52

375 Cauda mihi clypeus, gladius mihi cauda, securis,
lancea, funda, lapis, claua, sagitta, faces.
Cauda colit corpus, cutis est fidissima nutrix,
pulueris abstergens quicquid adhaesit eis.
Haec lauat, haec tergit, haec omnibus una ministrat,
380 ultima membrorum, prima labore suo.
Si bene pensetur quid honoris et utilitatis
contulerint dominae singula membra suae,
sola suo capiti membris sed et omnibus una
plus ualet, est et eis officiosa magis.
385 Omnibus una cauens fragilis discrimina sexus
publica ne pateant, cauda pudenda tegit.
Haec mea cauda mihi uario pro tempore confert,
quae tamen est certo tempore grata magis.
Tempora nam timeo quae sunt mihi iure timenda,
390 nec timet incassum qui mala nota timet.
Cumque quid et passa sim uel passura recordor,
haec ego sum semper dicere uisa mihi:
'Ecce dies ueniunt ueris, muscaeque resurgent,
quas sepeliuit adhuc cana pruina gelu,
395 cum calor aestatis nimio feruore per agros
sparserit omne pecus torrueritque greges;
musca, grauis pestis, qua nulla nocentior umquam

---

375 securis] securus *GoFr D ZQ* secutis *Vc*   377 cauda colit] cauda tollit *VbVd* qua
celat *F*ᵃᶜ que celat *F*ᵖᶜ; nutrix] tutrix *K ZQY*   378 adhaesit] adheret *D ZXQY*; eis] ei
γ- *TrHaLa*   379 haec²] hoc *Vd M* et *D X*; tergit] stergit *S HuMN*; omnibus una]
omnia sola γ- *TrHaLa*   381 pensetur] pensentur *Va Ha*; et] et quid *Fr* quid *CW om. S*
Ha   382 contulerint] contulerit *Go Z*ᵖᶜ*Y* contulerent *La*   383 membris] membrum *Vd Tr Q*; sed] est *Vd Q om. SMu Z*; et] in *X om. LF VcT CMDadd.D*ᵖᶜ *Q*   384 est]
et est *Vd La om. QY*; eis] erit *VbVc*   385 *om. Q; line repeated in alternative form*
Z₍₁₎Z₍₂₎; omnibus una cauens] impedit ipsa cito *X*; fragilis discrimina sexus] fragilis discrimine sexus α impedit ipsa cito *Y* sic impedit ipsa cito *Z₍₁₎*   388 quae] quod α qui
Hu; est] es *W om. Z*; grata] gratis *M* curta *fb*   389 tempora] tempore *L M*; nam] iam
H uel iam *add. X²* non *F SMuVaVbVdTGoBePkFrPmNe TrHaLa Q* nunc *Vc* namque
fb   390 nota] uota *H MuVdGoBeFrNe JRHuMNOPVe GI TrHaLa ZQY fb*
391 cumque quid et] quando quid *GI* cumque et *F* cum quod uel *D* cum quid uel *QY* cum
quid fine *Z*; sim uel] si uel *Fr* sim et *H GI* sum (sim *E*) tamen *LE* sum quodcum sum *F* uel
quid *Z*   392 haec ego sum semper] multotiens prodest *ZXQY*   393 ueniunt
ueris] uenient ueris *PVe Z* ueris ueniunt α ueniunt *Vb*; resurgent] resurgunt α β γ *GI TrHaLa*
Y resurgant *Q*   394 sepeliuit] castigat δ *ZXQY*; adhuc] ad hec *LE* ad hoc *T*; cana]
canina *Pm*ᵖᶜ *Tr* cauina *Ne* aspera *T*   396 sparserit] sperserit *H VbPm D TrHa*; torru-
eritque] terrueritque *AJCWRHuMNPDKVe ZXQY* torruerintque *Mu* corruerintque
SVaVbVcVdTBePkFrPmNe I TrHaLa corrueritque *Go* coegeritque *O*   397 nocen-
tior] nociuior *AJCWRHuMNPDVe* uiciuior *K*

SPECVLVM STVLTORVM

My tail is my shield, my tail is my sword, my axe, [375] my spear, sling, stone, club, arrow, torch. My tail cares for my body, faithfully cherishes my hide, wiping away all the dust that has stuck to it. It washes, it dries; this one member is the servant of all others—the least of members, but the most hard-working. [380] If one were to consider well what honour and usefulness each member furnishes to its mistress, then it alone is worth more than the head, and indeed all the members, and provides more service. Taking care that the marks of the weaker sex [385] are not publicly visible to all, my tail hides my private parts. This is what my tail affords me at various times, but at a certain time it is even more desirable. For I fear the times that I should rightly fear; he who fears well-known evils does not fear pointlessly. [390] When I remember what I have suffered or am to suffer, I have always seemed to say this to myself: 'See, the time of spring is coming, and the flies, which hoar-frost has buried in ice up to now, are coming back to life, when the heat of summer with its excessive ardour will scatter all the cattle through the fields [395] and burn up the flocks. The fly, a noxious plague, than which there was never anything in the world more baleful nor any

---

382 *singula membra*: also at *Miracles*, 950.

391 *passura recordor*: Ovid, *Heroides*, x. 79.

393 *resurgent* is less widely supported than 'resurgunt', but the future tense better matches the future perfects ('sparserit...torruerit') in 395–6. The present tense 'resurgunt' was probably induced by 'ueniunt'.

394 *sepeliuit*: Mozley prefers the δ reading 'castigat', but 'sepeliuit' is both more widely supported and also supplies an appropriate contrast to 'resurgent' (burial followed by resurrection). *cana pruina*: cf. Horace, *Odes*, i. 4. 4: 'nec prata canis albicant pruinis'.

54 SPECVLVM STVLTORVM

extitit in mundo uel magis atra lues,
dente graui miseras totum sparsura per orbem
400   percutiet pecudes; nec sinet ire pedes,
namque leui saltu tamquam per inane uolantes
morsibus et stimulis exagitabit eas.
Forte dies aderit in qua, ni fallor, egebit
uacca sua cauda quam modo spernit ita.
405   Illa dies caudam cunctis dabit esse salubrem,
et suus aestatem praeuenit augur hiems.
Illa dies caudae faciet meminisse iuuencas
et steriles uaccas emeritosque boues.
Illa dies caudae faciet meminisse Bicornem
410   qua mallet cauda non habuisse caput.
Illa dies caudas mundo faciet pretiosas,
quae plus sunt uiles quam uetus olla modo.
Illa dies dura multumque tremenda per orbem
tamquam iudicii plena timoris erit.
415   Illa dies caudas nostras numerabit, et illa
discernet pariter quae bona quaeue mala.
Illa dies caudas nostras discernet utrasque,
quae bene mundata quaeue lutosa nimis.
Haec est illa dies in qua, si forte iuuenca
420   posset habere duas, uellet habere decem.

---

398 atra] *illegible* Pm^{pc} arta α *J*   399 miseras] miseros *S* miseris *Q* muscas *Fr*
400 sinet] sinit β *Go JCR GI ZQY*; pedes] pedem *MN*   401 namque] nam
SMuVaVbVdTGoBePkPmNe TrHaLa non *Fr*; inane] prata *ZX* praua *QY*; uolantes] uolentes
VdBe D Z nolentes *La*   403–4 *om. QY*; *transp. after 406* β γ+ δ *ZX*   403 qua]
quo *SVaVbVcVdGoBePkFrPmNe TrHaLa Z*; ni] nisi *LE* β γ+ *GI Z om. M*; fallor] fallar *Ve X*
404 quam⸗ quid *Go* quem *Be La*; spernit] spreuit *TPm R*   405 illa] ille α *AJCWODKVe*
SMuVaVbVcVdGoBePkFrPmNe TrHaLa XQY; *after* 'caudam', *H writes* 'certe mihi grata
salubrem/ reddet et istius temporis ultor erit', *then deletes this and replaces with second half of*
405   407 *after 406* illa dies caudam certe mihi grata salubrem/ reddet et istius temporis ultor erit *GI*   407–8 *om. MuFr D^{pc}K Tr XQY*   407 illa] ille *SVaVbBePmNe*
HaLa; caudae] caude *P*; caudae faciet] faciet caude *Vc*; faciet] facies *LE* faciat *VdGo* fauet
D   408–9 que boues—caudae faciet] *om. Go*   409–10 *transp. after 422*
Z   409 illa] ille *LE Fr Ha*   411–14 *om. QY*   411 caudas mundo] mundo
caudas *D X* caudas modo *Fr*; faciet] faciat *MuVd K*   412 *after 411* qua sine qui fuerit
igne cremandus erit *add. H deleted* H^{pc}; plus sunt] sunt plus *H Vb GI*; olla] ulla *Go Z*
415–18 *transp. after 420 ZQY*   415–16 *transp. after 418 D*; *om. F*   415 numera-
bit] iuuabit Vb^{pc} monstrabit *Pm Ha*   416 discernet] discernit *MuFr CWRMO^{ac}*
417 discernet] discernit *GoFr CD Tr* discerneret *E*   418 bene mundata] bene man-
data *S* mundata bene α *P over erasure* bona mundana *G* uere mundata *Go*
419–20 *transp. after 422 SVaVbVcVdTBePkFrPmNe HaLa*; *transp. after 410 ZQY*; *om. Mu*
J X   419 illa] ista *ZQY*   420 posset] possit *LE M*

SPECVLVM STVLTORVM

55

blacker pest, will strike with its cruel tooth the wretched cattle so as to scatter them throughout the world; nor will it allow them to go on foot, [400] for with its bites and stings it will flick them up in a light jump, as if they are flying through the air. Perchance that day will come when, if I'm right, the cow will have need of the tail she now scorns. That day will make a tail a benefit to all, [405] and winter is the herald of the following summer. That day will make heifers mindful of their tails, and barren cows and worn-out oxen too. That day will make Bicornis mindful of her tail—on which she would rather be without her head than her tail. [410] That day will make tails highly valued in the world, although they are now rated lower than an old pot. That day of sorrow, striking terror through the world, will be as full of dread as Judgement Day. That day will number our tails, [415] and will judge which is good and which is bad. That day will judge between our tails, which is well cleaned and which is too dirty. This is the day when if by chance a heifer could have two tails, she would like to have ten. [420] This is the

398 *atra lues*: also at *Miracles*, 1634, 1729.

401 *leui saltu*: cf. Ovid, *Metamorphoses*, vii. 767. *per inane uolantes*: Prudentius, *Liber Cathemerinon*, x. 146.

403–4 These lines are transposed after 406 in βγδ*TrHaLaZX*, and are omitted entirely in *QY*. Probably they were at first omitted in the common ancestor of these manuscripts, then added in the margin by a corrector; in the ancestor of βγδ*TrHaLaZX* they were inserted in the wrong place, while in the common exemplar of *QY* they were overlooked.

405–26 Brunetta's speech is a parody of the 'dies irae' theme, which derives from the Bible (Zeph. 1: 15, 'dies irae dies illa', with 'dies' repeated five more times in verses 15–16). The Latin poem on this theme that was incorporated into the Requiem Mass is testified only from the 13th c. onwards, but may be much older. For medieval Latin poetic treatments of the theme, see Ermini, *Il 'Dies Irae'*. Nigel also uses the motif in a serious context in St Lawrence's long dialogue with the emperor Decius, *Lawrence*, 1351–6.

56   *SPECVLVM STVLTORVM*

Haec est illa dies ueniet qua durus oester,
   tortor uaccarum maximus atque boum.
Haec est illa dies quae muscas dente caninas
   morsibus et stimulis mittet in omne pecus.

425 Haec est illa dies quam praetimuisse futuram
   expedit armento, ne patiatur in hac.
O mihi! quam felix misera quae posset ab illa
   euasisse die, quam timet omne pecus!
Hanc etiam plus morte mea formido futuram,

430   qua nisi praeterita non ero tuta satis.
Namque graues muscae nimium feruorque diei
   multus erit, nec ibi quis latuisse potest.
Nec pecori tantum feruor muscaeque nocebunt,
   sed dominis pecorum consociisque gregum.

435 Haec est illa dies qua non aliena iuuabit
   cauda, nec alterius quid nocuisse potest.
Sed nec pastor ibi pecori taurusue iuuencae
   parue pari poterit ferre salutis opem.
Haec est illa dies, qua nil nisi cauda iuuabit,

440   uel loca quae musca tangere nulla potest.
Haec est illa dies de qua—si uera fatemur—
   pendet ab illius nostra salute salus.

421–2 *om. QY*   **421** haec] hic *VaVdBePkFrPm La*; est] enim *F*; illa] ille *VdBeFr*; ueniet qua] ueniet quo *BeFr Tr* uenit quo *Vd* ueniet que *S* ueniet quoque *MuVaVbGoPkPm Ha* ueniet queque *Ne* uenit quoque *La*   **422** maximus] pessimus γ+   **423** quae muscas] cua muscas *CWHuMND* muscas qua *K* quo muscas *G*; caninas] caminas *VdFr* canino *Mu* canum *Ne*   **424** mittet] mittit *MuVc ROP XQ* mettet *Ve*   **425–6** *om. F*   **425** praetimuisse] pretinuisse *VcTBePm QY* precinuisse *Va* pretenuisse *Go* presciuisse *Fr Z* pertimuisse *K* penituisse *Vd*; futuram] futurum *M* futura *Go Ve*   **426** armento] armenti *AJCWROVe Y*; hac] hoc *Vc GI*   **427** mihi] sibi α *X* uere *Ne*; quae] qui *EF ST XQY* quam *D* quis *MuVaVbVcVdGoBePkFrPmNe TrHaLa*; posset] possit α *S P XQY* poscit *Z*   **428** die] diem *MN*; quam] qua *SMuVaVbVcVdTGoBePkPmNe Ha* quo *Fr* quem *Z*   **429** etiam plus morte mea] etiam morte mea plus *D* et plus morte mea nunc *LE* plus morte mea (sua *F*^{ac}) nunc et *F*; futuram] futura *GoNe*   **430** praeterita] tunc munda δ munda *La* cum cauda *Skutsch*; satis] nimis satis *GI*^{ac} nimis *expuncted G*^{pc} *deleted I*²; *(whole line)* uitio quam nisi tunc non ero tuta satis *X*   **431** nimium feruorque] nimius feruorque *P Q* nimium furorque *Va* nimiumque feruorque *Ve* nimium feriorque *Fr* furor nimiumque *H GI* feruor nimiumque *B* animum feruorque *HuMN*   **432** multus] multis *I Ha*; ibi] ubi *GI* illi *Q*   **434** consociisque] cum sociisque *SPk* pastoribusque α β *AJCWROPDVe GI Tr XQY* prepositisque *HuMNK*   **435–6** *om.* γ *TrHa Z*   **436** nec] non *GI* uel *X*   **437–8** *om. QY*   **437** taurusue] tauroue *D* taurosue *Vc* taurusque *VaTFrPm Tr* tharusue *Vd*   **438** parue pari] puerpere *Vc* in nullo β *GI* quoque modo *X*   **439–40** *om. Ne D*   **440** uel] ad β *GI X*²*over erasure*; nulla] seua β *GI*; potest] solet *G*^{ac}*I* ualet *Mu*^{ac}   **441** *om. Fr*; fatemur] fatentur *VcT*   **442** illius] alius *ZY* alterius *Q*

SPECVLVM STVLTORVM 57

day on which will come the cruel gadfly, the greatest tormentor of cows and oxen. This is the day that will send out the dog-toothed fly with bites and stings against the whole herd. This is the day which it is well for the happy cattle to fear in advance, [425] lest it suffer on it. Ah me! how happy is she who could escape that miserable day, which all cattle fear! I fear its coming even more than my death, nor shall I be quite safe until that day has passed. [430] For the cruel flies and the excessive heat of the day will be great, and no one can find a hiding-place there. And the heat and the flies will torment not only the cattle but the cow-herds and companions of the flocks. This is the day on which no other cow's tail will do any good, [435] nor can anyone else's do harm. The herdsman will not be able to help the cattle, nor the bull the heifer, nor like help like. This is the day on which nothing but a tail will do any good—that, or the places that no fly can get at. [440] This is the day—if we speak truth about it—on whose safety our own safety depends. So

---

430 *qua nisi praeterita*: this is the reading of αβγ*TrHaZQY*; Skutsch ('Three rare words', p. 31) thought this was 'clearly a wilful alteration of the rather unintelligible *tunc munda*', which is the δ variant, but the opposite seems to me more likely. Skutsch's proposed emendation to 'cum cauda' seems to me unnecessary; Brunetta is saying that she will not be safe until 'illa dies' has gone by.

434 *consociisque*: This is the reading of γ; αβδ have 'pastōribusque' but the long o (cf. *Lawrence*, 261) is unmetrical at this point in the line. *HuMNK* seem to be attempting a metrical improvement.

436 *nec alterius quid*: for 'nil alienum'.

438 *ferre salutis opem*: A favourite phrase of Nigel's; see *SS*, 3412, 3284, 3302, and *Miracles*, 146, 248, 276, 1394. Cf. Bernard Silvestris, *Cosmographia*, ed. Wetherbee, *Megacosmos*, iii. 404.

442 A quotation of Vitalis of Blois, *Geta*, 138 (*Commedie*, iii. 198).

58   *SPECVLVM STVLTORVM*

Ergo licet tenear cauda grauiterque coarter,
non tamen effrangar ipsa dolore meo.

445   Malo per hos septem uel quinque dies cruciari,
(forsitan interea tristis abibit hiems)
quam praelonga nimis me feruida torreat aestas,
dilaceretque meam musca canina cutem." '

Qualiter Brunetta liberata est

'Talia dum memorat, modico recreata sopore,
450   flante leui Zephyro tempora uersa uidet.
Sol calet et superas clarus deuexus in auras
diffusis radiis temperat omne gelu.
Soluitur unda fluens, humus exhilarata tepescit,
aufugit et subito cana pruina solo.
455   Et status et facies siluis redduntur et aruis,
cuncta relaxantur carcere clausa prius.
Nec mora, consurgens caudam Brunetta retraxit,
acceleransque domum carpere coepit iter.
Quam procul ut uidit sanam remeare Bicornis,
460   ingemit, et tunso pectore tristis ait:'

Lamentatio Bicornis

' "Heu mihi! Quid feci? Quis me furor egit iniquus?
Quam nimis accelerans in mea damna fui!

---

443 tenear cauda] cauda tenear *α* teneat cauda *CWHuMN QY* teneor cauda *R*; coarter] coactus *F* coartar *K* coarthar *Go* cohartar *Ha* coharter *BeNe La* coarcer *PkPm* cohercer *SVdT CWHuMN* cohercet *QY* coarcet *Tr* coerceri *Fr*   **444** non tamen] sed non *D X*; tamen effrangar] effrangar adhuc *VaVbVcTGoPkPmNe HaLa* effranger adhuc *Mu* effrangor adhuc *VdBe Tr* effrangat adhuc *Fr* effrangatur *S*; effrangar] affrangar *R* effugar *H* effringar *Z* effrangat *QY*   **446** abibit] abiit *Mu* adhibit *VdPk*   **447** me] ne *X* uel ut *add. interlinear* X^2; torreat] terreat *L CVe Ha Q* torruat *P* correat *Ne* corruit *Tr* torruit *Z* feriat *Vc* **448** dilaceretque] dilaceratque *Vc ZQY*   **449** modico] medico *Go Ha Z*; sopore] sapore *Be M Z*   **450** uidet] uidit *R Z*   **451** calet] claret *K Ha* calcet *Vd*; superas] superat *S CM Tr ZQY* serras *MuGo* seras *VbVcTFrPm Ha* senis *Va*; clarus] claras *OP om. ZQY*; deuexus in auras] deuexit in auras *α X* deuexans in auras *Go* deuexas in aures *Fr* auras frigidas calefecit *QY* auras frigidasque calescat *Z*   **452** temperat] temporat *D Z* temperet *Q*   **454** aufugit] aufugat *Tr* effugit *P Z* affigit *QY* affugit *Ve* anstigat *Go*; solo] solo / uel gelu *La*   **455** *om. Z*; siluis] cibus *LE*; redduntur] redimitur *Mu GI*; et³] in *H Vd MNVe*   **459** uidit] uidet *Fr ACWHuMN ZY*   **460** ingemit] ingemuit *F H VdTGoBePkNe CWRPD TrLa* X^{ac}*Y* gemuit *O*; et] *om. F VdBe PD TrLa X add.* X^2; tunso] tunsa *Q* tonso *H SMuVdBePk ACWRHuMNOPVe GI Tr* conso *Ne* tonsa *Vb* tenso *FrPm* **462** quam] qua *LE* quo *F* que γ- *TrHaLa* quid *Q*; fui] rui *F ZQY* fugi *VaGoPm*

SPECVLVM STVLTORVM

59

although I am caught by my tail and am severely restrained, I shall not be broken by my grief. I prefer to be afflicted for these seven or five days [445] (perhaps bleak winter will depart in the interim) than that the long hot summer should scorch me beyond measure, and the dog-like fly should pierce my skin." '

How Brunetta Was Freed

'While she was saying this, and having been refreshed with a little sleep, she sees the weather change with the blowing of a gentle breeze. [450] The sun grows warm, and as it is carried into the upper part of the sky it counteracts all coldness with its spreading rays. The flowing water is released, the gladdened earth grows warm, and the hoary frost suddenly leaves the earth. Their normal condition and appearance are restored to the woods and fields; [455] everything that had formerly been shut in prison is released. Without delay Brunetta rose, withdrew her tail, and hastened off on her journey home. When Bicornis saw her from a way off coming back safe and sound. she groaned, and striking her breast sadly said:' [460]

The Lamentation of Bicornis

' "Ah me! What have I done? What evil fury drove me? How quickly did I speed to my own destruction! Oh, what cruel outcomes does

---

443 *grauiterque*: all manuscripts agree on this reading, but Mozley prints 'breuiterque' without signalling it as an emendation; presumably it is an error on his part.

446 *tristis... hiems*: Ovid, *Ars amatoria*, i. 409.

459 *Quam procul ut uidit*: Ovid, *Tristia*, iii. 9. 11.

461 Bicornis's lament parodies Ovid, *Heroides*, ix. 145: 'Ei mihi! quid feci? quo me furor egit amantem?'

60 SPECVLVM STVLTORVM

O quam perduros habet impatientia fines!
　Quamque solet praeceps exitus esse grauis!
465 Vae mihi! Vae miserae! Vae numquam non miserandae!
　Vae, cui nil nisi uae tempus in omne manet!
　Me miseram quod ego cunctis animantibus una
　　sum data ludibrium tempus in omne meum.
　Cur mihi cum cauda non est mea uita recisa,
470　　ut caput et cauda continuata forent?
　Cur non terra prius, cur non absorbuit unda,
　　fulminis aut missis ignibus usta fui?
　Quaeque nimis praeceps, cur non mea fata secuta
　　montibus e summis praecipitata rui?
475 Heu mihi! cur laquei circum mea guttura missi
　　uitam cum uitio non rapuere meo?
　Cur non mors subita uitam uel sonticus ille
　　morbus ademisset, qui uagus esse solet?
　Quid queror? Vna mihi superest medicina doloris:
480　　mors cita, quae sola soluere cuncta solet.
　Nec mora quin soluat: iam formidabilis aestas
　　imminet, exit hiems, uere uigente nouo.
　Viuet in exemplum populis moritura Bicornis,

---

463 perduros] preduros *SMuVaVbVdTGoBePkFrPmNe TrHaLa ZQY* **464** quamque] quam *CWHuMN* quamquam *Vb* quaque *Vd* **465** numquam] nonquam *S* umquam *MuVaVbVcVdGoBeFrPm Ha*; non miserandae] non miserando *CP* non miserende *Fr* ultra sanande *XQY* sanande *Z* **466** ue²] *om. GI add. in margin I²* **467** *line repeated in alternative form* $Z_{(1)}Z_{(2)}$; me miseram quod ego cunctis] uae mihi quod cunctis ego nunc *DK XQY* ue mihi quod ego nunc cunctis *AJCWHuMNO^{ac}PVe* ue mihi nunc quod ego cunctis *RO^{pc}* ue mihi ex cunctis ego $Z_{(1)}$; me] ue *Vc TrLa*; animantibus] in animantibus *Go* amirantibus *Pm* animalibus *Ha* $Z_{(1)}$ **468** ludibrium] ludibrio *JCWRHuMNOPDKVe Tr ZXQY* ludubrio *A* delubrium *GI* **469** est mea] est mihi *MuVaVdBePkFrPmNe TrHaLa* mihi est *Go* **472** *line repeated in alternative form* $Z_{(1)}Z_{(2)}$; fulminis] fluminis *F SMuVaVbVcVdGoBePkFrPmNe* δ *I TrHaLa XQY* flaminis *T* fluuiis *LE* $Z_{(1)}$ $Z_{(2)}$; missis] rutilis *SMuVaVbVcGoBePkFrPmNe HaLa* $Z_{(2)}$ rutibus *Vd* uitibus *T* **473** quaeque nimis praeceps] que nimis est preceps *Pm* que nimis preceps *VaVc* queque preceps nimis *Pk* quique nimis preceps *Ne* quique nimis est preceps *Go* qui nimis preceps *Be* quod nimis preceps *Vd La* quamque nimis preceps *T* heu mihi quid faciam *ZQY*; fata] sata *Ne* uel facta *add.* G^{pc} facta α β *SVdTPm AJCWHuMNPKVe ZX* uel fata *add.* K^{pc} alias fata *add.* $Pm²$; secuta] secura *VdGo* secuto *Fr* **475–8** *om. QY* **475** circum] certum *E Pm^{ac} Tr Z*; missi] misi *Fr D* missis *Go*; *(whole line)* heu mihi quid faciam et cur mea facta malorum *X* **477–8** uitam uel—ademisset] *om. Vc* **477** subita] subito *VbVcT Tr*; sonticus] senticus *Vd* saucius *T* sordidus *O* fontibus *Z* **478** ademisset] adhesisset β ademissis *MuGoPm* ademissit *Vd* adiuisset *Z* **479–80** *om.* γ *Ha*; *transp. after 481 O* **480** cita] ita *LE* scita *D* atra *K*; cita quae] citoque *Tr* itaque *Q* **481** quin] qui *SVdBePkNe* que *MuVaTGoPm TrHaLa* quam *Vc* quod iuuat *Fr*; soluat] *om. GI add. in margin I²* saluat *Vc* soluet *H T TrHa* **482** nouo] noua *Mu Q*

SPECVLVM STVLTORVM 61

impatience have! And how harsh is a rash conclusion! Woe is me! Woe to wretched me—never to be other than pitiable! [465] Woe to her for whom there remains nothing but woe for all time! Wretch that I am, who am now alone made a laughing-stock to all animals through my whole life. Why was my life not cut off with my tail, so that head and tail would be kept together? [470] Why did not the earth, why did not the wave first swallow me up, or why was I not burned up with lightning-bolts? I who was too hasty, why did I not pursue my death by rushing headlong from the mountain-tops? Ah me! Why did not snares placed round my throat [475] snatch away my life along with my wrongdoing? Why did not sudden death, or that critical illness which roams abroad, take away my life? Why do I lament? One remedy for my grief is left to me: a speedy death, which is usually the one way to solve everything. [480] Delay will solve nothing; already the terrible summer is at hand, winter is passing, and the new spring blooms. The dying Bicornis will

---

468 *ludibrium* is preferable to the δ reading 'ludibrio', as it avoids a double dative. *tempus in omne meum*: this phrase recurs as the second half of a pentameter at *SS*, 2882; *Miracles*, 2152, 2546. Variations using 'tuum' or 'suum' appear at *SS*, 796, 888, 1694, 3782, and with other disyllables at *SS*, 466, 2300.

471–2 Cf. Ovid, *Heroides*, iii. 63–4: 'devorer ante, precor, subito telluris hiatu,/ aut rutilo missi fulminis igne cremer.' The allusion to Ovid supports 'fulminis', the reading of βG, rather than 'fluminis'. It could also support either 'missis', the reading of αβδ*GITrZ*(1)*XQY*, or 'rutilis', the reading of *SMuVaVbVcGoBePkFrPmNeHaLaZ*(2). It is tempting to see 'rutilis' as a *difficilior lectio*, but the cross-branch evidence in favour of 'missis' is stronger.

477–8 *sonticus . . . / morbus*: epilepsy (Du Cange, s.v. 'Morbus sonticus').

SPECVLVM STVLTORVM

instruat ut stultos simplicitate sua.

485 Discant praecipites et quos mora nulla retardat,
ne nimis accelerent in sua damna manus.
Nil reputet modicum modico contenta uoluptas;
res de postfacto quod fuit ante docet.
Nec modicum quicquam reputet, si tempore quouis
490 fortuito casu perdere possit idem.
Cauda cauet capiti proprio, prohibetque timeri
cornua, dum metuunt posteriora sequi.
Quid queror incassum? Mando tamen ista modernis
qui post me uenient, haec duo uerba legant:
495 'Dum superest, nihil est nihiloque minus quod habemus;
cedat, et est magnum quod fuit ante nihil.'
Nil mea cauda fuit dum me comitata maneret,
maxima sed postquam desiit esse fuit.
Perdere cum timeas, magnum reputare memento
500 quicquid habes, modicum sit licet illud idem."
Desierat tandem mentis stimulata Bicornis
anxietate graui talia uerba loqui.'

Quid acciderit Bicorni

'Venerat interea tempus quo fertilis aestas
prata solet primo pingere flore nouo.

---

484 instruat ut] instruet ut *Mu* instruet et *AJCWRHuMNPDKVe X* instruat et *Tr* instruit et *Oᵖᶜ*; stultos] multos β *GI* stultus *VcGoFr Y*   **485** *om. Vc*; mora nulla] mors nulla α *corr. to* meus nulla *F²* mora nullus *La* nulla mora *H S*   **486** accelerent] accelerant *SVdGo M* accelerat *C*   **487** nil] *Mozley* non α β γ *ACJWRHuMNOPKVe GI TrHaLa ZXQY* ne *D*; reputet] reputat *Tr Z* reputent *Y* retinet *F*; contenta] contempta *F corr. F² MuVaVdGoBeFrPmNe Wʰᶜ Ha* temptata *Pk*; uoluptas] uoluntas *E X*   **488** res] sed α; quod] quid α β *S GI ZQY* que *MuVaVbVcVdTGoBeFrPmNe D HaLa X* qui *Pk*   **489** nec] non α *X*; quicquam reputet] quisquam reputet *VaVbVcVdTGoBePkFrNe TrHaLa* quisque reputet *Mu* quisquam reputes *Pm* reputet quicquam *D ZXY* reputet quicquid *Q*; si] se *VdBe La* cum *K*   **490** *fc excerpt 1 joins here*; fortuito] fortuitu *F P* fortuiti *Fr* fortuite *Z*; possit] posset *MuGoFr ROD* possis *T*   **491–2** *om. QY* **491** cauet] *Shackleton Bailey* nos *Fr* nocet *rest*; proprio] proprie *Go*; prohibetque] cohibetque *VaFr*   **492** dum] de *VdBePk*   **493** queror] queor *HuᵖᶜMN*; incassum] in casum *CWVe fc*   **495** dum superest] cum superest *O ft* dura super *S*; minus] nimis *GoBe*; habemus] habetur *DK XQY fc*   **496** cedat] cedit *D Y fc* cedant *E* cessit *Q* **497** dum me comitata] de me comutata *Vd* de me communicata *Pk* mihi dum coniuncta *AᵖᶜJCWHuMNOPDKVe La ZXQY fc* mihi cum coniuncta *R* mea dum coniuncta *Tr*; me] mea *Vc*; comitata] concomitata *Be* comutata *Pm* coniuncta *Va* (comitata *add. in margin*) ?comitatiua *Ne* commitancia *T*   **500** sit] sic *SVdBe Tr Y* sed *J*   **501** desierat] desiderat *BePkNe CWR La* desideret *Go* desirrat *Ve*; mentis] mente *Vc D* muscis *S* **503** *fg joins*; fertilis] sterilis *F GI*   **504** solet] solent *Pk GI* solo *S*; nouo] noue *MP*

SPECVLVM STVLTORVM

63

live as an example to the people, so that by her stupidity she may teach fools. Let the reckless, and those whom no delay holds back, [485] learn not to quicken their actions unduly to their own detriment. Let pleasure, content with a little, think nothing little; a thing reveals in the sequel what it was beforehand. Nor let pleasure think anything paltry, if at any time it is capable of losing it by a stroke of fortune. [490] The tail protects its own head, and prevents the horns from being feared, while they fear what comes behind. Why do I lament in vain?—yet I send this message to future posterity. Let them read these two words: 'While it lasts, what we have is nothing and less than nothing. [495] Let it disappear, and what was nothing before becomes important.' My tail was nothing while it was attached to me, but after it ceased to exist it was of great importance. Fearing to lose it, remember to think only that whatever you have is important, although it may only be little." [500] At length Bicornis ceased speaking these words, spurred on by deep mental anguish.'

What Happened to Bicornis

'Meanwhile, the time had come in which the fruitful summer is wont to decorate the fields with the first new flowers. Now it had clothed the

---

487 *Nil* appears to be an emendation by Mozley, although not signalled as such in his *apparatus criticus*. All MSS have 'non', except *D*, which has 'ne', but an object is needed for 'reputet'; 'modicum' is a complement. *modico contenta*: cf. Juvenal, *Saturae*, ix. 9.

491 *cauet*: see Introduction, p. lxxx for discussion.

495–8 Proverbial; see Singer, *Thesaurus*, s.v. 'Verlieren' 5. 14. 1 (xii. 184), and cf. Serlo of Wilton, *Poèmes latins*, ed. Öberg, p. 133, Appendix I. B. 4: 'Nescit homo, quid sit quod habet, si non prius absit.'

496 *quod fuit ante nihil*: Maximian, *Elegies*, i. 222.

504 Cf. Geoffrey of Vinsauf, *Poetria nova*, 791–2: 'Ergo sapit verbum si dicas: Tempora veris/ "Pingere" flore solum, "nasci" primordia florum.'

64 · SPECVLVM STVLTORVM

505 Induerat iam fronde nemus, iam gramine terram
texerat, intextis floribus arte pari.
Exierant uolucres hiemis de carcere fracto,
soluere finitimis digna tributa locis.
Verba negata sibi redimens philomena sonoris
510 uocibus insistit, personat omne nemus.
Quos natura uocat, cum turture uenit hirundo,
aduentusque sui tempora certa tenent.
Nuntius aurorae merulam comitatur alauda,
nec sua permutant tempora lege noua.
515 Semper idem repetens, ueteri noua tempora uoce
ostendit cuculus, nil nouitatis habens.
Concentu parili uocum concordia discors
intonat, et siluis organa mille sonant.
Certat odor florum cantus superare uolucrum;
520 organa uox superat, balsama uincit odor.
Dulce sonant siluae, redolent thymiamata campi,
floribus et fructu gignit amoma solum.
Aestuat aestiuo tellus feruore coacta,
soluitur in cineres quod fuit ante lutum.
525 Terra parit culices pariuntque cadauera uermes,
aera conturbat improba musca uolans.
Ardor agit pecudes, pecudum turbator oester

506 par.] pare *GI*   510 personat] personet *GoPm Ha QY* et personat
J   511 quos] quo α quod *SMuVaVbVdGoBePkFrPmNe J TrHa*; uocat] uetat
SMuVaVbVdGoPkFrPmNe Ha negat *T* necat *Be Tr* necat / uel uocat *La*   513 aurorae]
aurora *M* autore *Go* amore *VdNe K* amoris *VbVc*   514 permutant] permittant *Fᵃᶜ R X*
permittent *H* permittunt *Go*; tempora] tempore *VbVdBe Y*; lege] longe *CWHuMN* longa *Fr*
515 tempora] tempore *Be QY*; uoce] uite *GI*   516 ostendit cuculus] ostendat cuculus
Tr ascendit cuculus *Z* ostendit catulus *Fr*   517 concentu] contentu *VbGoBe GᵘᶜI* contenti *CW*; uocum] uotum *VbGoNe*; discors] concors *O Tr*   518 intonat] intonant *L Q*
intonatur *Vd*; et] in β *D GI ZXQY fc om. Vd*   519–20 *transp. after 522 Tr*
519 odor] ordo *La fc* ardor *Fr*   521 thymiamata campi] *om. D*   522 amoma]
amona *Banona VbPkAᵃᶜJᵃᶜVe Tr add. in margin Pᵖᶜ* anoua *La* annona *MuVaVcVdTGoBeFrPmNe*
CWᵖᶜR Ha ZXᵖᶜQY fg annona / uel anona uel amena *O* amonia *S* auena *Wᵃᶜ* amena α aroma
H Jᵖᶜ GI om. P<space left empty>   523 aestiuo] perstiuo *M*   524 cineres]
cineres / uel pulueres *Ha*   525 culices] *Skutsch* pulices *all MSS*; pariuntque] pere-
untque *CW* pariunt *Vc D Ha Q*   526 area] area *Vb fc* terram *Ha*   527 agit] ait
La urit *D X fc*; pecudum turbator] pecudum turbatur *B MuGoPm Tr QY* pariter conturbat
AJCWRHuMNODKVe X fc pariterque conturbat *fg* pariter conturbat / uel pecudum
turbat<or> *La* periret conturbat *P*

SPECVLVM STVLTORVM 65

wood with leaves, now it had covered the earth with grass [505] and flowers interwoven with equal artistry. The birds had left the broken prison of winter, to pay fitting tribute to the neighbouring regions. Philomel, making up for the speech denied her, pours her heart into melodious notes, and fills all the wood with music. [510] Summoned by nature, the swallow comes, along with the turtle-dove, and they keep to the established time of their arrival. The lark, herald of the dawn, accompanies the blackbird; they do not change their timetables for a new rule. Always repeating the same thing, the cuckoo signals the new season with an old voice [515] which has nothing new about it. The harmonious discord of voices resounds in well-matched harmony, and a thousand musical instruments echo in the woods. The odour of the flowers strives to outdo the song of the birds; the voice outdoes musical instruments, the scent surpasses balsam. [520] The woods resound sweetly, the fields smell of incense, and the earth gives forth fragrance from flowers and fruit. The earth burns under the pressure of summer heat, and what was mud beforehand is dissolved into ashes. The earth brings forth gnats and carcasses bring forth worms; [525] the evil fly disturbs the air in its flight. The heat drives the cattle onward; the

505 *Induerat...fronde nemus*: cf. *Carmina Burana*, no. cxl. 4. 1: 'Fronde nemus induitur.'

509–10 *Verba negata sibi*: Philomena was a beautiful girl who was brutally raped by her brother-in-law Tereus (see Ovid, *Metamorphoses*, vi. 424–676). Tereus then cut out her tongue to prevent her from accusing him, but she wove the story into a tapestry which she sent to her sister Procne. The two women took revenge on Tereus, and all three were then transformed into birds by the gods: Philomela became a swallow, Procne a nightingale, and Tereus a hoopoe. In the medieval tradition, the two women swapped places, and Philomena was identified with the nightingale. On the nightingale as a herald of spring, see Raby, 'Philomena praevia temporis amoeni'.

514 *lege noua*: also at *Miracles*, 914.

515–16 *Semper idem repetens*: the monotony of the cuckoo's song is proverbial; see Singer, *Thesaurus*, s.v. 'Kuckuck' 2 (vii. 221), and the lines added after 514 in MS *Ve*: 'Quamuis per multos cuculus cantauerit annos/ Discere nescit adhuc aliud uerbum nisi cucuck' (Werner, *Sprichwörter*, p. 75, Q27; Walther, *Proverbia*, 23426).

517 *Concentu parili*: Prudentius, *Liber cathemerinon*, v. 122. *concordia discors*: the phrase, and the notion, were a commonplace in classical Latin literature. See Horace, *Epistulae*, i. 12. 19; Ovid, *Metamorphoses*, i. 433; Lucan, *De bello civili*, i. 98. Medieval examples are Alan of Lille, *Anticlaudianus*, ii. 267, ed. Wetherbee, p. 278, and *De planctu Naturae*, xvii. 29, ed. Wetherbee, p. 198. The inversion of the phrase, 'discordia concors', is less frequently found.

525 *culices*: see Introduction, p. lxxx for discussion.

66   *SPECVLVM STVLTORVM*

aduolat et musca sordida, dente procax.
Per iuga, per colles, per deuia quaeque locorum,
530   diruptis stabulis soluitur omne pecus.
Insidet armento stimulo perdurus oester,
    assunt et uespes, immoderata lues,
saltibus et siluis currunt sine lege uagantes
    cum grege pastores, praecipitando gradum.
535   Vritur omne pecus, sudant animalia, passim
    spargitur armentum, diffugiuntque greges.
Brunettam sequitur pariter fugiendo Bicornis,
    quae quo tuta minus fortius urget iter.
Cui sua cauda manet muscis Brunetta resistit
540   fortiter, impendens pro uice saepe uicem.
Ventilat hinc uespes, alias dispergit oestros,
    dissipat et muscas, seque tuetur ab his.
Aggreditur tandem miseram nudamque Bicornem
    turbine multiplici turba proterua nimis.
545   Haec abit, illa uolat, fugit haec, comitatur et illa,
    hi stimulos acuunt, urget et illa pedes.
Quid faceret misera? Quo se lugubris et amens
    uerteret, in tantis nuda relicta malis?

528–31 *om.* α *GI*   **529** colles] collos *Go La* calles *Ve*   **531** insidet] insidit
TrHa institit *P* incidet *fc*; stimulo] stimulis *PK* stimula *Q*; perdurus] predurus β
SMuVbVdTGoBePkFrPmNe TrLa ZQY perdurat *X* perduro *D*   **532** *om. Vb*; assunt]
affuit *X* affert *Vd TrLa*; immoderata] non moderata *D X fc* in modo rita *Z*   **533** et] in
H GI Xcorr. X²Q; siluis] lignis *Mu* signis *SVaVbVdGoBePkFrNe Ha*; uagantes] uacantes
VaGoBePkNe HaLa   **536** *fg ends*; spargitur] spargit *Mu* spergitur *VbVd O QY* soper-
gitur *Ne*   **538** quae quo tuta minus] *Sedgwick* queque tuta minus *B Pm AJCRHuMNOP*
La queque minus tuta *Ve* queque nimis tuta *ZQY* quodque tuta minus α *I* quamque tuta
minus (tutam nimis *H*) *G H* que caudata minus *DK X fc* que quoque tuta (cuta *Go*) minus
SMuVaVbVcVdGoBePkFrNe que quoque tuta nimis *Ha* que quia tuta nimis *Tr* que quia tuta
minus *T* quoque tuta minus *W*; urget] urgit *Go X* uiget *Ve* agit /uel urget *Ha om. Pk*
539 resistit] recessit *X^{ac}* re *Ne*   **540** impendens] impediens *Ha Z*   **541** hinc]
hec *H GI* hic *Go R Ha* hoc *Vd*; alias] alas *Be^{pc} K La* alios *O* inde *D* cauda *ZXQY fc* seuos
MuGoFr; dispergit] disperget *CWO* disperdit *Fr* dispargit *Pm*   **542** seque] sepe *Xcorr.*
X² sed que *Fr*   **543–4** *transp. after 546 all MSS*   **543** miseram nudamque]
nudam miseramque *D ZXQ* unda miseramque *Y*   **545** haec¹] hic *GI* hoc *M*; abit] ait
Va abiit *Be W* habiit *Vd*; illa¹] ista *X* ille *VaPm Ha*; uolat] uolant α *SVaVbVcVdBePmNe*
AJWHuMNPKVe TrHaLa XQY; haec²] hic *VdBe?Pm RVe GI Ha*; comitatur] comitantur α
SVaVbVcBePmNe AJCWRHuMNOPDK La XY cominatur /uel comitatur *Ha* comutatur
Fr; illa²] illi δ *X* ille *VaPm*   **546** stimulos acuunt] stimulant mordent δ *Tr ZXQY fc*;
urget] *om. S* urgent *QY* uergit *GI* uiget *CWR* sternit γ- *TrHaLa*   **547** se lugubris et
amens] nescia lugubris amens α se lugubris sed et amens *OVe* se lugubris et amens se *J* se
furibunda bicornis *ZXQY fc*

SPECVLVM STVLTORVM 67

gadfly, tormentor of cattle, flies up, and also the dirty fly, sharp of tooth. Over ridges, over hills, through all the byways of the neighbourhood, all the cattle stream forth from their unlocked byres. [530] The vicious gadfly settles on the herd with its sting; the wasps are there too, an unmitigated pest. The shepherds hasten with their flocks, wandering aimlessly through groves and woods, with quickened pace. All the cattle are scorched, the animals sweat, [535] the herd is scattered everywhere, the flocks are dispersed. Bicornis follows Brunetta, fleeing like her, and hastens her steps the more vigorously in that she is the more vulnerable. Brunetta, who still has her tail, resists the flies vigorously, often giving as good as she got. [540] She whisks away the wasps on one side, gets rid of the gadflies on the other, and scatters the flies, protecting herself from them. At length a specially aggressive swarm approaches the naked and wretched Bicornis in a multitudinous cloud. She moves away, it flies after, she flees, it goes with her; [545] they sharpen their stings, while she quickens her pace. What could the wretch do? Where might she turn, doleful and demented, left exposed

---

533 *saltibus et siluis*: cf. Vergil, *Georgics*, iii. 40 and *Aeneid*, iv. 72.

538 The number of variants testifies to the scribal difficulty with the first half of this line. Sedgwick's proposed emendation, 'quae, quo tuta minus...' ('who, in that she was less protected...'), is an elegant solution to the difficulty ('Textual criticism', p. 292). *tuta minus*: 'less safe', 'vulnerable'. See n. to line 2.

543–4 These lines are placed after 546 in all manuscripts. See Introduction, p. lxxx.

544 *turba proterua*: Ovid, *Heroides*, v. 136.

545 *illa uolat*: Ovid, *Heroides*, vi. 66. *comitatur*: see Introduction, n. 246.

547–8 *lugubris et amens*: Ovid, *Metamorphoses*, ii. 334.

68   SPECVLVM STVLTORVM

Quod potuit fecit: licuit dum currere, cursu
550   certauit celeri praecipitique pede.
Praeuenit ala pedem, uincitque uolans gradientem;
    plus pede currentis penna uolantis habet.
Arma gerunt pacem, qui pugnaturus inermis
    aduenit ex facili succubuisse potest.
555 Conueniunt muscae, uespes glomerantur in unum,
    toruus oester adest, cuspide, dente nocens.
Praecipiti cursu terras dilapsa per omnes,
    donec deficeret, institit ipsa pedes.
Nec minus egit eam caudae pudor ille retrorsum
560   quam stimuli quibus est obsita tota simul.
Ergo resupina tandem sub colle iugoso
    corruit in terram praecipitata tamen.
Cumque foret morti iam iam uicina, resumptis
    uiribus, ad modicum extulit illa caput,
565 aspiciensque prope comites de morte gementes
    Brunettamque suam, talia dixit eis.'

Planctus Bicornis

'"Quam grauis ista dies, quam sit memoranda modernis
    casibus ex nostris discere quisque potest.
Nec mihi mors grauis est, quoniam, si uita superstes
570   esset, adhuc grauior haec mihi morte foret.
Dulce mori miseris, mors est mihi mite leuamen,
    morte nihil miseris mitius esse potest.

---

549 dum currere] discurrere α *K Y*ac decurrere *H VdBePkNe HuMND GI TrLa XQY*pc
fc deterrere *Z*; cursu] cursum *Mu CD Ha*   550 *fc* excerpt *1* ends here; celeri] crebro
CWHuMNODK ZXQY cerebro *AJRPVe*; praecipitique] precipiteque *JCWMNOVe Tr* pre-
cipitque *Q* precipueque *P* preciperique *Go*   551 uincitque] uincensque *Go* uincit *T*
La   552 penna] ala γ *HaLa* alam *Tr*   553 inermis] in armis
ZY   554 potest] solet *D ZXQY*   557 praecipiti] precipita *ACWHuMNPVe*
precipito *B R* precipit *Q*; terras] terra *CW* certas *Go*   559 nec] non *GI* nunc *T*; egit]
eget *Fr La* egeret *Ne*; ille] illa *Vc* iste *Fr HuMND X*; retrorsum] retrosum *Vd* retorsum *Pk*
Ve recursum *Go* rerecorsum /uel retrorsum *La*   560 est] *om. VbT*; obsita] consita
*W*ac*HuMNDK QY* obsta *Va*   561 *om. Vc*; colle] collo *F*ac *CWR Ha* calle *Va Q*; iugoso]
uigoso *M* nigoso *L* rugoso *VdTBe CWO TrLa Z*   564 extulit] sustulit α
γ+   565 comites] socios *D X* comitem *F*; morte] more *LE* prope γ *Ha*   566 eis]
ei *F Va*   567 sit memoranda] sic moderanda /uel sit moderata *La*; memoranda]
metuenda *R* modeanda *TGo* moderanda *PkFr*   569 quoniam] ?quod *Vd* quam *CW Ha*
nam et *Vc* cui *Be La*   570 haec] hac α β *SMuVaVbVcVdTBePkFrPmNe TrHaLa QY*
ac *GI* hic *K* hoc *Z om. Go*   571–2 mors est—nihil miseris] *om. Va*   571 mihi]
his *X om. Fr D*   572 *om. Fr*

SPECVLVM STVLTORVM

to such great evils? She did what she could; while it was possible to flee, she fought back with a swift course and a nimble foot. [550] The wing outstrips the foot, and what flies beats what walks; the wing of the flying creature is worth more than the foot of the runner. Arms ensure peace; the one who comes unarmed to a battle can easily be overcome. The flies come together, the wasps form a swarm; [555] the fierce gad-fly is there, wounding with its sting and tooth. She concentrated on running, fleeing with a rapid course through the whole countryside until she collapsed. And the shame of her tail at her rear drove her on as much as the stings with which at the same time she was assailed all over. [560] So, at last, she fell from a hilly ridge and tumbled to earth, lying on her back. And as she was at the very door of death, she gathered her strength and raised her head a little. Seeing nearby her companions mourning her death, [565] and her Brunetta, she spoke to them as follows:'

The Lament of Bicornis

'"How woeful is this day, how much it is to be remembered by posterity, anyone can learn from my fate. Nor is death grievous to me, since, if life were to survive, this would be even harder to me than death. [570] To wretches death is sweet; death is a kind relief to me; nothing can be kinder than death to the wretched. Death is no burden, but

---

564 *extulit illa caput*: Ovid, *Metamorphoses*, x. 419.
571 *Dulce mori miseris*: Maximian, *Elegies*, i. 115. *mite leuamen*: Ovid, *Heroides*, iii. 62.

70 SPECVLVM STVLTORVM

Non est mors oneri, sed plus conducit honori,
cum mors est talis quod cauet illa malis.

575 Mors inuita dabit requiem quam uita negauit;
nil mihi morte perit, sed releuamen erit.
Exemplum multis uixi, moriorque futurum
omnibus exemplum, non habitura modum.""

Confessio Bicornis

'"Discite quam prope sit et quam uicina ruinae
580 gloria discreta quae ratione caret.
Impetus euertit quicquid fortuna ministrat
prospera, nil stabile cui dedit ille statum.
Discite quam nihil est quicquid peritura uoluptas
possidet et falso praedicat esse suum.
585 Nil proprium natura dedit, communia quaeque
instituit fieri, quo meliora forent.
Discite quae nostrae fuerint discrimina caudae,
quodque necis causam contulit illa mihi."
Plura loqui uoluit, sed lingua deficiente
590 uix tantum potuit dicere "Bruna, uale!"
Pastores igitur, ne fama periret in aeuum,
signarunt tali grammate busta loci:'

Epitaphium Bicornis

'"Quae dum stulta fuit doctos docuisse probatur,
haec postquam sapuit uermibus esca datur.""'

---

573 conducit] conducet *D X*   574 cauet] caret *Vc Z* uenit *R*; illa] ipsa *T δ X* ista *Go*   575 negauit] negabit α β *MuVaVcGoFrPmNe GI* negat *Vd*   576 *om. H*; perit] *om. M* graue *X*; releuamen] reuelamen *Fr*   577 multis uixi] uixi multis α *H GI La* multis uix *Ve*; moriorque] moriarque α maiusque *Vc*; futurum] futuris *Va* futurus *Vc O*   578 exemplum] exemplis *H*   579 ruinae] ruina *Vc D La*   580 discreta] mundana δ *TrLa ZXY fb* mundata *Q*   582 prospera] prospere *Ne Ha*; dedit ille] dedit illa *F VcT ROPDKVe I Tr ZX*   583–4 *om. H*   583 discite] dicite *M Q*   584 *om. Vc*; falso] false *T R ZXQ*   585–6 *om. QY*   585 quaeque] queque ministrat *Be Tr*   586 quo] que *Vc D Tr X*; forent] foret *Fr X*   587 discite] dicite *QY*; nostrae] mee *MuGoPm* me *Va* uite *Fr*   588 causam] cause α(*F*ᵃᶜ) caudam *Go*   590 tantum] tamen *E H D GI Ha* tandem *Vc*; potuit dicere] hec potuit dicere *GI* dicere potuit *Go* uoluit dicere *Pk*   591 igitur] ergo *VdBePm*ᵃᶜ *TrLa*   592 signarunt] signarent *VdBe TrLa*; loci] loqui *RM Tr*   594 *P is out (rejoins at 667)*; *see line 55*   haec] hoc *M GI* hic *LE SVdGoBeNe*

SPECVLVM STVLTORVM

rather a benefit, since death is of a nature to keep us from harm. Death, despite itself, will bestow the rest that life denied. [575] I lose nothing by death; rather it will be a relief. I have been an example to many in my life, and in my death there shall be no end to my role as a future example to all." '

The Confession of Bicornis

' "Learn, how close and near to ruin is glory which is devoid of prudent wisdom. [580] Rashness overturns whatever favourable fortune affords, allowing it no stability. Learn that whatever transient pleasure has in its grasp, and falsely claims as its own, is nothing. Nature gave nothing as an individual possession; she ordained all things in common, [585] so they would be the better for it. Learn what were the perils of my tail, and that it has conferred on me the cause of my death." She wanted to say more, but her tongue faltered and she could with difficulty say only "Bruna, farewell!" [590] So the shepherds, lest her fame perish for ever, carved a tomb on the spot with this inscription:'

Bicornis's Epitaph

' "While she was foolish, she is proven to have taught the wise; but having acquired wisdom, she is given as food to worms." '

573–4 Cf. Publilius Syrus, *Sententiae*, 67: 'Bona mors est homini vitae quae exstinguit mala'.

577 Mozley prints 'futuris', which is found only in *Va*; the overwhelming manuscript evidence is in favour of 'futurum' (modifying 'exemplum').

578 *non habitura modum*: also in *Miracles*, 340.

583–6 The allusion is to the idea that according to natural law, which medieval thinkers considered to be prior to positive or customary law both in time and in importance, God originally created all things for men in common; private property is the creation of positive law, and is a response to man's sin—to the cupidity and avarice that would destroy the fabric of society if there were no distinction of mine and thine. The principle was incorporated into canon law: the summarizing heading of Gratian, *Decretum*, D. 8 c. 1, ed. Friedberg, i. 12–13, is as follows: 'Iure divino omnia sunt communia omnibus; iure vero constitutionis hoc meum, illud alterius est.' Gratian then quotes in support Augustine, *In Iohannis Evangelium Tractatus CXXIV*, tract. vi. 25 (ed. Willems, CCSL xxxvi. 66). For other patristic views on this subject, see Langholm, *Economics in the Medieval Schools*, pp. 71, 74–6.

589–90 Cf. Ovid, *Amores*, ii. 6. 48: 'clamavit moriens lingua: "Corinna, vale." '

SPECVLVM STVLTORVM

Reductio Galieni

595 'Haec igitur, Burnelle, tibi quae uidimus ipsi
diximus, exemplis ut docearis ab his.
Sufficiat quod habes, quoniam, si uera fatemur,
stulta petis, saluo semper honore tuo.
Nec tamen id fieri quouis medicamine posse
600 credideris; nihil est; stulte, redito domum.
Si quot habent medici spatiosi climata mundi
haec tibi iurassent, nil nisi uerba forent.
Non tamen id renuo quin possit crescere multum
haec tua cauda tibi, sed noua nulla dari.
605 Fracta uel elisa medicorum cura reformat,
funditus abscisa sic remanere solent.
Mortua cum uiuis nulla ratione cohaerent,
caesa nec abscisa cura iuuare potest.
Vnde satis longa poterit tua crescere cauda,
610 dummodo cum reliqua foedera carne tenet.
Et tamen in curis et sumptibus enumerandis,
ut decet et debet, copia larga subest.
Ardua praegnantem poscunt medicamina bursam,
res et opes magnas uulnera magna uolunt.'

---

595 haec] hic *L* hoc *G* nec *Vb*; igitur] ergo *MuVaVdGoBeFrPm JVe TrLa X* ego *T* modo *R* tibi *E*; Burnelle] brune *S*; tibi quae] tibi que nos *R* iam que nos *E* tibi quod *O* tibi qui *Z* tibi modo que *Tr* que modo *S* modo que γ- *HaLa*; ipsi] ipse *B Q*   596 exemplis] exemplum *Go GI* exemplis plus *Fr*; docearis] doceatis *Vb* mouearis *K* doceris *Va*   599 id] illud *HuMN* ad *Fr* hoc *T*; medicamine] modicamine *Fr D*   600 *line repeated in alternative form* $Z_{(1)}Z_{(2)}$; credideris] crederis *D* credidis *CW*; nihil] mihi *L Vc I*; est] *om. Vc I* $Z_{(2)}$; stulte redito domum] stultus es ito domum *L G* stultius ito domum *E* es stultus ito domum *I* stultus ito domum *F* stultus adesto domi *H* stultus es esto domi *B* tutius ire domum *AJCWRHuMNDKVe* $Z_{(1)}XQY$ totius ire domum *O*; stulte redito] stulte redito /[uel] tutius ire *La*; recito] redite *Vd* redire *Fr*; domum] domi *Tr*   601 *line repeated in alternative form* $Z_{(1)}Z_{(2)}$; quot] quod *SVdFr O Tr* $Z_{(2)}$ quid *MuVaVbVcTGoPkPmNe HaLa*; spatiosi] spatiora *D* spatiosa *Vd MO* $Z_{(2)}$ spatioso *VcFr Ha* speciosi *T*; climata] climate *MuVaVbVcVdTPkFrPmNe HaLa* cliate *Go*; *(whole line)* si cuncti medici mundi necnon sapientes $Z_{(1)}XQY$ 602 haec] hoc *VcVd GI* hic *Ne* hii *Be* et *Tr* nec *Z*; iurassent] nil essent *MuVaVbVdTGoBePkFrPmNe Ha* nil esset *Vc* narrassent *Ve*   603 id] hoc *GI* illud *Vd*; renuo] dico *VbVc R*; possit] posset α *MuVcTFrPm R Tr*   607 uiuis] minus *Be* uiuus /uel uiuis *La*   608 nec] sed non *H* uel γ+ *RD Z*; iuuare] iurare *M*; potest] nequit γ+ *Z*   609 unde satis] ut satis *Pm* dum satis est *QY*; poterit] possit *Go* poteris *Pm*   610 dummodo cum] dummodo non *Y* si tamen in γ+ ut dum *Z*; carne] cauda *GI*   611 *om. VaVc*; et¹] en *AJCWRHuNOKVe* si α β *SMuVbVdTGoBePkFrPmNe GI HaLa ZQY* sed *D Tr X*

SPECVLVM STVLTORVM

Galen's Conclusion

'These things, which I saw with my own eyes, [595] I have told you, Burnellus, so that you may learn from these examples. Let what you have be sufficient, for, to tell the truth, and with all respect to you, you are hankering after foolishness. Nor should you think it can be done by any kind of medicine. It is nothing—go back home, you fool! [600] If as many doctors as the corners of the wide world contain had sworn to do it, it would be nothing but words. Yet I do not deny that your present tail could grow a lot, I only deny that a new one could be bestowed. A doctor's care can repair what is broken or crushed, [605] but what is completely amputated stays that way. Dead things do not rightly bond with living ones; medicine cannot do anything for things cut off or amputated. So your tail could grow very long, so long as it retained its link to the rest of your body. [610] And yet in reckoning up the cures and their costs, as is right and proper, a large sum of money is involved. Complicated medicines demand a bulging purse, and serious wounds require great wealth and substance.'

Heading before 595: *Reductio*: 'Summary, epitome' (*DMLBS* 3).

595 *Burnelle*: 'Burnellus', meaning 'Brownie', is a typical name for an ass (like 'Fido' for a dog). It was used in popular philosophy to refer to a representative individual ass rather than the asinine genus (as 'Socrates' was used for a man). See Strecker, 'Henricus Septimellensis', pp. 119–20, and Abelard, *Dialectica*, ed. de Rijk, Tract. iii, p. 347. The name therefore became a popular synonym for 'asellus' in contemporary parlance; see Werner, *Sprichwörter*, p. 40, I 45 ('In glacie ludit brunellus, quem deus odit'); Henry of Settimello, *Elegia*, ii. 238, and *Carmina Burana*, no. vi. 18, 'brunelli chordas incitant', part of a description of a topsy-turvy world, as one sign of which asses play the lyre (with reference to the topos of 'asinus ad lyram'). For a summary of various examples of the name, see also Waltenberger, '*Socrates Burnelllus est*', pp. 87–9 and nn. 27–35.

600 *stulte redito domum*: the manuscript variants converge on this as the reading most likely to underlie the majority of them, with 'stulte' misread as 'stultus' (final -e taken as an abbreviation for -us?) and various subsequent attempts to repair the damage to grammar and metre (stultus es, stultius, es stultus, stultus adesto, etc.)

74   *SPECVLVM STVLTORVM*

Consilium Galieni ironice

615 'Nonne tibi satis est, unam si creuerit ulnam
      longior ex tanto quam fuit ante tibi?'
      Talibus auditis modicum subrisit asellus,
      sic tamen audirent quod fora tota sonum.
      Cui Galienus ait: 'Festinans perge Salernum,
620   inde relaturus cura quod ista petit.
      Perge redique celer, nocuit differre paratis;
      quatuor his quintum si potes adde pedem.
      Sumptibus ergo tibi nisi tu defeceris ipse,
      non tibi deficiet cura laborque meus.
625   Sumptibus insistas, nos artibus experiemur,
      si ualeant nostrae quod ualuere manus.
      Accelerans igitur, usus duplomate, longum
      abbreuiabis iter, nam uia longa nimis.
      Pluribus es notus necnon dilectus amicis,
630   qui tibi subuenient magnaque dona dabunt.
      Forsitan ex facili poterunt species reperiri,
      nec tamen ex facili credimus illa legi.
      Vasa sed et tecum portabis idonea multa,
      in quibus et referas hic habitura locum.
635   Cura laborque simul solet exactissimus esse,
      ne male depereant lecta locare bene.
      Cuncta locata bene uasisque recondita dignis
      tractari poterunt tutius atque geri.
      Mentis hebes quamuis non sis, in pelle notabis

---

615 unam si] si unam *VdBe*; creuerit] creuit *X* crederit *M* tenuerit *Vb*   618–81 *om.*
Va   618 sic] si *Vd Ha* sic ut *Go*; quod] ut *DK XQY* per *Go*   619 Salernum]
solernum *Vb*   621 *line repeated in alternative form* $Z_{(1)}Z_{(2)}$; nocuit differre paratis]
noli tardare pedester *AJCWRHuMNODKVe La* $Z_{(1)}XQY$ nocuit differre rumper *Go*
623–4 *om. Ha*   624–5 *om. Q*   624 deficiet] deficient *Vc R* deficiat *T*
625 nos] non *Vd*; artibus] actibus *Fr*   626 *om. Z*   ualeant] ualeat *AJCHuMNKVe*
Y; ualuere] soluere *X* uoluere *VbVcGoPkFrPmNe D Ha*   627 igitur usus duplomate]
ergo usum renuens tibi *X* igitur usus diplomate β *O GI*   629 es] est *MuBe CWD* et *Fr*;
dilectus] dilectis *Fr D*; amicis] amicus *MuVc K Tr*   630 subuenient] subueniunt *R La*
subueniant *T Q* subueniat *Mu*   631–2 poterunt—ex facili] *om. Ne*   631 poter-
unt] poterit *H* poteris *Vc* poterant *Go Tr* potuerunt *Vd* poterint *Fr* potuit *Ha*   633 tecum]
tectum *CWMN*[ac] totum *D*   634 *line repeated in alternative form* $Z_{(1)}Z_{(2)}$; referas] referes *AJCWRHuMNOKVe La X* referet *D*; hic] hec *MuTGoFrPm Ha X* huc *Y* hinc $Z_{(2)}$;
habitura locum] labitura locum *Vc* nominanda tibi $Z_{(2)}XQ$ 636 depereant] deperiant
VcFr dispereant *K*; locare] locata *ZX* locate *R* letare *GoPkPmNe* letare / uel locare *Ha*; bene]
male *ZQY*   637 locata] locare *GI* locuta *Go*; dignis] digne *Vb* $G^{ac}I$

SPECVLVM STVLTORVM

Galen's Ironical Advice

'Is it not enough for you if it grows an ell [615] longer than it was before?' When he heard this, the ass smiled a little, so that the whole town heard the sound.

Galen said to him: 'Hurry off to Salerno, to fetch from there what this treatment requires. [620] Go and come back quickly; to those who are ready, delay is harmful. If you can, add a fifth leg to these four! If you do not fall short in your outlay, my skill and effort will not fail you. If you take care of the outlay, I shall find out through my skills [625] what my powers are worth—if they have any worth. So, making haste, and travelling by night and day, you will shorten the whole journey, for the road is very long. You are known and loved by many friends, who will help you and give you substantial gifts. [630] Perhaps these medicines will easily be found, but I don't think they will be easily assembled. But you must also carry with you a lot of suitable containers, in which you are to bring these things back, so they may be stored here. You should exercise the most scrupulous care and effort [635] to put the things in a safe place once they are collected, lest they are destroyed. When they are all safely placed and stowed in suitable containers, they can be handled and carried more safely. Although you are not stupid, you must note down on parchment (since you know how to write) what medicine is needed.

617 *Talibus auditis*: a very frequent opening for a hexameter, both in Nigel and in other medieval poetry; see *Lateinisches Hexameter-Lexikon*, v. 347.

619 Salerno was a famous centre of medical teaching in the Middle Ages, although it seems that it did not formally become a university until the 13th c. See Kristeller, 'The school of Salerno', and cf. Geoffrey of Vinsauf, *Poetria nova*, 1008–12: 'In morbis sanat medica virtute Salernum/ Aegros. In causis Bononia legibus armat/ Nudos; Parisius in artibus illos/ Panes, unde cibat robustos. Aurelianis/ Educat in cunis auctorum lacte tenellos.'

621 *Perge redique celer*: also at *Miracles*, 532. *nocuit differre paratis*: Lucan, *De bello civili*, i. 281; used as an 'auctoritas' by Walter of Châtillon, *Poems*, no. xlii. 14. 4, and no. xliii. 14. 4. The δ variant ('noli tardare pedester') is clearly a *facilior lectio*, and in addition the αβγ variant has wider support. For discussion, see Introduction, p. cxxii.

624 *cura laborque*: a poetic cliché (cf. lines 635, 642, 1542), found in Lucan, *De bello civili*, ix. 621; Martial, *Epigrammata*, v. 21. 4, v. 24. 10; Petrus Pictor, *Carmina*, ed. van Acker, x. 5; John of Hauville, *Architrenius*, ed. Wetherbee, v. 483, and numerous less well-known Latin poets.

626 *ualuere manus*: Ovid, *Heroides*, viii. 6.

627 *duplomate*: a 'duploma' (also spelled 'diploma') was an official document (also known as 'evectio' and 'tratatoria') issued by a public authority, licensing the holder to travel on, and use the amenities of, the public roads, which were not otherwise open to general use. The system, known as the 'cursus publicus', goes back to Roman times; it is succinctly described by Jones, *The Later Roman Empire*, ii. 830–4. See Forcellini, s.vv. 'diploma' and 'evectio' 2, and Du Cange, s.v. 'duploma'. The phrase 'utens/usus duplomate' thus acquired the secondary meaning 'with all speed, at the double, post-haste' (referring to the advantages of extra speed afforded by the diploma), and also 'travelling by night and day', and so 'doubling' one's journey; see Justinian, *Digest* 45. 1. 137. 2, 'diplomate diebus ac noctibus…iter continuare',

76 SPECVLVM STVLTORVM

640   (scribere nam nosti) qua specie sit opus.
    Haec sunt quae referes uariis signata sigillis,
       ne pereant obiter cura laborque tuus:
    marmoris aruinam, furni septemplicis umbram,
       quod peperit mulo mula subacta suo;
645   anseris et milui modicum de lacte recenti,
       de lincis cursu, deque timore lupi;
    de canis et leporis septenni foedere drachmam;
       oscula quae niso misit alauda suo;
    pauonis propria libram de uoce sonora,
650   ante tamen cauda quam sit adepta sibi;
    de non contexta rubra sine stamine mappa,
       nam risus asini tu dabis ipse tibi;
    allecis uel apum croceo de spermate libram,
       de ciroli iecore, sanguine, siue pede;
655   Natalis Domini modicum de nocte salubri,
       quae nimis est longa iure ualebit ad hoc.
    In reditu, de Monte Iouis de uertice summo
       accipies libras quatuor asse minus.
    Alpibus in mediis Sancti de nocte Iohannis,
660   de niue quae cecidit fac simul inde feras;

---

640 scribere] scribe *Pm Ha*; nam] namque *VcNe* qua *Ha*; nosti] nosci *BeNe*   **642** obiter] obitus *H* ob iter *F* obicit *B AJCWRHuMNOVe* instent *K* subito *SMuVbVcVdTGoBePkFrPmNe TrHaLa* cures *D ZQY* om. *X*   **643** aruinam] aruina *L Mu D*   **644** quod] que *SVbVcVdBeNe TrHaLa* qui *Pk*; suo] sua *D* suis *G* **646** *om. Z*; lincis] linxis *D X* lucis β *SVbBePk AJCWHuMNO GI La* liceris *K* luteris *Ve* lune *L*   **647** *line repeated in alternative form Z*(1) *Z*(2); septenni] septennis *MuVbVdBePkFrPmNe TrHaLa*[ac] septem *Vc* sepius *Go* septenum *QY* septimum *Z*(1) septimam *Z*(2); foedere drachmam] federe dragma *T Z*(2) federa dragmam *G* pondus amore *QY* pondus amare *Z*(1)   **649** libram] misit *M* liberam *ZQY*; uoce] uocis *Y* nocte *Go D*   **650** sit] *om. M Z*; adepta] adempta β *SMuVbVcVdBePkPm ACWHuMNOK TrLa X* uel adulta *add. in margin X*[pc] adulta α; sibi] tibi *H Mu GI Z*   **651** stamine] flamine *AJMNO QY* stagmine *SPkPmNe* sagmine *Ha* stramine *Be I* sanguine *GoFr*   **653** allecis] alectis *BePk La*; apum] copri *Vc* aptum *Z* opum *Q*   **654** ciroli] crioli *Fr* cirobi *Ve* silicis *D Tr X* cirole *MN* ceruuli *Ne* aroli *Q*; siue] sine *Vb JW*   **656** *om. Q*; ad hoc] ad hec *H MuVbVcFrPmNe JMNK Ha* ei *Tr*   **658** accipies] accipias *H MuVcVdTGoFr RK GI HaLa ZQY*; asse] esse *Vd ZQ*; minus] nimis *Be corr. Be*[pc] *M Q*   **659** alpibus] apibus *HuMN* alphibus *Z*   **660** quae] qui *Pm D Ha* quod *B Z* quo *W*; fac] tu *AJCWRHuMNODKVe GI X* tu fac *La*; feras] feres α

SPECVLVM STVLTORVM   77

[640] These are what you should bring back, sealed with diverse seals, so that your care and effort are not wiped out on the journey. The fat from some marble, the shade from a sevenfold oven, the offspring of a female mule mated with a male one, a little fresh milk from a goose and a kite, [645] some of the speed of a lynx, and of a wolf's fear, a dram of a seven-year truce between a dog and a hare, the kisses which a lark sent to her sparrowhawk friend; a pound of the peacock's piercing voice, but before he has got himself a tail; [650] some of a red unwoven cloth without a warp; an ass's laugh you will, of course, provide yourself; a pound of yellow sperm from a herring or a bee; some of a mite's liver, blood, or foot; a little of holy Christmas night [655] (since it's very long, there will be enough for the purpose). In your return, you'll take four pounds, minus an ounce, from the top of the Great St Bernard Pass. Bring back from thence a little of the snow that fell in the Alps on midsummer eve. [660] The tail of a red snake

also quoted in Forcellini, s.v. 'diploma'. See also, in *DMLBS* s.v. 'diploma', the quotation from a gloss on this passage of the *Digest* in the *Liber pauperum* of Vacarius (on Vacarius, and his connection with Canterbury, see n. to line 1201): 'duploma dicitur tempus duplicatum, cum quis faciat de duobus [?duabus] dietis unam' (ed. de Zulueta, p. 268). See also John of Salisbury, *Entheticus minor*, ed. van Laarhoven, 143–4: 'Accelera gressus, cauto duplomate pergens/ ad mare, quo Morini [the inhabitants of Flanders] litora nostra petunt', and Peter of Blois, *Epistolae*, no. lii (PL ccvii. 159B): 'Dominus rex in Gasconiam tendit, ego autem diplomate utens eum e uestigio sequor.' At this point in PL ccvii, a note by Pierre de Goussainville, the 17th-c. editor of Peter of Blois's letters, glosses 'duploma' as 'duplum iter, seu itineris festinatio' and adds similar quotations from Peter of Blois, *Epistolae*, no. lix (PL ccvii. 175B), and also from Ralph de Diceto, *Ymagines historiarum*, under the years 1172 (i. 351), 1179 (i. 433), and 1184 (ii. 23–4); see also under the year 1191 (ii. 97): 'Quod audiens Lundoniensis episcopus, utens fere duplomate, cum festinatione qua potuit uenit ad cancellarium.' A gloss in Bodley 496 (MS *H*) agrees with this generalized interpretation: 'Diploma id est 2 x locucio'. My translation opts for the more specific 'travelling by night and day' because other manuscripts of *SS* gloss 'utens duplomate' in this line 'id est continuacio diei et noctis' (*Go Ha*), or 'i.e. diei et noctis' (*Pm*).

643–62 For other parodic recipes, see Lehmann, *Parodie*, pp. 68, 172, 177, 253.

643 *furni septemplicis*: cf. Dan. 3: 19: 'Et precepit ut succenderetur fornax septuplum quam succendi consueverat.'

646 *lincis*: has cross-group support, and fits the context better than 'lucis', since lines 645–50 all refer to animals. The comment in Mozley's *apparatus criticus* ('uolucris, piscis, conj. Skutsch') is unintelligible, since there is no mention of this line in Skutsch's 'Three rare words'.

651 *rubra...mappa*: Juvenal, *Saturae*, v. 27.

654 *ciroli*: 'cirolus' = 'a mite'. A rare word; see *DMLBS* s.v., referring to Migliorini, '*Cirolus*'.

657 *Monte Iouis*: the Great St Bernard Pass. Its name was derived from the temple erected on the pass by the Romans, which was still in use in the Middle Ages. It was one of the main routes used by pilgrims passing between Italy and northern Europe. See Tyler, *The Alpine Passes*, pp. 68–72; Parks, *English Traveller*, p. 188. John, one of the Canterbury monks who travelled to the papal curia in 1188 (see Introduction, p. xlv), described in a letter to the convent at home the terrifying experience of travel over the Mons Iouis (*Epistolae Cantuarienses*, no. cxcvii).

659 *Sancti de nocte Iohannis*: Midsummer Day, 24 June, the nativity of St John the Baptist.

SPECVLVM STVLTORVM

serpentisque rubrae necnon et cauda colubrae
utilis est ualde, nec tamen illud eme.
Haec bene collecta sed et ista recentia quaeque
impones humeris sarcinulisque tuis.'

665 Talia dicenti supplex respondit asellus,
poplite deflexo uertice pronus humi:
'Cuncta libens faciam, celer ibo celerque reuertar,
nam mea res agitur, non aliena mihi.
Non ero tardus ad hoc, quamuis piger esse solebam,
670 si dederit Dominus prospera fata mihi.
En ego progredior, benedic mihi progredienti,
ut mihi sit tota prospera, uita, uia!'
Mox idioma suum uertens Galienus et orans
subridensque parum sic benedixit ei.

Benedictio Galieni data Burnello

675 'Omnipotens odia tibi mille det et tua cauda
obtineat per se milia dena sibi!
Sit tibi potus aqua! Sit magnus carduus esca,
marmora stramenta, tegmina ros et aqua!
Grando, niues, pluuiae tecum comitentur ubique,
680 protegat et noctu cana pruina gelu!
Saepius exosus ueniat post terga molossus!'

---

661 rubrae] rubri *SMuVbVcVdTGoBePkFrPmNe D TrHaLa ZXQ* rubi *K*; et] tibi
HuMN de *R Q*; colubrae] colubri *MuVbVcTGoFrPm*pc*Ne RDK HaLa ZXQY* colubris
*SVdBePkPm*ac *Tr* salubre *L*ac   **662** illud] istud α   **663** haec] hoc *I* et *T*; collecta]
collata *H GI*; sed et ista] sed ista *LE* sed et ipsa *MuVbVdTGoBePkFrPmNe TrHaLa Z*
pariter *AJHuMNDVe QY* pariterque *CWROK X*; recentia] recensia *CHuMN* retencia
BeNe   **664** impones] imponas *Ve* imponis *BePk La*   **666** poplite] pollice *Y*
publice *Go ZQ*; deflexo] defixo *SMuVbVdGoBePkFrPmNe TrLa* deuictio *Z*; humi] humo
α   **667** *P rejoins*   **669–70** *om. Ve*   **669** ero] ego *LE B S AJMND GI XQY*
om. T; ad hoc] ad hec *H VbBeFrPmNe JHuMN Ha X* adhuc *Mu om. Vc Z*   **670** fata]
facta *Pm. La*ac *Z* cuncta *AJCWRHuMNOPDK X*   **671** en] si *Ne D Q* cum
Vd   **672** sit] sint *F Mu*; tota] pariter α; uia] uiat *E* uia / uel mea *La*   **673–4** suum
uertens—subridens] *om. Vd*   **673** et orans] adorans *T ZQY*   **675** et] *om.*
T   **676** *om. H add. in marg.* *H²*; dena] dona *DVe La*; sibi] tibi *Tr Q*   **677** carduus]
cardinus *T AM* cardinis *MuPmNe RVe Tr Y* carduus /[uel] cardinis *La*   **678** *om. J*;
ros] mos *M* rus *Fr* res [uel] ros *La*   **679** pluuiae tecum] puluis te *SMuVcTGoFrPmNe*
puluis tecum *VbPk Ha* puluis te nunc *VdBe Tr*; pluuiae] puluis / uel pluuie *La*; comitentur]
comitetu̶r *Fr* concomitatur *Mu* concomitentur *Go* commutatur *Vd*   **680** protegat]
protogat *Q* proroget *VbVcT Ha Z* progat *Vd* prorogat *BePkFrPm*ac; noctu cana] nocui canina
MN noctu canina *Vd Tr* noctu canna *T* noctem cana *Z* noceat cana *H* cauta cana *Pk*

SPECVLVM STVLTORVM
79

and of a serpent is very useful, but don't buy it. When all these have been gathered together—all of them fresh—you should load them on your back in your bags.'

To this speech the ass replied with a supplication, [665] with bended knee and head bent down to the earth: 'I'll happily do it all; I'll go and come back quickly, for it is my business that is in question, not someone else's. Although I used to be lazy, I won't be slow about this, if the Lord grants me good fortune. [670] Off I go! Bless me as I set out, so that the road and my life may be fortunate!' Galen, switching into Latin for the prayer, and smiling a little, gave him this blessing:

The Blessing that Galen Gave Burnellus

'May the Almighty grant you a thousand enmities [675] and may your tail win tens of thousands for itself! May your drink be water, a giant thistle your food! May your bed be marble, and dew and rain your coverings! May hail, snow, and rain go with you everywhere, and may the white hoar-frost protect you from the cold at night! [680] May the hated cur be often at your heels!' Kissing him, the ass said 'Amen!' The

---

661–2 On the ancient belief in the medicinal power of snakes, see Pliny, *Natural History*, xxix. 21–2; Dracontius, *De laudibus Dei*, ii. 262–4; and *Satisfactio*, 65–8.

668 *nam mea res agitur*: cf. Horace, *Epistulae*, i. 18. 84 (with 'tua').

673 *idioma... uertens*: Raymo thinks this means that Galen switches from Greek to Latin, but there is no indication that he has previously been speaking Greek, and more probably he was speaking English with the unlettered donkey. In this case, a switch into Latin would have the effect of disguising the true nature of his 'blessing' from the ass.

677–82 These lines read like a parody of the first two of eleven hexameter verses inserted into c. xxv of the *Tractatus novus de penitentia* of William of Auvergne in BnF lat. 8433, which advise the penitent: 'Sit tibi potus aqua, cibus aridus, aspera vestis,/ Dorso virga, brevis somnus durumque cubile' (Hauréau, *Notices et extraits*, i. 374). Hauréau notes the occurrence of these verses in seven other manuscripts (ibid.; see also v. 33), and Walther, *Initia* 18341, records the existence of 30 manuscripts, so the verses must have circulated separately.

680 *protegat*: 'protegere' usually takes 'a/ab' when meaning 'to protect from' (*DMLBS* 6).

80

SPECVLVM STVLTORVM

Oscula dando tamen, dixit asellus, 'Amen!'
Ingeminantis 'Amen' uox est audita per urbem,
murmuriique sonum percipit omne forum.

Qualiter Burnellus profectus est

685 Festinans igitur, ueniens in limine portae
haesit, et eliso corruit ipse pede.
'Signa reuertendi sunt haec,' dixere propinqui;
riserunt alii; dixit et ipse sibi:
'Debile principium melior fortuna sequetur.
690 Restat iter longum, non remanebit ita.
Dura satis didici postquam sum fusus ab aluo,
unde satis possum plurima dura pati.
Non est deliciis assueta uel ebrietati
haec mea persona, quae mala ferre solet.
695 Carduus et lappa constant mihi carior esca,
sufficit ad potum nam pluuialis aqua.
In salsamentis non est meditatio mentis,
in tenui uictu corpora nostra uigent.
Sum piger et tardus, sed certe tardior essem
700 si mea nonnumquam lauta diaeta foret.
Sed neque qui debet sumptus impendere multos
expedit ut crebro uina Falerna bibat.
Quid mihi cum uino? quo desipiunt sapientes,
multaque contingunt quo mediante mala.

---

682 *Va rejoins*; dando] danda *VdFrPm* **683** *om.* *Z*; ingeminantis] ingeminatis *W* ingeminans *GI* ingeminantes *MuVd* ingeminentis *Fr Tr*; urbem] urba *M* orbem *LE* β *SMuVaVbVdGoBePkPmNe RVe GI TrHaLa QY* **684** murmuriique] murmuris atque *SMuVaVbVcTGoPkFrPmNe JO Ha* murmur atque *VdBe* murmur et atque *Tr* mumureumque *R Z* murmuriique [*uel*] murmurii atque *La* **685** igitur] ergo *VcFr*; limine] lumine *VaVd* liminem *Be* lumen? *Go*; portae] forti *GI* **687** reuertendi] reuertenti *Fr ZQY*; dixere] dixisse *ZY* uicina *Q*; propinqui] *sic I²over erasure* parenti *G* **689** debile] flebile *Vc Z*; sequetur] *sic I²* sequatur *H Fr NK G* sequitur *Ve* **690** remanebit] remeabit *OVe* **691** ab] *om.* *M* **693** assueta] consueta *TGo*; ebrietati] ebrietate *VcPk R La ZX* **695** carduus] cardinis *MuVbBeNe HuNVe Y* cardius *Pm* cardinus *T*; constant] constat *D Q fb* sunt hec *SMuVaVbVdTGoPkFrPm TrHaLa* sunt hic *BeNe* **696** nam] sat *SMuVbPk TrHa* satis *VaVcVdGoBeFrPmNe* et *T* modo *La* **700** nonnumquam] quandoque γ *TrHa* quandoque [*uel*] nonnunquam *La*; lauta] lata *SMuVaVbVdTGoBePkPmNe TrHa Z*; foret] forent *Z^{ac}Y* **701** multos] multas *LE* multus *Go* **702** Falerna] salerna *SMuVaVbVcVdTGoBePkPm CWHuMNODVe G TrHaLa XQY fb* silerna *Ne* solerna *Fr P* **703-4** desipiunt sapientes—contingunt quo] *om.* *Mu* **703** desipiunt] despiunt *E* decipiunt *CWHuMN Q*; sapientes] sapientis *CW* **704** contingunt] contingant *L Tr*; quo] hoc β *D GI*

SPECVLVM STVLTORVM

81

utterance of his echoing 'Amen!' was heard throughout the town, and the whole marketplace was filled with the sound of the murmur.

How Burnellus Set Out

As he hurried off, he stopped when he came to the threshold, [685] caught his foot, and stumbled. 'This is a sign that he should turn back', said the bystanders. Others laughed, while he himself said: 'A better fortune will follow a feeble start. The way ahead is long, but it will get shorter. [690] I've been well schooled in hardships since I was born, so that I can well suffer more hardships. My body is not accustomed to delicate food or intoxicating drink, but is used to bear privations. The thistle and the burr are my favourite food; [695] rainwater is good enough for my drink. I do not hanker after fancy sauces; my body thrives on plain food. I am lazy and slow, but I'd be slower for sure if my diet was ever rich. [700] Nor is it a good thing for the man who has to pay a lot of expenses to drink Falernian wine frequently. What have I got to do with wine?—through which the wise grow foolish, and by whose agency many evils befall. My parents were accustomed to carry it on their shoulders, not in their stomach;

---

684 *murmurii*: for 'murmurium' as an alternative form of 'murmur', see Du Cange and *DMLBS*.

685–8 An omen of ill-luck (or less frequently, good luck) according to ancient superstition; see Bächtold-Stäubli s.v. 'Stolpern' (viii. 494–5), and for examples, Augustine, *De doctrina christiana*, ii. XX, line 32 (ed. Martin, CCSL xxxii, p. 55): 'redire domum, si procedens offenderit', and John of Salisbury, *Policraticus*, i. 13 (ed. Webb, i. 55, lines 9–10): 'Si egrediens limen calcaueris, aut in uia offenderis, pedem contine' ('If as you go out you trip on the threshold, or stumble on the road, stop'). Cf. Ovid, *Heroides*, xiii. 87–90, where Protesilaus stumbles on the threshold as he leaves for Troy; his wife Laodamia is dismayed, but prays that this may be an omen of his safe return. There may also be an ironic allusion here to the proverb that says the ass never returns to a place where he once fell (see Singer, *Thesaurus*, s.v. 'Esel' 10. 4 (iii. 72)).

689 Proverbial; see Walther, *Proverbia*, 5210; quoted twice in the *Becket Correspondence*, i. 608 (no. cxxvi), and ii. 1138 (no. cclxiv). The ultimate source is Ovid, *Metamorphoses*, vii. 518 (with 'flebile' instead of 'debile').

691 *fusus ab aluo*: also in *Miracles*, 1365.

697 *salsamentis*: 'salsamentum = 'sauce, condiment, seasoning' (*DMLBS* 2).

703–4 For numerous proverbs warning against the evil effects of drinking wine, see Singer, *Thesaurus*, s.v. 'Wein' 1. 11–16 (xii. 431–7).

703 Cf. *Babio*, 65: 'Quid mihi cum Croceo?' (*Commedie*, ii. 252)

82   *SPECVLVM STVLTORVM*

705   Hoc humeris non uentre suo gestare parentes
        consueuere mei; sit procul ergo merum!
        Ergo gestabo sed non gustabo Lyaeum,
        arripiat ne me cotidiana febris.
        Contra naturam uinum si forte bibissem,
710   mox mihi quartanam gigneret aut scabiem.
        Quatuor ex causis teneor uitare Falernum,
        quamuis sensus hebes exacuatur eo:
        sumptibus ut propriis parcam, ne febre laborem,
        et ne desipiam degeneremque simul.
715   Qui uitare malum poterit nec uult manifestum
        plangendus minus est, si male cedit ei.'

Qualiter Burnellus uenit Salernum

        Postquam bissenas confecerat ergo diaetas,
        ad quae tendebat moenia summa uidet.
        Moxque genu flexo, sursum sua brachia tendens,
720   uota Deo supplex soluit et orat ita:
        'Omnipotens Dominus meritis sancti Iuliani
        det ueniam nobis hospitiumque bonum!
        Sit procul omne malum, pontes, sportaeque gemellae,
        partibus in nostris quae satis esse solent!
725   Rusticus aut saccus non inueniatur in urbe!
        Absque molendino sit locus iste, precor!
        Sint hebetes stimuli surdi mutique molossi,

---

705 hoc] hic *F* hec *L SMu*; suo] suum *CW* sub *Vb*   **707** Lyaeum] lieum *EF B SMuVaVtVcVdTGoBePkPmNe JCWODK GI TrHaLa ZXQ* leeum *L* lienum *APVe* leenum *H* alieum *Fr*   **708–11** *transp. after 728 HuMN*   **708** arripiat] arripiet *Mu* arripit *Fr* surripiat *D X*   **709** uinum si forte] si uinum forte *X* si forte uina *MuVaVbVcVdTGoBePkPmNe TrHaLa* si forsan uina *Fr*   **711** Falernum] phalernum *Tr* ualernum *MuBe* falarnum *H* salernum *VaVbVcVdTPkFrPmNe HaLa* solernum *Go* lyaeum *RN Y* lieum *JCWHuMOK ZXQ fb* lienum *APDVe*   **712** *om. R Z*; exacuatur] exacuetur *α* β(*Hᵖᶜ*) *SMuVaVbVcGoBePkFrPmNe CWHuMN GI Tr* euacuatur *Q*   **713** ut] et *SVbVdPk Laᵃᶜ*   **714** desipiam] desideam *D* deficiam *K* decipiam *M Tr Y* despina *Z*   **715** malum poterit] poterit malum *Be fb*; manifestum] manifeste *α*   **716** plangendus] plangendo *VdBe*; minus] nimis *VaVb*; est] *om. Tr Z*; cedit] cedat *SVbVcVdBePkNe δ TrHaLa X fb* credat *Fⁿᶜ* cedet *ft*   **717** confecerat ergo] confecerit ergo *I* confecerat ipsa *F* conficerat ergo *Z* cum fecerit *Y* cum fecerat *VbVdPk Q* fecerat sudore *X* iam fecerat (facerat *Mu*) ergo *MuVaVcTFrPmNe* nam fecerat ergo *Ha* perfecerat ergo *Tr* iam fert ergo *Go*   **718** ad quae] atque *VaVc ZQY* acque *Vd*; uidet] uidit *T* uidet *Laᵃᶜ* uidit *Laᵖᶜ*   **719** moxque] mox *R Ha*   **720** orat] erat *Fr* ait *D X*   **721** dominus] deus *Mu RVe Y* d<*illegible*>itis *P*   **722–1598** *transp. after 2476 Pm*   **723** pontes] potens *MuVcPm QYXᵃᶜ* pontens *Xᵖᶜ* pestes *Laᵖᶜ*; sportaeque] sponteque *Vd La* porteque δ *QY*   **725** inueniatur] inueniantur *H D X* ueniatur *MuVa*; urbe] orbe *Ve GI*   **727** stimuli] stimuli / uel famuli *La*; mutique] mutuque *M*

SPECVLVM STVLTORVM

[705] so no wine for me! So I'll carry but not taste wine, lest raging fever take hold of me. If I happened, in contradiction of my nature, to drink wine, it would quickly produce a quartan ague, or the mange. [710] For four reasons I am obliged to avoid wine—although my dull brain may be sharpened by it: so that I save money, so that I do not suffer from fever, and so that I do not go to seed and grow foolish. Anyone who can avoid an obvious evil and refuses to do so [715] is the less to be lamented over if it goes badly for him.'

How Burnellus Came to Salerno

So after he had travelled for twelve days, he saw the high city-ramparts which were his goal. Straightway, on bended knee, raising his arms on high, he poured forth petitions to God in the following prayer: [720] 'May Almighty God, through the merits of St Julian, grant me mercy and a good lodging! Save me from every evil—bridges and double panniers, of which there are a lot in my country! Let there be not a peasant or a sack in town! [725] May this place be without a mill, I beg! Let the goads be blunt and the dogs deaf and dumb, and may the puppy's

---

710 *quartanam*: *sc.* febrem, a fever recurring every fourth day, as is characteristic of malaria.

712 Cf. Singer, *Thesaurus*, s.v. 'Wein' 1. 7. 3 (xii. 428): 'Bacchus sumatur modice, sensus cumulatur' ('Das Florileg von S. Omer', ed. Voigt, 21). Cf. Werner, *Sprichwörter*, p. 2, A 24: 'Acuit ingenium vinum moderamine sumptum.'

717 *bissenas diaetas*: the distance from Cremona (which we are later told is the ass's home town: see n. to line 1576 below) to Salerno is approximately 450 miles; to travel this distance in 12 days seems ambitious, but it was quite possible for a traveller on horse- or mule-back to average 35 miles a day. See Parks, *English Traveller*, pp. 180–5. However, Cremona has not been mentioned at this stage of the poem, and Burnellus's return journey suggests that he was making for France or England (see n. to line 829), which is impossible to reconcile with this passage. In 1188, the Canterbury monks who travelled to the papal curia at Rome took a maximum of 49 days (Parks, p. 183), and it would have taken even longer to reach Salerno.

721 St Julian was the patron saint of hospitality; he was invoked by travellers on a journey who were hoping to find safe lodging.

722 *ueniam nobis*: Mozley has 'nobis ueniam', but this is the reading of *R* alone.

84   SPECVLVM STVLTORVM

sitque procul catuli uox inimica mihi!
Hospes ruricola mihi sit, cui semper abundet
730   carduus hirsutus et pluuialis aqua.
Sint species uiles, sit et emptor rarus in urbe,
      quilibet existat uenditor aeris egens!
Sint merces multae, sit multum cara moneta;
      sit tempus pluuidum, sitque lutosa uia.
735   Prospera sint cuncta, sint cuncta salubria nobis,
      ut nostrum citius expediatur iter.'
Talia commemorans, postquam peruenit in urbem,
      se dedit hospitio membraque fessa toro.
Surgens mane forum species empturus adiuit,
740   quas non inueniens tristis abire parat.
Quattuor ergo dies circumlustrauit in urbe,
      orbe quod in toto non fuit usque petens.

Qualiter Burnellus deceptus est a mercatore

Talia quaerentem mercator Londoniensis
      uidit, et aduertens quis foret inquit ei,
745   'Nuntius es magnus, quisquis te miserit istuc;
      maxima namque petis et pretiosa nimis.
Et sapiens et diues erat, quicumque ministrum
      huc ita te misit, res manifesta docet.
Nam facies uultusque tuus satis indicat unde

---

728 sitque] *sic I^2 over erasure* sintque *F H^{ac} VaVbVdGoBePkPm C GI^{ac}?* TrLa XQY sint et Fr sint *Mu Ha* sit tibi *Ne*   **729** abundet] habundat *SVaVbVcVdTGoBePkFrNe K TrHaLa Z* habundant *MuPm R*   **730** carduus] cardinis *Vb HuNVe Tr* cardinus *T* cardus *Pm*   **731–4** *om. QY*   **731** sint] sunt *Z* sit *G*; rarus] raro *Vb* carus *Fr Tr* ratus *T*   **733** sint] sit *ZX*; multae] multa *ZX*   **734** tempus] templus *G*; pluuidum] pluidum β *SVaVbVcTGoPkPm Ha* pluuide *D* pluuie *X*   **735** $sint^2$ cuncta^2] *om. Z*   **736** nostrum] nobis *HuMN*   **737** in] ad β *GI*   **739** surgens] surgensque $C^{ac}W$ sergens *M* surge *Vd*; forum] fori *B GI*   **740** parat] cepit *X* uel parat *add. in margin X^2 perit Q*   **742** *line repeated in alternative form* $Z_{(1)}Z_{(2)}$, $La_{(1)}La_{(2)}$ orbe quod] urbe quod *F FrPm Ha* orbeque *MuVaGoNe*; toto] tota *F Ha*; usque] ipse *SMuVaVbVcVdTGoBePkFrPm TrHaLa$_{(1)}$* $Z_{(1)}$ ipso *Ne*; petens] potens *L Pk*; *(whole line)* nec tamen inuenit que cupiebat ibi (ei *C* ibo *Q*) δ *La$_{(2)}$* $Z_{(2)}$XQY add. as an alternative in upper margin G^{pc}*   **743** quaerentem] querenti *MuVaVdGoBePkFrPmNe P TrHaLa*; Londoniensis] lundoniensis *Z* landorniensis *La* lundon:gensis *Y* lundanigensis *Q* lodoniensis *Va* ludoniensis *TPkFr*   **744** uidit] uidens *CW*; foret] fuit δ *X*   **745** es] est *VcGo WK*; miserit] misit *HaLa* miserat *X*; istuc] istic *AfCWHuNOPDKVe* illic *M* illuc *FrNe Q* istac *VbVc* huc istuc *Ha*   **747** et^1] est *AfCWHuMNOPDKVe XQY* ut *S*   **749** tuus] *om. M*

SPECVLVM STVLTORVM 85

hostile bark be far from me! Let me have a countryman as host, with whom there is a constant supply of hairy thistles and rainwater. [730] Let medicines be cheap, and buyers hard to come by, and any vendor be short of ready money! Let goods be plentiful, and money high in value; let the weather be rainy and the road be muddy. Let everything be favourable and beneficial to me, [735] so that my journey may soon be over.' Running through these things, he entered the town and got himself to a lodging and his weary limbs to bed. Rising early, he went to the market to buy medicines, but not finding them, he departed sadly. [740] For four days he toured the city, constantly seeking what did not exist anywhere in the whole world.

How Burnellus Was Deceived by a Merchant

While he was looking for these things, a London merchant saw him, and seeing who he was, said to him: 'You are a great messenger, whoever sent you here, [745] for you seek very great and costly things. It is plain to see that whoever sent you here as his servant was both wise and rich. For your face and appearance show well whence you have come

---

736 *expediatur*: 'expedire' = 'to expedite, hasten progress' (*DMLBS*).

740 *tristis abire*: Avianus, *Fabulae*, xiii. 7.

748 *res manifesta*: also at *SS*, 1254; *Lawrence*, 705; *Miracles*, 326, 574, 1242, 1739, 1740, 2374.

86 SPECVLVM STVLTORVM

750 ueneris aut quis sis, nec latuisse potes.
Magnus es, et quamuis peregrino tectus amictu,
in propria patria non peregrinus eris.
O quam sollicita pro te domus est tua tota!—
proque tuo reditu uota precesque facit.

755 Anglia me genuit, Londonis ciuibus ortus
praesulis huc ueni nuntius ipse mei.
Cui quia plus aequo nasum natura retraxit,
institit arte malum posse leuare suum.
Quatuor ergo uiros partes transmisit in istas

760 praesul ob hanc causam conditione grauem.
Annus et annus abit ex quo peruenimus istuc,
tresque uiae comites mors tulit una meos.
Emimus hic species quas si fortuna dedisset
posse referre domum maxima cura foret.

765 Quicquid in hac urbe uenisti quaerere, totum
signatum teneo depositumque domi.
Sumptibus assumptis alieni debitor aeris
artor, et in patriam non licet ire meam.
Vror amore tamen patriae, tantoque reuerti

770 acrius exopto quo magis ire uetor.
Litera certa mihi patris de funere uenit,
fama sed et dominum fingit obisse meum.

---

750 aut] et *Go Z*; nec latuisse potes] nec latuisse potest *a Vc R La* res manifesta docet *D X* res patet ipsa palam *ZQY*   **751** magnus es et] magnus et es *GI* es magnus *D ZXQY*; peregrino] peregrini *Go AJCWRHuMNPDKVe X* pegrini *O*   **753** pro te domus est] domus est pro te *a D* pro te est domus *Vc* pro te domus *Go*   **754** tuo] tua *Q om. Fr* **755** me] que *F J*; ortus] ortum *DK*   **756** huc] hic *E R* hunc *Z*   **757** cui quia] cuique *MuVaVbFrPmNe Ha* cui *a Go* qui quia *Q*; aequo] dimidio *a* iuste *X*   **758** malum] nasum *VbGo*   **759** uiros] uires *F Z* uiro *Ve*; in] ad *T AJCWRHuNOPDKVe X* a *M* **760** ob] ab *Pm Z*   **761** *line repeated in alternative form* $Z_{(1)}Z_{(2)}$, $La_{(1)}La_{(2)}$; abit] abiit $La_{(2)}$; istuc] istac *AJCWHuMNOPDKVe* $La_{(2)}$; *(whole line)* ex quo uenimus huc (huc uel $Z_{(2)}$) iam (est *del.* $Z_{(2)}$) ter transiit annus *Pk* $Z_{(2)}$ ex quo uenimus (peruenimus *Vb*ᵖᶜ) huc iam ter pertransiit annus *SVb* ex quo peruenimus (uenimus *VdBeNe Tr*) huc iam pertransiit (pertransiuit *Tr*) annus *MuVaVdTGoBeFrPmNe TrHa* ex quo huc uenimus iam integer transiit annus *Vc* ex quo uenimus huc iam partis transiit annus $La_{(1)}$ **762** una] ipsa *DK X* dira *S*; meos] meus *Go Tr om. Ne*   **763** emimus hic] eminus his *I* hic emerem *a* hic teneo δ *X*   **764** referre] preferre *CW* referri *M* referro *Q* redire *P*; cura foret] lucra darent *a* cara forent *X*   **767** alieni] alienus *HuMN* alienis *Ne*   **768** et] *om.* LᵃᶜE **769** uror] uxor *M La* utor *Q*   **770–2** *om. QY*   **770** acrius *Mozley* anxius *all MSS*; exopto] excepto *X corr.* X^2; uetor] notor *Tr* negor *X* uel uetor *add. in margin* X^2 **771** patris de] de patris *a*   **772** et] ad *RM om. a*; fingit] dicit *a* clamat γ+ *Z*; obisse] obesse *AJD GI* abisse *VbGo Z*

SPECVLVM STVLTORVM   87

and who you are, and you cannot go incognito. [750] You are a great person, and although you are covered by the cloak of a foreigner, in your own country you won't be a foreigner. Oh, how anxious is your whole household on your behalf! It utters prayers and entreaties for your return. England gave me birth; born a citizen of London, [755] I came here myself as a messenger for my bishop. Since Nature stunted his nose more than is proper, he set his mind to redressing his defect by art. So the bishop sent four men to these parts for this cause, weighty in character. [760] Two years have gone by since we came here, and death has carried off three of my travelling companions. We have purchased here medicines, which, if fortune were favourable, would be a great trouble to take home. Whatever you came to look for in this town, [765] I have it all under seal and stored at home. From the expenses I have incurred, I am encumbered by debt to someone else, and am unable to return to my native land. Yet I burn with love of my country, and the more I am prevented from setting out, the more keenly do I desire to return. [770] A reliable letter has reached me concerning my father's death, but only rumour claims that my master has died too.

755–6 The merchant does not mention the bishop of London's name; when *SS* was dated to 1179–80, it was assumed that the reference was to Gilbert Foliot, bishop 1163–87. However my redating of *SS* to the 1190s means that the bishop in question must be Richard FitzNigel, bishop of London, December 1189–98. Richard is well-known as the author of the *Dialogus de scaccario* (ed. Amt), an account of the workings of the royal exchequer; in the opening of this work he defends the role of the 'courtly' clerics who are heavily criticized in Nigel's *Tractatus*. Nigel may have known Richard FitzNigel through his Ely connections (see Introduction, pp. lxii–lxiii): Richard's father Nigel was bishop of Ely (1133–69), and the young Richard was educated by the Ely monks. Unfortunately, history does not record whether either Gilbert or Richard had a snub nose.

761 *Annus et annus*: 'two years'. The expression derives from vulgar Latin; see Plater and White, *Grammar of the Vulgate*, pp. 26–7. 'iam ter pertransiit annus', which forms part of the variant version of this line in *SVb*, is a direct echo of *Pamphilus* 181 (*Commedie*, iii. 76); it is also recognizably at the back of the other γ readings, with 'ter' omitted and 'pertransiit' variously misread.

763 *emimus hic*: Mozley prefers δ's 'hic teneo', which seems a weaker reading; α's 'hic emerem' is wrong, but supports the βγ variant. See Introduction, p. lxxxiv.

767 *sumptibus assumptis*: also at *Miracles*, 625. 'assumere' = 'to undertake, take upon oneself' (*DMLBS* 5).

770 *acrius*: Mozley's conjecture; see Introduction, p. lxxx.

88 SPECVLVM STVLTORVM

Vitrea uasa decem mihi sunt, tenus ore repleta
his aliisque simul quae tua charta notat.

775 Si pretium dederis quo res mihi constitit ipsa,
cras potes in patriam diues abire tuam.

Vlterius pretio peregrinus de peregrino
absit ut accipiam, rem tibi dando meam,

Hoc tamen excepto, quia te puto religiosum,

780 ut liceat precibus participare tuis.'

Illico Burnellus pretium numerauit, et illa
nugis uasa decem plena recepit ibi.

Quoque magis fieret stabilis contractus utrimque,
nomen uendentis poscit, et ille refert:

785 'Londoniis natus Gila de matre parentis
nomine Truffator nuncupor ipse mei.

Gula mihi soror est, multis notissima regnis;
Est et Truffa mihi foedere iuncta tori.

Nec minus ipse tuum nomen mihi dicere dignum

790 duxeris, ut memori mente tenere queam.'

Inanis iactantia Burnelli

'Nomine Burnellus dicor,' respondit asellus,
'notus ubique satis nomine reque simul.

Principibus regni necnon et regibus ipsis
seruio, seruili conditione carens.

795 Et pater et proauus regum de more ministri

---

773 tenus ore] et cuncta δ *ZXQY*   774 aliisque] aliis *MuFr* absque *T*; charta] cura
β *GI*; notat] docet *D X* notat pretium *Y* rocat *Fr*   775 quo] quod γ+; ipsa] ista
CW   776 potes in] posses *D X* poteris *Vc Z* potes *Y* potest in *Go*; diues abire] si uis
redire /uel diues abire *Ha*; abire] adire *Go MND ZXQY* inire *Vc*   777 pretio] pretium *S D ZQY*   779 excepto] accepto β *MuFr* exopto *R*; quia] quod α que *M* qua
Fr   780 ut liceat] me licet /uel ut liceat *La*; ut] me γ *TrHa*; precibus] *om. L*; partici-
pare] precipitare *LE* pretipitare *T*   781 et illa] et ille *Fr Ha* in illa *Z om. M*
782 uasa...plena] plena...uasa γ+   783 quoque] quodque *GI* utque *ZXQY*;
utrimque] utrumque *Vc R* utrique *Pm*ᵃᶜ uterque *MuVaVbTGoBePkFrPm*ᵖᶜ*Ne TrHaLa*
utrisque *Z* uter *Vd*   784 uendentis] uenditoris *R* poscentis *GI*; poscit] possit *M*
*TrLa*ᵃᶜ   785 Gila] gilla *H* giila *La* gualdo *S* gula *MuVaVbVcVdTBePkFrPmNe TrHa*
illa *Ve* uocor *Go*   786 nomine] nom *D* nomen *Fr Q*   787 Gula] goula *Vd* bula *L*
B A GI Y boula *MuVaVbTGoBePkPmNe HaLa* bolla *Fr* boudla *Vc* oula? *J* gulaque *Tr*; mul-
tis] mulieris *Be La* mulier *Tr* mulieruum *Vd*   788 foedere] federa *R GI*; tori] toro *Fr*
AJCWRHuMNOPDVe Tr XQY   789 dignum] uelis *ZY* uilis *Q*   790 duxeris
ut] dixeris ut *Fr R GI* ut quidem *QY* ut quidnam *Z*; queam] quedam *MD*   791 nomine
Burnellus dicor] nomen brunellus dicor *Tr Z* domine burnellus dicor *FrPm*ᵃᶜ *GI* nomen burnellus mihi stat δ *X*   795 et¹] est *LE M X* sunt *F*; proauus] pauus *HuM*

SPECVLVM STVLTORVM   89

I have ten glass jars, filled to the brim with the things your list specifies, and others besides. If you just pay what they cost me, [775] tomorrow you can return to your country a rich man. Heaven forbid that I, a stranger myself, should take from another stranger more than cost-price; I'm virtually giving it away. One thing though: since I take you to be a member of a religious order, allow me to figure in your prayers.' [780] Burnellus counted out the money on the spot, and there received ten jars full of junk. And so that the bargain might be the more firmly established on both sides, he asked the name of the seller, and he replied: 'I was born in London, my mother is Guile, [785] and I am called Trickster, after my father. Gluttony is my sister, well-known in many lands, and Fraud is joined to me in marriage. You should think it equally proper to tell me your name, so that I can hold it in my memory.' [790]

Burnellus's Idle Boast

'I am called Burnellus,' said the ass, 'well known everywhere in word and deed alike. While not a serf, I serve the nobles of the realm, and the kings themselves. My father and grandfather have always been royal servants likewise, [795] and will be all their days. I entered the king's

779 *religiosum*: 'religiosus' = 'a member of a monastic community' or 'a pious person' (*DMLBS* 2, 3a).

787 *Gŭla* is metrically unacceptable, but it is hard to see how to emend it (see Introduction, pp. lxxx–lxxxi).

SPECVLVM STVLTORVM

semper erant et erunt tempus in omne suum.
Regis in obsequium successi iure paterno;
    indiget officio curia tota meo.
Obuius ipse mihi si rex quandoque feratur,
800   cedit, et incedo rege ferente locum.
Est tamen una mihi multum contraria pestis,
    rusticus immitis, exitiale malum.
Semper enim stimulos gerit aut nodosa flagella,
    aut graditur canibus cinctus utrumque latus.
805   Huic pater exosus meus extitit atque parentes
    deque meo genere quicquid in orbe fuit.
Principis et procerum mores satis approbo, quorum
    risus, uerba, iocus, dulcis amica decens.
Rex mihi dicit, "aue" per eum dum transeo; "uae! uae!"
810   furcifer ingeminat rusticus, orbis onus.
Impetat hunc scabies, hunc cotidiana perurat,
    ne possit uel eques ipse uel ire pedes.
Faucibus insideat mala gutta caputque fatiget,
    defluat et uenter nocte dieque suus.
815   Durus ei dominus longum succedat in aeuum,
    rixentur semper uxor et ipse simul.
Hunc pedis a planta summotenus ore perurant
    ulcera, quae scateant uermibus atque lue.

---

796 suum] meum *ROVe X*   **797** obsequium] obsequio *F* obsequiis *D X*
798 meo] mea *Mu*ᵃᶜ*Va* meam *Fr*   **799–801** si rex—una mihi *om. Go*   **800** et]
om. M   **801** una] ulla *SVaVbVdBePkFrPm TrLa Z* (una *add. Z*²) uilla *Ne* illa *Mu*; multum] uilium *VdBe* multumque *Pk*   **802** immitis] non mitis *MN* inuutus *H* imitutus *T*
immunis *Fr* inuictis *Pm*   **804** cinctus] cunctus *LE* tinctus *Ve* circa *Tr* circum *VdPk*
certum *Be* cinctus...latus /uel certum actus *La*   **805** huic] hinc *T J Tr*
806 orbe] urbe *M La* orobe *Mu*   **807–10** *om. QY; transp. after 816 Z*   **807** *om.*
Vc   **808** iocus] iocos *VcT*; decens] docens *Z* decent *AJWRHuMNOPKVe* docent *C*
dicent *D*   **809** dicit aue] dixit aue *F om. sp. left empty S*; eum dum] eundem *H*
eum du *HuMN* eum de *VaPkNe*   **810** furcifer...rusticus] rusticus...furcifer
SMuVaVbVcTPkPmNe TrHaLa Z rusticus...forcifer *Fr* rusticus...frutifer *Vd* rusticus...fructifer *Be* rusticus...fortiter *Go*; furcifer] fructifer *AJCWRO*ᵃᶜ*P* fercifer *O*ᵖᶜ fursifer
I; orbis] urbis *HuMN Z*   **811** impetat] impetunt *Fr* imperet *SVd La* imperat *BePk*
impigat *VbVc* imparet *Tr*; hunc¹] hinc *Tr* huic *VdBe La*; perurat] perurant *RP*   **812–**
17 *om. ROPVe*   **812** possit] posset *VdT CWHuMN GI*; ipse uel ire] ire uel ipse
MuVaVtVdTGoBePkFrPmNe TrHaLa nec uel ipse *Vc*   **813** insideat] insidiat *H Mu J*
I Tr ZY incideat *E K* incidiat *Q*; fatiget] fatigat *Go Ha Q*   **815** succedat] succedit
Fr Ha succendat *Va*   **816–18** *om. QY*   **816** rixentur] rixantur *LE Go*
817 *om. Z*

SPECVLVM STVLTORVM

91

service by right of succession from my father; the whole court relies on my offices. If the king himself meets me occasionally when he is out riding, he moves aside, and I proceed, with the king giving way. [800] But there is one pest which is a great vexation to me: the cruel peasant, a deadly evil. For he always carries goads or knotted whips, or he goes about surrounded by dogs on every side. To him, my father was hateful, my relatives too, [805] and all members of my family throughout the world. I greatly approve the behaviour of the king and nobles— laughter, fine talk, amusement, and a charming and lovely lady-friend. The king says "Good-day!" when I pass him, but the peasant repeats "Giddy-up, giddy-up!"—jailbait and burden on society that he is! [810] May the mange attack him, and fever burn him up, so that he can neither ride nor walk! May arthritis lodge in his throat and give him a headache, and may his stomach suffer from the trots, both day and night! May he have a cruel master all his life, [815] and may he and his wife quarrel non-stop! May ulcers corrode him from the sole of his

---

800 *ferente locum*: I have found no parallels to the expression 'ferre locum', but presumably it is intended as an equivalent for 'dare locum', 'to give way'. Cf. line 3494.

808 Mozley places a comma after 'dulcis', taking it to modify 'iocus', but the mid-line caesura suggests that the syntactic break comes after 'iocus'.

810–22 The ass's hostility to peasants is sufficiently motivated by the treatment he has received from his human master, but satire against peasants is also a staple of medieval Latin and vernacular literature, whose clerical authors ridicule rustic ignorance and boorishness. See Novati, *Carmina medii aevi*, pp. 25–38; Lehmann, *Parodie*, pp. 76–7, 80, 147–8; Coulton, *The Medieval Village*, p. 91.

811–22 A parody of an ecclesiastical excommunication. For other examples, see Lehmann, *Parodie*, pp. 154–8; Alan of Lille, *De planctu Naturae*, xviii. 17–19 (ed. Wetherbee, pp. 214–17); *Map Poems*, 'Raptor mei pilei', pp. 75–6.

811 *cotidiana*: sc. febris.

813 *gutta*: 'arthritic ailment' (*DMLBS* 6a). For arthritis of the jaw, see https://www.nras.org.uk/jaw-problems.

814 *nocte dieque*: also at *SS*, 1196, 2142, 2376, 3886; *Lawrence*, 1199; *Miracles*, 1408, 2478.

817 *pedis a planta*: cf. Job 2: 7; Isa. 1: 6, and n. to lines 2557–8.

92   *SPECVLVM STVLTORVM*

Hunc ego commendo Sathanae, de stercore cuius
820   dicitur esse satus, quod probat ipse satis.
Hunc ego si possem totum delere per orbem,
nullus ei fieret urbe uel orbe locus.'

Qualiter Burnellus rediit

His igitur dictis, patrias Burnellus ad oras
laetus et exultans mane redire parat.
825   Crastina lux aderat, Burnellus onustus ab urbe
exit et exsoluit uota precesque Deo.

Qualiter Burnellus incidit in canes

Casibus in laetis quam sit uicina ruina
et lapsus facilis nemo uidere potest.
Iam prope Lugdunum ueniens callemque secutus
830   per sata transibat, nil meditando mali.
Quem procul aspiciens quidam de Fratribus Albis,
quorum uicinam contigit esse casam,
quatuor immensos mordaci dente molossos
immittens in eum, talia dixit ei:
835   'Per sata nostra uia tibi num directa uidetur?
Num nimis arta fuit publica strata tibi?
Forsitan errasti, sed numquid quatuor isti
non poterunt rectam te docuisse uiam?
Per crepitas nostras, melior tibi torta platea
840   calle foret recto sum nisi stultus ego.

818–19 *om. D*   819–20 *om. Fr*   819 ego] ergo *L Ne*   820–1 *om. Tr*
820 esse͞ ipse *D X*   822 urbe uel orbe] orbe uel urbe *Vc ZQY* urbi uel orbe *Go*
823–82 *transp. after* 935 *Z*   823 igitur] ergo *VaVc RMP*; oras] horas *CW GI*
824 man͞e] mare *HuMN*   827 quam] quantum *fb*   828 facilis] facile *H GI* faciles *D*   829 secutus] securus *Vd Ha*   831 aspiciens] aspexit *γ+*   832 uicinam] uicinam /uel uicinia *La*; casam] causam *TGo*   833 immensos] immensas *Fr*
ingentes *α*   834 dixit] dicit *MuVaVbVcVdGoBePkFrPm Ha* dici *Ne*   835 uia
tibi] tibi uia *Mu DK XQY*; tibi num] numquid tibi *VbVcTGo*; num directa uidetur] recta
numquam uideretur *Vd* recta numquam uidetur *Be*; num directa] directa num *La*; num] non
AJCWRMNOPVe numquam *FrNe Tr* numquid *SMuVaPkPm Ha* unde *L* minus *Z*; directa]
recta *SMuVaVbVcTPkPmNe TrHa* recte *GoFr* ducere *Z*   836 num] nam *R Tr* non
SVdBePk M La uel *MuVaTGoFrPmNe Ha* unde *Vb* aut *Vc*; nimis] minus *Z om. X add. X²*;
fuit...tibi] tibi...fuit *D X*; strata] stra *GI corr. I²*   838 poterunt] poterant *F GoFr O*
Z poterint *T*; te] de *I corr. I²*   839–40 *om. QY*   839 torta] certa *TFr Tr* trita
HuMN corta *Go Ve* curta *Be* tota *Z* torta /[uel] trita *La*   840 calle foret recto] recto
calle foret *γ TrHa Z* recta calle foret *La* calle foret recta *β GI*; sum] sim *F β*
MuVbVcVdTGoBePkFrNe GI TrHaLa X sui *Z* num *AJCWHuMNPDVe* nam *OK* non *R*

SPECVLVM STVLTORVM

93

foot to the crown of his head, seething with worms and pus! I commend him to Satan, from whose shit he is said to have sprung, as he himself gives ample proof. [820] If I could wipe him out throughout the world, there would be no place for him anywhere.'

How Burnellus Returned

Having said this, Burnellus, happy and joyful, gets ready to return next day to his native shores. The next day came, and the laden Burnellus left the city, [825] pouring forth prayers and entreaties to God.

How Burnellus Fell among Dogs

In fortunate circumstances no one can see how near disaster is and how easy is a fall! Now, approaching Lyon, he was passing through a wheatfield, following the path, and thinking no harm. [830] A Cistercian monk, whose house happened to be nearby, saw him in the distance, and sent out against him four huge sharp-toothed dogs, saying to him: 'Does your direct route seem to you to lie through our crops? [835] Was the high road too narrow for you? Perhaps you have lost your way; well, surely these four will be able to teach you the right road! By my sandals,

819–20 Cf. *Ysengrimus*, vii. 230 (referring to the pigs who are attacking the wolf): 'Pessima que potuit monstra cacare Satan'; 'the worst monsters that Satan could shit'. The idea that peasants spring from Satan's shit is also found in the *Roman de Renart* (ed. Roques) Br. I, 532–3: 'Mes povres hom qui n'a avoir/ fu faiz de la merde au deauble.'

823 *His igitur dictis*: a frequent way of beginning a hexameter; see *Lateinisches Hexameter-Lexikon*, ii. 505, and *Lawrence*, 2319.

825 *Crastina lux aderat*: *Ysengrimus*, iv. 811; also at *Miracles*, 547. Cf. 'Tertia lux aderat', at *Lawrence*, 583, and *Miracles*, 313.

829 *prope Lugdunum*: later in the poem, Burnellus claims to be Italian (1228–9) and is said to reside at Cremona, in north Italy (1576, 3559). Here, however, he is represented as travelling home ('patrias... ad oras', 823) from Salerno via Lyon and the Rhône valley (1035, 1063, 1068, 1081, 1095), which was one of the possible routes from Italy to England, using the Great St Bernard Pass (Parks, *English Traveller*, p. 188; see also the map at pp. 48–9). Cf. line 656, where Galienus assumes that on return from Salerno ('In reditu') he will use the Great St Bernard. If the ass were returning from Salerno to Cremona by land, he would not pass through the Alps at all. It seems that at this stage Nigel might have been thinking of Burnellus as English, and probably as based at Canterbury, whose proximity to Dover made it a natural jumping-off place for a journey to the Continent.

831 *quidam de Fratribus Albis*: Raymo takes this to mean that Fromundus is a 'conversus'; that is, one of the lay brothers who performed the everyday labour of the monastery, and who were largely illiterate. However, since the Cistercian order reinstated agricultural labour as a regular part of the monk's daily routine (*Instituta* V, ed. Waddell, *Narrative and Legislative Texts*, p. 459), there is no reason why Fromundus should not have been an ordinary monk. As a Benedictine monk himself, Nigel is a priori likely to have been hostile to the Cistercians, given the animosity that existed between the two orders in the 12th c. (see n. to lines 2111–82), but his hostility will have been intensified by dislike for the Cistercian Baldwin of Ford, who as archbishop of Canterbury was head of the Christ Church community. See Introduction, p. xliv.

94   *SPECVLVM STVLTORVM*

Per sata nostra uia quam sit directa docebo,
  hi nisi deficiant quatuor ecce mihi.'
Dixit, et instigans clamosa uoce molossos
  undique correptum fecit inire fugam.
845 Serius hic, illi citius currendo retentum
  morsibus attrectant praecipitantque solo.
Ante tamen morsu nimium Grimbaldus iniquo
  arripiens caudam dimidiarat eam.
Funditus oblitus quidnam portaret et illud
850 quod sua praecipue uitrea uasa forent,
ex quo corripuit canis hunc caudamque momordit,
  seque suumque simul praecipitauit onus.

Infortunium Burnelli

Omnia uasa simul casu periere sub uno;
  rem fragilem potuit frangere causa leuis.
855 Parta labore graui leuiter cecidere, dolorem
  perpetuum domino parturiendo suo.
Illa remanserunt tantum quae nulla fuerunt;
  nil nisi uasorum fragmina sola manent.
In tenues auras substantia tota recessit;

---

843 clamosa] clamorosa *MuVaT Z*   844 correptum] correctum *S* correptam *Fr Tr*
X   845 serius] *sic X corr. to* sepius *X*² seuus *LE* seruus *Z* segnius *F Ha*; hic] hunc *D*
ZXQY hinc *Mu*; illi] ille *VaVc* illinc *Mu*; retentum] recentum *B BeFr* retetum *La*
846 *om. Vc*   attrectant] attractant *MuTPm*ᵃᶜ *JOD X* attractat *Fr* attrectent *H* aurectant /
[*uel*] arreptant *La*; solo] soli *AJCWHuMNP* sola *Ve*   848 arripiens] arripians *Be* eripiens *AJCWHuMNOPDKVe ZQY*; dimidiarat] dimidiaret *DO*ᵃᶜ*Ve* dimidiabat *O*ᵖᶜ dimidiauit
SMuVaVbVcVdTGoBePkPmNe TrHaLaQ dimidiat *Fr*; eam] ei *SMuVaVbVcGoBePkFrPmNe*
TrHaLa equi? *E*   849–1386 *om. B* (*lost leaves*)   850 quod sua praecipue] precipue sua quod *SMuVaVbVcVdTBePkPmNe TrLa* precipueque sua *Go* precipue sua *Fr* quid
sua precipue *ZQY*; (*whole line*) Precipue uitrea sua quod uasa forent *Ha*   851 hunc]
om. VaVc hanc *GI* hinc *Mu*; momordit] momordet *Y* remordit *VdTBe J Tr* immordit
La   852 *om. I*; seque suumque simul] se simul atque suum *D X* seque simulque suum
R seque suum simul *Va* sed que suum simul *Tr* seque suum simulque *Z*; onus] ita
LE   853 periere] perire *VaVbVdGoPkFrPm*ᵃᶜ *MN I Y* subire *Tr* subiere *Be* uel perire
*add. Be*²   854 rem fragilem potuit] rem potuit fragilem *D* res potuit fragiles *X* rem
fragilem poterit *VcVdBe Tr*   855 parta] porta *Q* ducta *X* parca *H P Tr* parca .i. furia
infernalis *add. in margin H*; leuiter] pariter *O*; cecidere] periere *SMuVcTGoBe TrLa ft*
pariere *PkPm Ha* perire *VaVbVdFrNe*; dolorem] laborem *Vc P*   856 parturiendo]
parturienda *SVaVbVcVdGoBePkPmNe La* parturrendo *Ve* perturienda *Tr* partuendo *M* par-
turiere *P Ha*   857 tantum quae] tantum quod *AJCWRHuMNOPVe* tantumque *Fr*
que tantum *D ZXQY* que tamquam *H GI*   859 auras] aures *Go AJCWP Tr X corr. X*²
duras *Vd*

SPECVLVM STVLTORVM 95

a crooked highway would be better for you than a straight footpath, unless I'm a fool. [840] I'll teach you how direct the path through our fields is, if these four don't let me down.' So he said, and urging on the dogs with loud voice, he put Burnellus to flight, beset on every side. He ran more slowly, the dogs more quickly; [845] they grab hold of him, seizing him in their teeth and throwing him to the ground. But first, Grimbaldus had seized his tail and with a specially cruel bite had reduced it to half its length. Completely forgetting what he was carrying, and in particular that his jars were made of glass [850], when the dog seized him and bit off his tail, he dashed both himself and his load to the ground.

Burnellus's Misfortune

All his jars were broken in a single fall; a flimsy cause was enough to break a fragile object. What had been acquired with great effort was easily destroyed, [855] generating endless grief to its possessor. Only those things which were nothing remained; nothing is left but the fragments of the jars. The whole cargo vanished into thin air, and his hope and his labour were brought to nought at the same time.

96   *SPECVLVM STVLTORVM*

860   deperiere simul spesque laborque suus.
      Hinc queritur caudam Grimbaldo dimidiatam;
      hinc dolet expensas deperiisse suas.
      Angit utrumque malum, misero satis esset et unum,
      acrius ille gemit quem duo damna grauant.
865   An labor an sumptus an cauda recisa dolori
      debeat esse magis, dinumerare nequit.
      Nam labor est cassus, sumptus periere, recisam
      nemo potest caudam restituisse sibi.
      Anxietas animi crescit stimulata dolore,
870   alternantque uices hinc dolor, inde pudor.
      Plus tamen affligit pudor hunc, comitante dolore,
      quam faceret solus absque pudore dolor.
      Totus in ore canum miser et miserabilis ille
      uoluitur, et sola uix sibi uita manet.
875   Nec prius a misero se continuere molossi
      donec Fromundus uix cohiberet eos.
      Frater Fromundus, fratrum de more suorum,
      non ferus, immo fera dissimulando diu,
      ut solet illius gentis genus illud iniquum,
880   uix etiam tandem tendere coepit eo.
      Non tamen accelerans, ut cum pulsatur ad ollam
      assolet, ad mensam uentre docente uiam,

---

860 deperiere] deperirere *Pm Ve* deperire *VaPkFrNe* de periore *E* disperiere *CW*ᵃᶜ*HuM̃NDK X* deperire solent *Vb*; spesque laborque] spes labor atque *D ZXQY* speciesque laborque *L*; suus] uie α   862 *om. H*; dolet] dolor *Go R*; deperiisse] disperiisse *DK* deperiisse *Go*   863–4 *om. QY*   863 angit] anget *Tr X* auget *RD fb* luget *Ve*; misero] miserum *F TGo*; et] *Mozley in all MSS*; unum] uno α *H* γ+ *RDVe GI ZX fb* 864 acrius] arcius *MuVc Z* anxius *AJCWRHuMNOPKVe* alcius *D X*; grauant] grauat *SMu*   865 dolori] dolore *R* labori *SMuVaVbVcVdGoBePkPmNe TrHaLa* labore *TFr*   867 periere] perire *VaVbVdBePkFrPmNe MN I TrLa*   868 nemo potest] non poterit *HuMNK* non poterat *D* non potest *CW*ᵃᶜ ne potest *La*; restituisse] retinuisse *GI*; sibi] mihi *H* suam *D X*   869 stimulata] simulata *GI* stimulante *CW*; dolore] dolere / uel dolore *La*   870–1 *om. T D*   870 alternantque] alternasque *S* alternatque *R Z* alternuntque *Go*; inde] hincque *K* uel inde *add. interlinear K*ᵖᶜ   871 affligit] affligat *Va*ᵃᶜ afflixit *VbVc*; hunc] huc *Pm* hinc *H AJCWRHuMNOPKVe GI QY*   872 pudore dolor] dolore pudor *H MO GI X*   874 sola] soli *AJCWRHu*ᵃᶜ*MNOVe* solum *P* saltim *La*   875 a misero] amisso *HuMN* a miseris *Go*; continuere] continere *VdBePk TrLa* contunere *Ne*   876–7 uix—Fromundus] *om. I*   880 tandem] caudam /[uel] tandem *La*; eo] ei *QY* iter *H* γ *GI TrHa Z* ita *X* iter / uel eo *La*   881 ut] nisi *H*ᵖᶜ nec *EF H*ᵃᶜ *AJCWHuMNOPVe GI Tr X* ni *R*; cum pulsatur] cum (cumque *I²*) pulsat *I* cum pulsatus *CWHuMNOPVe* conpulsatur *BePkNe TrLa*   882 assolet] ac solet *VaPkFrPm* ad solet *Vd* assidet *S* ut solet α δ *GI XQY* uel solet *H* et solet *MuTGoNe* ad /uel ut solet *La*

SPECVLVM STVLTORVM

[860] On the one hand he bewailed the tail that Grimbaldus had halved; on the other he grieved at the loss of the money he had spent. Both misfortunes torment him; one would be enough for a poor wretch, and he who is burdened with two disasters laments all the more vigorously. Whether his effort or his money or his truncated tail is a greater cause of grief, [865] he cannot determine. For his effort is wasted, his money lost, and no one can restore his truncated tail to him. His mental anguish grows under the stimulus of his grief, and grief and shame alternate with each other. [870] Yet shame coupled with grief afflicts him more than grief alone would do in the absence of shame. The pitiable wretch is rolled about completely in the mouths of the dogs, and life itself barely remains in him. Nor did the dogs hold themselves back from the wretch, [875] until Fromundus with difficulty restrained them. Brother Fromundus—in the manner of his brethren, not a wild beast, but long concealing bestial characteristics, as that evil breed of men customarily does—finally and reluctantly set about making his way to the spot. [880] He did not, however, approach in haste, as he does when the dinner-bell is struck, and the stomach teaches the way to the table, but

862 *expensas*: 'expensae' = 'expenses, money spent' (*DMLBS* 3d).

870 *hinc dolor, inde pudor*: also at *SS*, 1285; variations at *SS*, 2972 (with 'timor' as the first alternative), and *Miracles*, 2172 (with 'amor' as the first alternative).

873 *miser et miserabilis*: Rev. 3: 17.

878 *dissimulando diu*: also in *Miracles*, 461, 2483.

881–2 The speed with which monks go to the dinner table is similarly ridiculed in *Ysengrimus*, i. 433–4.

98   *SPECVLVM STVLTORVM*

sed pede spondaico gressu gradiens asinino,
ut solet ad laudes nocte uenire, uenit,
885 extendensque manum, dicto benedicite, 'ha! ha!'
dixit, et amouit corripuitque canes.

Responsio Burnelli

Cui Burnellus ait: 'Numquam sis tu benedictus,
sed maledicaris tempus in omne tuum!
Num Benedictus ita docuit uos, in peregrinos
890 instigare canes? Num Benedictus ita?
Hic est ordo nouus, haec est noua regula, frater,
obseruanda tibi, tradita iure nouo?
Numquid Cisterci canon fuit iste repertus,
uenit et hinc ad uos ordinis iste rigor?
895 Numquid in hoc anno qui conuenere sub uno
istud praeceptum constituere patres?
Summi pontificis canibus uexare ministrum
nescio si uobis regula uestra iubet.
Nescio si uobis liceat morti dare quemquam,
900 praecipue causa non praeeunte necis.
Pontificis summi medicamina maxima portans
huc ego perueni, nil meditando mali.
Per sata transiui, fateor, peregrinus et hospes;
quo tamen erraui callis apertus erat.
905 Semita magna fuit quam rebar et esse plateam,

883–935 *transp. after* 992 *Z*   885 dicto] dico *G*; ha ha] ua ua *SMuVaVbVdTGoBePkPmNe* ba ba *VcFr* ua ua /uel ba ba *Ha* ua ua /uel ha ha *La* bana *Tr* faua *Z*   886 dixit] dixitque *MuGo*; amouit] ammonit *L H Va CR XQY* ammonuit *MuGo Tr*   887 numquam] *sic P over erasure* num *G*; sis tu] tu sis *MuVbTBeFrPm RVe GITrXY*   889 num]non γ- *GI TrHa* non /uel num *La*; uos] nos *VbFr*   890 num] non γ- *TrHa* non /uel num *La*   891 nouus] manus *LE*; haec] hic *VaVdPkPmNe*; est²] *om. F R*   893–4 *om. Ha*   893 Cisterci] cistersi *HuMN* sistersi *K* cistarsi *QY*; iste] ista *Tr* ipse *R* ille α *M ZY*   894 et hinc] et hunc *H* et huc *X* ad huc *ZY* ab hinc *Q* et hic *MuVaVbVdTBePkFrPmNe TrLa*; uos] nos *MuPkFr Ve Tr*   895–6 *om. QY*   896 praeceptum] precepit *HuMN*   898 *om. H MuVaPm I add. in margin Va^{pc}Pm^{pc} I²*   898–901 *om. T*   900 praeeunte] pretereunte *LE* preente *F* preeunde *Go*   902 meditando] ratus ipse α *H* γ *GI TrHaLa ZQY*   903 fateor] feteor *M*   904 callis] callus *H HuMN* talis *Vd* tallis *Ve*   905 quam rebar et esse plateam] que rebar et esse plateam *Ha* quam rebar esse plateam *H T CW GI* cum rebar et esse plateam *Vc* quod rebar esse plateam *MuVaVbVdPm* quod rebar et esse plateam *BePkFrNe La* quod rebar esse placebam *Go* querebam et ipse plateam *S* quam rebar et omne plateam *Tr* necnon satis ampla platea *ZQY*

SPECVLVM STVLTORVM 99

with a spondaic foot, walking at an ass's pace, as he usually came to Lauds in the night. Stretching out his hand, having said 'Bless you!', he shouted 'Hey! hey!' [885] and called off the dogs and scolded them.

Burnellus's Reply

Burnellus answered: 'May you never be blessed, but cursed all your days! Is that what Benedict taught you, to set the dogs on strangers? Benedict taught you, I say? [890] Is this a new order, is this a new Rule, brother, newly given to you to observe? Was this a Rule discovered at Cîteaux? And was it from there that you got this harshness in your order? Did the abbots who assembled together this year [895] establish this regulation? I don't know if your Rule orders you to savage the Pope's servant with dogs. I don't know if you're permitted to kill any-one, especially when there is no cause for their death. [900] I came here with no evil intentions, carrying important medicines of the Pope. I confess that I passed through your cornfields, as a stranger and a guest, but the path along which I was going was open to all. It was a wide track which I thought was the highway, [905] both because it was very broad

---

889 *Benedictus*: The Cistercians aimed to restore the original rigour of the Benedictine Rule. See n. to lines 2111–82 below, and also Bernard of Clairvaux, *De praecepto et dispensatione*, xvi, line 49 (*Sancti Bernardi Opera*, iii. 286); Bruun, ed., *Cistercian Order*, p. 80.

895–6 Raymo suggests that these lines allude to the decretum of the Third Lateran Council of March 1179 which forbade the molestation of travellers (Mansi, xxii. 229–30, c. xxii). This decretum is reported by Gervase of Canterbury (*Chronicle*, i. 292), Roger of Howden (*Chronica*, ii. 184–5; *Gesta*, i. 233), and William of Newburgh, *Historia*, iii. 3 (i. 216; trans. Stevenson, p. 510). However, Raymo's explanation does not fit the text: Burnellus is not suggesting that the assembly of 'patres' forbade the molestation of travellers but rather that they recommended it, and also that this new rule ('noua regula'; 891) was introduced by the Cistercians in particular; that being so, the assembly of 'fathers' which took place 'this year' (895) is most probably to be identified as one of the annual chapter meetings which were characteristic of the Cistercian order (*Instituta*, Prologue, ed. Waddell, *Narrative and Legislative Texts*, p. 454; *Carta Caritatis Posterior*, ibid. p. 501; Bruun, ed., *Cistercian Order* pp. 29, 31, 90).

902 *meditando mali*: Langosch (review, p. 283) prefers this δ reading to the αβγ variant 'ratus ipse' (as does Mozley), on the grounds that 'reor' with the sense 'suspecting' ('ahnend') would be highly unusual. Cf. 'meditando mali' at line 830.

SPECVLVM STVLTORVM

100

tum quia lata nimis, tum quia trita satis.
Error inest facto non praemeditata uoluntas;
si qua fuit culpa, non nisi parua fuit.
Culpa leuis tanto non est plectenda rigore;

910   mitior in minimis debuit esse modus.
Quamuis culpa foret, etiam dignissima plecti,
hoc plectenda modo non fuit illa tamen.
Criminis ad pondus deberet poena rependi,
maior poena suo crimine crimen habet.

915   Summi pontificis ego nuntius atque minister
pacificus ueni, deuia forte sequens.
Pontificis summi timor et reuerentia uestrum
debuit ex aliqua parte leuare malum,
quod tamen auxerunt; non est in partibus istis

920   qui timeat Dominum pontificemue suum.
Non mihi sed Domino grauis est iniuria facta;
nostram papa, suam uindicet ipse Deus.
In dominum papam transgressio facta redundat,
laesa sed est tanto curia tota malo.

925   Horrendum facinus, tam detestabile factum,
tam grauis excessus numquid inultus erit?
In domini papae contemptu tam manifesto
Roma nisi fuerit usa rigore suo,

---

906 tum quia[1]] tumque *VaFrPm M GI ZQY* cum quia *Vd* tamen quia *Go*; tum quia[2]] tumque *Pm GI* cum quia *Vd* tum quoque *VaFr*   **907** uoluntas] uoluptas *LE H TGo CWHuMN Ha*[ac]   **908** si qua] si que *MuVaPmNe* sique *Go* sed quia *Z* sed que *Ha*; fuit culpa] culpa tamen *SMuVaVbVcVdTGoBePkPmNe HaLa* culpa *Fr*   **909** tanto non est] non est tanto *a Vc ROVe fb* non tanto *P* tanto non *Fr*   **910** debuit] debet /[*uel*] debuit *La*   **911–12** *om. ZQY*   **911** etiam dignissima] in indignissima *VdBe*   **912** hoc] hec *H VaGoFrNe GI Ha* hac *Be*; modo...illa tamen] modo...ipsa tamen *R* tamen...illo modo *H VaVdBeFrNe TrHaLa* tamen...illa modo *SMuVbVcTGoPkPm GI*   **913** criminis] germinis *HuMN* quamuis *T*   **916–17** *transp. Vd*   **916** pacificus] paficus *I* pontificus *VdFr La*   **917–18** *om. QY*   **917** pontificis] pacificis *VdBe* pontificus *Fr*; timor] metus *H GI*; uestrum] nostrum *H SMuVaBePkNe GI*   **918** *om. Vc*   **919** quod tamen auxerunt] si fatear uerum *XY* si fateor uerum *ZQ*; quod] quid *M* que *VdBe TrLa* qui *Pk*   **920–1** *transp. I corr. I*[2]   **920** *om. Vc*; pontificemue] pontificemque *F H MuVaVbVdTGoBePkFrPmNe D GI TrHaLa XQ*   **922** nostram papa suam] nostra papa suam *C* nostram pape suam *Tr* papa suam nostram *K* nostram personam *Ha* postquam papam suam *P* iniuriam factam *GI* incommodum tantum *ZQY*; uindicet] iudicet *SMuVaVbVdTGoBePkFrPmNe La* uindicet / uel iudicet *Ha*   **923–4** *lines repeated in alternative form Z*(1)*Z*(2)   **923** transgressio facta] specialiter ista *Z*(1)*QY*; redundat] redundant *QY*   **924** laesa sed est] leditur et *AJCWROPDKVe X* leditur in *HuMN*; (*whole line*) lesus et est grauiter uulnus utrumque patet *Z*(2)*QY*   **926** *transp. after 929 Mu*; numquid] an *T* nunquam *Fr Z*; inultus] inutilis *T* inulto *Fr* multus /[*uel*] inultus *La*   **927–8** *om. QY*   **927** domini papae] domini papam *Tr* dominum papam *Fr Z*; contemptu tam manifesto] contemptu tam manifestum *H D* contemptum facta putantur *X*

SPECVLVM STVLTORVM

and because it was very well-trodden. The mistake lies in the deed, not a premeditated intention; if there was any blame involved, it was only trivial. A light fault is not to be punished with such great harshness; moderation should take a gentler line on trifles. [910] Even if it were a fault, and even if it were worthy of punishment, yet it should not have been punished in that way. Punishment ought to be meted out in proportion to the crime; a punishment that is greater than the crime is itself a crime. I came here peacefully, as the messenger and servant of the Pope, [915] and I happened to be following the backroads. Fear and reverence for the Pope ought to have inhibited your malice to some extent, but they increased it; there is no one in these parts who seems to fear the Lord and His Pope. [920] A serious injury has been done, not to me but to the Lord; the Pope will avenge the injury to me, and God, the injury to Himself. The crime committed redounds on the Lord Pope—nay, the whole curia has been injured by this great wrong. Shall this abominable outrage, so loathsome a deed, [925] such a serious insult, be unavenged? When there is such obvious contempt for the Pope, unless Rome exercises severity so that the shame may be

908 *qua*: see *OLD* s. v. qui¹, indef. adj. (fem. nom. sg.) C. 24, after 'si' = 'any'.

915 Burnellus is claiming to be one of the papal legates who were appointed by the pope to supervise the implementation of canon law and papal policy in countries distant from Rome. They 'functioned as prosecutors, empowered to bring action against those who violated church law, and at the same time as judges, commissioned to hear and decide cases in the pope's name and with the force of papal authority' (Brundage, *Medieval Canon Law*, p. 42). William of Longchamp was a papal legate from 1190 to 1194, and in a letter of 2 December 1191, Pope Celestine III wrote an indignant letter to the English archbishops and bishops protesting at William's deposition from the justiciarship and ill-treatment; if reports of this are true, the Pope orders that those responsible (including John, count of Mortain) are to be excommunicated (Roger of Howden, *Chronica*, iii. 151–2; trans. Riley, ii. 242–3). At this point in his narrative, Nigel may have had in mind this example of the Pope's defence of one of his legates.

923 *redundat*: 'redundare in' = 'to redound upon' (*DMLBS* 5b).

925 *detestabile factum*: Juvenal, *Saturae*, xiii. 126.

926 *excessus* = 'insult, outrage' (*DMLBS* 6).

102   *SPECVLVM STVLTORVM*

ut breue sit dedecus, longum sit decus amicis,
930   hostibus eueniant dedecus atque decus,
non erit ulterius quaeuis metuenda potestas,
sed quod cuique libet iure licebit ei.
Dedecus in dominum papam damnumque redundat,
cetera sustineo uulnera solus ego.
935   Damnum marcarum plusquam duo millia constat,
sumptibus exceptis atque labore uiae.
Dedecus at quanti sit nescio, nouerit ille
ad quem spectat honor, spectat et istud onus.
Dedecus est magnum, damnum graue, praesul utrumque
940   puniet ad libitum, plus tamen istud eo.

929–30 *om.* α *D GI XQY*   929 ut breue sit dedecus] dedecus ut breue sit *K*;
longum sit decus] longumque decus sit γ+ *KVe* longum decus est et *R*; amicis] amicus *Fr*
antiquis / uel amicis *La*   930 eueniant] eueniat *VcTFr HuN* euenient *S*; dedecus] *om.*
HuMN; atque decus] hautque decus *Hu*ᵃᶜ*N*ᵃᶜ*K* hancque decus *Hu*ᵖᶜ*N*ᵖᶜ hanc non que decus
M atque pudor γ+ *Z*   931 metuenda] metuanda *C* intuenda /[*uel*] metuenda
La   932 quod cuique libet] quod cuique libet /uel quocumque *Ha* quodcumque libet
E quodcumque iubet *D* quod cuilibet *AJCWOP fb* quid cuilibet *Mu* quid cuique libet *T*
quot cuique libet *Be* quod cuique *H Ve*   933 *line repeated in alternative form* Z(1)Z(2);
papam damnumque] papam damnaque *T* papam domumque *Fr* papam tam grande
*HuMNDK X add. in longer gloss on whole line A*² nostrum papamque Z(1)*QY*; *(whole line)* in
dominum nostrum papam dedecusque redundat *AJCWROPVe*   934–1037 *missing*
*(leaf torn away, so that only the beginning of lines 967–83, and ending of lines 1013–37, are
legible) T*   936–92 *transp. after 822 Z*   936 atque] absque δ *La ZXQY*
937–40 *om. QY*   937 dedecus at quanti sit] dedecus ac quanti sit *GI* dedecus hoc
quanti sit *D X* quanti sit dedecus at (hoc *R*) *AJCWROPVe* quanti dedecus hoc sit *Hu*ᵖᶜ*MNK*
quanti dedecus est ego *SMuVaVdGoBePkFrPmNe TrHaLa Z* quanti dedecoris ego *VbVc*;
nouerit] nouit *VdBe La* sed nouit *Tr*   938 *om. Z*; honor] honos α *GI om. Vc*; spectat²]
spectet *F SVaVbVcVdBePkNe D GI TrLa*; istud] illud *H MuVaVb*ᵖᶜ*VdGoFrPm*
939 dedecus est] est dedecus *AJCWRHuMNOPVe*; damnum graue] damnumque graue *Ha*
graue damnum *H GI* sed summus *AJRHuMNOPDKVe X* sed summis *CW*   940 plus
tamen istud eo] plus illud ego *Z* criminis ultor erit δ *X*; eo] ego *F H MuVcTrHa GI*; *H adds
in R margin .s.* [=scilicet] dampnum [tagged to 'istud']

929–30 *dedecus* = 'shame, disgrace' ... *decus* = 'glory, honour'. In classical Latin, the first
syllable of 'dēdecus' is scanned long, while the first syllable of 'děcus' is scanned short. In
line 929 as printed by Mozley and Raymo, however, 'dēdecus' is scanned with a short first
syllable ('Ūt brěuě sīt dēdēcŭs lōngūmquě děcŭs sīt ămīcīs'). Sedgwick ('Textual criticism',
p. 292) commented on the unusual scansion of 'dedecus' in several examples in lines 929–37
(although it is scanned correctly elsewhere), but he was commenting on Wright's edition,
which was based on only two δ manuscripts (*A* and *C*); in Mozley and Raymo's edition the
problem is avoided by the choice of other variants, except in line 929. The conjectural
emendation proposed by Sedgwick (ibid.), 'dēdecŭs ŭt brěuě sīt', is in fact the reading of *K*
(whose scribe is, however, prone to emendation on metrical grounds). The situation is placed
in a new light by Carsten Wollin's observation that lines 929–30 of *SS* echo a marginal note
in two manuscripts of Alexander Neckam's *De commendatione vini* (Cambridge, UL, Gg. 6.
42 and Paris, BnF, lat. 11867), which reads, under the heading 'Serlo', 'Et breve sit dedecus

SPECVLVM STVLTORVM   103

short-lived and glory to its friends may be lasting, while [brief] glory
and [long] disgrace come to its enemies, [930] then no power of any
sort will any longer be feared, and whatever anyone desires will be lawful for him. The shame and harm redounds on the Lord Pope; the
other wounds I bear alone. There is a loss of more than 2,000 marks,
[935] not counting the cost and labour of the journey. What the cost of
the dishonour is, I don't know; he whose honour is concerned, and
whom this insult therefore concerns, he knows. The dishonour is great,
the damage serious, the Pope will punish both as he wishes, but the
latter more than the former. [940] I leave both honour and damage to the

et longum decus amicus. Hostibus eveniat dedecus atque decus. In nobis amor, in reliquis sit
amor' (see *Serlon de Wilton: Poèmes latins*, ed. Öberg, Appendix I. A. 2, p. 124, and pp. 33–4
on the manuscripts). The quotation is strikingly close to *SS*, and if, as seems very possible,
the attribution is to Serlo of Wilton, it must have been Nigel who was the borrower, since
Serlo died in 1181. Serlo's verses also appear, in slightly altered form, in Geoffrey of
Vinsauf's *Summa de coloribus rhetoricis*, which was edited in full for the first time by Carsten
Wollin, where they offer examples of 'egregie dicere' ('elegant style') achieved by deliberately altered vowel length ('Die erste Poetik Galfrids von Vinsauf', pp. 434–5, l 63. 770–5;
also p. 441 on the connection with *SS*). So the 'a' of 'amor', usually short, is lengthened:
'Producat sillabam corripiendum, vt hic: Corripiant alii, nos producamus "amorem": Āmŏr
ŭt īn nōbīs, īn rĕlīquīs sīt ămōr' ('It lengthens a syllable which should be short, as here: Let
others shorten, but let me lengthen "amor", so that love in me is long, though in others it is
short.') Conversely, 'dedecus' is given as an example of shortening a long vowel: 'Āssĭt ēī
dĕdĕcūs, quī uūlt, ŭt sīt mĭchī dĕcūs!/ Quī sprēvīt dĕcūs, dĕdĕcūs āssīt ēī!' ('Let shame be
on him who wishes it, so long as honour is [long] on me! May shame be [long] on him who
has spurned [long] honour.') Wollin does not explain the thought here, nor how it relates to
Nigel's lines, but Öberg's notes to Serlo's verses provide an illuminating parallel from
Gervais of Melkley: 'Quandoque contingit quod illa (dictio), quae brevis est per naturam,
subtilitate quadam producitur vel aequivoco, ut patet in hoc versu: In nobis amor, in reliquis
sit amor. hoc scilicet exili similitudine ut, sicut prima huius dictionis "amor" hic longa fit,
longum modo significet amorem vel, si vultis ut dicam, consignificet longitudinem.
Similiter: Qui spernunt decus, dedecus assit eis' (*Serlon de Wilton: Poèmes latins*, p. 67). That
is, the unusual vowel quantity matches the semantic content, reflecting the length or shortness of the psychological condition in question. Wollin concludes that the lines in future
editions of *SS* should read 'Ŭt brĕuĕ sīt dĕdĕcūs, lōngūm sīt dĕcūs ămīcīs:/ Hōstĭbŭs
ēvĕnīānt dĕdĕcŭs ātquĕ dĕcŭs.' The change in vowel length symbolically replicates the
change in the wish: that to friends, shame should be short and honour long, but to enemies,
the reverse. This in fact corresponds to the version of lines 929–30 in a substantial segment
of the manuscripts (929: ut breue sit dedecus] *sic H ACJWRHuMNOPVe* γ+ *Z*; longum sit
decus] *sic H ACJWHuMNOP*; 930: atque decus] *sic H ACJWROPVe*. Out: α *B D GI
UXQY*). If this explanation of the altered scansion of 'dedecus' is judged implausible, an
alternative would be to adopt the reading of *K*, or to read 'ut breue sit damnum', anticipating
the pairing of 'damnum' and 'dedecus' in lines 933–42.

  939 *utrumque* implies that two crimes are in question here, viz. the 'dedecus' and 'damnum' that are the subject of lines 933–7. Mozley prints the δ reading, 'sed summus', which
makes less good sense. 'Damnum graue' seems the preferable alternative.

  940 *plus tamen istud eo*: this is more widely supported and also makes better sense than δ's
'criminis ultor erit': the injury (loss of property) will be more severely punished than the
dishonourable treatment of the Pope's legate.

SPECVLVM STVLTORVM

Praesulis arbitrio decus hoc damnumque relinquo,
    ipse tamen proprii uulneris ultor ero.
Magnus Burnellus quo sum ter consule natus
    in me commissi criminis ultor erit.

945 Curia Romana, quae dignis digna rependit,
    pro meritis dignis praemia digna dabit.
Causa grauis, grauior persona, grauissima damna
    esse patet, magnum singula pondus habent.
In dominum papam specialiter ista redundant,

950   laesus et est grauiter; uulnus utrumque patet.
Quod grauius dicet, citius leuiusque remittet;
    quod leuius, poena sub grauiore cadet.
Laesus honor lacrimis poterit precibusque piari,
    ne nimis ulcisci se uideatur in hoc.

955 Damna sed illata nulla ratione remittet;
    mitis erit, redimi si patiatur ea.
Dummodo soluendo fuerit Cistercius ordo,
    nil sibi de toto deperiisse potest.
Aut decimas soluent et braccis lege perenni,

960   quamuis inuiti, posteriora tegent,

941–4 *om.* δ *X*　　941 decus hoc] decus hec *Be* dedecus *Va Ha ZQY*　　942 ero]
ego *H S Tr* erit *Vb GI*　　943 ter] tibi *VaVcBePkFrPm*　　944 criminis] uulneris
SMuVaVbVcVdGoBePkFrPmNe TrHaLa　　946 *line repeated Va*(1)*Va*(2); dabit] rependit
Va(1) dabit *Va*(2)　　948 patet] patent *H GI X*　　949–54 *om. QY*　　949–50 *om. Z*
949 in] et *MN* en *Hu*; redundant] redundat *MuVb*　　950 grauiter] pariter *a*
951–2 *X^2 adds in margin*: uel quod leuius dicet cicius leuiusque remittet/ quod grauius pena
sub grauiore cadet　　951 grauius] grauiusque *D* uel leuius *X^2*; dicet] ducet *Vc* dicet uel
decet *Ha* dicit *Z*; remittet] remittit *Ha Z*　　952 quod] quid *M* et *a*; leuius] leuis *Vd*
grauius *add. interlinearX^2*; grauiore] grauiora *Vc* grauiori *Fr Z* leuiore *DK X add. interlinear*
X^2; cadet] cadit *MuGo* cadat *Vc Z*　　953 honor] honos *a SVaNe Z* honus *La* onos *PkPm*
onus *VdGoBeFr Ha* enim *Mu*　　955 illata] illius *AJCWRHuMNODKVe X* in huius
P　　957 *line repeated in alternative form* Z(1)Z(2); soluendo fuerit] non pereat solus
SMuVaVbVcVdGoBePkFrPmNe TrHaLa Z(1); soluendo] soluendus *AJCRHuMNPKVe*
959 soluent et] soluent aut *H DK GI X* soluant et *MuVdFr AJCWHuMNOVe Ha QY* soluant aut *RP Z*　　960 inuiti] inuite *GI*

945–6 Cf. Prudentius, *Contra Symmachum*, ii. 750: 'his ego pro meritis quae praemia
digna rependam'. Cf. line 1108.

951–2 This reads like nonsense, which is what the scribe *X^2* obviously thought, as he reversed
the relation of crime and punishment. Is it deliberately nonsensical, with comic intention?

959–60 *decimas soluent*: in principle, monks were liable both to receive tithes payable on
land donated to them and worked by others, and to pay tithes on the produce of their demesne
land, which was cultivated by themselves. However, in the course of time, and increasingly
during the 12th c., monastic houses were granted exemption from the obligation to pay
tithes, especially in the case of the new orders which were bringing remote and inhospitable
areas of land under cultivation for the first time (*novalia*), and gaining little more than the
bare necessities as a result. The new orders were also inclined to renounce any income from
tithes due on lands that were donated to them, in order to avoid entanglement in worldly

SPECVLVM STVLTORVM   105

will of the Pope; but I will avenge my own injury. The great Burnellus, thrice consul, who is my progenitor, will be the avenger of the crime committed against me. The Roman curia, which pays back like with like, [945] will give worthy rewards to worthy merits. The offence is serious, the person more so, and the injuries are clearly most serious of all; everything is of great weight. These things redound on the Lord Pope in particular; he is seriously injured, and both his injuries are manifest. [950] The one he judges more serious, he will the more speedily and easily forgive; the more trivial one will incur a more serious punishment. His wounded honour can be expiated with tears and prayers, lest his vengeance in this respect seem excessive. But the losses inflicted he will not forgive on any account; [955] he'll be gentle [enough], if he allows compensation to be made for them. So long as the Cistercian order makes payment, he won't have lost everything. Either they shall pay tithes, and—however reluctantly—they shall cover their backsides with breeches, by an unchanging law, [960] nor

concerns and also to avoid encroaching on the rights of others. For a full study of this whole complicated situation, see Constable, *Monastic Tithes*. In 1132 Pope Innocent II exempted the Cistercian houses associated with St Bernard of Clairvaux's congregation from paying tithes on land cultivated by themselves (PL clxxix. 123, no. lxxii). Further extensions of this privilege were granted on a case-by-case basis, and by the 1180s it was granted to the order as a whole (Constable, *Monastic Tithes*, pp. 241–2, 251–4; Bruun, ed., *Cistercian Order*, p. 115). The Cistercians were not the only monastic body to be exempted from the payment of tithes, but the increasing wealth that accrued from their successful agricultural activities made their exemption seem grossly unfair, especially in comparison with smaller and poorer houses of (say) Benedictines, or when the transfer of property to them deprived previous owners of tithes that they were accustomed to receive. Resentment against the Cistercians on this score was widespread, particularly since, on the other hand, they defended their right to receive tithes from property which had been gifted to them, despite the fact that their statutes explicitly forbade them to receive revenues from ecclesiastical sources such as churches, altars, and tithes (*Exordium parvum* XV, ed. Waddell, *Narrative and Legislative Texts*, p. 434; *Instituta* IX, ibid. p. 460; *Statuta* 1190. 1B, ed. Waddell, *Statutes*, p. 174. See also Knowles, *Monastic Order*, pp. 354–5; Constable, *Monastic Tithes*, pp. 136–44, 186–97; Bruun, ed., *Cistercian Order*, p. 81). As early as the 1130s, Peter the Venerable wrote both to Pope Innocent II and to the chapter-general at Cîteaux, complaining about the order's freedom from tithes (*Letters* xxxiii–xxxv, ed. Constable, i. 107–16; Constable, 'Cluniac Tithes', pp. 609–17; id., *Monastic Tithes*, pp. 276–7). See also the letter from Pope Alexander III to the Cistercian general chapter, *c*.1178–9, in Wiederhold, 'Papsturkunden in Frankreich', pp. 60–2. Later in Alexander's long pontificate, however, he relaxed his policy on this matter (Constable, *Monastic Tithes*, pp. 294–306). In 1174 × 1181, Peter of Blois (acting as secretary of Archbishop Richard of Canterbury) wrote to the abbot and chapter of Cîteaux, earnestly requesting them to renounce voluntarily their exemption from tithes (Peter of Blois, *Epistolae*, no. lxxxii, PL ccvii. 252–5; summarized in *English Episcopal Acta ii. Canterbury 1162–1190*, ed. Cheney and Jones, no. 106, and partially translated in Constable, *Monastic Tithes*, pp. 292–3). The Fourth Lateran Council of 1215 revoked the exemption from tithes on all lands to be acquired in the future, though it still held good for those acquired earlier. An 'endeavour to interpret the earlier privilege as applying only to lands which the monks had been the first to bring under cultivation (*novalia*) was quashed', but it was allowed to apply to all land so reclaimed after 1215 (Knowles, *Monastic Order*, pp. 355–6).

106   *SPECVLVM STVLTORVM*

claustra nec exibunt, perdentque noualia passim,
    aut tria marcarum millia plena dabunt.
Sortem cum poena soluent tria millia plena,
    et nisi festinent soluere, mille dabunt.

965 Sed quid erit de me? Quaenam uindicta sequetur?
    Qualiter ulciscar sic laceratus ego?
Papa quidem statuet ne quis de fratribus extra
    saepta sui claustri quolibet ire queat.
Quam si quis fuerit legem trangressus eorum,

970   haec tria perpetuo iure sequantur eum:
numquam uina bibat, nisi cruda legumina gustet,
    sitque grauis culpae poena perennis ei.
Haec de iure poli faciet mihi papa libenter;
    sed de iure fori quid genus omne meum?

975 Istud erit quod ego faciam statuisse per orbem,
    si fuerit tanto tempore uita comes.
Istos conuersos (quos peruersos magis esse
    constat, ut ex factis nomina certa trahant)
ecclesiae portam quisquis conspexerit extra,

980   mox oculos dextros auferat atque pedes.

---

961 nec] non *JCWHuMNK*; perdentque] perduntque *GI* perdantque *P Ha* perque decem *K*; passim] possim *LE*   **963–4** *om. H Fr ROPVe X*   **963** *om. QY*; sortem] *sic Pover erasure* sorte *Pm Ha* mortem *G*; millia] *om. I*ᵃᶜ; poena] plena *Ha* pene *Z*; soluent] soluant *Vc Ha*   **965** sequetur] sequatur *Mu JO Tr*   **966** ulciscar] ultus ero *SMuVaVbVcVdGoBePkFrPmNe TrHaLa Z*   **967** quidem] quid *E Va* quidam *Tr*; statuet] statuit *FrNe HuMNOD*   **968** saepta] cepta *QY*; claustri] claustra *VaFr* claustro *Go*   **969** fuerit] fuerat *EF*   **970** perpetuo] *sic P²* perpetua *G* perpetue *Q* precipio *Go*; sequantur] sequentur *a ROPDVe SMuVaVbVcVdGoBePkFrPmNe TrHaLa ZX*   **971** nisi cruda] nec cocta *a* nec cruda *D X* nec nisi cruda *Go* nisi ruda *Fr*; gustet] gustat *MuFr O*   **972** sitque] sicque *SVcBePkFr P I QY* sit *La*; culpae] culpa *AJCWRHuMNPKVe QY*; ei] erit *H Vc GI*   **973** haec] hoc *F H* γ+(*Mu*ᵖᶜ) *AJCWHuMNDK GI TrHaLa ZQY*   **974** quid] quod *JD*; genus] decus *a* egenus *Y*; meum] malum *Vd R*   **975** *om. sp. left empty Vc*   **977** istos conuersos] istis conuersis *SMuVaVbVcVdTGoBePkPmNe HaLa* istos peruersus *Fr*   **978** certa] certe *Vd* uera *D X*; trahant] trahunt *SMu CWO Z* habent *QY*   **979** conspexerit] *sic Pover erasure* confecerit *G* perrexerit *D X*   **980** mox] mors *SPk*; oculos] oculo *HuN*; auferat] auferetur *Mu* auferet *VaVcGoBePkPmNe OP TrHaLa Q* aufert *VdFr*

Walter Map taunted the Cistercians by saying that like the Pharisee in Luke 18: 11–13, they boast 'we are not as other men', but unlike the Pharisee, they do *not* go on to say 'we give tithes of all that we possess' (*De nugis curialium*, dist. i. 25, pp. 88–9). John of Salisbury attacked the monastic 'wolves in sheep's clothing', who are clearly Cistercians, who 'urge princes to deprive churches of their lawful rights because of the vices of [their priests]. They rob churches of tithes and first fruits and do not scruple to accept churches from the hands of laymen without the bishops' having been consulted...I only marvel...how it is that they do not blush to usurp or withhold tithes and rights which belong to others. Perchance they

SPECVLVM STVLTORVM

shall they leave their cloisters, and they shall lose all their new fields, or they shall pay 3,000 marks. They shall pay a full 3,000 as capital, plus a fine, and if they're not quick about their payment, they'll pay another thousand. But what about me? What punishment shall follow? [965] How shall I be avenged for being thus mutilated? The Pope shall decree that none of the brethren may go anywhere outside the confines of his cloisters. And if any of them offends against this law, these three things shall be imposed on him by an eternal law: [970] he shall never drink wine, he shall eat nothing but raw beans, and this punishment for his serious crime shall be endless. The Pope will gladly do these things for me, by divine law, but what will all my kind do by secular law? This is what I shall get established worldwide [975]—if I live long enough. If anyone sees outside of the church door those "converts" (who are rather perverts, if they were to bear the name that matches their deeds), he will at once take away their right eye and foot. [980] And unless a bell hangs from his neck, his penis will be removed, together with its

---

will say, "We are men of religion." But surely to pay tithes is part of religion' (*Policraticus*, vii. 21, ed. Webb, ii. 192, 194, 196–7; trans. Dickinson (corrected), pp. 313, 315, 317). Gerald of Wales compared the Cistercian reversal of their initial rejection of tithes to a dog returning to its vomit (*Speculum ecclesiae*, dist. iii. 21, *Opera*, iv. 256). *braccis*: the Cistercians were notorious for their principled failure to wear drawers beneath their habits; see n. to lines 2139–56. *lege perenni*: Dracontius, *De laudibus Dei*, i. 737, ii. 20; John of Salisbury, *Entheticus maior*, ed. van Laarhoven, 569, 1041.

961 *noualia*: land cleared and tilled for the first time (*DMLBS* 3a); see preceding note.

963 *Sortem*: 'capital (of a debt)' (*DMLBS* 7). *poena* = 'emenda'; see Du Cange s.v. 'poena fiscalis', and cf. *DMLBS* s.v. 'emenda' 4, 'fine, mulct'.

968 *quolibet ire*: Ovid, *Tristia*, iii. 8. 22.

971 *nisi*: a preceding 'non' ('non nisi') is understood from 'nunquam'. Cf. lines 2097, 3171.

973–4 *iure poli... iure fori*: Niermeyer glosses 'ius poli' as 'divine law' (that is, the law that applies universally to all societies) and 'ius fori' as 'secular law' (that is, the law as formulated within a particular society).

976 *si fuerit tanto tempore uita comes*: 'if I live that long'; 'vita comite' = 'while alive'. See *DMLBS* s.vv. 'comes' 1b; 3 'vita' 3d. Cf. 4 Kgs. (2 Kgs.) 4: 16: 'in hac eadem hora, si vita comes fuerit, habebis in utero filium'.

977–8 *Conuersi* were lay brothers who carried out most of the manual labour necessary to support the monastic economy. Although 'the institution of the lay brotherhood was not original to the Cistercians,... they developed it to its fullest extent'; in particular, the *conuersi* were placed in charge of the monastic granges which 'formed the basis of the Cistercian agrarian economy' (Bruun, ed., *Cistercian Order*, pp. 84–5). The *conuersi* took vows of celibacy like the monks, and their efficiency and (unpaid) hard work were 'critical to the success of the Cistercian grange agriculture' (ibid. pp. 119–20). Burnellus's insistence that the *conuersi* should not be seen 'outside of the monastery' (979–81) presumably means 'outside the monastery lands'. *conuersos... peruersos*: The same play on words at the expense of monastic lay-brothers is to be found in the 11th-c. satirist Sextus Amarcius (*Satires*, i. 131–3): 'Quid de conuersis, quos recto et nomine vero/ Appellare volens perversos dicere debet,/ Christe, feram?' ('Christ, what shall I say about lay brothers ["converts"] whom one wishing to name rightly and truly ought to call perverts?', trans. Pepin). On the need for 'nomina' ('uerba') to match 'facta' ('res'), see n. to line 153.

108   SPECVLVM STVLTORVM

Et nisi campana collo dependeat una,
    mentula tollatur quodque cohaeret ei.
Dentur eis braccae, uinum tollatur in aeuum,
    damneturque caro, piscis, et oua simul.
985 Sufficiant cunctis duo cocta legumina tantum,
    uel potius cruda, sit nisi festa dies.
Haec ego cuncta meos faciam stabilire parentes,
    ne sit in aeternum res habitura modum.
Haec etiam papa mihi confirmabit in aeuum,
990 subscribetque suas curia tota notas.'

Simulatio fratris Fromundi

Talibus auditis, timuit Fromundus et ultra
    quam credi poterat obstupefactus ait:
'Si sciat haec abbas, nec eum res tanta latebit,
    culleus aut certe mors mihi certa manet.
995 Quis furor impegit canibus uexare ministrum
    pontificis summi? Non ita rebar ego.
Nunc opus est facto, sed et hoc nimis accelerato,
    nunc opus auxilio consilioque mihi.
Constat enim quod si uiuens discesserit iste,
1000 res nulla poterit conditione tegi.
Blanditiis opus est multis insistere, donec
    una dies ueniat quae sit ad istud opus.

981–2 *om. QY*   **982** tollatur] collatur *Fr Z* collator *Tr*; quodque cohaeret] quodque coherit *CW* et quicquid adheret *GI*; *H adds in margin* mentula .i. domus uoluptatis. *Vc* glosses 'mentula' as 'uirga uirilis' and 'quodque coheret ei' as 'testiculi'.   **983** eis] ei *Vb D QY* et eis *Fr*; tollatur] collatur *Fr C Tr*   **984** damneturque] damnaturque *AJCWRHuMNO* demneturque *Z* dematurque *SMuVaVcVdGoBePkFrPmNe TrHaLa* demanturque *Vb*   **985** sufficiant] sufficiat *H SVdBePkNe GI La* sufficiunt *Fr* sufficient *QY*; cocta] tacta *QY*ᵃᶜ *om. VcGo*   **986** uel potius] que quasi sint *D X*; sit] sed *GI*   **987** ego] *sic I²over erasure* sic *G* ergo *QY*   **988** *om. GI* (*add. in margin I²*); ne] ni *CW* nec *ZQY*   **989** papa mihi] mihi papa *Vc Z* papa sic δ *X*   **990** subscribetque] subscribatque *E VdGo RD Tr Z* subscribitque *Fr GI*   **992** quam] qua *I*; poterat] poterit *AJCWRHuMNOPKVe* potuit *D X*   **993–1048** *transp. after 1102 Z*   **993** haec] hoc *SMuVaVbVcVdGoBePkFrPmNe M GI TrHaLa ZY* hic *Q*; eum] *om. HuMN*; res tanta] tanta res *Fr*; latebit] latescit *ZQY*   **995–6** *transp. GI corr. I²*   **996** non ita rebar ego] non ita robar ego *E* nam ita rebar ego *D* gratia nulla fuit *X*   **997** nunc] non /uel nunc *Ha*; et] ad *Go R X in Mu om. Vb*; hoc] hec *M* hic *VaVbVdBePkFrPmNe TrHaLa om. Z*; nimis] minus *CW om. Fr*   **998** *om. O*   **999** uiuens] uiuus *MuVd* ueniens *O*ᵃᶜ *Z* ueniet *O*ᵖᶜ; discesserit] discrescerit *CW* discessit et *Go*   **1000** res] sed *CW*   **1002** ueniat] uenerit α *Ha* ueniet *MuVdFr Tr*

SPECVLVM STVLTORVM

appendages. Breeches will be given them, and wine taken away from them for good, while meat, fish, and eggs will all be forbidden. Two dishes of cooked beans alone shall be enough for all of them [985]—or rather raw ones, unless it's a feast-day. I'll make my relatives ratify these rules, so that there shall be no limit set to them, for all eternity. The Pope too will endorse them for me for all time, and the whole curia shall witness the bull.' [990]

The Deception of Brother Fromundus

When he heard this, Fromundus was afraid, and stupefied beyond belief, he said: 'If the abbot learns this—and the affair won't remain hidden from him—I'm looking at concrete overshoes or certain death for sure. What madness led me to harry the Pope's messenger with dogs? [995] I didn't know that's how it was. Something must be done, and double-quick too; now I need help and advice. For it's clear that if he leaves here alive, the affair cannot be concealed by any means. [1000] It is necessary to pile on the charm, until the time comes for the job. He's got to be got rid of, so that our whole breed isn't ruined, and our

---

990 *notas*: 'nota' = 'legal document' (*DMLBS* 9b).

991–2 *ultra / quam credi poterat*: cf. Gen. 27: 33.

994 *culleus*: literally, a leather bag in which, in Roman times, parricides were sewn up and thrown from the Tarpeian Rock into the Tiber (*OLD* s.v. 3).

995 *Quis furor impegit*: also in *Lawrence*, 2249.

SPECVLVM STVLTORVM

Tollere de medio decet hunc, ne tota per istum
gens pereat nostra depereantque loca.

1005 Sed nimis astute tantum scelus est faciendum,
et procul a populo conuenit istud agi.

Nam si fama loquax quicquam cognouerit inde,
peius erit multo quam fuit ante malum.

Plus etiam fratres mihi sunt quam fama timori,
1010 nam furor illorum nescit habere modum.

Fama potest aliquo saltem moderamine flecti,
illos cum furiunt flectere nemo potest.

Fratribus atque foro par est committere quicquam
prodere quod timeam uel latuisse uelim.

1015 Vna fori facies, fratrum sunt mille, quid ergo?
Quod cupis occultum reddere nemo sciat.

Menstrua namque fides faciem cum tempore mutat;
ne credas fidei, sit nisi fida tibi.

Qui se multorum fidei committere curat,
1020 auguror hunc leuiter posse carere fide.

Res erit arcana, quae sunt facienda seorsum
nemo sciat; satis est solus ut ipse sciam.

Quid moror? Accedam supplex ueniamque precabor,
reddere promittam perdita quaeque prius.

1025 Decipiam stultum, socium simulabo fidelem,
committet sese credulus ille mihi.'

Dixit, et accessit supplex, ueniaque petita
plus quam perdiderat reddere spondet ei;

Hospitiique mora longos releuare labores
1030 obtulit et molli membra fouere toro.

1003 tollere de medio decet hunc] tolle hunc decet de medio *Vd* tollere hunc decet
de medio *BePk*; decet] docet *H*; istum] istam *Va* ipsum δ *GI ZXQY*   **1004** *om. sp.*
left empty Vc   **1007** nam] quam *VdBe TrLa om. QY*; quicquam] quicquid *VdFrNe*
HuMNDK XY quodquam *Ve*   **1008** multo] multum *P I*; fuit] fuerit *VcVd*
1010 illorum] istorum *ZQY*   **1011–12** *om. QY*   **1013–16** *om.   Vc*
1014 prodere] perdere *F Fr R*; quod] quid *QY*   **1015–18** *om. QY*   **1016** cupis]
cupit *ROPVe fb* capis *La*   **1017** menstrua] monstrua *CWD*; mutat] mittat *E* mutet *Mu*
O   **1018** credas] credis *MN*; nisi] mihi *H ACWRHuMNP G*   **1020** *om. La,*
add. in margin La^{pc}   **1021** erit] erat *TrHa*   **1022** *om. T*; sciat] sciet α *D X*; solus
ut] ut solus *Vc ACWHuMNO^{ac}PVe Q* solus quod *Vb*; sciam] sciat *Go Z*   **1023** moror]
meror *M* morar /[*uel*] moror *La*; precabor] rogabo γ- *TrHaLa*   **1024** perdita] perdere
Fr R   **1025** decipiam] accipiam δ *QY*; simulabo] similabo *LE C* simulando *H Mu*
1026 ille] ipse γ+ *R* esse *F*   **1028** *om. Vc*   **1029** releuare] reuelare *VaVdTPkPm*
M La Z corr. Z² pre ualore Go

SPECVLVM STVLTORVM

houses destroyed, because of him. And a crime of this magnitude has got to be committed cunningly [1005] and out of the public eye, for if tongue-wagging rumour knows anything of it, the disaster will be much worse than before. Also, I fear my brothers more than gossip, for their rage knows no limit. [1010] Rumour can at least be quietened down by some good management, whereas no one can quieten them down when they are in a rage. To confide to my brothers something that I'm afraid to reveal or would like to remain a secret is the same as confiding it to the whole town. The town has one face, the monks a thousand: what then? [1015]—Let no one know what you want to keep hidden. For shifting faith changes its face with time; put no trust in good faith, unless it's faithful to you. I reckon that anyone who cares to entrust himself to the good faith of a multitude will quickly find good faith in short supply. [1020] The affair will be secret; no one shall know what is to be done in private. It's enough that I alone know it. What am I waiting for? I'll approach him as a suppliant and beg for mercy, promising to restore everything he has lost. I'll deceive the fool, and pretend to be a faithful friend; [1025] gullible as he is, he will trust himself to me.' So saying, he went to him as a suppliant, asked for mercy, and promised to restore to him more than he had lost. He offered to relieve his long exertions with a stay in a guest-house, and to rest his limbs in a soft bed. [1030] He promises money, doctors,

---

1007 *fama loquax*: Ovid, *Metamorphoses*, ix. 137, *Ex Ponto*, ii. 9. 3; Lucan, *De bello civili*, viii. 782; William of Blois, *Alda*, 557, *Commedie*, vi. 106; Walter of Châtillon, *Alexandreis*, ix. 31; Joseph of Exeter, *Ylias*, i. 307.

1012 *flectere nemo potest*: John of Salisbury, *Entheticus maior*, ed. van Laarhoven, 474.

1019–20 For proverbs warning against trust, see Singer, *Thesaurus*, s.v. 'Trauen' 2. 1. 3 (xi. 409–10).

1021 *Res erit arcana*: the first line of Hugh Primas's poem on his old coat (*Gedichte*, ed. Meyer, xii. 1).

1024 *perdita quaeque prius*: also at *Miracles*, 916.

1026 *credulus ille*: Ovid, *Heroides*, v. 106.

1029 Cf. Ovid, *Metamorphoses*, xv. 16: 'requie longum relevasse laborem'.

1030 *membra fouere toro*: repeated at *SS*, 2080, 2892. Cf. Maximian, *Elegies*, i. 40 ('membra fovere cibo'). Closer is John of Salisbury, *Entheticus minor*, ed. van Laarhoven, 52: 'membra fovenda thoro'.

112   *SPECVLVM STVLTORVM*

Spondet opes, medicos, genialia festa, salubris
    aeris accessum, quicquid et ipse uelit.
Nil deerit uotis, simul et semel omne quod optat
    accidet, accedat ipse uidere locum.

1035   Nam prope Lugdunum, Rodani conterminus undis,
    est situs arboribus consitus ille locus.
Est alter Paradisus ibi, quia quicquid habere
    mens humana cupit terra beata parit.
Ipse loci dominus domui disponet, ut eius

1040   sederit arbitrio, nemo rebellis erit;
seruiet ad nutum famulus uenietque uocatus,
    quaque placebit ei quisque sequetur eum;
ipse modum dicet sibi quo seruire clientes
    hos uelit aut illos, nemo resistet ei.

1045   Nec nouus hospes erit nec ut aduena cras rediturus,
    sed quasi perpetuus ciuis in urbe sua.
Postulat, adiurat, hortatur, et omnia spondet,
    uimque facit precibus, uoce manuque trahens.

1031–2 *om. QY*   **1031** opes medicos] opus medicos *M* apes medicas *LE* apes medicos *Tr*; genialia] generalia *H* γ+ δ *GI X*   **1032** aeris] aeris et *LE*   **1033–4** *transp. Fr*
1033 simul et semel] semel et simul *H S GI QY* simul et celer α; omne] esse *L Tr*
1034 accidet] accidit *LE Vb Ha* accedet *Fr Z*; accedat] accedat *QY* accidit *Z*   **1035** conterminus] cum terminus *S BePk Tr* cum cerminus *Vd* cum terminis *H G* conterminis *Pm C*
terminus *R* continuus *Ha* continuis *Z* exterius *Fr*; undis] undas *VdGo Tr* unde *Fr*
1036 *after 1035, T inserts two spurious lines, of which only the last few words are visible:* … pariter
et amenis plenus/ … satis est solus ut ipse sciam. *T then continues, at top of fo. 166ʳ, with lines
1023–4 (repeated), first half of 1025, then 1036 and following lines.*   consitus] conscitus *H Q*
consutus *AHuMN* causitus *LE* situs et *MuGoPm* situs *Fr* non conscitus *Z*
1039 domui] domini *VaNe D GI* domum *VcTPm Ha* donum *Vd La*; disponet] disponit
H ZQ disposuit *Va*; ut] et γ+   **1040** sederit arbitrio] cederit arbitrio *F*
AfCWRHuNO^{pc}PVe X crederit arbitrio *MO^{ac}* cesserit arbitrio *K* sesserit arbitrio *D* arbitrii
uotis *SMuVaVcTGoBePkFrPm TrHaLa* arbitrii uocis *Vd* arbitrii rotis *Vb* arbitrii uoci
Ne   **1042** quaque] quisque *Go* δ *X* quidque *Tr* quodque *Be* quoque *VcVd GI Z*;
quisque] quisquis *H Fr Tr*; sequetur] sequatur *M Ha* sequitur *Fr*; eum] eam *I* eum /uel idem
Ha   **1043** *U joins. First folio (fo. 1ʳ/13ʳ) is heavily rubbed and largely illegible up to line
1067*   dicet] dictat *LF* dicat *E* dicit *ZQ*; seruire] sub iure *Pm^{ac} Ha* alias seruire *add. Pm^{pc}*
1044 hos] hoc *Go GI* has *Q*; illos] istos *La ZQY om. Fr*; resistet] resistit *F Fr COD ZQY*
resistat *SVaTBeNe TrLa*   **1045** ut] nec *TGo om. SMuVaVbVcVdBePkFrPmNe
TrHaLa*; cras rediturus] transgrediturus *TNe Tr* transcenditurus *FrPm Ha*; cras] quas *F* sic
L trans *SVaGoBePk om. Vd*   **1047** adiurat] adiuuat *Pk* et iurat *T Q* et imperat *Pm Ha*
admore *Fr*   **1048** uimque facit] omnia dat *P over erasure*; uoce manuque] manu
uoceque *VaVdBeFr Tr* manuque uocemque *Pm* uoce namque *Go*

SPECVLVM STVLTORVM 113

convivial dinners, fresh air, whatever he wants. All his wishes will be granted; everything he desires will be instantly realized, if he comes to visit the house. For it is situated near to Lyon, bordering the waters of the Rhône, [1035] thickly planted with trees. It's a second paradise there, for whatever the human mind wishes to have, the blessed earth brings forth. As master of the establishment, he [Burnellus] will arrange everything in the house to suit his will; no one will disobey. [1040] A servant will be at his beck and call, and will come when summoned; in whatever way he pleases, everyone will serve him. He himself shall dictate the way in which he wants these servants or those to look after him; no one will refuse him. Nor shall he be a newly arrived guest, nor a stranger who is to depart tomorrow, [1045] but like a permanent citizen in his own city. He [Fromundus] begs, he entreats, he urges, promising everything; he uses force along with prayers, drawing him on with hand and words alike.

1035–8 Description of an earthly paradise (*locus amoenus*) which offered every kind of delight to the senses was one of the most highly favoured rhetorical motifs of Latin poetry from classical times down to the 16th c. See Curtius, *European Literature*, pp. 195–200.

1045–6 Modelled on Eph. 2: 19: 'Ergo iam non estis hospites, et advenae: sed estis cives sanctorum...'.

114   *SPECVLVM STVLTORVM*

Dissimulatio Burnelli

Annuit ille libens, tamen hac sub conditione,
1050   tollat ut e medio mors inopina canes;
comperiensque dolos Fromundi, dissimulare
rem studet, et risu palliat ora leui.
Dixit et ipse sibi secum duo uerba, nec illa
sic tamen audiret ut suus hospes ea.
1055   'En aliud ducens aliud meditatur asellus,
euentus uarios dissona uota tenent.
Saepe solet uitio uirtus uelocior esse,
praeuenit et morbum cura diserta grauem.
Fraude cadunt fraudes, falluntur et artibus artes,
1060   obruiturque dolus praeueniente dolo.'
Nec mora, Fromundus, correpto fuste, molossis
omnibus extinctis, accelerauit iter.
Cumque super ripam Rodani graderetur asellus,
et prope Fromundus subsequeretur eum,
1065   cernens Burnellus quantum foret aptus iniquis
saltibus et subitis mortibus ille locus,
impulsu subito summa de rupe reiectum
Fromundum Rodani fecit ad ima uehi.
Interceptus aquis mortem gustauit in undis;

1049–1102 *transp. after 1153* Z   1049 libens] *om. VaGoPm*; conditione] condicione
libens *VaGoPm*   1050 ut] ne *Go* et *Ve La om. Fr*; e] de *PkFr om. Tr*   1051 dolos]
dolus *Fr* dolus /uel fraudes *Ha*; dissimulare] dissimulari *VdBe La* dissimulaui
Tr   1052 rem studet et] student re *Vd* studet re *Be La* studereque *Tr*; studet] studet /
uel suadet *Ha*; palliat] palleat *H Vd GI Tr QY* pallia *D* polliat *Va*; ora] hora *GIᵃᶜ Tr QY* ore
Z   1054 sic] si *MuFr R Ha QY*; ut] quod α; hospes] hostes *Be Tr*   1055 aliud¹]
alius *GI*; ducens] minans α *H* δ *GI UXQY* dicens *MuVaVcBeFrPm TrHaLa*
Z   1056 uota] tota *I* uoce *Vd La*   1057 uelocior] uolocior *H* pernicior *Dᵃᶜ X* uel
uelocior *add. in margin* Xᵖᶜ   1058 diserta] deserta *F SVbVcVdGoBeFrPm CD Tr fb*
deserta /uel diserta *La*   1059 falluntur] fallantur *G*   1061–2 *om. QY*
1061 mora] mea *GI corr. I²*; correpto] correpte *Go* correpta *La* correptis *H T*
AʒRHuMNOPDK GI UX corruptis *Ve* correptus *CW om.* Z; fuste] faste *X* morte *U*; molos-
sis] molossos *GoPkFr* molossus *Vd Tr*   1062 extinctis] ex cunctis *G* exterritis
MuVaVdBePkFrPmNe TrHaLa; *(whole line)* disponit socium fallere fraude suum δ
UX   1063 cumque] dumque *VdTBe*   1065 quantum] quam *MuGoFr* quia *Va*;
iniquis] iniquus *E VaVcVdPkFr OP Tr*   1066 mortibus] moribus *GI corr. I²* morsibus
Tr   1067 *Fr begins this line* 'Impulsu subitos', *then switches to 1066b* ('moribus ille
locus'), *then starts 1067 afresh* (*Fr*(2)); summa] summe *Fr*(2) rupe] ripe *CW* ripa *T P*; reiectum]
reiectam Z deiectum *H* proiectum *Vc O* retectum *Be TrLa*   1068 uehi] rui α
1069–70 *om. P Tr*; *after 1069*, *ZQY add a line* (1070a): Et dare que uoluit premia dantur ei
(*QY omit 1071 in compensation*).

SPECVLVM STVLTORVM   115

Burnellus's Pretence

He willingly agreed, but on this condition, that a sudden death should put an end to the dogs; [1050] detecting Fromundus's trickery, he took care to show nothing, disguising his expression with a gentle smile. He spoke a few words to himself, in such a way that his host wouldn't hear them: 'The ass-driver thinks one thing, and the ass, another; [1055] their different intentions have different outcomes. Virtue is often quicker than vice, and skilled treatment prevents a serious illness. Deceit is thwarted by deceit, and tricks are cheated by tricks; guile is overcome by the guile that anticipates it.' [1060] Without delay, Fromundus seized a stick, killed the dogs, and set off in haste. While the ass was walking along the bank of the Rhône, and Fromundus was following close behind him, Burnellus, seeing how suitable the place was for disastrous falls [1065] and sudden death, with a sudden shove threw Fromundus from a high rock and hurled him to the bottom of the Rhône. Engulfed by the water, he tasted death in the waves; deceitfully

---

1051–2 Cf. *Lidia*, 309: 'Palliat illa dolum subridens' (*Commedie*, vi. 234).

1055 Proverbial. See Walther, *Proverbia*, 20293, and Singer, *Thesaurus*, s.v. 'Esel' 8. 1 (iii. pp. 68–9) and s.v. 'Gedanke' 10. 2–10. 5 (iv. 251–2). After 1054, *Ve* adds a line: 'Altera mens asini mens altera qui regit illum' (Werner, *Sprichwörter*, p. 3, A 61). Cf. *Fecunda ratis*, ed. Voigt, i. 258: 'Idem animus non est asino pueroque minanti', and *Ysengrimus*, iv. 368: 'Optat sic asinus, tendit agaso secus' ('The ass wants one thing, the ass-driver has other ideas'). *ducens*: there is cross-group support for 'mĭnans' from αβδ, but its short first syllable is metrically unacceptable, so I have preferred 'ducens', the γ variant. Cf. Introduction, p. xci.

1059–60 The idea is a commonplace; cf. Venantius Fortunatus, *Carmina*, ii. 2. 8: 'arte ut artem falleret' (*Opera Poetica*, ed. Leo, p. 28); *Miles gloriosus* 335–6: 'Sic laqueum laqueo, sic fraudem fraude resoluit/ Miles' (*Commedie*, iv. 88), and see n. to line 1107 below.

1061–2 *correpto fuste molossis/ omnibus extinctis*: for discussion of the variants in these two lines, see Introduction, pp. cxxii–cxxiii.

1069 *mortem gustauit*: also *Lawrence*, 1653.

SPECVLVM STVLTORVM

1070 euomuitque dolos pocula dante dolo.
Sic dolus et fraudes casu periere sub uno
lusus et est propriis artibus ipse prior.

Canticum Burnelli

Tunc cecinit carmen resonum Burnellus, et altis
uocibus exultans ora resoluit ita.
1075 'Cantemus, socii! festum celebremus, aselli!
Vocibus et uotis organa nostra sonent.
Exultent asini, laeti modulentur aselli,
laude sonent celebri tympana, sistra, chori!
Grimbaldus periit sociique sui perierunt;
1080 mors hostes rapuit quatuor una meos.
Fromundus cecidit Rodani submersus in undis,
lusus et est subito legibus ipse suis.
Incidit in laqueos frater Fromundus iniquos,
quos tamen ipse sibi texuit arte sua.
1085 Qui uoluit sapiens stultum delere scienter,
stultus et ignorans praecipitauit eum.
Corruit in foueam praeceps Fromundus, in illam
quam manibus propriis foderat ipse prius.
Ne uia longa foret, saltu Fromundus in uno
1090 compleuit cursum nescius ipse suum.

1070 *om. Be*; pocula dante dolo] pocula dante deo *H G* fraudes casu periere *Z*(1)*QY. Z repeats this line, with the accepted reading* 'pocula dante dolo', *after lines 1071–2 (in reverse order):* 1070a, 1072, 1071, 1070) 1070–1 *om.* δ *U* 1071 *om. QY*; periere perire *VaVdPkFr I La* perererere *Go* 1074–5 *om. GI*; 1075 *add. I²* 1075 celebremus] celebrantes *I²* celebramus *Tr* resonemus *La* 1075/1078 *transp. D (1078, 1075)* 1076–7 *om.* α *H TFrPm D UX; add. in margin Pm²ᶜ add. in lower margin U²* 1076 sonent] sonant *Ve GI Ha* sonenet *Va* 1077 *om. Vc;* asini] socii *GI*; modulentur] modulantur *CW* modulemur *Ve* 1078 sonent] sonant *Ve Z*; celebri] celebi *Tr* celeri *T La*; tympana] tympona *Be O La* tympanum *Vd*; sistra] cistra *L H AHuMN* cistara *Z* cystra *P Y* tistra *Ve* citra *O* cithra *UQ* nostri *D* nostra *X*; chori] thori *Pk TrLa Z* 1080 hostes] socios *K X* socio *D*; meos] suos *D X* 1081 cecidit] cecidit /uel periit *Ha*; submersus] submersis *E Vd* siue mersus *Z* mersus *T* 1082 *om. Z* 1084 ipse sibi texuit arte sua] arte sua texuit ante sibi α; sibi] sui *VdBePkNe La* 1085 *line repeated in alternative form Z*(1)*Z*(2); qui] quem *AJCWRHuMNOPKVe U fb* qua *QY* quo *Z*(1)*Z*(2); sapiens stultum delere scienter] stolidum sapiens morti dare fraude *T Z*(2); stultum delere scienter] stultum delere scientis *P* stultum de se scienter *MN* stolidum morti (morte *MuBeᵃᶜFr*) dare fraude (fraudem *Pm*) *SMuVaVbVcVdBePkFrPmNe TrHaLa* stolido morti dare fraudes *Go* stultum fraudasse scienter *Z*(1)*QY* 1087 praeceps] frater *D ZX*; illam] istam *UZQY* 1088 manibus propriis] propriis manibus *D X*; prius] sibi *ST Cᵃᶜ X* suis *P* 1089–92 *om. QY* 1090 *om. Vc*; nescius] nesciens *MuTNe*

SPECVLVM STVLTORVM

117

offering a chalice, he vomited up his deceit. [1070] So his deceit and fraud perished in a single fall, and he himself was the first to be fooled by his own tricks.

Burnellus's Song

Then Burnellus sang a loud song, and in thundering tones uttered the following song of triumph: 'Let us sing, friends! Let us celebrate a feast, o asses! [1075] Let our instruments sound in songs and prayers! Let asses rejoice, let donkeys sing in joy, and let timbrels, trumpets, singers sound forth in festive praise. Grimbaldus has perished and his fellows likewise; a common death has carried off my four enemies. [1080] Fromundus has fallen and is drowned in the waters of the Rhône, suddenly tricked by his own kind of practice. Brother Fromundus fell into the evil snares which he himself had laid by his cunning. The wise man who wanted cunningly to kill the fool [1085] was himself thrown down by the ignorant fool. Fromundus fell headlong into the ditch, the same ditch that he had earlier dug himself with his own hands. So that the way should not be long, Fromundus unwittingly finished his journey in a single bound. [1090] His leap was sudden, the rock fell away sheer, the river water greedy for prey, the

---

1072 After 1072, *F* adds 4 lines: 'Fallite fallentes ex magna parte prophanum/ sunt genus in laqueos quos posuere cadant/ iustus uterque fuit neque enim lex equior ulla [est]/ quam necis artifices arte perire sua' ('Deceive deceivers; they are mostly a wicked race. Let them fall into the traps they have set... both were just, for there is no law more just than that those who plot murder should perish by their own device'). The first two lines quote Ovid, *Ars amatoria*, i. 645–6; the second two quote *Ars amatoria*, i. 655–6, which refer to the tyrant Phalaris who roasted alive the maker of the metal bull designed for that purpose (see n. to lines 2569–70); they are also quoted in the introductory *Epistle* to *SS* (§39), which is lacking in the two other α manuscripts (*LE*), and probably made its first appearance in *F* (or a cognate).

1074 *ora resoluit*: a Vergilian phrase; see *Georgics*, iv. 452 and *Aeneid*, iii. 457; other examples in *Lateinisches Hexameter-Lexikon*, iv. 67–8. Also *SS*, 3778; *Lawrence*, 314, 718, 1108; *Miracles*, 432.

1075 An echo of the opening of a famous hymn by Sedulius: 'Cantemus, socii, Domino, cantemus honorem' (*Hymnus* i. 1, *Opera*, CSEL x. 155).

1078 *sistra*: 'sistrum' = 'a sort of trumpet' (*DMLBS* 2). Cf. 2 Kgs. (2 Sam.) 6: 5.

1082 Cf. Ovid, *Heroides*, v. 134: 'et poteras falli legibus ipse tuis'.

1083 *Incidit in laqueos*: also at *Miracles*, 654.

1087–8 Cf. the common biblical idea that he who digs a ditch ('fovea') is the first to fall into it; see Ps. 7: 16; Eccles. 10: 8; Ecclus. 27: 29; Prov. 26: 27.

118 *SPECVLVM STVLTORVM*

Saltus erat subitus, rupes praerupta deorsum,
fluminis unda rapax, alueus absque uadis.
Quem numquam didicit saltum docuisse probatur;
non opus est alio, sufficit unus ei.

1095 Exultet Rodanus celebri de laude triumphi!
Fromundus cecidit, florida psallat humus!'
Mortuus est igitur postquam Fromundus et undis
extractus, patrio sunt data membra solo;
cuius busta uidens cum pertransiret asellus,

1100 fleuit, et inciso marmore scripsit ita.

Epitaphium fratris Fromundi

'Fratribus exemplum frater Fromundus in aeuum
hunc titulum uiuo cepit ab hoste suo;
quem celer ac sapiens tardum stultumque parabat
fallere praeueniens ipse fefellit eum.

1105 Sic tardus celerem, sic sic stultus sapientem
in saltu celeri desipuisse dedit.
Sic fraus fraude perit, sic ars deluditur arte,
sic dolus et fraudes praemia digna ferunt.
Saltum Fromundi fratres memorentur iniqui,

1110 prosit ut a simili nota figura mali.'

1091 saltus] saltibus *CW* stultus *MuGoFr*; subitus] subtus *BeFr*   1092 unda] una *Z*
om. MN; alueus] abiens *HuMN*   1094 alio] alia *Mu* aliud *QY*   1095 exultet]
exultat *Go La*; celebri] celebris *SMuVaVbVcVdTGoBePkFrNe TrHaLa* celebris celebris
Pm   1096 psallat] phallat *HuMN* spallat *L*   1097 et undis] in undis *H MuFrPm*
DK GI TrLa X in aquis *CWHuMN*   1098 patrio] patris *Go* proprio *F CWK* primo *Vd*
D   1099 cuius] eius *ZQY*; uidens] uides *CW om. Z*; pertransiret] pertransisset *C*
pertransierat *Z*   1102 titulum] titulit *GI*   1103–53 *transp. after 882 Z*
1103–4 *om. QY*   1103 quem] quod *LE I* qui *Mu Z*; celer ac] celer et *T A^{pc}HuMNDK*
ZX celis ac *Pk* celerat *Go A^{ac}CRPVe U* celarat *W*; tardum stultumque] tardus stultumque
VaGoPm tardus stultusque *H* tarde stultumque *Be* tarde stultaque *Tr* tarda stultoque *Fr* tardum stolidumque *T* stultum tardumque δ *X* stultum fatuumque *U* stultumque tardumque
fb; parabat] parauit *Tr* pararat *U* peraddat *ACWHuMNVe* peraddit *OP* putauit *R* sperabat
Go   1105–6 *transp. after 1108 ZQY*   1105 sic¹] sit *FrNe*; sic sic stultus] sic sic
stultum *Vd* sic sit stultus *Be La* sicut stultus *Mu* sic stultus *Fr Z* sic et stultus *Go* sic stultus
sic *X*   1106 saltu] saltum *DVe*; celeri] celer *VdBe La* celerem *DVe X*; desipuisse]
decipuisse *H GI Z* dissipuisse *D* preueniendo *X*   1108 ferunt] ferent *Mu D* fuerunt
Vc   1109 saltum] saltus α *H MuVaVbVcVdTGoBePkPmNe* δ *GI TrHaLa UXQY*
salta *Fr* stultum *Z*; memorentur] memorantur *VdTFr R Z* meorentur *Vb*   1110 prosit]
par sit α possit *SMuVaVcVdTGoPkPmNe Ha* ne sinit *Vb* cessent *Fr*; ut] et *S U* uel *Ne om.*
VbGo; a simili] assimili *VaVbVdPmNe* a sibi *Z*

SPECVLVM STVLTORVM

channel deep. He never learned diving, but he gave a lesson in it. One such [lesson] is enough for him; there is no need for another. Let the Rhône rejoice in festive praise for the victory! [1095] Fromundus fell; let the blossoming earth rejoice!' So after the dead Fromundus was pulled out of the water, his body was given to his native earth. The ass, seeing his tomb as he passed by, wept, and cut the following inscription on the marble: [1100]

The Epitaph of Brother Fromundus

'Brother Fromundus, an example to his brethren for all time to come, was given this epitaph by the enemy who outlived him—the slow and foolish one whom he, the quick and clever one, was preparing to trick, and who tricked him first. So the slow made a fool of the swift one in his swift leap, the fool made a fool of the wise man. [1105] So fraud was destroyed by fraud, cunning was tricked by cunning, and guile and trickery have their just rewards. Let Fromundus's wicked brethren remember his leap, so they may learn from its similarity [to this one] how to recognize an obvious example of misfortune.' [1110]

1103 *tardum stultumque*: this order of the adjectives has wider support, and also provides a neater contrast with the preceding adjective pair: celer/tardus, sapiens/stultus.

1107 *sic ars deluditur arte*: *Disticha Catonis*, i. 26. 2. Often used by medieval poets (for example, Walter of Châtillon, *Poems*, no. xxxv. 5. 6–7) to describe Christ's tricking of the devil in the Redemption, in imitation of Venantius Fortunatus, 'arte ut artem falleret' (see n. to lines 1059–60 above).

1108 *praemia digna*: cf. line 946 and n.

1109 Only *S* reads 'saltum', but the singular is obviously more appropriate than the plural.

1110 Mozley prints 'par sit' but I cannot make sense of this; although most of the support for 'prosit' comes from δ, it at least yields a satisfactory meaning.

120   *SPECVLVM STVLTORVM*

His igitur gestis patrias Burnellus ad oras
   festinat celeri corpore, mente, pede.
Sed quia pauper erat, expensa deficiente,
   mendicando suum saepe retardat iter.

1115 Saepe suos casus secum memorando retractat,
   dixerat et dudum quid Galienus ei,
quoque magis pensat propriae discrimina sortis
   se magis accusat, sic sibi saepe loquens:
'Non sum Burnellus sapiens, sed iners et asellus
1120   semper, et in primis stultus hebesque nimis;
stultus ego natus, sum stultus et ante creatus,
   quamque diu fuero non nisi stultus ero.
Stultus et ipse pater meus et stultissima mater,
   dat mihi natura desipuisse mea.
1125 Quod natura dedit, quod tractu temporis haesit,
   haeret et est remanens, nec remouetur idem.
Vah! quid ego? Quis ego? Qualis? Quantumque pudendus?
   Si bene perpendam, nescio quid sit ego.
En ego consumpsi pariter cum corpore sumptus,
1130   cumque labore meo tempus et omne meum.
Iamque satis senui nec adhuc nisi desipuisse
   me fateor, facto res facit ipsa fidem.

1111 igitur] ergo *MuVaVcTFrPmGo R*   1112–13 corpore—sed quia *om. Be*
1112 celeri] celere *GI*   1113 quia] quod *HuMN*   1114 suum] suam *Ve* cibum
D X   1116–1744 *om. I (missing leaves)*   1116 dixerat] dixerit α; et] ut *H G*;
quid] quod *VdBeFr PD HaLa X*   1117 quoque] quodque *H Vd J U* quo facto *Fr*;
discrimina] discrimine *H D G*   1118 se] sed *Vd Tr*; sic] sit *VdGo Ve* fit *Be*
1119 sed] et *D Tr om. La*   1120 semper et in primis] semper in primis *Fr* semper in
euum *Vd* semper inops *Ha* ad fatua pronus *X* semper et imprudens *Be Tr Z*   1122 non]
nil *Vd* nec *Be TrLa*   1123 et²] est α *H SMuVaVbVcVdTBePkPmNe G TrHaLa X om.*
Go   1124 mihi natura] natura mihi α *H G ACJWRHuMNOPKVe UQYZ* natura
meum γ+; mea] meum α *H G QY* mecum *Z* mihi γ+   1125 quod²] que *GoPk*; tractu]
tracta *LE La*   1126 haeret] erat *Go*; nec] et *T*   1127–8 *lines repeated in alternative form Z*(1)*Z*(2)   1127 uah quid ego] apparat quis ego /uel uach quis ego [*uel*] quid
ego *La*; uah] uaht *Hu* apparet γ *Ha Z*(1) appareat *Tr* ualet *Y* uel *Z*(2) *om. Q*; quid ego] quis ego
AJHuNK Q quis *M om.* γ *TrHa Z*(1); quis] quid *AJCWHuMNK Q*; qualis quantumque]
qualis quantumcumque *Z*(1) quantum qualisque *T C* qualis quamcumque *BePk Ha*
1128 quid sit] quis sit *MuVaVdBePkPmNe HaLa* quis sim *VbTGoFr R* quis sum *Vc Z*(1)
sum quid *D X* sim quid *OPK Tr* quid sim *H*ᵖᶜ *CWVe* quid fit *E*   1129 en] cum *C* si *Mu*
Z sic *O*   1130 tempus et omne] et omne tempus *Pm* tempus in omne *T* tempus ad
omne *K* temptusque omne [*sic*] *Go* tempus et ipse *H AJCWRHuMNOPDVe G* UXQY corpus et ipse *Z*; meum] mecum *G Z* bonum *Ne*   1131 iamque satis] iam satis *La fb*
namque satis *Vb* iam satis est *D X*; adhuc] ad hoc *VdBePkPm Tr* ob hoc α; nisi desipuisse]
non desipuisse *MN* nec desipuisse *Q* dissipuisse nisi *Go*

SPECVLVM STVLTORVM 121

So when this was over, Burnellus hastens to his native shores with eager body, mind and feet. But because he was poor, and his money had run out, his journey is often delayed by begging. Often does he think over his adventures to himself, [1115] and what Galen had said to him before, and the more he thinks about the perils that had befallen him, the more he accuses himself, often saying to himself: 'I am not Burnellus the wise, but always a stupid donkey, who is, above all, foolish and dim-witted. [1120] A fool I was born, a fool created, and as long as I last I shall be nothing but a fool. A fool was my father, and my mother a downright idiot; Nature gave me my foolishness. What Nature gave, what has stayed fixed through the passing of time, [1125] clings fast and remains; it won't be got rid of! Oh! What am I? Who am I, of what nature? and how disgraceful? If I consider it well, I don't know what I am. See, I have used up my money and my bodily strength as well, my time and my labour likewise. [1130] I'm now getting on in years, and I confess that I have done nothing but be a fool; the facts

1111 *His igitur gestis*: also *Lawrence*, 1857, 2269; *Miracles*, 2061.

1124 *mihi natura*: this line is the last in a group of six that (unusually) have leonine rhymes (Burnellus/asellus; primis/nimis; natus/creatus; fuero/ero; pater/mater; natura/mea). This gives strong support to DX, the manuscripts reading 'mihi natura'. The scribe of D is very sensitive to metrical matters and may be responsible for this correction to the text himself, which was then copied by X (see Introduction, pp. xcvi, cvi).

122   SPECVLVM STVLTORVM

In sene sensus hebes multum solet esse pudori;
  ni sensus sapiant, est pudor esse senem.
1135 Vertitur in risus iuuenum delira senectus,
  nec redimunt damnum tempora lapsa suum;
  quantumcumque senex sapiat, tamen ecce iuuentus
  semper delirum somniat esse senem.
Et si deliret quisquam pariterque senescat,
1140 iudicio iuuenum nil nisi stultus erit.
Hoc habet innatum multis comitata senectus,
  quo plus desipiat plus sapuisse putat.
Nosse satis potui uerbis uultuque magistri
  quam mea uota forent a ratione procul.
1145 Ha! quotiens uoluit ea quae nocitura putabat
  dissuadere mihi, si licuisset ei.
Sed furor infelix et mens mea caeca futuri
  spreuit et irrisit utile quodque magis.
Et quid erit propriam cum mane reuertar ad urbem,
1150 nondum mutata conditione mea?
Error posterior peior quandoque priore
  esse solet; uereor posteriora mea.
Nonne reuertentem praeses populusque uidebit?
  Nonne meos casus curia tota sciet?

1133 multum] nihil *Q*   1134 sensus sapiant] sensus sapiat *R La* sensu sapiens *Mu*
sensus sapiens *VaTGoFrPm*   1135 risus] risum *VdT DK Tr X fb*   1136 nec] ni
Be Tr nil *Vd La*; redimunt] rediment *a Vd R X* redimant *Be Tr* redemunt *Fr*; lapsa] lassa
QY   1137–8 *om. QY*   1137 quantumcumque] quantumque *Vd J*; sapiat] sapi-
ant *P* sapit *Mu* aspicit *Fr*; tamen] tantum? *P* cum *Pk La*; ecce] ipsa *Vb G Z* ipse *CW* illa *a H*
X ista *Vc* nuda *MuVaT* uda *SGoBePk La* unda *PmNe TrHa* leta *Vd* uidet *Fr*   1138 esse]
ecce *MN*   1139 et si] quod si *F H* γ *G HaLa U* quod nisi *LE* quam si *Tr*; deliret]
delirat *a Vd R*; quisquam pariterque] pariter quisquamque *SMuVaGoBePkPmNe TrHaLa U*
pariter quisquam qui *Vd* pariter quisquam *Fr* pariter quisquando *VbVcT*; senescat] senectat
MN senescit *H* γ+ *ZQY*   1142 desipiat] decipiat *Be Z*; putat] putet *a*
*SMu*ᵖᶜ*VaV3VcTGoBePkPmNe AJCWR*ᵖᶜ*HuMNOPDVe G TrHa*ᵖᶜ*La XY*   1143 nosse]
nosce *LE H Mu Ha*; potui] potuit *VdBe Ve*; uultuque] multumque *QY*; magistri] magister *G*
Tr magistro *Q*   1145 ha] nam *D X* hic *ZQY*; uoluit] ualuit *MuVa*; nocitura] noscitura
W uocitatur *S* natura *MuFr*; putabat] putabit *Ve* sciebat *D X*   1147 futuri] futurum
VdBe Tr   1148 spreuit] spernit *H MN UXQY*; irrisit] irrisum *L* recisit *Va* misit *Z*;
magis] mihi *H G*   1149 ad] in *Mu AJCWMNOPKVe UXQY*   1150 nondum
mutata] non demutata *ACJWHuMNOPDKVe ZQY* de non mutata *H* ue non mutata *G* non
emendata γ+ non denudata *U*   1151 priore] priori *H D UZX*   1152 uereor]
uerior *F G Z*   1153 reuertentem] reuertente *MuGo*; praeses] preces *E Z*ᵃᶜ preceps *L*
presens *SVdBePk TrLa U* presul *P*; uidebit] uidebunt *T AJCWRHuMNOPKVe*
UZQY   1154–3882 *follow 1048 Z*   1154 *om. H*

SPECVLVM STVLTORVM   123

bear witness to it. A dull brain is very shameful in an old man; unless one is wise of mind, it's a disgrace to be old. Foolish old age is made the sport of the young, [1135] and the passing of time does not take away the stigma. However wise an old man is, young men always imagine he's a foolish dodderer. And if anyone is both stupid and old, in the opinion of the young he will be nothing but an idiot. [1140] With many people, old age has this innate characteristic: that the more foolish it is, the wiser it thinks itself. I could have recognized from my master's words and expression how remote my desires were from reason. Ah! how often would he have dissuaded me from those things he thought harmful to me, [1145] if he had been able. But my unhappy madness, and my blindness to the future, scorned and made mock of everything that was most useful. And how will it be when I return to town tomorrow, with my state unchanged? [1150] Sometimes a later error is worse than an earlier one; I fear what comes behind. Won't the mayor and the people see me when I return? Won't the whole court know of my adventures? They will say to me, "Look, he's come back to the town in the

---

1147 Cf. Lucan, *De bello civili*, ii. 14–15: 'sit caeca futuri/ Mens hominum fati'.
1151 An echo of Matt. 27: 64: 'erit novissimus error pejor priore'. Cf. *Lawrence*, 741.

124   SPECVLVM STVLTORVM

1155 Diceturque mihi, "Qualis discessit ab urbe,
     ecce reuersus adest nil nouitatis habens!"
     Ista quidem dici possent, si quod modo non est,
     integra cauda foret ceu fuit ante mihi.
     Ergo quid inspecto tanto discrimine dicent?
1160 Num poterunt risus continuisse suos?
     Risus ero populis, risus totius et urbis,
     risus erit magno cauda recisa foro.
     Si non ante fuit populi Burnellus in ore,
     tunc erit, et digito quisque notabit eum.
1165 Quosque loqui prohibet claustri censura, tacentes
     clamabunt digitis "cauda recisa fuit".
     Sicque loquax digitus redimendo silentia uerbi
     nutibus et signis lingua tacentis erit.
     Mille tibi tollent caudas totidemque remittent,
1170 nec tamen accrescet uel semel una tibi.
     Mille tibi uicibus nouiter plantata resurget
     crescere quam faciet officiosa manus.
     Si de tot uicibus posses, Burnelle, uel unam
     surripuisse tibi, quantus et ipse fores!
1175 Est melius quod non redeam mutilatus in urbem,
     donec prisca tegam crimina sorte noua.

1155 diceturque mihi] dicetque mihi *Z* dicetur de me *SMuVaVbVcTGoBePkFrPmNe TrHaLa* dicetur ad me *Vd*; discessit] recessit *L D* decessit *O G*   1157 possent] possunt *F TFr C La* possem *Vd*; si quod] si quid *Vc* si que *T AJRHuMNOPDKVe XQY* si quo *CW* sed quod *a* sed que *Z*   1158 ceu] seu *LE SVaPkPmNe* Tr^{ac}HaLa *UQ* ut *δ G ZXY* 1159 inspecto] inspectos *VaVc*; dicent] dicent mihi *Va* dicet *Vd La*   1160 num] non *E* γ+ *O ZX*; risus] risos *Be La*   1161 ero] erit *Va G*; et] in *Mu* sic et *T*; urbis] orbis *a VbVdPkNe G Tr QY* omnis *Z*   1162 magno] toti *SMuVaVbVdTGoBePkFrPmNe TrHaLa Z* toto *Vc*   1163–6 *om. Y, add. in lower margin* Y^{pc}   1164 *om. H*; et] in *Fr G* et ir. *Z*   1165 claustri] claustra *Vd G Tr* claustro *Ne La*; censura] cesura *HuM* clausura *Ha*   1166 *om. T*; digitis] digito *δ UZXQY*   1167–76 *om. QY* 1167 digitus] digitis *E MuGoFr G Z*; uerbi] uerbo *E* uerba *Z om. Vd*   1168–9 *transp. after 1185 U*, *1168 replaced by* monstrabit signis tollent caudas totidemque   1168 nutibus et] monstrabit *H^{pc} δ X*; signis] digitis *Vd^{pc} D X*; lingua tacentis erit] lingua silentis erit *T* dedecus omne meum *ACJWRHuNOPKVe U* dedicus omne meum *MD* 1169–72 *om. δ X*   1169 tollent caudas] tollant caudas *TrHa* caudas tollent *MuT* mittent caudas *Vc* tollent caudam *a Z*   1170 accrescet] accrescent *G* accescet *Fr* accrescit *MuVa^{ac}Vc HaLa Z*; uel semel] semel uel *SVc*; una] cona /uel cauda *La*   1171–2 *om. Z* 1172 *fc excerpt 2 joins here*   1173 posses] posset *CW* preses *H* preces *G* poteris *F* possis *Va*; unam] una *LE J*   1174 *om. Fr*   1175 est melius quod non redeam] ast ego numquam sic redeam *H G* dum melius quam sit redeam *S Ha* dum melius quod sit redeam *Va* dii (ay *MuVd* ey *Vc*) melius quam sic (sit *Mu om. Vd*) redeam *MuVbVcVdGoBePkFrPmNe TrLa* cui melius quam sic redeam *T* dedecus est redeam si sic *a* ibo priusquam sic redeam *Z*   1176 crimina] crimine *Be TrHa*; sorte] forte *F CWHu X* fore *MN* sorta *Tr*

SPECVLVM STVLTORVM

125

state he left it, [1155] without having anything new!" They could say that, if only—as is not the case—my tail was whole as it was before. So what will they say when they have seen this great disaster? Will they be able to hold back their laughter? [1160] I'll be a laughing-stock to the people, a laughing-stock for the whole town, and my truncated tail will be a laughing-stock in the central marketplace. If Burnellus was not on everyone's lips before, he will be now, and everyone will point their finger at him. Those whom the monastic restriction forbids to speak [1165] will silently cry out with their fingers "his tail was cut off". So the eloquent finger, making up for verbal silence with nods and signs, will be the tongue of the non-speaker. A thousand tails will they take away from you, and return the same number, but not even one will grow on you. [1170] The newly planted tail which their busy hands will make grow will spring up a thousand times for you. If out of all these occasions, Burnellus, you could have got just one tail for yourself, how great you would be! It is better that I don't return to town mutilated, [1175] until I can cover over old defects with a new condition. My body

1165–8 *censura* = 'ecclesiastical disciplinary justice' (Niermeyer). *digitis*: on monastic sign language, see n. to line 2188.

126   *SPECVLVM STVLTORVM*

Corpus adhuc sanum superest patiensque laborum,
 nondum centenus sum, nisi fallor ego.
Sum leuis et fortis nec adhuc uirtute solutus,
1180 sensus hebes studiis exacuendus erit.
Peruigiles studii longa de nocte labores
 et caput et corpus hoc bene ferre potest.
Restat et annorum numerus de iure legendus
 plurimus, usque patri comparer ipse meo.
1185 Nec sub ueste leui tenuis terrere diaeta
 me poterit certe, uel reuocare domum.
Nec mihi uirga grauis puerorum more nocebit;
 a puero didici multa flagella pati.
Pes uagus a studii non me reuocabit amore,
1190 quin magis accrescet ex grauitate mea.
Aetatis grauitas mihi de leuitate cauebit,
 consuetudo frequens alleuiabit onus.
Nec pudor annorum, quamuis puerilia discam
 iam senior, coget deseruisse scholas.
1195 Nec timor impediet uel desperatio, coeptis
 quo minus insistam nocte dieque meis.
Vtque nihil timeam, labor improbus omnia uincet,
 et Deus audaces ipse iuuare solet.

1177–1234 *om. Va* [*229–92 follow in MS*] 1177 adhuc] ad hunc *E* ad hec *H J* ad
hoc *VdTPkPm La*; sanum superest] superest sanum *H Vb G Q* superest *Fr Z* sanum semper
X; laborum] laborem *fc* 1178 centenus] centennis *Ha Z* septennis *H J G ?*senectus
La; fallor] fallar *SMuVcT AJCWRHuMND HaLa ZX* faller *U* 1180–1 *transp. after*
1182, with order reversed (*1179, 1182, 1181, 1180, 1183*) *U* 1182 hoc] hec *SBe CW*
fc 1184 *om. H; line repeated in corrected form* $W_{(1)}W_{(2)}$; plurimus] plurimos *Fr* pluri-
mis *Pm* pluribus *Go* restat ut *R* in $W_{(1)}$pc; usque] ut *MuVbVcVdTGoBePkFrPmNe TrHaLa*
atque $W_{(1)}$ *corr.* $W_{(2)}$; patri] pater *E GoFr*; comparer] comparar *Z* comparet *Pm* compater
VdTGo C $W_{(1)}W_{(2)}Ve$ *Q fc* 1185–6 *om.* δ *XQY* 1185 sub] cum *H*
SMuVbVcVdTBePkFrNe G TrHaLa UZ fc tamen *GoPm*; tenuis] tenuisse *Go*; terrere] terre
SVd 1186 *after* 1185, *U inserts* 1168–9 (*see above*): nutibus et signis lingua tacentis
erit/ mille tibi tollent caudas totidemque remittent; domum] domi α 1187 nec] non δ
U^2X; mihi] tibi *U corr.* U^2; uirga] briga *U corr.* U^2; *corrected version of line add. in lower margin*
U^2 1189–90 *om. QY* 1189 non me] me non *DK UX fc* 1190 quin] qui
α *H SVbVdGoBePkNe* δ *G TrHaLa UZX fc* quod *MuTPm*; accrescet] accrescit *MuVdGoBe*
O HaLa accessit *Tr* 1191 cauebit] carebit *CW* tacebit *Fr* 1192 (*whole line*)
alleuiabit onus consuetudo frequens *H SMuVdGoBePkFrPmNe AJCWHuMNOPDKVe G*
TrHaLa UZXQY fc alleuiabit onus sollicitudo frequens *Vc* 1194 senior coget] coget
senior *AJOPKVe* cogit senior *CWRHuMN* senior cogitet α; (*whole line*) coget cum sit honor
incoluisse scolas *D X* 1195–6 *om. QY* 1195 nec] non δ *X*; uel] nec α *Mu* nil
Fr; coeptis] ceptus *Mu* libris *X fc* 1196 meis] magis uel meis *La* 1197 utque]
ut quoque *TFr*; timeam] caueam *VbVc*; uincet] uincit *SMuVbV*ac*VdTPkFrPmNe RD G Ha*
UZXQ uicit *GoBe TrLa* uincent *M* 1198 audaces] audentes α *H S U*

SPECVLVM STVLTORVM   127

is still healthy and capable of hard work, and I am not yet a hundred, if I am not mistaken. I am nimble and strong, and not devoid of strength; my dull brain must be sharpened by study. [1180] My head and my body can easily bear the sleepless toil of study through the long night. A goodly number of years is still to be counted out before I equal my father. Nor can flimsy clothing or scanty food terrify me [1185] or send me back home. The heavy rod won't harm me as it does boys; from childhood I have learned to bear many blows. Wanderlust will not distract me from love of study; rather it will be increased by my solemn nature. [1190] The solemnity of age will keep me from frivolity, and repeated habit will make the burden light. Nor will shame at my years, although I learn childish things when already an old man, force me to desert the schools. Neither fear nor despair shall stop me [1195] from pressing on night and day with what I have begun. Let me fear nothing—"relentless work overcomes everything", and God himself

1177 *patiensque laborum*: Ovid, *Tristia*, i. 5. 71.

1184 *ūsquĕ pătrī*: Nigel scans the inflected forms of 'pater' with both a long and a short first syllable (as here). For the short forms, see *pătris* at *SS*, 1265, 1495, 1845, 2550; *Lawrence*, 1623, 1667; *Miracles*, 1060, 1069, 1070, 1146, 1496, 1787; *pătri* at *Miracles*, 1054, 1145, 2390; *pătres* at *SS*, 1500; and *pătrum* at *Lawrence*, 469, 1086; *Miracles*, 510, 1020. For the long forms, see *pātris* at *SS*, 206, 1312; *Lawrence*, 1340, 1727, 2201; *Epigrams*, no. xiii. 1; *pātri* at *SS*, 1314, 1809, 1891, 1927; *Lawrence*, 2203; and *pātrum* at *Lawrence*, 1616. Cf. n. to line 2600.

1190 *quin*: only *VcFr* read 'quin' but it makes better sense than the majority reading 'qui'. For 'quin' meaning 'rather', see *OLD* 2.

1192 On the scansion of 'cōnsuētūdŏ frĕquēns' and its problematic position in most manuscripts as the second half of the pentameter (where one would expect the first foot to be a dactyl), see Hall, 'Notes', p. 436: 'ancient dactylic poets accommodated *consuetudo* and similar forms by treating the *u* following the *s* as consonantal and making a single long syllable of -*sve*-'. Hall goes on to say of *SS*, 1192: 'I would bet money that the original there read *consuetudo frequens alleuiabit onus.*' This is in fact the reading of *αRVbT*, which I have adopted. Cf. similar scansion of 'consuetudo' at lines 55, 1356, 2392.

1197 *labor improbus omnia uincet*: 'Hard work will conquer everything.' Cf. Vergil, *Georgics*, i. 145–6: 'labor omnia uicit/ improbus'. Cf. *Pamphilus*, 71 (*Commedie*, iii. 66); John of Salisbury, *Metalogicon*, i. 6 (ed. Hall, p. 23) and iv. 30 (ed. Hall, p. 167).

1198 Cf. Vergil, *Aeneid*, x. 284: 'audentis Fortuna iuuat'.

128   SPECVLVM STVLTORVM

Parisius ueniam studioque uacando decenni
1200   artibus insistam, nec remorabor iter.
Postea Boloniam Domino ducente reuertar,
legales apices conciliare mihi.
Pagina diuina necnon decreta laborum
finis erunt, fuerit si mihi uita comes.
1205   Sicque, meum nomen alio praeeunte, Magister
Burnellus dicar nomine reque simul.
Si quis Burnellum non addens forte Magistrum
dixerit, ille mihi publicus hostis erit.
Nominis ergo mei fama praeeunte celebri,
1210   subsequar orator publicus, absque pari.
Obuius adueniet populo comitante senatus;
plebs ruet et dicet "Ecce Magister adest!"
Praesulis et fratrum concors sententia nostro
se uolet auxilio consilioque regi.

1199 ueniam] *om.* L conueniam *Tr*; uacando] uacandi *Mu* uocando *F Ne Z* uacabo *DK X fc* uocabo *La*   **1200** nec] non δ *X*; remorabor] rememorabor *SFr* memorabor *CW G*   **1201** postea] post hec *MuVbVcVdGoBePkFrPmNe TrHaLa* post hoc *T*; Boloniam] bolonia *J* bononiam *H^pc SMuVbVcVdTGoBePkPmNe CWHuMNDK HaLa ZXQ fc* bano- niam *Fr Tr* coloniam *ROVe* uolumina *Y^pc*   **1202** legales] regales *VdBe Tr* bagales *La*   **1203** necnon] ueterum *Vb* mecum *VdBe Tr* ne cum *Pk* ueterum non *Vc*   **1204** finis] fines *GoFr*; erunt] erit *Be HuD Tr*   **1205** sicque] sitque *VbT RO G Ha ZQ* sique *La*; meum nomen] mecum nomen Z nomen meum *MuBe Ha* meum *Vd*; alio] nullo *SMuVbVcVdTGoBePkFrPmNe TrHaLa Z*   **1206** dicar] dicat *E Be* dicor *T K*   **1208** dixerit] dixit *BePm Tr*   **1209–10** *om. QY*   **1209** fama praeeunte celebri] fama pereunte celebri *T* fama celebri preeunte *D X* celebri fama preeunte *S*   **1210** subsequar] subsequor *Tr* obsequar *F Ne Z* sequar *Mu*   **1211** adueniet] adueniat *Vd TrLa* aduenit *Fr Z*

1199 *Parisius*: although it was not formally organized as a university until the beginning of the 13th c., Paris was a famous site of teaching and learning from the mid-12th c. onwards (Rashdall, *Universities of Europe*, i. 62–72, 271–98; see also Baldwin, 'Masters at Paris', and Barrow, *Clergy in the Medieval World*, pp. 201–4). John of Salisbury gives a personal account of his studies there under Peter Abelard and others (*Metalogicon*, ii. 10, ed. Hall, pp. 70–3; trans. Hall, pp. 198–201). John of Hauville gives a glowing eulogy of Paris at the end of book ii of *Architrenius*, calling it 'the second palace of Phoebus, Apollonian in its citizenry, Chrysaean in its wealth, a Greece in its libraries, an India in its schools, a Rome for poets, an Attica for philosophers, the flower of the world, balm of creation, a Sidon in its splendor, its feasts and its drinking' (483–7, ed. and trans. Wetherbee).
        1200 *artibus*: the seven liberal arts comprised the trivium (grammar, rhetoric, dialectic), followed by the quadrivium (music, arithmetic, geometry and astronomy).
        1201 *Boloniam*: Bologna was famed as a leading centre for legal studies from the end of the 11th c. on. The *Corpus iuris civilis* of Justinian, rediscovered via a manuscript that came to Bologna *c.*1080, stimulated the study of Roman law; a little later, the study of canon law was initiated by the appearance in the mid-12th c. of Gratian's *Decretum*, which rapidly

SPECVLVM STVLTORVM   129

helps the brave. I shall go to Paris and devote myself to the arts, pursuing study for a decade; I shall journey without delay. [1200] Afterwards, God willing, I shall return to Bologna, in order to master the law. Theology and canon law will be the climax of my labours, if I live that long. So I'll have a title added to my name, [1205] and shall be called "Master Burnellus", in both name and fact. If anybody should happen to say "Burnellus" and doesn't add "Master", he'll be my avowed enemy. So, the dazzling renown of my name will go before me, and I shall succeed as public orator, without equal. [1210] The senate and people will come to meet me; the common folk will run forward, crying "Behold, the Master is here!" The united opinion of the bishop and the monks will willingly be governed by my advice and assistance.

became the standard textbook in the field. Gratian's work was augmented by the numerous decretals ('decreta') issued by the papal courts and church councils in subsequent years. See Rashdall, *Universities of Europe*, i. 87–175; Pedersen, *The First Universities*, pp. 125–8; Brundage, *Medieval Canon Law*, pp. 44–50, 53–6, 160, 165, 190–202. These developments in canon law studies will have been made familiar at Canterbury with the arrival of Vacarius, a Roman lawyer trained in Bologna and author of an abridgement of Justinian's works, who was, according to Gervase of Canterbury (*Actus pontificum Cantuariensium, Historical Works*, ed. Stubbs, ii. 384–5) brought to England in the mid-12th c. by Theobald, archbishop of Canterbury, to assist in a legal dispute. See also the references to Vacarius in John of Salisbury, *Policraticus*, viii. 22 (ed. Webb, ii. 399); Roger of Howden, *Chronica*, iv. 75; and Robert of Torigni, *Chronicle*, s. a. 1149 (ed. Bisson, i. 152–3) . For attempts to reconstruct Vacarius's career, and the role he played in the development of legal studies in England (whether in Oxford, Lincoln, or Northampton), see Southern, 'Master Vacarius'; id., 'From schools to university', pp. 8–10, and the recent thorough review of the evidence (with further bibliography) in Landau, 'The origins of legal science'.

 1202 *conciliare* = 'to win, obtain' (*DMLBS* 2). Cf. *SS*, 1777.

 1203 *Pagina diuina*: theology. *decreta*: prescriptions of canon law; see n. on line 1201.

 1204 *fuerit si mihi uita comes*: see n. to line 976.

 1205 *Magister*: The admission of a student to the mastership was a formal recognition that he had completed a formal education and was licensed to teach. 'The mastership in the philosophical faculty became the natural goal of every student's ambition and the usual if not essential preliminary to study in the higher faculties. Hence the enormous multiplication of masters' (Rashdall, *Universities of Europe*, i. 283–9, quotation at 289). On the growth in numbers of those claiming the title 'magister' from the 1130s on, rising sharply in the 1170s and later, see Barrow, *Clergy in the Medieval World*, pp. 209–10 (and n. 2), 231–2. The mastership was frequently the basis for a successful career in the Church, and also, in England, for employment in royal administration (Baldwin, 'The penetration of university personnel'; id.,'Masters at Paris', pp. 151–8). The pride taken in the title by its holders was often ridiculed by satirists; see Mann, *Chaucer and Medieval Estates Satire*, pp. 39–40.

130   SPECVLVM STVLTORVM

1215   Illud erit stabile quod nos statuemus in urbe,
        uerba sed et nostra legis ad instar erunt.
        Quod minus in cauda, quod et aequo maius in aure
        tunc fuerit, redimet nomen honore suo.
        Maius erit lucrum nostrum quam damna fuerunt;
1220   gloria finalis crimina cuncta teget.'

Qualiter Burnellus uadit Parisius, et de eius comite in uia

        Talia dum replicat, comes est sociatus eunti,
        Parisius tendens sarcinulasque ferens.
        Cui Burnellus 'aue' dicto dedit oscula, quaerens
        quis sit et unde satus, quo citus ire uelit.
1225   Ille refert 'Siculus ego sum, cupiensque doceri
        Parisius propero; sit uia tuta, precor!'
        Cui Burnellus ait 'Tria sunt communia nobis,
        uotum, causa, solum; sit uia quarta, peto.'
        Annuit Arnoldus, socioque ferenda petenti
1230   capsas et libros tradidit ille suos.
        Inde simul dextris sociali foedere iunctis
        Parisius properant pectore, uoce, pede.
        Dumque simul pergunt, socio Burnellus eunti
        quis sit et unde refert, quae sibi causa uiae,
1235   quos tulerit casus, quae sit discrimina passus,
        qualiter acciderint illa uel illa sibi;
        qualiter a patria primo discessit, et ad quid,
        consilium dederit quod Galienus ei;

1215 statuemus] statuimus *Go Z*   **1217** quod] quid *Be CW* qui *Pk*; maius] magis *L Fr CWMNPD G Ha X*   **1220** cuncta] nostra *HuMN*; teget] tegit *LE* reget *Tr*   **1222** sarcinulasque] sarniculasque *M* sarcinulaque *Ve* sarcinolasque *Mu Z* **1223–6** *om. G*   **1223** cui] cur *Ve* tunc *D X fc* qui *F Be*; aue] ait *Vd AJCWROVe Tr Y* ne *M* ue *HuN* ei *D fc*; dicto] dictus *Tr* primo *D fc*; dedit oscula quaerens] dat oscula querens *Vc* dans oscula querit *D X fc*   **1224** satus] sacus *Y* fatus *X* satus /uel seniatus(?) uel natus *Ha* natus *H RK La fc* satis *F* status *MuGoBeFrPm DVe* fatus *X*; citus] scitus *Tr* situs *ZY* pro citus *Q* cito *Fr D* pronus *X fc*   **1226** uia] uita *CW*; precor] rogo *SMuVbVcVdTGoBePkFrPmNe TrHaLa*   **1227** sunt] *om. CW*   **1228** uotum causa] uotam eam *Be* uotum tam *Pm* uocum causa *Ne*; peto] precor *SMuVbVcVdTGoBePkFrPmNe D TrHaLa X*   **1231** dextris…iunctis] iunctis…dextris *MuVbVcVdTGoBePkFrPmNe TrHaLa*   **1233** dumque] cumque *Vb ROPVe*   **1234** sit] *om. R Ha* **1235–6** *transp. VdBe TrLa*; *om. Fr*   **1235** *Va* rejoins; sit] sunt *CR* sint *Pk P UZ* sic *Tr* fuit *Ve*   **1236** illa²] ille *H G* ista *E UZQY*; *(whole line)* qualiter uel illa sibi acciderint *L*   **1237** discessit] dissesserit *F Mu* disscesserit *Go* decessit *W UX*   **1238** *fc excerpt 2 ends here*; consilium] concilium *H ZX*; dederit] dederat *RK U*

SPECVLVM STVLTORVM

131

What I decree in the city will stand firm, [1215] and my words will have the force of law. What I am lacking in my tail, and have to excess in my ears, will then be compensated for by the honour of my name. My profit will be greater than were my losses, and my final glory will blot out every misdeed!' [1220]

How Burnellus Went to Paris, and about His Travelling Companion

While he was musing in this way, a companion joined him on the road, heading for Paris and laden with baggage. Burnellus greeted him with a hello and a kiss, and asked who he was, where he was born, and whither he was hastening. He replied: 'I am a Sicilian, and, wanting to be educated, I am off to Paris; [1225] heaven grant me a safe journey!' Burnellus replied: 'We have three things in common—our goal, the reason for it, and our country; let our journey be the fourth, if you please.' Arnold agreed, and gave his companion his book-boxes to carry, as he offered. [1230] Then, having joined their right hands in friendly agreement, they set off for Paris with active hearts, tongues, and feet. While they walk together, Burnellus told his travel-companion who he was and where he came from, what was the reason for his journey, what accidents had befallen him, what dangers he had undergone, [1235], and how this or that had happened to him; how he first left his home country and to what end, and what advice Galen had given him;

1225–6 Students from all over Europe flocked to Paris in the 12th c., drawn by the fame of its teachers. See Budinsky, *Die Universität Paris und die Fremden*, pp. 178–206, on the Italians; for other foreigners, see Lesne, *Les Écoles*, p. 207, and Gabriel, 'English masters', pp. 51–3. The English masters were especially numerous; see Baldwin, 'Masters at Paris', pp. 149–50. 'No English student in the period 1066–1190 chose to stay in England for his higher studies if he could go abroad; and all the schoolmasters whom we can name in England during this period had studied in a foreign school' (Southern, 'From schools to university', p. 3).

1228 *solum*: this is the first indication in the poem that Burnellus is Italian; not until line 1576 do we learn that his home town is Cremona in northern Italy.

132   SPECVLVM STVLTORVM

        Brunettae casus uarios, causamque Bicornis,
1240   actibus expositis tempus utrumque notans;
        qualiter accepit a Truffatore Salerni,
        Londoniis orto, uitrea uasa decem;
        qua ratione canes frater Fromundus in illum
        miserit, et quantum perdidit ipse miser;
1245   inde canum mortem narrat saltumque sequentem
        fratris Fromundi iudiciumque Dei.
        Addidit et titulos bustali marmore scriptos,
        nunc quoque Parisius qua ratione petat.
        Talia dicenti casusque suos memoranti
1250   reddidit Arnoldus talia dicta sibi.

Narratio Arnoldi de filio presbiteri et pullo gallinae

        'Quam uariis uicibus humanae res uariantur,
        non est res facilis dinumerasse mihi.
        Quam minima causa magnum discrimen oriri
        possit, ab effectu res manifesta docet.
1255   Contigit Apuliae celebri res digna relatu,
        tempore Willelmi principis huius aui.
        Presbiter urbanus quidam, digressus ab urbe
        longius, agrestem coepit habere casam;
        cui bene temporibus cunctis sua rura colenti
1260   multotiens segetum copia multa fuit.
        Fecerat et natos propria de coniuge, dici
        coniux presbiteri si licet absque nota;

1239–40 *om.* P   **1239** causamque] casumque α *SMuVaVbVdTGoBePkFrPmNe R TrHaLa Z* casusque *Vc QX*   **1240** notans] notant *H G*   **1245–6** *om.* P **1245** canum mortem] tamen mortem *Be Tr* causam mortis *H*; saltumque] casumque *SMuVaVbVcVdTBePkFrPmNe TrHaLa* casuque *Go*   **1247** addidit] addit *VaT X corr.* *X²* reddidit *Mu*   **1249–502** *om.* QY   **1250** reddidit] reddit *T La*; Arnoldus] alnoldus uel alnodus *Ha*   **1251** humanae res] res humane *Vc C*; uariantur] uarientur *H SVbVcVdGoBePkFrPmNe G TrHaLa X*   **1252** dinumerasse] dinumerare *RD UX* dinumerasse uel dinumerare *Ha*   **1253** quam] qua *E* quo *Vd La* omni *Z*; minima] nimia *SGo*   **1255** celebri] cerebri *C* celebra *Go* celebris *Vd*; relatu] relata *O Tr* **1256** Willelmi] wilhelmi *O Ha* guillermi *S* gwillelmi *MuPk R* gwilhelmi *VcGo Z* guillelmi *Ne Tr* guinelli *Va* gwuillelmus *U* Gwillimi *Vd* Guillimi *Be* guillini *Fr* Guielli *Pm* gallieni *La* gauelii *T*; aui] anni *SVaFrNe D Tr corr. Tr²* aui /uel anni *Ha* eui *Z*   **1257** quidam] quidem *VbPm U* quondam *Go*; digressus] disgressus *Go HuMNᵖᶜ* discressus *VaNe* discedens *VdBe La*   **1259** cui] qui *Go G Ha Z*   **1260** multa] magna *OD X*   **1262** si licet] si ualet *SMuVaVbVcVdTBePkFrPmNe TrHaLa Z* si uellet *Go* scilicet *G U*

SPECVLVM STVLTORVM 133

the adventures of Brunetta and the story of Bicornis, explaining what they did and the fate of both; [1240] how he received ten glass jars from Trickster, a Londoner at Salerno; why brother Fromundus set the dogs on him, and how much he, poor wretch, had lost. Then he recounted the death of the dogs and the subsequent leap [1245] of brother Fromundus and God's judgement on him. He added the epitaph written on the marble tomb, and why he too was now making for Paris. When he had said all this and related his adventures, Arnold replied as follows. [1250]

Arnold's Story of the Priest's Son and the Hen's Chick

'It's no easy matter for me to enumerate the many different turns of events which alter the pattern of human affairs. From how small a cause a great disaster can arise, is something that clear examples teach us in action. There befell in Apulia, [1255] in the time of William, grandfather of the present prince, an event worthy to gain the fame of retelling. A certain town priest went some way out of town and settled on a country farm. He cultivated his acres well through all the seasons of the year, and his harvest of grain was often abundant. [1260] He had brought forth sons by his wife—if a priest's wife can be so called without infamy. One of them, a certain Gundulf, whom I've seen myself,

---

1239–40 These lines are omitted in *P*, because they refer to the story of the two cows, which forms part of the major omission of lines 55–666 in the original copying of the manuscript; lines 205–594 were added only at the very end of the poem.

1255 *res digna relatu*: also at *Miracles*, 1509, 1739, 2113.

1256 *tempore Willelmi principis huius aui*: the kings of Sicily/dukes of Apulia in the second half of the 12th c. were William I (the Bad), 1154–66; William II (the Good), 1166–89; Tancred (1190–4); and William III (1194). The 'grandfather of the present prince' implies a sequence of three rulers, which must therefore begin (counting backwards) either with Tancred or with William III; since William III was a small child whose reign lasted only a few months, the most likely candidate for 'the present prince' is Tancred (who was not, however, the grandson of either William). See further Introduction, p. liii.

1261 The rules on celibacy for the clergy (especially those above the rank of subdeacon) were not strictly enforced at this period, and many parish priests had a wife or concubine. In addition, the sons born from these relationships often inherited their fathers' churches. See Poole, *From Domesday Book to Magna Carta*, pp. 225–6, and Barrow, *Clergy in the Medieval World*, pp. 135–47, 338–9, 345. Progressive church councils attempted to curb the prevailing laxity; see Brooke, 'Gregorian reform in action'; id., 'Married men among the English higher clergy'; for a detailed account of numerous papal decretals dealing with the problems arising from such cases, see Duggan, 'Equity and compassion', pp. 60–8. Clerical celibacy became a controversial subject of debate in the late 12th c. (summarized in Baldwin, 'A campaign', and *Masters, Princes, and Merchants*, i. 337–43). Although not prescribed in the early Christian church, the rule of sexual continence, at least for those above the rank of subdeacon, had gained ground, especially after the Gregorian reform of the 11th c.; in the 12th c., however, there were opposing moves in support of allowing clerical marriage, in order to avoid 'the

134   *SPECVLVM STVLTORVM*

quorum Gundulfum quendam, quem uidimus ipsi,
    cum puer esset adhuc, contigit esse domi.
1265 Cumque foret frugum custos patris, ostia seruans,
    consueuit uirgam saepe tenere manu.
Accidit ergo semel, pullis comitantibus eius,
    Coppa quod intraret horrea, grana legens.
Cumque suam matrem pulli sequerentur egentes,
1270 ostia presserunt improbitate sua;
quos puer elata uirga quam forte tenebat
    caedere praesumpsit atque fugare foras.
Qui, quoniam turbatus erat, plus institit aequo,
    transgressus uerbis uerberibusque modum.
1275 Ira furore minus modico distare uidetur
    cum nimis excedit in grauitate modum.
Ira quid expediat, dum non discernit, inique
    plurima dispensat praecipitando gradum.
Saepe leui iactu constat iactura perennis,
1280 atque leui puncto pignora cara cadunt.
Cumque puer uirgam nimis exerceret in iram,
    contigit ut pulli tibia fracta foret.
Tibia fracta diu pullo pariterque parenti
    tristitiae causa non mediocris erat.
1285 Hinc dolor inde pudor pullum stimulabat in iram,
    ut cuperet puero reddere posse uicem.
Tempore crescente caro consolidata recreuit,
    obduxitque cutis uulnera ueste noua.

1265 cumque] cum *VdBe TrHaLa Z*   **1268** Coppa quod] cospa quod *G* cappa quod *Tr Z* coppa cum *H* cappo quod *La* capoque *T*   **1269** cumque] cum *VdBe La*; matrem pulli] pulli matrem α; sequerentur] sequeretur *F Be* sequentur *T*; egentes] agentes *H G*   **1271** elata] eleta *HuMN*   **1273** plus] magis α   **1274** modum] modis *CWHuMN Z* domum *VaVc* simul *U*   **1275–6** *om.* δ *X; transp. after 1278* γ-*TrHaLa Z*   **1275** ira] in *S Z*; minus] nimis *VcGoFrPm*; modico] modice *La om. Z* **1276** excedit] excedat *S om. (erased) U*, excederet *add. in lower margin* U^2 **1279** iactu] iactura *L* tactu *VbVd Tr* saltu *N* sactu *M*   **1280** puncto] pincto *K* puncta *Go* pugna *U*   **1281** cumque] cum *VdBe La*; exerceret] exercet *VaVbGoBePk TrLa* **1282** foret] fuit *H G* manet / uel foret *Ha*   **1285** inde] hincque *AJWRHuMNOPKVe*; stimulabat] stimulabant *Ha* stimulabunt *Go* simulabat *F* stimulauit δ *X*   **1286** cuperet] caperet *VdGo*; posse] sepe γ *HaLa Z*   **1287** crescente] labente γ *TrLa Z* labentes *Ha*; caro consolidata recreuit] caro consilidata recreuit *HuN* caro solidata recreuit *VcFr* sua caro consolidata *D* caro separat solidari *X* caro cepit consolidari X^2

SPECVLVM STVLTORVM

lived at home, since he was still a child. And since he used to guard his father's grain, watching the doors, [1265] he often used to have a stick in his hand. And so it happened one day that Coppa, her chicks alongside her, came into the barn, pecking up grain. And as the hungry chicks followed their mother, they crowded through the door in their boldness. [1270] The boy, raising the stick which he happened to be holding, went so far as to strike them and drive them outside. And since he was agitated, he went further than he should have done, passing the bounds of moderation in words and blows. Anger is evidently not much different from fury [1275] when it goes beyond moderation in its harshness. When anger loses sight of what is expedient, it commits many wrongs in its headlong rush. Often a permanent loss results from a careless throw, and valuable stakes are lost in a fleeting moment. [1280] While the boy wielded his stick too angrily, it happened that a chick's leg was broken. The broken leg was the cause of no little grief to the chick and likewise its mother for a long time after. On the one hand, the pain, on the other, the disgrace, drove the chick to anger, [1285] and to the desire to be able to get even with the boy. As time passed, the flesh joined together and healed, and the skin concealed the

well-known ills of prostitution, concubinage, and sodomy' (Baldwin, *Masters, Princes, and Merchants*, i. 337). Gerald of Wales claimed that he had heard Peter Comestor (who died *c.*1179) declare that the rule of clerical celibacy was invented by the devil in order to provoke clerical vice (*Gemma Ecclesiastica*, dist. ii, c. 6, *Opera*, ii. 185–8; trans. Hagen, p. 145). In Gerald's opinion, although the marriage of subdeacons could be licensed in special circumstances by the pope, the question of marriage for priests could be settled only by a general church council; in the event, the decision went the other way and the Lateran Council of 1215 reconfirmed the rule of clerical celibacy.

1268 *Coppa*: A traditional name for a hen (like 'Dobbin' for a horse); the French equivalent, Coupee, is the name of a hen murdered by the fox Reynard; see *Roman de Renart*, ed. Roques, Br 1. 399.

1274 Cf. Ovid, *Heroides*, xx. 70–1, and *SS*, 1852, 2094; *Lawrence*, 889–94, 1448, 1725. The writers of medieval Latin *passiones* were fond of this wordplay.

1277–8 Cf. *Disticha Catonis*, ii. 4. 2: 'impedit ira animum, ne possis cernere verum'.

1279 *iactura perennis*: also in *Miracles*, 101.

1280 *leui puncto*: cf. 'in puncto', 'in a moment' (*DMLBS* 6). 'Punctum' can also mean a dice-spot, but this is rare (Lewis and Short, punctum B.1.b(γ)).

136   *SPECVLVM STVLTORVM*

Ossa diu fracta iam dedidicere dolorem,
1290   uulneris inflicti corde tenente notam.
Vulneris exterius satis est obducta cicatrix;
    cruda sed interius uulnera corda tenent.
Iam proscripta diu proprias remeauit ad oras
    tibia, sed facti mens memor exul agit.
1295   Pes graditur recte, femur est sine uulnere, sura
    nil sapit elisum, tibia sana coit.
Claudicat ast animus, pectus sine uulnere languet,
    cor queritur, mens est ulcere plena graui.
Vltio suspensa, sine qua mens laesa quietis
1300   nil habet, expectat peruigil ante fores.
Nulla quies mentis laesae nullumque leuamen,
    dum suspensa manet ultio digna mali;
non capit ex tractu longo mens laesa leuamen,
    nil nisi uindicta pectora laesa leuat.
1305   Non mergus stagnum, fugientem non lupus agnum,
    turba canum leporem, uel fera capta fugam,
nec plus piscis aquam, nec auet plus nisus alaudam,
    quam mens uindictam laesa uidere citam.
Sic quoque Gundulfi pullus cupiebat iniqui

1289 iam dedidicere dolorem] iam dedicere dolorem *L* iam dediscere dolorem *Ha* iam didicere dolorem *H GoFr G* iam didicere laborem dolorem *S* iam non sensere dolorem *Mu* iam iam didicere dolorem (dolere *T*) *VaVbVcVdTBePkPmNe TrLa* iam iam dicere dolorem *Z* iam nunc didicere dolorem *U* multum doluere dolore *AJHuMNOPDKVe* multo doluere dolore *X* multum doluere dolere *CW* nimium doluere dolore *R*   1290 inflicti] inflictu *Tr* inflectu *Vd* inflicta *La Z* inflicer *Hu*; tenente] tenere *α*   1292 corda tenent] corda tenet *SVa* cor retinet *D X*   1293 proscripta] proscrita *D* prescripta *MNO* proscriptu *Vd*; proprias] patrias *D X*   1294 facti] fracti *VdBe G* fracta *Tr U*; agit] ait *VbGoNe Z*   1295–6 *transp. Tr*   1295 sura] sanum δ *Tr U²over erasure X* sanum /uel sura *La* sua *SVc* fixa *La Z*   1297 ast] ac *Be Tr* et *S* est *GoPk J G Ha*; uulnere] pectore *α H^{ac} G*   1298 cor queritur] conqueritur *T M* cor quam cur *Go*   1299 laesa quietis] lesa querentis /uel lassa quietis *Ha*; quietis] quieti *AJCWRHuMNPVe*   1301 nullumque] nullumue *LE*   1302–3 *om. F* γ+ δ *UZX*   1303 non] nunc *LE*   1304 *om. D*;   leuat] lauat *Vb* lenit *Ve* iuuat *α* sanat *H P G*; *(whole line)* dum sua damna nimis cernit multa diu *X*   1305 non...non] nunc...nunc *LE* nec...nec *FI;* mergus] mersus *HuMN*; stagnum] sta *<space left empty> S* stannum *Vd La* amnem *Vc* canum *MuVaGoPkFrPmNe* chamum *Vb* tantum *Z*; lupus] lepus *Be Ha*   1306 uel] et *α* nil *P om. Ha^{ac}* quam forte *Ha^{pc}*; *(whole line)* neque canis leporem iunctus et ipse fugam *Z*   1307 nec auet] nec aues *L* nec auem *OK* nec aue *ACWRMNPVe U* ne aue *Hu* nec amat *H G* sed nec *D X* cupit aut *SMuVaVbVdGoBePkFrPmNe TrHaLa Z* cupit nec *Vc*; alaudam] alauda *LE* alandam *Tr*   1308 *om. VdGo Z*; uindictam] uindicta *Fr C om. U, add. in margin U²*; laesa] lesam *Va* lese *Mu*; uidere] uide *HuMN*; citam] sitam *E CW* totam *La* suam *Tr* cupit *ODR X glossed* 'idest cupit' *ACHuMNKW*   1309 cupiebat] capiebat *MuFr La*; iniqui] inique *F H S Z*

SPECVLVM STVLTORVM

137

wound with a fresh covering. Long ago broken, the bones forgot their pain, but the heart still kept the record of the inflicted wound. [1290] The scar of the outer wound was quite healed over, but within, the wounds nursed by the heart were raw. The displaced leg had long since returned to its home, but the mind, brooding on the deed, languished in exile. The foot walks straight, the thigh is undamaged, [1295] the calf unharmed, the leg knits together and is whole. But the spirit limps, the breast aches although unwounded, the heart complains, the mind is full of a painful ulcer. Delayed revenge, without which the wounded mind knows no rest, waits vigilantly at the doors. [1300] There is no rest and no relief for the wounded mind, while the fitting vengeance for a wrong is delayed. The wounded mind gets no relief from the passing of time; nothing but vengeance soothes the wounded breast. The diver-bird does not more greatly desire the pool, the wolf desire the fleeing lamb, [1305] the pack of dogs desire the hare, the captured animal desire escape, the fish desire water, nor the sparrowhawk the lark, than the wounded mind desires to see speedy vengeance. So likewise the

---

1300 *peruigil ante fores*: Avianus, *Fabulae* i. 4.

138   *SPECVLVM STVLTORVM*

1310   sumere uindictam, si locus esset ei.
Creuerat in gallum sextum iam pullus in annum,
     fungens defuncti patris honore sui.
Creuerat et multum iam iam Gundulfus in altum,
     iamque suo patri substituendus erat.
1315   Iam nihil obstabat, iam nil deerat nisi solus
     ordo sacerdotis nuper habendus ei.
Praesul enim uictus precibus meritisque beati
     Ruffini uota censuit esse rata,
constituitque diem quo sanctificatio tanta
1320   debuit impendi more modoque loci.
Sabbata Natalem Domini praeeuntia festum
     terminus est positus, urbs Caraballa locus.
Gundulfum prouehi cupiunt gaudentque parentes,
     iamque parant festis munera digna suis.
1325   Ante diem festum genialia festa parentes
     ut faciant ueniunt conueniuntque simul.
Aula patet cunctis onerantque cibaria mensas
     indulgentque nimis potibus atque cibis.
Bacchus adest festo, patulo diffusus in auro,
1330   exhilarans populum sanctificansque locum.
Nox aderat qua mane citus Gundulfus ad urbem
     profecturus erat, sanctificandus ibi.

1311–13 sextum iam—et multum] *om. J*   **1311** sextum iam pullus in annum] iam lustrum fecerat ille (ipse *S*) γ+ *Z*; in²] et α; preteriit *add. at end of line U²*   **1312** fungens] fugens *E* fringens *Fr* functus *D U*   **1313** et] in *BeNe Ve*   **1317** uictus] uetus *U corr. U²*   **1318** *om. Ve*; censuit] sensuit *CWD UZX*   **1320** more modoque] more locoque *R* modo moreque *MuGo*   **1321** sabbata] sabbato *MuGoFrPm*; natalem] natalis *H TFr D G Z* natale *F SMuVaVbVcVdGoBePkPmNe K TrHaLa*; festum] *om. (erased) U*, festum *and* precedencia festum *add. in margin U²*; *(whole line)* sabata anterius precedens festa natalis *X*   **1322** urbs] est γ- *TrHa Z* est urbs *La om. S*; Caraballa] caraballa *ROVe HaLa* carballa *Pk* canturabella *S* tarabella *Vbᵖᶜ AJCWHuMNP G X* tarcaballa *Va* terraballa *Mu* tarabala *F VcNe* tarabalsa *Pm* tharaballa *T* tarabelsa *H* tarebella *Vbᵃᶜ DK* carnabilla *Go* tarabesa *U*   **1323–6** cupiunt—ueniunt] *om. Vd*   **1323** cupiunt] capiunt *Fr Z*   **1324–5** *om.* γ(*see 1323–6 for Vd*) *Ha Z*   **1325** genialia] generalia *H ẟ G TrLa UX*; parentes] parantes *F X*   **1326** faciant] faciunt *Fr Tr* facient *Z*   **1327** onerantque] onerant α *AJCWRHuNOPD Mu Ha X* onera *M* honorantque *SPk La* ornantque *Vb* seruantque *U*; mensas] menas *Aᵃᶜ* mensis *JCWHuMNOPKVe Uᵃᶜ*   **1328** indulgentque] indulgetque *H Vd* indulgent α   **1329** patulo] patulus *MN* poculo *K Tr*   **1330** exhilarans] exultans *VdBe Tr* exultans /uel exhilarans *La* **1331** qua] quam *H Go HuMN* quo *Vc* que *P* quasi *Pk*; citus] cito *Fr X*; ad] in *RVe* **1332** profecturus] profectus *TrLa*

SPECVLVM STVLTORVM

chick wanted to take vengeance on the wicked Gundulf, if the chance came his way.' [1310]

'Now the chick had reached his sixth year, and taken on the status of his dead father. Gundulf too had grown tall, and was now to take over from his father. There was no impediment; nothing was lacking [1315] except that he should be invested with the order of priesthood. The bishop, swayed by his entreaties and the merits of the blessed Rufinus, decreed that his wishes should be fulfilled, and fixed the day on which the consecration should be carried out in the manner and the custom of the region. [1320] The Saturday preceding Christmas was the date fixed, the town of Carabella the place. Gundulf's relatives, anxious for his advancement, are delighted, and prepare gifts worthy of his cele-brations. Before the festal day, his relatives come [1325] and get together to hold a celebratory feast. The hall is open to everyone; food loads the tables, and they overindulge in food and drink. Bacchus graces the feast, poured out into gold goblets, gladdening the company and blessing the house. [1330] It was the night before the morning on which Gundulf was to set out without delay for the town where he was

---

1316 After 1316, *Ve* adds two spurious lines: 'Presulis albini uel martiris ossa rufini/ Rome si quis habet uertere cuncta ualet' ('Anyone who has the bones of Bishop Albinus or of the martyr Rufinus, he can control everything in Rome').

1317–18 Canon law forbade the ordination of illegitimate children. A papal dispensation, sometimes delegated to (for example) a papal legate or bishop, was necessary to waive this prohibition, and was harder to obtain for the sons of priests than for the offspring of unmar-ried lay people, unless, according to Gratian, they were monks or regular canons or of superior moral quality to their fathers (*Decretum* D. 56 c. 1, ed. Friedberg, i. 219; see also D. 56 c. 13, ibid. i. 223). See Génestal, *Histoire de la légitimation des enfants naturels*, ch. II, especially pp. 71–4; Schimmelpfennig, '*Ex fornicatione nati*', especially pp. 21–7; Wertheimer, 'Illegitimate birth and the English clergy'. *beati/ Ruffini*: i.e. gold. On the parodic saints Rufinus and Albinus, see Introduction, pp. lxxiv–lxxv, and cf. *Epistolae Cantuarienses*, no. ccxxxiv. For other appearances of these pseudo-saints in Goliardic literature, see Lehmann, *Parodie*, pp. 25–9, and Yunck, *Lineage of Lady Meed*, pp. 81, 119, 126. They play a prominent role in the *Tractatus Garsiae* (ed. Thomson; cf. Yunck, pp. 71–6), an extremely popular 11th-c. satire on the venality of the papal curia.

1321 Ordinations were traditionally (since the time of Pope Gregory VII) held in one of the four Ember Weeks, one in each season of the year, weeks in which Wednesday, Friday, and Saturday were devoted to prayer and fasting. 'Because it was felt that ordinands should be prepared for ordination by fasting, the last day of ember days was thought to be especially appropriate' (Reynolds, 'Ordination', p. 48). The winter Ember Week occurred in the week before Christmas Eve, and this is chosen for Gundulf's ordination. Ironically, Gundulf and his family prepare for the ceremony, not by fasting, but by a drunken orgy.

1322 *Caraballa*: probably a reference to the town and *comune* of Carapelle, on the river of the same name, in the province of Foggia in Puglia. See Fossati, *Dizionario grafico-itinerario d'Italia*, p. 1152, and for the present day, *The Times Comprehensive Atlas of the World* (15th edn.), p. 80, P5.

140   *SPECVLVM STVLTORVM*

Ad gallicantus primos iter arripiendum
esse uolunt, aberat nam locus ille procul.
1335 Mandatur famulis tempus, praescribitur hora,
qua profecturus mane citandus erit;
scilicet ut studeant cantus audire priores
quos dederit gallus nuntius ante diem.
Sufficietque satis si tunc surrexerit ille,
1340 nam nox longa nimis, nec graue restat iter.
Gallus ut haec uerba uigili percepit in aure
gaudet et exultat pectore, uoce tacens.
Tanta quidem super his fuit exultatio cordis,
ora quod a laude uix cohibere potest.
1345 Quodque praeoptabat multum differre tacendo
uocibus explosis accelerare parat.
Quam dolor excludit immittunt gaudia uocem,
haec sua plectra monent, hic reticere iubet.
Inter utrumque manens neutri consentit, utroque
1350 uincitur, et uincit, uoce tacente tamen.
Iam nox tota fere fuerat consumpta bibendo,
cum iam fessa mero dant sua membra toro.
Tempora nocturna studio delusa bibentum
nec bene distincta praeteriere cito.
1355 Nec mora potantum potuit noctem remorari,

1333 primos] post *Mu* primum *T* primus *FrNe Ha* psalmos *Be* spalmos
Go   1334 aberat] aderat *SMuVaVdTGoBePkFrPmNe JCWRHuMNVe TrHaLa U* et
erat *Vb*; nam] non *Vc U* iam *Ne Ve*; locus…procul] procul…locus *D X*   1335 *line
repeated Vc*; famulis] famulus *HuN*; tempus] cunctis *SMuVaVbVcVdGoBePkFrPmNe
TrHaLa Z* cunctisque *T*; praescribitur] proscribitur *F H* prefigitur γ+ *Z*   1336 erit]
erat γ+ *RD UZX*   1337 studeant] studeat *GoPm*   1338 *transp. after 1344
HuMN*; dederit] dedit *F* dederat *MuFr*   1339 surrexerit] surrexit *La* recesserit *U*, *del.
and* surrexerit *add. in margin U²*   1340 nox] uox *VaVdFr La*;   1341 percepit]
precepit *MN*   1343 quidem] tamen *D X*   1344 *om. Va*; a laude] alauda *HuN*
alaude *MK La Z*   1345 praeoptabat] preoptabit *Tr* precipitabat *L* precipitat *E* preop-
tauit *G* peroptabat *Vc D X* portabat *Ha*   1346 parat] parit *MuᵖᶜVdGoBePkPmNe
TrHa*   1347 excludit] exclusit *X* includit γ- *TrHa Z*; immittunt] immutant *LE Fr
AJCWHuOPDVe U* inuitant *F H SMuVbVcVdTGoBePkPmNe TrHaLa ZX* mutant *Va*
mutauit *G*   1348 haec] hoc *MP* nec *Vd*; monent] mouent *SMuVaVbVcVdBePkFrPmNe
RO Tr* mouet *Go*; hic] hi *F* hec *SVc D Ha X* dolor *Fr*; reticere] recitere *VdBeNe* recitare *Z*
retinere *T*; iubet] iubent *G X*   1349 neutri] uentri *FrNe J* neutro *PD Z* uenter *Mu*
neuter *F VbT R* neutrum *Tr*; consentit] consensit *H G*; utroque] utrique *LE* utrumque *S*
uterque *T*   1351 nox tota fere] nox tota fero *M* nox fere tota *MuPkNe* tota nox fere *Go*
uox tota fere *VbVd*   1352 mero] modo *PkNe*   1353 bibentum] bibendum *LE*
potantum *G om. F*   1354 nec] ne *C* non *UX*; praeteriere] preterire *GoPkFr*
1355 potantum] potentum *Ha* post tantum *MuVbVcGoFrPm* post cantum *VaNe*; potuit]
patuit *VaGoFr* poterit *D*; noctem] nectem *HuN* nocte *CW Ha*

SPECVLVM STVLTORVM

141

to be consecrated. They want to start the journey at the first cockcrow, for the place was a long way off. The time was enjoined on the servants, the hour was determined [1335] at which he was to be summoned to set out on the morrow. That is, they were to listen out for the first crowings uttered by the cock to herald the approaching day. It would be soon enough for him to get up then, for the night was a long one, and the journey not difficult.' [1340]

'When the cock heard these words with attentive ear, he rejoiced and exulted in his heart, though he kept silence. So great was his exultation of heart, indeed, that he could hardly restrain his mouth from jubilation. What he hoped to delay by silence, [1345] he was threatening to precipitate by letting sound burst forth. His joy called forth the utterance which his resentment suppressed; the former urged him to crow, the latter bade him keep quiet. Poised between the two, he gives way to neither; he is overcome by, and overcomes, both—yet stays silent.' [1350]

'Now almost the whole night had been passed in drinking, when their limbs, weary with wine, are laid on the bed. The nocturnal hours, ignored by the zeal of the drinkers, passed quickly, without being well distinguished. The drinkers lingered, but they could not make the night do so, [1355] or prevent it binding them by its customary law.

1340 Shackleton Bailey ('Textual notes', p. 283) objected to 'nec' on the grounds that 'nec graue restat iter' contradicts line 1334, where the journey is said to be a long one; he suggests substituting 'et', a reading not found in any manuscript. Another way out of the difficulty would be to suggest that the journey will be long but not difficult ('graue'). The long winter night is convenient for the plot, since it explains why the servants are not surprised that the cock has not yet crowed; cf. lines 1411–14.

142   SPECVLVM STVLTORVM

quin non consueta lege ligaret eos.
Affuit interea cantandi temporis hora,
   sed cantor uocem supprimit atque sonum.
Nox silet et cantor, poti siluere ministri,
1360   pocula, nox, somnus quos uigilare uetant.
Admiransque diu gallina silentia galli
   et quod ab officio cederet ipse suo,
leniter accedens sponso suggessit in aure
   quod iam transissent tempus et hora simul.
1365   Cui respondit ita, "Noli uexare, quiesce!
   Semper eris stulta; stulta, recede, precor!
Vae cui stulta comes sociali foedere nupsit!
   Non erit illius absque dolore torus."
Nec minus illa tamen nimis importuna marito
1370   institit ut noctis tempora certa notet.
Ille sed econtra tentans cohibere loquacem
   porrigit inde preces, intonat inde minas.
Illa tamen iurat, nisi tanta silentia soluat
   ille, quod illa canet concutietque domum;
1375   impatiensque morae raucas de gutture uoces
   promit quaque potest uoce sonare sonat.
Qua tamen audita, quidam respondit eidem
   "Desine, Coppa, precor, nam nihil est quod agis.
Quamuis gallina nocturno tempore cantet,
1380   non ideo citius lux oriunda uenit."

1356 qu:n] qui *H G* quod *K U* cum *Mu Tr*; eos] eas *GoPm*   1358 sed] si *E*;
supprimit] subrimit *AJ* surripuit *CW* subripit *R* obrimit *P*   1359 nox] uox *MuVbVc*
AJCWRHuMNOPDVe Tr UZ; poti] potus α *T Ve X* potu *H G* toti *Go*   1360 nox] uox
Fr D X nox *add. interlinear* X^2 mox *U*; somnus] sompnis *Go D*   1362 cederet] cederit
Tr cedere *Vc* rederet *Va* crederet *Vd X* uel cederet *corr. interlinear* X^2; ipse] ipsa *P* ille
VbVcVdGoBePkNe TrHaLa   1363 leniter] leuiter *SMuVaVbVdGoBeFrNe J TrLa*
cernitur *Vc* lenis *Ha*; suggessit] subiecit *SMuVaVbVdTGoBePkFrPmNe TrHaLa*
Z   1364 *om. D*; quod] qui *Be Tr*; transissent] transisset *MuVaVbVcVdTGoBePkFrPm*
OP TrHaLa pertransisset *Ne*; et] *om. LE add.* E^{pc} 1365 cui] qui *Vc JROPVe G Tr X*
qui /[*uel*] cui *La*; respondit] respondet *HuMNK* respondens *Fr*   1366 *om. Vd*
1368 erit] erat *Be TrLa*   1370 notet] notat *E Fr* nocet *BeNe N Tr* uocet *Vd*
1372 inde^2] ipse *SMuVaVbVcVdTGoBePkPmNe TrHaLa Z* ille *Fr*   1373 tanta] cauta
Be Tr   1374 canet] canat *Go P* cauet *La U*   1376 promit] profert δ *X*; quaque]
quamque *H G* quam *C* qua *VdBe TrHa Z* quemque *La* quoque *Fr*; potest uoce] uoce potest
MuVaPm uoce ponit *Go* uoce pater *Fr*; sonare] sonore *D* sonora *T KVe X* seruare
Tr   1378 Coppa] cappa *TrLa* capo *add. in margin La*   1379 cantet] cantat *R*
canet *Mu* tacet *GoPm*

SPECVLVM STVLTORVM 143

Meanwhile the hour for crowing had arrived, but the crower suppressed both voice and sound. Night was silent, so was the crower, and silent were the drunken servants, prevented from watchfulness by drink, night, and sleep. [1360] The hen was for some time surprised at the cock's silence, and his abandonment of his duty. Softly approaching her husband, she whispered in his ear that the moment and the hour had already passed. He answered her thus: "Don't be a nuisance, be quiet! [1365] You'll always be foolish; go away, fool, I beg you! Woe to anyone who has married a foolish wife! His bed will never be free of grief." But no less did she importunately urge her husband that he should signal the fixed stages of the night. [1370] He, in response, in the attempt to stop her nagging, now offered entreaties, now thundered out threats. She, however, swore that unless he broke this silence, she would crow and rouse the house. Impatient of delay, she produced hoarse noises from her throat, [1375] and made what squawks she could. Hearing them, one of them answered her, "Cease, Coppa, I beg, for you are accomplishing nothing. Although a hen crows in the night, the dawn won't come any quicker." [1380] Meanwhile, night fades, and

---

1359 *poti*: 'potus', adj., = 'intoxicated, drunken'; see *OLD* s.v. 'poto' 4b and 'potus -a -um'.
1371 *econtra* = 'on the other hand, in rejoinder' (*DMLBS* 2).
1372 *intonat... minas*: cf. Ovid, *Amores*, i. 7. 46.
1375 *impatiensque morae*: Lucan, *De bello civili*, vi. 424; Prudentius, *Psychomachia*, 116.
1376 *quaque potest uoce*: cf. Ovid, *Heroides*, xi. 86.

144 SPECVLVM STVLTORVM

Nox ruit interea, domus ebrietate profunda
    tota sepulta iacet, dormit et ipse uigil.
Omnia somnus iners operit, Gundulfus et ipse
    dormit, et in somnis somnia grata uidet.'

Somnium Gundulfi

1385   'Ordine suscepto iam se putat esse reuersum,
    indutusque sacris iam celebrare parat;
cantorisque uidet niueo sub tegmine gallum
    obtinuisse uices atque tenere chorum.
Introitus missae, quem gallus uoce sonora
1390   omnibus inuitis intulit, iste fuit:
"Omnia quae, Domine, nobis fecisse uideris,
    iudicio iusto facta fuisse liquet."
Cumque calix magnus uinoque repletus adesset,
    hausit et a fundo uiscera tota tulit.
1395   Cumque calix saperet absumptus et ipse fuisset,
    cetera perfecit ordine cuncta suo.
Sed finem missae, cum cantor debuit "Ite"
    dicere, conticuit, signa nec ulla dedit.
Talibus obstupuit uisis Gundulfus, et altis
1400   uocibus exclamans, "Est," ait, "estne dies?"
Cui respondentes famuli dixere, uolenti
    surgere, "Sustineas; tempus adesse tuum
nondum cantauit gallus, qui tempora noctis
    nouit et assignat singula uoce sua.

1381 nox] mox *H* γ+ *AJCWHuMNOP*ᵖᶜ*DKVe G*ᵃᶜ uox *Z*; ruit] silet γ+ *Z*   1383 *om.*
Fr   1384 *om. Ne*; uidet] uidit *LE*   1386 indutusque] indutus α indictisque *H G*
iudiciisque *Tr*; parat] cupit *H G* putat γ *Ha Z* putat /uel parat *La*   1387 *B*
rejoins   1388 chorum] thorum *F VdGo JVe Tr*   1391 domine nobis] dominus
nobis α nobis dominus *Va* dure nobis *R* nobis domine *D X* domine nobis *Z*   1392 liq-
uet] liquent β *Vd G*   1393 cumque] cum *H AJCWHuMNO*ᵖᶜ*P X*; uinoque repletus]
uinoque repleto *R* uino completus *SVaVbVcVdGoBePkPmNe TrHa Z* uino repletus
MuFr   1394–5 *om. Vd*   1394 a fundo] affundo *VaVbPkNe HuMN* e fundo *Mu*
La effundo *Go* affudit *Ha* fundo *Fr*   1395 cumque] cum *Ve X*; calix] *om.* U, liquor *add.*
in margin U²; absumptus] absorptus *SMuVaVbVcTGoBePkPmNe HaLa Z* obsorptus *Fr*
consumptus *D* assumptus *Tr U*; et] *om. MuVa*   1396 cetera] cum tria
SMuVaVbVcVdGoBePkPmNe cumque tria *Ha* cum cetera *La* cum quoque *Z* omnia *T*
cunctaque *Fr*   1397 cantor] dicere *HuMN*; ite] ire *VbGo* iste *Vc Ha*   1399 obstu-
puit] obstipuit *O Tr U*; uisis] uisus *E CDVe*   1400 exclamans] exclamansque *VdPkNe*;
est¹] ast *T om. VdPkNe Tr*; dies] ait *VbVc*   1402 sustineas] festinas *SVcNe Ha* festinans *VoVdBe Tr Z* festinans /uel sustineas *La* festina *MuVaGoFrPm* festinat *Pk* festines *T*
1404–5 *om. R X*   1404 singula] tempora γ+ tempore *Z*

SPECVLVM STVLTORVM

145

the house lies buried in deep drunkenness; the watchman himself is asleep. Motionless sleep blankets everything; Gundulf himself sleeps, and in his slumbers sees pleasant visions.'

Gundulf's Dream

'Now he thinks he has been ordained and returned home, [1385] and now he is clothed in his vestments and is getting ready to celebrate Mass. He sees that the cock, in a snow-white surplice, has taken the place of the chanter and is leading the choir. The introit of the Mass, which the cock inflicted on his reluctant hearers with ear-splitting voice, was this: [1390] "All those things which, O Lord, You are seen to have done to us, were plainly done by a just judgement." And when the massive chalice filled with wine appeared, he drained it, consuming its contents to the dregs. And when the wine had been tasted and consumed, [1395] he completed everything else in its proper order. But when the chanter ought to have concluded the Mass by saying "Go", he was silent, and gave no signal. Seeing this, Gundulf was amazed, and cried out loudly "Is it—is it day?" [1400] The servants answered him, when he wanted to get up, "Be patient; the cock has not yet crowed your hour, and he knows the stages of the night and marks each of them with his crowing. Even if we wanted to suppress the passing

1381 *Nox ruit*: a Vergilian phrase; see *Aeneid*, vi. 539, viii. 369.

1386 *sacris*: *sc.* uestibus.

1391–2 *Introitus missae*: the Introit for the twentieth Sunday after Pentecost (based on Daniel 3: 31) is 'Omnia quae fecisti nobis, Domine, in vero iudicio fecisti, quia peccavimus tibi et mandatis tuis non obedivimus'. MS *X* (BL Cotton Vespasian E. XII, fo. 36ʳ) adds some musical notation in the margin. The text is chosen here, not to fix the date, but to emphasize that Gundulf is about to undergo God's 'just judgement' for his boyhood crime.

1394 Shackleton Bailey ('Textual notes', p. 283) suggested 'luit' as a replacement for 'tulit', comparing *Aeneid*, i. 738–9, but the meaning is not much clearer: 'He [Gundulf] washed his innards with the dregs'? I have retained 'tulit', and take the 'uiscera' to refer to the 'innards' of the cup, translating as follows: 'he drained it, consuming its contents to the dregs'.

146   *SPECVLVM STVLTORVM*

1405 Quamuis uellemus furari tempora, nobis
    inuitis gallus significaret ea.
Nouit enim melius quam nos discrimina noctis,
    pars quota transierit, pars quota restat adhuc.
Committamus ei surgendi tempora noctis,
1410   qui non dormitat sit uigil ille tuus.
Nox est longa nimis, superest pars plurima nobis;
    uerte latus, dormi, non breue tempus habes.
Nox hiemalis enim tribus est par longa diebus,
    nec sub momento dissiluisse potest.
1415 Nos uigiles erimus, gallo mediante fideli,
    qui quamuis uellet subticuisse nequit."
Gallus ad haec tacite gallinae dixit in aure
    "Obses ego uobis nec fideiussor ero!
Vt poterit, fiat, lex est quam tessera dictat;
1420   qui iacet ille bibat, qui bibit ille luat."
Dum loqueretur ita, clarum iam mane fenestras
    intrat, et ad rimas lux manifesta ruit.
Iam Phoebus radios toto diffuderat orbe,
    iam bobus iunctis uertit arator humum.

1405 nobis] uobis *Va J*   **1406** significaret] signaret /uel significaret *La*
1407–9 *transp. and new line 1409a added after 1408 (1407 om., 1409, 1408, 1409a)*
SMuVaVbVcVdTGoBePkFrNe HaLa Z. Tr has original 1407, but similarly continues with
1409, 1408, 1409a. Pm copies 1409 after 1406, repeats 1404–5 then deletes them and proceeds with
1408, 1409a, 1410   **1408** transierit] transierat *Ha* transiret *PkFr X*   **1409a** hic
erit innocuus qui non sibi tempora dictat *S* hic erit (erat *Vd*) innocuus (innocuas *Fr*) qui non
sibi (semper *Fr*) tempora uitat (uicat *La*) uitet *Vb*) *MuVaVbVdTGoBePkFrPmNe TrHaLa Z*
hic erit innocuus qui non nisi tempora notat *Vc*   **1409–10** *om.* δ *X*   **1409** sur-
gendi] surgenda *F Vc* surgentes β *G* surgentis *L* surgente *E* surgenti *U*   **1411** nox]
non *G TrHa* hox *Z*; plurima] maxima *F* δ *X*; nobis] noctis *Fr X*   **1413** enim] *om. MuFr*
Z; tribus est par longa] par tribus est longa *Mu* tribus perlonga *S* tribus est perlonga *ZX* que
est perlonga *D*   **1414** sub] ob *RO* sibi *Mu*; dissiluisse] desiluisse *P* preteriisse γ+ iam
preteriisse *Z*   **1416** qui] quod *MuVaGoPm Tr*; subticuisse] substituisse *F J La*
subtacuisse *Go* succubuisse *Pk*   **1417** ad haec] adhuc *H Va K* ad hoc *MuGo M*;
1418 ego uobis] nobis ero *H* in hoc uobis *SMuVaVbVcVdTGoPkFrPmNe TrHa Z* in hoc
nobis *Be*; ego] in hoc /uel ego *La*   **1419–20** *om. F*   **1419** poterit fiat] fiat poterit
X poterat fiat *VbGoFr* potuit fiat *VdBe TrLa*; lex] lux γ- *TrHaLa Z*; quam tessera dictat]
quam cessara dictat *Va* quam tessara dictat *Pm* quem tessera dictat *Be* quam tassera dicunt *Z*
quam crathera dicat *T* quam thessara dicat *Ne* quasi tessera dictat *X* quam chessina dictat *Ha*
quam cesseriat durat dictat *Fr* ut uindicet isto *E om. sp. left empty L*; dictat] dicta *H* dicat *D*
*Va*ac *La*ac ducat *Mu* alias dictat *add. Mu*pc durat *Go*   **1420** iacet] iacit *H La* iaceat *P* tacet
HuMN placet *T*; ille bibat] hic iaceat *AJCWRMNODKVe UX* iaceat *P*; bibit] bibat *Fr G Z*;
ille²] iste *HuMN*; luat] bibat δ *UX* iacet *E om. L*   **1421** loqueretur] loquerentur *F*
SVaVbVdPm La Z   **1423** Phoebus] phebet *VaVb U* phebis *Go*   **1424** uertit]
uergit α β *AJCWRHuMN* uerrit *Be K* regit *U*

SPECVLVM STVLTORVM   147

hours, [1405] the cock would signal them to us willy-nilly. He knows the stages of the night better than we do—how great a part has passed, how great a part still remains. So let's leave to him the hour of the night for getting up; let him, who does not sleep, be your watchman. [1410] The night is very long, most of it is still to come. Turn over, sleep, you have ample time. A winter night is as long as three [winter] days, and it can't have flashed by in a moment. We'll keep watch, with the aid of our faithful cock, [1415] who could not have kept silent if he'd wanted to." At this, the cock quietly said in his wife's ear, "I won't be your surety or your guarantor! Let it be as it may be, the law is as the dice dictates: let him who throws, drink, let him who drinks, pay." [1420] As he spoke, clear day came in through the windows, and bright light poured in at the cracks. Now Phoebus had scattered his rays over the whole earth, and now the ploughman was ploughing the earth with his team of oxen. Gundulf got up and struck his breast with his hands,

1409 Only γ has 'surgendi', which must be the right reading.

1414 *dissiluisse*: 'dissilire' = 'to break bounds, run away' (Niermeyer).

1418 That is, 'I wouldn't bet on it (what the servant has just predicted)'.

1419 Equivalent to the proverb 'the die is cast'. See Singer, *Thesaurus*, s.v. 'Würfel' 5. 1 (xiii. 325).

1420 For proverbs meaning 'whoever drinks, must pay for it (that is, what he drinks)', see Singer, *Thesaurus*, s.v. 'Zahlen' 3. 1 (nos. 41–4, 46, 48–9) (xiii. 339), and Walther, *Proverbia*, 5233 ('Debita vir reddat, qui vina libens bibit et dat').

1421–2 Cf. Persius, *Saturae*, iii. 1–2: 'iam clarum mane fenestras/ intrat et angustas extendit lumine rimas'.

148   *SPECVLVM STVLTORVM*

1425   Gundulfus surgens, et palmis pectora tundens,
            "En," ait, "en mallem mortuus esse modo!"
        Et nimis accelerans, strato femoralia linquens,
            protinus ad stabulum sternere currit equum.
        Frenum cum sella transacta nocte bubulci
1430   transtulerant, solito nec fuit illa loco.
        Insilit ille tamen, frenum redimente capistro,
            nec redit ad patrem quo benedicat ei.
        Fortiter elisus cursu dum transuolat urbem,
            corruit in terram, lapsus aberrat equus.
1435   Institit ergo pedes, sed cum peruenit in urbem,
            ordinibus factis serior hora fuit.
        Omnibus expletis praesul secesserat aris,
            nec locus exstabat nec fuit hora super.
        Lectio tota fuit perlecta, legensque "Tu autem",
1440   dixerat, et pueri uox resonarat "Amen".
        Quid faceret Gundulfus ad haec? Medicina dolori
            restabat nulla quam remeare domum.
        Ergo domum propere tristis multoque pudore
            confusus rediit, flensque gemensque satis.
1445   Hinc pater inde parens cum tota prole parentum,
            Gundulfum plangunt pectore, uoce, manu.
        Confusi redeunt qui conuenere parentes,
            in lacrimas etenim gaudia uersa uident.

1425 palmis] palmas *U* pugnis α; tundens] fundens *F* tondens *Fr OR*   1426 *om.*
Go; en²] in *LE* an *T D*   1429 sella] cella *LF MuVc P G*ᵃᶜ *Tr X*   1430 solito]
subito *F*   1431 insilit] insulit *G* insiluit *Go* insiliit *MN* insilet *U*; ille] iste *HuMN* inde
R ipse *MuFr* esse *Ha*; capistro] capistra *LE* capistrum *Mu* capistro *Z*   1432 quo]
quod *SMvVaVbVcVdTBePkFrPmNe HaLa Z* que *Go* qui δ *Tr X*   1433 elisus cursu]
elisum cursu *B* elisum cursum *G* illisus cursu *Fr P*; urbem] orbem *LE* β(*H*ᵖᶜ)
SVaVbVcGoBePkFrPmNe G La ZX   1434–5 *om. HuMN X*   1434 lapsus] largus *AJCWROPDKVe U*; aberrat] oberrat *H SMuVaVbVcVdGoPkPmNe TrHa* errat *D*
1435 in] ad *F STNe Z om. Go*   1437 secesserat] recesserat *F* secesserit *H* successerat
Va O excesserat *G* secerat *M corr. M²*; aris] horis *Go O*ᵖᶜ atro *Fr om. Vd*   1438 exstabat]
astabat *R X*   1440 resonarat] resonabat *H T* resonaret *VdBe OD Tr X* resonorat *S*
resonuit *Va* resonauit *Fr* resonauerit *Pm* resonat *La*   1441 ad haec] adhuc *H K Ha* ad
hoc *L Pk M* ob hoc *Vc* erat *Ve*; dolori] doloris *VcT CD Ha X*   1442 restabat nulla]
nulla restabat *TrLa* nullaque restabat *U* unica restabat α β γ *G Ha* unica exstabat *Z* restat non
alia (aliud *X*) *D X*; quam] que α *SMuVaVbVcGoBePkFrPmNe HaLa Z* nulla *Tr* que n *Vd*
hec *T*   1443 propere] prope *P*ᵃᶜ*Ve* properat β *VaFrPm G*; multoque] multumque *Mu*
*AJCWRHuMNO*ᵃᶜ*PDKVe X* multo *Fr*; pudore] dolore α *MuVaVbVcTGoBePkFrPmNe*
TrHa Z dolori *Vd* dolore /uel pudore *La*   1444 rediit] rediens β *G*; gemensque]
gemens *La* gemendo *D X*   1446–7 pectore—redeunt] *om. X*

SPECVLVM STVLTORVM 149

[1425] saying "Ah, would that I were dead at this moment!" And rushing off, leaving his breeches on the bed, he ran straight to the stable to saddle his horse. The ploughmen had moved the bridle and the saddle the previous night, so that it wasn't in its usual place. [1430] But he jumped on, using the halter in place of a bridle, and didn't turn back for his father to bless him. Coming a violent cropper in his mad dash through the town, he plunges to the ground; his horse escapes and runs loose. He pressed on on foot, but when he came to the town, [1435] the hour was later than the completion of the ordinations. Everything was finished and the bishop had left the altar; no place or time remained. The whole lesson had been read, the reader had said the "Tu autem", and the acolyte had echoed "Amen". [1440] What could Gundulf do about it? There was no remedy for his misery but to return home. So without delay he returned, miserable and vexed by great shame, weeping and groaning greatly. Here his father, there his mother and all their children [1445] express their grief for Gundulf with heart, voice and hands. The relatives who had gathered together went home in confusion, seeing their rejoicing turned to tears. One accuses the watchmen, another blames the drinkers, one reviles the

---

1425 *palmis pectora tundens*: also at *SS*, 3299; *Miracles*, 273. Cf. Ovid, *Ars amatoria*, i. 535.

1434 *lapsus*: past participle of 'labor', 'to escape'; see *OLD* 5.

1439 *Tu autem*: The phrase 'Tu autem Domine miserere nobis' was used to conclude lections in the Divine Office. See also n. to line 3663 below.

1442 *nulla* = 'nulla alia'.

1443 The δ reading 'multumque' has a claim to be the *difficilior*, with 'multoque' a variant induced by the ablative noun 'pudore', but 'multoque' is supported by three separate manuscript groups (αβγ).

1446 *pectore, uoce, manu*: also at *SS*, 2256, 3374; *Miracles*, 2210. With variations of 'manu' at *SS*, 1232 and 1342.

150 SPECVLVM STVLTORVM

Arguit hic uigiles, causatur et ille bibentes,
1450   impetit hic gallum, damnat et ille merum.
Talibus auditis, nido gallina relicto
exiit et gallo talia uerba refert.'

Querimonia gallinae

'"Gundulfus noster rediit frustratus ab urbe
tristis, et in lacrimas totus abire parat.
1455   Et pater et genetrix fratres miseraeque sorores
in lacrimas abeunt; omnia luctus habet.
Quamuis Gundulfus laqueo suspensus obisset,
non possent eius funera flere magis;
imponuntque tibi culpam discriminis huius,
1460   sis quasi totius causa caputque mali."'

Sententia galli

'Talia dicenti gallus respondit "Iniquum
non puto, sed dignam pro uice reddo uicem.
Pullus eram quando, Gundulfo percutiente
tibia fracta fuit, ipse recordor adhuc.
1465   Materiam prior ipse mihi causamque doloris
intulit, indicio tibia fracta manet.
Ipse prior risit, dum uulnera nostra dolerent,
nunc ego derisus rideo lege pari.
Sic uariat fortuna uices, sic gaudia luctus
1470   occupat, excelsa sic cecidisse solent.

1449 causatur] cantor *Vb* causat *Be Tr* causant *Vd*   1452 exiit] exilit *Mu* exit
VaVbVdGoBePkPmNe La exigit *Z*; uerba] dicta *TGoFrPm*   1454 lacrimas] lacrimis
MD X   1455 genetrix] mater *MuVaVbVcVdTGoBePkFrPmNe TrHaLa Z*
1456 abeunt] *om. J Z*; habet] habent *MuVaGoFr AJCWRHuMNPVe TrHa X*
1457 quamuis] et si γ+ *Z*; laqueo] laqueus *E*; obisset] abisset *Pm WᵃᶜRP La* abiisset
Go   1458 possent] posset *C* possunt *La U*   1459 imponuntque] imponunt
VbVdBe Tr imponitque *H*; tibi culpam] tibi culpas *MN* tibi culpans *Hu* culpam tibi *VcGoPk*
culpam tibi nunc *Vb* culpamque tibi *VdBe Tr*; huius] eius *F H G*   1460 *om. Vd*; sis] si
is *HuMN* et *Z*   1461 talia dicenti] talibus auditis α; respondit] respondet *P Z*;
iniquum] iniquam *Go AJCWRMNOP U* inique *Tr*   1462 dignam] dignum *Fr DK X*
digna *Vd*; reddo] redde *H VdFr La* reddere *Go* ferre *K* dare *AJCWRHuMNOPDVe G*
X   1463 eram] erat *Vd CW* ero *Vc*; quando] quondam β *SMuVaVbVcTBePkFrPmNe*
δ *G TrHaLa UZX* quodam *VdGo*   1465 prior ipse] ipse prior *VcPk*; prior] prius *D*
UX; mihi] *om. HuMN*   1467 dum] cum *D X*; dolerent] dolorem *T D* manerent
X   1468 derisus] *Shackleton Bailey* delusum α derisum *rest*

SPECVLVM STVLTORVM

151

cock, another curses the wine. [1450] Hearing this, the hen left her nest and went out to speak to the cock as follows:'

The Hen's Complaint

' "Our Gundulf has come back disappointed from the town, and is getting ready to leave, sad and all in tears. His father and mother, his brothers and wretched sisters, [1455] are going away in tears; grief reigns everywhere. Even if Gundulf had been hanged on the gallows and died, they couldn't have wept more for his death. They lay the blame for this disaster on you; you are the effective cause and source of the whole misfortune." ' [1460]

The Cock's Judgement

'To these words the cock replied: "I don't think it wrong, rather I dole out a fair tit for tat. When I was a chick, my leg was broken by a blow from Gundulf, and I still remember it. He first inflicted on me the grounds and cause for resentment, [1465] and my broken leg remains as a sign of it. He laughed first, while my wounds were giving pain, now I, the laughed at, by the same law laugh at him. So fortune turns things about, so grief takes the place of joy, and lofty things usually tumble. [1470]

1454 *et in lacrimas totus abire parat*: also in *Miracles*, 2376.

1456 *omnia luctus*: Ovid, *Heroides*, viii. 75.

1460 *caputque mali*: also in *Miracles*, 1178.

1462 *sed* is rather awkward here, but the manuscript evidence is in favour of 'iniquum' and 'dignam reddo uicem'. Cf. 1883–4, 1906.

1468 *derisus*: Shackleton Bailey's emendation to the nominative form ('Textual notes', p. 283) expresses the paradoxical reversal (the mocked turned mocker) more sharply.

1469 Prudentius, *Contra Symmachum*, ii. 318: 'sic variat natura vices'.

1469–70 *gaudia luctus/ occupat*: cf. Prov. 14: 13: 'extrema gaudii luctus occupat' ('mourning taketh hold of the end of joy').

152 SPECVLVM STVLTORVM

Exoptata diu dulcis medicina dolorum,
    sero licet ueniat, grata uenire solet.
Numquam sera uenit morbi medicina cruenti,
    quolibet antidoto dummodo curet eum.

1475 Quae uenit ex facili, nullo praeeunte labore,
    ultio delicti, dulcior illa uenit.
Laetus ab hoste meo uictor sine caede triumpho,
    ultus et est animus ore tacente meo.
Bella gerant alii, sint nostra silentia nobis,

1480   uoce tubisque tonent, nos tacuisse iuuat.
Quo leuius nobis cessit uictoria belli,
    uictoris tanto gloria maior erit.
Non opus est armis, ubi uox suppressa triumphat;
    qui bene dissimulat et tacet, ille sapit.

1485 Hostibus ergo meis lacrimae pro sanguine stillent,
    uulneris obtineant ira dolorque uices.
Vulnus enim cordis dolor est, grauiusque perurit
    intima quam gladius exteriora secat.
Exterioris enim leuis est medicina doloris,

1490   sed uix aut numquam saucia corda uigent.
Serius admittit animus solatia laesus
    quam medicinales saucia membra manus."
Vix ea fatus erat gallus, cum morte soluti
    cesserunt pariter hinc pater inde parens.

1495 Mox, patre defuncto, patris est Gundulfus ab aede
    pulsus, et externis tradita tota domus.
Gundulfusque miser, pauper, mendicus et omni
    auxilio uacuus cessit ab urbe procul.

1471 dolorum] doloris *MuVaTGoPm* *CRO* *X*   1472 sero] sera β
MuVaVbVdTGoBePkFrPmNe *G* *TrHaLa*   1473 sera] sero *Vc* *JD* *UZX*; cruenti]
querenti *Vd* *Tr* cruentis *T*   1474 curet] curat *T K* cruret *G* caret *Fr*   1476 illa]
ille *Fr* ista *HuMN* inde *Go*   1477 victor] uicto *D X*; sine] sum *VbBe P*; caede] cedo *Vc*
R cedet *Be* corde *F*; triumpho] triumphi *Vc MNDK X*   1479 gerant] gerunt *VdBeFr*
R *TrHa* *Z*; sint] sunt *G* *Ha* sic *Fr* *R*   1480 tubisque] tubeque *CW*; tonent] tonant *Vd*
P *U* tonant tonent *Z* sonent *L* *H* *MuVaTGoFrPm* *G* *X* tenent *Ha*   1481–2 cessit—
uictoris *om.* *Vd*   1482 uictoris] uictori *VaPk*   1485 stillent] stillant *VdFr* *G*
*La*ᵃᶜ   1486 uices] uicem δ *X*   1488 exteriora] exteriorque *AJCWROPVe* *U*
interiora *SMuVaVbVcVdGoBePkFrPmNe* *D* *TrHa*   1492 medicinales] medicinalis
MuVdBeFr *TrHaLa* medicinale *S*   1493 uix] uis *HuMN*; fatus] fassus α; soluti] saluti
Go *La*   1496 externis] exterius *SVaVbVdGoBePkFrNe* *AJCWRMNO*ᵃᶜ*PDK* *TrLa* *U*
extremis *X*   1497 mendicus] medicus *F* *Va* medico *Go*; et] in *Go* *Ve*

SPECVLVM STVLTORVM 153

The sweet remedy for my suffering, long desired, even if it comes late, is pleasing when it comes. The medicine for a cruel disease never comes too late, so long as it cures it by some antidote. The vengeance for a crime which comes easily, with no preceding effort, [1475] is the sweeter when it comes. I triumph as victor over my enemy without a battle, and my mind is avenged through the silence of my mouth. Let others wage war, let silence be for me; let them bellow forth with voice and trumpet, my salvation is to have kept silent. [1480] The more easily victory in the battle came to me, the greater will be the glory of the victor. There is no need for arms where a suppressed voice triumphs; he who dissimulates well and is silent is a wise man. So let tears drop from my enemies in place of blood, [1485] and let anger and grief do duty in place of a wound. For grief of heart is a wound, and burns one's innards more fiercely than a sword pierces one's outward parts. Healing for an outward injury is easy, but wounded hearts are with difficulty or never made strong again. [1490] The wounded spirit responds to comfort more slowly than wounded limbs do to the physician's touch." '

'Hardly had the cock spoken, when both the father and the mother alike passed away and were swallowed up by death. Soon, his father being dead, Gundulf was evicted from his father's abode, [1495] and the house was given over to strangers. The wretched Gundulf, poor, a beggar, and destitute of any assistance, went far away from the town. But this remarkable event lived on in the memory of many, and fathers

---

1479 *Bella gerant alii*: Ovid, *Heroides*, xiii. 84.

1484 Cf. Publilius Syrus, *Sententiae*, 562: 'Qui bene dissimulat citius inimico nocet'. After this line, MS *F* adds two lines from Ovid's *Remedia amoris* (697–8), advising a male lover who wishes to break off a relationship not to criticize his mistress's faults, lest she amend them and deprive him of an excuse for separation: 'Qui silet esse [*read* est] sanus [Ovid: 'firmus'] qui dicit multa puelle/ probra satisfieri postulat ipse sibi' ('He who keeps silence is sane; he who reproaches a woman is asking that he should be satisfied').

1493 *Vix ea fatus erat*: a Vergilian cliché; see *Aeneid*, i. 586, iii. 655, vi. 190, viii. 520, xii. 650. Also at *SS*, 3483; *Lawrence*, 1469.

154   SPECVLVM STVLTORVM

Mansit apud multos tamen hoc memorabile factum,
1500   hocque patres natis saepe referre solent,
ut memores facti sic se moderentur ubique,
ne de post facto paenituisse queant.'

Qualiter Burnellus uenit Parisius et quid fecerit ibi

Talia cum pariter gradientes plura referrent,
Parisius subeunt hospitiumque petunt.
1505   Corpora fessa quies recreat, tenuisque diaetae
damna recompensat mensa calixque frequens.
Ossa, cutem, neruos, quae uel labor aut uia longa
quassarat, refouent balnea, cura, quies;
Burnellusque sibi minuit crinesque totondit,
1510   induit et tunica se meliore sua.
Pexus et ablutus tandem progressus in urbem
intrat in ecclesiam, uota precesque facit.
Inde scholas adiens secum deliberat utrum
expediat potius illa uel ista sibi.
1515   Et quia subtiles sensu considerat Anglos,
pluribus ex causis se sociauit eis.
Moribus egregii, uerbo uultuque uenusti,
ingenio pollent consilioque uigent.
Dona pluunt populis et detestantur auaros,
1520   fercula multiplicant et sine lege bibunt.

1499 tamen] *om. Go*; hoc] hec *HuMN*; factum] *om. VdBe*   1500 hocque] hecque *H D* hoc γ *Ha Z*; patres] patris *D Z* patris es *Go* patre *Vd*   1501 sic] *om.* γ *HaLa U*; se] se et *Go* sese *VbT U*   1503 *QY rejoin*; cum] iam *B* dum *SMuVaVbVcVdTGoBeFrPmNe OP TrHaLa UZ* de *Pk*   1504 subeunt] ueniunt *Go* δ *X*   1505 diaetae] dieta *HaLa*   1506 recompensat] recompensant *MuVcVdTFr RD*; mensa calixque] mensaque *F*   1508 quassarat] quassarunt *H TrHa* quassarant *VcFr O Q* quasserant *Z* quassauerant *T* quasserat *E Go X*; refouent] et refouent *X* refoueant *E* refouet *G La* reuocant *K* renouent *Go* remouent *Fr*   1509 totondit] retondit *SMuVaVbVcVdGoPkFrPmNe TrHa* recondit *Be La*   1510 induit et] induitque *MuVaGoFrPm* induit *T*; tunica] roba *D X*; meliore] meliori *Pk DK* meliora *LE*   1514 expediat] exediat *Va* expedient *C* expediant *B TBeFr AJWRHuMNOPDKVe G Tr*; illa uel ista] ista uel illa *R Ha UX* illa uel illa γ *D TrLa* ista uel ista *C*; sibi] scola α   1517 uerbo] uerbis *P* uerba *QY*; uultuque] multumque *VdBe TrLa*ac; uenusti] uenisti *E G Q* uenusto *Be*   1519 auaros] auaris *AJCWHuMNP* auarum *O*   1520 *om. P*; bibunt] bibant *Va La*

SPECVLVM STVLTORVM   155

are often accustomed to relate it to their children, [1500] so that when they remember this event they might always keep a rein on themselves, lest they might later regret what they had done.'

How Burnellus Came to Paris and What He Did There

Recounting many things of this sort as they marched along, they reach Paris and look for a lodging. Rest restores their weary bodies, [1505] and food and plenty of drink repair the damages of their meagre diet. The bones, skin, and sinews which had been battered by exercise and by the long journey were revived by baths, pampering, and sleep. Burnellus had himself bled and had his hair cut; then he dressed himself in his best gown. [1510] Washed and combed, he goes out into the town; he enters a church, and makes his devotions. Then he sets out for the schools, meditating to himself on whether this one or that one would serve his purpose. And because he thinks that the English are quick-witted, [1515] he joined their company, for a number of reasons. They are distinguished for their morals, attractive in speech and appearance; they are strong in natural intelligence and are also blessed with worldly wisdom. They shower everyone with gifts and hate skinflints; they eat a lot, and drink without restraint. [1520] 'Wasshail', and

---

1509 *minuit*: 'minuere' = 'to let blood'; see Niermeyer.

1513–16 As at other universities, students and masters at the university of Paris were organized into loose groups according to their country of origin, which later evolved into the formalized bodies known as 'nations'. Gabriel, 'English masters', shows that there were large numbers of English students in Paris in the second half of the 12th c., forming a 'casual association of Insular scholars' (p. 95); this passage in *SS* is itself evidence for the existence of such a national group in the late 12th c., although official evidence of the Nations in Paris cannot be traced back further than the early 13th c., when the University of Paris was legally established (Rashdall, *Universities of Europe*, i. 311–20; Kibre, *The Nations in the Mediaeval Universities*, pp. 3, 65–6).

1515–24 This flattering view of the English is corroborated by a poem attributed to Alexander Neckam (Inc. 'Qualiter Anglorum possem describere gentem'), which says they are faithful friends, characterized by open-handed generosity, a love of food and drink, intelligence ('ingenium'), and pleasing morals (Esposito, 'On some unpublished poems', pp. 456–7).

1520 *sine lege bibunt*: for 12th-c. allusions to the English as heavy drinkers, see the references to William of Malmesbury, Geoffrey of Monmouth, Wace, Gaimar, and Jordan Fantosme (most of them also citing the drinking toasts 'washeil' and 'drinkheil'), in Weiss, ' "History" in Anglo-Norman Romance', pp. 282–3. John of Salisbury comments that their assiduous drinking has made the English 'famous among the foreign nations' (*Letters*, no. xxxiii, i. 56); Richard FitzNigel refers to the 'innate tendency to drunkenness' of the English (*Dialogus de Scaccario*, ed. Amt, p. 131); John of Hauville describes a drunken party, led by an 'English Ajax', enlivened by repeated cries of 'wesseil' (*Architrenius*, ed. Wetherbee, ii. 302–4, 310–26). See also Gerald of Wales, *Speculum ecclesiae*, dist. iii. 13 (*Opera*, iv. 209).

156   *SPECVLVM STVLTORVM*

Washeyl et drinkheyl necnon persona secunda,
   haec tria sunt uitia quae comitantur eos.
His tribus exceptis nihil est quod in his reprehendas;
   haec tria si tollas, cetera cuncta placent.
1525   Nec tamen haec ita sunt semper reprobanda quod illis
   esse locus nequeat tempore siue loco.
Nam duo praecipue sunt exclusiua dolorum
   laetitiaeque uias insinuare solent;
tertia res cohibet, quo dicitur esse referta
1530   Gallia fermentum ne nocuisse queat.
Hinc comes Angligenis prudens desiderat esse,
   possit ut illorum conditione frui.
Est in eis etiam quiddam (seu publica fama
   somniat) adiungi cur magis optet eis:
1535   si de conuictu mores formantur eisdem,
   cur nihil accrescat si comes esse queat?

1521–4 *om. T*   **1521** washeyl et drinkheil] wosheil et drynkheil *E* wosheyl et drynkheil *L* wessail et dringail *A* wessayl et drinkhayl *CWHuMN* wessayl et drinthayl *Ve* wassaille et drinkhaile *J* wessayl et drynckayl *O* wassayl et drynkhel *K* wesail et dunchail *R* washayl et drynchail *X* wesseil et drinchail *P* washeyl et drinkheyl *Q* wasseil et drincheyl *Y* uuesseil et drintulel *Be* wessayle et drinkhayle *D* uueseil et drincwel *S* uuesseil et drincuuel *Pk* wesseyl et drincuuel *Ne* uuasseil et drin?? *Vd* vnckil et trincwiel *Mu* weiesseil et drineuuel *Va* wesseyl cum drincheyl (dringkhayle *H*) β weyssheil et drinkheil *Ha* wesseyle cum drinkheyle *G* whassayllis et drunchel? *U* warsseyl et drinxeyl? *Z* uielessen et trinkuiel *Vb* ess uil und trink uil *Vc* wesselis et drinchal *Tr* uues et lul drincauel *Go* veresal et dermemies *Fr* uueshil et drineuuel *Pm* weyssail et dringaill *La* uuassel et drincuuel *add. in margin La*   **1522–3** *om Ha*   **1522** eos] eis β *OP Tr Z*   **1523–4** *om. OD*   **1523** est] *om. Fr Z*; reprehendas] reprehendes *L* reprehendis *VdFr* reprehendum *ZQY*   **1524** *transp. after 1534 Z*   **1525–6** *om. Q*   **1525** nec tamen haec] nec tamen nec *Y* non tamen hec *T* nec hec *S* nec tamen *U* necnon hic *Mu* necnon hec *VaVbGoFrPmNe TrHa* necnon hoc *Pk* necnon *VdBe*; ita] tria *F* β *D G Tr X*   **1526** esse] ecce *MN*   **1527** dolorum] doloris *VbVcFr R Z*   **1528** *om. Ha*   **1529** tertia] tua *VaNe* tempora *MuGoPm* cum tertia *Fr*; cohibet] cohibent *Mu* prohibet *VcT*; quo] que *Mu RDM UZ* qua *SVaVbVcVdTGoBePkPmNe* P^{pc} *HaLa Q* qui *J* quod *Fr*; referta] notata α *X* refracta uacat *Go*   **1530** *sic U²* over erasure Gallia fermentum] sallia fermentum *HuMN* gallia frumentum *S Ve* gallina fermentum *Go* feruentes febres *X*; queat] queant *T K ZX*   **1531** esse] eius *CW*   **1533** est] et *SFr*; quiddam] quedam β *D G Ha* quoddam *SMuVeVcVdTBePkPmNe RO TrLa ZQY* quodam *Fr Ve* quondam *Go* quid nam *X*; seu] ceu *H VcVdT La^{pc} Z* sed *F U* nam *AJHuMNDK La^{ac}* cum *CWROVe* en *QY* in *Go* quod *Mu P om. X*   **1534** cur] quo α cui *Go*; optet] optat α γ- *O TrHaLa Q*; eis] eos *AJCWRHuMNPVe G*   **1535** *line repeated in alternative form* Z(1)Z(2); de] pro *SMuVaVbVcVdTBePkFrPmNe HaLa* Z(2) pre *Go*; mores formantur] mores formant *Ve* quisquam formetur *SVaVbVcVdTGoBePkFrPmNe Ha* quis conformetur *Mu* quisquis formetur *Z*(2); mores] quisquam / uel mores *La*; formantur] formentur *La*; eisdem] eiusdem *L* eidem *VdGoBe Hu* easdem *Z*(1)   **1536** cur nihil accrescat] accrescat sibi quid *S* accrescat si quid *Pm* accrescat siquidem *MuVaVbVcTGoBePkNe TrHaLa* accrescit siquidem *Fr* accrescat siquidam *Vd* tunc generosus ero *X*

SPECVLVM STVLTORVM   157

'drinkhail', and a bit of skirt on the side—these are the three vices that
dog their heels. These three aside, there's nothing in them that you
could criticize; take away these three, and all the rest is fine. Nor are
these things always so deplorable [1525] that there can't be room for
them, given the right time and place. For two of them are very good at
drowning sorrows, and set one on the primrose path to happiness. And
the third keeps in check the corruption with which France is said to be
permeated, so that it can do no harm. [1530] So he wisely desires to be
a companion of the English, so that he can share their way of life.
There's also something else they have (or else public gossip is mere
fantasy), which is a stronger reason for becoming one of them: if com-
panionship fosters likeness in them, [1535] why shouldn't something
[i.e. Burnellus's tail] grow, if he is their companion? If nature furnishes

1530 *fermentum*: 'corruption, corrupting vice' (*DMLBS* 2; see especially the quotation of
Mark 8: 15). Raymo takes lines 1529–30 to refer to the therapeutic effects of sexual inter-
course, but it seems rather to be saying that heterosexual practice has the virtue of keeping
homosexuality at bay.

1533 *quiddam*: the allusion is to the popular medieval joking insult that Englishmen had
tails. See, for example, *Ysengrimus*, iii. 659, and the reference to 'the king of the English and
his tail-bearing men' in Richard of Devizes, *Chronicle*, pp. 18–19, and for detailed accounts
of the development of the topos, Neilson, *Caudatus Anglicus*, and Rickard, '*Anglois coué*'.
Burnellus hopes that association with the English will encourage his tail to grow back.

158 SPECVLVM STVLTORVM

Si quid eis praeter sortem natura ministrat,
ante retroue bonum cur nihil inde ferat?
Accelerans igitur studio studiosus adhaesit,
1540 ut discat lepide grammaticeque loqui.
Sed quia sensus hebes, ceruix praedura, magistri
dogmata non recipit, cura laborque perit.
Iam pertransierat Burnellus tempora multa,
et prope completus septimus annus erat,
1545 cum nihil ex toto, quocumque docente magistro
aut socio, potuit dicere praeter 'hy ha'.
Quod natura dedit, quod secum detulit illuc,
hoc habet, hoc illi nemo tulisse potest.
Cura magistrorum, multumque diuque laborans,
1550 demum defecit, uicta labore graui.
Dorso se baculus, lateri se uirga frequenter
applicat, et ferulam sustinuere manus.
Semper 'hy ha' repetit, nihil est quod dicere possit
affectus quouis uerbere praeter 'hy ha'.
1555 Vellicat hic aurem, nasum quatit ille recuruum,
excutit hic dentes, perforat ille cutem.
Hic secat, hic urit, hinc soluitur, inde ligatur,
intonat iste minas, porrigit ille preces.

1538 retroue] ue retro *ROPVe*; cur] non γ+; *(whole line)* siue malumue bonum hi nihil
inde ferunt *X* 1539 studiosus] studiosis *ACW QY* 1540 lepide] logice
SVcVdTBe Ha loyce *MuVaVbGoPkFrPmNe Tr* loyce /uel lepide *La* limpide
W 1541 magistri] magister *MD* magistrum *Go* 1543 multa] multa /uel longa
Ha 1545 quocumque] quodcumque *AJCWRHuMNODVe X* 1546 aut] uel *D*
X; potuit] poterit *Vc P* poterat *La*; dicere] discere *F H ACRHuMNOKVe G UY* et discere
J; hy ha] yha *H SMuVaVbVcVdTBePkFrPmNe TrHaLa QY* hy ya *Go* ya *AJHuMNOPDKVe*
hi ha *G* hy a *CW X* hya *U* iha *B* a b *R after 1546, 1563 transp. Tr* 1547 illuc] illic *LE*
B SMuVaVbVdTGoBePkFrPmNe CP TrHa QY illud *R G La U* 1548 hoc...hoc]
hec...hec *SVaVbVdGoFrPm M Ha* hoc...hec *N*; illi] ille *C* illic *S* isti *HuMN* sibi
Vc 1549 multumque] multum *GoFr Ha Y*; diuque laborans] diu laborans *Z* diuque
laborat *CWHuMNK* diuque laborabat *Q* diu laborabat *AOPVe Y* diu laborabit *J* diu laborando *D X* diu laboratus *G* diu studuisset *R* 1550 uicta] uita *LE PD X* uicte *Mu*
iuncta *Va* 1551 baculus] baculos *Q* baculis *Go Tr* balulos *Y* 1552 sustinuere]
sustinere *Fr D* 1553 hy ha] yha *H SMuVaVbVcVdTGoBePkFrNe TrLa QY* hia *C* ya
AJHuMNOPDKVe hya *W Ha UX* iha *B G* y. h. *Pm* a b *R*; dicere] discere *EF H*
SMuVaVbVcVdTGoBePkFrPm O G La UQY 1554 hy ha] hya *CW UX* ya
AJHuMNOPDKVe Ha yha *H SMuVaVbVcVdTGoBePkFrNe TrLa QY* iha *B G* y. h. *Pm* a b *R*
1555 quatit ille] querit iste *Hu^{pc}MN* querit ille *T O^{ac}* catit ille *SPkPmNe* cutit ille *Go* cauat
ille *Mu* tacit ille *Va* cedit ille *VdBe* sat? *Fr*; quatit] quatit /uel iacit *Ha* cedit /uel quatit *La*;
recuruum] retortum *B G* retrorsum *H Mu* 1556 *om. Vc*; perforat] perforet *Go Ha*
proferat *Tr* 1557 hinc] hic *MuGoFr JO U* huic *Vd* 1558 iste] ille *Fr UX*; ille]
iste *HuMND U*

SPECVLVM STVLTORVM 159

them with something beyond the common lot, why should he not reap the benefit of it, at either his front or his back end?

So without delay he diligently applied himself to study, so that he might learn to speak Latin fluently. [1540] But because he was dull-brained and stiff-necked, he could not take in the teacher's rules, and his trouble and toil went for nothing. Eventually Burnellus had spent a good deal of time, and the seventh year was almost over, and he could say nothing at all, whichever teacher or friend taught him, [1545] except 'heehaw'. What Nature gave him, what he carried there with him, *that* he retains, *that* no one could take away from him. The effort of his teachers, struggling hard and long, at length gave out, defeated by the hard toil. [1550] The stick was often applied to his back, the rod to his sides, and often did his hands feel the cane. Always he repeated 'heehaw'. Whatever blows were inflicted on him, there was nothing he could say except 'heehaw'. One pulls his ear, another slapped his curved nose; [1555] one knocked out his teeth, another cut his flesh. One cuts, one burns; now he is bound, now loosed. One thunders out threats, another offers cajolery. So Art and Nature struggle with each

---

1538 *ante*: Raymo suggests that this refers to 'caps with long tails' which were 'a normal part of student dress in the Middle Ages', but this seems improbable. I take it to mean that it refers to a possible improvement in Burnellus's mental agility.

1540 *lepide*: 'logice (loyce)' is a tempting variant, but it is confined to γ. *grammatice* here means 'in Latin' (Niermeyer, Du Cange), rather than 'grammatically' (*DMLBS*). Du Cange cites *Ysengrimus* iii. 382, where Reynard makes some old shoes seem more numerous than they are by counting them three times in three different languages, 'Ungarice, Turce, grammaticeque...semel omnia quaque loquela'.

1544 *septimus annus*: such lengthy studies were the norm at this period; Peter of Blois criticized a canon of Chartres for giving up his studies after only four years (*Epistolae*, no. lxxxi, PL ccvii. 250D). John of Salisbury calculates that his studies in France occupied almost twelve years (*Metalogicon*, ii. 10. 82–3, ed. Hall, p. 72; trans. Hall, p. 201). See also Haseldine's Introduction to Hall's *Metalogicon* translation, pp. 21–3, 33–43, for discussion of this passage.

1551–2 These lines contradict Rashdall's claim (*Universities of Europe*, iii. 358–9) that corporal punishment was not practised at the medieval universities, and was inflicted only on schoolboys in the early stages of learning. Ben Parsons agrees that there was 'little attempt to deploy corporal punishment in a university setting until the end of the Middle Ages' (*Punishment and Medieval Education*, p. 109), and provides ample illustration of Rashdall's point that it is Grammatica, representing elementary study, who traditionally holds a rod in medieval art and sculpture (ibid. pp. 79–90). Perhaps Burnellus is punished so heavily because although studying at university, he is only at the stage of a beginner.

1558 Repeats line 1372, with the two halves of the line in reverse order.

160   *SPECVLVM STVLTORVM*

Sic in eo certant ars et natura uicissim;
1560   ars rogat, illa iubet, haec abit, illa manet.
Quorum principia constat uitiosa fuisse,
aut uix aut numquam conualuisse ualent.
A puero didicit Burnellus 'hy ha'; nihil ultra
quam quod natura dat retinere potest.
1565   Quod fuit innatum seruat natura, quod artis
sic abit ut uento puluis abire solet.
Perdidit expensas, periit labor omnis et omne
quod fuit impensum conditione pari.
Spes quoque deperiit caudae superinstituendae,
1570   sensit et Anglorum carmina falsa fore.

Confessio Burnelli prae angustia

Ergo recordatus tandem Burnellus ineptae
damna iuuentutis se reprehendit ita:
'Heu mihi, quid uixi? Quis me furor egit ut istas
aggrederer partes Parisiique scholas?
1575   Quid mihi cum studio cunctoque labore petito?
Nonne satis potuit esse Cremona mihi?
Alpibus emensis et post mea terga relictis,
stultus in extremis partibus orbis agor.
Vt quid in has partes patriaque domoque relictis

1560 illa¹] ille *MN Y*; haec] hic *Pm D*   **1561** constat] constant β *AJCWRHuMNVe
Gfb*; uitiosa] preciosa *VdBe TrLa*ᵃᶜ *fb*ᵃᶜ   **1563** hy ha] yha *H SMuVaVbVcVdTGoBePkFrNe
TrHaLa Y* hia *C* ya *AJHuMNOPDKVe* iha *B G* hya *W UX* y. h. *Pm* a b *R om. Q*
1564 quam quod] quod quia *D* quicquid *Be Tr*   **1565** *(whole line)* quod prestat non
erant semper per uim uiolentam *X*ᵃᶜ quod—erant *deleted X*ᵖᶜ quod fuit innatum seruat natura
quod ars dat *add. in margin X*ᵖᶜ *followed by repeated line 1566*   **1567** periit labor omnis]
periitque labor sed δ *La UQY* periit labor sed *Z* periit labor *X* ars? *add. above line X*ᵖᶜ periit
omnis *S* pereiit labor omnis *Go* perit labor omnis *MuFr*   **1569** caudae (cause *M*)
superinstituendae]   superinstituende   caude   *La*   cauda   superinficienda   α
SMuVaVcVdTBePkFrPmNe G TrHa ZQY tam superinficienda *Go* cauda superinsicienda *B
Vb* cauda superinstituenda *H*   **1570** sensit] sentit δ *La*ᵖᶜ *UZXQY*; Anglorum] angelo-
rum *Pm J*; carmina] crimina β γ+ *AJCWHuMNOPDKVe G UXQY*; falsa] fessa
SMuVaVbVcVdTGoPkFrPmNe Ha fesse *La* fossa *Be*   **1573** mihi] *om. Fr Z*; quid]
quod *VdBeFr J TrLa*; ut] in *H Ve* ad *D*   **1574** aggrederer] aggreder *J* aggredior *H Tr*
aggrediar *Pm*.   **1575** *om. sp. left empty Vc*; cunctoque] cunctaque *TrLa Q* tantoque α *O*
totoque *CW*; petito] quesito *O* petita *TBe TrLa*   **1576** Cremona] ruina β remona *X*
crenona *G* cremonia *Va* tremonia *Ve* tremore *Tr* querela *U*ᵃᶜ Cremo *add. in margin U*²
1577 emensis] emenses *Vd* immensis *OVe UQ*   **1578–9** *om. SVd C*; *transp. after 1582 Vc*
1579 *om. U, add. in lower margin U*²; *marked for insertion after 1581*; *line repeated but without
change Z*₍₁₎*Z*₍₂₎; patriaque] patria α *VaFr Ha* patrioque *Z*₍₁₎*Z*₍₂₎

SPECVLVM STVLTORVM

other within him; Art requests, Nature commands; Art retreats, Nature stays put. [1560] Those things whose origins were evidently corrupt are rarely or never able to thrive. From childhood Burnellus had learned to say 'heehaw', and he could not retain anything other than what Nature gave him. Nature preserves what was inborn; [1565] what came from Art departed, just as the dust flies away in the wind. He lost his expenditure; all his effort and all he had spent were alike brought to nothing. His hope of reinstating his tail likewise came to naught, and he realized that the stories about the English were false. [1570]

Burnellus's Confession in His Distress

So, turning over in his mind the disasters of his wasted youth, he reproached himself thus: 'Ah me, what has been the point of my life? What madness drove me to come to this region, and to the schools of Paris? What had I to do with study and all this self-imposed toil? [1575] Could not Cremona satisfy me? Like a fool I traversed the Alps, and, leaving them behind me, went on to the utmost limits of the world. Why did I leave my home and native land and cross the Rhône into

---

1560 Cf. John of Salisbury, *Entheticus maior*, ed. van Laarhoven, 540: 'Angit hic, illa fovet, hic fugit, illa manet.'

1561–2 Proverbial; see Singer, *Thesaurus*, s.v. 'Anfang' 2. 3. 3 (i. 138–9).

1566 Cf. Prudentius, *Hamartigenia*, 387–8: 'velut excitus difflato pulvere ventus/ praeterit'.

1570 That is, Burnellus finds that the English do not really have tails.

1576 This is the first time that Cremona has been specified as Burnellus's home town; cf. line 3559. For the geographical confusion this causes, see n. to line 829.

1577 *emensis*: 'emetior' is a deponent verb, but the past participle was sometimes used with passive meaning ('traversed'), particularly in later writers. See *OLD* s.v.; *TLL* v. 2. 480. 37.

162 SPECVLVM STVLTORVM

1580 trans Rodanum ueni, regna uidere noua?
Quae mihi cura fuit per tanta pericula mortis
   cernere Francigenas Parisiique scholas,
nosse uel Angligenas largos Gallosue tenaces,
   hos calices, illos multiplicare minas?
1585 Appulus huc ueni, sed Gallicus ecce reuertor;
   Burnellusque tamen qui fuit ante manet.
Hic nihil addidici, modicumque quod ante sciebam
   hic ego me totum dedidicisse scio.
Gallica uerba duo tantum retinere loquique
1590 si possem, certe gratia magna foret.
Quod si forte tria uel multum quatuor essent
   par Iouis aut maior crederer esse Ioue;
Italiam facerem tanto trepidare timore
   quod mihi rex ipse certa tributa daret.
1595 Tunc ego Parisius in uanum non adiissem,
   si subiecta foret sic mea terra mihi.
Non modo uadit ita; longe mea stamina Parcae
   neuerunt aliter quam mea uota forent.
Dura mihi certe multum mea fata fuerunt,
1600 quae mala multa mihi nilque dedere boni.

1580–81 *marked (wrongly) for reversal U*   1580 Rodanum] radanum *Z* iordanum
GoBe corr. Be² *Tr* iordanem *Vd*   1582–3 Parisiique—Angligenas] *om. H*
1583 nosse] nosce *MuGo C Tr* noscere *F* posse *K*; largos] largo *Tr* argos
SVaVbVcTGoBePkFrPmNe Ha Z argos /uel angos *La* agros *Mu* uugaros *Vd*; Gallosue]
Gallosque *MuVcTGoPmNe* δ *Ha UZ* gallos ut *E*   1584 hos calices] hoc calices *MN*
hoc calidos *Q* heu calidos *SMuVaVbVcVdGoBePkFrPmNe TrHa* heu callidas *T* hos uel calidos /uel calices *La*   1585 huc] hic *E T HuMN X*; gallicus] gallus α *La*; reuertor]
reuertar *BeFr R Tr ZQ*   1586 qui] quod α   1587 addidici] addici *O G Ha Z*
didici *F S*; modicumque quod] modicum quod *GoFr C* modicum quod et *RVe*   1588 *om.
U, add. in lower margin U²*; hic] hoc *Fr P Tr Z*; dedidicisse] didicisse *Ne* dedicisse *SVdBe JC
G Ha X corr. X²*   1589 tantum] tanto *GoPm*   1591 quod] quid β *G X* qui *Be Tr*;
uel multum] multum si γ+ *Z* uel ad ultima *G* ad ultima *H* scirem uel *R*; essent] essem β *VcT
R G X* esset *Ne*   1592 Iouis] ioui *T Z* ioue *Fr*; crederer] cederer *Vb* credere *Fr J X*
crederet *Y* trude *Tr*   1596 si] sic *Be Tr*; sic] sit *Va* si *Fr Ha*   1597 longe] longo
SVaVdGoBePkFrNe AJCWHuMNPVe TrLa UZY longa β *MuVc R Ha*; stamina] scamina
Ve Q stagmina *SBePkNe La* sagina *Vd* famina α β *G X*; Parcae] parco *Ve* parte β *GoFr
AJCWRHuMNOᵖᶜD UXY* per te *LF* parthe *MuVaVdPkNe Ha* parche *Be La* parhte *S* pro
Tr   1598 neuerunt] uenerunt α β *T* δ(*Oᵃᶜ*) *G Laᵖᶜ UZXY* nouerunt
SMuVaVdBePkFrPmNe TrHaLaᵃᶜ neuererunt *Vb* non erunt *Go*; aliter] alia *D Xᵖᶜ* alter *Be M*
pariter *H* taliter *Go*; uota] fata α *MuVc*   1599–2476 *transp. after 721 Pm*
1599–1600 multum mea fata—mala *om. Va*   1599 *copied after 1597, del., rewritten
after 1598 and then corr. U*; mea fata] mihi fata *F* mea sata *BePk La* sed fata *AJCWROPKVe
ZQY* sed facta *HuMN* mea facta *Mu* facta *U* fata *U²over erasure* uota fata *Fr* mea scita *SVbVd
Tr* quasi semper fata *D*

SPECVLVM STVLTORVM   163

these regions, to see new kingdoms? [1580] Why was I anxious to set
eyes on the French and the Parisian schools, in the midst of so many
deadly perils, or to know that the English are generous, the French
miserly, the English revel in drinking, and the French in threats?
I came here as an Apulian, but I'm going back as a Frenchman [1585]—
yet the former Burnellus remains the same. I have learned nothing
here, and the little I knew before, I know I have here forgotten completely. If I could retain and speak only two words of French, that
indeed would be a great blessing. [1590] And if they were three or at
most four, I would be held the equal of Jove or Jove's superior. I would
make Italy tremble with such great fear that the king himself would
give me fixed tribute. Then I would not have come to Paris in vain,
[1595] if my country were thus placed under my sway. That's not how
it is now; the Fates have spun my thread very differently from how
I wished. My destiny was certainly very hard to me, giving me many ills
and no good [1600]—that's quite clear, since in the whole world there

---

1585 *Appulus*: Cremona is not in Apulia, but in northern Italy. However, this claim agrees
with Burnellus's earlier claim to share a national origin with the Sicilian Arnoldus (see line
1228), since the duchy of Apulia formed part of the patrimony of the kings of Sicily.
  1591 *multum*: 'at most' (Mozley, 'Latinity', p. 8; see also Blaise s.v. 'multum', and Ecclus.
18: 8: 'Numerus dierum hominum ut multum centum anni').
  1597–8 *Parcae*: the Three Fates of Greek mythology: Clotho spins the thread of life,
Lachesis measures it out, and Atropos severs it. *neuerunt* must have been very early and very
easily corrupted to 'uenerunt' and 'nouerunt'; only *Vc O*¹ (a marginal correction) and *Q* have
the correct reading (glossed 'filauerunt' in the margin in *O*). The correcting hand in *O* similarly alters 'parte' to 'parce' and adds a gloss: 'Cloto colum baiulat lachesis trahit atropos
occat' (the rest illegible). This is a mnemonic verse with wide circulation; see Walther,
Proverbia, 2879b, and *Jankyn's Book*, ed. Lawler and Hanna, ii. 518.

164   *SPECVLVM STVLTORVM*

Quod satis apparet, quia toto peior in orbe
   non est conditio conditione mea.
Sensus hebes meus est et saxo durior omni,
   durius hoc pectus est adamante meum.

1605 Cor, caput, et cerebrum sunt ponderis atque metalli
   eiusdem, plumbo nam grauiora magis.
Ferrea crura mihi, latus est quasi lamina ferri,
   non est in toto corpore uena puto.
Aenea ceu peluis cutis est mea, quae tamen ictus

1610   excipit incassum, nam nihil inde dolet.
Non ego uerberibus, non per maledicta perire
   possum, malleolis uix puto posse mori.
Cur mea me mater maledicta fudit ab aluo?
   Cur gladio iugulum non dedit ipsa meum?

1615 Tristis abortiuum si me peperisset, in aeuum
   quam fortunata quamque beata foret!
Cur lupus esuriens partes non uenit in illas,
   tolleret ut partum dum tener esset adhuc?—
Cui mea me mater primis deuouit in annis,

1620   atque uenire citum saepe rogauit eum;
huic ego pro certo non solum praeda futurus,
   esca sed et rabidis auguror esse lupis.
Nam celer euentus, si fas est credere famae,
   maternis precibus semper adesse solet.'

1603 hebes meus] meus ebes *Ha ZQY* mis ebes *Vd* ebes *Vc*   **1604** hoc] hic *MN Q*
hec *Be*   **1606** nam] iam *CW* sunt γ+ *U*   **1607** crura] cura *M La*; mihi] mea *Ha*
om. Pm; latus est] pectus γ *TrHa* pectus /[*uel*] latus est *La*   **1608** puto] meo δ puto
[*uel*] meo *La*   **1609** ceu] seu *GoBePkFrNe JCWHuMNVe G TrHaLa U* uel seu *Q* sub
α en *X*; peltis] puluis *RMPVe* poluis *O* pellis β *TGoPk CW G* peltis *LE SMuVaVbVdBeFrPmNe*
TrHa ZX peltis /uel peluis *La* plantis *F*   **1610** dolet] dolent α   **1612** possum]
possem *VdBe*; posse] esse *VaVd*   **1613** maledicta] maledicto α β *Fr? AJWRHuMNODK*
G Y maledictio *C* maledictum *X*; fudit] fuit *Q* subdit *Be corr. Be² La*; aluo] alio *Be corr.*
Be²   **1615** *om. Mu*   **1617** in] ad α *HuMN*; illas] istas *ZQY*   **1618** tolleret]
tollerat *Vc Z* tollet *Vd*; ut] et *SMuVaVbVdBePkNe AJCWROPKVe Tr UQY*   **1619** cui]
cur *AJCWRHuMNPDVe La UXQ* cum *Z*; me mater] mater me *H G* mater *La*; primis]
primus *Fr MN* prius *Be Tr* prius /uel primis *La*; deuouit] non deuouit *Fr* deuenit *Ve QY*
donauit *K*; annis] armis *HuMN* ampnis *D*   **1620** *om. Ne*; citum] scitum *VbGoPk Tr*
satum *VdBe Tr* satum /uel citum *La*   **1621** futurus] futuris *L R* futurum
Go   **1622** rabidis] rapidis α β *VbVcT ACWRHuMNOPDKVe G UXQ* rapidus *JY*

SPECVLVM STVLTORVM 165

is no condition worse than mine. My brain is dull and solider than any rock, and my breast is harder than steel. My heart, head, and brain are of the same weight and metal, [1605] for they are heavier than lead. My legs are of iron, my flanks are like sheets of iron; I don't think there's a vein in my whole body. My flesh is like a brass jar, which is impervious to blows, for it does not feel them. [1610] I cannot perish through blows nor through curses—I hardly think that hammers could kill me. Why did my mother bring me forth from her accursed womb? Why did she not offer my throat to the knife? If to her sorrow she had miscarried, [1615] how fortunate and blessed would she be for all time to come! Why did the hungry wolf not come to that neighbourhood, so that it might carry off the newborn child while it was still a weakling?—the wolf, to whom my mother cursed me in my early years, and often begged him to come quickly. [1620] Surely I believe I won't simply fall prey to him, but will be eaten by ravening wolves. For, if what they say is to be believed, a mother's prayers are always swiftly answered.'

1608 Langosch (review, p. 283) preferred 'meo', as better incorporated into the syntactic structure of the sentence, whereas 'puto' is a mere filler; however 'puto' has wide cross-group support in the manuscripts.

1613 Cf. the opening line of a popular poem on a hermaphrodite by Hildebert of Tours: 'Dum mea me mater gravida gestaret in alvo' (*Carmina*, xxiii, ed. Scott, p. 15; Walther, *Initia*, 3053, inc. 'Cum', 4902, inc. 'Dum').

1617–21 This is an obvious allusion to the first fable of Avianus, in which a peasant woman scolds her crying child and swears that if it does not keep quiet, it will be given to the wolf as food ('Rustica deflentem parvum iuraverat olim,/ Ni taceat, rabido quod foret esca lupo'; i. 1–2). Overhearing this, a credulous wolf waits all day for the fulfilment of this promise, and complains bitterly when this expectation proves false. The allusion supports the reading 'rabidis' (rather than 'rapidis') in line 1622.

1619 *deuouit*: 'deuouere' = 'to curse' (*OLD* 3).

1622 Shackleton Bailey ('Textual notes', pp. 283–4) makes the case for 'rabidis' as original (cf. 'rabidos canes' at 364), although it is confined to fourteen γ and associated manuscripts.

166

SPECVLVM STVLTORVM

Somnium Burnelli

1625 'Quoque magis moueor, me certa pericula terrent,
praeterita nocte somnia uisa mihi.
Nam pater et mater Domino pro me prece fusa
orabant, et in haec uerba fuere preces:
"Esto, Deus, nobis clemens et ab ore luporum
1630 eripe Burnellum, facque redire domum.
Sanus et incolumis patrias peregrinus ad oras
Burnellus redeat, liber ab ore lupi.
Non leo, non pardus, nec peste nocentior omni
rusticus obsistat uel dominetur ei.
1635 Transeat immunis per compita quaeque uiarum,
olfactu careat bestia quaeque suo.
Sit canis elinguis, catulo non calleat auris;
currere ne possit sit mala gutta lupo.
Quem quia nos aliis plus formidamus, ab ipso
1640 protege Burnellum, facque redire domum."
Vnde per antiphrasim quia somnia saepe resolui
consueuere, magis mens mea uisa timet.
Qualia cernuntur nocturno somnia uisu,
talia non debent mane sequente sequi,
1645 sed uice conuersa sunt exponenda uicissim
atque per antiphrasim somnia, crede mihi.
Si bona uidisti, tunc aspera multa sequentur;
si mala, non dubites prospera multa sequi.
Sic mea consueuit exponere somnia mater,
1650 sicut erat prudens atque diserta nimis.
Mater ob hanc causam litem cum patre frequenter
instituit, super his plurima uerba serens;

1625 terrent] certent /uel terrent *La* **1627** pro me prece] prece pro me
VaVd **1628** fuere] fudere *F* fecuere *Fr* **1629** deus nobis clemens] deus clem-
ens nobis α *Vb R* nobis deus clemens *VdTGoBe O TrLa* nobis clemens deus *Vc*; et] *om. Be G
Tr*; luporum] leonum *MN* **1631** incolumis] incolumus *E* incolomis *MuVa* incolimus
Fr **1632** *om. Vc sp. left empty* **1633** non¹] nam *MN*; non²] nec *RK* sed *J*; nec]
non α **1634** uel] nec *G* nil *VcVd* **1637** sit] sed *C*ᵃᶜ*W* sic *VdFr La*; calleat] caleat
Fr pareat *AJCWHuMNO*ᵖᶜ*PK Y* pereat *U* pariat *D* pateat *RO*ᵃᶜ*Ve Q* **1638** ne] non
VbTBe OK TrLa nec *G* **1639** quia nos] quia non *Vd QY* quoque nos *OP*ᵖᶜ*Ve* quoque
plus *O*ᵃᶜ **1642** mens mea uisa] uisa mens mea *VaPk* mens uisa mea *Pm*
1644 sequente] sequenti *W X* **1645–8** *om. D* **1645** conuersa] uersa *Fr Tr Q*
1646 crede] credo *AJCWHuMN X* credere *Va* **1647** uidisti] uidistis β *G*; sequuntur]
sequuntur *STGoPm G ZY fb* sequantur *Fr* sequetur *La* **1650** sicut] sic *GoPm*;
diserta] deserta *F Be O TrLa* discreta *Go* **1651** ob] ad *LE* **1652** serens] ferens
VaVdGoBe RVe

SPECVLVM STVLTORVM

Burnellus's Dream

'What disturbs me more is my fear of serious dangers, [1625] and the dream I had last night. My father and mother were praying to God for me with outpoured entreaty, and this was their prayer: "Be merciful to us, God, and deliver Burnellus from the jaws of the wolves, and make him come home. [1630] Let the wandering Burnellus return safe and sound to his native land, free from the jaws of the wolf. Let not the lion, the leopard, nor (most noxious plague of all) the peasant stand in his way or overpower him. Let him pass freely through all crossroads, [1635] and let every beast fail to pick up his scent. Let the dogs be mute, let the puppy's ear be deaf; let the wolf have gout so that it can't run—and since we fear him more than the rest, protect Burnellus from him, and make him come home." [1640] Wherefore, since dreams are often interpreted by contraries, my mind fears my dream the more. The dreams that are seen in nocturnal vision are not what are bound to follow on the next day. Rather, dreams are to be interpreted inside out [1645] and by their opposites, believe me. If you saw good things, bad things will follow; if you saw evils, you should not doubt that many blessings will follow. That's how my mother used to interpret dreams, as someone very wise and experienced. [1650] My mother often used to quarrel with my father on account of this, producing many speeches about it, while he always took the opposite view to my mother, and he

---

1641–2 Both John of Salisbury (*Policraticus*, ii. 17, ed. Webb, i. 97–101; trans. Pike, pp. 84–7) and Peter of Blois (*Epistolae*, no. lxv, PL ccvii. 190–5) express vigorous opposition to the belief that dreams presage the future in any way whatever.

168   *SPECVLVM STVLTORVM*

       ipse tamen matri semper contraria sensit,
         et sua dicebat dogmata falsa fore,
1655   utpote qui fuerat astrorum lege peritus,
         A puero doctus signa notare poli.'

Sententia Burnelli de faciendo episcopo

       'Sed quodcumque mei super his sensere parentes,
         mens mea tota tremit, plena timore nouo.
       Cur tamen haec timeam? Cum non sint iure timenda
1660   quae nequeunt alio stare uel ire modo.
       Fata, nec id dubito, quicquid statuere futurum
         eueniet; contra nemo uenire potest.
       Rebus in humanis ceu decreuere futurum
         fata, quod eueniat semper oportet ita.
1665   Nemo sui fati uel deuitare tenorem
         uel mutare potest; ergo nec ipse mei.
       Et tamen ignoro quae sunt mea fata futura,
         prospera uel dura, seu mala siue bona.
       Pontificem forsan me constituere futurum,
1670   inque mea patria sedis honore frui.
       Nam miranda solent magis his contingere mundo,
         quam mihi contingat pontificale decus.
       Et si contingat me pontificalibus uti,
         quo poterit capitis mitra sedere loco?
1675   Auribus erectis, ceu mos est pontificalis,
         nullus erit mitrae de ratione locus.
       Praesulis in mitra non est sua tota potestas,

1654 *om.* G   1655 astrorum] accorum *SVd* actorum *VaBePkNe Tr*
1656 poli] polo *Fr Z*   1657 sed] et *R S*; quodcumque] quicumque *S La* quecumque
MuVaVbVcVdTGoBePkFrNe Ha Z quemcumque *Pm* quantumque *Tr*; sensere] censere
VaVbVcVdTGoBePkFrPmNe G Ha UX   1658 tremit] cremit *Pk* cernit *Go Tr*
1659 haec] hoc *Vc N G U* hic *VbVdTBe K La Z*; sint] sunt *GoBe Tr* sit *F Vc La*
1660 alio] aliquo α *D*   1661 fata] fora *Go* facta *T Uᵃᶜ*; quicquid] quicquam *H G* sed
quid *R*   1662 eueniet] euenit *VdGo* euenerit *La*   1663 ceu] seu α *B
SVaGoBePkFrPmNe AJCWRHuMNP Tr QY* est *D* quod *G*   1664 quod] que *Mu U*;
eueniat] eueniet α *T* eueniunt *Tr X* eueniant *MuVbPm Ha Z* eueniunt *Fr U* eueneant
Go   1666 mutare] uitare β *G X* inuitare *Ne*   1667 et tamen] atamen *TGo* et
cum *Pk* et *Fr*; sunt] sint α *SMuVaVbVcVdBePkFrPmNe Tr*   1668 seu mala siue bona]
seu mala sine bona *CWP* seu mala fine bona *Va* uel bona siue mala *R U* seu bona siue mala
SFr D   1671 solent magis] magis solent *F Vc* solent plus *Vb*; his] *om. F QY*
1673 *om. Vc sp. left empty; om. Pmᵃᶜ, add. in margin Pmᵖᶜ*   1674 capitis] capiti γ
TrHa   1675 ceu] seu α *B SVaBePkPm JMNPVe TrLa XQY* uel seu *add. Cᵖᶜ* ut *U* sed
Go quod *G* si *D*   1677 sua] *om. U add. Uᵖᶜ*

SPECVLVM STVLTORVM 169

said that all her precepts were false, he being one who was learned in the law of the stars, [1655] and had been taught how to read the signs of the heavens from childhood.'

Burnellus's Ideas about Being Made a Bishop

'But whatever my parents thought about these things, my whole mind trembles, filled with a new fear. But why should I fear these things?—since it is not right to fear those things which cannot be or turn out otherwise. [1660] Whatever the Fates have decreed will be, will—I don't doubt it—come to pass; no one can withstand it. As the Fates have decreed it shall be in human affairs, so it must always happen. No one can evade or change the course of his destiny; [1665] so I cannot evade or change mine. And yet I don't know what my destiny is to be—fortunate or harsh, evil or good. Perhaps they have determined that I shall be a bishop, and that I shall enjoy the honour of a see in my home country. [1670] For greater wonders than this often come to pass—[greater] than the pontifical honour falling to my lot. And if the use of the pontifical regalia were to come my way, where on my head will the mitre be able to perch? When my ears are erect, as is the pontifical manner, [1675] there will be no room for the mitre. The bishop's power does not all reside in his mitre, although he wears the sacred signs of

---

1663 *Rebus in humanis*: for other examples of this phrase as the opening of a hexameter, see *Lateinisches Hexameter-Lexikon*, iv. 466. Also *SS*, 2043; *Lawrence*, 1259, 1265, 1995; *Miracles*, 1635.

1670 *sedis*: 'sedes' = '(episcopal) see' (Niermeyer).

1673, 1687–92 *pontificalibus*: the *pontificalia* are the distinctive insignia worn by a bishop, in addition to the usual liturgical garments, when officiating at Mass or other sacraments. See Bock, *Geschichte der liturgischen Gewänder*, ii. 1–236; Braun, *Die liturgische Gewandung*, pp. 359–676. The full list given by Bock comprises 15 items (see ii. 129), of which David Knowles specifies seven as having been granted to English abbots: staff, ring, sandals, gloves, tunicle, dalmatic, and mitre. Burnellus mentions only the mitre and the ring. When the right of wearing the pontificals was granted to an abbot, it was, until *c*.1150, 'a sign that the Curia considered the monastery to be a papal *Eigenkirche* [that is, removed from the jurisdiction of the local bishop, and placed under the direct control of the pope]; after that date, it was often merely an isolated favour' (Knowles, *Monastic Order*, p. 711; see also p. 586). Although of little practical benefit to the recipient, the grant was highly valued as a sign of papal favour and protection against the power of local bishops (Sweet, 'Apostolic See', pp. 476–84); throughout the Middle Ages, abbots also attached great importance to the prestige and status that the wearing of the mitre conferred (Heale, 'Mitres and arms', pp. 99–109). The practice was both criticized and ridiculed; see the short poem by Marbod of Rennes, 'De abbate usurpante pontificalia' (Inc. 'Abbas sola gerens insignia pontificalia'), PL clxxi. 1656; if such an abbot claims to be both abbot and bishop, he resembles a centaur, but if he pretends to be a bishop while remaining an abbot, he is like the ass in the lion's skin ('Permanet ergo latens

170 SPECVLVM STVLTORVM

quamuis officii signa sacrata gerat.
Inter eos igitur non est discretio mitrae,
1680   immo potestatis quae comitatur eam.
Mitra caput nostrum sine munere pontificali
nulla deaurabit, auxiliante Deo.
Mitra nec ascendet caput hoc neque cornua sumam,
si non affuerit quod solet inde sequi.
1685   Cetera cum desint quae sunt comitantia mitrae,
quid iuuat hac sterili conditione frui?
Plenus praesul ero, quia pontificalibus uti
nolo uelut mulus, sed uolo sicut equus.
Annulus abbatis et mitra sophistica semper
1690   sit procul a nobis, et decus absque Deo!
Abbatum steriles mitras, quas nulla sequuntur
chrismatis officia, non probo, sintque procul.
Gignere cum nequeat, sua sic genitalia gestat
mulus et est sterilis tempus in omne suum.

1678 quamuis] quamuis et α quam *Y* quantum *Q*; sacrata] sacra *L Z*; gerat] geres *MN*
gerit *Fr* ferat *XQ* regat *T*   1679 *after 1678* abbates quidam poterunt mitras bene
ferre/ a quibus est longe pontificalis apex *DK Tr*; discretio] distinctio *R Q*   1680 comitatur] comitantur *VdGoBePkPm TrLa*   1681 munere] nomine γ *TrHa* nomine /uel
munere *La* numine *H*^pc *QY* murmure *O*   1683 ascendet] ascendit *F MN Tr* ascendat
Fr ascordet *T*; hoc] hec *HuN* hic *M* om. *Ha Z*; neque] nec *MuVbGo HuK XQY* ni *WN*;
sumam] summa *L Go QY* summum *G* sumet *T* sumant *Z*   1685 desint] desunt
MuVaVbVcVdPkPmNe O TrHaLa desinit *Go* desunung *Fr* defuit *E*; mitrae] mitram
SMuVbVcVdTGoBePkFrPmNe TrHa mitra *Va La*   1686 om. *Z*; hac...conditione]
hoc...conditione *GoBeFr Tr* hec...conditione *Vd* hoc...editione *F*   1688 uelut]
sicut α *Vc D Q*   1689 abbatis] oblatus /alias ab *Ha*   1690 sit] sint *T P U* sic *Vc*
hoc *Fr*   1691 abbatum] ablatum /uel ob *Ha*; sequuntur] sequentur *H G*
1693 cum] non *O Tr*; nequeat] nequeant *H Ha ZQY*; genitalia gestat] genitalia mulus β *X*
genitalia gestant *QY* genitalia portat *MuVaVbVcVdTGoBePkPm La* gentilia portat *Ne* genitalia portant *Fr Ha* genitalia pareat *Tr* insignia portans *G*   1694–5 *om. G*
1694 mulus] malus *Fr* gestat β *X*

---

sub pelle leonis asellus'). See also 'De abbatibus mitris utentibus et deliciose viventibus' (Inc.
'Forma fuit quondam Cluniacus religionis'), *Anglo-Latin Satirical Poets*, ed. Wright, ii. 230–1;
cf. Rigg, *Anglo-Latin Literature*, p. 66. The joking comparison to the testicles on a sterile
mule seems to have been a popular one: when Peter of Blois's brother William, abbot of Santa
Maria di Maniaci in Sicily, was granted the right to wear pontificals (mitre, ring, and sandals)
by the pope, Peter wrote to him in dismay, urging him either to give up this right or to resign
the abbacy: 'Ambigenae non generant, teste Hippocrate, quod igitur genitalia in mulo faciunt, hoc sandalia in abbate' (*Epistolae*, no. xc, PL ccvii. 283B). After line 1692, manuscripts
Vb and *Vc* add 'ut duo testiculi sunt membra superflua muli/ sic caput abbatis portat duo
cornua gratis' ('as two testicles are superfluous members on a mule, so an abbot's head carries
two horns to no purpose'). Manuscripts *RVe* add extra lines after 1708 which make the same
point: 'abbatis tantum capiti ualet infula quantum/ testiculos mulo pendere quisque uelit' *R*
('testiculi mulo licet appensi sibi culo' *Ve*) ('The mitre on an abbot's head is worth as much
as if someone were to hang testicles on a mule'). The comparison is also found in the late

SPECVLVM STVLTORVM
171

his office. So it is not the mitre that distinguishes them, but the power that goes with it. [1680] God willing, the mitre will not decorate my head without the pontifical dignity. The mitre shall not crown my head, nor shall I wear its horns, if its usual consequence is lacking. When the other things that go with the mitre are lacking, [1685] what's the good of being in this sterile condition? I'll be a bishop in the full sense, for I don't want to wield the pontifical regalia like a mule, but like a horse. Not for me the meaningless ring and mitre of an abbot, the honour without God's backing! [1690] I don't approve of the futile mitres of abbots, which are not accompanied by the power of consecration— away with them! Since he can't bear offspring, the mule has genitals but is perpetually sterile. Those who have the name but are without the

fourteenth-century Latin prose satire *Laberintus*, attributed by its editor Thomas Haye to Edmund Bramfeld (d. 1393), L200, pp. 146–7.

The right to wear the pontificals was the focus of long-standing friction between Christ Church Canterbury and the neighbouring abbey of St Augustine's. Gervase of Canterbury gives a summary of the opposing positions in the dispute in one of the two *Imaginationes* that preface his *Chronicle* (i. 68–83). The abbots of St Augustine's had been granted the right to wear the mitre, episcopal ring, and sandals at an early date (Gervase, i. 78) but had ceased to insist on it in the mid-11th c., because of the opposition of the archbishops, whose authority it impugned. However, in 1177, when Roger, newly elected abbot of St Augustine's, requested the customary blessing of Archbishop Richard on his appointment, it was granted only on condition that he professed obedience to the archbishop at the same time. A counterproposal, that the words 'salvis utriusque privilegiis ecclesiae' be added to Roger's profession, was rejected, and Roger then sought the aid of Pope Alexander III, requesting 'ut in contumeliam archiepiscopi abbati [Roger] conferret insignia'; he returned to Canterbury in 1178 'elatus admodum anulo et mitra' (Gervase, *Chronicle*, i. 275). A formal settlement of the dispute was reached between Archbishop Richard and Abbot Roger in 1182 (Thorne, *Chronica*, col. 1836; Elmham, *Historia*, pp. 449–52), and in 1185 Archbishop Baldwin visited St Augustine's and was respectfully received. Gervase (*Chronicle*, i. 326) relates that in welcoming Baldwin, Roger reverently removed his mitre, and would not replace it until Baldwin ordered him to do so.

Nigel's witticisms about the 'sterility' of those who wear the pontificals without having real episcopal power can therefore be seen as a jibe at the expense of St Augustine's. The archbishop of Canterbury, who was the titular head of the Christ Church community, was of course fully entitled to wear the pontificals and to exercise episcopal powers; the abbot of St Augustine's, in contrast, lacked the power that the insignia symbolized.

1683 *cornua*: the double points on the crown of a bishop's mitre were often referred to as 'horns'. See *Carmina Burana*, no. xxxix. 4. 1: 'Episcopi cornuti'; Walter of Châtillon, *Poems*, no. lvi. 18. 1 (= *Carmina Burana*, no. xlii. 18. 1): 'Redeunt a curia capite cornuto'; *Apocalipsis Goliae*, ed. Strecker, st. 33. 1–4: 'Ve gentis mutile cornutis ducibus,/ ... non pastor ovium, sed pastus ovibus'; Gerald of Wales, *Speculum Ecclesiae*, dist. iii. 7 (*Opera*, iv. 164): 'abbas ... cornutus' (speaking of an abbot who had been made a bishop).

1692 *chrismatis officia*: chrism is a consecrated oil used in various liturgical rituals and sacraments, especially baptism, confirmation, and ordination. In the Western church it was usually consecrated by a bishop on Maundy Thursday (see *The Oxford Dictionary of the Christian Church*, s.v. chrism). The wearing of the *pontificalia* without possessing the episcopal right to consecrate the chrism makes the abbot 'sterile', in Nigel's view.

1694 *mulus et est sterilis*: cf. the quotations in the note to lines 1673, 1687–92 above.

172   SPECVLVM STVLTORVM

1695 Cum rem non habeant, sua sic insignia portant
   hi qui nomen habent officioque carent.
   Absit ut ascendam uel talia cornua sumam
   qualia sumpserunt ille uel ille sibi.
   Integer et plene totus uolo pontificari,
1700 et non sic sine re nomen habere rei.
   Nomen habent sine re qui sic sibi cornua sumunt,
   et nihil ulterius exhibuisse ualent.
   Absit ut hoc faciam uel sic mihi cornua sumam,
   cornua multiplici praemutilata modo.
1705 Auribus esse meis contentus malo duabus
   quam duo sic nasci cornua posse mihi.
   In quibus excellunt quoniam patiuntur eclipsim,
   mulus et abbates sunt in honore pares;
   qui ne pontifices fiant sunt apocopati,
1710 ut sint abbates syncopa mitra facit;
   re sine nomen habent, insignia menstrua portant,
   in quibus effectus nominis omnis abest.
   Non ita Burnellus capiet sibi nomen honoris,
   nec sinet imponi menstrua membra sibi,
1715 munus ab obsequio uel lingua praeambula uoti
   aut immunda manus non maculabit eum.
   Non erit intrusus, foedo cum Simone foedus

1695–6 sua sic insignia—nomen habent *om. Ha* **1695** cum] cur *HuMN*
1696 hi qui] hique *Vd D* hi quoque *X*; habent] habeant *Go Z* **1698–1703** *om. F*
1700 et non sic] et sic non *SMuVaVbVdTGoBePkFrPmNe TrHaLa* et non sit *U* et si non *Vc*
ut non sit δ *Y* ut sic nec *Q* **1701** sibi] sua *H O* ibi *VbGo* **1702** et] quod *LE*;
exhibuisse] exhabuisse *VdBeNe* **1703** hoc] hec *MuPk MN Ha* hic *BeNe La*
1705 meis] *om. L*; contentus] contentum *H G* contemptum *B*; duabus] duobus *MuGoFr*
TrHa **1706** nasci] uasa *G Tr* uesci *T* **1707** quoniam] quam *H* quantum *D* et
plus γ+ *Z* **1709** ne] me *HuMN* ue *VcVdGoBePk Ha ZY* ue /uel ne *La* nunc *R*; fiant]
fiunt *RVe* omnes *S om.* γ- *TrHaLa*; sunt] sic *H J G* sicut *MN QY* sunt protinus γ- *TrHaLa*
uelut *Z*; apocopati] apocapati *LE Tr* apocupati *Fr* **1710–11** *om. H G* **1710** ut]
Mozley nec *Be* ni *U* et *Fr* me *Q* ne *rest*; sint] sunt *HaLa* **1711** re sine nomen habent]
re sine nomine habent *Fr* re sine nomine hunc *Z* rem non nomen habent *Vc* rem sine nomen
habent *Go U* pre sine nomen *T* nomen habent sine re *AJCWRHuMNOPDVe Y* nomen
habent sine *Q*; menstrua] monstrua *B SMuVbVcTBePkPmNe AJCWOPDVe TrHaLa UZX*
mostrua *Va* monstra *Vd*? nomina *Fr* **1712** abest] habet α **1713** capiet] rapiet α
capiat *Ha* cupiet *Ve* capit *P* **1714** nec] non α ne *Vb OVe*; menstrua membra] cornua
uana δ monstrua membra *L* β *SMuVaVcVdTGoBePkPmNe G Ha UXY* monstrua
membra /uel cornua uana *La* **1715** munus] minus *LE S JO Ha* muus *Vd* nunus
Q omnis *Fr*; uoti] uoci *VcFrPm AJCWRK HaLa* uotis *Tr transp. to end of line 1700 T*
1716–17 non maculabit—intrusus] *om. X* **1717** foedo cum] cum fedo
SMuVaVbVcVdTBePkPmNe TrHaLa cum fodo *Fr* cum sede *Go* sede cum *U*

SPECVLVM STVLTORVM 173

function bear their titles in the same sort of way, [1695] since they're lacking any substance. Heaven forbid that I should be promoted or wear a mitre of this sort—or of the sort that one or another has accepted. I want to be a whole and fully complete bishop, and not to have the name of something without the thing. [1700] Those who assume a mitre in this way have the name without the thing, and are unable to show anything more. Heaven forbid that I should do this, or adopt a mitre of this sort—a mitre truncated in so many ways. I'd rather be content with my two ears, [1705] than that the two mitre-points should sprout on me in this way. Abbots are equal to a mule in honour, since they suffer a mutilation in the things that mark them out. They are cut short so that they don't become bishops—the castrated mitre makes them abbots. [1710] They have the name without the thing, and wear empty decorations which lack all the substance of the name. Not thus shall Burnellus win for himself a title to honour— he will not allow useless excrescences to be placed on him. He will not be defiled by a bribe of service, or a tongue that smoothes the way to his desire, [1715] or an unclean hand. He will not be railroaded in, nor will

---

1700 *sine re nomen*: Ovid, *Amores*, iii. 3. 23. Cf. n. to line 153.

1711 *menstrua*: the usual meaning of 'menstruus' is 'monthly'. Mozley ('Latinity', p. 18) glosses this example as 'uncertain, changeable, ambiguous', but without citing any parallel examples for this meaning outside of *SS*. This meaning fits the occurrence of 'menstrua' at 1017, but not at 1711; the variant reading at 1714, 'cornua uana' is possible but seems rather weak. 'Monstrua', which many manuscripts favour here and at 1714, is an otherwise non-attested adjective, but if it could be supposed that Nigel is coining an adjective 'monstruus', meaning 'monstrous' from the noun 'monstrum', it would fit the context better.

1717–32 *cum Simone*: cf. lines 2643, 2647. 'Simony' is the buying or selling of ecclesiastical preferment by giving donations or bribes to the ecclesiastical or lay patrons who had the power to grant it. It takes its name from the biblical figure Simon Magus (the Sorcerer), a recent convert to Christianity who was impressed by the miracles performed by other Christians, and offered payment to the apostle Peter if he would give him the power of the Holy Ghost, by the ceremony of 'laying on of hands'. Peter indignantly refused the assumption that 'the gift of God' might be bought with money (Acts 8: 9–24). In the Middle Ages, the selling of ecclesiastical benefices was an important potential source of revenue, which church reformers, supported by a wealth of moral and satiric literature, strove to eradicate (Yunck, *Lineage of Lady Meed*, pp. 47–61).

174   *SPECVLVM STVLTORVM*

non paciscetur, praemia nulla dabit,
sed neque promittet, quia numquam cauteriatam

1720   mentem sed sanam praesulis esse decet.
Non prece uel pretio sed nec terrore potentum
        Burnello ueniet pontificale decus.
Ingrediar simplex et sana mente; sin autem,
        praesul in aeternum non ero, crede mihi.

1725   Ordine legitimo gradiar cleroque uocante
        ingrediar, ne quis me reprobare queat;
ne, postquam fuero tanto donatus honore,
        dicere quis possit, improperando mihi:
"Sic ascendisti, sic es promotus et a me,

1730   sic es et ingressus, pastor, ouile tuum.
Vt praesul fieres, pepigisti talia nobis;
        esto memor uerbi, cur facis haec uel ita?"
Pontificis uita liber est, quem iure legendum
        sumere quisque sibi debet, eamque sequi.

1735   Pontificis mores clerus populusque fidelis
        debet in exemplum semper habere sibi.
Nil in eo uitii nil non uirtutis haberi
        condecet, ut forma sit gregis ipse sui.
Non leuiter liget aut soluat; quaecumque potestas

1740   fit pretiosa minus ex leuitate sui.

1718 paciscetur] paciscitur *Q* paciscetur *Vb A Y* pacificetur *CW*   **1720** mentem
sed] mentemque *E Ve*; decet] debet *A²over erasure JPVe* docet *Go*   **1721** uel] nec *R La*
non *Ne X* sed *Fr O*   **1723** ingrediar] ingrediat *Go Z*; *(whole line)* si non ingrediar
simplex sana quoque mente *K*   **1725** legitimo] legitime *TNe*; gradiar] grediar *H*
gradier *Mu* gradiar *Fr Tr* gradiat *Z*; uocante] uacante *JR*   **1727** donatus] dotatus *H*
Go D G ditatus *ZQ* dicatus *Y*; honore] honori *AC^{pc}JWRHuMNOPKVe X* ero
Vc   **1729** es] est *VaVd*   **1730** es et] et es *SVaVdTGoBePkFrPmNe HaLa* es *F*
VbVc OD et *Mu Tr*   **1732** esto memor uerbi] estor memor uerbi *F* esto memor *S* illius
esto memor *MuVaVbVcVdTBePkFrPmNe TrHaLa* illos esto memor *Go*; cur] ut *EF* quid *L*;
haec] hoc *SVbVc C G X* hic *VaBeFr MK TrLa*; ita] ista *MuVd^{ac}Pm*   **1733** quem] quam
VaVcTGoPm M quod *Tr*   **1734** eamque] eumque *Mu R U* eaque *Vd*   **1735** pon-
tificis] pontificisque *MuGoPm*   **1736** debet] debent *QY*; sibi] sui *H G X* suum *U*
1737 nil²] uel *Vd δ*   **1738** condecet] cum decet *SBePkFrNe* eum decet *Va* quidam *Q*;
forma] fama *H G* fueram *Mu*; sit] sic *Fr La* sed *Mu*   **1739** liget aut soluat] liget aut
soluet *D Tr* ligat aut soluat *Fr R* leget aut soluit *Mu* liget ut soluat *Go* ligans aut soluens *U*
liget aut soluatque *Z*; quaecumque] queque *a B γ+ A^{ac}JCWRHuMNO^{ac}P ZXQ* quisque *Ve*
eiusque *H* sic queque *G* quia queque *Y* nam *U*   **1740** fit] sit *H Pk CWD* erit *Go*;
minus] nimis *GoFr A^{ac}JCD*; ex] et *Fr* de β *G*; leuitate] uilitate / uel leuitate *G*; sui] sua *K Z*

SPECVLVM STVLTORVM 175

he tolerate an alliance with filthy simony; he'll give no gifts nor promise any, for a bishop's mind should be whole, not blemished. [1720] Neither by entreaty nor by bribery, nor through fear of the powerful shall the pontifical honour come to Burnellus. Uncorrupted and whole of mind I shall take it on; otherwise I shall never be a bishop, believe me. I shall proceed in lawful order, and shall take up office at the clergy's summons, [1725] so that no one can reproach me—so that no one, after I have been granted so great an honour, can say, to my reproach: "This is how you were elevated, this is how you were promoted, and by my means; this, shepherd, is how you entered your sheepfold. [1730] You promised such-and-such to us in order to become a bishop; remember what you said; why do you do this or that?" A bishop's life is a book, which anyone ought by rights to be able to pick up and read, and imitate it. The clergy and the faithful laity ought always to have the bishop's character [1735] as an example to them. It is not fitting for there to be any vice or anything other than virtue in him, so that he is a model to his flock. He should not lightly bind or loose; any power is less valued if frivolously used. [1740] Artless, not artful, smooth-tongued, not

1721 *prece uel pretio*: a common phrase (like 'for love or money'), which provided much opportunity for poetic wordplay. See *Lawrence*, 1346; *Miracles*, 761, 763–4, 1952, 2130–2, 2141; *Paul*, 671; John of Salisbury, *Entheticus maior* (ed. van Laarhoven), 474; Walter of Châtillon, *Poems*, no. xliii. 26. 3.

1727–32 Cf. *Tractatus*, ed. Boutemy, pp. 177–8, where Nigel imagines interrogating a bishop on the means by which he was elected ('vide si per ostium ascendisti in ovile ovium, alioquin fur es et latro').

1738 *forma... gregis*: Cf. 1 Pet. 5: 3: 'forma facti gregis'. Also echoed in *Lawrence*, 166; *Miracles*, 66.

176 *SPECVLVM STVLTORVM*

Simplex non duplex, blandus non blaesus, honori
non oneri studeat ciuibus esse suis.
Qui sua largiri debet, non hunc aliena
quolibet obtentu diripuisse decet.

1745 Nam nisi sit simplex oculus mentis, tenebrosum
totum corpus erit totaque uita sequens.
Si quod habet mundus totus uirtutis in unum
pontificem ueniat, uix reor esse satis.
Quique tenetur ad hoc sit ut omnibus omnia factus,

1750 quidnam uirtutis debet abesse sibi?
Non odium uel amor hebetent rationis acumen,
non oculum cordis faex nebulosa tegat.
Non caro, non sanguis quae sunt facienda reuelet
primum pontifici, Spiritus immo Dei.

1755 Nil faciat quod amor carnis uel suaserit ira,
haec quia praecipitat, ille trahendo ligat.
Sit baculus claudo, sit caeco lumen, egenti
copia, spes lapso, consiliumque reo.
Introeant ad eum dolor et gemitus uiduarum,

1760 pauperis et lacrimam iudicet esse suam.

1741 non blaesus] uel blesus *Va* non besus *Be* non lesus *Pk JCW Tr* illesus *M* nblesus *Hu*
om. <space left empty> N 1742 oneri studeat] studeat oneri α onere studeat *Mu* onori
studeat *Va* enim studeat *Pm* 1743 qui] hic *SVaVbVcVdTGoBePkFrPmNe HaLa Z*
hec *Mu Tr*; non hunc] nunc habens *G* non habens *Z* non habent *VdPm Y* 1745 *I*
rejoins; nam] non *R Y*; sit] *om. LE*; oculus mentis] oculis mentis *MuVaVdPkFrPmNe Ha Z*
ocultam metis *Go* oculus metus *T* 1747 si] sed *LE*; quod] quid *SVcTGoFr Ha QY*;
habet] *om. L*; totus] totum *SMuVaVbVdTGoBePkFrPmNe D TrHaLa* 1748 ueniat]
ueniet *Vc QYᵖᶜ* ueniant *Mu J* leuiat *Tr* 1749 ad hoc] ad hec *SMuVbVdPkNe HaLa* ad
hic *Q* ab huc *Go* adhuc *Fr HuMN*; sit ut omnibus omnia factus] uel sicut et uia duxque *add.*
in margin La; ut] *om. H Mu Q* in *Tr*; omnia factus] omni factus *Go* et uia duxque δ *U²over*
erasure 1750 quidnam uirtutis] nil ergo (igitur *D*) uitii δ (*A over erasure*); debet]
debent *Uᵃᶜ*; abesse] adesse β δ *GI UZY*; (*whole line*) uel nil ergo uicii debet adesse sibi *add.*
in margin La 1752 oculum] oculos *VaVcFrPm* oculis *Go* ocultum *Vd*; faex nebulosa]
fex nebulosa /uel nox tenebrosa *La*; nebulosa] tenebrosa *MuVaVbVcTGoBe*(nebulosa *add.*
Beᵖᶜ)*FrPmNe Ha UZ* tenebrosa uel nebulosa *Pk* 1753 sunt] sint α *Q*; reuelet] reuelat
Fr I 1754 pontifici] pontificis *Vc La* propositi *Z* 1755 faciat] faciet *R Ha*;
amor carnis] amor carius *Go* carnis amor β *X* amor cordis *Mu*; uel] ue *GI* que *Ve om. Aᵃᶜ C*;
suaserit ira] sanguis oportet /[*uel*] suaserit ira *followed by line 1756 in margin La*; suaserit]
suaserat *U* suadet *LF* suadeat *E PVe* suaderit *AᵃᶜJCW GI* suaderat *Y* sanguinis β
SMuVaTGoPm ZX sanguis *VbVcVdBePkFrNe TrHa*; ira] optat β *VdTFr ZX* optet
SMuVaVbVcGoBePkPm Ha oportet *Ne* esset *Tr* 1756 *om. VdBe Laᵃᶜ*; haec quia pre-
cipitat] *add. in margin Laᵖᶜ* (*illegible after* 'precipitat'); haec] hic *VcTNe*; quia] quoque α tria
Va; ille] istε *HuMND* illa *MuFr Q* 1757 sit¹] sic *VaVdFrPmNe Tr*; sit²] sic *VaVdFrNe*
Tr sine *J* 1758 spes] pes α *K om. S*; consiliumque] conciliumque *H Z* consilioque *D*
consilium *Fr* 1759 introeant] intereant *H* intrent et *S* et ueniant (ueniat *D*) δ *GI U*
1760 *om. Vd La*, *add. in margin Laᵖᶜ*; lacrimam] lacrimas *Mu P* lacrima *Pm* lacrimans *Fr*;
esse] ipse *Va Tr U* ipsi *Be*; suam] suas *MuFr*

SPECVLVM STVLTORVM 177

smarmy, he should try to be a blessing, not a burden to his people. It's not right that the one who ought to give away his own possessions should carry off other people's by some pretext or other. For unless the eye of the mind is pure, [1745] the whole body will be darkened, and the life that ensues. If all the virtue in the world were to enter into one bishop, I hardly think it would be enough. For what virtue can be lacking in one who is bound to this, that he should be all things to all men? [1750] Neither hate nor love should blunt the sharpness of his thinking, nor cloudy sediment obscure the eye of his heart. Neither flesh nor blood should first reveal to the bishop what is to be done, but rather the Spirit of God. He should do nothing under the persuasion of fleshly love or anger [1755]—for anger makes him too hasty, and love clings to him and drags him back. Let him be a staff to the lame, a light to the blind, abundance to the needy, hope to the fallen, and counsel to the guilty. Let the grief and lamentations of widows enter into him, and let him think the poor man's tear his own. [1760] Let the orphans' cause

1741–2 *blaesus*: literally, 'stammering, lisping'; here used to indicate affectedly ingratiating speech. See *DMLBS* sense b, and for examples of its use in this sense, Gerald of Wales, *Speculum duorum*, ed. Lefèvre et al., Part i, 443 (p. 28), and Part ii, 186 (p. 88; purportedly quoting Martial). *honori/ non oneri*: see n. to line 145.

1745–6 Matt. 6: 22–3: 'Lucerna corporis tui est oculus tuus. Si oculus tuus fuerit simplex, totum corpus tuum lucidum erit. Si autem oculus tuus fuerit nequam, totum corpus tuum tenebrosum erit.'

1749 *omnibus omnia factus*: 1 Cor. 9: 22. Also at *SS*, 2507 (with 'facta'); *Miracles*, 69.

1757 Job 29: 15: 'oculus fui caeco, et pes claudo'.

1759–61 *uiduarum...pupillorum*: widows and orphans are often paired in biblical phraseology as examples of the poor. See, for some examples, Exod. 22: 22; Deut. 10: 18; Ps. 145 (146): 9; Jer. 7: 6; Jas. 1:27. These lines closely resemble Isa. 1: 23, on the rulers who 'diligunt munera et sequuntur retributiones. Pupillo non iudicant, et causa viduae non ingreditur ad illos.' This verse was frequently echoed by patristic and medieval writers; see, for example, John of Salisbury, *Policraticus*, v. 16 (ed. Webb, i. 352), on sheriffs and justices: 'diligunt munera et sequuntur retributiones, nec liberant pauperem a potente, aduenae et pupillo non iudicant, et causa uiduae non ingreditur ad eos'. Like Nigel, St Bernard turns the negative into a positive: 'Causa viduae intret ad te, causa pauperis et eius qui non habet quod det' (*De consideratione*, i. 13, *Sancti Bernardi Opera*, iii. 408, line 23).

178 SPECVLVM STVLTORVM

Causa pupillorum sua sit, sibi credat adeptum
quod non abstulerit pauper ab aede sua.
Non inopem spernat, uultum uenerando potentum;
est hominis faciem cernere, corda Dei.

1765 Non sit captator famae popularis ineptae,
non studeat mundo sed placuisse Deo.
Namque quid est aliud quam uentus et aura recedens
laus populi, celebris fama, fauorque breuis?
Quid iuuat ad famam populi sibi conciliandam

1770 tollere pauperibus diuitibusque dare?
De lacrimis inopum uentrem satiare potentum
nescio quem laudis debet habere locum.
Sanius est famam, dum non de iure laborat,
spernere quam redimi conditione graui.

1775 Multi dum laudes hominum uenerantur ad horam
infames fieri promeruere diu.
Ad laudes hominum uanas sibi conciliandas,
qui nimis aspirat insipienter agit.'

Stulta gloriatio Burnelli

'Ergo cum fuero praesul promotus in urbe,
1780 in toto mundo par mihi nullus erit.
Obuius exibit populus mihi totus ab urbe,
dicet et obstipo uertice "Praesul, aue!"
Quid mea tunc mater, cum me benedicere clerum
uiderit et populum, dicere quaeso potest?

1761 sua] una *CW*; sibi] *om. D Ha*; adeptum] adeptam *Pk* adoptum *F* ademptum *B MuVaVbTGøFrPm* δ *GI HaLa UZXQY* ablatum *Vc*   1762 *om. Vd*; quod] qui *Be Tr* et *Pk*; abstulerit] abstulit *VaPmNe* obstulerit *Be*   1763 uultum] multum *Pk R*   1765 captator] captorum *GI*   1766 studeat mundo] mundo studeat γ+   1767 namque] nam *H VcFr*; quid] quod *ND*   1768 breuis] sequens *K* suus *Vd Tr* suusque *Be* breuisque *La*   1769 quid] quod *GI*; conciliandam] conciliandum *O* concilianda *E* conciliendam *B AJ* consiliandam *F H CWRPDVe TrHa UXQ* consiliendam *GI Y* consiliandum *Mu*   1771 uentrem] uentres *α*; satiare] sociare *F*; potentum] potuntum *Pk* petentum *F*   1772 quem] quid *MuVaGoPmNe Ha U*   1773 laborat] laboret *EF Vc*   1774 redimi] redemi *MuFr*   1775 hominum] homines *GI*; uenerantur] uenatur *F* uenantur *LE SVbVcVdTBePkPmNe TrHaLa* moueantur *Mu*   1776 *transp. after 1787 Z*   1777 uanas] nimias β *VbVcVdPm AJCWRHuMNPDK TrHaLa UZXfb* nimium *Ve* minas *MuVaGoBePkNe GI QY* uenias *T* aymas *S* animus *Fr*; sibi] ergo *VdBe* tibi *Pk om. Z*   1778 *om. Z*; insipienter] non sapienter δ *GI fb*   1779 ergo] ego *BeNe CW Tr*   1781 populus mihi] mihi populus *VcFr*; ab] in *H R X* ex *Z*   1782 et] *om. LE*; obstipo] ab stipo *J* inflexo *SMuVbVcVdTGoBePkFrPmNe TrHaLa* inflexio *Va*   1783 quid] quod *LE Fr*; me] *om. I add. I²*

SPECVLVM STVLTORVM

be his own, and let him think he possesses only what the poor man has not taken away from his house. Let him not spurn the poor man, while worshipping the presence of the mighty; men see the face, but God sees hearts. Let him not be a popular seeker of foolish fame; [1765] he should not aim to please the world, but God. For what is the people's praise, a famous reputation, and brief popularity, other than wind and fleeting breath? What is the good of taking from the poor and giving to the rich in order to win a popular reputation for oneself? [1770] I don't know what praise should be given for stuffing the belly of the powerful out of the tears of the poor. It's wiser to scorn reputation, when it has ill effects, than that it should be won by suffering. Many who seek men's praises for the moment [1775] have deserved to be infamous for a long time. He who desires to win the vain praises of men is acting foolishly.'

Burnellus's Foolish Boasting

'So when I shall be appointed bishop in the town, there'll be no one equal to me in the world. [1780] All the people will come out from the town to meet me, and will say, with bowed head, "Hail, bishop!" What, I ask, will my mother be able to say when she sees the clergy and the people blessing me? Filled with delight, she will bless the day, the season,

---

1761 Shackleton Bailey ('Textual notes', p. 284) thinks that the right reading here is 'ademptum' ('taken away, carried off') rather than 'adeptum' ('acquired, obtained, got possession of'), but I find it hard to make sense of 'ademptum' here. The thought is that the poor man has a right to any of the bishop's property he wishes to lay hold of (see n. to lines 583–6), and the bishop can call his own only what is left. Langosch's translation (*Narrenspiegel*, 1759–60) makes 'pauper' the subject of the main verb, which obscures the thought even further.

1764 Cf. 1 Kgs. (1 Sam.) 16: 7.

1782 *obstipo uertice*: cf. Horace, *Saturae*, ii. 5. 92.

180   SPECVLVM STVLTORVM

1785 Exhilarata diem tempus benedicet et horam
qua peperit natum me benedicta suum;
et pater ipse meus quanto gaudebit honore,
cum dominum dicent pontificisque patrem!'

Reuersio Burnelli in se

'Forsitan emeritos patrem matremque uidere
1790 rusticus accedet excutietque caput,
dicet et occulto (quoniam uersutior usque
ad mare non poterit esse repertus eo):
"Magna puer uidi, sed adhuc maiora uidebo
si fuero sospes et mihi uita comes.
1795 Tempora Burnelli modo sunt; quandoque fuerunt
alterius; uicis est non habuisse uicem.
Praesule defuncto modo plurima sunt in honore
quae tunc alterius conditionis erant.
Eius et ipsa parens, quae nunc communia spernit,
1800 auguror assuetum prona subibit onus,
deferet et saccum pater eius, ut ante solebat,
desinet et dici praesulis esse pater.
Plurima multotiens quae uidimus atque uidemus
sustineamus adhuc, nec moueamur in his."'

Narratio Burnelli de ingratitudine praepositi ciuitatis

1805 'Est quoque quod timeo, quoniam de iure timere
debeo, nam modicum quid nocuisse potest.

1785 benedicet] benedicat *Go Tr*   **1787** ipse] ille δ *GI UZQY*; quanto] quando *Y*
tanto γ+   **1788** dicent] dicunt *CW Q* dicens *Be I*   **1789** emeritos] emeritis *LE*
Vd   **1790** accedet] accedat *La Z* excedet *SVbTGo* excidet *VaVc* excidit *Fr* exodet
VdBePm Tr exedet *MuPkNe Ha* (*glossed* 'i. adiet')   **1791** occulto] occulte α *VcVdT R*
UX occulta *Q* oculo *Va*   **1794** mihi uita] uita mihi *CW* mihi uia *D*   **1795** modo]
non *VaVd om. La*; quandoque] et quandoque *La* et nostra γ *TrHa Z*   **1796** alterius
uicis est non] alteriusque uicis est β *STZX* alteriusque uices est *MuVaVbVcVdGoBePkFrPmNe*
TrHa   **1797** praesule defuncto modo plurima] presule defuncto mea plurima *Go* presule defuncto non plurima *Pm* presule burnello (burnelle *Y*) modo plurima *ZQY* pontificis
tanti nunc tempora δ *GI U* pontificis tanti modo tempora *add. in margin La*   **1798** quae]
qui *Ne K* quin *Va*; tunc] prius δ *GI U*; erant] erunt α *H SVbVcVdBePkNe TrHa X*
1799 eius] quis *GI*; parens] mater α; nunc] tunc *Vb om. S*   **1800** assuetum] assueta
GI; subibit] subiuit *Go Tr*   **1801** deferet] deferat *Fr RO Q* defeceret *Z* differet *Go D*
defert *MuPk*   **1802** esse] ecce *J* ipse *SMuVaVbVcVdTGoBePkFrNe K TrHa X* ipse
[*uel*] esse *La* tempore *Pm*   **1803** quae] quia β *SMuVaVbVcTGoBePkFrPmNe TrHaLa X*
quam *UY* quem? *Q*   **1804** nec] ne α β *SMuVaVbVcVdGoPkFrPmNe GI TrHaLa*
UZXQY om. Be; moueamur] moneamur *J* moueatur *Go Tr*   **1806** *om. Ve*; nam] non *D*
GI Tr ZY iam *Go*; quid] quod *VaGo GI Z* quis *O*

SPECVLVM STVLTORVM

181

and the hour [1785] on which she had the good fortune to bear me as her son. And my father, how much honour will he enjoy, when they call him "sir" and father of a bishop?'

Burnellus Returns to Himself

'Perhaps the peasant will come to see my old father and mother, and will shake his head, [1790] saying secretly (for none more cunning than he can be found throughout the land), "I saw great things when a boy, but still greater shall I see, if I survive and life remains to me. Burnellus's time has come; once it was another's. [1795] The absence of change constitutes a change. The bishop being dead, many things are now honoured which then were the opposite. His mother herself, who now despises common things, will, I foretell, bend to the accustomed load, [1800] and his father will bear a sack, as he did before, and will cease to be called a bishop's father. The things we have seen many times, and see now, let us still endure, and not be agitated by them."'

Burnellus's Story of the Ingratitude of the Sheriff of the Town

'There's also something I fear, since I ought rightly to fear, [1805] for a little thing can do harm. The sheriff of the town, unless he happens

182 SPECVLVM STVLTORVM

Vrbis praepositus, fuerit nisi forte coactus,
    non me suscipiet, congrua causa subest.
Namque meo patri saccum summamque farinae
1810   surripuit furto, res bene nota fuit.
Rumor erat celebris, uicinia tota sciebat,
    urbs est tota mihi testis, et ipse Deus.
Condixere sibi nostri genitoris in aulam
    tres pariter ciues, tertius ille fuit.
1815   Nequiter et noctu uenientes tollere plura
    proposuere sibi si licuisset eis.
Primus equum tulit, alter ouem, tulit ille farinam
    qui modo praepositus extat in urbe sua.
Egressique domum, cum iam remeare pararent,
1820   certantes subita dissiluisse fuga,
nescio siue pedum strepitu casuue molossi
    exciti ueniunt praepediuntque uiam.
Acceleransque pater praeuenit eos, et in arta
    uincula coniecit compedibusque dedit.
1825   Mane quidem facto ciues uenere uocati,
    hique quibus fuerant tradita iura fori.
Carcere producti manibus pedibusque solutis
    stabant, quisque suum turpe tenebat onus;
quos timor exsangues, quos et pudor ipse parentum
1830   fecerat elingues immemoresque sui.

1809 mec patri] patri modo *D* modo patri *VbBe Tr* meo *Vd* 1811–14 *om.*
Tr 1811 uicinia] uicina *E VbFr D Z* uicinis *Pk Ha* nam curia *Vd* incuris *Be* incuria *Ne*
incuriis [*uel*] uicinia *La*; tota] nota *LE* 1812 tota mihi] mihi tota *Vc Ve* tota modo *E*
1813 condixere] conduxere *Vc AJCWHuMNP Z* condiccere *Y* cum dixere *SVaVbGoFrNe*;
genitoris] ianitoris *ROP* 1814 ciues] fures *H δ GI UZXQY* ciues /uel fures *La*; ille]
iste *HuMN* ipse *X* 1815 uenientes] uenientis *GoPm*
1816 proposuere] preposuere *J* proposuisse *L P*; *(whole line)* si licuisset eis proposuere
(proposuisse *Ve*) sibi *ROVe* 1817 tulit¹] sic *GI*; ouem] auem *TFr*; tulit²] *om. SVaVc*;
ille] iste *HuMN* ipse *Tr* 1818 praepositus] propositus *E Y* 1819 pararent]
parant? *J* pararet *Pk* parent *FrPm Z* 1820 subita] subito *Go Z*; fuga] fugam *Ha Z*
1821 siue] sine *SVa JCW* si ne *Vb* si *MuVc K* 1822 exciti] extiti *Pk La* excitati *T Tr*
exterriti *H SMuVaPm Ha* territi *Fr*; uiam] fugam *SMuVaVbVdTGoBePkFrPm TrHaLa Z*
fudam *Ne* 1823 acceleransque] accelerans *Go Oᵖᶜ* deceleransque *T*; pater] pariter
Go O 1824 coniecit] cum iecit *GoPkPmNe Tr* tamen iecit *VaVdBe*; compedibusque]
cum pedibusque *GoPk* tamen pedibusque *Vd* 1825 uenere] ueniere *H Vc* conuenere
Mu uenire *Va Z* ferire *Go* 1826 hique] hi que *E* hii quoque *S* hii *Va RO Ha* hiis
Ve; iura] iure *D Tr* iuxta *J* 1827 producti] produci *J I*; solutis] salutis *T* soluti
MuVc 1828 stabant] stabunt *Q* stabat *Go Z*; turpe] turbe *JD* nempe *Vd* tempore *Be*;
onus] opus *CWHuMNDK Q* uel opus *add. in margin* *Xᵖᶜ* 1829–30 quos et pudor—
elingues] *om. Vd La, add. in margin* *Laᵖᶜ* 1829 quos² et] quosque *Fr* quis et *Tr* simul
et *α*; ipse] ille *L Tr* esse *F*; parentum] parentes *L*

SPECVLVM STVLTORVM

183

to be compelled to, will not receive me, and there's good reason. For he stole a sack and a load of flour from my father; the fact was well known. [1810] The rumour was rife, the whole neighbourhood knew; the whole town, and God Himself is my witness. Three townsfolk conspired together against my father's hall; he was the third. They planned to come at night and with criminal intent and carry off many things, [1815] if they got away with it. The first one took a horse, the second a sheep; the one who is now sheriff of his town took flour. Having left the house, they were now getting ready to return home, trying to scatter in immediate flight, [1820] when the dogs arrived—I don't know whether aroused by chance or by the noise of feet—and blocked their exit. My father, hastening to the spot, stopped their getaway, threw them in tight-bound chains and placed them in shackles. When it was morning, the citizens were summoned and assembled, [1825] together with those to whom the secular law was entrusted. Brought out of jail, with their hands and feet free, they stood, each one bearing his shameful burden. Fear had made them pale, shame for their relatives had deprived them of speech and presence of mind. [1830] For long they denied everything,

1807 *praepositus*: 'sheriff' (Niermeyer 12).
1809 *summa*: 'a measure (liquid or solid)' (Niermeyer, s.v. 'sagma').
1819 For 'egredior' with the accusative, see *OLD* 4.
1826 *iura fori*: see Niermeyer, s.v. 'forum' 2, and cf. n. to lines 973–4.
1827 *manibus pedibusque solutis*: prisoners had their hands released from shackles before they were brought before a justice, though according to Bracton (*De legibus*, ii. 403) their feet could still be shackled to prevent their escaping.

184 SPECVLVM STVLTORVM

Infitiando diu tandem coepere fateri,
    quos tamen ante satis constitit esse reos.
Crimina confessos populus decreuit iniquos
    in cruce suspendi, quam meruere sibi.

1835 Tota nocte cruces famuli funesque parabant,
    debuit et mane quisque subire suam—
cum mihi quae mecum miseratio creuit ab aluo
    suggessit, miseris ut misererer eis;
non tamen oblitus uulgi memorabile uerbum,

1840   quod solet ex tali conditione sequi:
"Inter mille uiros erit ille nocentior hostis
    quem te constiterit surripuisse cruci."
Sed tamen his spretis tandem miseratio mentem
    uicit et euicit me pietatis amor.

1845 Clauibus ergo patris clam sumptis clamque relatis
    rem grandem feci quamque recordor adhuc.
Carceris e fundo fures de nocte, solutis
    compedibus, solus et sine teste tuli.
Nam si forte nefas tantum sciretur in urbe,

1850   protinus inflicta debita poena foret.
Sicque recedentes nostro mediante labore
    euasere simul uerbera, uerba, cruces.
Quosque meis humeris, ne forsitan alter adesset
    conscius, exposui trans uada transque uias.

1855 Tres simul atque semel ne quis remaneret eorum
    impositos humeris longius ipse tuli.
Nec, postquam ferre didici mala pondera, pondus
    me memini tale tamque tulisse graue.

1831 infitiando] inficiando *Ne Z* inficiendo *F MuVdTGoBePkFrPm HaLa QY* infaciendo
Va insistendo δ *GI Tr U²over erasure*   1833 populus] populos *MuGoFrZ*   1836 et]
ut *VdBe TrLa*   1837 cum] tum *RK* tunc *T D* tum /uel tunc *Ha*; quae] qui *RD* quo *W*
om. *Vd*   1838 ut] et *Vc Z*; misererer] miserer *PkNe J U* miserere *Z* miseretur *H*
miseret *Tr*   1839 memorabile] miserabile *Q* miserabile /uel memorabile *La*
1840 quod] quid *Vd* qui *BePk*   1841 ille] ipse *MuVaVbVcVdGoBePkPmNe TrLa* sibi
T; nocentior] nociuior *α*   1842 constiterit] constituit *GoPm X*   1843 spretis]
sumptis *AJCWPVe GI UQY* scitis *D* scriptis *Be Z* scriptis /uel spretis *La*   1844 uicit]
uincit *H MuVaTGoFrPm*ᵃᶜ   1845 relatis] relictis *UZQY*   1847 e fundo] effundo
SVaVbTGoPkPmNe HuMN TrLa   1852 uerbera uerba] uerba uerbera *VdBe* uerbere
uerbaque *Z*   1853 quosque] quos *CW*; forsitan] forsan *G*ᵃᶜ*I*; ne] me *Go Tr*
1854 transque] tresque *SVaVbVcVdGoBePkFrPmNe TrHa* tresue *Z*; uias] uicos *LE* uices *F*
ripas *H*   1855 om. *X*; semel] om. *PVe*   1857 ferre didici] didici ferre *VbT D La*
ferre dici *QY* ferre didicere *Ve* didici *K*   1858 tamque] namque *C* tamquam *MuVdPm*
La Y nunquam *Go* quemque *Z*

SPECVLVM STVLTORVM   185

but at length began to confess—although it was quite clear at the out-set that they were guilty. When they had confessed their crimes, the people decreed that the reprobates should be hanged on the gallows that they had deserved as their fate. All night long the servants got ready the gallows and ropes, [1835] and next morning each was to mount his own—when the pity which from birth grew up alongside me suggested that I should take pity on those wretches. I did not forget the memorable popular saying, which is the usual consequence of such a situation [1840]: "Out of a thousand men your worst enemy will be the man whom you have saved from the gallows." But nevertheless, I paid no attention to this; pity conquered my mind and love of mercy constrained me. So, having secretly taken my father's keys and secretly returned them, [1845] I did a momentous deed, which I still remem-ber. I unlocked the fetters and released the thieves at night from the depths of the prison, alone and without any witness. For if by chance such a crime were to be known in the town, the due penalty would be inflicted without delay. [1850] So, getting away with the help of my efforts, they escaped at once blows, condemnations, the gallows. So that no one else should know, I carried all of them out on my back, through wet and dry. Three together, and all at the same time, so that none of them should be left behind, [1855] did I carry on my shoulders for a long time. And since I first learned to carry burdensome weights, I do not remember that I ever carried one like this or so heavy. Each

1837–8 Job 31: 18: 'Ab infantia mea creuit mecum miseratio'. *miseratio...miseris misere-rer*: a favourite type of wordplay; see *SS*, 3603–5; *Miracles*, 249–51, 270, 1913. Cf. Hugh Primas, *Gedichte*, ed. Meyer, vii. 31 'miseris misereri'; Walter of Châtillon, *Poems*, no. lviii. 12.1 'miseranter miseror miseros'; id., *Alexandreis*, iv. 421 'docens miseris misereri'; Henry of Settimello, *Elegia*, i. 43 'Sum miser et miseri nullus miserans miseretur.'

1841–2 Proverbial. See Walther, *Proverbia*, 11214: 'Hostem semper emit, alium qui de cruce demit' (a slightly different version of this proverb follows lines 1842 in MS *Ve*); see also Singer, *Thesaurus*, s.vv. 'Dieb' 10. 2 (ii. 213–14); 'Hängen' 16 (v. 401–2); 'Helfen' 1. 12 (vi. 12). Cf. Béroul, *Tristan*, 42–3: 'Qui de forches traient larron,/ Ja pus nes amera nul jor'.

1855 The picture of Burnellus groaning beneath the weight of three thieves has a coun-terpart in a story told by Gerald of Wales to ridicule the obtuseness and doctrinal ignorance of Hubert Walter, archbishop of Canterbury: in a sermon preached on Palm Sunday, the archbishop is said to have tried to impress his audience by stressing that the ass who bore Jesus into Jerusalem carried not one man alone, but all three persons of the Trinity—Father, Son, and Holy Ghost (*De invectionibus*, i. 5, *Opera* iii. 30–1; ed. Davies, p. 101; trans. Butler, *Autobiography*, p. 283). Gerald dates this incident to the year of Richard I's death, i.e. 1199, which does not fit the dating of *SS* to the early 1190s (and at any rate, before the death of William of Longchamp in 1197). Some such story may, however, have been a joke among the monks of Canterbury, which was adopted by Gerald to make fun of Hubert Walter. Gerald often repeats and reattributes his anecdotes. If Nigel did intend an allusion to this anecdote, it would account for the otherwise unnecessary inclusion of *three* thieves in Burnellus's story (since it is the ingratitude of only one of them that he fears).

186   SPECVLVM STVLTORVM

Quisque satis per se fuerat graue pondus, in unum
1860   quanto collecti plus nocuere mihi!
Annis quingentis si uixero, ponderis huius
prae grauitate mihi corpore peior ero.
Ponderis illius, quia me tulit inde deorsum,
quin memor existam non erit ulla dies.
1865   Malo tamen miseros nostro seruasse labore
quam non seruatos exposuisse cruci.
Cumque uale facerent et fletibus ora rigarent,
talia prostrati uix ualuere loqui:
"Ecce tui, domine Burnelle, per omnia serui
1870   hic et in aeternum tres sumus ecce tui.
Tu dare nos poteris, tu uendere, tuque uocare
quo tibi cumque placet, et ueniemus eo.
Tu tribus his miseris ueniam uitamque dedisti,
sed data non nostra sed tua semper erit.
1875   Nostrum quisque tibi seruus remanebit in aeuum,
tempore nec quouis desinet esse tuus.
Iure tuus debet, tuus, immo tuissimus esse,
quem tu saluasti carcere, fune, cruce.
Quemque tuis humeris dignatus es ipse magister
1880   et dominus ferre, non erit ille tuus?
Absit ut ille tuus non sit, qui nec suus esse
posset in aeternum, si tibi uelle foret.
Et si uita comes fuerit, nos retribuemus
hac tibi condignam pro uice iure uicem.

1859 quisque] quique *U* quisquis *S MN* quodque *D*; per se fuerat graue] per se graue
ferat *S* fuerat per se graue *Va Q*   1860 quanto] quando *VbFr* tanto β quarto *K*
1862 mihi] sui *LE* sua *F* meo *Mu* rei *Vb*   1863 *line repeated in alternative form*
La(1)*La*(2)   quia] quod α qui *CD U*; inde] ille α β *Y* esse *U* usque *Z*; *(whole line)* pondera
magna tuli sed me posuere deorsum γ+ *La*(1)   1864 ulla] illa α *Pk GI* ultra *CW*
1865 nostro] nostros *B Q*   1870 et] est *Ve om. LE Va*   1871 nos] non *Vd*
J   1872 quo tibi cumque placet] quod tibi cumque placet *Go* quo circumque placet *GI*
quo cui placebit et *D* quocumque placet *S* tibi add. interlinear *S*²   1873 ueniam uita-
mque] uitam ueniamque *Vc R UQ*   1874 erit] erunt *F D GI*   1875 remanebit]
permanebit *MuVaGoFrPm* remeabit *S* manebit *T*   1876 *om. GI*; nec] ne *VdFr U*; des-
inet] desinit *Fr Tr*   1877 tuus immo tuissimus] immo tuissimus *Go* debet immo
tuissimus *Q* seruus certissimus δ *GI U*²*over erasure*   1878 fune cruce] fune cruci *P*
cruce fune *Mu*ᵃᶜ*Va* fame cruce *Go*   1879 es] est *H T om. S*   1880 ille] ipse
MuVaTGoFr.*Pm* *C*ᶜ *Ha* *U*   1883 nos] non *Ne J*   1884 hac] ac α
MuVaVdGoBePkPmNe TrHa U at *Vb M* hanc *T RKVe* et *S* hunc *H* hoc *Z*; condignam]
condigna *L*

SPECVLVM STVLTORVM
187

one by himself would have been a heavy enough burden; how much more did they oppress me when joined into one! [1860] If I live five hundred years, I shall still suffer in my body from the heaviness of this load. There will be no day on which I do not remember that load, for it bore me down. And yet I would rather have saved the wretches by my efforts [1865] than not to have saved them and exposed them to the gallows. When they said goodbye, with tears wetting their faces, prostrate, they were hardly able to speak the following: "Behold, lord Burnellus, your servants in all things; behold, we three are yours, here and for eternity. [1870] You can give us away, you can sell us and call us wherever it pleases you, and we shall come. You have given pardon and life to these three wretches, but the life you have given will not be ours but yours for ever. Each of us will be your servant to eternity, [1875] nor will he cease to be yours at any time. Rightly should the one whom you saved from prison, from the rope, from the gallows, be yours—yours to the nth degree. And will not he be yours whom you, master and lord, deigned to carry on your shoulders? [1880] Heaven forbid that he should not be yours, for he could not to all eternity be his own man, if it were not your wish. And if we live long enough, we shall fittingly pay you back for this good turn with another one that is worthy

---

1867 *fletibus ora rigarent*: cf. Ovid, *Metamorphoses*, xi. 419, and Vergil, *Aeneid*, ix. 251.
1876 *desinet esse tuus*: *Babio*, 70: 'desinet esse tua' (*Commedie*, ii. 252).
1877 *tuissimus*: for similar comic formations of non-existent superlatives, see Walter of Châtillon, *Poems*, no. xlix. 19. 3: 'clerissimi', and the 13th-c. *Lamentations of Matheolus* (line 139): 'hostissimus'.

188   *SPECVLVM STVLTORVM*

1885 Quam bene reddemus tanti benefacta laboris,
       si Dominus dederit posse referre uicem!
     Detque Deus nobis tempusque locumque, nec ante
       quam tibi reddamus det potuisse mori."
     Ista satis memini quoniam dixere ruentes
1890   saepius in terram, "Tres sumus ecce tui!"
     Neue nefas patri populoque pateret et urbi,
       his ita dilapsis, mox ego uincla tuli.
     Et (mea culpa, miser, miser, et mea maxima culpa)
       caelitus asserui singula rupta fore,
1895 quodque Dei sanctus ueniens Leonardus eorum
       uincula soluisset quodque tulisset ea.
     Hinc igitur uereor ne uulgi uerba secundum
       praepositus reddat facta priora mihi,
     proque bonis satagat mala reddere, meque prioris
1900   ob causam meriti nolit habere parem.
     Non desperarem super his, nec iure timerem,
       conscius admissi criminis ipse sui,
     insita si misero generosi sanguinis illi
       naturae studio stilla uel una foret.
1905 Nam solet hoc proprium generosi sanguinis esse,
       condignam meritis reddere uelle uicem.
     Contra naturam niti moresque caninos
       quam sit difficile dicere nemo potest.
     Stigmata naturae seruilis conditionis
1910   tollere nec medicus nec medicina potest.
     Semper ab effectu quae sit natura uel unde
       uenerit ostendit, nec latuisse potest.'

1885–6 *om.* δ *XQ*   1885 tanti] tanta *F*; benefacta] benefacti *S* benefacto *TFrPm Ha* beneficio *MuVa* beneficia *Vb*   1887 *om. La*, *add. in margin after 1883 and repeated after 1886 La*pc; tempusque] empusque *M* tempus *GoPm*; locumque] locusque *VdBe TrLa* locum *Fr*; ante] uite *QY* annum *Tr*   1891 neue] neque *H D* reue *X* nonne *E La* ne *I UZQY* sed ne *VbVc*   1892 dilapsis] delapsis *Pm Ha* de lapsis *F*   1893 miser² et] miser est *Vc* et *VaVdBePm TrLa* miser *L* necnon δ *GI UX*   1894 singula] cingula *Q* singula [uel] uincla *La*   1895 quodque] quique *BePk* quod *Fr*   1897 igitur] ergo *GoPm AJCWRHuMNOKVe GI La UQY* et ego *Z* ego *P*   1898 facta] fracta *Be La*ac; priora] priori *VdPkPmNe La*pc   1900 parem] patrem *LE B* γ+ *D ZX*pc patris *F* 1901 desperarem] desparam *J* desperacem *Go* desperare *Tr Z*; timerem] timere *Tr Z* timorem *Be C*   1902 admissi] admisi *CWHuMND*; ipse] esse α; sui] mei *H* fui *Be R La* frui *Vd*   1904–5 *om. Mu*   1905 nam] non *Ne G Y*; proprium] primum α; esse] *om. F*   1906 condignam] condignum *GI*   1907 niti] uici *VdGo* uoti *Ha*   1909–10 *transp. after 1912 D*; *om. F*   1909 stigmata naturae] stingmata nature *Hu* scurruta nostra *Mu* scurrata nature *VaPm* stemata nature *TrLa* stimata nostrorum *Go* scemata nature *VdBe* scismata *Pk*   1911 effectu] affectu *JRK* effectum *M*

SPECVLVM STVLTORVM 189

of it. How well we shall repay the benefits of this great effort, [1885] if the Lord grants the power to make repayment! May God grant us time and place, and may He grant that we do not die before we repay you." These words I remember well, since they repeated many times, falling to the earth, "Behold, we three are yours!" [1890] And so that this crime should be concealed from my father, the people and town, when they had escaped in this way, I straightway took the chains, and (my fault, wretch that I am, my own most grievous fault) I declared that they were broken by divine intervention, and that Leonard, saint of God, had come, [1895] released their chains and carried them [the chains] off. For this reason, therefore, I am afraid that the sheriff will repay me for my former deeds in accordance with the popular saying: he will try to return evil for good, and will not want to have me as his equal on account of my former merit. [1900] I would not despair of this, nor would I rightly fear, since I am privy to the crime he committed, if even one drop of noble blood had been implanted in the wretch by Nature's care. For this is the characteristic of noble blood, [1905] to wish to make a fitting return for merits. No one can describe how difficult it is to struggle against Nature and dog-like behaviour. Neither doctor nor medicine can take away the defects of a naturally churlish condition. [1910] Nature always shows in its manifestations what it is or whence it came, and it cannot be hidden.'

1895–6 St Leonard was a Frankish saint, who was credited with the miraculous release of prisoners. For details of numerous examples of this type of miracle, effected by the intercession of other saints, holy men, and women, see Loomis, *White Magic*, p. 89 and n. 278 on pp. 200–1.

1899 *satagat*: 'satagere' = 'to try' (Niermeyer).

1909 *Mu*'s 'scurruta' must be related to 'scurra', defined variously in Du Cange and *DMLBS* as 'jester, buffoon'; 'disreputable person, scoundrel, vagabond'; and 'servant, messenger', but here it is not even clear whether 'scurruta' is a noun or an adjective; an interlinear gloss in *Mu* reads 'servi<l?>ia', which suggests a connection with 'seruilis' later in the same line.

190   *SPECVLVM STVLTORVM*

Discessus Burnelli a ciuitate Parisiensi

Talia Burnellus secum meditatus ab urbe
    Parisius statuit mane referre pedem.
1915   Ergo uale facto sociis et flentibus illis
    omnibus exit, abit, acceleratque gradum.
Montis in ascensu positus, post terga relictam
    Parisius cernens, obstupefactus ait:
'Sancta Maria, Deus, crux Christi, me benedicat!
1920   Hac in ualle situs quis locus esse potest?
Haec est Roma, puto, magnis circumdata muris!
    Vrbs ita turrita quid nisi Roma foret?
Atque quid esse potest aliud quam Mons Iouis iste?
    Sancta Maria Deus! Est ita Roma prope?
1925   Vrbs in qua studui, cuius modo nomen ab ore
    fugit et a corde, uae mihi, talis erat?
Ergo domum repetens, patri matrique roganti
    quonam profitear me studuisse loco?
Me fore trutannum, me nil didicisse parentes
1930   dicent et sumptus deperiisse suos.
Ergo reuertar ego, nomen quod nescio discam,
    ne rudis in patria praedicer esse mea.
Non nihil illud erit, cum nomina certa locorum
    dixero, confirmans me tenuisse scholas;
1935   et si nesciero uel nomina sola referre,
    quicquid ego dicam credere nemo uolet.'

1917 relictam] relictum *Y* relicta *Go Z*   **1918** Parisius] parisium β *ACJWRHuMNODVe GI XQY* parusius *T* pariseus *Fr*   **1919** Christi] *om. MN add. M*ᵖᶜ; benedicat] benedicit *J* benedicant *GoPm*   **1920** *om. HuMN*; hac] ac *VbBePk La* at *Ne*   **1922** turrita] turrida *VdBe Tr* currita *J*; quid] que *MuVaVcTFrPmNe* quis *GoBePk Tr*   **1923** aliud] alius *Be TrLa* ad *D*; Iouis] roma *QY*   **1924** est ita Roma prope] est roma ita prope *F C* est ita prope roma *PK*   **1925** studui] studii *MN XQ*   **1926** uae] ne *BePk*; talis erat] talis erit *Fr Z* qualis erat β qualis ego δ *GI Tr U*²*over erasureX* talis erat [*uel*] qualis ego *La*   **1928** quonam] quo iam *Pm* quanam *Q* que nam *Go* quoniam *T Ve* quo non *R*; profitear] profiteor *H Fr CD Tr X* profitearis *Pm*   **1931** reuertar] reuertor *H Go*   **1932** rudis] rudus *Fr D*   **1933** certa] certe β *Go AJCWHuNOPVe GI QY* certo *M*   **1934** confirmans] confingens α *SVaVbVcTBePkFrPmNe* δ *GI TrHa UZ* cum fingens *Va* confringens *QY* consurgens *MuGo La*   **1935** nomina] omnia *H Ne*   **1936** uolet] ualet *VdT D ZQ* uellet *Fr Tr* uelit *Ha*

SPECVLVM STVLTORVM

Burnellus's Departure from the City of Paris

Reflecting on these things to himself, Burnellus decided to leave the city of Paris on foot next morning. So, having said goodbye to his comrades, all in tears, [1915] he departed and hastened off. Stationed on the hillside he saw Paris left behind him, and said in amazement: 'Bless me, Saint Mary, God, Christ's cross! What can this place be, situated in this valley? [1920] This is Rome, I think, surrounded with mighty walls. What could this turreted city be but Rome? And what can this be other than the Great St Bernard Pass? Saint Mary, God, is Rome so near? Alas, was the town in which I studied, whose name has now fled my lips [1925] and my mind, like this? So when I go home and my father and mother ask me, in what place shall I say I have studied? My parents will say I am a fraud, that I have learned nothing, and that their money has been wasted. [1930] So I'll return, I shall learn the name I don't know, lest I'm called an ignoramus back home. That will not be nothing, when I repeat the exact names of the places, confirming that I've been to the schools. And if I can't repeat even the single names, [1935] no one will be willing to believe anything I say.'

1921–2 *magnis circumdata muris...Vrbs...turrita*: the ass thinks he is looking down at Rome from the Great St Bernard Pass (1923), but is actually looking at the great walls of Paris. Small parts of the city were surrounded by walls from Roman times onwards, but it was Philip Augustus who commanded the citizens, on the eve of his departure to the crusade in 1190, in 'to enclose the city of Paris, which he dearly loved, with a superb wall suitably fitted with turrets and gates. All this was completed in a short time' (Baldwin, *Paris, 1200*, p. 25, quoting the words of the royal historiographer Rigord of St-Denis). The first half of the wall to be built 'proceeded around the Right Bank for 2,600 meters in straight segments, containing thirty-nine turrets and five gates' (Baldwin, ibid., and see his Map 1 on pp. 14–15). This work was 'well under way' when work on the walls surrounding the Left Bank began around 1200 (Baldwin, p. 26; on the imposing construction of the walls, see ibid. pp. 27–8). This fits my proposed dating of *SS* post-1190. Burnellus seems to be equally mistaken in thinking that he has climbed up to the Great St Bernard Pass. Not only is he still 'in the midst of the Alps' 12 days later (1950–2), but his encounter with a pilgrim heading for Rome and coming from the city of Vienne suggests rather that he is following the route down the Rhône valley and then eastwards to the Mont Cenis Pass (see n. to lines 1951–2).

1929 *trutannum*: 'trutannus' = 'swindler' (Niermeyer).

SPECVLVM STVLTORVM

De silentio Burnelli

Talia dicenti, iamiamque redire uolenti
rusticus adueniens obuius inquit ei:
'Parisius quae causa tibi, Burnelle, petendi?
1940   An docuisse uenis, an didicisse tibi?'
Nomine Parisius statim Burnellus adepto
uertit iter, retinens nomen in ore suo.
Quod ne perdat item casu studioue loquendi,
accidat et rursum sicut et ante sibi,
1945   nil omnino loqui statuit ter quinque diebus
excepto solo nomine Parisius;
quicquid contingat, quicumque salutet euntem,
nil respondebit, sed quasi mutus erit.

Qualiter Burnellus uiolauit silentium suum

Contigit interea quod, cum completa fuisset
1950   religione sub hac iam duodena dies,
quidam Romipeta peregrinus ab urbe Vienna
Alpibus in mediis se sociauit ei,
accedensque prope dixit: 'Reuerende magister,
sit Dominus tecum! Sit tibi mane bonum!
1955   Prospera tota dies succedat, uespere clarum,
hospitium gratum, noxque quieta tibi!'
Sed Burnellus, adhuc indicta silentia seruans,
nil respondit ei uerba nec ulla dedit;
sed tamen inclinat supplex, uerboque salutis
1960   nutibus et signis annuit, ore tacens.

1937 iamque] iam *VdTBeNe Ve Y*   **1938** obuuius inquit] talia dixit γ *TrHa* talia dixit /uel obuius inquit *La*   **1939** tibi] fuit *B X* fruit *H*ac *om. Be*; petendi] petenti γ-*AJCWRHuMNPDKVe TrHaLa UZQY* potenti *GI*   **1940** uenis] uelis *T D* leuis *Go*   **1941** nomine] nomen *Z* nonne *SVdPm*   **1943** item] iter *SMu*ac*VbT* iterum *Vd*; studioue] studioque *D Z*   **1944** accidat] accidit *H TPkFrNe X*; et[1]] ut *R Ha*; ante sibi] ante fuit *T* ante fuit /uel sibi *K*   **1945** ter] sibi *QY* iterare *T*   **1947–8** *om. U*; *add. in lower margin U*[2]   **1947** salutet] salutat *VdTGo HuMND La Z*; euntem] eundem *Vd D GI* eum *Z*   **1948** respondebit] respondebat *Go P* respondit *Vd*   **1951** Vienna] uicina *AJCWRHuMNOPVe Tr X* uerona *Fr* uigenna *Z* propinqua *DK*   **1952** mediis] medio *GI*   **1953** dixit] dixi *L*; reuerende] uenerande β *X*   **1957** adhuc] ad hec *H K* ad hoc *VaTPkPm*   **1958** uerba nec ulla] uerbaque nulla *MuVaVbVdTGoBePkFrPmNe P TrHaLa* uerba que nulla *Vc*   **1959** sed] se *FrPm*; uerboque] uerbumque *D* et uerba *SMuVaVbVcVdGoBePkFrPmNe TrHaLa Z* ad uerba *T*

SPECVLVM STVLTORVM 193

Burnellus's Silence

As he said this and any moment was about to return, a passing peasant met him and said, 'What reason do you have for going to Paris, Burnellus? Do you come to teach? or to learn yourself?' [1940] Having caught the name 'Paris', Burnellus at once changed direction, keeping the name on his lips. And lest he lose it again by chance or by concentration on speaking, and the same thing happen to him as before, he decided to utter nothing at all for a fortnight [1945] except the name 'Paris' alone. Whatever might happen, whoever might greet him on the way, he will answer nothing, but will be as if dumb.

How Burnellus Broke His Silence

It befell meanwhile that, when the twelfth day of this observance was passed, [1950] a certain pilgrim on the way to Rome from the city of Vienne, joined him in the midst of the Alps. Approaching, he said, 'Reverend sir, the Lord be with you! May your morning be good, may a prosperous day follow on, the evening be fine, [1955] your lodging comfortable, and the night peaceful for you!' But Burnellus, still keeping his imposed silence, made no reply to him nor uttered any words. However he bowed humbly, and silently acknowledged the greeting with nods and signs. [1960] They entered the hospice together, where

---

1951–2 For comment on the variants 'uienna/uicina/propinqua', see Introduction, pp. xcvi, cxxiii. Travellers to Italy who wished to avoid the Great St Bernard Pass (which was at this date dangerous in the depths of winter) would instead go south down the Rhône valley as far as Vienne, which lay on the east bank of the Rhône. 'From Vienne...roads led eastwards...to the Mont Cenis pass...This was the main route to Italy for the traveller who wished to travel on southwards from Dijon through Burgundy before making the Alpine crossing' (Spufford, *Power and Profit*, pp. 155, 158, 165–9, and see the map on p. 159). The Mont Cenis pass was also closed in winter, but for a shorter period.

194   *SPECVLVM STVLTORVM*

Hospitium subiere simul, quo fessa diurno
   membra labore suo nocte dedere toro.
Cumque 'Pater Noster' peregrinus in ore frequenter
   uolueret, exorans sollicitansque Deum,
1965 euigilans Burnellus ait: 'Solum quod habebam
   uerbum surripuit uox peregrina mihi.
Syllaba consimilis uerbi totiens repetiti
   surripuit uerbum quod fuit ante meum.
Quique "Pater Noster" totiens iterauit, eodem
1970 me nimis intentum reddidit ille sibi.
Perque suum simile uerbum peregrinus inique
   me supplantauit, et mea uerba tulit.
Sanius est, memini, socialia foedera rumpi
   quam cum collega foedus inisse malo.
1975 Hoc satis ante mihi damni praesaga futuri
   mens mea praedixit uera propheta nimis.
Verbum pro uerbo proprium mutans alieno,
   destruo septenni parta labore graui.
Verbum quod periit nostrum uerbo peregrini
1980 par fuit in parte principioque sui.
Finis erat dispar, quem si meminisse ualerem
   me satis inferior Iupiter ipse foret.
Centum uel mille solidos si diues haberem,
   uellem sub tali conditione dare.

1961 subiere] subire *VbTGoBePkFrPmNe JCWD Tr ZY*; quo] que *D* quoque *GI* quo simul *Pk*   1962 membra] *om. U, add. in margin U²*   1963 cumque] cum *VdTBe La* tunc *U*   1964 uolueret] uoluerit *H I Z* uoluerat *U*   1966–7 *om. U, add. in lower margin U²*   1968 *line repeated in alternative form* $Z_{(1)}Z_{(2)}$; *(whole line)* nomen surripuit (subrupuit *A* subripuit *WP*) urbis (urbs *JCVe* uerbis *D*) ubi studui (studuit *K*) δ *GI* $UZ_{(1)}QY$ 1969 quique] quoniamque *Y* cumque *D* cuique *Z* quodque *MuVaTFrPm* quidque *Go* quisque *Tr* qui *Vd Ha*; iterauit] iteratur *Y* repetiuit *Vc Q*; eodem] in ore *R* eundem *SMuVaVbVcVdGoBePkPmNe TrLa* eundo *Fr Ha* eidem *T*   1970 me nimis] ne nimis *VdPm* meminis *F* me minus *P GI*   1971 simile uerbum] uerbum simile *VdBeNe TrLa*; peregrinus inique] uerbum peregrinus *VdBe TrLa* peregrinus iniret *Pk* 1973–4 socialia—collega *om. Vc*   1973 memini] nemini *B Mu* meum *Vd*; socialia] solacia *Vd CW Ha*; foedera] federe *Be La*ᵃᶜ federalia *U*   1975 hoc] hec α β *MuVbVc ZQ* hic *VdBe P La*; damni] damna *F Vd ZQY* damnis *T* damnum *Mu Tr* mea mens *Vc*; praesaga] presago *Fr Ve* prestigo *Tr*; futuri] futurum *VdGo Tr Q*   1978–9 *om. U, add. in lower margin U²*   1978 destruo] liqui *SVaVbVcVdTBePkNe TrHaLa* loqui *MuGoFrPm*; parta] parca *P Tr*   1979 periit] peperit *AJCWRHuMNPKVe GI U²Y* deperit *O*; uerbo]uerbum *VbRHa*   1981 quem]quodβ*SMuVaVbVcVdTGoBePkPmNe* δ *GI TrHaLa UZXQY* que *Fr*; ualerem] ualeret *Va* ualorem *Fr Z*   1982 ipse] ille δ tempore *Z*   1983 haberem]haberet *Go Z*   1984 dare]dari α *B SVaVcGoBePkPmNe*

SPECVLVM STVLTORVM 195

at night they consigned to bed the limbs worn out by the day's toil. And as the pilgrim frequently repeated the Pater Noster aloud, praying and beseeching God, Burnellus lay awake, saying, [1965] 'The pilgrim's voice has stolen from me the only word I had. The similar syllable of this word, so often repeated, has stolen away the word I had earlier. In repeating "Pater Noster" so many times, he thereby made me concentrate too much on him. [1970] Through his similar word, the pilgrim wickedly tripped me up, and took my word. It's wiser, I know, to break social bonds than to make an alliance with an evil companion. My mind, foreseeing my future loss, [1975] gave me good warning of this beforehand—too true a prophet. Changing my own word for another's, I destroy the profits of seven years' hard labour. My word which vanished was like the pilgrim's word in part and at its beginning. [1980] The ending was dissimilar, and if I could remember it, Jupiter himself would be inferior to me. If I were rich enough to have a hundred or even a thousand shillings, I'd willingly give them away on that condition [i.e. remembering

---

1961 *Hospitium*: if the assumption that Burnellus and the pilgrim are travelling through the Mont Cenis pass is correct (see n. to lines 1951–2), this is probably a reference to the hospice at the top of the pass, which was refounded in the 11th c. 'and richly endowed by the counts of Savoy' (Spufford, *Power and Profit*, p. 212).

1968 *meum*: Mozley has 'mihi', but this reading is found only in *H*; 'meum' is attested in αβγ*TrHaLaZ*(2)*X* (δ has a completely different version of this line).

1973–4 Cf. Prov. 13: 20, 2 Thess. 3: 6, and *Disticha Catonis*, Prol. 6: 'Cum bonis ambula'.

1975 *damni praesaga futuri*: cf. Vergil, *Aeneid*, x. 843.

1982 After 1982, *Ne* adds two lines which are a quotation from Proverbs 19: 4: 'Diuitie addunt amicos plurimos/ A paupere autem et hii quos habuit separantur ('Riches bring many friends, but from the poor man even those [friends] that he had are taken away').

1983 *solidos*: literally 'shillings' (*DMLBS* s.v. 'solidus' 3).

196   *SPECVLVM STVLTORVM*

1985   Nominis amissi uix syllaba prima remansit,
         quod superest reliquum desiit esse meum.'

Consolatio Burnelli ad se ipsum

     'Est aliquid melius quam nil tenuisse; tenebo
         quod superest, tantum syllaba prima, mihi.
     Partem pro toto poni docuere diserti,
1990   dummodo pars maneat sufficit una mihi.
     Nec totum superest, ubi pars est una recisa,
         nec totum periit, parte manente sui.
     Praestat de toto partem retinere uel unam,
         qualemcumque tamen quam retinere nihil.
1995   Plures non poteram forsan retinere, sed unam,
         pluribus elapsis, hanc retinebo bene.
     Artibus ex septem si syllaba sola supersit,
         hoc mihi non nihil est nec reor esse parum.
     Et quia multotiens errare scientia multos
2000   fecit et inflatos praestitit esse magis,
     littera ne lapsum pariatque scientia damnum,
         sufficit una mihi syllaba, nolo magis.
     Taedia nonnumquam generosa scientia gignit,
         et faciunt apices moribus esse graues.
2005   Saepius in paucis melius natura ministrat,
         exserit et uires fortius ipsa suas.
     Contenti paucis studiis breuitate iuuantur,
         opprimit et sensum sollicitudo frequens.

1985 amissi] admissi *VdNe Ve GI La* omissi *Y* admisse *Mu*[ac]   **1986** quod] quid
TBe U   **1987** aliquid] aliud *S U*   **1988** quod] *D²* quae *AJCWRHuMNOPKVe*
U qui *Be*   **1989–1990** *om. GI*   **1990** pars maneat] *ed.* pars permaneat *Z* sic
maneat β *X* me maneat α *MuVaVbVcVdBePkFrPmNe La ACJWHuMNODKVe UY* remaneat *T R* me manet *P* me manant *S* non maneat *Tr* hec maneat *Ha* immaneant *Q* maneat
Go   **1991–2** ubi pars—periit] *om. Q*   **1991** ubi] uerbi *LE* uerbum *F*
1993 uel] sed *HuMNDK*   **1994–5** *om. F HuMNDK; transp. after 1996 Tr*
1994 tamen] talem *AJCWPVe GI* causam *Be Tr*; retinere] reticere *AJCWROPVe*; nihil] mihi
Vd AJCWROPVe GI U corr. U²   **1996** *om. Vb*   **1998** hoc] hec *MuVaTGo Z* hac
Q hic *VbVdBePm Tr*; nec] non *Vc GI*   **1999** quia] quid *GI*; errare] exstare *MuFr Z*
extare *SVaTBe*(*add.* uel superbire *Be²*)*PkPmNe Ha* extare / uel superbire *La* superbire *Vd*;
multos] multis *E S*   **2000** magis] graues δ *GI UZQY*   **2001–4** *om. HuMNDK*
2001–2 *om. Pm*   **2002** nolo] uolo *MuVd* nulla *Tr*   **2006–7** *om. T*
2006 exerit] exierit *S* exurit *MuVaGoFrPmNe* exercet *Vd* exeret *Be* excutit *GI* eerit *M*; uires]
uiros *E Ve*; ipsa] ipse *SVbGoFr JCWHuMNOD GI ZQ*   **2008** sollicitudo frequens]
sollicitando grauis *Be Tr* sollicitudo grauis /[uel] frequens *La*

SPECVLVM STVLTORVM 197

the second syllable]. Barely the first syllable of the lost name has remained; [1985] the rest has passed out of my possession.'

Burnellus's Consolation to Himself

'It's better to have kept something than nothing; what remains to me, the first syllable only, I'll keep. The learned have taught that a part can be put for a whole; one is enough for me, so long as it remains. [1990] The whole does not survive, when a part is cut off, but neither is the whole destroyed, when a part of it remains. It is better to retain even a part of the whole, of whatever sort, than to retain nothing. Perhaps I was unable to retain several, but one, [1995] when several have vanished, I shall retain successfully. If out of the whole seven arts a single syllable remains, this is not nothing to me, nor do I think it is of small account. And because knowledge has often led many astray, and caused them to be more puffed up, [2000] lest learning may bring about a fault, and knowledge harm, one syllable is enough for me, I wish for no more. Sometimes learning, though noble, produces boredom, and letters create austerity of character. Often, Nature operates better in small things, [2005] and exerts her forces more powerfully. Those who are content with little study take pleasure in its brevity, while constant

---

1987 Cf. the moral of the anecdote related in Nigel's *Tractatus*, ed. Boutemy, p. 167, quoted in n. to line 257.

1988 *quod* is more widely attested than δ's 'quae', which may be a hyper-correction influenced by 'syllaba'.

1989 'Pars pro toto' is the definition of the rhetorical figure known as synecdoche (e.g. 'the crown' for 'the monarchy'); see Donatus, *Ars grammatica*, iii. 6 (*Grammatici latini*, ed. Keil, iv. 400).

1990 *pars maneat*: Mozley prints the reading of βX, 'sic maneat', which is rather vague in meaning. Of the other variants, 'remaneat' is the best in sense, but its initial short syllable does not scan. Z's 'pars permaneat' looks like a conflation of two alternatives, either of which would fit the requirements of metre and sense. The self-conscious repetition of 'pars' in these lines suggests that that was the original reading, perhaps lost through misreading of an abbreviation.

1999–2000 For 'scientia' as a source of pride, see also *Tractatus*, ed. Boutemy, p. 205: 'quia scientia inflat, timendum est ne inde corruas per superbiam unde ascendere debuisti'. Cf. Walter of Châtillon, *Poems*, no. xlii ('Missus sum in vineam'), st. 18, an ironic rejection of knowledge in favour of wealth: 'Adde, quod Superbia sequitur doctores./ Inflati scientia respuunt minores./ Ex hoc iam impletum est quod dicunt auctores:/ "inquinat egregios adiuncta superbia mores"' (quoting Claudian, *Panegyricus de Quarto Consulatu Honorii Augusti*, 305). John of Hauville acknowledges that the learned may be suspected of pride, but claims that this is a false impression (*Architrenius*, ed. Wetherbee, iii. 379–400); however, he goes on to admit that there *are* some superficial philosophers who are swollen with self-conceit and scorn others (ibid. 401–30).

2000 δ's variant is the result of eyeskip from 'esse magis' at the end of 2000 to 'esse graues' at the end of 2004.

198 SPECVLVM STVLTORVM

Scire quidem multa, nisi sit bene scire, scienti,
2010   ut uerum fatear, non honor est sed onus.
Paucula de multis multi rapuere, scientes
    ut uideantur in his omnibus esse suis.
Est quoque scire labor, labor est etiam retinere;
    est didicisse labor, est docuisse labor.
2015   Quoque magis moueor, quia nulla scientia mortem
    qualibet arte sua dedocuisse potest.
Nonne timor mortis toto dominatur in orbe?
    Omnibus et solis istud inesse solet.
Omnia lance pari partitur et omnibus uno
2020   pondere distribuit dura sed aequa nimis.
Hanc ego non possum nisi praetimuisse futuram,
    ex improuiso ne mihi dicat, "Abi." '

Compunctio Burnelli

'Hinc ego disposui me tradere religioni,
    ut ualeat saluus spiritus esse meus.
2025   Vtque senex redimam iuuenilia tempora, uitam
    fas est ut satagam corripuisse meam.
Quod superest modicum uitae, ne tota deorsum
    defluat, hoc opto claudere fine bono.
Est melius sero quam numquam paenituisse,

2009 nisi sit] nisi scit *Fr MR XY corr. X²* non sit *D* nisi *S*   **2010** fatear] fateor *Fr RVe Tr UZ*; est] *om. X corr. X²*   **2011–12** *om. γ+ La, add. in margin La^{pc}*   **2013–14** labor est—didicisse labor *om. Vd Ha*   **2013** labor labor] labor *Va O U*(labor² *add. in margin U²) fb* labor et *AJCWHuMNPVe GI Tr* labor et id *D* labor sed et *K* labor et labor *Y*   **2014** est¹] et *F MuVa O ZQ*; est² docuisse] estque docere *SMuVaVbVdTGoBePkFrNe HaLa* est que docere *Vc* est quoque docere *Pm*   **2015** quoque] quodque *GoFr Ve* quaque *Q*; quia] que *Vd Ve*; nulla] ulla *GI*; mortem] morte *EF*   **2016** *om. Go*; qualibet] quelibet *GI XQY* quamlibet *B* qualiter *C*; dedocuisse] dedecuisse *ST* me docuisse *K* redocuisse *VdBe*   **2017** nonne] nam *fb*; mortis] *om. U, add. in margin U²*   **2018** istud] illud *Go UQ*; solet] potest *β* potest uel solet *GI*   **2019** *om. O*; lance] laute *Fr Ve Q* laute / [*uel*] lance *La* caute *Pm* forte *Go*; partitur] pariter *Ne* paribus *ARMNPDKVe GI UZQY fb* peribet *JC^{uc}W* periret *C²*   **2021** hanc]hac *Hfb*;nisi]non *αβSMuVbVcVdTGoBePkFrPm RDK TrHaLa XQ* nec *GI Y* nunc *U om. VaNe Z*; praetimuisse] pertimuisse *VbVc* precinuisse *T O Y* pretinuisse *Go UQ fb* pretimisse *Vd*; futuram] futura *Go J*   **2022** ne] ut *Ha X*; mihi dicat] dicat mihi *VcPm fb*; abi] ibi *H T* obi *R* ubi *Go Ve* abi /uel aue *La*   **2023** hinc] huic *Vd J* hunc *Go* hanc *Ha* < >uc *Tr*   **2024** ut ualeat] ualeat ut *QY*; saluus] salus *MP* sanus *SMuVbVcVdTBePkFrPmNe Ha* sanius *VaGo* solus *Tr*   **2025** utque] usque *MuFr* ut qui *VdBe*; iuuenilia] iuuenalia *H Mu A* iuuenialia *U* iuuencula *α*   **2027** quod] quos *HuMN* et *AJCWOPVe GI XQY*; superest] superam *GI*; uitae ne] uita ne *Go GI* uite nec *MN* uitaue *X*   **2028** hoc] hanc *LE X*

SPECVLVM STVLTORVM

activity wears out the brain. To know many things without knowing them well is not an honour to the one who knows them, but a disadvantage, to tell the truth. [2010] Many have snatched up scraps about many things, so that they might seem knowledgeable in all these things to their associates. To know is an effort, to retain knowledge is also an effort; it's an effort to learn, an effort to teach. And what troubles me more is that no science [2015] can take death off the syllabus by any art. Does not the fear of death rule throughout the whole world? In each and all this is found. It shares out everything with an even balance, and distributes to everyone with a single weight, harsh but just. [2020] I can do no other than fear its arrival in advance, lest it say to me unexpectedly "Depart!" '

Burnellus's Remorse

'For this reason I have decided to devote myself to the religious life, so that my soul may be saved. So that in old age I may redeem my youthful years, [2025] it's right that I should try to correct my life. What small amount of life remains I wish to conclude with a good end, lest it slip away entirely. It's better to repent late than never; he who is

---

2010   *non honor est sed onus*: see n. to line 145.
2026   *corripuisse*: 'corripere' = 'to correct, set right' (*DMLBS* 2b).
2028   *claudere fine bono*: *Babio*, 472 (*Commedie*, ii. 298).

SPECVLVM STVLTORVM

2030
quem pudet erroris paenituisse decet.
Et si mane fuit uel tota dies nebulosa,
obscurum redimat uespera clara diem.
Quod male dispersit incircumspecta iuuentus,
spes in flore suo prodiga facta sui,

2035
damna iuuentutis redimens annosa senectus
colligat in fructu floribus usa suis.
Spes fuit in flore, sed flos defloruit, a spe
spes cecidit, fructu deficiente suo.
Spes abiit floris, spes una nouissima fructus

2040
dum superest, aliquid utilitatis agat.
De re tam certa nil morte latentius ipsa,
omnes ipsa latet, omnibus ipsa patet.
Rebus in humanis mors est res publica nobis,
in qua quisque uicem proprietatis habet.

2045
Si qua tamen propria res est uel publica, morte
nulla magis propria, publica nulla magis.
Ergo quid hic facio? Quorsum deseruio mundo?
Mors mihi cras dicet "En ego! surge, ueni."
Nil igitur superest nisi tantum religioni

2050
me conferre; procul sit, precor, ergo mora!'

Sententia Burnelli de diuersis religionibus existentibus

'Sed quia diuersae species sunt religionis,
nescio praecipue quae sit habenda mihi.'

2030 pudet] pendet *Go* pudor *T U*; decet] docet *T GI U*   **2031** uel tota] tota uel *Fr Q*   **2033** incircumspecta] incircumscripta *O*ᵃᶜ *X* incircumscripta /uel specta *Ha*   **2034** *om. Fr*; spes] *Skutsch* mens α ens β *SMuVaVbVdTGoBePkPmNe AJCWHuMNOPDKVe GI TrHaLa ZXQY* eius *R* eius et *Vc* quos *U*   **2035** annosa] animosa *ROVe*   **2037** flos defloruit] flos effloruit *MuTGoPm Ha* flore defloruit *BePk La* spes defloruit *U* spes deperit *F*   **2038** *om. O*; cecidit] recedit *fb*; suo] bono *AJCWRHuMNPDKVe* suo /uel bono *La*   **2039** fructus] fractus *MN*   **2041** nil] ne *XQ* uel *GoPm*   **2042** *om. Vd*; omnes] omnibus *F Go GI UQ* omnis *Mu JD Y*   **2043** in] *om. fb*; est res] res est *Vc K*   **2045–6** res est—magis propria] *om. O*   **2045** est] *om. H Fr*   **2047** *line repeated in alternative form* *Z*(1)*Z*(2); hic] hoc *K U* hec *S* hinc *Z*(2) *om. Fr*; facio] fructum *Tr om. Z*(2); quorsum deseruio mundo] quorsum declino mundo /uel nisi quod deseruio mundo *La*; quorsum] quo rursum *Pk* nisi quod δ *GI Tr UX fb* cur sic *H MuVaFrPm Ha* cur et sic *Go* quid sic *T* nil quam *Z*(1)*QY*; deseruio] disceruio *J* declino *VdBe*   **2048** surge] surgo *ZQY*   **2049** *om. U, add. in lower margin U²*   **2050** procul sit] sit procul *T* procul sic *Be Ve*   **2051** *fh, fm, and fn excerpt 2 join here*; species sunt] sunt species *SVaVcTGoFrPm CO*ᵃᶜ*P fm*

SPECVLVM STVLTORVM

ashamed of his wrongdoing rightly repents. [2030] And if the morning—
or the whole day—was cloudy, let a cloudless evening compensate for
the murky day. What careless youth has wrongly scattered, hope in its
flower made prodigal of itself, old age should repair the losses of youth,
[2035] by gathering it up in fruit, using its own flowers. There was
hope in the flower, but the hope withered; hope left the hope, when its
fruit was lacking. The hope of the flower has vanished; let one last hope
of fruit be of some use, while it remains. [2040] For a thing so certain,
nothing is more hidden than death; it is hidden from everyone, and yet
obvious to everyone. In human affairs, death is our common property,
in which everyone gets their turn at ownership. If indeed any property
is either private or public, [2045] nothing is more private than death,
nothing more public. So what am I doing here? To what end do I serve
the world? Tomorrow death will say to me, "Here I am! Rise, come!"
So there is nothing left but to devote myself to the religious life; heaven
forbid therefore that I should delay!' [2050]

Burnellus's Opinion of the Different Religious Orders in Existence

'But because there are different types of religious order, I don't know
which in particular should be mine.'

2034 *spes*: on this conjecture, see Introduction, p. lxxxi.
2041–2 Cf. Bernard of Clairvaux, *Epistolae*, no. cv (*Sancti Bernardi Opera*, vii. 264): 'Nil
mortalibus vel morte certius, vel incertius hora mortis.'
2043 *Rebus in humanis*: see n. to line 1663.
2045 *qua*: see n. to line 908.
2051 The survey of monastic orders has parallels in other 12th-c. satirists, most notably
in a lengthy section of Walter Map's *De nugis curialium* (dist. i. 16–28). This covers the
Carthusians (c. 16, recapitulated in c. 28); the Grandmontines (c. 17, recapitulated in c. 26);
the Templars (cc. 18–22); the Hospitallers (c. 23); the Cistercians (cc. 24–25); and the
Gilbertines of Sempringham (c. 27). Map's attitude is not consistently satiric: the chapters
on the Templars contain several fanciful tales of 'wonders', and the Templars are acknowledged
to live 'harmlessly enough' in Britain, so that the stories of their behaviour elsewhere may be
lies (c. 22, pp. 68–9). The accounts of the Carthusians, Grandmontines, and Gilbertines are
confined to factual information on their customs. The Hospitallers are admitted to have been
good at first, although they have succumbed to covetousness and have bribed the papal curia
in order to win privileges for themselves at the expense of the secular clergy (c. 23, pp. 70–3;
Map's self-interest is in evidence here). Map's most scathing satire is directed against the
Cistercians, who are charged with luxury, greed, avarice, fraudulent practices, and indecency.
Particular points of agreement with Burnellus's description of the Cistercians are noted
where relevant below.

202 *SPECVLVM STVLTORVM*

De Templariis

'Si cruce signatus rubea me confero Templo,
    trans mare me mittent soluere uota Deo.
2055 Seruus ero, seruum facient procul esse seorsum,
    seruiet et forsan in regione Tyri.
Non tamen ibo pedes, sed equo, qui pastus auena
    crassus, et ad calces sit tener atque leuis,
quique pedem seruans et fractis gressibus errans
2060 molliter incedat, regula namque iubet.
Scandere trottantem prohibet quoque regula, nolo
    quod pro me careat ordo rigore suo.
Ingrediar miles ne candida pallia desint,

2053–464 *om. Fr.*   **2053** confero] consecro *fm fn*   **2055** facient] faciunt *D* faciant *T fh*; seorsum] deorsum *F S*   **2056** seruiet] seruiam *Vd* seruiat *fh*; Tyri] teri *MN*   **2057** auena] auenis *L* annona *fn*   **2058** et] *om. fh fm fn*; calces] calles *S* culeos *fm fn*; sit] sic *Tr* sed *Ve U*   **2059** quique] cumque *GI* cuique *Z*; pedem seruans] pede seruas *LE*   **2060** incedat] incedet *F D* incedat ut *Z*; namque] nostra β *SMuVaVbVcVdTGoBePkPmNe* δ *GI TrLa UZXQY fh fm fn* mea *Ha*   **2061** trottantem] trotandem *S* trotante *Vd* set tanto *D* tractantem *E Tr fh fm fn* crotantem *Q* cunctantem *T*; nolo] uolo *VdBe Ha*   **2062** quod] quos *fh fm fn* qui *Pk;* pro] per *AJWRHuMNOPDKVe GI HaLa*   **2063** ingrediar] ingredior *Go R*; ne] nec *R Z* quia *SVaVbVcVdTGoPkPmNe Ha fh fm fn* quia /uel ne *La* qui *MuBe Tr*; desint] desunt *ZY* defert *SMuVaVbVcVdTGoBePkPmNe TrHaLa fh fm fn*

John of Salisbury comments on various religious orders in the *Policraticus*, vii. 21 and 23. In c. 23, he praises the Carthusians and the Grandmontines for their austerity and self-discipline (ed. Webb, ii. 204–5, trans. Pike, pp. 281–2). In c. 21, however, while professing admiration for those Carthusians, Cistercians, Cluniacs, and regular canons who follow the example of their founders, as well as for the Templars and Hospitallers who live blamelessly, he singles out for criticism those monastic hypocrites who 'come in sheep's clothing, but within they are ravening wolves' (ed. Webb, ii. 191–3; trans. Dickinson, pp. 313–14). This biblical quotation (Matt. 7: 15) was often applied to the Cistercians in the 12th c., and in what follows John displays his self-interest as a secular priest in attacking those recognizably Cistercian practices which infringe the rights and revenues of the secular clergy, especially in regard to their appropriation of tithes (see n. to lines 959–60 above). The Templars similarly incur his wrath because they hold benefices and enjoy the revenues from them (ed. Webb, ii. 198; trans. Dickinson, p. 319).

Burnellus's survey similarly betrays Nigel's self-interested point of view. Much of it is not satiric at all, being taken up with straightforward accounts of the customs of the individual orders (evaluated from a donkey's point of view), and there are even laudatory comments. The real villains of the piece here are the secular canons, who are the butt of a violent tirade which is, as Raymo noted, 'unparalleled in contemporary satire', and is self-evidently prompted by the Canterbury community's hostility to the proposed collegiate foundation at Hackington (see Introduction, pp. xliv–l). The account of the Cistercians as 'false brethren' is nearly as acerbic in tone, and can similarly be linked with Nigel's hostility to Archbishop Baldwin (ibid.). The inclusion of the survey of monastic orders was very probably motivated by the desire to incorporate these two attacks on the enemies of the Canterbury monks into *SS.*

2053 The Templars were a military order, founded by Hugh of Payns *c.*1120, to provide protection for the pilgrims flocking to Jerusalem after its capture by the First Crusade in 1099, and to battle against the Muslims in the Holy Land (Forey, *Military Orders*, p. 6; Barber, *New Knighthood*, pp. 6–9). Although the Templars, like the other military orders,

SPECVLVM STVLTORVM

About the Templars

'If I devote myself to the Temple, signed with a red cross, they will send me across the sea to fulfil my vow to God. I shall be a servant, and they will make their servant be far away; [2055] perhaps he will serve in the region of Tyre. Yet I shan't travel on foot, but on a horse, oat-fed and fat, and sensitive and responsive to the touch of my heels. He will move smoothly, controlling his pace and ambling with gentle steps, for the Rule orders it. [2060] The Rule also forbids me to mount a trotting horse, and I don't want the Rule to lose its rigour through me. I shall become a knight, so that the white tunics won't be lacking, but then I must go

were laymen, they took the monastic vows of poverty, chastity, and obedience (Forey, *Military Orders*, pp. 6, 189). They took their name from their original base in Jerusalem on the Temple Mount, adjacent to the al-Aqsa mosque, which was believed to have been the site of the Temple of Solomon (Forey, *Military Orders*, p. 6; Barber, *New Knighthood*, pp. 7, 90–3). After Saladin's victory at the battle of Hattin in 1187, and subsequent recapture of Jerusalem, the Templars lost their headquarters on the Temple Mount and retreated to Tyre, 'the most important city left in the kingdom of Jerusalem', which was saved from Saladin by 'the chance arrival of a fleet under the German crusader, Conrad of Montferrat' (Barber, *New Knighthood*, pp. 114–16). This would explain why Burnellus imagines serving as a Templar 'in regione Tyri', rather than in Jerusalem. In 1191, the Templar headquarters were transferred to Acre, which was captured from the Muslims by the forces of the Third Crusade under the leadership of Richard I (the Lionheart) and Philip II of France (Barber, *New Knighthood*, pp. 117–18; Riley-Smith, *Knights Hospitallers*, pp. 43–6). *cruce signatus rubea*: the knights of the Templar order (as opposed to the more numerous sergeants) wore white tunics (signifying chastity); Pope Eugenius III (probably in 1147) granted them the privilege of wearing a red cross (signifying blood) (Barber, *New Knighthood*, pp. 16, 66).

2059 *fractis gressibus*: as used of a manner of human walking, 'fractus' means 'soft, effeminate, enfeebled' ('mincing'?); see *OLD* s.v. 'fractus' 4; *DMLBS* s.v. 'frangere' 13b; *TLL* s.v. 'frangere', vi. 1. 1252. 57–9. Peter Chrysologus uses 'fractis gressibus' to describe the seductive manner of Herodias's dance (*serm.* clxxiv, PL lii, 654A). However, in relation to a horse, it has a more specialized sense: John of Salisbury uses the phrase in *Policraticus*, vii. 18 (ed. Webb, ii. 169. 25–6) when speaking of a horse of unknown calibre which some sharp salesman is trying to pass off as a future ambler ('gradarius'), 'walking gently with delicate steps' ('fractis gressibus mollius incedentem'). An ambler was (and is) a horse that was trained to use a gait more comfortable for riding over long distances than the bouncing movement of the normal trot, in which the legs move in diagonal pairs (two/four time); hence the reference in line 2061 to the trot as the prohibited motion. The ambling gait took various forms, but the one intended here probably involved moving the pair of legs on each side at the same time, at a walking pace (Chenevix-Trench, *A History of Horsemanship*, p. 67). See Deb Bennett, *Conquerors*, pp. 32–6, with useful drawings illustrating the leg movements in the walk, amble, trot, and canter, on p. 34. The Templar Rule strictly curtailed the speed at which horses were normally ridden, in order to save them from becoming overworked; see *La Règle du Temple*, ed. Curzon, ch. 315 (trans. Upton-Ward): 'No brother should run his horse if it is not rested, nor gallop without permission, and especially the one he is not using; he may go out for pleasure at a pace [walk] or amble' ('le pas ou l'embleure se puet aler desduire'); cf. chs. 95, 128, 137. The Templars customarily used an ambler (palfrey) to ride to the battlefield, and switched to a warhorse (destrier) for the battle itself (see Matthew Bennett in *The Rule of the Templars*, p. 183, who also cites the *Chanson de Roland*, ed. Whitehead, 1000–1: 'laissent les muls e tuz les palefreiz/ Es destrers muntent, si chevalchent estreiz'). Burnellus is hoping for a fat and lazy animal (see lines 2057–8) which will be easy to ride.

2063–4 Burnellus may seem to be stating the obvious, but it was not inevitable that anyone who joined the Templars would fight in the Holy Land. The Templars maintained convents

204 SPECVLVM STVLTORVM

sed tunc ad bellum non rediturus eo.
2065   De cute corrigiam nostra Saladinus habebit
et comedet carnes bestia saeua meas.
Incircumcisi gladius mea uiscera fundet,
detracto corio cetera tradet humo.'

De Hospitalariis

'Rursum si fuero crucis Hospitalarius albae,
2070   ad Libanum mittar, ligna referre domum.
Cum lacrimis pergam scutica caedente trinodi,
et uenter uacuus et cophinellus erit.

2064 rediturus] redditurus *I X*; eo] ero *Go RO*   **2065** corrigiam] corrigia *TGo* corrigam *Tr*; nostra] nostram *Mu Ha* noster *Tr Z*; Saladinus] soladinus *Va J La* saladinis *Mu*^{ac} salodinus *AWHuMN GI U* solodinus *C Tr* soldinus *Ve* sandalinus *Pm* saledinus *fm* soldidinus *fh* saldidinus *fn* saldanus *Q* soldanus *LE Mu*^{pc}*Go ROK Ha ZX*   **2066** comedet] comedit *F* comedat *Be Q* commodat *Go* corrodet *Pk*; saeua] seui *Z* sana *MuGo*   **2067** fundet] scindet *VdBe Tr* scindet /uel fundet *La*   **2068** corio] correo *D* coreo *VaVd Ha ZQ fm*; tradet] tradat *R* trahet *Q* dabit *O* tendet *fm*   **2069** rursum] < >ursus *Tr Q* rursus *H R* cursum *Go* sursum *U*; crucis] *om. U, add. in margin U*^{2} **2070** Libanum] clibanum *α VaTPm* libernum *Z*; mittar] mittent *T* mitterer *Z* mittat *fh fn;* ligna referre domum] lingua referre domi *C* scindere ligna domus *SMuVaVbVcVdGoBePkPmNe TrHaLa Z fh fm fn* scindere ligna *T*   **2071** scutica] scuta *Mu* sentita *VaPm* strucita *Tr* scucita *La* sicut *LE* securi *T*; caedente] cedenda *MuVaVbVdPkNe HaLa fh fn* cedende *Tr* cedendi *BeGo* cedendo *T* tendenda *Pm* cendenda *fm* sedente *U* tridente *C*; trinodi] trimordi *AJCWHuMNOPKVe GI* trinordi *U*^{2} timor<di?> *D* ternodi *Z* termodi *Q* remordi *R Tr* renodi *fh* feroci *T*   **2072** et cophinellus] *Skutsch* et prophinellus *LE* et prope nullus *D* et profinellus *F β S AJHuMNP UZXQY* uel prope nullus *add. X*^{pc} et profunellus *Ve* et prosinellus *CWO GI* et profamellus *Pk* et prosamellus erit /uel famelicus et erit *Ha* et famelicus *MuVdGoBePmNe* et famellicus *Va* famelicus et *Tr* atque famellus *VbVc* famelicus /uel prosinellus *La* et flamellus *fh fm fn* et fatigatus *T* et quasi uellus *R* et prosoletus *K* (*marginal gloss:* prosoletus dicitur transicio de longe ad peregrinacionem)

---

all over Western Europe, which served as administrative centres and reserves of manpower. 'The majority of Templars and Hospitallers lived in Western Europe and most...spent the whole of their careers residing peacefully in the West' (Forey, *Military Orders*, pp. 190–1). Henry II made them generous grants of land in England, and the Templar *Inquisitio* of 1185 records a donation of land made to them by Theobald, archbishop of Canterbury (1139–61); see *Records of the Templars*, ed. Lees, p. 25. By the 1190s, when *SS* was written, there were numerous Templar houses, the main one being the New Temple Church in London (Lord, *The Knights Templar in Britain*, pp. 22, 33–49 and accompanying plates). For indulgences granted by successive archbishops of Canterbury to those who visited this church on the day of its dedication (10 Feb. 1185) and who gave alms to it, see *English Episcopal Acta ii. Canterbury 1162–1190*, ed. Cheney and Jones, nos. 42, 317.

2065 *Saladinus*: Saladin first became known in the West for his destruction of the Templar castle at Jacob's Ford in 1179, but his victory in the battle of Hattin (over an army including Templars and Hospitallers), which enabled the recapture of Jerusalem in 1187, made his name into a household word (see Introduction, n. 116). In 1188, Saladin gained even greater notoriety

SPECVLVM STVLTORVM   205

to war, not to return. Saladin will make a shoelace out of my hide, [2065] and a wild beast will eat my flesh. The sword of the uncircumcised will pierce my entrails, he will remove my hide and consign the rest to the earth.'

About the Hospitallers

'Again, if I become a Hospitaller of the White Cross, I shall be sent to Lebanon, to bring home wood. [2070] With tears I shall proceed under the blows of the triple-knotted lash, and my belly and my hay basket will be empty. Although many things may come into my mind, nothing will

through the general levy of the infamous 'Saladin tithe', which was designed to finance English participation in the Third Crusade. The widespread resentment at this tithe was exacerbated in Canterbury by the fact that Henry II, with Archbishop Baldwin's approval, ordered the sequestration of profits from the donations made by pilgrims to Becket's shrine in order to pay what was due (*Epistolae Cantuarienses*, nos. clviii, clxvii; Tyerman, *England and the Crusades*, p. 75; Mitchell, *Taxation in Medieval England*, pp. 10, 12–14, 64–5, 87, 90, 119–22, 169–71). Gervase of Canterbury compared Archbishop Baldwin to Saladin: just as Saladin claimed that his recapture of Jerusalem proved that the God he worshipped was 'just and good', so Baldwin's supporters claimed that the death of the Canterbury monks at the papal curia who had been prosecuting the monastery's case against the proposed college of canons at Hackington showed the hand of God (Gervase, *Chronicle*, i. 430–1).

2067–8 Saladin regularly executed all Templars and Hospitallers who were taken prisoner in battle (Riley-Smith, *Knights Hospitallers*, p. 39).

2067 *Incircumcisi*: circumcision is not obligatory in Islam, but it is a widespread practice, and Nigel seems to have been mistaken on this point.

2069 The Order of the Hospital of St John originated in a hospital whose foundation is of uncertain date, but which was already caring for pilgrims in Jerusalem when the city was captured by the First Crusade in 1099 (Riley-Smith, *Hospitallers*, p. 19; *Knights Hospitallers*, pp. 4, 16–18). The Hospitallers were at first devoted to the service of the poor and the sick, but by the middle of the 12th c. they had taken on military functions (Forey, *Military Orders*, pp. 18–19; Riley-Smith, *Knights Hospitallers*, pp. 29–32). After the fall of Jerusalem in 1187, and the Christian recapture of Acre in 1191, they, like the Templars, transferred their headquarters to Acre, situated in historic Lebanon (Barber, *New Knighthood*, p. 118; Riley-Smith, *Knights Hospitallers*, pp. 45–50, 113). The Hospitallers 'began to receive gifts of land in England and in Scotland in the 1130s and 1140s, including the property at Clerkenwell, just outside the north walls of London, which was to be the site of the priory headquarters. Although in the 12th c. the Templars seem to have been more favoured by English benefactors, the Hospitallers had twenty-eight commanderies by the turn of the thirteenth century' (Riley-Smith, *Hospitallers*, pp. 79–80). *crucis...albae*: in 1130 Pope Innocent II approved a coat of arms for the knights of the order, a silver cross on a red background.

2071–2 *scutica caedente...uenter uacuus*: the Hospitallers usually ate twice a day, and were allowed cooked meat or fish, eggs, bread, and wine. The reference here may be to the punishment for certain types of misbehaviour, which consisted of beating, a diet of bread and water, and eating one's food on the ground, without a napkin (Riley-Smith, *Knights Hospitallers*, p. 123). *cophinellus*: on this conjecture, see Introduction, p. lxxxi.

206   *SPECVLVM STVLTORVM*

Multa licet subeant mihi, nil de iure licebit
   praeter mentiri magnificando domum.
2075 Et si transgressus fuero semel atque secundo,
   "Vade foras" dicent diripientque crucem.'

De Nigris Monachis

'Esse Niger Monachus si forte uelim Cluniaci
   oua fabasque nigras cum sale saepe dabunt.
Surgere me facient media de nocte, uolentem
2080 amplius in calido membra fouere toro.
Quodque magis nollem, uellent me psallere sursum
   et geminare meos in diapente tonos.
Vox est rauca nimis, quamuis sit et ipsa sonora,
   pectus et obstrusum tussis anhela grauat.
2085 Psallere si nolim, facient me ferre lucernam,
   debita reddentes praemia mane mihi.

2073 subeant] libeant *H F X* subeam *K* possideant *fh*; licebit] decebit *fh*
2074 domum] deum *H Va* deum /uel demum *La*   2076 diripientque] diripiantque
VdBe TrLa dirupiendo *Go*   2077 niger] magis *J Ha Y*; Cluniaci] cluniati *Q* clunaci *T*
J clunati *Pk* cluniace *Ha* cluniacensi *X* clunacensi *CWHuMN* cluniacensis *K* clunacensis *X*
2078 oua] qua *Ne D La*ᵃᶜ nam *Go*; fabasque] fabas *MuVaGo GI*; nigras] magnas *Pk*
Tr   2079 facient] facerent *LE* β *D X* faciunt *Mu* faciant *VdGo Ha Z*; uolentem]
uolente *RPK Ha* ualentem *Mu* uolantem *Tr*   2081 quodque] quique *GoBe corr. Be*²
quamque *Tr fn*; nollem] nolle *Be Ha* timeo *T*; uellent] pellent *R* facient *K* uellem
MuVaVdPkPm fh fn nollem *Q* uelle *Vc Ve* molle faciant *T add.* grauem *P*ᵖᶜ *om. VbGo*; psallere]
surgere *GI* psalle *A*; sursum] rursum *fh*   2082 meos] meis *fn*   2084 et] *om. LE*;
obstrusum] obstrusi *Q* obtrusum *H SPk JCWHuMNOD Ha Z* obtusum *VbVcVdT U* obscurum *R illegible I*; anhela] et anhela *fm*   2085 nolim] uelim *VdTGoBe*; facient] faciet *Vd*
facerent α *GoPm Y* faciunt *La fm*; lucernam] laternam *T D Z*   2086 mane] magna [*uel*]
mane *add. interlinear La*

2073 *subeant*: for 'subire' meaning 'to suggest itself (of a thought or idea)', see *DMLBS*
9b. However, it customarily takes the accusative rather than the dative as here.
2075 For serious sins, Hospitallers were deprived of their habit and expelled from the
order (Forey, *Military Orders*, p. 196; Riley-Smith, *Knights Hospitallers*, pp. 123–4).
2077–110 *Cluniaci*: the Burgundian monastery of Cluny was the source of a major reform-
ing movement in the 10th and 11th cc. Although it did not secede from its Benedictine origins and become a separate order, its influence spread throughout France, and by the 12th c.
it stood at the head of a network of satellite monasteries, 'bound together by a common
acceptance of the customs and uses of Cluny and by the decrees of successive abbots'
(Knowles, *Monastic Order*, p. 148; see also pp. 146–8 for a summary of the different kinds of
relationship between the mother house and its dependents). Christ Church Canterbury was
not a Cluniac house, but the earliest Cluniac foundation in England (1077) at Lewes, Sussex,
was not far away, and by 1160 there were nearly 40 Cluniac houses in the country (Knowles,
Monastic Order, pp. 154–8 and Table III on p. 723).

SPECVLVM STVLTORVM 207

be permitted me as of right except lies which glorify the house. And if I transgress once or twice, [2075] they will say "Get out!" and tear off my cross.'

About the Black Monks

'If I were to wish to be a Black Monk at Cluny, they will often give me eggs and black beans with salt. They will make me get up in the middle of the night, when I want to cosset my body longer in a warm bed. [2080] And what I would dislike more, they would want me to raise psalms on high and to repeat my braying in harmony. My voice is very harsh, although it is loud, and a rasping cough oppresses my constricted chest. If I don't want to sing, they'll make me carry the lamp, [2085] giving me my due reward in the morning. I should often eat meat

---

2078 On the Cluniac diet, see nn. to lines 2087–8 and 2111–12.

2081 Devotion to the liturgy was the glory of Cluny (see de Valous, *Le Monachisme clunisien*, i. 238). Over the centuries, no effort was spared to make the melodies more beautiful, the vestments richer, and the ceremonies more elaborate. In the poetic debate between a Cistercian (Zoilus) and a Benedictine (Maurus) (Inc. 'Nuper ductu serio'), Zoilus jeers at the Benedictines for singing away like birds in spring, while the Cistercians labour productively in the fields (*Map Poems*, p. 245, lines 83–8). *psallere*: 'The number of psalms chanted daily at Cluny was a hundred and twenty-four in the first half of the tenth century . . . and reached a maximum in the second half of the eleventh century of about two hundred and fifteen during Lent, the most heavily loaded time of the year . . . This was more than five times the number prescribed in the Rule' (n. to *Statuta Petri Venerabilis* xxxi, ed. Constable, p. 66). Peter the Venerable's *Statutes* reduced this number by omitting the so-called 'familiar psalms' on special feast-days (ibid.). See also Knowles, 'The monastic horarium', pp. 713–16, and the timetables on pp. 721–2.

2082 *diapente*: a musical interval of a fifth (see *DMLBS* s. v.). To duplicate the psalm tone by singing a fifth higher was one version of medieval discant or parallel organum. Burnellus has a naturally high voice, so this is the most suitable option for him; see Fuller, 'Discant and the theory of fifthing'.

2084 *obstrusum*: 'blocked, congested' (*DMLBS* 1). *tussis anhela*: Vergil, *Georgics*, iii. 497.

2085 Burnellus seems to be referring to the duties of the *circatores*, two senior monks who patrolled the monastery by day and night (with lanterns) to observe and report breaches of discipline, such as speaking during the hours of silence (Feiss, '*Circatores*'). Raymo's note refers to Ulrich, *Consuetudines Cluniacenses*, ii. 8 (PL cxlix. 706), which instructs the lantern-bearer to check whether any monk is sleeping during the readings in the night services; if so, and the light does not wake him after being shone in his face three times, the lantern is to be placed at his feet and when he awakes he is to carry it round himself.

2086 A reference to the confession of faults in chapter each morning (Ulrich, *Consuetudines Cluniacenses*, ii. 12, PL cxlix. 706–7).

208 · SPECVLVM STVLTORVM

Multotiens carnes et pinguia saepe uorarem
    in feria sexta, nam licet illud ibi.
Pellicias portant et plura recondita seruant,
2090   quae non sunt sociis omnia nota suis.
Sed neque sunt dominis abbatibus omnia nota,
    quamuis uel cupiant praecipiantque satis.
Quod si contingat stabilita silentia solui,
    corripient uerbis uerberibusque simul;
2095   sed si percutiam, uino stimulante uel ira,
    me grauibus culpis carceribusque dabunt.
Qui nisi claustrali multumque diuque labore
    expertis tribuunt exteriora loca.
Non amor abbatis ibi nec cognatio quaeuis
2100   contra claustrales obtinuisse potest.
Ordinis aut morum numquam dispendia quisquam
    fratribus ex nigris sustinuisse ualet.
Non uendunt uel emunt sua praedia uel prioratus,
    omnia sed gratis distribuuntur ibi.

2087 saepe] queque *K*; uorarem] uocarem *MuGoNe* uorem *fm* uorare *AJCWRHuMNPDK GI TrLa UZQY* rorare *Ve* uorari *O* notarem *VaVbVcVdBePkPm fh fn* uitarem *Ha* negarent *S* 2088 sexta] quarta β *JK X* quinta *SMuVaVbVcGoBePkPmNe TrHaLa fh fm fn*; nam licet illud ibi] nam licet illud mihi *Vb* nam licet istud ibi *fm* non licet istud ibi *fh* non licent ista ibi *fn* non licet illud ibi β *TrHa X* sepe licebit eis (ibi *Y*) δ *GI UZQY* 2089 pellicias] pollicias *Go* pellicia *VdTBe TrHaLa fh fm fn*; plura] multa *SMuVaVbVcVdTGoBePkPmNe TrHaLa fm fn* multis *fh*; recondita] recandita *E* 2090 omnia] omnibus *LE CW* 2092 uel] id α hec *D* nil *O Z*; praecipiantque] precipitantque *VaVd R ZY*; satis] suis *Ve* solus *fm* solis *fh fn* 2093 silentia] licentia *X corr. X²* 2094 corripient] corripiant *Vd Ha* corripientque *Go* 2095 sed] et δ 2097 qui] que *fh*; multumque diuque labore] multumque diu laborarem *AJ GI Tr UQY* multumque diu laborare *OPVe* multum longumque laborem *D* multumque diues labore *Z*; *(whole line)* simplicibus claustra (claustrum *HuK*) durum magnumque (longumque *K*) laborem *HuMNK* 2098 expertis] experto β *O X* expertos *D* ex partes *T* 2099 *after 2098 transp.* 2103–4 *K*; nec] hec *E* uel *SMuVaVbVcVdTGoBePkPmNe TrHaLa fh fm fn* 2102 ualet] uelet *J* ualent β potest α *SVb D* 2103 uendunt] comodant *ACWOP* comedant *JVe* comedunt *R GI UY*; sua praedia uel prioratus] cum symone predia gratis *HuMNK*; praedia] premia *MuVaVbVcVdTGoBePkPmNe HaLa Z fh fm fn*; *(whole line)* predia multa satis ibi gratis distribuuntur *D* 2104 omnia sed gratis] atque prioratus *HuMNK*; ibi] eis β *X*; *(whole line)* atque prioratus non comodant uel emunt *D*

2087–8 *carnes et pinguia*: the rich diet of the Benedictines was notorious (see the comment of Gerald of Wales, cited in the note below to lines 2111–12). In the debate between a Cistercian (Zoilus) and a Benedictine (Maurus) referred to in the n. to line 2081, Zoilus itemizes in elaborate detail the delicacies on the Benedictine tables, including fat ('sagimen'; see *DMLBS* 1b), which is 'almost meat, the next-best-thing to meat' ('pene caro'). Maurus replies that 'pinguia' are served only on feast-days, and the surplus food is given to guests,

SPECVLVM STVLTORVM   209

and fats on Fridays, for that is allowed there. They wear sheepskins, and keep hidden many things which are not all known to their companions. [2090] Nor are they all known to the lord abbots, although they wish and order it well enough. If the imposed silence should happen to be broken, they punish with words and blows together. But if I strike a blow, under the stimulus of wine or anger, [2095] they will consign me to heavy penalties and imprisonments. They give outside postings only to those who have been long and thoroughly tried by the discipline of the cloister. Neither the abbot's favour, nor any blood-relationship can prevail against the monks' interest. [2100] None of the Black Monks can bear a loss to the order or to its customs. They do not buy or sell their estates or their priories; everything there is distributed without payment. The number of dependent cells, which many think a disadvantage or a disgrace,

the sick, and the poor (*Map Poems*, pp. 247–8, lines 133–88). Peter the Venerable's *Statutes* strictly forbid meat, except for the sick (*Statuta Petri Venerabilis*, xii, ed. Constable, p. 51), and also forbid fat (suet and lard) on Fridays (ibid. x, ed. Constable, pp. 49–50) and in Advent, apart from the first Sunday (ibid. xv, ed. Constable, p. 54; see also n.).

2088 For 'feria sexta' meaning 'Friday', see *DMLBS* s. v. 'feria' 3f.

2089 *Pellicias portant*: Peter the Venerable's *Statutes* prohibit Cluniac monks from wearing fur other than sheep- or goat-skins (*Statuta Petri Venerabilis*, xvii, ed. Constable, pp. 55–6). The Cistercians criticized the Cluniacs for wearing sheepskins in addition to their woollen tunics and cowls. See for example St Bernard's Letter to his nephew Robert, who was thinking of leaving the Cistercians and returning to Cluny, where he had been an oblate: 'Does salvation rest rather in soft raiment and high living than in frugal fare and moderate clothing? If warm and comfortable furs ("pelliciae lenes et calidae"), if fine and precious cloth, if long sleeves and ample hoods, if dainty coverlets and soft woollen shirts make a saint, why do I delay and not follow you at once?' (*Sancti Bernardi Opera*, vii. 9; trans. Scott James, p. 8). Walter Map accuses the Cistercians of taunting the Black Monks for their lambskins ('cum de pelliciis nigros derideant'); *De nugis curialium*, dist. i. 25, pp. 84–5. For Peter the Venerable's defence of Cluniac practice in this respect, see his *Letters*, xxviii, ed. Constable, i. 62–4.

2093 Peter the Venerable's *Statutes* lay down rules for the times and places when strict silence in the monastery must be observed (*Statuta Petri Venerabilis*. xix–xxii, ed. Constable, pp. 57–60).

2094 On the monastic practice of flogging as a punishment for various offences, see *Rule of St Benedict*, c. xxviii; Ulrich, *Consuetudines Cluniacenses*, iii. 3, PL cxlix. 734; *Statuta Petri Venerabilis*, lxiii and n., ed. Constable, p. 95, and Smith, 'Discipline, compassion and monastic ideals'. *uerbis uerberibusque*: the collocation is conventional. On the gradations of monastic punishments, see the *Epistle to William*, n. 28.

2096 *carceribusque*: on imprisonment as a punishment for rebellious monks, see Ulrich, *Consuetudines Cluniacenses*, iii. 3, PL cxlix. 736. Flogging and incarceration were also prescribed as punishments at Christ Church Canterbury by the *Constitutions of Lanfranc*, cc. xciii, xcix–c, ed. Knowles and Brooke, pp. 134–5, 148–51.

2097 *nisi* = 'non nisi'. Cf. lines 971, 3171.

2103–4 See the prohibition against selling or exchanging for a pledge monastic lands or treasures in Peter the Venerable's *Statutes* (*Stauta Petri Venerabilis*, xliv, ed. Constable, p. 76).

210   *SPECVLVM STVLTORVM*

2105   Cellarum numerus, quem damno dedecorique
      esse putant multi, commoda multa parit.
      Si quam de membris nebulam contingit oriri,
      hanc caput absorbet nobilitate sua.
      Quamque semel culpam uindex sententia punit,
2110   ulterius cuiquam non licet inde loqui.'

De Albis Monachis

      'Si fuero Monachus Albus, generalia dura
      et pulmenta duo sed bene cocta dabunt.
      Hoc odiunt quod ego sine fine fideliter odi,
      scilicet ut prope se rusticus arua colat.
2115   Agrorum cupidi numquam metas sibi poni
      uicinis uellent, pestis iniqua, suis.

2105–6 *om.* δ **2105** quem] quoniam *H X* que *F Vd* quam *MuVcGoPm Ha* quid *fm fn* nec *U*; damno] damna *H GI ZQY fm fn* damnum *Vc* domino *Vd La* damnaque *U*; dedecorique] dedecorumque *H GI ZQY* dedecorque *MuGo* dedecoreque *VdBe TrLa fh fm fn* dedecoroque *Pk^{ac} Pm* decoroque *Pk^{pc}* dedecorisque *U*   **2106** multi] multis *B SMuVaVbVcVdTGoBePkPmNe TrHaLa fh fm fn* multas *H*; multa] mala *VdBe TrLa*; parit] perit *Be Z* poterit *Q*   **2107** quam] quem β *S Ha* qua *QY*; nebulam] nebula *H Pm fn*; contingit] contingat *MuVaVbVcVdTGoBePkPmNe TrLa*   **2108** *om. fh*; hanc] aut *SMuVaVbVdGoBePkPmNe TrHa fm fn*   **2109–10** *om.* δ *GI U*   **2109** quamque] quam *VdBe TrLa* quamquam *fm* omnia que *Z*; culpam] culpa *fh fm fn* cappa *T*; uindex] iudex *ZXY* iudicis *Q*   **2110** *after 2109, Z adds a new line (2109a):* inter eos nullus hanc iterabit item *ZQY; this line replaces 2110 in QY*   **2111** generalia] et generalia *Vb Ve*   **2112** et] in *S* hi α β δ *GI La UZXQY*   **2113** hoc] hac *Q* hanc *fm*; sine fine fideliter] fideliter sine fine *C fm* sine fide fideliter *D*   **2114** prope] propria *K* proprie *Va fn*; se] me β *X* sit *T om. VaGo fh fm fn*   **2115** poni] ponit *fm*

2105 *cellarum*: 'cella' = 'daughter house subordinate to house of religion' (*DMLBS* 4b), in this instance, subordinate to Cluny; see n. to lines 2077–110 above. *damno dedecorique*: Horace, *Saturae*, i. 2. 52–3.

2111–82 The origins of the Cistercian order date back to the very end of the 11th c., when a group of Benedictine monks left the Burgundian abbey of Molesmes and sought permission to establish a new community where they might 'adhere more strictly and perfectly to the Rule of the most blessed Benedict' (*Exordium parvum*, c. 2, ed. and trans. Waddell, *Narrative and Legislative Texts*, p. 419). This aspiration became, as Chrysogonus Waddell puts it, 'a *leit motiv* sustained throughout the whole of the *E[xordium] P[arvum]*' (ibid. c. 1 n. 3, p. 419), the account of the new foundation's beginnings, written by Stephen Harding, its second abbot. The new monastery was situated in an uninhabited region called Cîteaux, where hard manual labour was necessary to clear and cultivate the site. Hardship inspired admiration and emulation; the new order grew rapidly, its popularity bolstered by the membership of Bernard, abbot of Clairvaux, one of the most charismatic and influential figures of the 12th c. On this early history, see Bruun, ed., *Cistercian Order*, pp. 25–33, and Constance Berman's new interpretation, *The Cistercian Evolution*. By 1153 there were over 300 Cistercian houses (Knowles, *Monastic Order*, p. 218), many of them in England (ibid. pp. 246–52).

The Cistercian critique of Benedictine luxury understandably aroused defensive hostility in the older order, and gave rise to a voluminous polemical literature in the course of the 12th c. See Wilmart, 'Une riposte de l'ancien monachisme', and Leclercq, 'Nouvelle réponse', for bibliography on the Cluniac/Cistercian confrontation.

SPECVLVM STVLTORVM

[2105] brings many benefits. If any cloud happens to arise from the members, the head swallows it up in its nobility. And the fault that retributive judgement once punishes, it is not permitted to anyone to speak of further.' [2110]

About the White Monks

'If I become a White Monk, they will give me hard rations, with two dishes of beans and vegetables, but well cooked. They hate the thing that I have incessantly and unwaveringly hated—that is, that the peasant should cultivate the fields in their vicinity. Greedy for land, they are never willing, [2115] wicked pest, that their neighbours should set

---

2111–12 *generalia...pulmenta*: in line with their commitment to return to the simplicity of the original Rule of St Benedict, the Cistercians were served with two dishes of cooked food a day, and a third consisting of fresh fruit or young vegetables. One of the cooked dishes was usually of beans and the other of cooked vegetables, possibly flavoured with small quantities of eggs, cheese, or other foods. In the Benedictine Rule (c. 39), these two cooked dishes are called 'pulmentaria' (cf. *Instituta* XIX, ed. Waddell, *Narrative and Legislative Texts*, p. 464, and *Ecclesiastica Officia cisterciens*, ed. Choisselet and Vernet, p. 450 n. 171); they were also often known as 'generals' (*generalia*), since they were communal dishes of food served in quantities sufficient for all the monks. They were frequently accompanied by extra, more appetising, dishes known as pittances (*pietantie*), which would be served in amounts suitable for only one or two persons (Harvey, *Living and Dying*, pp. 10–12; ead., 'Monastic pittances', pp. 215–17). See also Niermeyer, s.v. 'generale'. John of Hauville praises the Cistercians for their simple food and abstinence from 'corrupting delicacies'; if a 'third dish' (i.e. a pittance) is served, it consists of cabbage boiled in water (*Architrenius*, ed. Wetherbee, ii. 380–90).

Since two *pulmentaria* are the norm specified by the Rule, it may seem odd that Nigel thinks it worthwhile to mention them as Cistercian practice, but it seems that Benedictine houses had become lax in this respect, and the Cistercians criticized them for this. Peter the Venerable defended the three or four *pulmentaria* served at Cluny, on the grounds that the Rule allowed for variations according to need (*Letters*, xxviii, ed. Constable, i. 67–8). Nevertheless, Gerald of Wales expressed indignant surprise at finding no fewer than 16 different dishes, containing fish 'roast and boiled, stuffed and fried', and eggs varied with 'flavourings and condiments', served up when he was a guest at the Trinity feast in Christ Church Canterbury in 1179 (*De rebus a se gestis*, ii. 5, *Opera*, i. 51–2; trans. Butler, *Autobiography*, pp. 71–2). Gerald repeats this account in his *Speculum ecclesiae*, dist. ii. 4 (*Opera*, iv. 40–2).

2113–16 Walter Map relates several anecdotes illustrating the fraudulent practices, including the shifting of boundary markers, by which the Cistercians allegedly expanded their land holdings (*De nugis curialium*, dist. i. 25, pp. 104–9). Gerald of Wales tells an anecdote about a boundary dispute between French Cistercians and 'a certain knight'; *Itinerarium Kambriae*, i. 12 (*Opera*, vi. 96; trans. Thorpe, pp. 153–4). Joseph Lynch paints a more sympathetic picture of the situation that might have led to this apparent land-grabbing: 'The basic idea of consolidating property for the sake of spiritual isolation and economic convenience was well known in the twelfth century. The ascetic, separatist orders of the time, like the Cistercians and the Carthusians, sought as a matter of policy to own entire blocks of land. They systematically removed all outsiders possessing rights and properties within the boundaries of their blocks. They did this primarily for the sake of separation from worldly affairs, but there were economic advantages as well, for such consolidated territories could be exploited effectively by *conversi* and granges. Furthermore, a religious house that had exclusive possession of a property stood less chance of being involved in litigation about that property' (Lynch, *Simoniacal Entry into Religious Life*, p. 17).

212 SPECVLVM STVLTORVM

Lac lanamque greges ouium pecorumque ministrant
    quod satis est, quamuis nil satis esse putent.
Paucis contenti non cessant quaerere magna,
2120   et cum possideant omnia semper egent.
Otia sectari non me patientur ibidem,
    sed bene me pascent in nouitate mea.
Omnibus iniungunt operas, ne desidiosus
    aut quandoque uacans inueniatur ibi.
2125 Sabbata rara colunt, male respondente coquina;
    est ibi uirga frequens atque diaeta grauis.
Non comedunt carnes, nisi cum permiserit abbas
    praepositusue loci de pietate sua.
Et quia quadrupedum prohibet sua regula carnes
2130   nec sinit his uesci pro grauitate sui,
quae uolat aut currit cupiunt carnem bipedalem,
    non quia sit melior sed quia rara magis.
Cum tamen illud agunt, testis uicinia fumi
    non erit aut facti conscia facta sui.
2135 Carnibus absumptis uestigia nulla uidebis,
    ne clament "her, her", ossa sepulta iacent.

2117 lac lanamque] *Mozley* lac lanam *Ne* his lac lana *K* lac et lana α β
SMuVaVbVcVdTGoBePkPm AJCWRHuMNOPDVe GI TrHaLa UZXQY fh fm fn; greges]
gregis *THa*; ministrant] ministrat α *BGoPmAJCWRHuMNKVeGIUQY* 2118 quod]
qui *VdBe* corr. *Be²*; satis¹] *om. L*; putent] putant α *VdGo TrHa UZX fm* putet *Ne* potest *D*
2119 magna] magis *MuVcGoPm* multa *Ve* 2121 otia] otio *Ve* ostia *L*; non me] me non
fh fm fn 2123 operas] opera *Vb Q*; desidiosus] desidiosos *Go* desidiosas *fm* insidiosus *fh*
2124 *om. Go*; quandoque] quicumque *fh fm fn*; uacans] uocans *Vd* uagans *ZQY* bachus *Va*;
inueniatur] inuenietur *fh fm fn* 2125 sabbata] sabbato *VdNe*; rara] raro
SMuVaVbVcVdTGoBePkPmNe RVe TrHaLa ZXQY fh fm fn; male] mala *fm fn* me *Z*
2126 uirga] uirgo *fm* nigra *QY* nuga *VdBe* nuga / uel iurga *La* 2127 *om. fh*
fm fn 2130 nec] non *Va* ne *Vc fm*; his] *om. fh*; pro] pre *SMuVaVbVcVdTBePkPmNe*
TrHaLa ZX fh fm fn p *Go*; sui] sua *F XQ* 2131–4 *om. fh* 2131 quae] quod *D*
aut *fm fn*; cupiunt carnem] capiunt carnem *F MuVaVbVdGoBePkPmNe HaLa fm fn* capiunt
carnes *T* querunt carnem *H* cupiunt *R* carnem cupiunt *UX* 2132 sit] sed *LE*; melior]
memor *fn* 2133 illud] id *HuMNP*ᵃᶜ; testis] tristis *HuMNK Tr*; uicinia fumi] uicina
fumi *VdPkPm La* uicinia sumi *Va HuMN* uicinia summi *Go* uicina futuri *H*ᵖᶜ uicina finiri *fm*
fn uicina sui *Vc* uicinia furni *Mu*ᵃᶜ*T* alias fumi *add. in margin Mu*ᵖᶜ 2134 facta] uera *F*
2135 carnibus] carnis *fn*; absumptis] assumptis *VdBePkPmNe Ve Ha U fh*; uidebis] relinqu-
unt β 2136 ne] nec *SMuVaVbVcVdGoBePkPmNe J TrHaLa Z fh fm fn* non *T*; cla-
ment] clamet *C* clamat *Vd* clamant *ST RO TrHaLa UZ*; her her] here here *U* herhe *Go* hyer
hyer *LE H* hier hier *B* heer her *F* heu heu *GI*; iacent] latent / uel uorant *Ha*

2117–18 *Lac lanamque*: for the emendation, see Introduction, p. lxxxi. All the monastic
orders practised sheep farming on a large scale, but the Cistercians were 'sheep farmers *par
excellence*...Their importance as sheep farmers is best demonstrated by the fact that in

SPECVLVM STVLTORVM · 213

boundaries for them. Their flocks of sheep and cattle provide plenty of milk and wool, although they don't think anything is plenty. Content with little, they never cease to strive for a lot, and although possessing all things, they are always needy. [2120] There, they will not allow me to indulge in leisure, but they will feed me well in my novitiate. They impose labour on everyone, lest anyone lazy, or occasionally idle, should be found there. They rarely celebrate the Sabbath, the kitchen not being up to it; [2125] the rod is frequent there and the diet harsh. They don't eat meat, except when the abbot and the prior of the house have allowed it as an act of mercy. And because their rule forbids the flesh of quadrupeds, and, in its severity, does not allow their consumption, [2130] they yearn for the flesh of bipeds, flying or running, not because it is better but because it is rarer. But when they do this, the neighbourhood will not be a witness of the smoke nor become aware of their deed. Once the meat has been consumed, you won't see any traces; [2135] the bones will be buried so that they don't cry "here, here!"

1193–4 when ransom had to be raised for Richard I the whole of the wool of the Cistercians and Praemonstratensians for that year was taken' (Power, *The Wool Trade*, p. 33; see also Knowles, *Monastic Order*, pp. 352–3, and Whitwell, 'English monasteries and the wool trade', pp. 1–7).

2120 This is a sardonic reversal of 2 Cor. 6: 10: 'tanquam nihil habentes, et omnia possidentes'.

2122 *nouitate*: 'nouitas' = 'novitiate' (*DMLBS* 5b). Like the *Rule of St Benedict* (c. 37), the Cistercian *Statutes* assume that the young need to eat three times a day, rather than twice, as the adult monks do; they therefore prohibit the admission of under-age youths to the order (*Statuta*, 1184. 2 and 1190. 30, ed. Waddell, *Statutes*, pp. 112–13, 202).

2125 *respondente*: 'respondere' = 'to be equal to, measure up to' (*DMLBS* s.v. 9).

2126 *uirga frequens*: minor faults were punished by a diet of bread and water; more serious transgressions were punished with flogging. See, for example, *Statuta* 1196. 24 and 1196. 26, ed. Waddell, *Statutes*, pp. 359–61.

2127–36 The Benedictine Rule (c. 39) had forbidden the consumption of the meat of quadrupeds, except by the sick. The Cistercians at first repeated this rule (*Statuta* 1158. 11, ed. Waddell, *Statutes* p. 70; *Instituta* XXIV, ed. Waddell, *Narrative and Legislative Texts*, p. 466), but later forbade meat-eating on Saturdays even for the sick (*Statuta* 1185. 3, ed. Waddell, *Statutes*, p. 121). In contrast, the Benedictines had given way to laxity on this point: 'it was an unusually strict house where meat in some form was not…consumed quite frequently' (Harvey, *Living and Dying*, p. 11). Rather than accusing the Cistercians of similar laxity, Nigel produces a comic justification by pretending that the Rule did not mean to exclude the meat of bipeds. Similarly, Walter Map, having stated that the Cistercians do not eat meat, goes on to undermine this claim by saying that in that case, it is not clear what becomes of the parts of their pigs that they do not sell, or what they do with their large flocks of fowls (*De nugis curialium*, dist. i. 24, pp. 76–7).

2136 The reference is to the murder of Edmund, a 9th-c. king of East Anglia, who was killed by a Viking army in 869, and whose severed head miraculously called out 'here, here!' to those who were looking for him. See Abbo of Fleury, *Life of St Edmund*, c. 12, in *Three Lives of English Saints*, ed. Winterbottom, p. 81.

SPECVLVM STVLTORVM

Tres etiam tunicas de iure duasque cucullas
omnes accipiunt et scapulare breue.
Taedia de nocte femoralia nulla iacenti
2140   in lecto facient; sit procul iste timor.
Nescia braccarum genitalia membra deorsum
nocte dieque simul libera semper erunt.
Ergo quid facerem, ueniens si uentus ab Austro
nudaret subito posteriora mea?
2145   Qua facie tantum quis sustinuisse pudorem
possit et ad claustrum postea ferre pedem?
Quod si contingat mea nuda pudenda uideri,
numquam de reliquo monachus albus ero.
Dispensare tamen mecum poterunt et oportet,
2150   ne pila quam porto sit manifesta foro.
Nonne pusillorum uitari scandala debent?

2137 cucullas] cuculla *Ve* cacullas *M* gugullas *VdPm Ha fm*   2138 scapulare] capu-
lare *SBePkPmNe*   2139 nocte] nocta *fm*   2140 facient] faciunt *MuVd U fh* faciant *T Z*; iste] ille *HuMNKVe ZQY*   2141 nescia] bestia *Vd* nescise *Tr* ueste *T* nescio
fh   2143 ueniens] *om. U, add. in margin for insertion after* uentus *U²*   2144 nudaret]
nil daret *M* nudaretur *fm*   2145–6 *om.* δ   2145 qua facie] de facili
SMuVaVbVcVdTGoBePkPmNe TrHaLa fh fm fn; tantum] tamen *E*   2146 possit]
posset *Vc Z*   2147 quod] quid *ZX* qui *Be corr. Be²*   2148 numquam de reliquo]
numquam post illud /uel numquam de reliquo *La*; numquam] numquid *AJCWOPVe GI
UZXQY*; de reliquo] de cetero β post illud *SMuVaVbVcGoBePkPmNe D TrHa fh fm fn* post
illud numquam *Vd* post *T*; monachus albus ero] albus ero monachus *D* monachus sic albus
ero *T*; *(whole line) om.* non albus monachus postea dictus (ductus *N*) ero *HuMNK*
2149 tamen] *om. MuGo Z*; poterunt] potuerunt *Ve* poterant *Go* poterint *fm fn* poterit *La fh*;
et oportet] tamen abbas et ordo *Mu* abbas et ordo *VaPm* et abbas et ordo *Ha* cum abbas et
ordo *Go* et ordo *Ne*; *(whole line)* dispensare possunt tamen abbas simul ordo *T*   2150 ne
pila quam porto] ne pisa quam porto *R* ne qua pila fero *SVaVbVcTGoBePkPm Ha fm fn* ne
qua pila sero *Vd* neque pila fero *MuNe* ne pila quam fore *Tr* ne contra pila fero *fh*; sit] sint
MuVaVbVcGoBePkPmNe TrHa^{ac} fh fm fn; *(whole line)* ne qua pila fero sint manifesta foro /uel
ne pila quam porto sit manifesta foro *La*   2151–2 *om. SMuVaVbVdTGoBePkPmNe
TrHaLa* δ *fh fm fn*   2151 nonne] pila β *GI ZXQY*; debent] debet *GI X* debunt *E*

2137–8 The Cistercian *Instituta* give only a very general directive that clothing should be
plain and ordinary (*Instituta* IV, ed. Waddell, *Narrative and Legislative Texts*, p. 459), echoing
the *Rule of St Benedict*, c. 55. The monks should have two robes or tunics, two cowls, and a
scapular for work. The cowl (*cuculla*) was originally a simple square hood, which later became
attached to a full-length cloak (also known as *cuculla*) worn over the tunic. The scapular was
a sleeveless length of cloth with a central opening for the head, which hung down at front and
back and protected the tunic during work (like an apron). See France, *The Cistercians in
Medieval Art*, pp. 72–3. 'Breue' suggests that the scapular reached only to the knees, not the
feet. The early Cistercians rejected the capacious cowls with wide sleeves (*frocci*), furs, linen
shirts, ample hoods with capes (*caputia*), and drawers, which were 'contrary to the Rule in all
its purity' (*Exordium parvum* 15, ed. Waddell, *Narrative and Legislative Texts*, p. 434). From

SPECVLVM STVLTORVM   215

Also, they are all entitled to three tunics, two cowls, and a short scapular. No underpants incommode them when they lie in bed at night; no fear of that. [2140] Down below, their genitals, innocent of underpants, will be constantly at liberty, night and day alike. So what should I do, if a wind blowing up from the south, were suddenly to expose my backside? What face could anyone put on so great a shame, [2145] and how could he go back to the cloister afterwards? So if it happens that my private parts were seen naked, I'll never be a White Monk in future. They can make a special dispensation in my case, and so they should, lest the pestle I carry about is revealed in public. [2150] Should not stumbling-blocks for little ones be avoided? So mine should be, for

the same motive, the Cistercians abandoned the black habits of the Benedictines, preferring garments of undyed wool, which was cheaper and could be woven from the fleece of their own sheep. In practice, this meant that the wool could have any one of a range of colours from white to creamy yellow, grey, or brown, according to the sheep's natural colour, but the contrast with the black Benedictine habit meant that the Cistercians were generally identified as 'White Monks' (France, *The Cistercians in Medieval Art*, pp. 78–82). Unlike Walter Map, who accuses the Cistercians of being provided with 'numbers of comfortable habits', of a quality suitable to be dyed a royal scarlet (*De nugis curialium*, dist. i. 25, pp. 84–5), Nigel merely increases the Rule's prescribed number of tunics from two to three, and says nothing about their luxurious quality.

2139–56 The Benedictine Rule states that breeches should be worn under the monastic habit only when travelling, but it seems that this restriction had fallen into disuse and most monks wore them at all times. In accordance with their strict obedience to the Rule, the Cistercians seem to have given up wearing breeches altogether, which 'proved an inexhaustible source of material for coarse pleasantry' (Knowles, *Monastic Order*, p. 678). Walter Map tells a comic story about a Cistercian who happened to fall over in the street as the king was riding by; the wind blew up the monk's habit and exposed his bare behind to the king's view (*De nugis curialium*, dist. i. 25, pp. 102–3). The custom is also mocked in the two verbal sparring matches between a Cistercian and a Benedictine in *Map Poems*, 'Dum Saturno conjuge', p. 241, lines 141–4, and 'Nuper ductu serio', p. 244, lines 52–3, 63–4, and in a satiric poem on the Cistercians, 'Sompno et silentio', ibid. pp. 56–7, lines 49–50 ('Carent femoralibus partes turpiores,/ Veneris ut usibus sint paratiores').

2149 *Dispensare*: 'to exempt' (Niermeyer 5); esp. eccl., 'to allow by special dispensation (with 'cum' in reference to person)' (*DMLBS* 3c).

2150 *pĭla*: with a short vowel, as here, means 'ball' in classical Latin, and this is how Langosch translates it here, without, however, explaining what he thinks it might mean. In her translation of *SS*, Albini points out the problematic vowel quantity, but comments, rightly, that the context shows that the word must be used in an obscene sense (i.e. 'penis'), and thinks it must therefore be identified with classical Latin 'pīla', 'pillar, column'. *DMLBS* records two other examples of 'pīla': as an alternative form of 'pīlum' 3 meaning 'pestle', and also of 'pīlum' 4 meaning (1) 'javelin', and (2) 'pointed stake, pile', which would fit the context equally well if not better. Since 'pīla' in any of these three senses is more likely to have been encountered in prose rather than verse, ignorance of the correct quantity is explicable.

2151 An allusion to Matt. 18: 6: 'Qui autem scandalizauerit unum de pusillis istis qui in me credunt, expedit ei ut suspendatur mola asinaria in collo eius, et demergatur in profundum maris.' The 'mola asinaria' is a millstone turned by an ass; Burnellus might therefore see it as an appropriate punishment for someone who *offends* an ass.

216   *SPECVLVM STVLTORVM*

Ergo meum certe, namque pusillus ego.

Membra pudenda magis, magis est texisse necesse,
     atque minus dignis maior habendus honos.

2155 Est in fratre suo sua uel texisse pudenda
     uel detexisse; qui tegit, ille sapit.

Tu tibi quod non uis fieri ne feceris ulli,
     quod cupis ut faciat quis tibi, fac et ei.

Frater ab effectu non solo nomine dici
2160 frater habet; sine re nomen inane tenet.

Sunt etiam multi quos falso nomine fratres
     dicimus, et scimus hostibus esse pares.

Fratribus in falsis quia multa pericula Paulus
     passus erat, scriptis inserit ista suis.

2165 Plurima falsorum sunt uera pericula fratrum,
     et uenit a falsis fratribus omne malum.

Quisque sibi caueat a fratre suo, nec in illo
     ponere praesumat spemue fidemue sibi.

Rara fides fratrum, quia, cum sit quisque fidelis,
2170 se probat infidum, dum caret ipse fide.

Frater carnalis nec non et spiritualis
     fallitur, et fratrem fallit uterque suum.

Si tibi contingat fratrem reperire fidelem,
     sit tibi pars animae dimidiumque tuae.

2175 Nam tot sunt falsi, tot ficti, totque ferales,

2152 meum] uicum *GI Y* uitam *Q*; ego] ero *XY*   **2153** magis²] agis *fn* maius α simul *Be om. Vd I corr. I²*; est] *om. LE S Tr*   **2154–5** *om. U, add. in lower margin U²* **2154** dignis] dignus *Go U²*; maior] maius *Pm* minor *fm*; honos] hones *F* onus *QY* **2155–6** *om. Vc*   **2155** in fratre] inferre *SPk fh fm fn*   **2156** qui] quem *GI* que *U* **2159** frater] affer *fm fn*; non] nec *fh*; solo] solum *SMuVaVbVcVdTGoBePkPmNe TrHaLa Q fh fm fn*   **2160** frater habet] debet nam *SMuVaVbVcVdTGoBePkPmNe TrHaLa fh fm fn*   **2161** sunt] sint *E*; etiam] etenim *fm* et *fn*   **2163** *om. Z*   **2164** scriptis] scriptus *E*; inserit] inseruit *Pk* inserat *F Q* narrat ut *MuVaTGoPmNe Ha* prohibet *VbVc* notuit *fh fm fn* indicat *VdBe TrLa*; ista] ille *D* ipse *VaT* ipsa *Q* ita *S*; *after 2164, Z adds new 2164a*: scriptis narrat ut ista suis   **2165** uera] uere *O Tr* magna *B* nam *Va* **2167** quisque] quisquis *Go Y*; nec in illo] nec in ille *Go* neque ille *H* nec in ullo *U* nec illo *fh*; nec] non α   **2168** spemue fidemue] spemque fidemque δ *GI Tr UQY* spemue fidemque *T* spem uel fidemue *S*   **2170** infidum] infidis *S* insidiis *MuVaGoPm* infidus *Pk fm fn* mundus *Ne*; dum] cum *Ve Z*; fide] fidem *fh*   **2171** et] *om. TPk*   **2172** fratrem fallit] fallit frater *SMuVaVbVcVdTGoBePkPm TrHaLa fh fm fn* fallunt frater *Ne*; uterque] utrumque *VdBe TrLa*ᵃᶜ   **2173** *after 2172, 2095–6 repeated D*   **2174** sit] si *VdBeNe* hic *Va*; tuae] tui *ACᵖᶜWHuMNK* tui *add. interlinear La*ᵖᶜ sue *Pk* mee *D*ᵖᶜ **2175** falsi] ficti *Vc* δ *GI UQY* filii *Go*; tot ficti] *om. fh*; ficti] fures *Ve* furti *ACWHuMNOPDK GI UQY* futuri *J* uicti *La Z* falsi *Vc R*

SPECVLVM STVLTORVM   217

I am little. The more shameful members are, the more necessary it is to cover them, and more reverence is due to the less worthy. It's for one's brother to cover up or to reveal one's shameful secrets; [2155] the one who covers them up is wise. You shouldn't do to anyone what you don't want to be done to yourself; what you want anyone to do to you, you should do to him. A brother gets to be called brother from the deed, not from the name alone; without the substance, he has an empty name. [2160] There are also many whom we call brothers by a false name, knowing them to be equivalent to enemies. Because Paul had endured many perils from false brethren, he put this in his writings. There are many true perils from false brethren, [2165] and every evil comes from false brethren. Let everyone beware of his brother, and not presume to place any hope or trust in him. Faith among brethren is rare, for even though anyone is faithful, he shows himself untrustworthy when he himself lacks trust. [2170] A brother in the flesh is deceived, and a brother in the spirit likewise, and each deceives his brother. If it should befall you to find a faithful brother, let him be part of your soul and half of it. For so many are deceitful, so many false, so many wild beasts, [2175] that the world cannot count them. They are

2155–6 This seems to be a comic echo of the injunction in the *Disticha Catonis*, iii. 3. 2: 'quantumcumque potes, celato crimen amici', with the 'pudenda' taken in a bodily sense.

2157–8 Tobias 4: 16; Matt. 7: 12; Luke 6: 31. Quoted in the *Rule of St Benedict*, c. 4, and the Cistercian *Instituta*, XI, ed. Waddell, *Narrative and Legislative Texts*, p. 461. Walter Map pointedly claims that the Cistercians care nothing for the precept 'do not do to others what you do not wish to be done to you' (*De nugis curialium*, dist. i. 25, pp. 86–7).

2160 *sine re nomen*: see nn. to lines 153 and 1700 above.

2163 For St Paul's warning against 'false brethren', see 2 Cor. 11: 26. In dwelling on Cistercian treachery, Nigel is obviously targetting Archbishop Baldwin (see Introduction, pp. xliv, xlix).

2174 *pars animae dimidiumque tuae*: see Introduction, pp. xliii–xliv, n. 79.

2175 For αβγ's 'falsi…ficti', δ has 'ficti…furti'. It is not clear why Mozley chose to reject αβγ's perfectly acceptable readings, especially since the choice required him to replace δ's 'furti' (referring to deeds) with conjectural 'fures' (referring to persons). His *apparatus criticus* attributes the conjectural 'fures' to Skutsch, but does not record its appearance in *Ve*, and there is no mention of this line in Skutsch's 'Three rare words' (nor in Sedgwick's 'Textual criticism'). *ferales*: 'savage (of wild beasts)' (Niermeyer).

218

SPECVLVM STVLTORVM

quod iam mundus eos dinumerare nequit.
Qui sunt in claustro tamquam Sathan in Paradiso,
in quo constat eum iuris habere nihil.
Talia me terrent, dum religionis ad arcem
2180 tendo, nec attendo quoue uel unde ruo.
Forsitan et uanus timor est, uanoque moueri
multotiens hominum corda timore solent.'

De ordine Grandimontis

'Grandimontanam uitam cum ueste professus
si fuero, uereor asperiora pati.
2185 Hi cum nil habeant nec se patiantur habere,
ex nihilo semper sufficienter habent.
Abdita claustra colunt et nulla silentia seruant,
nescit signa manus, libera lingua manet.
Non fundos nec agros nec pascua lata requirunt,
2190 nec facit ad saccos annua lana decem;

2176 quod] quot *fh*; eos] uix eos *fm*; dinumerare nequit] uix numerare potest β *VcTr X* uix numerare nequit *S Va Vd Go Be Pk Ne Ha* uix numerare queat *Mu Vb T Pm fh fn* dinumerasse nequit *F* numerare queat *fm* **2178** *om. D add. in margin D^pc*; eum] eis β **2179** terrent] torrent *fm*; dum] de *Pk Ne fh fm fn*; ad arcem] arce *fn* ad artem *S T Go Be Pk Pm JD Tr* inarme *fh* **2180** ruo] ruam *Vc* tuo *fh fm fn om. Pk Ne* **2181** uanus timor] timor uanus *Mu Va Go Ha* bonus timor *Tr*; uanoque] uaneque *Va* fauoque *Mu* nouoque *S Tr* **2182** hominum corda] hominem corda *JVe GI* corda hominum *Va*; timore] timere *F S Mu Va Vd T Go Pk Pm Ne AJCWRMNPDKVe Ha U fh fm fn* **2183** ueste] forte *H X* festo *Vc* **2185** patiantur] patientur *Mu Ha Y* **2188** signa] siqua *fn*; lingua] ligna *F fn*; manet] manus *Vb Vc* **2189** nec²] non *LE H S Vb Vc Vd Be Pk Ne D Tr Ha La om. M*; lata] luta *Vc* loca *QY* **2190** facit ad] faceret *S Va Vb Vc Vd T Go Be Pk Pm Ne Ha La fh fm fn* faciunt *Mu*; saccos] saccas *LE*; annua] omnia *Go* anima *Tr QY^ac*

2179–80 *religionis ad arcem/ tendo*: the 'peak' of religion is the archbishopric of Canterbury. Nigel (in the person of Burnellus) is afraid that his harsh attack on 'false brethren' will gain him enmity in high places.

2183–226 The Grandmontines originated in the late 11th c. as a group of hermits based at Muret in the Limousin, attracted by the charismatic figure of Stephen of Muret (d. 1124). In the mid-12th c., the community was obliged by loss of their land to move to Grandmont, north of Limoges (Hutchison, *Hermit Monks of Grandmont*, pp. 27–65;). The new order grew rapidly, and by 1189, when Stephen was canonized, it numbered approximately 150 dependencies (ibid. pp. 98–9; see also Graham and Clapham, 'The Order of Grandmont and its houses in England', pp. 159–71). The order was patronized by both the French king, Philip Augustus, and King Henry II of England (Hutchison, *Hermit Monks of Grandmont*, pp. 57–63). The first Grandmontine house in England (in Eskdale, North Yorkshire) was not founded until *c.*1200, and there were never more than three, but the Limousin was part of Aquitaine, which had passed into English possession with Henry's marriage to Eleanor of Aquitaine in 1154 (Graham and Clapham, 'The Order of Grandmont and its houses in England', pp. 169–80). Walter Map comments on Henry's generosity to the order (*De nugis curialium*, dist. i. 26, pp. 114–15), which the king held in such esteem that in 1170, when he was seriously ill, he gave orders that he should be buried at Grandmont; on this occasion he

SPECVLVM STVLTORVM 219

present in the cloister like Satan in Paradise, in which he clearly had no right. Such things frighten me, while I aim at the height of religious life, and I pay no attention to where I'm rushing or whence. [2180] And perhaps this fear is vain; the hearts of men are often troubled by vain fear.'

About the Grandmontine Order

'If I were to adopt the life and habit of a Grandmontine, I fear that I shall suffer hardships. They, since they have nothing and do not allow themselves to have anything, [2185] are always satisfied with nothing. They inhabit secluded monasteries, and do not observe silence; their hands know no signs, their tongue is unrestrained. They do not desire farms or fields or broad meadows, nor does their annual wool amount to ten sacks. [2190] They have not learned to grade their wool by a

recovered, but when he drew up his will in 1182 he left the order 3,000 silver marks, equivalent to £2,000 (Gerald of Wales, *De principis instructione*, dist. ii. 17, ed. Bartlett, pp. 504–5; Warren, *Henry II*, pp. 148, 212). For further details on the relations between the Angevin kings and the Grandmontines, see Hallam, 'Henry II, Richard I and the Order of Grandmont'.

2184–7 True to their eremitical ideal, the Grandmontines sought out remote and harsh locations ('abdita claustra'), and lived a life of extreme austerity (hence 'uereor asperiora pati'). Around 1184, the site of Grandmont was described by the seventh prior Gerard Itier as 'stern and cold, infertile and rocky, misty and exposed to the winds... The land around the monastery scarcely ever suffices to provide necessities, for the soil is so infertile, sterile and barren... those who dwell there lead a hard life' (*Explanatio super Librum Sententiarum beati Stephani*, ed. Becquet, CCCM viii, p. 431, lines 171–87; trans. Hutchison, *Hermit Monks of Grandmont*, pp. 52–3).

2187 *Abdita claustra*: Sextus Amarcius, *Satires*, i. 134. *nulla silentia seruant*: Nigel seems to have been misinformed on this point. The Grandmontine Rule, which was given papal approval in 1156, in fact ordered continual silence to be observed in the church, in the cloister, in the refectory, and in the dormitory, and in addition from compline until the end of morning chapter. At other times and places, speech should be restricted to essentials only (*Regula Stephani Muretensis*, c. 47, ed. Becquet, CCCM viii). Meyer ('De scismate Grandimontanorum', p. 54 n. 2) suggested that Nigel's 'nulla' should be emended to 'multa' or 'muta' (as at Ovid, *Metamorphoses*, vii. 184), but line 2188 ('libera lingua manet') makes it clear that 'nulla' is what Nigel meant (and this is confirmed by line 2429, where the ass says that the Grandimontines 'speak everywhere'). As Meyer notes, the text of *SS* used by Guiot de Provins already had the reading 'nulla' (*Bible*, ed. Orr, 1517: 'il ne tiennent pas silence').

2188 *nescit signa manus*: during the hours of compulsory silence, medieval monks communicated with each other when necessary by using an established system of signs made with their hands. See Sherlock, *Monastic Sign Language*; Jarecki, *Signa loquendi*; Bruce, *Silence and Sign Language*; Barakat, *The Cistercian Sign Language*.

2189–96 The Grandmontine Rule (*Regula Stephani Muretensis*, ed. Becquet, CCCM viii) strictly prohibited the possession of lands (c. iv), churches and their perquisites (c. v), cattle or other animals (cc. vi, vii), tithes (c. xxxii), revenues (c. xxiii), and dealings in markets (c. xv), in order to ensure as complete a separation from worldly affairs as possible (see also the summary of these prohibitions in c. lxiv). The monks were also forbidden to engage in lawsuits (c. xxxi), ironically in view of their later history (see n. to lines 2211–20 below). Fairly soon, however, these impossibly strict regulations were relaxed (Hutchison, *Hermit Monks of Grandmont*, pp. 105–6).

2190 *facit ad*: 'facere ad' = 'to amount to, reach (a specified amount)' (*OLD* 8).

SPECVLVM STVLTORVM

uellera nec triplici positu distinguere norunt,
idem saccus habet pectora, colla, latus.
Non macerant nudas sicco cum subere pelles,
nec faciunt pingues in nemus ire sues.
2195 Non mare conscendunt ratibus quo retia laxent
piscibus, aut hamis insidiantur eis.
Qualia uel quando comedunt, si lauta diaeta
uel tenuis sit eis, non mihi scire licet.
Si pluit e coelo semper quod habent quasi manna,
2200 quid plus praestaret area lata sibi?

2191 nec] sed *CW X* non *H D*; positu] potu *CW* posita *SMuVaVbVcVdTGoBePkPmNe Ve TrHaLa fh fm fn* posit *R*; *(whole line)* non in tres partes distinguere uellera norunt *K* **2192** saccus habet] saccos habent *Go* saccos habet *fh* **2193** non] nec *LE*; nudas] nudis *JCWHuMNK* nudos *Y* nodos *O* idas *LE* udas *F* uda β udos *La*ᵃᶜ *SMuVbVcVdGoBePkPmNe HaLa*ᵖᶜ *fm fn* unda *T* undas *Va*; sicco cum subere] siccas cum subere *T* sicco cum subare *Ha* sicca cum subere *Vd* sicco cum fallere *Tr* ficto cum subere *LE B SVaVbPm ZQY* ficta cum subere *H* fuco cum subere *F* assumpto uellere δ *GI UX* **2194** in nemus] inuenimus *VdGo*; ire] ite *Be Tr* terre *Ne*; sues] suos *S D* senes *Vd* **2195** mare] mane *MNO*; conscendunt] concendunt *JD Y* contendunt *Ve Q*; ratibus] retibus *SMuGo RO*ᵃᶜ*Ve La*; quo] que α *T* quos *S* quoque *H* ut *D*; laxent] laxant *F STGo AJCWRHuMNP GI TrHa Z fm fn* laxarit *Ve* **2196** hamis] alias *SMuVaVbVcVdT GoBePkPmNe Ha* alias / uel hamis *La* aluis *fm* auis *fn* auibus *fh*; insidiantur *Vc ACWHuMNPKVe GI* insideantur *H* **2197** uel] ut *fn* om. *Pk*; quando] quanta *La*ᵖᶜ quantum β *XQ*; si lauta] se lata [*uel*] si lauta *La*; lauta] lenta *S* lata *MuVaVbVdTGoBePkPmNe TrHa Z fh fm fn* **2198** tenuis] tinus / uel ?comire *Ha*; sit eis] fit eis *VaVbVdBePkPmNe TrHaLa* om. *S*; licet] licuet /[*uel*] liquet *La* **2199** si] ni *VdBe La*; e coelo] ei cele *Go* a celo *T Tr* e sero *D*; semper quod habent] desuper quod habent *D Tr* quod habent semper *P*ᵖᶜ quod semper habent *Z* semper habent *Mu* **2200** om. *Z*; quid] quis *H fh fm fn* qui *S* quod *GI*; praestaret] prestarent *VaPk*; area] aera *fh fm* arra *fn* area grata *J*; sibi] breui α *AJCWHuNOPDKVe GI UXQY* breuis *R* boni *SMuVaVbVcVdTGoBePkPmNe TrHaLa fh fm fn* broui *M*

2191–2 *triplici positu*: that is, by separating it into three parts. The contrast is with the Cistercian practice of dividing the wool from their sheep into three separate parts, graded by quality, and priced differentially. Other monastic orders, especially the Premonstratensians and the Gilbertines, also engaged in sheep farming, but did not practise the threefold grading of the wool; see Knowles, *Religious Orders*, i. 66–7.

2193 *sicco cum subere*: the αβγ variants support this reading, even when the scribes clearly do not understand and garble it; δ's 'assumpto uellere' is a reversion to an easier reading. Cork-oak ('suber') played (and plays) an important role in the process of tanning hides. Mike Watt, of the leather-working firm Rural Kind (Carmarthenshire), kindly supplied me with the following information (personal communication, 2.9.2017): 'Oak bark and other tree barks have certainly been used in the process of tanning leather for centuries. Barks are high in tannins—which when soaked in a pit with animal skins, permanently alter the protein

SPECVLVM STVLTORVM 221

threefold discrimination; the same sack holds belly, neck, and sides. They don't soak the stripped hides with dried cork-oak bark, nor do they drive fat pigs into the woods. They don't put out to sea in boats from which they cast nets for fish, [2195] or ensnare them with hooks. What or when they eat, whether their diet is luxurious or sparse, I am not allowed to know. If what they have rains down continually from heaven, like manna, what more use would a wide threshing-floor be to them? [2200] If they live like men and not like angels, why are they thus

structure of the hide, making it more durable and less susceptible to decomposition, creating what we recognise as leather. The inner bark of cork oak (quercus suber) is high in tannins. With regard to the reference to "dry" oak bark; the tannins in bark are water soluble, which is why the hides and bark are steeped in a pit of water for the tannins to be released. However this also means that for bark to retain its tannins it needs to be kept *dry*, otherwise the tannins leach out of the bark and essentially create an ineffective mulch (if you imagine the dry bark as the equivalent of a dry tea bag!). Prior to the tanning process, the bark is also ground up into fine bark chips, and this can only really be done when the bark is dry. So "they macerate (soak) the skins/hides with dry oak[bark]" makes complete sense. With regard to "nudas" (naked) hides, as against "udas" (wet) hides. I would suggest that "nudas" is probably correct and I think this refers to the fact that the hides are stripped of hair prior to the tanning process. Prior to tanning, the hides are "fleshed"—removing the flesh from the inside of the skin, and then soaked in a lime solution to remove the hair/wool. Once this is done the resulting hides are pale, almost translucent-looking, skins and they are naked. "Wet" hides only make sense if it is related to the soaking process, but this is already covered by "macerant", so I think nudas/naked seems perfect.'

For an instructive video of the entire tanning process, as practised in the last remaining oak-bark tannery in the UK, see http://www.jfjbaker.co.uk/the-process/.

2198 *non mihi scire licet*: cf. Ovid, *Heroides*, i. 57–8.

222   SPECVLVM STVLTORVM

Si uiuunt ut homo nec sunt uelut angelus ipsi,
    a studiis hominum cur prohibentur ita?
Et si sunt homines mortales conditione,
    cur non humana uiuere lege licet?
2205   Quod fit in occulto raro sine suspicione
    esse potest homini, sit licet absque nota.
Si satagunt corpus carnemque domare rebellem,
    commodius facerent et meliore modo.
Non reprehendo tamen super his nec iudico quemquam,
2210   seruus enim domino statque caditque suo.

2201 nec] ne *GI*; sunt] sut *J*; uelut] sicut *O* ut *Vc UQ fh*; ipsi] ipse *R* christi *Va* ipso *fh om.*
Ne   2202 prohibentur] prohibetur *LE* prohibenter *B*   2203 sunt] sint *OPVe U*
2204 licet] licent *Go* decet *T Z*   2205 fit] sit *GoBe J* sic *S*   2206 *om. fm*; hom-
ini] hominum *E* β *SMuVaVbVcVdTGoBePkPmNe TrHaLa ZXQY fh*; sit licet] scilicet *VaVb*
ZQ fn sed nec *Vc* sic licet *Be X* nec licet δ *GI Tr U* si licet *SMuVdGoPkPmNe Ha* nec si licet
La sciet esse *Y* sit *fh*   2207 satagunt] satagant *VbVcT R U*; carnemque] carnem *Go D*
2208 meliore] meliori *F TGo CWDVe* meliora *TrHa Z* moliori *Q*   2209 reprehendo]
reprehenso *fn*; his] hoc *SMuVaVbVcVdTGoBePkPmNe TrHa fh fm fn* hic *La om.* Hu*MN*;
nec] non *Ne fm*; iudico] iudice *fn*; quemquam] quicquam *MuPm*   2210 domino] dominus *GI*; statque caditque] stat caditque *Vc Ha* statque cadit *Vd* stat cadit atque *D X* statque
raditque *Go*

2201–4 *angelus*: the Grandmontine Rule enjoins the brethren to remember that they have
left behind all servants, as part of their worldly affairs, and they must therefore treat each
other with fraternal meekness, as if ministering to angels; 'credibile est enim eos sine dubio,
si in hac perseuerauerint, fore saluandos, sicque pares angelis futuros. Porro si cuilibet absurdum et inconueniens uideatur dici tamquam angelis, cum homines sint, et utique peccatores,
dicatur expressius, non solum tamquam angelis, sed etiam quasi Deo...' ('for it can be
believed without doubt that if they persevere in this, they will be saved, and so will be equal
to the angels. Furthermore, if it seems to anyone absurd and inappropriate that it should be
said "as the angels", let it be said more clearly, "not only as the angels, but also as God"'
(*Regula Stephani Muretensis*, c. lix, ed. Becquet, CCCM viii, p. 96). Nigel may be referring to
this section of the Rule; however, it is also quite likely that he had in mind a story told in the
Lives of the desert fathers (*Vitas patrum*, v. 27, PL lxxiii. 916D–917A) about a monk called
Iohannes who expressed the wish to be 'securus sicut angeli sunt securi nihil operantes, sed
sine intermissione servientes Deum' ('carefree as the angels are carefree, not working but
serving God without intermission'). To fulfil this aim, he took off his clothes and went out
into the desert ('in eremo'). After a week of starvation he returned and sought entry; asked
who he was, he replied 'I am Iohannes' but was met with the answer 'Iohannes has become an
angel and is no longer among men'. Iohannes persisted and finally was told 'If you are a man,
you must work again in order to live. If however you are an angel, why do you wish to enter
the [monastic] cell?' Humbled, Iohannes asked pardon for his sin. Since the Benedictine
Rule recommends that the *Vitas patrum* should be read after meals in the monastic refectory
(cc. 42, 73), it is entirely likely that Nigel knew this story. It was also turned into a rhythmic
verse (Inc. 'In gestis [or 'uitis'] patrum ueterum') whose popularity is attested by its survival
in eleven manuscripts, including Cambridge, University Library, Gg.5.35, the famous
Carmina Cantabrigiensia (ed. Strecker, no. 42), copied in the mid-11th c. at Saint Augustine's
Abbey, Canterbury (ed. Ziolkowski, pp. xxvi–xxviii). Interestingly, in the last line of the
poem, Iohannes promises that since he could not be an angel, he has learned to be a good man

SPECVLVM STVLTORVM 223

restrained from human pursuits? And if they are mortal men in condition, why is it not permissible to live by human law? What is done in secret rarely escapes human suspicion, [2205] even if it is blameless. If they try to tame the body and the unruly flesh, they should do it more pleasantly and in a better way. But I don't criticize or judge anyone on this; for a servant stands and falls with his master. [2210] They trouble the public law courts with quarrels and various lawsuits, and a simple

('uir bonus'), and from an early date the Grandmontines were familiarly known as 'Bonshommes' (Hutchison, *Hermit Monks of Grandmont*, p. 45). The poem pre-dates the foundation of the Grandmontine order, so that no direct reference can be intended, but a later reader might well have interpreted the phrase that way, and seen the poem as a comic deflation of the exaggerated eremitical pretensions of the order.

2206 *nota*: 'reproach, disgrace' (Lewis and Short B.2.b; *OLD* 4c).

2208 *commodius*: 'commode' = 'agreeably, comfortably, pleasantly' (*OLD* 5–6).

2209–10 Rom. 14: 4: 'Tu quis es, qui iudicas alienum servum? Domino suo stat, aut cadit.' Cf. *Tractatus*, ed. Boutemy, p. 153: 'Nolo...servum alienum judicare, suo enim domino stet aut cadit.'

224   SPECVLVM STVLTORVM

Litibus et causis uariis fora publica uexant,
et teritur longo tempore causa breuis.
Sumptibus insistunt, nil proprietatis habentes,
fitque trilustralis causa sepulta diu.
2215 In duo diuisi multumque diuque laborant,
atque superuacuis sumptibus usque uacant.
Nam uice conuersa laico dictante, sacerdos
exhibet officii iura sacrata sui.
Motus ob hanc causam Mons est Romamque profectus,
2220 sed nec ibi meruit sumere causa modum.
Plurima fuderunt, sed Mons est pinguis et uber,
qui de lacte suo cuncta ministrat eis.
Et quem nullus arat, serit, aut metit, ordine miro
pullulat ad uotum quicquid habere uolunt.

2211–12 *om. QY*; *transp. after 2214 Z*   2211 causis] canis *Go fn*   2212 teritur] trahitur *α* fertur *Go*   2213 *om. Vc*   2214 fitque trilustralis] fit quoque claustralis *α* fitque claustralis *H* fitque trislustralis *S* fitque ter lustralis *Mu* eritque claustralis *Go* fitque claustralis *T* fit trilustralis *La* fitque relustralis *fh*   2215–24 *om. QY*
2215 diuisi] diuisum *fn*   2216 superuacuis] superuacui *Va* seruatui *fh fm fn*; usque] usa *AꝰCWOPDVe GI U*   2217 uice] uita *fm*; conuersa] conuerso *Be La* uersa *Z fh* conuersi *fm*   2218 iura] uota *δ GI Uᵃᶜ* uita *β Tr U²*   2219 Mons] mox *SMuVaVbVcVdTGoBePkPmNe R HaLa Z fh fm fn* motus *H* mens *DVe*; profectus] perfectus *F* prospectus *HuMN* prouectus *D* professus *S*   2220 nec ibi] ibi nec *fh*; causa] citra *fh fm fn*; modum] finem *VdBe Tr* finem / uel modum *La*   2222 qui] sed *HuMN* si *DK*; suo] sua *Va* modo *VdBe*; cuncta] emicta *T om. Vd*; ministrat] miserat *Go*   2224 uotum] forum *Mu* notum *VaTr*

2211–20 The Grandmontines were divided into two bodies ('In duo diuisi'), choir monks, who were educated and were responsible for religious worship, and lay brothers (*conversi*), who performed the practical and administrative tasks necessary for the daily running of the community, and also handled all transactions with the outside world. In the use of lay brothers, they resembled the Cistercians and Carthusians, but whereas in the latter orders the *conversi* resided in separate buildings and played a subordinate role in the community, the Grandmontine *conversi* shared the same living quarters, ate in the same refectory, slept in the same dormitory, attended the conventual chapter, and even had an equal share in electing the prior (*Regula Stephani Muretensis*, c. lx, ed. Becquet, CCCM viii, pp. 96–7). Furthermore, in the day-to-day affairs which were their responsibility, they enjoyed complete autonomy and took orders from nobody (*Regula*, c. liv, ed. Becquet, CCCM viii, pp. 92–3; Hutchison, *Hermit Monks of Grandmont*, pp. 68–74, 95, 110). These arrangements were meant to ensure that the *clerici* were totally insulated from worldly concerns (*Regula*, c. liv, ed. Becquet, CCCM viii, p. 92), but eventually they led to great dissension between the two bodies. The uneducated *conversi* dominated and even bullied the educated *clerici*, obliging them, for example, to hold church services at times that fitted in with their manual work. If the *clerici* protested, the lay brothers retaliated by withholding the food and clothing that according to the Rule only they were entitled to dispense (*Regula*, c. lv, ed. Becquet, CCCM viii, p. 93). In 1185, the *conversi* rebelled against prior William, barricaded him in his room, and elected

SPECVLVM STVLTORVM 225

case is dragged out at length. Having no property, they yet run up expenses, and a long-buried case turns into a marathon. Divided into two, they work hard and long, [2215] and continually put themselves to unnecessary expenses. For in a reversal of order the lay-brother rules, while the cleric performs the sacred duties of his office. Disturbed on this account, Grandmont went to Rome, but there too the lawsuit had no end. [2220] Their outlay was large, but the Mount is fat and rich, providing them with all things from its milk, and although no one ploughs it, sows it, or reaps it, it miraculously brings forth at

their own prior, Stephen. The quarrel was referred to the papal curia, and in 1186, Pope Urban III issued the first of a series of papal bulls which attempted to settle the dispute and establish the overall authority of the *clerici* and the prior. These attempts were unsuccessful, as were later interventions by Urban and his successors. In 1187, King Philip Augustus entered the fray by convoking an assembly, which produced a proposal of 18 regulations clarifying the distribution of authority in the convent. In 1188, Pope Clement III responded to this regal initiative by ordering the election of a new prior, and endorsing Urban's revised version of the Rule. An uneasy peace was thus reached, but the problems continued and the dispute rumbled on until well into the 13th c. For a detailed account of the dispute, with analysis of contemporary documents, see Wilhelm Meyer, 'De scismate Grandimontanorum'; see also Hutchison, *Hermit Monks of Grandmont*, pp. 67–91. Meyer also prints four contemporary Latin poems which (predictably) take the part of the *clerici* and bewail their ill-treatment.

As noted above, there were no Grandmontine houses in England before 1200, but the Continental members of the order were divided into two groups, one known as *fratres Gallici* (who favoured the *clerici*, and were supported by Philip Augustus), and the other known as *fratres Anglici* (who favoured the lay-brothers, and were supported by Henry II of England). Both groups were French, but the latter group was based in Aquitaine, an English possession. (Meyer, 'De scismate Grandimontanorum', pp. 73–5; Hutchison, *Hermit Monks of Grandmont*, p. 62). Nigel doubtless obtained his information on the order and the dispute from the entourage of Henry II.

2211 *fora*: 'forum' = 'law-court' (*OLD* 6).

2214 *trilustralis*: literally '15 years long'.

2221–4 Paradoxically, the Grandmontines' eagerness to renounce worldly possessions and live a life of extreme austerity incited admirers to shower them with donations, which were accepted (Meyer, 'De scismate Grandimontanorum', pp. 58–9). The new acquisitions were handled by the lay-brothers and thus expanded their power.

226   *SPECVLVM STVLTORVM*

2225   Ergo quid est quod homo qui uiuit ut angelus intus
        pulsatur totiens exteriore foro?'

De ordine Carthusiae

        'Quid si Carthusiam me conuertendo reuertar?
        Pellibus et tunicis pluribus utar ibi.
        Cella mihi dabitur quam solam solus habebo,
2230   nemo mihi socius, nemo minister erit.
        Solus enim psallam, solusque cibaria sumam,
            Et sine luce meum solus adibo torum.
        Semper solus ero cella retinente trimembri,
            in qua continuo pes meus alter erit.
2235   Semper erunt praesto, pulmento conficiendo,
            in cella propria ligna, legumen, aqua.
        Visere me ueniet prior ordinis, atque frequenter
            panis erit calidi portio magna mihi.
        His ouium, pecorum, nemoris terraeque feracis,

2225–6 *om. Z*   **2225** est quod] est *A Ve GI UQY* est quid *F* extat *R*; qui uiuit] uiuit
quod *X* uiuit *fm*; ut] uelut *A*ᵃᶜ? *GI Y* et *H*   **2226** pulsatur] pulsatus *W* pulsetur
SMuVaVbVcVdTGoBePkPmNe TrHaLa fh fm fn; exteriore] exteriora *Vd D* exteriori
MuVaVbVcPm; foro] suo *CWHuMN GI* sequi *D*   **2227** quid] qui
MuVaVbVcVdBePkNe Ha Z fh fm fn < >ui *Pm La* < >um *T*; Carthusiam me] cartusia me *C*
charusiam me *R* cartusum me *T* me carthusiam *fm*; conuertendo] conuertendo /uel comit-
tendo *Ha*; reuertar] reuerter *K Q*   **2228** ibi] ubi *fh*   **2232** adibo] adhibo *SVaPm Q*
2233–6 *om. QY*   **2233–4** *transp. C*   **2233** solus ero] solus erit *D* ero solus
SMuVaVbVcVdTGoBePkPmNe TrHaLa Z fh fm fn; retinente] retinenti *MuGo*; trimembri]
trimembra *P* termembri *fm* membri *Go*   **2234** continuo] continue δ continua
fm   **2235** erunt] erint *A U* erit *LE* β ero *F GI*; praesto] presta *fh*; pulmento] pulmentum *D Z* pulmenta *F T KVe fm fn*   **2236** cella propria] propria cella α *fh fm*
fn   **2237–8** *transp. after 2250 Z*   **2237** ueniet] uenit *Mu* ueniat *Vd* uenient *T*
sepe *add. in margin U*²; frequenter] minister *LE* sequester *T* frequens *Z*   **2239–40** *om.*
QY   **2239** his] hii *Va M*; nemoris] nemorum *H RO Z* ne moris *M* memoris *E VdGoPm*;
feracis] ferarum *R fh fm fn* fe *Tr* fera *Ne* ferocis *Ve*

2227–56 The Carthusian Order originated in 1084 when Bruno of Cologne and six followers dedicated themselves to an eremitical style of life in the Alps near Grenoble. Over the
next century their example inspired the formation of similar communities throughout France,
which gradually became institutionally formalized into a monastic order. However, it was
only in the late 12th c., probably around 1180, that the first Carthusian house was founded in
England, at Witham in Somerset, by Henry II (Thompson, *Carthusian Order*, pp. 3–102).
The daily routine of Carthusian life in the early years was described in accounts by Guibert
of Nogent (*Vita*, i. 11), by Peter the Venerable (*De miraculis*, ii. 27 (28), ed. Bouthillier, pp.
149–52), and, most important, in the *Consuetudines* drawn up by Guigo I, fifth prior of La
Grande Chartreuse. The details of Nigel's account in these lines agree remarkably closely

SPECVLVM STVLTORVM 227

will whatever they want. So why is it that a man, who lives like an angel inwardly, [2225] is so often battered about in the public court?'

About the Carthusian Order

'What if my change of life takes me to the Charterhouse? There I shall have the use of several sheepskins and tunics. A cell will be given to me, which I shall have to myself alone; no one will be my companion, no one my servant. [2230] Alone I shall chant, alone I shall take my food, and alone I shall go, lightless, to my bed. I shall always be alone within the confines of my tripartite cell, in which the only stranger's foot will always be mine. Wood, beans, and water will always be ready in my cell, [2235] for making a mash. The prior of the order will come to visit me, and I'll often have a piece of warm bread. A certain quantity of

with these early descriptions (references in the rest of this section are, first, to the relevant line(s) of *SS*, and second, to the relevant chapter of Guigo's *Consuetudines*).

In contrast to the other monastic orders, the Carthusians did not always worship and eat as a community; instead, in order to maximize the silence necessary for contemplation, each monk spent most of the day in his individual cell (2229–34), which included kitchen facilities, water, and wood for fire, so that he could prepare his own food (2235–6; *Consuetudines*, c. xxviii. 5). The monastic hours were sung in solitude, except for matins and vespers when the community assembled (2231; *Consuetudines*, c. xxix. 6). Again in contrast to the other monastic orders, Mass was not celebrated daily but only on Sundays and feast-days (2245–6; see Guigo's explanation of this practice in *Consuetudines*, c. xiv. 5). Their austere lifestyle completely excluded meat (*SS*, 2251), even for the sick (despite *SS*, 2252); however, fish was allowed for the sick or when it was donated to the community (2244; *Consuetudines*, c. xxviii. 3, c. xli. 5). On Mondays, Wednesdays, and Fridays, they ate only bread and water (2243; *Consuetudines*, c. xxxiii. 1). They were well supplied with clothing (necessary in a mountain climate), including two tunics and two sheepskins (2229; *Consuetudines*, c. xxviii. 1), but beneath them they wore a hair shirt (2241–2; *Consuetudines*, c. xxviii. 1). Strict limits were imposed on the amount of land, livestock, and revenues they were allowed to possess (2249–50; *Consuetudines*, c. xli. 1), and they were not permitted to increase their income by begging (2247–8; *Consuetudines*, c. xix. 2, c. lxxix. 2; cf. Thompson, *Carthusian Order*, pp. 15–16, 92).

For the implications of this passage for the dating of *SS*, see Introduction, p. li.

2233 *cella...trimembri*: Carthusian cells were traditionally divided into separate compartments for different activities (Raymo specifies eating, sleeping, and praying, and refers to Thompson, *Carthusian Order*, p. 33, but this only says that in the early days of the Order the cells were not so divided). At Mount Grace priory in North Yorkshire, a reconstructed cell shows this tripartite division on the ground floor, with a workroom above.

2234 That is, no one else will enter.

2235 *pulmento conficiendo*: on this Latin construction (replacement of a gerund followed by an accusative noun, here 'pulmentum conficiendo', by a gerundive in agreement with a noun), and its use for an action which is 'in progress or repetitive or contemplated'), see Woodcock, *New Latin Syntax*, 206 and Note 1 (pp. 160–1). Cf. 'a pascendo grege' in line 2675.

2237 The prior visited novices in their cells, in order to provide instruction in Carthusian practices (*Consuetudines*, c. xxii. 4).

228   *SPECVLVM STVLTORVM*

2240   uiuere qua possunt, portio certa datur.
Interior uestis, quam lana caprina ministrat,
    carnem castigat asperitate sua.
Qualibet hebdomada ter pane cibantur et unda;
    non comedunt pisces, sit nisi festa dies.
2245   Et semel in mense uel bis de iure uenire
    ad missas poterunt, si uacat atque uolunt.
Contenti propriis, nec diuitibus nec egenis
    esse uolunt oneri, cras, hodie, nec heri.
Non licet augere numerum pecorum uel agrorum,
2250   taxatur certo canone quicquid habent.
Carnis in aeternum cuncti prohibentur ab esu,
    praeter eum si quem tabida lepra tenet.
Ad fora non ueniunt, quo litem lite resoluant.
Nec populi uanum depopulantur "Aue":
2255   hospitis aduentu gaudent, mutantque diaetam,
    dant quod habent hilari pectore, uoce, manu.'

2240 uiuere qua] unde qua *E* uiuere qui *Pm GI* uiuere quo *R* uiuere quam *Ve* uiuere que *Be* uiuereque *fm* uiuere que *fh fn*; possunt] possint *RP* possum *J*   **2241–6** *transp. after 2238 Z*   **2241** quam] qua *D* cum *fh fm fn*; ministrat] ministra *Be Tr*   **2243** ter pane] pane ter *fm* pane *VdTBe TrLa*; cibantur] cibatur *HuMNDK Q*   **2244** *om. Z*; non] nec α β *SMuVaVbVcVdTGoBePkPmNe K TrHaLa X fh fm fn*; pisces] carnes δ *GI Tr U²over erasure*; sit nisi] sit tibi *F* nisi sit *fn*   **2246** missas] missam *H* δ mensas *Vb*; uacat] uacant *Mu fm*   **2247–50** *om. QY*   **2248** hodie nec] hodie uel *VdT Z* hora nec *fm* hora uenit *fh fn* hodiernus *D*   **2249** non] nec *LE*; uel] nec *F Go om. Va*   **2250** taxatur] texatur *Be* taxantur *CW* taxatur ergo *J*   **2251** cuncti] cuncta *fm* cunctis *fh*; esu] usu *Mu K fh fm*   **2252–5** *om. QY*   **2252** praeter eum] totus? cum *fm* preter cum *fn*; tabida] tabidam *Pm* calida *D* rabida *MuVaVdTGoBePk Tr* rapida *Ve* rabida / [*uel*] tabida *La*   **2253** *om. Vc*; fora] forum *Tfn*; lite] scire *AJCWRHuMNOPDVe GI U* iura *S* iure *MuVaVbVdTGoBePkPmNe TrHaLa Z fh fm fn*   **2255** *om. line left empty, 2255 inser. after 2285 S*   **2256** uoce] uoceque *Ve Z*

SPECVLVM STVLTORVM   229

sheep, cattle, forest, and fertile land is given to them to live off. [2240] An inner garment made of goat's hair chastens the flesh with its harshness. Three times a week they are fed with bread and water; they do not eat fish except on a feast-day. And once or twice in the month they can licitly come to Mass, [2245] if there is time and they wish it. Content with their own possessions, they do not want to be a burden to rich or poor, yesterday, today, or tomorrow. They are not allowed to increase the number of their cattle or lands; whatever they have is valued according to a fixed scale. [2250] They are all permanently forbidden to eat meat, except for anyone who is a victim of wasting leprosy. They don't go to the courts, to settle strife with strife. Nor do they spurn the vain salutation of the populace: at the arrival of a guest they rejoice, and change their diet, [2255] giving what they have with cheerful heart, voice, and hand.'

2238 This is probably a reference to the 'torta', a small cake or bread roll, which was dispensed to the monks after supper on Sundays and feast-days for them to take back to their cells (Thompson, *Carthusian Order*, p. 38; *Consuetudines*, c. vii. 10).

2253 *litem lite resoluant*: cf. Horace, *Saturae*, ii. 3. 103: 'litem quod lite resolvat'.

2254 *depopulantur*: the precise meaning of this line is hard to grasp, but it seems best to take it together with the following couplet: 'they do not spurn the greetings of the people' and in fact they welcome visitors. 'depopulor' occurs with its usual meaning 'to destroy' in *Miracles*, 1008, 1616.

2255–6 In fact, 'Carthusian hospitality was very restricted' (Thompson, *Carthusian Order*, pp. 26–7), both because of the remote and barren territory in which the early community lived, which meant they had little food to spare, and in order to guard against secular temptations. Guests who were not monks or clerics were confined to the lay-brothers' quarters (*Consuetudines*, c. x. 1, cc. xviii–xx, c. xxxvi). *hospitis aduentu*: also in *Miracles*, 1682.

230   SPECVLVM STVLTORVM

De Nigris Canonicis

'Est et item uita Nigrorum Canonicorum
iudicio populi digna decensque Deo.
Mollibus induti, non spernunt pinguibus uti,
2260   inque refectorio carnibus atque mero.
Quid caro peccauit plus quam faba, pisa, legumen,
ne possit comedi conditione pari?
Quem nos causamur non est in carne reatus,
sed comedente male nec cohibente gulam.
2265   Causa datur uino, debetur culpa bibenti,
cum caput aut membra cetera mane dolent.
Ne pariat psalmus uel lectio taedia longa,

2257 est et item uita] *add. [uel]* est et recta uia *R* est et recta uia *Ve* < >st enim uita *Tr*; et item] etiam *Vd* et enim *VaBe²* et iter *BePk* iterum *T D* et ita *fh fm fn* **2258** decensque] decusque *CHuMNDK* decusque /uel decensque *W* dicensque *E Vd Ve Tr* decorisque *fh fm fn* decens est *Pk* **2259** non spernunt] non semper *AJCWRHuMNOPKVe U* semperque *QY* possunt quoque *D* non s<*erasure*> *G* spernunt *om. I add. I²* **2260** refectorio] refectoria *Tr* refectoriis *Mu* refertorio *Go*; carnibus] carnes *fh* **2261** quid] quod *Go P Tr Y* **2262** ne] non *LE* nec *Be*; possit] posset *VbPk AJCWRHuMNOKVe* possunt *F* **2263** quem] quam β *MuVaVdBePkPmNe AOPVe GI HaLa UQY fh fm fn* que *LE* qua *R* **2264** nec] ne *MN*; cohibente] prohibente *SMuVaVbVcVdTGoBePkPmNe R TrHaLa ZX fh fm fn* **2265** bibenti] bibente *fm* **2266** *line repeated in alternative form* Z(1)Z(2); cum] dum *O UZ*(1); aut] et *P* atque *Z*(1) infirmum *SMuVaVbVcGoBePkPmNe TrHaLa Z*(2) *fh fm fn* infinum *Vd* egrotat *T*; membra cetera] cetera membra β *SMuVaVbVcVdTGoBePkPmNe TrHaLa Z*(1)Z(2) *fh fm fn*; mane] *om. SMuVaVbVcVdTGoBePkPmNe TrHaLa Z*(2) *fh fm fn* **2267** ne] non α; pariat] pereat *AJCWHuPDVe GI UQ* periat *Tr Y add. as corr. Be²* pareat *Go Z*; uel lectio taedia] nec lectio tedia *X* uel lectio tedio *Ve QY* nec littera tedia *F* uel tedia lectio *fm*; lectio] letum *fh*

2257–86 Canons are of two main sorts: secular canons, whose name indicates that they live in the world (Latin *seculum* = 'the world'), and regular canons, whose name indicates that they live according to a rule (Latin *regula* = 'rule'). On secular canons, see further n. to lines 2315–54. Both types of canons take their inspiration from the life of the apostles, as described in Acts 2: 44–5 and 4: 32–5; that is, renouncing individual possessions and sharing all things in common (*Praeceptum*, ed. Verheijen, i–iii). The regular canons interpreted this more strictly, living and eating together in a community which was funded as a whole (*Praeceptum*, ed. Verheijen, iv), whereas secular canons had individual incomes from prebends, and lived separately. Unlike monks, canons were not vowed to strict claustration. The 'black canons' are Augustinians; that is, they follow the so-called Rule of St Augustine (see below) or one of its derivatives. Other types of regular canons include Premonstratensians (see n. to lines 2287–314) and Gilbertines (see n. to lines 2401–12). Canonries were widespread on the Continent at a very early date, and after the Norman Conquest they appeared in England, proliferating until by the mid-12th c. this was 'incomparably the most numerous religious order in England' (Dickinson, *Austin Canons*, pp. 59, 91–162; cf. Barrow, *Clergy in the Medieval World*, pp. 107–9).

The 'Rule of St Augustine' in its most fundamental form comprises two brief texts, designated by their editor, Luc Verheijen, as the *Praeceptum* and the *Ordo monasterii*, the first of

SPECVLVM STVLTORVM

About the Black Canons

'The life of the Black Canons is also worthy in the judgement of the people and fit for God. Clothed in soft garments, they do not scorn the consumption of fat and meat, with wine, in the refectory. [2260] What is more sinful about meat than beans, peas, pulses, that it can't be eaten in the same conditions? The fault we criticize is not in the meat, but in the one who fails to restrain his greed and eats wickedly. The crime is attributed to the wine, but the blame ought to be given to the drinker, [2265] when the head and other members suffer the next morning. So that the chant and the lessons don't cause long weariness, they always exercise restraint in chanting and reading. Nor do they attempt to raise

which was very probably composed by Augustine of Hippo himself, while the second probably emanated from his milieu. The *Praeceptum* is a series of very general admonitions on the behaviour suitable to the communal life; the *Ordo* is an extremely brief set of instructions concerning liturgical observances and the daily life of the monastery. The long and complicated history of these two texts, which circulated in combined and separate forms, as well as in versions adapted for female religious, has been painstakingly reconstructed by Luc Verheijen on the basis of 274 manuscripts (Verheijen, *La Règle de Saint Augustin*, i. 11–34; ii. 175–218); for his critical editions of these two texts, see i. 148–52 (*Ordo*) and 417–47 (*Praeceptum*). Verheijen's text of the *Praeceptum* is translated by R. Canning, with Introduction and Commentary by T. J. van Bavel. See also George Lawless, *Augustine of Hippo and his Monastic Rule*, with texts and translations of both *Praeceptum* and *Ordo* at pp. 74–103. Over time the basic Rule was supplemented or replaced by customary observances that varied from one place to another (see Dickinson, *Austin Canons*, Appendix I, pp. 269–72). This makes generalization difficult, but Nigel's account of the canonical life accurately reflects the common-sense balance that these observances struck between austerity and luxury. Like monks, regular canons recited the eight daily services that make up the Divine Office, but without the elaborate ritual of the monks (Dickinson, *Austin Canons*, pp. 185, 273). Meat was allowed three or four times a week (ibid. pp. 181–2), and wine on Saturday and Sunday (ibid. p. 273). They wore linen undergarments, rather than the woollen ones worn by monks, since their rule prescribed simply that their dress must be plain and clean (ibid. p. 184). For the same reason, its colour was not strictly determined, but Nigel describes its most familiar form: a black cassock lined with sheepskin, with a white surplice over it, and a large black cope over all, from which they were known as 'black canons' (ibid. p. 185). Nigel's insistence that the inner spiritual state is more important than external behaviour (2283–6) echoes the canonical custumals, and also other satirical poetry; see Sextus Amarcius, *Satires*, iii. 744–7: 'Velat eum [sc. monachum] vestis pullo fuscata colore,/ Ut despectibilis mundo videatur inopsque;/ Esto, sed interius si non vult candidus esse,/ Extera nigredo nil confert, credite nobis', and 'Dum Saturno conjuge', where the Cluniac contrasts his 'raven-black garment' with his 'dove-like heart' (*Map Poems*, p. 239, lines 69–70). It may, however, be possible to glimpse a tinge of Chaucerian irony (e.g. in lines 2261–2, 2269–70) in Nigel's enthusiastic approval of the less demanding life of the canons.

2263 *causamur*: 'causari' = 'to complain about' (Niermeyer).

2265 *causa*: 'crime, offence' (Niermeyer 3). Cf. *Disticha Catonis*, ii. 21 .2: 'nam crimen vini nullum est, sed culpa bibentis'. Peter of Blois's second poem in defence of wine against beer similarly asks why wine should be blamed for Lot's incest with his daughters; 'non ibi uini/ culpa, set in uino non habuisse modum./ Peccauit potor, non potus' (*Carmina*, ed. Wollin, CCCM cxxviii, i. 7, lines 17–19, p. 285).

232   SPECVLVM STVLTORVM

       in psallendo tenent inque legendo modum.
       Nec nituntur ad hoc ut uocibus immoderatis
2270   ardua praeualeant rumpere tecta domus.
       Candida sed pura, subtili stamine texta,
       (mundis munda placent), linea uestis eis.
       Vestis honesta quidem, quae nec cum carne rebelli
       uel cute bella gerat asperitate sui;
2275   exteriora tamen clauduntur scemate nigro,
       ut color alternus aptior esse queat.
       Lumina ne laedat albedo nigredo repugnat
       inque timore nigro gaudia candor habet.
       Sic arcus coeli gemino splendore refulget,
2280   sic pilus est pardo candidus atque niger;
       pallia cornici dat penna subalbida nigrae,
       candida sic picas et nigra penna tegit.
       Si uestis bicolor carnem sine corde colorat,
       mens erit absque nota, ueste tenente notam.
2285   Quid refert quales ueniant in ueste colores,
       si mens unicolor interiora regat?'

2268 modum] modo *fm*   2269 nec] ne *HuMN*; hoc] hec *H SMuVbVd La X*
2270 praeualeant] preualuant *fm*   2271 *om. Z*; pura] plura *F H VdBe La*; stamine]
tegmine *SMuVaVbVcVdTPkPmNe Ha fh fm fn* tegmine /[*uel*] stamine *La* tegumine *Be* tec-
mine *Go*; texta] texa *T N* tecta *Go Ve*   2272 mundis] mundus *GoBeNe D*; placent]
placet *B SMuVbVdBePkPmNe AJCWROPDKVe TrLa UZX fh fm fn*   2274 uel] ue *C*
aut *O* nec *R* uel [*uel*] nec *La* ut *AJWPVe GI U* et *ZQY*; gerat] gerit *VcT ZQY* ierat *X*; sui]
sua *VaVbVcVdTGoBePkPmNe TrHaLa Q fh fm* serua *Mu*   2275 tamen] quidem
MuVaVbVcVdTGoBePkPmNe TrHaLa fm fn suo quidem *fh*; clauduntur] claudentur *H*
AJCWRHuHuMNOPVe GI ZXQY claudenter *B* teguntur *fh fm fn*; scemate] stemate *WMN*
cemate *B D* temate *S* scomate *Mu* themate *VdBePkNe AJROPVe GI TrLa UQY fh fm fn*
2276 alternus] alterius *LE H SMuVcVdPkPm*ac *AJCWRHuMNPDKVe GI Tr UZQY fh fm*
fn alterius /[*uel*] alternis *La* interius *O*; queat] potest *fh fm fn*   2277 ne] non *CW U*;
laedat] ledant *Go O Ha* lodat *M*; albedo] albo δ *GI La U²over erasureQY*; nigredo] nigre-
doque *fh*   2279–82 *om. QY*   2279 *om. Vd*; splendore] fulgore *D GI* candore *Vc R*
2280 pilus] plus *Mu*ac*Va*; est] in *F Vc*   2281 pallia] pellia *Z* pallida *fm*; subalbida]
albida *Vd* albida /uel subalbida *La*; nigrae] nigro *C* nigri *Vc D Z*   2282 *om. T*; sic] si
fh fm fn; nigra] magna *fh*; tegit] teget *CWMN* cogit *fh fm fn*   2283 si] sic
SMuVaVdTGoBePkNe WHuMNDK TrHaLa U fh fm fn sit *Pm C* sed *VbVc GI*; uestis]
nescis *Pm* uestibus *fh*; bicolor] wicolor *Vc* uicolor *Tr* omnicolor *fh*; corde] sorde *H* code *fh*
carne /uel corde *Ha*   2284 erit] erat *CW*; ueste] mente *SMuVaVbVcVdTGoBePkPmNe*
Ha fh fm fn; notam] notat *F*   2285 quid] quidque *SMuVcGoPkPm HaLa fm* quicquid
VaVbT Tr Z quodque *VdBeNe fh fn*; ueniant] ueniat *Va* ueniunt *O*; colores] calores *Mu*
Tr   2286 *after 2285 transp. 2255 S*; regat] ligat *D* tegat *MuTGoPmNe R fm* negat *Q*
regat /uel tegat *Ha* tenet *fn*

SPECVLVM STVLTORVM

the house rafters with unrestrained voices. [2270] Pure things please the pure; a linen garment, white and clean, woven with a fine thread, pleases them. A decent garment indeed, which wages no war on the rebellious flesh or skin with its harshness. But their outside is enveloped in a black habit, [2275] so that the different colour may be more appropriate. The blackness repels the eye, lest the whiteness dazzle it, and the whiteness provides pleasure within the fearful black. So the rainbow shines with double splendour; so the coat of the leopard is light and dark. [2280] So a white feather clothes the black crow, and white and black plumage covers magpies. If a two-tone garment colours the flesh but not the heart, the mind will be blameless, the garment bearing the blame. What does it matter what colours appear in their clothing, [2285] if a single-coloured mind rules their inward selves?'

2272 *mundis munda*: Titus 1: 15.

2275 *scemate*: 'scema' = 'monastic habit' ('scema, vel schema, proprie usurpatur pro habitu monachico', Du Cange; *DMLBS* s.v. 'schema').

2281 Crows can develop some white feathers as the result of a genetic condition known as leucism, and also because of old age.

234 SPECVLVM STVLTORVM

De ordine Praemonstratensi

'Praemonstratenses rursus, qui uestibus albis
induti ueniunt, simplicitate placent.
His color unus adest niueo candore refulgens,
2290   hos semper simplex uestis ouina tegit.
Omnibus abiectis duris pro mollibus uti
uestibus ad praesens hoc statuere modo.
Vellere partito, quod colli nuda tegebat,
in proprios usus constituere suos.
2295   Ne caro luxuriet, ueruecis uellere crispo
corpora castigant asperitate graui.
Damna tamen lini, lana redimente suaui,
ordine cogente sustinuisse decet.
Ordinis austerus rigor est, quia carnibus uti
2300   hos in conuentu tempus in omne uetat.
Dispensando tamen sacer ordo salubribus usus
consiliis, super his alleuiauit onus,
pinguia concedens quae sunt affinia carni,

2287 Praemonstratenses] Premostratenses *LE HuMN* Premonstratensis *Mu*; rursus qui]
rursus quia *LE B VdBePkPmNe TrHaLa ZX* rursusque *F H MuVaVbGo* rursum quoque *Vc*
rursus quam *I* russus qui *D* cursus qui *AJCWHuMNPVe* cursusque *QY* cursus in *U* mer-
susque *S* minus quoque *fm* misus? quoque *fn* niueis quoque *fh*   2288 simplicitate pla-
cent] placent simplicitate *fn* simplicitate tenent *CW*   2289 his] is *QY*; unus] nimis *Be*
La om. Tr; candore] splendore *LE*   2290 hos] has *fh fm fn*; semper simplex uestis]
simplex semper uestis *Tr* simplex uestis pellis *S* simplex omnis uestis *MuTGoNe Ha fh* simplex omnis nescis *Pm* simplex omnes uestis *VaVbVcVdBePk La fn* simplex omnis uestes *fm*;
ouina] ouinalis *L* omnia *MuVaVbTr fh*   2291–2 duris pro—ad praesens *om. Q*
2291 abiectis] adiectis *JMPVe Z fh fm fn* obiectis *Be;* duris] dura *AJCWRPVe GI*; pro] pre
Ve his *S* hi *MuVaVbVcVdTBePkPmNe TrHaLa fh fm fn* hi sed *Go*   2292 hoc] hec
MuGo Ve X fh fm fn hic *Be La* hi *VbVcVd*   2293–4 *om. ZQY*   2293 colli] colla
Vc Tr tolli *Ne*; tegebat] protexit *AJCWROPDVe* retexit *GI*   2295 ne] nec *Go Ha*;
luxuriet] luxuriat *fh*   2296 corpora] corpore *F*; asperitate] asperita *J* asperite
fn   2297–8 *om. QY*   2297 *om. Z*; damna tamen lini] *om. U, add. U²*; suaui] suam
VdGo fh sua *Pk*   2300 hos] his *F* β *SMuVaVbVcVdTGoBePkPmNe* δ *TrHaLa GI
UXQY fh fm fn* hi *Z*; uetat] uetet *Go QY* decet *fh fm fn* negat *U*   2301 salubribus]
solubribus *Be* salubrius *H ACWOPDVe GI Tr QY fn* salubrimus *J* salubrios *R* salubrior *U*
2302 alleuiauit] alleuiabit *S CWHuMNODK GI UZXQY* alleuiat *VaPk*

2287–314 The Premonstratensians were (and are) an order of regular canons (see n. to
lines 2257–86), founded *c.*1120 by St Norbert of Xanten, who gathered round himself a group
of followers at Prémontré, in the diocese of Laon. In 1126, Norbert left to become archbishop of Magdeburg, and Hugh de Fosses took his place as abbot. Initially the community
followed the Rule of St Augustine, but in the 1130s Hugh wrote a new set of *consuetudines* for
the order, drawing freely on Cistercian practices (on the early history of the order, see Colvin,

SPECVLVM STVLTORVM   235

About the Premonstratensian Order

'Then again, the Premonstatensians, who go about dressed in white clothing, please by their uniformity. One colour, gleaming snowy white, is theirs; a single-coloured woollen garment is their constant covering. [2290] All harsh clothes having been laid aside in favour of soft ones, they have determined this for the present. Having divided up the fleece, they have allotted to their own use the bit that covered the skin of the neck. So that the flesh is not indulged, they chasten their bodies with the harsh roughness of a wether's curly fleece. [2295] It's fitting to endure the lack of linen, as the order requires, when soft wool makes up for it. The rigour of the order is harsh, for it forbids them ever to consume meat in the convent. [2300] But the holy order, giving dispensation to practices by wise counsels, will lift the burden in this respect, allowing fats, which are meat's concomitants, on condition

White Canons, ch. 1). In the mid-12th c. these statutes were revised (Les Statuts de Prémontré au milieu du XIIᵉ siècle, ed. Lefèvre and Grauwen), and this is the Rule that would have been in force when SS was written. Like the Cistercians, the Premonstratensians were organized in a network of dependent houses, whose practices were regulated by general chapter meetings, held annually, and by a system of abbatial visitations. Also like the Cistercians, they were served by lay-brothers (conversi), and were successful sheep-farmers. The order expanded rapidly, not only in France and the Low Countries, where nearly 100 monasteries were in existence by the 1140s (Colvin, White Canons, p. 28), but also in England; Colvin's table of English abbeys lists 28 which were founded before 1200 (ibid. p. 26; cf. p. 37). Henry II's justiciar, Rannulf de Glanville, and his relatives founded several Premonstratensian houses around 1180–90, and other foundations around the same period 'exemplify the connection ... between the order and prominent members of the royal administration' (Mortimer, 'Religious and secular motives', pp. 77, 81–2; quotation at p. 82).

2289–98 uestis ouina: for 'ouinus' meaning 'woollen', see DMLBS 2. The Premonstratensians wore habits of white wool, as prescribed by St Norbert, who gave various justifications for this choice: penitents were clothed in wool, and the angels who witnessed Christ's resurrection were clothed in white (Vita S. Norberti, PL clxx. 1293). The most elaborate set of reasons for the white clothing is given by Adam of Dryburgh (c.1140–c.1212), a Premonstratensian abbey in Scotland (De ordine, habitu et professione canonicorum ordinis Praemonstratensis, PL cxcviii. 467–79 [sermones ii–iv]). The Premonstratensians did not wear linen undergarments, except for their drawers (Les Statuts de Prémontré au milieu du XIIᵉ siècle, ed. Lefèvre and Grauwen, dist. iv. 14).

2303–14 In fact, the Premonstratensian statutes forbade both meat and fats, except for the sick (Les Statuts de Prémontré au milieu du XIIᵉ siècle, ed. Lefèvre and Grauwen, dist. iv. 12: 'intra monasteria nostra pulmenta sint semper et ubique sine carne et sine sagmine'). Either Nigel was misinformed on this point, or Premonstratensian practice in England was lax.

236 SPECVLVM STVLTORVM

sic tamen ut numquam sit manifesta caro.

2305 Bellum cum carne, pacem cum pinguibus esse,
pacis amatores hoc statuere modo,
carnis honestatem sic conseruare uolentes,
ne contra carnem lex inhonesta foret.
Si foret exclusa penitus caro, carnis honestas
2310 laesam se posset de ratione queri.
Si foret in totum sine conditione recepta,
saepe daret causam materiamque mali.
Vnde nec admissa penitus, nec tota repulsa
exulat, in patria menstrua facta sua.'

De Canonicis Secularibus

2315 'Sunt et canonici seculares quique uocati;
nomen ab officio promeruere suo.
His quodcumque libet lex est licitumque, sub isto
canone constituit uiuere tota cohors.
Hi nihil excipiunt, nec dicunt despiciendum
2320 quicquid in obsequio corporis esse potest.

2304 sic] sit *Go D U fm fn*; numquam] raro *CWHuMNDK X* unquam *J Go*; caro] raro *fm fn* **2305–12** *om. QY* **2310–11** *om.* δ *GI U* **2310** se] si *E Vc La* **2311** foret] forte *VbGo*; totum] toto *Go fh* **2312** causam] curam *SMuVaVbVcVdGoBePkPmNe HaLa Z fh fm fn*; materiamque] materiaque *E* materiaque materiamque *J* iure de iamque *T* **2313–14** *om. Z* **2313** repulsa] *om. fm* **2314** patria] patriam *fn*; menstrua] monstrua *Vc DO Ha UX* **2315** et] qui *ZQY*; seculares quique uocati] seculares quoque uocati *Vc* seculares qui uocitati *X* qui secularesque uocati *B S ACWHuMN GI* secularesque uocati *T PVe fb* seculares atque uocati *R* quo secularesque uocati *J* seculares sunt uocitati *ZQY* quidam secularesque uocati *MuVdGoBePkPm TrHaLa* quidam seculares uocati *Ne fn* quidem seculares uocati *fh fm* quidam scolaresque uocati *Va* quidem secularesque uocati *Vb* quorum nomen metra spernunt *DK* **2316** *after 2315* ne longent breuia longaque (longaue *K*) corripiant/ sed errante (erranteque *K*) metro sunt canonici seculares *DK*; nomen] non *fb fn*; promeruere] promerure *M* qui meruere *DK* promeruisse *Mu* **2317** lex est licitumque] lex et licitumque *VdBe TrLa* lex noua lutumque *AJCWPVe GI* lex noua licetque *HuMNO* noua lex licitumque *RD* lex et (et *illegible U*) lutumque *UQY*; isto] ipso *F G^{ac}I*; *(whole line)* his noua lex quodcumque libet licet atque sub isto *K* **2318** *om. Vc* **2319** excipiunt] despiciunt *fh fn* eripiunt *Vd La* **2320** quicquid] quid *S La*; obsequio] obsequium *fm*

2315–54 On the distinction between secular and regular canons, see n. to lines 2257–86 above; for the historical background, see Barrow, *Clergy in the Medieval World*, pp. 269–309. Nigel's lengthy tirade against this clerical body contains nothing in the way of factual detail, and is clearly an exaggerated polemic inspired by his personal prejudices as a Canterbury monk whose way of life was threatened by the proposal to establish a college of canons at Hackington.

SPECVLVM STVLTORVM

that meat is never apparent. The lovers of peace have thus decided that there shall be war against meat, but a truce with fats, [2305] wishing thus to preserve the honour of meat, lest there should be a dishonourable law against meat. If meat were totally excluded, the honour of the flesh could reasonably claim it had been wounded. [2310] If it were totally and unconditionally allowed, it would often provide the cause and material for evil. So, neither completely allowed nor entirely neglected, it is an exile, made a temporary resident in its home country.'

About Secular Canons

'There are also those called secular canons, [2315] who have earned their name from their function. For them, whatever pleases them is lawful and legitimate; this is the canon under which the whole pack of them has determined to live. They do not rule out or hold in contempt anything which ministers to the flesh. [2320] And this thing in particular

---

2315 On the two lines added at this point by *D* and *K*, objecting to the scansion, see Introduction, pp. xcvi and cliv, n. 344.

2316 'Secularis' literally means 'worldly'; as applied to canons it means that they live 'in the world', rather than in a religious community; Nigel here interprets it in a pejorative sense, meaning 'dedicated to worldly things'.

2317 *quodcumque libet*: also in *Lawrence*, 562.

238   SPECVLVM STVLTORVM

Illud praecipue tamen instituere tenendum
    omnibus in tota posteritate sua:
lex uetus ut suasit, ne quilibet absque sua sit,
    et quod quisque suas possit habere duas.
2325 Hi sunt qui mundum cum flore cadente tenentes,
    ne cito marcescat, saepe rigare student.
Hi sunt qui faciunt quicquid petulantia carnis
    imperat, ut uitiis sit uia prona suis.
Totus in errorem mundus praeeuntibus istis
2330 ducitur, hi praeeunt praecipitesque ruunt.
Hi mundum non mundus eos habet, atque deorsum
    hi quia compellunt, funditus ille cadit.
Hi fundamenta fidei subuertere prompti
    moribus expugnant quae facienda docent.
2335 Hi sunt pontificum per quos uigor, ordo, potestas
    nutat, et ecclesiae fit status absque statu.
Languet et exspirat per eos reuerentia cleri,
    deficit in nihilum religionis honos.
Horum consilio reges meditantur iniqua,
2340 et quae debuerant stringere laxa tenent.

2322 tota] toto *Vd fh*; posteritate] prosperitate *S Z fb^{ac}* posterioritate *X fh fn*; sua] suo
fh   2323 suasit] sua sit α *H VdNe D TrHa*; ne] nec *Go TrHa* quod *Y om. Q*; quilibet]
qualibet *Ve* cui libet *Q* quidam *S* quisque *fn*   2324 possit] posset *Vd Z* potest *Q*; duas]
suas *fh fn*   2325 cadente] tenente *D GI*   2326 marcescat] marcescant *T fb fh fm*
marcescescat *Be*; saepe] cito *S* usque *MuVaVbVcVdTGoBePkPmNe HaLa fh fm* absque *fn*;
rigare] rigore *TrHa fn* uigare *Z*   2327–8 *transp. after 2346 Tr*   2327 faciunt
quicquid] quicquid faciunt quicquid *fh fn*   2328 imperat] impetrat *H X*
2329 errorem] errore *E Ne*; istis] illis δ *GI Ha^{ac} UZXQY fb*   2330 praeeunt] preuiunt *L*
pereunt *VdBe Ve La fh fm fn*; praecipitesque] precipites *Pm* precipites que *fh*   2332 *om.*
fh; hi] hunc *VbVc*; quia] quoque α qui *Z om. T*; cadit] cadet *ACWRHuMNPDKVe GI*
2333 fundamenta] fundamentum δ *U fb*   2334 expugnant] impugnant *Mu fn*;
facienda] faciendo *K Tr*; docent] decent *SVbVdGo Z fh fm* decet *T*   2335 pontificum]
pontifices *H Ha*; uigor ordo] rigor ordo *T* ordoque *Vc* ordo *F* uigor *Vd*   2336 nutat et]
mutat et *SVdGoBePkPmNe TrLa Z fm* mutatur *Va* mussat et *Vc* micat et *QY*; fit] sic *S T* sit
VdGoBePkNe TrLa   2338 *line repeated in alternative form Z(1)Z(2)*; in nihilum] in nihil
T et nihilum *Vd* inter eos *Z(1)QY*; religionis honos] *om. D^{ac}*, religionis honos uel honor *add.*
D^{pc}; honos] honor *VaGoPm CW Ha X fm* honus *Vd La^{ac}* onus *SMuVbVcPk La^{pc} U^{ac}Z(1)Q fh*
fn om. Tr   2339 consilio] concilio *H Z fb* consilia *Ne*; iniqua] inique *Go* iniquo *Tr Z*
2340 debuerant] debuerent *LE* deberent *T*

2321–4 Raymo claims that John of Salisbury also charges the secular canons with sexual
licence, but he has been misled by Pike's inaccurate translation of the passage of *Policraticus*
that he cites as evidence (vii. 23, ed. Webb, ii. 207–8; trans. Pike, pp. 283–4). John himself was
a canon of Exeter (*Fasti Ecclesiae Anglicanae*, x. 56), probably by 1160, and later (by 1164) a
canon of Salisbury (ibid. iv. 125), and in this passage of *Policraticus* he is comparing monks
and regular canons with 'seculares', 'such as myself'. If, he says, members of the secular

SPECVLVM STVLTORVM 239

they have set up as something to be observed by all for all time: that, as the old law commanded, no male should be without a female, and that each male can have two females. They hold to the world, and lest its drooping flower [2325] should quickly wither, they take care to water it frequently. These are they who do whatever the wantonness of the flesh commands, so that the path to their vices may be smooth. They lead the whole world into error; they go first and take a headlong tumble. [2330] The world does not possess them but rather they the world, and because they drive it downwards, it topples from its foundations. Ready to undermine the foundations of the faith, what they recommend in their teaching they demolish in their practice. It is through them that the force, rule, and power of bishops falters [2335] and the order of the church becomes disordered. Through them, respect for the clergy grows faint and dies, and the glory of religious life dwindles to nothing. By their counsel kings plan wicked deeds, and give free rein to what they should hold back. [2340] They are the evil associates of bishops

clergy followed the observances to which even unwilling monks are bound (such as fasting, vigils, vegetarianism, silence, obedience, and so on), they would be regarded with admiration and awe. The difference between the two orders does not lie in clothing, but in behaviour. 'There are those in ordinary clothing whom I do not dare to call "secular" since there is nothing worthy to be called "secular" in such a man, unless he is bound to the world by the pull of wicked love' ('Sunt tamen in habitu communi quos seculares non audeo nominare, cum nichil seculare sit dicendus in talibus, nisi quod seculo nequam amoris federatur affectu'). John is practising the etymological logic so popular in the Middle Ages, and pointing out the inappropriateness of the name 'secular' to those who are *not* worldly. In other words, he is rejecting the pejorative sense of the word that Nigel deploys in line 2316. Nevertheless, John concludes, he is content to follow common usage and call this group 'seculares'. Pike translates the quoted passage as follows: 'Yet there are those found in the common garb, some of whom I would not venture to call seculars since there is nothing in such individuals that ought to be called secular, unless it be the bond formed by the secular passion of carnal love.' It is love for the world ('seculo'), not carnal love or amorous passion, that is in question here, and it is considered only hypothetically, not as an actual feature of the secular clergy.

2326 Cf. *Lawrence*, 544: 'ne marcescant, nouiter plantata rigare'.
2327 *petulantia carnis*: also at *Miracles*, 1035.

240   *SPECVLVM STVLTORVM*

Pontificum latera sunt hi regumque sinistra,
    pes errans, mendax lingua, recurua manus,
cor duplex, simulatus amor, sine numine nomen,
    ira latens, uera motio, falsa quies,
2345   bursa carens fundo, praedae sine nomine praedo,
    lanx mendax ueri, uera statera doli,
lex sine lege Dei, canon sine canone Christi,
    praeuia causa mali, pagina plena doli.
Hi sunt iustitiam qui prostituere pudicam,
2350   falsa loqui linguas qui docuere suas;
qui dum labentem mundum retinere laborant,
    cum labente labant, cumque ruente ruunt;
quorum uita labor, uia lubrica, gloria stercus,
    finis in incerto, praemia certa dolor.
2355   Quod bene dum secum quidam meditantur eorum,
    talibus a studiis se cohibere student,
qui pariter mundi foeno cum flore relicto
    omnia quae mundi sunt nihil esse putant.
In medio fornacis agunt, flammaeque uorantis
2360   in giro stadium constituere suum.

2341–4 *om. Tr*   **2341** *om. Vc*; sinistra] sinister β(*H*ᵖᶜ) *D* sinistri *S*   **2343** *line repeated in alternative form after 2344 Z*(1)*Z*(2) (*Z*(1), 2344, *Z*(2)); cor] cur *AC GI QY*; simulatus] simulatur *J* stimulatus *Ne Z*(2) geminatus *U om. Z*(1)*QY*; sine numine nomen] est sub tegmine uestis *Z*(1) est magis sub tegmine uestis *QY*; numine] mumine *E* uiuere β *MuVd AJC*ᵃᶜ*WRHuMNOPDKVe UX fb* munere *VaVcPkNe C*ᵖᶜ *G La fh*   **2344** uera motio] uetera nocio *Ha* fallit est quia *ZQY*   **2345–8** *om. T*   **2345** praedae] prae *M* preda *Ha fh* predo *UQY fb fm* prece *Vb*; praedo] preda *fh*   **2346** lanx] laus *F H SMuVaVbVcVdGoBePkPmNe CW*ᵃᶜ *TrHaLa ZQY fh fm fn*; uera] ueri *Vd* ueta *M* uiri *fn*; statera] strata *Ne* statura *fn*; doli] mali *MuVaVbVcVdGoBePkPmNe TrHaLa fh fm fn* **2347–8** *om. SMuVaVbVcVdGoBePkPmNe R TrHaLa Q fh fm fn*   **2347** canone] nomine *F*   **2349** prostituere] prestituere *H* perstituere *Tr* constituere *R* statuere *S* prostrauere *fh*   **2350** docuere] docuisse *LE*   **2351–677** *om. U* (*missing leaves*) **2351** *om. fh fn*; laborant] laborans *Pk Z*   **2352** cum¹] cumque *AJCWRHuMNOPDKVe Tr X fb* qui cum *fh fn* (= *jump from 2351 to 2352*); labente] cadente *Vc*; labant] labunt *H F* labent *AJCWRHuMNOPDVe GI Tr ZXQY fb* cadunt *MuVaVbVcVdTGoBePkPmNe HaLa fh fm fn om. S*; cumque] cumque ipsi *S* cum *VdBe La*; ruente] cadente α *SMuVbVcVdTGoBePkPmNe HaLa ZY fh fm fn* labente *Q*; ruent] ruent δ *GI Tr fb* uiuunt *Vc*   **2353** uia] uita *H TPk*; gloria] stat quasi δ *Tr fb* sit quasi *GI ZQY*; stercus] stultus *fh fn*   **2354** in incerto] meror *Vc* incerto *fm* incerta *fh* in incerte *Va* in introitu *Tr* in cruce *fn* in mente *VdBe La;* certa] terra *SVaVdPkNe Ha*ᵃᶜ*La fh fn* carens certus *Vc* circa *J* **2356** cohibere] cohibente *F*   **2357** mundi] ex mundi *Go* mundo *VdBe La om. GI*; foeno cum] cum feno α fens cum *J* pariter cum *Go* fenum cum *fh*   **2360** in giro] *Mozley* in girum α *SMuVaVbVcVdTGoBePkPmNe HaLa Z fh fm fn* ignitum β *ACWRHuMNOPDKVe GI Tr XQY* ignium *J*; stadium] studium *MuVaVcTGo RD fn* studium / uel stadium *Ha*

SPECVLVM STVLTORVM   241

and kings—a wandering foot, a lying tongue, a grasping hand, a double
heart, counterfeit love, a godless name, a concealed wrath, a real turbulence and a false calm, a bottomless purse, a robber without the name
of robbery, [2345] a lying scale of truth and a truthful measure of
fraud, law without the law of God, and canon without the rule of
Christ, the preceding cause of evil, a page on which guile is written.
They are the ones who have prostituted virgin justice, and have taught
their tongues to utter falsehoods. [2350] While they endeavour to prop
up the tottering world, they stagger when it staggers and fall when it
falls. Their life is toil, their path slippery, their glory is shit and their
end doubtful, grief their sure reward. [But] some of them, taking
thought on all this, [2355] make efforts to refrain from such pursuits.
Having abandoned the world's flower along with its hay, they think
everything worldly is as naught. They walk in the midst of the furnace,
and take their positions within the circle of the devouring flame. [2360]

2347–8 The omission of these lines in γ can be explained by eyeskip from 'doli' in line
2346 to 'doli' in line 2348; the substitution of 'mali' for 'doli' must have taken place subsequently. Raymo suggests that line 2347 is echoed in Gower's *Mirour de l'Omme*, 21157–8:
'Ensi comme Moigne, ensi Canoun/ Ne tient la regle du canoun', but the wordplay is too
obvious to make the specific influence plausible.
2353 *gloria stercus*: 1 Macc. 2: 62: 'Et a verbis viri peccatoris ne timueritis, quia gloria eius
stercus et vermis est.' Cf. John of Salisbury, *Letters*, no. ccii (ii. 298): 'quorum...gloria ignis,
stercus et vermis'.

242　　　*SPECVLVM STVLTORVM*

Nec tamen uruntur, quia quos refrigerat intus
　　spiritus exterior flamma cremare nequit.
Decoquit hos mundus et sicut in igne camini
　　aurum flamma probat sic Deus urit eos.

2365　In mediis flammis et in ignibus esse nec uri
　　non est naturae sed deitatis opus.
Cum propria carne certamina longa tenere
　　res est difficilis et metuenda nimis.
Nam caro mortalis leuis est et cerea flecti

2370　quo natura uetus et uitiosa trahit.'

De monialibus

'Est et adhuc ordo uelatarum mulierum,
　　quas etiam nonnas dicimus esse sacras;
qui de uirginibus uiduisque coactus in unum
　　ordo satis notus pluribus esse solet.

2375　Horas canonicas solito de more frequentant,
　　soluentes pensum nocte dieque suum.
Vocibus altisonis adeo modulamine dulci
　　cantant, sirenes quod cecinisse putes.
Corpore serpentes, sirenes uoce, dracones

2380　pectore, Susanna smigmate, corde Paris.

2361 nec] non *Vc OVe*; tamen] *om. VbVc*; uruntur] utuntur *Pk Y* comburuntur *VbVc*
urimur *fh*　　**2363** decoquit] decoquet *VaPm* dequoquit *T La*ᵃᶜ ne coquit *H* de quoquid
Vd de quod *sp. left empty D* de corr. to dico *in margin D*ᵖᶜ; et sicut in] etiam si in *Go* et sic in *I*
et sit in *X* et uelut in α miseros uelut *QY*　　**2364** aurum] aura *LE* aut *fb* durum *M*
Ha　　**2364–5** sic Deus—mediis flammis *om. Va*　　**2365** et] *om. VdBe La*; in²] *om.*
VcTGoPm Ha fb　　**2369** nam] non *SMuVaVdGoBePkPmNe TrHaLa*ᵃᶜ *Z fm fn*; leuis
est et cerea] leuis et cerea *Ha* leuis est et terea *OP fb* leuis est terrea *Ve* leuis est etiam cito β
poterit cito cerea *D* poterit cito terrea *QY* leuis est et tenera *X* leuis est et seria *Mu Z fm* leuis
est et cera *Go fh fn* leuis ad singula *T*; flecti] reflecti *fh* reflati *fn*　　**2370** quo natura] qua
natura *Q* que natura *Be Ha* que mentem *K*; uetus] uentus *CWHuN* uelit β uenit *X* semper
K; et] ad *fh fn*　　**2371** et] *om. F VdGo CR Tr X fn*; uelatarum] uelatorum *Q* uetularum
fh fn　　**2372** etiam nonnas] etiam nummas *R* etiam minimas *Vb* nunnas etiam *MuPm*
nunnas *Go* feminas etiam *T*　　**2373** *om. fh fn*; qui de] que de β *Mu X* quedam *R*; uidu-
isque] uiduis *T*; coactus] coactis *LF* β *AJCPVe Ha XQY* coacus *W*　　**2374** satis] sacer
SGo D; notus] natus *fh*　　**2377–82** *transp. after 2386* α　　**2377** adeo] ac *H* ideo
fm　　**2378** cantant] cantent *VaPm*; sirenes] sirentes *MN*; putes] putas *Vd* puter *HuMN*
par his *R*　　**2379–80** dracones—smigmate] *om. Q*　　**2379** corpore] pectore α
2380 pectore] corpore α pectora *T*; Susanna] susanne *H fh*; smigmate] dogmate
SMuVaVbVcVdTGoBePkPmNe HaLa Z fh fm fn stigmate *Tr*; Paris] pares *L H S CW* puris
fh fn

SPECVLVM STVLTORVM 243

Yet they do not burn, because the outward flame cannot burn those whom the spirit inwardly cools. The world is their crucible, and God burns them just as the flame refines gold in the fire of the furnace. To be in the midst of flames and not to be burned [2365]—this is not the work of nature but of God. To wage lengthy battles with one's own flesh is a difficult task and a fearful one. For mortal flesh is frail and like wax is easily turned in whatever direction nature, old and corrupt, draws it.' [2370]

About Nuns

'There remains the order of veiled women whom we call holy nuns; assembled together from virgins and widows, the order is well known to many. They celebrate the canonical hours in the usual way, [2375] fulfilling their duty by night and day. In high voices they sing with such sweet melody that you would think they were sirens singing. They are serpents in body, sirens in voice, dragons in courage, Susannah in cleanliness, Paris in heart. [2380] But they have one characteristic

---

2363 *Decoquit*: 'decoquere' = 'to smelt, refine' (metal); see *DMLBS* 4b.
2364 Cf. 1 Pet. 1: 7.
2369 *cerea flecti*: cf. Horace, *Ars poetica*, 163: 'cereus in vitium flecti'.
2371–400 Sally Thompson's study of English nunneries after the Norman Conquest lists over 120 nunneries in existence in the 12th c. (*Women Religious*, pp. 217–31), spanning the whole range of monastic orders. See also the list in Gilchrist, *Gender and Material Culture*, pp. 36–50. Thompson surveys Cluniacs, Cistercians, the (mixed) order of Fontevrault, and the canonical orders. Nigel's treatment, however, lumps all the different orders together and characterizes them according to the general medieval stereotypes of women: they weep copiously (2381–4); they are sexually incontinent (2395–400); they are quarrelsome (2392–4). As was common in portraits of secular women, Nigel indulges in prurient allusions to the 'white limbs' hidden beneath their black robes (2390), and as he does with the Cistercians, he makes a salacious joke out of their possible lack of drawers (2391–2). Their singing is also interpreted as a sexual attraction (2377–80; cf. n. to lines 2411–12). None of these remarks shows detailed knowledge of 12th-c. nuns and their behaviour (as indeed is only to be expected from a Benedictine monk), other than their black robes and close-cropped hair.
2375 *frequentant*: 'frequentare' = 'to celebrate (ritual)' (Niermeyer).
2380 *smigmate*: 'smigma' = 'ointment', used as an equivalent of soap (*OLD* s.v. 'smegma' 1). Cf. the story of Susanna, Dan. 13: 17 (Sus. 17): 'Dixit ergo puellis: Afferte mihi oleum, et smigmata, et ostia pomarii claudite, ut lauer.' *Paris*: as the adulterous lover of Menelaus's wife Helen, Paris here represents unbridled sexuality, in contrast to Susanna, representative of chastity.

244 SPECVLVM STVLTORVM

Sed tamen illud habent, unum quod cuncta refellit:
 ante Deum lacrimas quae sine lege fluunt.
His Dominum placant semper ueniamque merentur,
 his sua cuncta lauant crimina, quicquid agunt.
2385 Omnibus aure tenus licet his nutrire capillos
 sed non ulterius, regula namque uetat.
Vtuntur niueis agni de corpore sumptis
 pellibus intonsis, pallia nigra gerunt.
Hae caput abscondunt omnes sub tegmine nigro,
2390 sub tunicis nigris candida membra latent.
Cingula nulla ferunt sed nec femoralibus uti
 consuetudo fuit, nescio si modo sit.
Numquam rixantur, nisi cum locus exigit aut res,
 sed neque percutiunt, sit nisi causa grauis.
2395 Harum sunt quaedam steriles, quaedam parientes,
 uirgineoque tamen nomine cuncta tegunt.
Quae pastoralis baculi donatur honore,
 illa quidem melius fertiliusque parit.
Vix etiam quaeuis sterilis reperitur in illis,
2400 donec eis aetas talia posse negat.'

2381 tamen] cum *VdPk*; illud] id *CW*   2382 fluunt] refluunt *fm* pluunt *fh*
2384 sua] suis *fh*; crimina] criminis *fm;* agunt] agant *α SMuVaVbVcVdBePkPmNe TrHaLa Q*
2385 aure tenus] aure tenens *Tr* auertenus *Ve* ante tenus *VdBe La* antetenus *fh* antenus
fn   2386 *om. Z*; namque] uera *fh fn*   2387 niueis] uineis *GoPmNe La*^{ac}
2388 intonsis] insuntis consis *Go* et tonsis *Tr* intensis *Vd Ha*; gerunt] ferunt α ferent *K*
2389 hae] hec *SVa MN* hi *GI*; abscondunt] ostendunt *fh fn*; nigro] sacro *F*   2390 can-
dida] cetera α   2391 cingula] singula *L Vd K Z*; ferunt sed nec] *om. L*; femoralibus]
femuralibus *Mu* femoralia *fn*   2392 *(whole line)* illis usque modo consuetudo fuit α
2394 percutiunt] percussint *VdBe La*   2395 harum] horum *T Q om. CWHuMNDK*;
sunt quaedam] quedam sunt α sunt *ROPVe fb*; steriles] steriles et δ *fb*; quaedam²] quedam
sunt *Tr* quodam *fn*; parientes] parturientes δ *Tr fb*   2396 uirgineoque] uirgineo *D* uirgineo quoque *fh fn* uirginitatis *Vc*; tamen] cum *fn*; nomine] nomina *Vd Tr*   2397 bac-
uli] waculi *Vc* baculo *fm*; donatur] dotatur *H*^{pc} δ *GI ZX* donantur *VdPm QY* uocatur
Tr   2400 eis] eius *Z fh*; negat] neget *QY*

2381–4 Copious weeping has a double relevance to nuns: it is a stereotypical characteristic
of women, as shown by the proverb 'Fallere flere nere/ statuit deus in muliere' ('Deceit,
weeping, spinning, were fixed in women by God'; Walther, *Proverbia*, 8751), and it is the
proper function of the monastic orders: St Jerome's saying, 'Monachus autem non doctoris
habet sed plangentis officium, qui uel se uel mundum lugeat' ('The duty of the monk is not
teaching but weeping, to mourn for himself or the world'; *Adversus Vigilantium*, xv. 14–16,
CCSL lxxixC. 28), was very widely quoted by medieval writers (sometimes with 'lugentis' or
'dolentis' in place of 'plangentis'). A computer search in *Patrologia Latina* turns up over a
dozen entries, including such well-known authors as Abelard and St Bernard.

SPECVLVM STVLTORVM 245

which renders all the rest void: the tears which are uncontrollably poured out before God. With these they continually appease God and earn mercy; with these they wash away whatever sins they commit. All of them are allowed to grow their hair down to their ears, [2385] but no further, for the Rule forbids it. They use white unclipped sheepskins taken from the body of a lamb, and wear black habits. They all hide their head with a black covering; their white limbs are hidden beneath black habits. [2390] They wear no girdles, nor was it their custom to wear knickers—I don't know if it is now. They never quarrel, unless occasion and cause demand it, nor do they strike a blow unless there is a serious reason. Some of those are barren, some fertile, [2395] but they cloak everything with the name of virginity. The one who is endowed with the honour of the pastoral rod [i.e. the abbess], she indeed gives birth more fruitfully and often. Hardly any among them is found who is sterile, until age denies them the possibility.' [2400]

2390–2 Hinting at the beauties hidden beneath female clothing was a convention in descriptions of lovely women. See Alan of Lille, *De planctu Naturae*, ed. Wetherbee, i. 4, where Alan teasingly refers to the secret beauties hidden under the goddess Nature's robe; John of Hauville, *Architrenius*, ed. Wetherbee, ii. 66–7, where the visible beauties enable the beholder to deduce the quality of those that are hidden; Geoffrey of Vinsauf, *Poetria nova*, 594–5: 'Taceo de partibus infra:/ Aptius hic loquitur animus quam lingua.'

2393–4 On anger and quarrelsomeness as stereotypically female characteristics, see Mann, *Chaucer and Medieval Estates Satire*, pp. 122–3 and n. 82.

2395–400 Most of the evidence on the sexual incontinence of nuns in Power, *Medieval English Nunneries*, pp. 436–74, post-dates *SS*. However, she refers to an example in the notorious case reported in Roger of Howden's *Gesta* (i. 135–6) under the year 1177: the prioress of Amesbury had borne three children after taking the habit, and had infected her nuns with similar laxity. The prioress was expelled, and nuns from Fontevrault were brought over to reform the convent life; those of the nuns who repented were allowed to stay, if they followed the rule of Fontevrault.

246 SPECVLVM STVLTORVM

De ordine de Simplingham

'Est et adhuc alius nuper nouus ordo repertus,
  quem bene, nam bonus est, commemorare decet.
Hic apud Anglorum fines exortus, ab ipso
  nomen habet natus quo fuit ipse loco.
2405 Simplingham dictus, de simplicitate uocatus—
  siue per antiphrasim ordo uocatur ita.
Canonicos laicosque simul duplicesque sorores
  quadrifido positu continet una domus.
Canonici missas tantum, reliquumque sorores
2410 explent, officii debita iura sui.
Corpora non uoces murus disiungit, in unum
  psallunt directo psalmatis absque melo.'

Nouus ordo Burnelli factus de aliis ordinibus

'Talia dum mecum tacitus considero, uitam
  nescio quam possim constituisse mihi.

2401–12 *om. QY*   **2401** et] *om. F MuVcVdGo*; nuper nouus ordo] nouus nuper ordo *Mu* nuper ordo nouus *fm*   **2402** quem] que *F Vd C*; decet] debet *fm* licet *fh*   **2403** fines] finis *Vd* fratres *Tr Z* ciues *fh fn*   **2404** natus] nactus *VaBe Tr*; loco] locas *fm^{ac}* locos *Vb*   **2405** de] a *LE HuMNDK GI*   **2406** siue] sim *AJCWOP* atque *HuMND GI* sicque *K* simple *X* qui *T*   **2407–8** *om.* δ *GI Tr*   **2408–9** *om. L SMuVaVbVcVdTGoBePkPmNe HaLa Z fh fm fn; replaced by 2 new lines*, *T*: continet iste locus deuotione pares/ qui summis uotis nituntur ad hoc sed que   **2408** quadrifido positu] quas simul in unum β *X*; una] illa *F B*   **2409** *om. fm*; missas] missam *H X* missa *J*   **2410** iura] iuraque *Z* uita *Ha fn*   **2412** psallunt] psallant *O Z* psallit *GI* pallunt *M*; directo] directe *T R*; psalmatis] plasmatis *LE Go* psalmitis *R fh*; absque] atque *D I*; melo] mero *AJCWROPVe* metro *HuM?NDK GI* molo *Mu* malo *Go* melo /uel malo *Ha*   **2413** *after 2412 HuMNDK GI add 244 lines* (see Appendix B: Interpolation on the Mendicant Friars); talia] talem *fh*   **2414** possim] possum β *SMuTGo CWRHuMNDK GI Tr ZX* possem α *Vc*; constituisse] continuisse *LE*

2401–12 *nouus ordo*: the 'new order' was instituted *c.*1131, when Gilbert, parish priest of Sempringham in Lincolnshire, installed seven women in a cloistered enclosure attached to his parish church. The nuns followed the Benedictine Rule, but the order owed much to the support of the Cistercian abbot Bernard of Clairvaux (see n. to lines 2411–12). As at Cîteaux, the nuns were supported by lay-brothers and lay-sisters who performed the necessary manual work; soon after, they were joined by canons, who served as chaplains and administrators, and followed a Rule derived from Augustinian and Premonstratensian practices (see Graham, *S. Gilbert of Sempringham and the Gilbertines*, and Brian Golding, *Gilbert of Sempringham and the Gilbertine Order*, ch. 2, pp. 71–137, 'The Making of the Rule').

The Gilbertines doubtless earned Nigel's approval by their support of Thomas Becket in his quarrel with Henry II; they helped him to escape from England in 1164 (Golding, *Gilbert of Sempringham*, pp. 38–40). See also *Becket Correspondence*, i. 180–3 (no. xliv).

2407–8 Nigel accurately describes the 'fourfold' membership of the order: canons, lay-brothers, nuns, and lay-sisters.

2410 *debita iura*: also at *Miracles*, 936.

SPECVLVM STVLTORVM 247

About the Order of Simplingham

'There is still another order, a new one, recently invented, which it is fitting to mention, for it's a good one. This one arose among the English, and takes its name from the place where it was born. It is called Simplingham, named after "simplicity" [2405]—or else the order is so called by antiphrasis. One house contains canons and lay-brothers and two sorts of sisters all at the same time, in a fourfold structure. The canons perform the Masses only, the sisters perform the rest, the due obligations of their office. [2410] A wall divides their bodies, but not their voices; they chant the psalms together plainly, without harmony.'

The New Order of Burnellus, Made from the Other Orders

'When I quietly reflect on these things, I don't know what life to settle on for myself. So I think it safer and also more prudent for

2411–12 In order to guard against the obvious dangers of a mixed community, great care was taken to keep the men and the women separate at all times (except when the canons administered Extreme Unction to a dying nun). They had separate living quarters; food and money were passed through a turntable window, and a wall in the church kept them apart during religious services (*Monasticon anglicanum*, vol. vi. 2, p. xix (*Institutiones*, c. ii); *Vita Sancti Gilberti* c. 16, in *The Book of St Gilbert*, ed. Foreville and Keir, p. 46; Golding, *Gilbert of Sempringham*, pp. 126–32). See also Walter Map, *De nugis curialium*, dist. i. 27 (pp. 116–17), who states that 'nothing sinister is as yet reported of them', but 'there is fear of it'. This fear was justified, not only by the notorious episode of the nun of Watton (see Constable, 'Ailred of Rievaulx and the Nun of Watton'), but also by an incident reported by Gerald of Wales (see below). *directo* (adverbial) 'According to the method of performance, we may distinguish three different types of psalmody: *direct*, *antiphonal*, and *responsorial*. In direct psalmody, the verses of the psalms are sung [in a monotone] straight through with no textual additions' and no melodic variations (Hoppin, *Medieval Music*, p. 81). A papal bull confirming Gilbertine privileges, issued by Alexander III in 1178, endorses this mode of performance for the nuns: 'Moniales quoque in omnibus illum modum officii sui in ecclesia servent qui a *dilecto in domino filio* Gileberto primo priore ordinis de Sempingham [*sic*] institutus et a beato Bernardo quondam Clarevallis abbate et aliis religiosis personis primo fuerat approbatus, scilicet non musice cantando sed honeste *et moderate* psallendo atque legendo' ('The nuns also in church should observe in all things that form of the Office that was instituted by Gilbert, beloved son of the Lord, first prior of the order of Sempringham, and which was approved by blessed Bernard, sometime abbot of Clairvaux, along with many other religious, that is, [the nuns perform the Office] not by singing musically but by chanting and reading in a dignified and restrained manner'). See Cheney, 'Papal privileges for Gilbertine houses', pp. 59–60. (Cheney's text is a reconstruction based on MS Bodley, Laud misc. 642, fos. 2ᵛ–3ʳ, but the manuscript version differs in the passage quoted above only in the substitution of 'supradicto sancto' for the first of the italicized phrases above and of 'moderate ac distincte' for the second.) The prohibition is mentioned by John of Salisbury, *Policraticus* i. 6 (ed. Webb, i. 43; trans. Pike, pp. 33–4). The reasons behind this injunction may be discerned in the incident reported by Gerald of Wales, *Speculum ecclesiae*, dist. iii. 11 (*Opera*, iv. 184–5): despite the intervening wall in church, a nun and a canon, each of whom possessed a distinctively beautiful voice, were attracted to each other, contrived a secret meeting, and eloped together.

2413 *tacitus considero*: cf. Gen. 37: 11.

248   SPECVLVM STVLTORVM

2415   Tutius ergo puto nec non consultius esse
        ut statuam leges ordinis ipse noui,
        qui meus ordo meo nomen de nomine sumat,
        nomen in aeternum uiuat ut inde meum.
        Sic igitur fiet, de quolibet ordine sumam
2420   quod melius fuerit commodiusque mihi.
        Ordine de Templi sumamus equos gradientes
        leniter, ut lenis sit meus ordo mihi.
        Vt mihi mentiri liceat quocumque locorum
        fratribus ex aliis hoc retinere uolo.
2425   Vt feria sexta liceat mihi pinguibus uti,
        hoc Cluniacensis conferat ordo mihi.
        Fratribus ex albis satis est et sufficit illud
        ut liceat braccis nocte carere meis.
        Grandimontanos in eo quod ubique loquuntur
2430   multum commendo, quod retinere uolo.
        Carthusiae fratres in eo decerno sequendos,
        missa quod in mense sufficit una satis.
        Canonicos nigros carnes comedendo sequemur,
        ne quid ab hypocrisi contrahat ordo meus.
2435   Praemonstratenses statuo de iure sequendos

2416 leges] regulam *F*   2417–18 *transp. after 2420* α β *SMuVaVbVcVdTGoBePkPmNe TrHaLa ZXQY fh fm fn*   2417 qui] quod *MuVaTGoPkPm fh fn*; meo nomen de nomine sumat] non nomen de nomine sumare *S* nomen meo de nomine sumare *Go* meum sumat de nomine nomen *HuMNDK*   2418 uiuat] ueniat *Vd* uiuet *T fh fn*; ut] et α *H SMuVaVbVcVdTGoBePkPmNe HaLa fm fn*   2419–20 *om.* δ *GI*   2419 fiet] fiat *VdGoBe TrLa*   2422 leniter] leuiter *SMuVaVbVcVdTGoBeNe JHuMN TrHaLa fh fn*; lenis] leuis *H SMuVaVbVcVdTGoBeNe JHuMN TrLa fh* leuius *Ha* lenius *PkPm*[ac]; sit] si *fh* fit *Z*   2423 quocumque] quoque *Vd* ubique *fh*   2424–7 hoc retinere—ex albis] *om. Ne*   2424 aliis] albis *L H*; hoc] haec *E Pm* hic *VdBe*   2425 feria sexta] feriis sextis *HuMND* feria quarta β *JK X*   2426 conferat] conferet *E B T X* tribuat *Z* 2427 albis] aliis β *Va* δ *GI XQY*; et] ut *CWHuMN om. fm fn*; illud] idem *X* mihi *fn* 2428 liceat] liqueat *VdBe TrLa*   2429 Grandimontanos] Grandimontanes *H* Grandimontenses *MuVbVcVdGo fm* Grandimontensis *SVaBePkPmNe TrHa fn* Grandimontes *La* Grandimontanenses *T* Grandimontanum *fh*; ubique loquuntur] ubicumque loquuntur *SNe GI Q* loquuntur ubique *Va* ubique locantur *La*[ac] ubique locorum *Tr* ubique *T* multa loquuntur δ   2430 quod retinere] quodque (quosque *R* quoque *GI*) tenere β *SMuVaVbVcVdTGoBePkPmNe TrHaLa* δ *GI ZXQY fh fm fn*   2431 *om. GI*; decerno] discerno α *AJCWRODVe XQY* cerno *Vc*   2432–5 *om. La*   2432 mense] mensa *T Tr*; sufficit] suffit *fn*; satis] mihi *K fm*   2433–4 *transp. after 2436* α 2433 canonicos] canonicosque *F*; carnes] carnem α carnis *Tr* sequar carnes *Go*; comedendo] comedentes *Go* commendo *J Tr*; sequemur] sequamur *SMuVdTBePkPmNe ROVe Ha Z fm fn* seque *G* sequentur *Tr om. Go*   2435 Praemonstratenses] Premostratenses *LE*; statuo] statuto *Va* statui *LE* statuam *Z* status *QY*; de] quoque *LE om. fn*

SPECVLVM STVLTORVM 249

me [2415] to lay down the rules of a new order myself. My order will take this name from mine; thus my name will live for ever. And this is how it will be done: from each order I shall take whatever is best and most agreeable to me. [2420] From the order of the Temple let us take the gentle-paced horses, so that my order may be gentle to me. And from the other brothers I want to retain this, that I am allowed to tell lies anywhere. Let the Cluniac order give me the right to consume fats on Friday. [2425] From the White Monks all that's needed is that I should be allowed to dispense with my pants at night. I much approve of the Grandmontines in that they speak everywhere, and I want to retain that. [2430] I decree that the brothers of the Charterhouse are to be imitated in that one Mass a month is enough for them. We shall imitate the Black Canons in eating meat, lest my order is contaminated by hypocrisy. I decree that the Premonstratensians are rightly to be imitated [2435] in their soft tunic and multiple habits. From the

250   *SPECVLVM STVLTORVM*

in molli tunica multiplicique toga.
Ordine de reliquo placet ut persona secunda
foedere perpetuo sit mihi iuncta comes.
Hic fuit ordo prior et conditus in Paradiso;
2440   hunc Deus instituit, et benedixit ei.
Hunc in perpetuum decreuimus esse tenendum,
cuius erat genitor cum genetrice mea;
et genus omne meum semper fuit ordinis huius,
quo genus humanum deficiente cadet.
2445   Ordine de sacro uelatarum mulierum
accipiam zonam semper abesse meam;
cingula lata mihi non sunt bona, sed neque uentri
conueniunt grosso cingula stricta meo.
Est et adhuc aliud in eis quod in ordine nostro
2450   apponi uolumus, cum locus aptus erit.
Quid de Simplingham, quantum, uel qualia sumam,
nescio, nam noua res me dubitare facit.
Hoc tamen ad praesens nulla ratione remittam,
namque necesse nimis fratribus esse reor,
2455   quod numquam nisi clam nulloque sciente sorori
cum quocumque suo fratre manere licet.
Sunt etiam quaedam quae si non nunc meminisse
possumus ad praesens, postea tempus erit.
Ergo nil restat nisi confirmatio sola
2460   pontificis summi, quam dabit ipse libens.

2437 ut] nunc *Vc om. H Tr*   **2439** prior] primus *T CW*[ac]   **2441** *om. Vb O*;
decreuimus] discernimus *F* decernimus *SVdBe TrLa* de criminis *D* nos uolumus *Go*
2442 genitor] genitrix *fh*; genetrice mea] genitore meo *fh*   **2444** cadet] cadit α *Go C Tr*
Z caret *T*   **2445** uelatarum] sacratarum β *SMuVaVbVdTGoBePkPmNe AJCWROPVe*
GI TrHaLa ZXQY fh fm fn   **2446** zonam...meam] et ouam...meam *E* zona...mea
β sanam...meam *Mu fh* zonam...mihi *Tr*; abesse] adesse *fh*   **2447** cingula] singula
Go K; non] ut non *L*; sunt] sint *L*; bona] *om. LE*; uentri] uenti *N* uenter *Vb fh*   **2448** *om.*
Z; grosso] grossa *Tr Q* gresso *X*; cingula] singula *L K*   **2449** et adhuc aliud] adhuc
et aliud *VaGoPm* et adhuc alius *Z* adhuc aliud *Vd CW* aliud adhuc *T*; in eis] in eo *O* meis
Be La om. L   **2450** erit] fuerit *fn*   **2451–8** *om. QY*   **2451** uel] et
SMuVaVcVdTGoBePkPmNe HaLa fh quoque *Tr*   **2452** nam] an *Vc* sed
fm   **2453** hoc] hec *F T* hic *VdBe La*   **2454** namque] nam *B AJCWVe GI*; nimis]
minus *L* nimia *I* fuit *fm*   **2455** nulloque] nullaque *MuVbVdGoPmNe* δ *GI Ha ZX fh*
fn; sciente sorori] sciente sororum β *SMuVbVdGoBePkPmNe AJCWRHuMNODKVe GI*
TrHaLa ZX fh fm fn sciente sororem *Va* sciente locorum *Vc* sorore scienti *P*   **2457** *after*
2456 *HuMNDK add 14 lines* (see Appendix B); etiam] et *fm*; quae] bona que
SMuVaVbVcVdTGoBePkPmNe TrHaLa fh bona *fm fn*; si non nunc] si modo non α si nunc
non *R* quamuis non *K* si non hic β *X* si non *SMuVaVbVcVdTGoBePkPmNe TrHaLa Z fh fn*
non *T* quasi *Vc* nunc si non *fm*   **2460** *om. Y*; libens] mihi α labens *Go*

SPECVLVM STVLTORVM 251

remaining order [the secular canons], it pleases me that a mistress should be joined to me as my companion by a perpetual bond. This was the first religious order, founded in Paradise; God instituted this and blessed it. [2440] This order we have decreed shall be observed for ever; my father and mother were members of it, and all my race were always of this order, without which human kind would wither and perish. From the holy order of veiled women, [2445] I shall choose that I never have a belt; loose belts are not good, but a tight belt does not suit my fat belly. And there is something else which I want to be added to my order, when the place is suitable. [2450] What I should take from Simplingham, how much, or which features, I don't know, for the novelty of it makes me doubtful. But this, for the time being, I shall not leave out on any account, for I think it very necessary to the brethren, that no sister should be allowed to be with her brother except in secret, without anyone knowing. [2455] There are some other things too, but if I can't remember them now, there will be time later. So nothing remains except only the pope's approval, which he will give gladly. [2460]

2455 The variant reading 'nullaque sciente sororum' arises from scribal failure to look beyond the end of the line and to realize that 'sorori' does not belong with this phrase but depends on 'licet', and that 'nulloque sciente' is a self-contained unit.

252 SPECVLVM STVLTORVM

Nam qui iusta petunt, nulla ratione repulsam
a domino papa sustinuisse solent.
Illuc ergo decet primo diuertere, papam
et fratres humili sollicitare prece.'

Quomodo Burnellus obuiauit Galieno

2465   Talia dicenti ueniens Galienus ab urbe
obuius accessit, uidit, et inquit ei:
'Numquid non es tu noster Burnellus?' Et ille:
'Heu mihi! Sum certe; care magister, aue!
Ille dolens ego sum Burnellus ab urbe Cremona,
2470   quem bene tu nosti, si meminisse placet.
Ecce senem cernis fractumque labore decenni,
qui iuuenis quondam fortis et acer eram.
Quam mala multa tuli pridem! Sed me tamen unum
funditus absumpsit, sollicitudo scholae.
2475   Rusticus atque schola duo sunt tormenta, dolores
intus et exterius quae mihi ferre solent.
Rusticus exterius pungit, ferit atque flagellat,
at schola depascit uiscera, corda, latus.
Saxa sed et lapides mallem portare molares
2480   quam sic assiduis inuigilare scholis.
Quam mala fila mihi neuerunt fata, nec ultra
uel citra possum quam statuere mihi.

2461 repulsam] repulsa *T C X fm* pulsam *Z*   2462 solent] ualent *GI*
2463 illuc] illic *F*   2464 *fh and fn excerpt 2 end here*; sollicitare] solicitate *VaGoPk*
2465 *Fr rejoins*; dicenti] dicente *H GoFr*   2467 es] est *E D* eras *Ne*   2468 heu]
en *AJCWHuMNOPDVe Tr* ey *R*; mihi] ego *D Tr*   2470 *om. T*; tu] si *SVbPk om. X*; si]
sed *LE*   2471 *fn excerpt 1 joins here*; fractumque] stratumque *T* fructumque *Fr fn*
2474 absumpsit] assumpsit *SVaBePk GI TrLa Z* asumpsit *PmNe* exhausit *Vd*
2475 dolores] doloris α β *SMuVaVbVdTBePkFrPmNe AJCWRHuMNPDKVe GI TrHaLa
ZXQY fm fn* dolorum *O* laboris *Go*   2476–7 quae mihi ferre—Rusticus exterius *om.
TGo Ve ZQ*   2476 mihi ferre solent] mihi ferie solent *Ne* cruciare solent α nocuere
mihi *CWHuMNDK GI Tr* me nocere solent *AJP Y* macerare solent *RO* nocuisse solent *X*
2477 *om. Vc*; flagellat] flagella *A?CWRHuMNPK I*   2478 at] *Skutsch* sed α β γ *HaLa
ZX fm fn* dat δ *GI Tr QY*; depascit] sed pascit *ACWRHuMNOPDVe GI Tr QY* sed passit *J*
2479 mallem] uellem *P fn*   2480 sic] sit *SNe fn*; assiduis] assiduus *Mu J*
2481–2 *om. T*   2481 fila] filia *Z* uila *Go* fata *LE* δ *GI Tr XQY om. Fr*; neuerunt] *B*ᵃᶜ
uenerunt *H* uenerunt mea *Vd* nerunt me *F* nerunt mea *Va*ᵖᶜ*VbVcBe Ha Z* netunt mea *fn*
norunt mea *SMuPkPmNe fm* norunt me *Go* uerum mea (me *QY*) δ *GI Tr XQY* fuerunt mea
L fuerant mea *E* ferunt mea *La* erunt mea *Fr*; fata] facta *AJCWHuMNDVe GI ZXQY* uel
fata *add. in margin X*ᵖᶜ; nec] non *J* uel *F K fn* sed β *X*   2482 uel citra] nec ultra *S* nec
citra *MuVaVbVcVdGoBePkFrPmNe HaLa Z fm fn*; possum] possim *Mu* passum *Tr fm*
nequeo β *X*; quam] quem *Tr* quod *CWHuMND*   *fm* ends here, with 'Et tantum de illo'; *fn
excerpt 1 ends here*

SPECVLVM STVLTORVM

253

For those who seek what is just do not receive a refusal from the Lord Pope on any account. So I must go there first, to beseech the Pope and the brethren with humble prayer.'

How Burnellus Met Galen

As he said this, Galen, coming out of the city, [2465] met him, saw him, and said to him: 'Are not you our Burnellus?' And he replied, 'Alas! I certainly am; greetings, dear master! I am that poor Burnellus from the town of Cremona whom you knew well, if it pleases you to remember. [2470] See, you behold me old, and broken by ten years' labour, I who was once a strong and energetic youth. How many evils I suffered in former days! But one completely ruined me—the concern for study. The peasant and the school are two tortures [2475] which inflict outward and inward suffering on me. The peasant pierces me outwardly, strikes and whips me, but the school eats up my entrails, heart, and flanks. I would rather carry rocks and millstones than sweat away in constant study like that. [2480] What an evil thread the fates have spun for me, and I cannot fall short of what they have decreed for me, nor go beyond it. My mind tosses in doubts and torments, and my mind loses

2475 *tormenta dolores*: the reading 'doloris' in most of the manuscripts may have been prompted by the echo of Ovid, *Metamorphoses*, xiv. 716. Also in *Lawrence*, 1208 (with 'dolores'), 1479 (with 'dolori'), 2091 (with 'doloris'). For Skutsch's emendation to 'dolores', see Introduction, p. lxxxii.

2478 According to Mozley's *apparatus criticus*, 'at' is a conjecture by Skutsch (not, however, to be found in 'Three rare words'), which elegantly accounts for both the variants 'sed' and 'dat'.

2481 As at line 1598, 'neuerunt' has provoked considerable scribal confusion; only *B* has the correct reading (and the initial 'n' in *B* seems to have been corrected from a 'u').

254 SPECVLVM STVLTORVM

Fluctuat in dubiis animus meus inque dolendis,
praeque dolore meo mens mea mente caret.

2485 Namque tot et tanta miseri sunt scandala mundi,
tot regum scelera pontificumque mala,
tot quoque sunt mortes in religione, tot extra
pessima praeque sui sorde tacenda mihi,
quod dum flens recolo mundi mala prospicioque

2490 quis sit, quis fuerit, quis status orbis erit,
ignis ut a facie subito noua cera liquescit,
et solis radio nix glaciesque fluunt,
sic ego deficio sic defluo sicque resoluor,
totus et in lacrimas fontis ad instar eo.

2495 Quarum praecipua, quarum praemaxima causa est
curia Romana quod modo uadit ita;
quae regum domina, quae regnantum diadema,
quae decus atque decor urbis et orbis erat;
quae solis radius, noctis carbunculus ardens,

2500 malleus erroris, poena parata malis,

2483–3258 *om.* α; *F has the remaining lines in the following order:* 3279–432, 3259–78, 3323–8 *(repeated, = F(2)),* 3435–44, 3447–8　　2483–4 *transp. Vd*; meus inque—dolore meo *om. Go*　　2483 dolendis] dolendus *W Ha Q* dolendo *Vc*　　2484–5 *transp. Z* 2485 tanta] tanti *VdBe TrLa*; miseri] misera *RP* miser *Pk*　　2487 tot quoque] totque *Ha Y fb* quod quoque *Go*; tot²] totque *Fr et Oᵃᶜ* uel *Oᵖᶜ* quot *VcNe om. T*　　2488 pessima praeque] pre nimiaque β *SMuVaVbVcVdTBePkPmNe TrHaLa Z* pre nimia quod *Fr* pramiaque *Go* pessima postque *HuMN* pessimaque *fb*; sorde] corde *Sᵃᶜ* sorte *fb* surdo *Fr* sardo *Tr*　　2489 dum flens] dum fles *Vd* dum deflens *Mu* deflens *VaVbVcGoPkPmNe* defluens *Fr*; dum] sum *D* cum *Z* bene *N* dum /uel de *Ha*　　2490 fuerit] fuerat *MuVaTGoPm* 2492 et] ex *CR*　　2493–4 *om. Vd*　　2493 sic defluo] *om. Z fb*　　2494 lacrimas] lacrimis *Tr fb*; eo] ego *H MN X* ero *R*　　2495 quarum praemaxima causa est] quarumque maxima causa est *MuVaVbVdGoBePkPmNe HaLa* quarumque maxima causa *SVc* quarumcumque maxima causa *Fr* quorum quoque maxima causa est *T* quarum est praemaxima causa *X* quarum praemaxima causa *RPK Q* duarum premaxima causa est *Tr* 2496 quod] que β γ *R HaLa ZXQY* qui *Tr*; modo] non *fb*　　2497 regnantum] regnatum *Fr Z*

2491–2 Raymo's notes describe these lines as a conflation of Ps. 67 (68): 3 ('sicut fluit cera a facie ignis') and Wisd. 2: 3 ('et sicut nebula dissolvetur quae fugata est a radiis solis'). The image of melting wax is common in the Bible (see Ps. 21 (22): 15; 57 (58): 9; 96 (97): 5; Mic. 1: 4, and cf. *Lawrence*, 1088), and Ps. 67 certainly accounts for the phrase 'a facie ignis', but the combination of this image with the melting of snow and ice (not 'cloud') at the appearance of the sun has a closer parallel in Ovid, *Metamorphoses*, iii. 487–9: 'sed ut intabescere flavae/ igne levi cerae matutinaeque pruinae/ sole tepente solent'. Raymo also sees line 2491 as the source of Eberhard the German, *Laborintus* (ed. Faral), 913–14: '... vultus/ Defluit, ut cera liquitur igne nova', but only the adjective 'nova' provides a verbal link with *SS*. Closer to *SS* is the 13th-c. *commedia, De uxore cerdonis,* 22–3 (*Commedie,* vi. 458): 'Intabescit amans glacies ut sole repente,/ Ignis ut a facie cera liquere solet', where wax and ice appear together;

SPECVLVM STVLTORVM 255

its reason through grief. For so numerous and so great are the scandals of the wretched world, [2485] so many the crimes of kings and the wickednesses of bishops, so many too are the deaths within religion, so many evils without, which because of their foulness cannot be mentioned, that when I with weeping recall the evils of the world, and consider what the state of the world is, what it has been, and what it will be, [2490] as new wax suddenly melts before fire, and snow and ice thaw in the ray of the sun, so I weaken and melt and am totally dissolved in tears, taking on the likeness of a fountain. The principal, the greatest cause of this, [2495] is that this is now the case with the Roman curia: she who was the mistress of kings, the crown of rulers, the glory and honour of the City and the world, a beam of the sun, the blazing carbuncle of night, the hammer of error, a punishment ready for wrongs, [2500] the sword of justice, the abundant oil of mercy, a generous hand

the first half-line of the hexameter ('Ignis ut a facie') echoes *SS*, and 'repente' repeats 'subito' (but may be a mistake for 'tepente'), while 'intabescit' echoes Ovid. In short, Nigel's combination of the wax image with frost more likely goes back to Ovid; the link with Eberhard is dubious, since the fundamental idea of melting wax may simply be proverbial (see Singer, *Thesaurus*, s.v. Wachs 1.4, xii. 302), and Nigel's influence is more clearly apparent in *De uxore cerdonis*.

2495–558 *curia Romana*: the papal court at Rome was a vast legal bureaucracy, and 'as the ultimate appeals judge of the Latin church was one of the principal sources of papal power. In addition, the fees and costs collected from litigants furnished an important source of revenues for members of the curia and accounted for a large part of the prosperity of medieval Rome' (Brundage, *Medieval Canon Law*, p. 123; see also Yunck, *Lineage of Lady Meed*, pp. 85–92). However, even a sympathizer such as St Bernard of Clairvaux admonished his former pupil Pope Eugenius III (1145–53) against the excessive amount of time spent in dealing with litigation (Brundage, pp. 123–4), and understandably, the litigants themselves were resentful at the amount of time and money that had to be expended in travelling to Rome and waiting to have their case heard (ibid. p. 127). As a result, impassioned criticism of the Roman curia became a staple of medieval satire in both verse and prose. (See Yunck, *Lineage of Lady Meed*, pp. 67–81, 93–117, and Benzinger, *Invectiva in Romam*, especially pp. 100–15.) Classic examples of contemporary satire on papal avarice and corruption are the poems of Walter of Châtillon (see *Poems*, no. lvi (= *Carmina Burana*, no. xlii); no. lix. 8–11; no. lxiii; no. lxiv) and the parodic *Gospel according to the Mark of Silver*, which survives in several different versions (printed in Lehmann, *Parodie*, pp. 183–8, and Bayless, *Parody*, pp. 321–3, discussed on pp. 136–42). Walter Map explains the name R.O.M.A. as 'Radix Omnium Malorum Avaricia' (*De nugis curialium*, dist. ii. 17 (pp. 168–9)). For the attitude of the Canterbury monastery to the papal curia, see Introduction, pp. lxxiv–lxxv.

2497 *regnantum diadema*: cf. Isa. 62: 3.

2498 *decus atque decor*: a frequent punning pair in Nigel; see *SS*, 2551; *Miracles*, 262, 595, 1412, 1432, 2533; *Paul*, 236. Cf. Walter of Châtillon, *Poems*, no. lviii. 15. 1: 'O decus et demonum decor, Antichriste'.

256   *SPECVLVM STVLTORVM*

iustitiae gladius, oleum pietatis abundans,
  larga manus inopi, dextra referta bonis,
flos nouus et nullo marcescens temporis aestu,
  fons sine defectu, balsama larga fluens,

2505 religionis apex, pacis concordia, morum
  gloria, fax fidei, regula recta boni,
uexillum patriae, sed et omnibus omnia facta
  debuit esse caput, sicut origo fuit.

Sed conuersa retro rediit, fideique prioris

2510   immemor in caudam fecit abire caput.
Si caput a capio uel dixeris a capiendo,
  tunc est ipsa caput, omnia namque capit.
Sic declinando, "capio, capis", ad capiendum
  retia laxauit, retia longa nimis;

2515 quod de praeterito "cepi" formare futurum
  non ualet ad praesens, nec uidet unde locum.

Quondam larga sui proprii nec auara cruoris,
  fundere consueuit seque suumque suis,
nunc uice conuersa faciens sitit, atque cruorem

2520   fundat ut alterius, ebibit ipsa suum.
Sic causam mortis quae debuit esse salutis
  fecit, et in populo prodiga fudit eum.
Vasaque commutans ex hoc transfudit in illud,
  sub mellis specie pocula felle linit.

2502 inopi] inopis β *AJCWRHuOPDVe GI XQY fb* inopum *Mu* miseris *K om.*
MN   **2503** nullo marcescens] nulla marcescens *Z* nullo marcens *Fr* nullus marcessu
GI in illo marcescens *Vb*   **2504** fons] flos *fb*   **2505** morum] motum *SVaPkPm*
Ha motus *Go* uotum *VdBe* uel motum *add. in margin Be*[2] uocum /uel motum *La*
2506 *om. Vc*; fax] pax *H* uas *MuGoFrNe Ha* fas *VaVbTBePkPm TrLa* fons *Vd*; recta] tecta
QY certa *Z*   **2507** et] *om. VaFr GI QY*; omnia] ordine δ *Tr X fb*   **2508** sicut]
sicut et *Pm* sic et *fb*   **2509** prioris] pudoris δ *GI ZQY*   **2510** in caudam] in
cauda *Be TrLa* in causa *Fr* incautum *Mu* caudam *Z*; fecit] facit *Va K*   **2511–12** *om. O*
2514 laxauit] laxat *fb*; longa] larga γ+   **2515** quod] hec γ *HaLa* et *Tr*; cepi] cepit
MuVaTGoFrNe Ha   **2516** uidet] uidit *CVe*; unde] inde *DK* bene *O Q*; *(whole line)*
sed (si *Vc* nam *Z*) nequit ad presens nec (non *Tr*) ualet inde dolet γ+ *Z*   **2517** sui] fuit
γ- *TrHaLa Z om. O*; auara] amara *GI*   **2518–19** *om. P*   **2518** *om.*
Vc   **2519** conuersa] uersa *Tr Z fb*; faciens] sitiens β *SMuVbVcVdTGoBePkFrPmNe*
AJHuWMNODKVe GI TrHaLa ZXQY fb sities *C* sciens *Va*   **2520** fundat] fundit
BeNe R Tr X; ut] et *R* in *SVaVdGoBePkPmNe Ha*[pc]*La* uel *HuMN Tr*; ebibit] ebibat *Fr RO*
GI X ebibet *D*; ipsa] illa *SMuVaVbVcVdGoBePkFrPmNe TrHaLa*   **2521** causam]
causa *MuVaTGoFrPm* tamen *J La*; quae] qui β(*H*[pc]) *GI XY*   **2522** prodiga] prodigia
VaFr CW[ac] prodigat *M*; eum] eam γ+ *Z*; *S ends abruptly*   **2523** illud] illis
AJCWRHuMNO[ac]*PDVe GI Y*   **2524** *line repeated in alternative form* $Z_{(1)}Z_{(2)}$; linit]
luit β *X* luat *AJCWROPVe GI* $Z_{(1)}QY$ habet *D*; *(whole line)* pocula pro (cum *MuVaGoFr*) melle
felle (felleque *Pm* fella *Ha*) referta (refecta *Pm* referte *Vc*) sua (suo *TPk* $Z_{(2)}$) γ- *TrHaLa* $Z_{(2)}$

SPECVLVM STVLTORVM   257

to the poor, a hand filled with good things, a fresh flower which did not wither with seasonal heat, a never-failing fountain, pouring forth abundant balsams, the pinnacle of religion, the harmony of peace, the glory of morals, [2505] the torch of faith, the right rule of good, the banner of the country—indeed, all things to all men—ought to be the head, as she was in the beginning. But, facing about, she has gone backwards, and forgetful of her former good faith has turned her head into her tail. [2510] If you derive "caput" from "capis" or from "capiendo", then she is the head, for she takes everything. She conjugates the verb like this: "I take, then you take", and has stretched out her nets for taking—nets of great length. For from the past tense, "I have taken", [2515] she is unable these days to form a future, and sees no way to doing so. Once generous with her property and not greedy for blood, she used to pour forth herself and her goods for her people. Now, on the contrary, she is thirsty, and so that she may shed another's blood, she swallows up her own. [2520] So she makes a cause of death what ought to be a cause of salvation, and has generously spread it among the people. Changing cups around, she has poured from one into the other; under the appearance of honey, she defiles the cups with poison.

2501 *referta bonis*: also at *SS*, 2936; *Miracles*, 348.

2502 *larga manus*: cf. 1 Macc. 3: 30.

2507 See n. to line 1749.

2508–10 Raymo (p. 127 n. 50) sees an echo of these lines in Boccaccio's *Decameron*, Day v, Novella 3 (ed. Branca, iv. 463): 'In Roma, la quale come è oggi coda così già fu capo del mondo...', but the designation of Rome as 'caput mundi' (or 'caput orbis') goes back to antiquity (see, for example, Ovid, *Amores*, i. 15. 26, and Lucan, *De bello civili*, ii. 655–6), and is found in medieval writers such as Walter of Châtillon (see next note). The 'caput/cauda' inversion is also a conventional trope (see n. to line 20 above). Raymo's claim that one of Boccaccio's letters explicitly refers to *SS* is unfounded (see Introduction, n. 294).

2511–16 *caput...capio...capiendo*: cf. Walter of Châtillon, *Poems*, no. lvi. 4. 1: 'Roma caput mundi est, sed nil capit mundum' (= *Carmina Burana*, no. xlii. 4. 1). Punning wordplay of this type is a frequent device in Goliardic satire, as are the grammatical transformations; see Yunck, *Lineage of Lady Meed*, p. 104; Mann, 'Satiric subject and satiric object', pp. 69–73; Walter of Châtillon, *Poems*, no. xli. 1. 1–4 ('Ecce mundus demundatur,/ totus enim uacuatur/ mundus a mundicia./ Nihil habet mundi mundus...'); no. lv. 1. 46 ('carum care...caro cari,/ careamus carie'); *Map Poems*, 'A legis doctoribus', p. 43, line 20 ('nec jam dona gratiae gratus habet gratis').

2519–20, 2526–30 The greed of the curia for money is often represented as an insatiable thirst in contemporary satire; Yunck (*Lineage of Lady Meed*, p. 96) quotes a popular quatrain: 'Roma sitit; sciensque bibit, bibit atque bibendo/ Plus bibit et sitit et bibit et sitit et siciendo/ Non minuetur ei sitis immense rabiei,/ Ni prius in Roma distillent aurea poma' (Walther, *Initia*, 16864; see *Beiträge*, ed. Werner, no. ccccv, p. 55; cf. no. ccci, p. 121). Other examples of the metaphor are given by Yunck, p. 96, n. 27. See also *Lawrence*, 559–60; Walter of Châtillon, *Poems*, no. xxxix. 2. 4; no. xliii. 18. 3–4; no. xliv. 6–7; no. l. 10. 3; no. lx. 17. 2. The metaphor goes back to Horace, *Epistulae*, ii. 2. 146–8, and Ovid, *Fasti*, i. 215–16.

2519 *faciens* is only in *R*, but the majority reading 'sitiens' is a superfluous repetition of 'sitit'.

258   *SPECVLVM STVLTORVM*

2525 Ipsa tamen semper in se sitibunda manebit,
      cumque bibat semper, semper auara sitit.
Cuius in os patulum, quamuis foret aes mare magnum
      influeretque simul, non satiaret eam.
Vae! barathro uentris, nequeunt extinguere cuius
2530   fercula nulla famem, pocula nulla sitim.
Vae! cui nil satis est, et quem sua reddit egenum
      copia, nec totus sufficit orbis ei.
Sustinet aeris egens quicquid peccatur, auari
      quicquid delirant bursa referta luet.
2535 Bursa referta reos soluit, peccata relaxat,
      quae non peccantes euacuata ligat.
Nil tam difficile, nil tam graue, nil ita prauum
      quod non emendet bursa referta bene.
Haec facit ut licite fiat quodcumque libebit,
2540   reddit et illicitum quod licet arte pari.
Cum sua non mundet, aliorum crimina mundat,
      cernere quae propria uulnera sola nequit.
Sic dolor in capite facit omnia membra dolere,
      toxicat et modicum dolia magna uirus.
2545 Sic ouis una gregem totum maculat maculosa,

2525–6 in se sitibunda—bibat semper *om. Ve*   2525 semper in se] in se semper β
MuFr semper sitiens *Vc* in se *T*   2526 bibat] bibit *Mu La*; auara] auare *D* amara *Go*
GI   2527 in os patulum] in os paculum *VaGoBe La Z* in os paculum *Ne* inops pocu-
lum *Vd* inopis poculum *QY*; aes] et *H VaBe Tr* est *Ve* os *D G Ha X* ens *T* esse *Pk* es et *Z om.*
Vc I(erased)   2528 non] nec *D T*; eam] eum *Vb Q*   2529 uae] de γ- *CR HaLa*
ZQY ut *GI*; cuius] eius *T Z*   2531 quem] que *TGo*   2533 peccatur] peccetur *B*
VaVbVcVdBePkFrPmNe GI HaLa^pc *XQY* pecietur *H* portetur *Mu* petetur *Go* pexetur *Z*
paciatur *Tr* pacietur *T*; auari] *Sedgwick* auarum β *VbVcVdTGoBePkPmNe RP GI HaLa*
ZQY auarus *Mu* auaris *Fr Tr* amarum *AJCWHuNODKVe X fb* amari *M* egenum *Va*
2534 bursa referta] *ed.* cetera bursa β *ACJWRHuMNOPKVe MuVaVbVcVdTBePkFrPmNe*
GI TrHaLa ZQY certa bursa *X* omnia bursa *D* cordi bursa *Go*; luet] luat *B H X* luent
Va   2535 referta] refecta *CW om. Ve*   2536 quae] quod *VdBe La*; peccantes]
peccantis *B AJCWRHuMNO*^pc?*PDVe GI QY*   2537 nil tam difficile] est nil tam facile
GI   2538 *om. H*; emendet] emendat *GoFr* δ *GI fb*; referta] refecta *CW X* repleta
Go   2539 haec] hoc *H Vc*; licite fiat] licite faciat *MuVaVdTGoBePkFrPmNe TrHaLa*
licite faciet *Vc* faciat licite *Vb*; quodcumque] quidcumque *Vd* quicumque *La* quecumque
GoPk quotcumque *Ha*; libebit] licebit *H* *MuVaVbVdTGoBePkFrPmNe O*
TrHaLa   2541 aliorum] aliarum *VdBe La* maioris *Tr*   2542 cernere quae] cer-
nereque *GoPk CWMN* cerneque *Va* cernere non *D* cernere quod *Mu* cernere *Pm*
GI   2544 *om. Fr; fp joins here*; toxicat et] toxigat et *J* coxicat et *Go* et uirus *HuNDK* et
unus *M*; uirus] grauat *HuMN* grauiter *D* necat *K* urens *Ne*   2545 totum maculat
maculosa] maculat maculosa simulque *Vc*; totum] totam *Fr R*; maculat] maculando δ *GI Tr*
QY fb maculosa β *X* maculant *Go*; maculosa] respergit *B* δ *GI Tr XQY fb* respersit *H*

SPECVLVM STVLTORVM 259

Yet she herself will remain perpetually thirsty, [2525] and although she drinks continually, she continually thirsts with greed. Even if the mighty sea were money and flowed all at once into her gaping mouth, it would not satisfy her. Woe! to the abyss of her stomach, whose hunger no food can extinguish, no drinks her thirst. [2530] Woe! to her for whom nothing is enough, and whose wealth makes her needy, and for whom the whole world is not enough. The one who lacks money bears the penalty of all his sins, while whatever the greedy do wrong, the well-filled purse will pay for. A well-filled purse absolves the guilty, forgives sins, [2535] an empty one binds the innocent. Nothing is so difficult, nothing so serious, nothing so wicked, that a well-filled purse cannot put right. This brings it about that whatever you want can be lawfully done, and it makes the lawful illicit by a similar art. [2540] It cleanses others' sins, although it does not cleanse its own, unable to see its own defects alone. So a pain in the head makes all the members ache, and a little venom poisons large vessels. Thus does a single contaminated sheep defile the whole flock, [2545] and a huge mass takes

2533–4 *auari*: is Sedgwick's conjecture ('Textual criticism', p. 293), to provide a subject for 'delirant'. *quicquid delirant*: Horace, *Epistulae*, i. 2. 14. *bursa referta*: the majority reading is 'cetera bursa', but this does not yield any obvious meaning. 'Referta' is my proposed emendation, anticipating 'bursa referta' in line 2535, which is again repeated in line 2538.

2535 *peccata relaxat*: cf. Walter of Châtillon, *Poems*, no. lxiv. 16. 1 (= *Carmina Burana*, no. xli. 16. 1): 'Nos peccata relaxamus.'

2543 Proverbial; for many examples, see Singer, *Thesaurus*, s.v. 'Haupt' 1. 3–1. 4 (v. 431–5). See also Walter of Châtillon, *Poems*, no. xxxvii. 7. 3–5; no. xl. 5. 4; no. lvi. 3. 3 (= *Carmina Burana*, no. xlii. 3. 3).

2545 A conventional image; see Juvenal, *Saturae*, ii. 79–80; *Rule of St Benedict*, c. 28; Bernard of Clairvaux, *Epistolae*, no. cccxxv (*Sancti Bernardi Opera*, viii. 262). *maculat maculosa* is the reading of γ. Mozley adopts the δ version of this line ('maculando respergit'). For comment, see Introduction, p. xci.

260   *SPECVLVM STVLTORVM*

et trahit ex modico maxima massa luem.
Sic sapit ex fonte, quamuis procul inde remotus,
 riuus, et ex igne fumus odorem habet.
Ex morbo capitis artus traxere dolorem,
2550 peccatumque patris plangit origo sequens.
Virtutum quondam decus et decor, in uitiorum
 est conuersa caput, quae caput orbis erat.
Non mihi sufficeret longaeui Nestoris aetas,
 singula si memorem quae memoranda forent.
2555 Sed sit ut ad summam tituloque referre sub uno
 quae sit uox populi, quae solet esse Dei,
a summo capitis in ea pedis usque deorsum
 ad plantam sanum nil superesse reor.'

De regibus

'Rursus si regum mores uitamque reuoluam,
2560 quid nisi maioris causa doloris erunt?
Quorum uita dolor, quorum dominatio dura,
 quorum uerba uelut uentus et aura leuis.

2546 modico] morbo β *X* monito *P*; maxima] magna *fb*; luem] malum *CWHuMND*
mali *K* 2547 sic] et *fp* 2548 *line repeated in alternative form* $Z_{(1)}Z_{(2)}$; et] *om.*
VaVdBePkPm fp; ex igne fumus odorem habet] *ed.* ex igne fumus odoris habet β δ exinde
fumus odoris habet *GI* odorem fumus ab igne trahit *MuVbVcVdTBeFr La* odoremque
fumus ab igne trahit *VaPkPmNe Ha* $Z_{(2)}$ *fp*; odorem] odores $Z_{(1)}$; *(whole line)* riueis odorem
que fumus ignem trahit *Go* fluuius odorem fumus ab igne cadit *Tr* 2549 ex] et *fp*
2551 decus] dedecus *VaFr*; decor] decorem *VdBe La* dedecor *Q*; in] hec *HuMNDK* sic *T om.*
VdBe AJCWPVe GI TrLa QY 2552 caput²] capit *fp* 2553 sufficeret] sufficiet
VaVbVcVdBePkPmNe GI HaLa Y fp sufficiat *MuTFr Tr* sufficit *Go* 2555–8 *om.* δ
2555 sed sit] sufficit *H Y* sed sic *XQ* sic sed *GI* sic sit *Z*; ad summam] assumam *GI ZQY*;
tituloque] tituboque *GI*; *(whole line)* sed (si *Vd* sic *La*) liceat summam (summo *Fr* sumam
VdGoBe) titulo tractare sub uno (unam *MuVa*) γ- *TrHaLa fp* 2556 quae sit uox populi quae] nam sicut populi uox (nox *MuGo*) γ- *TrHaLa fp*; Dei] diei *fp* 2557 a summo]
assummo *fp*; capitis in ea] capitisque mei *GI*; in ea] in ora *H* tanti *VbVc* mea *Y* mei *Q* pariter
MuVaTGoBeFrPmNe TrHa fp a *Pk om. Vd La*; pedis] redis *Pm fp* 2558 plantam]
planctum *ZY* 2559 reuoluam] resoluam *Vc* reuoluem *Go D* reuolutam *Vd*
2560 erunt] erit *H CR Z* erant *W* 2562 leuis] breuis *MuVaVbVcVdGoBePkFrPmNe*
HaLa fp breuis erit *Tr*

2546 An echo of 1 Cor. 5: 6: 'nescitis quia modicum fermentum totam massam cor-
rumpit?' Cf. *Lawrence*, 851; *Miracles*, 2327–8; *Tractatus*, pp. 168, 177.

2548 *odorem*: Mozley has 'odoris', but the genitive is difficult to account for syntactically.

2554 *singula si memorem*: also in *Miracles*, 31, but more frequently in a form closer
to Horace, *Saturae*, i. 8. 40, 'singula quid memorem'; see *Lawrence*, 1041, 1357, 1589,
Miracles, 69.

SPECVLVM STVLTORVM   261

corruption from a small part. So a river tastes of its source, although it is a long way off, and smoke has the smell of the fire. From the head's sickness the limbs have become ill, and the subsequent offspring bewail the sin of the father. [2550] Once the glory and honour of virtues, she is changed into the head of vices, she who was once the head of the world. If I were to rehearse all the things that should be said, the years of aged Nestor would not be enough for me, but to put in a nutshell and in a single statement [2555] what the people's opinion is, which is usually God's: from the top of her head down to the sole of her foot, I judge that there is nothing sound in her.'

About Kings

'Again, if I meditate on the morals and life of kings, what will they be except a cause of greater grief? [2560] Their life is pain, their rule harsh, their words like wind and fleeting air. Although man is created

---

2556 *uox populi... [uox] Dei*: this well-known phrase is found in a letter of Alcuin to Charlemagne, *Epistolae*, no. cxxxii (ed. Dümmler, p. 199): 'Nec audiendi qui solent dicere: "Vox populi, vox Dei", cum tumultuositas vulgi semper insanie proxima sit.' In his *Gesta pontificum Anglorum* (*c.*1125), i. 14. 5, William of Malmesbury quotes 'Vox populi uox Dei' as Oda's reluctant consent to election as archbishop of Canterbury in the mid-10th c. (ed. Winterbottom and Thomson, i. 26). It is also quoted by Eadmer (a monk of Christ Church Canterbury) as an expression of popular support for Archbishop Anselm in a dispute with King William Rufus (*Historia novorum in Anglia*, ed. Rule, p. 61; trans. Bosanquet, p. 63). The ultimate origins of the saying seem to be unknown.
2557–8 Isa. 1: 6: 'A planta pedis usque ad verticem, non est in eo sanitas.' Cf. n. to line 817.
2560 *causa doloris*: also at *Miracles*, 1112.
2562 *aura leuis*: also at *Lawrence*, 24.

SPECVLVM STVLTORVM

Cumque creatus homo sit ad instar imaginis eius
    qui dedit ex nihilo cuncta creata fore,
2565   pluris habent homine reges animantia terrae,
    et genus humanum uilius esse putant.
In cruce suspendi pro sumpta carne ferarum
    quam plures faciunt saepe dolore graui.
Quid grauius Siculi possent statuisse tyranni
2570   quam pro morte ferae quod moriatur homo?
Qui sic regna regunt, qui sic sine remige regnant,
    uix regum tantum nomina sola tenent.
Quamuis regna sua sibi sint subiecta, tributa

2563 creatus] reatus *La*[ac] *Z*; sit] sic *Vc Ve I*; eius] eris *Go* huius *VdBe La*   **2564** qui]
quod *fp*; fore] forte *Vd fp*   **2565** *om. La*; pluris] plures *DVe* plurius *Tr*; habent] sunt *H*
habuit *Go* hunc *fp*; homine] omne *QY* homines *JR*; reges] regis *VcVd QY*; terrae] forte
MuVaVbVcVdGoBePkFrPmNe TrHa Z fp om. T   **2567** sumpta carne] suspicione β *Y*
suipercione *Q* saluacione *MuVaVbVcTGoPkFrPmNe HaLa Z fp* saluatore *VdBe*
2568 *om. X, add. in marg.* *X*[pc]; dolore] dolere *DVe*; *(whole line)* nec (ne *T*) fera (uera *Go*)
consuleret (consulitur *H XY* consuliter *B* consuletur *Tr Q*) consule (consulo *HaLa* con-
sulere *Z*) queso (queo *Ne*) feras (foras *Vd* ueras *Go*) β γ- *TrHaLa ZXQY fp*   **2569** siculi]
seculi *VdTBeFr CKVe GI TrHaLa QY* uituli *Go*; possent] possunt *MuTGoPm fp* posset
La   **2571** regna] regna regna *fp*; sic[2]] *om. VdBe La*   **2573** sibi sint] sibi sunt *Fr*
CWRHuMN Ha fuerit *X*

2563–70 After the Conquest, the Normans introduced laws under which the forests of
England became royal game parks and the animals and birds in them were by law protected
for hunting. Violation of these forest laws was severely punished. See Poole, *From Domesday
Book to Magna Carta*, pp. 29–35; Grant, *Royal Forests*, pp. 3–24. In terms very similar to
Nigel's, Peter of Blois protested against the laws which licensed animals to devour the crops
and fruits of the poor, many of whom, who was created in the image of God ('homo qui
ad imaginem et similitudinem Dei creatus est'; cf. *SS*, 2563) is castrated, blinded, or loses
hands or feet, on the mere suspicion of poaching (*Canon episcopalis*, PL ccvii. 1110C). John
of Salisbury likewise complained that kings have subjected 'God's image to exquisite torture
in enforcing their claim to wild beasts; for a beast's [sake] they have not feared to destroy
man, whom the Only Begotten Son of God [has] redeemed with his blood.' Wild animals,
John asserts, are the lawful property of whoever lays hold of them (*Policraticus*, i. 4; ed. Webb,
i. 30; trans. Pike, p. 22). Peter the Chanter and Thomas of Chobham took the same view
(Baldwin, *Masters, Princes, and Merchants*, i. 246–7, 319–20). The abolition of the forest laws
was finally approved by Henry III in the Forest Charter of 1217.

2563 *ad instar imaginis eius*: cf. Gen. 1: 27.

2568 *dolore graui*: also at *SS*, 2960, 3866; *Miracles*, 2502.

2569–70 The Greek *'turannos'* simply meant ruler, but in antiquity, the rulers of Sicily
had already acquired a reputation for cruelty. Horace uses the notorious torments inflicted
on their victims as a standard of comparison (*Epistulae*, i. 2. 58–9: 'invidia Siculi non inve-
nere tyranni/ maius tormentum'; 'Sicilian tyrants invented no torture worse than envy').
This dictum on envy is repeated by John of Salisbury, *Policraticus*, vii. 24, ed. Webb, ii. 212,
trans. Pike, p. 287. Celebrated Sicilian tyrants were Phalaris, ruler of Agrigento *c.*570–554 BC,
for whom Perillus invented the brazen bull in which victims were burned alive, and Dionysius
the Elder, ruler of Syracuse *c.*432–367 BC, whose cruelty is the subject of an anecdote in John
of Salisbury's influential discussion of tyranny at the end of the *Policraticus* (vii. 25, ed.

SPECVLVM STVLTORVM

263

in the likeness of His image Who granted that all things should be created out of nothing, kings value animals above men [2565] and think the human race is worth less. They often cause many to be hanged on the gallows, with harsh pain, for taking the flesh of wild animals. What more cruel could Sicilian tyrants have decreed, than that a man should die for the death of a wild beast? [2570] Those who rule kingdoms thus, who thus reign without a governor, have hardly more than the bare name of a king. Although their kingdoms are under their sway, the

Webb, ii. 222–3, trans. Dickinson, pp. 328–9). For other references to ancient Sicilian tyranny, see *Policraticus* viii. 6, ed. Webb, ii. 256, trans. Pike, p. 320, and viii. 23, ed. Webb, ii. 408, trans. Dickinson, p. 407. Otto of Freising made the connection between ancient and contemporary Sicilian tyranny explicit: 'For Sicily is said to have been the nurse first of the Cyclopes and afterwards of tyrants, *even down to the present day*; the former always fed upon the flesh of men, the latter on their sufferings' (*Chronica*, ed. Hofmeister, ii. 19, p. 90; trans. Mierow, pp. 175–6; apart from the italicized phrase, this sentence is based on Orosius). Later (*Chronica*, vii. 23; trans. p. 432), Otto cites examples of tyranny in the behaviour of Roger II, the contemporary king of Sicily. Other 12th-c. writers shared this view of Roger as a tyrant whose self-interested exercise of power was evident not only in his domineering treatment of his subjects, but especially in his cavalier disrespect for ecclesiastical authority, which seemed to English writers such as Thomas Becket and John of Salisbury to match Henry II's bullying attitude to the church. Becket probably has Roger in mind when he says 'Sweet to every tyrant is the bitter servitude of the Church...It has already come to pass that our king follows the Sicilians, or rather goes ahead of them in this matter' (*Becket Correspondence*, i. 602–3, no. cxxv). John of Salisbury says of Roger that 'after the fashion of tyrants, [he] had reduced the church in his kingdom to slavery, and instead of allowing any freedom of election named in advance the candidate to be elected, so disposing of all ecclesiastical offices like palace appointments' (*Historia pontificalis*, xxxii, ed. Chibnall, p. 65). Cf. John's comments on the machinations of the Sicilians against the Church in his *Letters*, ii. 376–7 (no. ccxix), ii. 560–1 (no. cclxxii), ii. 600–1 (no. cclxxviii). For a full documentation of this view of Roger, see Wieruszowski, 'Roger II of Sicily, *Rex-Tyrannus*'. Wieruszowski recognizes that there is a case to be made in Roger's defence, as does Loud ('Royal control of the church'), but there is no doubt that for many contemporaries, references to 'Sicilian tyranny' would immediately bring Roger to mind.

2571 *remige*: in classical Latin, 'remex' means 'helmsman, steersman'; Osbern of Gloucester, a 12th-c. English lexicographer, derives the word from 'rego', 'to rule', and glosses it 'ille qui regit' (*Derivationes*, ii. 594; see *DMLBS* 1b, which also has examples of the metaphorical application of the term to Christ, 'Christo remige').

264 SPECVLVM STVLTORVM

dent populi, trepidet terra timore suo,
2575 non tamen hi regnant, quoniam regnare timeri
non est, aut dura lege ligare suos.
Quos non rectores sed raptores bene dici
constat, et ex facto nomen habere suo.
Quorum nulla fides, et qui confidit in ipsis
2580 errat et arbitrio desipit ipse meo.
Quorum fictus amor, quorum uia nulla fidelis,
quorum lingua dolo plena, cruore manus.
In quorum manibus crebro tractantur iniqua,
dextera muneribus esse referta solet.
2585 Munera respiciunt, quae dum uenerantur abesse
iustitiam faciunt iudiciumque procul.
Quicquid enim faciunt uel dicunt uel meditantur,
si bene discutias, omnia munus olent.
Quod nisi praecedat, comitetur, siue sequatur,
2590 ut uaccam uitulus, non procul immo prope,
nil habitus, nil ordo tibi, nec opinio uitae,
quilibet aut titulus plusue minusue dabit.
Munera conturbant reges rursusque serenant,
munera dant pacem, munera bella parant.
2595 Munera pontifices subuertunt, munera reges,
munera ius statuunt destituuntque simul.
Munera stultorum linguas dant esse disertas,
munera cum clamant cetera quaeque tacent.
Munera peruertunt leges, decreta refellunt,
2600 euacuant patrum iura rigore suo.

2574 trepidet] trepident *Tr QY*^{ac}   2575 quoniam] quo nam *T* quem *Mu* quam
VdBeNe TrLa fp   2576 dura] duram *fp*; lege] lego *fp*   2578 et] *om. GoFr*; suo]
suum /uel suo *K*   2580 et] in *Tr Z*; desipit] decipit *H Q* deficit γ- *TrHaLa* deficiet
fp   2582 cruore] timore *Fr* amore *fp*   2583–4 *transp. after 2644* β δ *GI TrHaLa*
ZXQY; *transp. here Mozley. om.* γ- *fp (they end at 2602)*   2585 uenerantur] fenantur
Mu uenantur *VaVbVcVdTBePkFrPm HaLa*^{pc} *fp* ueniantur *Ne La*^{ac} *Z* uideantur *Tr*
2587 faciunt] *om. fp*   2588 bene] beati *fp*; discutias] discuties *VcFr Ha Q*; munus]
nummus *T* minus *fp*   2589 siue] sine *JP Tr*; sequatur] sequetur *Fr K* sequitur *Q*
2591 nil²] uel *Z fp*   2592 titulus] uitulus *VdBe TrLa*; plusue minusue] plus nouimusue
fp   2593 conturbant] perturbant *P* conturbat *fp*; serenant] serenat *fp* senant *Z* reseruant *AJCWHuMNOPVe GI XQY fb* reformant *RDK*   2594 *om. Pm*
2596 statuunt] faciunt *Va* subruunt *fp*; destituuntque] discuciuntque *Vd* discuciuntque /uel
destituunt *Ha* deficiuntque *Q*   2598–9 *transp. Ve*   2598 cum clamant] dum clamant *H Vb RP* conclamant *VaVdGoBePkFrPmNe HaLa fp* clamant *Z*   2599 refel-
lunt] refellit *D* reuellant *Go* reuellunt *La Z* repellunt β *X* reflent *fp*   2600 euacuant]
euuacuunt *Fr* munera euacuant *Vc* euacuantque *Mozley*; patrum] patrem *Va DVe*? parum *Z*
peccatum? *Q*; iura] iure *Vd D* iura in *fb*; rigore] uigore β *XY*

SPECVLVM STVLTORVM   265

people pay tribute, the earth trembles in fear of them, yet they do not reign, for to reign is not to be feared [2575] or to bind one's people by a harsh law. They ought not to be called rulers but robbers, and have the name from their actions. There is no trust in them, and whoever trusts in them goes astray and acts foolishly, in my opinion. [2580] Their love is feigned, their paths are treacherous, their tongue is full of guile, their hands full of blood. Iniquities are often perpetrated at their hands, and their fist is stuffed with bribes. They have regard for bribes, and in honouring them, [2585] banish justice and law a long way off. Whatever they do or say or think, if you examine it closely, it all smells of money. Unless it precedes, accompanies, or follows, as a calf does the cow, not at a distance but closely, [2590] no habit, no order, nor fame of life, nor any title will give you more or less. Bribes unsettle kings and make them calm again; bribes give peace, bribes brew war. Bribes pervert bishops, bribes pervert kings, [2595] bribes make the law and unmake it as well. Bribes make the tongues of fools eloquent; when bribes are shouting out, everything else shuts up. Bribes pervert laws, revoke decrees, and empty ancestral laws of their rigour. [2600]

2583–4 Close to Ps. 25 (26): 10.

2585–651 This tirade against the corrupting power of 'munera' is an example of a wide-spread topos of medieval literature, in which the power of money is often represented in quasi-personified form (Nummus, Aurum, Pecunia, Bursa, and so on). See Yunck, *Lineage of Lady Meed*, pp. 80–1, 110, 123, 170–84, and specifically on 'munera', pp. 133–9, and Murray, *Reason and Society*, pp. 71–7 (cf. also *Lawrence*, 563–72). The use of 'munera' to signify bribery goes back to biblical sources; see Ps. 14 (15): 5 and Isa. 1: 23.

2588 *discutias*: 'discutere' = 'to examine, inquire' (Niermeyer 1).

2591 *opinio*: 'reputation, good name' (*OLD* 5; *DMLBS* 4).

2600 *euacuant*: all manuscripts have 'euacuant' (except for *Fr*, which reads 'euacuunt', and *Vc*, which reads 'munera euacuant'). Mozley emended to 'euacuantque' presumably on metrical grounds, assuming that 'patrum' has a short first syllable. However, although the first syllable of nominative 'pater' is short, Nigel scans the inflected forms both long and short; see n. to line 1184.

266 SPECVLVM STVLTORVM

Munera palpare faciunt delicta potentum,
    utque magis uigeant facta nefanda tegunt.
Munera – sed taceo, ne forte tegenda reuelem –
    in manibus sanctis esse reperta solent.

2605 Munera declarant quidnam meditantur auari,
    quidue uelit fieri mens maculosa uiri.
Munera quid ualeant sedes pastore uacantes,
    credere si fas est, saepe docere solent.
Munera dulce malum, uirus insanabile sanis

2610 mentibus, aegrotis mortis imago recens.
Munera semper habent aliquid portantia uocem,
    uerborumque uices ore tacente gerunt.
Munera iudicii libram moderantur et ipsam
    protinus inflectunt quo data pensa trahunt.

2615 Munera mortifero dant pocula plena ueneno,
    excaecant oculos praecipitantque gradus.
Omnia uincit amor, sed amorem munera uincunt,
    quod siquis dubitat, ponderet haec et eum.
Munera uirtutum suffocant germina, sanctos

2620 irritant, reprobos mortis ad ima trahunt.
Munera corrumpunt mores pariuntque recepta
    damna pudicitiae, dona cupita procis.
Munera pontifices extollunt, munera reges,
    munera dant apices exhilarantque duces.

2625 Munera suffodiunt turres montesque coaequant
    uallibus et pariunt absque cruore necem.
Munera praecedunt, quotiens mala multa sequuntur,
    munera cum ueniunt proxima causa subest.

2601–2 *om. QY*   **2602** *MuVaVbVcTGoPkFrPmNe fp end here; after 2602, VdBe
repeat 2595, then end; om. Ve*   **2603** tegenda] tangenda *PVe* tacendo *RO* tacenda *M
fb* pudenda *K*   **2604** in] que *C Ha* que in *JW La*   **2607–10** *om. QY*
2607 uacantes] uocantes *W* uacante *Ha Z* carentes *Tr*   **2609** uirus] sunt *K* uirtus *MN*
unus *La*; insanabile] sanabile *H AJCWROPVe GI Tr ZX*   **2611** *om. I*; uocem] *Skutsch*
secum β δ *G TrHaLa ZXQY*   **2612** uices…gerunt] uices…gemunt *Tr* ciues…gerunt
*K*ac ciues…gemunt *AJCWRHuMNOPDVe GI ZQY*   **2613–14** *om. QY*
2613 ipsam] illam *GI* ab ipso *Z* in ipsam *Ve*   **2618** dubitat] dubitet δ *GI TrHaLa
ZXQY*; eum] ea β *AJCWROPDVe GI TrHaLa ZXQY*   **2619–20** *om.* δ
TrHaLa   **2621–2** *om. QY*; *2621 om., 2622 transp. after 2626 Z*   **2622** procis]
precis *OP* pretum *Tr* parit *Ha*   **2627–32** *om. QY*   **2627** praecedunt] precedent
GI procedunt *Z*; sequuntur] sequentur *MODVe X*

SPECVLVM STVLTORVM   267

Bribes cause the crimes of the mighty to be given the kid-glove treatment, and conceal wicked deeds so that they flourish more vigorously. Bribes—but I am silent, lest I happen to reveal things that should be concealed—are often to be found in holy hands. Bribes speak aloud whatever the greedy are thinking, [2605] or whatever the corrupted mind of men wishes to be done. Bribes—if this is credible—often teach what sees lacking a bishop are worth. Bribes are a sweet evil, an incurable poison to healthy minds, to the sick a vivid image of death. [2610] Bribes which have something to bring always have a voice, and although speechless, perform the functions of words. Bribes govern the scale of justice and quickly tilt it in whichever direction the weight of gifts inclines. Bribes offer cups filled with deadly poison; [2615] they blind eyes and trip up feet. Love conquers all things, but bribes conquer love; if anyone doubts this, let him weigh them and it. Bribes stifle the seeds of virtue, they vex the righteous, and drag the wicked to the abyss of death. [2620] Bribes corrupt morals, and bring about the frequent loss of chastity, the gift desired by lovers. Bribes elevate bishops to office, and kings as well; bribes bestow crowns, and give happiness to magnates. Bribes undermine fortresses, level mountains with valleys, [2625] and produce death without bloodshed. Bribes are in the vanguard whenever a crowd of evils follows; when bribes appear, a lawsuit

2601 *palpare*: 'to treat gently' (*DMLBS* 3).

2609 Cf. Ovid, *Amores*, ii. 9. 26: 'dulce puella malum'.

2610 *mortis imago*: also in *Lawrence*, 508; *Miracles*, 795, 2402. Originally biblical; see Jer. 2: 6.

2611 *uocem*: Skutsch's conjecture (according to Mozley's *apparatus criticus*, but not in 'Three rare words'). The manuscripts have 'secum', which leaves 'aliquid' confusingly vague, and either 'habent' or 'portantia' without an object.

2614 *data pensa trahunt*: cf. Ovid, *Metamorphoses*, xiii. 511.

2616 Cf. Deut. 16: 19: 'munera excaecant oculos sapientum'.

2617 *Omnia uincit amor*: Vergil, *Eclogues*, x. 69. Also quoted in *Lawrence*, 616–17. Cf. *Miles gloriosus*, 71: 'Me tibi vincit amor et te michi vinciat aurum' (*Commedie*, iv. 64). The phrase was proverbial; see Walther, *Proverbia*, 20097–9.

2624 *apices*: 'crowns' (*OLD* 1b).

268 SPECVLVM STVLTORVM

Munera si cessent, cessabunt iurgia, lites,
2630 Mars cadet et Veneris nullus amicus erit.
Munera si cessent, sine sanguine tempore pacis,
quod numquam potuit, Roma subacta ruet.
Munera si cessent, primatum pallia multo
constabunt leuius et meliore foro.
2635 Munera si cessent, abbatum cornua longa
ponderis et pretii iure minoris erunt.
Munera si cessent, regis reuocatus ab aula
monachus in claustrum limina sacra teret.
Munera si cessent, grex cum pastore quiescet,
2640 iunctus et amborum spiritus unus erit.
Munera si cessent, Deus in cellas Cluniaci
forte reuertetur et remanebit ibi.
Munera si cessent, Iudam cum Simone clerus
tollet et e medio coget abire sui.
2645 Munera si cessent, miseris mortalibus ultra
clamor nec luctus nec dolor ullus erit.
Munera si cessent, pariter cum Simone Iudas
decidet et loculos perdet uterque suos.
Munera subuersum faciunt de rege tyrannum,
2650 conuertuntque suas in sua membra manus.
Plebs sine doctrina, populus sine lege, cruentis
moribus, accelerat pronus in omne nefas.
Gens grauis esuriens carnem sitiensque cruorem
armat inarmatas ad scelus omne manus.
2655 Ille timor Domini reges qui terruit olim
et populos periit nomine reque simul.
Quid Dominum loqueris? Deus est post terga relictus.
Non opus est alio, sit sibi quisque Deus.
Regis ad exemplum populus lasciuit ineptus,

2629–30 *om.* Z   **2630** cadet] cadit *D Ha X fb*   **2631–2** *om. HuMN*
2632 ruet] cadet *GI* uel ruet *add. in marg.* G^{pc} **2633–6** *om.* C   **2633–4** *om.* Y;
transp. after 2642 Z   **2634** leuius] melius *Tr Q* melius leuiui *La*   **2635–8** *disordered
(2637, 2635, 2638, 2636)* Z   **2636–40** *disordered (2636, 2639, 2637, 2638, 2640)* X
2636 iure] longe β *X*   **2638** limina] lumina *MVe* munera *X* summa *La*
2639 quiescet] quiescit *R Ha ZQ*   **2640** iunctus] intus β inctus *C*   **2641–2** *om.*
QY; *transp. after 2632 Z*   **2641** cellas] cellam *HaLa*   **2645–6** *om. H HaLa Q*
2648 perdet] pendet *Ve Tr*   **2651–4** *transp. after 2657 Z*   **2652** moribus] morsibus β *X* motibus *Z*   **2654** inarmatas] inarmata *GI* in armatis *D* et armatas *Ve* inarma-
tos *Ha Y* inornatos *Q*   **2657** dominum] domino *Tr* demum *RVe*   **2658** sibi] tibi
RM Ha   **2659** ad] in *P Q*; lasciuit] lasciuius *GI*

SPECVLVM STVLTORVM

is imminent. If bribes cease, quarrels will cease, and disputes; Mars will topple, and Venus will have no friends. [2630] If bribes cease, Rome will be conquered and fall without bloodshed and in peacetime—which was never before possible. If bribes cease, archbishops' robes will be cheaper and a better bargain. If bribes cease, the abbots' long horns [2635] will rightly weigh and cost less. If bribes cease, the monk will be recalled from the king's court, and will tread the sacred ground of the cloister. If bribes cease, the flock will lie down with the shepherd, and one spirit of unity will be in both. [2640] If bribes cease, God will perhaps return to the cells of Cluny and remain there. If bribes cease, the clergy will dismiss both Judas and Simon and expel them from their company. If bribes cease, there will be no more lamentation [2645] nor weeping nor grief in wretched mortals. If bribes cease, Judas and Simon will perish, and both will lose their money bags. Bribes pervert the king and turn him into a tyrant, turning his hands against his own limbs. [2650] A people without teaching, a people without law, bloody in character, rushes headlong towards every wickedness. A harsh race, hungering for flesh and thirsting for blood, arms unarmed hands for every crime. That fear of the Lord, which once terrified the kings and people, [2655] has perished in name and actuality alike. Why speak of God? God is left behind; everyone is his own God, there is no need of another. The foolish people go astray through the king's example, and

2633 *pallia*: 'pallium', the cloak sent by the pope to archbishops as a sign of their office (*DMLBS* 4; Niermeyer 4).

2634 *leuius*: 'leuis' = 'low' (of price or value); usually with 'pretium' (*DMLBS* 9). *meliore foro*: 'forum bonum' = 'cheap price' (cf. French 'bon marché') (*DMLBS* 4b).

2637 *reuocatus ab aula*: cf. Lucan, *De bello civili*, x. 504.

2643, 2647 *cum Simone*: see nn. to lines 1715–32 above.

2644 *tollet et e medio*: also in *Miracles*, 1072 (with 'tollit').

2645–6 Rev. 21: 4: 'mors ultra non erit, neque luctus, neque clamor, neque dolor erit ultra'.

2652 *pronus in omne nefas*: cf. Lucan, *De bello civili*, vi. 147. For 'omne nefas' at the close of a pentameter, see *Miracles*, 1164.

2653 *sitiensque cruorem*: also in *Lawrence*, 1977.

2654 *ad scelus omne*: also in *Miracles*, 116.

2659 *Regis ad exemplum*: Claudian, *Panegyricus de Quarto Consulatu Honorii Augusti*, 300.

270   *SPECVLVM STVLTORVM*

2660   ueruecisque pedes sors facit una pares.
        Ecce tot et tantas patiuntur saecula strages,
          posteriorque dies deteriora parit.
        Nec superest redimat neque qui saluos faciat nos,
          sed sperata salus funditus omnis abest.'

De episcopis et prelatis

2665   'Non alios igitur super his nisi temporis huius
          pontifices sacros auguror esse reos,
        qui se pastores legemque tenere fatentur,
          nec tamen haec faciunt quae facienda docent;
        qui potius fures quam pastores uocitari
2670   teste Deo debent, de quibus illud ait:
        "Aduenient multi pseudo falsique prophetae,
          et satagent multos fallere fraude sua.
        Qui quamuis ueniant ouium sub ueste, rapaces
          sanguinis hos auidos noueris esse lupos."
2675   A pascendo grege, non depascendo, merentur
          pastores ouium nomen habere suum.
        Nomen ab officio sumptum uertere seorsum,
          ut non pastores sint gregis, immo lupi.
        Tres sunt praecipue prope qui uersantur ouile,
2680   quorum quisque gregi proximus esse studet;
        primus enim pastor est, mercenarius alter,
          tertius insidians dicitur esse lupus.
        Primus oues gratis pascit, mercede secundus,
          tertius ut perdat diripiatque gregem.
2685   Pastores igitur, quia gratis nulla ministrant,

2660 ueruecisque] ueruecesque *QY* feruentesque *Z*   **2663** neque] ne *D* nec *Tr* nec /uel neque *Ha*; faciat] faciet *RO* facit *La Z*; nos] *om. P fb*   **2664** abest] adest *MN* **2665** non] nos *H Ve*   **2666** auguror] augurior *CW* arguor *R*; reos] suos *HaLa* **2667** qui] non *Ha* < >on *La*; se] si β *ACWOPVe GI TrHaLa ZQY* sic *J*   **2668** nec] non *Ve Z*; haec] hoc *H M*   **2669** qui] hii *HaLa*   **2670** de quibus illud] ipsemet istud *CWHuMNDK*   **2673** ueniant] ueniunt *CRO* uenient *Z*   **2675** a] e *HaLa*; pascendo] poscendo *R Y* uastando *Z*; grege] gregem *RO Ha XZQ*   **2677** seorsum] deorsum *GI TrHaLa ZQY* leorsum *J*   **2678** *U rejoins*   **2679** ouile] oliue *QY* ouili *corr. in margin Y²*   **2683–4** *om. O*   **2683** secundus] sed alter *CWHuMNK* **2684** diripiatque] decipiatque β *UX*   **2685** quia] qui β *DK ZXQ*

2660 Literally, 'one fate makes their feet equal'. The idea seems to be that the people follow their ruler as, proverbially, one sheep follows another; see Singer, *Thesaurus*, s.v. 'Schaf' 18 (x. 7–8).

SPECVLVM STVLTORVM   271

sheep-like, their feet follow the same path. [2660] See, how many and how great the troubles that the world suffers, and every succeeding day brings forth worse things. There is no one who can rescue us or save us; the salvation we long for is nowhere to be seen.'

About Bishops and Prelates

'No one other than the holy bishops bears the blame for these things at the present time, in my opinion. [2665] They profess themselves pastors and guardians of the law, but they do not practise the practices they preach. They ought to be called thieves rather than shepherds, by the testimony of God, who said of them: [2670] "There will come many false prophets, who will try to deceive many with their trickery. Although they come in sheep's clothing, you should know that they are greedy wolves, ravening for blood." The shepherds of the sheep deserve to bear their name from feeding their flock, not from feeding off it. [2675] They have turned upside down the name derived from their function, so that they are not shepherds of the flock, but wolves. There are three in particular who are found in the vicinity of the sheep-fold, each of whom tries to get nearest to the sheep: [2680] the first is the shepherd, the second the hireling, the third is the treacherous wolf. The first feeds the sheep without payment, the second for hire, the third so that he may destroy and carry off the sheep. So the bishops, who do nothing for free, [2685] have nothing in common with the first of these. And since they feed for the love of payment, similarity of situation aligns them with the function of the second. They have nothing

---

2662 Cf. 2 Pet. 2: 20: 'facta sunt eis posteriora deteriora prioribus'.

2663 Cf. Walter of Châtillon, *Poems*, no. lxvii. 3. 5–6: 'dum non habet redemptorem/ nec qui saluum faciat'.

2668 Cf. *Tractatus*, ed. Boutemy, p. 188, where Nigel reminds William of Longchamp that when he was consecrated a bishop, he promised to teach his flock 'by word and example'.

2671–4 Matt. 7: 15 and 24: 24. This biblical passage was often applied to the Cistercians (see *Ysengrimus*, ed. Mann, Introduction, pp. 141–2, and the passages from John of Salisbury quoted in the nn. to lines 959–60 and 2051 above), and it is not difficult to imagine that Archbishop Baldwin is the deceitful 'pontifex' that Nigel is taking aim at here.

2675–6 Cf. Ezek. 34: 2. The mock-derivation of 'pastor' from 'pascor' rather than 'pasco' was popular in Goliardic verse; see *Apocalipsis Goliae*, ed. Strecker, st. 33. 4: 'non pastor ovium, sed pastus ovibus', and Walter of Châtillon, *Poems*, no. xlix. 10 ('pastores prelatique,/ amatores muneris,/ cum non pascant, set pascantur,/ non a "pasco" deriuantur,/ set a "pascor, pasceris"'); no. lv. 8. 4–6, and no. lx. 12. 1. *A pascendo grege*: on the Latin construction, see n. to line 2235.

2681–2 John 10: 11–13. John of Salisbury develops this threefold categorization (adding a thief to the wolf) in connection with the contemporary priesthood; *Policraticus*, viii. 17, ed. Webb, ii. 352, trans. Dickinson, pp. 343–4.

272 SPECVLVM STVLTORVM

nil sibi cum primo proprietatis habent.
Et quoniam pascunt mercedis amore, secundi
officio similis sors facit esse pares.
Nil sibi cum primo, sed habent coniuncta secundo
2690 plurima, de reliquo quaestio nulla manet.
Ergo lupis similes comedunt cum sanguine carnes,
matris et ex utero uiscera rapta uorant.
More lupi ueniunt pastores temporis huius,
morte gregem primum perdere quisque suum.
2695 Quodque uident fragile frangunt, quod debile spernunt,
quod crassum comedunt, proiciuntque macrum.
Lac gregis et lanam quaerunt misereque subactas
undique dispersas depopulantur oues.
Nec satis istud eis, quod depraedantur ouile
2700 disperguntque gregem diripiuntque sibi,
sit nisi quem sitiunt calidum sorbere cruorem
inque gregis iugulum mittere posse manum.
Qualiter introeant pastores temporis huius
in caulas ouium, quo duce, quaque uia,
2705 ingressi quid agant et quam studiose ministrent
in grege suscepto, non mihi, crede foro.
Pastorum uitam si discutiamus ad unguem,
plurima quae faciunt plena ruboris erunt.
In specula positi, qua circumquaque uideri
2710 seque uidere ualent, lumina clausa tenent.
Sanguinis et carnis curam non despicientes,
solliciti curant seque suosque simul.
Quem sibi praecipue deberent praeposuisse
uix ualet extremo delituisse loco.

2686 primo] primis β *GI UXQY* **2687** et] sed β *GI UZXQY*; secundi] secundis β
secundo *R GI ZQY* **2688** similis] *Shackleton Bailey* similes β δ *GI TrHaLa UZXQY*
2692 et] *om. K Z* **2696** *om. Z*; proiciuntque macrum] quod leue proiciunt *Mozley*
quod uile (quod uidunt uile *La*) despiciunt *H AJRHuMNOPDVe GI TrHaLa UQY* uileque
despiciunt *CWK* **2697** misereque] miscere *AJCWRHuMNOPDVe GI Tr UZQY*
miscereque *H*ᵖᶜ **2700** gregem] greges δ *GI TrHaLa UZQY* **2701** sit] sic *H*
RVe TrLa ZQ sint /uel sunt *Ha*; quem] quod *HuMN* quid *R* qui *Ha* quoniam *Z*; sitiunt]
faciunt *HaLa* **2703** qualiter] qualibus *HaLa* **2704** quaque] quaue β *Y* quoue *Q*
2705 et quam studiose] studiose quamque *K* et quid studiose *O* et studiose *QY*; ministrent]
ministrant *PD HaLa Z* **2709** specula...qua] speculo...quo *H AJCWRHuMNPDK*
TrLa UZ specula...quo *OVe* speculo...qua *Y* speculo...qui *Q*; specula] specula /uel lo
Ha **2710** seque] neque *P²over erasure* **2712** curant] curent *Tr*
QY **2713** praeposuisse] proposuisse *HuMN Z* **2714** delituisse] dilatuisse *Z*
dilicuisse *QY* delicuisse *Ve La* dilituisse *Ha*

SPECVLVM STVLTORVM 273

in common with the first, but many features of the second—as for the third, there's no doubt. [2690] Like wolves, they eat flesh and blood, devouring the entrails torn from the mother's womb. The shepherds these days come in the guise of the wolf, each one seeking above all the destruction of his flock. What they see to be fragile they smash; what is weak they spurn, [2695] what is fat, they devour; what is lean, they discard. They seek the flock's milk and wool, and ravage the wretchedly oppressed sheep, scattered in every direction. Nor is it enough for them to pillage the sheepfold, scatter the sheep, and take plunder for themselves, [2700] unless they also drink the hot blood they thirst for and raise their hand against the throat of the sheep. Don't believe me, believe the public, on how the shepherds nowadays enter the sheepfolds, under what guidance, and by what route, what they do once they have entered, and how eagerly they serve the flock [2705] for which they have taken responsibility. If we were to discuss the life of bishops in detail, many things they do will appear shameful. Placed on a watchtower, from whence they can see and be seen on all sides, they keep their eyes closed. [2710] Not despising a care for flesh and blood, they attentively look after both themselves and their family. The one whom they especially ought to have promoted barely manages to skulk in some remote corner. He who gave what might alleviate another's hunger now burns, freezes, and is needy, thirsts, hungers, and is full of

---

2688 *similis*: see Introduction, p. lxxxii.

2696 *proiciuntque macrum*: the majority reading, 'quŏd uīlĕ dēspĭcĭŭnt', is unmetrical as the second half of a pentameter; *CWK*'s 'uīlĕquĕ dēspĭcĭŭnt' looks like an attempt at repair. The reading of *B X*, 'prŏīcĭūntquĕ mācrŭm' is metrical if it is accepted that Nigel regularly did not lengthen a syllable if the second consonant of a following pair was -r. For examples, see 1386 'īndūtūsquĕ săcrīs'; 1192 'cōnsuĕtūdŏ frĕquēns; 1678 sīgnă săcrātă gĕrāt'; 1854 'trāns uădă trānsquĕ uĭās'; 2236 'īn cēllā prŏpriā'. Obviously a balancing phrase that began with 'quod' would be preferable, but Mozley's conjecture 'quod leue despiciunt' is unsatisfactory; 'leue' is an unsatisfactory opposite of 'crassum'.

2711–12 Cf. the criticism of clerical nepotism in *SS*, *Epistle to William*, §§13, 21, and lines 2837–8; *Miracles*, 1811–14, 1885–6, 1910, 1915–16, 2213–16. For discussion of the widespread practice of clerical nepotism, see Barrow, *Clergy in the Medieval World*, pp. 128–35, and cf. Introduction, p. lxi. Promotion of the interests of relatives also extended to the secular sphere: see the charters recording William of Longchamp's arrangements for the marriage of his nephew to a baronial heiress (probably to be dated 31 Dec. 1189 × Oct. 1191), *English Episcopal Acta xxxi. Ely 1109–1197*, ed. Karn, nos. 142–3. The editors comment: 'The scale of the transaction somewhat sets this apart, but the bishop of Ely [i.e. William] made provision for many members of his family' (p. 184).

274 SPECVLVM STVLTORVM

2715 Vritur alget eget sitit esurit, ulcere plenus,
qui dedit unde suam cuique leuare famem.
Praesulis ad mensam tot fercula, totque ferentes,
tot uini cyati, tot sine lege scyphi;
totque domus domini, tot circumquaque ministri,
2720 tot stantes pueri, totque meando uagi;
tot iuuenes compti uariisque modis redimiti,
totque senes docti gesta priora loqui;
et quasi castrorum regum statione soluta,
discurrunt acies, corpore mente leues.
2725 Dumque bibit dominus, quidam sua brachia tendit,
atque genu flexo pronus adorat eum.
Splendida tota domus, duplici radiante metallo,
in quibus offertur hostia sacra Deo.
Sed quae pontificis sunt usibus appropriata,
2730 non sunt de uili materiaque rudi.
Non norunt recte partiri qui statuerunt
aurea pontifici, stagnea uasa Deo.
Praesul in argento totus discumbit et auro,
uix quoque fictilibus utitur aula Dei.
2735 Ecclesias uacuas, altaria nuda, crucesque
detractis spoliis stare uidere potes.
Regia pontificis sublimibus alta columnis,

2715 alget] olet *ZY*   2716 qui] quis *R* cui /uel qui *Ha*; cuique leuare] quit releuare
R quique leuare *QY*   2718 tot uini cyati] tot uini crati *H XQ* tot uini crateri *Z* uestibus
ornati δ *TrHaLa U²over erasure*   2719 domus] domos *QY*   2722 *om.* *D*; gesta]
gestaque *GI*   2723 et] ut β *X*; soluta] saluta *QY*   2725 dumque] dum *Ha*
cumque *H ROP Tr*; quidam sua brachia tendit] quidam brachia sua tendit *Ha* tendit sua
brachia mundus (mondus *U* seruus *X*) β *GI UZXQY*; quidam] quidem *CDK*   2728 *om.*
GI   2729 sed] sunt *GI*; quae] quia *H D*   2731 qui] que *JHuMNPD Ha*
2733 et] in *JMN GI*   2735–6 *om.* *ZQY*   2735 uacuas] laceras *AJRHuMNODKVe*
GI TrHa U lateras *CWP La*   2737 regia] splendida δ *TrHaLa U²over erasure*; alta]
aula δ *TrHaLa U²over erasure Z*; columnis] calumpnis *ZQY*

2718 For discussion of this line, see Introduction, p. cxxiii.

2737 Modelled on the first line of Ovid, *Metamorphoses*, ii: 'Regia Solis erat sublimibus
alta columnis.'

2737–42 Like all great households of the period, that of the archbishop of Canterbury was
peripatetic, since revenues from its estates were paid in kind and consumed on the spot.
Consequently, in addition to the palace next to Canterbury cathedral, the archbishops owned
a string of other palaces on their manors, where they resided when necessary or convenient.
Those in use in the 12th c. included Charing, Gillingham, Otford, Teynham, Wingham,
Wrotham (all in Kent), and Croydon (in Surrey). For time spent by Archbishop Baldwin at

SPECVLVM STVLTORVM

275

sores. [2715] At the bishop's table there are so many dishes, so many servants, so many measures of wine, so many limitless glasses, so many officers of the household, so many servants everywhere, so many pages standing by, so many moving about, [2720] so many youths, adorned and garlanded in various ways, so many old men trained to recite deeds of old. And as if a royal army camp were let loose, the troops of servants run about, lively in mind and body. And while the master drinks, someone holds out his arms [2725] and with bended knee bows down and worships him. The whole house glitters, shining with gold and silver, in which the sacred Host is offered to God. But the things reserved to the bishop's use are not of base or coarse material. [2730] Those who allotted golden vessels to the bishop, and tin vessels to God, did not know how to make a right distribution. The bishop sits down to gold and silver, while God's house hardly gets earthenware. You can see churches stand empty, altars bare, [2735] and crosses stripped of treasures. The bishop's lofty palace, with its soaring columns, gleams with the marble that supports it, both inside and out. So many are the

the first five of these palaces, see the itinerary in *English Episcopal Acta Canterbury ii. 1162–1190*, ed. Cheney and Jones, pp. 280–3. The contrast with the subsequent archbishop, Hubert Walter, who when away from Canterbury spent most of his time at Westminster, is striking (*English Episcopal Acta iii. Canterbury 1193–1205*, ed. Cheney and John, pp. 309–15). Nigel's remarks may also be a response to the rebuilding of the Old Palace at Canterbury between 1193 and 1228. Largely thanks to the efforts of Henry VIII in appropriating monastic possessions, little remains of most of these early buildings today, so that it is not possible to judge the accuracy of Nigel's description of their interior splendour, but some 12th-c. criticisms of the luxurious lifestyles of contemporary bishops, and in particular of their splendid palaces, are assembled by Mortet, 'Hugue de Fouilloi, Pierre le Chantre, Alexandre Neckam'. In the first half of the 12th c., Henry of Blois, younger brother of King Stephen and bishop of Winchester, built or enlarged many episcopal palaces and castles, including Winchester Palace in London, Wolvesey Palace, Bishop's Waltham, and Merdon, all in Hampshire, and Farnham Castle in Surrey. See Biddle and Keene, 'Winchester in the eleventh and twelfth centuries', pp. 323–8; Biddle, 'Wolvesey: The *domus quasi palatium* of Henry de Blois'; id., *Wolvesey: The Old Bishop's Palace*, pp. 6–10 and the plan on pp. 24–5; Riall, *Henry of Blois, Bishop of Winchester*; id., 'The new castles of Henry de Blois'. Many of these constructions were demolished in 1155 by Henry II, who feared that the fortified buildings might be used against him, but the residential quarters were spared and the castles rebuilt after Henry of Blois returned from exile in 1158. Gerald of Wales speaks with awe of Henry's magnificent lifestyle and his 'palatia sumptuosissima' (*Vita S. Remigii*, c. xxvii, *Opera*, vii. 45). *marmore fulta*: on the use of Tournai marble and Purbeck marble in Henry of Blois's palaces, see Riall, *Henry of Blois*, pp. 10, 13, 24, and Fig. 5.

On the history and location of these and other palaces and their present-day remains, see, in addition to the items cited above, Thompson, *Medieval Bishops' Houses* (especially Appendix 3), and The Gatehouse website list of post-conquest pre-Reformation bishops' houses and palaces of England and Wales, at www.gatehouse-gazetteer.info/indexs/bispal.html (accessed 16/11/2020).

276   SPECVLVM STVLTORVM

intus et exterius marmore fulta, nitet.
Tot sunt pontifici tunicae, tot pallia, cappae,
2740   ipse quod ignoret nec numerare queat.
Praesulis e digitis gemmarum pendet et auri
septem diuitibus quod satis esset opum.
Praesul amat marcam plus quam distinguere Marcum,
plus et amat lucrum quam sapuisse Lucam.
2745   Sic hodie, sic cras sibi credita non data certe
dispensant, Domino dissimulante diu.
Qualiter atque quibus curam credant animarum,
(quod magis est aliis omnibus) ecce patet.
Ante puer patrem primum matremque uocare
2750   quam sciat aut possit stare uel ire pedes,
suscipit ecclesiae claues animasque regendas,
in cunis positus dummodo uagit adhuc.
Quid dicet Petrus cum me Robekinus ad astra
aut Wileminus aget duxque comesque meus?
2755   Petro, non puero, claues Deus ecclesiarum
tradidit atque suas iussit habere uices.
In manibus, Domine, Robekini uel Wilemini
ne me tradideris, sit tibi cura mei.
Sed neque me tradam, quamuis mihi forte, quod absit,
2760   praesul uim faciat exagitetque diu.
Tristis ob hanc causam prius appellabo, Petrumque,

2738 marmore] marmora *CHuMNP*; nitet] nitent β *R*   **2740** ipse quod] ipseque
NVe; ignoret] ignorat *ROKVe Z*; nec] uel β *AJCHuMNOVe GI TrHaLa UXQY* ne *P*
2741–2 *transp. after* 2743 *Z*   **2741** e] in β *X*   **2743–4** *om.* β *GI QY*; *om. A U,
add. in lower marg. A*^pc *U*² **2744** *om. Z*; et amat] amat et *AJWHuMNDKVe TrHaLa
U*²*X* amat ipse *C* amat et ipse *C*^pc; sapuisse] *Sedgwick facit ipse* δ *TrHaLa U*²*X*   **2745** sibi]
sic *J La*   **2746** *G ends imperfectly here (missing leaves)*; dispensant] dispensat *RDVe Z*
2747–3258 *om. I*   **2747** credant] credunt *Tr Z*   **2748** magis] magis / uel maius
Ha; ecce] esse *H R U*   **2749** primum] proprium β   **2753** me] *om. Ha X*
2755 non] de *W* nec *HaLa*; claues deus] deus claues *P Ha Q*   **2756** suas] dedit δ
TrHaLa U fb   **2757** domine] domini *H Ha*   **2758** ne me] non me *JO* nonne *R*
ne tu *U*   **2759** forte] fore *AJ Tr* cura *Q*   **2760** faciat] faciet *CWRHuMN Ha*

2743–4 The manuscript attestation of these lines is slender. These puns are popular in
satiric literature (Lehmann, *Parodie*, pp. 35–8; Yunck, *Lineage of Lady Meed*, pp. 94, 107, 125
and n. 75), and the lines may be a scribal addition. *distinguere*: 'to analyse' (in the manner of
an *explication de texte*); cf. *DMLBS* 4. *sapuisse facit ipse*: all MSS. According to Mozley's
apparatus criticus, 'sapuisse' is a conjecture by Sedgwick, but it is not in his 'Textual criticism'.
    2746 *dissimulante*: 'dissimulare' = 'to ignore, disregard' (*DMLBS* 2).

SPECVLVM STVLTORVM 277

bishop's tunics, so many his gowns, his hoods, that he himself does not know how many and cannot count them. [2740] On the bishop's fingers hang gold and jewels which would be wealth enough for seven rich men. The bishop loves a mark better than analysing Mark; he loves lucre better than knowing Luke. This is how they dispense what has been entrusted, not given, to them, both today and tomorrow, [2745] and all the while God pays no attention. How and to whom they commit the cure of souls—which is more important than all the rest—is evident. Before a boy knows how to name his father and mother, or can stand or walk, [2750] he takes on the keys of the church and the guidance of souls, while he is still howling in the cradle. What will Peter say, when little Bobby or little Willy leads me to heaven as my guide and companion? God gave the keys of the church to Peter, not to a child, [2755] and bade him take charge of its fate. Lord, do not let me fall into the hands of little Bobby or little Willy; have a care for me. And I won't let myself do so either, unless—which heaven forbid—the bishop inflicts force on me and harasses me for a long time. [2760] Saddened by this, I shall first lodge a complaint, and shall go on foot to Peter and

---

2749–84 The Third Lateran Council of 1179 attempted to put an end to this practice by decreeing that no one should be made a bishop under the age of 30, and no one should receive lower orders that entailed the cure of souls before they were at least 25 years old (c. 3, Mansi, xxii. 218–19). Bernard of Clairvaux had complained of 'scholares pueri et impuberes adolescentuli' who were promoted to church dignities because of their high birth ('ob sanguinis dignitatem'), 'et de sub ferula transferentur ad principandum presbyteris, laetiores interim quod virgas evaserint, quam quod meruerint principatum' (*Epistolae*, no. xlii, *Tractatus de moribus et officiis episcoporum, Sancti Bernardi Opera*, vii. 121). In 12th-c. England there were numerous complaints about children being given church livings and bishoprics. John of Hauville criticized the presumption of young boys who take on the care of souls when they are 'scarcely weaned' (*Architrenius*, ed. Wetherbee, v. 51–6). In 1138, Richard of Belmeis laid claim to the archdeaconry of Middlesex which his uncle Richard, bishop of London (1108–27), had bestowed on him while he was 'still a child' ('nondum plene pubes'), his place having been filled by a substitute who did not want to relinquish it, as Ralph de Diceto reports (*Abbreviationes*, i. 251–2). William of Newburgh (*Historia*, iii. 5; i. 225–6) accused Roger, late bishop of York, of having bestowed parishes on 'imberbes, et quosdam etiam agentes sub ferula, aptos magis pro aetate "Aedificare casas, plostello adjungere mures,/ Ludere par impar, equitare in arundine longa" [Horace, *Saturae*, ii. 3. 247] quam personas in ecclesia gerere magnatorum' ('beardless boys, and some still under the rod [i.e. at school], more suited from their age "to build toy-houses, to harness mice to little carts, to play odds and evens, to ride on a long stick" than to act the part of dignitaries in church'). In 1194, Pope Celestine III wrote to Geoffrey, bishop of York, listing various charges made against him, among them that he presented livings to 'boys and disreputable people' ('pueris et minus honestis personis') (Roger of Howden, *Chronica*, iii. 280).

2761 *appellabo*: 'appellare' = 'to appeal to a judge, lodge a complaint, bring an action (against someone)' (Niermeyer 1–2; *DMLBS* 4).

278   *SPECVLVM STVLTORVM*

eius et haeredem solus adibo pedes.
Cum nutrice sua Romam Robekinus adibit,
     quem noua siue uetus sportula tecta feret.
2765   Missus et in peram ueniet Wileminus in urbem,
     curia Romana tota uidebit eum.
Nec uacuis manibus aderunt nec uentre soluto,
     sed quasi parturiens et prope tempus agens.
Accedent propius uenientque uidere sepulchrum,
2770   quod semper uacuum permanet atque capax.
Quod deest aetati tenerae supplebit eorum
     gratia, consortes quos habuere uiae.
Praestabunt annos pater et pedagogus eisdem,
     quotquot opus fuerit, si tamen esset opus.
2775   Qui dedit ecclesias, numquid non contulit annos
     et mores quales talibus esse decet?
A simili reliquum potuit, qui contulit unum,
     iure pari licuit illud et illud ei.
Impubes pueros pastores ecclesiarum
2780   uidimus effectos pontificesue sacros.
Sicut ait quidam de quodam pontificando,
     cum princeps regni sollicitaret eum,
"Est puer, et nondum discernere possumus utrum
     foemina uel mas sit, et modo praesul erit!"
2785   Talibus est hodie cleri populique potestas
     atque domus Domini cura regenda data.
Talibus ecclesia Christi suffulta columnis
     decidet, ante suam praeiugulata diem.
Si quaeris quid agat praesul festinus in urbe,
2790   assumptis canibus in nemus ire parat,
aut ut aues auibus capiat uel piscibus hamum
     mittat et esocem hinc trahat inde lupum.

2764 siue] sine *WHuMN La*; uetus] *om. HaLa*; feret] foret *La U* ferent *Z*   **2767** uentre] uente *HuN*   **2771** deest] desit *DVe*   **2772** habuere uiae] uix habuere *Z* habuere uite *HaLa*   **2777** reliquum] requiem *HaLa*; potuit] patuit *Q om. HaLa* **2779** impubes] *sic RO* impuberes *rest*   **2780** pontificesue] pontificesque *M Ha UZX* **2781** sicut ait] sic dixit δ *TrHaLa*   **2787** *om. La Q*   **2788** suam] diem *CK* sitam *H* sunt *Tr*; praeiugulata] preuigilata *H X* priuigilata *B*; diem] suam *CK*   **2789** praesul festinus] festinus praesul *AJCWRHuMNODKVe TrHaLa*; in] ab β *UZQY*   **2791** auibus capiat] capiat auibus β *K X* auibus capit *Z*; uel] aut *D Z*   **2792** mittat] mittit *Ha U* mutat *D La*; esocem] esorem β *AJCWRMNODK Tr UXQ* esotem *Ve* esosem *Y*; hinc] hic *J* nunc *R* quod β *X*; trahat] trahit *AJCWRMNOVe TrHaLa UZY*

SPECVLVM STVLTORVM

279

his heir. Little Bobby will go to Rome with his nurse, carried in a covered basket, new or old. And stuffed into a shoulder bag, little Willy will come to the city, [2765] and the whole Roman curia will see him. They will not come with empty hands nor having given birth, but as if in labour and drawing near their time. They will approach nearer, and will go to see the sepulchre which always remains empty and spacious. [2770] What their tender years lack, the grace of those who are their travelling-companions will supply. Their father and their teacher will give them whatever years are needed, if need there is. Did not he who gave the churches also bestow years [2775] and morals fitting for such as these? He who gave the one could give the rest likewise; both the one and the other were allowed him by equal right. We have seen beardless boys made church pastors and holy bishops. [2780] This is what some-one said about a certain episcopal candidate, when the king of the realm asked him: "He is a child, and we can't yet tell whether he is male or female, and now he's to be a bishop!" To such is given power over clergy and people, [2785] and the duty of governing the house of God. Supported by such columns, the church of Christ will fall, murdered before its time. If you ask what the busy bishop is doing in town, he is taking his dogs and getting ready to go to the wood, [2790] either so that he may catch birds with birds, or so that he may throw a hook to fish and draw up now a salmon, now a pike. A heron has been glimpsed

2763–70 On the venality of the Roman curia, see n. to lines 2495–558 above. The permanently 'empty sepulchre' is the empty money-chest of the curia, which the 'pregnant' purse of the would-be bishop is destined to fill.

2765 *peram*: 'pera' = a wallet or satchel in which to carry books, provisions, etc., usually hung from the shoulder (*DMLBS*).

2779 *Impubes*: the majority of the manuscripts read 'īmpŭbĕrēs', which is unmetrical. *R* and *O* have the correct form.

2781 *pontificando*: 'pontificare' = 'to be a bishop' (Niermeyer 2; *DMLBS* 1).

2789–99 On the clerical passion for hunting, and attempts to restrain it, see Baldwin, *Masters, Princes, and Merchants*, i. 226–7.

2792 *esocem*: Sedgwick's conjecture ('Textual criticism', p. 293) is confirmed by the read-ing of *PHaLaZ*. 'Esox' is 'a kind of pike'; the word is found in Pliny, *Natural History*, ix. 4. 4. It is here translated 'salmon' to avoid repetition, since 'lupus' also means 'pike'. According to the two verse citations in *TLL* (Paulinus of Périgueux, Venantius Fortunatus), the first syllable is scanned short, but it is scanned long in Ekkehard (*Carmina*, no. lx. 114).

SPECVLVM STVLTORVM

280

Ardea uisa fuit fluuiali proxima ripae,
iactet ut accipitrem praesul ab urbe ruit.

2795 Siluarum saltus plus quam loca sancta frequentat,
latratusque canum canone pluris habet.

Plus cane percusso dolet anxius aut aue laesa
quam si decedat clericus unus ei.

Saepe dies tota causis cedit sine causa,
2800 officiisque sacris sufficit hora breuis.

Litibus impensa breuis est quaeuis mora longa,
moxque quod est Domini taedia magna parit.

Acrius insistit lepori canis, irrequietus
donec et officium compleat ipse suum,

2805 quam sua persoluant, cum tempus et hora requirit,
pontifices nostri debita pensa Deo.

Qui si pro Domino paterentur quod patiuntur
propter res uiles deliciasque breues,

nullus eos dubitet uiuos, in carne manentes,
2810 esse Dei sanctos martyribusque pares.

Nec tamen ista pati pudet hos aut poenitet horum
quamuis saepe grauet sustinuisse iugum.

Nam Deus illorum, pro quo patiuntur ad horam
haec mala, pro meritis praemia digna dabit.'

De abbatibus

2815 'Quodque magis miror, abbates atque priores
conuentusque sacri, quos suus ordo ligat,

canone posthabito, quem sunt seruare professi
quemque patres sancti constituere sibi,

ecce retro redeunt sorbentque quod euomuerunt,
2820 ut canis ad uomitum, susque reuersa lutum.

2793 *om. J*; uisa] nisi *QY*; fluuiali] fuuiali *W* femali *Hu^{ac?}MN*; ripae] rupe *CWMN*
2794 iactet] iacet *J HaLa*; ut] et *Ve Tr Z*; ruit] ruet *O* fuit *MN*   **2795** plus quam]
postquam *UX*; frequentat] frequentant *CRO*   **2796** habet] habent *R U*
2798 decedat] decidit *Z* discedat *AJCWHuMNPDVe TrHaLa^{pc}*   **2799** cedit] cedet *R*
Tr sedat *U*   **2802** moxque quod est] moxque est *J* uoxque queuis *Ha* hora breuis
Sedgwick; magna] longa *HaLa*   **2803** acrius] arcius δ *TrHaLa UZQY*; irrequietus] ire
quietus *AJCWPDKVe TrLa QY* ille quietus *Z* ira quietus *R*   **2805** quam] qui *QY*
2807 quod] que β *Ha UX* ut *QY* aut *Z*   **2809** dubitet] dubitat *QY*   **2810** sanc-
tos] socios *CW* sanctis *Z*   **2812** grauet] grauat *AJCWRHuMNOPDVe Tr* graue *K*
2814 haec] hic *O ZQY*   **2815** miror] miror quod *AJCWO^{ac}PVe TrLa UQY* mirorque
Ha   **2816** sacri] sacer *RHuMNO TrHaLa*   **2817** posthabito] postposito *ZQY*
plus habito *Ve*

SPECVLVM STVLTORVM 281

near the riverbank—the bishop rushes out of town to fly his hawk. He haunts the forest glades more than sacred ground, [2795] and prefers canine barking to canon law. He is more upset and sorrowful when a dog is struck or a bird injured than if one of his clergy dies. Often the whole day passes in causeless lawsuits, while a brief hour is sufficient for the holy office. [2800] However long the time spent on lawsuits is, it is [too] short, whereas what pertains to God quickly produces great boredom. More keenly does the dog pursue the hare, unresting until its task is done, than our bishops fulfil the duties owed to God, when season and hour require them. [2805] If they suffered for God's sake what they suffer for base things and fleeting pleasures, no one would doubt that they were saints of God and the equals of the martyrs, while alive and still in the flesh. [2810] Yet they are not ashamed to suffer these things nor do they repent, although it often burdens them to have taken on this yoke. For their God, for whom they now suffer these evils, will give them fit rewards for their merits.'

About Abbots

'And what causes me greater wonderment, abbots and priors of the holy community, [2815] who are bound by their order, disregarding the rule which they have vowed to keep, and which the holy fathers established for them—see, they return and guzzle up what they have spewed out, like a dog to its vomit, or a sow who has gone back to the mud. [2820] Outwardly they lay claim to the appearance of religion but

---

2796 *canum canone*: for similar wordplay on 'canis' and 'canon', see *Apocalipsis Goliae*, ed. Strecker, st. 49. 1–3: 'Decanus canis est archidiaconi,/ cuius sunt canones latratus dissoni,/ canens de canone discors est canoni.'

2802 *moxque quod est*: for discussion see Introduction, n. 171.

2819–20 Prov. 26: 11 (dog returning to its vomit) and 2 Pet. 2: 22 (dog returning to vomit and pig to mud). *sorbentque quod euomuerunt*: see *Anglo-Latin Satirical Poets*, ed. Wright, ii. 203, line 20. The verses that Wright prints here under the title 'Invectio in monachos' are an amalgamation of separate items (see Rigg, *Anglo-Latin Literature*, pp. 65–6, and 'Medieval Latin Poetic Anthologies (I)', p. 302); the above quotation occurs in the third of these items, a poem beginning 'Quae monachi quaerunt' (Walther, *Initia*, 15005), which survives in BL, Cotton Titus A. XX, MS *C* of the present edition of *SS*, which was used by Wright. See Boutemy, 'Deux poèmes inconnus', pp. 262–9, for details of these manuscripts, and an *apparatus criticus* of variant readings which enables improvement of Wright's inadequate text.

282 SPECVLVM STVLTORVM

Exterius faciem praetendunt religionis,
    interiusque gerunt pectora plena dolo.
Qui duce Bernardo gradiuntur uel Benedicto,
    aut Augustini sub leuiore iugo,
2825 omnes sunt fures, quocumque charactere sancto
    signati ueniant magnificentque Deum.
Ne credas uerbis, ne credas uestibus albis,
    uix etenim factis est adhibenda fides.
Quorum uox lenis uox Iacob creditur esse
2830   cetera sunt Esau, brachia, colla, manus.
Rursus in Aegyptum quem deseruere reuersi,
    dulce sibi reputant a Pharaone premi.
Carnis ad illecebras nullo retinente ruentes
    in foueam mortis carne trahente cadunt.
2835 Inuidiae stimulis uexantur, et ambitionis
    aestibus assiduis, praecipueque tribus.
Primus ut ascendant labor est, sequiturque parentum
    indiscretus amor, cura quiete carens.
Hac omnes ardent, hac omnes febre laborant,
2840   haec tenet imperium, postpositura Deum.
Hinc, ut opes habeant summa uirtute laborant,
    possideantque breui tempore parta diu.
Olim paupertas rebusque carere caducis
    religiosorum gloria magna fuit.
2845 Nunc nisi possideant, animarum damna suarum,
    res et opes magnas, pascua, prata, greges,
esse putant miseri, quia mundo pauper haberi
    inter eos hodie creditur esse scelus.
Pauper erat Christus, quem sic imitando sequuntur
2850   pauperis ut sine re nomen habere queant.
Sicque uolunt dici quod nolunt esse, putantes

2824 Augustini] augustino *AJCWRHuMNOPDVe TrHaLa UZ*; leuiore] leuiori
CWHu HaLa X   2826 ueniant] uenient *ZQ*   2831 quem] quam *H R X*
2832 premi] primi *H RHuMN X*   2833 *line repeated in alternative form* $Z_{(1)}Z_{(2)}$; carnis ad] carnis in *O* carnes et *Y* carnes ad $Z_{(1)}$ carius ad $Z_{(2)}$; illecebras] celebres $Z_{(2)}$
2834–5 *transp. after 2837 Z*   2835 ambitionis] ambitiosis *H HuMN QY*
2837 labor est] laborem *Tr* laborque *HaLa*   2838 *om. Y*; cura] crura *HuMND^{ac}K*;
carens] carent *AJCWHuMNPDKVe Tr* caret *O HaLa*   2839 hac[1]] ac *CW*; hac[2]] ac
CWHuMN Z huc *Tr*; febre] fere *RP Tr*   2842 parta] parca *H Tr* prata *Z*
2848 scelus] nefas δ *TrHaLa UZQY fb*   2851 uolunt...nolunt] nolunt...uolunt *fb*;
nolunt] uolunt quod *Tr* uolunt *ZQ*

SPECVLVM STVLTORVM
283

inwardly their hearts are full of guile. Those who march under Bernard's leadership and those under Benedict's, and those under the lighter yoke of Augustine—they are all thieves, with whatever holy brand-mark [2825] they come stamped, praising God. Do not trust their words, do not trust their white robes—indeed you should hardly found any trust on their actions. Their gentle voice is believed to be the voice of Jacob, but the rest is Esau's—arms, neck, and hands. [2830] They have returned once more to the Egypt they had left, and think it sweet to be oppressed by Pharaoh. Rushing to the pleasures of the flesh with no one holding them back, they are lured on by the flesh and fall into the pit of death. They are tormented by the pangs of envy [2835] and the constant seething of ambition, and by three things in particular: the first is the effort to rise in life, after which come the indiscriminate love of their relatives, and an anxiety that knows no peace. This is the fever that sets them all on fire and makes them sweat; this holds sway, pushing God into second place. [2840] Thus they toil away with all their strength so that they may get riches, and possess for a brief time what has been long in the winning. In the old days, poverty and the lack of temporal possessions was the great glory of those in religious life. Now, unless they possess (what is harmful to their souls) [2845] great property and wealth, pastures, meadows, flocks, they think themselves wretched, for to be thought poor in the world is today considered to be a crime among them. Christ was poor, whom they imitate in such a way that they can have the name of poverty without the actuality. [2850] Thus they want to be *called* what they do not want to *be*, thinking that they can deceive the God Who sees all. They have

2823–4 That is, whether the abbots/priors are Cistercian (indicated by the reference to Bernard of Clairvaux), Benedictines, or Augustinian canons.

2827 White robes suggest a Cistercian, indicating that the target here is again Archbishop Baldwin.

2829–30 Gen. 27: 22. Jacob and Esau are types of good and evil respectively.

2837–8 On clerical nepotism, see n. to lines 2711–12.

284   *SPECVLVM STVLTORVM*

omnia cernentem fallere posse Deum.
Omnibus abiectis inopis uestigia Christi
    uerbis, non factis, se statuere sequi.
2855 Spreuerunt mundum, sed tali conditione
    ut semel abiectus semper adesse queat.
Ne quid eis desit spreuerunt omnia; felix
    quisquis, ut ipse metat plurima, pauca serit.
Cum lupus ex habitu non est suspectus ouili,
2860   dentis ab effectu quo timeatur habet.
Simpliciter graditur uulpis uultuque modesto
    et nihil in facie suspicionis habet,
corde sed astuto uincens animalia multa,
    semper in insidiis tota dolosa manet.
2865 Quo magis ascendit caelo uicinior alto
    accipiter, praedam fortius inde capit.
Fortius ut feriat aries retrocedit, et ictus
    suscipit obstipo uertice datque simul.
Sic faciunt hodie quos mundus religiosos
2870   aestimat et sanctos praedicat esse uiros.
De quibus ad praesens, quamuis mihi multa supersint,
    plura loqui timeo, ne reprehendar ego.'

De laicis

'Sed quid de laicis dicam? Si publica quaedam
    dixero quae didici, publicus hostis ero.
2875 Nuper cum profugus fugerem festinus ab urbe,
    Bernardum fugiens, uerbera saeua timens,
abdita quaerebam loca, quae non posset adire
    ille meus dominus, rusticus ille miser,
qui me quaerebat per deuia quaeque locorum,
2880   cum canibus multis multa minando mihi.
Iurabatque satis quod si possem reperiri
    illud iter luerem tempus in omne meum,

2856 adesse] abesse *Ve QY*   **2858** plurima] *om. fb*; pauca] pauca sed *fb* parta *U*
2859–3097 *copied a second time on fos. 138ʳ–138ᵛ* = *P*(2)   **2859** ex] *om. M*
2861–2 *om. H La add. in margin La*ᵖᶜ   **2861** graditur] creditur *fb*; uulpis] uulpes
JROPP(2)*K TrHa ZXQ*   **2865** ascendit] ascendet *H X*   **2867** aries] aues *CW*
2869 sic] sicque *fb*   **2873** publica] publicam *P*(2) *La*   **2875** cum] tamen *QY*
om. H   **2877** quaerebam] qurebam *J* querelam *WM*   **2882** *om. Ha*; luerem]
lugerem *QY*

SPECVLVM STVLTORVM   285

decided to cast off everything and follow the steps of the indigent
Christ—in words, not in deeds. They have rejected the world, but in
such a way [2855] that once cast aside, it can be always present. Lest
they may lack anything, they have rejected everything; happy is he who
sows a little so that he may reap a lot. Although the wolf is not suspected because of his sheep's clothing, he still has the teeth which
ought to make him feared. [2860] The fox approaches innocently and
with a gentle expression, and has nothing suspicious in its appearance,
but outdoing many animals in mental cunning, it is thoroughly deceitful and always laying traps. The higher the hawk ascends, the nearer to
lofty heaven, [2865] the more powerfully it seizes its prey from this
vantage-point. The ram retreats so that it may charge more strongly,
and with lowered head receives a blow and inflicts one at the same time.
Those whom the world believes to be religious, and declares to be holy
men, act in the same way. [2870] Although I still have a lot remaining,
I fear to say more about them at the moment, in case I am blamed.'

About the Laity

'But what shall I say about the laity? If I speak publicly certain things
I have heard, I shall be a public enemy. Once, when I was leaving the city
in haste as a fugitive fleeing from Bernard, [2875] in fear of his savage
blows, I was seeking out-of-the-way places, which my master, that
wretched peasant, who was seeking me with a host of dogs and profuse
threats, through all the byways of the region, could not come near.
[2880] He swore vigorously that if I could be found, I would pay for
that exodus for the rest of my life, and that he would inscribe that flight

---

2859–62 Cf. *Tractatus*, ed. Boutemy, p. 170: ambitious clerics adopt a life of ostentatious
asceticism, wearing poor clothing, 'ut lupus rapacitatis et vulpis astutiae sub pelle ovina
delitescat'.

2867 Cf. *Tractatus*, ed. Boutemy, p. 170: [clerical hypocrites] 'quasi aries gradu retrogrado
feruntur ut fortius impingant', and *Policraticus*, vii. 18. 7 (ed. Webb, ii. 167): 'more (ut dicitur) arietis ut fortius feriat recedentis'.

2871–2 Nigel uses this conventional disclaimer as a pretext; his real reason for abandoning any satirical attacks on the laity is that his main targets are kings, bishops, and abbots—in
other words, the figures involved in the threat to the monastic community of Christ Church
(see Introduction, pp. lxxiv–lxxv).

2882 See n. to line 468.

286 SPECVLVM STVLTORVM

quodque fugam dorso mihi scriberet ipse legendam
taliter ut numquam non meminisse foret.

2885 Me quoque stertentem laetus quandoque putabat
admota propius prendere posse manu.

Sed celer exiliens Bernardum pone sequentem
ridebam dominum conscius ipse meum.

Saepe supinatum per posteriora coegi,

2890 calce repercussum, stertere more meo.

Aestus erat, lassusque fui uoluique sub umbra
ilicis optato membra fouere toro.

Carmina quae nuper me composuisse iuuabat
scribere conabar tutus ab hoste meo.

2895 Et locus et tempus, studio nimis apta, uolentem
scribere cogebant improbitate sua.

Venter erat plenus, pes lassus, pagina prompta
exceptura noua carmina digna nota.

Cumque manus calamum ferrumque teneret acutum

2900 exciperetque nouos pellis ouina tonos,
nescio quem prope me ramos super ilicis altae
audio garritum percipioque sonum.

Nec mora, tanta locum uolucrum uaga turba repleuit,
silua quod, ampla prius, tunc tamen arta foret.

2905 Intonat omne nemus, uolucrum dispersa per auras
uox abit in caelum concutiendo solum.

Ipse mihi timui coepique timendo coactus
dicere "Quid sibi uult hoc nouitatis opus?"

Terreor aspectu; nec mirum; tum quia notus

2883 ipse] esse δ *TrLa UZQY om. Ha*   2885 stertentem] sternentem *MRD*ᵃᶜ
stercentem *JHu* stertem *Z*   2886 admota] ad metam *Ha Z*; propius] proprius *CW*;
prendere] pendere *HuMN*   2887 pone] prope *H* pede *CW* pene *ROPVe HaLa*
2890–92 *transp. after 2897 Z*   2890 stertere] sternere *CWHuMNDK* stercore *Q*
2891 aestus] estas *AJCRMO*ᵃᶜ*P*(₂)*DVe TrHaLa* *U*²*over erasure* estat *HuN*; uoluique] noluique
C La   2893 iuuabat] uidebar *JCWRHuMNOPP*(₂)*DKVe TrHaLa* *U*²*over erasure X*
uidebat *A*   2894–6 tutus ab hoste—scribere cogebant] *om. H*   2894–5 *transp. Z*
2895–6 *om. U, add. in lower margin* *U*²   2896 cogebant] conebant *HaLa*
2898 exceptura] excerptura *AJOPVe La U* exterptura *Tr*; nota] notum *J* uota *La U*
2899 ferrumque teneret] ferrum uideret *HaLa*   2901 quem] quam *H D Ha XQ*; me]
om. H R; ramos super] sub ramos *AJHuMNPP*(₂) *Tr* sub ramis *CWRODKVe HaLa X* ramos
sub *U*²*over erasure QY* ramis sub *Z*   2902 percipioque] precipioque *MN*
2903 nec] ne *MN*   2906 abit] habet *La* habet /uel abit *Ha*   2907 timendo]
timere β *UZQY om. Ha*   2908 dicere] discere *H HuN*; hoc] hec *HuMN*

SPECVLVM STVLTORVM 287

for all to read on my back in such a way that it would never be forgotten. And sometimes he thought, with joy, [2885] that he could seize me with outstretched hand as I was snoring. But I was aware of him, and quickly jumping up, I laughed at my master Bernard, following behind. Often I caused him to bray like me, flat on his back, sent flying by my hoof. [2890] It was hot, I was tired, and wanted to rest my limbs on the welcome couch beneath the shade of a holm-oak. Safe from my enemy, I was trying to write down the poems it was once my amusement to compose. Place and time, highly suitable for study, [2895] boldly urged me to write, as I wished to do. My belly was full, my feet tired, the page ready to receive the new poems in elegant writing. But as my hand held the pen and the sharp blade, and the parchment was receiving the new notes, [2900] I heard a sound, a sort of chattering noise, close by me, on the branches of the tall holm-oak. And all at once, so great a crowd of fluttering birds filled the place that the wood, which before had seemed spacious, now seemed cramped. The whole woodland echoed, as the noise of the birds filled the air, [2905] bouncing off the ground and rising up to heaven. I feared for myself, and under the pressure of fear I began to say to myself, "What does this strange event mean?" The sight terrified me, and no wonder, for the place was an unfamiliar one

2891 *Aestus erat*: the memorable opening words of Ovid's most pornographic poem: *Amores*, i. 5.1.

2894 *tutus ab hoste*: Ovid, *Heroides*, xi. 44.

2896 *improbitate*: 'improbitas' = 'persistence' (*DMLBS* 3b).

2898 *exceptura* (the reading of β supported by some δ manuscripts) is preferable to 'excerptura' in meaning, is better supported by the manuscripts, and is confirmed by 'exciperet' at 2900.

2899 The 'sharp metal' is the knife which medieval scribes customarily held in their left hand while writing, using it to sharpen the nib of their pen, or, occasionally, to scrape away errors from the parchment as they copied. See D'Haenens, 'Écrire, un couteau dans la main gauche' (with plentiful illustrations); Leclercq, 'Pour l'histoire du canif et de la lime'; Scott, 'Representations of scribal activity'. Corpus Christi College Cambridge 200, a manuscript from Christ Curch Canterbury which contains Archbishop Baldwin's *De sacramento altaris*, begins on p. 1 with a historiated initial showing Baldwin writing the work, with a pen in his right hand and a knife in his left hand (the manuscript is available online via Parker on the Web, at <parker.stanford.edu>; see James, *Ancient Libraries*, pp. 26 (no. 94), 507, for the Canterbury connection. Cf. Ovid, *Heroides*, xi. 3: 'dextra tenet calamum, strictum tenet altera ferrum' (where, however, the 'ferrum' is the drawn sword with which Canace will kill herself).

2903 *uolucrum uaga turba*: the sudden arrival of the huge flock of birds which settle on a tree is reminiscent of Chretien de Troyes, *Yvain*, lines 459–77.

288 SPECVLVM STVLTORVM

2910 non erat ille locus, tum quia solus eram.
Auribus erectis et fixo corpore toto
prostratus iacui murmuris absque sono.
Pectora tundebam tacitus ueniamque precabar
uoto non uerbo, supplice corde meo.
2915 Paene timore graui uentrem sine uentre resolui
contigit, et dubito ne sit et an sit ita.
Namque graues uenti tempestatesque morosae
imbribus exiguis delituisse solent.
Murmure sedato tenuere silentia tandem,
2920 et quotquot fuerant conticuere simul.
Agminis in medio, tota reticente caterua,
surrexit solus coruus, adorsus ita.'

Sententia corui

'"Dilecti fratres dominique mei speciales,
si placet, audite me, quia pauca loquar,
2925 non quia sim melior uobis uel stemmate maior,
utpote de uili cespite natus ego,
uel quod plus sapiam, cum sit sapientia prima,
teste Dauid magno, scire timere Deum,
sed quia sum maior natu senioribus istis
2930 omnibus, annorum tempore teste mihi.
Me Noe septennem prudens induxit in arcam,
cum tegeret montes altior unda fluens.
Postea fluxerunt quamplurima saecula nobis,
pluribus ignota saecula, ualde bona.
2935 Quorum dum recolo mecum tacitusque recordor
quam bona tunc fuerint quamque referta bonis

2911 et fixo] et fixis *La* fixo pede β *X*   2913 tundebam] tondebam *R Ha*
2914 supplice] supplici *H Ve Ha* simplice *CWHuMNK* simplici *D*   2915–16 *om. QY*
2915 paene] pone *C La* preque *Ha Z*; uentrem] uentum *CVe*; sine uentre] mihi forte *K* sine
uento *O U*   2916 dubito] subito *HuMND*   2917 morosae] morosi *MN* mirose
Tr nemorose *ZQY*   2918–20 delituisse solent—quotquot fuerant] *om.* δ(*P*(2)) *TrHaLa*
UZQY   2918 exiguis] ex ignis *H M Tr*   2920 conticuere] conticuereque *Tr*
contiguere *J* continuere *H X* concutiere *U*   2921 reticente] retinente *R Ha*
2923 dilecti] delicti *MN*   2925 sim] sum *JCWHuMNDK TrHa X*; melior uobis] uobis
melior β; uel stemmate maior] uel (aut *Ha* et *U*) sanctior unus δ(*P*(2)) *TrHaLa UZXQY*
2927 quod] quia *RD U²XQ*   2928 scire] fore *AJCWRHuMNOPP*(2))*DVe TrHaLa U²*
om. K   2934 saecula] specula *C X*

SPECVLVM STVLTORVM

289

and I was alone. [2910] With ears erect, and my whole body tense, I lay prostrate without uttering a sound. Silently I beat my breast, and begged for mercy—mentally, not verbally, my heart making entreaty. It almost happened—though I'm not sure whether it did or not—that in my great fear my bowels involuntarily opened without discharging anything solid. [2915] For violent winds and lengthy storms often vanish with a little rain. The noise died down, and silence reigned at last; all those present fell silent. [2920] In the middle of the throng, the whole troop remaining silent, a solitary raven rose and spoke as follows.'

The Opinion of the Raven

' "Beloved brethren, my dear friends, hear me, if you please, for I shall be brief, not because I am better than you or of nobler ancestry, [2925] born as I was of base stock, or because I know more (since the foundation of wisdom, as the great David witnesses, is to know how to fear God), but because I am greater in age than all these greybeards, as the passage of years is my witness. [2930] The far-sighted Noah kept me in the Ark for seven years, while the sea rose high enough to cover the mountain tops. Afterwards many centuries rolled by me—centuries unknown to many, but happy ones. And when I recall them in my mind, and silently remember [2935] how happy they were, how filled with good things in comparison with present times, I am sad and troubled,

---

2916 *ne sit et an sit ita*: cf. *SS*, 3844: 'quae sit et an sit ita'; also *Miracles*, 1794, and cf. *Miracles*, 202, 'quid sit et an sit homo'.

2917–18 Proverbial; see n. to line 357. *morosae* with a long first syllable 'morosus' means 'hard to please, difficult, exacting', which does not fit the context, but this is 'mŏrōsus' meaning 'protracted, lengthy' (*OLD* s.v. 'morosus²'; cf. Niermeyer, s.v.).

2923 *speciales*: 'specialis' = 'intimate, familiar' (Niermeyer); (as noun) 'close or intimate friend' (*DMLBS* 4c).

2924 *pauca loquar*: Vergil, *Aeneid*, iv. 337.

2927–8 Ps. 110 (111): 10.

2931 *septennem...arcam*: 'septennis' means 'lasting seven years' (*DMLBS* 2), which is difficult to relate to the ark of Noah (Gen. 6–7). The length of time it took to make the ark is not specified; seven *days* after its completion, the rain began. The rains stopped and the ark came to rest on the seventh *day* of the seventh *month*. In addition to the above details, Noah is ordered to introduce seven males and seven females of clean animals, and also of all birds. But none of this explains why the ark itself is called 'septennis'.

290   *SPECVLVM STVLTORVM*

horum respectu quae sunt modo, tristis et amens
   tempora festinae mortis adesse reor.
Namque senescentis mundi decus omne recessit
2940   et sua quaeque suum deseruere statum.
Sidera, terra, mare, solito priuata tenore,
   legibus antiquis dedidicere regi;
et si praeterita praesentibus annumeremus,
   nulla cohaerebunt corpore membra suo.
2945 Ordine transposito uariantur saecula quaeque,
   alter et est hodie quam fuit orbis heri.
Contra naturam rerum natura ministrat,
   deserit et cursum noxque diesque suum.
Hinc homines morbi perimunt, animalia pestes,
2950   hinc quoque languore praemoriuntur aues.
In promptu causa est: quoniam peccauimus omnes,
   nec superest qui se iudicet esse reum.
Omnes sunt iusti, nullus peccauit, iniquum
   nil ego commisi, tu nihil, ille nihil,
2955 'Non ego gustaui' cuncti dixere ministri;
   et tamen absorptum constitit esse camum.
Esto quod apponat aliquis sua crimina flere
   et de commissis paenituisse uelit,
pectore contrito statuat sua facta fateri
2960   crimina cum lacrimis cumque dolore graui—
cui sua secure poterit secreta fateri
   omnibus ex nobis? Nescio, crede mihi.
Mille mihi fratres numeres totidemque sorores,
   mille sed et matres sint mihi totque patres,
2965 omnibus ex illis secreti conscius unus,
   unicus atque meus consiliator erit?

2937 sunt] sint *B AJWRHuNPD TrLa U* sit *CM*   **2938** reor] precor β *QY*
2939 namque] nam *B ARVe TrHa U*   **2940** et] sed *R Tr*   **2942** antiquis]
antique *P*(2); dedidicere] didicere *C* dedicere *RVe TrHa X* dediceri *D*ᵃᶜ dididicere *D*ᵖᶜ tunc
dedicere *Z*   **2944** corpore] corpori *D* corpora *La Y*   **2950** languore] languorem
Ve La   **2951** promptu] prompto *PP*(2) prompta *Ve Q*; est] *om. RMPP*(2)
2953 iniquum] iniquus *AJPP*(2)*Ve TrHaLa U*² inique *R*   **2954** commisi] commissi *K X*
2956 absorptum] absorbitum *Z* absortum *H*ᵃᶜ δ(*P*(2)) *Tr XY*; camum] *Skutsch* cadum
Sedgwick ciphum *K* canem β *AJCWRHuMNOPP*(2)*DVe TrHaLa UZXQY*
2959 facta] cuncta β *X*   **2960–1** *om. Ha U, add. in lower margin U*²   **2961** cui]
cum *D* qui *TrLa Z*   **2962** *after 2961, Q adds an extra line, of which the first half repeats*
2960: Crimina cum lacrimis cum iam habitum? est; nobis] uobis *JO Tr*   **2964** sint]
sunt *H D* fiunt *Ha*

SPECVLVM STVLTORVM   291

and think that the day of my speedy death is at hand. For all the glory of the world has departed as it grows old, and all its features have abandoned its proper station. [2940] The stars, the earth, the sea, bereft of their accustomed course, have ceased to be ruled by their ancient laws. And if we weigh up the past with the present, coherence between the body and its members will disappear. The passage of the ages is disrupted by a reversal of order, [2945] and the world today is not what it was yesterday. Nature works against the nature of things, and night and day abandon their course. So men are killed by disease, and beasts by pestilence, and birds die of sickness before their time. [2950] The cause is plain to see: since we have all sinned, and there is no one alive who holds himself guilty. Everyone is just, no one has sinned; I have done nothing wrong, nor have you, nor has he. 'I didn't touch it,' said all the servants, [2955] and yet it's clear that the beer was drunk. Suppose that someone does resolve to weep for his wrongdoing, and is willing to repent of what he has done—suppose he decides to confess the crimes he has committed, with a contrite heart, with tears and deep sorrow [2960]—to whom, out of all of us, can he safely confess his secrets? Believe me, I don't know. You may count my brothers by the thousand, and my sisters too—even suppose I had a thousand mothers and as many fathers—shall one out of all of them be privy to my secret [2965] and be my sole counsellor? If I tell my crimes to the raven, the raven

---

2939 *senescentis mundi*: also in Nigel's *Epigrams*, no. xi. 1.

2943 *annumeremus*: 'annumerare' = literally, 'to count, reckon (among)'; here, meaning something like 'to estimate'.

2956 *camum*: for discussion of this conjecture, see Introduction, p. lxxxii.

2957 *apponat*: 'apponere' = 'to undertake (something), proceed to do (something)' (Niermeyer; *DMLBS* 6b).

SPECVLVM STVLTORVM

292

Dixero si coruo coruus mea crimina dicet
cornici, cornix per fora tota canet.
Si me prodidero gallo, gallina, quod absit,

2970   prodigium pullis me dabit esse suis.
Mors mihi, si taceo, mors est si dixero quicquam;
me duo dura premunt, hinc timor inde pudor.
Lingua sacerdotum, quoniam secreta reuelat,
cogit ut inuiti confiteamur eis.

2975   Nulla lues grauior quam cum secreta reuelat
factus secreti conscius ille tui.
Qui cadit in gladio semel est plangendus, at ille
tempore perpetuo quem sua lingua necat.
Vos igitur qui uel facitis fieriue uidetis

2980   plurima quae non sunt enumeranda modo,
quid cui dicatis, ne postea poeniteatis,
quique per exemplum discite, quaeso, meum.
Qui sciat, atque uelit crebro releuare cadentem
et magis afflictos exhilarare magis,

2985   qui mox quassatum calamum non conterat, immo
alliget et sanet sustineatque diu;
qui grauiter lapsis ignoscens compatiatur
seque reformidet talia posse pati;
qui semper fragilis quam sit caro praemeditetur,

2990   et leuis ad lapsum conditione graui;
qui grauiter laesus non exardescat in iram,
nec mox uindictam poscat ab hoste suo,
sed pius et patiens omnem prius ipse remittat
criminis offensam quam roget alter eum;

2995   qui sibi sufficiens nec opum cupidus nec honorum
respuat oblata proprietate carens;
quem nec amor mundi uexet nec causa parentum,

2968 tota] cuncta δ(*P*(2)) *TrHaLa UZQY*
*HuRMNO La*ᵃᶜ *UY add. in lower margin U*²   2974 cogit] contigit *J Ha*; confiteamur]
confideamur *C* confiteantur *D La*   2976 ille] ipse δ(*P*(2)) *TrHaLa UZQY*
2977 at] et *JRMOPP*(2)*Ve TrLa* sed *CWHuND Ha illegible A*   2979 fieriue] fierique β
ACJWRHuMNODKVe TrHaLa UXQY   2982 *om. P Tr*; quique] cuique *HaLa*
2983 atque] aut *H Tr ZQY*; releuare] reuelare *N TrHaLa*ᵃᶜ *ZQ*   2984 *om. (line left empty) Ha*   2985 calamum] thalamum *H Tr* clauum *R*; non] nemo *QY*
2990 graui] grauis β   2991 exardescat] exardescit δ(*P*(2)) *TrHaLa Q*   2993 et] ac
AJCWHuMNDK aut *O*   2994 roget] rogat *HaLa Z*

SPECVLVM STVLTORVM 293

will tell them to the crow, and the crow will squawk them through every marketplace. If I betray myself to the cock, the hen—perish the thought!—will hold me up as a spectacle to her chicks. [2970] It's death to me to be silent, and death to say anything. Two evils oppress me—fear on one hand, and shame on the other. The tale-telling tongue of the priests obliges us to confess to them only reluctantly. There is no greater calamity than for someone who is privy to your secret to reveal your confidences. [2975] The man who falls by the sword is to be wept for once, but the man who is slain by his tongue is to be wept for all his days." '

' "So you, who either do, or see being done, many things which are not to be spelled out in detail now, [2980] learn, one and all, by my example, I beg you, what you should say to whom, in case you regret it afterwards. He who has the knowledge and the will to raise the fallen many times, and to bring greater cheer to those who are more greatly afflicted; he who does not straightway trample the broken reed, [2985] but binds it up and heals and supports it over time; he who pardons and has pity for those who have seriously erred, and fears that he may suffer the same fate; he who is always aware of how weak is the flesh, and how liable to fall in adversity; [2990] he who when deeply injured does not flare up in anger, nor demand immediate vengeance on his enemy, but mercifully and patiently forgives the whole injury of the crime before the other asks him; he who is self-sufficient, greedy neither of wealth nor of honours, [2995] and rejects gifts although he lacks wealth; he who is troubled neither by love of the world nor by the interest of his relatives, who is not swayed by proffered gifts (sweet evil!); he who

2971 This line echoes the moral of the beast fable of the ape at the lion's court: 'Et loqui pena est et reticere tormentum' (*Romulus vulgaris*, iii. 20, ed. Hervieux, *Fabulistes latins*, ii. 223, and *Romulus Nilantii*, ii. 20, ibid., ii. 538). On the problematic relations between speech and silence in *SS*, see Mann, *From Aesop to Reynard*, pp. 116–21.

2979 *fieriue*: this reading occurs only in *P* and *Z*, but 'fierique', the majority reading, does not follow logically from 'uel'.

2985 *mox* is the reading of all the manuscripts. Mozley emended to 'modo', attributing this reading to Sedgwick (but it is not to be found in the latter's 'Textual criticism'). If 'mox' is taken with 'conterat' rather than 'quassatum', the sense is unproblematic. *quassatum calamum non conterat*: Isa. 42: 3.

2990 *leuis ad lapsum*: also in *Miracles*, 1175.

2996 *proprietate*: 'proprietas' = 'riches, wealth' (Niermeyer 4).

2997 *causa* in the first instance means '(legal) case, action, plea' (*DMLBS* 1), and then more generally 'affair, matter' (*DMLBS* 2). Here it seems to refer to whatever promotes the interest of the relatives. On clerical nepotism, see the n. to lines 2711–12.

SPECVLVM STVLTORVM

uel data supplantent munera, dulce malum;
qui nec amet uel agat quod quis iusto reprehendat;

3000   cui sit idem secum uiuere quod sine se –
si fuerit talis tantusque repertus in orbe
confessor, fateor, cuncta fatebor ei.

Exemplum uobis ego sum, cui garrula quondam
lingua fuit damno, teste colore meo.

3005   Dum tacui dilectus eram, sed prodiga lingua
reddidit exosum; uae tibi, lingua loquax!

O quam diues eram multisque beatus amicis,
donec surripuit me mea lingua mihi!

Felix si statua Martis taciturnior essem,

3010   mansissetque mihi qui fuit ante color,
quod semel admisi, longum damnatus in aeuum,
lugeo perpetuo tempore tristis ego.

Gratia, fama, decor, mihi sunt sublata loquenti,
surripuit totum lingua diserta nimis.

3015   Lingua loquax nocuit, fateor, quia, si tacuissem,
cuncta remansissent insita dona prius.

Inter aues omnes formosior unus habebar,
et magis acceptus omnibus unus eram.

Vox mea, clara prius, misero uix rauca remansit,

3020   criminis admissi testis et ipsa mei.

Perpetuata foret mea gloria si tacuissem,
sed quia non tacui tota repente ruit.

Vnde mei memores linguam cohibete loquacem,
ne iugulet dominum prodiga facta suum.

3025   Pauca loquar, salua dominorum pace meorum,
uera tamen, ueris si licet esse locum.

Non est mirandum, quamuis aduersa frequenter
nobis contingant et mala plura premant;

2999 amet] amat *O La*; uel] nec *DK HaLa UZ*; iusto] iuste *H R HaLa XQ*   3000 cui] qui *J HaLa*; sit] scit *C* sic *TrLa*   3001 orbe] urbe *CW Q*   3007 beatus] beatis *HuND*^{pc} *Z* bonis *Q*   3009 Martis] iouis *PP*(2) mortis *Tr Q* marchis *La* 3011 admisi] amisi *H* δ(*P*(2)) *HaLa UZX* amici *Tr*; damnatus] damnatur *H* δ(*P*(2)) *TrLa UZXQY* dominetur *Ha*   3014 nimis] minus *B AWRHuMNOK UQY* 3015 tacuissem] tacuisse *H M*   3019 uix] uox *PP*(2) *U*   3020 admissi] admisi *HuMND*; mei] mihi *CWHuMNDK*   3021 perpetuata] perpetua *H D Tr Z* perpetu-aque *ROP*(2)*Ve* perhennisque *P*; mea] me *La U corr. U*^{2} 3023 cohibete] cohibere *H Ve Tr U* cohibite *R*   3028 plura] multa *OD*; premant] premunt *AJCWRHuMNOP*(2)*DVe Tr UZQY*

SPECVLVM STVLTORVM 295

neither approves nor performs what anyone might rightly criticize, and to whom it's all the same if one lives with him as without him [3000]— if such and so great a confessor were found in the world, to him shall I, I confess, confess everything." '

' "I, whose garrulous tongue was formerly my ruin—as my colour bears witness—am an example to you. While I kept silence, I was beloved, but my unbridled tongue [3005] made me hateful. Woe to you, chattering tongue! Oh, how rich I was and blessed with many friends, until my tongue snatched me away from myself. Happy would I be, if I had been more silent than a statue of Mars, and my original colour had remained. [3010] In sadness, condemned to the end of time, I mourn perpetually a single guilty act. Popularity, reputation, beauty were lost to me by speaking, and my too eloquent tongue took away the lot. I confess, my chattering tongue did the damage, for if I had been silent, [3015] all my former native gifts would not have been lost." '

' "Among all birds I alone was judged most beautiful, and I alone was more pleasing than the rest. My voice, once melodious, is reduced to a bare squawk—wretch that I am!—and is itself the witness to the sin I committed. [3020] My glory would have endured for ever if I had been silent, but because I was not silent it all vanished in a moment. So, remembering me, you should curb your chattering tongue, lest it run away with itself and be the death of its owner. I shall say little, saving your lordships' reverence, [3025] but I shall say truth, if room is allowed to truth. It's no wonder if adversities often befall us, and many

---

3004–22 The story of the garrulous raven, who was originally white, with a melodious voice, but was turned black as a punishment for revealing to the god Phoebus that his mistress Coronis was unfaithful, is related in Ovid, *Metamorphoses*, ii. 531–632.

3004 *lingua fuit damno*: Ovid, *Metamorphoses*, ii. 540.

3007 Cf. the first line of a poem by Hildebert of Tours, 'Nuper eram locuples multisque beatus amicis' (*Carmina*, xxii, ed. Scott, p. 11).

3009 *statua ...taciturnior*: cf. Horace, *Epistulae*, ii. 2. 83.

3011 *admisi*: 'I was guilty of, committed, perpetrated' (*OLD* s.v. 'admitto' 13).

SPECVLVM STVLTORVM

296

nos sumus in causa, si causam quaerimus, ipsi,
3030   cur tot in aduersis deficiamus ita.
Nos sata destruimus, nos semina diripientes
    tollimus, et plenos depopulamur agros.
Ne faciant fructum flores, mox arbore natos
    unguibus et rostris dilaceramus eos.
3035 Caedibus assiduis insistimus atque rapinis,
    ad bona difficiles, luxuriosa cohors.
Aestimat excussam tuto se deposuisse
    rusticus annonam, poste tenente seram.
Sed gallus ueniens, tota comitante sequela,
3040   quantumcumque placet tollit et inde fugit.
Nec satis est sumpsisse satis, totam nisi massam
    dispergat pedibus per loca cuncta domus.
Nisus et accipiter, postquam fuerit bene pastus,
    auolat et dominum spernit adire suum;
3045 nec pueri lacrimas sese reuocantis et illi
    brachia tendentis respicit, immo fugit.
Qua totiens pastus, totiens portatus, amicam
    spernit ut hostilem captus ab hoste manum.
Certa licet quamuis obiecta pericula mortis
3050   immineant pueris, non miserentur eis;
dumque sequuntur eos per deuia quaeque locorum,
    saepe quidem siluis, saepe necantur aquis.
Sic bene pro meritis nostros uexamus amicos,
    reddimus atque bona pro uice saepe mala.
3055 Psittacus in thalamum domina redeunte puellas
    prodit, et illarum uerba tacenda refert.
Quod fuerant secum tacite timideque locutae

3029 causam] tamen *JVe*   3030 cur] cui *HuMN*; in] *om. H La*   3033 natos] natus *D* multos *HaLa*   3035 insistimus] assistimus *D Tr*   3036 difficiles] deficiles *Ve* difficilis *Ha Q*   3037 tuto] tute *R HaLa* tutam *P* cuto *Ve*   3038 *om. La*; poste] posse *Tr UQY* peste *CW*   3040 quantumcumque] quantumque *J La* 3041 satis] sibi *HaLa*   3044 auolat] aduolat *AJCWHuMNDVe La UXY* aduelat *Q*; et] ad *P* et ad *P*(₂)   3046 tendentis] tendentes *D QY*; respicit] despicit *HaLa* respuit *CD*ᵃᶜ *X* euolat *P*; immo] atque *AJCWRHuMNOPP*(₂)*DVe HaLa UZXQY*   3047 qua] quam *R TrHa* quo *HuMN*   3049 obiecta] abiecta *K Q*   3051 dumque] cumque *RDVe Tr*   3053 nostros uexamus] nostros ueneramur *R* nostros ridemus *K* nostrosque ridemus *Tr* nostros beamus *D* nostros beamur *P* nostrosque beamur *AJWHuMNP*(₂)*Ve La ZQY* nostrisque beamur *U* nostrosque beamus *B CO Ha*   3055 domina] domino *R Tr*   3056 refert] profert *CW*

SPECVLVM STVLTORVM 297

evils oppress us. If we look for a reason, we ourselves are the reason why we founder thus in so many adversities. [3030] We destroy the crops, we tear up the seeds and carry them off, laying waste the abundant fields. To prevent the flowers bearing fruit, as soon as they have blossomed on the tree we tear them to shreds with our claws and beaks. We busy ourselves with continual destruction and plunder, [3035] a depraved bunch, resistant to good. The peasant thinks he has stored the grain he has threshed safely, the door being barred. But along comes the cock, accompanied by his whole retinue, takes whatever he wants and makes off. [3040] Nor is it enough that he steals from the grain, unless he also scatters the whole pile with his feet through every corner of the building. The sparrowhawk and the falcon, after they have been well fed, fly away and refuse to return to their masters. Nor do they pay any regard to the tears of the boy who calls them back, [3045] stretching out his arms to them—no, they fly off. They spurn the friendly hand which has so often fed and carried them, as one who has been captured by an enemy flees the enemy's hand. However many the grave perils of death which threaten the boys, they do not pity them. [3050] As they pursue them through every neck of the woods, they often meet their death in the woods or the waters." '

' "In this way we often punish our friends for their virtues, and pay back a good turn with a bad one. The parrot tells tales of the maidservants when the lady of the house returns to the chamber, [3055] and repeats their words, which were better kept quiet. What they had

---

3041–2 Cf. Boethius, *De consolatione*, iii. m. 2. 24: 'sparsas pedibus proterit escas'.

3043 *ancipiter* = classical Latin 'accipiter', 'hawk, sparrowhawk'.

3055–60 These lines are reminiscent of the widely disseminated story of the three parrots (Mann, *From Aesop to Reynard*, pp. 211–12, and nn. 45–7), but as in Ovid's story of the raven, it is the misbehaviour of the mistress, rather than her maidservants, which is reported by the birds.

298   *SPECVLVM STVLTORVM*

auribus et tutis, et sine teste loco,
nescius ille loqui, sed nescius immo tacere,

3060   profert plus aequo psittacus oris habens.
Hinc auibus crebro miscent aconita puellae,
discat ut ante mori quam didicisse loqui.
Sunt et aues aliae quae toto tempore uitae
religiosorum claustra beata colunt;

3065   quae quot eis faciant discrimina saepe per annum,
non ego sufficio dinumerare modo.
Hinc est quod populus odio nos odit iniquo,
reddit et exactam pro uice saepe uicem.
Hinc est cotidie quod nobis insidiantur,

3070   tollit et e medio nos inimica manus.
Hinc laqueos nobis ponunt, hinc retia tendunt,
hinc lapis, inde parit missa sagitta necem.
Hinc inuiscatis pedibus retinemur et alis,
fallimur et dulci saepe tonante tono.

3075   Ista nec immerito patimur luimusque coacti
plurima quae gratis facta fuisse liquet." '

Responsio galli

'Talia dicenti gallus respondit: "Amice,
pone modum uerbis; sunt satis ista; tace.
Sunt discreta minus tua uerba minusque diserta,

3080   nec sapit in nostro pectore sermo tuus.
In sermone tuo nimis es diffusus, abundans
uerbis non sensu, quod solet esse senum.
Olim lingua tibi damnosa fuisse refertur,
sed nec adhuc quicquam profuit illa tibi.

3085   Plurima uidisti uelut is qui tempore longo
uixit et inspexit saecula multa retro.

3058 loco] locis *RO* malo *Mozley*   **3059** nescius²] nesciens *CW* nescimus *Tr*; immo]
ille *PP*(2) *Z*   **3061** miscent aconita] miscent et aconita *H* miscent acoma *Tr* miscent
aconipta *Ve* dixerunt queque *ZQY*   **3062** discat ut] discat et *CWHuMN* discant et *D*
discunt *R*   **3065** quot] quod *Tr ZY* tot *HaLa*; faciant] faciunt *RPP*(2)*D*   **3070** nos]
om. U, add. in margin U²   **3071** nobis ponunt] ponunt nobis *RK*   **3073** *om. O*;
retinemur] retinetur *C Tr* tenemur *D* retinentur *JVe La Y*   **3074** saepe] sepeque *CW*
3075 nec] non *CW*   **3078** modum] modis *MN* mdum *Tr*   **3079** diserta] deserta
O discreta *H Y*ᵃᶜ   **3080** sapit] capit *B AJCWHuMNOPP*(2)*DKVe TrLa U*(corr. in
margin *U²*)*QY*ᵃᶜ cadit *Y*ᵖᶜ cadit /uel capit *Ha*   **3081** diffusus] diffusus /uel se *Ha*
diffuse *La*   **3082** esse] *om. J Z*; senum] sanum *O Ha* sonum *U*

SPECVLVM STVLTORVM 299

spoken among themselves, quietly and cautiously, to trustworthy listeners, with no one to overhear, the parrot, big-mouth that he is, [3060] incapable of speech but even more incapable of silence, makes public. For this reason the maids often mix poisonous potions for the birds, so that they may learn to die before they have learned to speak. There are other birds too, who all their lives inhabit the blessed cloisters of the monks, and I am incapable of enumerating now the dangers they inflict on them on many occasions through the year. [3065] Hence people hate us with a vicious hatred, and often pay us back in equal kind. Hence it is that they daily set traps for us, and that their hostile hand is our undoing. [3070] Hence they set snares for us, and spread nets, hence the stone or loosened arrow is the bearer of death. Hence we are held down by limed feet and wings, and are often tricked by the sweet-sounding music. And we do not suffer these things undeservedly, but are forced to pay the penalty [3075] for many things which it is evident were voluntary actions." '

The Cock's Reply

'To these words the cock replied: "Friend, put a limit on your words; that's enough, shut up. Your words are neither well judged nor well expressed, and your speech strikes no chord in our hearts. [3080] You are too unbridled in your speech, overflowing with words rather than sense, as is often the way with old men. It is said that your tongue once did you harm, but it's not done you any good to this day. You have seen many things, as one who has lived long [3085] and can look back on many centuries. So it's no wonder if your now doting old age rambles

---

3058 *loco*: this is the reading of all the manuscripts except *RO*, which have 'locis'. Mozley conjectured 'malo' but the emendation is unnecessary. See Introduction, n. 171.

3061 *miscent aconita*: Ovid, *Metamorphoses*, i. 147.

3073–4 These lines refer to two ways of catching birds that were common in the medieval period. In the first, birdlime, a sticky substance, is applied to places where the birds commonly perch; they are then unable to fly away. In the second, the bird-catcher lures the birds to him by playing a pipe that imitates birdsong.

300   *SPECVLVM STVLTORVM*

Vnde nec est mirum si iam delira senectus
    erret et existat mens ratione carens.
In sene decrescunt semper, crescentibus annis,
3090   hinc mentis ratio, corporis inde uigor.
In sene deliro sensus patiuntur eclipsim,
    quem constat casu non ratione regi;
turbato cerebro turbantur et omnia membra,
    deficiuntque sibi lumina, lingua, manus.
3095   Hinc est quod sceleris nos arguis et reprehendis,
    tamquam sis solus iustus et absque nota.
Iustus es et certe toto spectabilis orbe,
    quodque satis sine me praedicat arca Noe.
Nonne reuersurum Noe te dimisit ab arca?
3100   Quae te detinuit causa cadauer erat.
Te gula, te uenter, te uicit inepta uoluptas,
    proderes ut dominum perfidus ipse tuum.
Si uitam mores actusque tuos bene penses,
    in toto mundo par tibi nullus erit.
3105   A teneris annis didicisti perfidus esse,
    non potes illud adhuc deseruisse senex.
Ventris ob ingluuiem uilemque cadaueris escam
    a puero constat te uiolasse fidem.
Nam bene pro meritis dominum male deseruisti,
3110   tempore quo fuerat deseruisse nefas,
contraherent de te maculam ne cetera quaeque;
    perfidus existi, non rediturus item.
O quam dissimilis tibi sum, quantumque repugnant
    moribus et factis omnia nostra tuis!
3115   Nactus enim dominum quemcumque, fidelis eidem
    tempore perpetuo seruio, seruo fidem.
Proueniunt etiam per me nonnulla per annum

3088 erret] errat *R Tr*   **3090** corporis] temporis *Z*   **3092** ratione] recte *X corr. X²*   **3095** sceleris] scelerum *Tr* celeris *J La* sterilis *Z*   **3102** proderes ut] proderis ut *H R* ut fugeres *K*   **3103** mores actusque tuos] moresque tuos actus *AJCWHuMNOPDK TrHaLa ZQY*; penses] pensas *R Y*   **3104** toto mundo] mundo toto *HaLa*   **3106** potes] potest *TrLa*   **3109** nam] non *QY*; deseruisti] deseruisse *H Z*   **3110** quo] ue *Ve* quod *ACWRHuMN La*   **3113** quantumque] quantumcumque *Ha* quantocumque *Q* quantacumque *Y* (a *expunct.?*)   **3117** proueniunt] proueniant *Ve* peruveniunt *H RO UX* prouenitur *HuMN*; nonnulla] non *MN*

SPECVLVM STVLTORVM   301

and your mind has lost its grip on reason. In old age, as the years mount up, mental judgement and bodily vigour continually dwindle. [3090] In a doting old man the faculties suffer an eclipse, for he is clearly ruled by chance rather than reason. Once the brain is disordered, so are all the members, and eyes, tongue, and hand fail him. It's for this reason that you accuse us of wrongdoing, and criticize us, [3095] as if you alone are just and without a blemish. Sure, you're just, and an example to the whole world—as Noah's Ark testifies well enough, without my help. Didn't Noah send you out from the Ark with the idea that you should return? What detained you was a dead body. [3100] Your stomach, your belly, your aberrant desire overcame you, so that you treacherously betrayed your master. If you weigh up carefully your life, your morals, and your actions, there is no one like you in all the world. From your tenderest years you have learned deceit, [3105] and you still cannot leave it off now you are an old man. It's evident that you have since boyhood broken faith for the sake of your belly's greed and the wretched food of a corpse. And it was a good thing that you evilly abandoned your master in return for his kindness, at a time when it was a crime to abandon him, [3110] so that the others were not contaminated by you; a traitor you left, never to return." '

' "Oh, how unlike you am I, and how different are my morals and actions from yours. For, once I have acquired a master, I serve him faithfully [3115] for all time, and keep faith. What's more, numerous benefits are furnished by me in the course of the year to rich and poor

---

3094 *lumina, lingua, manus*: also in *Miracles*, 2467.

3099–100 The explanation that the raven did not return to the Ark because it was feeding on drowned corpses is non-biblical, but it is found as far back as Augustine, *Contra Faustum*, xii. 20 (ed. Zycha, p. 348); Prudentius, *Tituli historiarum*, iii, and Avitus, *Poemata*, iv (*De diluuio mundi*), 565–8 (*Opera*, ed. Peiper, p. 251); it also appears in such widely known sources as the *Glossa ordinaria* (*Genesis* viii. 7, PL cxiii. 109B) and Peter Comestor's *Historia scholastica* (*Genesis*, c. xxxiv, PL cxcviii. 1085B), which Nigel annotated; see Introduction, p. xxxii n. 9. Gervase of Canterbury, explaining that the friends of the monastery dared not comment on the king's order to elect William, bishop of Monreale, as archbishop of Canterbury, says this is 'propter *quosdam corvini generis monachos* [i.e. prior Osbern and three confederates] *qui in die necessitatis ab archa avolaverant*, conventus sui proditores effecti, qui hucusque in conventu specie tenus latitabant' (Gervase, *Chronicle*, i. 494–5; my italics).

3107 *Ventris ob ingluuiem*: Henry of Settimello uses an almost identical phrase (with 'ad' instead of 'ob') when speaking of the greed of the vulture, the crow, and the 'corvus niger' (*Elegia*, i. 137–8). The *Elegia* seem to have been composed at much the same time as *SS*, making it difficult to establish who is the borrower; see the discussion of internal indications of date in Fossati's edition, pp. xiii–xvi.

3114 *moribus et factis*: for other examples of this phrase as the opening of a hexameter, see *Lateinisches Hexameter-Lexikon*, iii. 421–2. Also *Epigrams*, no. ii.16.

SPECVLVM STVLTORVM

302

commoda, pauperibus diuitibusque simul.
Per me pluma datur, qua fessa labore diurno,
3120   ut uires reparent, molliter ossa cubant.
Per me praecipue medicorum cura iuuatur,
et datur infirmis apta diaeta suis.
Per me debilibus desperatisque salubris
esca datur, pulli deliciosa caro.
3125   Pinguis et eunuchus, nostra de stirpe creatus,
fortibus et sanis fortior esca datur.
Belli perpetui, belli quod fine carebit,
quod nullus hominum pacificare potest,
inter claustrales quod semper durat et oua,
3130   de lumbis nostris coepit origo prior.
Tempore nocturno uigili uigilantior omni
horarum signo tempora uoce mea.
Ipse pigros pueros nec surgere mane uolentes
excito nec patior incaluisse toro.
3135   Plura sed et per me constant collata fuisse
commoda, quae non sunt enumeranda modo.
Non tamen ingratus uel inofficiosus eisdem,
quos mihi sors dominos contulit, esse uolo.
Namque malignari si uellem, sique, quod absit,
3140   nescirem labiis ponere frena meis,
multi de medio fierent dignasque subirent
poenas pro meritis carceris atque crucis.
Nocte sub obscura quae fiunt multa nefanda,
et quae nocte nigra sunt nigriora satis,
3145   quid faciat dominus, quid dicat seruus iniquus,
si fora nouissent omnia sicut ego,

3119–21 qua fessa—me praecipue] *om. J*   3120 cubant] cubent *B D U*
3122–4 apta dieta—datur pulli] *om.* δ *TrHaLa UZQY*   3125 et eunuchus] erat cibus
ZQY; nostra de] de nostra *AJCWHuMNOPDKVe TrHaLa*   3126 *om. X*; fortior] fortius *Ha*ᵃᶜ*La*   3127–9 *om.*, 3130 *transp. after 3134a (3126, 3131–4, 3134a (see below),
3130, 3135)* δ *TrHaLa*   3129 *replaced by 3134a U²over erasure; 3130 also over
erasure U²*   3131 uigili] *om. M*   3132 uoce mea] uoce meo *O* uoto meo *D La*
3134 nec] non *HuMN after 3134 (after 3128 U)* et per quam (quem *Ha* qua *Ve*) pingues
pulli (pulli pingues *La*) procreantur et oua (3134a)/ de lumbis nostris cepit origo prior
(= *3130*) δ *TrHaLa U²over erasure;* plura] plurima *JD*   3136 enumeranda] enumer-
ando *AJ* connumeranda *H Z* enumerata *Tr*   3138 sors] *om. Z*; dominos] domino *QY*
dominus *La*; uolo] nolo *QY*   3139 sique] sed que *Z* que *HaLa*   3140 frena]
fienda uel frena *Ha*   3143 quae] qua *TrHa UZQY*   3144 sunt] sint *R*

SPECVLVM STVLTORVM   303

alike. By me is bestowed the feather, on which the limbs wearied by
daily toil may rest softly and repair their strength. [3120] By me medical care is greatly assisted and an appropriate diet is given to the sick.
By me wholesome food, delicious chicken meat, is given to the weak
and dying. The fat capon, born of my race, [3125] is given as stronger
food to those who are strong and healthy. The earliest origin of the
perpetual war—the war without end, which no man can pacify—that is
waged continually between monks and eggs, had its beginning in my
loins. [3130] At night, more vigilant than any watchman, I signal the
passing hours with my voice. I rouse the lazy boys who don't want to
get up in the morning, and I don't let them stay warm in bed. It's clear
that I have provided many other benefits [3135] which can't be specified now. But I don't want to be ungrateful or undutiful to those whom
fate has made my masters. For if I wanted to speak slander, and if—
which heaven forbid!—I didn't know how to put a rein on my tongue,
[3140] many people would come to a sticky end and would suffer the
penalties of prison or the gallows which befitted their deserts. Many
crimes which are committed in the darkness of night, and which are far
blacker than black night—what the master does, what the wicked servant says [3145]—if the whole town knew as well as I do, the morrow
might well see many men, and many women too, hanged on the gallows.

3120 *molliter ossa cubant*: Ovid, *Heroides*, vii. 162.

SPECVLVM STVLTORVM

saepe uiros multos multas etiam mulieres
in cruce suspensos mane uidere foret.
Rusticus uxori tacitus quod dicit in aure,
3150   ipse licet nolit, me latuisse nequit.
Dii nolint quod me contingat laedere quemquam,
uel scelus alterius prodere uoce mea.
Absit ut assimiler coruo, qui prodidit illum
qui sibi praecipue causa salutis erat.
3155   Iuppiter ante precor in me sua fulmina mittat,
deuoret et terra meque genusque meum,
me prius unda maris absorbeat, inque profundum
gurgitis inferni praecipitatus eam,
quam commissa mihi quaeuis secreta reuelem,
3160   exeat aut sermo prauus ab ore meo.
Cum quibus est uita cuiuis communis habenda,
hos nisi commendet, laudet, honoret, amet,
desipit, et statuae similis, quamuis sine sensu
corporis humani, sensile corpus habet.
3165   Hic meus est animus, haec est sententia uera,
haec pro me solo dixero solus ego.
Nisus et accipiter pro se reliquique loquantur,
qui satis aetatis uocis et oris habent.
Ruricolis subici mea me fortuna coegit,
3170   et procul a regum iussit abesse domo.
Hinc nisi uim passus uenio delatus in aulam,
insita cum fuerit lignea cauda mihi.
Nisus et accipiter quoniam uersantur in aula
intersunt regum consiliisque ducum.
3175   His loca secreta strepituque carentia uulgi
et procul a turbis incoluisse datur.
Principis in thalamo positi statuuntur in alto,
ut de sublimi multa uidere queant.

3147 etiam] necnon *CWHuMNDK*   3148 suspensos] suspensas β *La*ᵃᶜ *ZXQY*
3149 quod] quid *RP Ha Q*; dicit] dicet *Ve Tr ZY* dicat *Ha Q*   3151 dii nolint] dii
nolunt *AJCWRHuMNOPD TrHaLa UZXQ* hii nolunt *Ve* nolint dii *K* si nolint *H*
3156 meum] suum /uel meum *Ha*   3157 unda] *om. M*; inque] hincque *Y* meque *Tr U*
3161–4 *om. QY*   3161 cuiuis] cuius *B AJCWHuMNOPDKVe Tr UZ* ciuis *H* cuique
La X cuiquam *Ha*   3162 nisi] mihi *JHuMN Tr Z* ni *CW*   3163 desipit] decipit
MD Tr despicit *X*   3167 nisus] nisi *MN*   3171 nisi] mihi *U* ubi *HaLa*
3172–3 *om. ROPVe Tr*   3174 consiliisque] conciliisque *ZQ*

SPECVLVM STVLTORVM 305

What the peasant speaks quietly in his wife's ear, he can't conceal from me, whether he likes it or not. [3150] The gods forbid that it should be my fate to harm anyone, or to betray another's crime with my voice. Let me not be like the raven, who betrayed the one who was the major source of his well-being. May Jupiter hurl his thunderbolts against me first, [3155] and the earth swallow up me and my kin, may the wave of the sea engulf me and may I tumble headlong into the depth of hell's abyss, before I reveal any secrets committed to me, or any wicked speech comes out of my mouth. [3160] Anyone who does not praise, speak well of, honour, and love those people with whom he is obliged to live, is a fool, and lacks a human being's understanding, statue-like, although possessing a sentient body. This is what I think, this is my true opinion, [3165] and this I will say for my part, speaking for myself alone. Let the sparrowhawk and the falcon and the rest speak for themselves, since they're old enough and have tongue and voice for it. My fortune obliged me to be subjected to farmers, and constrained me to live far away from royal palaces. [3170] Hence I only enter the hall when forcibly carried there, when a wooden tail has been stuck into me. Since the sparrowhawk and the falcon live in the hall, they are party to the discussions of kings and dukes. To them it is granted to inhabit secret places, free from the noise of common people [3175] and far from the throng. They are placed high up in the prince's chamber, so that they can see many things from their perch. The

---

3154 *causa salutis*: also at *Miracles*, 1015.

3155–60 A fusion of Vergil, *Aeneid*, iv. 24–5 ('sed mihi vel tellus optem prius ima dehis-cat/ vel pater omnipotens adigat me fulmine ad umbras') and Ovid, *Heroides*, iii. 63 ('devorer ante, precor, subito telluris hiatu').

3162 *laudet, honoret, amet*: also in *Miracles*, 1214.

3164 *sensile* = 'capable of sensation, sentient' (*DMLBS* s.v. 'sensilis' 1).

3171 *nisi*: = 'non nisi'. Cf. lines 971, 2097.

306   SPECVLVM STVLTORVM

Angulus extremus thalami, locus aptus agendis
3180   rebus in occultis, intitulatur eis.
Illic consilia crebro capiuntur iniqua,
    illic temptari pessima quaeque solent.
Gratior interdum pueris simul atque puellis
    angulus est aula, nox tenebrosa die.
3185   Hic solet abscondi furtum, quod uentre soluto
    egrediens tempus uim tulit ante suum.
Hic quoque consueuit fieri confessio, nulli
    facta sacerdotum nec facienda, reor.
Hic aconita latent longo quaesita labore,
3190   hicque nouercarum carmina dira uigent.
Vt puer accipitrem ueniens de nocte profunda
    uisitet infirmum, postulat ille locus.
Hic locus astmaticos sanat curatque caducos
    et facit in noctem saepe uenire diem.
3195   Haec igitur loca sunt quibus est odiosa lucerna,
    et uitii titulo praemia laudis habent.
Nisus et accipiter, loca qui male sancta frequentant,
    rem bene nouerunt quae sit et unde loquor.
Hi duo praecipue, si uellent dicere uerum,
3200   mira quidem possent dicere, uera tamen." '

Responsio nisi

'Talibus auditis nisus respondit, "Iniquum
    arbitror, officium deseruisse suum.
Nos sumus ingenui, generoso stemmate nati,
    non decet os nostrum turpia uerba loqui.

3181 illic] illuc *UQY*ᵖᶜ; consilia] consilio *J* concilia *ZQ*   3182 illic] illuc *UQY*ᵖᶜ; quaeque] sepe δ *TrHaLa UZQY*   3183 atque] *om. TrHa*   3187 nulli] nulla *O Q* mali *H*   3188 nec] ne *Ve Tr* ue *P*   3189 aconita] atonita *R La* attonita *Ha* anoconita *X*; latent] lateret *Tr* latet *HaLa*   3193–4 *transp. O*   3193 sanat curatque] curat sanatque *HaLa Z*   3195 haec] hic *AJCWHuMNPVe U* hec β *RODK TrHaLa ZXQY*   3196 et] ut *CW U*   3197 qui male sancta frequentant] *Mozley* qui malefata frequentant *Skutsch* que mala fata (facta *X* multa *U*) frequentant β *UXQY* que mala (male *R Ha*) facta sequantur δ *TrHaLa* mala sacraque frequentant *Z*   3198 unde] uis unde *QY*ᵃᶜ   3200 possent] possunt *H D*; tamen] tantum /uel tamen *La* 3201 respondit] respondet *AJCWRHuMNPD La*   3203 ingenui] ingenii *AMN HaLa ZX*; generoso] generosi *CW*

SPECVLVM STVLTORVM

307

remotest corner of the chamber, a place suitable for business that has to be conducted in private, is assigned to them. [3180] There wicked plots are often hatched, and vile deeds set in train. Sometimes, the corner is more agreeable than the hall to young lads, and girls too, and dark night more agreeable than day. Here is often hidden the secret love, which, when the womb opens up [3185] and it emerges, suffers an untimely end. Here too are confessions made which have been uttered to no priest, nor ought to be, as I think. Here lurk poisons, sought with long effort, here flourish the baleful spells of stepmothers. [3190] This place requires a boy to come at dead of night to visit a sick hawk. This place cures asthmatics and heals epileptics, and often makes dawn at night. These are the places where a lamp is unwelcome, [3195] and which earn the rewards of praise by their claim to wickedness. The sparrow-hawk and the falcon, who frequent these unholy places, know well what the case is and what I speak of. Those two in particular, if they are willing to tell the truth, can speak wondrous things, but true." ' [3200]

The Sparrowhawk's Reply

'Having heard this, the sparrowhawk replied: "I think it wrong to neglect one's duty. We are aristocrats, born of a noble family; it's not fitting for our mouth to utter base words. Whatever the young lads do,

---

3179 *Angulus extremus thalami*: prized hawks were kept indoors, on a special perch in the corner of a room; see Holmes, *Daily Living*, p. 232, citing Alexander Neckam, *De nominibus utensilium*, ed. Scheler, p. 65, where a perch for a hawk or falcon is listed as a regular item of furniture 'in camera sive in thalamo' (ibid. p. 64). An example of this occurs in the mini-romance included in Andreas Capellanus, *De amore*, where a British knight undertakes a quest to bring back 'the victorious hawk which is said to sit on a golden perch in Arthur's court'; he eventually finds the hawk on its perch in Arthur's palace (ii. 8. 35–40, ed. and trans. Walsh, pp. 270–1, 278–9). On Henry II's passion for hawking, see Oggins, *The Kings and their Hawks*, pp. 54–63.

3185–6 An allusion to abortion, which destroys the evidence of sexual misdemeanours.

3193 These sicknesses are 'cured' because they were only a pretext for visiting the dark corner where the hawk was kept.

3197 For discussion of this line see Introduction, pp. lxxxii–lxxxiii.

3203 *generoso stemmate nati*: cf. *SS*, 3289: 'generoso stemmate nata'; *Lawrence*, 1997: 'generosos stemate natum'; *Miracles*, 1125: 'generosi stematis ortum'.

308 SPECVLVM STVLTORVM

3205　Quicquid agant pueri, nobis patientia facti
　　　tempore perpetuo quod sit habenda puto.
　　　Si ludunt pueri, cum non laedamur ab ipsis,
　　　cur laedamus eos? Sit procul iste furor.
　　　Qui sua non dubitant nobis secreta fateri,
3210　　ne prodamus eos, iure tenemur eis.
　　　Nos pueri pascunt, nos portant, nosque reportant,
　　　nos quoque conseruant sedulitate sua.
　　　Redditur exosus merito delator, amico
　　　criminis est crimen imposuisse suo.
3215　Cum taceant oculi qui res uidere stupendas,
　　　cur quod non uidit garrula lingua refert?
　　　Absit ut os oculis hac conditione ministret,
　　　alter ut ambobus causa sit unde ruant.
　　　Os male si prauum laxes, cum sit tamen unum,
3220　　quid prodest oculos continuisse duos?
　　　Os igitur prauum taceat, quoadusque loquantur
　　　aures aut oculi pesue manusue sibi.
　　　Soluere tunc poterit indicta silentia lingua,
　　　cum prius audierit cetera membra loqui.
3225　Si prius ediderint oculus quod uidit et auris
　　　ante quod audiuit pesque manusque mea,
　　　libera tunc linguae sua uox reddetur in omnes
　　　de quibus ad praesens quaestio mota fuit—
　　　hoc tamen adiecto, quod si sibi forte cauere
3230　　nec membris ualeat, muta sit usque queat.
　　　Nam nihil in mundo, cum sint nequissima multa,
　　　hoc uitio nequam nequius esse potest." '

Voluntas et ratio Burnelli

　　　'Talia dicente niso mea lumina clausit
　　　somnus, et incepi stertere more meo.
3235　A sonitu uolucres uerna uelocius aura

3205 agant] agunt *R Tr*　　　3206 quod] quid *R Tr*　　　3207 laedamur] ledantur *W Tr*
3208 sit] sic *MN*　　　3210 *om. La*　　　3211 pascunt...portant] portant... pascunt
UQ　　　3216 quod] quia *HuMN* que *U* cum *X*; uidit] uidet *K Tr UZQ* uideat *R*
3217 ministret] ministrent *MN* ministrat *La*　　　3218 ruant] ruent β ruat *AJCWPD*
TrHaLa UZY ruet *U*　　　3221 igitur] *om. HaLa*; loquantur] loquatur *D TrLa UQY*
3225 ediderint] ediderit *AJWRHuMNOPDKVe TrHa UZXQY* edidit *C* aude edderit *La*
3227 linguae] lingua *ZQ*　　　3229 si sibi] sibi si *D* sibi *R HaLa*　　　3233–458 *om. QY*
3233 dicente] decente *J* dicenti *HaLa*　　　3234 incepi] cepi *B AJPVe TrHaLa UZ*;
more] modo *CW om. D*　　　3235 uerna] uernaque *B AJCWRHuMNOPDVe TrHaLa*
UZX sumptaque *H*

SPECVLVM STVLTORVM

309

I think we should exercise forbearance [3205] towards their deed for all time to come. If the lads have their fun, and we're not harmed by them, why should we do them any harm? Away with such rashness! We are rightly bound not to betray those who do not hesitate to confess their secrets to us. [3210] The lads feed us, carry us out, carry us back, and look after us with care. The telltale is rightly hated; it's a crime to impute a crime to one's friend. When the eyes which saw amazing things are silent, [3215] why does the chattering tongue relate what it did not see? Heaven forbid that the mouth should serve the eyes in such a way that either of them should be the reason why both come to ruin. What's the use of restraining your two eyes, if you stupidly give rein to your wicked tongue, although there's only one of it? [3220] So let the wicked tongue be silent, until the ears or the eyes, or the hand or the foot, speak to it. Then the tongue can break the silence imposed on it, when it has heard the other members speak first. If the eye should first divulge what it has seen, [3225] and the ear what it has heard, or my foot or my hand, then the tongue will be given its free utterance against all those who have been the topic of the present conversation— this in addition, that if it is not capable of looking after itself or the other members, it should be dumb until it can do so. [3230] For I think nothing in the world more evil than this evil vice, although there are evils a-plenty." '

Burnellus's Desire and Decision

'As the hawk said this, sleep closed my eyes, and I began to snore in my habitual way. The birds, alarmed by the sound, [3235] suddenly

SPECVLVM STVLTORVM

excitae subito disparuere loco.
Talia, mi doctor, mecum dum saepe recordor,
    artor et in curas distrahor ipse graues.
Cumque nihil stabile maneat sub sole creatum,
3240   quis neget instabilem quemlibet esse statum?
En! ego qui fueram iuuenis patiensque laborum
    et fortis, modo sum fractus et ipse senex.
Cumque satis constet centum uixisse per annos,
    uix mihi iam uideor tres habuisse dies.
3245 Omnia testantur solum superesse sepulchrum;
    sique dies superest, auguror esse breuem.
Viuere uelle diu nihil est, nisi uelle—quod absit!—
    uiuere peccato; uita sit ergo breuis.
Cum sine peccato non sit nascentis ab aluo
3250   una dies pueri, quid rear esse mihi,
qui semper pecco numquamque miser resipisco,
    non metuens hominem despiciensque Deum?
Nec tamen ignorans pecco, sed praua scienter
    et prudens facio flagitiosus ego.
3255 Dumque miser meditor loquor aut operor mala, semper
    posteriore die deteriora sequor.
Prauus heri, peior hodie, cras pessimus, ultra
    quonam progrediar, pronus in omne malum?
Hinc est quod statui me tradere religioni,
3260   cuius ero primus doctor et auctor ego.
Hanc ego quamcitius, Domino praestante, subibo,
    sollicitus uitae de breuitate meae.
Hac quoque de causa Romam deuotus adibo,
    ut confirmetur hic nouus ordo mihi.

3239 sole] orbe *R* celo *P Tr Z*   3240 neget] negat *La Z*   3241 fueram] filam *M*; laborum] laborans *Tr Z*   3242 et fortis] hesterno *H* esterno *B U*; modo sum] mensum *Tr* non sum *Z om. HaLa*; fractus] factus β *AJCWHuMNOPDKVe TrHaLa UZX* 3243 constet] constat *RO Z*   3245 omnia] omnia /uel omina *La*   3250 quid rear] quid reor *AJROPKVe TrHaLa ZX fb* quod reor *CWMND*; mihi] mei β 3251 pecco] miser pecco *Z* peccato *AD* pecto *J La*ac; numquamque] nunquam *HaLa Z fb* 3253 nec] non *P Ha fb*; pecco] pecto *J La*ac   3254 flagitiosus] religiosus δ *TrHaLa Z fb* uel religiosus *add. in margin* *X*pc   3255 dumque] cumque *RVe Tr Z*; aut] ac *B AJOPVe UZ* et *R TrHa om. La*; semper] queque *CMNK X* quoque *W* quique *D* 3256 posteriore] posteriora *RP Ha Z*   3258 quonam] quo non *fb*; progrediar] progredior *TrHaLa UZ fb*   3259 *LEF I rejoin, but F transposes lines 3259–78 after lines 3279–432*; statui] statuo δ *TrHaLa Z*; tradere] reddere α *I*   3260 auctor] actor *CWHuMND* 3262–3 *om. Ha*   3264 nouus] meus α *I*

SPECVLVM STVLTORVM 311

vanished from the place, more swiftly than a spring breeze. While I often think on these things, O teacher, I am distressed and troubled by deep anxieties. Since no created thing under the sun remains stable, who can deny that every condition is unstable? [3240] See! I, who was young and strong and able to bear hard work, am now a broken old man. Although there's no doubt that I've lived a hundred years, I hardly seem to myself to have passed three days. Everything testifies that only the grave remains, [3245] and if any life remains, I foresee it will be short. To want to live long is nothing other than to want to live in sin—perish the thought!—so let my life be short. Since a day in the life of a newborn child is not without sin, what shall I think of myself, [3250] who am continually sinning and never, wretch that I am, reform, not fearing man, and despising God? Nor do I sin in ignorance, but like the reprobate that I am I commit wicked acts wittingly and of malice aforethought. And while I wretchedly think and speak and perform evil, [3255] I always pursue worse on the following day. Bad yesterday, worse today, worst tomorrow, whither can I go next, in my slide to wickedness?'

'It's on this account that I have decided to devote myself to the religious life, whose teacher and founder I shall be. [3260] God willing, I shall enter it without delay, since I am anxious about the shortness of my life. For this reason too I shall make a pious journey to Rome, so that my new order may be approved there. Nor do I think the Pope will

---

3245 Job 17: 1.
3256 *deteriora sequor*: Ovid, *Metamorphoses*, vii. 21.

312   *SPECVLVM STVLTORVM*

3265   Nec mihi difficilem super his credo fore papam;
         assensum facilem curia tota dabit.
         Et si forte uelis uitam mutare, magister,
         consulo ne quoquam longius ire pares.
         Nec te discipulo pudeat tua colla, magister,
3270   subdere pro Domino proque salute tua.
         Istud contingit in religione frequenter,
         quod maior seruit praeficiturque minor.
         Digna sub indignis uiuunt, rosa sub saliuncis,
         lilia sub tribulis; ne mouearis in his.
3275   Opprimit ingenuum seruus stultusque disertum,
         iniustus iustum, nox tenebrosa polum.
         Quod magis abiectum uel quod minus utile cernunt,
         maiori studio magnificare solent.
         Exemplumque meae matris meditantur in actu,
3280   quod fuerat solita saepe referre mihi.'

De tribus sororibus fatalibus

         'Ibant tres hominum curas releuare sorores,
         quas nos fatales dicimus esse deas.
         Vnus erat cultus tribus his eademque uoluntas,
         naturae uitiis ferre salutis opem.
3285   Et quod auara minus dederat uel prodiga multum,
         his emendandi plurima cura fuit.
         Dum graderentur ita casu reperere puellam
         colle sub umbroso quae Ioue digna foret.
         Nam formosa nimis, generoso stemmate nata,
3290   aequabat uultus nobilitate genus.

3265 difficilem] difficile *H J*; his] *om. U*, hoc *add. interlinear U²*   3268 ne quoquam] nequaquam *ZX* ne quemquam *Ve* ne quodquam *U*; pares] paras *Tr Z*   3269 tua] te *W* tota *HaLa Z*   3272 quod] qui *CW*; seruit] fuerit *CWHuMN*   3273 uiuunt rosa sub] uiuit rosa sub α *I* uiuuntque rosa *AJCWHuMNOVe X* minuitque rosa *Ha* minuit rosa *La* uiuuntque rose *U* uiuunt quia rosa *P* ueniuntque rose *D* rosa sepe ruit *Z* ueniuntque rosa *Tr*; saliuncis] saliuntis *TrLa U* salientis *Ve* salutis *M* salincis *X* saluncis *P* salamentis *Ha*   3274 lilia] alia *HaLa*   3275 ingenuum] ingenium *JRMNO*ᵃᶜ*DVe I TrHaLa UZX*   3276 polum] diem α *I* *P*ᵃᶜ *U*   3279–432 *transp. before 3259–78 F; after 3278, F repeats 3323–8* (F₍₂₎), *followed by 3435–44, 3447–8*   3279 meditantur] meditatur *F D Ha* meditantis *Tr* meditemur *LE I* meditabor *Z*   3280 fuerat] fuerit α *C I* fuit *P*; solita] soluta *MN*   3281 releuare] reuelare *H J La Z*   3282 nos] non *Tr* modo *P Z*   3285 auara] aura *B R*   3287 dum] cum *L?E H P I X*; reperere] uidere *LE K I* reperire *MN ZX* reperire /uel reperiere *Ha* reperare *La*   3288 colle] collo *D I* cella *U*; quae] quo *TrLa*

SPECVLVM STVLTORVM 313

be difficult about this, [3265] and the whole papal court will easily give assent. And if by chance you, O teacher, wish to change your life, I advise you to stop right here. And do not be ashamed, teacher, to bow your neck to your pupil, for the sake of God and your salvation. [3270] This often occurs in religious life, that the greater serves and the lesser is placed in command. Worthy things are subordinated to unworthy, the rose to thorns, lilies to thistles—so don't get worked up about this. The slave oppresses the noble, and the fool the learned man, [3275] the unjust the just man, and dark night the heavens. Whatever men see is baser or least useful, they are accustomed to honour with greater enthusiasm. They give practical application to a story of my mother's, which she often used to relate to me.' [3280]

About the Three Sister-Fates

'The three sisters whom we call the goddesses of destiny were travelling about to alleviate the sorrows of humankind. All three had one attire, and one desire: to bring a remedy to the defects of Nature. And what she had meanly scanted or prodigally lavished, [3285] it was their prime concern to redress. While they were travelling thus, by chance they found at the foot of a shady hill a girl worthy of Jupiter. For she was exceedingly beautiful, and born of a noble family; her ancestry matched her face in nobility. [3290] For her sake the gods—if she were

---

3268 That is, he need look no further, as he can join Burnellus's new order.

3273 *saliuncis*: 'saliunca', 'identified with various thorny or spiny plants' (*DMLBS* 2); thus, 'in figurative contexts as type of worthless or undesirable plant, frequently contrasted with *rosa*' (*DMLBS* 3). For the contrast with the rose, cf. Vergil, *Eclogues*, v. 17; *Carmina Burana*, no. x. 21.

3281 This story rests on the Scandinavian legends of three female Fates, known as Norns, who travelled about the country and foretold to people their future destiny. In some versions of the story, the first two Norns dispense benefits, while the third maliciously tries to negate their benevolence; see Grimm, *Teutonic Mythology*, trans. Stallybrass, i. 407–17, iv. 1400; Bek-Pedersen, *The Norns in Old Norse Mythology*, pp. 84–8, and for one such version (the story of Olaf), Saxo Grammaticus, *Gesta Danorum*, ed. Friis-Jensen, vi. 4. 12 (ii. 376–7). Nigel's version of the story, in which the third Fate obstructs the benevolent intentions of the others towards the first two girls, and showers gifts on the undeserving peasant girl, gives an unusual twist to the story in order to turn it into a satire on the unjust distribution of wealth and honours to the undeserving (see Introduction, pp. lix–lxi, cxxvi).

3283 *cultus*: 'adornment, costume' (*DMLBS* 2).

3289 See n. to line 3203.

SPECVLVM STVLTORVM

Propter eam superi, superis si nota fuisset,
mouissent magno praelia magna Ioui.
Iuppiter ipse polo quam uirgine se caruisse
septenni spacio mallet et exul agi.

3295 Nil tribuisse magis potuit natura decoris,
si Styga iurasset uel Ioue nata foret.
Planctibus illa tamen tantis lacrimisque uacabat
quod circumpositam saepe rigaret humum.
Nunc faciem caedens, nunc palmis pectora tundens

3300 non requiescebat, unguibus ora secans.
Hac igitur uisa geminae uoluere sorores
ferre salutis opem, si licuisset eis;
instabantque duae, dominam sociamque rogantes
ut saltem sineret mitius esse malum.

3305 Illa sed e contra uultu uerbisque renitens
obstitit et surda pertulit aure preces.
Sed ne sollicitas super his timidasque sorores
et quasi contemptas redderet, inquit eis:
"Venimus, ut nostis, nos tres inuisere mundum

3310 ut ferremus opem, sed quibus esset opus.
Non opus est isti, quia quam natura beauit
in quantum potuit et quibus ausa fuit,
cui genus et speciem formae tribuit specialem,
ut sit utrumque nimis alterutrumque satis,

3315 quae maiora sibi uel quae meliora daremus
quam natura dedit officiosa satis?
Muneribus geminis quibus est ditata uel uno
utatur, nostra non eget illa manu.
Cui natura satis et sufficientia praestat

3320 debet id et nobis et satis esse sibi.
Forsitan auxilium si praestaremus eidem,

3291 eam] *om. L I*; fuisset] fuissent *DVe*   3293 ipse] ipso *LE I* ille *HaLa*
3296 si Styga iurasset] si de saturno *D* quam si saturno *K*; Ioue] noua *Tr Z*   3298 *om.*
Ha; rigaret] rigabat *F*   3299 tundens] tendens *N X* tondens *R Ha*   3300 non]
nunc *H Z*   3306 pertulit] protulit *Ve La*   3307 timidasque] timidaque *F* tumi-
dasque *C*^{pc} tundasque *MN*   3308 contemptas] conceptas *E*   3310 *om. La*; sed]
si *F Ha*; esset opus] opus esset *AJCW* opus erat *OPVe TrHa* opus erit *Z* extat opus *R*
3311 quia] quoque *LE I*   3314–19 *om.* β δ *TrHaLa UZX*   3316 satis] nimis *F*
3318 nostra] nostro *F*   3320 id et] et id α *RD I X*   3321–601 *transp. after 3896*
MN

SPECVLVM STVLTORVM   315

known to the gods—would have instigated great battles with great Jupiter. Jupiter himself would rather have done without heaven for seven years, and be driven out as an exile, than have done without the girl. Nature could not have given her more beauty [3295] if she had sworn by the Styx or if she were Jupiter's daughter. Yet she was plunged in lamentation and such great weeping that she was wetting the ground around her. Now clawing her face, now beating her breast with her hands, she was never still, tearing her face with her nails. [3300] When they saw her, two of the sisters wanted to come to her aid, if they could. Eagerly they begged their lady and companion that she would at least permit some alleviation of her distress. But she, on the contrary, refused, setting her face and words against it, [3305] and suffered all their prayers with a deaf ear. But so that she should not seem to despise her sisters, and make them cowed and troubled over this, she said to them: "We three have come to visit the world, as you know, so that we may bring assistance, but to those who have need of it. [3310] This one has no need, for to her whom Nature has blessed as much and in such ways as she could and dared—to whom she gave ancestry and outstanding beauty of appearance, so that either of them by itself would be enough, and both together a superabundance—what might we give her that would be greater or better [3315] than the ample gifts of beneficent Nature? If she uses even one of the two gifts with which she is endowed, she will not need our help. When Nature and wealth give anyone enough, that ought to be enough for them and us. [3320] Perhaps, if we lent her aid, she could easily be worse off. Improvement

---

3295–6 The Styx was the river of Hades, by which the gods themselves feared to swear falsely (Vergil, *Aeneid*, vi. 323–4).

316   *SPECVLVM STVLTORVM*

posset de facili deteriora pati.
Obfuit augmentum multis, meliusque fuisset
    uiuere contentos simplicitate sua
3325 quaerere quam supra uires proprias aliena
    et uetitis pariter illicitisque frui.
Naturae studio quae non comitantur et usu
    succumbunt leuiter deficiuntque cito.
Non patitur natura diu contraria iungi
3330   nec sibi uim ferri; uult ratione regi.ˮ
Dixit, et abscedens flentem tristemque reliquit,
    non immutato qui fuit ante statu.
Cumque recedentes feruentior ureret aestus
    artaretque nimis hinc calor, inde labor,
3335 uicini nemoris umbras petiere, uolentes
    arentem gelido fonte leuare sitim.
Iam nemus attigerant, sed et ecce puella uenusta
    inque toro posita sola iacebat ibi;
quae cum numinibus assurgere laeta pararet
3340   non potuit multa mole retenta pedum.
Quod potuit fecit, sua brachia prona tetendit,
    obtulit et lepide uerba salutis eis.
Edocuitque uiam nemoris, qua parte serenus
    fons erat et uiuas parturiebat aquas.
3345 Addidit et dicens, “Irem comes ipsa libenter
    uobiscum, sinerent si mea fata mihi.
Sed pedis et femorum tum pondere tumque dolore
    haereo continuo corpore fixa toro.
Huc ut obumbrarer alieno fulta ducatu,

3323–8 *repeated after 3278 F*(2)   3325 quaerere] *om.* α(*F*(2)) *I* quere *Ha* sumere *Z*;
aliena] alienas *Z* aliena uenari α(*F*(2)) *I*   3327 et] in *F*(2) *K*   3330 ferri] fieri α
ROPKVe I Tr Z   3331 abscedens] abcedens *L* β *R I X* ascendens *O Z*   3332 *om. Z*
3333–58 *this folio is badly rubbed in U and much is illegible*   3334 calor] color *CW*; inde]
hincque *Tr Z*   3335 petiere] petire *La ZX* retinere *F*   3337 et] *om. F P Ha X*;
uenusta] iuuenca *Ve om. Tr Z*   3338 ibi] ei *Tr Z* ita *HaLa*   3339 pararet] parasset *AJCWRHuMNPDKVe TrHa UZ* posset *O La*   3341 sua] *om. Ve Z*
3345 addidit] abdidit *Tr* addit *F*; et] hec *LE I*; irem comes ipsa] irem comes ipse *E* et ipsa
comes irem *F* uere comesque *Tr* irem comesque *AJCWHuMNO*ᵃᶜ*PDVe HaLa X* effectum
comesque *Z*   3346 sinerent] sinerem *M* finerent *E*   3347 pedis] pedes *CK Ha*;
femorum] femoris *RO Z*; tum…tumque] cum…cumque *F RO I TrHaLa*   3348 cor-
pore] tempore α *I Ve* et corpore *X*   3349 huc] hic α *I* hoc *O* his *H*; obumbrarer] obumbrarem α *I* umbrarer *RO*ᵃᶜ*PVe Z* in umbrarer *O*ᵖᶜ umbraret *Tr* obumbraret *U*; alieno] aliena
H K Z alienum *Ve*

SPECVLVM STVLTORVM

317

of circumstances has done harm to many, and it would have been better for them to live content in their unpretentiousness than to seek to move out of their own sphere [3325] and to enjoy things that are both forbidden and illicit. Whatever is not in line with the course and practice of Nature easily falters and quickly fails. Nature does not suffer contraries to be yoked together for long, nor does she suffer violence to herself; she desires to be ruled by Reason." ' [3330]

'She ended, and departed, leaving her weeping and sad, her former state unchanged. Since the day's heat burned more fiercely as they went, and they were oppressed both by heat and by their exertion, they sought the shade of a neighbouring grove, [3335] wishing to slake their parching thirst from a cold stream. Now they had reached the grove— and lo and behold, a beautiful girl, placed on a couch, lay there alone. As she gladly tried to rise to meet the goddesses, she was held back by the heavy weight of her feet, and could not do so. [3340] What she could do, she did: leaning forward, she stretched out her arms, and courteously offered them words of greeting. She explained to them the layout of the grove, in which part there was a clear spring which brought forth sparkling waters. She added: "I would willingly go with you myself, [3345] if my fate allowed me. But I am permanently tied to my bed, held fast by my body, by the weight and pain of my feet and legs. It was with the support of another's steps, not my own, that I was

---

3329 Boethius, *De consolatione*, ii. pr. 6: 'natura respuit, ut contraria quaeque iungantur'.
3300 *unguibus ora secans*: cf. *Miracles*, 1498 (with 'secat'). The phrase 'unguibus ora' occurs in Vergil, *Aeneid*, iv. 673, xi. 86, xii. 871, and Ovid, *Metamorphoses*, xii. 563
3336 Cf. Ovid, *Heroides*, iv. 174: 'arentem quae levet unda sitim'.
3345 *Addidit et dicens*: 2 Chr. 2: 12.

318   SPECVLVM STVLTORVM

3350 non proprio, ueni sumque relicta mihi."
Talibus auditis geminae fleuere sorores,
quaerentes dominam flectere flendo suam.
Cumque nimis flerent multumque diuque rogarent
quatenus huic saltem redderet ipsa gradum
3355 ut pedibus niti propriis possetque reuerti
sana, nec ulterius aegra tenere torum,
illa nihil mota sed nec miserata sorores
ibat, et exorsa taliter inquit eis:
"Vt decet et debet, multa pietate moueri
3360 uos bene conspicio uotaque uestra scio.
Sunt pia sed iusta non sunt, quapropter oportet
iure repellantur quae ratione carent.
Virginis illius pro qua me sollicitastis
quae sit conditio cernite, quisue status.
3365 Pondere pressa pedum prohibetur figere gressum,
haeret et assiduo pondere mersa toro.
In membris aliis uiget, et specialia dona,
si bene pensetis, insita multa manent.
Hinc sensu mentis, hinc pollet acumine uocis,
3370 moribus et studiis hinc uacat, inde uiget.
Gratia tanta sibi manuum concessa uidetur
quod uix aut numquam possit habere parem.
In tribus excellit, cum sit pulcherrima uultu,
pectore, uoce, manu, sunt satis ista sibi.
3375 Sola decem posset satis exhibuisse puellis
ex manibus solis; sola quid ergo iacet?
Non opus est igitur ditari munere nostro,
cui natura potens tot pretiosa dedit.
Officio priuata pedum si languet in uno,

3350 proprio] proprie *Tr Z*   3352 quaerentes] querantes *Z* querendo *H X*; domi-
nam] sociam α *I*   3353 diuque] diu *TrLa*   3355 propriis possetque] posset propriisque *LF I U* propriis posset *R* propriis possitque *HaLa*   3359–412 *om. U (lost
leaves)*   3360 bene conspicio] uideo bene nunc δ *TrHaLa*; *(whole line)* uos uideo sed
non sunt bona uestra sua *Z*   3361 sed iusta non sunt] sed non sunt iusta *F B* et iusta non
sunt *ND* non sunt sed iusta *LE I*   3362 repellantur] refellantur α *I* expellantur *MN*
3363 sollicitastis] sollicitatis *H MOD* sollicitasti *F* sollicistastis *J*   3364 quisue] queue
HuMN   3366 et] *om. Tr Z*; pondere] pondus *LE I*; mersa] merso *La* mensa *X* pressa
DK iuncta *F* inerte *LE I*   3367 uiget et] uigent β δ *TrHaLa ZX*   3369 hinc²]
hic *JVe*; pollet] possit *H*; uocis] uisus *LE I* uotis *H*   3372 quod] que α *I*; possit] posset
F β O   3375 posset] possit *Tr Z*; puellis] puellas *F β Z*   3378–9 *transp. Z*
3378 *(whole line)* quam sic ditauit gratia totque dedit α *I*

SPECVLVM STVLTORVM

319

brought here to lie in the shade, and was left to myself." [3350] Hearing this, the two sisters wept, trying to persuade their lady by their weeping. And as they wept copiously and begged hard and long, that she should at least give the girl the power to walk, so that she might go home cured, relying on her own feet, [3355] and no longer lie sick on her bed, she, neither moved nor showing pity on her sisters, set off, and addressed them thus: "I see well that you are moved by great compassion, as is right and proper, and I know your wishes. [3360] They are compassionate but not just, on which account it is necessary that they should be rightly rejected, as lacking reason. See what is the condition, what is the state, of that girl on whose behalf you have importuned me. Burdened by the weight of her feet she is prevented from taking a step, [3365] and overcome by this weight, is permanently tied to her bed. She is healthy in her other members, and, if you consider carefully her particular gifts, there are still many of them. So, she is distinguished for mental intelligence, and for incisiveness of speech; she cultivates virtue and the life of the mind, and is strong in both. [3370] It is evident that such great beauty has been given to her hands that it could rarely or never have an equal. Loveliest of face, she excels in three things—in soul, voice, and hand; these are enough for her. She alone could have furnished enough for ten girls [3375] with her hands alone; so why does she lie alone? So there is no need to enrich with our gift the one to whom mighty Nature has given so many treasures.

3357 *nihil mota*: cf. Boethius, *De consolatione*, i. pr. 5.
3369 *acumine*: 'acumen' = 'incisiveness, pointedness (of language)' (*OLD* 4b).
3378 *natura potens*: Boethius, *De consolatione*, iii. m. 2. 2.

320　　SPECVLVM STVLTORVM

3380　in tribus aut certe quatuor ipsa uiget."
Talibus auditis lacrimas tenuere sorores,
　restantemque sibi corripuere uiam.
Serior hora deas monet indulgere quieti,
　alternaque uice nocte leuare diem.
3385　Cumque forent positae, sese iam compositurae,
　urbis in introitu quae prope forte fuit,
exiit in biuium uentrem purgare puella
　rustica, nil reuerens inuerecunda deas.
Vestibus elatis retro nimiumque reiectis,
3390　poplite deflexo, curua resedit humi.
Vna manus foenum, panis tenet altera frustum,
　utraque dat dominae debita pensa suae.
Sed neque pro populo cessauit praetereunte,
　nec propter posita numina sacra prope.
3395　Erubuere duae uisum, uultumque tegentes,
　uestibus obiectis arripuere fugam.
Tertia subsistens reuocansque duas fugientes,
　"Vt quid" ait, "fugitis? sistite, quaeso, gradum.
Quaenam causa mali? Num somnia uana timetis?
3400　Quod modo uidistis alter horizon erat;
non habuit melius quam quod nobis manifestum
　fecit et ostendit simplicitate sua.
Si natura potens miserae meliora dedisset,
　non ita monstrasset cornua luna noua.
3405　Hic opus, hic opus est, non parcere, sed misereri,
　et festinando ferre leuamen ei.

3382 corripuere] arripuere *LE I Ha*　　3384 alternaque] alterna pro *LE I*
3385 compositurae] compositiuri *F* composuere *AJCWRHuMNPKVe TrHaLa ZX* compusuere *D*　　3386 urbis] uerbis *D Tr*; quae] qui *LE I*　　3388 reuerens] renuens
CWHuMN　　3389 reiectis] reiectit *MN* reiectus *I* reiectas *Z* reiectis / uel re<*illegible*>is
La　　3390 curua] curue *Ve Tr* crure β *AJCWRHuMNOPDK HaLa X* cruce *Z*; resedit]
recedit *O I Tr Z*; humi] humo *H I Z*　　3391 panis] pannis *H HuMN*; frustum] frustrum β *K La* frustam *APVe* frustram *Hu* crustam *MN*　　3392 *om. R; (whole line)*
neutra uacat domine seruit utraque sue α *I*　　3393–4 cessauit praetereunte—propter
posita] *om. O*　　3393 sed] et α *I*　　3396 obiectis] abiectis *TrHa ZX*　　3397 *om.*
Ve; subsistens] subsistit α *I*　　3399 causa] tam *Ve La*; num] non *R* nostri *La om.* <*space
left empty*> *Tr*; uana] mala *X* uera *Ha Z om. Tr*; timetis] uidetis δ *TrHaLa ZX*
3401 nobis] uobis α *B AO I Ha* modo *H* modo sic *X*　　3404 monstrasset] monstraret
CWK　　3405–32 *are mostly illegible in I (last folio, badly rubbed)*　　3405–6 *om.*
ZX　　3405 non] *om. LE reading uncertain I*　　3406 festinando] festinato α *reading*
uncertain I

SPECVLVM STVLTORVM 321

If she is feeble in one thing, being deprived of the use of her feet, she is strong in three or four others." [3380] Hearing this, the sisters held back their tears, and set out on the remainder of their journey.'

'The late hour prompted the goddesses to take some rest, and to repair the labours of the day with night, turn and turn about. When they had settled, and were about to lay themselves to rest, [3385] at the entrance to a town which happened to be near by, a peasant girl came out to the crossroads to empty her bowels, shamelessly showing no respect to the goddesses. With her clothes lifted up and thrown well back from her posterior, her knees bent, hunched over, she squatted on the ground. [3390] One hand held a piece of hay, the other a hunk of bread, both performing their due office to their mistress. Nor did she leave off for the sake of the people passing by, nor on account of the goddesses positioned nearby. Two of them blushed, and covering their faces, [3395] picked up their skirts and ran off. The third stayed put, and called back the two fugitives. "Why", she said, "are you running away? Stop, I beg. What's wrong? Are you afraid of empty dreams? What you have just seen was another horizon. [3400] She had nothing better than what she made manifest to us and revealed in her naivety. If mighty Nature had been more generous to the wretch, the new moon would not have shown its horns like this. Here, here it is necessary not to hold back, but to have pity, [3405] and speedily to give her relief. Here, here it is necessary for us to show largesse in abundance, and to give great gifts with a lavish hand. To her, rich Nature has left

---

3391 Hay was used in medieval times to perform the functions of modern toilet paper. Cf. *Ysengrimus*, v. 609–10.

3404 *monstrasset cornua luna noua*: that is, the girl's behind (cf. the modern expression 'mooning').

SPECVLVM STVLTORVM

322

Hic opus, hic opus est, ut diffundamus abunde,
et demus larga munera magna manu.
Huic nihil omnino diues natura reliquit,
haec eget, hic opus est ut faciamus opem.
Ista sua numquam uirtute resurgeret; isti
est pietatis opus ferre salutis opem.
Si cadat ista semel, non est qui subleuet illam
nec quicquam proprium quo releuetur habet,
pauper, inops, et egens, quam sic natura creauit
insita quod miserae gratia nulla manet.
Non quem fortuna, sed quem natura beauit
munere uirtutum diuitis omen habet.
Contra naturam nihil inseruisse ualemus
nec uolumus, nisi quod de ratione licet.
Intus et exterius eadem natura manebit
quae prius extiterat, sed status alter erit.
Quodque nequit fieri, naturam degenerare
nolumus, iniustas non decet esse deas.
Res et opes adici possunt extraque liniri
naturae salua proprietate sua.
Nos igitur, quibus est super his collata potestas,
demus abundanti munera magna manu,
diuitias et opes, census, fundos et honores,
praedia montana, pascua, prata, greges.
Vrbis et istius dominam statuamus eandem,
ut nihil in nostro munere desit ei."

Haec mea multotiens genitrix narrare solebat,
cuius me certe non meminisse pudet.
Talibus exemplis in religione frequenter
multa solent fieri quae ratione carent.
Hic modus esse solet in religione, magister,

3410

3415

3420

3425

3430

3435

3408 et] ut *CW*   3410 haec] hic *O La* hoc *W*; eget] egit *Tr* eger *F* aget *MN*
3413 *U rejoins*; subleuet] subleuat *H Z*; illam] eam *ACW HaLa Z* ipsam *R Tr*   3414 quic-
quam] quicquid *LE P I*   3416 quod] quid *O Tr Z* que *D*; miserae] miseris *Tr Z*
3418 omen] omne *RO*ᵃᶜ   3420 de] *om. CWDP* ex *X*   3422 status] satis *F*
3423 quodque] quidque *O Tr* quod *X*   3426 naturae] natura *H HaLa* nature propria *F*
3427 quibus est super his] super his quibus est *LE reading uncertain I*
3428 magna] larga *α H reading uncertain I*   3432–48 *blurred and rubbed I*
3432 ut] et *Ha UX; F returns to 3259; after 3278 repeats 3323–8, then continues from*
3435   3434 *om. O*   3437 hic] his *CHuMN*

SPECVLVM STVLTORVM 323

absolutely nothing; she is in need, here we must give assistance. [3410] She would never rise by her own powers; to her, it is a work of mercy to give aid. If she should once fall, there is no one to raise her up, and she has nothing of her own by which she may be lifted up, poor, helpless, and needy, whom Nature created such [3415] that no inborn grace is found in the wretch. It is the one whom Nature, not Fortune, has blessed with the gift of virtues who has true wealth. We are incapable of implanting anything against Nature's will, nor do we wish to, if Reason does not allow it. [3420] Both internally and externally Nature will remain the same as it was before; but her circumstances will change. We don't wish for the impossible, for Nature to be weakened—which is impossible; goddesses should not be unjust. Property and wealth can be added on and plastered over from without, [3425] while Nature's characteristics remain intact. So let us, on whom this power is bestowed, give great gifts with generous hand—riches, wealth, money, lands and honours, mountain farms, pastures, meadows, cattle. [3430] And let us make her mistress of this city, so that she may lack nothing of what we have to give." '

'Many a time did my mother, whom I am not embarrassed to recall, tell me this story. On models such as this, many things often come about in religious life [3435] which are not in accord with reason.

3412 *pietatis opus* (also 3548, 3662, 3872): a favourite phrase of Christian Latin writers; see Prudentius, *Hamartigenia*, 628, *Psychomachia*, 239; Prosper, *Liber Epigrammatum*, lxv. 3, lxxxiii. 2 (ed. Horsting, pp. 125, 139); Dracontius, *De laudibus Dei*, ii. 50, *Satisfactio* 290, 298; Venantius Fortunatus, *Carmina*, ii. 8. 3; John of Salisbury, *Entheticus maior* (ed. van Laarhoven), 322.

3418 *omen*: 'substance, power, authority', as contrasted with 'nomen', the mere name (*DMLBS* 3).

SPECVLVM STVLTORVM

324

istud oportebit te quoque saepe pati.
Istud ubique uiget, haec sunt specialia multis,

3440   hic praelatorum mos malus esse solet.
Haec sunt quae faciunt inconuenientia multa,
et ne conueniant pastor ouesque gregis,
haec sunt quae pariunt in religione ruinas,
scandala, contemptum, schismata, damna, dolum.

3445   Cetera cum possit multis obnoxia uirtus,
contemptum proprium dissimulare nequit.
Nil grauius laedit mentem, nil altius urit,
quam cum uirtutum munera spreta iacent.
Cetera cum soleant etiam cum tempore labi,

3450   hoc animum numquam deseruisse solet.
Vulneris hoc genus est quod per medicamina crescit
et grauius tractu temporis ulcus habet.
Aspidis hoc animo facit instillare uenenum,
cui nihil antidotum praeualuisse potest.

3455   Contemptum proprium qui ferre potest patienter,
cetera de facili sustinuisse potest.
Omnia cum soleat uictrix patientia ferre,
uicta sub hoc onere succubuisse solet.'

Imprecatio Burnelli contra uolentes sibi mala

Talia dicenti subito de nare sinistra

3460   frigidus erupit sanguis, et ipse breuis.
Quo statim uiso dixit Burnellus: 'Iniquum
portendunt aliquid talia signa mihi.
Olim, nocte prius quam caudam mane molossi
surripuere meam, contigit istud idem.

3465   Prospera det Dominus mihi nunc et ab omine duro

3438 istud] illud δ *TrHaLa UZ*   3439 *om. La*; istud] illud δ *TrHa Z*   3440 hic]
hec *a I*; mos malus esse solet] consuetudo frequens *a I*   3442 gregis] greges *O Tr*
3444–5 contemptum schismata—obnoxia uirtus *om. Z*   3444 scandala] scanda *L I*
scisma *K*; schismata] scandala *K*   3445–6 *om. a I*   3446 *run on to* 3444a *Z*
3447 mentem] militem *LE I*   3448 *LEF I end here*   3451 est] *om. H Z*
3455–6 *om. D*   3457 uictrix] nutrix *C X*   3459 *QY rejoin*; subito] niso *QY*;
nare] *om. HuMN*; sinistra] sinistro *Tr Z*   3460 erupit] erupuit *M Tr* eripuit *R*
3462 portendunt] protendunt *JRHuMNPKVe QY* pretendunt *H D Tr UZ* pretendit *CW*
portentum *Ha* portendunt /[uel] portentum *La*; aliquid] aliquod *H X*   3464 contigit]
contingit *ZY*; istud] illud δ *TrHaLa ZQY*   3465 det] dat *ZY*; ab omine] ab homine *H*
*AJCWHuMNO*ᵖᶜ*PDKVe TrHaLa* ab omni *Z* homine *QY* de mare *R* ab emulo? *U*

SPECVLVM STVLTORVM 325

This is often the way in religious life, O teacher, and you too will often have to put up with it. That is the general rule; these characteristics are shared by many, and this is generally the evil practice of bishops. [3440] This is what produces many improprieties, and sets the pastor and his flock at odds with each other. These are the things that produce disasters in religious life, scandals, contempt, schisms, injuries, guile. Although virtue can disregard other things which are harmful to many, [3445] it cannot disregard its own contemptuous treatment. Nothing wounds the mind more grievously, nothing burns more deeply, than when virtue's gifts are scorned. Although other things wear off over time, this never leaves the mind. [3450] This is a type of wound that gets worse with treatment, and becomes a bigger sore with the passage of time. This causes snake poison to drip into the mind, and no antidote has power against it. Anyone who can patiently bear his own contempt [3455] can easily endure other things. Although patience conquers by bearing everything, beneath this burden she falls conquered.'

Burnellus's Curse against Those Who Wish Him Evil

As he said this, cold blood suddenly and briefly burst out of his left nostril. [3460] Seeing this, Burnellus at once said: 'This sign portends some evil to me. The same thing happened once before, on the night before the dogs tore off my tail. May God grant me good fortune now, and rescue me from bad luck! [3465] May this blood betoken good,

---

3457 *uictrix patientia*: an allusion to the well-known medieval proverb 'patientia uincit' ('patience conquers'). See Walther, *Proverbia*, 16974, 20833f, 24454.

3459–60 A nosebleed could be interpreted as a portent of good or bad luck (though if it was from the left nostril, the latter); see Bächtold-Stäubli, s.v. 'Nase', 3(a), 'Nasenblüten' (vi. 972–3).

326   SPECVLVM STVLTORVM

eruat! Inque bonum sit cruor iste, precor!
Omine mane suo currens lepus et capra clauda
    obuia sint illis qui mala nostra uolunt!
Noctua prima precor sit auis quae mane sereno
3470   exeat, occurrens hostibus atra meis!
Obuia nens ueniat lanam de uellere nigro
    deque colo taxi foemina nuda pedes!
Mane senex caluus et uespere crine soluto
    hostis in occursum curua feratur anus.
3475 Obuius occurrat utriusque coloris eisdem
    obstipo monachus uertice, uoce carens.
Pauperis aut uiduae ueniens de funere tristi
    presbiter iratus ipse salutet eos.
Ad laeuam bufo transuersus corpore toto
3480   his prior occurrat et ferat ipse pedem.
Quique solet dici pestisque nocentior esse
    rusticus occurrat hostibus ipse meis.'

Qualiter Bernardus superuenit, dominus Burnelli

Vix ea fatus ita cum rusticus ecce cruentus
    intrat et acclaudens ostia dixit ita:
3485 'O Burnelle, mihi multos quaesite per annos,
    et nunc fortuitu uixque reperte tamen!
En ego! Bernardus, dominus tuus! en ego certe
    sub quo praeterita crimina cuncta lues.
Huc ades, accede! Mecum gradieris ad urbem
3490   unde recessisti nocte patrando dolum.
Et nouus annus erat et sabbata sacra fuerunt,

3466 inque] hincque *O Y*; iste] ipse *Ve* atque *HaLa*   3467 omine] *Sedgwick* omni *all MSS*   3468 sint] sunt *DK*   3470 occurrens] occurrat *K La*; atra] atque *ZQY* 3471 nens] mens *H Ve Tr ZQY* ne *M Ha* neue *N*   3472 deque] de quo *CW* et que *P*; colo] calo *Tr* talo *AJCWRO*ᵃᶜ*PVe HaLa ZQY* dolo *H* collo *D U*²   3475 utriusque] utrique *JCWOP Ha* uterque *HuMNVe Tr*; eisdem] eiusdem *CWHuMN*   3477 aut] ac *ZQY*   3478 salutet] salutat *R Y*   3479 bufo] buffo *AHuMNO* burfo *J* ousso *Tr* (*u expuncted?*)   3480 ipse] ipse /uel ipsi *Ha*   3481 esse] omni δ *TrHaLa ZX* 3483 ita] erat *H R X*   3484 intrat] intrans *R Tr*   3486 uixque] uix *Ha Z* 3490 dolum] malum /uel dolum *K*

3467–82 *omine*: for the conjecture, see Introduction, p. lxxxiii. The allusion is to the super-stitious belief that the first person, animal, or thing that one encountered in the day brought one good or bad luck. Grimm's *Teutonic Mythology* (trans. Stallybrass, iii. 1119–35, iv. 1637–40) gives many examples of this sort, some of which appear in Burnellus's list, and also in lists of

SPECVLVM STVLTORVM 327

I pray! May the running hare and the limping goat, bearing their own ill omen, tomorrow meet those who wish me ill! I beg that the ominous owl may be the first bird to fly out in bright day and encounter my enemies. [3470] Let them meet a barefoot woman spinning wool from a black fleece on a distaff of yew! Let a bald old man cross my enemy's path in the morning, and in the evening a hunchbacked old woman with flowing hair. May they meet a dumb monk, of either colour, [3475] his head bent. May an angry priest, coming from the sad funeral of a pauper or a widow, give them greeting. May a toad, his whole body turned to the left, be first to come to meet them. [3480] And may my enemies encounter the one who is said to be an even more harmful pest—the peasant.'

How Bernard, Burnellus's Master, Came Along

Hardly had he said this when, blow me, the bloodthirsty peasant enters, and slamming shut the doors, says: 'Oh Burnellus, whom I have sought for many years, [3485] and now found, albeit by chance and with difficulty! It's me, Bernard, your master! I'm the one under whose hands you shall pay for all your past misdeeds. Come here, approach! You shall go with me to the city you ran away from in the night, practising deception. [3490] It was the New Year; and the holy Sabbath, when you

---

examples provided by John of Salisbury (*Policraticus*, i. 13, ed. Webb, i. 55–61; trans. Pike, pp. 45–50), and Peter of Blois (*Epistolae*, no. lxv, PL ccvii. 195), both of whom are sceptical of such superstitions. Examples mentioned by both John and Peter are the hare (*SS*, 3467; Grimm, *Teutonic Mythology,* trans. Stallybrass, iii. 1126, iv. 1639, 1762. 55), a woman with her hair unbound (*SS*, 3473–4; Grimm, iii. 1124), and a monk (*SS*, 3476; Grimm, iv. 1638). John of Salisbury also mentions the goat (*SS*, 3467), the owl (*SS*, 3469; Grimm, iii. 1135, iv. 1643), a priest (*SS*, 3477–8; Grimm, iii. 1125, iv. 1638), and a toad (*SS*, 3479–80; Grimm, iii. 1132). Grimm cites examples of a woman spinning (*SS*, 3472; Grimm, iii. 1124, iv. 1638), and of a bird-flight on the left side (*SS*, 3479; Grimm, iv. 1640, 1771). The other examples, and the picturesque details (such as the black wool and the distaff of yew) may be Nigel's own.

3484 *acclaudens*: 'acclaudere' = 'to close' (*DMLBS* 1). Raymo takes this to be the door of the 'Alpine inn' referred to at line 1961, but see 2465–6, where Burnellus meets Galen outside on the road leading out of an unspecified town. The only earlier reference to location is at line 1961, 'in mediis Alpibus', and probably refers to a travellers' hospice at the top of an Alpine pass (see n.). The long account of Burnellus's views on monastic orders and social classes allows the reader to suppose that his journey has been continued in the meantime.

328   SPECVLVM STVLTORVM

tempore quo scelus hoc ausus es atque nefas.
Et, bene si recolo, postquam me deseruisti,
    quatuor aut quinque lustra dedere locum.

3495 Iam senio fractus iam uiribus atque uigore
    corporis effractus diceris esse senex.
Absit ut ulterius quicquam nisi forte coactus
    siue libens facias, absque labore tamen.
Vsibus addictus tantummodo cotidianis

3500 nil facies, nisi quod paucula ligna feres,
sportellasque meas geminas duplicesque farinae
    saccos, meque super; nec graue pondus ego.'
Dixit, et iniecto capiti de more capistro
    duxit et abduxit, fuste docente uiam;

3505 Et ne forte fugam rursus meditetur iniquam,
    subtrahat et domino debita pensa suo,
funditus abscidit aurem Bernardus utramque,
    cautior ut fieret cauteriatus ita.

Animaduersio Burnelli

Tunc Burnellus ait Bernardo: 'Nunc scio uere,
3510 uertice cum cauda conueniente mea,
quod mihi sit uerus sanctusque propheta locutus
    Parisius dudum, dum meditarer ibi.
Hic quasi praeterita narrauit saepe futura,
    multaque praedixit non memoranda modo.

3515 Quicquid enim factum uel dixerit esse futurum,
    fecerunt uerbis facta secuta fidem.
Saepius ille mihi de te quoque multa locutus
    plurima praedixit quae memorabor adhuc.
Nam nihil in terram cecidit quaecumque locutus,

3520 nec sunt priuata pondere uerba suo.
Saepe meos casus et quae uentura super me

3496 effractus] effectus β UY affectus Q effracto Z; diceris] disceris HuN La^{ac} cerneris K   3497 ulterius] alterius D ZQ   3499 addictus] addictis HaLa adductus H JKVe UX abdictis Tr addamus QY   3500 facies] facias Ha Q; ligna] lingua CW 3501 sportellasque meas] sportellas eneas δ TrHaLa   3504 docente] ducente HaLa 3509 nunc] non /uel nunc Ha   3514 memoranda] memorando A Ve   3515 dixerit] diceret β dixerat OK   3516 uerbis facta] factis uerba AJCWRHuM(barely legible)NDVe TrHaLa UZQY orbis fa<erasure> ta O   3518–19 om. δ TrHaLa XY add. in lower marg. Y^{pc}   3520 suo] sua Ve Tr UQ

SPECVLVM STVLTORVM 329

ventured on this crime and wickedness. And, if I remember well, since you deserted me, twenty or twenty-five years have gone by. Now I am weakened with age, now you, feeble in strength and vigour, [3495] have the name of an old man. Heaven forbid that you should do any more— unless perhaps compelled to, or willingly, but without hardship. You'll only be devoted to my daily needs and will do nothing, except carry a few logs, [3500] and my two paniers, and two sacks of flour, and me on top—I don't weigh much.' Having spoken, he threw the halter over his head in the accustomed manner and led him off, teaching him the way with a stick. And so that he should not contemplate a wicked escape again, [3505] and deprive his master of the duties he owed him, Bernard cut off both his ears in their entirety, so that he might be more cautious when thus cauterized.

Burnellus's Punishment

Then Burnellus said to Bernard: 'Now I know for sure, when my head matches my tail, [3510] what a true and holy prophet once told me in Paris, while I was studying there. He often recounted the future as if it were the past, and predicted many things that cannot be mentioned now. Whatever he said had happened or was going to happen, [3515] the subsequent events bore out his words. Often he said many things to me about you, and foretold many things which I shall still bear in mind. For nothing in the world, of whatever he said, has failed to come to pass, nor have his words been deprived of their weight. [3520] Often he prophetically described to me my adventures and what things he had

---

3494 *dedere locum*: 'dare locum' = 'to give place, make way' (*OLD* s.v. 'locus' 12d).

3507–8 Cf. Avianus, *Fabulae*, xxx, where a farmer cuts off the ears of a pig which has been eating his crops, in hopes that, remembering the pain, the pig will stay away from the crops in future.

3516 *fecerunt uerbis facta...fidem*: for variations on this idea, see *Miracles*, 318, 706, 1241, 1296, 1710, 2343.

3519 *cecidit*: 'cadere' = 'to fail, come to nothing' (*OLD* 12c, *DMLBS* 6b). Cf. 1 Kgs. (1 Sam.) 3: 19: 'et non cecidit ex omnibus verbis eius in terram'.

3520 Cf. Ovid, *Heroides*, iii. 98: 'mea pro nullo pondere verba cadunt'.

330   *SPECVLVM STVLTORVM*

uiderat exposuit praescius ille mihi.
Prospera quinque mihi praedixit adesse futura,
    postquam praeterita quinque sinistra forent.
3525 Quatuor ex quinque iam praeteriere sinistris
    quae mihi praedixit ille propheta meus.
Quinta mihi superest, sed et ipsa nouissima, plaga,
    quam sum passurus perpetiorque modo.
Vltimus ille dolor erit ultimus ille dolorum
3530 terminus, et tanti meta laboris adest.
Vltima plaga mihi finem requiemque laborum
    conferet, et uoto perfruar ipse meo.
Namque meis iam quinque malis modo sic superatis
    mox totidem uenient prospera fata mihi.
3535 Rusticus hic nequam, uelut extitit ante dolorum
    principium nobis, sic quoque finis erit.
Prima mali causa contrarius atque rebellis
    a puero coepit rusticus esse mihi.
Prima status nostri per eum mihi quaestio mota,
3540 namque prius toto tempore liber eram.
Callidus ille prior sibi me seruire coegit,
    fecerat et multum ferre laboris onus.
Sed uice conuersa finem uexatio nostra
    unde prius coepit est habitura suum.
3545 Non ego, crede mihi, sed rusticus ille malignus
    praestitit exemplum principiumque mali.
Vnde suis meritis condigna rependere certe
    non erit indignum sed pietatis opus.
Lex antiqua iubet pro membro reddere membrum,
3550 dentem dente, pedem restituisse pede.
Sic ego Bernardo faciam, nisi forte, quod absit,
    fata uocent alias quam mea uota uelint.

3522 ille] ipse *H Q*   **3523** praedixit adesse] predixerat esse *JO* dixit adesse *Q*
3525 praeteriere] preteriore *W* preterire *La Y* preteriisse *Q*   **3526** *om. Tr*
3529 ultimus¹] ulterius *ZX*; dolorum] doloris *O Tr* dolor *J*   **3531** laborum] laborem
La malorum *B UQY* laboris *O TrHa*   **3535–8** *om. P*   **3535** dolorum] doloris *O
Tr*   **3539** nostri] *om. ZQY*; per eum—mota] *om. J*; mihi quaestio mota] que ruina
patebat *U*; mota] mota est β *ACMNOPVe ZXQY* nota est *W* mota sit / uel est *K*   **3542** *A
ends here (missing leaves).*   **3545** crede] credo *R Tr*   **3548** indignum] condignum
/uel in *Ha*   **3550** dentem] dentem pro *H D*; pedem…pede] pede…pedem *H R
Ha*   **3551** ego] ergo *HaLa*   **3552** uocent] nocent *CWVe Tr X* nocens *HaLa*
notent *B HuMNPK UY* uetent *Z*; alias] aliud *P X* aliis *Tr*; uelint] uolent *H* uolunt *D X*

SPECVLVM STVLTORVM

331

seen were to befall me. He foretold that five pieces of good luck would come to me, after five misfortunes were past. Now four out of the five misfortunes [3525] which that prophet of mine foretold me have passed. The fifth disaster remains, but it is the last that I am to suffer, and I now endure it patiently. That will be the last grief, the end of all griefs, and the conclusion of my great suffering. [3530] The last disaster will bring me an end and respite from hardships, and I shall enjoy my desire. For when my five misfortunes have thus been surmounted, soon the equivalent number of lucky events will come to me. This wicked peasant, as he was earlier the beginning of my griefs, [3535] will be their end. From my boyhood, the hostile and rebellious peasant has been to me the prime cause of evil. It was at his instigation that my status was first called in question, since I had previously always been a free man. [3540] That trickster first forced me to be his servant, and made me bear many a burden of labour. But, by a turnabout, my torment is to have its end whence it took its beginning. Not I, believe me, but that wicked peasant [3545] has provided an example and a source of evil. So to repay his merits with their deserts will certainly not be unfitting but a deed of kindness. The old law orders a limb to be given for a limb, a tooth for a tooth, and a foot to be forfeited for a foot. [3550] So shall I do to Bernard, unless perhaps—heaven forbid!—the fates summon otherwise than my wishes would have it. Oh, if Bernard saw

---

3542 *ferre laboris onus*: Ovid, *Heroides*, xix. 166.
3549–50 Exod. 21: 23.
3552 *alias*: 'otherwise' (*DMLBS* 3a).

332   *SPECVLVM STVLTORVM*

O si Bernardus quae sunt uentura uideret,
    et quam Burnellum gloria magna manet,
3555   non ita me premeret uirga baculoque feriret,
    nec ferrum faceret in latus ire meum;
sed potius prostratus humi uestigia nostra
    pronus adoraret porrigeretque preces.'
Talia Burnello secum meditante, Cremonam
3560   intrat et est domino subditus ipse suo.

De Bernardo

Contigit interea Bernardo res memoranda,
    quae satis in tota nota Cremona fuit.
Fama frequens populi ne tempore gesta senescant
    annorum senio consuluisse solet.
3565   Fama frequens populi rerum facies rediuiuas
    suscitat, et ueteres res facit esse nouas.
Damna uetustatis morituraque tempora nobis
    fama frequens redimit, gesta priora docens.

3553 uentura] futura *Ha Z*   3557 potius prostratus humi] potius prostratus humo
H prostratus humi pocius (poscius *M*) *HuMN*   3562 *(whole line)* quam nouit ueram
tota cremena satis *D*   3563–4 *transp. after 3566 JWRHuMNOPDK TrHaLa U; om. Z*
3563 tempore] tempora *H HuMN Tr UY*; senescant] senescat *QY*   3565 *om. O*
3565–6 *om.*   *C*   *QY*   3567–74 *om.*   *Z*   3567 morituraque] moritura *B*
JCWHuMNPDVe TrHaLa UQY

3561–866 The story of the grateful animals and the ungrateful man does not belong to the
body of western European beast narratives that derive from Aesopic fable. It is in origin an
oriental tale, part of the famous collection of animal narratives known variously as the
Pañcatantra, *Kalila and Dimna*, or the *Fables of Bidpai*. Originally written in Sanskrit, this
collection was translated, adapted, and added to, in many languages (for example, Syriac,
Greek, Persian, Hebrew, Latin; see the table of the various versions in Keith-Falconer's
translation of *Kalilah and Dimnah* from Syriac, p. lxxxvi, and Hertel, *Das Pañcatantra*, for an
account of its development). The tale of the grateful animals first appears in the eighth-
century Arabic version by Abdullah Ibn Al-Muquaffa' (*Le Livre de Kalila et Dimna*, trans.
Miquel), from which it passed into the late version of the Sanskrit *Pañcatantra* (1199) on
which the Penguin Classics translation by Chandra Rajan is based (see Rajan, p. xxii). The
arrival of this particular tale in England is recorded by Matthew Paris, monk of St Albans,
whose *Chronica maiora* (ii. 413–16) includes it under the year 1195, where a marginal note
labels it as a 'story of King Richard which he told to Warin, abbot of St Albans, and he
[Warin] told to us'. The 'ungrateful man' of Matthew's story is named as Vitalis, a Venetian
merchant; the man who rescues him from the pit is an unnamed 'poor man'. Only two animals, lion and serpent, fall into the pit with the rich man, and the jewel which the serpent
brings to the poor man as reward does not have the miraculous property of returning to the
original owner whenever it is sold; otherwise the story is very close to the version told by
Nigel in *SS*. According to Matthew, Richard I frequently related this story as a reproach to
those 'ingrates' who were unwilling to take the Cross in defence of the Holy Land, and since

SPECVLVM STVLTORVM 333

what is to happen, and what great glory awaits Burnellus, he would not harry me with the rod and strike me with his stick in this way, [3555] nor would he drive iron into my side, but rather, prostrate and face down on the ground, he would worship my footsteps and offer up prayers.' Thinking such thoughts to himself, Burnellus enters Cremona and his master's service. [3560]

About Bernard

Meanwhile, there befell Bernard a notable adventure, which was very well known in all Cremona. The common gossip of the people, lest deeds grow old with passing time, provides a remedy for the feebleness of the years; the people's common gossip freshens up the shape of events so that they live again, [3565] making old things new. Common gossip repairs the ravages of age and preserves times about to be lost to

---

Canterbury was the first place he visited after returning to England in 1194, it seems entirely plausible that Nigel heard the story from the king himself (see Introduction, pp. lxxi–lxxiii). It is also entirely likely that Richard himself first heard the story in the Norman kingdom of Sicily, where he had spent the winter of 1190–1 on his way to the Holy Land, and where 'Arabic as well as Greek and Latin culture flourished side by side in the 12th-c.' (Chesnutt, 'The Grateful Animals', p. 51; for a Greek version of *Kalila and Dimna* that could have served as the conduit of transmission from Arabic to Latin, see ibid. pp. 41, 51). Cf. also John of Salisbury mentioning what he learned 'during a stay in Apulia from a Greek translator who knew Latin pretty well' (*Metalogicon*, i. 15, ed. Hall, p. 37; trans. Hall, p. 156). On the close relations between Sicily and England at this period, see Appendix E below.

The story of the grateful animals is also found in the misleadingly named *Novus Aesopus* by a certain Baldo, where it is one of 23 fables from *Kalila and Dimna*, alongside 12 of Aesopic origin. Nothing is known of Baldo besides his name, but circumstantial evidence suggests that he can be located in southern Italy (supporting the hypothesis of a Sicilian connection). His dates are also uncertain, and may be 12th or 13th century. Baldo marks the first incursion of *Kalila and Dimna* into continental Europe; his work was quickly followed by a Hebrew version, which was translated into Latin by John of Capua, a converted Jew, under the title *Directorium humanae vitae* (ed. Gessler), and by another Latin version, heavily indebted to John of Capua, by Raymond of Bézières (ed. Hervieux, *Fabulistes latins*, v. 379–775). These Latin prose versions of the whole work are 13th-c. and thus cannot have influenced Nigel. Meanwhile, as Chesnutt's very able analysis of the dissemination of the tale of the grateful animals shows, *SS* itself is the likeliest source of the later versions in Latin and English; viz., in the late 13th-c. *Compilatio singularis exemplorum* (ed. Hilka, pp. 21–3), in the 14th-c. *Anglo-Latin Gesta Romanorum* (ed. Bright, c. lxxxiii, pp. 545–63), and, at the end of the 14th c., in Gower's *Confessio Amantis* (ed. Macaulay, v. 4937–5162); divergences in narrative detail are plausibly accounted for as deliberate variations introduced by the author in question. See Introduction, pp. cxxxiv–cxli.

3563 *Fama frequens*: cf. Cicero, *De inventione*, ii. 55.
3567–8 Translating 'redimit' twice.

334 SPECVLVM STVLTORVM

Tres habuit pueros pauper Bernardus alendos,
3570   quarta fuit coniux, quintus asellus erat;
ille domus dominique sui substantia tota
    solus erat, quamuis parua parumque ualens.
Ad fora ligna trahens sese dominumque domumque,
    quinque labore suo solus alebat eos.
3575 Contigit ergo semel quod cum Bernardus ab urbe
    in nemus exisset ipse comesque suus,
audirent hominis uelut existentis in antro
    uox foret exclamans auxiliumque petens.
Haesit et obstupuit primo Bernardus, at inde
3580   imposuit fronti signa sacrata crucis,
discernensque modum clamoris, uocis acumen
    corporis humani comperit esse sonum;
designansque locum quo uox diffusa per auras
    clarius auditur, ire parabat eo.
3585 Sicque sonus uocis, uox uerbi nuntia tandem
    nosse dat expressa uerba quid ipsa uelint.
Nobilis atque potens, uir magnus ab urbe Cremona
    forte Dryanus erat, diues et ipse nimis,
qui cum saepe canes sequeretur amore ferarum
3590   in foueam lapsum contigit esse semel.
Os erat angustum foueae, sed lata deorsum
    atque profunda nimis et tenebrosa fuit.
Corruerantque simul in eam leo, simia, serpens,
    cum quibus et quartus ipse Dryanus erat.
3595 His tribus in foueam lapsis, collapsus et ipse,
    hospes et inuitus coeperat esse comes.
Quisque sibi timuit tacuitque, timore coactus,
    praeter eum cui uox aucta timore fuit.
Quarta dies aderat ex quo clamore lugubri
3600   quaesierat uana uoce salutis opem.
Qua tamen excitus uenit Bernardus et illum

3574 quinque] quique *Ha* cumque *HuMN*   3577 audirent] audiret *P Z* audierat *U*
3578 exclamans] eclamans *JVe La* et clamans *Ha*   3579 primo] prius *QY*; at] ac
JCWKVe ab *O* et *R ZQY*   3581 discernensque] discernens *R Z*   3586 expressa]
expresse *K La Z*; quid] quod *H HuMN Q*   3589 *om. J*; ferarum] fratrum *U*, ferarum
add. in margin U^2 3593 corruerantque] corruerant *R Ha* corrueratque *U*
3596 inuitus] iniuncus *QY*   3597 quisque] quisquis *HuMN*   3599 quo] qua *H Q*
3600 uoce] uace *Tr* nece *HaLa*   3601 tamen] cum *J QY* tunc *D*; excitus] exitus *DVe*
exutus *Ha*; et] ad *P Z*

SPECVLVM STVLTORVM 335

us, teaching of earlier deeds. Bernard, a poor man, had three children
to feed; his wife made four, and the ass was the fifth. [3570] He [the ass]
alone was the whole wealth of the household and his master, although
it [the wealth] was small and worth little. Carrying wood to market, he
provided food for himself, his master, and the household—all five of
them by his labour. So it happened once that when Bernard had gone
out from the town [3575] into the woodland, his companion with him,
they heard a voice, as it were of a man in a cave, crying out and begging
for help. Bernard first stopped in amazement, and then marked his
forehead with the sacred sign of the Cross; [3580] identifying the
nature of the clamour, he discovered the pitch of the voice to be the
sound made by a human being. Noting the place where the voice, echo–
ing through the air, was heard most clearly, he set out in that direction.
As the sound presaged the voice, so the voice presaged the word, [3585]
and at length made known what the distinct words mean. As it hap–
pened, it was Dryanus, a powerful nobleman, a great man from the
town of Cremona, and exceedingly wealthy. He often followed his dogs
in pursuit of game, and on this occasion it happened that he fell into a
pit. [3590] The mouth of the pit was narrow, but lower down it was
wide, very deep, and dark. There had fallen in at the same time a lion,
an ape, and a snake, with whom Dryanus made a fourth. These three
having fallen into the pit, and he having tumbled in too, [3595] he was
their guest and unwilling companion. Each feared for himself, and
under the pressure of fear was silent, except for him, whose voice was
louder from fear. For four days he had sought rescue with dismal
clamour and fruitless cry. [3600] But Bernard was attracted by it, came,
and asked him to explain who he was and where from. He replied: 'I'm

SPECVLVM STVLTORVM

poscit ut exponat quis sit et unde; refert
ille 'Dryanus ego miser et miserabilis hic sum,
qui nuper fueram maior in urbe mea.

3605 Quisquis es, accede; fer opem miserumque misertus
extrahe; pro certo praemia magna feres.
Quicquid in humanis rebus mihi competit, illud
pro mercede tua dimidiabo tibi.
Quoque magis possis securior esse, deorum

3610 per sacrosancta numina iuro tibi.'
Talibus auditis spe lucri ductus ad antrum
rusticus accedens accelerauit opus.
Vimine contextum funem dimittit, at illum
simia corripiens exit abitque cito.

3615 Tunc ita Bernardus Sathanae phantasmate lusum
se reputans dixit 'Vah! quid ineptus ago?
Ecce quod extraxi, dum debuit esse Dryanus,
daemone fallente simia magna fuit.
Est locus infaustus, uox daemonis, arsque maligna

3620 me male subuertit, meque fefellit ita.
Ergo reuertar ego, signo crucis intitulatus,
ne quodcumque malum possit obesse mihi.'
Talia dicentem magno clamore Dryanus
aduocat, adiurat, multiplicatque preces;

3625 et ne delusum sese phantasmate credat
commemorat sanctos et sacra uerba refert.
Postulat ut funem rursus dimittat in antrum,
praemia ne pereant percipienda sibi.
Vicit amor lucri rursumque remittit ad ima

3630 funem, sed frustra, spe pereunte sua.
Funibus immissis serpens exiuit ab antro

3602–896 *transp. after 3320 MN*　　　**3602** refert] dolet *DK* foret *X*　　　**3603** ego]
ait *JCWRHuMNOPDKVe TrHaLa Z*; hic] huc *H* huius *HaLa*　　　**3605** miserumque]
miseroque *R* miserique *Tr Q*　　　**3607** competit illud] compit illud *J* contigit umquam
H X　　　**3609–10** *om. K Ha add. in margin* K^{pc}　　　**3609** quoque] quodque *P Tr*
3613 dimittit at] dimittit ad *UZQY* dimisit ad *JCWRHuMNOPDKVe HaLa* dimisit in *Tr*
3614 corripiens] quem sumens *DK* quam capiens *H* preripiens *X*　　　**3617** quod] quid
R Tr QY quot *B*　　　**3619** arsque] atque *Ha Q*　　　**3621** signo] sigo *Ha* sum *U*, signo
add. in upper margin U^2　　　**3622** obesse] abesse *TrHa*　　　**3623** dicentem] dicente
HuMNK La dicenti *Ha*; Dryanus] dianus *U*　　　**3627** funem] finem *HuMN*
3629 uicit] uincit *CWRHuMNDK*; lucri] lucrum *CWHuMND*; rursumque remittit] rursum remittat *R Q* rursus remittit *La* rursumque dimittit *Ve Ha*　　　**3630** spe] sepe *CW*
3631 immissis] emissis *P U*

SPECVLVM STVLTORVM   337

the wretched and miserable Dryanus, who was once a great man in my city. Whoever you are, come here; lend your aid, have pity on a wretch [3605] and pull him out. Assuredly you will have a great reward. I will give you half of all my worldly possessions in recompense. And so that you may be sure of this, I swear it to you by the all-holy gods.' [3610] Hearing this, and led by the hope of profit, the peasant approached the pit and hastened to the task. He let down a rope, twined out of willow, but the ape seized it, got out, and quickly ran off. Then Bernard, thinking himself deceived by a demonic apparition, [3615] said 'Ah! fool, what am I doing? See, what I have released, which ought to have been Dryanus, through the devil's deception was a huge ape. There is a curse on this place; the devil's voice and wicked cunning led me astray and deceived me in this way. [3620] So I'll go home, signed with the sign of the Cross, lest I encounter some misfortune.' As he says this, Dryanus calls to him with mighty cries, beseeching him with more entreaties; and so that he should not think himself deluded by an apparition, [3625] he calls on the saints and recites the Scriptures. He asks him to lower the rope once more into the pit, lest he lose the rewards he is to receive. The love of profit won out, and again he sends the rope to the bottom, but in vain, his hope is extinguished. [3630] The rope having been let down, the snake came out of the pit, horrible

---

3604 *maior*: 'mayor' (*DMLBS* 10).

338 SPECVLVM STVLTORVM

horridus aspectu, delituitque cito.
Quo uiso Bernardus ait 'Tua dona, Dryane,
respuo, cuncta tua sint tibi, tuque procul!

3635 Daemonibus plenus locus hic, phantasmata terra
de gremio profert et noua monstra parit.'
Iamque recessisset fugiens sine spe redeundi,
spes nisi lucrandi detinuisset eum.
Spes et amor lucri cupidum uicere, Dryano

3640 quas promissa iuuant multiplicante preces.
Ordine quo supra, misero remanente Dryano,
funibus immissis exiit ante leo
quam uel eos posset subito discernere uisu,
uel celeri missos corripuisse manu.

3645 Palluit inspecta Bernardus ad ora leonis,
concutit et gelidus omnia membra timor,
nec remanere putat tutum nec uoce timorem
prodere nec celerem corripuisse fugam.
Si fugit, ecce! fame longa stimulante coactus

3650 circuit esuriens ore fremente leo;
si manet, exosus locus est quia daemone plenus,
exactoque die nox metuenda uenit.
Viribus elapsis sensum timor ebibit, artus
deficiunt, domino deficiente suo.

3655 Auget et ipsa metum uox exclamantis in antro,
importuna satis et miseranda nimis.
Spondet opes et agros, turrita palatia spondet –
quicquid spondere corde uel ore potest.
Iamque tot addiderat precibus promissa quod ipsa

3660 uox simul et uentus deficiebat ei.
Et pietate sua nisi plus innata cupido

3632 horridus] arridus *HuMN*; aspectu] apparuit *CW*   3635 phantasmata] fantas-
mate *CW*; terra] terre *JCWRHuMNOPDKVe TrHaLa UZY* certe *Q*   3636 de] in
Ve HaLa   3639 Dryano] drianum β *R Tr X* driane *P U*   3640–1 *om. P*
3640 quas] que *JCWRHuMNOVe TrHaLa ZX* magnis *D* cum *K*; multiplicante]
multiplicare β *UQY*   3641 remanente] reclamante *CW*   3643–4 *om.*
JCWRHuMNOPDKVe TrHaLa U   3645 ad ora] ab ore *D* ora *TrHaLa Q*
3649 fugit] fugat *D Ha*   3653 sensum] sensus *K La*   3654 *om. O*   3655 ipsa]
ipse *QY* hec *R*; metum] secum *B JCWRO^{ac}PVe TrHaLa UZXQY* sitim *O^{pc}*
3659 iamque] iam *MN*; promissa] uel ore *HaLa*; ipsa] ipse *Q*   3661 nisi] nil *O Z*;
(whole line) et si non pietas plus tunc quam praua cupido *D*

SPECVLVM STVLTORVM

to see, and quickly disappeared. Seeing him, Bernard said: 'I spurn your gifts, Dryanus! May all you have stay yours, and you be a long way off! This place is full of devils; the earth brings forth apparitions [3635] from its bosom and gives birth to new monsters.' And now he would have departed, fleeing without hope of return, had not the hope of making a profit held him back. Hope and love of profit conquered the greedy man, while Dryanus pours out more entreaties, bolstered by promises. [3640] In the same way as before, the rope was let down and the wretched Dryanus stayed put, while the lion came out, before Dryanus could either see it with a speedy glance or grasp it with a nimble hand as it dangled. Bernard turned pale when he saw the lion's face, [3645] and chill fear struck all his limbs. He does not think it safe either to stay there or to reveal his fear by crying out or to take to his heels. If he runs away, why! the hungry lion, driven by the pangs of his long hunger, is roaming around with growling jaws; [3650] if he stays put, the place is abominable, for it is full of devils, and once the day has passed, a fearful night will follow. His strength fails him, and fear drains his power of thought; his limbs give way as their master does likewise. The voice of the man calling out in the pit increases his fear, [3655] begging earnestly and in a pitiable plight. He promises wealth and land, he promises turreted palaces—whatever he can promise with heart or mouth. And now he had added so many promises to his entreaties, that his voice and his breath together failed him. [3660] And had not his innate greed, which was greater than his compassion, lured

---

3639 *Spes et amor*: also in *SS*, 3807; *Lawrence*, 17, 991, 1700, 1952; *Epigrams*, no. iii. 18, no. vi. 3; *Miracles*, 1110.
3640 *quas promissa iuuant... preces*: literally, 'prayers which are supported by promises'.
3649 *fame... stimulante*: Ovid, *Tristia*, i. 6. 9.

340 SPECVLVM STVLTORVM

Bernardum traheret ad pietatis opus,
dixissent pariter et uox et uita 'tu autem',
'supremumque uale' cuncta, Dryane, tibi.
3665 Sed quia cuncta facit uincitque pericla cupido,
conuertit cupidi uota uiamque uiri.
Ardet anhela sitis et spe fallente laborem
amplius accensa crescit auara fames.
Funibus immissis tandem Bernardus ab imo
3670 carceris horrendi triste leuauit onus.
Vtque solent crebro uarii contingere fines
casibus in uariis praecipueque malis,
cum prope iam putei foret egressurus ab ore,
inque pedem laetus depositurus humo,
3675 rupto fune miser rursum cecidisset ad ima,
ni cito Bernardi dextra tulisset opem.
Qui subito casu capiens retinensque ruentem
longius abstraxit restituitque suis.
Sic patriae domuique suae rebusque Dryanus
3680 redditus euasit damna, pericla, necem.
Quo facto Bernardus adest poscitque Dryanum
ut firmata fide pacta tenere uelit.
Quem quia mutata facie considerat, olim
facta recordatur, et sua pacta petit;
3685 et si non possit seruare per omnia pactum,
uel saltem pacti pars quota detur ei.
Ille sed econtra pactum negat huncque furoris
arguit et canibus arcet ab aede sua;
quoque magis cogat miserum reticere, minatur
3690 priuandum capitis proprietate sui.
Obstupefactus ad hoc uerbum Bernardus ab aula
festinans digito comprimit ora suo;
compertoque satis quod sit metuenda potestas,

3662–5 *om. ROPVe Tr* 3667 sitis] satis *H CWHuMNDK Tr* 3669 ab] ad *J Tr* 3673 putei] putet *HaLa* 3674 inque] *all MSS* iamque *Mozley* 3675 rupto] rupte *HuMN* 3676 cito] cita *B JROP TrLa Y*; opem] eum *UZQY* 3677 capiens] cupiens *Tr* rapiens β *X* 3681 poscitque] possitque *JHuMN* 3682 firmata fide] seruata fide *CW HaLa* formata fide *QY* seruando fidem *HuMNDK* 3683 facie] faciem *HuMN* 3685 possit] posset *R TrHa Q* 3689 quoque] quodque *D Ha* queque *Z*; cogat miserum] miserum cogat *CWHuMNDK X* 3690 sui] sua β *Ha X* 3691 hoc] hec *HuMN*

SPECVLVM STVLTORVM   341

Bernard to the deed of kindness, his voice and life would have uttered 'The End' together, and the world would have said a last goodbye to you, Dryanus. But because greed is all-powerful and overcomes perils, [3665] it changed the intentions and the steps of the greedy man. Panting thirst burns hot, and greedy hunger is kindled and grows greater when hope is not realized through effort. Letting down the rope, Bernard at last raised up the miserable burden from the depths of the horrible prison. [3670] And as there are often wont to be different endings to different adventures, especially nasty ones, when he was just at the mouth of the pit, and about to emerge, and just about to place his foot joyfully on the earth, the rope broke, and the wretch would have fallen to the bottom again [3675] if Bernard had not lent assistance with his hand; seizing him as he suddenly fell and holding him back as he plunged down, he laboriously pulled him out and restored him to his loved ones. So Dryanus, restored to his country, household, and possessions, escaped injury, danger, and death. [3680]

After this was accomplished, Bernard comes and asks Dryanus to keep the agreement he had confirmed with his promise. Noting that his looks are changed, he recalls what had happened earlier, and asks for what had been promised him—and if Dryanus cannot keep his promise in every respect, [3685] that at least some part of what had been promised should be given him. But he, in reply, denies the promise, accusing him of delirium, and drives him with dogs from his house. And so that he might more effectively force the wretch to keep silence, he threatens him with losing possession of his head. [3690] Stunned at these words, Bernard hurried out of the palace and buttoned his lip. Having learned well that power is to be feared, and that a rich man's

---

3663 *'tu autem'*: the phrase 'tu autem domine miserere nobis' was used to conclude lections in the Divine Office (cf. line 1439 above) and in the monastic refectory; there are also numerous examples of its marginal use for this purpose in 9th-c. *passionalia* and in manuscripts of 10th-c. authors such as Lantfred. It therefore developed a general meaning as a phrase signalling the conclusion of anything (like 'Amen'). See Henry, 'Le Tu Autem', and 'Encore le "Tu Autem"'. The earliest instance cited by Henry occurs in the Archpoet's 'Lingua balbus' (ed. Watenphul and Krefeld, i. 4. 4); Henry does not include the example at *Ysengrimus*, i. 927.

3664 *supremumque uale*: Ovid, *Metamorphoses*, vi. 509.

3667 *spe fallente laborem*: literally, 'when hope deceives/frustrates effort'.

3674 *inque*: see Introduction, p. lxxx, n. 171.

3678 *longius*: literally, 'lengthily'.

342   SPECVLVM STVLTORVM

atque quod interdum diuitis ira furor,
3695   tutius esse putat linguam cohibere, Dryanum
quam de promisso sollicitare suo.
Nam cui sunt etiam suspecta silentia, certe
uerba magis fieri suspiciosa solent.
Diuitis offensam non est incurrere tutum,
3700   cuius rara fides et metuendus amor.

De remuneratione leonis, simiae, et serpentis

Cumque die quarta siluam Bernardus adisset,
Burnello dominum more sequente suum,
en leo deposita solita feritate, ferinis
carnibus oblatis, annuit ore, pede.
3705   Sicque uicem meritis referens gratesque rependens,
et quacumque potest parte iuuare iuuans,
de grege ceruorum quod pinguius esse putabat
abstulit et domino contulit ipse suo.
Vertice submisso nec dum remeante leone
3710   uenit et in dorso simia ligna tulit,
lignorumque struem positam prope quam prius ipse
fecerat ex sicco, praemia monstrat ei.
Quam sibi tollendam se collegisse reuelat
nutibus et signis officiosa suis.
3715   Nec semel aut iterum fuit hoc iterare, sed omni
quo Bernardus adest constituere die.
Haec duo cotidie, carnes et ligna parata,
in nemus adueniens accipiebat ibi.
Sed neque serpenti labor est impensus inanis,
3720   munere qui modico maxima dona dedit;

3698 fieri] *om. HaLa*   3700 rara] rata *CWD*   3701 quarta] quarto *X*; adisset] adiret *JCWRHuMNOPDKVe TrHa^{pc}La UZQY*   3703 en] heri *QY* hinc *Z*   3705–6 *om. Tr*   3706 quacumque] sic quaque β *JWRHuMNOPKVe Ha X* sic quaue *C* sic quoque *La* sic quam *Y* sic qua *QZ* quocumque *U*; iuuans] *Mozley* iuuat *all MSS*   3707 de] ne *HuMN*; quod]que *HuMN*   3708 abstulit] attulit *JCWRHuMNOPDKVe TrHaLa X*   3709 remeante] remanente *CWHuMNDK* retineante *B*   3710 tulit] ferens *JCWRHuMNOPDKVe TrHaLa*   3711 ipse] ipsa *PK HaLa* et ipse *Z*   3713 *om. Tr*   3715 aut] et *JCWO^{pc}PVe TrHaLa*; fuit] sinit *Z* fecit *CWK* facit *HuMN* fecerunt *D*; hoc] hos *QY* hec *Ve X* ista *D*   3716 *(whole line)* in nemus adueniens accipiebat ibi *Z (i.e., line 3718 is repeated here).*   3717 ligna] lingua *CWHu*   3718 in nemus] iuuenis *MN* rusticus *D*; ibi] ei *HaLa*   3720 munere] munera *HaLa*; qui] quo *CWHuMND* pro *Z*

SPECVLVM STVLTORVM

343

anger sometimes rises to madness, he thinks it safer to restrain his tongue [3695] than to pester Dryanus about his promise. For if a man's silence is suspect, certainly his words are even more suspicious. It is not safe to incur the displeasure of a rich man, whose trustworthiness is spasmodic and whose love is to be feared. [3700]

Concerning the Recompense by the Lion, the Ape, and the Snake

When, four days later, Bernard went to the wood, with Burnellus following his master as usual, behold! the lion, laying aside his customary ferocity, brings him game, beckoning him with voice and paw. And in this way he made return for his service, and paid thanks, [3705] assisting him in whatever way he can. From the herd of deer he took whatever he thought fleshiest and brought it to his master. Before the lion departed, the ape came with lowered head, carrying wood on his back, [3710] and showed him a pile of logs placed nearby, which he had made earlier from dry [timber] as a reward for him. By nods and signs, he courteously indicated that he had collected it for him to take away. Nor was this to be repeated once or twice, but they put it into practice on every day [3715] that Bernard came. Daily, when he came to the wood, he received these two gifts, the meat and the gathered logs. Nor was the effort expended on the serpent in vain, since with a small gift he bestowed great benefits. [3720] For on a single occasion he approached,

---

3701 *quarta*: all manuscripts except *X* have the feminine form of the adjective. 'Dies' in medieval Latin is treated as of either gender; Nigel occasionally treats it as masculine (see lines 266, 1319, 1325), but more usually as feminine (see lines 36, 322, 403, 567, 986, 1002, 1864, etc.).

3706 *iuuans*: see Introduction, p. lxxxiii.

3716 *constituere*: contracted form of 'constituerunt', 3rd person plural, perfect tense of 'constituere', 'to establish, agree upon'.

344   *SPECVLVM STVLTORVM*

nam semel accedens supplex similisque uolenti,
    si posset, grates uoce referre sua,
faucibus inclusam gemmam dimisit ab ore,
    imposuitque manu suscipientis eam.

3725   Neue moram faciens faceret collata minoris
    ponderis et precii dona timore sui;
protinus effugiens doni dantisque fauorem
    auget, et obtentu fit fuga grata suo.
Cuius enim non est praesentia grata uidenti,
3730   dona parum sapiunt et sua uerba minus.
Talia Bernardus cernens sensumque ferarum
    factaque dinumerans, hinc stupet, inde probat.
Carnes, ligna, lapis, quae dant leo, simia, serpens,
    moribus ingenuas praedicat esse feras.
3735   Bestia pro meritis dum praemia digna rependit,
    arguit ingratos immemoresque boni.
Quod bene Bernardus, male respondente Dryano
    pro meritis tantis, se didicisse probat.
Munere donatus tanto Bernardus ad urbem
3740   festinat, laeto corde iuuante pedem;
atque sui lapidis uires cognoscere quaerens
    artifices lapidum sollicitare studet.
Sed lapis ignotus nec in urbe repertus eadem
    antea scire negat insita dona sibi.
3745   Quem tamen aeris egens tandem distraxit et auri
    pondere pro triplici fecit abesse sibi.
Cumque domum rediens uellet numerare monetam,
    quam retinere magis quam numerare iuuat,
quem modo uendiderat lapidem, pretiumque tenebat,
3750   impositum loculis comperit esse suis.
Quem retinere uolens timuit, quia principis illum

3722 *om.* U, *add. in lower margin* U²; posset] possit O Tr; grates] gratis CWʰᶜ
3724 imposuitque] supposuitque HuMNDK inspueritque R; manu] manum QY; suscipien-
tis] suscipientes J Y suscipiens et Z   **3725** neue] neque H nec D Q ne U; faceret] facerent B facere CW facerat Z   **3726** timore] tenore JRHuMNOK TrHa tenere
CWPDVe tumorem La   **3728** fit] sic CW Tr sit U   **3729** uidenti] uidete
Wʰᶜ HuMN uideri K   **3730** minus] nimis HuMN La   **3731** sensumque] cen-
sumque JO X fb   **3734** ingenuas] ingenuis RVe ingeniis Tr   **3739** donatus]
dotatus WRHuMND   **3740** pedem] pede CM Q   **3744** negat] negant R
3745–6 *om.* HaLa   **3745** distraxit] destruxit CW ZQY detraxit Ve distruxit X; et
auri] in aurum Z in auri Ve Q   **3746** pondere] spondere HuMN   **3747** rediens]
ueniens R Ha   **3750** impositum] suppositum CWHuMNDK   **3751** timuit
quia] timuitque HaLa

SPECVLVM STVLTORVM 345

submissively and seeming to want to give thanks with his voice if he could, and dropped from his mouth a jewel held in his jaw, placing it in the hand of the receiver. Nor would he, by loitering, make the gift bestowed of less worth [3725] and value through fear of him; by retreating at once, he increased the appreciation of both gift and giver, and the gift is made pleasing by his departure. For when anyone's presence is not pleasing to the beholder, his gifts win little favour and his words less. [3730] Seeing all this, and registering the understanding shown by the animals and what they had done, Bernard is filled with astonishment on one hand and admiration on the other. The meat, logs, jewel given by the lion, ape, and serpent, show them to be beasts of noble character. In paying worthy rewards for services rendered, [3735] the animals implicitly reproached those who are ungrateful and forgetful of a good turn. This, Bernard showed he had learned well, when Dryanus gave such a bad response to such great services. Having been presented with this great gift, Bernard hurried off to town, his steps lightened by his joyful heart, [3740] and, seeking to know the powers of his stone, he makes assiduous enquiries of jewellers. But being unknown, and never before found in that town, the stone makes it impossible to know its properties. However, needing money, he eventually sold it, [3745] and parted with it for three times its weight in gold. When, on his return home, he wanted to count his money— which it gives him even more pleasure to have than to count—he found the stone he had just sold, and the payment for which he possessed, nestling in his purse. [3750] He wanted to keep it but was afraid to,

---

3728 *obtentu*: 'obtentus' = 'offering' (*DMLBS* 1c). An instance of the rhetorical figure of hypallage (exchange of cases): the grammatical subject is 'fuga', but the logical subject is 'obtentus'.

3745 *distraxit*: 'distrahere' = 'to sell' (Niermeyer; *DMLBS* 10).

346 SPECVLVM STVLTORVM

emerat eunuchus, uir bene notus ei.
Vnde celer ueniens, simulans errore retentum,
reddidit emptori fida timore manus.

3755 Vix Bernardus erat intra sua tecta receptus,
cum lapis in loculis ecce reuersus adest.
Reddidit eunucho rursus uelut ante relatum,
sed redeunte domum rursus et ipse redit.
Iamque reuersus adest totiens quotiensque relatus,

3760 et uice conuersa res uariata fuit,
quod murmur populi regis peruenit ad aures
et rumor lapidis se referentis ita.
Qui nouitate rei ductus praecepit adesse
non lapidem solum sed simul hunc et eos.

3765 Partibus accitis, mixtus cum diuite pauper
intrat, et ingressus atria lata replet.
Sub damno capitis, sub conditionis et urbis,
subque fide Christi, quaque tenentur ei,
rex iubet ut si quis factum factique tenorem

3770 nouerit, impune dicat et absque metu;
quae sit causa latens, quanam ratione lapillum
collatum totiens nil retinere queat;
unde sit allatus uel qua regione repertus,
quod sit ei nomen, gloria si qua latet.

3775 Surgit ad hanc uocem poscensque silentia solus
Bernardus regis procidit ante pedes;
exurgensque statim, positoque timore, resumptis
uiribus ebibitis, ora resoluit ita:
'Quatuor in puteum nuper cecidere profundum,

3780 ex quibus unus homo tresque fuere ferae.
Exitus omnis eis fuit interdictus et esset

3754 reddidit] reddit *Ha Z*; fida] feda *QY* peda *Z*　　　3756 ecce] esse *CW*; reuersus]
receptus　*CWHuMN*　repertus　*DK*　　　3759 iamque]　namque　*DK*　*ZQY*
3761–825 *transp. after 3853 O*　　　3761 *om. Z*　　　3762 rumor] minor *HaLa*; referentis]
reserentis *HuMN* referemus *Tr*　　　3764 hunc] *om. Ha Z*　　　3765 accitis] accisitis *C*
acutis *D La* attitis *P* a cunctis *Z* acutis /uel auditis *Ha*　　　3766 ingressus] ingressis
HuMNK　　　3767 conditionis] conditione *O Z*　　　3768 subque] sedque *HuMN*;
tenentur] tenetur *HuMNDK* teneretur *C* tenerentur *H*　　　3771 quanam] quenam *H*
qua non *O*ac *Tr U* qua uel *O*pc　　　3772 nil] non *OP*　　　3773 regione] racione *K*
Ha racione regione *La*　　　3777 positoque] positeque *D* positorum *Y* posito *ZQ*
3778 ebibitis] ebitis *QY*; ora] ore *CWD* hora *Z*　　　3781 esset] esset /uel erat *Ha*

SPECVLVM STVLTORVM

because it had been bought by a eunuch of the prince, a man well known to him. So he quickly returned, pretending that it had been kept by mistake, and the hand made honest by fear returned it to the purchaser. Hardly was Bernard back in his house, [3755] than, lo and behold, the stone is back in his purse. Again he took it back to the eunuch as before, but when he returned home it once more returned too. And now, so often had it been taken back, and so often had it returned, and the action been cancelled by its opposite, [3760] that the people's talk, and the gossip about the stone that returned itself in this way, had reached the ears of the king. Intrigued by the unusual nature of the occurrence, he ordered not only the stone but also Bernard and the people to appear before him. The regions having been summoned, rich and poor alike enter, [3765] and once inside, they fill the spacious hall. On pain of death, of loss of rank and citizenship, on the Christian faith, by which they are bound to him, the king orders that if anyone knows of the occurrence and its course, let him speak with impunity and without fear [3770]—what is the hidden cause, for what reason nothing can retain the stone handed over so many times, where it came from or in what region it was found, and what its name, and if it has any secret reputation.

Bernard alone rises at this speech, and begging silence, [3775] throws himself before the king's feet. Rising immediately, and casting aside his fear, recovering his temporarily vanished strength, he spoke as follows: 'Once, four beings fell into a deep pit, of which one was a man and three were wild animals. [3780] Egress was completely debarred them, and would have been so for all time, had it not been for

---

3763 *nouitate rei*: also in *Miracles*, 1102, 1110, 2652.
3774 *qua*: see n. to line 908.

348 SPECVLVM STVLTORVM

tempus in omne suum, ni mea cura foret;
namque loci talis puteus fuit, ordine tali
dispositus, caeca nocte tegente diem,

3785 quod semel illapsus semper remaneret ibidem,
si non alterius cura leuasset eum.

Dum nemus ingrederer, solo comitatus asello,
auribus insonuit uox miseranda meis,
quam dum persequerer multo discrimine tandem

3790 assequor, inquirens quaeue uel unde foret.
Quae mihi respondit quoniam foret illa Dryani,
qui iam factus erat quatriduanus ibi.

In puteum lapsi fuerant leo, simia, serpens,
hospes et ipse tribus quartus adauctus erat.

3795 Sed tamen id tacuit, ne me terreret eorum
nomine prolato, corriperemque fugam.

Sed de postfacto res est patefacta, fuitque
nota satis misero teste labore meo.

Anxius ille nimis mortisque timore coactus,

3800 hinc spondebat opes, inde petebat opem.
Iurauitque mihi per numina summa, suumque
baptismum, Christi per caput atque pedes;
per sanctum Iacobum, per Thomam Cantuariensem,
quos etiam nudo uouit adire pede,

3805 quod mihi res et opes, sed et omnia dimidiaret,
si meus inde labor tollere posset eum.

Spes et amor lucri multum suasere, Dryano
multiplicante preces, ut misererer ei.

Sed plus teste Deo uicit miseratio mentem

3810 et dolor et gemitus quam sua dona meam,
iunctaque cum lacrimis tandem miseratio mentis

3782 ni] si *MN* in *J XQ*   3783 namque] nam *ZQY*; talis] calis *N* positu β
positus *U* positi *X*   3784 caeca] una *WHuMNDK* tota *Q*   3785–6 *om. B*
JCWRHuMNOPDKVe TrHaLa UZQY   3785 illapsus] *Mozley* illapsum *H X*
3791 quoniam] quam *La* quod uox *QY* uox *Z*; foret] fuit *R U* forte *P*   3794 adauctus]
adductus *MN Ha* adauctas *Ve* et auxtus *Z*   3796 prolato] probato *CW QY* prolata *U*;
corriperemque] corripereque *C* arriperemque *HaLa*   3797 patefacta] patefacto *Q*
manifesta *JCWRHuMNOPDKVe TrHaLa*   3802 baptismum] baptisma *B*
JCWHuMNOPDVe TrHaLa UXQY fc suumque per baptisma *Z*   3803–4 *transp. O*
3804 uouit] uenit *D fc*; pede] pe *M* pedes *JO La*   3807 suasere] suadere *HuMN*
HaLa fc   3808 ut] et *HaLa*; misererer] miserer *C* miseretur *Tr* miserabar *HaLa*
3810–11 *om. B JCWRHuMNOPDKVe TrHaLa UZQY*

SPECVLVM STVLTORVM 349

my assistance. For the pit was in such a place, and shaped in such a way, with black night obscuring the daylight, that he who once fell in would remain there forever, [3785] if someone else's efforts did not raise him up. As I entered the wood, accompanied only by my donkey, a pitiful cry echoed in my ears. I followed and at length, with great difficulty, came up with it, and asked what and from where it was. [3790] It answered me that it was the voice of Dryanus, who had been there four days now. A lion, an ape, and a snake had fallen into the pit, and he as an added fourth was guest to the three of them. Yet he suppressed this information, lest he might terrify me [3795] by mentioning their names and I might run away. But the truth appeared from what then happened, and was made clear enough to my poor self, as my efforts showed. Under great stress, and driven by fear of death, on the one hand he promised wealth and on the other he begged for aid. [3800] He swore to me by the highest gods, by his baptism and the head and feet of Christ, by Saint James, by Thomas of Canterbury, to whom he vowed he would make barefooted pilgrimage, that he would share with me his wealth and possessions—indeed, everything [3805]—if my efforts could raise him out of there. The hope and love of gain were a powerful persuasion, as Dryanus multiplied entreaties that I should take pity on him, but—as God is my witness—compassion and his misery and groans swayed my mind more powerfully than his gifts. [3810] And eventually, my heart's pity, joined with his tears, swayed and overcame me. What I accomplished through my ingenuity, and

---

3785 *H* and *X* are the only witnesses to lines 3785–6, and both read 'illapsum', presumably taking 'quod' to be a (neuter) relative pronoun ('that which') rather than a conjunction; Mozley correctly points out that 'eum' in 3786 refers to the subject of the verb 'remaneret', and 'illapsus' therefore requires the masculine nominative ending.

3803 St James of Compostela and St Thomas Becket. For this line to be metrical, '-uar-' needs to be pronounced as a single short syllable; on 'u' as a half-consonant, see Stotz, *Handbuch*, iii. 147 (§ 111.1), and cf. n. to line 1192.

3807 *Spes et amor*: see n. to line 3639.

350   *SPECVLVM STVLTORVM*

persuadendo simul uimque ferendo mihi.
Artibus ergo meis, multo comitante labore,
    quid factum fuerit facta loquuntur adhuc.

3815 Quod leo, quod serpens, quod simia non perierunt,
    non ego Bernardus causa, sed ille fuit.

Nam, nisi propter eum, quia cetera turba latebat,
    qua prece, quo pretio, curque grauarer ego?

Quatuor extraxi, fuit ille nouissimus horum,
3820   cum quibus et primum nollet habere locum.

Vltimus exiuit sed uix tardeque Dryanus,
    non quia tardus ego, sed grauis ille fuit.

Ergo grauem dixi, quem multo tum grauiorem
    optarem stricto iure fuisse meo.

3825 Rupta forent utinam mea uincula cuncta repente,
    et me frustrassent arsque laborque meus.

Funibus abruptis puteus clausisset iniquum,
    texissetque suum nox tenebrosa caput.

Reddidit obsequium dignum mihi cura ferarum,
3830   et maiora dedit dona labore meo.

Nam leo cotidie carnes de caede ferarum
    praestat, et aduentum praeuenit ipse meum.

Simia ligna legit, quae tuto lecta reponit
    inque loco certo praeparat illa mihi.

3835 Haec quotiens quantumque uolo mihi tollere tollo,
    tamquam pro meritis certa tributa meis.

Hunc etiam lapidem serpentis ab ore recepi,

3812 simul…mihi] mihi…simul *CWHuMNPDK*; *(whole line)* persuadendo mihi quam bona cuncta sua *ZQY*   3813 artibus] auribus *W*ᵃᶜ*HuMN* uiribus *D fc* 3814 quid] quod *JCWHuMNOPDKVe TrHaLa U*; loquuntur] loquetur *X* loquentur *OPVe Tr U*; adhuc] ad hoc *XY*   3817 quia] qui *MN*   3818 grauarer] grauaret *MN* 3820 quibus] primus quilibet *HaLa*; primum nollet] premium uellet *X* primum uellet *Ha Z* primum noluit *La*   3821 *om. O*   3822 ille] ipse *UZ*   3823 tum] tamen *H JHuMNOPVe TrHaLa Z* cum *RD QY*   3825 rupta] sumpta *HuMN* sumpta rupta *W*; cuncta repente] penultima cuncta *HuMNDK*   3826–53 *transp. after 3760 O* 3826 frustrassent] frustassent *HuMN* frustraret *Z* frustraret *P*; arsque] ars et *Z* timor *HaLa*   3827 abruptis] obruptis *Tr Z*; puteus] puteum *HaLa Z* petens *J* 3828 nox] uox *CM* nos *J*   3830–1 *om. DOPVe; transp. after 3832 Ha fc; lines repeated in alternative form* $Z_{(1)}Z_{(2)}$ 3830 *(whole line)* sit (sic *Tr* $Z_{(2)}$)) fera non fera sit (fit *Tr om.* $Z_{(2)}$)) premia digna ferens *R Tr* $Z_{(2)}$ 3831 *(whole line)* nam leo preclarus (preclaras *Tr*) carnes referendo (ferendo *Tr*) ferinas (ferines $Z_{(1)}$) *R Tr* $Z_{(1)}$ 3832 ipse] ipsa *OVe Ha*   3833 tuto] tuta *CHuMN* irito *Ve*   3835 haec] hoc *R UZ*; quantumque] quantumcumque *C* quantumue *P* quantum *QY* quemcumque *Z*; tollo] tollit *CWHuMND* tollunt *K*

SPECVLVM STVLTORVM

with the aid of a lot of effort, the facts declare to this day. Not I, Bernard, but he, was the reason why the lion, the snake, and the ape did not perish. [3815] For, since the rest of them were hidden, why should I have been worked on by any entreaty of promise of reward except on his account? I brought four of them out, and he was the last of them, not wanting to take first place among them. [3820] Last, but with difficulty and slowly, Dryanus emerged—not because I was slow, but because he was heavy. Heavy I call him, but in all honesty I could wish he'd been much heavier. Would that all my ropes had suddenly broken, [3825] and my ingenuity and effort had disappointed me! If the rope had broken, the pit would have swallowed up the villain, and dark night would have closed over his head. The solicitude of the wild animals rendered me worthy recompense, and gave me gifts greater than my service. [3830] For the lion, anticipating my arrival, daily provides meat from wild animals he has killed. The ape gathers wood, and when it's gathered stows it safely, making it ready for me in a safe place. From this I take whatever I want as often as I want, [3835] as an unfailing tribute for my services. From the mouth of the snake I also received this stone, which is the subject of the present discussion. Whether it

---

3824 *stricto iure*: 'by strict letter of the law' (*OLD* s.v. 'strictus' 3b).

352   SPECVLVM STVLTORVM

propter quem praesens quaestio mota fuit.
Cui tamen an alia quam quod nequeat retineri
3840   insita sit uirtus, nescio, teste Deo.
Haec ita sunt, domine mi rex; aliterque locutum
quam fuerit seruum non reor esse tuum.
Ipse uelim sine me quaeras faciasque requiri,
uera rei series quae sit et an sit ita.
3845   Praemia ueridicus capiam, falsumque locutus
si fuero, gladio uel cruce plectar ego.'

Sententia regis pro Bernardo

Talibus auditis, rex iussit adesse Dryanum;
nec mora, iussus adest, infitiatur opus.
Sed quia de facto regi constabat, et ipsa
3850   res fuit indiciis certificata tribus,
protulit edictum, uel consentire Dryanum
ut cum Bernardo dimidiaret opes,
uel quod per triduum putei loca nota subiret,
adiunctus tribus his cum quibus ante fuit.
3855   In commune placet cunctis sententia regis,
Bernardoque satis res ita gesta placet.
Maluit ergo sua se dimidiare Dryanus
et seruare simul pacta fidemque suam
quam se fortunae tali committere, totum
3860   quae sibi surriperet dimidiando nihil.
Dimidians igitur Bernardo cuncta, Dryanus
tristis et inuitus dimidiata dedit.
Nec minus ingrati nomenque notamque perennem
incurrit facti conditione sui.

3838 mota] facta *H ZQY fc*   3839 cui] qui *O HaLa*   3841 aliterque] alterque
CWMN Z alacrique *Tr*   3842 fuerit] fuerat *H Tr UX*   3843 uelim] uolo *ZQY*
3845 locutus] locutum *HaLa* loc< > *Z (leaf cut away)*   3847 adesse] adire *CW*
3848 iussus] missus *CMN*; infitiatur opus] inficietur opus *U* insisitatur *H* rege iubente suo
JCWRHuMNOPDKVe TrHaLa QY fc rege iubente < > *Z (leaf cut away)*   3849 sed]
et *JCWRHuMNOPDKVe TrHaLa*   3853 loca nota] loce nota *Y* nota loca *CW; lines
3761–825 transp. to follow this line in O*   3854 adiunctus] adiunctis *K Z*   3855 in]
an *CWHuMN*   3856–7 res ita gesta—ergo sua] *om. HaLa*   3857 se] *om. HuMNO*
3858–61 *om. DP*   3861 igitur] itaque *CWHuMNK* ergo *U*   3862 dimidiata]
dimidianda *H X*   3863–72 *om. HuMN*   3863 nomenque] nomen *JCWROPDVe*
TrHaLa U   3864 *BH U* end here

SPECVLVM STVLTORVM

353

has any other power than that it cannot be kept, I do not know, as God is my witness. [3840] This is how things are, my lord king; I do not think your servant has spoken any other than it was. I ask you to make enquiries of others than me, and to have it investigated what was the true course of events and whether it was thus. If I have told the truth, let me be rewarded, if I have spoken falsely, [3845] let me be punished with the sword or the gallows.'

The King's Verdict in Favour of Bernard

Having heard this, the king ordered Dryanus to be summoned. The order given, he at once appears, and denies the deed. But because the king was clear about the affair, and the event was authenticated by three pieces of evidence, [3850] he issued a decree that Dryanus should consent either to share half his wealth with Bernard, or that he should go into the familiar pit for three days, along with the three he had been with before. The king's verdict is generally pleasing to all, [3855] and Bernard is happy that the matter should be managed thus. So Dryanus preferred to divide his possessions, and to keep at once his promises and his good faith, than to surrender himself to such a chance, which would share nothing but take everything from him. [3860] So Dryanus shared everything with Bernard, and sadly and reluctantly gave him half. And nonetheless he acquired the name and eternal reputation of an ingrate by virtue of his deed.

3848 *nec mora, iussus adest*: also at *Miracles*, 526.

SPECVLVM STVLTORVM

354

3865 Ex tunc Bernardus fit diues, flente Dryano,
quod sic perdiderat tanta, dolore graui.
Taliter ecce luunt ingrati saepe, quod ipsi
non reddunt digna praemia pro meritis.

Expedit idcirco melius quandoque dedisse
3870 corde libenti quam detinuisse manum.
Maxime pro meritis impendere praemia digna
est pietatis opus, et iubet ista Deus.
Non hominis labor aut opus usque moretur apud te
mane, quod hinc non sit clamor in aure Dei.
3875 Et noua lex dicit quod quilibet est bene dignus
uir mercede sua, teste labore suo.
Ergo qui non dat, dum tempus postulat aut res,
suscitat ipse sibi damna nociua nimis.
Cedat in exemplum cunctis uiuentibus ista
3880 Burnelli uita, nam docet auctor ita.
Non quod uerba sonant sed quicquid mystice signant
Scrutetur lector caute quid ipsa uelint.
Designare sibi poterit tunc forte uidere
plura pericla mali iure cauenda sibi.
3885 Nam sunt nonnulli transcendere magna uolentes,
et nituntur ad hoc nocte dieque simul,
qui dum magna petunt et semper ad ardua tendunt,
saepe repente ruunt, saepeque deficiunt.
Contra naturam uel sortem quaerere quicquam,
3890 nemo potest illud reddere uel facere,
Burnello teste, qui, dum quaesiuit inepta,

3865 fit diues] *om. La Z*   3866 quod] quos *C* qui *ZQY*; dolore] labore *R Tr*
3867 ecce] ergo *CWP X* ipsi *Ha*   3870 manum] manu *HaLa*; *(whole line)* gratuito
corde quam tenuisse manu *ZQY*   3871 maxime pro] saltem pro *DK* proque bonis
ZQY   3872 est] et *JD*   3873 moretur] moratur *HuMN*   3874 sit clamor]
clamet *QY* fit *Ha*   3877 dum] cum *JCWHuMNODKVe La ZXQY*   3878 sibi]
mihi *MN* sui *HaLa*   3879 uiuentibus] uenientibus *M QY*   3879–80 *om. J*
3880 nam] non *Tr Z*   3882 *(whole line)* discretus lector denotet (denotat *Z*) illa (ille
Z) sibi *ZQY*; *Z ends here*   3883 designare sibi] designari sibi *X* et cum signauerit *D QY*
que bene cum uideat *K*   3887 qui dum] quidam *QY*; semper ad ardua tendunt] talia
certa (certe *R* circa *JW X*) laborant *JCWROVe Tr X* tali iure (iura *Ha*pc) laborant *Ha* tali cura
laborant *La* talia certa labo *P* circa uana laborant *QY*   3888 saepe] atque *QY*
3889 quicquam] quicquid *HuMN*   3890 illud] recte *QY*   3891 quaesiuit] qui
fuit *QY*; inepta] inepte *HuMNDK QY*

SPECVLVM STVLTORVM

355

From then on Bernard was rich, and Dryanus lamented [3865] with deep sorrow that he had thus lost so much. See, this is how ingrates often pay for not bestowing worthy rewards on services rendered. So it's better on occasion to have given a gift with a willing heart than to have stayed one's hand. [3870] To pay due recompense for services is a deed of the greatest piety, commanded by God. Let not a man's toil or assistance hang on you until the morrow, that there be no complaint of it in the ear of God. The New Testament says that a man is worthy of the hire [3875] to which his labour entitles him. So whoever does not give, when time and cause require it, creates injurious harms for himself. Let this life of Burnellus be an example to all, for this is its author's teaching. [3880] Let the reader pay careful attention, not to what the words say, but to their hidden meaning, to what they are driving at. Then perhaps he will be able to detect and see many risks of misfortune which he ought to beware of. For there are some who wish to climb to greatness, [3885] and strive after this both night and day, but while they seek greatness and strive for the heights, often they suddenly fall and often fail. To seek something against the will of Nature or Fate is what no one can either grant or accomplish. [3890] Burnellus is a witness: seeking foolish things, he always remained what he was at

---

3875–6 Luke 10: 7.
3877 *dum tempus postulat aut res: Disticha Catonis*, ii. 5. 2.

SPECVLVM STVLTORVM

semper permansit quod prius ipse fuit.
Est igitur felix aliena pericula cautum
quem faciunt, formant et ratione regi.

3895 Plura loqui possem sed nolo scribere plura,
sufficiant ista carmina tam modica.
Deprecor ergo pia prece, si quid lector in illis
inueniat uitium uel ratione carens,
corrigat ipse pie, me commendando Marie

3900 felici Nato, quod roget omnis homo!

3892 prius...fuit] fuit...prius *JROPVe TrHaLa fb*   3893 igitur felix] felix igitur
R felix *HaLa*; cautum] cauere *QY*   3894 quem] que *QY*; faciunt formant et] nequeunt
regere nec *QY*   3896 *Lines 3321–691 transp. to follow this line in M and N*; sufficiant]
sufficiunt *JCWVe TrLa QY*   3897 quid] quod *MNDK QY*   3898 uitium] uitii *R*
Tr, uel] seu *HaLa*   3900 roget] rogat *Ha* reget *MN X*; amen *add. JHuMNDK TrLa*;
(whole line) atque pio nato (nata *Y*) sit cui laus et honor *D QY*

SPECVLVM STVLTORVM 357

the outset. So, happy is the man who is made prudent by another's perils, and is taught to be ruled by moderation. I could say more, but I don't want to write more; [3895] let these few verses be enough. So with sincere prayer I beg, if in these verses the reader finds any fault or silliness, let him kindly correct it, commending me to the Blessed Son of Mary, which should be the prayer of every man! [3900]

3893–4 Raymo claims this line is echoed by the 13th-c. writer Albert of Stade (*Troilus*, ed. Gärtner, iv. 583), but Albert, like Nigel, is simply quoting a well-known proverb: 'Felix quem faciunt aliena pericula cautum'; see Walther, *Proverbia*, 8952; Walther, *Nachträge*, 36887a.

APPENDIX A

Manuscript Descriptions and Early Printed Editions

MAIN MANUSCRIPTS

I have collated the 41 medieval manuscripts of *SS*, and have personally examined those in London (*A*, *B*, *C*, *K*, *U*, *X*), Oxford (*E*, *F*, *G*, *H*, *I*, *W*), Brussels (*O*, *P*), and Munich (*Mu*). For the remainder I have had to rely on photographic copies supplied in the form of microfilms, CDs, or electronic downloads. Of the fragments, I have collated all except *fq*, in the printed versions in the case of *ft* and *fu*, and in person in the case of *fm* and *fn*. The travel restrictions imposed by the Covid pandemic prevented further visits even to the more accessible Continental libraries. These short manuscript descriptions are not therefore intended to give a palaeographical or codicological account of each item (for which reference should be made to the catalogue entries cited at the end of each entry); instead they concentrate on the evidence of date, geographical location, and ownership history, as evidence for the long popularity and wide diffusion of *SS*. They also give some details of major lacunae and textual dislocation, since these features potentially have some bearing on the question of the poem's development. That is, if these gaps and dislocations can be traced to a physical origin, they do not constitute evidence of different versions of the poem, but simply the accidents of transmission over a period of several centuries.

References to the bibliographical or digital sources from which the information is taken are provided at the end of each entry. Since almost all these sources are cited only here, they are not included in the main Bibliography and the references are given here in full. For the reader's convenience, I have cited links to digitized versions of manuscripts and manuscript catalogues where they are readily available; it should be noticed, however, that digitization is proceeding apace these days and this information should not therefore be taken as complete or final.

The abbreviation 'RMT' after a manuscript date means that Professor Rodney Thomson, who kindly examined sample photos of each manuscript on my behalf, has corrected a date given by Mozley or a manuscript catalogue.

360   APPENDIX A

A London, British Library, Harley 2422, fos. 2^r–81^v (Mozley's A)

Parchment. s. xiii^2.

Contents: *SS* (ends at 3542), with *Epistle*.

History: England. William Oakley (s. xv–xvi) inscribed 'Willmus Ukelej' (fo. 1^v). The name John Paschall (s. xvii) appears on fos. 41^v, 42^v, 54^v. There is a note in the hand of John Covel (1638–1722), chaplain of the Levant Company at Constantinople 1670–76, later Master of Christ's College, Cambridge, and the number XXVIII (fo. 1^v), corresponding to the numbering of his catalogue (Add. 22911, fos. 180–3), where this manuscript is no. 28 in the Latin section; it was sold, together with Covel's other manuscripts, to Edward Harley on 27 Feb. 1715/6.

The Harley Collection, formed by Robert Harley (1661–1724), 1st earl of Oxford and Mortimer, politician, and Edward Harley (1689–1741), 2nd earl of Oxford and Mortimer, book collector and patron of the arts, was bequeathed to Edward's widow, Henrietta Cavendish, during her lifetime and thereafter to their daughter, Margaret Cavendish Bentinck, duchess of Portland. The Harley manuscripts were sold by the Countess and the Duchess in 1753 to the nation for £10,000 under the Act of Parliament that also established the British Museum; they form one of the foundation collections of the British Library.

BL online *Catalogue of Illuminated Manuscripts* (includes a reproduction of fo. 64^r).

B London, British Library, Arundel 23, fos. 1^r–66^v (Mozley's B)

Parchment. s. xv med. Fos. 1^r–76^v are written in a humanist hand by the English scribe Thomas Candour, who also copied BL, Cotton Julius A. VII (digitized), fos. 55^r–65^r, containing John of Salisbury's *Entheticus in Policraticum* on fos. 55^r–60^v and the verse prologue to Nigel's *Tractatus* on fos. 60^v–65^r.

Contents: *SS* (ends at 3864), with *Epistle*; two of Nigel's other works (see Introduction, p. xxxii, n. 9), a life of St Eustace; Herbert of Bosham's *Catalogus Eruditorum beati Thomae*. *SS* lacks lines 849–1386, the result of a missing quire (the manuscript is quired in 10s, with 27 lines to a page; the catchword 'Funditus' on fo. 21^v shows that the following quire originally began with line 849, and the missing 537 lines would fill 20 pages = 10 folios).

MANUSCRIPT DESCRIPTIONS   361

History: The name of a former owner, Thomas Jakes (d. 1516), appears on fo. 67ᵛ in a late fifteenth-/early sixteenth-century hand. Jakes was Clerk of the Warrants of the Inner Temple; 'men in his profession built up their own personal collections of books' (Connolly, p. 68), as can be seen from the bequests in his will. As well as Arundel 23, Jakes owned Cambridge University Library, Ff.5.35, containing a copy of Mandeville's *Travels* and the C text of *Piers Plowman*, and BL, Cotton Nero C. I, containing *Statutes of the Realm* and the *Modus tenendi Parliamentum* (Boffey, pp. 126–7 and n. 43). He married Elizabeth Frowyk, widow of the Chief Justice of the Common Pleas Sir Thomas Frowyk, who brought into his possession BL, Additional 37659 and Additional 37657. Jakes's will directed his wife to give the Frowyk books to the Inner Temple, in memory of himself, Elizabeth, and Sir Thomas (*ODNB*, s. Frowyk, Sir Thomas; Connolly, pp. 59, 68–9).

BL online Catalogue of Manuscripts.
Julia Boffey, *Manuscripts of English Courtly Love Lyrics* (Cambridge, 1985).
Margaret Connolly, *Sixteenth-Century Readers, Fifteenth-Century Books: Continuities of Reading* (Cambridge, 2019).
David Rundle, 'The Scribe Thomas Candour and the Making of Poggio Bracciolini's English Reputation', *English Manuscript Studies 1100–1700*, xii (2005), 1–25.

Be Berlin, Staatsbibliothek zu Berlin, Preussischer Kulturbesitz, theol. qu. 214, fos. 181ʳ–234ʳ (not known to Mozley)

Paper. s. xv.

Contents: A composite manuscript, containing a miscellany, including *SS* (ending at line 2602), with *Epistle*, in part 3, accompanied by the 'Liber de vita et moribus antiquorum philosophorum et poetarum' formerly attributed to Walter Burley (see below, p. 396).

History: Formerly owned by the convent of Crutched Friars ('cruciferi') of Falkenhagen in the countship of Lippe.

Valentin Rose, *Die Handschriften-Verzeichnisse der königlichen Bibliothek zu Berlin*, xiii, Verzeichnis der lateinischen Handschriften, ii. 3 (Berlin, 1905), no. 924, pp. 1133–5.

C London, British Library, Cotton Titus A. XX, fos. 4ʳ–50ᵛ (Mozley's C)

Parchment. Internal indications and script favour a date between 1367 and 1400.

362 APPENDIX A

Contents: A miscellany of Latin verse, including *SS* (without *Epistle*); has links with Bodley 851, Bodley 496, and other manuscripts (Rigg, 1977, pp. 327–8).

History: Formerly owned by John Leland and later by William Camden, whose books passed into the Cotton library. Mozley (*SS*, p. 9) thought that the attribution of some poems in the manuscript to Robert Baston, prior of Scarborough Abbey in the early fourteenth century, and two descriptive poems of Norfolk by an anonymous monk of Peterborough suggested a northern origin. However A. G. Rigg pointed out that the attributions to Baston were in the handwriting of John Bale (who borrowed the manuscript from Leland), and only one is evidentially based (the author's name in the last 4 lines) (Rigg, 1978, pp. 323, 327). Fifteenth-century accounts recording purchases of food and stationery written on the flyleaves suggest the manuscript came from a large monastic house in the vicinity of London. The connections with Rawlinson B. 214, which was written at Waltham Abbey, Essex, one of the most important Augustinian houses in the country, suggest that Titus A.XX might come from the same monastery, but there are other good candidates (e.g. St Albans) in the London area (Rigg, 1977, p. 293). Rigg thinks the 'codex Camdeianus' referred to in a note by Richard James (Cotton librarian 1624–38) in Cotton Vespasian E. XII (see the entry for MS *X* below) is Titus A. XX, as it has matching readings (Rigg, 1977, p. 294).

A. G. Rigg, 'Antiquaries and Authors: The Supposed Works of Robert Baston, O. Carm.', in M. B. Parkes and Andrew G. Watson, eds., *Medieval Scribes, Manuscripts and Libraries: Essays Presented to N. R. Ker* (London, 1978), pp. 317–31.
—— 'Medieval Latin Poetic Anthologies (I)', *Mediaeval Studies*, xxxix (1977), 281–330.

D Dublin, Trinity College Library, 440, pp. 1–130 (paginated) (Mozley's D)

Parchment. Colker's *Catalogue* dates it to the early 15th c., but Rodney Thomson judges it to be mid-14th c.

Contents: *SS*, followed by *Epistle*. Contains the Interpolation on the Mendicant Orders. At the end of *SS*, 'Explicit Burnellus perfecte Lullay' (p. 125); at the end of the *Epistle*, a colophon: 'Hic locus e[st] mete. Venit Explicit ergo valete'.

History: Belonged to a monk of the Benedictine cathedral priory of St Cuthbert, Durham. On the verso of the flyleaf is an owner's inscription,

MANUSCRIPT DESCRIPTIONS 363

'Constat dompno Petro le/ (in smaller script) monacho Dun'lm'. According to Neil Ker, Peter Lee was warden of Durham College, the Oxford residence of monks from the Durham cathedral priory, in 1523 (N. R. Ker, *Medieval Libraries of Great Britain: A List of Surviving Books* (2nd edn., London, 1964), pp. 62, 256. There is a gap at this point in the list of wardens of Durham College given in *A History of the County of Oxford: Volume 2*, ed. William Page (London, 1907), pp. 68–70 (*British History Online* http://www.british-history. ac.uk/vch/oxon/vol2/pp68-70), but according to Andrew G. Watson's *Supplement* to Ker's Second Edition (p. 92), Lee incepted 1522, and *fl.* 1510–27.

> Marvin L. Colker, *Trinity College Dublin, Descriptive Catalogue of the Mediaeval and Renaissance Latin Manuscripts* (2 vols., Dublin, 1991), ii. 871.

E Oxford, Bodleian Library, Bodley 761 (S.C. 2535), fos. 160ʳ–180ʳ (Mozley's E)

Paper. s. xiv. Written in three hands of about 1360–70 in England.

Contents: A Latin and French miscellany, containing historical and medical items. Includes *SS*, which (like MS *L*) lacks the *Epistle*, and (like MSS *LF*) 2483–3258, and ends at 3448. For a proposed explanation of the lacunae, see Introduction, pp. lxxi–lxxviii. *SS* is headed by the rubric: 'Burnelli speculum merito liber iste vocatur/ Cuius sub specie stultorum vita notatur' (also found in *L* and *F*).

History: Indicated by various notes linking the manuscript with the Bohun family (Thompson, pp. xiv–xvi), including, on fo. 91, a copy of a notarial deed awarding a pension to Thomas de Walmesford, a canon of Godchester (or Good Easter) in Essex, 10 Feb. 1355/6, who had earlier (in 1328 and 1334) been presented to two Essex livings by John de Bohun, earl of Hereford.

For a full description of the contents of this manuscript, see *Chronicon Galfridi Le Baker de Swynebroke*, ed. Edward Maunde Thompson (Oxford, 1889), pp. xii–xv; P. Meyer, 'Notice du MS. Bodley 761 de la Bibliothèque Bodléienne (Oxford)', *Romania*, xxxvii (1908), 509–28.

> *A Summary Catalogue of Western Manuscripts in the Bodleian Library at Oxford which have not hitherto been catalogued in the Quarto Series*, ed. Falconer Madan and H. H. E. Craster, ii. 1 (Oxford, 1922), no. 2535.

F Oxford, Bodleian Library, Bodley 851 (S.C. 3041), fos. 97ᵛ–115ᵛ (Mozley's F)

364   APPENDIX A

Parchment. A composite manuscript, made up of three main parts. Written in the latter part of the fourteenth century; extended and compiled in the early fifteenth century. Several hands; *SS* is by hand A. Like *LE*, *F* lacks 2483–3258, but it also displaces 3259–78 to follow 3432, then repeats 3323–8, and ends with 3435–44, 3347–8, resulting in the following order: 1–2482/ 3279–432 (including 3323–8)/ 3259–78/ 3323–8 (again)/ 3435–44/ 3347–8. The *Epistle* follows *SS*. See Introduction, pp. lxxiii–lxxiv on these changes. As in *LE*, *SS* is prefaced by a rubric: 'Speculum Burnelli merito liber iste vocatur/ Cuius sub specie stultorum vita notatur'. At the end of the poem is a colophon (fo. 114^r): 'Burnelli dicta multo moderamine ficta/ Spernere qui querit semper asellus erit'; Rigg quotes this colophon in his analysis of Bodley 851 (Rigg, 1978, p. 400) but neither there nor in his analysis of Titus A. XX (Rigg, 1979) does he notice that it forms the last two lines of the six that follow *SS* in Titus A. XX (my MS *X*; see below).

Because this manuscript contains the so-called 'Z text' of *Piers Plowman*, it has been much discussed, and there is some disagreement over its features, which does not, however, substantially affect *SS*. What follows is an attempt to summarize the general consensus that emerges from the following accounts:

Ralph Hanna III, 'MS. Bodley 851 and the Dissemination of *Piers Plowman*', pp. 195–202, 312–14 in Hanna, *Pursuing History: Middle English Manuscripts and their Texts* (Stanford, CA, 1996). (First published in *The Yearbook of Langland Studies*, vii (1993), 14–25.)

Ralph Hanna III and Traugott Lawler, *Jankyn's Book of Wikked Wyves*, vol. i (Athens, GA and London, 1997).

George Kane, 'The "Z" Version of *Piers Plowman*', *Speculum*, lx (1985), 910–30.

Kathryn Kerby-Fulton, *Books under Suspicion: Censorship and Tolerance of Revelatory Writing in Late Medieval England* (Notre Dame, IN, 2006).

Kathryn Kerby-Fulton, 'Confronting the Scribe-Poet Binary. The Z-Text, Writing Office Redaction, and the Oxford Reading Circles', in Kathryn Kerby-Fulton, John J. Thompson, and Sarah Baechle, eds., *New Directions in Medieval Manuscript Studies and Reading Practices: Essays in Honor of Derek Pearsall* (Notre Dame, IN, 2014), pp. 489–515.

Kathryn Kerby-Fulton, 'Oxford', in David Wallace, ed., *Europe: A Literary History, 1348–1418* (2 vols., Oxford, 2016), i. 208–26.

A. G. Rigg, 'Medieval Latin Poetic Anthologies (II)', *Mediaeval Studies*, xl (1978), 387–407.

A. G. Rigg, 'Medieval Latin Poetic Anthologies (III)', *Mediaeval Studies*, xli (1979), 468–505.

William Langland. The Z Version, ed. A. G. Rigg and Charlotte Brewer (Toronto, 1983), pp. 2–5.

MANUSCRIPT DESCRIPTIONS 365

Contents: I. (= Hanna's part 3) Walter Map, *De Nugis Curialium*; II. (= Hanna's part 4) a miscellany of Latin *comediae* and poems, which includes *SS* (with *Epistle*); III. (= Hanna's part 5) *Piers Plowman* (the so-called 'Z text', followed by the end of *Piers Plowman* A, and *Piers Plowman* C). Parts I and II were written primarily by Hand A, with some interventions from Hands B and C at the beginning of Part II (Rigg, 1978, p. 389); Part III was written by Hand X, which was also responsible for some additions and corrections in Parts I and II (Hanna and Lawler, 1997, p. 102, n. 172), including *SS* (Kerby-Fulton, 2014, p. 512, n. 31). Rigg, 1978 provides the fullest description of the contents of the manuscript. Hanna 1996 gives the most detailed analysis of its physical make-up; on the basis of quire signatures, catchwords, signs of wear and tear on leaves which were formerly the first and last of separate booklets, and spaces left blank at the end of major text sections, he concludes that 'Bodley 851 was built up over time, as a sequence of discrete booklets, two of which (parts 3 and 4) show ample evidence of a lengthy existence as separate loose quires' (pp. 196–7, quotation on p. 197).

History: A bookplate on fo. 6ᵛ reads 'Iste liber constat Fratri Iohanni de WELLIS Monacho Rameseye', showing that at least Part I belonged to John Wells, monk of Ramsey Abbey, Huntingdonshire, a well-known anti-Wycliffite and scholar of Gloucester College, Oxford, who died in Perugia in 1388. Hanna (1996, pp. 198, 200) thought that Hand A is very possibly that of Wells, and that parts 3 (the *De nugis*) and 4 (the anthology) in Part II might have been copied at Oxford, but that the Z-text, because of relations with other *Piers Plowman* manuscripts, was probably copied 'at the abbey [of Ramsey] or in its neighborhood' (ibid. p. 200) and that Bodley 851 was compiled at Ramsey. Hanna states that the bookplate could belong to part 3 or part 4 or both or neither; Rigg had already acknowledged that the bookplate could refer to any of the seven stages in the manuscript's history which he outlines (Rigg, 1978, p. 390). Rigg initially associated Bodley 851 with Ramsey, although he said it could have circulated elsewhere, 'perhaps in Oxford' (Rigg, 1978, pp. 392–4), but Rigg and Brewer (1983, pp. 4–5) proposed that Part III (a), the Z-text, was written in Oxford, perhaps at Gloucester College, the Oxford residence for Benedictines from Ramsey and Glastonbury. This would explain its textual connections (in Walter Map's *De coniuge non ducenda*) with Cambridge, Trinity College O.9.38 and London, British Library, Cotton Vespasian E. XII (my MS *X*). Bodley 851 shares three other items besides *SS* with these

366 APPENDIX A

manuscripts and Cotton Titus A. XX (my MS *C*); see Rigg, 1979, pp. 501–5. Kerby-Fulton (2014, p. 497) endorsed the suggestion of Gloucester College: 'Monks from Ramsey were going back and forth all the time to Oxford's Benedictine college of Gloucester, where in fact the owner of Bodley 851, John Wells, was prior of students for thirteen years (ibid.).' Kerby-Fulton also cites a personal communication from Malcolm Parkes, leaning towards Oxford provenance, in view of ownership evidence among later Oxford students, one of whom gave it to the Bodleian in 1601. Benedictines often brought books from their abbeys to Oxford, and normally added *ex libris* inscriptions, like the Wells example, to books of this sort. See also Kerby-Fulton, 2016, pp. 214–15. The professionally made bookplate was most probably produced in London.

Fr Frankfurt am Main, Universitätsbibliothek, Barth. 62, fos. 150^r–162^v (not known to Mozley)

Paper. s. xv$^{3/4}$. A composite manuscript (six main hands).

Contents: A large Latin miscellany, including school texts (e.g. *Disticha Catonis*, Alan's *Liber Parabolarum, Floretus*), *SS* (ends at 2602), with *Epistle*. Lines 2053–2464 (the survey of monastic orders) are lacking; for a possible explanation, see Introduction, p. lxxi. A line is left empty after 2052, which ends 'habenda mihi] ut habetur alibi post pamphilum'. This seems to imply that the missing lines 2053–464 appear later in the MS, after *Pamphilus*—but *Pamphilus* does not appear in this MS, so the reference may be to the exemplar.

History: The dialect of the manuscript's German contents links it with West Germany. It is a former possession of the vicar of the Bartholomaeusstift, Jakob Rudesheim (a fifteenth-century inscription on fo. 1^r: 'Iste liber est ex testamento domini Jacobi Rudessheym qui debet tradi in elemosinam quia vendi non potuit. [added by another hand] Sed modo pertinet (ecclesie sancti bartholomei ad liberiam).').

Gerhardt Powitz and Herbert Buck, *Die Handschriften des Bartholomaeusstifts und des Karmelitklosters in Frankfurt am Main* (Frankfurt a. M., 1974), pp. 128–34. (Catalogue available online in www.manuscripta-mediaevalia.de)

G Oxford, Bodleian Library, Digby 27 (S.C. 1628), fos. 1^r–61^v (Mozley's G)

Parchment. s. xv.

MANUSCRIPT DESCRIPTIONS   367

Contents: *SS* (ends at 2746), with *Epistle*, and a few minor items. Contains the Interpolation on the Mendicant Orders. On the missing leaves, see Introduction, pp. lxviii, ciii. Lines 405–26 are displaced to fo. 20^r (where they follow line 766) instead of fo. 13^r, but the mistake was noted by the original scribe, who wrote corrective notes on fo. 12^v and fo. 20^r, with catchwords to indicate the correct sequence. This manuscript is related to MS *I* (see Introduction, pp. ci–ciii).

History: One of the manuscripts that belonged to Thomas Allen of Gloucester Hall (*d.* 1633), who was Kenelm Digby's tutor.

W. D. Macray, *Bodleian Quarto Catalogues* IX, *Digby Manuscripts* (1883), with Notes on Macray's Descriptions of the Manuscripts by R. W. Hunt and A. G. Watson; Appendix: An Edition of Thomas Allen's Catalogue of his Manuscripts by A. G. Watson (Oxford, 1999).

Andrew G. Watson, 'Thomas Allen of Oxford and his manuscripts', in M. B. Parkes and Andrew G. Watson, eds., *Medieval Scribes, Manuscripts & Libraries: Essays Presented to N. R. Ker* (London, 1978), pp. 279–314.

Go [Erfurt], Forschungsbibliothek Gotha, Chart. B 517, fos. 136^r–195^v (Mozley's k)

Paper. Fascicle III (which contains *SS*, ending at 2602, with *Epistle*) is written in one hand; the scribe is identical with that of fascicle VI, i.e. Matthias Czemler of Zeypsch. Both fascicles originate in s. xv$^{1/4}$ (evidence of watermarks and script).

Contents: A very large composite manuscript (seven fascicles), with theological and scientific texts as well as *SS*.

History: At least part of this manuscript comes from Bohemia/ Moravia. In the eighteenth century it belonged to the library of Ludwig Bernhard von Zech.

Elisabeth Wunderle, *Katalog der mittelalterlichen lateinischen Papierhandschriften, aus den Sammlungen der Herzog-von-Sachsen-Coburg-und-Gotha'schen Stiftung für Kunst und Wissenschaft* (Wiesbaden, 2002), pp. 338–49. Wunderle's catalogue is available online in the Münchener DigitalisierungsZentrum (MDZ). See also manuscripta-mediaevalia.de.

The manuscript is digitized and available online at https://dhb.thulb. uni-jena.de.

H Oxford, Bodleian Library, Bodley 496 (S.C. 2159), fos. 146^r–192^r (Mozley's H)

368   APPENDIX A

Paper. s. xv med.

Contents: Comprises two fifteenth-century manuscripts, the first of which is a large Latin miscellany, including the *Historia Alexandri* of Quilichinus of Spoleto, the *Apocalipsis Goliae* and other Goliardic poems, and the elegiac *Romulus*, as well as *SS* (which ends at 3864), with *Epistle*. *SS* concludes with a colophon: 'Sit meritas operis oracio sancta legentes/ Que iungit superis nos toto robore mentis.' Underneath it, 'Corpus scriptoris careat grauitate doloris', and under that, the scribe's initials, 'T. G.', which correspond to the name 'T. Graunt' on fos. 203ᵛ and 236ᵛ. Also includes a hexametric poem on the life of monks, apparently composed by John Matthew, monk of Glastonbury, in 1431, at the desire of the abbot Nicholas Frome (1420–65), and a poem by 'Stoon', a Carthusian monk, in praise of Richard Fleming, bishop of Lincoln (d. 1431), quoting his epitaph.

History: The manuscript was presented to the Bodleian by Sir George More in 1604 (see https://medieval.bodleian.ox.ac.uk/catalog/ for other manuscripts donated by Sir George).

A Summary Catalogue of Western Manuscripts in the Bodleian Library at Oxford which have not hitherto been catalogued in the Quarto Series, ed. Falconer Madan and H. H. E. Craster, ii. 1 (Oxford, 1922), no. 2159.

Ha Halle, Universitäts- und Landesbibliothek, Stolb.-Wern. Za 89, fos. 1ʳ–47ᵛ (known to Mozley only when *SS* was in press; see *SS*, p. 128)

Paper. s. xv (evidence of watermarks, colophon). See item 3's explicit: 'ultimam rosam id est Pater noster. Sic est finis huius deuote contemplacionis et Serti contextionis, finite anno 1466 per C[ONRADUM] G[ESSELEN] peccatorem indeuotissimum et huius contemplacionis inexpertum' (Blaschka, p. 720). The entire manuscript is written by one scribe.

Contents: A Latin miscellany, including *SS* (with *Epistle*), which is the first item, Albertano of Brescia's *Liber consolacionis et consilii*, and other minor items. *SS* ends with a colophon: 'Explicit Speculum Stultorum quod communiter et vulgariter inititulatur brunellus. In multis probandum quoniam corrigit et instruit signanter religiosos' (Blaschka, p. 718).

History: The contents list begins: 'Liber Conradi Gesselen, in quo continentur infrascripti...'. A Konrad Gesselen is known as the

MANUSCRIPT DESCRIPTIONS 369

author of a Low German Cisiojanus (a metrical composition of 24 hexameters designed as a mnemonic for saints' feast days). He also appears in the fifteenth-century records of the University of Rostock.

Anton Blaschka, 'Monumentum Thorunense', *Wissenschaftliche Zeitschrift der Martin-Luther-Universität Halle-Wittenberg*, vii, Gesellschafts- und Sprach-wissenschaftliche Reihe (1957–58), 715–26; id., 'Die neue Handschrift U des Speculum Stultorum', ibid. 727–37. The second of these articles gives detailed lists of lines omitted in Ha, and its variant readings, but since the comparison is with Thomas Wright's defective edition, and Blaschka did not know of all the surviving manuscripts of *SS*, these lists are superseded by my *apparatus criticus*. Blaschka assigned this MS the sigil U but Mozley and Raymo had already assigned this sigil to Sloane 1831B. Blaschka's foliation is one number out.

Hu Huntington Library, San Marino, California, MS HM 80250, fos. 168^v–184^r (not known to Mozley)

Parchment. s. xiv^1.

Contents: William Durandus, *Rationale de divinis officiis*, works by Anselm of Bec, short works by St Augustine; *SS* (with *Epistle*). Contains the Interpolation on the Mendicant Orders.

History: Textually, *Hu* is closely related to *M* and *N*, the two Lincoln manuscripts. An inscription by 'Thome Wynter' at the base of the table of contents on the front flyleaf presents the work in 1482 to a monastic or cathedral library. The manuscript later belonged to the library of the Barons Monson in Burton, Lincolnshire, as is shown by their armorial bookplate on the inside front cover and shelfmarks on the front flyleaf; it was probably acquired by William John Monson, 6th Baron Monson (1796–1826). In 2013 (2 July), it was sold at Sotheby's to Maggs Bros, acting for the Huntington Library, apparently by the Monson family or one of their descendants.

Huntington Library online catalogue.

I Oxford, Bodleian Library, Bodley 780 (S.C. 2583), fos. 1^r–33^v (Mozley's I)

Parchment. s. xv. English.

Contents: *SS* and *Epistle* only. Contains the Interpolation on the Mendicant Orders. Lacks 1116–744 (missing leaves); omits 2747–3258

370 APPENDIX A

(like *G*); copies 3259–448 from an exemplar closely related to *L*; ends at 3448 (like *LEF*). See Introduction, pp. lxviii, ci–ciii.

History: On fo. 1ʳ, 'Donum Jacobj Lee militis', *c.*1611; on fo. 33ᵛ, a fifteenth-century owner's note: 'Iste liber constat Thomas Seruaylle'.

A Summary Catalogue of Western Manuscripts in the Bodleian Library at Oxford which have not hitherto been catalogued in the Quarto Series, ed. Falconer Madan and H. H. E. Craster, ii. 1 (Oxford, 1922), no. 2583.

J Oxford, All Souls College, 37, fos. 171ʳ–196ʳ (Mozley's J)

Parchment. s. xv in.

Contents: A composite manuscript. Hand B, which is responsible for *SS* and *Epistle*, is 'a good bookhand', but despite the neat and elegant script, the scribe does not seem to know Latin well and often writes nonsensical words.

History: An All Souls *ex libris*, 'datus per Henricum Penworth[a]m' (a priest and canon, who on his death in 1438 bequeathed books to the value of 40 marks to Archbishop Chichele for All Souls College; see A. B. Emden, *A Biographical Register of the University of Oxford to A.D. 1500* (3 vols., Oxford, 1957–9), iii. 1459–60. At the end of *SS*, there is the following note: 'Precium scripture .v.s & iiij.d.'

R. M. Thomson, *The University and College Libraries of Oxford* (Corpus of Medieval British Library Catalogues; 2 vols., Oxford, 2015), i. 91.

Andrew G. Watson, *A Descriptive Catalogue of the Medieval Manuscripts of All Souls College, Oxford* (Oxford, 1997), pp. 73–5.

K London, British Library, Additional 38665, fos. 85ʳ–156ʳ (Mozley's K)

Parchment. Mostly s. xv[1].

Contents: A Latin miscellany (includes the *Disticha Catonis* and the elegiac Romulus). Contains *SS*, with *Epistle*. Contains the Interpolation on the Mendicant Orders. The manuscript contains marginal pen drawings of Burnellus wearing a bishop's mitre (see Frontispiece for an example). The four drawings on fos. 87ᵛ, 107ʳ, 114ᵛ, and 132ʳ can be viewed in the British Library's Online Gallery (search <Brunellus>), and printed out.

History: Written largely in the hand of John Streech, a canon of the Augustinian priory of Kenilworth (cf. Add. 35295, which was written about 1422). Many of the items included relate to the Augustinians,

MANUSCRIPT DESCRIPTIONS 371

and on fo. 55ʳ is the colophon 'involvens pannis puerum miserere Iohannis. Streech'.

BL online Catalogue of Manuscripts.

L London, Lambeth Palace Library, 357, fos. 78ʳ–111ʳ (Mozley's L)

Parchment. s. xv¹ (RMT).

Contents: Rolle, other religious texts, various Augustinian documents. *SS* (without *Epistle*), ends at 3448, and lacks 2483–3258. As in *EF*, *SS* is prefaced by a rubric: 'Burnelli speculum merito liber iste vocatur/ Cuius sub specie stultorum vita notatur'. At the end is a colophon: 'Qui scripsit Amen sit benedictus Amen Johannes Batte'.

History: The manuscript is written in several hands, and comes from Duleek, the Irish cell of the Augustininan priory of Llanthony 'as is seen from the presence in it of the Office of St Kenan', who was Llanthony's patron saint (James, *Catalogue*, p. 478).

Montague Rhodes James and Claude Jenkins, *A Descriptive Catalogue of the Manuscripts in the Library of Lambeth Palace*, 5 vols. in 1 (continuous pagination) (Cambridge, 1930–2); the catalogue is available online, in slightly rearranged format, at http://archives.lambethpalacelibrary.org.uk/.

La Sankt Paul im Lavanttal (Kärnten), Stiftsbibliothek, Codex 239/4, fos. 101ʳ–151ᵛ, 161ʳ–184ᵛ (not known to Mozley)

Paper. s. xv med.

Contents: Latin miscellany, of school-text type (Prosper of Aquitaine, *Floretus*, Maximian). *SS* with *Epistle*. There is a break in the poem following line 2592 at the bottom of fo. 151ᵛ; the folios intervening between this point and fo. 161ʳ, where *SS* resumes, were originally left blank (see Introduction, p. c, n. 200). Some of the blank folios were later filled by various unconnected items: on fo. 152ʳ, the fable 'De Catulo et Asello' (no. xvii of the popular collection now known as the elegiac *Romulus, L'Esopus attribuito a Gualtiero Anglico*, ed. Paola Busdraghi (Genoa, 2005), p. 80, Inc. 'Murmuris et caude studio testatus amorem'); on fos. 152ᵛ–153ʳ, a series of quotations from classical and medieval authors against talking too much; on fo. 153ᵛ, three longer quotations, beginning with a definition of the qualities needed by a good king or judge, taken from the commentary on Justinian's *Codex* by the fourteenth-century jurist Lucas de Penna.

372 APPENDIX A

History: Originally from the collegiate church of Spital am Pyrhn in Carinthia (founded as a hospital in 1190 and converted to a collegiate church in 1418). The Benedictine abbey of St Paul im Lavanttal, 'located on the southern tip of Austria near Slovenia, was founded in 1091 from the famous German reform abbey of Hirsau. Although of important religious and cultural influence, it was dissolved in 1782 and its manuscript collection disseminated in various directions. In 1807, however, the Benedictine community of Sankt Blasien in Schwarzwald requested permission to resettle in Austria. First moving to the vacant Augustinian monastery of Spital am Pyhrn, they moved again in 1809 to the abandoned buildings of Sankt Paul, bringing with them not only the manuscripts of Sankt Blasien but those of Spital am Pyhrn as well' (Hill Museum and Manuscript Library website).

Hill Museum and Manuscript Library website, at https://w3id.org/vhmml/readingRoom/view/12801.

Christine Glassner, *Inventar der Handschriften des Benediktinerstiftes St. Paul im Lavanttal bis ca. 1600* (Vienna, 2002), online at https://manuscripta.at/stpaul/inv/.

M Lincoln, Cathedral Chapter Library, 105, fos. 91^r–116^v (Mozley's M)

Parchment. s. xiv. Two originally separate volumes.

Contents: *SS* (with *Epistle*) is the only major item in Part 2. Contains the Interpolation on the Mendicant Orders. On the close textual relations between *Hu*, *M*, and *N*, see Introduction, pp. xciv–xcvi.

In *M* and *N*, but in no other manuscript, there is a major displacement of text: lines 3602–896 follow line 3320, so that the resulting order is 3320/ 3602–896/ 3321–3601/ 3897–3900. In *N*, line 3602 follows directly on line 3320, but (what looks like) a different hand has added the opening words of line 3321 in the margin to direct the reader to go there for the continuation of the text; in *M* (as Mozley notes in his *apparatus criticus*, *SS*, p. 138), the scribe leaves a line vacant after line 3320, but otherwise the copying continues without a break, and there is no sign of embarrassment at the textual confusion the displaced text creates (see Introduction, pp. lxix, xciv, xcvi). The error is most probably the result of displaced leaves in the common ancestor; if it had quires of 4, and an average of 35–6 lines to a page, the displacement of a quire (8×35–6) would account for the transposition of these 285 lines.

Hand 2 (fos. 91^r–98^v) is an anglicana hand; Hand 3 (fos. 99^r–118^v) begins by imitating Hand 2 but gradually becomes more formal.

MANUSCRIPT DESCRIPTIONS   373

History: 'At the head of f. 5ʳ, in a rough late fifteenth-century hand, "liber cantarii domini Nicholai de Cantilupo Lincolniensis". At the head of f. 62ᵛ is pencilled "Liber domini Cantilupo", perhaps in an earlier hand. The Cantelupe Chantry in Lincoln cathedral was founded in 1360 by Joan, widow of Nicholas third baron Cantelupe, Lord of Gresley, Notts., who died in 1355' (Thomson, p. 79; see also p. xviii). 'A man of notable religious conviction, [Cantelupe] went on pilgrimage overseas in September 1333 ... He also founded Cantilupe College in Lincoln Cathedral close, whose priests celebrated at the altar of St Nicholas within the cathedral' (*ODNB*, 'Cantilupe [Cantelupe], Nicholas, third Lord Cantilupe (*c.*1301–1355)'). Thomson concludes that this manuscript belonged to Cantelupe and became the property of his Chantry after 1360 (p. 79).

R. M. Thomson, *Catalogue of the Manuscripts of Lincoln Cathedral Chapter Library* (Woodbridge, 1989), pp. 78–9.

Mu Munich, Bayerische Staatsbibliothek, clm 23820, fos. 243ʳ–282ᵛ (Mozley's m)

Paper. s. xv med. (The date of 1462, given by Halm, refers to a scribal colophon relating only to the Petrarch section of the manuscript.)

Contents: A miscellany, containing Petrarch, *De remediis fortunae prosperae*, *Historia Griseldis*, and other works, a work by Leonard of Chios (*c.*1365–1459) on the loss of Constantinople, as well as *SS* (ends at 2602) with *Epistle*.

History: The volume was apparently bound in Erfurt, as Carolin Schreiber of the Bayerische Staatsbibliothek in Munich kindly informs me: 'one of the stamps seems to be the "Mondsichelmadonna" from two Erfurt bookbinder's workshops, cf. https://www.hist-einband. de/de/werkzeugdetails.html?entityID=s018834. I see a rosette and a stamp with "Maria" from the same workshop(s) on the binding, so that seems fairly reliable. The manuscript seems to have been in the possession oft the Kollegiatstift St. Martin und Castulus in Landshut/ Bavaria by 1735: cf. Catalogus librorum insignis et Electoralis Ecclesiae Collegiatae Ss. Martini et Castuli Landishuti, descriptus 12ma. Aug. Anno 1735—BSB Cbm Cat. 535: Fachkatalog der Handschriften und Drucke der Bibliothek des Kollegiatstifts St. Martin und Castulus Landshut (Landshut, 1735.—72 fol.). An entry in this catalogue "Fran. Petrarchae de remedys fortunae prosperae prologus, MS" (cf. Decima cl. Miscellaneorum' Nr. 4, 53a) was identified with Clm 28320 by

374   APPENDIX A

Glauche (p. 97). Glauche implies that Clm 23820 comes from the same source as Clm 23821, which has a Landshut binding. Both volumes may come from the book collection of a Martin Angerbeck (d. 1520), sub-provost in Moosburg/Bavaria.'

Karl Halm, Georg von Laubmann, and Wilhelm Meyer, *Catalogus codicum latinorum Bibliothecae Regiae Monacensis*, 2nd edn., vol. ii. 4 (Munich, 1881); vol. iv. 4 in the series *Catalogus codicum manuscriptorum Bibliothecae Regiae Monacensis*. See https://daten.digitale-sammlungen.de/~db/bsb00008255/images/index.html.

Günter Glauche, *Auf den Spuren Schmellers: Die Aufstellung der lateinischen Handschriften in der Bayerischen Staatsbibliothek. Nachlese zu einer bestandsgeschichtlichen Pionierarbeit* (Munich, 2017), p. 97, online at: http://publikationen.badw.de/de/044794532).

N Lincoln, Cathedral Chapter Library, 191, fos. 228^v–255^r (Mozley's N)

Parchment. s. xiv. A single English bookhand throughout.

Contents: Latin religious texts, *SS* (with *Epistle*). Contains the Interpolation on the Mendicant Orders. Like *M*, to which it is closely related, *N* transposes 3602–896 after 3320 and omits 3863–72 (see above).

History: This manuscript was at Lincoln by the early fifteenth century (Thomson, p. 154). Textually, *N* is close to *Hu*, but *Hu* does not have the displacement of lines 3602–896 that *N* shares with *M*.

R. M. Thomson, *Catalogue of the Manuscripts of Lincoln Cathedral Chapter Library* (Woodbridge, 1989), pp. 153–4.

Ne Lobkowicz Library, Nelahozeves Castle, Czech Republic, Sig. VI Fb 29, pp. 87–125 (formerly Roudnice Lobkowicz Library) (not known to Mozley)

Paper. s. xv. Date taken from the list in Walther's *Initia*, in the entry for *SS* (number 18944). Soňa Černocká, Lobkowicz Library and Archives Curator, kindly informs me that the manuscript was created *c.* 1452–56.

Contents: 'Liber Quadripartitus' (an alternative title for the fable collection titled *Speculum sapientiae* ('Ps-Cyril', now ascribed to the Italian Dominican Giovanni da Messina; see Kaeppeli, no. 699, and Creytens, p. 272, no. 89), which is found in company with *SS* in other manuscripts; see notes on *T* and *Vb* below); *SS* (ends at 2602), with

MANUSCRIPT DESCRIPTIONS 375

Epistle, followed by the *Occultus Erfordensis* (a history of Erfurt) attributed to Nicholas of Bibra.

History: The manuscript was part of a collection created by Bohuslav Hassenstein, a fifteenth-century humanist and member of the Lobkowicz family, a noble dynasty of Bohemia, into whose possession Hassenstein's collection passed. It was kept at the principal Lobkowicz residence, Roudnice Castle. In 1941 the books were confiscated by the Nazis and passed into the administrative care of the University Library of Prague; under the Communists, they were distributed to various libraries and depositories in Bohemia. In 1992 they were returned to the Lobkowicz family, and a new library was created to hold them at Nelahozeves Castle, a Lobkowicz possession. Because of this chequered history, there is no printed catalogue, but steps are now being taken to catalogue the collection.

Raymond Creytens, 'Les Écrivains dominicains dans la chronique d'Albert de Castello (1516)', *Archivum Fratrum Praedicatorum*, xxx (1960), 226–313.
Thomas Kaeppeli and Emilio Panella, *Scriptores Ordinis Praedicatorum Medii Aevi* (4 vols., Rome, 1970–3), i. 251.
Der '*Occultus Erfordensis*' des Nicolaus von Bibra: Kritische Edition mit Einführung, Kommentar and deutscher Übersetzung, ed. Christine Mundhenk (Weimar, 1997), pp. 98–9. (When Mundhenk's book was published, the manuscript was still on deposit at the National Library in Prague.)

O Brussels, KBR, 2695–719, fos. 34^r–93^v (Mozley's O)

Paper. s. xiv–xv. A composite manuscript of three parts bound together; *SS* (without *Epistle*) is in Part A, written by several fifteenth-century hands, writing variously Continental *cursiva* or *hybrida*; see *Codices Boethiani*, ii. 118–19. Lines 3761–825 were omitted from fo. 91^v by the scribe, but he quickly noticed the error and corrected it by copying these lines after line 3853 on fo. 92^{r-v}, and adding detailed instructions directing the reader to go to fo. 92 and then back to fo. 91^v for lines 3826–53. The foliation in the manuscript is one lower than that in Van den Gheyn's *Catalogue*.

Contents: Part A is a large Latin miscellany, containing, for example, saints' lives and excerpts from Godfrey of Viterbo's *Pantheon*, Ovid's *Metamorphoses*, Walter of Châtillon's *Alexandreis*.

History: Belonged to the monastery of Stavelot (modern Belgium). A note on fo. 1^r reads 'Liber monasterii Stabulen[sis]'.

376 APPENDIX A

Codices Boethiani, ed. Lesley Smith et al. (2 vols., London, 2001), ii. 118–19.
J. van den Gheyn *et al.*, *Catalogue des manuscrits de la Bibliothèque royale de Belgique* (13 vols., Brussels, 1901–19), v. 111–12.

P Brussels, KBR, 1701–4, fos. 122^v–138^v (Mozley's P)

Paper. s. xv. (colophon and watermarks).

Contents: Peter Riga, *Aurora*, and *SS*, without *Epistle*. The text omits lines 55–666, but adds 205–594 on fo. 136rb, following the end of the poem at fo. 136ra, so that only 56–204 and 595–666 are completely lacking. Lines 2859–3097 appear in the expected place (fo. 132^{r-v}), but are also repeated on fo. 138^{r-v} after the end of the poem and the addition of lines 205–94. For an attempt to account for these features, see Introduction, pp. lxix–lxxi.

History: On fo. 122^v appears the following note: 'Io. Dalsche presbyter scripsit hunc librum', and on fo. 136^r: 'Explicit speculum stultorum scriptum a Iohanne Dalsche presbytero anno Domini M°iiii°xv° crastino beati Sixti pape finitum'. The manuscript belonged to the house of canons regular of the Holy Cross (Crutched Friars) in Cologne; an inscription on fo. 2^r reads 'Liber M. Petri Riga qui dicitur Aurora. a. Item speculum stultorum metrice. b. Et pertinet fratribus Sanctae Crucis in Colonia'.

J. van den Gheyn *et al.*, *Catalogue des manuscrits de la Bibliothèque royale de Belgique* (13 vols., Brussels, 1901–19), i. 84–5.

Pk Prague, Archiv Prazského Hradu, Knihovna Metropolitni Kapituly, M. CXXI (catalogue 1482), fos. 43^r–86^v (not known to Mozley)

Paper. s. xv (RMT).

Contents: *SS* (ends at 2602), with *Epistle*; the *Occultus Erfordensis* (a history of Erfurt) attributed to Nicholas of Bibra, *Asinarius*, and Cato's *Distichs*.

History: Unknown.

Der 'Occultus Erfordensis' des Nicolaus von Bibra: Kritische Edition mit Einführung, Kommentar and deutscher Übersetzung, ed. Christine Mundhenk (Weimar, 1997), pp. 101–2.
Antonio Podlaha, *Catalogus Codicum Manuscriptorum qui in archivio capituli metropolitani pragensis asservantur* (Prague, 1923), pp. 342–3.

Pm Prague, Knihovna Národního muzea, XIV. D. 4, fos. 144^r–180^v (not known to Mozley)

Paper. s. xv$^{1/4}$.

MANUSCRIPT DESCRIPTIONS 377

Contents: *SS* (ends at 2602), with *Epistle*; Pierre Bersuire, *Reductorium morale*; *Occultus Erfordensis* (a history of Erfurt) attributed to Nicholas of Bibra (mistitled, as a result of the contents list, Registrum rerum naturalium, que comparantur homini, virtutibus et viciis). As a result of a displaced quire, lines 1599–2476 follow line 721 in *SS* (see Introduction, p. lxix).

History: 'Explicit Brunellus maior, qui speculum stultorum dicitur, finitus in carnisprivio [Shrove Tuesday] in scola Pragensi'. Owner's inscription: 'istum librum legauit magister Jaksso pro ecclesia Crumpnoviensi [= Český Krumlov]', with a shelfmark, 'N. 104', on the spine.

F. M. Bartoš, *Soupis rukopisů národního musea* (*Catalogus codicum manuscriptorum Musaei Nationalis Pragensis*) (2 vols., Prague, 1926–7), ii. 298–9; catalogue available online at biblio.hiu.cas.cz.
For description, see also manuscriptorium.com.

Q Copenhagen, Det Kongelige Bibliotek, GKS 1634 quarto, fos. 85^r–133^r (Mozley's Q)

Paper. s. xv. Originally two parts; various hands (see Voigt, p. 6).

Contents: *SS*, without *Epistle*, and a huge miscellany of Latin texts (Vergil's *Eclogues*, Ovid, *De remedio amoris*, *Asinarius*, *Geta*, *Rapularius*, *Ovidius de lupo*, inc. 'Saepe quidam lupus', *Pamphilus*, Henry of Settimello, Petrarch, *Historia Griseldis*, etc.) including those used as school texts (e.g. Avianus, Theodulus, Maximian, 'Cato', *Facetus* 'Moribus et vita', *De contemptu mundi*, inc. 'Cartula nostra'). As in *Y*, *SS* omits lines 1249–502 (the story of Gundulf) and 3233–458 (the story of the Three Fates), as well as lines 2401–12 (the order of Simplingham/Sempringham). For discussion of these omissions, see Introduction, pp. lxxi, cx–cxi.

SS is titled 'Brunellus azinus'; after an explicit, 'Finit feliciter', there are four lines of verse:

> Ecce poeta datur sic accipe quod fabulatur
> Non nimium deuores fabulas sed discito mores
> Quod tibi de cauda brunelli dogmaque lauda
> Hiis fabulose datis sit tibi docma satis

History: The date of 1468 is given on fo. 84^v, and two scribes identify themselves at fo. 156^v ('Hinricus', with a date of 1470) and fo. 175^v ('Didericus scolaris diotzesis verdensis'); (Voigt, p. 6; Wetzel, pp. 180, 182, 184). The

378 APPENDIX A

manuscript formerly belonged to Bordesholm Priory (dedicated to St Mary), a house of Augustinian canons, as is shown by its classmark (G.XXVII), corresponding to the Bordesholm catalogue of 1488, and the letter S imprinted on the cover, probably referring to Prior Sudo (Jørgensen, p. 351; Voigt, p. 6; Wetzel, pp. 121, 173). When the priory was suppressed in the seventeenth century, part of the Bordesholm manuscripts were transferred to Gottorf Castle, the main seat of the dukes of Schleswig-Holstein, while a smaller portion went to the University of Kiel. In 1749 the Gottorf manuscripts were taken to Copenhagen and mostly incorporated into the Royal Library (Voigt, pp. 5–6).

For details of the manuscript and its contents, see Voigt, pp. 5–7; Wetzel, pp. 173–91.

Ellen Jørgensen, *Catalogus codicum latinorum medii aevi Bibliothecae Regiae Hafniensis* (Copenhagen, 1926); available online.

Ernst Voigt, 'Kleinere lateinische Denkmäler der Thiersage aus dem zwölften bis vierzehnten Jahrhundert', *Quellen und Forschungen zur Sprach- und Culturgeschichte der germanischen Völker*, xxv (1878).

August Wetzel, 'Die Reste der Bordesholmer Bibliothek in Kopenhagen', pp. 117–202 in Emil Steffenhagen and August Wetzel, *Die Klosterbibliothek zu Bordesholm und die Gottorfer Bibliothek: Drei bibliographische Untersuchungen* (Kiel, 1884); available online at dibiki.ub.uni-kiel.de. Wetzel's contribution originally appeared in the *Zeitschrift der Gesellschaft für Schleswig-Holstein-Lauenburgische Geschichte*, xiv (1884).

R Città del Vaticano, Biblioteca Apostolica Vaticana, reg. lat. 1379, fos. 1^r–70^r (Mozley's R)

Paper. s. xv$^{1/4}$.

Contents: *SS* (followed by *Epistle*) and Henry of Settimello's *Elegia*.

History: Colophon on fo. 67^r: 'Explicit Speculum Stultorum per manum fratris H. de Palude.' The manuscript belonged to Alexander Pétau (1610–47), son of the French scholar and book collector Paul Pétau, from whom it passed into the collection of Queen Christina of Sweden in 1650. After her death in Rome in 1689, it was bought by Cardinal Pietro Ottobuoni, later Pope Alexander VIII (1689–91), for the Vatican collection. The name of an early owner (Arnoldus Doesborch) appears on fo. 54^r. Digitized version of the manuscript available at digivatlib.it/view/MSS_Reg.lat.1379.

Ludwig Konrad Bethmann, 'Nachrichten über die von ihm für die "Monumenta germaniae historica" benutzten Sammlungen von Handschriften und

MANUSCRIPT DESCRIPTIONS 379

Urkunden Italiens, aus dem Jahre 1854', *Archiv der Gesellschaft für ältere deutsche Geschichtskunde*, xiii (1874), p. 319; available online.

Eva Nilsson Nylander, ' "Ingens est codicum numerus": I fondi reginensi', in Claudia Montuschi, ed., *La Vaticana nel Seicento (1590–1700): Una biblioteca di biblioteche* (Città del Vaticano, 2014), pp. 395–426.

J. Bignami Odier, 'Le Fonds de la Reine à la Bibliothèque Vaticane', *Collectanea Vaticana in honorem Anselmi M. Card. Albareda a Biblioteca Apostolica edita*, Studi e Testi, 219–20 (Città del Vaticano, 1962), i. 159–89.

S Paris, Bibliothèque nationale de France, lat. 16519, fos. 51^r–106^v (Mozley's S)

Parchment. Dated 1391.

Contents: *SS* (with *Epistle*), ends at 2522, at the bottom of fo. 106^v; *Formula Novitiorum* of the thirteenth-century Franciscan David of Augsburg; Hugh of St-Victor, *De institutione novitiorum*.

History: A manuscript of the abbey of Saint-Denis, written in 1391, according to an inscription on fo. 1^r: 'iste liber est de conventu sancti Dionysii in Francia quem fecit scribi frater Reginaldus de Betencuria ad usum fratris Radulphi de Pratellis et ad beneplacitum domni abbatis. Anno Domini Mmo CCCmo nonagesimo primo'. Renaud de Bétencourt was a monk of Saint-Denis, who composed an ambitious *Tabula librorum*, a programme of reading for the purpose of spiritual improvement. The *Tabula* describes the contents of ten projected volumes devoted to this programme, two of which can be identified with surviving manuscripts. Unsurprisingly, the *Speculum Stultorum* is not included in this serious religious programme, but it seems that Renaud may have been misled by the *Epistle* into thinking its character more edifying than it is, to judge by the title given to *SS* on fo. 51^r of the manuscript: 'Incipit speculum stultorum in quo quisque potest suos defectos cognoscere et cognitos corrigere' (echoing *Epistle* 5). Other manuscripts commissioned by Renaud similarly rely on the introduction to a work to characterize it (Nebbiai-Dalla Guarda, 'La "Tabula Librorum" ', p. 112).

Digitized version online at https://gallica.bnf.fr/ark:/12148/btv1b52504757k; catalogue details online at https://archivesetmanuscrits.bnf.fr/ark:/12148/cc76952r.

Donatella Nebbiai-Dalla Guarda, 'La "Tabula Librorum" de Renaud de Bétancourt', *Archives d'histoire doctrinale et littéraire du Moyen Âge*, liv (1987), 103–70. Detailed description of BnF lat. 16519 on pp. 160–1;

380　　APPENDIX A

discussion on pp. 107, 111–12, 117 n. 2. The manuscript later passed into the possession of Cardinal Richelieu, and afterwards of the Sorbonne Library, whence it was incorporated into the BnF collection.

Donatella Nebbiai-Dalla Guarda, 'Des rois et des moines: Livres et lecteurs à l'abbaye de Saint-Denis (XIIIe–XVe siècles)', in Françoise Autrand, Claude Gauvard, and Jean-Marie Moeglin, eds., *Saint-Denis et la royauté: Études offerts à Bernard Guenée*, ed. (Paris, 1999), pp. 355–74.

André Vernet, 'Un programme de lectures spirituelles à l'abbaye de Saint-Denis à la fin du XIVe siècle', *Bulletin de la Société des Antiquaires de France*, 1972 (1970), 208–14.

T Wrocław, Biblioteka Uniwersytecka we Wrocławiu (University Library), IV.Q.126, fos. 154^r–183^r (Mozley's T)

Paper. s. xv². A composite manuscript, written by several hands. On fo. 28^v a scribal note reads: 'per Georgium Schlyffir de brega (?berga) filium carnificis in Cracouia feria sexta ante palmarum anno domini 1475'. The section of the manuscript containing *SS* is written in a very careless hand, with many interlinear glosses and alternative readings in the margin.

Contents: *SS* (with *Epistle*); ends at 2602; numerous other Latin texts, including *Asinarius*; Avianus; the *Speculum sapientiae* of Giovanni da Messina (see **Ne** above); '*Ovidius de lupo*', inc. 'Saepe quidam lupus'; 'Brunellus', inc. 'Instabat festiva dies'; *De contemptu mundi*', inc. 'Cartula nostra'. For details of the manuscript and its contents, see Ernst Voigt, 'Kleinere lateinische Denkmäler der Thiersage aus dem zwölften bis vierzehnten Jahrhundert', *Quellen und Forschungen zur Sprach- und Culturgeschichte der germanischen Völker*, xxv (1878), pp. 7–8. A full description is contained in the so-called 'Göber's catalogue': O. Günther, J. Klapper, and K. Rother, 'Katalog der Handschriften der Universitätsbibliothek Breslau', 26 vols. [handwritten catalogue, in German], Biblioteka Uniwersytecka we Wrocławiu, Akc., available online at manuscripta.pl.

History: The manuscript belonged to the Corpus Christi community of the Knights of Malta in Wrocław, as is shown by a shelfmark on the front cover, and a later ex libris: *Ex bibliotheca Corporis Xsti Vratislav*.

Tr Trento, Biblioteca comunale, W 3154, fos. 211^r–235^v (Mozley's s)

Paper. A composite manuscript; Part IV, containing *SS*, is s. xv^1.

Contents: *SS* with *Epistle*; other Latin texts, including Vegetius, *Epitoma rei militaris*; Guido delle Colonne, *Historia destructionis Troiae*; Quilichinus of Spoleto, *Historia Alexandri Magni*.

MANUSCRIPT DESCRIPTIONS 381

History: Belonged to Johannes Hinderbach, prince-bishop of Trento (1466–86), whose marginal notes are to be found in the margins of *SS*; it remained in the episcopal library until 1805, when it was taken to the Hofbibliothek (now the Austrian National Library) in Vienna. The Viennese classmark, 3154/18.Salisb.2, is preserved on the inner front cover. In 1919 the manuscript was restored to Italy and deposited in the Biblioteca comunale of Trento.

Adriana Paolini, *I manoscritti medievali della Biblioteca comunale di Trento* (Florence, 2006). [Paolini gives the folio refs as 210^r–43^r but according to Silvano Groff, the Trento librarian, fos. 210^{rv} and 236^r–243^v are blank].

Online catalogue: bdt.bibcom.trento.it/Manoscritti. The manuscript is digitized and available on the same website.

U London, British Library, Sloane 1831 B, fos. 1^r–47^v (Mozley's U)

Parchment. s. xv

Contents: *SS* (without *Epistle*); the manuscript is badly mutilated and contains only *SS* lines 1043–2350, 2678–3358, 3413–864; followed by the *Apocalipsis Goliae* (incomplete).

For an attempt to account for the lost text, see Boutemy, pp. 511–12 (but note that his line-numbering refers to Wright's edition of the poem). There are three major lacunae: lines 1–1042, 2351–677, 3359–412. Fo. 1^r carries an older folio number 13, and this older numbering continues throughout. This means that the beginning of the manuscript has lost at least twelve folios, which is the regular number in each quire in **U**, and since it averages 26 lines to a page, this would account for the loss of some 624 lines (24 × 26). That still leaves over 400 lines unaccounted for, and Boutemy speculated that it had also lost, at a different stage, its first gathering, large enough to contain the *Epistle to William* in addition to the first 400+ lines. The loss of lines 2351–677 occurs between fos. 25^v and 26^r, which represent the outer leaves of a quire, as can be seen by the catchword 'Dampna tamen' (the beginning of line 2297) at the bottom of fo. 24^v, which ends with line 2296, and the catchword 'non norunt' (the beginning of line 2731) at the bottom of fo. 26^v. The ten missing folios of this quire would, however, have accommodated far more than the 326 lines absent from the normal text of *SS* at this point, and in consequence Boutemy speculated that **U** originally contained the Interpolation on the Mendicant Friars found in *MNDKGI*. Finally, the lacuna at 3359–412 is, as Boutemy says,

382 APPENDIX A

'easily explicable by the loss of one sheet', which would have been the first of a quire (as shown by the catchword 'Vt decet' (the beginning of line 3359) at the bottom of fo. 38^v; the other half of the bifolium will have been fo. 49, since the text of the *Apocalipsis Goliae* (which follows the end of *SS* on fo. 47^v) breaks off incomplete on fo. 48^v.

Mozley's statement (*SS*, p. 14) that this manuscript contains the *Epistle to William* is incorrect.

After the original copying, the scribe made extensive corrections, probably using a manuscript from the δ branch of the stemma. Mozley's theory that he was using two manuscripts at the same time (*SS*, p. 21) is, however, unlikely (see Introduction, pp. cix–cx).

History: formerly owned by Edward Browne, MD (1644–1708), President of the College of Physicians (see *ODNB*), who owned several Sloane manuscripts (see BL online catalogue), inherited from his father, Sir Thomas Browne, MD (author of *Religio medici*).

André Boutemy, 'The manuscript tradition of the *Speculum Stultorum*', *Speculum*, viii (1933), 510–19.
BL online Catalogue of Manuscripts.

Va Vienna, Österreichische Nationalbibliothek, 3487, fos. 1^r–43^r (Mozley's V)

Paper. s. xv (RMT).

Contents: *SS* only (ends at 2602), with *Epistle*. Fos. 43^v–44^v are ruled but blank; remaining folios blank. *SS* lacks lines 618–81 and 1177–1234, probably as a result of the loss of two folios during the process of (mis)binding: fo. 11^v ends at 617, fo. 12$^{r–v}$ contains 33–96, fo. 13 resumes at line 682; fo. 20^v ends at 1176, fo. 21$^{r–v}$ contains lines 229–92, fo. 22^r resumes at line 1235. That is, fo. 12 should properly be between fo. 4^v and fo. 5^r, and fo. 21 should be between fo. 6^v and fo. 7^r. Since the manuscript averages 30–3 lines a page, the text lost in each case amounts to recto and verso of a single leaf. It is significant that in each case the loss of text occurs at the point of textual disjunction: that is, between fos. 11^v and 12^r, and between fos. 20^v and 21^r. In the absence of catchwords, it is not possible to determine the quiring of this manuscript, and current restrictions on travel prevent physical analysis.

History: unknown.

ÖNB online catalogue. Digitized version of the manuscript available online on the ÖNB website (onb.ac.at).

MANUSCRIPT DESCRIPTIONS 383

Vb Vienna, Österreichische Nationalbibliothek, 12531, fos. 85ʳ–133ʳ
(Mozley's z)

Paper. A colophon at the end of the *Speculum sapientiae* gives the date
as 1422: 'Laus sit deo finito libro Sub anno domini MᵒCCCCXXII
dominica post Galli'. On fo. 196ᵛ the date of 1433 is given.

Contents: *SS* (ends at 2602) with *Epistle*, which is incomplete (see
Introduction, p. lxix); 'Cato novus', the *Speculum sapientiae* now
ascribed to Giovanni da Messina (see *Ne* above), Petrarch, *Historia
Griseldis*, the *Occultus Erfordensis* (a history of Erfurt) attributed to
Nicholas of Bibra, and other Latin texts, with some medical recipes
and household tips in German.

History: Owned by Wenzel von Iglau, notary of Olmütz (Olomouc):
'Libellus wenceslau de Iglauia Notarij Olomucensis In quo Nouus
katho historia Quadripartita Speculum stultorum et Ocultus continentur' (fo. 1ʳ). Later owned by the library of the university of Olmütz,
the oldest university in Moravia, established in 1573 as a public university led by the Jesuit order in Olmütz, which was at that time the
capital of Moravia and the seat of the episcopacy.

ÖNB online catalogue.
*Der 'Occultus Erfordensis' des Nicolaus von Bibra: Kritische Edition mit
Einführung, Kommentar and deutscher Übersetzung*, ed. Christine Mundhenk
(Weimar, 1997), p. 103.

Vc Vienna, Österreichische Nationalbibliothek, 3283, fos. 1ʳ–87ʳ
(Mozley's t)

Paper. Colophon on fo. 87ʳ gives date of completion as 1478: 'Finitus
tractatus metricus sub anno domini i.c. 1478 die (visitacionis *deleted*)
marie presentacionis Brunellus'. (Mozley wrongly gives the date as
1468.)

Contents: *SS* (ends at 2602) and *Epistle* (written in different hands).

History: unknown.

ÖNB online catalogue. Digitized version of the manuscript available online on
the ÖNB website (onb.ac.at).

Vd Vienna, Österreichische Nationalbibliothek, 3467, fos. 1ʳ–56ʳ
(Mozley's u)

384   APPENDIX A

Paper. s. xv. A composite manuscript.

Contents: *SS* (ends at 2602) with *Epistle* in an abridged form (see Appendix C); the *Occultus Erfordensis* (a history of Erfurt) attributed to Nicholas of Bibra.

History: The manuscript was previously owned by the Universitätsbibliothek, Vienna.

ÖNB online catalogue. Digitized version of the manuscript available online on the ÖNB website (onb.ac.at).
Der 'Occultus Erfordensis' des Nicolaus von Bibra: Kritische Edition mit Einführung, Kommentar and deutscher Übersetzung, ed. Christine Mundhenk (Weimar, 1997), p. 103.

Ve Vienna, Österreichische Nationalbibliothek, 3529, fos. 1^r–74^v (Mozley's x)

Paper. s. xv.

Contents: A large Latin miscellany, mostly historical works or travel literature. *SS* (complete) with *Epistle*. Colophon: 'Hic explicit liber qui dicitur speculum stultorum/ Speculum Stultorum reperitur copia quorum'.

History: Cologne, Fraterhaus (Brethren of the Common Life), St Michael Weidenbach (founded 1417). This community was part of the *devotio moderna* movement. The Brethren supported themselves by producing books, copying, decorating, and binding them (Löffler, pp. 116–20). Löffler stated (p. 120) that surviving examples of the Fraterhaus's productions were very few, but *Ve* is presumably one of them.

Klemens Löffler, 'Das Fraterhaus Weidenbach in Köln', *Annalen des historischen Vereins für den Niederrhein, insbesondere die alte Erzdiözese Köln*, cii (1918), 99–128.
ÖNB online catalogue (onb.ac.at).

W Oxford, Bodleian Library, Lat. misc. c. 75 (*olim* Phillips 3119), fos. 1^r–23^v (not known to Mozley)

Parchment. A composite volume of seven fragments of seven different manuscripts, all of which belonged to the sixteenth-century antiquary John Bale. *SS* is in Part A, which, judging by the script, is probably an Oxford manuscript, written by a fourteenth-century rounded semi-cursive hand.

MANUSCRIPT DESCRIPTIONS 385

Contents: Besides *SS* (with *Epistle*), Part A also contains three short poems on the fall of Troy. Lines 1515 and 1517–18 of *SS*, on the intellectual and moral excellence of the English, are underlined, and a marginal note reads 'Nota condiciones anglorum'. In lines 1530–1, 'Gallia' and 'comes Angligenis' are underlined, as are lines 1582–5 on national characteristics.

History: Later owners are Sir Gregory Page-Turner of Battlesden, Beds. (sold on 19 October 1824, lot 2716) and Sir Thomas Phillips; in 1973 it was bought by the Bodleian Library.

For a full description of this manuscript, its contents, and its history, see *Bibliotheca Phillippica*, n. s. 8, *Catalogue of Manuscripts on Vellum, Paper and Papyrus* [Sotheby's sale on Wednesday 28 November 1973], item no. 610.

X London, British Library, Cotton Vespasian E. XII, fos. 10^v–77^r (Mozley's X)

Parchment. s. xv^2. Written continuously by one fifteenth-century Oxford hand.

Contents: A large Latin miscellany, containing *SS* (with *Epistle*) and other Latin works, including the *Apocalipsis Goliae* and *Predicatio Goliae*, Petrarch's *Historia Griseldis*, *De coniuge non ducenda*, Martin of Braga's *Formula vitae honestae*, and Seneca, *De remediis fortuitorum bonorum*. On fo. 13^v, *SS* is ascribed to John of Salisbury: 'Libellum istum qui dicitur speculum stultorum composuit Saresburiensis sacre theologie doctor eximius sicud patet in Epistola Blesensi directa Saresburyensi regraciantis sibi pro libello quem composuit de nugis curialium et iste Saresburiensis morabatur cum Thoma cantuariensi'.

History: an inscription on fo. 1^v indicates that the manuscript belonged to John Russell, scholar of New College Oxford 1447, Fellow 1449, sub-warden 1461, chancellor of the University 1483–death, bishop of Lincoln 1480–death, chancellor of England 1483–5, died 1494. On Russell as a scribe and owner of manuscripts, see further M. B. Parkes, *English Cursive Book Hands 1250–1500* (Oxford, 1969; corr. edn. London, 1979), pl. 18 (ii), and Index.

There are 3 sets of annotations: (1) the main scribe making alterations and supplying variants (see my *apparatus criticus* for the variants in *SS*); (2) a more florid hand, probably also the main scribe's, adds missing lines and stanzas on some folios (but not in *SS*); (3) a smaller

386   APPENDIX A

hand, perhaps Russell's, has added proverbs at the top of early pages of
SS. Richard James, Sir Robert Cotton's librarian, added the foliation
and also numbered leaves by tens on the verso (beginning incorrectly
on fo. 13^v).

Six lines of verse and an explicit follow the end of *SS* on fo. 77^r:

> Christe uagas asini nugas crimenque driani
> A nobis tenebras mentis et ammoneas
> Ac de pressura mundi nos sorteque dura
> Saluos custodi regnaque redde poli
> Burnelli dicta multo moderamine ficta
> Spernere qui querit semper asellus erit
> Explicit Speculum Stultorum. Amen.

A marginal note in Richard James's handwriting comments:
'Hexastichon istud non habet Codex Camdeianus [= Titus A. XX, my
manuscript *C*; see entry on this manuscript above] nec in exemplaribus
impressis reperitur'. Rigg (1977, p. 294) comments on James's note,
but he does not notice the connection with Bodley 851 (see my notes
on MS *F* above). James also made a marginal note to line 3484 on
fo. 76^r, adding the variant reading 'rege iubente suo', found in
Titus A. XX (and other δ manuscripts), which he likewise attributes to
the 'ms Camd.' (Rigg (1979), p. 497).

For a full description of the manuscript and its contents, see
A. G. Rigg, 'Medieval Latin Poetic Anthologies (III)', *Mediaeval
Studies*, xli (1979), 468–505.

A. G. Rigg, 'Medieval Latin Poetic Anthologies (I)', *Mediaeval Studies*, xxxix
(1977), 281–330.

Y Wolfenbüttel, Herzog-August Bibliothek, Helmst. 616, fos. 93^r–137^v
(Mozley's Y)

Paper. Dated 1419 (on fo. 138^r, a half-erased inscription: 'Anno Domini
m cccc xix ipso die beati Lamberti... canonicus ecclesie Lubicensis').

Contents: A Latin miscellany (including *Anticlaudianus*, *Disticha
Catonis*, *Novus Cato*, and sermons); *SS* (without *Epistle*). Like *Q*, Y
lacks lines 1249–502 (the story of Gundulf), 3233–458 (the story of the
Three Fates), and 2401–12 (on the order of Simplingham/Sempringham);
it also has many smaller omissions. See Introduction, pp. lxxi, cx–cxi
for discussion.

MANUSCRIPT DESCRIPTIONS 387

History: Originally Lübeck (see ownership inscription above), later owned by the humanist scholar and church reformer Matthias Flacius Illyricus (1520–75), who entered on the first flyleaf the titles of some of the items contained in it (Heinemann, ii. 78–9; Hartmann, p. 237). In 1597, Matthias's library was purchased by Heinrich Julius, Duke of Brunswick-Luneburg, for the imposing ducal library at Wolfenbüttel which had been created by his father Julius (Hartmann, p. 83). In 1618 Heinrich Julius's son Friedrich Ulrich transferred the whole ducal collection to the university of Helmstedt, which had been founded by his grandfather Julius; in 1810, the university was closed down and most of the books were eventually returned to Wolfenbüttel (Milde; Werner, pp. 249, 257).

Otto von Heinemann, *Die Handschriften der Herzoglichen Bibliothek zu Wolfenbüttel*, Abth. 1, *Die Helmstedter Handschriften* (Wolfenbüttel, 1886); available online at Wolfenbütteler Digitale Bibliothek-drucke.

Wolfgang Milde, 'The Library at Wolfenbüttel, from 1550 to 1618', *The Modern Language Review*, lxvi (1971), 101–12.

Martina Hartmann, *Humanismus und Kirchenkritik: Matthias Flacius Illyricus als Erforscher des Mittelalters* (Stuttgart, 2001).

Arnold Werner, 'Die Wanderung der Bücher', in *Das Athen der Welfen: Die Reformuniversität Helmstedt 1576–1810*, ed. Jens Bruning and Ulricke Gleixner (Wolfenbuttel, 2010), pp. 248–57.

Z Leipzig, Universitäts-Bibliothek, 1591, fos. 1ʳ–62ᵛ (Mozley's Z)

Paper. s. xv (*c.*1475).

Contents: *SS* only (ends at 3882), without *Epistle*. Frequently alternative versions of lines are given; see Introduction, pp. cxiii–cxiv. The scribe uses a (would-be) classical Latin spelling: e.g. 'quum' for 'cum', 'quur' for 'cur', 'dominae' for 'domine' (vocative), 'saed' for 'sed', 'perfoecit' for 'perfecit' 'oequum' for 'equum', etc.

History: German (Magdeburg). This manuscript is written by the same hand as Leipzig UB 1592 (containing the *Elegia* of Henry of Settimello), which has an inscription on fo. 1ʳ: 'Conradus Balderdecanus... capitulum ecclesie sanctorum Petri et Pauli Noue Civitatis Magdeburgensis, dominus Johannes...canonicus eiusdem ecclesie', and on fo. 1ᵛ, 'Ex Magdeburgo anno domini 1475' (part of a model letterform). The two manuscripts also have covers of waste parchment taken from the same liturgical manuscript.

388   APPENDIX A

The text of *SS* is severely dislocated between lines 823 and 1153, as a result of misplaced folia at an earlier stage of transmission. The original must have had a quire of six, with the text distributed as follows: 1 (recto and verso) 823–82; 2 (recto and verso) 883–935; 3 (recto and verso) 936–92 ||middle of quire|| 4 (recto and verso) 993–1048; 5 (recto and verso) 1049–1102; 6 (recto and verso) 1103–53.

The first and third bifolia (1+4, and 3+6) changed places at some point, resulting in the following textual order: 1 (recto and verso) 936–92; 2 (recto and verso) 883–935; 3 (recto and verso) 823–82; 4 (recto and verso) 1103–53; 5 (recto and verso) 1049–1102; 6 (recto and verso) 993–1048. The dislocation occurred at an earlier stage of copying, as the points of textual change occur in mid-folio in *Z*. Additionally, it is clear that the manuscript in which the dislocation occurred had 25–29 lines to a page, whereas *Z* has on average 30–32.

Digitized version of the manuscript available online at https://www.ub.uni-leipzig.de/forschungsbibliothek/digitale-sammlungen/mittelalterliche-handschriften/

For description of the manuscript, its contents, and its history, see http://www.manuscripta-mediaevalia.de/?INFO_projectinfo/leipzig1#|5.

FRAGMENTS AND EXTRACTS

fb Bonn, Universitåts- und Landesbibliothek, S 220, fos. 252^v–258^v, 356^v–358^v

Paper. 15th c. (1465/ 1470) (not known to Mozley)

Contents: A composite manuscript, assembled *c.*1470 in the abbey of Maria Laach. Part IV is a large florilegium which contains two sets of extracts from *SS*: (1) 13–14, 45–8, 57–8, 79–80, 93–4, 113–14, 125–6, 137–8, 161–2, 165–6, 171–2, 203–4, 285–6, 291–2, 295–6, 309–12, 317–18, 349–50, 355–6, 363–6, 571–2, 703–4, 711–16, 827–8, 854, 907–10, 1220, 1561–2, 1647–50, 1733–4, 1733 (*sic*), 1735–6, 1765–78, 2013–14, 2017–22, 2029–32, 2035–8, 2041–8, 2283–6, 2315–16, 2319–22, 2325–31, 2333–48, 2351–4, 2364–72, 2374, 2377–80, 2385–6, 2393–6, 2399–400, 2415–16, 2485–2508, 2511–14, 2517–21, 2533–5, 2537–8, 2543–6, 2559–64, 2571–4, 2577–82, 2587–95, 2597–604, 2613–17, 2629–31, 2637–9, 2645–6, 2649, 2655–9, 2661–4, 2755–6, 2827–8, 2843–54, 2858–72, 3231–2, 3249–54, 3257–60, 3889–94;

MANUSCRIPT DESCRIPTIONS   389

(2) 51–2, 55–6, 78, 91–2, 105–6, 131–4, 167–70, 185–6, 253–4, 257, 259–60, 301–4, 307–8, 345–8, 353–4, 359–62, 381–2, 386–90, 579–80, 607–8, 613–14, 695–8, 701–2, 779–80, 855–6, 863–4, 911–14, 931–2, 946–8, 1011–18, 1020–2, 1056–60, 1085–8, 1103–5, 1107–8, 1131–6, 1180–1, 1187–8, 1301, 1304, 1487–8, 3697–700, 3729–38, 3867–78.

Its textual alignment with group δ is sufficiently evident from the fact that its quotations are culled from the fullest version of the poem; where there is no agreement with δ, the variants are often unique readings, and even where there is agreement it is often the case that it could have arisen by coincident variation.

The first set of extracts from *SS* is immediately followed by extracts from Nicholas of Bibra, *Liber Occultus*, on fos. 258ᵛ–263ᵛ.

History: The twelfth-century abbey of Maria Laach. A contents list which includes the *Liber moralium antiquorum poetarum et barbarorum quorundam* (= Part IV), also indicates ownership: *Liber monasterii beate Marie in Lacu*.

Jürgen Geiss, *Katalog der mittelalterlichen Handschriften der Universitäts- und Landesbibliothek Bonn* (Berlin and Boston, 2015), pp. 24–6; catalogue available online.

fc Canterbury Cathedral Archives CCA-DCc/AddMS/127/4 (not known to Mozley)

Parchment. s. xv.

Contents: This is not an excerpt but a fragment, comprising two bifolia used in rebinding later volumes. The first bifolium is written on both recto and verso; the outer folios contain lines 490–519 and 1208–38, and the inner folios contain lines 520–50 and lines 1172–1207. That is, the recto and verso of each individual folio contain consecutive portions of text, but the text on the inner folios is not consecutive from left to right, showing that this bifolium was part of a quire which has lost its inner bifolia. The text averages 31 lines to a page, and since the missing stretch of text consists of 622 lines, it can be assumed that the lost portion of the quire consisted of 10 folios (20 pages, or 5 bifolia), making up a quire of 12.

The second bifolium is less easily accounted for: one half contains *SS* lines 3797–822 on the recto, and lines 3829–52 on the verso, while the other half is blank on both recto and verso. It contains a consecutive stretch of text, allowing for the fact that physical damage to the

390 APPENDIX A

bifolium has resulted in the loss of 6–7 lines at the bottom of the page. Lines 3797–852 occur very near the conclusion of the poem, which ends at line 3900 in its fullest version (3864 in a slightly shorter version). Since lines 3853–900 do not follow on the other half of the bifolium, nor does it contain preceding text, the written part must represent the initial leaf (or almost initial) of a final quire, folded so that the blank half-leaves would form blank end-leaves. One last bifolium, inserted inside this present one, could have accommodated the final 40-odd lines needed to conclude the poem.

History: Canterbury cathedral archives have kindly supplied the following comments on the collection of fragments: 'These were found as flyleaves or covers of business books for church courts from the 1560s to 1580s. These books were probably supplied ready-bound by local stationers who would have got their binding leaves from the unwanted books of the Cathedral priory or St Augustine's libraries. When the bindings were extracted, no record was kept of which volumes they came from. Not all the fragments may have been bindings; some are probably bits of books that might have escaped total destruction. This item was probably catalogued some time ago, being imported from a legacy database which itself is likely to have been based on a card index. The wide date span suggests that it is a rough estimate only. The MS looks to be degraded rather than burnt; heat causes them to shrivel up and become charred. Rather, it is more likely to be the product of wear and tear, and abraded edges are a common problem where sheets were reused in bindings.'

Textually, fc's most noticeable affinities are with *DX*, or with one of these two manuscripts (see Introduction, p. cvi for discussion of the relation between them). In line 1223, for example, fc agrees with *DX* in reading 'Tunc' and 'dans oscula querit', but with *D* alone in reading 'ei' and 'primo'. Conversely, at 1195, it is the only manuscript to agree with *X* in reading 'libris' instead of 'coeptis', and at 1224, it is likewise the only one to agree with *X* in reading 'pronus' in place of 'citus'.

N. R. Ker *et al.*, *Medieval Manuscripts in British Libraries* (5 vols., Oxford, 1969–2002), ii. 322, 324.

fg Paris, Bibliothèque de Sainte Geneviève, 3196, fos. 115^r–116^r (Mozley's e)

Paper. s. xv

MANUSCRIPT DESCRIPTIONS 391

Contents: a large miscellany of excerpts from medieval and some classical authors. The excerpt from *SS* comprises lines 503–36 (the description of the coming of spring). The reading 'pariterque conturbat' in line 527 aligns this manuscript with the stemmatic group δ.

History: formerly belonged to François Pynart, a monk at Clairvaux, whose name appears inside the cover and on the first folio.

The manuscript is digitized and available online (https://archive. org/details/MS3196).

CALAMES (Catalogue en ligne des Archives et des Manuscrits de l'Enseignement Supérieur), Bibliothèque de Sainte Geneviève.

fh Giessen, Universitätsbibliothek 1251, fos. 51ᵛ–52ᵛ (not known to Mozley)

Paper. A composite manuscript: *SS* in Part IV, which is s. xv⁴ᐟ⁴.

Contents: *SS* lines 2051–464 (survey of the monastic orders), along with Henry of Settimello's *Elegia*. Its readings are generally aligned with γ, but in particular it is often in agreement only with *fm* or *fn* or both.

History: copied in the archdiocese of Mainz (?).

J. Valentinus Adrian, *Catalogus codicum manuscriptorum bibliothecae academicae Gissensis* (Frankfurt a. M., 1840).
The manuscript is digitized and available online; see http://digisam.ub. uni-giessen.de/ubg-ihd-hm.

fm Munich, Bayerische Staatsbibliothek, clm 237, fos. 218ʳ–220ᵛ (Mozley's n)

Paper. s. xv.

Contents: A vast anthology of Latin poetry (e.g. Geoffrey of Vinsauf, *Poetria nova*; Alan of Lille, *Anticlaudianus* and *De planctu naturae*; *Rapularius*; Avianus; elegiac *Romulus*; Henry of Settimello, *Elegia*; Maximian; Ovid, *De pulice*; Bede, *De metrica*). Includes lines 2051–482 of *SS* (survey of monastic orders)

History: According to Boutemy (p. 514), the manuscript 'belonged to Hartmann Schedel, and was copied by him at Leipzig while studying at the university in 1460, as is attested by the numerous notes which he added to the manuscript'. Its readings show general alignment with γ, but in particular with *fh* and *fn*.

392   APPENDIX A

Karl Halm, Georg von Laubmann, Wilhelm Meyer, *Catalogus codicum latino-rum Bibliothecae Regiae Monacensis* (2nd edn., vol. i.1, Munich, 1892).
André Boutemy, 'The manuscript tradition of the *Speculum Stultorum*', *Speculum*, viii (1933), 510–19.
A digitized version of the manuscript is available in the Münchener Digitalisierungszentrum.

fn Munich, Bayerische Staatsbibliothek, clm 14529, fos. 154^v, 160^r–166^r (Mozley's o)

Paper. 1465–6.

Contents: A miscellany of school texts, *auctoritates*, and other edifying matter (e.g. Alan of Lille, *Parabolae*; Henry of Settimello, *Elegia*; *Cato antiquus et novus*, a florilegium of classical authors); see Knödler, pp. 222–8. Includes *SS*, lines 2471–82 (Burnellus is old and broken by his peasant master and by the schools), and 2051–464 (survey of monastic orders). The manuscript title for the *SS* excerpts is *Querela Brunelli*. The readings of *fn* show general alignment with γ, but in particular with *fh* and *fm*.

History: The owner and scribe was Johann Tegernpeck, the abbot (1471–93) of St Emmeram in Regensburg. Like the scribe of *fm*, he made his copy while studying at the University of Leipzig in 1465–6 (Boutemy, p. 514; Knödler, pp. 219, 222–8).

Karl Halm, Georg von Laubmann, Wilhelm Meyer, *Catalogus codicum latino-rum Bibliothecae Regiae Monacensis* (2nd edn., vol. ii.2, Munich, 1876).
André Boutemy, 'The manuscript tradition of the *Speculum Stultorum*', *Speculum*, viii (1933), 510–19.
Julia Knödler, 'Schul- und Studienhandschriften des 15. Jahrhunderts aus St. Emmeram als Quellen zur spätmittelalterlichen Bildungsgeschichte unter besonderer Berücksichtigung studentischer Musterbriefe', in *Gelehrtes Leben im Kloster: Sankt Emmeram als Bildungszentrum im Spätmittelalter*, ed. Peter Schmid and Rainer Scharf (Munich, 2012), pp. 213–41.
A detailed online description is available in manuscripta-mediaevalia.de (search shelfmark). A digitized version of the manuscript is available in Münchener Digitalisierungszentrum.

fp Prague, Narodni Knihovna, III. D. 17, unnumbered guard-leaf, r–v (= 469) (Mozley's p)

The date of 1397 appears on fo. 19^r of the manuscript.

Contents: A large Latin miscellany, whose guard-leaf contains *SS* lines 2544–602 (part of the satire on the Roman curia and the power of

MANUSCRIPT DESCRIPTIONS 393

'munera'). Its readings show general alignment with γ, as is indicated by the fact that a colophon reading 'Explicit Albertanus dom. Wenceslay dicti Skala vicarii dom. Hermanni ecclesie Pragensis et supra' follows line 2602, showing that this was the last leaf of the poem in the manuscript from which it was taken.

For description, see manuscriptorium.com.

fq Prague, Narodni Knihovna, X. D. 9, fos. 94ᵛ–96ᵛ (=1888) (Mozley's q)

Contents: fos. 1a–83b Processus Belial alias peccatorum consolatio by Jacobus de Teramo, with an explicit: Et sic finitus est a. d. 1394 die VII mensis Octobris. Scriptus et finitus est presens liber a. d.... (rasura) in vigil. ss. Philippi et Jacobi apost. per L. de N.

fos. 84a–94b Historia Joseph translata de arabico in latinum per Alfuncium de Hispania, quam scripsit in Egypto existens in carcere Zoldani a. d. 1336.

fos. 94ᵛ–96ᵛ *SS*: *Epistle* and lines 1–2 only; rest of manuscript missing.

Not collated.

For description, see manuscriptorium.com.

ft Trier, Stadtbibliothek 1898, fo. 90ʳ⁻ᵛ (not known to Mozley)

s. xv med.

Contents: A florilegium, consulted in the printed version edited by Franz Brunhölzl, 'Florilegium Treverense', *Mittellateinisches Jahrbuch*, iii (1966),129–617; the excerpts from *SS* appear on pp. 188–9 (lines 1621–48). Contains *SS* lines 495–500, 715–16, 1057–8, 1151–2, 165–6, 301–2, 855–6, 1013–14, 95–6, 60a–b (see Notes), 115–16, 131–2. Its readings show general alignment with γ; see especially the two additional lines after line 60, which are shared with *MuVcTGoPmNe*.

fu Uppsala, Universitets-Bibliothek, Lat. 931, fos. 86ʳ–86ᵛ (not known to Mozley)

Paper. 1463 (date on fo. 56ᵛ, fo. 86ʳ). Written by one hand.

Contents: A florilegium which includes 35 lines of didactic verse, printed by Tönnes Kleberg, 'Eine spätmittelalterliche Proverbiasammlung der Universitätsbibliothek zu Uppsala (Cod. Ups. lat. 931)', *Eranos*, lviii (1960), 210–13. Robert R. Raymo identified 29 of these lines as taken

394   APPENDIX A

from *SS* (lines 285–96, 301–8, 311–15, 317–20); 'A Note on Uppsala Ms. Lat. 931', *Eranos*, lix (1962), 169. Raymo's comments on the stemmatic affiliation of this fragment are based on Mozley's faulty *apparatus criticus* and need correction: lines 309–10 are omitted, not 310–11, and only in *MK*, not *MKF*, probably as a result of eyeskip provoked by 'Casibus in laetis'. The remaining variants show a connection with γ rather than δ: 'bono' rather than 'pio' at 292; 'prospera' rather than *MND*'s 'aspera' at 302; 'praesciuisse' (*TGoFr*) at 305, rather than 'praetimuisse' in δ; 'uterque' in *VcPk* as well as *D* at 313; 'sero' (αβγ) rather than 'raro' (δ) at 317.

The final six lines read as follows:

> Post ualidas hyemes post longaque tempora brume
> Succedant iterum uernalia tempora mundo.
> Gaudia post fletum, post gaudia semino luctum,
>   Post lucem tenebrae, post tenebrosa iubar.
> Fflorent quos ditat infirme pulsio uene
>   Urine sedimen stercoreusque color.

NB qu(ocum)que in line 13 of the excerpt is very probably a mistaken expansion of qn̄que, the usual abbreviation for 'quandoque' (*SS* line 301).

Online searches reveal that the first two lines come from Venantius Fortunatus, *Carmina*, lib. ix. 3, lines 3 and 5 (ed. F. Leo, MGH auct. ant. IV.1 (Berlin, 1881)), while the last four lines derive from Eberhard the German, *Laborintus*, lines 99–100 and 109–10 (ed. E. Faral, *Les Arts poétiques du XIIe et du XIIIe siècle* (Paris, 1962), p. 341). In Venantius, 'post longaque tempora' is a variant of the reading in Leo's edition, 'ac tristia frigora'. In the last line of the Eberhard quotation, Faral reads 'sterculeusque', with a proposed correction to 'stercoreusque' in a footnote.

EARLY PRINTED EDITIONS

Mozley consulted the following early printed editions:

1. Editio Princeps. Utrecht, by Nicolaus Ketelaer and Gerardus de Leempt, *c.*1474. (ISTC iw00063000)
2. Paris, by Guy Marchant, *c.*1483–4. (ISCT iw00064000)
3. Leipzig, by Conrad Kachelofen, *c.*1490. (ISTC iw00066000)
4. Cologne, by Cornelis de Zierikzee, 28 Feb., 1499. Available online, from the Universitäts- und Landesbibliothek,

MANUSCRIPT DESCRIPTIONS 395

Darmstadt, at http://tudigit.ulb.tu-darmstadt.de/show/
inc-ii-179. (ISTC iw00067000)
5, 6. Frankfurt, by G. Draud, 1602, 1605.
7. Wolfenbüttel, 1662.

According to Mozley, 1, 2, and 7 are closely related to *R* or some
manuscript closely akin to it; 3, 4, 5, and 6 have a close relationship
with the γ group.

The *Incunabula Short Title Catalogue* also lists an edition published
at Paris by Philippe Pigouchet, *c.* 1490. (ISTC iw00065000). See the
ISTC for further details.

EXCLUDED WITNESSES

Ja Oxford, Bodleian Library, James 15, fos. 4^r–73^r (Mozley's h)

A paper manuscript copied by Richard James, Sir Robert Cotton's
librarian, between 1620 and 1630. Contains *SS*, with *Epistle*, and some
Goliardica. Listed by Mozley in the Mozley–Raymo edition, but not
included in his stemma or textual apparatus. Not collated.

PROSE PARAPHRASES

Mozley also included in his list of manuscripts the prose paraphrase of *SS*
found in Vienna, Nationalbibliothek, MS 4459, fos. 2^r–26^v, which he labels
y. Another copy of this prose paraphrase (unknown to Mozley, although
cited in Walther's *Initia*) is contained in MS Darmstadt 2525, fos. 33^r–61^v.
The paraphrase represents the full-length version of the poem. Both copies end with the colophon 'Explicit Speculum Stultorum reperitur copia
quorum/ Rome colonie necnon ubique locorum'. On the medieval practice of turning poems into prose in order to make them more accessible to
contemporary readers, see Paul Gerhard Schmidt, 'Prosaauflösung im
lateinischen Mittelalter', in *Philologie als Kulturwissenschaft. Studien zur
Literatur und Geschichte des Mittelalters*, ed. Ludger Grentzmann, Hubert
Herkommer, and Dieter Wuttke (Göttingen, 1987), pp. 38–44.

The prose paraphrases are too far removed from the poetic original
to be collated and included in the *apparatus criticus* in this edition. The
same is true of Munich, Bayerische Staatsbibliothek, MS clm 14129,
fos. 288^r–298^v (Mozley's l), which contains the so-called *Liber de moribus egregiisque dictis omnium philosophorum et poetarum* (Inc. 'Cum ex

396   APPENDIX A

honesta vita gentilium'). This is a voluminous prose compendium of various moralizing texts, including *SS*. A résumé of the poem's narrative is followed by excerpts of its moralizing passages (e.g. 'de medicis', 'de miserabili statu curie romane'). I have collated the relevant portion of clm 14129, but its text is too far distant from the original of *SS* to make it worthwhile to include it in the *apparatus criticus*.

On clm 14129, see Elisabeth Wunderle, *Katalog der lateinischen Handschriften der Bayerischen Staatsbibliothek München: Die Handschriften aus St Emmeran in Regensburg*, vol. 1: *CLM 14000–14130* (Wiesbaden, 1995).

On the *Liber de moribus egregiisque dictis*, and the need to distinguish it from the work with an almost identical title (*Liber de vita et moribus philosophorum*), formerly attributed to Walter Burley ('Inc. 'De [vita et moribus] philosophorum veterum tractaturus'), see Jan Prelog, 'Die Handschriften und Drucke von Walter Burleys Liber de vita et moribus philosophorum', *Codices manuscripti*, ix (1983), 1–18. On the changed attribution, see Mario Grignaschi, 'Lo Pseudo Walter Burley e il "Liber de Vita et Moribus Philosophorum"', *Medieovo*, xvi (1990), 131–90, 'Corrigenda et addenda sulla questione dello pseudo Burleo', ibid. 325–54, and *A Companion to Walter Burley: Late Medieval Logician and Metaphysician*, ed. Alessandro D. Conti (Leiden, 2013), pp. 41–2.

Other manuscripts of the the *Liber de moribus egregiisque dictis* listed by Prelog are as follows:

Berlin, Staatsbibliothek zu Berlin, Preussischer Kulturbesitz, lat. fol. 460, fos. 1^r–421^v

Munich, Bayerische Staatsbibliothek, clm 26781, fos. 22^r–122^v

Vienna, Österreichische Nationalbibliothek, 3337, fos. 1^r–228^v

LOST WITNESSES

The following seven manuscripts are recorded in the library catalogues edited by James, *Ancient Libraries of Canterbury and Dover*:

Henry of Eastry's catalogue (Christ Church): 545 (p. 67); 709 (p. 77); 1434 (p. 122).

Catalogue of St Augustine's Abbey: 485 (p. 251); 871 (p. 290); 1541 (p. 374); 1557 (p. 378); for further details, see Barker-Benfield's edition of this catalogue as listed in the main Bibliography, BA I.485e (i. 670–1),

MANUSCRIPT DESCRIPTIONS 397

BA I.871a (ii. 902–3), BA I. 1541c (ii. 1446–7), BA. I. 1557k–l (ii. 1470–1).

A further two are listed in Stoneman's catalogue of Dover Priory: 105g (p. 75); 106g (p. 76).

None of the above have been identified with surviving manuscripts.

Walther's *Initia*, no. 18944, lists 'Breslau R. 379', which was lost/destroyed in the war (see manuscripta.pl).

APPENDIX B

Interpolation on the Mendicant Friars

This interpolation appears in only seven of the 41 complete manuscripts of *SS*, which are linked by textual affiliation into three groups (see Introduction, pp. xciv–xcvii, ci–ciii): *MNHu, DK,* and *GI. M, N, Hu,* and *D* date from the fourteenth century, *K, G,* and *I* from the fifteenth. All seven are of English origin, and six (all except *I*) have early associations with English religious institutions (see Manuscript Descriptions in Appendix A). Since the opening lines of the interpolation clearly refer to the suppression of new mendicant orders by the Council of Lyon in 1274 (see n. to lines 2–6), the interpolation must post-date 1274, and probably 1298, when the Carmelites and Augustinians finally won confirmation of their exemption from the decree of suppression, and it could have been written well into the fourteenth century.

Textually, *K* is clearly differentiated from the other six manuscripts. In several places, it has extra lines which are lacking in *HuMNDGI* (23–4, 73–4, 85–8, 135–6, 139–40, 203–6); in other places, it supplies its own version of whole lines (84, 137–8, 144, 149–50, 210, 213). In the main body of *SS*, the scribe of *K* can be recognized as an intelligent 'improver' of the text (see Introduction, p. xcvi); it might therefore seem that there is a reasonable case for omitting *K*'s additional lines, and preferring the versions of the other manuscripts where there are two alternatives. However, *K*'s readings are often clearly superior in sense, while the readings of *HuMN* are often unacceptable, and the contaminated history of *GI* deprives them of full authority. Consequently, while basing the text on agreement between the different manuscript groups, I have thought it worthwhile to treat *K*'s version of the Interpolation as worth recording for its own sake, and have printed its extra lines in italics.

Mozley and Raymo's edition includes the Interpolation in Appendix A (*SS*, pp. 183–8). but without an *apparatus criticus*. The text is said to be 'mainly from *G*', but the printed text is closer to *K*; not only does it include *K*'s extra lines and unique variations of individual lines, but it also opts for *K*'s variants of individual words (e.g. 62 'inesse' for 'ut esse', 117 'statuere' for 'statuerunt', 128 'uocat' for 'docet', 146 'nusquam' for 'nunquam', 215 'Octonianus' for 'Octouianus'). Conversely, *G*'s omissions (e.g. at 55–64) are not reproduced in Mozley's text. No

INTERPOLATION ON THE MENDICANT FRIARS   399

other manuscripts are specified in the Appendix, and neither here nor in their Introduction is it mentioned that the interpolation is contained in *M* and *N*; n. 53 of the Introduction (p. 127) says it is found in the four manuscripts *DGIK* (*Hu* was unknown to Mozley and Raymo).

Headings: the headings in the manuscripts vary in line with the manuscript groups, but are rather haphazardly situated in the text. I have therefore reported them in the *apparatus criticus* but inserted my own simplified versions in the text.

APPENDIX B

DE QUATVOR ORDINIBVS MENDICANTIVM

Sunt quoque mendicae multe modo religiones
sed priscis plures temporibus fuerant—
sicut euangelia temptarunt scribere multi,
sed cepit tantum quatuor ecclesia.
5   Sic quia mendicis mundus frustra quasi fluxit
ad similem numerum papa redegit eos.
Suffecere tubae legi tantummodo binae,
argentum non est omne quod amplius est.
Istorum primos Iacobinos Francia dicit,
10   quod prius ecclesiam suscipiunt Iacobi.
Hic ordo primus ut praedicet est stabilitus,
ex actu tali nomen honoris habens.
Sanctus Dominicus primus fundator eorum
est, quem sancta satis celebrat ecclesia.
15   Sanctus Franciscus fratres dedit inde minores,
quamuis cordatos Gallia dicat eos.
Hi quia se primis reputabant inferiores
hoc elegerunt nomen habere sibi.

---

after line 2412] de quatuor ordinibus mendicantium *HuMN* de ordine mendicantium *K* de ordinibus mendicantibus *D* de iacobinis fratribus *I²* *om. GI*   **1** mendicae] mendices *D*; modo] uero *HuMN*; religioni] *end not visible M*   **2** priscis] piscis *M*   **3** sicut] sunt *HuMN D GI*; temptarunt] quam multi *D* ceu multi *HuMN GI*; multi] nisi *HuMN D GI*   **4** sed cepit tantum] accepitque nisi *HuMND GI*   **5** quia] quoque *GI*; fluxit] *end not visible M*   **7** suffecere] sufficere *K*   **after 8** de fratribus predicatoribus *HuMN* de predicatoribus *D* de iacobinis seu *G om. K I*   **9** dicit] dedit *K*   **10** quod] *Mozley* quo *all MSS*; Iacobi] *end not visible M*   **11** primus] prius *D*   **12** habens] habet *D*   **14** quem sancta satis] quam sancta satis *M* satis hunc sancta *GI*   **after 15** de fratribus minoribus *I²* de minoribus *D* (*illegible Hu*)   **16** quamuis cordatos] quam concordatos *D*   **17** primis] primus *D^pc*   **18** hoc] hos *HuN*; elegerunt] elegere *GI*   **after 18** de augustinianis et carmelitis *N D* (*illegible Hu*) de fratribus augustinianis et carmelitis *M*

---

1 For 'religio' = 'religious order', see Niermeyer 5, *DMLBS* 4.

2–6 At Lyon in 1274, the General Council of the Latin Church took note of the many new religious orders, especially mendicants, that had proliferated in recent years, despite the prohibition against their formation which had been issued by the Fourth Lateran Council in 1215. The Council of 1274 (c. xxiii, Mansi, xxiv. 96–7) decreed the suppression of the new orders, even those that had previously won papal approval. The Franciscans and Dominicans were exempted from this decree because of their manifest importance to the life of the Church; the Carmelites and Augustinians were granted a stay of execution on the grounds that they pre-dated the ban of 1215, and in 1298 their right to survive was confirmed (Andrews, *The Other Friars*, pp. 1–2, 18–21, 90–1, 207–8). Other orders, such as the Sack Friars and Pied Friars, were forbidden to take on new recruits, so that eventually they would die out by natural wastage (ibid. pp. 20, 207–11, 231).

7–8 'And the Lord spake unto Moses, saying: Make thee two trumpets of silver; of a whole piece shalt thou make them: that thou mayest use them for the calling of the assembly, and for

INTERPOLATION ON THE MENDICANT FRIARS 401

ON THE FOUR ORDERS OF THE MENDICANTS

Nowadays there are also many mendicant orders, but in former times there were more, just as many tried to write gospels, but the Church accepted only four. So because the world was uselessly overflowing, as it were, with mendicants, [5] the pope reduced them to a similar number. Two trumpets were enough under the law; not everything more than that number is silver. France calls the first of these Jacobins, because they first supported the church of St James. [10] This order was first founded in order to preach, bearing the honourable name of this activity. St Dominic is their first founder, whom Holy Church holds in high esteem. St Francis next founded the Minorites, [15] although France calls them the Cordeliers. Because they thought themselves inferior to the first ones, they chose to have this name for

the journeying of the camps' (Num. 10: 1–2). The two silver trumpets were used to summon the Israelites together in preparation for their march through the wilderness. Line 8 comments that if there had been more than two, they would not have been of silver. Similarly, if there were more than four mendicant orders, the extra ones would not be of high quality.

9–10 *primos*: as Knowles remarked, historians have tended to treat the Franciscans as the earlier of the first two mendicant orders, but both were formally approved at the Fourth Lateran Council of 1215, and as well as being senior to Francis by more than ten years, Dominic had for many years been leader of a group of priests dedicated to combating heresy. The Friars Preachers also reached England in 1221, three years before the Minorites (Knowles, *Religious Orders*, i. 146; Hinnebusch, *The Early English Friars Preachers*, pp. 3–4). The author of the Interpolation is therefore justified in claiming precedence for the Dominicans. *ecclesiam...Iacobi*: in 1218 Jean Barastre gave the Dominican order a house in Paris with a chapel which was dedicated to St James the Great; it gave its name to the rue Saint-Jacques and to the French Dominicans, who became known as the 'Jacobins' after this, their main monastery. (St James = Latin Sanctus Iacobus, French Saint Jacques).

11–12 The official title of the Dominicans is the Ordo Praedicatorum.

13 Dominic Guzman, a Spaniard born in Castile *c*.1170, was at first an Augustinian canon, but in the early 13th c., confronted with widespread heresy in southern France, he assembled a group of friends to preach against it. In 1215 they were officially instated as the Order of Preachers, adhering to an adapted version of the Rule of St Augustine.

15 According to the *Scripta Leonis* (c. xv, ed. Brooke, pp. 114–15), St Francis explained the name 'Fratres Minores' as implying that the Franciscans ought to be humble. Later in the *Scripta Leonis* (c. lxvii, ed. Brooke, pp. 202–5), St Francis is said to have claimed that when Christ said, 'What ye have done unto one of the least of these my brethren, ye have done unto me', although he was speaking of 'all the holy poor, he was especially predicting the Order of Friars Minor' (trans. Brooke). (The Latin quotation is a conflation of Matt. 25: 40 and 25: 45: 'Quod uni ex hiis minoribus fratribus meis fecistis, mihi fecistis'.) Accordingly, when Francis submitted the first version of his Rule for papal approval, he particularly requested that his followers should be called 'Fratres Minores'. See also *1 Cel.* xv (38), *Fontes Franciscani*, pp. 312–13, trans. Armstrong, *Francis*, i. 217; *2 Cel.* xli (71), *Fontes Franciscani*, p. 510, trans. Armstrong, *Francis*, ii. 295; Moorman, *History of the Franciscan Order*, p. 17.

16 *cordatos*: in place of a leather belt, the Franciscans wore a simple rope girdle; in the part of the girdle that hung down below the waist, it had three knots, signifying their threefold vow of obedience, poverty, and chastity (*Regula bullata*, c. i, *Fontes Franciscani*, pp. 171–2, trans. Armstrong, *Francis*, i. 100).

402 APPENDIX B

Post ambos uani surgunt Augustiniani
20 et Carmelitae consociantur eis,
quos mendicandi uexat tantummodo feruor,
spirituum cura nulla molestat eos.
Pauperibus Salomon periuria concomitari
annuit, et constat sic aliquando fore.
25 Quatuor hos omnes recte reputo fugiendos,
nam nequam uita tot uariare domos.
Plus uero querulus, plus recto semper adulans,
quae sapiens uitat sponte pericla subit.
Mendax mendicus modicum distare uidetur
30 nomine, re raro dissociata sibi.
Alliciunt tamen haec quod in his addiscere multa
possem, quodque michi sufficiunt modica.
Sic exercitium mentem racione bearet,
paupertas carni debita frena daret.
35 Et sic a reliquis distarem religiosis,
quis deus est uenter, mens asinina nimis;
qui plus acceptant salmonem quam Salomonem,
et multum bibere, scribere uero nichil;
qui modicum libros, multum libras uenerantur,
40 non aras sed haras, non inopes sed opes.

De ordine Praedicatorum uel de Iacobinis

Prae cunctis uellem Iacobinis associari
si non obstarent multa timenda michi.

---

19 ambos] istos *GI*; Augustiniani] augustiani *M*   **after 22** inuectiua contra quatuor ordines simul *HuMN*   **23–4** *sic K om. HuMN D GI*   **24** annuit] *Mozley* innuit *K*   **25** omnes] *om. N add. N*[pc]; recte reputo] recte preputo *D* reputo recte *K* **26** domos] domans *K*   **27** semper] pauper *HuMN D GI*; adulans] adulas *GI* **29** uidetur] uidentur *HuMN K GI*   **30** re] reque *GI*   **after 30** allectiua ad quatuor ordines simul *HuMN*   **31–40** *om. GI*   **31** tamen hec] haec me *K*; in] ab *D*   **32** modica] comoda *K*   **33** exercitium mentem] exercium mentem *N* exersicium mentem *Hu* exercitum mentem mentem *D*   **34** *om. N*   **35** sic] si *D*; religiosis] religionis *MN*   **36** quis] uel quibus *add. M*[pc]*N*[pc] *K*[pc]; est] uel quibus *D* **40** aras sed haras] *Mozley* haras sed aras *M*[pc] aras sed aras *HuM*[ac]*ND K*   **after 40** inuectio contra predicatores *D* de ordine predicatorum vel de Iacobinis quod idem est *K* inuectiua in speciali contra predicatores *HuN* allectiua ad ordinem predicatorum *added in lower margin M*[2]

INTERPOLATION ON THE MENDICANT FRIARS 403

themselves. After these two arose the vain Augustinians, and the Carmelites are joined with them. [20] The fervour for begging torments them so greatly that no care for souls troubles them. *Solomon acknowledges that perjury is found among the poor, and it is clear that this is sometimes the case.* I think that all these four should rightly be shunned, [25] for it is a wicked life to change so many houses. The one who complains more than is justified, the one who always praises more than is right, falls prey to dangers which the wise man avoids. 'Liar' [*mendax*] and 'beggar' [*mendicus*] seem to differ little in name, and are rarely dissociated from each other in fact. [30] They attract me [Burnellus] because I could learn many things among them, and because I am contented with little. So exercise would benefit my mind with moderation, and poverty would give the due restraints to the flesh. And so I would differ from the other men of religion, [35] for whom the stomach is God, and the mind all too asinine, who are more receptive to salmon than to Solomon, and to drinking a lot but writing nothing, who revere books [*libros*] little but pounds [*libras*] a lot, not altars [*aras*] but pigsties [*haras*], not the poor but riches. [40]

Of the Order of Preachers or Jacobins

Above them all I should wish to be associated with the Jacobins, if there were not many frightening things to put me off. My tongue is rough,

23–4 'Mendicitatem et divitias ne dederis mihi; tribue tantum victui meo necessaria . . . ne forte . . . egestate compulsus, furer, et periurem nomen Dei mei' (Prov. 30: 8–9). The AV does not use the word 'perjury'; the last part of verse 9 runs 'and take the name of my God in vain'.

31 *Alliciunt me*: Burnellus is claiming his natural qualifications for the mendicant life, as he had earlier claimed suitability for life as a scholar.

36 *deus est uenter*: Phil. 3: 19.

37–40 This punning wordplay is characteristic of medieval Latin satire; see nn. to *SS*, 2511–16, 2743–4, 2796.

40 For 'hara' = 'pigsty', see *DMLBS*. *M*'s correction is on the right lines, but is made to the wrong member of the pair.

404 APPENDIX B

Est mea lingua rudis, uox horrida, mens sine sensu,
    sic despectus ab his semper ineptus ero.
45   Nullus enim nisi qui bene praedicat aut bene cantat
    aut qui consiliis praeminet eximiis,
uel tractus de gente bona uel multa reportans
    uiuere cum tantis absque pudore potest.
Sub celebri ueste fatuus reputabor asellus,
50   paupertatis onus non honor esse ualens.
Sed me solatur quod quaeuis curia partim
    per me perue meos stabit, ut acta docent.
Et trabeae regis aequalis erit mea uestis,
    ut me magnificet talia quisque uidens.
55   Hoc quoque prae cunctis quae nunc occurrere possunt
    allicit elinguem, quod caput ecclesiae
clausit eis ora, ne contra facta malorum
    qui male iam possunt dicere quid ualeant.
Sicque Dei uerbum iacet arta lege ligatum,
60   ut non tangat ibi quo magis esset opus.
Sicque minas hominum metuens uelut opto silebo,
    ut sic terrena uiuere pace queam.
Heu tam diuitibus damnatio certa paratur,
    ut uia non pateat ulla salutis eis.

De ordine Fratrum Minorum

65   Non michi concordat cum cordis ordo minorum,
    ne concessa negans me fatuum statuam.

---

43 est] et *D*; mens] uox *HuMN*   **45** aut] uel *K*   **46** praeminet] premium *HuMN* eminet *GI*   **48** tantis] sanctis *HuMN D* fratribus *K*   **49** sub] a *GI*; reputabor] repetarer *GI*   **50** ualens] ualet *GI*   **after 50** inuectiua in speciali contra predicatores *M* allectiua ad (contra ad *Hu*) ordinem predicatorum *HuN*   **52** acta docent] afficiam *GI*   **53** mea] mihi *GI*   **54** uidens] uidet *HuMN D GI*   **55–64** *om. GI*   **after 55** allectiua ad ordinem predicatorum *M*   **56** caput ecclesiae] modo lege noua *K* id est papa *add. D in margin*   **57** clausit eis ora] taliter artantur *K*   **58** possunt] *Mozley* presunt *HuMN DK*; quid] quod *D*   **61** opto] apto *HuMN*   **62** ut] et *HuMN*; uiuere pace] pace uiuere *D*   **after 64** de ordine fratrum minorum *K* de minoribus *HuMN* inuectio contra minores *D*

45–6 As a natural concomitant of their preaching against heresy, the Dominicans devoted themselves to the study of theology, and their convents were important centres of teaching and learning (Knowles, *Religious Orders*, i. 151–2). However, Burnellus's claim about their singing ability is inaccurate; in fact they contented themselves with simple unelaborated

INTERPOLATION ON THE MENDICANT FRIARS 405

my voice harsh, my mind without understanding, so I shall always be despised by them as foolish. For no one can live with such exalted beings without disgrace unless he preaches well, or sings well, [45] or is distinguished for his excellent counsels, or comes from a good family or brings with him much wealth. In the celebrated habit I shall be thought a foolish ass, worthy to be the burden, not the glory, of poverty. [50] But it consoles me that any court will partly be supported by me and my relatives, as deeds teach. And my coat will be equal to a royal robe, so that anyone seeing it will revere me. Above all other things that can now come to mind, [55] this also attracts someone deprived of speech, that the head of the church shut their mouths, lest they should be able to say anything against the deeds of the evil who may act wickedly. So the word of God lies bound by a strict law, so that it may not have an impact where there is most need. [60] So, fearing the threats of men, I shall be silent as I wish, so that in this way I may live in peace on earth. Alas! such sure damnation awaits the rich, so that no way of salvation is open to them.

Of the Order of the Minorites

The *cord*ed order of Minorites does not ac*cord* with me, [65] lest I should make myself foolish by denying what has been granted. If one

---

chant (ibid. i. 151). The claim that they value birth and wealth may be a comment on the amount of support they received from royalty and the upper classes (see Hinnebusch, *The Early English Friars Preachers*, pp. 72–102, 253–8).

50 *onus non honor*: see nn. to *SS*, 145, 511–16.

51–4 This is probably an allusion to the prominent role of the Dominicans as 'household chaplains and confessors to the great' in England; 'for some two hundred years without a break the post of royal confessor was given to the friars. In this office the Preachers all but held a monopoly' (Knowles, *Religious Orders*, i. 167). The English Dominicans 'took a prominent role in the life of their country, serving the King as confessors, messengers, ambassadors, judges, or counsellors' (Hinnebusch, *The Early English Friars Preachers*, p. 458; for details, see pp. 458–91).

55–64 These lines seem to refer to the fact that the Dominicans 'were forbidden to censure clergy or monks in their public utterances' (Hinnebusch, *The Early English Friars Preachers*, p. 284). The Dominican Constitutions of 1228 prescribe that 'Our brethren should be careful not to upset religious or the clergy when they preach, by "setting their mouths against heaven" [Ps. 72: 9]. If they see anything in them which needs correcting, they should try to put it right by taking them aside and pleading with them as with fathers' (*Early Dominicans: Selected Writings*, ed. Tugwell, p. 468). See also Humbert of Romans (5th Master General of the Dominican Order, 1254–63), *Opera*, ii. 371: 'Item, caveat in sermone derisiones praesentium, vel derogationes absentium. specialiter autem vitam clericorum, vel religiosorum coram populo nunquam arguat; nec eos directe, vel indirecte, quasi sub pallio, notet; quia de talibus non sequitur aedificatio, sed frequenter scandalum, et turbatio plurium.'

56 *elinguem* is glossed 'id est me', to explain the accusative, in *M* and *D*.

406 APPENDIX B

Si quaeratur ab his qui sunt, quod nomen eorum,
  'sum minor hoc', quisquis absque pudore feret.
Cum quo si conferre uelis, mox magnificat se
70   maiorem dicens ordinibus reliquis.
Quo teneam nodo mutantem Protea uultum?
  Nunc minor est et nunc maior ut esse cupit.
Nunc satyrum, nunc agrestem Cyclopa mouetur,
  et nunc pigmeus, nunc Polyphemus erit.
75 Hos igitur miror se uelle uocare 'minores',
  cum sic praeferri prae reliquis studeant.
Lucifer astrorum dum despexit dominantem,
  surgere ne possit corruit in puteum.
Sic se iactantem reprobat dominus Phariseum
80   asseruit quia se dissimilem reliquis.
Sic qui se dicunt cunctis aliis meliores,
  est casus magnus plus metuendus eis.
Haec gens Franciscum se iactat habere patronum,
  si uerum dicant ergo sequantur eum.
85 *Hic non in summum se trusit pontificatum*
  nec Christi tunicam diuidit ecclesiam.
Eius sequaces in primis regula summo
  papae submittit ecclesiaeque sacrae.
Non caput ecclesiae conturbauit sacer ille,
90   non intrudere se quemue suum studuit.
In primis summo deuote pontifici se
  ut debet subicit ecclesiaeque sacrae.
Aes non admisit contentus tegmine solo,

---

68 quisquis] quisque *D* **69** uelis] uelim *HuM N D* **70** dicens] dicit
GI **71** nodo] modo *GI*; mutantem] unitatem *D* **72** ut esse] inesse
K **73–4** *sic K om. HuMN D GI* **75** miror] minor *MN* **76** sic] se *GI*;
praeferri] preferre *GI* **77** dominantem] paritatem *HuMN DK* **82** est casus
magnus plus] angelicus casus sit *GI*; est] et *D* **83** iactat] dicit *GI* **84** *whole
line*] *sic K* sanctum pro (sic *G* sit *I*) certo si sequerentur (sequeretur *GI*) eum *HuMN D
GI* **85–8** *sic K om. HuMN D GI* **89** conturbauit] conturbat *K*; sacer] satis
HuMN **90** se] *om. K*; quemue] queue *GI* **91** deuote] deuoti *D*; pontifici] pontifice *M*; se] *om. M* **93** admisit] amisit *MN*

---

71 A line from Horace, *Epistulae*, i. 1. 90; however, in Horace this line reads 'Quo teneam
vultus mutantem Protea nodo?' The rearranged word-order in the version quoted here is
found in the *Florilegium Gallicum*, fo. 86rb (see Duggan's note in *Becket Correspondence*,
p. 1016). Proteus was a sea-god who could change shape at will.

74 The giant encountered by Ulysses in Homer's *Odyssey*, Book xiii.

79–80 The boastful Pharisee who thanked God that he was not sinful like other men
appears in one of Christ's parables; Luke 18:9–14.

85–8 Having dedicated himself to a life of religious poverty in 1206 (see n. to lines 93–6),
St Francis attracted an increasing number of followers, and in 1209 he sought papal approval

INTERPOLATION ON THE MENDICANT FRIARS   407

asks them who they are, what is their name, 'I am less [*minor*] than this other', replies each one shamelessly. If you want to compare him with the other, he at once aggrandizes himself, saying he is greater than the other orders. [70] In what knot shall I hold this face-changing Proteus? Now he is lesser, and now he wants to be greater. *Now he is turned into a satyr, now a savage Cyclops, and now he will be a pygmy, now Polyphemus.* Therefore I marvel that they want to be called 'Minor', [75] when they strive in this way to take precedence over the others. When Lucifer scorned the ruler of the stars [God], he fell into the pit [of hell] so that he might not rise aloft. So the Lord reproved the Pharisee who was boasting of himself because he claimed that he was unlike others. [80] So those who call themselves better than everyone else should be the more afraid of a mighty fall. This race boasts of owning Francis as their patron; if they speak truly, let them therefore imitate him. *He did not thrust himself into the highest pontificate, [85] nor did he divide the Church, Christ's robe. His rule in the early days subordinated his followers to the pope and to Holy Church.* That holy man did not harass the head of the Church, nor did he try to intrude himself, or any of his followers. [90] In the early times he devoutly subjected himself, as he ought, to the mighty pope and to Holy Church. He did not allow money, content

for a simple Rule (no longer extant) outlining their way of life. This first Rule was replaced by several revised versions in subsequent years, as the expansion of the Order into Spain, France, and Germany as well as throughout Italy necessitated change; it was not until 1223 that a final version, the so-called *Regula bullata*, was approved by Honorius III (Moorman, *History of the Franciscan Order*, pp. 31, 50–8; text of the *Regula bullata* is in *Fontes Franciscani*, pp. 171–81, trans. Armstrong, *Francis*, i. 99–106). In the following year, a group of Friars Minor set out on a mission to England, where they met with such success that some ten years later 34 friaries had been founded in England and Scotland (Knowles, *Religious Orders*, i. 130–2; Moorman, *History of the Franciscan Order*, pp. 72–4, 171–3; Gurney Salter, *The Coming of the Friars Minor*).

86 When Christ was despoiled of his robe at the Crucifixion, it was found to be seamless, so the soldiers cast lots for it rather than cut it up; so, if the Church is Christ's robe, it too should not be torn apart (John 19: 23–4). Ironically in view of this claim, the final version of the Franciscan Rule approved in 1223 (see preceding n.) was a compromise between sharply dissenting factions in the Order (Moorman, *History of the Franciscan Order*, pp. 54–6).

93–6 According to the early lives of St Francis, he was inspired to dedicate himself to a life of poverty by hearing the Gospel passage in which Christ sent out his disciples to preach the kingdom of God, instructing them not to carry gold or silver or money, nor a staff for the journey; nor should they have two tunics, nor wear shoes (Luke 9: 3, 10: 1–8; Matt. 10: 9–10). He immediately put these prescriptions into practice, abandoning shoes, staff, and money, and contenting himself with a single tunic and a rope in place of a leather belt (*1 Cel.* ix (22), *Fontes Franciscani*, pp. 296–7, trans. Armstrong, *Francis*, i. 201–2; Bonaventura, *Legenda maior Sancti Francisci*, c. iii (1), *Fontes Franciscani*, pp. 794–5, trans. Armstrong, *Francis*, ii. 542). The same prescriptions were then incorporated into the so-called *Regula non bullata* of the Franciscan order (1221), together with the injunction that the disciples should not choose their own food but accept whatever was offered to them by those with whom they lodged in their travels (Luke 10: 7–8; *Regula non bullata*, c. ii and c. xiv, *Fontes Franciscani*, pp. 186–7 and 197–8, trans. Armstrong, *Francis*, i. 64–5 and 72–3).

408 APPENDIX B

et simplex uictus sufficiebat ei.
95 Regula Francisci sub praecepto prohibet ne
aes quisquam per se uel medium capiat.
Sic mortale facit praeceptum transgrediendo
aes, quocumque modo sumere quisque uolet.
Ergo si uita Sancti uideatur auita,
100 quis Franciscita sit modo cernis ita.
Hoc tamen est gratum, quod semper habere paratum
possem congenitum de propriis habitum.
Et placet hoc etiam quod cingit cordula corpus
taliter ut nodi tangere non ualeant.
105 Pendet pars nodosa nimis motura uidentes,
cingit pars plena nil nocitura michi.
Nunc etiam pedibus nudis incedo libenter;
ne grauet hoc soleae sufficienter agent.
Vt pulchras dominas inflammatas michi reddam,
110 opto nudentur tibia crura femur.

De fratribus Augustinianis

Augustinensis auertatur procul ordo,
ex aliis totum quicquid habet capiens.
Hi fuerant quondam deserti uasta colentes,
contentique satis simplicitate sua.
115 Post attendentes Iacobinos atque minores
mundo praeclaros et celebres fieri,

---

98 uolet] *sic all MSS* uelit *Mozley*   **99** sancti] sanctis *GI*; auita] unita *GI* id est antiqua *add. D*   **102** possem congenitum] possunt congenium *GI*   **103** cingit] tingit *D*   **104** non] hee *M*   **106** plana] plena *D*   **108** ne grauet] nec grauat *GI*   **109** pulchras dominas] mulieres sic *K*   **110** nudentur] uidentur *G I*   **after 110** de augustinianis *HuMN* inuectio contra augustinianos *D* de fratribus augustiniencis *K om. G I*   **112** totum] totum totum *M* tamen totum *HuN*   **114** *om. D*; contentique] contenti quod *M*; satis] gratis *GI*

97–8 Already in the mid-12th c., mechanisms were set up which enabled the Franciscans to circumvent the strict prohibitions of the order against accepting gifts of money or handling their own financial affairs. Even more alarming to hardliners, there were a growing number of instances where friars accepted gifts of money for their own personal use (Moorman, *History of the Franciscan Order*, pp. 185–7).

INTERPOLATION ON THE MENDICANT FRIARS   409

with a garment only, and simple food was enough for him. The Franciscan Rule forbids in its charter [95] that anyone should accept money, either himself or by a middleman. So it makes money a mortal sin, transgressing the rule, in whatever way anyone wants to receive it. So if the life of the Saint seems of ancestral authority, you now see who is a Franciscan. [100] This, however, is attractive, that I can always have ready a habit produced from my own resources. And this too pleases me, that the cord circles my body in such a way that the knots cannot touch [me]. The knotted part hangs down, so as to affect the beholders, [105] while the smooth part encircles but does not incommode me. Now too I go happily with bare feet; so that this causes no discomfort, sandals are sufficiently effective. So that I may make beautiful women aroused by me, I choose that my thighs, legs, and hip should go naked. [110]

Of the Augustinian brothers

Let the Augustinian order be kept at a distance, receiving from others everything it possesses! They were once inhabitants of the desert wastes, quite content with their simplicity. Later, observing that the Jacobins and Minorites [115] were honoured and celebrated in the world, they decided, so that they might be like both, to make a corrupt

---

99–103 These lines suddenly break into dissyllabic leonine rhyme. The meaning of lines 99–100 seems to be that, if the accounts of Francis's refusal to take money are authoritative, then the present-day friars are not true Franciscans. The meaning of lines 102–3 is obscure, but Burnellus may be saying that his grey coat qualifies him as a Franciscan (see line 120 and n.).

107–8 Following the Gospel Prescriptions (see n. to lines 93–6), Franciscans went barefoot, but were allowed to wear sandals if necessary (Gurney Salter, *The Coming of the Friars Minor*, p. 49; Cutts, *Scenes and Characters*, p. 42).

109–10 Franciscans did in fact wear breeches; St Francis repeatedly said that a mendicant should own nothing except a habit, a cord belt, and breeches (*Scripta Leonis*, cc. lxvi, lxix, lxxiv, ed. Brooke, pp. 202–3, 206–7, 216–17). However, the temptation to repeat the ridicule directed at the Cistercians on this point was evidently too good to pass by.

113 The Augustinian friars drew their existence from the informal and experimental groups of hermits which appeared in northern and central Italy from the 11th c. on. In 1256, Pope Alexander IV united five of these groups (the Tuscan Hermits, the Bonites, the Brettini, the Williamites, and the hermits of Montefavale) into a single order of hermit friars. The last two of these groups soon left this 'Great Union', while the remainder adopted the constitution and habits of the Tuscan Hermits (Andrews, *The Other Friars*, pp. 71–2, 84).

APPENDIX B

ut simul ambobus similes essent, statuere
  ex his corruptum compositum facere,
  ex primis tunicam sumentes cum scapulari;
120 grisea de reliquis sumpta cuculla fuit.
  Post haec cordatis similes ne desuper essent,
  a papa precibus obtinuere suis,
  compulsique suas denigrauere cucullas;
  sic color est alius formaque prima manet.
125 Viliter in causa cum uicti taliter essent,
  nomine sub decoris id statuere tegi,
  capas dicentes caputia cum propriae sint,
  sicut Franciscus, huius origo, docet.
  Nulla nociua magis Iacobinis gens reperitur,
130 nam dat uterque color his mala multa nimis.
  Ad loca suspecta si noctibus ire placebit,
  exterius sumunt candida sola sibi.
  Quos si deprendi contingit, se Iacobinos
  dicunt, hoc habitu testificante suo.
135 *Cumque uidere uolet uetitas, solum capit album,*
  et sic in sanctos scandala multa mouet.
  In uillis patriae cum mendicant ut oportet,
  fallitur ex nigro simplicitas populi,
  quae cinctum de non cincto discernere nescit,
140 *quis manicas habeat, quis manicis careat.*
  Sic persaepe ferunt quae debentur Iacobinis,
  sic res, sic famam surripiendo bonis.
  A monachis albis carnes ad uota uorare,
  dummodo delator non uideat, capiunt.

---

117 statuerunt] statuere *K* 119 scapulari] scapulare *I* 121 post haec] post
hoc *M* postea *GI*; cordatis] cordati *HuMN D* 123–5 *transp. HuMN* (125 – 123 –
124) 123 denigrauere] denigrare *K* 125–8 *om. GI* 126 statuere] stu-
duere *HuMN D* **after 126** de (a *HuN*) regula francisci unde habuerunt originem
HuMN 127 caputia] caputie *D* 128 docet] donet *D* uocat *K* 130 multa]
cuncta *GI* 131 si] de *GI*; placebit] licebit *D GI* 133 si] se *G*; contingit] contingat *GI* 134 habitu] habitum *D* 135–6 *sic K om. HuMN D
GI* 135 cumque] *Mozley* cum *K*; capit] *Mozley* capud *K* 137 *whole line*] sic *K*
quando mendicant laicos fallit nigra uestis *HuMN D GI* 138 *whole line*] sic *K* seque
ferunt alios teste colore nigro *HuMN D* seque ferunt teste colore nigro alios *GI* 139–
40 *sic K om. HuMN D GI* 142 sic … sic] hinc … hinc *D*; res … famam] formam … res
K; surripiendo] surripuere *K*; bonis] bonam *GI* 143 albis] *om. GI*; ad uota] discunt
ad uota *GI* 144 capiunt] capiant *GI*; (*whole line*) sumunt delator dummodo non
uideat *K*

INTERPOLATION ON THE MENDICANT FRIARS   411

combination of them, adopting from the former a tunic with scapular; from the others a grey cowl was taken over. [120] Afterwards, by their entreaties they obtained from the pope that they should not resemble the Franciscans in their outer layer, and under compulsion they darkened their cowls. So the first shape remains but the colour is different. When they were disgracefully beaten in court over this, [125] they decided to conceal it under the name of propriety, calling the cowls hoods, since they are appropriate, as Francis, their founder, teaches. No race is more harmful to the Jacobins, for both colours bring many evils to them. [130] If they want to go to shady places at night, they take only the white ones on the outside. If it happens that they are caught, they declare themselves to be Jacobins, as their habit testifies. *And when he wants to visit forbidden women, he takes the white one only,* [135] *and thus he creates many scandals to the detriment of the holy men. In the country towns when they beg, as is necessary, the people's naivety is deceived by the black—not being able to differentiate belted from unbelted, or who has sleeves and who has none.* [140] So they often take what is due to the Jacobins in this way, taking goods and reputation from the virtuous. From the white monks they borrow meat-eating to their heart's content, so long as the informer does not see. From the black monks

119–42 Before the Great Union, the separate hermit groups had a variety of different clothing, but in 1256 papal bulls decreed that their outer garments should be black, with black leather belts, covering a white tunic. This would distinguish them both from the Franciscans, who wore grey, and from the Dominicans, who wore a white tunic and scapular with a black cloak and hood on top (Hinnebusch, *The Early English Friars Preachers*, p. 244). However, the Augustinians were allowed to remove their outer black garment in hot weather, and even when they wore it, the white garment could still be glimpsed underneath, so that confusion was still possible. Further papal injunctions attempted to strengthen the rule in favour of black, but dress 'long remained a contentious issue' (Andrews, *The Other Friars*, pp. 89–90), as these lines of the Interpolation confirm. The author implies that the Augustinians deliberately remove their identifying black outer garment when engaged in shady pursuits, thus throwing the blame on the Dominicans, but when they are begging, they cash in on the good reputation of the Dominicans by wearing black again.

120 *grisea*: the Franciscan habit was originally grey (hence their name 'Greyfriars'), which continued to be the official colour until the 18th c. (Moorman, *History of the Franciscan Order*, p. 149 and n. 4). *cuculla* (= 'cowl'). Originally an outer garment prescribed to be worn by Benedictine monks (Rule of St Benedict c. lv), the term was also used to designate the small hood attached to the Franciscan habit (since they were allowed only one tunic, without an outer cloak), and the separate hood worn by Augustinian friars (see lines 127–8).

121 *cordatis*: see n. to line 16 above.

135–40 In addition to *K*'s extra lines (135–6, 139–40), I have printed its version of lines 137–8, since the version of these lines in the other manuscripts is weaker in sense.

139 *cinctum*: the black leather belt of the Augustinians was a feature that distinguished them from the Dominicans (see n. to lines 119–42).

144 The Augustinians followed the general prescriptions of the Rule of St Augustine (see n. to *SS*, 2257–86): holding all property in common, fasting and abstinence, humble clothing, chastity, obedience, discipline, and fraternal forbearance with each other. Meat-eating was forbidden. *delator* = 'informer'. In a religious community, it refers to a member who was assigned the task of observing the behaviour of its members and denouncing anyone who broke the rules.

APPENDIX B

145 A nigris monachis mirum hoc sumpsisse uidentur,
    ut nunquam carnes et quasi semper edant.
    Nam tritas clausas sectasque sophistice cunctas
    sicque boues crassas et sine carne uorant.
    Munera uel festa plus istos quam bona uita,
150   uel quam doctrinae gratia, gratificant.
    His quis fundator primus sit quisue patronus
    aestimo quod nullus dicere nouit homo.
    Nam quidam primum Paulum fingunt heremitam,
    quidam Baptistam, quod nichil esse liquet.
155 Immo nec magnus Augustinus ualet esse,
    de tribus his pariter certa probat ratio.
    Hi sancti non sic uixerunt nec statuissent
    uitam praeter eam quam uoluere sequi.
    Normam praefixit nigris monachis Benedictus,
160   iuxta quam uixit inter eos monachus.
    Sic loca Robertus fundat Cistercia sanctus,
    dans albos monachos albus et ipse simul.
    Dominicusque suos, Franciscus uero minores
    sic fundant ut eis nomine conueniant.
165 Est satis insanus dicens Augustinianum
    fratrem dictorum quemque fuisse trium.

De fratribus Carmelitis

    Ad Carmelitas quid me de iure moueret,
    quos constat sine re nomen habere suum?
    Hi faex et cauda cunctarum religionum,

145–8 *om. GI*   **145** monachis] nimis *HuMN D*; mirum hoc] *Mozley* hoc mirum *HuMN D K*   **146** nunquam] nusquam *K*   **147** nam] non *HuMN* ; sectasque] sectaque *M*   **149** (*whole line*) istos mundana mundo caros tria reddunt *K*   **150** quam] qui *GI*; gratificant] gratificat *GI*; (*whole line*) fictio doctrinae munera magna dapes *K*   **152** aestimo quod] est ideo *GI*   **153** quidam] quisquis *D*; primum Paulum] paulum primum *K*; fingunt] cingunt *M* singunt *HuN*   **156** his] hic *M* hoc *HuN GI*; certa probat] una patet *K*   **157** statuissent] statuerunt *GI*   **158** praeter eam] preterea *GI*   **159** normam] formam *M*; monachis] sanctus *GI*   **161** sic] et *GI*   **162** albus] albet *G*   **163** Dominicusque] dominicosque *GI*   **164** fundant] fundat *K*; nomine] *sic HuMN K GI* nomina *D*   **166** quemque] quamquam *D*   **after 166** de carmelitis *HuMN D* de fratribus carmelitis *K om. GI*   **167** quid] qui *GI*; moueret] mouebant *GI*   **168** quos] quorum *M*

INTERPOLATION ON THE MENDICANT FRIARS   413

they seem to have taken this miracle, [145] that they never and almost always eat meat. For they devour emaciated, incarcerated, chopped-up oxen, and so both 'fat' and 'meatless'. Gifts or feasts please them more than a virtuous life or than the benefit of teaching. [150] I think that nobody can tell who was their first founder or patron. For some say it was Paul the first hermit, some the Baptist, which is clearly rubbish. But neither can it be the great Augustine. [155] Sound reason judges equally about these three. These saints did not live thus, nor would they have established a life other than the one that they wanted to follow. Benedict set up a Rule for the black monks, according to which he lived as a monk among them. [160] So St Robert founded Cîteaux, himself a white monk creating white monks. And Dominic founded his followers, Francis his minorites, in such a way that they resemble them in their name. He who says that the Augustinian friar [165] was any one of the three above is totally insane.

Of the Carmelite brothers

What would rightly impel me to the Carmelites, who clearly have no substance to their name? They are the dregs and tail-end of all religious

151 The Augustinian friars were acutely aware that their obscure early history meant that they lacked an important and identifiable founder-figure, and as time went on they tried to repair this lack by focusing on St Augustine, whom they implausibly claimed as 'both patron and founder of their order' (Andrews, *The Other Friars*, p. 159). This claim brought them into conflict with the Augustinian regular canons, whose house at Pavia was proud of its possession of Augustine's body. In the 14th c., a series of Austin friars composed texts which developed a fake history of their order, claiming that it pre-dated the order of canons regular, and that they had a right to share custody of Augustine's relics. The dispute lasted for more than two centuries (Andrews, *The Other Friars*, pp. 158–62).

161 *Robertus*: Robert of Molesmes was the leader of the group of monks who left the Burgundian abbey of Molesmes in order to live a life more strictly conforming to the Benedictine Rule, the eventual result of which was the establishment of the Cistercian order (see n. to *SS*, 2111–82).

414 APPENDIX B

170   qui tantum nomen religionis habent.
         Est mons Carmelus heremi quo uiuere cepit
            gens cui diuisa cuique cauerna fuit.
         His erat ecclesia de Virgine matre Maria
            quo conuenerunt quando placebat eis.
175   Inter eos tandem Sathanas sua semina sparsit,
            et ne concordent schismate uexat eos.
         Albertus legatus eis pro lite premenda
            summi pontificis mittitur a latere;
         qui quosdam pellit, normam certamque quibusdam
180   uiuendi tradit, quos remanere sinit.
         Committit crimen post completoria uerbum
            dicens, praeceptum transgrediendo suum.
         Sed cautela iuuat post sompnum dicere, quamuis
            hoc contra mentem praecipientis erat.
185   Post cum carpetis stragulis spernendo cauernas
            exiliunt muros, multa patrando mala.
         Se tamen intitulant ex his quae deseruerunt,
            quae sunt mons heremus atque capella sacra.
         Et Carmelitas se dicunt aut Heremitas
190   aut fratres certe Virginis egregiae.
         Ast Albertinos melius se dicere possent,
            cuius eis solis regula sumpta manet.
         Iam sua carpeta mutauerunt radiata,
            ne contemnentur, in clamides niueas.
195   Nunc est scarletum quod carpetum fuit ante,

---

170 tantum] tamen *I*   **171** quo uiuere cepit] quod et ima recarpit *GI*   **172** cuique] cuiusque *K*   **173** his erat ecclesia] hisque capella fuit *K*   **175** sparsit] seuit *GI* perpsit *D*   **176** schismate] cismate *GI* sosmate *N*   **178** a latere] alacriter *GI*   **180** tradit] tribuit *GI*; sinit] fuit *K* sciuit *I*   **185** post cum carpetis] postea carpeta *GI*   **186** muros] mures *HuMN DK*   **187** se] sed *D GI*   **190** certe] tene *GI*   **191** possent] possunt *GI*   **192** manet] fuit *GI*   **194** contemnentur] contemnantur *HuMN D GI*; niueas] nimias *I*   **195** fuit ante] fuerat tunc *HuMN DK*

171–2 The Carmelites originated, at an uncertain date, as a group of hermits living on Mount Carmel in the Holy Land. As hermits, they lived as solitaries (like the Carthusians). A 12th-c. Jewish writer named Benjamin of Tudela records the existence of 'Christian monks' who 'inhabit some of the Carmel caves' (Andrews, *The Other Friars*, p. 10).

175–80 The 'proto-Carmelites' were transformed into a monastic community only in the early 13th c. 'Hermits identified as living at "the spring of Elijah" on Mount Carmel petitioned Albert of Vercelli, the Latin patriarch of Jerusalem (1205–14), whose see, after the battle of Hattin in 1187 and the loss of the holy city, had been transferred to the port of Acre

INTERPOLATION ON THE MENDICANT FRIARS   415

orders, who have only the name of religion. [170] Mount Carmel is where the desert race first lived, separate from each other, each with their own cell. Theirs was the church of the Virgin Mother Mary, where they assembled when they wished. At length Satan scattered his seeds among them [175] and troubled them with schism, to destroy their harmony. The legate Albert was sent to them from the pope's side, to suppppress the dispute; he expelled some, and gave a fixed rule of life to some whom he allowed to remain. [180] Anyone speaking a word after compline commits a crime, transgressing his precept. But craftiness takes pleasure in speaking after sleep, although this was against the intention of their legislator. Later, scorning the caves with their coarse fabrics, [185] they leaped over the walls, bringing about many evils. But they call themselves after those things they left behind, that is, the desert and the holy chapel. And they call themselves the eremitical Carmelites, and the brethren of the blessed Virgin. [190] But they could more properly call themselves Albertines, whose rule, adapted by them alone, still survives. Now they have changed their striped cloaks into snowy-white tunics, so that they should not be despised. What was hessian before is now scarlet; [195] this is how the

and the strip of coast still remaining in Christian hands', for a simple rule for the religious life (Andrews, *The Other Friars*, p. 11). Although this first rule does not survive, it has been reconstructed from later texts: it prescribed celibacy, a mixture of eremitical and communal elements (solitary contemplation in individual cells, tempered by daily Mass and weekly chapter meetings), the holding of all property in common, fasting, avoidance of meat, and silence from vespers until terce the following day. Papal approval was granted to this first rule of life by Pope Honorius III in 1226 (Andrews, *The Other Friars*, pp. 11–13).

182–3 On the rule concerning silence, see the preceding note.

185–6 The Carmelites began to leave the East 'as the security of the Holy Land became increasingly doubtful'. They were in Cyprus in 1238, Sicily in 1240/2, and were brought to England in 1242 by Richard de Grey, Earl of Cornwall and brother of Henry III, on his return from Syria (Andrews, *The Other Friars*, p. 14; Gurney Salter, *The Coming of the Friars Minor*, p. 125). For a list of Carmelite houses in England before the Reformation, with dates of their foundation, see Sheppard, *The English Carmelites*, p. 107.

190 The Carmelites were specially devoted to the Virgin Mary, and called themselves 'Hermits of the Blessed Virgin of Mount Carmel' (Andrews, *The Other Friars*, pp. 52–5).

193–4 The early Carmelites wore a tunic and scapular (a sleeveless outer garment) with a grey capuce or hood attached. Over this they wore a mantle with alternating light and dark stripes, woven from one piece of cloth; in Paris they were known as *barrés*. However in 1284 the general chapter of Pavia appointed proctors to petition the papal curia for permission to change their garment, on the grounds that the striped fabric was expensive and difficult to get hold of, and was also a cause of ridicule, preventing recruitment to the order. They chose instead a white mantle, which gave rise to their English name, 'Whitefriars' (Andrews, *The Other Friars*, pp. 20–21).

195 *scarletum*: a rich woollen cloth (initially, of any colour, not necessarily red); see *DMLBS* s. v. scarlatus 1.

APPENDIX B

sic humilis caeli gaudia pauper emit.
Cum dimiserunt heremum montemque, capellam
et uestem primam, nomen inane gerunt.
Si Carmelitae cupiant omnino uocari,
200   quid uere nomen significet uideant.
'Car' carnes comedit sed clam, 'me' moechus habetur,
'li' nutrit lites, 'ta' sacra uerba tacet.
Heliam dicunt isti necnon Heliseum
radicem sanctam primo fuisse suam.
205   *Vt non degenerent circumcidantur oportet*
quos tamen abscidi plus foret expediens.
Conuenit ambobus his ac Augustinianis
unum commune principium dubium.
Ignoratur enim quis sit fundator eorum
210   quis primus frater aut heremita fuit.
Si fons ignotus necnon suspectus habetur,
dici de riuis quae bona iure queunt?
Acephali ne sint aliquos signabo patronos,
qui magis his deceant nomine reque simul.
215   Augustus Caesar sit primis Octouianus
et Carmelitis impius ille Nabal.
Ad Carmelitas per se redeo michi caros,
finem sortiri de quibus haud facile.
Cellam cum lecto diuisam quisque tenebit,
220   liber cum sola solus ut esse queat.
Ad libitum carnes ibi deuorat et mala plura
committit quae nunc commemorare pudet.
Nam sunt tam sancti quod carnes tempore nullo
tangunt praeter quam quando latere putant.

---

197 dimiserunt] demiserunt *MN*; capellam] capella *G*   **198** et uestem primam] et primam (prima *G*) uestem *GI*   *after* **198** de patronis augustinorum et carmelitarum *HuMN*   **199** cupiant] cupiunt *K* capiant *D*   **200** uere] uerum *GI* **201** comedit] comedunt *GI*   **202** nutrit lites] lites nutrit *GI*   **203–6** *sic K om.* *HuMN D GI*   **208** commune principium] principium commune *G*   **209** sit fundator] primus frater *K*   **210** *whole line*] aut heremita quidem uel stabilitor erat *K* **213** aliquos] alios *GI*; signabo] signando *GI*; (*whole line*) hinc his ne capite careant *K* **214** qui magis his deceant] tales ut cumque *HuMN D* talibus utuntur *GI*; nomine] homine *M* **215** Cesar] primus *HuMN D GI*; primis] primus *K I*; Octouianus] octonianus *K* **216** Nabal] naballis *D*   *after* **216** redit ad carmelitas *HuMN D* **217** per se redeo] redeo per se *GI*   **218** haud] hanc *D*   **220** liber cum] gliscens *GI*; ut esse] adesse *D*   **221** carnes] canes *M*

INTERPOLATION ON THE MENDICANT FRIARS 417

humble pauper buys the joys of heaven. Since they have abandoned the desert and the mount, the chapel and their first vestment, they bear an empty name. If they absolutely insist on being called Carmelites, they should take note what the name really means: [200] 'Car'—'eats meat [*carnem*] but in secret'; 'me'—'is a fornicator' [*moechus*]; 'li'—'fosters quarrels' [*lites*]; 'ta'—'does not speak [*tacet*] the sacred words'. *They say that Elijah and also Elisha were their first holy founders. So that they do not degenerate, it is necessary for them to be cut back, [205] but it would be more expedient for them to be cut off altogether.* They and the Augustinians share one common dubious origin, for it is unknown who was their founder, who was the first brother or hermit. [210] If the source is unknown and also suspect, what good can rightly be said of its streams? So that they are not left without a head, I will indicate patrons which fit them better both in name and in deed. Let Octavian Augustus Caesar be for the former [Augustinians], [215] and that cruel Nabal for the Carmelites. I return to the Carmelites, dear to me, about whom it is not easy to make an end. Each of them will have a divided cell with a bed, so he can be freely alone with a single girl. [220] There he devours meat to his heart's content, and commits many sins which it is shameful to mention now. For they are so holy that they never touch meat at any time except when they think it is hidden. When they are outside,

197 Although many brethren moved to the West, Carmelite houses survived, on Mount Carmel itself, at Acre, and at Tyre, until the fall of Acre in 1291, when the remaining house on Mount Carmel was destroyed (Andrews, *The Other Friars*, p. 23).

203–4 The myth that the origins of the Carmelite order could be traced back to Elijah and Elisha is already contained in the opening rubric of the 1281 constitutions (quoted by Zermatten, 'The Carmelite Rule', pp. 377–8) and was energetically propagated by 14th-c. historians of the order (Andrews, *The Other Friars*, pp. 56–60; cf. Chaucer, *Summoner's Tale*, 1890–3).

216 Nabal was a rich landowner in Carmel, who churlishly rejected King David's request of hospitality for his shearers; Nabal's wife Abigail appeased David's anger, but God struck Nabal dead, whereupon David took Abigail as his wife (1 Sam. 25).

221–2 Meat-eating was permitted by Pope Eugenius IV in 1432, but the practice was 'in any case long established' (Andrews, *The Other Friars*, p. 64; cf. Zermatten, 'The Carmelite Rule', p. 384).

418 APPENDIX B

225 Extra cum fuerint, ludos spectacula quaerunt
ecclesiaeque sacrae limina raro terunt.
His magis interne mulieres atque tabernae
et mendicare quam sacra uerba dare.
Iam sua Carmelus dispersit ubique uenena,
230 et magnas urbes inficiendo replet.
Quae nunc urbs aut quis uicus uel quod modo pratum
quo non istorum luxuriae pateant?
A socio licite qui uult se quisque sequestrat,
ut uia prona malis undique detur eis.
235 Inter eos pugna plus quam patientia uincit,
plus uis quam uirtus, plus ratione rigor.

Quamuis ludendo sim forsan falsa locutus,
fratribus his sanctis non minus afficior.
Est unum solum quod tot mala iure repensat,
240 illa quod impune pro libito faciam.
Nulla michi culpa tantum uel fama resistet,
ad quemcumque gradum quominus aptus ero.
Nam uelut in poenis furiunt ratione remota,
sic dispensando iura sopita iacent.

Interpolation after line 2456 in MSS Hu, M, N, D, and K

1 Semper honorari desidero cum Iacobinis
pro quo conabor cuncta tacere mala.
Ex reliquis habitum fermentatos simul actus
sumere, pro lucris expediens, reputo.
5 Augustinenses mihi nil praestare ualebunt;
ex aliis namque quicquid habent capiunt.

229 ubique] uerba *D* 230 replet] replent *GI* 231 quis uicus] uicus quis *G*;
quod modo] quoque *MN* quod quoque *Hu D* **after 236** allectiua ficta ad carmelitas
HuMN D 237–8 *om. GI* 238 minus] nimis *D* 239 quod] quot
K 241 tantum] grandis *D* fraudis *K*; resistet] resistit *GI* resiccet *D* 242 quom-
inus] que minus *D* 243 nam uelut in poenis furiunt] nam uelut in penis furint *D* iam
uelut imponis fuerint *GI* **after line 2456]** *HuMN DK no variants*; *om. GI*

INTERPOLATION ON THE MENDICANT FRIARS 419

they seek out theatrical plays, [225] and rarely cross the thresholds of holy church. They are more familiar with women, taverns, and begging than with uttering sacred words. Now Carmel has spread its poison everywhere, and fills great cities with its corruption. [230] What city or what village or what meadow is there now where their excesses are not on display? Anyone who wishes is permitted to separate himself from a companion, so that the way to sins may be made easy for them. Among them, aggression, rather than patience, conquers, [235] force rather than virtue, rigour rather than reason.

Although I have perhaps spoken falsehoods in jest, I [Burnellus] am not less attached to these holy brethren. There is only one thing that rightly repays so many ills, which I shall willingly perform without punishment. [240] For no blame or gossip will exclude me from whatever ranks I shall be suited to. For just as they rage immoderately in punishment, so the laws lie dormant on the production of payment.

Interpolation after line 2456

I want to be always honoured with the Jacobins, for the sake of which I shall try to keep silent about all their misdeeds. As for the rest, I think to take on their habit and their corrupt deeds, taking advantage of their wealth. The Augustinians will give me nothing, [5] because they take from others whatever they have. But following their example, it pleases

225–6 The relaxation of the Rule by Eugenius IV meant that the friars were no longer confined to their individual cells (Andrews, *The Other Friars*, p. 64; Zermatten, 'The Carmelite Rule', p. 384).

225 *ludos spectacula*: it is not clear whether the friars are attending dramatic performances as spectators or as participants; 'miracles or "clerk plays"... seem to have been written, directed, and probably performed by members of the minor clergy' in the 13th and 14th centuries (Twycross and Carpenter, *Masks and Masking*, p. 191). The Decretals of Gregory IX (1234) forbade clerical participation in unruly types of 'ludi theatrales', while allowing serious liturgical drama (ibid. p. 41), but they 'seem on occasion to have been invoked against ordinary religious drama performed in church or churchyard' (ibid. pp. 40 n. 114, 192). For further examples of clerical involvement in (and disapproval of) theatrical activity, see Owst, *Literature and Pulpit*, pp. 480–5, especially p. 482. The original motive behind this involvement may be glimpsed in the medieval religious tale reported by Rosemary Woolf (*The English Mystery Plays*, p. 36), in which two friars, while travelling through the country, hear laughter and applause in a nearby meadow and deducing that 'spectacula... quae nos miracula appellare consuevimus' were taking place, immediately went there to preach.

Interpolation 2
These lines are not printed in Appendix A of the Mozley–Raymo edition (or even referred to elsewhere).

APPENDIX B

Exemplo tamen istorum mihi complacet unum
  ex plerisque bonis conglomerare malum.
Carmelitarum mihi cunctae conditiones
  sunt satis acceptae sed tamen una magis:
si quid lucrari potero uictus uel amictus,
  nullo participe, solus habere queo;
buccellam solus comedam, nulli dabo partem
  assideat quamuis contio tota mihi,

11–12 Since the Carmelites, like the Carthusians, did not eat as a community, Burnellus
looks forward to having no competition for whatever food is available.

INTERPOLATION ON THE MENDICANT FRIARS 421

me to heap up one evil from many goods. All the features of the Carmelites are quite pleasing to me, but one in particular: [10] if I am able to acquire any food or clothing I can have it to myself, with no one sharing. I shall eat my titbit alone; I shall give no one a share, although the whole convent sits around me.

APPENDIX C

Epistola ad Willelmum in Österreichische Nationalbibliothek
3467, fols. 1ʳ–3ʳ

1 Dilecto et cetera

4 Titulus libri Speculum Stultorum dicitur 5 ut insipientes aliena
inspecta stultitia tamquam in speculo propriam corrigant 7 et ex trabe
conspecta in oculo alieno festucam eiciant de proprio

9 Introducitur autem asinus animal stolidum uolens caudam aliam et
ampliorem quam natura contulerat sibi inseri <non> respiciens quid
necessitatis exposcat sed quid inepta cupiditas suadeat

10 Asinus iste religiosum significat qui tamquam asinus ad onera
portanda domini seruicio est deputatus qui non contentus condicione
sua sicut nec asinus cauda amplius affectans

11 et ad illud <omnibus> modis anhelans ut 12 caudam ueterem posset euellere et nouam inser<er>e id est uitam claustralem in qua debet
usque in finem perseuerare ut saluus fieret omnino fastidit et prolix-
iorem caudam 13 uidelicet prioratum uel abbatiam sibi posset apprehendere ubi amicorum copiam sequelam posset prius inserere et postea
quasi caudam post se quocumque ierit trahere

14 Medicus uero ille audito quid asinus petat petitionem habet pro
friuolo 15 unde ab inceptis suadet desistere et naturalibus contentari
16 et ut ei hec efficacius persuadeat assumpta parabola de duabus uaccis quid contigerit narrat

17 quomodo due uacce tempore hiemali in quodam prato lutoso de
nocte remorate sunt et post comestionem iacentes ueniente gelu acriori
portandas caudas[1] lutosas terre que limosa erat adheserunt et mane
redire uolentes caudas a terra euellere non potuerunt

18 Vnde altera illarum nimis impatiens illecta nihilominus amore
uituli^{pc} caudam suam amputauit suadens socie ut similiter faceret

19 Sed illa magis circumspecta socie sue consilio acquiescere supersedit expectans temporis beneficium et sic per discretionem se nouit in
angustiis temperare

20 Hec due uacce duo genera hominum significant in religione uiuentium

---

[1] caudas *add. in margin*

EPISTOLA AD WILLELMUM IN VIENNA 3467

21 Sunt enim quidam nimis precipites et indiscreti qui aduersitate aliqua superueniente id est amicorum suorum teneritudine quadam sicut uacca uituli[pc] amore capti et exercitati caudam suam statim abscidunt id est memoriam mortis qua se a muscis hoc est demonibus deberent protegere

24 Alii autem sunt qui maturiori reguntur consilio et quod maxime prudentie est fortuitos casus inopinatorum mentiuntur euentuum

25 Illud sapientis pre oculis interioribus habentes A casu describe diem non solis ab orti Non attendentes faciem scorpionis sed caudam

26 Hi sunt qui rerum exitus plusquam principia ponderant

31 Galienus uero uolens ut asinus saperet et intelligeret ac nouissima prouideret dissuasione prius usus est sed considerans quod stulto aliquid contra uoluntatem dissuadere uel suadere ualde sit difficile **32** cum eum uidet in proposito suo ita pertinaciter persistere iuxta Salomonem qui ait Responde stulto iuxta stultitiam suam precepit ei ut quedam perquireret que impossibile erat reperiri **33** quasi manifeste[pc] diceret consilio non acquiescis exemplo non instrueris necesse est ut labore erudiaris **34** multis enim uexatio dedit intellectum quos prosperitas nunquam potuit erudire

35 Asinus igitur qui uadit emere uana ille est qui uanitatem quam desiderat assequitur circumquaque discurrit gratiam hominum que quasi uitrum fragile est nunc adulationibus allicit nunc muneribus astringit **36** totque laboribus et erumnis efficitur pro nihilo quod longo minori pretio possit sibi regnum celorum comparasse **37** unde plerumque illud quod prius habuit perdi\<di\>t sicut asinus qui dum caudam suam prolongere laborauit ueterem ex toto amisit

38 Item frater Fromundus qui canes misit in asinum et postea min\<i\>s eius perterritus simulauit se in omnibus satisfacturum cogitans quomodo eum clanculo de medio tolleret et postea ab eo in rodanum est precipitatus **39** eos significat qui fratres aut homines simplices de sua astutia decipere attemptant sepius ipsi in laqueos incidunt quos alios abscondunt Iuxta illud non est lex equior illa quam necis artifices arte perire sua

40 Verba que asinus loquitur secundum animum sui intentum nunc fatua nunc discreta meditationes cordis significant inutiles **41** qui dies suos in uanitate consumunt circa seria desides et negligentes circa friuola soliciti et precipites quorum opera que sequuntur ostendunt dicente scriptura A fructibus eorum cognoscetis eos

42 Item de filio presbiteri et pullo galline qui postea pro tibia fracta reddidit talionem pro se satis lucet

43 Hoc enim hodie ex consuetudine uersum est in naturam ut qui leduntur in pueritia tempus retributionis usque ad annos senectutis

APPENDIX C

retinent in memoria nec acceptam obliuiscuntur iniuriam quousque manifesta fuerit expiata perpetua pena[2]

44 Preterea asinus qui parum scolas frequentauit de studio transiens nomen urbis non ualuit retinere in qua moram fecerat septennem illos significat qui cum sensus habeant ebetes ad scripturarum apices intelligendos tamen ut uideantur in utroque test\<amen\>to eruditi libros legunt quos non intelligunt **45** quorum nomina eis perlectis non meminerunt **48** Sepius enim contingit ut qui artibus uacant simulant se scire quod nesciunt **45b** cupientes ut ab hominibus multa et magna scire uideantur

Explicit prologus bonus   Incipit Brunellus   Assit in principio sancta Maria

---

[2] 'pena' *add. interlinear.*

APPENDIX D

Borrowings from the *Speculum Stultorum* in Gower's *Vox Clamantis*

See Introduction, pp. cxl–cxli, for Gower's direct allusions to *SS*. His frequent borrowings from Nigel's poem are set out in Raymo's article, 'Gower's *Vox Clamantis* and the *Speculum Stultorum*'. However Raymo's references are to the superseded edition of Thomas Wright, and since Wright does not provide line numbers of any sort, Raymo cites by page number and line number on the page. I think it therefore worthwhile to repeat the references to the parallels, using line numbers from the present edition.

At the outset it should be noted that Raymo claims for himself some borrowings which had already been identified by Macaulay, as he makes clear in some cases by listing them in his footnote 4 as Macaulay's, but including them among the examples he himself has observed (see lines i. 205–6, 556, 603). I have corrected the attributions in the following lists.

The borrowings identified by Macaulay in his notes are as follows: *VC* i. 79–80 = *SS*, 1037–8; *VC* i. 205–7 = *SS*, 61–2, 83; *VC* i. 211 = *SS*, 133; *VC* i. 213–14 = *SS*, 139–40; *VC* i. 603 = *SS*, 556[a]; *VC* i. 615–16 = *SS*, 397–8; *VC* i. 635 = *SS*, 423; *VC* i. 637–8 = *SS*, 437–40; *VC* ii. 15 = *SS*, 14.

The extra borrowings identified by Raymo are as follows: *VC* i. 92 = *SS*, 510[b]; *VC* i. 93–4 = *SS*, 515; *VC* i. 217 = *SS*, 159; *VC* i. 364 = *SS*, 696[a]; *VC* i. 511 = *SS*, 529–30; *VC* i. 601–2 = *SS*, 555, 526[a]; *VC* i. 605 = *SS*, 533[b]; *VC* i. 620–2 = *SS*, 394–6[a]; *VC* i. 628 = *SS*, 528[a]; *VC* i. 667–8 = *SS*, 413–14; *VC* i. 669 = *SS*, 441; *VC* i. 1331 = *SS*, 1301; *VC* ii. 33 = *SS*, 1133; *VC* ii. 193–4 = *SS*, 581–2; *VC* iii. 103 = *SS*, 1329; *VC* iii. 107–8 = *SS*, 1327–8; *VC* iii. 503 = *SS*, 113; *VC* iii. 508–10 = *SS*, 1479[a], 1480–2; *VC* iii. 513 = *SS*, 1483; *VC* iii. 521 = *SS*, 463–4; *VC* iii. 535 = *SS*, 1251; *VC* iii. 537 = *SS*, 1253–4; *VC* iii. 539–40 = *SS*, 285–6; *VC* iii. 540 = *SS*, 293; *VC* iii. 543 = *SS*, 287; *VC* iii. 551 = *SS*, 309; *VC* iii. 557 = *SS*, 311; *VC* iii. 559–60 = *SS*, 827–8; *VC* iii. 561–6 = *SS*, 487–90, 485–6; *VC* iii. 1309 = *SS*, 1471–2; *VC* iii. 1371–4 = *SS*, 49–52; *VC* iii. 1631–2 = *SS*, 55–6; *VC* iv. 173 = *SS*, 1167; *VC* iv. 501 = *SS*, 677[a]; *VC* iv. 614 = *SS*, 854; *VC* iv. 721 = *SS*, 2213[b]; *VC* iv. 747–8 = *SS*, 977–8; *VC* v. 429–30 = *SS*, 1367–8; *VC* vi. 713 = *SS*, 553[a]; *VC* vi. 371 = *SS*, 579; *VC* vi. 1081 = *SS*, 195[a]; *VC* vii. 373–4 = *SS*, 583–4; *VC* vii. 1021 = *SS*, 573.

426 APPENDIX D

For general similarities which are not verbatim borrowings, cf. *VC* i. 2076 and *SS*, 1151–2; *VC* iv. 79–82 and *SS*, 881–4; *VC* vii. 247–8 and *SS*, 37–8.

I have omitted Raymo's comparison of *VC* vi. 789 with *SS*, 3893–4 since this is simply a quotation of a familiar proverb (see n. on these lines), and also his comparison of *VC* iii. 11 ('Cristus erat pauper') with *SS*, 2849 ('Pauper erat Christus'), as not sufficiently distinctive.

Gower draws heavily on the story of the two cows and the story of Gundulf and the cock. Interestingly, as Raymo points out (p. 320), his quotations are drawn from every section of *SS* except the story of the Grateful Animals and the Ungrateful Man, which is the story he retells in the *Confessio Amantis*.

APPENDIX E

England and Sicily

One of the most puzzling features of the *Speculum Stultorum* is its geographical ambiguity. When Burnellus sets out for Salerno, his starting point is not specified, and it could well be England. On the way home, having got as far as the vicinity of Lyon, in the Rhône valley, he loses his medicines and decides to make for Paris; he then meets Arnold, a Sicilian ('Siculus ego sum'; 1225), who tells him the story of Gundulf, which he says took place in the time of 'William, grandfather of the present prince'. To the reader's surprise, Brunellus immediately declares that he is of the same nationality (1228), and this claim is confirmed a little later when he refers to himself as 'Apulian' (1585), since the duchy of Apulia formed part of the patrimony of the kings of Sicily. What has prompted this sudden appearance of Sicily in a poem that had seemed to be set in northern Europe? If there is some special satiric point to these details, it is no longer possible to grasp its significance, but it is worth noting that Sicily was not so far removed from English experience in the second half of the twelfth century as might be supposed. There was in fact a considerable amount of to-ing and fro-ing between Sicily and Canterbury in particular, and Nigel would have had no lack of opportunities to acquaint himself with this other Norman kingdom.[1]

John of Salisbury's boast of his extensive Italian travels on business of various kinds is well known: 'I have on ten occasions crossed the Alpine ridges, and on two passed down the length of Apulia; on many occasions I have executed business in the Roman Curia for my masters and friends.'[2] In the *Policraticus*, he refers to a three-month stay in Benevento (in Campania) with Pope Adrian IV,[3] and in a letter to Peter of Celle, he makes jocular reference to his preference for any wine other than 'the wine of Falerno or Palermo or of Greece, which the chancellor of the king of Sicily used to give me to the peril of my life and my salvation'.[4] The chancellor in question was Robert of Selby (Salesby), an Englishman by birth, who held this office in the chancery

---

[1] For general surveys of English–Sicilian relations at this period, see Haskins, 'England and Sicily', and Jamison, 'The Sicilian Norman Kingdom'.

[2] *Metalogicon*, iii. Prol. ed. Hall, p. 101; trans. Hall, p. 237. See also John of Salisbury, *Letters*, i. 253–6, Appendix 1, documenting his visits to the papal curia.

[3] *Policraticus*, vi. 24, ed. Webb, ii. 67; trans. Dickinson, p. 252.

[4] *Letters*, i. 57–8 (no. xxxiii); trans. ibid.

428 APPENDIX E

of Roger II of Sicily for over ten years, and 'dispensed a lavish hospitality to his fellow countrymen'.[5]

Another Englishman who served in Roger II's administration was Thomas Brown, who went to Norman Sicily after the death of Henry I (1135).[6] The *Dialogus de scaccario* says of Thomas: 'Magnus hic erat in magni regis Siculi curia consiliis providus et in regiis secretis pene precipuus'; however, with the accession of a new king (that is, William the Bad, who acceded in 1154), 'qui ignorabat illum', Brown was forced by court machinations to leave Sicily, and, says Richard FitzNigel in the contemporary *Dialogue of the Exchequer*,

> although he could have found the highest honour in any number of kingdoms, he chose to return to his native soil and to his hereditary liege-lord [Henry II]. Having been received by the king in a manner befitting both, because he had supervised great matters in Sicily, here too he was assigned to the important business of the exchequer. Thus he attained a place and an office of great dignity, and along with the barons he is also concerned with all the important business of the exchequer.[7]

The role of English administrators in the royal court of Sicily continued into the reign of William I ('the Bad'), when an Englishman called Richard Palmer began his rise to prominence. Already in 1157, Richard was nominated bishop-elect of Syracuse, but his involvement in government took precedence over his ecclesiastical duties and he delayed his election until 1169. 'In the king's last years he is called royal *consularis et familiaris* and he was one of the three familiars whom the king appointed on his deathbed (1166) to advise Queen Margaret during the regency for the young William II' ('the Good').[8] Richard was an opponent of Margaret's chief counsellor Stephen of Perche, and after Stephen's downfall in 1168,[9] Richard 'was one of the three or four longest-serving members of the king's inner council, which ran the government throughout the reign of William II (*r.* 1166–1189)'.[10] He also enjoyed high esteem in his native England: he earned the gratitude of Thomas Becket, for example, by his charitable welcome of Becket's fellow exiles

---

[5] Haskins, 'England and Sicily', p. 437; Abulafia, 'Selby [Salesby], Robert of (*fl.* 1137–1151)', *ODNB*.

[6] Matthew, 'Brown, Thomas (*d.* 1180)', *ODNB*.

[7] *Dialogus de scaccario* (ed. and trans. Amt), pp. 52–5. See also pp. 26–9.

[8] Matthew, 'Richard [Richard Palmer] (*d.* 1195)', *ODNB*.

[9] On this 'palace revolution', see 'Stephen des Routres, of Perche', Appendix I, *Becket Correspondence*, ii. 1389–90, and letter no. clix, i. 736, n. 1.

[10] See Matthew's *ODNB* entry, cited in n. 8.

ENGLAND AND SICILY

and kinsmen in Sicily.[11] However, Becket also entertained suspicions that Richard was 'corrupted by the hope of gaining the bishopric of Lincoln', and therefore tried to win Henry II's favour by supporting Becket's persecutors with money and advice, while they on their part competed to win the favour of William II by promising him 'the king of England's daughter [Joanna] in marriage'.[12] In 1176, Richard was one of the party that travelled to France to meet Joanna and escort her to Sicily for her marriage. In 1183 he was translated to the archbishopric of Messina, but he still involved himself in public affairs. In 1190, he was 'a prominent member of the delegation sent by the city of Messina to negotiate with Richard I while he was staying in the city'.

Richard Palmer was an old friend and associate of Peter of Blois, who had begun his career in 1166 as the tutor of the 12-year-old King William II ('the Good').[13] William's mother Margaret, acting as regent, had appealed to her French relatives for help in her new governmental responsibilities; Peter and his brother Guillaume were members of a group of 37 who were sent to Sicily in response to this appeal, 'ready to take over the administration of a country with a unique combination of Arab, Norman, and Sicilian people, of whose habits and expectations the newcomers knew nothing'.[14] Peter became keeper of the royal seal as well as tutor to the king, while his brother William became abbot of Santa Maria di Maniaci near Maletto.[15] But the foreign advisers were soon ousted, and in the autumn of 1168 Peter, with most of the newcomers, was forced to flee the country in fear of his life, and after a brief period in his native France, found employment in the household of Richard, archbishop of Canterbury (1173/4). Thereafter he managed to find further administrative posts in England, eventually (in 1182) becoming archdeacon of Bath. Probably around 1175, Peter was urged by Richard Palmer to return to Sicily, but he vigorously rejected the invitation, on the grounds that the Sicilian weather was unendurable, the food inedible, the Sicilians themselves deceitful and treacherous, and the eruptions of Etna resembled the horrors of hell. Instead, he urged Richard to return to England, where he would be welcomed by the king, and to live out his life in the land of his birth.[16]

---

[11] See Becket's letter to Richard Palmer in 1169, *Becket Correspondence*, ii. 970–3 (no. ccxxii): 'You have received our fellow exiles and blood relations.' Cf. the earlier, affectionately worded letter to Palmer written *c*.Dec. 1167, ibid. i. 736–9 (no. clix).

[12] Ibid. ii. 945 (no. ccxvi).

[13] See Cotts, *The Clerical Dilemma*, pp. 138–41.

[14] Southern, 'Blois, Peter of (1125×30–1212)', *ODNB*. See also *Becket Correspondence*, Appendix 1, ii. 1389–90, 'Stephen des Routres, of Perche'.

[15] He later resigned this abbacy and returned to France, as his brother Peter had urged him to do (*Epistolae*, nos. xc, xciii, PL ccvi. 281–5, 291–3).

[16] *Epistolae*, no. xlvi, PL ccvii. 133–7. Cf. Peter's unfavourable comparison of life in Sicily with life in his native France, *Epistolae*, no. xciii, PL ccvii. 292C.

430   APPENDIX E

Churchmen as well as administrators were exchanged between England and Sicily. Herbert Hoscam (d. 1180), bishop of Conza in Campania, was of English birth, while Simon of Puglia, dean of York and bishop of Exeter, was 'valde carus et familiaris' to Henry II.[17]

Finally, King Richard I's personal knowledge of Sicily should also be mentioned in this connection. As noted in the Introduction (pp. xxx, lxxii), Richard spent the winter of 1190 in Sicily on his way to the Holy Land to fight the Third Crusade. After the death of King William II, his illegitimate cousin Tancred had seized power, and had imprisoned Queen Joanna, William's widow and Richard I's sister. Tancred also withheld the money bequeathed to her in William's will. Richard demanded that his sister be released and given her inheritance; she was released in September but without the inheritance. Meanwhile the people of Messina revolted in protest against the presence of foreign troops, and Richard attacked and captured the city in October 1190. A treaty with Tancred was finally signed in March 1191; Tancred agreed to make financial reparations to Joanna, and he also agreed that Richard's nephew Arthur of Brittany (a mere infant at the time) should be married to one of his daughters when Arthur came of age. This marriage would have further cemented relations between England and Sicily, but as a result of Tancred's death in 1194 and the seizure of the kingdom of Sicily by the Hohenstaufen emperor Henry VI, husband of Roger II's daughter Constance, the plan came to nothing.[18]

The second half of the twelfth century was, therefore, a time when contacts between England and Sicily were especially frequent and intimate, and the monks of Canterbury, with their involvement in royal and papal affairs, were well placed to accumulate knowledge of Sicilian society.

---

[17] Gerald of Wales, De vita Galfridi, i. 12, Opera, iv. p. 383. Speaking of Geoffrey, the illegitimate son of Henry II, who is the subject of this vita, Gerald says that he 'quendam clericum suum, virum bonum et liberalem copiose litteratum et jurisperitum, magistrum Simonem scilicet Calabriae oriundum, qui pluribus jam annis ei in omni fortuna sua fideliter astiterat, et regi quoque patri suo valde carus et familiaris extiterat, ad curiam Romanam transmisit'. Simon is also mentioned in the Epistolae Cantuarienses (no. ccxcii, p. 276) as representing the interests of the king and Archbishop Baldwin at the Roman curia in 1189. Haskins ('England and Sicily', p. 437) also mentions 'Walter Offamil' and his brother Bartholomew, bishop of Agrigento, as examples of Englishmen holding high church office in Sicily, but there is in fact no evidence to support Walter's English nationality. See Loewenthal, 'For the biography of Walter Ophamil', and Mann, 'Why are names so important?', pp. 177–9.

[18] See Gillingham, Richard I, pp. 130–44.

BIBLIOGRAPHY

PRIMARY SOURCES

Translations follow after the edition of the original sources.

Abbo of Fleury, *Life of St Edmund*, in *Three Lives of English Saints*, ed. Michael Winterbottom (Toronto, 1972).

Abelard, Peter, *Dialectica: First Complete Edition of the Parisian Manuscript*, ed. L. M. de Rijk (2nd edn., Assen, 1970).

Adam of Dryburgh, *De ordine, habitu et professione canonicorum ordinis Praemonstratensis*, PL cxcviii. 443–610.

Alan of Lille: *Alano di Lilla. Liber Parabolarum*, ed. Oronzo Limone (Lecce, 1993).

—— trans. Ronald E. Pepin as *The Proverbs of Alan*, in *An English Translation of Auctores Octo, a Medieval Reader* (Lewiston, NY, 1999), pp. 149–75.

—— *De fide catholica contra haereticos*, PL ccx. 305–430.

—— *Literary Works*, ed. and trans. Winthrop Wetherbee (DOML 22; Cambridge, MA, 2013). [includes *Anticlaudianus* and *De planctu Naturae*]

Albert of Stade: *Albert von Stade, Troilus*, ed. Thomas Gärtner (Hildesheim, 2007).

Alcuin, *Epistolae*, ed. Ernst Dümmler (MGH, Epp. ii; Berlin, 1895).

Alexander Neckam, *De nominibus utensilium*, ed. A. Scheler, in 'Trois traités de lexicographie latine du XIIe et du XIIIe siècle: II', *Jahrbuch für romanische und englische Literatur*, vii (1866), 58–74, 155–73.

Andreas Capellanus, *De amore: Andreas Capellanus On Love*, ed. and trans. P. G. Walsh (London, 1982).

Anglo-Latin Satirical Poets and Epigrammatists of the Twelfth Century, The, ed. Thomas Wright (RS lix; 2 vols., London, 1872).

Annales Wintonienses: Annales Monasterii de Wintonia, ed. Henry Richards Luard, *Annales Monastici*, 2 (RS xxxvi.2; London, 1865).

Apocalipsis Goliae: Die Apokalypse des Golias, ed. Karl Strecker (Rome, 1928).

Archpoet: *Die Gedichte des Archipoeta*, ed. Heinrich Watenphul and Heinrich Krefeld (Heidelberg, 1958).

Augustine, *Contra Faustum*, ed. Joseph Zycha (CSEL xxv; Prague, Vienna, and Leipzig, 1881).

—— *De doctrina christiana*, ed. J. Martin (CCSL xxxii; Turnhout, 1962).

—— *In Iohannis Euangelium Tractatus CXXIV*, ed. Radbod Willems (CCSL xxxvi; Turnhout, 1954).

Avianus: *Aviani Fabulae*, ed. Antonio Guaglianone (Turin, 1958); also in *Minor Latin Poets*, ed. and trans. J. Wight Duff and Arnold Duff (2 vols., Cambridge, MA, 1934), ii. 669–749.

—— Alexander Neckam, *Novus Auianus*, ed. Thomas A.-P. Klein, *Favolisti latini medievali*, vii (Genoa, 1998).

432 BIBLIOGRAPHY

—— *L'Anti-Aviano*, ed. Simona Tamanza, *Favolisti latini medievali*, vii (Genoa, 1998).

—— *Astensis poetae Novus Avianus*, ed. Loriano Zurli, trad. and comm. Armando Bisanti, *Favolisti latini medievali*, v (Genoa, 1994).

—— *Il Novus Avianus di Venezia*, ed. Caterina Mordeglia; *Il Novus Avianus di Darmstadt*, ed. Elisabetta Vernetti, *Favolisti latini medievali*, xi (Genoa, 2004).

—— *Il Novus Avianus di Vienna*, ed. Emanuela Salvadori, *Favolisti latini medievali*, xii (Genoa, 2005).

Avitus, *Opera*, ed. Rudolph Peiper (MGH Auct. Ant.; Berlin, 1883).

Babio, ed. Andrea Dessì Fulgheri, in *Commedie*, ii. 129–301.

Baldo: *Beiträge zur lateinischen Erzählungsliteratur des Mittelalters* (I. Der Novus Aesopus des Baldo; II. Eine lateinische Übersetzung der griechischen Version des Kalila-Buchs), ed. Alfons Hilka, Abhandlungen der Gesellschaft der Wissenschaften zu Göttingen, philologisch-historische klasse, NS xxi. 3 (1928).

Baldwin of Ford: *Baudouin de Ford, Traités: Pain de Cîteaux 35–40*, ed. Robert Thomas (Chimay, Belgium, 1973–5).

—— *Spiritual Tractates*, trans. David N. Bell (2 vols., Kalamazoo, MI, 1986).

Bernard of Clairvaux: *Sancti Bernardi Opera*, ed. Jean Leclercq, C. H. Talbot, and H. M. Rochais (8 vols. in 9, Rome, 1957–77).

—— *The Letters of St. Bernard of Clairvaux*, trans. Bruno Scott James (Chicago, 1953).

Bernard Silvestris, *Cosmographia*, in *Bernard Silvestris, Poetic Works*, ed. and trans. Winthrop Wetherbee (Cambridge, MA, 2015).

Béroul, *The Romance of Tristran*, ed. and trans. Norris J. Lacy (New York and London, 1989).

Boccaccio, *Decamerone*, ed. Vittore Branca, in *Tutte le opere di Giovanni Boccaccio*, ed. Vittore Branca, (10 vols., Milan, 1964–98), iv.

—— *Epistole e lettere*, ed. Ginetta Auzzas, in *Tutte le opere di Giovanni Boccaccio*, ed. Vittore Branca, v. 1

—— *Epistolarum quae supersunt*, ed. Aldo Francesco Massèra, in Giovanni Boccaccio, *Opere latine minori* (Bari, 1928).

—— *Le lettere autografe di Giovanni Boccaccio del codice Laurenziano XXIX, 8*, ed. Guido Traversari (Castelfiorentino, 1905).

Boethius, *De topicis differentiis*, ed. Dimitrios Z. Nikitas (Athens, 1990).

—— trans. Eleanor Stump as *Boethius's De topicis differentiis* (Ithaca, NY, and London, 1978).

—— *In Topica Ciceronis Commentariorum Libri Sex*, PL lxiv. 1089–1174.

—— trans. Eleanor Stump as *Boethius's In Ciceronis Topica* (Ithaca, NY, and London, 1988).

Bonaventura, *Legenda maiora Sancti Francisci*, in *Fontes Franciscani*, pp. 777–911.

—— ed. and trans. in Armstrong, as 'The Major Legend', *Francis*, ii. 525–649.

Book of St Gilbert, The, ed. Raymonde Foreville and Gillian Keir (OMT, 1987).

BIBLIOGRAPHY 433

Bracton, Henry de, *De legibus et consuetudinibus Angliae*, ed. and trans. Sir Travers Twiss (RS lxx; 6 vols., London, 1878–83).

Busdraghi, Paola, ed., *L'Esopus attribuito a Gualtiero Anglico* (Genoa, 2005) ['elegiac *Romulus*'].

Carmina Burana, vol. i(1), ed. Alfons Hilka and Otto Schumann, *Die moralisch-satirischen Dichtungen* (Heidelberg, 1930); vol. i(2) [nos. 56–186], ed. Alfons Hilka and Otto Schumann, *Die Liebeslieder* (Heidelberg, 1941).

Carmina Cantabrigiensia: Die Cambridger Lieder, ed. Karl Strecker (MGH Scriptores rerum germanicarum in usum scholarum separatim editi; Berlin, 1926).

—— *The Cambridge Songs (Carmina Cantabrigiensia)*, ed. and trans. Jan M. Ziolkowski (Tempe, AZ, 1998).

Chanson de Roland, La, ed. F. Whitehead (Oxford, 1965).

Chartes et documents pour servir à l'histoire de l'abbaye de Saint-Maxent, ed. A. Richard, Archives historiques de Poitou, xvi (1886).

Chaucer, Geoffrey, *The Canterbury Tales*, ed. Jill Mann (London, 2005).

Chretien de Troyes, *Le Roman de Perceval ou Le Conte du Graal*, ed. Keith Busby (Tübingen, 1993).

—— *Yvain (Le chevalier au lion)*, ed. T. B. W. Reid (Manchester, 1942; corr. edn. 1967).

Compilatio singularis exemplorum, ed. A. Hilka, in 'Neue Beiträge zur Erzählungsliteratur des Mittelalters', *Jahresbericht der schlesischen Gesellschaft für vaterländische Cultur*, xc (1912), 1–24.

—— 'Geschichten aus der "Compilatio singularis exemplorum"', ed. Carsten Wollin, *Mittellateinisches Jahrbuch*, xli (2006), 77–92.

De uxore cerdonis, ed. Ferruccio Bertini, in *Commedie*, vi. 429–503.

Dracontius: *Blossii Aemilii Dracontii Carmina*, in MGH Auct. Ant. xiv, ed. Friedrich Vollmer (Berlin, 1905).

Eadmer, *Historia novorum in Anglia*, ed. Martin Rule (RS lxxxi; London, 1884).

—— trans. Geoffrey Bosanquet as *Eadmer's History of Recent Events in England* (Philadelphia, PA, 1965).

Eberhard Alemannus, *Laborintus*, in *Les Arts poétiques du XIIe et du XIIIe siècle*, ed. Edmond Faral (Paris, 1962), pp. 336–77.

Ecclesiastica Officia cisterciens du XIIème siècle, Les, ed. Danièle Choisselet and Placide Vernet (Reiningue, 1989).

Egbert of Liège: *Egberts von Lüttich Fecunda ratis*, ed. Ernst Voigt (Halle a. S., 1889).

'elegiac *Romulus*', see Busdraghi.

Elmham, Thomas of, *Historia Monasterii S. Augustini Cantuariensis*, ed. Charles Hardwick (London, 1858).

English Episcopal Acta ii. Canterbury 1162–1190, ed. C. R. Cheney and Bridgett E. A. Jones (Oxford, 1986).

434 BIBLIOGRAPHY

English Episcopal Acta iii. Canterbury 1193–1205, ed. C. R. Cheney and Eric John (Oxford, 1986).

English Episcopal Acta xvii. Coventry and Lichfield 1183–1208, ed. M. J. Franklin (Oxford, 1998).

English Episcopal Acta xxxi. Ely 1109–1197, ed. Nicholas Karn (Oxford, 2005).

Epistolae Cantuarienses, The Letters of the Prior and Convent of Christ Church, Canterbury, in *Chronicles and Memorials of the Reign of Richard I*, vol. ii, ed. William Stubbs (RS xxxviii; 2 vols., London, 1864–5). [Cited by number of Epistle.]

Favolisti latini medievali e umanistici, gen. ed. Ferruccio Bertini, Università di Genova, Pubblicazioni del Dipartimento di Archeologia, Filologia Classica e loro Tradizioni (14 vols., Genoa, 1984–2009).

Firminus Verris, *Dictionarius: Dictionnaire latin-français de Firmin le Ver*, ed. Brian Merrilees and William Edwards (Turnhout, 1994).

Fontes Franciscani, ed. Enrico Menestò, Stefano Brufani, *et al.* (Assisi, 1995).

Francis of Assisi: Early Documents, ed. and trans. Regis J. Armstrong, J. A. Wayne Hellmann, and William J. Short (4 vols., New York, 1999–2002).

Geoffrey of Vinsauf, *Poetria nova*, in *Les Arts poétiques du XIIe et du XIIIe siècle*, ed. Edmond Faral (Paris, 1962), pp. 194–262. [Cited by line number.]

—— *Poetria nova*, trans. Margaret F. Nims (rev. edn., Toronto, 2010).

—— *Summa de coloribus rhetoricis*, ed. Carsten Wollin, in 'Die erste Poetik Galfrids von Vinsauf: Eine vorläufige Edition der "Summa de coloribus rethoricis" ', *Mittellateinisches Jahrbuch*, xlix (2014), 393–442.

Gerald of Wales, *The Autobiography of Giraldus Cambrensis*, ed. and trans. H. E. Butler (London, 1937; reissued with a guide to further reading by John Gillingham, Woodbridge, 2005 [selected passages from a number of Gerald's works, arranged in chronological order to form an 'autobiography']).

—— *De invectionibus*, ed. J. S. Brewer, in *Giraldi Cambrensis Opera*, iii (1863), 3–96.

—— *De invectionibus*, ed. W. S. Davies, *Y Cymmrodor* xxx (1920).

—— *De principis instructione. Instruction for a Ruler*, ed. and trans. Robert Bartlett (OMT, 2018).

—— *De rebus a se gestis*, ed. J. S. Brewer, in *Giraldi Cambrensis Opera*, i (1861), 1–122.

—— *De vita Galfridi archiepiscopi Eboracensis*, ed. J. S. Brewer, in *Giraldi Cambrensis Opera*, iv (1873), 355–431.

—— *Gemma ecclesiastica*, ed. J. S. Brewer, in *Giraldi Cambrensis Opera*, ii (1862).

—— trans. John J. Hagen as *The Jewel of the Church* (Leiden, 1979).

—— *Giraldi Cambrensis Opera*, ed. J. S. Brewer, J. F. Dimock, and G. F. Warner (RS xxi; 8 vols., London, 1861–91).

BIBLIOGRAPHY
435

—— *Itinerarium Kambriae*, ed. J. F. Dimock, in *Giraldi Cambrensis Opera*, vi (1868), 1–152.

—— trans. Lewis Thorpe as *The Journey through Wales: The Description of Wales* (Harmondsworth, 1978).

—— *Speculum duorum or A Mirror of Two Men*, ed. Yves Lefèvre, R. B. C. Huygens, and Michael Richter, trans. Brian Dawson (Cardiff, 1974).

—— *Speculum ecclesiae*, ed. J. S. Brewer, in *Giraldi Cambrensis Opera*, iv (1873), 1–354.

—— *Speculum ecclesiae*, excerpts, ed. R. Pauli, in MGH SS. xxvii. 418–21.

—— *Symbolum electorum*, ed. J. S. Brewer, in *Giraldi Cambrensis Opera*, i (1861), 197–395.

—— *Topographia hibernica*, ed. J. F. Dimock, in *Giraldi Cambrensis Opera*, v (1867), 3–204.

—— *Vita S. Remigii*, ed. J. F. Dimock, in *Giraldi Cambrensis Opera*, vii (1877), 1–78.

Gervase of Canterbury, *Actus Pontificum Cantuariensium*, in *The Historical Works of Gervase of Canterbury*, ed. William Stubbs (RS lxxiii; 2 vols., London, 1879–80), ii. 325–414.

—— *The Chronicle of the Reigns of Stephen, Henry II., and Richard I.*, in *The Historical Works of Gervase of Canterbury*, ed. Stubbs, vol. i.

Gesta Romanorum: The Anglo-Latin Gesta Romanorum, ed. and trans. Philippa Bright (OMT, 2019).

Geta, ed. Ferruccio Bertini, in *Commedie*, iii. 139–242.

Glossa ordinaria, PL cxiii.

Gower, John, *Confessio Amantis*, ed. G. C. Macaulay (EETS e.s. lxxxi–lxxxii; 2 vols., London, 1900–1).

—— *Mirour de l'Omme*, in *The Complete Works of John Gower*, ed. G. C. Macaulay, i: *The French Works* (Oxford, 1899).

—— *Vox Clamantis*, in *The Complete Works of John Gower*, ed. G. C. Macaulay, iv: *The Latin Works* (Oxford, 1902).

Grammatici Latini, ed. H. Keil (7 vols., Leipzig, 1857–80).

Grandmont: *Regula Venerabilis Viri Stephani Muretensis*, in *Scriptores Ordinis Grandimontensis*, ed. J. Becquet (CCCM viii; Turnhout, 1968).

Guibert de Nogent, *Autobiographie*, ed. Edmond-René Labande (Paris, 1981).

—— *Guibertus de Nouigento, De sanctis et eorum pigneribus*, ed. R. B. C. Huygens (CCCM cxxvii; Turnhout, 1993), pp. 79–175.

—— *Monodies and On the Relics of Saints*, trans. Joseph McAlhany and Jay Rubenstein (London, 2011).

Guigo I, *Consuetudines: Guiges Ier, Prieur de Chartreuse, Coutumes de Chartreuse* [with French translation], ed. 'par un Chartreux' (SC cccxiii; Paris, 1984).

Guiot de Provins, *Bible*, in *Les Oeuvres de Guiot de Provins, poète lyrique et satirique*, ed. John Orr (Manchester, 1915).

Gurney Salter, E., *The Coming of the Friars Minor to England and Germany, Being the Chronicles of Brother Thomas of Eccleston and Brother Jordan of*

436 BIBLIOGRAPHY

Giano, Translated from the Critical Editions of A. G. Little and H. Bohmer (London, 1926).

Haye, Thomas, ed., *Der Laberintus des Edmund Bramfield: Eine Satire auf der römische Kurie* (Beihefte zum Mittellateinischen Jahrbuch, xix; Stuttgart, 2017).

Henry of Settimello: Arrigo da Settimello, *Elegia*, ed. Clara Fossati (Florence, 2011).

Henryson, Robert, *The Poems of Robert Henryson*, ed. Denton Fox (Oxford, 1981).

Hervieux, Léopold, ed., *Les Fabulistes latins* (5 vols., vols. i–ii in 2nd edn., Paris, 1893–9).

Hildebert of Tours: *Hildeberti Cenomannensis episcopi Carmina minora*, ed. A. Brian Scott (Bibliotheca Teubneriana; Leipzig, 1969).

Holtzmann, Walther, *Papsturkunden in England*, vol. ii, Abhandlungen der Gesellschaft der Wissenschaften zu Göttingen, philologisch-historische klasse, series iii. 14–15 (1935–6).

—— *Papsturkunden in England*, vol. iii, Abhandlungen der Akademie der Wissenschaften in Göttingen, philologisch-historische klasse, series iii. 33 (1952).

Hugo Falcandus: *The History of the Tyrants of Sicily by Hugo Falcandus 1154–69*, ed. Graham A. Loud and Thomas Wiedemann (Manchester, 1998).

Hugh Primas: *Hugh Primas and the Archpoet*, trans. and ed. Fleur Adcock (Cambridge, 1994).

—— *Die Oxforder Gedichte des Primas*, ed. Wilhelm Meyer (Berlin, 1907).

Humbert of Romans, *Opera de vita regulari*, ed. Joachim Joseph Berthier (2 vols., Rome, 1888–9).

Jankyn's Book of Wikked Wyves, ed. Ralph Hanna and Traugott Lawler, 2 vols.: vol. i: *The Primary Texts: Walter Map's "Dissuasio"* (Athens, GA, 1997); vol. ii: *Seven Commentaries on Walter Map's "Dissuasio Valerii"* (Athens, GA, 2014).

Jerome, St: *Adversus Vigilantium*, in *S. Hieronymi Presbyteri Opera*, ed. J.-L. Feiertag (CCSL lxxixC; Turnhout, 2005).

—— *Sancti Eusebii Hieronymi Epistulae*, ed. I. Hilberg (CSEL 54–6; 3 vols., Vienna, 1910–18).

Jocelin of Brakelond, *The Chronicle of Jocelin of Brakelond*, ed. and trans. H. E. Butler (London, 1949).

John of Capua, *Directorium humanae vitae: Beispiele der alten Weisen des Johann von Capua*, ed. Friedmar Gessler (Berlin, 1960).

John of Hauville: *Johannes de Hauvilla Architrenius*, ed. and trans. Winthrop Wetherbee (Cambridge, 1994).

John of Salisbury, *Entheticus maior and minor*, ed. and trans. Jan van Laarhoven (3 vols., Leiden, 1987). [Vol. i = Introduction, Texts, and (English) Translations; vol. ii = Commentaries and Notes; vol. iii = Bibliography, Dutch Translations, and Indexes.]

—— *Historia pontificalis*, ed. Marjorie Chibnall (OMT, 1986).

—— *The Letters of John of Salisbury* (OMT, 2 vols., i: *The Early Letters (1153–1161)* [numbers 1–135], ed. and trans. W. J. Millor, H. E. Butler,

BIBLIOGRAPHY 437

and C. N. L. Brooke (Oxford, 1986); ii: *The Later Letters (1163–1180)* [numbers 136–325], ed. and trans. W. J. Millor and C. N. L. Brooke (Oxford, 1979).

—— *Metalogicon*, ed. J. B. Hall (CCCM xcviii; Turnhout, 1991).

—— trans. J. B. Hall as *Metalogicon* (CCCM in Translation, CCCM xcviii; Turnhout, 2013).

—— *Policraticus: Ioannis Saresberiensis episcopi Carnotensis Policratici: sive, De nugis curialium et vestigiis philosophorum libri VIII*, ed. C. C. J. Webb (2 vols., Oxford, 1909).

—— *Policraticus*, Books I–IV, ed. K. S. B. Keats-Rohan (CCCM cviii; Turnhout, 1993).

—— trans. John Dickinson as *The Statesman's Book of John of Salisbury* [Books IV–VI, and selections from Books VII and VIII] (New York, 1963).

—— trans. Joseph B. Pike as *Frivolities of Courtiers and Footprints of Philosophers* [Books I–III, and selections from Books VII and VIII] (New York, 1972).

Joseph of Exeter, *Ylias: Joseph Iscanus Werke und Briefe*, ed. Ludwig Gompf (Leiden and Cologne, 1970).

—— trans. Gildas Roberts as *The Iliad of Dares Phrygius* (Cape Town, 1970).

Justinian, *Corpus Juris Civilis*, ed. Theodor Mommsen with the aid of Paul Krüger, Rudolph Schöll, and Wilhelm Kroll (3 vols., Frankfurt a. M., 1968–70); vol. i, *Digest*; vol. ii, *Codex*; vol. iii, *Novellae*. [Cited as recommended in Brundage, *Medieval Canon Law*, p. 203.]

—— *The Digest of Justinian*, trans. Alan Watson (4 vols., Philadelphia, 1985).

Kalila and Dimna: Kalilah and Dimnah or the Fables of Bidpai: Being an Account of their Literary History with an English Translation of the Later Syriac Version of the Same, and Notes, trans. I. G. N. Keith-Falconer (Cambridge, 1885).

—— *Ibn Al-Muquaffa', Le livre de Kalila et Dimna*, trans. André Miquel (Études arabes et islamiques: Textes et Traductions, i; Paris, 1957).

Lamentations of Matheolus: Jehan le Fèvre, *Les Lamentations de Matheolus et le Livre de Leesce de Jehan le Fèvre, de Ressons*, ed. A. G. Van Hamel (Bibliothèque de l'École des Hautes Études, 95–6, 2 vols., Paris, 1893–1905).

Lanfranc: *The Monastic Constitutions of Lanfranc*, ed. and trans. Dom David Knowles, rev. Christopher N. L. Brooke (OMT, rev. edn., 2002).

Lees, B. A., ed., *Records of the Templars in England in the Twelfth Century: The Inquest of 1185* (British Academy Records of the Social and Economic History of England and Wales, ix; London, 1935).

Lidia, ed. Isabella Gualandri and Giovanni Orlandi, in *Commedie*, vi. 111–318.

Marbod of Rennes, 'De abbate usurpante pontificalia', PL clxxi. 1656.

Matthew of Vendôme, 'Commendatio militis', PL ccv. 983.

Miles gloriosus, ed. Silvana Pareto, in *Commedie*, iv. 11–93.

Minor Latin Poets, ed. and trans. J. Wight Duff and Arnold Duff (2 vols., Cambridge, MA, 1934).

438 BIBLIOGRAPHY

Nigel of Longchamp, *Speculum Stultorum*:

—— *Speculum Stultorum*, ed. John H. Mozley and Robert R. Raymo (Berkeley, CA, 1960).

—— *Speculum Stultorum*, ed. Thomas Wright, in *The Anglo-Latin Satirical Poets and Epigrammatists of the Twelfth Century* (RS lix; 2 vols., London, 1872), i. 3–145.

—— *Speculum Stultorum*, ed. and trans. Francesca Albini (Genoa, 2003).

—— *The Book of Daun Burnel the Ass: Nigel Wireker's Speculum Stultorum*, trans. Graydon W. Regenos (Austin, TX, 1959).

—— *A Mirror for Fools: The Book of Burnel the Ass by Nigel Longchamp*, trans. J. H. Mozley (Oxford, 1961; repr. Notre Dame, IN, 1963).

—— *Narrenspiegel oder Burnellus, der Esel, der einen längeren Schwanz haben wollt*, trans. Karl Langosch (Leipzig, 1982).

—— 'The *Epistola ad Willelmum* of Nigel Longchamps', ed. J. H. Mozley, *Medium Ævum*, xxxix (1970), 13–20.

Nigel of Longchamp: Other Works

—— *Nigel of Canterbury: Miracles of the Virgin Mary, in Verse*, ed. Jan Ziolkowski (Toronto, 1986).

—— *The Passion of St. Lawrence, Epigrams and Marginal Poems*, ed. and trans. Jan M. Ziolkowski (Mittellateinische Studien und Texte, xiv; Leiden, 1994).

—— *Nigellus de Longchamps dit Wereker, Tractatus contra curiales et officiales clericos*, ed. André Boutemy (Paris, 1959).

—— *Tractatus Nigelli contra curiales et officiales clericos*, ed. Thomas Wright, in *The Anglo-Latin Satirical Poets and Epigrammatists of the Twelfth Century* (RS lix, 2 vols., London, 1872), i. 146–230.

—— *Vita Sancti Pauli Primi Eremitae*, ed. André Boutemy, 'Une vie inédite de Paul de Thèbes par Nigellus de Longchamps', *Revue belge de philologie et d'histoire*, x (1931), 931–63.

—— ed. Leo M. Kaiser, 'A critical edition of Nigel Wireker's *Vita Sancti Pauli Primi Eremitae*', *Classical Folia*, xiv (1960), 63–81.

Nouveau recueil complet des fabliaux, ed. Willem Noomen and Nico van den Boogaard (10 vols., Assen and Maastricht, 1983–98).

Novati, Francesco, ed., *Carmina medii aevi* (Florence, 1883).

Osbern of Gloucester: *Osberno, Derivationes*, ed. Ferrucio Bertini, Vincenzo Ussani Jr, *et al.* (2 vols., Spoleto, 1996).

Otto of Freising: *Ottonis episcopi Frisingensis Chronica sive de duabus civitatibus*, ed. Adolf Hofmeister (MGH SS rer. germ.; 2nd edn., Hanover, 1912).

—— trans. C. C. Mierow as *The Two Cities* (New York, 1928).

Owl and the Nightingale, The: Text and Translation, ed. Neil Cartlidge (Exeter, 2001).

Pamphilus, ed. Stefano Pittaluga, in *Commedie*, iii. 11–137.

Pañcatantra (see also *Kalila and Dimna*), *The Pañćatantra*, trans. Chandra Rajan (London, 2006). [Based on the redaction by Purnabhadra, AD 1199.]

BIBLIOGRAPHY 439

Peter of Blois: *Canon episcopalis* (= De institutione episcopi), PL ccvii. 1097–1112.

—— *Petri Blesensis Carmina*, ed. C. Wollin (CCCM cxxviii; Turnhout, 1998).

—— *Epistolae*, PL ccvii. 1–560.

——*The Later Letters of Peter of Blois*, ed. and trans. Elizabeth Revell (Auctores Britannici Medii Aevi, xiii; Oxford, 1993).

Peter Chrysologus, *Sermones*, PL lii. 183–666.

Peter Comestor, *Historia scholastica*, PL cxcviii.

Peter the Venerable: *The Letters of Peter the Venerable*, ed. Giles Constable (2 vols., Cambridge, MA, 1967).

—— *Petri Cluniacensis Abbatis De Miraculis Libri Duo*, ed. Denise Bouthillier (CCCM lxxxiii; Turnhout, 1988).

—— *Statuta Petri Venerabilis Abbatis Cluniacensis IX (1146/7)*, ed. Giles Constable, in *Consuetudines Benedictinae Variae (Saec. XI–Saec. XIV)* (CCM vi; Siegburg, 1975), pp. 19–106.

Petrus Pictor: *Petri Pictoris Carmina*, ed. Lieven van Acker (CCCM xxv; Turnhout, 1972).

Premonstratensians: *Les Statuts de Prémontré au milieu du XIIe siècle*, ed. P. F. Lefèvre and W. M. Grauwen (Bibliotheca Analectorum Praemonstratensium xii; Averbode, 1978).

Prosper of Aquitaine: Prosper Aquitanus, *Liber Epigrammatum*, ed. Albert G. A. Horsting (CSEL c; Salzburg, 2016).

Ralph de Diceto: *Abbreviationes chronicorum*, in *Historical Works*, ed. Stubbs, i. 3–263.

—— *The Historical Works of Master Ralph de Diceto*, ed. William Stubbs (RS lxviii; 2 vols., London, 1876).

—— *Opuscula*, in *Historical Works*, ed. Stubbs, ii. 177–285.

—— *Ymagines historiarum*, in *Historical Works*, ed. Stubbs, i. 291–440, ii. 3–174. [Cited by volume and page number.]

Raymond of Bézières, *Liber Kalilae et Dimnae*, in *Les Fabulistes latins*, ed. Léopold Hervieux (5 vols., vols. i–ii in 2nd edn., Paris, 1893–9), v. 382–775.

Richard of Devizes: *The Chronicle of Richard of Devizes of the Time of King Richard the First*, ed. and trans. John T. Appleby (London, 1963).

Richard FitzNigel, *Dialogus de Scaccario. The Dialogue of the Exchequer*, ed. Emilie Amt (with *Constitutio Domus Regis. The Disposition of the King's Household*, ed. S. D. Church) (OMT, 2007).

Robert of Torigni, *The Chronography of Robert of Torigni*, ed. Thomas Bisson (2 vols., OMT 2020), vol. i: *The Chronicle AD 1100–1186*.

—— trans. Joseph Stevenson as *The Chronicles of Robert de Monte* (London, 1856; repr. and repaginated Llanerch, 1991).

Roger of Howden, *Chronica Magistri Rogeri de Houedene*, ed. William Stubbs (RS li; 4 vols., London, 1868–71). [Cited by volume and page number.]

—— trans. Henry T. Riley as *The Annals of Roger de Howden*, (2 vols., London, 1853; facsimile reprint, 2 vols. in 4, Felinfach, 1994).

440 BIBLIOGRAPHY

—— *Gesta Regis Henrici Secundi Benedicti Abbatis. The Chronicle of the Reigns of Henry II. and Richard I. A.D. 1169–92; known commonly under the name of Benedict of Peterborough*, ed. William Stubbs (RS xlxix; 2 vols., London, 1867). [Cited by volume and page number. For the attribution to Roger of Howden, see Richard Sharpe, *A Handlist of Latin Writers of Great Britain and Ireland before 1540* (Turnhout, 1997), p. 591.]

Roger II and the Creation of the Kingdom of Sicily: Selected Sources, ed. and trans. Graham A. Loud (Manchester, 2012).

Le Roman de Renart, ed. Mario Roques, Première Branche (CFMA; Paris, 1970).

Rubisca: in *The Hisperica Famina II: Related Poems*, ed. and trans. Michael W. Herren (Toronto, 1987), pp. 94–103.

Rule of St Augustine: *La Règle de Saint Augustin*, ed. Luc Verheijen (Études Augustiniennes; 2 vols., Paris, 1967).

—— trans. Raymond Canning as *The Rule of Saint Augustine*, with Introduction and Commentary by Tarsicius J. van Bavel (Kalamazoo, MI, 1996) [first published 1984].

Saxo Grammaticus, *Gesta Danorum: The History of the Danes*, ed. Karsten Friis-Jensen, trans. Peter Fisher (2 vols., OMT, 2015).

Scripta Leonis, Rufini et Angeli Sociorum S. Francisci: The Writings of Leo, Rufino and Angelo Companions of St. Francis, ed. and trans. Rosalind D. Brooke (OMT, 1970).

Sedulius: *Sedulii Opera Omnia*, ed. Johann Huemer (CSEL x; Vienna, 1885).

Serlo of Wilton: *Serlon de Wilton: Poèmes latins*, ed. Jan Öberg (Stockholm, 1963).

Sextus Amarcius, *Satires* [ed. Karl Manitius], trans. Ronald E. Pepin (Cambridge, MA, 2011).

Talis of the Fyve Bestis, The, in *Six Scottish Courtly and Chivalric Poems, Including Lyndsay's Squyer Meldrum*, ed. Emily Wingfield and Rhiannon Purdie (Kalamazoo, MI, 2018).

Templars: *La Règle du Temple*, ed. Henri de Curzon (Paris, 1886).

—— trans. J. M. Upton-Ward as *The Rule of the Templars: The French Text of the Rule of the Order of the Knights Templar* (Woodbridge, 2002).

Thomas Becket: *The Correspondence of Thomas Becket Archbishop of Canterbury 1162–1170*, ed. and trans. Anne Duggan (2 vols., OMT, 2000).

—— *The Lives of Thomas Becket*, trans. Michael Staunton (Manchester, 2001).

Thomas of Celano, *Vita prima Sancti Francisci*, in *Fontes Franciscani*, pp. 275–424; trans. Armstrong, *Francis*, i. 180–308.

—— *Vita secunda Sancti Francisci*, in *Fontes Franciscani*, pp. 441–639; trans. Armstrong, *Francis*, ii. 239–393.

Thorne, William, *Chronica*, in *Historiae Anglicanae Scriptores Decem*, ed. Roger Twysden (London, 1652).

—— trans. A. H. Davis as *William Thorne's Chronicle of Saint Augustine's Abbey, Canterbury* (Oxford, 1934).

BIBLIOGRAPHY 441

Tractatus Garsiae: or the Translation of the Relics of SS. Gold and Silver, ed. Rodney M. Thomson (Leiden, 1973).

Tugwell, Simon, ed., *Early Dominicans: Selected Writings* (London, 1982).

Ulrich of Cluny, *Antiquiores Consuetudines Cluniacensis Monasterii*, PL cxlix. 633–778.

Vacarius: *The Liber Pauperum of Vacarius*, ed. F. de Zulueta (Selden Society; London, 1929).

Varnhagen, H., ed., 'Zwei lateinische metrische Versionen der Legende von Placidus-Eustachius. I. Die Version in Distichen', *Zeitschrift für deutsches Altertum und deutsche Literatur*, xxiv (1880), 241–54.

Venantius Fortunatus, *Opera Poetica*, ed. Friedrich Leo (MGH Auct. Ant.; Berlin, 1861).

Verheijen: see Rule of Saint Augustine

Vita S. Norberti, PL clxx. 1257–1344.

Vitas patrum, PL lxxii.

Voigt, Ernst, ed., 'Das Florileg von S. Omer', *Romanische Forschungen*, vi (1891), 557–74.

Waddell, Chrysogonus, ed., *Narrative and Legislative Texts from Early Cîteaux* (Cîteaux, 1999). [Cited by internal references, plus page number.]

—— *Twelfth-Century Statutes from the Cistercian General Chapter* (Cîteaux, 2002).

Walter of Châtillon: *Galteri de Castellione Alexandreis*, ed. Marvin L. Colker (Padua, 1978).

—— trans. R. Telfryn Pritchard as *Walter of Châtillon, The Alexandreis* (Toronto, 1986).

—— trans. David Townsend as *The Alexandreis of Walter of Châtillon* (Philadelphia, PA, 1996).

—— *The Shorter Poems*, ed. and trans. David Traill (OMT, 2013). [Cited by poem number, stanza number, and line number.]

Walter Map, *De nugis curialium*, ed. and trans. M. R. James, C. N. L. Brooke, and R. A. B. Mynors (OMT, 1983).

Werner, Jakob, ed., *Beiträge zur Kunde der lateinischen Literatur des Mittelalters* (2nd edn., Aarau, 1905; repr. Hildesheim, 1979).

Wiederhold, Wilhelm, 'Papsturkunden in Frankreich II', *Nachrichten von der königlichen Gesellschaft der Wissenschaften zu Göttingen, philologisch-historische klasse*, (Berlin, 1906), 1–98.

William of Auvergne, see Hauréau.

William of Blois, *Alda*, in *Commedie*, vi. 11–109.

William Longchamp, *Practica legum et decretorum*, ed. in Exupère Caillemer, *Le Droit civil dans les provinces anglo-normandes au XIIe siècle*, Mémoires de l'Académie des sciences, arts et belles-lettres de Caen (1883), 157–220.

William of Malmesbury, *Gesta Pontificum Anglorum*, ed. and trans. M. Winterbottom and R. M. Thomson (2 vols., OMT, 2007).

William of Newburgh, *Historia Rerum Anglicarum*, in *Chronicles of the Reigns of Stephen, Henry II., and Richard I.*, ed. Richard Howlett (RS lxxxii/i–ii;

442 BIBLIOGRAPHY

2 vols., London, 1884–5). [Cited by book and chapter of the *Historia*, with volume and page number if the chapter is a long one.]

—— trans. Joseph Stevenson as *The History of William of Newburgh* (London, 1856; facsimile reprint, Felinfach, 1996).

Ysengrimus: Text with Translation, Introduction, and Commentary, ed. Jill Mann (Leiden, 1987).

SECONDARY SOURCES

Abulafia, D. S. H., 'Selby [Salesby], Robert of (*fl.*1137–1151)', *ODNB*.

Andrews, Frances, *The Other Friars: The Carmelites, Augustinian, Sack, and Pied Friars in the Middle Ages* (Woodbridge, 2006).

Appleby, John T., *England without Richard, 1189–1199* (London, 1965).

Arbesmann, Rudolph, 'The concept of "Christus medicus" in St Augustine', *Traditio*, x (1954), 1–28.

Baist, Gottfried, 'Der dankbare Löwe', *Romanische Forschungen*, xxix (1911), 317–19.

Baldwin, John W., 'A campaign to reduce clerical celibacy at the turn of the twelfth and thirteenth centuries', *Études d'histoire du droit canonique dédiées à Gabriel Le Bras* (2 vols., Paris, 1965), ii. 1041–53.

—— 'Masters at Paris from 1179 to 1215: A social perspective', in *Renaissance and Renewal in the Twelfth Century*, ed. Robert L. Benson and Giles Constable with Carol D. Lanham (Toronto, 1982), pp. 138–72.

—— *Masters, Princes, and Merchants: The Social Views of Peter the Chanter and his Circle* (2 vols., Princeton, NJ, 1970).

—— *Paris, 1200* (Stanford, CA, 2010) [original French version, Paris, 2006].

—— 'The penetration of university personnel into French and English administration at the turn of the twelfth and thirteenth centuries', *Revue des études islamiques*, xliv (1976), 199–215.

Bale, John, *Index Britanniae Scriptorum: John Bale's Index of British and Other Writers*, ed. Reginald Lane Poole and Mary Bateson (Oxford, 1902); reissued with an Introduction by Caroline Brett and James P. Carley (Cambridge, 1990).

Balfour, David, 'The origins of the Longchamp family', *Medieval Prosopography*, xviii (1997), 73–92.

—— 'William Longchamp: Upward mobility and character assassination in twelfth-century England', PhD diss., University of Connecticut, 1996. [Available through <OpenCommons@uconn.edu/dissertations>.]

Barakat, Robert A., *The Cistercian Sign Language: A Study in Non-Verbal Communication* (Kalamazoo, MI, 1975).

Barber, Malcolm, 'Frontier warfare in the Latin kingdom of Jerusalem: The campaign of Jacob's Ford, 1178–79', in *The Crusades and their Sources: Essays Presented to Bernard Hamilton*, ed. John France and William G. Zajac (Aldershot, 1998), pp. 9–22.

—— *The New Knighthood: A History of the Order of the Temple* (Cambridge, 1995).

BIBLIOGRAPHY 443

Barker-Benfield, B. C., ed., *St Augustine's Abbey, Canterbury* (Corpus of British Medieval Library Catalogues, xiii; 3 vols. [continuously paginated], London, 2008).

Barlow, Frank, *The English Church 1066–1154* (London and New York, 1979).

—— *Thomas Becket* (London, 1986).

Barrow, Julia, *The Clergy in the Medieval World: Secular Clerics, their Families and Careers in North-Western Europe, c.800–c.1200* (Cambridge, 2015).

Bartlett, Robert, *Gerald of Wales 1146–1223* (Oxford, 1982); repr. with new pagination and supplementary bibliography, as *Gerald of Wales: A Voice of the Middle Ages* (Stroud, 2006) [page numbers in parentheses refer to the reprint].

Batany, Jean, 'Le Rôle du zoomorphisme dans le *Speculum Stultorum*', in *The Fox and Other Animals*, ed. Brian Levy and Paul Wackers, *Reinardus Special Volume* (Amsterdam, 1993), pp. 3–12.

Baxter, Ron, *Bestiaries and their Users in the Middle Ages* (Stroud, 1998).

Bayless, Martha, *Parody in the Middle Ages: The Latin Tradition* (Ann Arbor, MI, 1996).

Bek-Pedersen, Karen, *The Norns in Old Norse Mythology* (Edinburgh, 2011).

Bennett, Deb, *Conquerors: The Roots of New World Horsemanship* (Solvang, CA, 1998).

Bennett, Matthew, '*La Regle du Temple* as a military manual, or How to deliver a cavalry charge', Appendix in *The Rule of the Templars*, trans. J. M. Upton-Ward (Woodbridge, 2002), pp. 175–88.

Benzinger, Josef, *Invectiva in Romam: Romkritik im Mittelalter vom 9. bis zum 12. Jahrhundert* (Lübeck and Hamburg, 1968).

Berman, Constance H., *The Cistercian Evolution: The Invention of a Religious Order in Twelfth-Century Europe* (Philadelphia, PA, 2000).

—— 'The Cistercian mystery: How was the order formed and by whom? Can the Anglo-Norman sources elucidate the problem?', *Haskins Society Journal*, xiii (1999), 1–19.

Biddle, Martin, 'Wolvesey: The domus quasi palatium of Henry de Blois in Winchester', in *Chateau Gaillard: 3rd Conference on European Castle Studies Held at Battle, Sussex, 19–24 September, 1966*, ed. A. J. Taylor (London, 1969), pp. 28–36.

—— *Wolvesey: The Old Bishop's Palace, Winchester* (London, 1986).

—— and D. J. Keene, 'Winchester in the eleventh and twelfth centuries', in Martin Biddle, ed., *Winchester Studies*, 1: *Winchester in the Early Middle Ages* (Oxford, 1976), pp. 241–448.

Bock, F., *Geschichte der liturgischen Gewänder des Mittelalters* (3 vols., Bonn, 1859–71).

Boutemy, André, 'À propos d'un manuscrit du Tractatus contra Curiales et Officiales Clericos de Nigellus de Longchamps', *Revue belge de philologie et d'histoire*, xii (1933), 987–1003.

—— 'Deux poèmes inconnus de Serlon de Bayeux et une copie nouvelle de son poème contre les moines de Caen', *Le moyen âge*, li (1938), 241–69.

444 BIBLIOGRAPHY

—— 'The manuscript tradition of the *Speculum Stultorum*', *Speculum*, viii (1933), 510–19.

—— 'Sur le "prologue en prose" et la date du Speculum Stultorum', *Revue de l'université de Bruxelles*, xl (1934–5), 67–90.

—— 'Two obituaries of Christ Church, Canterbury', *English Historical Review*, l (1935), 292–9.

Braun, Joseph, *Die liturgische Gewandung im Occident und Orient nach Ursprung und Entwicklung, Verwendung und Symbolik* (Freiburg i. Bresgau, 1907).

Brooke, C. N. L., 'Gregorian reform in action: Clerical marriage in England, 1050–1200', *The Cambridge Historical Journal*, xii (1956), 1–21.

—— 'Married men among the English higher clergy, 1066–1200', *The Cambridge Historical Journal*, xii (1956), 187–8.

Bruce, Scott G., *Silence and Sign Language in Medieval Monasticism: The Cluniac Tradition, c.900–1200* (Cambridge, 2007).

Brundage, James A., *Medieval Canon Law* (London and New York, 1995).

Bruun, Mette Birkedal, ed., *The Cambridge Companion to the Cistercian Order* (Cambridge, 2013).

Budinsky, A., *Die Universität Paris und die Fremden an derselben im Mittelalter* (Berlin, 1876).

Burton, Janet, and Karen Stöber, eds., *The Regular Canons in the Medieval British Isles* (Turnhout, 2011).

Champeaux, L. Boivin, *Notice sur Guillaume de Long-Champ* (Évreux, 1885).

Cheney, C. R., *Hubert Walter* (London, 1967).

—— 'Papal privileges for Gilbertine houses', in id., *Medieval Texts and Studies* (Oxford, 1973), pp. 39–65.

—— see also *English Episcopal Acta*.

Chenevix-Trench, Charles, *A History of Horsemanship* (New York, 1970).

Chesnutt, Michael, 'The Grateful Animals and the Ungrateful Man: An oriental exemplum and its derivatives in medieval European literary tradition', *Fabula*, xxi (1980), 24–55.

Cian, Vittorio, 'Una chiosa al testo delle "Epistolae" giovanili di Giovanni Boccaccio', *Bulletino della società dantesca italiana*, NS xvii (1910), 138–40.

Collinson, Patrick, Nigel Ramsay, and Margaret Sparks, eds., *A History of Canterbury Cathedral* (Oxford, 1995).

Colvin, H. M., *The White Canons in England* (Oxford, 1951).

Constable, Giles, 'Ailred of Rievaulx and the Nun of Watton: An episode in the early history of the Gilbertine Order', in *Medieval Women*, ed. Derek Baker (Oxford, 1978), pp. 205–26.

—— 'Cluniac tithes and the controversy between Gigny and Le Miroir', *Revue bénédictine*, lxx (1960), 591–624.

—— 'The military orders', in id., *Crusaders and Crusading in the Twelfth Century* (Aldershot, 2008), pp. 165–82.

—— *Monastic Tithes from their Origins to the Twelfth Century* (Cambridge, 1964).

BIBLIOGRAPHY 445

Conway, Agnes Ethel, 'The family of William Longchamp, Bishop of Ely, Chancellor and Justiciar of England, 1190–1191', *Archaeologia Cantiana*, xxxvi (1923), 15–42.

Cotts, John D., *The Clerical Dilemma: Peter of Blois and Literate Culture in the Twelfth Century* (Washington, DC, 2009).

—— 'The critique of the secular clergy in Peter of Blois and Nigellus de Longchamps', *The Haskins Society Journal*, xiii (1999), 137–50.

Coulton, G. G., *The Medieval Village* (Cambridge, 1925; repr. online, 2010).

Crosby, Everett U., *Bishop and Chapter in Twelfth-Century England: A Study of the Mensa Episcopalis* (Cambridge, 1994).

Curtius, Ernst Robert, *European Literature and the Latin Middle Ages*, trans. Willard R. Trask (New York, 1953).

Cutts, Edward L., *Scenes and Characters of the Middle Ages* (3rd edn., London, 1911).

Dart, J., *The History and Antiquities of the Cathedral Church of Canterbury and the Once-Adjoining Monastery* (London, 1726).

Delisle, Léopold, 'Notes sur quelques manuscrits de la bibliothèque de Tours', *Bibliothèque de l'École des chartes*, xxix (1868), 596–611.

D'Haenens, Albert, 'Écrire, un couteau dans la main gauche: Un aspect de la physiologie de l'écriture occidentale aux XIe et XIIe siècles', in *Clio et son regard: Mélanges d'histoire, de l'histoire de l'art et d'archéologie offerts à Jacques Stiennon*, ed. Rita Lejeune and Joseph Deckers (Liège, 1982), pp. 129–41.

Dicke, Gerd, and Klaus Grubmüller, eds., *Die Fabeln des Mittelalters und der frühen Neuzeit: Ein Katalog der deutschen Versionen und ihrer lateinischen Entsprechungen* (Munich, 1987).

Dickinson, J. C., *The Origins of the Austin Canons and their Introduction into England* (London, 1950).

Dodwell, C. R., *The Canterbury School of Illumination 1066–1200* (Cambridge, 1954).

Duckworth, George E., *Vergil and Classical Hexameter Poetry: A Study in Metrical Variety* (Ann Arbor, MI, 1969).

Dugdale, William, *Monasticon anglicanum*, rev. edn by John Caley, Henry Ellis, and Bulkeley Bandinel (6 vols. in 8, London, 1817–30).

Duggan, Anne J., 'Classical quotations and allusions in the correspondence of Thomas Becket: An investigation of their sources', *Viator*, xxxii (2001), 1–22.

Duggan, Charles, 'Equity and compassion in papal marriage decretals to England', in *Love and Marriage in the Twelfth Century*, ed. W. van Hoecke and A. Welkenhuysen (Leuven, 1981), pp. 59–89.

Elliott, Dyan, *The Corrupter of Boys: Sodomy, Scandal, and the Medieval Clergy* (Philadelphia, PA, 2020).

Empson, William, *The Structure of Complex Words* (3rd edn., Totowa, NJ, 1979).

446 BIBLIOGRAPHY

Ermini, Filippo, *Il 'Dies Irae'* (Geneva, 1928).

Esposito, M., 'On some unpublished poems attributed to Alexander Neckam', *English Historical Review*, xxx (1915), 450–71.

Fasti Ecclesiae Anglicanae 1066–1300: iv, *Salisbury*, ed. Diana Greenway (London, 1991).

—— x: *Exeter*, ed. Diana Greenway (London, 2005).

Feiss, Hugh, '*Circatores*: From Benedict of Nursia to Humbert of Romans', *American Benedictine Review*, xl (1980), 346–79.

Fichtner, Gerhard, 'Christus als Arzt: Ursprünge und Wirkungen eines Motivs', *Frühmittelalterliche Studien*, xvi (1982), 1–17.

Fleming, Robin, 'Christchurch's sisters and brothers: An edition and discussion of Canterbury obituary lists', in *The Culture of Christendom: Essays in Medieval History in Commemoration of Denis L. T. Bethell*, ed. Marc Anthony Meyer (London, 1993), pp. 115–53.

Flinn, John, *Le Roman de Renart dans la littérature française et les littératures étrangères au moyen âge* (Toronto, 1963).

Forey, Alan, *The Military Orders from the Twelfth to the Early Fourteenth Centuries* (Basingstoke, Hampshire, 1992).

Fossati, Luigi, *Il Pragmapoledittico: Dizionario grafico-itinerario dei Comuni e delle Frazioni d'Italia* (Milan, 1905).

Foulet, Lucien, *Le Roman de Renard* (2nd edn., Paris, 1968).

France, James, *The Cistercians in Medieval Art* (Stroud, Gloucestershire, 1998).

Franklin, M. J., see *English Episcopal Acta*, xvii: *Coventry and Lichfield 1183–1208*

—— 'Nonant, Hugh de (d. 1198)', *ODNB*.

Fryde, E. B., D. E. Greenway, S. Porter, and I. Roy, eds., *Handbook of British Chronology* (3rd edn., London, 1986).

Fuller, Sarah, 'Discant and the theory of fifthing', *Acta musicologica*, l (1978), 241–75.

Gabriel, A. L., 'English masters and students in Paris during the XIIth century', *Analecta Praemonstratensia*, xxv (1949), 51–95.

Gameson, Richard, *The Earliest Books of Canterbury Cathedral: Manuscripts and Fragments to c. 1200* (London, 2008).

Génestal, R., *Histoire de la légitimation des enfants naturels en droit canonique* (Paris, 1905).

Gibson, Margaret, 'Normans and Angevins, 1070–1220', in *A History of Canterbury Cathedral*, ed. Patrick Collinson, Nigel Ramsay, and Margaret Sparks (Oxford, 1995), pp. 38–68.

Gilchrist, Roberta, *Gender and Material Culture: The Archaeology of Religious Women* (London and New York, 1994).

Gillingham, John, 'The kidnapped king: Richard I in Germany, 1192–1194', *German Historical Institute London Bulletin*, xxx (2008), 5–34.

—— *Richard I* (rev. edn., New Haven, CT, and London, 2002).

Golding, Brian, *Gilbert of Sempringham and the Gilbertine Order c.1130–c.1300* (Oxford, 1995).

BIBLIOGRAPHY 447

Gouron, André, 'Cessante causa cessat effectus: À la naissance de l'adage', *Comptes rendus des séances de l'Académie des Inscriptions et Belles-Lettres*, cxliii (1999), 299–309.

Grabes, Herbert, *The Mutable Glass: Mirror-Imagery in Titles and Texts of the Middle Ages and English Renaissance* (Cambridge, 1982).

Graham, Rose, *S. Gilbert of Sempringham and the Gilbertines: A History of the Only English Monastic Order* (London, 1901).

—— and A. W. Clapham, 'The Order of Grandmont and its houses in England', *Archaeologia*, lxxv (1926), 159–210.

Graham, Timothy, and Andrew G. Watson, *The Recovery of the Past in Early Elizabethan England: Documents by John Bale and John Joscelyn from the circle of Matthew Parker* (Cambridge, 1998).

Gransden, Antonia, *Historical Writing in England c.550–c.1307* (London, 1974).

Grant, Raymond, *The Royal Forests of England* (Stroud, Gloucestershire, 1991).

Greatrex, Joan, *Biographical Register of the English Cathedral Priories of the Province of Canterbury, c.1066 to 1540* (Oxford, 1997).

Grimm, Jacob, *Teutonic Mythology*, trans. James Steven Stallybrass (4th edn., 4 vols., London, 1882–8; repr. 1966).

Grondeux, Anne, 'La Notion de langue maternelle et son apparition au Moyen Âge', in *Zwischen Babel und Pfingsten: Sprachdifferenzen und Gesprächverständigung in der Vormoderne (8.–16. Jahrhundert)*, ed. Peter von Moos (Münster, 2008), pp. 339–56.

Hall, Catherine, 'The one-way trail: Some observations on CCC ms 101 and G&CC ms 427', *Transactions of the Cambridge Bibliographical Society*, xi (1998), 272–84.

Hall, J. B., 'Notes on the "Miracula Sancte Dei Genitricis Virginis Marie, Versifice" of Nigellus de Longo Campo', *Studi medievali*, ser. iii, xxix (1988), 423–43.

Hallam, Elizabeth M., 'Henry II, Richard I and the Order of Grandmont', *Journal of Medieval History*, i (1975), 165–86.

Harvey, Barbara, *Living and Dying in England 1100–1540: The Monastic Experience* (Oxford, 1993).

—— 'Monastic pittances in the Middle Ages', in *Food in Medieval England: Diet and Nutrition*, ed. C. M. Woolgar, D. Serjeantson, and T. Waldron (Oxford, 2006), pp. 215–27.

Haskins, Charles H., 'England and Sicily in the twelfth century', *English Historical Review*, xxvi (1911), 433–47, 641–65.

—— 'Henry II. as a patron of literature', in *Essays in Mediaeval History Presented to Thomas Frederick Tout*, ed. A. G. Little and F. M. Powicke (Manchester, 1925), pp. 71–7.

Hauréau, Barthélemy, *Notices et extraits de quelques manuscrits latins de la Bibliothèque nationale* (6 vols., Paris, 1890–3).

448 BIBLIOGRAPHY

Haye, Thomas, 'Der Catalogus testium veritatis des Matthias Flacius Illyricus—eine Einführung in die Literatur des Mittelalters?', *Archiv für Reformationsgeschichte*, lxxxiii (1992), 31–48.

Heale, Martin, 'Mitres and arms: Aspects of the self-representation of the monastic superior in late medieval England', in *Self-representation of Religious Communities: the British Isles in Context*, ed. Anne Müller and Karen Stöber (Berlin, 2009), pp. 99–122.

Henry, Albert, 'Encore le "Tu Autem"', *Bulletin du Cange*, xiv (1939), 107–11.

—— 'Le Tu Autem', *Bulletin du Cange*, xiv (1939), 37–9.

Hertel, Johannes, *Das Pañcatantra: Seine Geschichte unde seine Verbreitung* (Leipzig, 1914).

Hinnebusch, William A., *The Early English Friars Preachers* (Rome, 1951).

Holmes, Urban Tigner, Jr, *Daily Living in the Twelfth Century, Based on the Observations of Alexander Neckam in London and Paris* (Madison, WI, 1952).

Hoppin, Richard H., *Medieval Music* (New York and London, 1978).

Hornbeck, Patrick J., and Michael Van Dussen, eds., *Europe after Wyclif* (New York, 2017).

Huber-Rebenich, Gerlinde, 'Die Rezeption der mittellateinischen Satire bei Matthias Flacius Illyricus', in *Epochen der Satire: Traditionslinien einer literarische Gattung in Antike, Mittelalter und Renaissance*, ed. Thomas Haye and Franziska Schnoor (Munich, 2008), pp. 173–90.

Hudson, Anne, *Studies in the Transmission of Wyclif's Writings* (London and New York, 2008).

Hudson, John, 'Administration, family and perceptions of the past in late twelfth-century England: Richard FitzNigel and the Dialogue of the Exchequer', in *The Perception of the Past in Twelfth-Century Europe*, ed. Paul Magdalino (London and Rio Grande, OH, 1992), pp. 75–98.

Hutchison, Carole, *The Hermit Monks of Grandmont* (Kalamazoo, MI, 1989).

Iredale, Eric W., *Sempringham and Saint Gilbert and the Gilbertines* (Pointon, Lincolnshire, 1992).

James, Montague Rhodes, *The Ancient Libraries of Canterbury and Dover* (Cambridge, 1903; repr. Cambridge, 2011).

—— *A Descriptive Catalogue of the Manuscripts in the Library of Corpus Christi College, Cambridge* (2 vols., Cambridge, 1912).

—— *A Descriptive Catalogue of the Manuscripts in the Library of Gonville and Caius College* (2 vols., Cambridge, 1907–8).

Jamison, Evelyn, 'The Sicilian Norman kingdom in the mind of Anglo–Norman contemporaries', *Proceedings of the British Academy*, xxiv (1938), 237–85.

Janssen, Hendrikus Hubertus, 'Le caratteristiche della lingua poetica romana', in *La lingua poetica latina*, ed. Aldo Lunelli (2nd edn., Bologna, 1980), pp. 67–130.

Jarecki, Walter, *Signa loquendi: Die cluniacensischen Signa-Listen eingeleitet und herausgegeben* (Baden-Baden, 1981).

Jones, A. H. M., *The Later Roman Empire 284–602* (3 vols. and maps, Oxford, 1964; repr. in 2 vols., Bailtimore, MD, 1986 [continuously paginated]).

BIBLIOGRAPHY   449

Karn, Nicholas, 'The twelfth century', in *Ely: Bishops and Diocese 1109–2009*, ed. Peter Meadows (Woodbridge, 2010), pp. 1–25.

Kay, Richard, 'Gerald of Wales and the Fourth Lateran Council', *Viator*, xxix (1998), 79–93.

Ker, N. R., *Medieval Libraries of Great Britain: A List of Surviving Books* (2nd edn., London, 1964); Supplement by Andrew G. Watson (London, 1987).

Kibre, Pearl, *The Nations in the Mediaeval Universities* (Cambridge, MA, 1948).

Kidson, Peter, 'Gervase, Becket, and William of Sens', *Speculum*, lxviii (1993), 969–91.

Kleberg, Tönnes, 'Eine spätmittelalterliche Proverbiasammlung der Universitätsbibliothek zu Uppsala (Cod. Ups. lat. 931)', *Eranos*, lviii (1960), 210–13.

Klopsch, Paul, *Einführung in die mittellateinische Verslehre* (Darmstadt, 1972).

Knapp, Fritz Peter, '"Antworte dem Narren nach seiner Narrheit!": Das *Speculum Stultorum* des Nigellus von Canterbury', *Reinardus*, iii (1990), 45–68.

—— *Das lateinische Tierepos* (Erträge der Forschung, cxxi; Darmstadt, 1979).

—— 'Das mittelalterliche Tierepos: Zur Genese und Definition einer grossepischen Literaturgattung', *Sprachkunst*, x (1979), 53–68.

—— 'Über einige Formen der Komik im hochmittelalterlichen Tierepos', *Wolfram-Studien*, ed. Werner Schröder, vii (Berlin, 1982), pp. 32–54.

—— 'Von der antiken Fabel zum lateinischen Tierepos des Mittelalters', *Fondation Hardt. Entretiens sur l'antiquité classique*, xxx (1984), 253–306.

Knowles, David, *The Episcopal Colleagues of Thomas Becket* (Cambridge, [1951], corr. edn., 1970).

—— 'The monastic horarium 970–1120', *Downside Review*, li (1933), 706–25.

—— *The Monastic Order in England: A History of its Development from the Times of St Dunstan to the Fourth Lateran Council 940–1216* (2nd edn., Cambridge, 1963).

—— *The Religious Orders in England* (3 vols., Cambridge, 1948–59).

—— *The Historian and Character and Other Essays*, ed. C. N. L. Brooke and Giles Constable (Cambridge, 1964).

—— and R. Neville Hadcock, *Medieval Religious Houses: England and Wales* (London, 1953; rev. edn., Harlow, Essex, 1971).

——, C. N. L. Brooke, and Vera C. M. London, *The Heads of Religious Houses: England & Wales. I. 940–1216* (2nd edn., Cambridge, 2001).

Kristeller, Paul Oskar, 'The school of Salerno: Its development and its contribution to the history of learning', *Bulletin of the History of Medicine*, xvii (1945), 138–94.

Landau, Peter, 'The origins of legal science in England in the twelfth century: Lincoln, Oxford and the career of Vacarius', in *Readers, Texts and Compilers in the Earlier Middle Ages: Studies in Medieval Canon Law in Honour of Linda Fowler-Magerl*, ed. Martin Brett and Kathleen G. Cushing (Farnham, 2009), pp. 165–82.

450 BIBLIOGRAPHY

Landon, Lionel, *The Itinerary of King Richard I* (Publications of the Pipe Roll Society, li; London, 1935).

Langholm, Odd, *Economics in the Medieval Schools* (New York, 1992).

Lapidge, Michael, 'Poetic compounds in Late Latin and early medieval Latin Verse (300–900)', in *Litterarum dulces fructus: Studies in Early Medieval Latin Culture in Honour of Michael Herren for his 80th Birthday*, ed. S. Bruce (Turnhout, 2021), pp. 189–234.

—— 'Two notes on the "medieval" hexameter', in *Ingenio facilis: per Giovanni Orlandi (1938–2007)*, ed. Paolo Chiesa, Anna Maria Fagnoni, and Rossana E. Guglielmetti (Millennio medievale, cxi; Florence, 2017).

Lateinisches Hexameter-Lexikon: Dichterisches Formelgut von Ennius bis zum Archipoeta, ed. Otto Schumann (5 vols., Munich, 1979–82).

Lawless, George, *Augustine of Hippo and his Monastic Rule* (Oxford, 1990).

Leclercq, Jean, 'Nouvelle réponse de l'ancien monachisme aux critiques des cisterciens', *Revue bénédictine*, lxvii (1957), 77–94.

—— 'Pour l'histoire du canif et de la lime', *Scriptorium*, xxvi (1972), 294–300.

Lehmann, Paul, *Die Parodie im Mittelalter* (2nd edn., Stuttgart, 1963).

Lesne, Émile, *Les Écoles de la fin du VIIIe siècle à la fin du XIIe* (Lille, 1940).

Leumann, Manu, 'La lingua poetica latina', in *La lingua poetica latina*, ed. Aldo Lunelli (2nd edn., Bologna, 1980), pp. 131–78.

——, J. B. Hofmann, and A. Szantyr, *Lateinische Grammatik* (2 vols., Munich, 1965–77).

Lewis, C. S., *The Allegory of Love* (Oxford, 1936, repr. New York, 1958).

Liebermann, F., 'Raginald von Canterbury', *Neues Archiv*, xiii (1888), 519–56.

Lind, Levi Robert, 'Reginald of Canterbury and the rhymed hexameter', *Neophilologus*, xxv (1940), 273–5.

Loewenthal, L. J. A., 'For the biography of Walter Ophamil, Archbishop of Palermo', *English Historical Review*, lxxxvii (1972), 75–82.

Loomis, C. Grant, *White Magic: An Introduction to the Folklore of Christian Legend* (Cambridge, MA, 1948).

Lord, Evelyn, *The Knights Templar in Britain* (Harlow, 2002).

Loud, G. A., *The Latin Church in Norman Italy* (Cambridge, 2007).

—— 'Royal control of the church in the twelfth-century kingdom of Sicily', *Studies in Church History*, xviii (1982), 147–59.

Lynch, Joseph H., *Simoniacal Entry into Religious Life from 1000 to 1260: A Social, Economic and Legal Study* (Columbus, OH, 1976).

Macray, W. D., *Bodleian Quarto Catalogues IX: Digby Manuscripts* (1883), with Notes on Macray's Descriptions of the Manuscripts by R. W. Hunt and A. G. Watson; Appendix: An Edition of Thomas Allen's Catalogue of his Manuscripts by A. G. Watson (Oxford, 1999).

Mann, Jill, *Chaucer and Medieval Estates Satire: The Literature of Social Classes and the General Prologue to the Canterbury Tales* (Cambridge, 1973).

—— 'Does an author understand his own text? Nigel of Longchamp and the *Speculum Stultorum*', *The Journal of Medieval Latin*, xvii (2007), 1–37.

BIBLIOGRAPHY 451

—— *From Aesop to Reynard: Beast Literature in Medieval Britain* (Oxford, 2009).

—— ' "He knew nat Catoun": Medieval school-texts and Middle English literature', in *The Text in the Community: Essays on Medieval Works, Manuscripts, Authors and Readers*, ed. Jill Mann and Maura Nolan (Notre Dame, IN, 2006), pp. 41–74.

—— 'Satiric subject and satiric object in Goliardic literature', *Mittellateinisches Jahrbuch*, xv (1980), 63–86.

—— 'The *Speculum Stultorum* and the Nun's Priest's Tale', *Chaucer Review*, ix (1974–5), 262–82.

—— 'Why are names so important? *Ysengrimus* and some other works of beast literature', *Filologia mediolatina*, xxiii (2016), 167–84.

Manselli, Raoul, 'Giovanni di Salisbury e l'Italia del suo tempo', in *The World of John of Salisbury*, ed. Michael Wilks (Oxford, 1984), pp. 401–14.

Matthew, D. J. A., 'Brown, Thomas (*d.* 1180)', *ODNB*.

—— 'Richard [Richard Palmer] (*d.* 1195)', *ODNB*.

Meyer, P., 'Les Manuscrits français de Cambridge', *Romania*, xv (1886), 236–357.

Meyer, Wilhelm, 'De scismate Grandimontanorum (vier lateinische Rythmen von 1187)', *Nachrichten von der königlichen Gesellschaft der Wissenschaften zu Göttingen, philologisch-historische klasse* 1906, 49–100.

Migliorini, Bruno, '*Cirolus*', *Archivum Latinitatis Medii Aevi*, ix (1934), 256–8.

Mitchell, Sydney Knox, *Taxation in Medieval England* (New Haven, CT, 1951).

Moorman, John, *A History of the Franciscan Order from its Origins to the Year 1517* (Oxford, 1968).

Mortet, Victor, 'Hugue de Fouilloi, Pierre le Chantre, Alexandre Neckam et les critiques dirigées au douzième siècle contre le luxe des constructions', in *Mélanges d'histoire offerts à M. Charles Bémont* [no editor] (Paris, 1913), pp. 105–37.

Mortimer, Richard, 'Religious and secular motives for some English monastic foundations', in *Religious Motivation: Biographical and Sociological Problems for the Church Historian*, ed. Derek Baker (Studies in Church History, xv; Oxford, 1978), pp. 77–85.

Mozley, John Henry, 'The Latinity of Nigel de Longchamps', *Bulletin du Cange*, xiv (1939), 5–22.

—— 'Nigel Wireker or Wetekre?', *Modern Language Review*, xxvii (1932), 314–17.

—— 'On the text of the *Speculum Stultorum*', *Speculum*, iv (1929), 430–42.

—— 'On the text and manuscripts of the *Speculum Stultorum*: II', *Speculum*, v (1930), 251–63.

—— 'The unprinted poems of Nigel Wireker: An examination of *MS. Cotton Vespasian D xix*, fols. 1–53', *Speculum*, vii (1932), 398–423.

Murray, Alexander, *Reason and Society in the Middle Ages* (Oxford, 1978).

Neilson, George, *Caudatus Anglicus: A Mediaeval Slander* (Edinburgh, 1896).

452   BIBLIOGRAPHY

Norwich, John Julius, *The Kingdom in the Sun 1130–1194 (The Normans in Sicily*, vol. ii) (London, 1970).

O'Daly, Irene, 'Reading the *Historia Scholastica* at the close of the twelfth century: Nigel of Canterbury and Trinity College, Cambridge, MS B. 15. 5', *Journal of Ecclesiastical History*, lxxi (2020), 270–92.

Oggins, Robin S., *The Kings and their Hawks. Falconry in Medieval England* (New Haven, CT, 2004).

Orlandi, Giovanni, 'Caratteri della versificazione dattilica', in *Giovanni Orlandi: Scritti di Filologia Mediolatina*, ed. Paolo Chiesa, Anna Maria Fagnoni, Rossana E. Guglielmetti, and Giovanni Paolo Maggioni (Millennio medievale, lxxvii; Florence, 2008), pp. 345–59.

—— 'The hexameter in the "aetas Horatiana" ', ibid. pp. 373–89.

Owst, G. R., *Literature and Pulpit in Medieval England* (2nd edn., Oxford, 1966).

Oxford Dictionary of the Christian Church, The, ed. F. L. Cross (3rd edn., ed. E. A Livingstone, Oxford, 1997).

Parks, George B., *The English Traveller to Italy*, vol. i: *The Middle Ages (to 1525)* (Rome, 1954)

Parsons, Ben, *Punishment and Medieval Education* (Cambridge, 2018).

Pease, Arthur Stanley, 'Things without honor', *Classical Philology*, xxi (1926), 27–42.

Pedersen, Olaf, *The First Universities: Studium Generale and the Origins of University Education in Europe* (Cambridge, 1997).

Pepin, Ronald E., 'A note on curses, cures and omens in *Speculum Stultorum*', *Classica et mediaevalia*, xli (1990), 235–40.

Plater, W. E., and H. J. White, *A Grammar of the Vulgate* (Oxford, 1926).

Poole, A. L., *From Domesday Book to Magna Carta, 1087–1216* (2nd edn., Oxford, 1955).

Power, Eileen, *Medieval English Nunneries c. 1275 to 1535* (Cambridge, 1922).

—— *The Wool Trade in English Medieval History* (Oxford, 1941).

Quilligan, Maureen, *The Language of Allegory: Defining the Genre* (Ithaca, NY, and London, 1979).

Raby, F. J. E., 'Philomena praevia temporis amoeni', in *Mélanges Joseph de Ghellinck, S.J.* (2 vols., Gembloux, 1951), ii. 435–48.

Rashdall, Hastings, *The Universities of Europe in the Middle Ages* (2nd edn. by F. M. Powicke and A. B. Emden, 3 vols., Oxford, 1936).

Raymo, Robert R., 'Gower's *Vox Clamantis* and the *Speculum Stultorum*', *Modern Language Notes*, lxx (1955), 315–20.

—— 'A Note on Uppsala Ms. Lat. 931', *Eranos*, lix (1962), 169.

—— 'The Parlement of Foules 309–15', *Modern Language Notes*, lxxi (1956), 159–60.

Reynolds, Roger E., 'Ordination and the priesthood in the early Middle Ages and its depiction', in *A Companion to Priesthood and Holy Orders in the Middle Ages*, ed. Greg Peters and C. Colt Anderson (Leiden, 2016), pp. 43–69.

BIBLIOGRAPHY 453

Riall, Nicholas, *Henry of Blois, Bishop of Winchester: A Patron of the Twelfth-Century Renaissance* (Hampshire, 1994).

—— 'The new castles of Henry de Blois as bishop of Winchester: The case against Farnham, Surrey', *Medieval Archaeology*, xlvii (2003), 115–29.

Rickard, P., '*Anglois coué* and *L'Anglois qui couve*', *French Studies*, vii (1953), 48–55.

Rigg, A. G., *A History of Anglo-Latin Literature 1066–1422* (Cambridge, 1992).

—— 'Medieval Latin Poetic Anthologies (I)', *Mediaeval Studies*, xxxix (1977), 281–330.

—— 'Medieval Latin Poetic Anthologies (II)', *Mediaeval Studies*, xl (1978), 387–407.

—— 'Medieval Latin Poetic Anthologies (III)', *Mediaeval Studies*, xli (1979), 468–505.

—— 'Medieval Latin Poetic Anthologies (IV)', *Mediaeval Studies*, xliii (1981), 472–97.

—— 'Nigel of Canterbury: What was his name?', *Medium Ævum*, lvi (1987), 304–7.

Riley-Smith, Jonathan, *Hospitallers: The History of the Order of St John* (London and Rio Grande, OH, 1999).

—— *The Knights Hospitallers in the Levant, c. 1070–1309* (Basingstoke, 2012).

—— 'The Military Orders and the East, 1149–1291', in *Knighthoods of Christ: Essays on the History of the Crusades and the Knights Templar, Presented to Malcolm Barber*, ed. Norman Housley (Aldershot, 2007), pp. 137–49.

Roling, Bernd, 'Burnell the Ass: Nigel von Longchamp und die Wissenschaftskritik seiner Zeit', *Zeitschrift für Germanistik*, xxv (2015), 28–41.

Sanford, Eva Matthews, 'Quotations from Lucan in mediaeval Latin authors', *American Journal of Philology*, lv (1934), 1–19.

Scherer, Margaret R., *The Legends of Troy in Art and Literature* (New York and London, 1963).

Schimmelpfennig, Bernhard, '*Ex fornicatione nati*: Studies on the position of priests' sons from the twelfth to the fourteenth century', *Studies in Medieval and Renaissance History*, ii (1979), 1–50.

Schmidt, Paul Gerhard, 'Prosaauflösung im lateinischen Mittelalter', in *Philologie als Kuturwissenschaft: Studien zur Literatur und Geschichte des Mittelalters. Festschrift für Karl Stackmann zum 65. Geburtstag*, ed. Ludger Grenzmann, Hubert Herkommer, and Dieter Wuttke (Göttingen, 1987), pp. 38–44.

Scott, Kathleen, 'Representations of scribal activity in English manuscripts *c.*1400–*c.*1490: A mirror of the craft?', in *Pen in Hand: Medieval Scribal Portraits, Colophons and Tools*, ed. Michael Gullick (Walkern, Hertfordshire, 2006), pp. 115–49.

Sedgwick, Walter Bradbury, 'The textual criticism of mediaeval Latin poets', *Speculum*, v (1930), 288–305.

454 BIBLIOGRAPHY

Shackleton Bailey, D. R., 'Textual notes on some poems of Nigel de Longchamp', *Medium Ævum*, liii (1984), 282–90.

Sharpe, Richard, 'Richard Barre's *Compendium Veteris et Noui Testamenti*', *The Journal of Medieval Latin*, xiv (2004), 128–39.

Sheppard, Lancelot C., *The English Carmelites* (London, 1943).

Sherlock, David, *Monastic Sign Language in Medieval England* (Suffolk, 2016).

Skutsch, Otto, 'Three rare words from Nigel's *Speculum Stultorum*', *Archivum latinitatis medii aevi*, xi (1937), 29–31.

Smalley, Beryl, *The Becket Conflict and the Schools: A Study of Intellectuals in Politics in the Twelfth Century* (Oxford, 1973).

Smith, Katherine Allen, 'Discipline, compassion and monastic ideals of community, c.950–1250', *Journal of Medieval History*, xxxv (2009), 326–39.

Smith, R. A. L., *Canterbury Cathedral Priory: A Study in Monastic Administration* (Cambridge, 1969 [1943]).

Southern, R. W., 'Blois, Peter of (1125–1212)', *ODNB*.

—— 'From schools to university', in *The History of the University of Oxford*, vol. i, ed. J. I. Catto (Oxford, 1984), pp. 1–36.

—— 'Master Vacarius and the beginning of an English academic tradition', in *Medieval Learning and Literature: Essays Presented to Richard William Hunt*, ed. J. J. G. Alexander and M. T. Gibson (Oxford, 1976), pp. 257–86.

Spear, David S., 'Les Archidiacres de Rouen au cours de la période ducale', *Annales de Normandie*, xxxiv (1984), 15–50.

—— *The Personnel of the Norman Cathedrals during the Ducal Period 911–1204* (London, 2006).

Spufford, Peter, *Power and Profit: The Merchant in Medieval Europe* (London, 2002).

Stoneman, William P., ed., *Dover Priory* (Corpus of British Medieval Library Catalogues, v; London, 1999).

Stotz, Peter, *Handbuch zur lateinischen Sprache des Mittelalters* (5 vols., Munich, 1996–2004).

Strecker, Karl, 'Henricus Septimellensis und die zeitgenössische Literatur', *Studi medievali* NS ii (1929), 110–33.

—— 'Studien zu karolingischen Dichtern', *Neues Archiv*, xliv (1922), 209–51.

Summerlin, Danica, *The Canons of the Third Lateran Council of 1179: Their Origins and Reception* (Cambridge, 2019).

Sweet, Alfred H., 'The Apostolic See and the heads of English religious houses', *Speculum*, xxviii (1953), 468–84.

Sweetinburgh, Sheila, 'Caught in the cross-fire: Patronage and institutional politics in late twelfth-century Canterbury', in *Cathedrals, Communities and Conflict in the Anglo-Norman World*, ed. Paul Dalton, Charles Insley, and Louise J. Wilkinson (Woodbridge, 2011), pp. 187–202.

Thompson, E. Margaret, *The Carthusian Order in England* (London, 1930).

Thompson, Michael, *Medieval Bishops' Houses in England and Wales* (Aldershot, Hampshire, 1998).

BIBLIOGRAPHY 455

Thompson, Sally, *Women Religious. The Founding of English Nunneries after the Norman Conquest* (Oxford, 1991).

Thomson, R. M., *Catalogue of the Manuscripts of Lincoln Cathedral Chapter Library* (Woodbridge, 1989).

Times Comprehensive Atlas of the World, The (15th edn., London, 2018).

Turner, Ralph V., 'Changing perceptions of the new administrative class in Anglo-Norman and Angevin England: The *curiales* and their conservative critics', in id., *Judges, Administrators and the Common Law in Angevin England* (London, 1994), pp. 225–49.

—— 'Longchamp, William de (*d.* 1197)', *ODNB*.

—— *Men Raised from the Dust: Administrative Service and Upward Mobility in Angevin England* (Philadelphia, PA, 1988).

—— 'Richard Lionheart and English episcopal elections', *Albion*, xxix (1997), 1–13.

—— and Richard V. Heiser, *The Reign of Richard Lionheart, Ruler of the Angevin Empire, 1189–99* (Harlow, Essex, 2000).

Tuve, Rosemond, *Allegorical Imagery: Some Mediaeval Books and their Posterity* (Princeton, NJ, 1966).

Twycross, Meg, and Sarah Carpenter, *Masks and Masking in Medieval and Early Tudor England* (London and New York, [2002] 2016).

Tyerman, Christopher, *England and the Crusades 1095–1588* (Chicago, 1988).

Tyler, J. E., *The Alpine Passes: The Middle Ages (962–1250)* (Oxford, 1930).

Urry, William, *Canterbury under the Angevin Kings* (London, 1967).

Valous, Guy, de, *Le Monachisme clunisien des origines au XVe siècle* (2nd edn., 2 vols., Paris, 1970).

Vanderputten, Steven, 'Canterbury and Flanders in the late tenth century', *Anglo-Saxon England*, xxxv (2006), 219–44.

Van Dussen, Michael, *From England to Bohemia: Heresy and Communication in the Later Middle Ages* (Cambridge, 2012).

The Victoria County History of the County of Cambridge and the Isle of Ely, ed. L. F. Salzman, vol. ii (Oxford, 1948, repr. London, 1967).

Vincent, Nicholas, 'Albion adrift: The English presence in Paris and its environs after 1204', forthcoming in *Thirteenth-Century England*.

Vollmer, F., *Zur Geschichte des lateinischen Hexameters*, Sitzungsberichte der Bayerischen Akademie der Wissenschaften, phil.-hist. klasse (Munich, 1917).

Waltenberger, Michael, 'Socrates Brunellus est, oder: Aspekte asininer Narrativik. Zum Speculum Stultorum des Nigellus von Canterbury', in *Tierepik und Tierallegorese: Studien zur Poetologie und historischen Anthropologie vormoderner Literatur*, ed. Bernhard Jahn and Otto Neudeck (Frankfurt a. M., 2004), pp. 71–100.

Ward, H. L. D., *Catalogue of Romances in the Department of Manuscripts in the British Museum* (3 vols., London, 1883–1910).

Warren, W. L., *Henry II* (New Haven, CT, and London, 1973).

BIBLIOGRAPHY

Weiss, Judith, '"History" in Anglo-Norman romance: The presentation of the pre-Conquest past', in *The Long Twelfth-Century View of the Anglo-Saxon Past*, ed. Martin Brett and David A. Woodman (Aldershot, 2015), pp. 275–87.

Wertheimer, Laura, 'Illegitimate birth and the English clergy, 1198–1348', *Journal of Medieval History*, xxxi (2005), 211–29.

West, Francis, *The Justiciarship in England 1066–1232* (Cambridge, 1966).

Whitwell, Robert Jowitt, 'English monasteries and the wool trade in the 13th century', *Vierteljahrschrift für Social- und Wirtschaftsgeschichte*, ii (1904), 1–33.

Wieruszowski, Helene, 'Roger II of Sicily, *Rex-Tyrannus*, in twelfth-century political thought', *Speculum*, xxxviii (1963), 46–78.

Wilks, Michael, ed., *The World of John of Salisbury* (Oxford, 1984).

Wilmart, André, 'Une riposte de l'ancien monachisme au manifeste de Saint Bernard', *Revue bénédictine*, xlvi (1934), 296–344.

Wolff, Reinhold, 'Unterwegs vom mittelalterlichen Predigtmärlein zur Novelle der frühen Neuzeit: Die Erzählsammlung "Compilatio singularis exemplorum"', *Mittellateinisches Jahrbuch*, xli (2006), 53–76.

Woodcock, E. C., *A New Latin Syntax* (Bristol, 1959).

Woolf, Rosemary, *The English Mystery Plays* (Berkeley and Los Angeles, CA, 1972).

Yunck, John A., *The Lineage of Lady Meed: The Development of Mediaeval Venality Satire* (Notre Dame, IN, 1963).

Zermatten, Coralie, 'The Carmelite Rule', in *A Companion to Medieval Rules and Customaries*, ed. Krijn Pansters (Leiden, 2020), pp. 367–92.

INDEX OF QUOTATIONS
AND ALLUSIONS

References are keyed to the footnotes to the text of *SS*, cited by line number.

A. BIBLICAL QUOTATIONS AND ALLUSIONS

Genesis
- 1: 27 — 2563
- 6–7 — 2931
- 27: 22 — 2829–30
- 27: 33 — 991–2
- 37: 11 — 2413
- 44: 17 — 284

Exodus
- 21: 23 — 3549–50
- 22: 22 — 1759–61

Numbers
- 23: 27 — Ep. 16

Deuteronomy
- 10: 18 — 1759–61
- 16: 19 — 2616

1 Kings (1 Samuel)
- 3: 19 — 3519
- 16: 7 — 1764

2 Kings (2 Samuel)
- 6: 5 — 1078

4 Kings (2 Kings)
- 4: 16 — 976

2 Chronicles
- 2: 12 — 3345

Tobias
- 4: 16 — 2157–8

Job
- 2: 7 — 817
- 17: 1 — 3245
- 29: 15 — 1757
- 31: 18 — 1837–8

Psalms
- 7: 16 — Ep. 39, 1087–8
- 14 (15): 5 — 2585–651
- 21 (22): 15 — 2491–2
- 25 (26): 10 — 2583–4
- 57 (58): 9 — 2491–2
- 67 (68): 3 — 2491–2
- 77 (78): 33 — Ep. 41
- 96 (97): 5 — 2491–2
- 110 (111): 10 — 2927
- 145 (146): 9 — 1759–61

Proverbs
- 13: 20 — 1973–4

- 14:13 — 1469–70
- 19: 4 — 1982
- 26: 5 — Ep. 32
- 26: 11 — 2819–20
- 26: 27 — 1087–8

Ecclesiastes
- 10: 8 — 1087–8

Wisdom
- 2: 3 — 2491–2

Ecclesiasticus
- 18: 8 — 1591
- 27: 29 — 1087–8

Isaiah
- 1: 6 — 817, 2557–8
- 1: 23 — 1759–61, 2585–651
- 11: 2 — Ep. 24
- 42: 3 — 2985
- 62: 3 — 2497

Jeremiah
- 2: 6 — 2610
- 7: 6 — 1759–61

Lamentations
- 1: 6 — Ep. 23

Ezekiel
- 34: 2 — 2675–6

Daniel
- 3: 19 — 643
- 3: 31 — 1391–2
- 13: 17 — 2380

Micah
- 1: 4 — 2491–2

Zephaniah
- 1: 15 — 405–26

1 Maccabees
- 2: 62 — 2353
- 3: 30 — 2502

Matthew
- 6: 22–3 — 1745–6
- 7: 3 — Ep. 7
- 7: 12 — 2157–8
- 7: 15 — 2051, 2671–4
- 7: 16 — Ep. 41
- 18: 6 — 2151
- 23: 27 — 45–8

458   INDEX OF QUOTATIONS AND ALLUSIONS

Matthew (*cont.*)

24: 13	Ep. 12
24: 24	2671–4
27: 64	1151

Mark

8: 15	1530

Luke

6: 31	2157–8
10: 7	3875–6
18: 11–13	959–60

John

10: 11–13	2681–2

Acts

2: 44–5	2257–86
4: 32–5	2257–86
8: 9–24	1717–32
23: 3	45–8

Romans

14: 4	2209–10

1 Corinthians

5: 6	2546
9: 22	1749, 2507

2 Corinthians

6: 10	2120
11: 26	2163

Ephesians

2: 19	1045–6

2 Thessalonians

3: 6	1973–4

Philippians

3: 13	Ep. 24

Titus

1: 15	2272

Hebrews

2: 10	173–4
12: 12	316

James

1: 24	Ep. 7
1: 27	1759–61

1 Peter

1: 7	2364
5: 3	1738

2 Peter

2: 20	2662
2: 22	2819–20

Revelation (Apocalypse)

3: 17	873
21: 4	2645–6

B. ALLUSIONS TO CLASSICAL AND POST-CLASSICAL SOURCES AND PARALLELS

Historical writers are not included in this index; they are entered in the General Index.

Abbo of Fleury
Life of St Edmund

c. 12	2136

Abelard
Dialectica

Tract. iii	595

Alan of Lille
Anticlaudianus

ii. 267	517

De fide catholica

i. 31	255–6

De planctu Naturae

i. 4	2390–2
xvii. 29	517
xviii. 17–19	811–22

Liber Parabolarum

299	60
433–6	57–66

Alcuin
Epistolae

cxxxii	2556

Alexander Neckam

'Qualiter Anglorum'	1515–24

Andreas Capellanus
De amore

i. 6. 50	255–6
ii. 8. 35–40	3179

Apocalipsis Goliae

st. 33. 4	1683, 2675–6
st. 49. 1–3	2796

Archpoet
Gedichte

i. 4. 4	3663
iv. 24. 1–3	57–66

Augustine
Contra Faustum

xii. 20	3099–100

De doctrina christiana

ii. XX	685–8

In Iohannis Evangelium

tract. vi. 25	583–6

Avianus
Fabulae

Dedicatory Letter	5–12
I	1617–21
i. 4	1300
v	57–66
viii. 1–2	79–80

INDEX OF QUOTATIONS AND ALLUSIONS 459

xiii. 7   740
xxx   3507–8
Avitus
  De diluvio mundi
   565–8   3099–100
Babio
  65   703
  70   1876
  303–4   56
  472   2028
Becket, Thomas
  Correspondence
   cxviii   357
   cxxv   2569–70
Bernard of Clairvaux
  De consideratione
   i. 13   1759–61
  De praecepto et dispensatione
   xvi   889
  Epistolae
   xlii   2749–84
   cv   2041–2
   cccxxv   2545
  Letter to Robert   2089
Bernard Silvestris
  Cosmographia: Megacosmos
   iii. 404   438
Béroul
  Tristan
   42–3   1841–2
Boethius
  De consolatione Philosophiae
   i. pr. 5   3357
   ii. pr. 6   3329
   iii. m. 2. 2   3378
   iii. m. 2. 24   3041–2
   iii. pr. 9   49–50
  De topicis differentiis
   ii. 7. 24   253, 255–6
  In Ciceronis Topica
   ii   255–6
Bramfeld, Edmund
  Laberintus, L200   1673, 1687–92
Carmina Burana
  vi. 9–15   31–42
  vi. 18   595
  x. 21   3273
  xxxix. 4. 1   1683
  xli. 16. 1   2535
  xlii   2495–558
  xlii. 1. 4   57–66
  xlii. 3. 3   2543
  xlii. 4. 1   2511–16
  xlii. 13   153
  xlii. 18. 1   1683

xlii. 18. 3–4   45–8
cxl. 4. 1   505
Chrétien de Troyes
  Perceval
   5414   357
  Yvain
   459–77   2903
Cicero
  De inventione
   ii. 55   3563
Claudian
  De raptu Proserpinae
   ii. 298   39
  In Eutropium
   i. 181   60
  Panegyricus de quarto consulatu Honorii
   300   2659
   305   1999–2000
  De uxore cerdonis
   22–3   2491–2
Disticha Catonis
  Prol. 6   1973–4
  i. 21. 2   293–4
  i. 26. 2   1107
  i. 38. 1–2   293–4
  ii. 4. 2   1277–8
  ii. 5. 2   3877
  ii. 10. 1–2   293–4
  ii. 21–2   2265
  iii. 3. 2   2155–6
  iii. 17. 1   293–4
Donatus
  Ars grammatica
   i. 1   170
   iii. 6   1989
Dracontius
  De laudibus Dei
   i. 737   959–60
   ii. 20   959–60
   ii. 50   3412
   ii. 262–4   661–2
  Satisfactio
   65–8   661–2
   290, 298   3412
Eberhard the German
  Laborintus
   913–14   2491–2
Fecunda ratis
  i. 258   1055
'Forma fuit quondam Cluniacus religionis'   1673, 1687–92
Geoffrey of Vinsauf
  Poetria nova
   383   Ep. 25

460   INDEX OF QUOTATIONS AND ALLUSIONS

Geoffrey of Vinsauf (*cont.*)

594–5	2390–2
741–5	45–8
791–2	504
1008–12	619
1775–6	37–8

Summa de coloribus rhetoricis

63. 770–5	929–30

Gerald of Wales

De invectionibus

i. 5	1855

De principis instructione

ii. 17	2183–226

De rebus a se gestis

ii. 5	2111–12

De vita Galfridi

ii. Prol.	317

Gemma ecclesiastica

dist. ii 6	1261

Itinerarium Kambriae

i. 4	317
i. 12	2113–16

Letter to Stephen Langton	317
Preface to a sermon on St Stephen	317

Speculum ecclesiae

dist. ii. 4	2111–12
dist. iii. 7	1683
dist. iii. 11	2411–12
dist. iii. 13	1520
dist. iii. 21	959–60
dist. iv. 19	317

Symbolum electorum

dist. ii. 5	317

Topographia hibernica

dist. iii. 49	317

Vita S. Remigii c.xxvii	2737–42

Geta

138	442

Glossa ordinaria

Genesis viii. 7	3099–100

Gospel according to the Mark of Silver   2495–558

Gower, John

Mirour de l'Omme

21157–8	2347–8

Gratian

Decretum

D. 8 c. 1	583–6
D. 56 c. 1	1317–18
D. 56 c. 13	1317–18

Henry of Settimello

Elegia

i. 43	1837–8
i. 137–8	3107

ii. 238	595

Hildebert of Tours

Carmina

xxii. 1	3007
xxiii. 1	1613

Horace

Ars poetica

163	2369

Epistulae

i. 2. 14	2534
i. 2. 58–9	2569–70
i. 12.19	517
i. 18. 84	668
ii. 2. 83	3009
ii. 2. 146–8	2519–20, 2526–30

Odes

i. 3. 8	4
i. 4. 4	394

Saturae

i. 2. 52–3	2105
i. 8. 40	2554
ii. 3. 103	2253
ii. 3. 247	2749–84
ii. 5. 92	1782
ii. 6. 77–117	137–8

Hugh Primas

Gedichte

vii. 31	1837–8
xii. 1	1021

'In gestis patrum veterum'	2201–4

Jerome

Adversus Vigilantium

xv. 14–16	2381–4
Epistola cxlvii	Ep. 43

John of Hauville

Architrenius

i. 65–99	31–42
ii. 66–7	2390–2
ii. 302–4, 310–26	1520
ii. 380–90	2111–12
ii. 483–7	1199
iii. 379–430	1999–2000
v. 51–6	2749–84
v. 72–9	31–42
v. 483	624

John of Salisbury

Entheticus maior

40–64	31–42
322	3412
474	1012, 1721
540	1560
569, 1041	959–60

Entheticus minor

52	1030

INDEX OF QUOTATIONS AND ALLUSIONS 461

143–4	627	ii. 655–6	2508–10
196–7	57–66	vi. 147	2652
202	357	vi. 424	1375
Historia pontificalis		viii. 782	1007
xxxii	2569–70	ix. 379	293–4
Letters		ix. 621	624
xxxiii	1520	x. 504	2637
ccii	2353	Map, Walter	
ccix	2569–70	*De nugis curialium*	
ccxliv	20	dist. i. 16–28	2051
cclxii	2569–70	dist. i. 24	2127–36
cclxxviii	2569–70	dist. i. 25	959–60, 2089, 2113–16,
Metalogicon			2137–8, 2139–56, 2157–8
i. 3	31–42	dist. i. 26	2183–226
i. 6	1197	dist. i. 27	2411–12
i. 15	3561–866	dist. ii. 17	2495–558
ii. 10	1199, 1544	*Map Poems*	
iv. 30	1197	'A legis doctoribus', line 20	2511–16
Policraticus		'Dum Saturno coniuge'	
i. 4	2563–70	lines 69–70	2257–86
i. 6	2411–12	lines 141–4	2139–56
i. 13	685–8, 3467–82		
ii. 17	1641–2	'Nuper ductu serio'	
ii. 29	116	lines 52–3, 63–4	2139–56
v. 16	1759–61	lines 83–8	2081
vii. 18	2059, 2867	lines 133–88	2087–8
vii. 21	959–60, 2051	line 228	145
vii. 23	2051, 2321–4	'Raptor mei pilei'	811–22
vii. 24	2569–70	'Sompno et silentio'	
vii. 25	2569–70	lines 49–50	2139–56
viii. 6	2569–70	Marbod of Rennes	
viii. 17	2681–2	'De abbate usurpante	
viii. 22	1201	pontificalia'	1673, 1687–92
viii. 23	2569–70	Martial	
Joseph of Exeter		*Epigrammata*	
Ylias		v. 21. 4	624
i. 15–23	31–42	v. 24. 10	624
i. 307	1007	*Matheolus, Lamentations of*	
Justinian		139	1877
Digest		Matthew of Vendôme	
45. 1. 137. 2	627	*Commendatio militis*	37–8
Juvenal		Maximian	
Saturae		*Elegies*	
ii. 79–80	2545	i. 40	1030
v. 27	651	i. 115	571
ix. 9	487	i. 222	496
xiii. 126	925	v. 54	186
Lidia		v. 70	76
309	1051–2	*Miles gloriosus*	
Lucan		71	2617
De bello ciuili		335–6	1059–60
i. 98	517	Nigel of Longchamp	
i. 281	621	*Epigrams*	
ii. 14–15	1147	ii. 2, iii. 6–7	145

462 INDEX OF QUOTATIONS AND ALLUSIONS

Nigel of Longchamp (*cont.*)

ii. 12, 18	153
ii. 16	3114
iii. 18	3639
ivA. 7	153
ivB	153
vi. 3	3639
xi. 1	2939
xi. 25	3

Lawrence

17, 991, 1700, 1952	3639
24	2562
314, 718, 1108	1074
166	1738
337–8, 2238	153
508	2610
544	2326
559–60	2519–20, 2526–30
562	2317
563–72	2585–651
583	825
616–17	2617
705	748
741	1151
851	2546
889–94, 1448, 1725	1274
914–16	Ep. 32
1041, 1357, 1589	2554
1088	2491–2
1199	814
1208, 1479, 2091	2475
1259, 1265, 1995	1663, 2043
1346	1721
1351–6	405–26
1437	167
1469	1493
1653	1069
1857, 2269	1111
1977	2653
1997	3203, 3289
2249	995
2319	823

Miracles

31	2554
43	305
66	1738
69	1749, 2554
101	1279
116	2654
146, 248, 276, 1394	438
202	2916
249–51, 270, 1913	1837–8
262, 595, 1412, 1432, 2533	2498
273	1425
313	825

318, 706, 1241, 1296, 1710, 2343	3516
326, 574, 1242, 1739, 1740, 2374	748
340	578
348	2501
423	3
432	1074
461, 2483	878
526	3848
532	621
547	825
606	344
625	767
645	3
654	1083
663, 1621, 2431	145
732–8, 1018, 1769, 1875, 1891	153
761, 763–4, 1952, 2130–2, 2141	1721
795, 2402	2610
914	514
916	1024
936	2410
950	382
1015	3154
1035	2327
1072	2644
1102, 1110, 2652	3763
1110	3639
1112	2560
1125	3203, 3289
1137–8	186
1139	121
1164	2652
1175	2990
1178	1460
1214	3162
1365	691
1408, 2478	814, 1196, 2142, 2376, 3886
1498	3300
1509, 1739, 2113	1255
1606	186
1634, 1729	398
1635	1663, 2043
1682	2255–6
1794	2916
1811–14, 1885–6, 1910, 1915–16, 2213–16	2711–12
2061	1111
2152, 2546	468, 2882
2172	870
2210	1446
2327–8	2546
2376	1454
2467	3094

INDEX OF QUOTATIONS AND ALLUSIONS 463

2476	264
2502	2568
Paul	
149, 613	153
236	2498
671	1721
Tractatus	
p. 153	2209–10
p. 167	257, 1987
pp. 168, 177	2546
p. 170	2859–62, 2867
pp. 177–8	1727–32
p. 188	2668
p. 204	153
p. 205	1999–2000
Otto of Freising	
Chronica	
ii. 19	2569–70
vii. 23	2569–70
Ovid	
Amores	
i. 5. 1	2891
i. 7. 46	1372
i. 8. 3	153
i. 8. 106	167
i. 15. 26	2508–10
ii. 6. 48	589–60
ii. 9. 26	2609
iii. 3. 23	1700
Ars amatoria	
i. 409	446
i. 535	1425
i. 645–6	1072
i. 655–6	Ep. 39, 1072
ii. 123	23
Ex Ponto	
i. 3. 17	114
ii. 9. 3	1007
Fasti	
i. 215–16	2519–20,
	2526–30
vi. 771	299
Heroides	
i. 57–8	2198
i. 72	300
iii. 62	571
iii. 63–4	471–2
iii. 63	3155–60
iii. 98	3520
iv. 174	3336
v. 106	1026
v. 134	1082
v. 136	544
vi. 66	545
vii. 41	341

vii. 162	3120
viii. 6	626
viii. 75	1456
ix. 31	145
ix. 145	461
x. 79	391
xi. 3	2899
xi. 44	2894
xi. 86	1376
xiii. 84	1479
xiii. 87–90	685–8
xix. 166	3542
xx. 70–1	1274
Metamorphoses	
i. 147	3061
i. 433	517
ii. 1	2737
ii. 334	547–8
ii. 531–632	3004–22
ii. 540	3004
iii. 487–9	2491–2
vi. 424–676	509–10
vi. 509	3664
vii. 21	3256
vii. 518	689
vii. 767	401
ix. 137	1007
x. 419	564
xi. 419	1867
xii. 563	3300
xiii. 511	2614
xiii. 569–70	153
xiv. 716	2475
xv. 16	1029
Remedia amoris	
697–8	1484
Tristia	
i. 5. 71	1177
i. 6. 9	3649
iii. 8. 22	968
iii. 9.11	459
Pamphilus	
71	1197
181	761
480	357
Persius	
Saturae	
iii. 1–2	1421–2
Peter of Blois	
Canon episcopalis	2563–70
Carmina	
i. 7	2265
Epistolae	
lii	627
lix	627

464 INDEX OF QUOTATIONS AND ALLUSIONS

Peter of Blois (*cont.*)	
lxv	1641–2, 3467–82
lxxxi	1544
lxxxii	959–60
xc	1673, 1687–92
ci	20, 31–42
Peter Comestor	
Historia scholastica	
c. xxxiv	3099–10
Peter the Venerable	
Letters	
xxviii	2111–12
xxxiii–xxxv	959–60
Petrus Pictor	
Carmina	
x. 5	624
Phaedrus	
Fabulae	
i. Prol.	5–12
Pliny	
Natural History	
xxix. 21–2	661–2
Priscian	
Institutiones grammaticae	
i. 1	170
Prosper	
Liber epigrammatum	
lxv. 3, lxxxiii. 2	3412
Prudentius	
Contra Symmachum	
ii. 318	1469
ii. 750	945–6, 1108
Hamartigenia	
387–8	1566
628	3412
Liber cathemerinon	
v. 122	517
x. 146	401
Praefatio	
11–12	46
Psychomachia	
116	1375
239	3412
Tituli historiarum	
iii	3099–100
Publilius Syrus	
Sententiae	
67	571
141	291–2
562	1484
'Quae monaco quaerunt'	
20	2819–20
Roman de Renart	
i. 399	1268

i. 532–3	819–20
Romulus, elegiac	
Prologue 1–6	5–12
i. 3	14
v. 5–6	79–80
xii. 31–2	137–8
xviii. 23–4	359–60
Romulus Nilantii	
ii. 20	2971
Romulus vulgaris	
iii. 20	2971
Sedulius	
Hymnus	
i. 1	1075
Serlo of Wilton	
Poèmes	
lxxv	57–66
Appendix I. A. 2	929–30
Appendix I. B. 4	495–8
Sextus Amarcius	
Satires	
i. 131–3	977–8
i. 134	2187
iii. 744–7	2257–86
Statius	
Thebaid	
x. 704–5	289
Tractatus Garsiae	1317–18
Vacarius	
Liber pauperum	627
Venantius Fortunatus	
Carmina	
ii. 2. 8	1059–60, 1107
ii. 8. 3	3412
Vergil	
Aeneid	
i. 586	1493
i. 738–9	1394
iii. 457	1074
iii. 610	231
iii. 655	1493
iv. 24–5	3155–60
iv. 72	533
iv. 337	2924
iv. 673	3300
vi. 190	1493
vi. 323–4	3295–6
vi. 539	1381
viii. 369	1381
viii. 520	1493
ix. 251	1867
x. 284	1198
x. 843	1975
xi. 86	3300

INDEX OF QUOTATIONS AND ALLUSIONS 465

xii. 650	1493	lv. 8. 4–6	2675–6
xii. 871	3300	lvi	2495–558
Eclogues		lvi. 1. 4	57–66
v. 17	3273	lvi. 3. 3	2543
x. 69	2617	lvi. 4. 1	2511–16
Georgics		lvi. 13	153
i. 145–6	1197	lvi. 18. 1	1683
iii. 40	533	lvi. 18. 3–4	45–8
iii. 226	231	lviii. 12. 1	1837–8
iii. 497	2084	lviii. 15. 1	2498
iv. 452	1074	lix. 8–11	2495–558
Vitas patrum		lx.12. 1	2675–6
v. 27	2201–4	lx. 17. 2	2519–20, 2526–30
Walter of Châtillon		lxiii	2495–558
Alexandreis		lxiv	2495–558
iv. 421	1837–8	lxiv. 16. 1	2535
ix. 31	1007	lxvii. 3. 5–6	2663
Poems		William of Auvergne	
xxxv. 5. 6–7	1107	*Tractatus novus de penitentia*	677–82
xxxvii. 7. 3–5	2543	William of Blois	
xxxix. 2. 4	2519–20, 2526–30	*Alda*	
xl. 5. 4	2543	557	1007
xli. 1. 1–4	2511–16	*Ysengrimus*	
xlii. 14. 4	621	i. 433–4	881–2
xlii. 18	1999–2000	i. 927	3663
xliii. 14. 4	621	iii. 382	1540
xliii. 18. 3–4	2519–20, 2526–30	iii. 594–5	Ep. 25
xliii. 26. 3	1721	iii. 659	1533
xliv. 6–7	2519–20, 2526–30	iv. 368	1055
xliv. 18. 4	145	iv. 811	825
xlix. 10	2675–6	v. 512	37–8
xlix. 19. 3	1877	vi. 319	257
l. 10. 3	2519–20, 2526–30	vii. 230	819–20

INDEX OF BIBLICAL QUOTATIONS AND ALLUSIONS
IN THE INTERPOLATION

Numbers		Luke	
10: 1–2	7–8	9: 3	93–6
Proverbs		10: 1–8	93–6
30: 8–9	23–4	10: 9–18	93–6
Matthew		18: 9–14	79–80
10: 9–18	93–6	John	
25: 40	15	19: 23–4	86
25: 45	15	Philippians	
		3: 19	36

INDEX OF MANUSCRIPTS

The following index lists manuscripts mentioned in the Introduction or Notes, other than manuscripts of *SS*, which are listed in Manuscript Descriptions in Appendix A.

Bern, Burgerbibliothek 679:   cxxxviii

Cambridge:
Corpus Christi College 200:   287
Corpus Christi College 287:   xxxii
Corpus Christi College 441:   cxlii
Gonville and Caius College
    191/224:   xxxii
Gonville and Caius College
    427/427:   xxxii
Trinity College B. 15.5:   xxxii
University Library Gg. 5. 35:   33, 222
University Library Gg. 6. 42:   102

Edinburgh, National Library of Scotland,
    MS 16500 (the Asloan MS)   cxxxii,
    cxxxiv

London, British Library:
Arundel 23:   xxxii, clxii
Cotton Cleopatra B. III   lxii

Cotton Julius A. VII   xxxii, lxii
Cotton Nero C. IX   xxxi, xlviii,
    361
Cotton Vespasian D. XIX   xxxii, xxxiii,
    xxxiv
Cotton Vitellius A. XI   xxxii
Harley 219:   cxlii

Oxford, Bodleian Library:
Douce 95:   xxxii
Laud misc. 642:   247

Paris, Bibliothèque nationale de France:
lat. 8433:   79
lat. 11867:   102

Tours, Bibliothèque municipale,
    468:     cxxxviii

Uppsala, Universitets-Bibliotek, C
    523:     cxxxviii

GENERAL INDEX

This index includes historical personages and places, medieval historical works and their authors, modern authors, and general topics of interest, that are mentioned in the Notes, Introduction, or Appendices B and E. It does not include references to editors or translators of medieval texts, unless they are the subject of discussion. For works of literature and their authors that are cited in the notes, see the Index of Quotations and Allusions. They are not included here unless they are also cited or discussed in the Introduction. Appendix A is excluded from this index, since its many historical and bibliographical details would add excessively to its bulk, and they can be easily located *in situ*.

Abbo of Fleury 213
Abbo of St-Germain cl n.
Abdulla Ibn al-Muquaffa' cxxxv, 332
Abelard, Peter 128
Abigail 417
Abulafia, D. S. H. 428
Acre xxxii n., xl, 203, 205, 414, 417
Adam of Dryburgh 235
Adrian IV, Pope 427
Adrianus cxxxviii–cxxxix, cxli
Agamemnon 47
Agatha, sister of Nigel, monk of
    Canterbury xxxi, xxxiii n.
Agrigento 262
Alan, abbot of Tewkesbury lxii
Alan of Lille cxlix
al-Aqsa mosque 203
Albert of Stade 357
Albert of Vercelli, patriarch of
    Jerusalem 414
Albini, Francesca clxv, 215
Albinus, ps.-saint lxxv, 139
Alexander III, Pope 105, 171, 247
Alexander IV, Pope 409
Alexander Neckam 102
allegory lvi–lvii
Alps 93, 191, 193, 195, 327
ambler 203
Amesbury, prioress of 245
Andrews, Frances 400, 409, 411, 413–15,
    417, 419
Annales Wintonienses xlvii n.
Anselm, archbishop of Canterbury 261
Apocalipsis Goliae cxlvi n.
Appleby, John T. xxxviii n.
Apulia, dukes of liii, 133, 163, 427;
    see also Sicily, kings of
Aquitaine 218, 225; see also Eleanor of
Aquitaine, Richard, duke of, later Richard I,
    king of England xxxv, liv n.

Arator cxlvi
Arbesmann, Rudolph 31
Arthur of Brittany, nephew of Richard I,
    king of England 430
Augustine of Hippo, St 31, 231, 413
Augustinian canons 413
Augustinian friars 398, 400, 409–13
Augustinian Rule 230–1, 234, 246,
    401, 411
Auzzas, Ginetta cxlii n.
Avianus cxlv–cxlvi

Babio cxlvi
Baist, Gottfried cxxxviii n.
Baldo, author of the *Novus Aesopus* 333
Baldwin, archbishop of Canterbury xxxii n.,
    xxxv, xxxix n., xl, xlii–xlvi, xlviii, l,
    lii n., lxii, lxxiv, cxxvi, 93, 171, 202,
    205, 217, 271, 274–5, 287, 430
Baldwin, John W. 128–9, 131, 133, 135,
    191, 262, 279
Bale, John W. xxxiii n., lxiii, cxliv n.
Balfour, David xxxi, xxxiv n., xxxv n., lv n.
Barakat, Robert 219
Barastre, Jean 401
Barber, Malcolm lii n., 202–3, 205
Bardus cxli
Barlow, Frank lxxviii n.
Barrow, Julia 128–9, 133, 230, 236, 273
Bartholomew, bishop of Agrigento 430
Bartlett, Robert xxxvi n., xxxvii n., xl, 47
Baudri of Bourgueil clv
Bayless, Martha 255
beast epic cxxvii–cxxxi
beast fable cxxvii–cxxxi, 21
Becket, see Thomas Becket
Bek-Pedersen, Karen 313
Benedict, abbot of Peterborough lxii
Benedictine Rule 19, 99, 209–11, 213, 222,
    246, 259, 411, 413

GENERAL INDEX

Benedictines xliv, cxliii, 207–8, 215, 411;
  see also Cluniacs
Benevento 427
Benjamin of Tudela 414
Bennett, Deb 203
Bennett, Matthew 203
Benzinger, Josef 255
Berman, Constance H. 210
Bernard, Burnellus's master cxli, 327–55
Bernard, St, abbot of Clairvaux 105, 210, 247
Biddle, Martin 275
Bidpai, Fables of 332
bird debate lxxi, lxxiii, lxxv–lxxvii, lxxxiii,
  lxxxvii, cxi, cxxvi, cxxx–cxxxi
Blaschka, Anton lxvii
Boccaccio, Giovanni cxlii n.
Bock, F. 169
Boethius cxlv
Bohemia, Anne of, queen of England cxliv
Bologna 128–9
Bonaventura 407
Bonites 409
Boutemy, André xxxi n., xxxii n., xxxiv n., l,
  lii n., lvii n., lxii n., lxviii n., cxxv n.,
  18, 281
Bracton, Henry de 183
Bramfeld, Edmund 171
Braun, Joseph 169
Brettini 409
Bright, Philippa cxxxviii n.
Brooke, C. N. L. 133
Brown, Thomas 428
Bruce, Scott G. 219
Brunain 37
Brundage, James A. 41, 101, 129, 255
Bruno of Cologne 226
Bruun, Mette Birkedal 99, 105, 107, 210
Budinsky, A. 131
Burnellus (name) 73

Caelius Sedulius cxlvi
canons, regular cxliii, 202, 230–1, 236,
  243, 246
canons regular of St Anthony cxliii
canons, secular xliv, xlix–l, lxxiv, lxxviii,
  202, 230–1, 236–9
Canterbury 93, 129
  Old Palace at 274–5; *see also* Christ
    Church, Canterbury
Capuchonnés du Puy cxliii
Caraballa 139
Carmel, Mount 414, 417
Carmelite Rule 414
Carmelites 398, 400, 412–21

Carmina Burana cxlvi n.
Carpenter, Sarah 419
Carthusian *consuetudines* 226–8
Carthusians li, cxliii, 201–2, 211, 226–8
Cato 23, 45
Celestine III, Pope xliii n., lxxiv n., 101, 277
celibacy, *see* marriage, clerical
Champeaux, L. Boivin xxxi
Chanson de Roland 203
Charlemagne 261
Chartres, cathedral of 159
Chaucer, Geoffrey cxxxi–cxxxii, 417
Chaunticleer cxxxiv
Chenevix-Trench, Charles 203
Cheney, C. R. 247
Chesnutt, Michael lxxi, cxxxvi n., cxxxviii,
  333
child priests and bishops cxliii, 277
Chrétien de Troyes cxxxviii n., 287
chrism 171
Christ Church, Canterbury, library xxxii n.,
  lxii n., cxlii n.
  monks of xxx–xxxi, xxxii n., xl–xlviii, lxii,
    cxxvi, 83, 171, 202, 205, 236, 255, 285
  food at 211
Christina, queen of Sweden cxliii
Cian, Vittorio cxlii n.
Cicero 23
circatores 207
Cistercians xliv, xlvi, xlix, cxliii, 93, 99, 105–7,
  201–2, 207–15, 234–5, 243, 271, 283
  hostility to Cluniacs 209–11, 413
Cîteaux 210
  abbot of xlvi
  chapter general of xlvi, 99, 105
Clapham, A. W. 218
Claudian cxlv
Clement III, Pope xliii n., lxxiv, 225
Clerkenwell 205
clothing, mendicant 401, 407, 409, 411, 415
clothing, monastic 208–11, 209, 214–15,
  227, 231, 235, 239, 243
Cluniacs 202, 206–10, 243
Cluny, monastery of 210
Colvin, A. M. 234–5
Compilatio singularis exemplorum
  cxxxviii–cxxxix, cxli n., 333
Conrad of Montferrat xxxvi n., 203
Constable, Giles 105, 247
Constance, daughter of Roger II, first king
  of Sicily liii n., 430
conversi 93, 107, 224, 246
Conway, Agnes Ethel lxi n.
Coppa cxxxiii n., 135

GENERAL INDEX 469

Coppok cxxxiii
Cotts, John D. xlvi n., l n., lxxiv n.
Coulton, G. G. 91
Council, Fourth Lateran, 1215 105, 135
Council, Third Lateran, 1179 99, 277
Council of Lyon, 1274 398, 400
Coventry, expulsion of monks at xxxvii n.,
    xlvi–xlvii
Cows, story of xxviii–xxx, lii, lvi, lxx,
    cxxix–cxxxi, 7–9, 37–71, 132–3
Cremona cxxiii n., 83, 93, 131, 161, 163,
    333, 335
Crosby, Everett U. xlv n.
Crusade, First 202
Crusade, Third xxx, xxxv, xxxix n., liv,
    191, 205, 430
curia, papal lxxi, lxxiii–lxxiv, lxxxiii,
    lxxxvii, cxxvi, cxliii, 255, 430
Curtius, Ernst Robert 21, 23, 113
Cutts, Edward L. 409
Cyprianus Gallus cxlvi

Dart, J. xxxi n.
Delisle, Léopold cxxxviii n., cliv n.
D'Haenens, Albert 287
Dialogus de scaccario 87, 155, 428
Dicke, Gerd 25
Dickinson, J. C. 230–1
dies irae 55
Dionysius the Elder, Sicilian tryant 262
Disticha Catonis cxlv
Divine Office 149, 231, 341
Dominic, St 401, 413, 415
Dominicans 400–1, 403–5, 411
Dover 93
Dover Priory xxxvi n., lxii n., cxlii n.
Dracontius cxlvi
drama, religious 419
Dryanus cxxxvii–cxxxviii, 335–55
Duckworth, George E. cxlvii
Duggan, Anne J. 406
Duggan, Charles 133

Eadmer, monk of Christ Church,
    Canterbury 261
Ecbasis Captivi cxxvii n., cliv
Edmund, St, king of east Anglia 213
Eleanor of Aquitaine xlii n., 218
elegiac verse cxlvi–cliii
Elijah 417
Elisha 417
Elliott, Dyan lxxviii n.
Ely, bishops of xxxv n.
    monks of xlvii, lxii–lxiii, 87

Ember Weeks 139
Emma of Whiteacre xxxiii n.
Empson, William lvii
English Episcopal Acta xxxix n., lii n., lxxvii n.,
    lxxviii n., 105, 204, 273, 275
English, national characteristics of the
    155, 157
Epistolae Cantuarienses xl nn.–xlvii nn., lii n.,
    lxii n., lxxiv, lxxv n., 139
Ermini, Filippo 55
Eskdale 218
Esposito, M. 155
estates satire cxlii
Eugenius III, Pope 203
Eugenius IV, Pope 417, 419
Eugenius of Toledo cli

Fates, Three, story of lix, lxix, lxxi–lxxiv,
    cxi, cxxvi, 163, 313; see also Norns
Feiss, Hugh 207
Fichtner, Gerhard 31
Fleming, Robin xxxi n., xxxiii n.
Flinn, John xxviii n.
Florilegium Gallicum 406
Fontevrault, order of 243, 245
food, mendicant 407, 417
food, monastic 207–9, 210–11, 213, 227–8,
    231, 235
Forest Charter 262
Forey, Alan 202–6
Fossati, Luigi 139
Foulet, Lucien xxviii n.
France, James 214–15
Francis, St 401, 409, 413
Franciscan Rule 407
Franciscans 400–1, 404–9, 411
Franklin, M. J. xxxix n.
friars see Mendicant Orders
friends, old lviii–lix
Fuller, Sarah 407

Gabriel, A. L. 155
Gaimar 155
Galen xxvii–xxviii, lii, lvi, lxxiii,
    cxxviii–cxxix, cxxxi, cxxxiv, 13,
    29–79, 121, 131, 253, 327
Génestal, R. 139
Geoffrey, fourth son of Henry II, count of
    Brittany lv n.
Geoffrey, illegitimate son of Henry II,
    archdeacon of Rouen, later
    archbishop of York xxxvi, xxxix, xliii,
    liv n., 227, 430
Geoffrey of Monmouth 155

470   GENERAL INDEX

Gerald of Wales xxxvi–xxxvii, xxxviii n.,
  xxxix, liv n., lxi n., lxxvii–lxxviii,
  cxliii, 47
Gerard Camville, sheriff of
  Lincolnshire xxxix–xl
Gerard of Itier, prior of Grandmont 219
Gervase of Canterbury xxxvi n., xxxviii n.,
  xl–xli nn., xliii nn., xlv nn.–xlvii nn.,
  lii n., lxii n., 99, 129, 171, 205, 301
Gervais of Melkley 103
Gesta Romanorum, Anglo–Latin
  cxxxviii–cxl, 333
Geta cxlvi, cxlix
Gilbertines li, 201, 220, 230, 246–7
Gilbert Foliot, bishop of London 87
Gilchrist, Roberta 243
Gillingham, John xxxviii–xxxix nn., liv n., 430
Godfrey de Lucy, bishop of
  Winchester xxxix
Golding, Brian 246–7
Gospel According to the Mark of Silver 255
Gouron, André 41
Gower, John Confessio Amantis cxxxviii,
  cxli, 333
  Vox Clamantis cxl–cxli
Grabes, Herbert 3
Graham, Rose 218, 246
Graham, Timothy xxxii n.
Grandmont 219
Grandmontine Rule 219, 222
Grandmontines l–li, cxi, cxliii, 201–2, 218–25
Grant, Raymond 262
Grateful Animals and Ungrateful Man lii,
  lv n., lix, lxix, lxxi–lxxii, lxxxiii,
  lxxxvii, cxxvi, cxxxiv–cxli, 332–55
Gratian 128–9
Greatrex, Joan xxxi n.
Great St Bernard Pass 77, 93, 191
Gregory VI, Pope xxxvi n.
Gregory VII, Pope 139
Gregory VIII, Pope lxxiv n.
Gregory IX, Pope 419
Grenoble 226
Grimm, Jacob 313, 326–7
Grubmüller, Klaus 25
Guibert of Nogent 226
Guigo I, prior of La Grande Chartreuse 226
Guiot de Provins cxlii–cxliii, 215
Gundulf, story of xxvii–xxix, liii, lxxi, cx,
  cxxxi–cxxxiv, 133–53
Gurney Salter, E. 407, 409, 415
Guzman, Dominic, see Dominic, St

Hackington xliv, xlvi, l, lxxiv, 202, 205, 236
Hagenau xxxviii

Hall, Catherine xxxii n.
Hall, J. B. 127
Hallam, Elizabeth M. 219
Hanna, Ralph 163
Harvey, Barbara 211, 213
Haseldine, Julian 159
Haskins, Charles H. xxxvii n., 427–8, 430
Hattin, battle of 203–4, 414
Hauréau, Barthélemy 79
hawking 307
Haye, Thomas cxliv n., 171
Heale, Martin 169
Heiser, Richard V. xxxvi n.
Henry of Blois, bishop of Winchester 275
Henry of Eastry, prior of Christ Church,
  Canterbury cxlii
Henry, eldest son of Henry II, the 'Young
  King' lv
Henry VI, Holy Roman emperor, king of
  Sicily liii, 430
Henry II, king of England xliii, xlv n., li,
  liv–lv n., lxxiv, cxxvi, 204–5,
  218–19, 225, 246, 263, 307, 428–30
Henry III, king of England 262, 415
Henry VIII, king of England 275
Henry of Longchamp, abbot of
  Crowland lxi
Henry of Settimello cli
Henryson, Robert cxxxiii n., cxxxiv
Herodias 203
Hertel, Johannes 332
Hervieux, Léopold cxlii
Hildebert of Tours cxlvi, cliv–clv
Hinnebusch, William A. 401, 405, 411
Hippocrates 29
Hofmann, J. B. clix n., clx n.
Holmes, Urban Tigner 307
homosexuality lxxvii–lxxviii, 157
Honorius III, Pope 407, 415
Honorius, prior of Christ Church,
  Canterbury xlv, lxxiv–lxxv
Hoppin, Richard H. 247
Horace cxlv
Hornbeck, Patrick J. cxliv n.
Hoscam, Herbert, bishop of Conza 430
Hospitallers lii n., cxliii, 201–2, 204–6
Hrotswitha cliv
Huber-Rebenich cxliv n.
Hubert Walter, archbishop of Canterbury
  xxxii n., xli–xlii, xlv, xlviii n., 185, 275
Hudson, Anne cxliv n.
Hugh de Fosses, abbot of Prémontré 234
Hugh of Nonant, bishop of
  Coventry xxxvi, xxxviii–xxxix,
  xlvi–xlvii, lxi n., lxxvii

GENERAL INDEX

471

Hugh of Payns 202
Hugh Primas cxlvi, cliv n.
Hugh of Puiset, bishop of Durham xxxv
Humbert of Romans 405
hunting 262, 279
Hus, Jan cxliii–cxliv
Hutchison, Carole 218–19, 223–5

Igny, abbot of xlvi n.
illegitimacy 139
ingratitude lviii–lix, lxxii–lxxiii
Innocent II, Pope 105, 205
Interpolation, *see* Mendicant Orders
Isidore of Seville clix n.

Jacobins, *see* Dominicans
Jacob's Ford lii, 204
James of Compostela, St 349
James the Great, St 401
James, Montague Rhodes 287
James, Richard, Cotton librarian lxiii n.,
    clxiii
Jamison, Evelyn 427
Janssen, Hendrikus Hubertus
    clvi n.–clviii n.
Jarecki, Walter 219
Jerusalem lii, 202–5, 414
Joanna, sister of Richard I, king of
    England 429–30
Jocelin of Brakelond xli
Joel, Rabbi cxxxv n.
John of Capua cxxxv n., cxxxviii, 333
John, count of Mortain, later king of
    England xxxv, xxxviii n., xli,
    lv n., 101
John, monk of Christ Church
    Canterbury 77
John of Salisbury lxxviii n., cxlvi, 238, 427
Jones, A. H. M. 75
Jordan Fantosme 155
Joseph of Exeter cxlix, cli
Julian, St 83
Justinian 128–9
Juvenal cxlv, cliv
Juvencus cxlvi

Kachelofen, Conrad 23
Kalila and Dimna lxxi, cxxxv–cxli, 332
Karn, Nicholas xxxv n., xlv n.
Kay, Richard 47
Keene, D. J. 275
Keith-Falconer, I. G. N. 332
Kibre, Pearl 155
Klopsch, Paul cxlviii n., cxlix, clv n.
Knapp, Fritz Peter xxviii n., lvi

Knowles, David xliv n., lxi n., lxii, clxiii,
    105, 169, 206–7, 210, 213, 215, 220,
    401, 404–5, 407
Kristeller, Paul Oskar 75

Lambeth xlvi, lxxiv
Landau, Peter 129
Landon, Lionel xxxviii n., xliii n., xlvi n.,
    lxxii n.
Lanfranc, Constitutions of 209
Langholm, Odd 71
Langosch, Karl lxxx, clxiv–clxv, 99, 165,
    179, 215
Laodamia 81
Laon 234
Lapidge, Michael cxlviii n., cliv n., clvii n.
Lawler, Traugott 163
Lawless, George 231
Lebanon 205
Leclercq, Jean 210, 287
Lehmann, Paul 77, 91, 139, 255, 276
Lenticulus cxxxix–cxl
Leonard, St 189
Leopold VI, duke of Austria liii n.
Lesne, Émile 131
Leumann, Manu clvi n.–clvii n.,
    clix n.–clx n.
Lewis, C. S. lviii n.
*Liber de moribus egregiisque dictis
    omnium philosophorum et
    poetarum* clxii
Lidia cxlvi
Liebermann, F. clv n.
Limousin 218
Lincoln, bishopric of 429
Lind, Levi Robert clv n.
liturgy 143, 207, 247
locus amoenus 113
Loewenthal, L. J. A. 430
London, bishop of 87
Longchamp family xxxv n., lxi, 273
Longchamps, Normandy xxxiv n.
Loomis, C. Grant 189
Lord, Evelyn 204
Loud, G. A. 263
Louis VII, king of France lii, 37
Lucan cxxii, cxlv
Lucius III, Pope liv n.
Lucretius cxlv n., cl n.
Lynch, Joseph H. 211
Lyon 93; *see also* Council of

Macaulay, G. C. cxl, 425
Mados cxxxix
magister 129

472 GENERAL INDEX

Mann, Jill xxviii n., cxxviii n., cxxx n.,
 cxxxi n., cxxxiv n., cxliii n., 33, 129,
 245, 257, 293, 297, 430
Mansi, G. D. 99, 277, 400
Marbod of Rennes clv
Margaret, queen of Sicily 428–9
Marie de France cxxxi
marriage, clerical cxliii, 133
Massèra, Aldo Francesco cxlii n.
Matthew, D. J. A. 428
Matthew Paris, monk of St Albans lxxii,
 cxxxvi–cxxxix, cxli n., 332–3
Matthias Flacius Illyricus cxliv
Maurus 207–9
Maximian cxlv–cxlvi
Mendicant Orders, Interpolation on the
 xcviii, ci, cxvii, clxiv–clxv, 398–421
Messina, archbishopric of 429
 city of 430
Meyer, Wilhelm cliv n., 215, 225
Migliorini, Bruno 77
Minorites, see Franciscans
Mitchell, Sydney Knox 205
Molesmes 210, 413; see also Robert of
 Molesmes
monastic orders, survey of xlix, l–lii, lv, lvii,
 lxxi, lxxiii, cxlii–cxliv, 201–2, 327
Mont Cenis Pass 191, 193, 195
Monreale, archbishop of xl, xli n., xlviii n.
Montefavale, hermits of 409
Moorman, John 401, 407–8, 411
Mortet, Victor 275
Mortimer, Richard 235
Mount Grace 227
Mozley, J. H. xxxii n., xxxiii, lviii n., lxiii n.,
 lxvii, lxxii n., lxxix n., lxxx–lxxxiii,
 xci, xcii n., xciv n., xcv, xcvi n., cv,
 cix, cx n., cxvi–cxxv, clxii–clxv,
 clxix–clxx, 3, 5, 7, 9, 11, 13, 15, 17,
 173, 195, 197, 217, 253, 259–60,
 265, 273, 276, 293
munera lxxxviii, cxxvii, 265
Muret 218
Murray, Alexander 265

Nabal 417
Neilson, George 157
nepotism, clerical 7, 273, 283, 293
Nestor 22
Nicholas, monk of Ely lxii
Nigel, bishop of Ely 87
Nigel of Longchamp, life xxxi n., xxxiv, 18
 Epistle to William xxxi, lv–lxiii,
 lxxii–lxxiv, lxxviii, lxxxvii, cxxvi

other works xxxi–xxxii
 Passio S. Laurentii xxxi
 Tractatus xxx–xxxi, xxxvii–xxxix, xlvii
 prefatory poem to lxii
Noah's Ark 289, 301
Norbert of Xanten, St 234
Norns 313
Norwich, John Julius liii n.
Novati, Francesco 91
nuns 243–5

Oda, archbishop of Canterbury 261
O'Daly, Irene xxxii n., lv n.
Odo, abbot of Battle lxii
Odo of Cheriton cxlii n.
Oggins, Robin S. 307
Old Man of the Mountain, leader of the
 assassins xxxvi n.
ordination 139
Orlandi, Giovanni cxlviii n., cliv n.
Osbern of Gloucester 263
Osbern, prior of Christ Church,
 Canterbury 301
Otto of Freising 263
Ovid lxii, cxlv, cxlvii–cliv, clvii, clviii n.
Owl and the Nightingale, The cxxxi, cxxxiv
Owst, G. R. 419

palaces, episcopal 274–5
Palmer, Richard 428–9
Pamphilus cxlvi
Pañchatantra, see *Kalila and Dimna*
papal legates 101
Paris, city of liii–liv, cxxiii, 191
Paris, lover of Helen of Troy 243
Paris, university of xxxiv, 128–9, 131, 155
Parker, Matthew xxxii n.
Parks, George B. 77, 83
parrots, story of the three 297
Parsons, Ben 159
Pauli, Reinhold 47
peasants 91
Pease, Arthur Stanley 51
Pedersen, Olaf 129
Perillus 262
Persius cxlv
Pertelote cxxxiv
Peter, St 173
Peter Abelard, see Abelard, Peter
Peter of Blois xxxix n., xliv n., xlvi n., l n.,
 105, 429
Peter of Celle 427
Peter the Chanter 262
Peter Chrysologus 203

GENERAL INDEX

473

Peter Comestor xxxii n., lv n., 135
Peter Damian cxxxviii n.
Peter the Venerable 105, 209, 226
  Statuta 207–9
Phalaris, Sicilian tyrant 117, 262
Philip Augustus, (Philip II), king of
  France lii, liv, 191, 203, 218, 225
Philomena 65
Phoebus 147, 295
Pied Friars 400
Pierre de Goussainville 77
Pike, Joseph B. 238–9
Pipewell, council of xxxv
Poitou, Richard, count of, later Richard I,
  king of England xxxv, liv n.
pontificals 169–71
Pontigny, abbot of xlvi n.
Poole, A. L. 133, 262
Power, Eileen 213, 245
Premonstratensians cxliii, 213, 220, 230,
  234–6, 246
  statutes 235
Procne 65
Protesilaus 81
proverbs 11, 17, 25, 27, 29, 35, 43, 45, 47,
  63, 65, 81, 83, 111, 115, 147, 161,
  185, 244, 259, 267, 270, 289, 325,
  357
Prudentius cxlvi
psalm-singing 207, 247
Puglia, dukes of liii, 133, 163, 427;
  see also Sicily, kings of
Purchard of Reichenau cliv

Quilligan, Maureen lvi n.

Raby, F. J. E. 65
Rajan, Chandra 332
Ralph, abbot of Shrewsbury lxii
Ralph de Diceto xxxvi, xli n., 77, 277
Rannulf de Glanville, justiciar 235
Rashdall, Hastings 128–9, 155, 159
Raymo, Robert R. lxvii, lxxx, cxl, cxlii n.,
  clxiii–clxv, 23, 29, 79, 93, 99, 157,
  159, 202, 207, 238, 241, 254, 257,
  327, 357
Raymond of Bézières 333
Reginald of Bath xl–xli, xlix n.
Reginald of Canterbury clv
Regula S. Benedicti, see Benedictine Rule
Reynard the Fox xxvii, cxxviii
Reynolds, Roger E. 139
Rhône, river and valley 93, 191, 193
Riall, Nicholas 275

Richard, archbishop of Canterbury xxxii n.,
  105, 171, 429
Richard Barre xxxvi
Richard of Belmeis I, bishop of London
  (1108–27) 277
Richard of Belmeis II, archdeacon of
  Middlesex, later bishop of London
  (1152–62) 277
Richard of Devizes xxxvi n., xlii n., xlvii n.,
  xlix n., lxi nn., 157
Richard FitzNigel, bishop of London 87, 155
Richard de Grey, Earl of Cornwall 415
Richard I, king of England xxx, xxxv,
  xxxviii–xl, xlii, xlvi, xlvii n.,
  liv–lv, lxxii, cxxxvi–cxxxvii, 203,
  332–3, 430
  imprisonment in Austria xxxvii, liii n.
Richard II, king of England cxliv
Richard de Weynchepe, prior of
  Dover cxlii
Rickard, P. 157
Rigg, A. G. 170, 281
Rigord of St-Denis 191
Riley-Smith, Jonathan 203, 205–6
Robert, abbot of Thorney lxi
Robert of Longchamp, prior of Ely lxi
Robert of Molesmes 413
Robert of Selby 427
Robert of Torigni 129
Rochester, bishop of xlii–xliii
Roger, abbot of St Augustine's,
  Canterbury lxii, 171
Roger, archbishop of York lxxviii n., 277
Roger II, count of Pulia, later first king of
  Sicily liii n., 263, 428
Roger of Howden xxxv nn., xxxvi n.,
  xxxviii.–xl nn., lxi nn., 99, 101, 129,
  245, 277
Roger Norreys, prior of Canterbury, later
  abbot of Eynsham xlvi, lxii
Roman de Renart xxviii, cxxviii, cxxxiv
Rome 255, 257
Romulus, elegiac ci n., cxlvi
Romulus vulgaris cxxxviii n.
Rubisca 33
Rufinus, ps.-saint lxxv, 139

Sack Friars 400
St Albans lxxii, cxxxvi
St Augustine's, Canterbury xxxii n., clv,
  33, 171
Saladin lii n., 203–5
  Saladin tithe 204–5
Salerno 83, 85, 93

474 GENERAL INDEX

Sanford, Eva Matthews 45
Sarness Farm, Waltham xxxiii n.
Savaric, bishop of Bath xlii n.
Saxo Grammaticus 313
Scherer, Margaret R. 47
Schimmelpfennig, Bernhard 139
Scott, Kathleen 287
Sedgwick, Walter Bradbury lxxix n., lxxxii–
  lxxxiii, 67, 102, 217, 259, 276, 279, 293
Sempringham, Gilbert of 246
Sempringham, order of cxi, cxliii n.,
  246–7; see also Gilbertines
Serlo of Wilton cliv n.
Sextus Amarcius cxlvi
Shackleton Bailey, D. R. lxxx, lxxxii, 23,
  41, 145, 151, 165, 179
Sharpe, Richard xxxvi n., lv n.
sheep-farming, monastic 212–13, 220
Sheppard, Lancelot C. 415
Sherlock, David 219
Sicily lxxi–lxxii, 333, 427–30
Sicily, kings of liii, 133, 262–3, 427
sign language, monastic 125, 219
Silius Italicus cxlv n.
Simon of Puglia 430
simony 173, 269
Simplingham, see Sempringham
Skutsch, Otto lxxx–lxxxiii. 57, 217, 253, 267
Smith, Katherine Allen 209
Soissons, bishop of xlvi
Southern, R. W. 129, 131, 429
Spear, David S. liv n.
Spufford, Peter 193, 195
Statius cxlv n.
Stephen, St xlv
Stephen Harding, abbot of Cîteaux 210
Stephen of Muret, founder of the abbey of
  Grandmont 218
Stephen of Perche 428
Stephen, rebel prior of Grandmont 225
Stotz, Peter 23, 349
Strecker, Karl cliv n., 73
Stubbs, William xxxiv–xxxvi nn.,
  xxxviii–xl nn., xli, xlii n.,
  xliv–xlvii nn., lxii n., lxxiv–lxxv nn.
Styx, river of Hell 315
superstitions 81, 325–6
Susanna 243
Sweet, Alfred H. 169
Sweetinburgh, Sheila xliv
Syracuse 262
Szantyr, A. clix n., clx n.

Taillebourg liv n.
Talis of the Fyve Bestis cxxxii–cxxxiv
Tancred, king of Sicily liii, 133, 430

tanning 220–1
Temple Mount 203
Templars lii n., cxliii, 201–5
  Rule 203
Tereus 65
Theobald, archbishop of Canterbury 129, 204
Thomas Becket, St xliii, xliv n., xlv, xlviii n.,
  li, lxxviii n., 18, 205, 246, 263, 349,
  428–9
Thomas of Chobham 262
Thompson, E. Margaret li n., 226
Thompson, Michael 275
Thompson, Sally 243
Thomson, R. M. xcvi n.
Thorne, William 171
Tibullus clii
Times Comprehensive Atlas of the World,
  The 139
tithes 104–7, 204–5
Traill, David 24
Traversari, Guido cxlii n.
Trifels xxxviii
Troy 47
Turner, Ralph V. xxxi n., xxxv n., xxxvi n.,
  xxxviii n., xl n., lv n.
Tuscan Hermits 409
Tuve, Rosemond lvi n.
Twycross, Meg 419
Tyerman, Chrisopher 205
Tyler, J. E. 77
tyranny 262–3
Tyre 203, 417

Ulrich of Cluny 207, 209
Urban III, Pope xliv n., xlv n., xlvi n.,
  lxxiv n., 225
Urry, William xxxi n., xxxiii nn.

Vacarius 129
Van Dussen, Michael cxliv n.
Van den Vos Reinaerde xxviii n.
Vergil cxlv, cxlix, cli, cliv
Verheijen, Luc 230–1
Victoria County History lxi
Vienne cxxiii, 191, 193
Vincent, Nicholas liv n.
Vitalis cxxxvi–cxxxvii, 332
Vollmer, Friedrich cli n.

Wace 155
Waddell, Chrysogonus 210; see also
  Cistercians
Waltenberger, Michael 73
Walter, archbishop of Rouen xli n.
Walter of Châtillon cxxii, cxlvi,
  cxlix, cli

GENERAL INDEX

475

Walter, lover of Roger, archbishop of
York lxxviii n.
Walter Offamil 430
Walther, Hans lxvii
Ward, H. L. D. xxxii n., xxxiv n.
Warin, abbot of St Albans lxxii,
cxxxvi, 332
Warren, W. L. 219
washeil 155
Watson, Andrew G. xxxii n.
Watton, nun of 247
Weiske, Brigitte cxxxviii n.
Weiss, Judith 155
Wells, diocese of li
Wertheimer, Laura 139
West, Francis xxxv nn.
Westminster xlii, xlvi, 275
Whitwell, Robert Jowitt 213
Wibert, prior of Christ Church,
Canterbury xxxiii n.
Wiederhold, Wilhelm 105
Wieruszowski, Helene 263
William, archbishop of Sens lxxviii n.
William I, 'the Bad', king of Sicily liii,
133, 428
William II, 'the Good', king of Sicily liii,
133, 428–30
William III, king of Sicily liii, 133
William, bishop of Monreale 301
William of Blois, abbot of Santa Maria di
Maniaci, Sicily 170, 429
William of Longchamp xxxi, xxxiv–xliii,
xlvi–xlviii, liv–lv, lx–lxiii, 18, 273
as bishop of Ely xxxv, xlv n., xlvi–xlviii,
lxi, 271, 273

as justiciar xxxv, lxi
as papal legate xxxv, xlii–xliii, lxi, 101
enemies of xxxv–xxxvi, xxxix, xlvii, lxi,
lxxvii
alleged homosexuality lxxvii–lxxviii
William of Malmesbury 155, 261
William of Newburgh xxxvi n., xxxviii n.,
xli n., xlvii n., 99, 277
William, prior of Grandmont 224
Williamites 409
William Rufus, king of England 261
Wilmart, André 210
Winchester xxxvii–xxxviii, 275
Wireker, Witeker xxxii–xxxiii
Witham, Somerset li, 226
Wolff, Reinhold cxxxviii n.
Wollin, Carsten cxxxviii n., 102–3
women, medieval stereotypes of 243–5
Woodcock, E. C. 227
Woolf, Rosemary 419
Worcester xliii
Wright, Thomas clxii, clxix, 102, 281
Wycliffites cxliii

Ysengrimus the wolf xxx, cxviii
Ysengrimus xxviii n., cxxvii n., cxxviii,
cxxx–cxxxi, cxxxiii–cxxxiv, cxlvi,
cxlix, 271, 321
Yunck, John A. 139, 173, 255, 257,
265, 276

Zermatten, Coralie 417, 419
Ziolkowski, Jan xxxi n., xxxii n.,
xxxvii–xxxviii, liv, lxii n., clv n.
Zoilus 207–8